Third Edition

SYSTEMS ANALYSIS AND DESIGN

Kenneth E. Kendall

Rutgers University
School of Business-Camden
Camden, New Jersey
USA

Julie E. Kendall

Rutgers University
School of Business-Camden
Camden, New Jersey
USA

Prentice Hall, Englewood Cliffs, New Jersey 07632

Library of Congress Cataloging-in-Publication Data

Kendall, Kenneth E., 1948–
  Systems analysis and design / Kenneth E. Kendall, Julie E. Kendall.—3rd ed.
    p. cm.
  Includes bibliographical references and index.
  ISBN (invalid) 0-01-314883-x
    1. System design. 2. System analysis. I. Kendall, Julie E.,
  1952– . II. Title.
  QA76.9.S88K45   1994
  004.2'1—dc20   94-30969
                                                        CIP

Production Editor: Editorial Services of New England, Inc.
Project Manager: Alana Zdinak
Acquisition Editor: P. J. Boardman
Interior Design: Maureen Eide
Cover Designer: Wendy Helft
Design Director: Patricia Wosczyk
Copy Editor: Gina Russo
Proofreader: Julie DeSilva
Manufacturing Buyer: Paul Smolenski
Editorial Assistant: Amy Cohen

Cover art: Victor Vasarely, *Vega Nor,* 1969, Albright-Knox Art Gallery, Buffalo, NY

©1995, 1992, 1988 by Prentice-Hall, Inc.
A Simon & Schuster Company
Englewood Cliffs, New Jersey 07632

Printed in the United States of America
10 9 8 7 6 5 4 3

ISBN 0-13-148883-X

Prentice-Hall International (UK) Limited, London
Prentice-Hall of Australia Pty. Limited, Sydney
Prentice-Hall Canada Inc., Toronto
Prentice-Hall Hispanoamericana, S.A., Mexico
Prentice-Hall of India Private Limited, New Delhi
Prentice-Hall of Japan, Inc., Tokyo
Simon & Schuster Asia Pte. Ltd., Singapore
Editora Prentice-Hall do Brasil, Ltda., Rio de Janerio

To Edward J. Kendall and Julia A. Kendall,
whose lifelong example of working together inspired us

COMPANY
TRADEMARKS

CONTENTS

PART TWO
INFORMATION REQUIREMENTS ANALYSIS

CONSULTING OPPORTUNITIES

HyperCase Experiences

PREFACE

Information systems in particular, and the world in general, have changed dramatically since we wrote our second edition. The watchwords are *user empowerment,* regardless of where users are or when they want to communicate and compute. Information technology now empowers users to span time and space in remarkable ways. Users are now diverse and difficult to characterize in any standard way. In response, systems analysts are now in the unique and enviable position of being able to exercise full creativity and ingenuity in the types and sizes of applications and systems they develop, and the methods they can use to do so. Rather than taking one, limited, world view, analysts can vary their perspectives, and ultimately the systems they design.

We have come to understand through numerous discussions with professors, students, systems analysts, and other IS practitioners worldwide that the analyst's job has become so complex that it is absolutely essential that a variety of different methods, tools, and techniques are necessary if these challenges are to be met. We think that the communication and input generated through these discussions have helped us to develop a complete, up-to-date, and useful third edition.

One comment we always receive from students and their prospective employers alike is that they wish they "had more experience" solving complex organizational problems. To help fill that need, the book is available with a **HYPERCASE®** disk containing an original hypertext-based software that allows students to become immediately immersed in organizational life. Students will interview people, observe their office environments, analyze their prototypes, and review the documentation of their existing systems. HyperCase is an interactive, hypertext-based program that presents an organization called Maple Ridge Engineering in a highly graphical, colorful environment, for use on a personal computer. HyperCase permits professors to begin approaching the systems analysis and design class with exciting multimedia material. Carefully watching their use of time and managing multiple methods, students use the hypertext-based capabilities to create their own individual paths through the organization.

Maple Ridge Engineering (MRE) is drawn from the actual consulting experiences of the authors (Raymond Barnes, Richard Baskerville, Julie E. Kendall, and Kenneth E. Kendall). In each chapter there are special HyperCase Experiences that include assignments (and even some clues) to help students solve the difficult organizational problems they encounter at MRE. HyperCase has been fully classroom tested, and was also an award winner in the Decision Sciences Institute Innovative Instruction competition. HyperCase may be installed on a computer network, or be copied for use in class.

We recognize the importance of being able to see the world of information systems from many different perspectives. This capability has become so critical that we have included an entirely new chapter, **Object-Oriented Systems Analysis and Design**, which was written especially for our text by Richard L. Baskerville of Binghamton University. Chapter 22 has been fully classroom tested in Europe as well as the United States, and it offers a comprehensive and easy-to-follow introduction to the object-oriented approach.

In response to the team-oriented approaches that are becoming increasingly important and popular in all types of organizations around the world, we have added a number of **Group Projects** throughout the third edition. These have been carefully written to enable students to hone the skills required of them to work productively in groups on relevant systems analysis and design projects.

Additionally, we've added new examples from current, popular software packages that can help keep students and professors up to date on the latest popular tool packages that support systems analysis and design activities with increasing computer power. This feature permits readers to remain current by demonstrating the functionalities of several popular software packages, including Visible Analyst Workbench by Visible Systems, Delrina's FormFlow, Visio by Shapeware Corporation, Microsoft Project and XperCASE by Siemens.

Readers who have been with us from early editions will notice that in the third edition there is expanded coverage of data flow diagrams and data dictionaries, as well as a major new section on process specifications. The coverage on structure charts has been greatly expanded as well. These are all additions that you have requested over the years.

We believe that the importance of CASE tools for the work of the systems analyst can only increase. In order to help students learn proficiency with a CASE tool, Visible Systems Corporation has offered that the third edition of Kendall & Kendall be bundled with a new student version of **Visible Analyst Workbench (VAW).** This is the first time it has been economically feasible to make a relatively sophisticated, individual copy of a CASE tool available to students. This is an exciting change which will permit students to work wherever there is adequate hardware available, rather than being confined to the school's microcomputer laboratory. To contact Visible Systems Corporation, professors should call (617) 890-2273. Consult your Prentice Hall representative about this option.

In support of VAW is a new student workbook, *Visible Analyst Workbook*, written by Allen Schmidt, soon to be published by Prentice Hall. This book is closely keyed to the contents of the third edition of Kendall & Kendall, so that students can easily see how VAW reinforces the concepts and techniques they are learning in the text. Additionally, it demonstrates in clear, meaningful examples how to use Visible Analyst Workbench to its full potential. Numerous hands-on problems are provided as well.

In keeping with our belief that a variety of approaches is important, we have once again integrated the Central Pacific University (CPU) Case into every chapter of the third edition. The CPU case takes students through all phases of the systems development life cycle, demonstrating the capabilities of yet another popular CASE tool, **Excelerator**. This CASE tool also gives students an opportunity to solve problems on their own, using Excelerator and data from a specially prepared data disk (available to all instructors adopting the text) containing Excelerator exercises specifically keyed to each chapter of the book. The CPU case has been fully classroom tested with a variety of students over numerous terms. The case is detailed, rigorous, and rich enough to stand alone as a systems analysis and design project spanning one or two terms. Alternatively, the Central Pacific University case can be used as a way to teach the use of CASE tools in conjunction with the assignment of a one-term or two-term, real-world project outside the classroom.

A copy of the Excelerator CASE tool, for use in conjunction with this text, may be obtained through an educational grant program offered by INTERSOLV. Professors who use Kendall & Kendall's third edition of *Systems Analysis and Design*, and who have access to the necessary hardware to run Excelerator in class, are eligible to purchase a copy of Excelerator for use in their own school. Please write to INTERSOLV, 1 Main Street, Cambridge, MA, 02142 or call their representative, Carlene Dolan, at (617) 252-4504. Alternatively, you may fill in the application form provided in the instructor's manual.

The underlying philosophy of our book is that systems analysis and design is a process that integrates the use of many tools to systematically accomplish its goals of improving businesses through the implementation or modification of computerized information systems. The text is divided into five major parts: Systems Analysis Fundamentals (Part One), Information Requirements Analysis (Part Two), The Analysis Process (Part Three), The Essentials of Design (Part Four), and Software Engineering and Implementation (Part Five).

Part One (Chapters 1 through 3) stresses the basics that students need to know about what an analyst does; how organizations function and how information systems fit into them; how to determine whether a systems project is worthy of commitment; and how to manage a systems project using special software tools. **Alternative systems analysis and design methods** such as ETHICS are introduced. The three roles of the systems analyst as consultant, supporting expert, and agent of change also are introduced and explained.

Part Two (Chapters 4 through 8) emphasizes the use of systematic and structured methodologies. Attention to analysis helps analysts ensure that they are addressing the correct problem before designing the system. The presentation of each methodology (sampling, investigating hard data, interviewing, questionnaires, and observation) moves students closer to understanding what information users need and how needs can best be ascertained. Chapter 5 includes new material on **joint application design (JAD)** for ascertaining information requirements in concert with users. Chapter 7 is especially innovative and goes well beyond the typical text in showing how to accomplish systematic observation of decision makers. Chapter 8 is also innovative in its treatment of prototyping as another data-gathering technique that enables the analyst to solve the right problem by getting users involved from the start.

Part Three details the analysis process (Chapters 9 through 14). It builds on the previous two parts to move students into analysis of data flows, as well as structured and semistructured decisions. It provides step-by-step detail on how to use structured techniques to draw data-flow diagrams. Chapter 9 is innovative in its expanded coverage of **how to create child diagrams**; **how to develop both logical and physical data flow diagrams**; and **how to partition data flow diagrams**. Many **new examples from actual businesses** are provided. Chapter 10 now has new material on the **data repository** and **vertical balancing of data flow diagrams**. Chapter 11 now includes a new section devoted to developing process specifications. Another section discusses both physical and logical process specifications, and using process specifications for horizontal balancing. Examples include a video rental business; the systems involved in an auction house; and the information systems of an international mail order clothing business.

Other chapters in Part Three cover how to diagram structured decisions with the use of structured English, decision tables, and decision trees. Students then progress to a consideration of semistructured decisions that are featured in decision support systems. After analysis of decisions is accomplished, students learn how to ascertain the hardware and software needs of the organization. In addition, students are taught several methods for forecasting costs and benefits, which is necessary to the discussion of software and hardware. Next, students are supplied with the quantitative and qualitative techniques needed to compare costs and benefits of a proposed system. Chapter 14 features innovative material giving the **guidelines for using graphics presentation packages** to present the systems proposal. It stresses the importance of a professionally prepared, written and oral presentation of the systems proposal. The proposal is viewed as a persuasive document that is extremely important to the future acceptance and success of the system.

Part Four covers the essentials of design (Chapters 15 through 19). It begins with designing output, since many practitioners believe systems to be output driven. Particular attention is paid to relating output method to content, the effect of output on users, and designing good forms and screens. Chapter 15 features new material comparing advantages and disadvantages of **modern methods of output including specialty printers, screens, audio, microform, CD-ROM, and electronic output such as e-mail, faxes, and bulletin boards**. Innovative material in Chapter 16 includes a new section on **computer-assisted form design**. New sections cover **differences in mainframe and microcomputer screen design**; using icons in screen design; and **graphical user interface design**. Input design stresses the importance of a systematic approach to the design of screens and forms and the influence of analysts in getting users to use the system. How the user interacts with the computer and how to design an appropriate interface are also covered. The importance of user feedback and correct ergonomic design of computer workstations are innovative topics in Part Four. How to design accurate data-entry procedures that take full advantage of computer and human capabilities to assure entry of quality data is the key here.

Also in Part Four, new material in Chapter 17 details **how to use the entity-relationship diagram to determine record keys**, as well as providing **new guidelines for file/database relation design**. Students are shown the relevance of database design for the overall usefulness of the system, and how users actually use databases. Chapter 18 highlights **new material on**

graphical user interface (GUI) design as well as providing innovative approaches to **designing dialogs and customizing desktops**.

Finally, Part Five (Chapters 20, 21, and 22) introduces students to structured software engineering and documentation techniques as ways to implement a quality system. Chapter 20 includes a new section on the **important concepts of code generation and design reengineering.** Students are introduced to an exciting new tool from Siemens called **XperCASE** that automates these functions and helps address the growing needs of analysts for practical, flexible support. We also cover the most recent developments in structured techniques while also teaching students which techniques are appropriate for which situations. The material on structure charts has been greatly expanded, including details on how to use data flow diagrams to draw structure charts. In addition, expanded coverage of security is included. Testing, auditing, and maintenance of systems are discussed in the context of **total quality management (TQM).** Also in part Five, Chapter 21 introduces innovative tools for modeling networks, and now features a discussion of groupware. Part Five also introduces the student to implementing the information center and distributed systems. Both of these approaches require training users and choosing a conversion strategy, and are discussed in a step-by-step way. Techniques for evaluating the completed information systems project are covered systematically as well.

Part Five concludes with an entirely new chapter, which is Chapter 22 on **Object-Oriented Systems Analysis and Design**. This chapter introduces this important new approach and demonstrates through several examples and Consulting Opportunities how to use an object-oriented approach. An extended example of the problems associated with running a six-train, semi-automated monorail in a small theme park is used to make key concepts come alive. This new chapter on object-oriented systems analysis and design has been classroom tested internationally with excellent results.

The third edition includes all new **HyperCase Experiences** in every chapter. However, the unique hypertext features of HyperCase can best be realized by having students navigate through it independently or as teams, creating their own unique paths through the MRE organization and discussing their findings with their professor over the term. In this way, HyperCase can be used periodically throughout the semester in a much less structured, more creative way. For professors who prefer to take a more traditional approach, we have included detailed assignments in every chapter for students to complete. These lend more structure to students in navigating through the hypertext based case disk included with each text and challenges them to solve the complex organizational problems awaiting them in the interactive, graphical HyperCase world of MRE.

Once again, Kendall & Kendall, third edition, includes **the CPU case**, which is included in every chapter and requires the use of Excelerator (or another CASE tool). Each chapter has been updated (or expanded) to permit full coverage of important and timely topics. The third edition of *Systems Analysis and Design* provides hundreds of clear diagrams and shots of actual screens that show students how to solve problems. Many of these are accompanied by transparency masters available to instructors wishing to cover text material in depth in a classroom environment.

The third edition presents over sixty **Consulting Opportunities**, which can be used for stimulating in-class discussions or assigned as homework or take-home exam questions. Since not all systems are huge two-year or three-year projects, our book contains many Consulting Opportunities that can be solved quickly in twenty to thirty minutes of group discussion or individual writing. These minicases, written in a humorous manner to enliven the material, require students to synthesize what they have learned up to that point in the course, ask students to mature in their professional judgment, and expect students to articulate the reasoning behind their systems decisions.

Each of the twenty-two chapters provides an end-of-the-chapter summary that ties together the salient points of each chapter while providing an excellent review source for exams. New in this edition is the inclusion of Group Projects at the end of most chapters. Group Projects help students to learn to work together in a systems team to solve important problems that can best be solved through group interaction. The index is suitably expanded to allow easy access to material in the new third edition.

Many materials are available to help in the preparation of this course. Allen Schmidt has prepared an excellent **instructor's manual** to accompany the third edition of *Systems Analysis and Design*. It once again includes an innovative **data disk** with completed examples and partially completed exercises that instructors may import into Excelerator. Use of this disk provides students with hands-on experience with a CASE tool by completing Excelerator exercises assigned throughout the CPU case in the third edition. Allen Schmidt's book, *Working with Excelerator 1.9,* is available from Prentice Hall. Professor Schmidt's manual demonstrates easy, common-sense approaches for working with Excelerator 1.9 and it goes on to explain more advanced uses of the Excelerator CASE tool as well. The instructor's manual contains transparency masters for help with lecture preparation.

Systems analysis and design is taught in one or two semesters. Our book may be used in either situation. The text is appropriate for undergraduate (junior or senior) curriculum at a four-year university, graduate school, or community college. The level and length of the course can be varied and supplemented by using other materials, such as the casebook written to accompany this text.

Many colleges use one of two approaches for scheduling the course—the first is referred to as the ACM curriculum (Association for Computing Machinery), and the second as the DPMA curriculum (Data Processing Management Association). This third edition of *Systems Analysis and Design* is suitable for use in either the DPMA Model course CIS-06 Systems Development 1 (Single User Systems) and CIS-07 Systems Development 2 (Multi User Systems). It can also be used in courses following the ACM information systems curriculum for both IS05 Fundamentals of Information Systems Development, and IS08 Information Systems Development Tools and Techniques.

kendallk@camden.rutgers.edu
kendallj@camden.rutgers.edu

ACKNOWLEDGMENTS

Our students made this book possible. We have appreciated their enthusiasm, assistance, and humor throughout this project. Their insistence on depth and clarity have kept us working. In the time it took to write this book many of them have graduated, begun their careers, or returned to school for graduate studies. We wish them all well.

Our colleagues (here and around the world) have also made a substantial contribution to our thinking in shaping the third edition. Allen Schmidt deserves our undying gratitude for all of the thought and hard work he has put into this book. His unflagging optimism and clear vision make him a wonderful colleague. We are also thankful to our talented co-author Richard L. Baskerville. His clear and imaginative thinking has helped us throughout this project. Raymond J. Barnes also deserves hearty thanks. The contributions of our co-authors to this edition are many and remarkable on many different dimensions.

There are some very special people at Rutgers University-Camden who have supported us and encouraged us over the years, as well. We appreciate the help of Provost Walter K. Gordon and Dean Milton Leontiades.

We would like to thank John Fitzpatrick of ESI (Editorial Services of New England) for his dedicated work in keeping the project on track. We also give hearty thanks to Matt Tyndall, Kim McCabe, and John Lione for their inspiring and energetic art work. Thanks must go to our Editor, P.J. Boardman, for her thoughtful contribution to the project, and Alana Zdinak for her assistance with same.

Many of our reviewers, colleagues, and friends have been steady sources of inspiration throughout the writing of this book. They include Professors Nabil Adam, Ian O. Angell, David Avison, Srisakdi Charmonman, Roger Clark, Charles J. Coleman, Melissa Covelli, Gordon B. Davis, Gerry DeSanctis, Mark Dishaw, Dorothy G. Dologite, Bruce Fanning, Martha Grabowski, Paul Gray, Blake Ives, Dean James, Geoffrey Jones, Chin Kuo, Marian Kuras, Pentti Kerola, Oliver Karall, Han Chung Kwong, Deborah La Belle, Frank Land, Jonathan Liebenau, Ian McKillop, Bob Mockler, Enid Mumford, James Murphy, John Neter, Hans-Erik Nissen, Marc J. Schniederjans, Don Sherwood, Steve Smithson, Shelly Sofer, Malcolm Warner, and Clay Whybark.

Edward and Julia Kendall have demonstrated unwavering support, encouragement, and good humor throughout this project. We can scarcely repay them for all that they have given us. We are happy to dedicate this third edition to them.

1

ASSUMING THE ROLE
OF THE SYSTEMS ANALYST

INFORMATION AS AN ORGANIZATIONAL RESOURCE

Organizations have long recognized the importance of managing key resources such as labor and raw materials. Information has now moved to its rightful place as a key resource. Decision makers are beginning to understand that information is not just a by-product of conducting business; rather, it fuels business and can be the critical factor in determining the success or failure of a business.

Managing Information as a Resource

To maximize the usefulness of information, a business must manage it correctly, just as it manages other resources. Managers need to understand that costs are associated with the production, distribution, security, storage, and retrieval of all information. Although information is all around us, it is not free, and its strategic use for positioning a business competitively should not be taken for granted.

Managing Computer-Generated Information

The ready availability of computers has created an information explosion throughout society in general and business in particular. Managing computer-generated information differs in significant ways from handling manually produced data. Usually there is a greater quantity of computer information to administer. Costs of organizing and maintaining it can increase at alarming rates, and users often treat it less skeptically than information obtained in different ways. This chapter examines the fundamentals of different kinds of information systems, the varied roles of systems analysts, and the phases in the systems development life cycle, and, it introduces computer-assisted software engineering (CASE) tools.

SYSTEMS ANALYSIS AND DESIGN CONCEPTS

Information systems are developed for different purposes, depending on the needs of the business. Transaction processing systems (TPS) function at the operational level of the organization; office automation systems (OAS) and knowledge work systems (KWS) support work at the knowledge level. Higher-level systems include decision support systems (DSS) and management information systems (MIS). Expert systems apply the expertise of decision makers to solve specific, structured problems. On the strategic level of management we find executive support systems (ESS). Group decision support systems (GDSS) aid group-level decision making of a semistructured or unstructured variety.

Transaction Processing Systems

Transaction processing systems (TPS) are computerized information systems developed to process large amounts of data for routine business transactions such as payroll and inventory. TPS eliminate the tedium of necessary operational transactions and reduce the time once required to perform them manually, although people must still input data to computerized systems.

Transaction processing systems are boundary-spanning systems that permit the organization to interact with external environments. Because managers look to the data generated by the TPS for up-to-the-minute information about what is happening in their companies, it is essential to the day-to-day operations of business that these systems function smoothly and without interruption.

Office Automation Systems and Knowledge Work Systems

At the knowledge level of the organization are two classes of systems. Office automation systems (OAS) support data workers, who do not usually create new knowledge but rather use information for analysis to transform data or manipulate it in some way and then share it or formally disseminate it throughout the organization and, sometimes, beyond. Familiar aspects of OAS include word processing, spreadsheets, desktop publishing, electronic scheduling, and communication through voice mail, e-mail (electronic mail), and video conferencing.

Knowledge work systems (KWS) support professional workers such as scientists, engineers, and doctors by aiding them to create new knowledge and contribute it to their organization or to society at large.

Management Information Systems

Management information systems (MIS) do not replace transaction processing systems—rather, all MIS include transaction processing. MIS are computerized information systems that work because of the purposeful interaction between people and computers. By requiring people, software (computer programs), and hardware (computers, printers, etc.) to function in concert, management information systems support a broader spectrum of organizational tasks than transaction processing systems, including decision analysis and decision making.

In order to access information, users of the management information system share a common database. The database stores both data and models that help the user interpret and apply that data. Management information systems output information that is used in decision making. A management information system can also help unite some of the computerized information functions of a business, although it does not exist as a singular structure anywhere in the business.

Decision Support Systems

A higher-level class of computerized information systems is the decision support system (DSS). The DSS is similar to the traditional management information system in that they both depend on a database as a source of data. A decision support system departs from the traditional management information system in that it emphasizes the *support* of decision making in all of its phases, although the actual decision is still the exclusive province of the decision maker. Decision support systems are more closely tailored to the person or group using them than is a traditional management information system.

Expert Systems and Artificial Intelligence

Artificial intelligence (AI) can be considered the overarching field for expert systems. The general thrust of AI has been to develop machines that behave intelligently. Two avenues of research of AI are understanding natural language and analyzing the ability to reason through a problem to its logical conclusion. Expert systems use the approaches of AI reasoning to solve the problems put to them by business (and other) users.

Expert systems are a very special class of information system made practicable for use by business since the recent and widespread availability of hardware and software such as microcomputers and expert system shells. An expert system (also called a knowledge-based system) effectively captures and uses the knowledge of an expert for solving a particular problem experienced in an organization. Notice that unlike the DSS, which leaves the ultimate judgment to the decision maker, an expert system selects the best solution to a problem or a specific class of problems.

The basic components of an expert system are the knowledge base, an inference engine connecting the user with the system by processing queries via languages such as SQL (structured query language), and the user interface. People called knowledge engineers capture the expertise of experts, build a computer system in which to include expert knowledge, and then implement it. It is entirely possible that building and implementing expert systems will be the future work of many systems analysts.

The variety of information systems that analysts may develop are shown in Figure 1.1. Notice that the figure presents these systems from the bottom up, indicating that the operational, or lowest level of the organization, is supported by TPS, and the highest, or strategic level of semistructured and unstructured decisions, is supported by ESS at the top. This text uses the terms *management information system, information system, computerized information system,* and *computerized business information system* interchangeably to denote computerized information systems that support the broadest range of business activities through the information they produce.

Group Decision Support Systems

When groups need to work together to make semistructured or unstructured decisions, a group decision support system may afford a solution. Group decision support systems (GDSS) are used in special rooms equipped in a

FIGURE 1.1
A systems analyst may be
involved with any or all of
these systems.

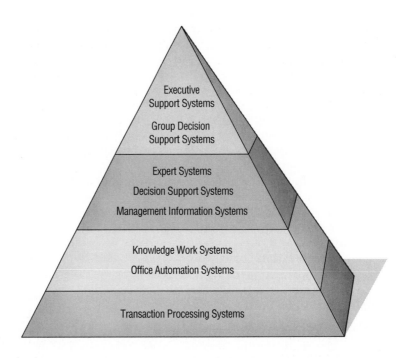

number of different configurations that permit group members to interact with electronic support—often in the form of specialized software—and a special group facilitator. Group decision support systems are intended to bring a group together to solve a problem with the help of various supports such as polling, questionnaires, brainstorming, and scenario creation. GDSS software can be designed to minimize typical negative group behaviors such as lack of participation due to fear of reprisal for expressing an unpopular or contested viewpoint, domination by vocal group members, and "group think" decision making. Sometimes GDSS are discussed under the more general term computer supported collaborative work (CSCW), which might include software support called "groupware" for team collaboration via networked computers.

Executive Support Systems

When executives turn to the computer, they are often looking for ways to help them make decisions on the strategic level. An executive support system (ESS) helps executives to organize their interactions with the external environment by providing graphics and communications support in accessible places such as boardrooms or personal corporate offices. Although ESS rely on the information generated by TPS and MIS, executive support systems help their users address unstructured decision problems, which are not application-specific, by creating an environment that is conducive to thinking about strategic problems in an informed way. ESS extend and support the capabilities of executives to make sense of their environments.

Need for Systems Analysis and Design

Systems analysis and design, as performed by systems analysts, seeks to systematically analyze data input or data flow, processing or transformation of data, data storage, and information output within the context of a particular business. Further, systems analysis and design is used to analyze, design, and implement improvements in the functioning of businesses that can be accomplished through the use of computerized information systems.

Installing a system without proper planning leads to great dissatisfaction and frequently causes the system to fall into disuse. Systems analysis and design lends structure to the analysis and design of information systems, a costly endeavor that might otherwise have been done in a haphazard way. It can be thought of as a series of processes systematically undertaken to improve a business through the use of computerized information systems. A large part of systems analysis and design involves working with current and eventual users of information systems.

End Users

Anyone who interacts with an information system in the context of his or her work in the organization can be called an *end user*. Over the years, the distinctions among users have become blurred. Further, any categories of users employed should not be thought of as exclusive.

However end users are classified, one fact about them remains pertinent to the systems analyst: Some kind of user involvement throughout the systems project is critical to the successful development of computerized information systems. Systems analysts, whose roles in the organization are discussed next, are the other essential component in developing useful information systems.

ROLE OF THE SYSTEMS ANALYST

The systems analyst systematically assesses how businesses function by examining the inputting and processing of data and the output of information with the intent of improving organizational processes. Many improvements involve better support of business functions through the use of computerized information systems. This definition emphasizes a systematic, methodical approach to analyzing, and potentially improving, what is occurring in the specific context created by a business.

Our definition of a systems analyst is necessarily broad. The analyst must be able to work with people of all descriptions and be experienced in working with computers. The analyst plays many roles, sometimes balancing several at the same time. The three primary roles of the systems analyst are: consultant, supporting expert, and agent of change.

Systems Analyst as a Consultant

The systems analyst frequently acts as a consultant to a business and thus may be hired specifically to address information systems issues within a business. This can be an advantage since outside consultants can bring with them a fresh perspective that other members of an organization do not possess. It also means that outside analysts are at a disadvantage because the true organizational culture can never be known to an outsider.

As an outside consultant, you will rely heavily on the systematic methods discussed throughout this text in order to analyze and design appropriate information systems for a particular business. Additionally, you will rely on information system users to help you understand the organizational culture from their viewpoints.

Systems Analyst as Supporting Expert

Another role that you may be required to play is that of supporting expert within a business where you are regularly employed in some systems capacity. In this role, the analyst draws on professional expertise concerning computer hardware and software and their uses in the business. This work is often not a full-blown systems project, but rather a small modification or decision affecting a single department.

As the support expert, you are not managing the project; you are merely serving as a resource for those who are. If you are a systems analyst employed by a manufacturing or service organization, many of your daily activities may be encompassed by this role.

Systems Analyst as Agent of Change

The most comprehensive and responsible role that the systems analyst takes on is that of agent of change, whether internal or external to the business. As an analyst, you are an agent of change whenever you perform any of the activities in the systems development life cycle (discussed in the next section) and are present in the business for an extended period of time (from two weeks all the way to more than a year). An agent of change can be defined as a person who serves as a catalyst for change, develops a plan for change, and works with others in facilitating that change.

Your presence in the business changes it. As a systems analyst, you must recognize this fact and use it as a starting point for your analysis. This is why you must interact with users and management (if they are not one and the same) from the very beginning of your project. Without their help, you cannot understand what is happening in an organization, and real change cannot take place.

If change (that is, improvements to the business that can be realized through information systems) seems warranted after analysis, the next step is to develop a plan for change along with the people who must enact the changes. Once a consensus is reached on the change to be made, you must constantly interact with those who are changing. You facilitate change by using your expertise with humans as well as with computers to bring about their integration in a human-machine information system.

As a systems analyst acting as an agent of change, you advocate a particular avenue of change involving the use of information systems. Additionally, you teach users the process of change, because you are aware that changes in the information system do not occur independently but cause changes in the rest of the organization as well.

Qualities of the Systems Analyst

From the foregoing descriptions of the roles the systems analyst plays, it is easy to see that the successful systems analyst must possess a wide range of qualities. Many different kinds of people are systems analysts, so any description is destined to fall short in some way. However, there are some qualities that most systems analysts seem to display.

Above all, the analyst is a problem solver. He or she is a person who views the analysis of problems as a challenge and who enjoys devising workable solutions. When necessary, the analyst must be able to systemati-

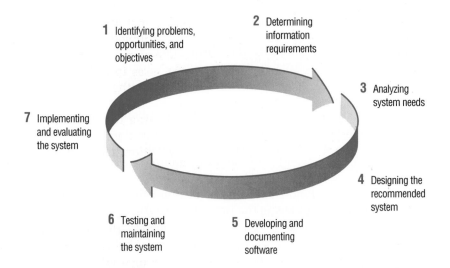

FIGURE 1.2
The seven phases of the
systems development life
cycle.

cally tackle the situation at hand through skillful application of tools, techniques, and experience. The analyst must also be a communicator capable of relating meaningfully to other people over extended periods of time. Systems analysts need enough computer experience to program, to understand the capabilities of computers, to glean information requirements from users, and to communicate what is needed to programmers.

The systems analyst must be a self-disciplined, self-motivated individual able to manage and coordinate innumerable project resources, including other people. Systems analysis is a demanding career but, in compensation, an ever-changing and always challenging one.

THE SYSTEMS DEVELOPMENT LIFE CYCLE

Throughout this chapter, we have referred to the systematic approach analysts take to the analysis and design of information systems. Much of this is embodied in what is called the *systems development life cycle* (SDLC). The SDLC is a phased approach to analysis and design which holds that systems are best developed through the use of a specific cycle of analyst and user activities.

Analysts disagree on exactly how many phases there are in the systems development life cycle but generally laud its organized approach. Here we have divided the cycle into seven phases, as shown in Figure 1.2. Although each phase is presented discretely, it is never accomplished as a separate step. Instead, several activities can occur simultaneously, and activities may be repeated. That is why it is more useful to think of the SDLC as accomplished in phases (with activities in full swing overlapping with others, and then tapering off) and not in separate steps.

Identifying Problems, Opportunities, and Objectives

In this first phase of the systems development life cycle, the analyst is concerned with identifying problems, opportunities, and objectives. This stage is critical to the success of the rest of the project, since no one wants to waste subsequent time addressing the wrong problem.

The first phase requires that the analyst look honestly at what is occurring in a business. Then, together with other organizational members, the analyst pinpoints problems. Often, these will be brought up by others, and they are the reason the analyst was initially called in.

Opportunities are situations that the analyst believes can be improved through the use of computerized information systems. Seizing opportunities may allow the business to gain a competitive edge or set an industry standard.

Identifying objectives is also an important component of the first phase. First, the analyst must discover what the business is trying to do. Then the analyst will be able to see if some aspect of information systems applications can help the business reach its objectives by addressing specific problems or opportunities.

The people involved in the first phase are the users, analysts, and systems managers coordinating the project. Activities in this phase consist of interviewing user management, summarizing the knowledge obtained, estimating the scope of the project, and documenting the results. The output of this phase is a feasibility report containing a problem definition and summarizing the objectives. Management must then make a decision whether to proceed with the proposed project. If the user group does not have sufficient funds in their budget, desires to tackle unrelated problems, or the problems do not require a computer system, a manual solution may be recommended, and the systems project does not proceed any further.

Determining Information Requirements

The next phase that the analyst enters is that of determining information requirements for the particular users involved. Among the tools used to define information requirements in the business are: sampling and investigating hard data, interviewing, questionnaires, observing decision makers' behavior and office environments, and even prototyping.

In this phase, the analyst is striving to understand what information users need to perform their jobs. You can see that several of the methods for determining information requirements involve interacting directly with users. This phase serves to fill in the picture that the analyst has of the organization and its objectives. Sometimes only the first two phases of the systems development life cycle are completed. This kind of study may have a different purpose and is typically carried out by a specialist called an information analyst (IA).

The people involved in this phase are the analysts and users, typically operations managers and operations workers. The systems analyst needs to know the details of current system functions: who (the people who are involved), what (the business activity), where (the environment in which the work takes place), when (the timing), and how (how the current procedures are performed) of the business under study. The analyst must then ask why the business uses the current system. There may be good reasons for doing business using the current methods, and these should be considered when designing any new system.

However, if the reason for current operations is "It's always been done that way," the analyst may wish to improve on the procedures. Business process reengineering may be of help in framing an approach for rethinking the business in a creative way. At the completion of this phase, the analyst should understand how the business functions and have complete information on the people, goals, data, and procedures involved.

Analyzing System Needs

The next phase that the systems analyst undertakes involves analyzing system needs. Again, special tools and techniques help the analyst make requirements determinations. One such tool is the use of data flow diagrams to chart the input, processes, and output of the business's functions in a structured graphical form. From the data flow diagrams, a data dictionary is developed that lists all of the data items used in the system, as well as their specifications—whether they are alphanumeric and how much space they take up when printed.

During this phase the systems analyst also analyzes the structured decisions made. Structured decisions are those for which the conditions, condition alternatives, actions, and action rules can be determined. There are three major methods for analysis of structured decisions: structured English, decision tables, and decision trees.

Not all decisions in organizations are structured, but it is still important for the systems analyst to understand them. Semistructured decisions (decisions made under risk) are often supported by decision support systems. When analyzing semistructured decisions, the analyst examines the decisions based on the degree of decision-making skill required, the degree of problem complexity, and the number of criteria considered when the decision is made.

Analysis of multiple-criteria decisions (decisions where many factors must be balanced) is also part of this phase. Many techniques are available for analyzing multiple-criteria decisions, including the tradeoff process and the use of weighting methods.

At this point in the systems development life cycle, the systems analyst prepares a systems proposal that summarizes what has been found, provides cost/benefit analyses of alternatives, and makes recommendations on what (if anything) should be done. If one of the recommendations is acceptable to management, the analyst proceeds along that course. Each systems problem is unique, and there is never just one correct solution. The manner in which a recommendation or solution is formulated depends on the individual qualities and professional training of each analyst.

Designing the Recommended System

In this phase of the systems development life cycle, the systems analyst uses the information collected earlier to accomplish the logical design of the information system. The analyst designs accurate data-entry procedures so that data going into the information system are correct. In addition, the analyst also provides for effective input to the information system by using techniques of good form and screen design.

Part of the logical design of the information system is devising the user interface. The interface connects the user with the system and is thus extremely important. Examples of user interfaces include a keyboard to type in questions and answers, on-screen menus to elicit user commands, and a mouse to select options.

The design phase also includes designing files or databases that will store much of the data needed by decision makers in the organization. A well-organized database is the basis for all information systems. In this phase the analyst also works with users to design output (either on-screen or printed) that meets their information needs.

Lastly, the analyst must design controls and backup procedures to protect the system and the data and produce program specification packets for programmers. Each packet should contain input and output layouts, file specifications, and processing details, and it may also include decision trees or tables, data flow diagrams, a system flowchart, and the names and functions of any prewritten code routines.

Developing and Documenting Software

In the fifth phase of the systems development life cycle, the analyst works with programmers to develop any original software that is needed. Some of the structured techniques for designing and documenting software include structure charts, the HIPO method, flowcharts, Nassi-Shneiderman charts, Warnier-Orr diagrams, and pseudocode. The systems analyst uses one or more of these devices to communicate to the programmer what needs to be programmed.

During this phase, the analyst also works with users to develop effective documentation for software, including procedure manuals. Documentation tells users how to use software and also what to do if software problems occur.

Programmers have a key role in this phase as they design, code, and remove syntactical errors from computer programs. If the program is to run in a mainframe environment, job control language (JCL) must be created. To ensure quality, a programmer may conduct either a design or a code walkthrough, explaining complex portions of the program to a team of other programmers.

Testing and Maintaining the System

Before the information system can be used, it must be tested. It is much less costly to catch problems before the system is signed over to users. Some of the testing is completed by programmers alone, some of it by systems analysts in conjunction with programmers. A series of tests to pinpoint problems is run first with sample data and eventually with actual data from the current system.

Maintenance of the system and its documentation begins in this phase and is carried out routinely throughout the life of the information system. Much of the programmer's routine work consists of maintenance, and businesses spend a great deal of money on maintenance. Many of the systematic procedures the analyst employs throughout the systems development life cycle can help ensure that maintenance is kept to a minimum.

Implementing and Evaluating the System

In this last phase of system development, the analyst helps implement the information system. This involves training users to handle the system. Some training is done by vendors, but oversight of training is the responsibility of the systems analyst. Additionally, the analyst needs to plan for a smooth conversion from the old system to the new one. This process includes converting files from old formats to new ones or building a database, installing equipment, and bringing the new system into production.

Evaluation is shown as part of this final phase of the systems development life cycle mostly for the sake of discussion. Actually, evaluation

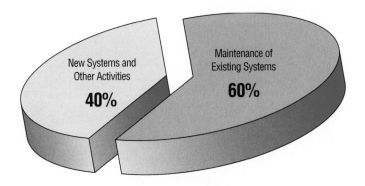

takes place during every phase. A key criterion that must be satisfied is whether the intended users are indeed using the system.

It should be noted that systems work is often cyclical. When an analyst finishes one phase of system development and proceeds to the next, the discovery of a problem may force the analyst to return to the previous phase and modify the work done there. For example, during the testing phase, the programmer may discover that the program does not work correctly, either because code was not written to support certain portions of the system design or the design was incomplete. In either event, the programs must be modified, and the analyst may have to change some of the system design materials. In turn, this may necessitate that the analyst meet with the user and reinvestigate how a specific business activity functions.

The Impact of Maintenance

After the system is installed, it must be maintained, meaning that the computer programs must be modified and kept up-to-date. Figure 1.3 illustrates the average amount of time spent on maintenance at a typical MIS installation. Estimates of the time spent by departments on maintenance have ranged from 48 to 60 percent of the total time spent developing systems.[1] Very little time remains for new system development. As the number of programs written increases, so does the amount of maintenance they require.

Maintenance is performed for two reasons. The first of these is to correct software errors. No matter how thoroughly the system is tested, bugs or errors creep into computer programs. Bugs in commercial microcomputer software are often documented as "known anomalies" and corrected when new versions of the software are released or in an interim release. In customized software, bugs must be corrected as they are detected.

The other reason for performing system maintenance is to enhance the software's capabilities in response to changing organizational needs, generally involving one of the following three situations:

1. *Users often request additional features after they become familiar with the computer system and its capabilities.* These requested features may be as simple as displaying additional totals on a report or as complicated as developing new software.

2. *The business changes over time.* Software must be modified to encompass such changes as new government or corporate reporting

1 S. Yoo and K. E. Kendall. "Pseudocode-Box Diagrams: An Approach to More Understandable, Productive, and Adaptable Software Design and Coding," *International Journal on Policy and Information,* Vol. 12, No. 1, June, 1988, pp. 39–51.

FIGURE 1.4
Resource consumption over
the system life.

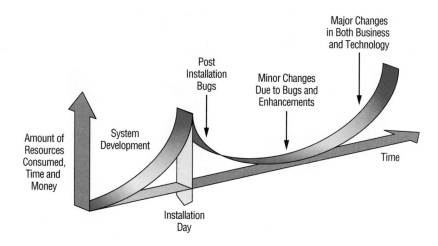

requirements arise, new client information needs to be produced,
and so on.

3. *Hardware and software are changing at an accelerated pace.* A system that uses older technology may be modified to use the capabilities of newer technology. An example of such a change is replacing a
mainframe terminal with a microcomputer workstation or a microcomputer with a desktop computer.

Figure 1.4 illustrates the amount of resources—usually time and money—
spent on system development and maintenance. The area under the curve
represents the total dollar amount spent. You can see that over time the
total cost of maintenance is likely to exceed that of system development.
At a certain point, it becomes more feasible to perform a new systems
study, since the cost of continued maintenance is clearly greater than that
of creating an entirely new information system.

In summary, maintenance is an ongoing process over the life cycle of
an information system. After the information system is installed, maintenance usually takes the form of correcting previously undetected program
errors. Once these are corrected, the system approaches a steady state, providing dependable service to its users. Maintenance during this period may
consist of removing a few previously undetected bugs and updating the system with a few minor enhancements. However, as time goes on and the business and technology change, the maintenance effort increases dramatically.

USING CASE TOOLS

Throughout this book we emphasize the need for a systematic, thorough
approach to the analysis, design, and implementation of information systems. We recognize that in order to be productive, systems analysts must
be organized, accurate, and complete in what they set out to do. Within the
last few years, analysts have begun to benefit from new productivity tools
that have been created explicitly to improve their routine work through the
use of automated support. These are called CASE tools for Computer
Aided Software Engineering tools. One popular CASE package is
Excelerator. Because it is microcomputer-based rather than limited to a
mainframe as its predecessors of the 1970s were, Excelerator has become
the cornerstone of many analysts' work.

Analysts rely on CASE tools to increase productivity, communicate more effectively with users, and integrate the work that they do on the system from the beginning to the end of the life cycle.

Increasing Analyst Productivity

Excelerator allows its users to draw and modify diagrams easily. By our definition, the analyst can thus become more productive simply by reducing the considerable time typically spent in manually drawing and redrawing data flow diagrams until they are acceptable.

A tools package such as Excelerator, XperCASE, or Visible Analyst also enhances group productivity by allowing analysts to share work easily with other team members, who can simply access the file on their microcomputer and review or modify what has been done. This reduces the time necessary to reproduce and distribute data flow diagrams among team members. It further allows members of the systems analysis team to work with the diagrams whenever they have the time rather than mandating a strict distribution and feedback response schedule.

CASE tools also facilitate interaction among team members by making diagramming a dynamic, iterative process rather than one in which changes are cumbersome and therefore tend to become a drain on productivity. In this instance, the CASE tool for drawing and recording data flow diagrams affords a record of the team's changing thinking regarding data flows.

Improving Analyst-User Communication

In order for the proposed system to come into being and actually be used, excellent communication among analysts and users throughout the systems development life cycle is essential. The success of the eventual system implementation rests on the capability of analysts and users to communicate in a meaningful way. So far, it has been the experience of analysts currently using the new CASE tools that their use fosters greater, more meaningful communication among users and analysts.

PROVIDING A MEANS OF COMMUNICATION. Analysts and users alike report that CASE tools afford them a means of communication about the system during its conceptualization, as shown in Figure 1.5. Through the use of automated support featuring on-screen output, clients can readily see how data flows and other system concepts are depicted and request corrections or changes that would have taken too much time with a manual system.

Whether a particular diagram will be adjudged useful by users or analysts at the end of the project is questionable. What is important is that such automated support for many life cycle design activities (often imperceptibly to users) serves as a means to an end by acting as a catalyst for analyst-user interaction. The same arguments used to support CASE tools' role in increasing productivity are equally valid in this arena: That is, the manual tasks of drawing, reproducing, and distributing take much less time, and so work in progress can be shared more easily with users.

Integrating Life Cycle Activities

The third reason for using CASE tools is to integrate activities and provide continuity from one phase to the next throughout the systems development life cycle.

FIGURE 1.5
Analysts can improve their
communication with users
with the help of computer-
generated diagrams.

CASE tools are especially useful when a particular phase of the life cycle requires several iterations of feedback and modification. Recall that user involvement is important during all phases. Integration of activities through the underlying use of workbench technologies makes it easier for users to understand how all of the life cycle phases are interrelated and interdependent.

Accurately Assessing Maintenance Changes

The fourth and possibly one of the most important reasons for using CASE tools is that they enable users to analyze and assess the impact of maintenance changes. For example, the size of an element such as a customer number may need to be made larger. The CASE tool will cross-reference every screen, report, and file within which the element is used, leading to a comprehensive maintenance plan.

UPPER AND LOWER CASE

CASE tools are classified as lower CASE, upper CASE, and integrated CASE, which combines both upper and lower CASE in one toolset. Although experts disagree about what precisely constitutes an upper CASE tool versus a lower CASE tool, it might be helpful to conceptualize upper CASE tools according to whom they support. Upper CASE tools primarily help analysts and designers. Lower CASE tools are used more often by programmers and workers who must implement the systems designed via upper CASE tools. Figure 1.6 lists some of the more popular CASE tools.

Upper CASE Tools

An upper CASE tool allows the analyst to create and modify the system design. All the information about the project is stored in an encyclopedia

FIGURE 1.6
Selected CASE tools.

Corporation	Product Name	Type of CASE Tool
Al Lee & Associates	Magec	Lower CASE
Anderson Consulting	Foundation	Integrated CASE
Cadre Technologies, Inc.	Teamwork	Upper CASE
CGI Systems, Inc.	PacBase	Integrated CASE
Computer Systems Advisers Inc.	POSE	Upper CASE
Intersolv	Excelerator	Upper CASE
	APS	Lower CASE
KnowledgeWare, Inc.	Application Development Workbench (ADW)	Integrated CASE
	Information Engineering Workbench (IEW)	Integrated CASE
Siemens AG	XperCASE	Integrated CASE
Synon, Inc.	Synon	Integrated CASE
System Software Associates, Inc.	AS/SET	Lower CASE
Texas Instruments	Information Engineering Facility (IEF)	Integrated CASE
Visible Systems Corp.	Visible Analyst	Upper CASE
Yourdon, Inc.	Analyst/Designer Toolkit	Upper CASE

called the CASE repository, a large collection of records, elements, diagrams, screens, reports, and other information, illustrated in Figure 1.7. Analysis reports may be produced using the repository information to show where the design is incomplete or contains errors.

Upper CASE tools can also help support the modeling of an organization's functional requirements, assist analysts and users in drawing the boundaries for a given project, and help them visualize how the project meshes with other parts of the organization. Additionally, some upper CASE tools can support prototyping of screen and report designs.

Lower CASE Tools

Lower CASE tools are used to generate computer source code, eliminating the need for programming the system. Code generation has several advantages:

1. The system may be produced more quickly than by writing computer programs. However, becoming familiar with the methodology used by the code generator often takes a great deal of time, so program generation may initially be slower. Additionally, the design must be thoroughly entered into the toolset, which may require a lengthy period of time.

2. The amount of time spent on maintenance decreases with code generation. There is no need to modify, test, and debug computer programs. Instead, the CASE design is modified, and the code is regenerated. Decreased time spent on maintenance results in more time to develop new systems and helps to relieve a backlog of projects under consideration for development.

3. Code may be generated in more than one computer language, so it is easier to migrate systems from one platform, such as a mainframe, to another, perhaps a microcomputer. For example, Excelerator can generate code in COBOL, C, BASIC, and PL/1 using the same repository.

FIGURE 1.7
The repository concept.

```
        ADD CUSTOMER

  NUMBER  XXXXXX

  NAME    XXXXXXXXXXX
  STREET  XXXXXXXXXXX
  CITY    XXXXXXXXXXX
  STATE   XX
  ZIP     XXXXX-XXXX
```

```
      SALES ANALYSIS REPORT
        ITEM          TOTAL
     DESCRIPTION      SALES
  XXXXXXXXXXXXX      ZZ,ZZ9
  XXXXXXXXXXXXX      ZZ,ZZ9
  XXXXXXXXXXXXX      ZZ,ZZ9
  XXXXXXXXXXXXX      ZZ,ZZ9
  XXXXXXXXXXXXX      ZZ,ZZ9
  XXXXXXXXXXXXX      ZZ,ZZ9
```

Screen and report design

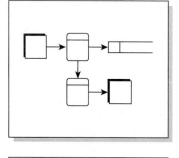 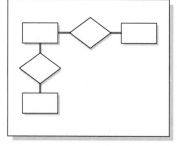

System Diagrams and Models

```
Item = Number +
       Description +
       Cost +
       Price +
       Quantity on hand +
       Quantity on  order +
       Reorder point +
       Monthly sales +
       Year to date sales
```

```
DO WHILE NOT End of file
   Read Item record
   IF Item is low in stock
      Print Purchase Order
      Update Item record
   ENDIF
ENDDO
```

Data Dictionary and Process Logic

System Requirements
• Add new customers
• Identify fast and slow selling items
• Enter customer orders
• Look up customer credit balance
• Maintain adequate inventory

Deliverables
• Add customer screen
• Item Analysis Report
• Customer order entry screen
• Customer inquiry screen
• Vendor purchase order program
• Seasonal forecasting

Project Management

4. Code generation provides a cost-effective way of tailoring systems purchased from third-party vendors to the needs of the organization. Often, modifying purchased software requires such great effort that the cost of doing so exceeds that of the software. With code generation software, purchasing CASE design and repository for the application enables the analyst to modify the design and generate the revised computer system.

5. Generated code is free of computer program errors. The only potential errors are design errors, which may be minimized by running CASE analysis reports to ensure that the system design is complete and correct.

Figure 1.8 illustrates the traditional systems development life cycle and the CASE life cycle. Notice that the program coding, testing, and debugging portions of the cycle are eliminated from the CASE life cycle.

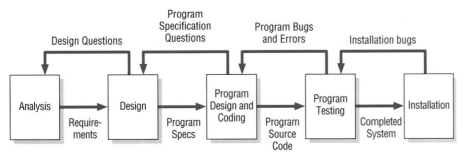

Traditional Systems Development Life Cycle

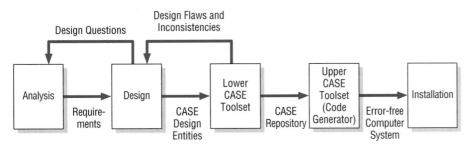

CASE Systems Development Life Cycle

FIGURE 1.8
Traditional versus CASE systems development life cycles.

SOFTWARE REVERSE ENGINEERING AND REENGINEERING

Software reverse engineering and reengineering are methods for extending the life of older programs, called legacy software. Both approaches use CARE (Computer Assisted Reengineering) software to analyze and restructure existing computer code. Several reverse engineering toolsets are available. These are summarized in Figure 1.9.

Note the term *reengineering* is used in a number of different engineering, programming, and business contexts. Often, it is used to mean "business process reengineering," which is a way of reorienting an organization around key processes. Systems analysts can play an important role in business process reengineering, since many of the necessary changes are possible only because of the availability of innovative information technology. Many analysts are now being educated in ways to facilitate organizational change.

Reverse engineering is the opposite of code generation. The computer source code is examined, analyzed, and converted into repository entities, as illustrated in Figure 1.10. The first step in software reverse engineering is to

Corporation	Product Name
Bachman Information Systems, Inc.	Analyst Capture
Cadre Technologies, Inc.	Teamwork
CGI Systems, Inc.	PacReverse
Intersolv	XL Recover
	Design Recovery
Siemens AG	XperCASE

FIGURE 1.9
Selected reverse engineering tools.

FIGURE 1.10
Reverse engineering
concepts.

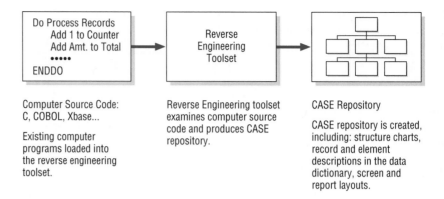

Computer Source Code:
C, COBOL, Xbase...

Existing computer
programs loaded into
the reverse engineering
toolset.

Reverse Engineering toolset
examines computer source
code and produces CASE
repository.

CASE Repository

CASE repository is created,
including: structure charts,
record and element
descriptions in the data
dictionary, screen and
report layouts.

load existing computer programs' code as written in COBOL, C, or another high-level language into the toolset. Depending on the reverse engineering toolset used, the code is analyzed and the toolset produces some or all of the following:

1. Data structures and elements, describing the files and records stored by the system.
2. Screen designs, if the program is on line.
3. Report layouts for batch programs.
4. A structure chart showing the hierarchy of the modules in the program.
5. Database design and relationships.

The design stored in the repository may be modified or incorporated into other CASE project information. When all the modifications are complete, the new system code may be regenerated. Reengineering refers to the complete process of converting program code to the CASE design, modifying the design, and regenerating the new program code.

The advantages of using a reverse engineering toolset are numerous:

1. The time required for system maintenance is reduced, freeing up time for new development.
2. Documentation, which may have been nonexistent or minimal for older programs, is produced.
3. Structured programs are created from unstructured or loosely structured computer code.
4. Future maintenance changes are easier to make, since changes may be made at the design level rather than the code level.
5. Analysis may be performed on the system to eliminate unused portions of computer code that may exist in older programs although it was made obsolete by revisions of the program throughout the years.

OBJECT-ORIENTED SYSTEMS ANALYSIS AND DESIGN

A new and very different approach to systems analysis and design is object-oriented (O-O) systems analysis and design. Object-oriented techniques, which are based on object-oriented programming concepts, can help respond to organizational demands for new systems that must undergo continuous maintenance, adaptation, and redesign. Basically, in object-oriented programming, objects are created that include not only code about data, but also instructions about the operations to be performed on it.

Using the Coad and Yourdon approach to O-O analysis, we employ a five-layer model consisting of: (1) the class/object layer, (2) the structure layer, (3) the attribute layer, (4) the service layer, and (5) the subject layer. Object-oriented analysis and design can be thought of as the development and assembly of these five layers into one all-encompassing design package. The design activities are grouped into the four major components of the final system: the problem component, the human interface component, the data management component, and the task management component.

Operational prototypes (discussed in Chapter 8) are frequently used during the design phase. Chapter 22 provides a practical explanation of object-oriented analysis and design which takes the structured analysis and design presented in the preceding twenty-one chapters as its point of departure.

NEED FOR STRUCTURED ANALYSIS AND DESIGN

Structured analysis and design provides a systematic approach to designing and building quality computer systems. Throughout the phases of analysis and design, the analyst should proceed step by step, obtaining feedback from users and analyzing the design for omissions and errors. Moving too quickly to the next phase may require that the analyst return to rework earlier portions of the design.

Figure 1.11 illustrates the cost of correcting an error detected in each of the phases. Notice that considerably more effort is required to correct an error in each succeeding phase. For example, suppose several elements were omitted when the analyst was examining the details of the data used within the system. If the analyst learned that these elements were missing after programs were written, the file, report, and screen layouts would have to be modified, as would the test data files, programs, and documentation. These corrections might take 100 hours, whereas, adding them to design materials and programs had the elements been part of the original design, at the outset might have taken only 4 hours. Look for suggestions throughout the following chapters that indicate where analysis should take place and how to determine whether the systems design is accurate and complete.

Analysts have at their disposal a number of microcomputer software tools that may be used to assist them in the development of systems. In addition to CASE and reverse engineering tools, the following may be used at various parts of the analysis and design life cycle: management software to optimize the allocation of people and project resources; prototyping software to rapidly create screens and reports for users to review and modify; form design tools to help design forms or source documents; and graphics and presentation software to assist in creating illustrations and producing a professional presentation to users.

ALTERNATIVE METHODOLOGIES

Although this text focuses on the most widely used approach in practice, there will be times when the analyst recognizes that the organization could benefit from the use of an alternative approach. Perhaps a systems

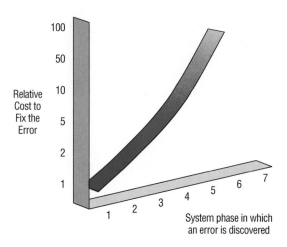

FIGURE 1.11
Cost to fix an error and the
phase where the error is
detected.

project using a structured approach has recently failed, or perhaps the organizational subcultures, comprised of several different user groups, seem more in step with an alternative method. We cannot do justice to these methods in a small space; each deserves and has inspired its own books and research. However, by mentioning these approaches here we hope to help you become aware that under certain circumstances, your organization may want to consider an alternative or supplement to structured analysis and design and the systems development life cycle.

Among the most popular alternatives are: prototyping, (distinct from the prototyping we discuss in Chapter 8) ETHICS, the project champion approach, Soft Systems Methodology, and Multiview. Prototyping, established in other disciplines and applied to IS, was offered as a response to the long development times associated with the systems development life cycle approach and to the uncertainty often surrounding user requirements. ETHICS was introduced as a sociotechnical methodology combining social and technical solutions. The project champions approach, a concept borrowed from marketing, adopts the strategy of involving one key person from each area affected by the system to ensure the system's success. Soft Systems Methodology was envisioned as a way to model a world that is often chaotic by using "rich pictures," ideographs that capture characteristic organizational narratives. Multiview was proposed as a way to organize and use elements of several competing methodologies.

SUMMARY

Information can be viewed as an organizational resource. As such, it must be managed carefully, just as other resources are. The availability of affordable computer power to organizations has meant an explosion of information, and consequently more attention must be paid to coping with the information generated.

All computerized information systems have as their basis a database that stores data necessary to support business functions. A transaction processing system (TPS) supports large-volume, routine business transactions such as payroll and inventory. Office automation systems (OAS) support data workers who use word processing, spreadsheets and so on to analyze, transform, or manipulate data. Knowledge work systems (KWS) support professionals such as scientists and engineers who create new knowledge. Management information systems (MIS) are computerized information systems that support a broader range of business functions than do transaction processing systems. Most often, MIS output reports to decision makers. Decision support systems (DSS) are information systems whose output is tailored to their users and which help support decision makers in making semistructured decisions. Expert systems capture the expertise of decision makers for use in solving a problem or a class of problems. Group decision support systems (GDSS) bring together group members in special electronic settings to help groups solve semistructured or unstructured problems. Executive support systems (ESS) help executives organize their interactions with the external environment by providing graphics and communications support in accessible locations.

Systems analysis and design is a systematic approach to identifying problems, opportunities, objectives, analyzing the information flows in organizations, and designing computerized information systems to solve a problem. As information proliferates, a systematic, planned approach to the introduction, modification, and maintenance of information systems is essential. Systems analysis and design provides this.

Systems analysts are required to take on many roles in the course of their work. Some of these roles are: (1) outside consultant to business, (2) supporting expert within a business, and (3) agent of change in both internal and external situations.

Analysts possess a wide range of skills. First and foremost, the analyst is a problem solver, someone who enjoys the challenge of analyzing a problem and devising a workable solution. Systems analysts require communication skills that allow them to relate meaningfully to many different kinds of people on a daily basis, as well as computer skills. End-user involvement is critical to their success.

Analysts proceed systematically. The framework for their systematic approach is provided in what is called the systems development life cycle (SDLC). This can be divided into seven sequential phases, although in reality the phases are interrelated and often are accomplished simultaneously. The seven phases are: identifying problems, opportunities, and objectives; determining information requirements; analyzing system needs; designing the recommended system; developing and documenting software; testing and maintaining the system; and implementing and evaluating the system.

Automated, microcomputer-based software packages for systems analysis and design are called CASE tools. The four reasons for adopting CASE tools are increasing analyst productivity, improving communication among analysts and users, integrating life cycle activities, and analyzing and assessing the impact of maintenance changes.

Analysts also use CARE (Computer Assisted Reengineering) approaches to do software reverse engineering and reengineering to extend the life of legacy software.

A new and different approach to systems analysis and design is object-oriented (O-O) systems analysis and design. These techniques are based on object-oriented programming concepts in which objects that are created include not only code about data, but also instructions about the operations to be performed on it.

When the organizational situation demands it, the analyst may depart from the SDLC to try an alternative methodology such as prototyping,

"Welcome to Maple Ridge Engineering, what we call MRE. We hope you'll enjoy serving as a systems consultant for us. Although I've worked here five years in different capacities, I've just been reassigned to serve as an administrative aide to Snowden Evans, the head of the new Training and Management Systems Department. We're certainly a diverse group. As you make your way through the company, be sure to use all of your skills, both technical and people-oriented, to understand who we are, and to identify the problems and conflicts that you think should be solved regarding our information systems.

"To bring you up to date, let me say that Maple Ridge Engineering is a medium-sized medical engineering company. Last year, our revenues exceeded $287 million. We employ about 335 people. There are about 150 administrative employees, management and clerical staff like myself; approximately 75 professional employees, including engineers, physicians, and systems analysts; and about 110 trade employees, such as draftsmen and technicians.

"There are four offices: You will visit us through HyperCase in our home office in Maple Ridge, Tennessee. We have three other branches in the southern United States as well: Atlanta, Georgia; Charlotte, North Carolina, and New Orleans, Louisiana. We'd love to have you visit when you're in the area.

"For now, if operating in a hypertext environment is a new experience for you, you may want to click the mouse on the rectangle labeled Run Tutorial on your HyperCase screen. The tutorial explains the basics about how hypertext material is linked together and how to navigate through it.

"To learn more about Maple Ridge Engineering as a company, or to find out how to interview our employees, who will use the systems you design, and how to observe their offices in our company, you may want to start by clicking your mouse on the rectangle labeled Case Introduction for an overview of who we are and some hints on how to quickly begin your consulting experience. To skip all of that and start consulting immediately, click the mouse on the rectangle labeled MRE Reception or read more about HyperCase in Chapter 2."

The MRE example is on the HyperCase disk that is affixed to the back cover of your book. It was designed to run on any IBM PC-compatible machine, 286 or higher. Insert the diskette into your PC. At the A:\> prompt, type INSTALL and then press ENTER.

ETHICS, the project Champion approach, Soft Systems Methodology, or Multiview.

KEYWORDS AND PHRASES

computer-generated information

transaction processing systems (TPS)

management information systems (MIS)

office automation systems (OAS)

knowledge work systems (KWS)

decision support systems (DSS)

artificial intelligence (AI)

expert systems

computer-generated	maintenance
executive support systems (ESS)	code generation
group decision support	migrate systems
systems (GDSS)	software reverse engineering
groupware	reengineering
systems analysis and design	CARE (Computer Assisted
systems analyst	Reengineering)
systems consultant	legacy software
supporting expert	object-oriented systems
agent of change	analysis and design
systems development life	ETHICS
cycle (SDLC)	Multiview
CASE tools	Prototyping
program specifications packet	Soft Systems Methodology
CASE repository	Project Champions

REVIEW QUESTIONS

1. Describe why information is most usefully thought of as an organizational resource rather than as an organizational by-product.
2. Define what is meant by a transaction processing system.
3. Explain the difference between office automation systems (OAS) and knowledge work systems (KWS).
4. Compare the definition of a management information system (MIS) to the definition of a decision support system (DSS).
5. Define the term *expert systems*. How do expert systems differ from decision support systems?
6. List the problems of group interaction that group decision support systems (GDSS) were designed to address.
7. List the advantages of using systems analysis and design techniques in approaching computerized information systems for business.
8. List three roles that the systems analyst is called upon to play. Provide a definition for each.
9. What personal qualities are helpful to the systems analyst? List them.
10. List and briefly define the seven phases of the systems development life cycle (SDLC).
11. Define software reverse engineering and reengineering as they apply to CARE (Computer Assisted Reengineering).
12. List the four reasons for adopting CASE tools.
13. Define the term *object-oriented systems analysis and design*.

SELECTED BIBLIOGRAPHY

Alavi, M. "An Assessment of the Prototyping Approach to Information Systems." *Communications of the ACM,* Vol. 26, No. 6, June 1984, pp. 556–563.

Avison, D. E. and A. T. Wood-Harper. *Multiview: An Exploration in Information Systems Development.* Oxford: Blackwell Scientific Publications, 1990.

Beath, C. M. "Supporting the Information Technology Champion." *MIS Quarterly,* Vol. 15, No. 3, September 1991, pp. 355–372.

Checkland, P. B. "Soft Systems Methodology." *Human Systems Management,* Vol. 8, No. 4, 1989, pp. 271–289.

Checkland, P. B. *Systems Thinking, Systems Practice.* Chichester, U.K.: John Wiley, 1981.

Coad, P. and E. Yourdon. *Object-Oriented Analysis,* 2nd ed. Englewood Cliffs, NJ: Yourdon, 1991.

Davis, G. B. and M. H. Olson. *Management Information Systems: Conceptual Foundation, Structure, and Development,* 2nd ed. New York. McGraw-Hill Book Company, 1985.

Holsapple, C. W. and A. B. Whinston. *Business Expert Systems.* Homewood, IL: Irwin, 1987.

Jackson, M. A. *Systems Development.* Englewood Cliffs, NJ: Prentice-Hall, 1983.

Kendall, K. E. "Behavioral Implications for Systems Analysis and Design: Prospects for the Nineties." *Journal of Management Systems,* Vol. 3, No. 1, 1991, pp. 1–4.

Laudon, K. C. and J. P. Laudon. *Management Information Systems,* 3rd ed. New York: McGraw-Hill Book Company, 1994.

Mumford, E. and M. Weir. *Computer Systems in Work Design—the ETHICS Method.* Associated Business Press, London, 1979.

Naumann, J. D. and A. M. Jenkins. "Prototyping. The New Paradigm for Systems Development." *MIS Quarterly,* Vol. 6, No. 3, September 1982, pp. 29–44.

Whitten, J. L. , L. D. Bentley and V. M. Barlow. *Systems Analysis & Design Methods,* 3rd ed. Homewood, IL: Irwin, 1994.

Yourdon, E. *Modern Structured Analysis.* Englewood Cliffs, NJ: Prentice Hall, 1989.

THE CASE OPENS

On a warm, sunny day in late October, Chip Puller parks his car and walks into his office at Central Pacific University. It felt good to be starting as a systems analyst, and he was looking forward to meeting the others staff.

In the office, Anna Liszt introduces herself. "We've been assigned to work as a team on a new project. Why don't I fill you in with the details, and then we can take a tour of the facilities."

"That sounds good to me," Chip replies. "How long have you been working here?"

"About five years," answers Anna. "I started as a programmer analyst, but the last few years have been dedicated to analysis and design. I'm hoping we'll find some ways to increase our productivity," Anna continues.

"Tell me about the new project," Chip says.

"Well, like so many organizations, we have a large number of microcomputers with different software packages installed on them. In the early 1980s there were only a few microcomputers and limited software, but there has been a rapid increase in recent years. The current system used to maintain software and hardware has been overwhelmed."

"What about the users? Who should I know? Who do you think will be important in helping us with the new system?" Chip asks.

"You'll meet everyone, but there are key people I've recently met, and I'll tell you what I've learned so you'll remember them when you meet them.

"Dot Matricks is manager of all microcomputer systems at Central Pacific. We seem to be able to work together well. She's very competent. She'd really like to be able to improve communication among users and analysts."

"It will be a pleasure to meet her," Chip speculates.

"Then there's Mike Crowe, the micro maintenance expert. Really seems to be the nicest guy. But too busy. We need to help lighten his load. The software counterpart to Mike is Cher Ware. She's a free spirit, but don't get me wrong, she knows her job," Anna says.

"She could be fun to work with," Chip says.

"Could be," Anna agrees. "You'll meet the financial analyst, Paige Prynter, too. I haven't figured her out yet."

"Maybe I can help," Chip says.

"Lastly, you should—I mean, you will—meet Hy Perteks, who does a great job running the Information Center. He'd like to see us be able to integrate our life cycle activities."

"It sounds promising," Chip says. " I think I'm going to like it here."

Exercise

E-1. From the introductory conversation Chip and Anna shared, which elements mentioned might suggest the use of CASE tools?

Allen Schmidt,
Julie E. Kendall, and
Kenneth E. Kendall

2

UNDERSTANDING ORGANIZATIONAL STYLE AND ITS IMPACT ON INFORMATION SYSTEMS

ORGANIZATIONAL FUNDAMENTALS

In order to analyze and design appropriate information systems, systems analysts need to comprehend the organizations they work in as systems shaped through interactions of three main forces: the levels of management, design of organizations, and organizational cultures.

Organizations are large systems composed of interrelated subsystems. The subsystems are influenced by three broad levels of management decision makers (operations, middle management, and strategic management) that cut horizontally across the organizational system. Organizational cultures and subcultures all influence the way people in subsystems interrelate. The foregoing topics and their implications for information systems development are considered in this chapter.

ORGANIZATIONS AS SYSTEMS

Organizations are usefully conceptualized as systems designed to accomplish predetermined goals and objectives through people and other resources that they employ. Organizations are composed of smaller, interrelated systems (departments, units, divisions, etc.) serving specialized functions. Typical functions include accounting, marketing, production, data processing, and management. Specialized functions (smaller systems) are eventually reintegrated through various mechanisms to form an effective organizational whole.

The significance of conceptualizing organizations as complex systems is that systems principles allow insight into how organizations work. It is of primary importance to understand the organization as a whole in order to ascertain information requirements properly and to design appropriate information systems. All systems are composed of subsystems (which include information systems); therefore, when studying an organization, we also examine how smaller systems are involved and how they function.

Interrelatedness and Interdependence of Systems

All systems and subsystems are interrelated and interdependent. This fact has important implications for organizations and systems analysts who seek to help them better achieve their goals. When any element of a system is changed or eliminated, the rest of the system's elements and subsystems are also impacted.

For example, suppose that the administrators of an organization decide not to hire personal secretaries any longer and to replace their functions via use of networked PCs. This decision has the potential to impact not only the secretaries and the administrators but also all of the organizational members who built up communications networks with the now-departed secretaries, the secretaries remaining in other organizational positions, and those in the organization already using microprocessors to handle secretarial functions.

Organizational Boundaries

Another aspect of organizations as systems is that all systems are contained by boundaries separating them from their environments. Organizational boundaries exist on a continuum ranging from extremely permeable to almost impermeable. In order to continue to adapt and survive, organizations must be able to import people, raw materials, and information through their boundaries (inputs), and exchange their finished products, services, or information with the outside world (outputs). However, if boundaries become too lax, the organization's competitive edge is endangered, and control over performance is diminished.

System Feedback for Planning and Control

Feedback is one form of system control. As systems, all organizations use planning and control to manage their resources effectively. Figure 2.1 shows how system outputs are used as feedback with which to compare performance to goals. This comparison in turn helps administrators formulate more specific goals as inputs. An instance of this is a manufacturing company that produces red, white, and blue weight-training sets as well as gun-metal-colored sets. The company finds that one year after the Olympics, very few red, white, and blue sets are purchased. Production managers use that information as feedback to make decisions about what quantities of each color to produce. Feedback in this instance is useful for planning and control.

However, the ideal system is one that self-corrects or self-regulates in such a way that decisions on typical occurrences are not required. An example is a computerized information system for production planning that takes into account current and projected demand and formulates a proposed solution as output. An Italian knitwear manufacturer that markets its clothing in the United States has just such a system. This company produces most of its sweaters in white, uses its computerized inventory information system to find out what colors are selling best, and then dyes sweaters in hot-selling colors immediately before shipping them. With a self-regulating information system, a manager can review the proposed production figures and make interventions only when exceptional factors, not accounted for in the computer's software formulation of the problem, are present.

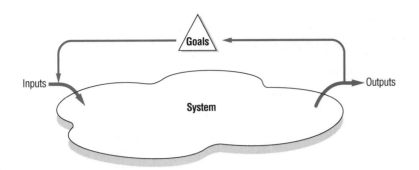

FIGURE 2.1
System outputs serve as
feedback that compares
performance to goals.

Environments for Organizational Systems

Feedback is received from within the organization and from the outside environments around it. Anything external to an organization's boundaries is considered to be an environment. Numerous environments, with varying degrees of stability, constitute the milieu in which organizations exist.

Among these are: (1) the environment of the community where the organization is physically located, which is shaped by the size of its population and its demographic profile, including factors such as education and average income; (2) the economic environment, influenced by market factors, including competition; and (3) the political environment, controlled through state and local governments. Although changes in environmental status can be planned for, they often cannot be directly controlled by the organization.

Openness and Closedness in Organizations

Related and similar to the concept of external boundary permeability is the concept of internal openness or closedness of organizations. Openness and closedness also exist on a continuum, since there is no such thing as an absolutely open or completely closed organization.

Openness refers to the free flow of information within the organization. Subsystems such as creative or art departments often are characterized as open, with a free flow of ideas among participants and very few restrictions on who gets what information at what time when a creative project is in its infancy.

At the opposite end of the continuum might be a defense department unit assigned to work on top-secret defense planning affecting national security. Each person needs to receive clearance, timely information is a necessity, and access to information is only on a "need to know" basis. This sort of unit is limited by numerous rules.

Using a systems overlay to understand organizations allows us to acknowledge the idea of systems composed of subsystems, their interrelatedness and their interdependence, the existence of boundaries that allow or prevent interaction between various departments and elements of other subsystems and environments, and the existence of internal environments characterized by degrees of openness and closedness, which might differ across departments, units, or even projects.

Taking a Systems Perspective

Taking a systems perspective allows systems analysts to start broadly clarifying and understanding the various businesses with which they will come

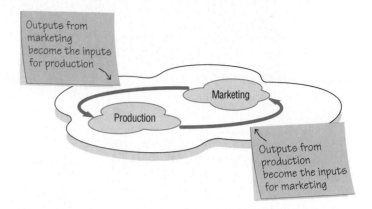

Outputs from marketing become the inputs for production

Outputs from production become the inputs for marketing

Marketing

Production

into contact. It is important that members of subsystems realize that their work is interrelated. Notice in Figure 2.2 that the outputs from the production subsystems serve as inputs for marketing, and that the outputs of marketing serve as new input for production. Neither subsystem can properly accomplish its goals without the other.

Problems occur when each manager possesses a different picture of the importance of his or her own functional subsystem. In Figure 2.3, you can see that the marketing manager's personal perspective shows the business as driven by marketing, with all other functional areas interrelated but not of central importance. By the same token, the perspective of a production manager positions production as central to the business, with all other functional areas driven by it.

The relative importance of functional areas as revealed in the personal perspectives of managers takes on added significance when managers rise to the top through the ranks, becoming strategic managers. They can create problems if they overemphasize their prior functional information requirements in relation to the broader needs of the strategic manager.

For example, if a production manager continues to stress production scheduling and performance of line workers, the broader aspects of forecasting and policy making may suffer. This tendency is a danger in all sorts of business—where engineers work up to become administrators of aerospace firms, college professors move from their departments to become deans, or programmers advance to become executives of software firms. Their tunnel vision often creates problems for the systems analyst trying to separate actual information requirements from desires for a particular kind of information.

DEPICTING SYSTEMS GRAPHICALLY

A system or subsystem as it exists within the corporate organization may be graphically depicted in several ways. The various graphical models show the boundaries of the system and the information used within the system.

Systems and the Context Level Data Flow Diagram

The first model is the context level data flow diagram (also called an environmental model). Data flow diagrams focus on the data flowing in and out of the system and the processing of the data. These basic components of every computer program may be described in detail and used to analyze the system for accuracy and completeness.

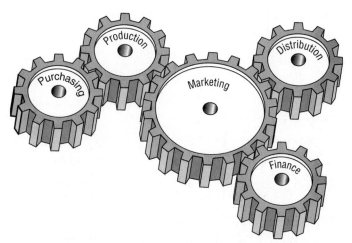

How a marketing manager may view the organization

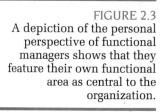

FIGURE 2.3
A depiction of the personal perspective of functional managers shows that they feature their own functional area as central to the organization.

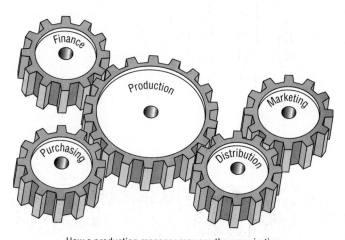

How a production manager may see the organization

The context level diagram employs only three symbols: (1) a rectangle with rounded corners, (2) a square with two shaded edges, and (3) an arrow, as shown in Figure 2.4. Processes transform incoming data into outgoing information, and the content level has only one process, representing the entire system. The external entity represents any entity that supplies or receives information from the system but is not a part of the system. This entity may be a person, a group of people, a corporate position or department, or other systems. The lines that connect the external entities to the process are called data flows and represent data.

An example of a context level data flow diagram is found in Figure 2.5. In this example, the most basic elements of an airline reservation system are represented.

The passenger (an entity) initiates a travel request (data flow). The context level diagram doesn't show enough detail to indicate exactly what happens (it isn't supposed to), but we can see that the passenger's preferences and the available flights are sent to the travel agent, who sends ticketing information back to the process. We can also see that the passenger reservation is sent to the airline.

In Chapter 9, we will see that a data flow contains much information. For example, the passenger reservation contains the passenger's name, airline,

FIGURE 2.4
The basic symbols of a data
flow diagram.

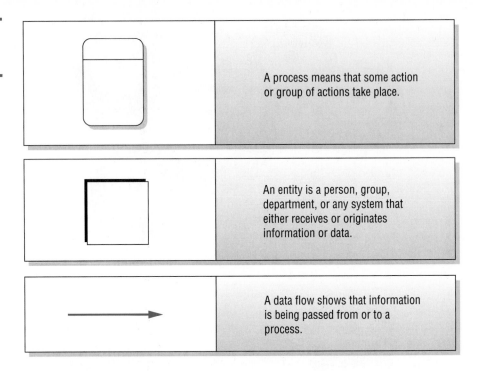

A process means that some action
or group of actions take place.

An entity is a person, group,
department, or any system that
either receives or originates
information or data.

A data flow shows that information
is being passed from or to a
process.

flight number(s), date(s) of travel, price, seating preference, etc. For now, however, we are concerned mainly with how a context level defines the boundaries of the system. In the preceding example, only reservations are part of the process. Other decisions that the airline would make (e.g., purchasing airplanes, changing schedules, pricing, etc.) are not part of *this* system.

FIGURE 2.5
A context level flow diagram
for an airline reservation
system.

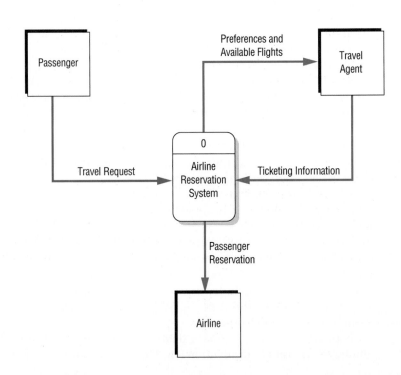

Systems and the Entity-Relationship Model

One way a systems analyst can define proper system boundaries is to use an entity-relationship model. The elements that make up an organizational system can be referred to as entities. An entity may be a person, a place, or a thing, such as a passenger on an airline, a destination, or a plane. Alternatively, an entity may be an event, such as the end of the month, a sales period, or a machine breakdown. A relationship is the association that describes the interaction between the entities.

The standard format for drawing an entity-relationship (or E-R) diagram, shown in Figure 2.6, uses only two symbols: a rectangle and a diamond. The rectangle is used to show an entity, while the diamond represents the relationship between that entity and another entity. The diagram is always drawn so that the primary entity is on top.

Figure 2.7 shows the four different types of E-R diagrams. The first is a one-to-one (1:1) relationship. Here, each EMPLOYEE is assigned only one PHONE EXTENSION, and each PHONE EXTENSION is unique to each EMPLOYEE. The second diagram shows a many-to-one (M:1) relationship. A DEPARTMENT can have many EMPLOYEEs, but an EMPLOYEE can belong to only one DEPARTMENT. The third type of E-R diagram shows a one-to-many (1:M) relationship. In this example, a TRAVEL DESTINATION can be booked by many PASSENGERS, but a PASSENGER will have only one final TRAVEL DESTINATION. The difference between the 1:M and the M:1 relationships occurs because of the varying nature of the primary entity, which always appears on top. Finally, the fourth diagram shows a many-to-many (M:N) relationship. A FLIGHT may carry many PASSENGERS and a PASSENGER may have many FLIGHTS in an itinerary.

Entity-relationship diagrams are often used by systems designers to help model the file or database. However, it is even more important that the systems analyst understand early on the entities and relationships in the organizational system. In sketching out some basic E-R diagrams, the analyst needs to:

1. List the entities in the organization in order to gain a better understanding of the organization.
2. Choose key entities in order to narrow the scope of the problem to manageable and meaningful dimension.

FIGURE 2.7
Entity-relationship diagrams
can be one-to-one (1:1),
one-to-many (1:M), many-to-
one (M:1), or many-to-many
(M:N).

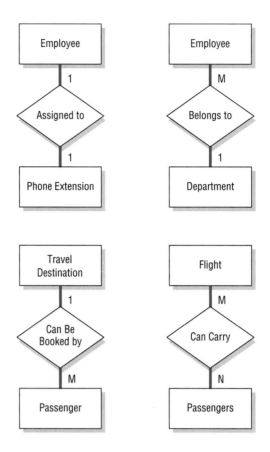

3. Identify what the primary entity should be.

4. Confirm the results of steps 1–3 through other data-gathering methods (investigation, interviewing, administering questionnaires, observation, and prototyping), as discussed in Chapters 4–8.

Take, for example, the case of Festival-on-the-Lake, an organization that produces summer theatre. Your role as systems analyst is to analyze the current overall system and design a ticket system. As you think about the situation, you list entities such as PATRON and SEATS, but you could also list entities such as PERFORMANCES, DATE, and even ACTORS and their UNDERSTUDIES.

You may gain a better picture of the organization by listing the entities, but soon you have to narrow the scope of the problem. Although they work in the theatre, the ACTORS and UNDERSTUDIES have no bearing on the reservation system. Furthermore SEATS, PERFORMANCE, and DATE could all be treated as attributes of a single entity called TICKETS.

The next step involves choosing the primary entity. In this example, the choice is PATRON. It is the PATRON who reserves TICKETS for a show; the TICKETS don't choose the PATRON. When the PATRON comes to the box office to pick up the TICKETS, the PATRON gives as an identifier the PATRON'S NAME, not one of the attributes of the TICKET such as seat number or performance.

In this example, choosing the primary entity may seem easy, but in other problems it might be difficult. Remember that each person in the organization sees it differently, as we pointed out earlier in this chapter.

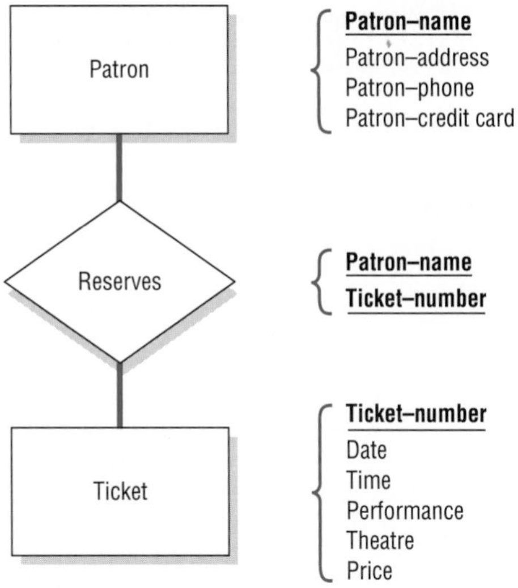

FIGURE 2.8
The Festival-on-the-Lake E-R
diagram is expanded to show
the attributes for each entity
and the relationship.

The entity-relationship diagram for the Festival-on-the-Lake project is shown in Figure 2.8. Notice that the E-R diagram can be expanded to include some of the attributes that describe each entity or relationship. The PATRON has attributes such as name, address, phone, and credit card number, which can be filed away for future mailings. The TICKET has attributes such as the ticket number, the date, the time, the performance, the theatre, and the price. The relationship between the two entities—the act of reserving the ticket—has attributes in common with the two entities: the patron's name and the ticket number.

It is critical that the systems analyst begin to draw E-R diagrams on entering the organization rather than wait until the database needs to be designed, because E-R diagrams help the analyst understand what business the organization is actually in, help determine the size of the problem, and help discern whether the right problem is being addressed. The E-R diagrams need to be confirmed or revised as the data-gathering process takes place.

Organizational factors that influence analysis and design of information systems include levels of management and organizational culture. We discuss each of these factors and their implications for analysis and design of information systems in the remaining sections of this chapter.

LEVELS OF MANAGEMENT

Management in organizations exists on three broad, horizontal levels: operational control, managerial planning and control, and strategic management, as shown in Figure 2.9. Each level carries its own responsibilities, and all work toward achieving organizational goals and objectives in their own ways.

Operations Management

Operational control forms the bottom tier of three-tiered management. Operations managers make decisions using predetermined rules that have predictable outcomes when implemented correctly.

Operations managers are the decision makers whose work is the most clear-cut because of the high degree of certainty in their decision-making environment. They make decisions that affect implementation in work scheduling, inventory control, shipping, receiving, and control of processes such as production. Operations managers oversee the operating details of the organization, ensuring that the basic tasks of the organization are accomplished on time and in accordance with organizational constraints.

Middle Management

Middle management forms the second, or intermediate, tier of the three-tiered management system. Middle managers make short-term planning and control decisions about how resources may best be allocated to meet organizational objectives.

Middle managers experience very little certainty in their decision-making environment. Their decisions range all the way from forecasting future resource requirements to solving employee problems that threaten productivity. Few of the decisions that middle managers make are as structured as those made by operations managers. The decision-making domain of middle managers can usefully be characterized as partly operational and partly strategic, with constant fluctuations.

Strategic Management

Strategic management composes the third level of three-tiered management control. Strategic managers look outward from the organization to the future, making decisions that will guide middle and operations managers in the months and years ahead.

Strategic managers work in a highly uncertain decision-making environment. Through statements of goals and determination of strategies and

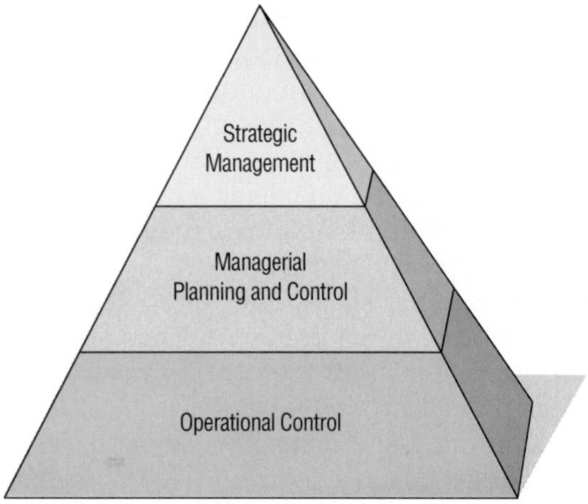

FIGURE 2.9
Management in organizations
exists on three horizontal
levels: operational control,
managerial planning and
control, and strategic
management.

policies to achieve them, strategic managers actually define the organization as a whole. Theirs is the broad picture, wherein the company decides to develop new product lines, divest itself of unprofitable ventures, acquire other compatible companies, or even allow itself to be sold.

There are sharp contrasts among the decision makers on many dimensions. For instance, strategic planners have multiple decision objectives while operations managers have single ones, and it often is difficult for high-level managers to identify problems, but easy for operations managers to do so. Strategic planners are faced with semistructured problems, whereas lower-level managers deal mostly with structured problems. The alternative solutions to a problem facing the strategic manager are often difficult to articulate, but the alternatives that operations manager work with are usually easy to enumerate. The nature of the decisions made by the various levels of management is entirely different. Strategic managers most often make one-time decisions, whereas the decisions made by operations managers tend to be repetitive. Finally, the decision style of strategic managers tends toward the heuristic, while operations managers tend to be mainly analytic in their style.

Implications for Information Systems Development

Each of the three management levels holds differing implications for developing management information systems. Some of the information requirements for managers are clear-cut, while others are fuzzy and overlap.

Operations managers need internal information that is of a repetitive, low-level nature. They are highly dependent on information that captures current performance, and are large users of on-line, real-time information resources. The need of operations managers for past performance information and periodic information is only moderate. They have little use for external information that allows future projections or creation of "what-if" scenarios.

Information systems designed for operations managers are valuable if they can provide information to help in controlling operations in a timely manner. Much of the information needed for operations is already being generated or can be easily pinpointed, but would be more useful if it were accessible from an on-line system.

On the next management level, middle managers, who both plan and control, are in need of both short- and longer-term information. Due to the troubleshooting nature of their jobs, middle managers experience extremely high needs for information in real time. In order to control properly, they also need current information on performance as measured against set standards.

Middle managers are highly dependent on internal information. In contrast to operations managers, they have a high need for historical information, along with information that allows prediction of future events and simulation of numerous possible scenarios.

Strategic managers differ somewhat from both middle and operations managers in their information requirements. They are highly dependent on information from external sources that supply news of market trends and the strategies of competing corporations.

Since the task of strategic managing demands projections into the uncertain future, strategic managers have a high need for information of a predictive nature and information that allows creation of many different "what-if" scenarios. Strategic managers also exhibit strong needs for periodically reported information as they seek to adapt to fast-moving changes.

Strategic planners need general, summarized information rather than the highly detailed, raw data required by low-level managers. Information for strategic planners may be older and estimated, whereas operational managers need current, accurate information. Finally, the strategic planner needs qualitative information, mainly from external sources, rather than the quantitative information from internal sources required by the operations manager.

ORGANIZATIONAL CULTURE

Organizational culture is a burgeoning area of research that has grown remarkably in the past decade. Just as it is appropriate to think of organizations as including many technologies, it is similarly appropriate to see them as hosts to multiple, often competing subcultures.

Since the area is relatively new, there is little agreement on what precisely constitutes an organizational subculture. It is agreed, however, that competing subcultures may be in conflict, attempting to gain adherents to their vision of what the organization should be.

Rather than thinking about culture as a whole, it is more useful to think about the researchable determinants of subcultures such as shared verbal and nonverbal symbolism. Verbal symbolism includes shared language used to construct, convey, and preserve subcultural myths, metaphors, visions, and humor. Nonverbal symbolism includes shared artifacts, rites, and ceremonies such as clothing; use, placement, and decoration of offices; and rituals for celebrating members' birthdays, promotions, and retirements.

Subcultures coexist within "official" organizational cultures. The officially sanctioned culture may prescribe a dress code, suitable ways to address superiors and coworkers, and proper ways to deal with the outside public. Subcultures may be powerful determinants of information requirements, availability, and use.

Organizational members may belong to one or more subcultures within the organization. Subcultures may exert powerful influence on member behavior, including sanctions for or against the use of information systems.

Understanding and recognizing predominant organizational subcultures may help the systems analyst overcome the resistance to change that arises when a new information system is installed. For example, the analyst might devise user training to address specific concerns of organizational subcultures. Identifying subcultures may also help in the design of decision support systems that are tailored for interaction with specific user groups.

SUMMARY

There are three broad organizational fundamentals to consider when analyzing and designing information systems. These are the concept of organizations as systems, the various levels of management, and the overall organizational culture.

Organizations are complex systems composed of interrelated and interdependent subsystems. Additionally, systems and subsystems are characterized by their internal environments on a continuum from open to closed; an open system allows free passage of resources (people, information, materials) through its boundaries. Closed systems do not permit free flow of input or output.

Entity-relationship diagrams help the systems analyst understand the entities and relationships that comprise the organizational system. The four different kinds of E-R diagrams are: a one-to-one relationship, a one-to-many relationship, a many-to-one, and a many-to-many relationship.

The three levels of managerial control are: operational, middle management, and strategic. The time horizon of decision making is different for each level.

Organizational cultures and subcultures are important determinants of how people use information and information systems. By grounding

"You seem to have already made a good start at MRE. Even though I can tell you a lot about the company, remember that there are a number of ways to orient yourself within it. You will want to interview users, observe their decision-making settings, and look at archival reports, charts, and diagrams. In order to do so, you can click on the telephone directory to get an appointment with an interviewee, click on the building map to go to a particular location, or click on organizational charts that show you the functional areas and formal hierarchical relationships at MRE.

"Many of the rules of corporate life apply within the MRE HyperCase. For instance, there are many public areas in which you are free to walk. However, if you want to tour a private corporate office, you must first book an appointment with one of our employees. Some secure areas are strictly off limits to you, just because you are an outsider and could pose a security risk.

"I don't think you'll find us excessively secretive, however, since you may assume that any employee who grants you an interview will also grant you access to the archival material in his or her files, as well as to current work. You'll be able to go about your consulting freely in most cases. If you get too curious or invade our privacy in some way, we'll let you know. We're not afraid to tell you what the limits are."

FIGURE 2.HC1
The reception room resembles a typical corporation. While you are in this HyperCase screen, find the directory if you want to visit someone.

"Unfortunately, some people in the company never seem to make themselves available to consultants. If you need to know more about these hard-to-get interviews, I suggest you be persistent. There are lots of ways to find out about the people and the systems of MRE, but much of the time creativity is what pays off. You will notice that the systems consultants who follow their hunches, sharpen their technical skills, and never stop thinking about piecing together the puzzles here at MRE are the ones who are the best.

"Remember to use multiple methods—interviewing, observation, and investigation—to understand what we at MRE are trying to tell you. Sometimes actions, documents, and offices actually speak louder than words!"

HYPERCASE QUESTIONS

1. What major organizational change recently took place a MRE? What department(s) were involved, and why was the change made?

2. What does the Management Systems Unit at MRE do? Who are their clients?

3. What are the goals and strategies of the Engineering and Systems division at MRE? What are the goals of the Training and Management Systems Department?

4. Would you categorize MRE as a service industry, a manufacturer, or both? What kind of "products" does MRE "produce" (i.e., do they offer material goods, services, or both)? Suggest how the type of industry MRE is affects the information system it uses.

5. What type of organizational structure does MRE have? What are the implications of this structure for MIS?

6. Describe in a paragraph the "politics" of the Training and Management Systems Department at MRE. Who is involved and what are some of the main issues?

information systems in the context of the organization as a larger system, it is possible to realize that numerous factors are important and should be taken into account when ascertaining information requirements and designing and implementing information systems.

KEYWORDS AND PHRASES

systems	closedness
interrelatedness	entity-relationship diagrams
interdependent	operations management
organizational boundaries	middle management
feedback	strategic management
environment	organizational culture
openness	

REVIEW QUESTIONS

1. What are the three groups of organizational fundamentals that carry implications for the development of information systems?
2. What is meant by saying that organizational subsystems are interrelated and interdependent?
3. Define the term *organizational boundary.*
4. What are the two main purposes for feedback in organizations?
5. Define *openness* in an organizational environment.
6. Define *closedness* in an organizational environment.
7. What is meant by the term *entity-relationship diagram?*
8. What two symbols are used to draw E-R diagrams?
9. List the four types of E-R diagrams.
10. List the three broad, horizontal levels of management in organizations.
11. How can understanding organizational subcultures help in the design of information systems?

PROBLEMS

1. "It's hard to focus on what we want to achieve. I look at what our real competitors, the convenience stores, are doing and think we should copy that. Then a hundred customers come in, and I listen to each of them, and they say we should keep our little store the same, with friendly clerks and old-fashioned cash registers. Then, when I pick up a copy of *SuperMarket News,* they say that the wave of the future is super grocery stores, with no individual prices marked and UPC scanners replacing clerks. I'm pulled in so many directions I can't really settle on a strategy for our grocery store," admits Geoff Walsham, owner and manager of Jiffy Geoff's Grocery Store.

   In a paragraph, apply the concept of permeable organizational boundaries to analyze Geoff's problem in focusing on organizational objectives.

2. Draw an entity-relationship diagram of a patient-doctor relationship.
   a. Which of the four types of E-R diagrams is it?
   b. In a sentence or two, explain why the patient–doctor relationship is diagrammed in this way.

3. You began drawing E-R diagrams soon after your entry into the health maintenance organization for which you're designing a system. Your team member is skeptical about using E-R diagrams before design of the database is begun.

   In a paragraph, persuade your team member that early use of E-R diagrams is worthwhile.

4. Sandy works as a manager for Arf-Arf Dog Food Company. Since there are several different suppliers of ingredients and their prices fluctuate, she has come up with several different formulations for the same dog food product, depending on the availability of particular ingredients from particular suppliers. She then orders ingredients accordingly. Even though she cannot predict when ingredients will become available at a particular price, her ordering of supplies can be considered routine.

    a. On what level of management is Sandy working? Explain in a paragraph.

    b. What attributes of her job would have to change before you would categorize her as working on a different level of management? List them.

5. Many of the people who work at Arf-Arf Dog Food Company laugh about Arf-Arf and about how silly it is that making dog food is such an important enterprise in the United States. However, other groups in the company are extremely proud of Arf-Arf's products and reputation for producing quality dog chow and they happily display industry awards they have received.

    a. In a paragraph, identify and give descriptive names to organizational subcultures that seem apparent at Arf-Arf.

GROUP PROJECT

1. With your group, draw a context level diagram of your school's or university's registration system. Label each entity and process. Discuss why there appear to be different ways to draw the diagram. Reach consensus as a group about the best way to draw the diagram and defend your choice in a paragraph. Now, working with your group's members, follow the appropriate steps for developing an E-R diagram and create one for your school or university registration system. Make sure your group indicates whether the relationship you depict are 1:1, 1:M, M:1, or M:N.

SELECTED BIBLIOGRAPHY

Burch, J. G., F. R. Strater, and G. Grudnitski. *Information Systems: Theory and Practice*, 3rd ed. New York: John Wiley & Sons, 1983.

Chen, P. "The Entity-Relationship Model—Towards a Unified View of Data." *ACM Transactions on Database Systems 1*. March 1976, pp. 9–36.

Davis, G. B., and M. H. Olson. *Management Information Systems, Conceptual Foundations, Structure, and Development*, 2nd ed. New York: McGraw-Hill Book Company, 1985.

Galbraith, J. R. *Organizational Design*. Reading, MA: Addison-Wesley, 1977.

Kendall, K. E., J. R. Buffington, and J. E., Kendall. "The Relationship of Organizational Subcultures to DSS User Satisfaction." *Human Systems Management*. March 1987.

PICTURING THE RELATIONSHIPS

"So the project involves more than simply performing maintenance work on the current programs," Chip says. "Are we using a formal methodology for analyzing and designing the new system?"

"Yes," replies Anna. "We are also using a CASE tool, Excelerator, to analyze and design the system.[1–2] We've recently installed the product on our microcomputer in the office." Anna motions to a large computer work area containing a microcomputer with attached laser printer and mainframe terminal.

"That's great!" exclaims Chip. "Have you used Excelerator on other projects?"

"No," Anna says. "This is the pilot project involving Excelerator. I've attended training sessions and I'm somewhat familiar with its operation. Are you familiar with Excelerator?"

"I've had some experience with it at school. I understand that's one of the reasons that I was hired for this position," answers Chip. "Let me see what you've done so far."

They both move to the microcomputer area, where Anna boots Excelerator. Working her way through the menus, she comes to a context level data flow diagram (see Figure E2.1). "It's very useful to begin thinking of the system this way," Anna says as they look at the diagram on the screen.

Chip agrees, saying, "I can very easily see what you think is happening with the system. For instance, I see that the external entity Management supplies hardware and software inquiries and receives the corresponding response in return. It shows the system within the larger organization."

"I've also drawn an E-R diagram of the system (see Figure E2.2), so I could start understanding the relationships between the data structures," Anna says as she brings up the entity-relationship diagram on the screen.

"Yes, the many-to-many and one-to-many relationships are very clear when you look at this," Chip says, viewing the screen. "You've got a good start here," Chip continues. "Let's get to work and see what needs to be done next."

Allen Schmidt,
Julie E. Kendall, and
Kenneth E. Kendall
44

[1] For more details on how to begin using Excelerator, see your Excelerator user's guides by Index Technology. For additional help, see *Working with Excelerator, Version 1.9,* by Allen Schmidt (Prentice-Hall, 1992).

[2] The Central Pacific University case can be adapted to other CASE tools. Alternatively, many of the exercises can be accomplished manually if CASE tools are unavailable.

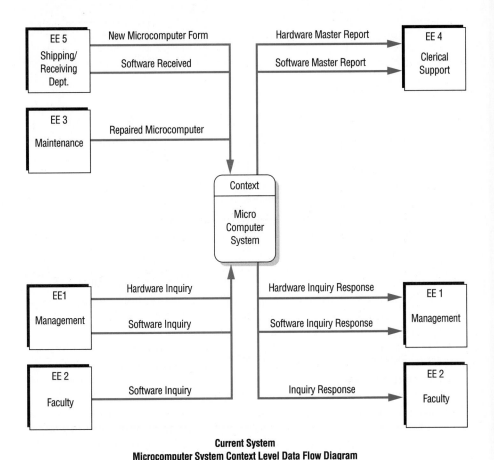

Current System
Microcomputer System Context Level Data Flow Diagram

FIGURE E2.1
Context level data flow diagram, Current System.

*Exercises**

💾 **E-1.** Use Excelerator to view and print the context level data flow diagram for the microcomputer systems, as Chip and Anna did.

💾 **E-2.** Use the DESCRIBE drawing option to view the description screen for the central process.

💾 **E-3.** Use Excelerator to view and print the entity-relationship diagram for the microcomputer system.

E-4. Explain why the external entities on the context level diagram are not found on the entity-relationship diagram.

E-5. Explain why the entities MANAGEMENT and FACULTY are found on both sides of the process on the context level diagram.

* Exercises preceded by a disk icon require the program Excelerator or another CASE tool. A disk is provided free of charge to any professor adopting this book. The examples on the disk may be imported into Excelerator and then used by students.

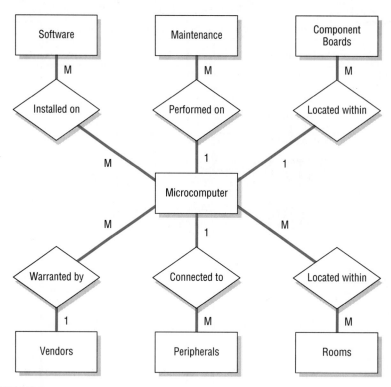

FIGURE E2.2
Entity-relationship diagram, Microcomputer System.

REFERENCE TEXTS

Excelerator Series, Application Guide, Excelerator Windows Version 1.0. Rockville, MD: INTERSOLV Inc., 1992.

Excelerator Series, Reference Guide, Excelerator Windows Data & Reports, Version 1.0. Rockville, MD: INTERSOLV Inc., 1992.

Excelerator Series, Reference Guide, Excelerator Windows Facilities and Functions, Version 1.0. Rockville, MD: INTERSOLV Inc., 1992.

Schmidt, Allen. *Working with Excelerator, Version 1.8.* Englewood Cliffs, NJ: Prentice-Hall, 1990.

Schmidt, Allen. *Working with Excelerator, Version 1.9.* Englewood Cliffs, NJ: Prentice-Hall, 1991.

3

DETERMINING FEASIBILITY AND MANAGING ANALYSIS AND DESIGN ACTIVITIES

PROJECT FUNDAMENTALS

Initiating projects, determining project feasibility, scheduling projects, and managing activities and team members for productivity are all important capabilities for the systems analyst to master. As such, they are considered project fundamentals.

A systems project begins with problems or opportunities for improvement within a business that often come up as the organization adapts to change. Changes that require a systems solution occur in the legal environment as well as in the industry's environment. Once a project is suggested, the systems analyst works quickly with decision makers to determine whether it is feasible. If a project is approved for a full systems study, the project activities are scheduled through the use of tools such as Gantt charts and PERT charts, so that the project can be completed on time. Part of assuring productivity of systems analysis team members is effectively managing their scheduled activities. This chapter is devoted to a discussion of these project fundamentals.

PROJECT INITIATION

Systems projects are initiated by many different sources for many reasons. Some of the projects suggested will survive various stages of evaluation to be worked on by you (or you and your team); others will not and/or should not get that far. Business people suggest systems projects for two broad reasons: (1) to experience problems that lend themselves to systems solutions and (2) to recognize opportunities for improvement through upgrading, altering, or installing new systems when they occur. Both of these situations can arise as the organization adapts to and copes with natural, evolutionary change.

47

Problems within the Organization

Managers do not like to conceive of their organization as having problems, let alone talk about them or share them with someone from outside. However, good managers realize that recognizing symptoms of problems or, at a later state, diagnosing the problems themselves and then confronting them is imperative if the business is to keep functioning at its highest potential.

Problems surface in many different ways. One way of conceptualizing what problems are and how they arise is to think of them as situations where goals have never been met or are no longer being met. Useful feedback gives information about the gap between actual and intended performance. In this way, feedback spotlights problems.

In some instances, problems that require the services of systems analysts are uncovered because performance measures are not being met. Problems (or symptoms of problems) with processes that are visible in output and that could require the help of a systems analyst include excessive errors and work performed too slowly, incompletely, incorrectly, or not at all.

Other symptoms of problems become evident when people do not meet baseline performance goals. Changes in employee behavior such as unusually high absenteeism, high job dissatisfaction, or high worker turnover should serve to alert managers to potential problems. Any of these, alone or in combination, might be sufficient reason to request the help of a systems analyst.

Although difficulties such as the above occur within the organization, feedback on how well the organization is meeting intended goals may come from outside, in the form of complaints or suggestions from customers, vendors, or suppliers, and lost or unexpectedly lower sales. This feedback from the external environment is extremely important and should not be ignored.

A summary of symptoms and approaches useful in problem detection is provided in Figure 3.1. Notice that checking output, observing or researching employee behavior, and listening to feedback from external sources are all valuable in problem finding.

When reacting to accounts of problems within the organization, the systems analyst plays the roles of consultant and supporting expert, as discussed in Chapter 1. As you might expect, roles for the systems analyst shift subtly when projects are initiated because the focus is on opportunities for improvement rather than the need to solve problems.

Opportunities for Improvement

The systems analyst serves as catalyst and supporting expert primarily by being able to see where processes can be improved. Optimistically, opportunities can be conceived of as the obverse of problems; yet in some cultures, crisis also means opportunity. What looms as a disturbing problem for a manager might be turned into an opportunity for improvement by an alert systems analyst.

Improvements to systems can be defined as changes that will result in incremental yet worthwhile benefits. There are many possibilities for improvements, including:

1. Speeding up a process.
2. Streamlining a process through elimination of unnecessary or duplicated steps.

To Identify Problems	Look for These Specific Signs:
Check output against performance criteria	• Too many errors • Work completed slowly • Work done incorrectly • Work done incompletely • Work not done at all
Observe behavior of employees	• High absenteeism • High job dissatisfaction • High job turnover

Listen to external feedback from:
   Vendors
   Customers
   Suppliers
	• Complaints
	• Suggestions for improvement
	• Loss of sales
	• Lower sales

FIGURE 3.1
Checking output, observing employee behavior, and listening to feedback are all ways to help the analyst pinpoint systems problems and opportunities.

3. Combining processes.

4. Reducing errors in input through changes of forms and VDT screens.

5. Reducing redundant output.

6. Improving integration of systems and subsystems.

7. Improving worker satisfaction with the system.

8. Improving ease of customer, supplier, and vendor interaction with the system.

It is well within the systems analyst's capabilities to notice opportunities for improvements. However, people who come into daily contact with the system may be even better sources of information about improvements that should be made. If improvements have already been suggested, your expertise is needed to help determine whether the improvement is worthwhile and how it can be implemented.

Although the list of improvements given above is long, it is not an exhaustive one. The difficult part of suggesting and implementing improvements is that they must be worth the discomfiture and cost of change.

Selection of Projects

Projects come from many different sources and for many reasons. Not all of them should be selected for further study. You must be clear in your own mind about the reasons for recommending a systems study on a project that seems to address a problem or bring about improvement. Consider the motivation that prompts proposal of the project. You need to be sure that the project under consideration is not being proposed simply to enhance your own political reputation or power or that of the person or group proposing it, since there is a high probability that such a project will be ill-conceived and eventually ill-accepted.

As outlined in Chapter 2, prospective projects need to be examined from a systems perspective, in such a way that you are considering the impact of the proposed change on the entire organization. Recall that the various subsystems of the organization are interrelated and interdependent, so that a change to one subsystem might affect all of the others. Even though the decision makers directly involved ultimately set the boundaries for the

FIGURE 3.2
Selecting systems projects
based on five criteria.

Criteria for Selection of Systems Projects
• Backing from management
• Appropriate timing of project commitment
• Possibility of improving attainment of organizational goals
• Practical in terms of resources for systems analyst and organization
• Project is worthwhile compared to other ways organization could invest resources

systems project, a systems project cannot be contemplated or selected in isolation from the rest of the organization.

Beyond these general considerations are the five specific criteria for project selection listed in Figure 3.2. The first and foremost is backing from management. Absolutely nothing can be accomplished without the endorsement of the people who eventually will foot the bill. This does not mean that you lack influence in directing the project or that people other than management can't be included. However, management backing is essential.

Another important criterion for project selection includes timing for you and the organization. Ask yourself and others involved if the business is presently capable of making a time commitment for installation of new systems or improvement to existing ones. You must also be able to commit all or a portion of your time for the duration.

A third criterion is the possibility of improving attainment of organizational goals. The project should put the organization on target, not deter it from its ultimate goals.

A fourth criterion is selecting a project that is practicable in terms of your resources and capabilities, as well as those of the business. Some projects will not fall within your realm of expertise, and you must be able to recognize these.

Finally, you need to come to a basic agreement with the organization about the worthiness of the systems project over any other possible project being considered. Remember that when a business commits to one project it is committing resources that thereby become unavailable for other projects. It is useful to view all possible projects as competing for the business resources of time, money, and people.

DETERMINING FEASIBILITY

Once the number of projects has been narrowed according to the criteria discussed previously, it is still necessary to determine if projects selected are feasible. Our definition of feasibility goes much deeper than common usage of the term. For systems projects *feasibility* is assessed in three principal ways: operationally, technically, and economically. A project must be feasible in all three ways to merit further development, as shown in Figure 3.3.

The feasibility study is not a full-blown systems study. Rather, the feasibility study is used to gather broad data for management that in turn enables them to make a decision on whether to proceed with a systems study.

Data for the feasibility study can be gathered through interviews, which are covered in detail in Chapter 5. The kind of interview required is directly related to the problem or opportunity being suggested. The systems analyst typically interviews those requesting help and those directly concerned with the decision-making process, typically, management.

FIGURE 3.3
Determining feasibility of a
systems project by judging
how it meets organizational
objectives.

FEASIBILITY Means That the Proposed Project:

- Helps the organization attain overall objectives
- Is possible to accomplish with present organizational resources in the following three areas:

  Technical Feasibility
  Add on to present system
  Technology available to meet users' needs

  Economic Feasibility
  Systems analysts' time
  Cost of systems study
  Cost of employees' time for study
  Estimated cost of hardware
  Cost of packaged software/software development

  Operational Feasibility
  Whether the system will operate when installed
  Whether the system will be used

While it is important to address the correct problem, the systems analyst should not spend too much time doing feasibility studies, since many projects will be requested and only a few can or should be executed. The feasibility study must be highly time-compressed, encompassing several activities in a short span of time.

Defining Objectives

Ascertaining the overall feasibility of a requested project means finding out what the organizational objectives are and then determining if the project serves to move the business toward its objectives in some way. The objectives of the project should be clarified through interviews with the person, group, or department proposing it. Additionally, a review of written work related to the requested project is also useful.

There are several acceptable objectives for systems projects. These include, but are not limited to:

1. Reducing errors and improving the accuracy of data input.
2. Reducing cost of system output by streamlining and eliminating duplicate or unnecessary reports.
3. Integrating business subsystems.
4. Upgrading customer services to gain a competitive edge.
5. Speeding up input.
6. Shortening data-processing time.
7. Automating manual procedures to improve them in some way (reduce errors, increase speed or accuracy, cut down on employee time required, etc.).

There also are some unacceptable objectives for systems projects. As mentioned before, these include undertaking a project solely to prove the prowess of the systems analysis team or purely to assert the superiority of one department over the other in terms of its power to command internal resources. It is also unacceptable to automate manual procedures for the sake of automation alone or to invest in new technology because of infatuation with the "bells and whistles" it provides over and above what the present system offers, without consideration of its true contribution to achievement of the organization's goals.

The objectives of the project need to be cleared formally on paper as well as informally by talking to people in the business. Find out what problem they believe the systems project would solve or what situation it would improve and what their expectations are for the proposed system.

Determining Resources

Resource determination for the feasibility study follows the same broad pattern discussed previously and will be revised and reevaluated if and when a formal systems study is commissioned. Resources will be discussed in relationship to three areas of feasibility: technical, economic, and operational.

TECHNICAL FEASIBILITY. A large part of determining resources has to do with assessing technical feasibility. The analyst must find out whether current technical resources can be upgraded or added to in a manner that fulfills the request under consideration. However, sometimes "add-ons" to existing systems are costly and not worthwhile, simply because they meet needs inefficiently. If existing systems cannot be added onto, then the next question becomes whether there is technology in existence that meets the specifications.

This is where the expertise of systems analysts is beneficial, since using their own experience and their contact with vendors they will be able to answer the question of technical feasibility. Usually the response to whether a particular technology is available and capable of meeting the users' requests is "yes," and then the question becomes an economic one.

ECONOMIC FEASIBILITY. Economic feasibility is the second part of resource determination. The basic resources to consider are: your time and that of the systems analysis team, the cost of doing a full systems study (including time of employees you will be working with), cost of the business employee time, estimated cost of hardware, and estimated cost of software and/or software development.

The concerned business must be able to see the value of the investment it is pondering before committing to an entire systems study. If short-term costs are not overshadowed by long-term gains or produce no immediate reduction in operating costs, then the system is not economically feasible, and the project should not proceed any further.

OPERATIONAL FEASIBILITY. Suppose for a moment that technical and economic resources are both judged adequate. The systems analyst must still consider the operational feasibility of the requested project. Operational feasibility is dependent on human resources available for the project and involves projecting whether the system will operate and be used once it is installed.

If users are virtually wed to the present system, see no problems with it, and generally are not involved in requesting a new system, resistance to implementing the new system will be strong. Chances for it ever becoming operational are low.

Alternatively, if users themselves have expressed a need for a system that is operational more of the time, in a more efficient and accessible manner, chances are better that the requested system will eventually be used. Much of the art of determining operational feasibility rests with the user interfaces that are chosen, as we shall see in Chapter 18.

At this point, determining operational feasibility requires creative imagination on the part of the systems analyst, as well as the powers of persuasion to let users know which interfaces are possible and which will satisfy their needs. The systems analyst must also carefully listen to what users really want and what it seems they will use. Ultimately, however, to a large extent assessing operational feasibility involves educated guesswork.

Judging Feasibility

From the foregoing discussion, it is evident that judging the feasibility of systems projects is never a clear-cut or easy task. Further, project feasibility is not a decision to be made by the systems analyst but instead by management. Decisions are based on feasibility data expertly and professionally gathered and presented by the analyst.

The systems analyst needs to be sure that all three areas of technical, economic, and operational feasibility are addressed in the preliminary study. The study of a requested systems project must be accomplished quickly so that the resources devoted to it are minimal, information output from the study is solid, and any existing interest in the project remains high. Remember that this is a preliminary study, which precedes the system study, and it must be executed rapidly and competently.

Projects that meet the criteria discussed in the project selection subsection, as well as the three criteria of technical, economic, and operational feasibility, should be chosen for a detailed systems study. At this point the systems analyst must act as a supporting expert, advising management that the requested systems project meets all of the selection criteria and has thus qualified as an excellent candidate for further study. Remember that a commitment from management at this juncture means only that a systems study may proceed, not that a proposed system is accepted. Generally, the process of feasibility assessment is effective in screening out projects that are inconsistent with the business's objectives, technically impossible, or economically unprofitable. While it is painstaking, studying feasibility is worthwhile and saves businesses and systems analysts a good deal of time and money in the long run.

ACTIVITY PLANNING AND CONTROL

Systems analysis and design involves many different types of activities that together make up a project. The systems analyst must manage the project carefully if the project is to be a successful one. Project management involves the general tasks of planning and control.

Planning includes all of the activities required to select a systems analysis team, assign members of the team to appropriate projects, estimate time required to complete each task, and schedule the project so that tasks are completed in a timely fashion. Control means using feedback to monitor the project. This includes comparing the plan for the project with its actual evolution. Control additionally means taking appropriate action to

"We could really make some changes. Shake up some people. Let them know we're with it. Technologically, I mean," said Malcolm Warner, vice president for AllFine Foods, a wholesale dairy products distributor. "That old system should be overhauled. I think we should just tell the staff that it's time to change."

"Yes, but what would we actually be improving?" Kim Han, assistant to the vice president, asks. "I mean, there aren't any substantial problems with the system input or output that I can see."

Malcolm snaps, "Kim, you're purposely not seeing my point. People out there see us as a stodgy firm. A new computer system could help change that. Change the look of our invoices. Send jazzier reports to the food store owners. Get some people excited about us as leaders in wholesale food distributing *and* computers."

"Well, from what I've seen over the years," Kim replies evenly, "a new system is very disruptive, even when the business really needs it. People dislike change, and if the system is performing the way it should, maybe there are other things we could do to update our image that wouldn't drive everyone nuts in the process. Besides, you're talking big bucks for a new gimmick."

Malcolm says, "I don't think just tossing it around here between the two of us is going to solve anything.

Check on it and get back to me. Wouldn't it be wonderful?"

A week later Kim enters Malcolm's office with several pages of interview notes in hand. "I've talked with most of the people who have extensive contact with the system. They're happy, Malcolm. And they're not just talking through their hats. They know what they're doing."

"I'm sure the managers would like to have a newer system than the guys at Quality Foods," Malcolm replies. "Did you talk to them?"

Kim says, "Yes. They're satisfied."

"And how about the people in systems? Did they say the technology to update our system is out there?" Malcolm inquired insistently.

"Yes. It can be done. That doesn't mean it should be," Kim says firmly.

As the systems analyst for AllFine Foods, how would you assess the feasibility of the systems project Malcolm is proposing? Based on what Kim has said about the managers, users, and systems people, what seems to be the operational feasibility of the proposed project? What about the economic feasibility? What about the technological feasibility? Based on what Kim and Malcolm have discussed, would you recommend that a full-blown systems study be done?

expedite or reschedule activities to finish on time, while motivating team members to complete the job properly.

Estimating Time Required

The systems analyst's first decision is to determine the amount of detail that goes into defining activities. The lowest level of detail is the systems development life cycle itself, while the highest extreme is to include every detailed step. The optimal answer to planning and scheduling lies somewhere in between.

A structured approach is useful here. In Figure 3.4, the systems analyst beginning a project has broken the process into three major phases: analysis, design, and implementation. Then the analysis phase is further broken down into data gathering, data flow and decision analysis, and proposal preparation. Design is broken down into data entry design, input and output design, and data organization. The implementation phase is divided into implementation and evaluation.

In subsequent steps the systems analyst needs to consider each of these tasks and break them down further, so planning and scheduling can take place. Figure 3.5 shows how the analysis phase is described in more detail. For example, data gathering is broken down into five activities, from conducting interviews to observing reactions to the prototype. This particular

Analysis	Data Gathering Data Flow and Decision Analysis Proposal Preparation
Design	Data Entry Design Input Design Output Design Data Organization
Implementation	Implementation Evaluation

Break apart the major activities into smaller ones.

project requires data flow analysis, but not decision analysis, so the systems analyst has penciled in "analyze data flow" as the single step in the middle phase. Finally, proposal preparation is broken down into three steps: perform cost/benefit analysis, prepare proposal, and present proposal.

The systems analyst, of course, has the option to break down steps further. For instance, the analyst could specify each of the persons to be interviewed. The amount of detail necessary depends on the project, but all critical steps need to appear in the plans.

Sometimes the most difficult part of project planning is the crucial step of estimating the time it takes to complete each task, or activity. There is no substitute for experience in estimating time requirements, and systems analysts who have had the opportunity of an apprenticeship are fortunate in this regard.

Planners have attempted to reduce the inherent uncertainty in determining time estimates by projecting most likely, pessimistic, and optimistic estimates and then using a weighted average formula to determine the expected time an activity will take. This approach offers little more in the way of confidence, however. Perhaps the best strategy for the systems analyst is to adhere to a structured approach in identifying activities and describing these activities in sufficient detail. In this manner, the systems analyst will at least be able to limit unpleasant surprises.

Using Gantt Charts for Project Scheduling

A Gantt chart is an easy way to schedule tasks. It is essentially a chart on which bars represent each task or activity. The length of each bar represents the relative length of the task.

Figure 3.6 is an example of a two-dimensional Gantt chart where time is indicated on the horizontal dimension and a description of activities makes up the vertical dimension.

In this example, the Gantt chart shows the information-gathering phase of the project. Notice on the Gantt chart that conducting interviews will take three weeks, administering the questionnaire will take four weeks, and so on. Activities A and C are to take place at the same time.

Special graphical devices described in the key can help the developer of the chart control the project. Figure 3.6 depicts the current state of the data-gathering project in the ninth week. The symbol signifies that it is week 9. The bars with darker shading represent projects or parts of projects that have been completed. This tells us that the systems analyst is behind in activity E but ahead in activity D. Action must be taken on the first

FIGURE 3.5
Refining the planning and
scheduling of analysis
activities by adding detailed
tasks and establishing the
time required to complete
these tasks.

Phase	Detailed Activity	Weeks Required
Data Gathering	Conduct Interviews	3
	Administer Questionnaires	4
	Read Company Reports	4
	Introduce Prototype	5
	Observe Reactions to Prototype	3
Data Flow and Decision Analysis	Analyze Data Flow	8
Proposal Preparation	Perform Cost/Benefit Analysis	3
	Prepare Proposal	2
	Present Proposal	2

Break these down further,

then estimate time required.

activity soon so that other activities or even the project itself will not be delayed as a result.

The main advantage of the Gantt chart is its simplicity. The systems analyst will find not only that this technique is easy to use but also that it lends itself to worthwhile communication with end users. Another advantage of using a Gantt chart is that the bars representing activities or tasks are drawn to scale; that is, the size of the bar indicates the relative length of time it will take to complete each task.

Using PERT Diagrams

PERT is an acronym for Program Evaluation and Review Techniques. A *program* (a synonym for a project) is represented by a network of nodes and arrows then evaluated to determine the critical activities, improve the schedule if necessary, and review progress once the project is undertaken. PERT was developed in the late 1950s for use in the U.S. Navy's Polaris nuclear submarine project. It reportedly saved the U.S. Navy two years' development time.

PERT is useful when activities can be done in parallel rather than in sequence. The systems analyst can benefit from PERT by applying it to systems projects on a smaller scale, especially when some team members can be working on certain activities at the same time that fellow members are working on other tasks.

Figure 3.7 compares a simple Gantt chart with a PERT diagram. The activities expressed as bars in the Gantt chart are represented by arrows in the PERT diagram. The length of the arrows has no direct relationship with the activity durations. Circles on the PERT diagram are called *events* and can be identified by numbers, letters, or any other arbitrary form of designation. The circular nodes are present to (1) recognize that an activity is completed and (2) indicate which activities need to be completed before a new activity may be undertaken (precedence).

In reality, activity C may not be started until activity A is completed. Precedence is not indicated at all in the Gantt chart, so it is not possi-

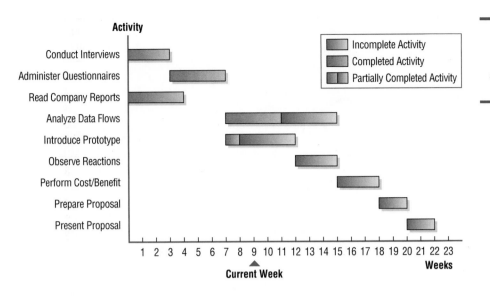

Activity

Conduct Interviews
Administer Questionnaires
Read Company Reports
Analyze Data Flows
Introduce Prototype
Observe Reactions
Perform Cost/Benefit
Prepare Proposal
Present Proposal

☐ Incomplete Activity
☐ Completed Activity
☐ Partially Completed Activity

1 2 3 4 5 6 7 8 9 10 11 12 13 14 15 16 17 18 19 20 21 22 23

▲ Current Week

Weeks

FIGURE 3.6
Using a two-dimensional
Gantt chart for planning
activities that can be accomplished in parallel.

ble to tell whether activity C is scheduled to start on day 5 on purpose or by coincidence.

A project has a beginning, a middle, and an end; the beginning is event 10 and the end is event 50. In order to find the length of the project, each path from beginning to end is identified, and the length of each path is calculated. In this example, path 10-20-40-50 has a length of 15 days, while path 10-30-40-50 has a length of 11 days. Even though one person may be working on path 10-20-40-50 and another on path 10-30-40-50, the project is not a race. The project requires that both sets of activities (or paths) be completed; consequently the project takes 15 days to complete.

The longest path is referred to as the *critical path*. Although the critical path is determined by calculating the longest path, it is defined as the path that will cause the whole project to fall behind if even one day's delay

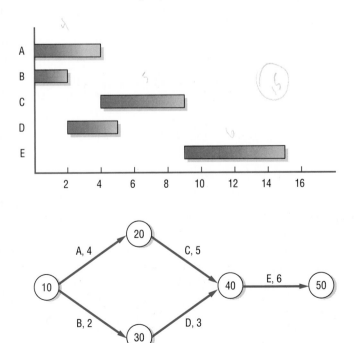

FIGURE 3.7
Gantt charts compared with
PERT diagrams for
scheduling activities.

A
B
C
D
E

2 4 6 8 10 12 14 16

20
A, 4   C, 5
10   40   E, 6   50
B, 2   D, 3
30

FIGURE 3.8
Precedence of activities is
important in determining the
length of the project when
using a PERT diagram.

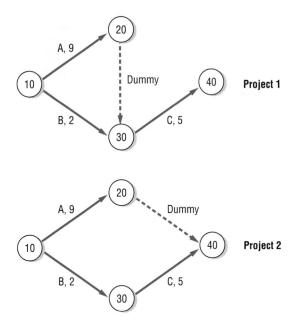

is encountered on it. Note that if you are delayed one day on path 10-20-40-50 the entire project will take longer, but if you are delayed one day on path 10-30-40-50, the entire project will not suffer. The leeway to fall behind somewhat on noncritical paths is called slack time.

Occasionally, PERT diagrams need pseudo activities, referred to as dummy activities, to preserve the logic or clarify the diagram. Figure 3.8 shows two PERT diagrams with dummies. Project 1 and project 2 are quite different, and the way the dummy is drawn makes the difference clear. In project 1, activity C can only be started if *both* A and B are finished, since all arrows coming into a node must be completed before leaving the node. In project 2, however, activity C requires only activity B's completion and can therefore be underway while activity A is still taking place.

Project 1 takes 14 days to complete, while project 2 takes only 9 days. The dummy in project 1 is necessary, of course, since it indicates a crucial precedence relationship. The dummy in project 2, on the other hand, is not required, and activity A could have been drawn from 10 to 40 and event 20 may be eliminated completely.

Therefore, there are many reasons for using a PERT diagram over a Gantt chart. The PERT diagram allows:

1. Easy identification of the order of precedence.
2. Easy identification of the critical path and thus critical activities.
3. Easy determination of slack time.

A PERT EXAMPLE. Suppose a systems analyst is trying to set up a realistic schedule for the data-gathering and proposal phases of the systems analysis and design life cycle. The systems analyst looks over the situation and lists activities that need to be accomplished along the way. This list, which appears in Figure 3.9, also shows that some activities must precede other activities. The time estimates were determined as discussed in an earlier section of this chapter.

Activity		Predecessor	Duration
A	Conduct Interviews	None	3
B	Administer Questionnaires	A	4
C	Read Company Reports	None	4
D	Analyze Data Flow	B, C	8
E	Introduce Prototype	B, C	5
F	Observe Reactions to Prototype	E	3
G	Perform Cost/Benefit Analysis	D	2
H	Prepare Proposal	G	2
I	Present Proposal	H	2

FIGURE 3.9
Listing activities for use in
drawing a PERT diagram.

DRAWING THE PERT DIAGRAM. In constructing the PERT diagram, the analyst looks first at those activities requiring no predecessor activities—in this case, A (conduct interviews) and C (read company reports). In the example in Figure 3.10, the analyst chose to number the nodes 10, 20, 30, and so on, and drew two arrows out of the beginning node 10. These arrows represent activities A and C and are labeled as such. Nodes numbered 20 and 30 are drawn at the end of these respective arrows. The next step is to look for any activity requiring only A as a predecessor; task B (administer questionnaires) is the only one, so it can be represented by an arrow drawn from node 20 to node 30.

Since activities D (analyze data flow) and E (introduce prototype) require both activities B and C to be finished before they are started, arrows labeled D and E are drawn from node 30, the event that recognizes the completion of both B and C. This process is continued until the entire PERT diagram is completed. Notice that the entire project ends at an event called "node 80."

IDENTIFYING THE CRITICAL PATH. Once the PERT diagram is drawn, it is possible to identify the critical path by calculating the sum of the activity times on each path and choosing the longest path. In this example, there are four paths: 10-20-30-50-60-70-80; 10-20-30-40-60-70-80; 10-30-50-60-70-80; and 10-30-40-60-70-80. The longest path is 10-20-30-50-60-70-80, which takes 22 days. It is essential that the systems analyst carefully monitor the activities on the critical path in order to keep the entire project on time or even shorten the project length if warranted.

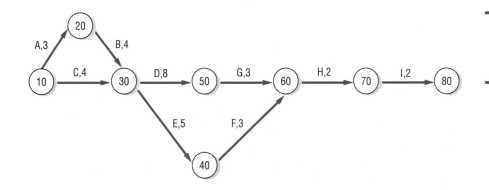

FIGURE 3.10
A completed PERT diagram
for the analysis phase of a
systems project.

59

FIGURE 3.11
A table showing the crash
time and cost of expediting.

Activity	Estimated Duration	Crash Time	Cost/Week
A	3	1	$800
B	4	2	500
C	4	2	400
D	8	6	1000
E	5	5	1000
F	3	3	800
G	3	3	800
H	2	2	400
I	2	1	600

Expediting

When all of the activities are identified and drawn as a PERT diagram, or whenever a project seems to be falling behind, a systems analyst has a chance to speed up the process to complete the project in the time desired. This process is referred to as expediting.

Figure 3.11 is essentially a table of time and money tradeoffs for our systems analyst project. Each activity is listed, along with the estimated time it takes to complete the activity. The third column, labeled "crash time," refers to the absolute minimum time in which an activity can be completed if additional money is funneled to that activity. The final column contains the cost of reducing the activity duration by 1 week.

Expediting can help reduce the time it takes to complete the entire project, but in order to do so the expedited activities have to be on the critical path. Which activity is expedited on the critical path depends on the cost, assuming the activity is not already at its crash time.

The maximum number of weeks each activity can be reduced is the difference between the expected time and its crash time. As an example, activity B, administering the questionnaires, could be reduced from 4 weeks to 2 weeks at the cost of $500 per week, but cannot be reduced to less than 2 weeks; activity H, preparing the proposal, cannot be reduced since it is already at its crash time.

The expediting analysis for our example is found in Figure 3.12. The expediting process takes place one step at a time, until it is impossible to expedite any further. The columns in the table include eligible activities (tasks which are on the critical path and can be reduced by expediting), the activity chosen (because it is the cheapest alternative), the current time it takes to complete each of the paths, the cost (of expediting the chosen activity), and, finally, the cumulative cost.

In the first step, the critical path is 10-20-30-50-60-70-80, so the eligible activities are A, B, D, or I. Activities G and H are also on the critical path, but they are already at their crash times and are consequently ineligible for expediting. The cheapest alternative is to expedite activity B by 1 week. This reduces the first path from 22 to 21 weeks and the second from 19 to 18 weeks, but does not affect the third and fourth paths since activity B is not on either path. The critical path, and therefore the entire project, is reduced from 22 to 21 weeks (circled on the table). We can repeat this reduction and reduce the project time by another week.

When activity B reaches its crash time, another activity must be chosen. Row 3 in the table shows that activities A, D, and I are eligible and

Eligible Activities	Activity Chosen	Time for Each Path ㉒ 18 18 18				Cost	Cumulative Cost
A, B, D, or I	B	㉑	18	19	16	$ 500	$ 500
A, B, D, or I	B	⑳	17	19	16	500	1000
A, D, or I	I	⑲	16	18	15	600	1600
A or D	A	⑱	15	⑱	15	800	2400
A and C, or D	D	⑰	15	⑰	15	1000	3400
A and C, or D	D	⑯	⑮	⑯	15	1000	4400
A and C	A	⑮	⑭	⑮	14	1200	5600

FIGURE 3.12
Using expediting to minimize project time.

activity I is the cheapest alternative. Reducing activity I not only reduces the critical path, but all paths, because it is common to all of them.

In the fourth step, activity A is chosen and it reduces paths 1 and 2, but the result is that there are now two critical paths. This implies that any further reduction of the project time will take place only if both of the critical paths are reduced at the same time. This is accomplished in the fifth and sixth steps by choosing either a combination of activities A and C (one activity from each of the critical paths) or activity D (an activity common to both critical paths). Reducing D by 2 weeks shortens the paths to 16, 16, 16, and 15 weeks, respectively (now there are three critical paths). Finally, when activity D reaches its crash time, the only available choice is a combination of activities A and C. The minimum project time is therefore 15 weeks, obtainable by reducing activity A by 2 weeks, activity B by 2 weeks, activity C by 1 week, activity D by 2 weeks, and activity I by 1 week at the total cost of $5,600.

Of course, the preceding situation describes all-out expediting to obtain the minimum project time at any cost. The systems analyst may be faced with a budget. In our example, a budget of $4,000 would result in expediting up to and including step 5; the project would be shortened to 17 weeks at a cost of $3,400. Another possible criterion could be the net amount one would save if the project were shortened. Suppose that in the preceding example the analyst would save $750 per week, mostly consisting of the opportunity to work on new projects sooner. In this case, expediting would take place until step 3, since step 4 (expediting activity A) would exceed the $750 limit.

Expediting can make or break a successful project. The systems analyst has to remain on top of the situation by managing the project throughout the entire systems development life cycle. Managing team members is another key area, as we will discuss in the next section.

COMPUTER-BASED PROJECT SCHEDULING

Using microcomputers for project scheduling has now become practical. DOS-based scheduling programs were unwieldy because the amount of keystrokes, the time needed to memorize those keystrokes, and the steep learning curve proved to be barriers to everyday computerized scheduling by the typical end user. Under a GUI (Graphical User Interface) environment, using project management software is less of a problem. Microsoft Project, Symantec's Timeline, and Computer Associates' CA-Super Project are three good examples of powerful programs.

An example of project management from Microsoft Project can be found in Figure 3.13. Here you can see that the expediting problem

Two-Minute Penalty for Delay of Project

The systems analysis team composed of Hy Sticking, Rip Shinpadd, Fiona Wrink, and yourself, is running into some time pressures that it didn't anticipate. Your team is rushing to get a system up and running for Kitchener, Ontario's professional hockey team, the Kitchener Redwings, before the hockey season begins. Once the season begins, it will be impossible to switch to computerized scheduling of hockey games, computerized ticketing, and automatic compilation of team statistics.

The systems analysis team is gathered around a table in Hy's office; each team member is holding a copy of the most recent PERT chart being used to control and monitor the project. Hy, your leader, speaks first, saying, "We need to make a decision on this today. Management would very much like to see a prototype for the ticketing system sooner than we have it here. That's not a bad idea, except you can see that some other activities need to be completed first."

Fiona says, "What you're saying is we should expedite the project. I'm all for it, except I know from other projects that interviewing the managers is going to be hard to do in the crash time."

"I think we can do it. We have another project lined up too," Rip interjects. "Expediting would probably be a good idea if we can swing it."

Hy turns his attention to the most recent PERT diagram and notes aloud the different activities on the critical path that can be effectively shortened. "I think we can reduce interviews by sampling managers, rather than talking to all of them. And if you take a look at the other activities remaining, we need to shorten the time it takes to contact the other hockey teams in the league by putting both Rip and Fiona on that."

Fiona and Rip agree that expediting the project would be worthwhile, and Hy proceeds to discuss with them in detail what it would take in terms of manhours and money to expedite three of the activities on the critical path.

As the fourth member of the systems analysis team, you have been quietly observing the proceedings. What is your overall perspective on the value of expediting a project? In this particular instance, management has requested an additional activity that is causing the team leader to suggest expediting in order to accommodate the request. In your view, is this an appropriate motivation for expediting? What are the potential impacts on the team and the project if expediting is undertaken?

completed earlier in this chapter is entered into Microsoft Project. New tasks can be entered into either the top or the bottom part of the screen, whichever is easier for the user. Let's assume that we want to enter the task "Analyze data flow" on the bottom half of the screen. First we enter the name of the activity, then its duration, 8d (including a qualifier: d for day, w for week, etc.), and the ID for any predecessors (in this case there are two). The ID, or identifier, is simply the number of the task. We don't have to enter a start date if we want the computer program to schedule it for us (as soon as possible, given the predecessors). The upper part of the table lists the activities in the order in which we entered them. To the right is a Gantt chart. The lighter bars appear in orange on the screen and indicates the critical path. The darker bars are shaded blue and are noncritical.

Figure 3.14 is another screen from Microsoft Project. The bottom half of the screen is the same, but the top half now shows a PERT diagram. Computer programs take the liberty of representing the tasks or activities with rectangles, rather than with arrows. Although this goes against the traditional conventions used in PERT diagrams, the software authors feel that it is easier to read tasks in rectangular boxes than to read them on arrows. A darker line, shown in red on the actual screen, indicates the critical path. Once activities are drawn on the screen, they can be repositioned using a mouse in order to enhance readability and communication with others. The dark box indicates that we are looking at that activity at the moment. The dotted vertical line on the right side of the screen shows the user where the page break will occur.

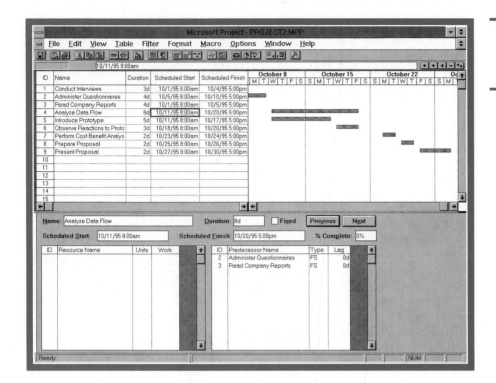

FIGURE 3.13
This screen from Microsoft
Project illustrates a
Gantt chart.

The icons at the top of the page are familiar to anyone who uses Word for Windows, Excel, or PowerPoint, three other Microsoft products.

Other approaches to scheduling include integrated personal information managers, or PIMs. Some examples of a PIM include ECCO by Arabesque, PackRat by Polaris Software, and Organizer by Lotus Corporation. These PIMs are useful because they are a repository for phone and fax numbers of business associates, daily, weekly, or monthly planners, and to-do lists. Some PIMs are designed to be shells that enable you to launch other programs and even allow you to store similar data from word processing and spreadsheet programs in "folders" organized around a particular topic. Some, like ECCO, are good at sharing data with other programs, while others include Gantt charts to aid in project management.

Figure 3.15 is a screen from Lotus Corporation's Organizer. Although the calendar shown is helpful in planning, it does not perform the analysis found in Gantt charts or PERT diagrams, so you could schedule more tasks than you can handle or even miss a deadline if you are not careful. The program is useful because it looks like familiar paper planners, you can print out the calendar easily, and you can drag and drop activities to and from the calendar. If you drag anything to the garbage can in the lower left corner, a tiny animated fire burns up the discarded item.

MANAGING ANALYSIS AND DESIGN ACTIVITIES

Along with managing time and resources, systems analysts must also manage people. Management is accomplished primarily through communicating accurately to team members who have been selected for their competency and compatibility. Goals for project productivity must be set, and members of systems analysis teams must be motivated to achieve them.

FIGURE 3.14
Computer-based project
management programs often
show activities as rectangles,
not arrows.

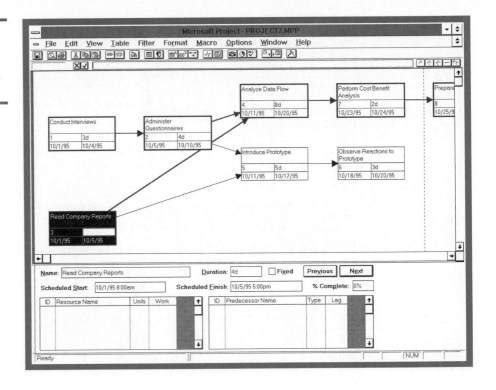

Communication Strategies for Managing Teams

Teams have their own personalities, a result of combining each individual team member with every other in a way that creates a totally new network of interactions. A way to organize your thinking about teams is to visualize them as always seeking a balance between accomplishing the work at hand and maintaining the relationships among team members.

In fact, teams will often have two leaders, not just one. Usually one person will emerge who leads members to accomplish tasks, and another person will emerge who is concerned with the social relationships among group members. Both are necessary for the team. These individuals have been labeled by other researchers as, respectively, task leader and socioe-motional leader. Every team is subject to tensions that are an outgrowth of seeking a balance between accomplishing tasks and maintaining relationships among team members.

For the team to continue its effectiveness, tensions must be continually resolved. Minimizing or ignoring tensions will lead to ineffectiveness and eventual disintegration of the team. Much of the tension release necessary can be gained through skillful use of feedback by all team members. However, all members need to agree that the way they interact (i.e., process) is important enough to merit some time. Productivity goals for processes are discussed in a later section.

Securing agreement on appropriate member interaction involves creating explicit and implicit norms (collective expectations, values, and ways of behaving) that guide members in their relationships. A team's norms belong to it and will not necessarily transfer from one team to another. These norms change over time and are better thought of as a process of interaction rather than a product.

Norms can be functional or dysfunctional. Just because a particular behavior is a norm for a team does not mean it is helping the team to

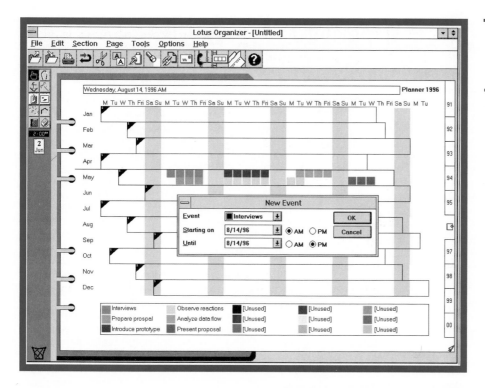

FIGURE 3.15
Organizer from Lotus
Corporation provides a sim-
ple way to manage projects.

achieve its goals. For example, an expectation that junior team members should do all project scheduling may be a team norm. By adhering to this norm, the team is putting extreme pressure on new members and not taking full advantage of the experience of the team. It is a norm that, if continued, could make team members waste precious resources.

Team members need to make norms explicit and periodically assess whether norms are functional or dysfunctional in helping the team achieve its goals. The overriding expectation for your team must be that change is the norm. Ask yourself whether team norms are helping or hindering the team's progress.

Setting Project Productivity Goals

When you have worked with your team members on various kinds of projects, you or your team leader will acquire an acumen for projecting what the team can achieve within a specific amount of time. The earlier section in this chapter on methods for estimating time required, coupled with experience, will enable the team to set worthwhile productivity goals.

Systems analysts are accustomed to thinking about productivity goals for employees who show tangible outputs such as number of blue-jeans sewn per hour, number of entries keyed in per minute, or number of items scanned per second. However, as manufacturing productivity rises, it is becoming clear that managerial productivity must keep pace. It is with this aim in mind that productivity goals for the systems analysis team are set.

Goals need to be formulated and agreed to by the team, based on team members' expertise, former performance, and the nature of the specific project. Goals will vary somewhat for each project undertaken, since sometimes an entire system will be installed, while other projects might involve limited modifications to a portion of an existing system.

CONSULTING OPPORTUNITY 3.3

Goal Tending

"Here's what I think we can accomplish in the next 5 weeks," says Hy, the leader of your systems analysis team, as he confidently pulls out a schedule listing each team member's name alongside a list of short-term goals. Just a week ago, your systems analysis team went through an intense meeting on expediting their project schedule for the Kitchener, Ontario Redwings, a hockey organization whose management is pressuring you to produce a prototype.

The three other members of the team look at the chart in surprise. Finally, one of the members, Rip, speaks: "I'm in shock. We each have so much to do as it is, and now this."

Hy replies defensively, "We've got to aim high, Rip. They're in the off-season. It's the only time to get them. If we set our goals too low, we won't finish the systems prototype, let alone the system itself, before another hockey season passes. The idea is to give the Kitchener Redwings the fighting edge through the use of their new system."

Fiona, another team member, enters the discussion saying, "Goodness knows their players can't give them that!" She pauses for the customary groan from the assembled group, then continues, "But seriously, these goals are killers. You could have at least asked us what we thought, Hy. We may even know *better* than you what's possible."

"This is a pressing problem, not a tea party, Fiona," Hy replies. "Polite polling of team members was out of the question. Something had to be done quickly. So I went ahead with these. I say we submit our schedule to management based on this. We can push back deadlines later if we have to. But this way they'll know we're committed to accomplishing a lot during off-season."

As a fourth team member listening to the foregoing exchange, what suggestions might you make to Hy that would help him improve his approach to goal formation and presentation? How well-motivated do you think the team will be if they share Fiona's view of Hy's goals? What are the possible ramifications of supplying management with overly optimistic goals? Think of both short-term and long-term effects.

Motivating Project Team Members

Although motivation is an extremely complex topic, it is a good one to consider, even if briefly, at this point. To oversimplify, recall that people join organizations to provide for some of their basic needs such as food, clothing, and shelter. But all humans also have higher-level needs that include affiliation, control, independence, and creativity. People are motivated to fulfill unmet needs on several levels.

Team members can be motivated, at least partially, through participation in goal setting, as described in the previous section. The very act of setting a challenging but achievable goal and then periodically measuring performance against the goal seems to work in motivating people. Goals act almost as magnets in attracting people to achievement.

Part of the reason goal setting motivates people is that team members know prior to any performance review exactly what is expected of them. The success of goal setting for motivating can also be ascribed to the fact that it affords the team member some autonomy in achieving the goals. While a goal is predetermined, the means to achieve it may not be. In this instance, team members are free to use their own expertise and experience to meet their goals.

Setting goals can also motivate team members by clarifying for them and others what must be done in order to get results. Team members are also motivated by goals because goals define the level of achievement that is expected of them. This simplifies the working atmosphere, but it also electrifies it with the possibility that what is expected can indeed be done.

Avoiding Project Failures

The early discussions that you have with management and others requesting a project, along with the feasibility studies you do, are usually the best defenses possible against taking on projects that have a high probability of failure. Your training and experience will improve your ability to judge the worthiness of projects and the motivations that prompt others to request projects. If you are part of an in-house systems analysis team, you must keep current with the political climate of the organization, as well as with financial and competitive situations.

Remember that you are not alone in the decision to begin a project. Although apprised of your team's recommendations, management will have the final say about whether a proposed project is worthy of further study (that is, further investment of resources). The decision process of your team must be open and stand up to scrutiny from those outside of it. The team should consider that their reputation and standing in the organization are inseparable from the projects they accept.

SUMMARY

The four major project fundamentals that the systems analyst must handle are: (1) project initiation, (2) determining project feasibility, (3) project scheduling, and (4) managing systems analysis team members. Projects may be requested by many different people within the business or by systems analysts themselves.

Selecting a project is a difficult decision, since more projects will be requested than can actually be done. Five important criteria for project selection are: (1) that the requested project be backed by management, (2) that it be timed appropriately for commitment of resources, (3) that it move the business toward attainment of its goals, (4) that it be practicable, and (5) that it be important enough to be considered over other possible projects.

If a requested project meets these criteria, then a feasibility study of its operational, technical, and economic merits can be done. Through the feasibility study, systems analysts gather data that enable management to decide whether to proceed with a full systems study.

Project planning includes the estimation of time required for each of the analyst's activities, scheduling them, and expediting them if necessary to ensure a project is completed on time. One technique available to the systems analyst for scheduling tasks is the Gantt chart, which displays activities as bars on a graph.

Computer-based project scheduling using microcomputers is now practical, due largely to the use of graphical user interfaces. Additionally, personal information managers (PIMs) can be used by analysts to do planning, create repositories for phone and fax numbers, or even launch other programs.

A second technique, called PERT (for Program Evaluation and Review Techniques), displays activities as arrows on a network. PERT helps the analyst determine the critical path and slack time, which is the information required for effective project control. When it is necessary to complete a project in less time, the analyst can reduce total project duration by identifying and expediting key activities.

Once a project has been judged feasible, the systems analyst must manage the team members, their activities, time, and resources. Most of

"I hope everyone you've encountered at MRE has treated you well. Here's a short review of some of the ways you can access our organization through HyperCase . The reception area at MRE contains the key links to the rest of our organization. Perhaps you've already discovered these on your own, but I wanted to remind you of them now, since I don't want to get so engrossed in the rest of our organizational problems that I forget to mention them.

"The telephone on the receptionist's desk has instructions about how to answer the phone in the rest of the organization. You have my permission to pick up the phone if it is ringing and no one else answers it.

"The people shaking hands in the doorway will take you on a 10-minute tour of our building. They'll even tell you some of the history of MRE to keep you entertained along the way. The empty doorway that you see is a link to the next room, which we call the East Atrium. You have probably noticed that all open doorways are links to adjacent rooms. Notice that the building map displayed in the reception area is dynamic, in that it is linked to all public rooms. As you know, you must have an employee escort you into a private office. You cannot go there on your own.

"By now you have probably noticed the three documents on the small table in the reception area. The little one is the MRE internal phone directory. Just click on an employee name, and if that person is in, he or she will grant you an interview and a tour of the office. I leave you to your own devices in figuring out what the other two documents are.

FIGURE 3.HC1
Click on key words in Hypercase and find out more detail.

"If you have had a chance to interview a few people and see how our company works, I'm sure you are becoming aware of some of the politics involved. But we are also worried about more technical issues, such as what constitutes feasibility for a training project and what does not."

HYPERCASE QUESTIONS

1. What criteria does the Training Unit use to judge the feasibility of a new project? List them.
2. List any changes or modifications to these criteria which you would recommend.
3. Snowden Evans has asked you to help prepare a proposal for a new project tracking system for the Training Unit. Briefly discuss the technical, economic, and operational feasibility of each alternative for a proposed project tracking system for the Training Unit.
4. Which option would you recommend? Use evidence from HyperCase to support your decision.

this is accomplished by communicating with team members. Teams are constantly seeking a balance between working on tasks and maintaining relationships within the team. Tensions arising from attempting to achieve this balance must be addressed. Often two leaders of a team will emerge—a task leader and a socioemotional leader. Members must periodically assess team norms in order to assure that the norms are functional rather than dysfunctional for the attainment of team goals.

It is important that the systems analysis team set reasonable productivity goals for tangible outputs and process activities. Project failures can usually be avoided by examining the motivations for requested projects, as well as your team's motives for recommending or avoiding a particular project.

KEYWORDS AND PHRASES

operational feasibility
technical feasibility
economic feasibility
Gantt chart
PERT diagrams
critical path
expediting
computer-based project
   scheduling

personal information managers (PIMs)
task leader
socioemotional leader
team norms
team process
productivity goals
team motivation

REVIEW QUESTIONS

1. What are the four major project fundamentals?
2. List three ways to find out about problems or opportunities that might call for a systems solution.

3. List the five criteria for systems project selection.

4. Define *technical feasibility*.

5. Define *economic feasibility*.

6. Define *operational feasibility*.

7. When is a two-dimensional Gantt chart more appropriate than a one-dimensional Gantt chart?

8. When is a PERT chart useful for systems projects?

9. List three advantages of a PERT chart over a Gantt chart for scheduling systems projects.

10. Define the term *critical path*.

11. When is expediting of systems projects done?

12. List the functions of microcomputer based project scheduling available in common software packages.

13. List the functions of some commonly used personal information manager (PIM) software.

14. List the two types of team leaders.

15. What is meant by *dysfunctional team norm*?

16. What is meant by "*team process*"?

17. What are three reason why goal setting seems to motivate systems analysis team members?

PROBLEMS

1. Dressman's Chocolates of St. Louis makes an assortment of chocolate candy and candy novelties. They have six in-city stores, five stores in major metropolitan airports, and a small mail-order branch. Dressman's has a small, computerized information system that tracks inventory in their plant, helps schedule production, and so on, but is not tied directly into their retail outlets. Their mail-order system is handled manually. Recently, several Dressman's stores experienced a rash of complaints from mail-order customers that their candy was spoiled upon arrival, that it did not come when promised, or that it never arrived; they also received several letters complaining that candy in various airports tasted stale. Finally, a few sales clerks in company stores reported being asked whether the firm would be willing to market a new, dietetic form of chocolate made with aspartame.

   You had been working for two weeks with Dressman's on some minor modifications for their inventory information system when you overheard two managers discussing these occurrences. List the possible opportunities or problems among them that might lend themselves to systems projects.

2. Where is most of the feedback on problems with Dressman's products coming from in problem 1? How reliable are the sources? Explain in a paragraph.

3. After getting to know them better, you have approached Dressman's management with some of your ideas on possible systems improvements that could address some of the problems or opportunities given in problem 1.

   a. In two paragraphs, provide your suggestions for systems projects. Make any realistic assumptions necessary.

b. Are there any problems or opportunities discussed in problem 1 that are *not* suitable? Explain your response.

4. The systems analysis consulting firm of Flow Associates is working on a systems design project for Wind and Waves Waterbeds, Inc.

Description	Task	Must Follow	Expected Time (Days)
Draw data flow	P	None	9
Draw decision tree	Q	P	12
Revise tree	R	Q	3
Write up project	S	R,Z	7
Organize data dictionary	T	P	11
Do output prototype	X	None	8
Revise output design	Y	X	14
Design database	Z	T,Y	5

a. Using the data from above, draw a Gantt chart to help Flow Associates organize their design project.

b. When is it appropriate to use a Gantt chart? What are the disadvantages? Explain in a paragraph.

5. Figure 3.EX1 is a PERT diagram based on the data from problem 4. List *all* paths and calculate and identify the critical path.

6. **a.** Based on problems 4 and 5 and the following data, minimize the time it takes to complete the project for Wind and Waves Waterbeds. Assume an unlimited budget (that is, expedite).

Task	Expected Time (Days)	Crash Time	Cost of Expediting
P	9	5	$ 50
Q	12	8	160
R	3	3	130
S	7	6	300
T	11	9	80
X	8	8	70
Y	14	8	200
Z	5	2	150

b. Minimize the time it takes to complete the project for Wind and Waves Waterbeds. Assume Flow Associates has a budget of $1,000.

c. Minimize the time it takes to complete the project for Wind and Waves Waterbeds. Assume that Flow Associates saves $200 per day and has an unlimited budget.

7. At the top of the next page are some estimates Wendy, the systems analyst, has prepared for training users of the new system her firm is installing for Fortuna Farms, a large dairy.

Activity	Must Follow	Expected Time (Days)
A	None	5
B	None	9
C	None	4
D	A	3
E	B	8
F	B	6
G	C	13
H	E	1
I	E	11
J	G	14

a. Draw a PERT diagram of Wendy's time estimates.

b. List *all* paths and calculate and identify the critical path.

8. a. Based on problem 7 and the data shown below, minimize the time it takes to complete the project for Fortuna Farms. Assume an unlimited budget (that is, expedite).

b. Minimize the time it takes to complete the project for Fortuna Farms. Assume that Wendy has a budget of $1,000.

c. Minimize the time it takes to complete the project for Fortuna Farms. Assume that Wendy saves $200 per day and has an unlimited budget.

Task	Expected Time (Days)	Crash Time	Cost of Expediting
A	5	3	$140
B	9	7	150
C	4	3	50
D	3	1	40
E	8	7	105
F	6	6	60
G	13	6	90
H	1	1	110
I	11	6	80
J	14	11	70
K	3	1	130
L	2	2	75
M	7	5	250

9. Recently, two analysts fresh out of college have joined your systems analyst group at the newly formed company, Mega Phone. When talking to you about the group, they mention that some things strike them as odd. One is that group members seem to look up to two group leaders, Bill and Penny, not just one.

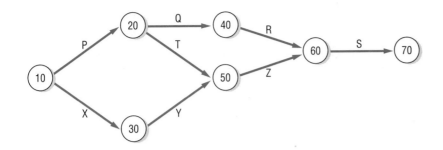

FIGURE 3.EX1
The PERT diagram from Flow
Associates.

Their observation is that Bill seems pretty relaxed, while Penny is always planning and scheduling activities. They have also observed that everyone "just seems to know what to do" when they get into a meeting, even though no instructions are given. Finally they have remarked on the openness of the group in addressing problems as they arise, instead of letting things get out of hand.

a. By way of explanation to the new team members, label the types of leaders Bill and Penny appear to be, respectively.

b. Explain the statement that "everyone just seems to know what to do." What is guiding their behavior?

c. What concept best describes the openness of the group that the new team members commented on?

GROUP PROJECT

1. With your group members, explore a computerized project manager such as Microsoft Project or Lotus Organizer. What features are available? Work with your group to list them. Have your group evaluate the usefulness of the software for managing a systems analysis and design team project. In a paragraph, state whether the software you are evaluating facilitates team member communication and management of team activities, time, and resources. State which particular features support these aspects of any project. Note whether the software falls short of these criteria in any regard.

SELECTED BIBLIOGRAPHY

Adam, E. E., Jr., and R. J. Ebert. *Production and Operations Management*, 3rd ed. Englewood Cliffs, NJ: Prentice-Hall, Inc., 1986.

Bales, R. F. *Personality and Interpersonal Behavior*. New York: Holt, Rinehart and Winston, 1970.

Gildersleeve, T. R. *Successful Data Processing for Systems Analysis*. Englewood Cliffs, NJ: Prentice-Hall, Inc., 1977.

Merry, U., and M. E. Allerhand. *Developing Teams and Organizations*. Reading, MA: Addison-Wesley, 1977.

Schein, E. H. *Process Consultation: Its Role in Organization Development*. Reading MA: Addison-Wesley, 1969.

Weinberg, G. M. *Rethinking Systems Analysis and Design*. Boston: Little, Brown and Company, Inc., 1982.

GETTING TO KNOW U

Chip enters Anna's office one weekend saying, "I think the project will be a good one, even though it's taking some long hours to get started."

Anna looks up from her screen and smiles, "I like what you've done in getting us organized. I hadn't realized Excelerator could help us this much with project management."

"Let me show you how easy it's going to be to keep track of our users," Chip says as he brings up a User Description screen about Dot Matricks, the manager of microcomputer systems at CPU. (See Figure E3.1.)

"See, we can put a description of her responsibilities in here, and any time we want to review it, we've got it stored."

Anna glances at the screen with interest. "This will help immensely. Much easier than remembering all of this ourselves. What else do you have there?"

"I've got a second screen on Dot with more details," replies Chip, bringing up that screen. (See Figure E3.2.)

Anna remarks, "Great. This will make it less of a chore to find a good time to meet for an interview. Now here's what I've been up to. Remember when we started looking at the old system to see what requirements users had? Well, here's a User Requirement description screen for preventive maintenance." (See Figure E3.3.)

"We will usually need a longer description of the user requirement, so you just page down, and as you can see, I've already added to the basics." Anna continues. (See Figure E3.4.) Anna glances at her watch.

User: DOT MATRICKS

Entity   Edit   Help

Alternate Name | MANAGER - MICROCOMPUTER SYSTEMS

Definition | RESPONSIBLE FOR ALL MICROCOMPUTER EQUIPMENT AND SOFTWARE
Location | ADMINISTRATION - ROOM 207

User Responsible For:

Type Name

Type	Name
DFD	MICROCOMPUTER CONTEXT DIAGRAM
DFD	MICROCOMPUTER DIAGRAM 0
REC	MICROCOMPUTER MASTER
REC	MICROCOMPUTER MAINTENANCE
REC	SOFTWARE MASTER
SCD	MICROCOMPUTER - ADD NEW MICRO
SCD	MICROCOMPUTER INQUIRY
SCD	MICROCOMPUTER - CHANGE SOFTWARE
RED	MICROCOMPUTER SOFTWARE CROSS-REF
RED	MICROCOMPUTER MASTER LIST

FIGURE E3.1
User description screen.

Allen Schmidt,
Julie E. Kendall, and
Kenneth E. Kendall

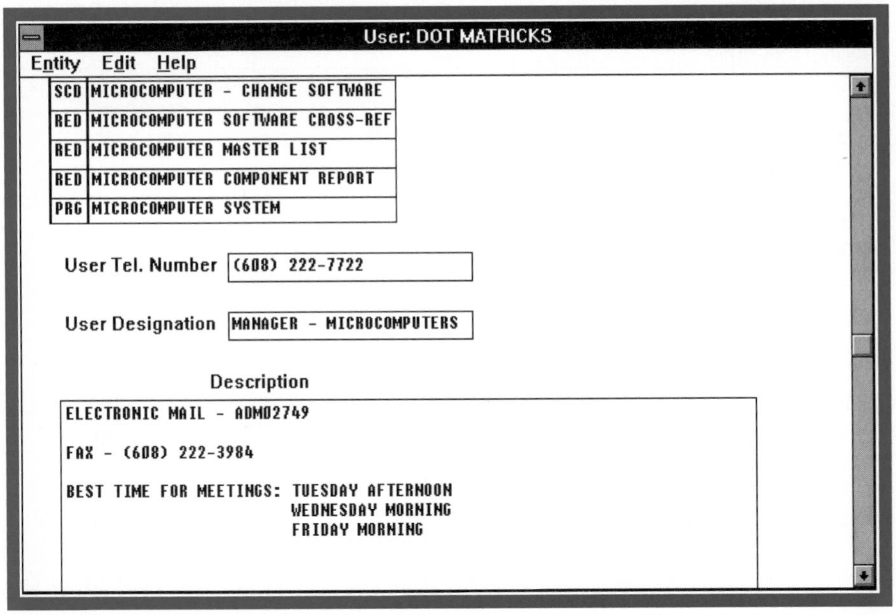

FIGURE E3.2
User description screen, second page.

"But now it's getting late. I think we've made a lot of progress in setting up our project. Let's call it a day, or should I say evening? Remember, I got us tickets for the football game."

Chip replies, "I haven't forgotten. Let me get my coat, and we'll walk over to the stadium together."

Walking across campus later, Chip says, "I'm excited. It's my first game here at CPU. What's the team mascot, anyway?"

"Chipmunks, of course," says Anna.

"And the team colors?" Chip asks, as they enter the stadium.

"Blue and white," Anna replied.

"Oh, *that's* why everyone's yelling, 'Go Big Blue!'" Chip says, listening to the roar of the crowd.

"Precisely," says Anna.

Exercises*

Use Excelerator to define the following User entities and User Requirements.

🖫 **E-1.**   Use Excelerator to view the information stored about Dot Matricks.

🖫 **E-2.**   Modify the User entry for Mike Crowe. Create and print the information summarized on the next page.

Allen Schmidt,
Julie E. Kendall, and
Kenneth E. Kendall

---

* Exercises preceded by a disk icon require the program Excelerator or another CASE tool. A disk is provided free of charge to any professor adopting this book. The examples on the disk may be imported into Excelerator and then used by students.

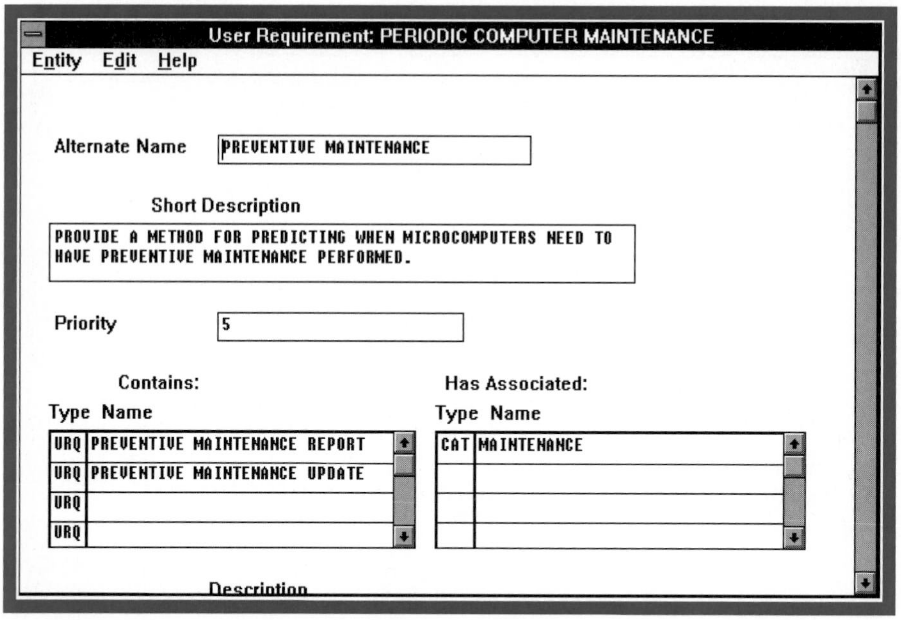

FIGURE E3.3
User Requirement description screen.

Electronic mail ID: DPT09374
FAX: (608) 222-6889
Phone number: (608) 222-0224
Location: Microcomputer Maintenance, Room 384
User Designation: Technical Support—Microcomputers
User Responsible For:
    RED Preventive Maintenance Report
    REC Maintenance Information
    REC Peripheral Equipment

⊟ **E-3.** Modify the User entry for Hy Perteks. Create and print the information summarized below.

Electronic mail ID: DPT09374
FAX: (608) 222-4711
Phone number: (608) 222-2988
Location: Information Center, Room 320
User Designation: Technical Specialist, Information Center
Best time for interviews: Tuesday, Thursday mornings
User Responsible For:
    SCD Software Location Inquiry
    REC Software Expert

```
┌─────────────────────────────────────────────────────────────┐
│ ─    User Requirement: PERIODIC COMPUTER MAINTENANCE          │
│ E̲ntity  E̲dit  H̲elp                                            │
│                                                            ▲  │
│   Priority        ┌5──────────────────────┐                  │
│                   └───────────────────────┘                  │
│                                                               │
│        Contains:                  Has Associated:            │
│   Type Name                       Type Name                  │
│  ┌────┬──────────────────────┐┬  ┌────┬─────────────────────┐┬│
│  │URQ │PREVENTIVE MAINTENANCE ││▲ │CAT │MAINTENANCE          ││▲│
│  │    │REPORT                │┤  │    │                     │┤ │
│  │URQ │PREVENTIVE MAINTENANCE ││  │    │                     ││ │
│  │    │UPDATE                │┤  │    │                     │┤ │
│  │URQ │                      ││  │    │                     ││ │
│  │URQ │                      ││▼ │    │                     ││▼│
│  └────┴──────────────────────┘┴  └────┴─────────────────────┘┴│
│                                                               │
│          Description                                          │
│  ┌──────────────────────────────────────────────────────┐    │
│  │THERE IS A STRONG NEED TO PERIODICALLY CLEAN ALL       │    │
│  │MICROCOMPUTERS AND THE PERIPHERALS ATTACHED TO THEM.   │    │
│  │THIS WILL KEEP THE HARDWARE IN SERVICE FOR LONGER      │    │
│  │PERIODS OF TIME AND PREVENT THE LOSS OF VALUABLE       │    │
│  │OPERATING TIME AT CRITICAL PERIODS.  ONCE THE          │    │
│  │MAINTENANCE HAS BEEN PERFORMED, THERE NEEDS TO BE A    │    │
│  │METHOD OF UPDATING HARDWARE RECORDS TO REFLECT THIS.   │    │
│  │                                                       │    │
│  │                                                    ▼  │    │
│  └──────────────────────────────────────────────────────┘    │
└─────────────────────────────────────────────────────────────┘
```

FIGURE E3.4
User requirement description, second screen.

E-4. Create a User entry for Cher Ware. Create an electronic mail ID, FAX and phone numbers, location, and other information. Print the entry.

E-5. Create User entries as described in problem 4 for Paige Prynter. Include best times for interviews and other pertinent information. Modify the User Requirement entities in exercises E-6 to E-8.

E-6. Cher Ware must have all new software added to the SOFTWARE MASTER file. The entity is ADD NEW SOFTWARE. Enter a priority of 5, and the associated entity CAT—SOFTWARE. Create a long description indicating that the all-new software must be keyed, edited for validity, and updated on the SOFTWARE MASTER file.

E-7. Dot Matricks needs to have a PENDING MICROCOMPUTER ORDER file updated as new microcomputers are received. The User Requirement entity is PENDING MICROCOMP. FILE. The priority is 7. An associated entity is CAT—MICROCOMPUTER INFORMATION. Create a long description of the process: The PENDING MICROCOMPUTER ORDER file is to be randomly obtained, using the order number. The number of microcomputers on order should be decreased by one, and the last update date replaced with the current date. The PENDING MICROCOM-PUTER ORDER record should be rewritten.

E-8. Mike Crowe would like to automate the Microcomputer Inventory process. Modify the AUTOMATE MICRO INVEN-TORY PROCESS User Requirement entity. The priority is an 8, indicating a lower priority. The following user requirements should be included: URQ—PRODUCE MACHINE LOCATION LIST AND URQ—UPDATE MACHINE LOCATIONS. The

Associated entity is CAT—MICROCOMPUTER INFORMA-TION. The lengthy description would reflect the need to periodically produce a listing of all locations, in order of building and then room number. Each room location would include the machines presumed to be present. Include a procedure for updating the machine records once the inventory has been completed.

E-9. Create User Requirement entities for the following situations:

a. Dot Matricks needs to know which component boards are located within each microcomputer.

b. Dot Matricks must provide an inquiry that will satisfy persons looking for a machine with specific graphics, printing, and other special capabilities.

c. Mike Crowe must know if a machine is covered under warranty.

d. Mike Crowe would like a "lemon" report, showing machines that frequently break down.

e. Cher Ware needs a comprehensive list of all software.

f. It is essential for Cher Ware to have a cross-reference listing of which software is located on which microcomputers.

g. Paige Prynter needs to know the total dollar amount of hard- ware inventory.

h. Paige Prynter needs figures on how much it would cost to upgrade a currently used piece of software, along with the total costs for each software package.

## 4

SAMPLING AND INVESTIGATING HARD DATA

Underlying all of the data-gathering methods of investigation, interviewing, and observing are the crucial decisions regarding what to examine and who to question or observe. The systems analyst can make these decisions based on a structured approach called sampling.

SAMPLING

Sampling is the process of systematically selecting representative elements of a population. When these selected elements are examined closely, it is assumed that the analysis will reveal useful information about the population as a whole.

The systems analyst has to make a decision on two key issues. First, there are many reports, forms, output documents, and memos that have been generated by members of the organization. Which of these should the systems analyst pay attention to and which should the systems analyst ignore?

Second, a great many employees can be affected by the proposed information system. Which people should the systems analyst interview, seek information from via questionnaires, and observe in the process of carrying out their decision-making roles?

The Need for Sampling

There are many reasons why a systems analyst would want to select a representative sample of data to examine or representative people to interview, question, or observe. They include:

1. Containing costs
2. Speeding up the data gathering
3. Improving effectiveness
4. Reducing bias

Examining every scrap of paper and talking with everyone in the organization would be far too costly for the systems analyst. Photocopying reports, asking employees for valuable time, and duplicating unnecessary questionnaires would result in much needless expense.

Sampling helps accelerate the process by gathering selected data rather than all data for the entire population. In addition, the systems analyst is spared the burden of analyzing data from the entire population.

Effectiveness in data gathering is an important consideration as well. Sampling can help improve effectiveness if more accurate information can be obtained. This is accomplished, for example, by talking to fewer employees but asking them more detailed questions. Additionally, if fewer people are interviewed the systems analyst can afford the time to follow up missing or incomplete data, thus improving the effectiveness of data gathering.

Finally, data-gathering bias can be reduced by sampling. When the systems analyst interviews an executive of the corporation, for example, the executive is involved with the project. The executive has given a certain amount of time to the project and would like it to succeed. When the systems analyst asks an opinion about a permanent feature of the installed information system, the executive interviewed may provide a biased evaluation since there is little possibility of changing it.

Sampling Design

The four steps that a systems analyst must follow to design a good sample are:

1. Determine the data to be collected or described.
2. Determine the population to be sampled.
3. Choose the type of sample.
4. Decide on the sample size.

These steps are described in detail in the following section.

DETERMINING THE DATA TO BE COLLECTED OR DESCRIBED. The systems analyst needs a realistic plan about what will be done with the data once it is collected. If irrelevant data is gathered, then time is wasted in the collection, storage, and analysis of useless data.

The duties and responsibilities of the systems analyst at this point are to identify the variables, attributes, and associated data items that need to be gathered in the sample. The objectives of the study must be considered, as well as the type of data-gathering method (investigation, interviews, questionnaires, observation) to be used. The kinds of information sought when using each of these methods will be discussed in more detail in this and subsequent chapters.

DETERMINING THE POPULATION TO BE SAMPLED. Next, the systems analyst must determine what the population is. In the case of hard data, the systems analyst needs to decide, for example, if the last two months are sufficient, or if an entire year's worth of reports are needed for analysis.

Similarly, when deciding who to interview, the systems analyst has to determine whether the population should include only one level in the organization, or all of the levels—or maybe even go outside of the system

	Not Based On Probability	**Based On Probability**
Sample elements are selected directly without restrictions	Convenience	Simple random
Sample elements are selected according to specific criteria	Purposive	Complex random (systematic, stratified, and cluster)

The systems analyst should use a complex random sample if possible.

FIGURE 4.1
Four main types of samples
the analyst has available.

to include the reactions of customers. These decisions will be explored further in the chapters on interviewing, questionnaires, and observation.

CHOOSING THE TYPE OF SAMPLE. The systems analyst has four main types of samples, as pictured in Figure 4.1. They are convenience, purposive, simple, and complex.

Convenience samples. Convenience samples are unrestricted, nonprobability samples. A sample could be called a convenience sample if, for example, the systems analyst put a notice in the company newsletter asking for everyone interested in the new sales performance reports to come to a meeting at 1:00 P.M. on Tuesday the 12th. Obviously, this sample is the easiest you could set up, but it is also the most unreliable.

Purposive samples. A systems analyst can choose a group of individuals who appear knowledgeable and interested in the new information system. This is an example of a purposive sample, based on the analyst's judgment. Here the systems analyst bases the sample on criteria (knowledge and interest in the new system) but it is still a nonprobability sample. Thus purposive sampling is only moderately reliable.

Simple random samples. If you choose to perform a simple random sample, you need to obtain a numbered list of the population to ensure that each document or person in the population has an equal chance of being selected. This, often is not practical, especially when sampling involves documents and reports.

Complex random samples. You can often accomplish the goals of sampling by choosing one of the approaches for complex random sampling. The approaches most appropriate for the systems analyst are: (1) systematic sampling, (2) stratified sampling, and (3) cluster sampling.

In the simplest method of probability sampling, systematic sampling, the systems analyst would, for example, choose to interview every kth person on a list of company employees. However, this method has certain disadvantages. You would not want to use it to select every kth day for a sample because of the potential periodicity problem. Furthermore, a systems analyst would not use this approach if the list were ordered (for example, a list of banks from the smallest to the largest) because bias would be introduced.

Stratified samples are perhaps the most important to the systems analyst. Stratification is the process of identifying subpopulations, or strata, and then selecting objects or people for sampling within these subpopulations. Stratification is often essential if the systems analyst is to gather data efficiently. For example, if you want to seek opinions from a wide range of employees on different levels of the organization, systematic sampling would select a disproportionate number of employees from the operational control level. A stratified sample would compensate for this. Stratification is also called for when the systems analyst wants to use different methods to collect data from different subgroups. For example, you may want to use a questionnaire to gather data from middle managers but use personal interviews to gather similar data from executives.

Sometimes the systems analyst must select a group of document or people to study. This is referred to as cluster sampling. Suppose an organization had twenty warehouses scattered across the country. You may want to select one or two of these warehouses under the assumption that they are typical of the remaining warehouses.

DECIDING ON THE SAMPLE SIZE. Obviously, if everyone in the population viewed the world the same way or each of the documents in a population contained exactly the same information as every other document, a sample size of one would be sufficient. Since this is not the case, it is necessary to set a sample size greater than one but less than the size of the population itself.

It is important to remember that the absolute number is more important in sampling than the percentage of the population. We can obtain satisfactory results sampling 20 people in 200 or 20 people in 2,000,000.

The sample size depends on many things, some set by the systems analyst, some determined by what we know about the population itself, and other important factors. The systems analyst can choose the acceptable interval estimate (that is, the degree of precision desired) and the standard error (by choosing the degree of precision desired) and the standard error (by choosing the degree of confidence).

Furthermore, the characteristics of the population may change the sample size. If the sales figures in a report range from $10,000 to $15,000 a small sample size would be sufficient to give you an accurate estimate of average sales. However, if the sales ranged from $1,000 to $100,000 then a much larger sample size would be required. Sample size is discussed in greater detail in the following section.

The Sample Size Decision

The sample size often depends on the cost involved or the time required by the systems analyst, or even the time available by people in the organization. This section gives the systems analyst some guidelines for determining the required sample size under ideal conditions.

DETERMINING SAMPLE SIZE WHEN SAMPLING DATA ON ATTRIBUTES. Sometimes the systems analyst might want to find out what proportion of people in an organization think a certain way or have certain characteristics. Other times the analyst may need to know what percentage of input forms have mistakes. This type of data can be referred to as attribute data.

The systems analyst needs to follow a series of steps, some of which are subjective judgments, to determine the required sample size. The following is the list of seven steps:

1. Determine the attribute you will be sampling.
2. Locate the database or reports where the attribute can be found.
3. Examine the attribute. Estimate p, the proportion of the population having the attribute.
4. Make the subjective decision regarding the acceptable interval estimate, i.
5. Choose the confidence level and look up the confidence coefficient (z value) in a table.
6. Calculate σ_p, the standard error of the proportion as follows:

$$\sigma_p = \frac{i}{z}$$

7. Determine the necessary sample size, n, using the following formula:

$$n = \frac{p\,(1-p)}{\sigma_p^2} + 1$$

The first step, of course, is to be determining which attribute you will be sampling. Once this is done, you can find out where this data is stored, perhaps in a database, on a form, or in a report.

It is important to estimate p, the proportion of the population having the attribute so that you set the appropriate sample size. Many textbooks on systems analysis suggest using a heuristic of 0.25 for $p(1-p)$. This almost always results in a sample size larger than necessary because 0.25 is the maximum value of $p(1-p)$, which occurs only when $p=0.50$. When $p=0.10$, as is more often the case, $p(1-p)$ becomes 0.09, resulting in a much smaller sample size.

Steps 4 and 5 are subjective decisions. The acceptable interval estimate of ± 0.10 means that you are willing to accept an error of no more than 0.10 in either direction from the actual proportion, p. The confidence level is the desired degree of certainty—say, for example, 95 percent. Once the confidence level is chosen, the confidence coefficient (also called a z value) can be looked up in a table like the on found in Figure 4.2.

Steps 6 and 7 complete the process by taking the parameters found or set in steps 3 through 5 and entering them into two equations to eventually solve for the required sample size.

	Confidence Level	Confidence Coefficient (z-value)
First decide on the confidence level,		
	99%	2.58
	98	2.33
	97	2.17
	96	2.05
	95	1.96
	90	1.65
	80	1.28
	50	0.67

then look up the z value.

FIGURE 4.2
A table of area under a normal curve can be used to look up a value once the systems analyst decides on the confidence level.

EXAMPLE

The foregoing steps can best be illustrated by an example. Suppose the A. Sembly Company, a large manufacturer of shelving products, asks you to determine what percentage of orders contain mistakes. You agree to do this and perform the following steps:

1. Determine that you will be looking for orders that contain mistakes in names, addresses, quantities, or model numbers.
2. Locate copies of order forms from the past six months.
3. Examine some of the order forms and conclude that only about 5 percent (0.05) contain errors.
4. Make a subjective decision that the acceptable interval estimate will be ±0.02.
5. Choose a confidence level of 95 percent. Look up the confidence coefficient (z value) in Figure 4.2. The z value equals 1.96.
6. Calculate σ_p as follows:

$$\sigma_p = \frac{i}{z}$$

$$= \frac{0.02}{1.96} = 0.0102$$

7. Determine the necessary sample size, n, as follows:

$$n = \frac{p(1-p)}{\sigma_p^2} + 1$$

$$= \frac{0.05(0.95)}{(0.0102)(0.0102)} + 1 = 458$$

The conclusion, then, is to set the sample size at 458. Obviously, a greater confidence level or a smaller acceptable interval estimate would require a larger sample size as shown below. If we keep the acceptable interval estimate the same but increase the confidence level to 99 percent (with a z value of 2.58), the standard error of the proportion is:

$$\sigma_p = \frac{i}{z}$$

$$= \frac{0.02}{2.58} = 0.0078$$

and necessary sample size is:

$$n = \frac{p(1-p)}{\sigma_p^2} + 1$$

$$= \frac{(0.05)(0.95)}{(0.0078)(0.0078)} + 1 = 782$$

If the confidence level stays at 95 percent (z value = 1.96) but the acceptable interval estimate is set to 0.01, then the standard error of the proportion is:

$$\sigma_p = \frac{i}{z}$$

$$= \frac{0.01}{1.96} = 0.0051$$

and the necessary sample size is:

$$n = \frac{p(1-p)}{\sigma_p^2} + 1$$

$$= \frac{(0.05)(0.95)}{(0.0051)(0.0051)} + 1 = 1827$$

DETERMINING SAMPLE SIZE WHEN SAMPLING DATA ON VARIABLES. A systems analyst may sometimes need to gather information on actual numbers such as gross sales, amount of items returned, or number of mistakes keyed in. Data of this type are referred to as variables.

The steps in determining the necessary sample size for variables is similar to the steps for attribute data. The steps are:

1. Determine the variable you will be sampling.
2. Locate the database or reports where the variable can be found.
3. Examine the variable to gain some idea about its magnitude and dispersion. Ideally, it would be useful to know the mean to determine a more appropriate acceptable interval estimate and the standard deviation, s, to determine sample size (in step 7).
4. Make a subjective decision regarding the acceptable interval estimate, i.
5. Choose a confidence level and look up the confidence coefficient (z value) in a table.
6. Calculate $\sigma_{\bar{x}}$ the standard error of the mean as follows:

$$\sigma_{\bar{x}} = \frac{i}{z}$$

7. Determine the necessary sample size, n, using the following formula:

$$n = \left(\frac{s}{\sigma_{\bar{x}}}\right)^2 + 1$$

Step 3 is difficult to do precisely. In order to estimate the mean and standard deviation accurately, you would actually have to sample the population. This is, of course, a chicken-or-egg problem because the systems analyst does not know which comes first. Consequently, it is not necessary to know precisely what are the mean and standard deviation. A reasonable estimate will do.

The importance of estimating the mean and standard deviation becomes obvious when you attempt to set the acceptable interval estimate. Suppose you were asked to determine the average gross sales for a small greeting card store ($3,500 per week) and a large grocery store ($70,000 per week). A desired interval estimate of $350 for the small greeting card store would be inappropriate for the large grocery store.

Further, the estimated dispersion is important because the smaller the dispersion (as measured by the standard deviation), the smaller the necessary sample size. For example, suppose you were trying to determine the average age of purchasers of compact discs. If you make the assumption that anyone from 10 to 100 years of age purchases compact discs, you would need a very large sample size. If, however, you estimate that generally the ages of compact-disc purchasers are between 13 and 23, you can get by with a much smaller sample size.

The formulas for determining the necessary sample size for variables are different from the formulas for attribute data. Since the systems analyst must take more care in estimating the magnitude and dispersion of a variable, it is slightly more difficult than determining the sample size for attribute data.

EXAMPLE

Another example from the A. Semble Company can be used to illustrate how to find the necessary sample size for variables. Now you are asked to determine the average dollar amount for an order. You agree to do this and perform the following steps:

1. Determine that you will be looking for the mean dollar amount for orders on shelving.
2. Locate copies of order forms from the past six months.
3. Examine some of the order forms and conclude that orders average about $1,500 with a standard deviation, s, of about $100.
4. Make a subjective decision that the acceptable interval estimate will be $5.00.
5. Chose a confidence level of 96 percent. Look up the confidence coefficient (z value) in Figure 4.2. The z value equals 2.05.
6. Calculate $\sigma_{\bar{x}}$ as follows:

$$\sigma_{\bar{x}} = \frac{i}{z}$$

$$= \frac{5.00}{2.05} = 2.44$$

7. Determine the necessary sample size, n, as follows:

$$n = \left(\frac{s}{\sigma_{\bar{x}}}\right)^2 + 1$$

$$= \left(\frac{100}{2.44}\right)^2 + 1$$

$$= 1680 + 1$$

$$= 1681$$

You therefore would want to sample 1681 orders to determine the mean dollar amount of orders.

As with sampling attribute data, a greater confidence level or a smaller acceptable interval estimate would require a larger sample size. If we keep the acceptable interval estimate the same but increase the confidence level to 99 percent (with a z value of 2.58), the standard error of the mean is:

$$\sigma_{\bar{x}} = \frac{i}{z}$$

$$= \frac{5.00}{2.58} = 1.94$$

and the necessary sample size is:

$$n = \left(\frac{s}{\sigma_{\bar{x}}}\right)^2 + 1$$

$$= \left(\frac{100}{1.94}\right)^2 + 1$$

$$= 2,658$$

If the confidence level stays at 96 percent (z value = 2.05) but the acceptable interval estimate is set to \$1.00, the standard error of the mean is:

$$\sigma_{\bar{x}} = \frac{i}{z}$$

$$= \frac{1.00}{2.05} = 0.488$$

and the necessary sample size is:

$$n = \left(\frac{s}{\sigma_{\bar{x}}}\right)^2 + 1$$

$$= \left(\frac{100}{0.488}\right)^2 + 1$$

$$= 41,992$$

This implies that accuracy to the nearest dollar would be far too costly in sampling, because sampling over 41,000 of anything is excessive.

DETERMINING SAMPLE SIZE WHEN SAMPLING QUALITATIVE DATA. A good deal of information cannot be obtained by searching through files. That information can best be obtained by interviewing people in the organization.

There are no magic formulas to help the systems analyst set the sample size for interviewing. The overriding variable that determines how many people the systems analyst should interview in depth is the time an interview takes. A true in-depth interview and follow-up interview is very time-consuming for both the interviewer and the participant.

A good rule of thumb is to interview at least three people on every level of the organization and at least one from each of the organization's functional areas (as described in Chapter 2). Remember also that one does not have to interview more people just because it is a larger organization. If the stratified sample is done properly, a small number of people will adequately represent the entire organization.

Trapping a Sample

"Real or fake? Fake or real? Who would have thought it, even five years ago?" howls Sam Pelt, a furrier what owns stores in New York, Washington, D.C., Beverly Hills, and Copenhagen. Sylva Foxx, a systems analyst with her own consulting firm, is talking with Sam for the first time. Currently, P & P, Ltd. (which stands for Pelt and Pelt's son) is using a microcomputer system that supports package software for a select customer mailing list, accounts payable and accounts receivable, and payroll.

Sam is interested in making some strategic decisions that will ultimately effect the goods purchasing for his four fur stores. He feels that while the computer might help, there are also other approaches to be considered.

Sam continues, "I think we should talk to each of the customers when they come in the door. Get their opinion. You know some of them are getting very upset about wearing fur from endangered species. They're very environment-minded. They prefer fake to real, if they can save a baby animal. Some even like fake better—call them 'fun furs.' And I can charge almost the same for a good look-alike.

"But it's a very fuzzy proposition. If I get too far away from my suppliers of pelts, I may not get what I want when I need it. They see the fake fur people as worms—worse then moths! If I deal with them, the real fur men might not talk to me. They can be animals. On the other hand, I feel strange showing fakes in my stores. All these years, we've prided ourselves on having only the genuine article."

Sam continues, in a nearly seamless monologue, "I want to talk to each and every employee, too."

Sylva glances at him furtively and begins to interrupt, "But that will take months, and purchasing may come apart at the seams unless they know soon what—"

Pelt continues, "I don't care how long it takes, if we get the right answers. But they have to be right. Not knowing how to solve this dilemma about fake furs is making me feel like a leopard without its spots."

Sylva talks to Sam Pelt for a while longer and then ends the interview by saying, "I'll talk it all over with the other analysts at the office and let you know what we come up with. I think we can outfox the other furriers if we use the computer to help us sample opinions, rather than trapping unsuspecting customers into giving an opinion. But I'll let you know what they say. This much is for sure, if we can sample and not talk to everybody before making a decision, every coat you sell will have a silver lining."

As one of the systems analysts who is part of Sylva Foxx's firm, suggest some ways that Sam Pelt can use the small computer system he has to sample adequately the opinions of his customers, store managers, buyers, and any others you feel will be instrumental in making the strategic decision regarding the stocking of fake furs in what has always been a real fur store. Suggest a type of sample for each group, and justify it. The constraints you are subject to include the need to act quickly so as to remain competitive, the need to retain a low profile so that competing furriers are unaware of your fact gathering, and the need to keep costs of the data gathering to a reasonable level.

KINDS OF INFORMATION SOUGHT IN INVESTIGATION

The systems analyst seeks facts and figures, financial information, organizational contexts, and document types and problems through the sampling and investigation of hard data as shown in Figure 4.3. Hard data accumulated in records supply information that cannot be obtained through other methods such as interviewing or observation.

Although hard data are produced by the organization as a generic product much like "to whom it may concern" material, the analyst needs to remember that meanings taken from hard data are constructed personally by organizational members. So it becomes important to ask who the documents were produced for originally, and why they have been kept. In other words, the role of the document in the organization needs to be understood. Generally, well-documented organizations may be more rigid than businesses with less documentation, since documentation may function to create one-way centralized control.

The analyst also needs to be aware that documents in an organization can serve as persuasive messages, since they offer information about how

FIGURE 4.3
Kinds of information sought
in investigation.

people are expected to behave. It also follows that organizational change is facilitated through the changing of documents.

Types of Hard Data

As the systems analyst works to understand the organization and its information requirements, it will become important to examine different types of hard data, which offer information unavailable through any other method of data gathering. Hard data reveal where the organization has been and where its members believe it is going. The analyst needs to examine both quantitative and qualitative hard data in order to piece together an accurate picture.

ANALYZING QUANTITATIVE DOCUMENTS. A variety of quantitive documents is available for interpretation in any business. These include reports used for decision making, performance reports, and various forms. All of these documents have a specific purpose and audience for which they are targeted.

Reports used for decision making. A systems analyst needs to obtain some of the documents that are used in running the business. These documents are often paper reports regarding the status of inventory, sales, or production. Many of these reports are not complex, but serve mainly as feedback for quick action. For example, a sales report may summarize the amount sold and type of sales. Additionally, sales reports might include graphical output comparing revenue and income over a set number of periods. This enables the decision maker to readily spot trends.

Production reports include recent costs, current inventory, recent labor, and plant information. Beyond these key reports, many summary reports are used by decision makers to provide background information, spot exceptions to normal occurrences, and afford strategic overviews of organizational plans.

Performance reports. Most performance reports take on the general form of actual versus intended performance. One important function of performance reports is to assess the size of the gap between actual and intended performance. It is also important to be able to determine if that gap is widening or narrowing as an overall trend in whatever performance is being measured. Figure 4.4 shows a clear improvement in sales

FIGURE 4.4
A performance report
showing improvement.

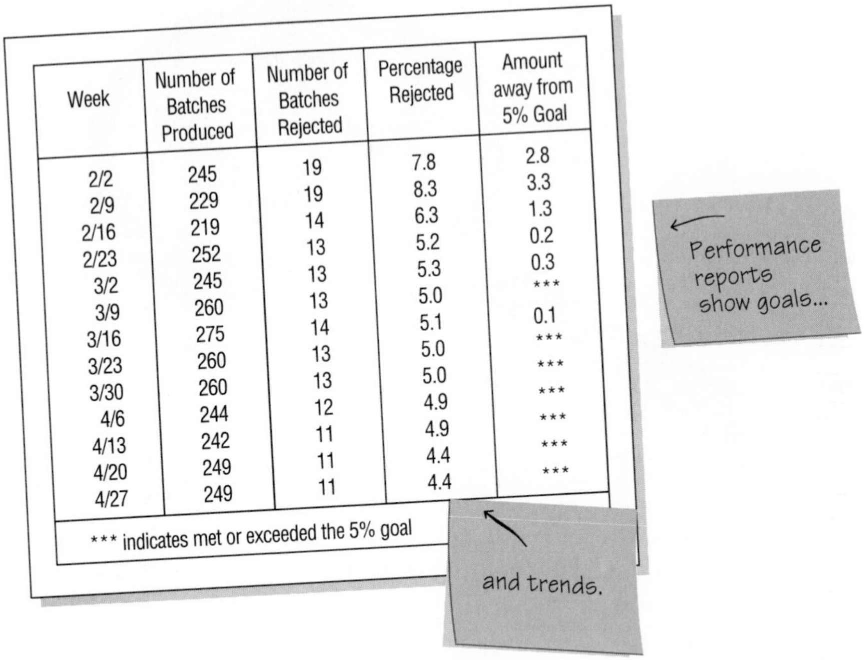

Week	Number of Batches Produced	Number of Batches Rejected	Percentage Rejected	Amount away from 5% Goal
2/2	245	19	7.8	2.8
2/9	229	19	8.3	3.3
2/16	219	14	6.3	1.3
2/23	252	13	5.2	0.2
3/2	245	13	5.3	0.3
3/9	260	13	5.0	***
3/16	275	14	5.1	0.1
3/23	260	13	5.0	***
3/30	260	13	5.0	***
4/6	244	12	4.9	***
4/13	242	11	4.9	***
4/20	249	11	4.4	***
4/27	249	11	4.4	***

*** indicates met or exceeded the 5% goal

Performance reports show goals...

and trends.

performance over six months. The analyst will want to note if performance measurement is available and adequate for key organizational areas.

Records. Records provide periodic updates of what is occurring in the business. If the record is updated in a timely fashion by a careful recorder, it can provide much used information to the analyst. Figure 4.5 is a manually completed payment record for apartment rental. Notice that there are several ways that the analyst can inspect a record, including

1. Checking for errors in amounts and totals.
2. Looking for opportunities for improving the recording form design.
3. Observing the number and type of transactions.
4. Watching for instances where the computer can simplify the work (that is, calculations and other data manipulation).

Data capture forms. Before you set out to change the information flows in the organization, you need to be able to understand the system that is currently in place. You or one of your team members may want to collect and catalog a blank copy of each form (official or unofficial) that is in use. (Sometimes businesses have a person already charged with forms management who would be your first source for forms in use.)

Blank forms, along with their instructions for completion and distribution, can be compared to filled-in forms to see if any data items are consistently left blank on the forms, whether the people who are supposed to receive the forms actually do get them, and if they follow standard procedures for using, storing, and discarding them.

Here is how to proceed when creating a catalog of forms to help you understand the information flow currently in use in the business:

FIGURE 4.5
A manually completed
payment record.

Check for errors.

Look for opportunities for improvement in design.

PROJ. NAME	OAK. FC	# 562	KEY SIGNATURE			15.00
					PRORATE	121.32

RENT POTENTIAL			1175/0	81299		DEPOSIT POTENTIAL						Days	Daily Rate	Totals	5.20

Base Rent	Refrigerator	Furniture	A/C	Util.	HMSR	T.V.	Maid	Total Rent	Security	Cleaning	31175/0	81299	31700 Tax	Days	Daily Rate	Totals
855		55						910			H/S dep.	H/S rent		4	30.33 1.30	910 3.9
									200	115					Deposits 31.63	340

TOTAL INITIAL PAYMENT REQUIRED: 1430.52

PAYMENT RECORD: Tot. 31175/0 + 81299 + Rent = 910

Memo Only	Date Due	Date Paid	Receipt Number	Paid to Noon	Total Rent	Security	Cleaning	31700 Tax	31175/0	81299 Dates	Other Amt.	Descr.	Amt.	Amount Paid	Balance Due
TV 10/3 MO!	8/28	8/28	106642	9/30	1031.32	202	115	44.20	25			414.82	15	1430.52	0
	10/1	10/3	107503	10/31	910									910	0
	11/1	11/1	10935	11/16	485.28									485.28	0
C1H/S9-16	11/17	11/8	11200	11/23	212.31									212.31	0
Bill 1 MO	11/24														
Prorated															
H/S should be															
created toward															
refund deposit															

Orig. Move-in Date _____ 8-28 _____ d _____ same _____ Exp. _____ x # _____ 1

BLDG. # _____   NAME _____ Kend _____   1st

Observe the number and type of transactions.

Watch for places the computer can simplify the work.

1. Collect examples of all of the forms in use, whether officially sanctioned by the business or not (official versus bootleg forms).
2. Note the type of form (whether printed in-house, handwritten, computer-generated in-house, printed externally and purchased, etc.).
3. Document the intended distribution pattern.
4. Compare the intended distribution pattern with who actually receives the form.

Although this procedure is time-consuming, it is useful. Another approach is to sample data capture forms that have already been completed. The analyst must keep in mind many particular questions, as illustrated in Figure 4.6. They include:

1. Is the form filled out in its entirety? If not, what items have been omitted, and are they consistently omitted? Why?
2. Are there forms that are never used? Why? (Check the design and appropriateness of the form for its purported function.)
3. Are *all* copies of forms circulated to the proper people or filed appropriately? If not, why not?
4. Are "unofficial" forms being used on a regular basis? (Their use might indicate a problem in standard procedures or may indicate political battles within the organization.)

FIGURE 4.6
Questions to ask about
official and bootleg forms that
are already filled out.

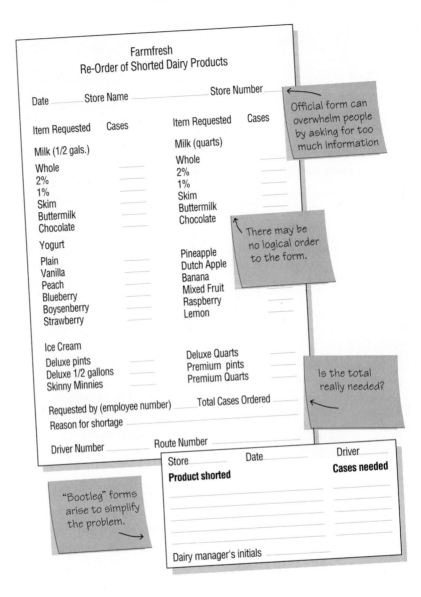

You can learn many things about an organization's information flow through examination of the form it uses. Some of the signs to watch for that may be symptomatic of larger problems include:

1. Data or information doesn't flow as intended (too many people, too few people, or the wrong people receive it).
2. Bottlenecks in the processing of forms result in slowed or stopped work.
3. Unnecessary duplication of work occurs because employees are unaware that information is already in existence on another form that they do not receive.
4. Employees lack understanding about the interrelatedness of information flow (that is, they do not know that their output work serves as input for another person).

ANALYZING QUALITATIVE DOCUMENTS. Many documents circulating within organizations are not quantitative. Although qualitative documents may not follow a predetermined form, analysis of them is critical to understanding how the organizational members engage in the process or organizing. Qualitative documents include memos, signs on bulletin boards and in work areas, procedure manuals, and policy handbooks. Many of these documents are rich in revealing the expectations for behavior of others that their writers hold.

Although many systems analysts are apprehensive about analyzing qualitative documents, they need not be. Several guidelines that can help analysts to take a systematic approach to this sort of analysis are:

1. Examine documents for key or guiding metaphors.
2. Look for insiders versus outsiders or an "us against them" mentality in documents.
3. List terms that characterize good or evil and appear repeatedly in documents.
4. Recognize a sense of humor, if present.

Each guideline is explained briefly in the following paragraphs. Guidelines should be viewed as a way to begin interpreting qualitative documents. Certainly there are other approaches that go much further in analysis than necessary for the systems analyst's purposes.

MEMO

To: All Night Shift Computer Operators
From: S. Leep, Night Manager
Date: 2/15/95
Re: Get Acquainted Party Tonight

It's a pleasure to welcome 2 new 11-7 computer operators, Twyla Tine and Al Knight. I'm sure they'll enjoy working here. Being together in the wee hours makes us feel like one big happy family. Remember for your breaks tonight that some of the crew has brought in food. Help yourself to the spread you find in the break room, and welcome to the clan, Twyla and Al.

Examining documents for key or guiding metaphors is done because language shapes behavior, and thus the metaphors we employ are critical. For example, an organization that discusses employees as "part of a great machine" or "cogs in a wheel" might be taking a mechanistic view of the organization. Notice that the guiding metaphor in the memo in Figure 4.7 is "We're one big happy family." The analyst can use this information to predict the kinds of metaphors that will be persuasive in the organization as well as to understand how a new system might be characterized metaphorically.

When the analyst finds language that pits one group or department against another or sets the business as a whole against competitors, it is possible to understand more clearly the politics that exist. Obviously, if one department is battling another, it may be impossible to gain their cooperation on a systems project until the politics are resolved in a satisfactory manner. By the same token, if the business is fiercely competitive in its remarks about other businesses in the industry, part of the thrust for the systems project may come from wanting to hold the competitive edge.

Listing the terms found in qualitative documents that characterize actions, groups, or events as good or evil allows the analyst to see what is considered good in the business and what is deemed bad or wrong. This knowledge allows insights into what group values are being espoused. For instance, if accumulating information without apparent reason is described in negative terms as depicted in Figure 4.8, then the analyst will want to ensure that system output is actually used and is not being accumulated "just in case."

The fourth guideline encourages the analyst to recognize the existence of a sense or senses of humor in the qualitative documents of the organization. Assessing use of humor provides a quick and accurate barometer of many organizational variables, including which subculture a person belongs to and what kind of morale exists. For example, conservative, traditionalist

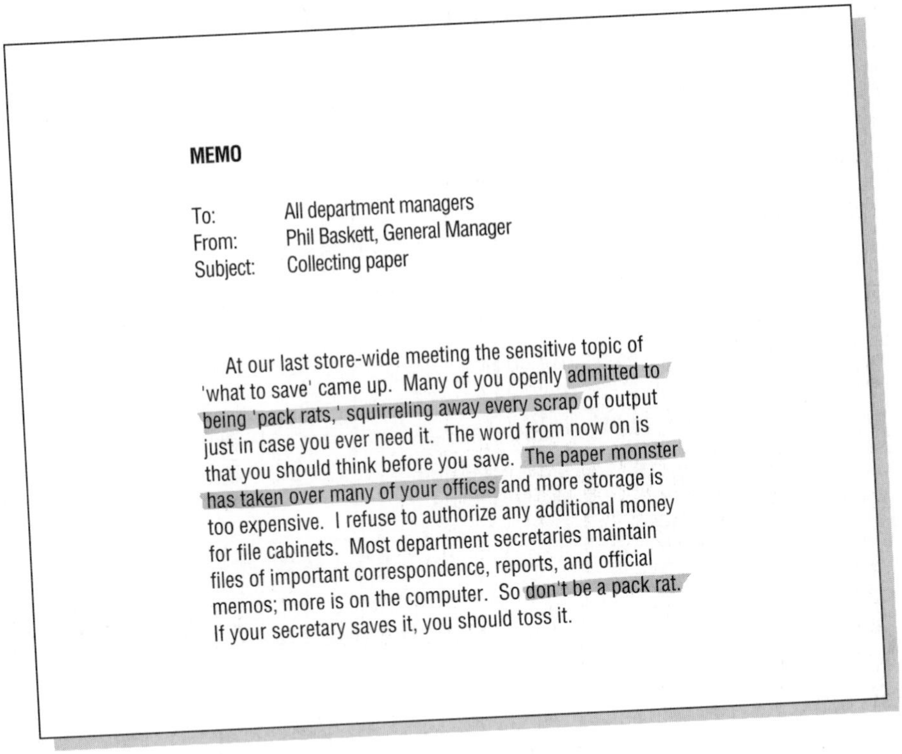

FIGURE 4.8
Analysis of memos reveals
values, attitudes, and beliefs
of organizational members
regarding use of information.

MEMO

To: All department managers
From: Phil Baskett, General Manager
Subject: Collecting paper

At our last store-wide meeting the sensitive topic of 'what to save' came up. Many of you openly admitted to being 'pack rats,' squirreling away every scrap of output just in case you ever need it. The word from now on is that you should think before you save. The paper monster has taken over many of your offices and more storage is too expensive. I refuse to authorize any additional money for file cabinets. Most department secretaries maintain files of important correspondence, reports, and official memos; more is on the computer. So don't be a pack rat. If your secretary saves it, you should toss it.

organizational members tend to relate formula jokes, with a beginning, middle, and ending punchline. People who are sensitive to others' communication needs tend to relate anecdotal, humorous stories that are self-deprecating. Additionally, if morale is low, "black" or "gallows" humor tends to be a common way of coping with organizational uncertainties.

Memos. When possible, analysts should sample memos sent throughout the business. However, sometimes memos are not kept or they are made available only to those who have "a need to know" as defined in organizational policy. Along with the four preceding guidelines, the analyst should also consider who sends memos and who receives them. Typically, most information flows downward and horizontally rather than upward in organizations. Memos reveal a lively, continuing dialog in the organization. Analysis of memo content will provide you with a clear idea of the values, attitudes, and beliefs of organizational members.

Signs on bulletin boards or in work areas. Although signs may seem incidental to what is happening in the organization, they serve as subtle reinforcers of values to those who read them, as depicted in Figure 4.9. Signs such as "Quality is forever," or "Safety first" give the analyst a feel for the official organizational culture. It is also instructive to note whom signs are intended for and to find out through interviews whether organizational members are held accountable for acting on the information posted.

Manuals. Other qualitative documents the analyst should examine are organizational manuals, including manuals for computer operating procedures. Manuals should be analyzed following the four guidelines spelled out

FIGURE 4.9
Posted signs reveal the official organizational culture.

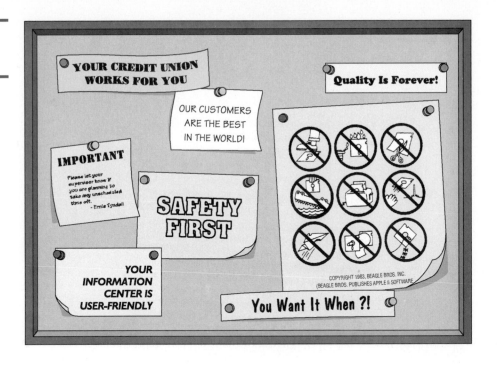

previously. Writers of manuals are allowed more elaboration in making a point than is typically accorded in memos or posted signs. Remember that manuals are the "ideal"—the way machines and people are *expected* to behave. Examining manuals systematically will give you a picture of the way things ought to happen. It is important to recall that manuals are rarely kept current and are sometimes relegated to a shelf, unused. Check to see if the manuals you are looking at are current and whether they are followed or forgotten.

Policy handbooks. The last type of qualitative document that we consider is the policy handbook. While these documents typically cover broad areas of employee and corporate behavior, you can be primarily concerned with those that address policies about computer services, use, access, and charges.

Policies are larger guidelines that spell out the organization's ideal of how members should conduct themselves in order to achieve strategic goals, as depicted in Figure 4.10. Once again, members may not even be aware of particular policies, or policies may be purposely sidestepped in the name of efficiency or simplicity. However, examining policies allows the systems analyst to gain an awareness of the values, attitudes, and beliefs that are guiding the corporation.

Abstracting Data from Archival Documents

Much of the data, both quantitative and qualitative, that you will need will not be in current use. Rather they will be stored in archives of some sort. Some material is kept because of government regulations, some because of accounting practices, and some because the business may have formerly been called upon to produce historical information.

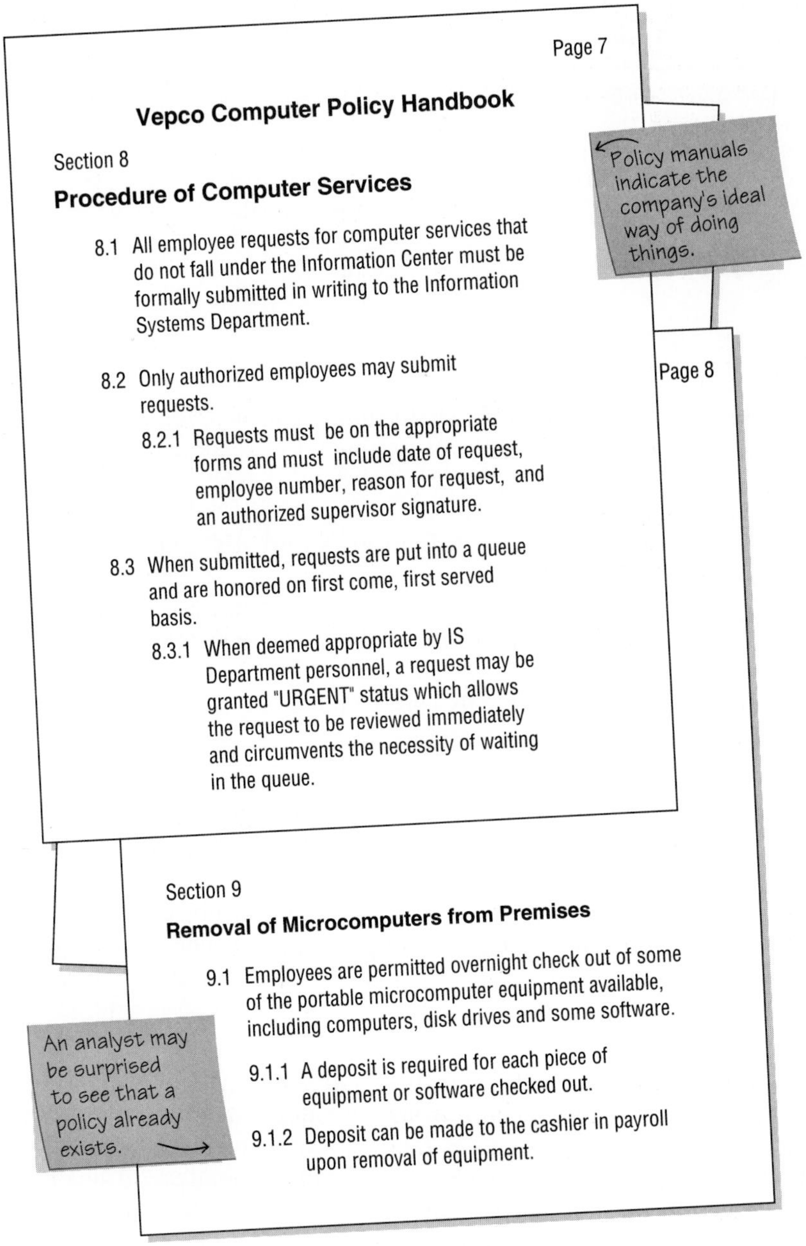

Vepco Computer Policy Handbook

Section 8

Procedure of Computer Services

8.1 All employee requests for computer services that do not fall under the Information Center must be formally submitted in writing to the Information Systems Department.

8.2 Only authorized employees may submit requests.

    8.2.1 Requests must be on the appropriate forms and must include date of request, employee number, reason for request, and an authorized supervisor signature.

8.3 When submitted, requests are put into a queue and are honored on first come, first served basis.

    8.3.1 When deemed appropriate by IS Department personnel, a request may be granted "URGENT" status which allows the request to be reviewed immediately and circumvents the necessity of waiting in the queue.

Policy manuals indicate the company's ideal way of doing things.

Page 8

Section 9

Removal of Microcomputers from Premises

9.1 Employees are permitted overnight check out of some of the portable microcomputer equipment available, including computers, disk drives and some software.

    9.1.1 A deposit is required for each piece of equipment or software checked out.

    9.1.2 Deposit can be made to the cashier in payroll upon removal of equipment.

An analyst may be surprised to see that a policy already exists. →

FIGURE 4.10
Policy manuals provide insights into the prescribed way of behaving in the organization.

Examples of archival data that may be of interest to the systems analyst include actuarial records, budgets, and sales reports. One common characteristic that all archival data share is that their collection was paid for by someone other than the systems analyst. This may or may not influence the content, but as a result archival data is a relatively low-cost informational source. Another advantage of archival data is that there is no overt changing of data, since its producer is unaware that he or she is being studied.

One disadvantage of using archival data is that the analyst may be uncertain about their meaning if only a limited subset of the data originally created exists. Another disadvantage of using archival data is that the records that survive (or that someone decided to keep) may *not* be the most

Advantages of Using Archival Data	Disadvantages of Using Archival Data
• Archival documents are already paid for— by someone else • Data are not changed since the producer is unaware of being studied	• Uncertainty exists if the data are only a subset of original data • The records that survive may not be the most important or meaningful • May be biased because someone originally decided what to file • New data are difficult to obtain from equivalent samples

important or meaningful. A third disadvantage of using archival data is that there is a large degree of built-in bias because someone has decided, for whatever reasons, to file the original data as well as to preserve some data and not others. Additionally, new data are difficult to obtain from the same or equivalent samples. Advantages and disadvantages of using archival data are summarized in Figure 4.11.

Even with all of the preceding cautions, there are some guidelines that can make abstracting data from archives worthwhile. They are:

1. Fragment the data into subclasses and make cross checks to reduce errors.

2. Compare reports on the same phenomenon by different analysts (or maybe even someone within the organization).

3. Realize the inherent bias associated with original decisions to file, keep, and/or destroy reports.

4. Use other methods such as interviewing and observation to fill out your organizational picture and supply a cross check.

SUMMARY

The process of systematically selecting representative elements of a population is called sampling. The purpose of sampling is to select and study documents such as invoices, sales reports, and memos; or perhaps to select and interview, give questionnaires to, or observe members of the organization. Sampling can reduce cost, speed data gathering, potentially make the study more effective, and possibly reduce the bias in the study.

A systems analyst must follow four steps in designing a good sample. First, there is a need for determining the population itself. Second, the type of sample must be decided upon. Third, the sample size is calculated. Finally, the data that needs to be collected or described must be planned.

The types of samples useful to a systems analyst are: convenience samples, purposive samples, simple random samples, and complex random samples. The last type includes the subcategories of systematic sampling and stratified sampling. There are several guidelines to follow when determining sample size. The systems analyst can make a subjective decision regarding acceptable interval estimates. Then a confidence level is chosen, and the necessary sample size can be calculated.

Systems analyst need to investigate hard data, including reports, documents, financial statements, procedure manuals, and memos. Hard data

reveal where the organization has been and where its members believe it is going. Both quantitative and qualitative documents need to be analyzed. Since documents are persuasive messages, it must be recognized that changing them might well change the organization.

There are many ways to analyze both quantitative and qualitative documents. However, it is important to remember that the investigation of archival data has drawbacks as well as advantages. Because many of these drawbacks can be overcome, archival investigation is worthwhile.

KEYWORDS AND PHRASES

sampling	attribute data
sample population	acceptable interval estimate
convenience sample	confidence level
purposive sample	variables
simple random sample	dispersion
complex random sample	hard data
systematic sampling	quantitative data
stratified sampling	qualitative data
cluster sampling	archival documents

REVIEW QUESTIONS

1. Define what is meant by sampling.
2. List four reasons why the systems analyst would want to sample data or select representative people to interview.
3. What are the four steps to follow in order to design a good sample?

"We're glad that you find MRE an interesting place to consult. According to the grapevine, you've been busy exploring the home office. I know, there's so much going on. We find it hard to keep track of everything ourselves. One thing we've made sure of over the years is that we try to use the methods that we believe in. Have you seen any of our reports? How about the data that was collected on one of Snowden's questionnaires? (He seems to favor questionnaires over any other method. Some people resent them, but I think you can learn a lot from the results.) Some people have been good about cooperating on these projects. Have you met Kathy Blandford yet?"

HYPERCASE QUESTIONS

1. Use clues from the case to evaluate the Training Unit's computer experience and feeling about a computerized project tracking system. What do you think the consensus is in the Training Unit toward a computerized tracking system?
2. What reports and statements are generated by the Training Unit during project development? List each with a brief description.
3. According to the interview results, what are the problems with the present project tracking system in the Training Unit?
4. Describe the "computer system conflict" at MRE. Who is involved? Why is there a conflict?
5. How does the Management Systems Unit keep track of project progress? Briefly describe the method or system.

4. Give an example of a convenience sample.
5. Define what is meant by taking a purposive sample.
6. Why is it often impractical to use a simple random sample for sampling documents and reports?
7. List the three approaches to complex random sampling.
8. Define what is meant by stratification of samples.
9. Give an example of attribute data.
10. What two changes can cause the analyst to use a larger sample size when sampling for attributes?
11. In what way does determining the sample size for variables differ from determining the sample size for attribute data?
12. What effect on sample size does using a greater confidence level have when sampling attribute data?
13. What is the overriding variable that determines how many people the systems analyst should interview in depth?
14. List three of the quantitative documents that the analyst should analyze when attempting to understand the organization.
15. List four qualitative documents that the analyst should analyze when attempting to understand the organization.

16. What are four guidelines for the systematic analysis of qualitative documents?

17. What are two advantages of using archival data as a source for understanding the organization?

18. What are four disadvantages of using archival data as a source for understanding the organization?

PROBLEMS

1. Dee Fektiv is concerned that too many forms are being filled out incorrectly. She feels that about 10 percent of all of the forms have an error.

   a. How large a sample size should Dee use to be 99 percent certain she will be within 0.02?

   b. Suppose Dee will accept a confidence level of 95 percent that she will be within 0.02. What will the sample size of forms be now?

2. Rhea Fund has asked you to determine the average number of rebates mailed on a daily basis. You examine some records and believe the average to be about 200, with a standard deviation of 20. You want to be more certain, so you decide to sample.

   a. How large should the sample size be if you want to be 99 percent certain that the number will be within 5 of the mean?

   b. How large should the sample size be if you change the confidence limit to 95 percent?

3. Phil Ittup, a member of your systems analysis group, has been assigned the task of interviewing organizational members for your systems study. The business, Fall Back Industries, has five layers of management. Also, production, accounting, marketing, systems, logistics, and top management are the functional areas that will be affected by the proposed system. Each level has about 40 people. Production has 80 people total, accounting has 35, marketing has 42, systems has 10, and logistics has 28. There are 5 people in top management.

   a. Draw up an interviewing sample for Phil to follow in choosing who to interview. Justify why you have recommended that he interview the number of people you have chosen. What factors influenced your decision?

   b. While waiting for you to make up your sample, Phil Ittup decided that, just to be on the safe side, he would skip sampling and interview each person. In a paragraph, explain to him why it is unwise for your systems analysis team not to follow a sampling strategy.

   c. Phil has finally asked you for a hard-and-fast rule for how many people to interview in the organization. If you know of one, state it. If there isn't one, explain why one does not exist.

4. "I see that you have quite a few papers there. What all do you have in there?" asks Betty Kant, head of the MIS task force that is the liaison group between your systems group and Sawder's Furniture Company. You are shuffling a large bundle of papers as you prepare to leave the building.

   "Well, I've got some financial statements, production reports from the last six months, and some performance reports that Sharon got me that

FIGURE 4.EX1
One user's idea of how to
complete the computer
usage log.

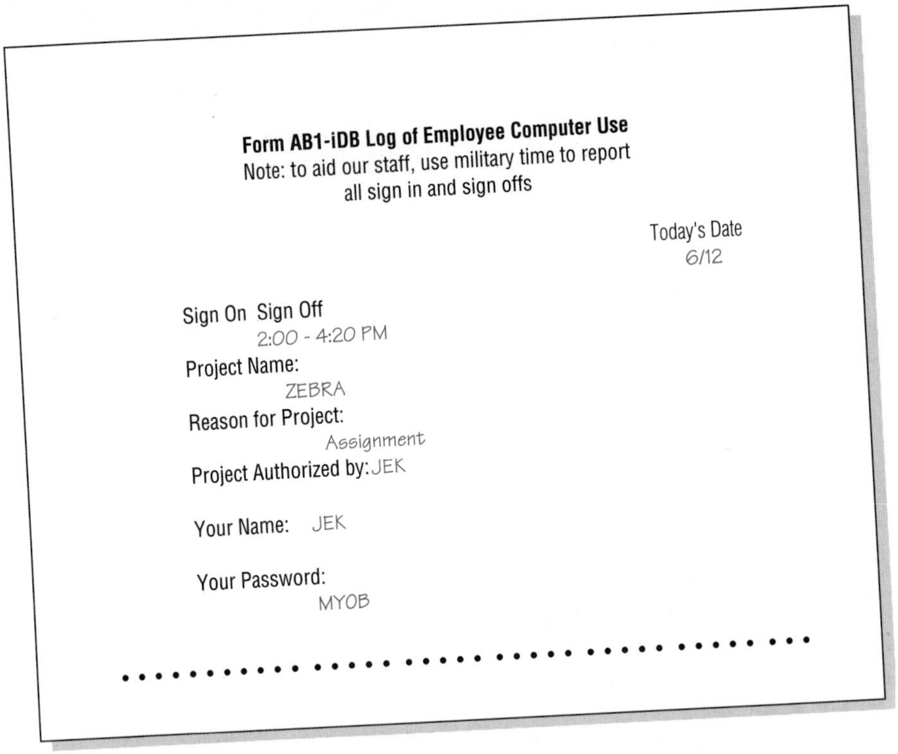

Form AB1-iDB Log of Employee Computer Use
Note: to aid our staff, use military time to report
all sign in and sign offs

Today's Date
6/12

Sign On Sign Off
2:00 - 4:20 PM
Project Name:
ZEBRA
Reason for Project:
Assignment
Project Authorized by: JEK

Your Name: JEK

Your Password:
MYOB

cover goals and work performance over the last six months," you reply as some of the papers fall to the floor. "Why do you ask?" Betty Kant takes the papers from you and puts them on the nearest desk. "Because you don't need all of this junk. You're here to do one thing, and that's talk to us, the users. Bet you can't read one thing in there that'll make a difference."

a. The only way to convince Betty Kant of the importance of each document is to tell her what you are looking for in each one. Use a paragraph to explain what each kind of document contributes to the systems analyst's understanding of the business.

b. While you are speaking with Betty, you realize that you actually need other quantitative documents as well. List any that you are missing.

5. Figure 4.EX1 and 4.EX2 are two filled-in pages that compose a larger computer usage log that the administrator of the information center has been using:

a. Analyze the way the log has been completed. Compare the data collected with the data the information center administrator intended to get from the form. List the omissions or errors users are making.

b. To what do you attribute the problems that people are having with filling out the log? Explain in a sentence or two the reason for each problem you found in 5a.

c. In a paragraph, explain why it is important to examine forms that have been completed, as well as blank ones that are in use.

6. You've sampled the memos that have been sent to several middle managers of Sawder's Furniture Company, which ships build-your-own particle board furniture across the country. Here is one that repeats a message found in several other memos.

Form AB1-iDB Log of Employee Computer Use
Note: to aid our staff, use military time to report all sign in and sign offs

Today's Date
FEB. 4

Sign On Sign Off
9:15 - 9:40
Project Name:
2378
Reason for Project:
?
Project Authorized by: _____

Your Name:
MIKE H.
Your Password:
TOIL-ON

To: Sid, Ernie, Carl   From: Imogene
Re: computer/printer supplies   Date: 11/10/88

It has come to my attention that I have been waging a war against requests for computer and printer supplies (diskettes, ribbons, paper, etc.) that are all out of proportion to what has been negotiated for in the current budget. Since we're all good soldiers here, I hope you will take whatever our supply sergeant says is standard issue. Please, no "midnight requisitioning" to make up for shortages. Thanks for being GI in this regard; it makes the battle easier for all of us.

a. What metaphor(s) is (are) being used? List the predominant metaphor and other phrases that play on that theme.

b. If you found repeated evidence of this kind of message in memos, what interpretation would you have? Use a paragraph to explain.

c. In a paragraph, describe how your systems analysis group can use the information from the memos to shape their systems project for Sawder's.

d. In interviews with Sid, Ernie, and Carl, there has been no mention of problems with obtaining enough computer and printer supplies. In a paragraph, discuss why such problems may not come up in interviews and the value of examining memos in addition to interviewing.

7. "Here's the main policy manual we've put together over the years for system users," says Al Bookbinder, as he blows the dust off it and hands the manual to you. Al is a document keeper for the systems department of Prechter and Gumbel, a large manufacturer of health and beauty aids. "Everything any user of any part of the system needs to know is in what I call the Blue Book. I mean it's chock a block with policies. It's so big, I'm the only one with a complete copy. It costs too much to reproduce it." You thank Al and take the manual with you. When you read through it, you are astonished at what it contains. Most pages begin with a message such as: "This page supersedes page 23.1 in manual Vol. II. Discard previous inserts; do not use."

    a. List your observations about the frequency of use of the "Blue Book."

    b. How user-friendly are the updates in the manual? Write a sentence explaining your answer.

    c. Write a paragraph commenting on the wisdom of having all important policies for all systems users in one book.

8. Arch Ives, a newly hired and rather shy systems analyst with your systems group, has come to you with an idea that he assures you will save the team time, and hence the business you're consulting with will save money. Arch proposes that, rather than doing time-consuming interviews or collecting current quantitative and qualitative documents, the team rely primarily on what it discovers in archival data. "They've kept everything. They even have their old reports from earlier systems projects. We don't have to talk with anyone, we can access the material all day, without seeing a soul."

    a. List the merits of what Arch is proposing.

    b. List the problems with what Arch is proposing.

    c. In a paragraph, explain tactfully to Arch why the systems team uses many different approaches to data gathering.

GROUP PROJECT

1. Assume that your group will serve as a systems analysis and design team for a project designed to computerize or enhance the computerization of all business aspects of a 15-year-old, national US trucking firm called Maverick Transport. Maverick is an LTL (less-than-a-truckload) carrier. Management work from the philosophy of JIT (just in time) in which they have created a partnership including the shipper, the receiver, and the carrier (Maverick Transport) for the purpose of transporting and delivering the materials required just in time for their use on the production line. Maverick maintains 626 tractors for hauling freight and has 45,000 square feet of warehouse space and 21,000 square feet of office space.

    a. Along with your group members, develop a list of sources of archival data that should be checked when analyzing the information requirements of Maverick.

    b. When this list is complete, devise a sampling scheme that would permit your group to get a clear picture of the company without having to read each document generated in its 15-year history.

SELECTED BIBLIOGRAPHY

Babbie, R. R. *Survey Research Methods.* Belmont, CA: Wadsworth Publishing Company, Inc., 1973.

Bormann, E. G. *Discussion and Group Methods: Theory and Practice,* 2nd ed. New York: Harper and Row, 1975.

Emory, C. W. *Business Research Method,* 3rd ed. Homewood, IL: Richard D. Irwin, Inc., 1985.

Johnson, B. M. *Communication—The Process of Organizing.* Boston: Allyn and Bacon, 1977.

Kendall, J. E., and K. E. Kendall. "Metaphors and Methodologies: Living Beyond the Systems Machine." *MIS Quarterly,* Vol. 17, No. 2, pp. 149–171, June 1993.

Kendall, J. E., and K. E. Kendall. "Metaphors and Their Meaning for Information Systems Development." *European Journal of Information Systems*, 1994.

Webb, E. J., D. T. Campbell, R. D. Schwartz, and L. Sechrest. *Unobtrusive Measures: Nonreactive Research in the Social Sciences.* Chicago: Rand McNally College Publishing Company, 1966.

MINDING THE MEMOS

"Anna, I've been busy gathering some memos to help us understand what's behind some of the changes people have requested to the system," says Chip as he hands over a sheaf of papers to Anna.

"Good idea," she replies, "but do you have any way to make them meaningful to us?"

Chip carefully rereads the memos shown in Figures E4.1, E4.2, E4.3, and E4.4.

"They tell an interesting story," Chip replies. "I can't wait for you to take a look."

Exercises

E-1. Analyze the four memos depicted in Figures E4.1-E4.4. Discuss how you analyzed them and, in a paragraph, describe what you have found.

E-2. In a paragraph, answer the following: Is any information missing from the memos? What is it? Where would you get it?

MEMO

Date: July 23, 1994
To: Cher Ware
From: Ed U. Cater *EUC*
Re: Microfocus COBOL in new lab

I would like to request that Microfocus COBOL be installed in the new lab. We have recently acquired the software via an academic grant.

This should be ready for the fall semester since we are planning to use the product for 9 programming classes, including several sections of 331, 335, and 336.

FIGURE E4.1
July 23rd memo from Ed U. Cater.

MEMO

Date: July 30, 1994
To: Cher Ware, Dot Matricks
From: Ed U. Cater *EUC*
Re: Microfocus COBOL problems

Thanks for your recent memo. On your advice I went to the new lab to start setting up student projects using Microfocus COBOL and found that the Workbench program will not execute.

Apparently there is not enough RAM memory for the product to execute. Is there any means of fixing the problem? Time is running short for us to set up projects and make student handouts.

Extreme urgency is needed in fixing the problem!!

FIGURE E4.2
July 30th memo from Ed U. Cater.

MEMO

Date: August 1, 1994
To: Ed U. Cater, Dot Matricks
From: Cher Ware *CW*
Re: Microfocus COBOL problems

Ed, I looked into your problem and found that Microfocus COBOL requires 3 MB of RAM memory to run the Workbench product. You may execute the COBOL compiler and some other features with less memory.

Please think about developing materials without the use of the Workbench product.

Let us know what you decide, and we'll modify the COBOL.BAT file.

FIGURE E4.3
August 1st memo from Cher Ware.

MEMO

Date:	August 5, 1994
To:	Cher Ware, Dot Matricks
From:	Ed U. Cater *EUC*
Re:	Re-installing Microfocus COBOL

First, thanks for your recent memo, Dot. However, our curriculum design requires that we use the full Workbench product. We are planning to use Excelerator to generate Microfocus COBOL code and then have the students complete the project.

Since code generation requires the full Workbench, I would like to know which machines are available that have 3 MB of RAM memory and then request that the software be installed on these machines.

These machines should be available on the main campus, hopefully in the Computer Sciences building or one nearby.

I don't mean to sound panicked, but time is running short. The students need this to complete the course. Please respond quickly!

FIGURE E4.4
August 5th memo from Ed U. Cater.

E-3. In a paragraph, discuss who you would contact to better understand the memos. Additionally, discuss how you would bring up the content of the memos so that they can be incorporated into the requirements determination phase.

5

INTERVIEWING

Before you interview someone else, you must in effect interview yourself. You need to know your biases and how they will affect your perceptions. Your education, intellect, upbringing, and emotions all serve as powerful filters for what you will be hearing in your interviews.

You need to think out the interview thoroughly before you go. Visualize why you are going, what you will ask, and what will make it a successful interview in your eyes. The other half of all this is the individual you will interview. You must anticipate how to make the interview fulfilling for him or her as well.

KINDS OF INFORMATION SOUGHT

An information-gathering interview is a directed conversation with a specific purpose that uses a question-and-answer format. In the interview you want to get the opinions of the interviewee and his or her feelings about the current state of the system, organizational and person goals, and informal procedures, as shown in Figure 5.1.

Above all, seek the opinions of the person you are interviewing. Opinions may be more important and more revealing than facts. For example, imagine asking the owner of a store how many customer refunds she typically gives each week. She replies, "About 20 to 25 a week." When you search the records and discover that the average is only 10.5 per week, you might conclude that the owner is overstating the facts and the problem.

Imagine instead that you ask the owner what her major concerns are, and she replies, "In my opinion, customer refunds are way too high. We must strive to get it right the first time." By seeking opinions rather than facts, you discover a key problem that the owner wants addressed.

In addition to opinions, you should try to capture the feelings of the interviewee. Remember that the interviewee knows the organization better than you do. You can understand the organization's culture more fully by listening to the feelings of the respondent. You can also determine the existing degree of optimism.

109

FIGURE 5.1
Kinds of information sought
in interviewing.

Expressed feelings help capture emotion and attitudes. If the owner of the store tells you, "I feel encouraged that you are working on this project," then you can take it as a positive sign that the project will go well. This information is available only through asking about feelings.

Goals are important information that can be gleaned from interviewing. Facts that you obtain from hard data may explain past performance, but goals project the organization's future. Try to find out as many of its goals as possible from interviewing. You may not be able to determine goals through any other data-gathering methods.

In the interview, you are setting up a relationship with someone who is probably a stranger to you. You need to build trust and understanding quickly, but at the same time you must maintain control of the interview. You also need to sell the system by providing needed information to your interviewee. The way to begin doing this is by planning for the interview before you go, so that conducting it is second nature to you. Fortunately, effective interviewing can be learned. As you practice, you will see yourself improving. Later in the chapter we discuss Joint Application Design (JAD) which can serve as an alternative to one-on-one interviewing in certain situations.

PLANNING THE INTERVIEW

Five Steps in Interview Preparation

The five major steps in interview preparation are shown in Figure 5.2. These steps include a range of activities from gathering basic background material to deciding who to interview.

READ BACKGROUND MATERIAL. Read and understand as much background information about the interviewees and their organization as possible. This material can often be obtained by a quick call to your contact person to ask for a current annual report, a corporate newsletter, and any publications sent out to explain the organization to the public. Check the library for any corporate information such as that in *Standard and Poor's.*

As you read through this material, be particularly sensitive to the *language* the organizational members use in describing themselves and their

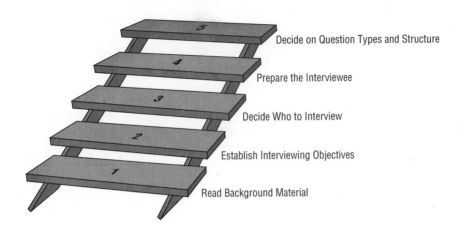

FIGURE 5.2
Steps the systems analyst
follows in planning the
interview.

Decide on Question Types and Structure

Prepare the Interviewee

Decide Who to Interview

Establish Interviewing Objectives

Read Background Material

organization. What you are trying to do is build up a common vocabulary that will eventually enable you to phrase interview questions in a way that is understandable to your interviewee. Another benefit of researching your organization is to maximize the time you spend in interviews rather than wasting time asking general background questions.

ESTABLISH INTERVIEWING OBJECTIVES. Use the background information you gathered as well as your own experience to establish interview objectives. There should be four to six key areas concerning information-processing and decision-making behavior about which you will want to ask questions. These areas include: information sources, information formats, decision-making frequency, qualities of information, and decision-making style.

DECIDE WHO TO INTERVIEW. When deciding who to interview, include key people at all levels who will be affected by the system in some manner. As discussed in Chapter 4, it is important to sample organizational members. Strive for balance so that as many user's needs are addressed as possible. Your organizational contact will also have some ideas about who should be interviewed.

PREPARE THE INTERVIEWEE. Prepare the person to be interviewed by calling ahead and allowing the interviewee time to think about the interview. Arrange time for phone calls and meetings. Interviews should be kept at 45 minutes to an hour at the most. No matter how willing your interviewees seem to extend the interview beyond this limit, remember that when they spend time with you, they are not doing their work. If interviews go over an hour, it is likely that the interviewees will resent the intrusion, whether or not they articulate their resentment.

DECIDE ON QUESTION TYPES AND STRUCTURE. Write questions to cover key areas of decision making discovered when you ascertained interview objectives. Proper questioning techniques are the heart of interviewing. Questions have some basic forms that you need to know. The two basic question types are open-ended and closed. Each question type can accomplish

FIGURE 5.3
Open-ended interview questions allow the respondent
open options for responding.
The examples were selected
from different interviews and
are not shown in any particular order.

Open-Ended Interview Questions
• What's your opinion of the present computer system?
• How do you view the goals of this department?
• How does this form relate to the work you do?
• What are some of the problems you experience in receiving information on time?
• What are some of the common errors made in data entry in this department?
• Describe the most frustrating computer system you've worked with.

something a little different from the other, and each has benefits and drawbacks. You need to think about the effect each question type will have.

It is possible to structure your interview in three different patterns: a
pyramid structure, a funnel structure, or a diamond structure. Each is
appropriate under different conditions, which will be discussed later in
the chapter.

The following discussion describes in detail some of the important
decisions the interviewer must make. These include which questions to
ask and how, whether to structure the interview, and how to document the
interview.

Question Types

OPEN-ENDED QUESTIONS. Open-ended questions include those such as
"What do you think about microcomputers for managers?" and "Please
explain how you make a scheduling decision." Consider the word *open-
ended*. "Open" actually describes the interviewee's options for responding.
They are open. The response can be two words or two paragraphs. Some
examples of open-ended questions can be found in Figure 5.3.

The benefits of using open-ended questions are numerous and
include:

1. Putting the interviewee at ease.
2. Allowing the interviewer to pick up on the interviewee's vocabulary,
   which reflects his or her education, values, attitudes, and beliefs.
3. Providing richness of detail.
4. Revealing avenues of further questioning that may have gone
   untapped.
5. Making it more interesting for the interviewee.
6. Allowing more spontaneity.
7. Making phrasing easier for the interviewer.
8. Using them in a pinch if the interviewer is caught unprepared.

As you can see, there are several advantages to using open-ended questions. However, the flip side is that there are also many drawbacks, which
include:

1. Asking questions that may result in too much irrelevant detail.
2. Possibly losing control of the interview.
3. Allowing responses that may take too much time for the amount of
   useful information gained.

Closed Interview Questions

- How many reports do you generate in a month?
- How long have you worked for Bakerloo Brothers?
- Which of the following sources of information is most valuable to you:
  - filled-out customer complaint forms
  - face-to-face interaction with customer
  - returned merchandise itself
- List your top two priorities for the marketing department.
- Who receives this output?

FIGURE 5.4
Closed interview questions limit the options the respondent has for responding. The examples were selected from different interviews and are not shown in any particular order.

4.   Potentially seeming that the interviewer is unprepared.

5.   Possibly giving the impression that the interviewer is on a "fishing expedition" with no real objective for the interview.

You must carefully consider the implications of using open-ended questions for interviewing.

CLOSED QUESTIONS. The alternative to open-ended questions is found in the other basic question type: closed questions that are of the basic form, "How many subordinates do you have?" The possible responses are closed to the interviewees, since they can only reply with a finite number such as "None," "One," or "Fifteen." Some examples of closed questions can be found in Figure 5.4.

A closed question limits the response available to the interviewee. You may be familiar with closed questions through multiple-choice exams in college. You are given a question and five responses, but you are not allowed to write down your own response and will be counted as correctly answering the question.

A special kind of closed question is the bipolar question. This limits the interviewee even further by only allowing a choice on either pole, such as yes or no, true or false, agree or disagree. Examples of bipolar questions can be found in Figure 5.5.

The benefits of using closed questions of either type include:

1.   Saving time

2.   Easily comparing interviews

3.   Getting to the point

4.   Keeping control over the interview

5.   Covering lots of ground quickly

6.   Getting to relevant data

Bipolar Interview Questions

- Do you use a microcomputer?
- Do you agree or disagree that automating teller functions would be worthwhile?
- Do you want to receive a computer printout of your account status every month?
- Does your accounting department offer automatic electronic funds transfer of payroll checks for hourly employees?
- Is this form complete?

FIGURE 5.5
Bipolar interview questions are a special kind of closed question. The examples were selected from different interviews and are not shown in any particular order.

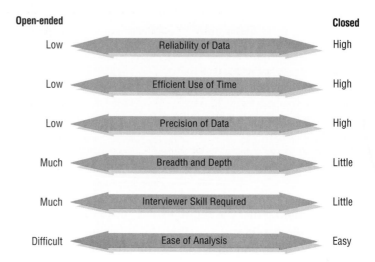

FIGURE 5.6
Attributes of open-ended and closed questions.

Open-ended		Closed
Low	Reliability of Data	High
Low	Efficient Use of Time	High
Low	Precision of Data	High
Much	Breadth and Depth	Little
Much	Interviewer Skill Required	Little
Difficult	Ease of Analysis	Easy

The drawbacks of using closed questions are substantial, however. They include:

1. Being boring for the interviewee.
2. Failing to obtain rich detail (due to the interviewer supplying the frame of reference for the interviewee).
3. Missing main ideas for the preceding reason.
4. Failing to build rapport between interviewer and interviewee.

So as the interviewer, you must think carefully about the question types you will use.

Both open-ended and closed questions have advantages and drawbacks, as shown in Figure 5.6. Notice that choosing one question type over the other actually involves a tradeoff; while an open-ended question affords breadth and depth of reply, responses to open-ended questions are difficult to analyze.

PROBES. A third type of question is the "probe" or "follow-up." The strongest probe is the simplest: the question "Why?" Other probes are, "Can you give me an example?" and "Will you elaborate on that for me?" Some examples of probing questions can be found in Figure 5.7. The purpose of the probe is to go beyond the initial answer to get more meaning, to clarify, and to draw out and expand on the interviewee's point. Probes may be either open-ended or closed questions.

It is essential to probe. Most beginning interviewers are reticent about probing and consequently accept superficial answers. They are usually grateful that employees have granted interviews and feel somewhat obligated to accept unqualified statements politely.

If done in a systematic and determined manner, your probing will be acknowledged as a sign that you are listening to what's being said, thinking it through, and responding appropriately. This can only help the situation. Rather than using a tough "investigative-reporter" type of approach, you should probe in a way that exhibits your thoroughness and desire to comprehend the interviewee's responses.

FIGURE 5.7
Probes allow the systems analyst to follow up questions to
get more detailed responses.
The examples were selected
from different interviews
and are not shown in
any particular order.

Probes
• Why?
• Give an example of your decision-making process.
• Please provide an illustration of the performance measures you mentioned earlier.
• What you said just now about using your IBM PC seems to conflict with your earlier opinions that managerial work can't be automated. Please clarify what you meant by each statement.
• What makes you feel that way?
• Tell me what happens, step by step, to the form the patient fills out.

Question Pitfalls

By wording your questions beforehand, you are able to correct any poor questions that you have written. Watch for troublesome question types that can ruin your data. They are called "leading questions" and "double-barreled questions."

AVOIDING LEADING QUESTIONS. Leading questions tend to lead the interviewee into a response that you seem to want. The response is then biased since you are setting up a kind of trap. An example is: "You agree with other managers that inventory control should be computerized, don't you?" You have made it very uncomfortable to disagree. An alternative, preferred phrasing could be, "What do you think of computerizing inventory control?" Your data will be more reliable and more valid, hence easier to understand and more useful.

AVOIDING DOUBLE-BARRELED QUESTIONS. Double-barreled questions are those that use only one question mark for what are actually two separate questions. A question such as "What decisions are made during a typical day and how do you make them?" is an example of a double-barreled question. If your interviewee responds to this type of question, your data may suffer.

A double-barreled question is a poor choice because interviewees may answer only one question (purposely or not), or you may mistake which question they are answering and draw the wrong conclusion. If you are lucky enough to discover your error, it still means orally retracing steps and straightening out the misunderstanding, which takes extra time. Most of this can be avoided by phrasing questions carefully beforehand.

Arranging Questions in a Logical Sequence

Just as there are two generally recognized ways of reasoning, inductive and deductive, there are two similar ways of organizing your interviews. A third way combines both inductive and deductive patterns.

USING A PYRAMID STRUCTURE. Inductive organization of interview questions can be visualized as having a pyramid shape. Using this form, the interviewer begins with very detailed, often closed, questions. The interviewer then expands the topics by allowing open-ended questions and more generalized responses, as shown in Figure 5.8.

Strongbodies, a large, local chain of sports clubs, has experienced phenomenal growth in the past 5 years. Management would like to refine their decision-making process for purchasing new body-building equipment. Currently, managers listen to customers, attend trade shows, look at advertisements, and put in requests for new equipment purchases based on their subjective perceptions. These are then approved or denied by Harry Mussels.

Harry is the first person you will interview. He is a 37-year-old division manager who runs five area clubs. He travels all over the city to their widespread locations. He keeps an office at the East location, although he is there less than a quarter of the time.

Additionally, when Harry is present at a club, he is busy answering business-related phone calls, solv-ing on-the-spot problems presented by managers, and interacting with club members. His time is short, and to compensate for that he has become an extremely well-organized, efficient divisional manager. He cannot grant you a lot of interview time. Yet his input is important, and he feels he would be the main beneficiary of the proposed system.

What types of interview questions might be most suitable for your interview with Harry? Why are they most appropriate? How will your choice of question type affect the amount of time you spend in preparation for interviewing Harry? What other techniques might you use to supplement information unavailable through that type of question?

A pyramid structure should be used if you believe your interviewee needs to warm up to the topic. It is also useful if the interviewee seems reluctant to address the topic. For example, if you are interviewing someone who has told you over the phone that he or she does not need to talk with you because that person already knows what is wrong with the forecasting model, you should probably structure the interview as a pyramid.

Utilizing a pyramid structure for question sequencing is also useful when you want an ending determination about the topic. Such is the case in the final question, "In general, how do you feel about forecasting?"

FIGURE 5.8

Pyramid structure for interviewing goes from specific to general questions.

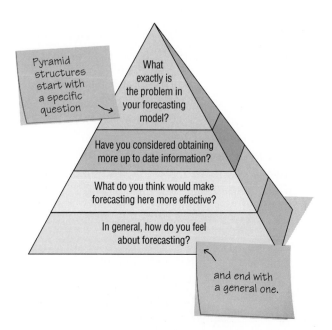

Pyramid structures start with a specific question

What exactly is the problem in your forecasting model?

Have you considered obtaining more up to date information?

What do you think would make forecasting here more effective?

In general, how do you feel about forecasting?

and end with a general one.

What are your reactions to the new computer system?

Funnel structures begin with a general question

What computers do you use?

What is the cost of the new computer system?

Is the new computer system worth the cost?

and end with a specific one.

USING A FUNNEL STRUCTURE. In the second kind of structure, the interviewer takes a deductive approach by beginning with generalized, open-ended questions and narrowing the possible responses by using closed questions. This interview structure can be thought of as funnel-shaped, like that depicted in Figure 5.9.

Using funnel structure provides an easy, nonthreatening way to begin an interview. Respondents will not feel pressured that they are giving a "wrong" response to an open-ended question. A funnel-shaped question sequence is also useful when the interviewee feels emotional about the topic and needs freedom to express those emotions. A benefit of using a funnel structure is that organizing the interview in such a manner may elicit so much detailed information that long sequences of closed questions and probes are unnecessary.

USING A DIAMOND-SHAPED STRUCTURE. Often a combination of the two above structures, resulting in a diamond-shaped interview structure, is best. This entails beginning in a very specific way, then examining general issues, and finally coming to a very specific conclusion, as shown in Figure 5.10.

The interviewer begins with easy, closed questions that provide a warmup to the interview process. In the middle of the interview, the interviewee is asked for opinions on broad topics that obviously have no "right" answer. The interviewer then narrows the questions again to get specific questions answered, thus providing closure for both the interviewee and the interviewer.

The diamond structure combines the strengths of the other two approaches but has the disadvantage of taking longer. The chief advantage of using a diamond-shaped structure is keeping your interviewee's interest and attention through a variety of questions. Remember that once you know how to ask the right questions at the right time, you have many options for sequencing them.

Structured Versus Unstructured Interviews

Many beginning interviewers believe that, because interviews are similar to conversations, they would be better off not structuring the questions or question sequences in their interviews. For a completely structured interview,

FIGURE 5.10
Diamond-shaped structure for
interviewing combines the
pyramid and funnel
structures.

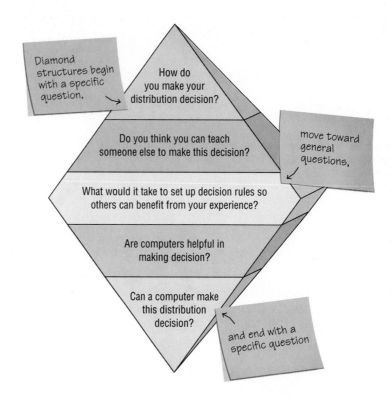

everything is planned out and the plan is strictly adhered to. Closed questions are at the core of a completely structured interview.

There are explicit tradeoffs involved for each of ten variables, as shown in Figure 5.11. Notice that while it is hard to evaluate an unstructured interview, it is easier to evaluate one that is structured; greater contact time is required to conduct an unstructured interview than a structured one; much training is needed to conduct a successful unstructured interview, limited training is required to conduct a completely structured interview, and so on.

Awareness of the tradeoffs between structured and unstructured interviews will enable you to make a better decision about which kind of interview is more appropriate for a particular situation. If you decide to follow the unstructured route, you should still prepare for the interview as discussed in the previous steps. For the unstructured approach we advocate, at minimum, a brief outline (including many questions worded precisely as they will be asked). Remember that *unstructured* here refers only to the order in which the questions are asked and does not imply a lack of other preparation.

The only way to tell if your question is appropriate is to word it exactly beforehand, then anticipate possible responses and how you will follow them. It is necessary for you to project what the other person might say. This takes considerable time and thought and is in itself an excellent argument for preparing several questions with various avenues to take during the course of the interview. This approach is actually a branching program—if the answer is "yes," you proceed one way; if "no," you take the other path of questioning.

Making a Record of the Interview

Record the most important aspects of your interview. You can use either a tape recorder or pen and paper notetaking, but it is important to make a permanent record during the actual interview.

Whether you take notes or use a tape recorder depends in part on who you are interviewing and what you will do with the information once the interview is over. Additionally, there are advantages and disadvantages inherent in each of the recording methods.

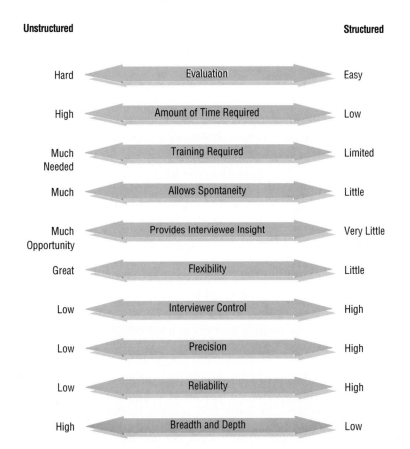

Unstructured — **Structured**

Hard	Evaluation	Easy
High	Amount of Time Required	Low
Much Needed	Training Required	Limited
Much	Allows Spontaneity	Little
Much Opportunity	Provides Interviewee Insight	Very Little
Great	Flexibility	Little
Low	Interviewer Control	High
Low	Precision	High
Low	Reliability	High
High	Breadth and Depth	Low

FIGURE 5.11

Attributes of unstructured and structured interviews to consider when deciding on an interview format.

119

Hitting the High Note

Late in the afternoon, you see Gabriel García, manager of Chumco's infant toy line, turning a corner in the corridor to return to his office. Gabriel, who is walking rather slowly, looks baffled. Your team member, Arthur Brown, just completed an interview with him about the possibility of having your systems analysis team design a decision support system to support Gabriel's process of deciding which new toys to produce. As project leader, you are curious about uncharacteristic behavior and want to learn his impression of the interview.

You easily catch up with Gabriel and ask if everything went all right in the interview. This is his reply:

"Yes, it was okay, I guess. We covered a lot of territory. It was a little strange, though. I'm not even sure I'll recognize the guy who interviewed me if I see him again. All I saw was the top of his head, his pad, and his pencil. He wrote down every word I spoke! I felt like I was in court. What are you going to do with all that information? Publish quotations? I hope it doesn't get back to the wrong people."

What important notetaking guidelines did Arthur apparently forget to follow? As project team leader, what assurances can you give Gabriel now that this has happened?

USING A TAPE RECORDER. Consider your interviewee when deciding how to record your interview. When you make an appointment, tell the interviewee that you would like to tape record the interview. Mention what you will do with the tape: Either it will be listened to by you and by the other team members and then destroyed, or it will be transcribed and used as information for system development. Be truthful about your intentions and reassuring about the confidentiality of any of the interviewee's remarks. If your interviewee refuses to allow you permission to tape record, graciously accept that constraint.

Tape recording has advantages and disadvantages. The advantages are that tape recording does the following:

1. Provides a completely accurate record of what each person said.
2. Frees the interviewer to listen and respond more rapidly.
3. Allows better eye contact and hence better development of rapport between interviewer and interviewee.
4. Allows replay of the interview for other team members.

The disadvantages of tape recording are also numerous. They include:

1. Possibly making the interviewee nervous and less apt to respond freely.
2. Possibly making the interviewer less apt to listen since it's all being recorded.
3. Difficulty in locating important passages on a long tape.
4. Increasing costs of data gathering because of the need to transcribe tapes.

The decision to tape record interviews is a professional one that you will have to make based on what you know about interviewing, the interviewee's outlook on taping, and the particular project. Evaluate tape recording each time it is chosen, just as you would evaluate any other procedure.

NOTETAKING. Notetaking may be your only way to record the interview if your interviewee refuses your request to tape record. It is important that you somehow record the interview as it takes place. The advantages of notetaking include:

1. Keeping the interviewer alert.
2. Aiding recall of important questions.
3. Helping recall of important interview trends.
4. Showing interviewer interest in the interview.
5. Demonstrating the interviewer's preparedness.

There are some very good reasons for notetaking, but it is not without drawbacks. The disadvantages include:

1. Losing vital eye contact (and therefore rapport) between interviewer and interviewee.
2. Losing the train of conversation.
3. Making the interviewee hesitant to speak when notes are being made.
4. Causing excessive attention to facts and too little attention to feelings and opinions.

In order to prepare for your interview properly, you must understand yourself and your own biases. Then research your interviewee and his or her organization, sketch out key areas for questioning, contact interviewees, write interview questions, and formulate an interview plan.

Before the Interview

The day preceding your interview, contact your interviewees to reconfirm times and places of interviews. Coordinate appointments with any other team members and gather necessary materials.

When you conduct interviews, dress appropriately, perhaps wearing what you would wear to interview for a job in the same organization. Since you will be controlling the interview, you must dress in a credible manner. Failing to dress appropriately could result in poor data gathering. Interviewee's responses to you are geared to their initial perceptions.

Arrive a little early for your interview. You can use the extra time to review your notes or start making observations about the organization. (See Chapter 7 for observation techniques.) Affirm with the interviewee that you are present and ready to begin the interview.

CONDUCTING THE ACTUAL INTERVIEW

Beginning the Interview

As you enter, firmly shake your interviewee's hand. This applies whether you are male or female. As in any other business situation, a handshake helps establish your credibility and trustworthiness. Remind the interviewee of your name and briefly outline once more why you are there and why you chose to interview him or her.

As you sit down, immediately take out your tape recorder and/or note pad. Remind your interviewee that you will record important points. Tell the interviewee what you will do with the data you collect and be reassuring about its confidentiality.

Now is the time to check whether your tape recorder and microphone are working properly. Some beginning interviewers are embarrassed to take time to check equipment, but the result of assuming that you're taping when you're not is disastrous. Your interviewee will respect your professionalism in guaranteeing that everything is in working order before you begin.

Depending on the structure you are following in your interview, you may begin with some very general, nonthreatening, open-ended questions. Opening an interview this way helps to relax you and your interviewee. It also provides a frame of reference for you that is helpful in tailoring your later questions. By listening closely to early responses, you can pick up on vocabulary and jargon (maybe they don't have "departments" but instead call them "units," for example) the relevant metaphors such as, "The EDP department is a zoo," or "Our scheduling system works like a well-oiled machine," or "We're one big happy family here." Recall from Chapter 2 that metaphors help reveal membership in organizational subcultures.

Early open-ended responses can also reveal attitudes, morals, and beliefs of the interviewee that will help you understand how he or she uses information and how he or she feels toward others in the organization. You must listen and respond appropriately to what your interviewee is saying.

As you proceed through your interview schedule, mention to your respondent what sort of detail you would like to receive in answers. For instance, if you feel you need depth on a question, encourage your interviewee to provide an example. If you have only passing interest in a topic, tell your respondent a "yes" or "no" is sufficient. You are in control of time usage in this kind of interview, and providing guidelines for length of response is helpful in maintaining interview balance.

All interview material should be covered in 45 minutes to an hour, and by now you are well aware of the planning and managing necessary to accomplish this. Closing the interview appropriately is just as important as opening it well.

During the interview, reflect back to some of your interviewee's responses through paraphrasing or summarizing in order to double check that you understand his or her meaning. If at any time you are unsure, you must ask for definitions or other clarification. Feigning knowledge only works against your ultimate objectives. The close of the interview is not the place to bring up all of these concerns. Rather, they are more naturally handled as they arise.

However, the end of the interview is a natural place to ask one key question: "Is there anything we haven't touched on that you feel is important for me to know?" Most of the time this is considered a formula question by the interviewee, and the response will be "No." However, you are interested in the small percentage of time that this question opens the proverbial floodgates and much new (and often surprising) data are presented.

As you conclude the interview, there are other procedures to follow. Summarize and feed back your overall impressions. Inform the interviewee about the subsequent steps to take and what you and other team members will do next. You may wish to ask the interviewee who to talk with next. Set up future appointment times for follow-up interviews, thank the interviewee for his or her time, and shake hands.

WRITING THE INTERVIEW REPORT

Although the interview itself is complete, your work on the interview data is just beginning. You need to capture the essence of the interview through a written report. It is imperative that you write the interview report as soon as possible after the interview. This is another way you can assure quality of interview data. The longer you wait to write up your interview, the more suspect the quality of your data becomes.

After this initial summary, go into more detail, noting main points of the interview and your own opinions. Figure 5.12 shows a sample interview report form that will aid you in capturing the interview essentials. It will help you in planning for your next interview as well.

Review the interview report with the respondent at a follow-up meeting. This helps clarify the meaning the interviewee had in mind and lets the interviewee know that you are interested enough to take the time to understand his or her point of view and perceptions.

JOINT APPLICATION DESIGN

No matter how adept you become as an interviewer, you will inevitably experience situations where one-one-one interviews do not seem to be as useful as you would like. Personal interviews are time-consuming, subject to error, and their data are prone to misinterpretation. An alternative approach to interviewing users one by one, called Joint Application Design (JAD), was developed by IBM. The motivation for using JAD is to cut the time (and hence the cost) required by personal interviews, to improve the quality of the results of information requirements assessment, and to create more user identification with new information systems as a result of the participative processes.

Although JAD can be substituted for personal interviews at any appropriate juncture during the systems development life cycle, Joint Application Design has usually been employed as a technique that allows you, as a systems analyst, to accomplish requirements analysis and design the user interface jointly with users in a group setting. Sometimes a group decision support system (GDSS) can be used, but it is not mandatory. The many intricacies of this approach can only be learned in a paid seminar demonstrating proprietary methods. However, we can convey enough

FIGURE 5.12

An interviewer's follow-up report documenting data gathered as well as the interviewer's reaction to them.

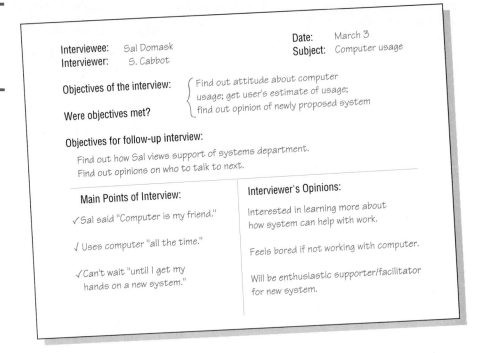

Interviewee: Sal Domask
Interviewer: S. Cabbot

Date: March 3
Subject: Computer usage

Objectives of the interview: { Find out attitude about computer usage; get user's estimate of usage; find out opinion of newly proposed system

Were objectives met?

Objectives for follow-up interview:
Find out how Sal views support of systems department.
Find out opinions on who to talk to next.

Main Points of Interview:

✓ Sal said "Computer is my friend."

✓ Uses computer "all the time."

✓ Can't wait "until I get my hands on a new system."

Interviewer's Opinions:

Interested in learning more about how system can help with work.

Feels bored if not working with computer.

Will be enthusiastic supporter/facilitator for new system.

information about JAD here so that you become aware of some of its benefits and drawbacks in comparison to one-on-one interviews.

Joint Application Design requires some specialized skills on the part of the analyst, and many skills and a firm commitment on the part of the organization and users who undertake to use this approach. However, in certain situations, JAD can be very effective and should be considered as an alternative to more traditional methods of systems analysis.

Conditions That Support the Use of JAD

The following list of conditions will help you decide when the use of JAD may be fruitful. Consider using Joint Application Design when:

1. User groups are restless and want something new, not a standard solution to a typical problem.

2. The organizational culture supports joint problem-solving behaviors among multiple levels of employees.

3. Analysts forecast that the number of ideas generated via one-on-one interviews will not be as plentiful as the number of ideas possible from an extended group exercise.

4. Organizational work flow permits the absence of key personnel during a two-to-four-day block of time.

Who Is Involved

Joint Application Design sessions include a variety of participants—analysts, users, executives, and so on—who will contribute differing backgrounds and skills to the sessions. Your primary concern here is that all project team members are committed to the JAD approach and become involved. Choose an executive sponsor, a senior person who will introduce and conclude the JAD session. Preferably, select an executive from the user group who has some sort of authority over the IS people working on the project. This person will be an important, visible symbol of organizational commitment to the systems project.

At least one IS analyst should be present, but the analyst usually takes a passive role—unlike traditional interviewing where the analyst controls the interaction. As the project analyst, you should be present during JAD to listen to what users say and what they require. Additionally, you will want to give an expert opinion about any disproportionate costs of solutions proposed during the JAD session itself. Without this kind of immediate feedback, unrealistic solutions with excessive costs may creep into the proposal and prove costly to discourage later on.

From eight to a dozen users can be chosen from any rank to participate in JAD sessions. Try to select users above the clerical level who can articulate what information they need to perform their jobs, as well as what they desire in a new or improved computer system. Some of the ideas on sampling from Chapter 4 can be put to good use here, since your goal is to get a representative sample of users without forming such a large group that it becomes unwieldy during group interactions.

The session leader should not be an expert in systems analysis and design but rather someone who has excellent communication skills to facilitate appropriate interactions. Consider having a full-time training department member serve as session leader. Note that you do not want to use a session leader who reports to another person in the group. To avoid this, an organization may want to retain an outside management consultant to serve as session leader. The point is to get a person who can bring the group's attention to bear on important systems issues, satisfactorily negotiate and resolve conflicts, and help group members reach consensus rather than rely on simple majority rule to make decisions.

Your JAD session should also include one or two observers who are analysts or technical experts from other functional areas to offer technical explanations and advice to the group during the sessions. Additionally, one scribe from the IS department should attend the JAD sessions to formally write down everything that is done. Ensure that the scribe publishes the record of JAD results rapidly once the group has met. Slow publication of results risks losing the time savings and momentum that are the prime motivations for using JAD in the first place. Consider selecting second scribe from a user department as well. Then the responsibility for recording systems issues can be left to the IS scribe, and the scribe from the user group can note business-related content.

Planning for the JAD Session

One of the keys to a successful JAD workshop is laying the groundwork through advance study and planning. The session leader chosen will work with an executive sponsor to determine the scope of the project which JAD must cover. Sometimes the project requires more than one JAD workshop, but some of the benefits of JAD erode if too many independent sessions are planned. Following the definition of the project scope, participants will be selected, and the session leader will learn the application by doing some interviews with key users. The purpose of the interviews is to gather information to facilitate understanding of what is happening in the business.

Where to Hold JAD Meetings

If it is at all possible, we recommend holding the two-to-four-day sessions offsite, away from the organization, in comfortable surroundings. Some groups use executive centers or even group decision support facilities available at major universities. The idea is to minimize daily distractions and responsibilities of the participants' regular work. The room itself should comfortably hold the twenty or so people invited. Minimal presentation support equipment includes two overhead projectors, a whiteboard, a flipchart, and easy access to a copier. Group decision support rooms will also provide networked microcomputers, a projection system, and software written to facilitate group interaction, while minimizing unproductive group behaviors.

Give adequate thought to the creature comforts of participants as well, since this will be an intense experience, quite different in nature from a typical day's work for most people. Plan for sufficient food, as well as ample refreshments during scheduled breaks before lunch and again in late afternoon.

Schedule your JAD session when all participants can commit to attending. Do not hold the sessions unless everyone who has been invited can actually attend. This is critical to the success of the sessions. Ensure that all participants receive an agenda before the meeting and consider holding an orientation meeting for a half-day one week or so before the workshop, so that those involved know what is expected of them. This allows you to move rapidly and act confidently once the actual meeting is convened.

Accomplishing a Structured Analysis of Project Activities

IBM recommends that the JAD sessions examine these points in the proposed systems project: planning, receiving, receipt processing/tracking, monitoring and assigning, processing, recording, sending, and evaluating. For each topic, the questions who, what, how, where, and why should also be asked and answered. Clearly, *ad hoc*, interactive systems such as decision support systems and other types of systems dependent on decision-maker style (including prototype systems) are not as easily analyzed with the structured approach of JAD.

As the analyst involved with the JAD sessions, you should receive the notes of the scribes and prepare a specifications document based on what happened at the meeting. Systematically present the management objectives as well as the scope and boundaries of the project. Specifics of the system, including details on screen and report layouts, should also be included. As a guide for what to include, use Chapter 14, which details the composition of a systems proposal. You can also look to the client organization for other guidelines to be followed in preparing this document.

Potential Benefits of Using JAD in Place of Traditional Interviewing

There are four major potential benefits that you, the users, and your systems analysis team should consider when you weigh the possibilities of using Joint Application Design. The first potential benefit is time savings over traditional one-on-one interviews. Some organizations have estimated that JAD sessions have provided a 15 percent time savings over the traditional approach. Hand-in-hand with time savings is the rapid development possible via JAD. Since user interviews are not accomplished serially over a period of weeks or months, the development can proceed much more quickly.

A third benefit to weigh is the possibility of improved ownership of the information system. As analysts, we are always striving to involve users in meaningful ways and to encourage users to take early ownership of the systems we are designing. Due to its interactive nature and high visibility, JAD helps users become involved early in systems projects and treats their feedback seriously. Working through a JAD session eventually helps reflect user ideas in the final design.

A final benefit of participating in JAD sessions is the creative development of designs. The interactive character of JAD has a great deal in common with brainstorming techniques that generate new ideas and new combinations of ideas because of the dynamic and stimulating environment. Designs can evolve through facilitated interactions, rather than in relative isolation.

Potential Drawbacks of Using JAD

There are four drawbacks or pitfalls that you should also weigh when making a decision on whether to do traditional one-on-one interviews or to use Joint Application Design. The first drawback is that JAD requires the commitment of a large block of time from all of the 18–20 participants. Since JAD requires a two-to-four-day commitment, it is not possible to do any other activities concurrently or to time shift any activities, as is typically done in one-on-one interviewing.

A second pitfall occurs if preparation for the JAD sessions is inadequate in any regard or if the follow-up report and documentation of specifications is incomplete. In these instances, resulting designs could be less than satisfactory. Many variables need to come together correctly for JAD to be successful. Conversely, many things can go wrong. The success of designs resulting from JAD sessions is less predictable than that achieved through standard interviews.

Finally, the necessary organizational skills and organizational culture may not be sufficiently developed to make the concerted effort required to be productive in a JAD setting. In the end, you will have to make the judgment about whether the organization is truly committed to, and prepared for, this approach.

SUMMARY

This chapter has covered the process of interviewing, which is one method systems analysts use for collecting data on information requirements. Systems analysts listen for goals, feelings, opinions, and informal procedures in interviews with organizational decision makers. They also sell the system during interviews. Interviews are preplanned question and answer dialogs between two people.

There are five steps to be taken in preplanning the interview:

1. Read background material
2. Establish interviewing objectives
3. Decide who to interview
4. Prepare the interviewee
5. Decide on question types and structure

Questions are of two basic types: open-ended or closed. Open-ended questions leave open all response options for the interviewee. Closed questions limit the possible options for response. Probes or follow-up questions can be either open-ended or closed, but they ask the respondent for a more detailed reply.

"Well, I did warn you that things weren't always smooth here at MRE. By now you've met many of our key employees and you are starting to understand the "lay of the land." Who would have thought that some innocent decisions about hardware, like whether to buy a COMTEX or Shiroma would cause such hostility? Well, live and learn, I always say. At least now you'll know what you're up against when you have to start recommending hardware!

"It's funny that not all questions are created equally. I myself favor asking open-ended questions, but when I have to answer them it is not always easy. Have you been taking the opportunity to view people's offices when you've been in there to do your interviews? You can learn a lot more by using a structured observation method such as STROBE."

HYPERCASE QUESTIONS

1. Using the interview questions posed in HyperCase, give five examples of open-ended questions and five examples of closed questions. Explain why your examples are correctly classified as either open-ended or closed question types.

2. List three probing questions that are part of the HyperCase interviews. In particular what did you learn by following up on the questions you asked Snowden Evans?

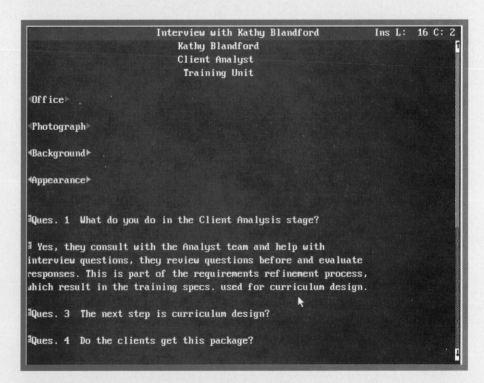

FIGURE 5.HC1
Pointing to a question in HyperCase will reveal an answer.

Interviews can be structured in three basic ways: pyramid, funnel, or diamond structure. Pyramid structures begin with detailed, closed questions and broadens to more generalized questions. Funnel-shaped structures begin with open-ended, general questions and then funnel down to more specific, closed questions. Diamond structures combine the strengths of the other two structures, but take longer to conduct. There are tradeoffs involved when deciding how structured to make interview questions and question sequences.

Interviews should be recorded via tape recorders or notes. After the interview, the interviewer should write a report listing the main points provided, as well as opinions about what was said. It is extremely important to document the interview soon after it has taken place.

To cut both the time and cost of personal interviews, analysts may want to consider Joint Application Design (JAD) as an alternative. Using JAD, analysts accomplish both requirements analysis and user interface design with users in a group setting. Careful assessment of the particular organizational setting will help the analyst judge whether JAD is a suitable alternative.

KEYWORDS AND PHRASES

interviewee opinions	probes
interviewee feelings	leading questions
interviewee goals	double-barreled questions
informal procedures	pyramid structure
open-ended questions	funnel structure
closed questions	diamond-shaped structure
bipolar closed questions	Joint Application Design (JAD)

REVIEW QUESTIONS

1. What kinds of information should be sought in interviews?
2. List the five steps in interview preparation.
3. Define what is meant by "open-ended" interview questions. Give eight benefits and five drawbacks of using them.
4. When are open-ended questions appropriate for use in interviewing?
5. Define what is meant by closed interview questions. Give six benefits and four drawbacks of using them.
6. When are closed questions appropriate for use in interviewing?
7. What is a probing question? What is the purpose of using a probing question in interviews?
8. What are leading questions? Why should they be avoided in interviews?
9. What are double-barreled questions? Why should they be avoided in interviews?
10. Define what is meant by pyramid structure. When is it useful to employ it in interviews?
11. Define what is meant by funnel structure. When is it useful to employ it in interviews?
12. Define what is meant by diamond-shaped structure. When is it useful to employ it in interviews?

13. What are the ten variables that become tradeoffs between structured and unstructured interviews?

14. What are the four advantages and four disadvantages of tape recording interviews?

15. What are the five advantages and four disadvantages of notetaking during interviews?

16. Define the phrase "Joint Application Design."

17. List the situations that warrant use of JAD in place of personal organizational interviews.

18. List the potential benefits of using Joint Application Design.

19. List the four potential drawbacks of using JAD as an alternative to personal interviews.

PROBLEMS

1. While going over your interview schedule, you notice several questions that seem inadequate. Here are the original questions for the sales manager of Sampson Paper Products, whose company has expressed a desire to computerize their sales information in order to refine their sales projections. Rewrite the questions in a more appropriate manner.

   1. Your subordinates told me that you have a high level of computer anxiety. Is that true?
   2. I'm new to this. What did I leave out?
   3. What are your most used sources of information on sales figures and how frequently do you use them?
   4. Do you agree with other sales managers that computerizing monthly sales and then doing trend analysis would be a major improvement?
   5. Isn't there a better way to project sales than the antiquated one you're using now?

2. As part of your systems analysis project to update the automated accounting functions for Chronos Corporation, a maker of digital watches, you will be interviewing Harry Straiter, their chief accountant. Write four to six interview objectives covering his use of information sources, information formats, decision-making frequency, desired qualities of information, and decision-making style.

   a. In a paragraph, write down how you will approach Harry to set up an interview.

   b. State which structure you will choose for this interview. Why?

   c. Harry has three subordinates who also use the system. Would you interview them also? Why or why not?

3. Here are five questions written by one of your systems analysis team members. Her interviewee is the local manager of LOWCO, an outlet of a national discount chain, who has asked you to work on a management information system to provide inventory information. Review these questions for your team member.

   1. When was the last time you thought seriously about your decision-making process?
   2. Who are the trouble makers in your store—I mean the ones that will show the most resistance to changes in the system that I have proposed?

3. Are there any decisions you need more information to make?

4. You don't have any major problems with the current inventory control system, do you?

5. Tell me a little about the output you'd like to see.

a. Rewrite each question to be more effective in eliciting information.

b. Order your questions in either a pyramid, funnel, or diamond-shaped structure, and label the structure used.

c. What guidelines can you give your team member for improving her interviewing questions for the future? Make a list of them.

4. Ever since you entered the door, your interviewee, Max Hugo, has been shuffling papers, looking at his watch, and lighting and snuffing out cigarettes. Based on what you know about interviews, you guess that Max is nervous because of the other work that he needs to do.

a. In a paragraph, describe how you would deal with this situation so that the interview can be accomplished with Max's full attention. (Max cannot reschedule the interview for a different day.)

5. Write a series of six closed questions that cover the subject of decision-making style for the accountant described in problem 2.

6. Write a series of open-ended questions that cover the subject of decision-making style for the accountant described in problem 2.

7. Examine the interview structure presented in the sequencing of the following questions:

1. How long have you been in this position?

2. What are your key responsibilities?

3. What reports do you receive?

4. How do you view the goals of your department?

5. How would you describe your decision-making process?

6. How can that process best be supported?

7. How frequently do you make those decisions?

8. Who is consulted when you make a decision?

9. What is the one decision you make that is essential to departmental functioning?

a. What structure is being used? How can you tell?

b. Restructure the interview by changing the sequence of the questions (you may omit some if necessary). Label the structure you have used.

8. This is the first interview report filed by one of your systems analysis team members:

"In my opinion, the interview went very well. The subject allowed me to talk with him for an hour and a half. He told me the whole history of the business, which was very interesting. The subject also mentioned that things have not changed all that much since he has been with the firm, which is about 16 years. We are meeting again soon to finish the interview, since we did not have time to go into the questions I prepared."

a. In two paragraphs, critique the interview report. Assume that you asked the team member to use the report form provided in Figure 5.12. What critical information is missing?

b. What information is extraneous to the interview report?

c. If what is reported actually occurred, what three suggestions do you have to help your teammate conduct a better interview next time?

GROUP PROJECTS

1. With your group members, role play a series of interviews with various end users at Maverick Transport (first introduced in the Chapter 4 Group Project). Each member of your group should choose one of the following roles: company president, information technology director, dispatcher, customer service agent, or truck driver. Those group members playing roles of Maverick Transport employees should attempt to briefly describe their job responsibilities, goals, and informational needs.

    Remaining group members should play the roles of systems analysts and devise interview questions for each employee. If there are enough people in your group, each analyst may be assigned to interview a different employee. Those playing the roles of systems analysts should work together to develop common questions that they will ask, as well as questions tailored to each individual employee. Be sure to include open-ended, closed, and probing questions in your interviews.

    Maverick Transport is attempting to change from outdated and unreliable technology to more state-of-the-art, dependable technology. The company is seeking to move from dumb terminals attached to a mainframe to using PCs in some way and is also interested in investigating a satellite system for tracking freight and drivers. Additionally, the company is interested in pursuing ways to cut down on the immense storage requirements and difficult access of troublesome, handwritten, multipart forms that accompany each shipment.

2. Conduct all five interviews in a role-playing exercise. If there are more than ten people in your group, permit two or more analysts to ask questions.

3. Debrief from the interviews, using the forms provided in this chapter.

4. Formulate follow-up questions for second interviews, based on what you found out from the debriefing reports. Your group should produce a written list of follow-up questions for each employee interviewed.

5. With your group write a plan for a JAD Session to take the place of personal interviews. Include relevant participants, suggested setting and so on.

SELECTED BIBLIOGRAPHY

Cash, C. J., and W. B. Stewart, Jr. *Interviewing Principles and Practices*, 4th ed. Dubuque, IA: Wm. C. Brown Company Publishers, 1986.

Di Salvo, V. *Business and Professional Communication*. Columbus, OH: Charles E. Merrill Publishing Company, 1977.

Gorden, R. *Interviewing: Strategy, Techniques and Tactics*. Homewood, IL: Dorsey Press, 1964.

Gane, C. *Rapid Systems Development*. New York: Rapid Systems Development, Inc., 1987.

Joint Application Design. GUIDE Publication GPP-147. Chicago: GUIDE International, 1986.

TELL ME MORE, I'LL LISTEN

"I've scheduled preliminary interviews with five key people. Since you've been so busy with Excelerator, I decided to do the first round of interviews myself," Anna tells Chip as they begin their morning meeting.

"That's fine with me," Chip says. "Just let me know when I can fill in. Who will you be talking to first? Dot?"

"No secret there, I guess," replies Anna. "She's critical to the success of the system. Her word is it when it comes to whether a project will fly or not."

"Who else?" asks Chip.

"I'll see who Dot refers me to, but I set up appointments with Mike Crowe, the maintenance expert; Cher Ware, the software specialist; and Paige Prynter, CPU's financial analyst."

"Don't forget Hy Perteks," says Chip.

"Right. The Information Center will be important to our project," says Anna. "Let me call and see when he's available."

After a brief phone conversation with Hy, Anna turns once again to Chip.

"He'll meet with me later today," Anna confirms.

"I can't wait to hear what they're thinking about the new system," says Chip. "Good luck."

INTERVIEWS WITH CPU STAFF MEMBERS

Interview One

> Respondent: Dorothy (Dot) Matricks, manager, microcomputer systems
> Interviewer: Anna Liszt
> Location: Dorothy's office

Anna: (*Extending her hand as she enters Dorothy's office*) Hello, Dorothy. It's good to see you once again. I think we last saw each other when they had the reception for the new president.

Dot: (*Rising from her desk, shakes hands with Anna*) Please, call me Dot. And I remember that reception, too. It was fun. Please, have a seat (*she indicates a chair beside her desk*) while I call Pat to put a hold on my phone calls. I didn't know at the time we'd be working together. But (*she continues with a laugh*), it seems sooner or later computer people find each other. I've heard through the grapevine that your group is contemplating helping us out of our quagmire here.

Anna: I'm not sure it's a "quagmire," but the administration has requested that the systems and programming group help you to manage your micros with a system of your own.

Dot: (*Sits back in her chair with a chuckle*) I couldn't be more delighted. That means that my efforts to get some help, or should I say my unabashed pleading, has not fallen on deaf ears. Tell me more.

Anna: I thought I'd keep this first interview short, about a half an hour to forty-five minutes (*glancing at her watch*). My overall objective is to find out about micro usage on campus currently, from your perspective. Later we can get into the system you use to manage the micros and its strengths and weaknesses.

Dot: It's easy enough to give an overview, since it's something I often communicate to people. Let me begin with a little history so you can understand where I'm coming from. We started getting involved with micros in the early eighties. We thought we were very high-tech to be buying them as fast as they were produced.

Anna: Yes. Not many schools or even businesses had a plan for implementing microcomputer systems.

Dot: Don't be misled by the haze of history. We purchased some micros early, mostly for the accounting area. But we didn't have a plan, except that we reacted to demand. The beginning was slow, but once hardware and software became available we grew explosively. Once a marketing professor saw what accounting was doing, he or she would say, "What's new for me? We don't want to deal with the mainframe unless we have to." And so we grew and grew. We now have about 820 micros with three or four pieces of equipment attached to each one. Do you believe there is a total of more than 4,000 tagged items in our inventory? By the end of next fall, 200 more micros will be added. You have probably noticed that we have a mix of brands. IBM is used primarily in the business courses, and Apple Macs are used in the art department. Science areas like to use both IBM and Apple, it seems. Many of our computers are IBM compatibles.

Anna: (*Nodding as she absorbs Dot's response*) That's a lot for anyone to manage. But you seem to be up-to-date on what you have in inventory. What system are you using now to keep track of it all?

Dot: I've been here since the beginning and I honestly believe we've done better than most, but still the database system we use is inadequate. Again, my analysis is that just like we outgrew our Apple IIs, we have outgrown our management system. But we are reluctant to fiddle with it too much.

Anna: Why?

Dot: Well, I guess it's because something is better than nothing, even if something is antiquated. We try to be resourceful. It all started in the mid-eighties. I, and the few other people who were assigned to the micros (on a part-time basis, back then), began to realize that something had to be done to prevent chaos. People were asking us for things, and we couldn't lay our hands on them. At the same time, computers were breaking down, and we did not know who had the service contract on them, if they had ever been serviced, and so on. We sensed disaster in the making. From our old mainframe experience, we started trying to organize what we had in a logical way. We all agreed to get a system running with a little off-the-shelf database package (which was not user-friendly, may I be the first to point out). We had very much of a family atmosphere at the time.

Anna: What functions did the package perform?

Dot: It was very basic information, which is what we desperately needed at the time. It sounds simple now, but we took some time and we were thrilled to have inventory information, including the type of equipment, the manufacturer, initial cost, room number where equipment was located, serial number, and equipment purchase date. Even that took extensive updating.

Anna: Is it the same system you run today?

Dot: Yes and no. Same software, but we've been through three updates.

Anna: What other improvements were made?

Dot: After using the system for a couple of years, we knew what we wanted. We added fields to capture the memory size on each micro and graphics boards were installed in the machines.

Anna: And is this the same system you are using now?

Dot: Yes. Yes it is. We can print a number of reports and some summary information. But don't get the wrong impression. The system as it stands is clearly inadequate. You won't get much argument on that point from anyone you interview. But we did what we could with what we had at the time. In fact, there are still a few of the original group here. I will admit that it's been interesting to watch the micros grow. It makes me feel like I had a hand in helping develop a very important area.

Anna: What do you see as the strengths of the current system?

Dot: Since I was in it from the start, I find it fairly easy to use. And it's flexible enough to produce a variety of reports. It's brought us quite far and it does provide the elementary information required to manage the micros.

Anna: Earlier you alluded to some limitations of the system. What are the specific weaknesses you were speaking about?

Dot: (*Reflecting before she speaks*) In a way, they are not weaknesses of the system per se, but changes in the types of micros we are seeing that the system was not far-sighted enough to accommodate. For instance, the number of internal boards and disk drives has increased markedly. A few machines have modems, some have different graphics boards, EGA and VGA, and many have hard drives, but some micros just have two floppy drives. Those drives also vary. Some use 5 1/4-inch disks and others use 3 1/2. We have no information on file regarding the components, and we are asked many questions each week, such as "Where can I find a machine with VGA graphics and a mouse?" Another problem is that we do not have a concise report of which peripherals are connected to the machines, so we do not have a handle on what type of keyboard, printer, mouse, or external drive unit each micro uses. Memory is also a mixed bag. Some machines have 640K, some have 1 meg, and some have other memory installed. You can imagine what it is like to try and find the right memory to run a particular software package. Sometimes we run the software and run into problems.

Anna: How *do* you track what software is installed on which machine?

Dot: Well, unfortunately, we don't have a good grasp of that. We started to track it, but as I mentioned, the whole micro area is growing so fast. We spend so much time putting out brush fires that we're losing the battle to keep track of the information we have.

Anna: Are there similar problems with maintaining the equipment?

Dot: You're getting the idea, now. We fix whatever we can as soon as possible. Some of the machines are shipped out on warranty. We don't even dream of preventive maintenance, even though we are agreed that it is important.

Anna: Really, I am interested in what you are dreaming about for the new system. What would you like it to accomplish?

Dot: That's easy for me to summarize. All of the weaknesses I've outlined should be addressed. I'd like it to have a dossier about each machine—its internal components, the peripherals attached to it. I would also like to have good cost and repair information maintained. As changes occur, we need to keep the files up to date.

Anna: Anything specifically related to software?

Dot: Software cross-referencing is a must.

Anna: One of the items I picked up on during our conversation today has been your dissatisfaction with the capability of the old system to keep pace with the micros' growth. How would any future plans affect the system we develop?

Dot: Certainly we will be adding significant numbers of machines every year. The requests for machines far exceed the budget for several years. We expect that new technology will be adding new components, such as optical disks, that must be added to the system. Also, the use of laptop and notebook micros that actually leave the premises with users will probably grow. Perhaps they will be checked out by individuals for teaching remote classes, research, curriculum development, and the like.

Anna: (*Glancing at her notes*) We've covered quite a bit, I think I am beginning to understand what the old system does and doesn't do, what you'd like to see in the new system, and what you project for growth in the coming years. Is there anything else that you think is important for me to know that I haven't asked?

Dot: It's an oversight of mine, but I should mention that we also have micros on our four satellite campuses in outlying areas. Those machines and all they entail need to be included in our system plans.

Anna: I know there are several people who can help with this project. Is there anyone in particular you would recommend that I talk to?

Dot: There are several people that you will want to seek out. They will be very useful to us. Mike Crowe is our maintenance expert. He's been here almost as long as I have. You will enjoy him very much. His counterpart in software is Cher Ware. She's easy to talk with. Don't forget to touch base with Paige Prynter. She's in charge of financial information about the micros. She'll have what you need in that area. And Hy Perteks runs the Information Center for us. Certainly you will want to see him before you're done.

Anna: Yes. In fact, they are already on my schedule. We must be thinking alike. As I summarize our interview for the systems team I may have some follow-up questions for you.

Dot: I'm delighted to be a part of this. Call me anytime.

Anna: (*Standing up and extending her hand to Dot*) Thanks very much for your time. The information you provided gave me a solid start. I will be back in touch.

Dot: (*Shaking hands and standing*) Let me know how I can help. My door is always open.

Interview Two

> Respondent: Mike Crowe, maintenance expert, microcomputers
> Interviewer: Anna Liszt
> Location: Mike's workroom, at a workbench

Anna: (*Entering his workroom and extending her hand*) Hello, Mike. I'm Anna from systems and programming. The administration asked my team to develop a system to keep track of maintenance costs, preventive maintenance, and other information about the micros. Dot said you'd be a good person to talk to.

Mike: (*Shakes hands heartily. Clears a spot for Anna to sit beside the workbench*) Hello Anna. What do you need to know?

Anna: I'd like to ask you some questions regarding the maintenance of the microcomputers.

Mike: (*Looks around a room strewn with open micros, cables, parts that defy description, tools, and general clutter*) As you can see, we're constantly working on the machines that have problems. Some of these are breakdowns, but a lot of the work is upgrading machines to include new capabilities. These things on the workbench are getting memory expansion; those over there are having graphics boards installed. Really sharp images, with VGA, EGA, Mono, multi freq, and a 16/8 bit bus operations. The micros stacked in boxes behind me are to be installed in Room 472. They'll be linked using Zipnet software and a Maxus XZ server with 1 meg of RAM and a zero wait state.

Anna: Tell me about your preventative maintenance program.

Mike: (*Laughs*) When we have time. We would like to periodically blow the dust off every machine, keyboard, and printer, and vacuum the CPUs. The disk drives should also be cleaned once in a while. Often we simply don't have the time to accomplish this work.

Anna: How many people are working on maintenance?

Mike: There's me, my assistant, and quite a few students who work part time for me.

Anna: How do you know when to perform the periodic maintenance?

Mike: Well, we don't have any exact way to do that. Normally we go from room to room, as we have time. When a room is completed we write it on a list. Let me show you the clipboard we use. We just keep it hanging on the wall. Since the students do a lot of the preventive maintenance, I'm not directly involved in each room. I spot-check their work. You know how kids are, though. Sometimes they forget to write which rooms they've completed and I have to get after 'em. But I rely on them. They're good for the most part.

Anna: What aspects of maintenance would you like the new system to help you with?

Mike: I've seen some systems at other places, and they can get pretty fancy. I don't think I need anything that complicated. I would like to know which machines are still under warranty. That's a big one. Right now, if a machine breaks down I have to look through stacks of information to find out the warranty period and when we bought the thing.

Anna: (*Nodding as she makes a note*) What else would be useful?

Mike: I'd like to know which machines are lemons. Which are constantly breaking down, I mean. I'd take those right out of the high usage areas. Knowing how often we had to repair the machine would be useful. It would be great to have a list of machines showing which ones need preventative maintenance the most. This would probably cut down on the number sent in for repairs.

Anna: Do all of the machines have the same preventive maintenance interval?

Mike: No. (*Mike's portable pager sounds. In response, he goes to the phone and has a short conversation about a microcomputer problem*) Now, where were we? Oh yes. The interval between maintenance. There is different timing for each machine. It would be good to keep that information on file somewhere.

Anna: Is there anything else you would like to add that I haven't covered?

Mike: Let me say it again, loud and clear. We need warranty information. Also, it would be good to get a report saying which machine needs preventative maintenance when. Putting it in order of room numbers where the machines are located would make it easy to find the things.

Anna: (*Standing and extending her hand to shake Mike's*) Thanks for your time, Mike. May I get back to you with any further questions and also have you review my interview summary?

Mike: (*Standing and shaking hands*) Sure. Just have the office page me and leave your number. If you build me a system like what I just described, I'll put it to good use.

Interview Three

Respondent: Cher Ware, software specialist, microcomputer systems
Interviewer: Anna Liszt
Location: Cher's office

Anna: (*Entering the open office and extending her hand to the woman perched on an old sofa to one side of the office*) How do you do? I'm Anna from systems and programming. Dot mentioned that you would be an important person to talk to about building a new system for managing the micros. I'd like to ask you some questions about the systems you have for managing software for the micros.

Cher: (*Gesturing to a spot on the sofa next to her and shaking hands with Anna*) Sure. I was expecting you. Dot told me all about you. She keeps us going. She is order itself. I'm happy to talk to you because I know that we need a system for managing our software. It's not like I haven't been trying to keep a grasp on all this, but we've had a fantastic explosion of software. It's growing like "The Thing that Ate Sacramento." I feel like we're living in a science fiction flick half the time. The software is clearly trying to gobble up our database capacity. Just to track it takes a lot.

Anna: (*Laughing*) Well, what are some of the basics about "The Thing," the software that's in use here at CPU?

Cher: Well, it started around the early part of the eighties. Or was it 1981? I lose track. The seventies were the best for me personally, but the nineties should be good too. What was your question?

Anna: How many software packages did you have in the early 1980s?

Cher: Early on, there were only a few. Some simple packages. A word processor, a database, a spreadsheet. Boy, when you think of how things have changed!

Anna: Can you contrast that to the number of packages that are in use now?

Cher: A humongous variety now. Lots and lots of versions of each of them, too. You don't see plain vanilla packages anymore, either. There are several word processors, several database, spreadsheet, and graphics packages. Then we have software for the science and math programs. Mac packages for the art department. And they're pretty jazzy, too. Not to mention the grammar checkers for the English profs. You know, I don't actually know how many packages there are.

Anna: How does the current system work for managing software?

Cher: It's simple database system that was developed years ago. We never expected to see the growth that we have. Almost since the beginning, our system hasn't been able to maintain all of the information that we need. Information is also missing. Let me say it better. Not all of the software packages have been captured by our system. Many times a professor gets software for class or research and forgets to tell us about it. I wish that I wasn't the last person on earth to know about nifty updates and new packages. If there was just one process for registering software with us that everyone had to follow, life would be rosier.

Anna: What process is followed when your office receives a new piece of software?

Cher: We inventory it, inform the professor that it has arrived, and key the information into the database. Then it is delivered to the lab or the prof that requested it.

Anna: What happens to the older version of the software, if there is one?

Cher: Chaos city. I mean we are talking nightmare time. Golden oldies should be deleted from the hard disks and scratched. But that's not the case. Often we have several versions of the same software in several different labs and campuses, even though we try not to let it happen. WonderWord is a good example. We have WonderWord 4.1, 5.0, and 5.1. The same is true of our DOS versions. But really, sometimes there's a good reason for having multiple versions, since not all of the equipment in all of the labs is upgraded to run new software.

Anna: Do site licenses add further complications?

Cher: You guessed it. Recently, we've been getting site licenses for some of the most commonly used software. Some of it is used on a LAN where there are many workstations and only one copy of the software. If there is no site license, then we need to know how many copies of a particular package we have and on which machines they're located.

Anna: How do you determine which machines or labs will have a new package installed?

Cher: We like to think we have that under control. The normal situation is to use the labs that are designated for that application. For example, DrAwsome is installed in Room 320, the art department's lab. It is an awesome package, by the way. Excelerator is installed in the information sciences lab. Some packages, like WonderWord, are installed in several labs. There are some exceptions to this, though. For instance, some of the scientific software now requires high-quality VGA graphics and a mouse. Typically, scientific packages would be installed in the science- and math-complex labs, but only the machines in the information sciences lab have the VGA and mouse to support them. So that's where the new scientific packages wind up.

Anna: Describe the problems you encounter when locating a machine for installation of new software.

Cher: Sometimes we have requirements for graphics and printers and don't really know which machines have the specific configuration needed. That kind of information is not maintained by either our system or the hardware system. Sometimes the machines don't have enough main memory, especially the older ones. Sometimes the hard disks are simply full. We usually investigate these cases, though. Lots of times students put their own games and stuff on machines. We take it off when it's noticed.

Anna: Explain what happens when you receive a request for the location of a particular software package.

Cher: We have a sorted listing of software by its name, which also contains the room number. We can't trust it completely, though, since it's often outdated and incomplete. Not all software is registered with our area, as I mentioned earlier. For example, last week a professor asked me where he could use the language "C." We informed him of the labs where it was supposed to be located, and later he called to tell us that he found it close to his office, on machines that weren't supposed to have "C."

Anna: Do you currently keep financial information pertaining to software?

Cher: Not on the same database. I know this is critical information that should be maintained, though. It would be extremely useful to know the total costs of each software package and category, such as word processors. It would also be great to have total cost available for an upgrade. The upgrades seem to happen so often that we can hardly install all of the packages and provide training before a new release is announced.

Anna: From what you've said today, I can see that you have an incredibly complex operation. You've been very helpful explaining how the software is managed and giving me ideas about what you would like to see the new system do. Is there anything that we have not covered that you would like to mention?

Cher: Well, talking to you reminded me of a lot of things I hadn't thought about for a while. I hope the new system can help out, especially in getting all software registered with our office. We'd also like to be able to tie into the hardware system to determine which machines will actually run the software we have.

Anna: (*Rises and extends her hand to shake Cher's*) I will be back in touch with you as the project continues. We should be able to help out. I'll ask you to review an interview summary in a few days. Thanks very much for your time.

Cher: (*Shaking hands and rising as Anna leaves*) My pleasure. We have a lot of fun here, even though it's crazy. I'm happy to help any way I can.

Interview Four

Respondent: Paige Prynter, financial analyst
Interviewer: Ann Liszt
Location: Paige's office

Anna: (*Knocking on Paige's door. As Paige opens the door she extends her hand to shake Paige's*) Hello Ms. Prynter. I'm Anna Liszt from systems and programming.

Paige: (*Shaking hands, then showing Anna to a chair opposite her desk*) I've been expecting you. Please have a seat. Dot told me you would be contacting me.

Anna: The administration has asked my group to help build a system to manage the microcomputers, and I am doing a series of interviews with key people who will use the information provided by the system.

Paige: The system is sorely needed. What do you need to know from me?

Anna: I'd like to ask you some questions about the financial needs regarding microcomputers used at CPU. More specifically, what types of reports are you currently receiving?

Paige: We get a report listing the cost of all the microcomputers and a total. That is about the extent of our financial information right now.

Anna: Would it be useful to have subtotals added to the reports?

Paige: Yes. That would be extremely useful for costs on each type of machine.

Anna: Do you receive financial information on software?

Paige: You've touched on an issue that is controversial these days. We receive absolutely no computerized information on software. And of course, the software has just snowballed. We have no idea of the total amount invested. What we scrape by with are outdated requisitions for software. We desperately need more information about software purchases in order to formulate better controls and put together reasonable budgets. We need subtotals by product and by category of software, such as word processing.

Anna: How do site licenses fit into the picture?

Paige: We would like to have the figure for the site license as a total and then not have to calculate the amount for each copy.

Anna: Your current needs are clearly pressing. But is there anything you would add to the system for the future?

Paige: Yes. We would like to input the cost of an upgrade to a particular software package and have the computer tell us how much it would cost for all of the currently installed software. We also need subtotals by product for both hardware and software, along with totals. It would also be useful to have totals for each of the satellite campuses.

Anna: You've answered all of the quesitons I have right now. Is there anything you would like to add?

Paige: Yes. We need to take an accurate inventory of the hardware periodically. Machines have an annoying habit of moving from one room to another over the course of a semester. But we need to know what we have and precisely where it is. You can imagine how time-consuming the inventory process is. Automating it would be highly desirable.

Anna: May I get back to you with a summary of our interview and also any further questions I might have?

Paige: Certainly. Just set up an appointment ahead of time again, and I will be glad to speak with you.

Anna: (*Rising and extending her hand to shake Paige's*) Thank you very much for your time. Your input will be valuable in helping to put together the new system.

Paige: (*Shaking Anna's hand and rising from her desk*) I hope that the new system will provide us with the vital information we need. I don't like to complain, but it's been a long time in coming. Please close the door behind you.

Interview Five

> Respondent: Hy Perteks, director, Information Center
> Interviewer: Anna Liszt
> Location: Hy's office in the Information Center

Anna: (*Walking past several students and faculty working on micros to get to Hy's open door; pausing at the entrance*) Hello, Hy. I'm Anna.

Hy: (*Getting up from a crowded desk to welcome her and extending his hand to shake Anna's*) I remember you. We were at that conference together about two years ago. Please come in and pull up a chair. I got your message, and Dot said you'd be by, too.

Anna: (*Sitting down in a chair by the side of Hy's desk*) She probably told you that the administration has asked my group to help with designing a system to manage the micros. I've been doing a series of interviews with key people, and it's time for me to find out about the needs you are experiencing here in the Information Center.

Hy: What we need so badly I can taste it is a centralized bank of information on the micros and the software we have.

Anna: Who is served by the Information Center?

Hy: Our clients come from every level of the university. We serve administrators, both on the managerial and support staff levels, and we also serve the needs of faculty for teaching and research. Our clients are pretty evenly split between those groups, with maybe a little lean toward the faculty.

Anna: What services do you provide them?

Hy: We do a lot of training, a lot. Every so often we offer classes in popular software packages. You've probably gotten some of our flyers announcing those classes. We answer (or try to answer) tons of technical questions as well. They usually are specific as to how to perform advanced tasks with the software. A third category of service we perform is helping users to adapt software to their particular application. We also help in figuring out which software would be most effective in solving their problems.

Anna: It seems that the staff here has to be fairly well-versed in many different areas. Do you have an expert in each software package?

Hy: No, although I personally am familiar with the basics of all the packages. I receive training in the operation of the software and work on small projects just to familiarize myself with new programs. When the nitty-gritty detailed technical questions arise, I dive into the manuals and other reference materials we have here in the IC library. But I'm not alone. I often call on specialists who are on the faculty to help with particularly thorny problems. At times I even call software vendors for help.

Anna: How often do you add new software packages?

Hy: More often than you would believe. We do upgrades, as well as altogether new software. For example, we recently purchased a math word processor and are scheduling classes for training. We are being absolutely deluged with requests from math and science faculty. They are so tickled that the package is here and running. There's never a dull moment. That's why I love the job.

Anna: What are some of the problems you are experiencing that might be dealt with more effectively via an improved microcomputer system?

Hy: I know there's a lot that can be done that we haven't, just because no one has taken the time. For one, we need to know what version of software a person is using. You wouldn't believe how critical this is in determining the solution to a technical question, such as how to create a macro or transfer files from one package to another. Lots of times the users just aren't sure of what version they're using. And we'd also like to know the phone numbers of software providers so we can quickly phone for assistance. Sometimes it's difficult to find an expert around the university for a particular program. I meet a lot of interesting people searching for help, though.

Anna: Other people have mentioned the need to know which software is located on which machine in which room. Is this important to you?

Hy: You bet. We get requests for training or someone wants to use software that isn't in the information center. If it's an oddball package, we don't know where it's located without lots of calling around.

Anna: You've told me a good deal in a short time. Is there anything else that you'd like to add that we haven't covered?

Hy: I know I talk a lot. But I mean well. Really, I think we've covered all of the bases. Let me just add that I would like to have a sense of how many people would be interested in training on software that we have now. I'd also like to know which software people want us to purchase. We can't get everything, but if they don't ask, I'll never know. That's a tall order, though. I'm not sure how to get that without surveying the entire university.

Anna: (*Rising and extending her hand to shake Hy's*) We'll try to include as much of what you've said as we can. Thanks for your time. May I get back to you with follow-up questions if they are needed?

Hy: (*Shaking her hand and rising to accompany her to the door*) No problem. Service is what we're here for. If you end up using a micro package as part of the solution, I can get involved even more.

Exercises

E-1. Assume that Chip conducted all of the initial interviews rather than Anna. In small groups, role-play the part of Chip and the interviewees. Assign students to analyze and comment on the differences in the results.

E-2. Analyze the five interviews. In a paragraph, discuss what type of structure each interview had.

E-3. List each interview, 1–5, and then write a paragraph for each, discussing ways that Anna might improve on her interviews for next time.

E-4. Analyze the questions used in the five interviews. In a paragraph, discuss the question types used and whether they were appropriate for getting needed information.

6

USING QUESTIONNAIRES

KINDS OF INFORMATION SOUGHT

Questionnaires are an information-gathering technique that allows systems analysts to study attitudes, beliefs, behaviors, and characteristics of several key people in the organization who may be affected by the current and proposed systems, as shown in Figure 6.1. Attitudes are what people in the organization say they want (in a new system, for instance); beliefs are what people think is actually true; behavior is what organizational members do; and characteristics are properties of people or things.

Responses gained through questionnaires using closed questions can be quantified. Responses to questionnaires using open-ended questions are analyzed and interpreted in other ways. Questions on attitudes and beliefs are notably sensitive to the wording chosen by the systems analyst.

Through the use of questionnaires, the analyst may be seeking to quantify what was found in interviews. Additionally, questionnaires may be used to determine how widespread or limited a sentiment expressed in an interview really is. Conversely, questionnaires can be used to survey a large sample of system users in order to sense problems or raise important issues before interviews are scheduled.

Throughout this chapter, we will compare and contrast questionnaires with interviews, which were covered in Chapter 5. There are many similarities between the two techniques, and perhaps the ideal would be to use them in conjunction with each other, either following up unclear questionnaire responses with an interview or designing the questionnaire based on what is discovered in the interview. However, each technique has its own specific functions, and it is not always necessary or desirable to use both.

FIGURE 6.1
Kinds of information sought
when using questionnaires.

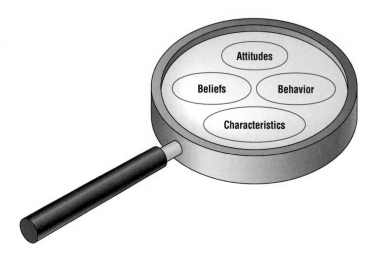

PLANNING FOR THE USE OF QUESTIONNAIRES

At first glance, questionnaires may seem to be a quick way to gather massive amounts of data about how users assess the current system, what problems they are experiencing with their work, and what people expect from a new or modified system. While it is true that you can gather lots of information through questionnaires without spending time in face-to-face interviews, developing a useful questionnaire takes extensive planning time in its own right.

You must first decide what you are attempting to gain through using a questionnaire. For instance, if you want to know what percentage of users prefer an information center as a means of learning about new software packages, then a questionnaire might be the right technique. If you want to do an in-depth analysis of a manager's decision-making process, then an interview is a better choice.

Here are some guidelines to help you decide whether use of questionnaires is appropriate. Consider using questionnaires if:

1. The people you need to question are widely dispersed (different branches of the same corporation).
2. A large number of people are involved in the systems project, and it is meaningful to know what proportion of a given group (for example, management) approves or disapproves of a particular feature of the proposed system.
3. You are doing an exploratory study and want to gauge overall opinion before the systems project is given any specific direction.
4. You wish to be certain that any problems with the current system are identified and addressed in follow-up interviews.

Once you have determined that you have good cause to use a questionnaire and have pinpointed the objectives to be fulfilled through its use, you can begin formulating questions.

Writing Questions

The biggest difference between the questions used for most interviews and those used on questionnaires is that interviewing permits interaction regarding the questions and their meanings. In an interview, the analyst has an opportunity to refine a question, define a muddy term, change the course of questioning, respond to a puzzled look, and generally control the context.

Little of this is possible on a questionnaire. What this means for the analyst is that questions must be transparently clear, the flow of the questionnaire cogent, the respondent's questions anticipated, and the administration of the questionnaire planned in detail.

The basic question types used on the questionnaire are open-ended and closed, as discussed for interviewing. Due to the constraints placed on questionnaires, some additional discussion of question types is warranted.

OPEN-ENDED QUESTIONS. Recall that open-ended questions (or statements) are those that leave all possible response options open to the respondent. For example, open-ended questions on a questionnaire might read, "Describe any problems you are currently experiencing with output reports," or "In your opinion, how helpful are the user manuals for the current system's accounting package?"

When you write open-ended questions for a questionnaire, anticipate what kind of response you will get. It is important that responses you receive are capable of correct interpretation. Otherwise, many resources will have been wasted in the development, administration, and interpretation of a useless questionnaire.

For instance, if you ask a question such as "How do you feel about the system?" the responses are apt to be too broad for accurate interpretation or comparison. So even when you write an open-ended question, it must be narrow enough to guide respondents to answer in a specific way. (Examples of open-ended questions can be found in Figure 6.2.)

For instance, if you really want to gather feelings toward the current system, you might couch your questions in the context of satisfaction versus dissatisfaction with the system. Further, you might suggest some system features to prompt respondents in recalling which features are of interest.

Open-ended questions are particularly well-suited to situations in which you want to get at organizational members' opinions about some aspect of the system, whether product or process. In such cases, you will want to use open-ended questions when it is impossible to list effectively all of the possible responses to the question.

Additionally, open-ended questions are useful in exploratory situations. These occur when the systems analyst is not able (because of diversity of opinion or far-flung employees) to determine precisely what problems exist with the current system. Responses to the open-ended questions will then be used to focus on cited problems more narrowly, via interviews with a handful of key decision makers.

CLOSED QUESTIONS. Recall that closed questions (or statements) are those that limit or close the response options available to the respondent. For example, in Figure 6.3, the statement "Below are the six software packages currently available in the Information Center. Please check the one package you personally use most frequently," is closed. Notice that respondents are not asked *why* the package is preferred, not are they asked to select more than one, even if that is a more representative response.

FIGURE 6.2
Open-ended questions used
for questionnaires.

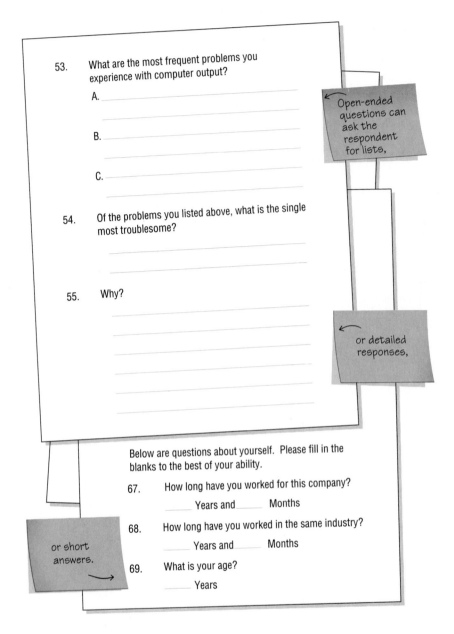

Closed questions should be used when the systems analyst is able to list effectively all of the possible responses to the question and when all responses listed mutually exclusive, so that choosing one precludes choosing any of the others.

Use closed questions when you want to survey a large sample of people. The reason for this becomes obvious when you start imagining how the data you are collecting will look. If you use only open-ended questions for hundreds of people, correct analysis and interpretation of their responses becomes impossible without aid of a computerized content analysis program.

There are tradeoffs involved in choosing either open-ended or closed questions for use on questionnaires. Figure 6.4 summarizes these tradeoffs. Notice that responses to open-ended questions can help analysts gain rich, exploratory insights, as well as breadth and depth on a topic. While open-ended questions can be written easily, responses to them are difficult and time-consuming to analyze.

FIGURE 6.3
Closed questions on
questionnaires can help
ensure responses.

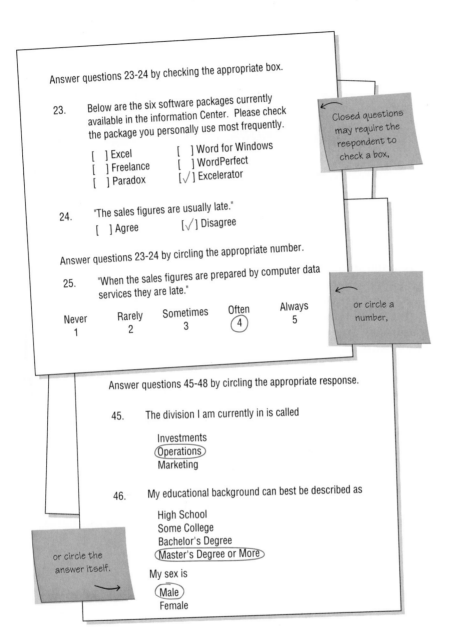

When we refer to the writing of closed questions with either ordered or unordered answers, we often refer to the process as scaling. The use of scales on questionnaires is discussed in detail in a later section.

CHOICE OF WORDS. Just as with interviews, the language of questionnaires is an extremely important aspect of their effectiveness. Even if the systems analyst has a standard set of questions concerning system development, it is wise to write them to reflect the business's own terminology.

Respondents appreciate the efforts of someone who bothers to write a questionnaire reflecting their own language usage. For instance, if the business uses the term *supervisors* not *managers*, or *units* rather than *departments*, incorporating the preferred terms into the questionnaire helps respondents relate to the meaning of the questions. Responses will be easier to interpret accurately and respondents will be more enthusiastic overall.

FIGURE 6.4
Tradeoffs between the use of
open-ended and closed
questions on questionnaires.

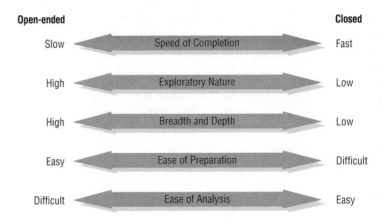

Open-ended		Closed
Slow	Speed of Completion	Fast
High	Exploratory Nature	Low
High	Breadth and Depth	Low
Easy	Ease of Preparation	Difficult
Difficult	Ease of Analysis	Easy

In order to double check whether language used on the questionnaire is that of the respondents, try some sample questions on a pilot group. Ask them to pay particular attention to the appropriateness of the wording and to change any words that do not ring true.

Here are some guidelines to use when choosing language for your questionnaire:

1. Use the language of respondents whenever possible. Keep wording simple.
2. Work at being specific rather than vague in wording. However, avoid overly specific questions as well.
3. Keep questions short.
4. Do not patronize respondents by talking down to them through low-level language choices.
5. Avoid bias in wording. This also means avoiding objectionable questions.
6. Target questions to the right respondents (that is, those who are capable of responding). Don't assume too much knowledge.
7. Ensure that questions are technically accurate before including them.

USING SCALES IN QUESTIONNAIRES

Scaling is the process of assigning numbers or other symbols to an attribute or characteristic for the purpose of measuring that attribute or characteristic. Scales are often arbitrary and may not be unique. For example, temperature is measured in a number of ways, the two most common being the Fahrenheit scale (where water freezes at 32 degrees and boils at 212 degrees) and the Celsius scale (where freezing occurs at 0 degrees and boiling at 100 degrees).

Scaling Fundamentals

REASONS FOR SCALING. The systems analyst may want to design scales to either (1) measure the attitudes or characteristics of the people answering the questionnaire or (2) have the respondents judge the subjects of the questionnaire. Let's look at how each of these types of scales can be applied. For our purposes, each will use the same set of questions about a number of sample monthly statement printouts for the Never Fail Bank of America.

If the analyst wants to measure attitudes or characteristics of the respondents, the responses can be combined or grouped to reflect that information. A number of people might fall into a group that doesn't want to change the monthly printouts at any cost, another group may want cleaner output, while a third group might want to add features such as sorting checks by number and category. Here we are trying to measure the differences among respondents, and it doesn't matter how each of the sample printouts was rated. Other examples of measuring characteristics or attitudes will be discussed later in this chapter.

If the systems analyst was interested in how each of the sample monthly statements fared, the respondents would serve as judges. In this case, it wouldn't matter how much respondents differ in their attitudes.

MEASUREMENT. There are four different forms of measurement scales, each form offering different degrees of accuracy. The form of measurement also dictates how to analyze the data collected. The four forms of measurement are:

1. Nominal
2. Ordinal
3. Interval
4. Ratio

Nominal scales are used to classify things. A question such as:

What type of program do you use the most?
1 = A WORD PROCESSOR
2 = A SPREADSHEET
3 = A DATABASE
4 = A GRAPHING PROGRAM

uses a nominal scale. Obviously, nominal scales are the weakest of the forms of measurement. Generally, all the analyst can do with them is obtain totals for each classification.

Ordinal scales, like nominal scales, allow classification. The difference, however, is that the ordinal scale also implies rank ordering. In this example, a systems analyst asks an end user to circle one of the numbers:

The support staff of the information center is:
1. EXTREMELY HELPFUL
2. VERY HELPFUL
3. MODERATELY HELPFUL
4. NOT VERY HELPFUL
5. NOT HELPFUL AT ALL

Ordinal scales are useful because one class is greater or less than another class. On the other hand, no assumption can be made that the difference between choices 1 and 2 is the same as the difference between choices 3 and 4.

Interval scales possess the characteristic that the intervals between each of the numbers are equal. Due to this characteristic, mathematical operations can be performed on the questionnaire data, resulting in a more complete analysis. Examples of interval scales are Fahrenheit and Celsius scales to measure temperature.

The foregoing example of the information center is definitely not that of an interval scale, but by anchoring the scale on either end, the analyst *may* want to make the assumption that the respondent perceives the intervals to be equal:

How useful is the support given by staff in the information center?

NOT USEFUL AT ALL				EXTREMELY USEFUL
1	2	3	4	5

If the systems analyst makes this assumption, more quantitative analysis is possible.

Ratio scales are similar to interval scales in that the intervals between numbers are assumed to be equal. Ratio scales, however, have an absolute zero. An example of a ratio scale is distance as measured by a ruler. Another example is the following:

Approximately how many hours do you spend on the computer daily?

0	2	4	6	8

Ratio scales will be used less often by the systems analyst.

As a guideline, a systems analyst should use:

1. A ratio scale when the intervals are equal and there is an absolute zero.

2. An interval scale when it can be assumed that the intervals are equal, but there is no absolute zero.

3. An ordinal scale when it is impossible to assume that the intervals are equal, but the classes can be ranked.

4. A nominal scale if the systems analyst wants to classify things but they cannot be ranked.

VALIDITY AND RELIABILITY. There are two measures of performance in constructing scales: validity and reliability. The systems analyst should be aware of these concerns.

Validity is the degree to which the question measures what the analyst intends to measure. For example, if the purpose of the questionnaire is to determine whether the organization is ready for a major change in computer operations, do the questions measure this?

Reliability measures consistency. If the questionnaire was administered once and then again under the same conditions and the same results were obtained, the instrument is said to have external consistency. If the questionnaire contains subparts and these parts have equivalent results, the instrument is said to have internal consistency. Both external and internal consistency are important.

Constructing Scales

The actual construction of scales is a serious task. Careless construction of scales can result in one of the following problems:

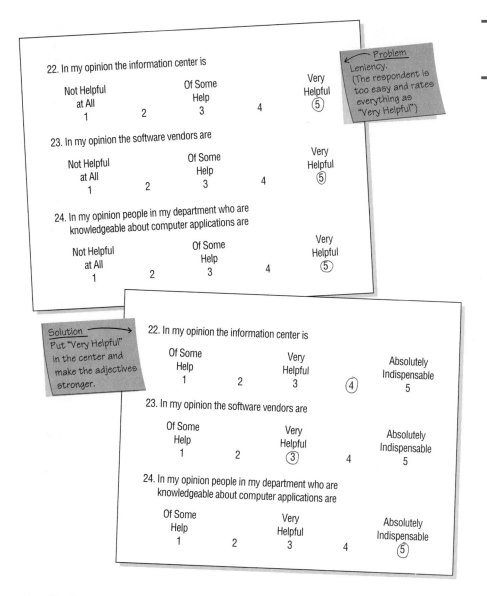

FIGURE 6.5
Correcting the problem of
respondent's leniency.

1. Leniency
2. Central tendency
3. Halo effect

Leniency is a problem caused by respondents who are easy raters. A systems analyst can avoid the problem of leniency by moving the "average" category to the left (or right) of center, as shown in Figure 6.5.

Central tendency is a problem that occurs when respondents rate everything as average. The analyst can improve the scale by either (1) making the differences smaller at the two ends, (2) adjusting the strength of the descriptors, or (3) creating a scale with more points. An example of correcting for central tendency can be found in Figure 6.6.

The halo effect is a problem that arises when the impression formed in one question carries into the next question. For example, if you are rating an employee about whom you have a very favorable impression, you may give a high rating in every category or trait, regardless of whether or not it is a strong point of the employee's. The solution is to place one trait

FIGURE 6.6
Correcting the problem of
respondent's central
tendency.

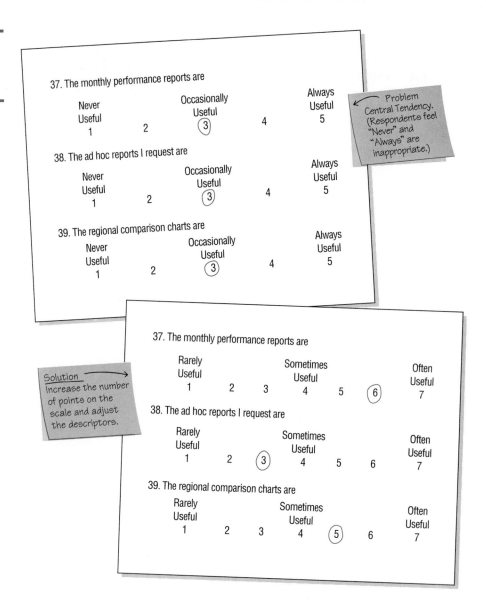

and several employees on each page, rather than one employee and several traits on a page. An example of correcting for the halo effect can be found in Figure 6.7.

DESIGNING AND ADMINISTERING THE QUESTIONNAIRE

Designing the Questionnaire

Many of the same principles that are relevant to the design of forms for data input (as covered in Chapter 16) are important here as well. Although the intent of the questionnaire is to gather information on attitudes, beliefs, behavior, and characteristics whose impact may substantially alter users' work, respondents are not always motivated to respond. Remember that organizational members as a whole tend to receive too many questionnaires, which are often ill-conceived and trivial.

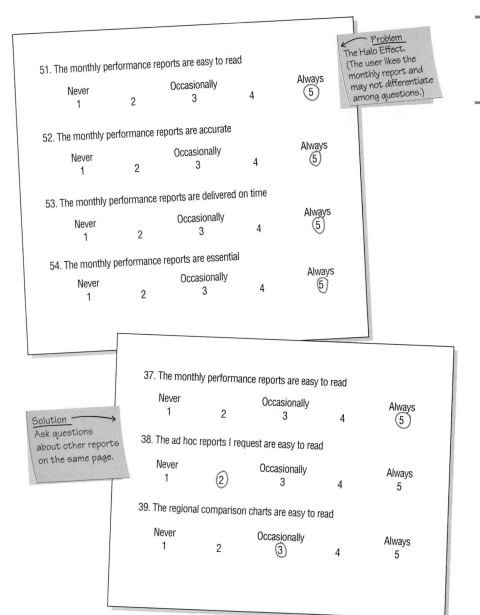

FIGURE 6.7
Correcting the problem of
respondent's answering
everything favorably due to a
halo effect.

A well-designed, relevant questionnaire can help overcome some of this resistance to respond. This section discusses the stylistic considerations that can help improve the response rate to questionnaires. It also presents the guidelines for ordering the content the best results.

QUESTIONNAIRE FORMAT

Allow ample white space. The most important consideration in designing the questionnaire format is to allow enough white space so that the respondent is drawn into the form. White space refers to blank space surrounding printed matter on a page. A questionnaire that is squeezed together without benefit of adequate white space is not as likely to be completed, even though it will take less paper to print. To further increase the response rate, use only white or off-white paper to print questionnaires.

The Unbearable Questionnaire

"I'm going to go into a depression or at least a slump if someone doesn't figure this out soon," say Penny Stox, office manager for Carbon, Carbon & Rippy, a large brokerage firm. Penny is sitting across a conference table from you and two of her most productive account executives, By Lowe and Sal Hy. All of you are mulling over the responses to a questionnaire that has been distributed among the firm's account executives, which is shown in Figure 6.C1.

"We need a crystal ball to understand these," By and Sal call out together.

"Maybe this reflects some sort of optimistic cycle, or something," Penny says as she reads more of the responses. Who designed this gem, anyway?"

"Rich Kleintz," By and Sal call out in unison.

"Well, as you can see, it's not telling us anything," Penny exclaims.

Penny and her staff are dissatisfied over the responses they have received on the unbearable questionnaire, and feel that the responses are unrealistic reflections of the amount of information account executives want. Why is this occuring and how can you change the scaling of the questions in order to avoid these problems?

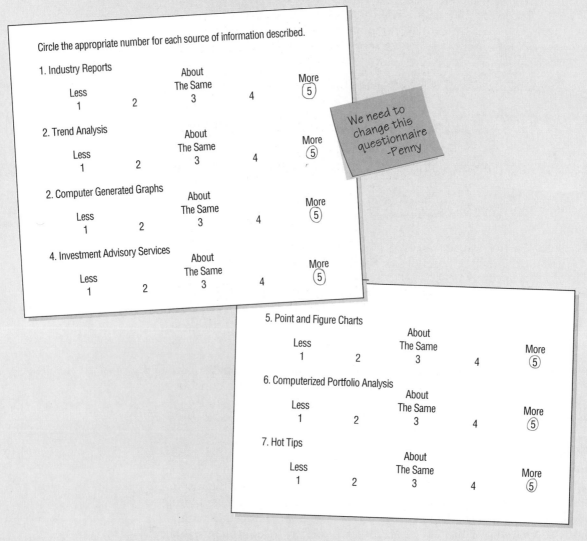

FIGURE 6.C1
Questionnaire developed for the brokerage firm of Carbon, Carbon, & Rippy by Rich Kleintz.

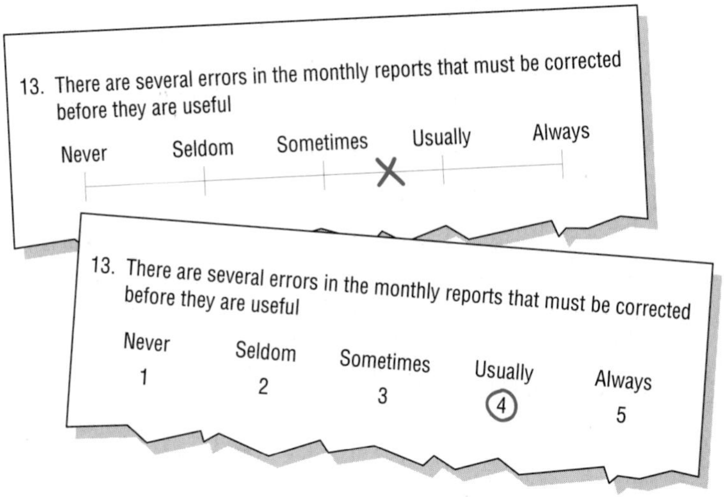

FIGURE 6.8
Improving accuracy of
responses by asking a
respondent to circle a
number.

Allow adequate space for responses. Above and beyond allowing white space to set off the printed material, allow adequate space for responses as well. If you expect respondents to write a paragraph in response to an open-ended question, you must leave three to five lines blank for them to do so.

Ask respondents to circle their answers. Another good practice for capturing a response correctly is to request that respondents circle their answers (or numbers if you are employing a scale). Figure 6.8 shows what can happen if respondents aren't encouraged to circle numbers. In this example, the analyst would have a difficult time trying to determine if the respondent meant to choose a 3 or 4.

It is also sometimes permissible to have respondents check a box [ ] created by a pair of brackets or check a space ( ) created with a pair of parentheses. However, care must be taken to allow enough space for people who make large checkmarks. Data tabulation and analysis become difficult if respondents inadvertently check through several boxes.

Use objectives to help determine format. Before you design the questionnaire, you need to articulate your objectives. For instance, if your objective is to poll as many organizational members as possible concerning an identified list of problems with the current system, it is probably best to use a response form that is machine readable. This will affect how you design the questionnaire and what kinds of instructions you will include.

Alternatively, if you desire written responses, you need to calculate the amount of space necessary for the length of response you want and then be sure to include that space on the form or on a separate answer sheet. You might need to plan for both numerical and written responses.

You may also wish to assign someone other than the respondents to enter the responses on the questionnaire. Although doing so presents a greater possibility of errors in interpretation, it does afford an opportunity to avoid mechanical data-entry errors that inexperienced respondents might make. Additionally, keep in mind that questionnaire sheets on which respondents can write directly are often easier for them to complete correctly than are machine-readable response forms.

FIGURE 6.9
Using a consistent format in
presenting questions and
responses.

In this section, please circle the number that best suggests your opinion about each topic.
Remember to circle only ONE number for each question.

10. Monthly reports of sales figures for our division reach me in time to make decisions

Never	Seldom	Sometimes	Usually	Always
1	2	3	4	5

11. I use the display screen to view monthly sales figures

Never	Seldom	Sometimes	Usually	Always
1	2	3	4	5

12. Monthly sales reports are valuable to me in making decisions

Never	Seldom	Sometimes	Usually	Always
1	2	3	4	5

13. There are several errors in the monthly reports that must be corrected before they are useful

Never	Seldom	Sometimes	Usually	Always
1	2	3	4	5

14. I think the monthly sales reports are irrelevant to most of those who receive them

Never	Seldom	Sometimes	Usually	Always
1	2	3	4	5

Be consistent in style. Organize the questionnaire consistently throughout. Put instructions in the same place in relation to question subsections, so respondents always know where to find instructions.

Be consistent as shown in Figure 6.9. If you use shaded boxes, use them in the same way from question to question. Following this format consistently allows respondents to get through the questionnaire quickly and reduces the chance of error.

Another major part of designing the questionnaire is deciding the order in which questions should appear. You will often need the input of a pilot group to help decide the most appropriate question order.

ORDER OF QUESTIONS. There is not one best way to order questions on the questionnaire. Once again, as you order questions you must think about your objectives in using the questionnaire and then determine the function of each question in helping you to achieve your objectives. It is also important to see the questionnaire through the respondent's eyes. If you are without the help of a pilot group, always ask yourself how respondents will feel about the order and placement of a particular question, and whether this is indeed how you want them to react.

Questions of importance to respondents go first. The first questions should deal with subjects that respondents view as being important. This approach makes for an intriguing start to the questionnaire and is a technique to get people quickly involved. Respondents should feel that by answering each question and completing the form, they can cause a change or have some impact. For example, if organizational members are keen on rating potential software packages for the proposed system, begin with questions on this subject.

This technique is quite different from the typical novice's approach, which is to begin by asking for demographic information such as job title, years with the company, number of subordinates, male or female, and years in school. Some people will find this style boringly similar to other forms they routinely fill out whereas, others may actually find it threatening, especially if you stressed confidentiality earlier but are now requesting data that will clearly allow identification of the respondent.

Cluster items of similar content together. When you build a frame of reference for respondents, take advantage of it by placing questions related to each other close together on the questionnaire. For example, all questions dealing with end-user computing might be grouped together in one sub-headed section of the questionnaire.

Some researchers have suggested that data are cleaner if questions appear randomly; however, this approach is not recommended here. Randomization in this case merely tries the patience of respondents who are likely to prefer being able to see for themselves that questionnaire construction is logical.

Employ respondents' associational tendencies. This consideration is similar to the guideline for clustering questions on similar topics. However, it goes even further by reminding the analyst to anticipate the kinds of associations that respondents make and then to use these associations in ordering questions.

For instance, if you ask, "How many subordinates do you have?" you will probably want to continue in that vein and ask about other formal organizational relationships as well. Further, the respondent may associate the formal organizational structure with the informal. If that is the case, it is appropriate to include questions about the informal relationships in the same section of the questionnaire. Figure 6.10 shows an associational ordering of questions.

Bring up less controversial items first. In your preliminary assessment of what is happening in the business, you will have run into some issues that are, for one reason or another, divisive to particular groups. If you believe that those issues still must be examined, try to put less controversial items before divisive or inflammatory items in a questionnaire.

For example, if you realize that computerization of manual tasks has long been a sore point with some employees but you want to find out how widespread this sentiment is, the questions should still be asked, but they should follow less upsetting ones.

FIGURE 6.10
Using an associational ordering of questions to enable
respondents to think about
unrelated subjects.

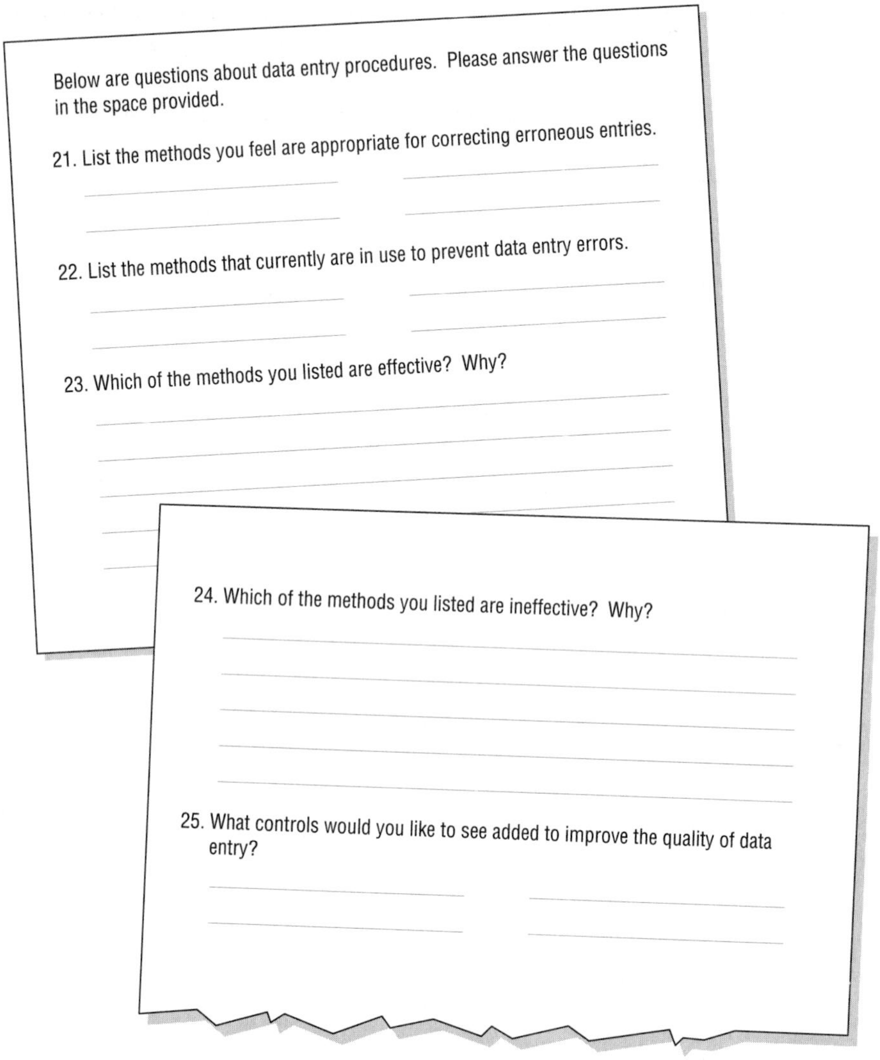

Below are questions about data entry procedures. Please answer the questions in the space provided.

21. List the methods you feel are appropriate for correcting erroneous entries.

22. List the methods that currently are in use to prevent data entry errors.

23. Which of the methods you listed are effective? Why?

24. Which of the methods you listed are ineffective? Why?

25. What controls would you like to see added to improve the quality of data entry?

Since your overall objective is to gather data on attitudes, beliefs, behaviors, and characteristics, you expect and seek some diversity among respondents; otherwise, a questionnaire would be extraneous. However, you want respondents to feel as unthreatened by and interested in the questions being asked as possible, without getting overwrought about a particular issue.

Administering the Questionnaire

RESPONDENTS. Deciding who will receive the questionnaire is done in conjunction with setting objectives for its results. Sampling, which was covered in Chapter 4, helps the systems analyst to determine what sort of representation is necessary and hence what kind of respondents should receive the questionnaire.

Recipients are often chosen as representative of the rank, length of service with the company, job duties, or special interest in the current or proposed system. Be sure to include enough respondents to allow for a reasonable sample in the event that some questionnaires are not returned or some response sheets are incorrectly completed and thus must be discarded.

METHODS OF ADMINISTERING THE QUESTIONNAIRE. The systems analyst has several options for administering the questionnaire, and the choice of administration method is often determined by the existing business situation. Options for administering the questionnaire include:

1. Convening all concerned respondents together at one time.
2. Personally handing out blank questionnaires and taking back completed ones.
3. Allowing respondents to self-administer the questionnaire at work and drop it in a centrally located box.
4. Mailing questionnaires to employees in branch or satellite sites and supplying a deadline, instructions, and return postage.

Each of these four methods has advantages and disadvantages. Collecting questionnaire data from a group gathered at one place in one time is helpful in that there is no wait time (except whatever time it takes to complete the form) involved before getting back the data. Additionally, the analyst is better able to control the data collection situation by guaranteeing that everyone receives the same instructions and that 100 percent of the forms will be returned.

A disadvantage of group data collection is that not all employees in the sample will be free at the scheduled time. Additionally, there may be some resentment at being asked to focus on the task of filling out the questionnaire when other work seems more pressing. Peer pressure in this context can work for or against the completion of the questionnaire. If key respondents seem favorable, the majority will catch on and react in the same way and vice versa.

The systems analyst can also guarantee a good response rate by personally handing out and collecting questionnaires, but analyst time becomes a problem when a large or widely dispersed group is sampled. Also, respondents may be skeptical that even though the questionnaire stressed confidentiality, the analyst is all too aware of who is turning in which form.

Allowing respondents to self-administer the questionnaire is done frequently. Response rates with this method are a little lower than with the other methods, since people may forget about the form, lose it, or purposely ignore it. However, self-administration allows people to feel that their anonymity is assured and may result in less guarded answers from some respondents.

One way to increase the response rate on self-administered forms is to set up a central drop box at an employee's desk and ask him or her to cross off the names of respondents who return a form. That way a particular person is not associated with a particular response form, but there is still subtle pressure to return the form.

The response rate for mailing, the fourth method of questionnaire administration, is notably poorer. Mailing a questionnaire does not involve the respondent in a personal way with the survey. However, it is often important to include remote organizational members just because they are not as involved with life at headquarters and will likely have a different perspective on current and prospective computer systems that should be taken into account.

SUMMARY

By using questionnaires, systems analysts can gather data on attitudes, beliefs, behaviors, and characteristics from key people in the organization. Questionnaires are useful if: people in the organization are widely

Order in the Courts

"I love my work," Tennys says, beginning the interview with a volley. "It's a lot like a game. I keep my eye on the ball and never look back," he continues. Tennyson "Tennys" Courts is a manager for Global Health Spas, Inc., which has popular health and recreation spas worldwide.

"Now that I've finished my M.B.A., I feel like I'm on top of the world with Global," Courts continues. "I think I can really help this outfit shape up with its computers and health spas."

Tenny's is attempting to help your systems group, which is developing a system to be used by all 80

outlets (where currently each group handles its paperwork in its own way). "Can I bounce this off of you?" he asks Terri Towell, one of your team of systems analysts. "It's a questionnaire I designed for distribution to all spa managers."

Ever the good sport, Terri tells Tennys that she'd love to take a look at the form. But back in the office, Terri puts the ball in your court. Systematically critique Tenny's technique as depicted in Figure 6.C2 and explain to him point by point what it needs to be a matchless questionnaire with a winning form.

QUESTIONNAIRE FOR ALL MANAGERS OF HEALTH SPAS

URGENTFILL OUT IMMEDIATELY AND RETURN

PERSONALLY TO YOUR DIVISION MANAGER. YOUR NEXT

PAYCHECK WILL BE WITHHELD UNTIL IT IS CONFIRMED

THAT YOU HAVE TURNED THIS IN.

In ten words or less, what complaints have you lodged about

the current computer system in the last six months to a year?

Are there others who feel the same way in your outlet as you

do? Who? List their names and positions.

1.   2.

3.   4.

5.

7.

Terri
* Please help*
me improve this
form.
*   -Tennys*

What is the biggest problem you have when communicating

your information requirements to headquarters? Describe it

briefly.

How much computer down time did you experience last year?

1 - 2 - 3 - 4 - 5 - 6 - 7- 8 - 9 - 10 -

Is there any computer equipment you never use?

Description   Serial Number

Do you want it removed? Agree   Neutral   Disagree

In your opinion, what's next as far as computers and Global

Spas are concerned?

Thanks for filling this out   • • • • • • • • • • • • • • •

FIGURE 6.C2
Questionnaire developed for managers of Global Health Spas by Tennys Courts.

dispersed, many people are involved with the systems project, exploratory work is necessary before recommending alternatives, or there is a need for problem sensing before interviews are conducted.

Once objectives for the questionnaire are articulated, the analyst can begin writing either open-ended or closed questions. Choice of wording is extremely important and should reflect the language of the organizational members. Ideally, the questions should be simple, specific, free of bias, not patronizing, technically accurate, and addressed to those who are knowledgeable.

Scaling is the process of assigning numbers or other symbols to an attribute or characteristic. The systems analyst may want to use scales either to measure the attitudes or characteristics of respondents or to have respondents act as judges for the subject of the questionnaire.

The four forms of measurement are nominal, ordinal, interval, and ratio scales. The form of measurement is often dictated by the data, and the analysis of data is in turn dictated to some degree by the form of measurement.

Systems analysts need to be concerned with validity and reliability. Validity means that the questionnaire measures what the systems analyst intended to measure. Reliability means that the results are consistent.

Analysts should be careful to avoid problems such as leniency, central tendency, and the halo effect when constructing scales.

Consistent control of the questionnaire format and style can result in a better response rate. Additionally, the meaningful ordering and clustering of questions is important for helping respondents understand the questionnaire.

KEYWORDS AND PHRASES

questionnaire	interval scale
respondents	ratio scale
open-ended questions	validity
closed questions	reliability
scaling	leniency
nominal scale	central tendency
ordinal scale	halo effect

REVIEW QUESTIONS

1. What kinds of information is the systems analyst seeking through the use of questionnaires?
2. List four situations that make the use of questionnaires appropriate.
3. What are the two basic question types used on questionnaires?
4. List two reasons why a systems analyst would use a closed question on a questionnaire.
5. List two reasons why a systems analyst would use an open-ended question on a questionnaire.
6. What are the seven guidelines for choosing language for the questionnaire?
7. Define what is meant by *scaling*.
8. What are two kinds of information that can be gained by the use of scales on questionnaires?
9. What are nominal scales used for?
10. What is the difference between nominal and ordinal scales?
11. Give an example of an interval scale.
12. When should the analyst use interval scales?
13. Describe the difference between interval and ratio scales.
14. Define reliability as it refers to the construction of scales.
15. Define validity as it refers to the construction of scales.
16. List three problems that can occur because of careless construction of scales.

"You've probably noticed by now that not everyone enjoys filling out questionnaires at MRE. We seem to get more questionnaires than most organizations. But I think it's because many of the employees, especially those from the old Training Unit, value the contributions of questionnaire data in our work with clients. When you examine the questionnaire that Snowden distributed, you'll probably want not only to look at the results, but also to critique it from a methods standpoint. I always feel strongly that we can improve our internal performance so that eventually we can better serve our clients. The next time we construct a questionnaire we want to be able to improve three things: the reliability and validity of the data, and the response rate that we get."

HYPERCASE QUESTIONS

1. What evidence of questionnaires have you found at MRE? Be specific about what you have found and where.
2. Critique the questionnaire that Snowden circulated. What can be done to it to improve its reliability, validity, and response rate? Provide three practical suggestions.
3. Write a short questionnaire to follow up on some aspects of the merger between Management Systems and the Training Unit at MRE that are still puzzling you. Be sure to observe all of the guidelines for good questionnaire design.

17. What are four actions that can be taken to ensure that the questionnaire format is conducive to a good response rate?
18. Which questions should be placed first on the questionnaire?
19. Why should questions on similar topics be clustered together?
20. What is an appropriate placement of controversial questions?
21. List four methods for administering the questionnaire.

PROBLEMS

1. Cab Wheeler is a newly hired systems analyst with your group. Cab has always felt that questionnaires are a waste. Now that you will be doing a systems project for MegaTrucks, Inc., a national trucking firm with branches and employees in 130 cities, you want to use a questionnaire to elicit some opinions about the current and proposed systems.
   a. Based on what you know about Cab and MegaTrucks, give three persuasive reasons why he should use a questionnaire for this study.
   b. Given your careful arguments, Cab has agreed to use a questionnaire but strongly urges that all questions be open-ended so as not to constrain the respondents. In a paragraph, persuade Cab that closed questions are useful as well. Be sure to point out tradeoffs involved with each question type.

2. "Everytime we get a consultant in here, they pass out some goofy questionnaire that has no meaning to us at all. Why don't they bother to personalize it, at least a little?" You are discussing the possibility of beginning a systems project with Pohattan Power Company (PPC) of Far Meltway, N.J.

   a. What steps will you follow to personalize a standardized questionnaire?

   b. What are the advantages of adapting a questionnaire to a particular organization? What are the disadvantages?

3. A sample question from the draft of the Pohattan Power Company questionnaire reads:

   I have been with the company:
   20-upwards years
   10-15 years upwards
   5-10 years upwards
   less than a year
   Check one that most applies

   a. What kind of a scale is the question's author using?

   b. What errors have been made in the construction of the question and possible responses?

   c. Rewrite the question to achieve clearer results.

   d. Where should the question you've written appear on the questionnaire?

4. Also included on the PPC questionnaire is the question: When a residential customer calls, I always use my computer terminal to get an answer.

Sometimes	Never	Always	Usually
1	2	3	4

   a. What type of scale is this intended to be?

   b. Rewrite the question and possible responses to achieve better results.

5. Another question used on the PPC draft questionnaire reads: My manual log of time spent on the computer matches the computer log all of the time:

Time				Time
0%	5%	25%	50%	100%

   a. What kind of scale does the question's author intend to use?

   b. Is the intended scale appropriate for the question? Why or why not?

   c. Rewrite the question to achieve clearer results.

6. Figure 6.EX1 is a questionnaire designed by an employee of Green Toe Textiles, which specializes in manufacturing men's socks. Di Wooly wrote the questionnaire because, as office manager at headquarters in Juniper, Tennessee, she is concerned with the proposed acquisition of a new computer system.

   a. Provide a one-sentence critique for each question given.

   b. In a paragraph, critique the layout and style in terms of white space used, room for responses, ease of responding, and so on.

FIGURE 6.EX1
Questionnaire developed by
Di Wooly.

Hi! All Employees

What's new? According to the grapevine, hear we're in for
a new computer. Here's some questions for you to think
about.
a. How long have you used the old computer?_____
b. How often does it go down?_____
c. Who repairs it for you? _____
d. When was the last time you suggested a new improvement
to the computer system and it was put into use?   What was
it? _____
e. When was the last time you suggested a new improvement to
the computer system and nobody used it? What was it? _____
f.   Do you use a CRT or printer or both?_____
g. How fast do you type? _____
h. How many people use the computer at your branch? Is there anyone not using the
computer now who would like to? _____

7. Based on what you surmise Ms. Wooly is trying to get at through the questionnaire, rewrite and reorder the questions (use both open-ended and closed questions) so that they follow good practice and result in useful information for the systems analysts.

   a. Indicate next to each question that you write whether it is open-ended or closed, and write a sentence indicating why you have written the quesiton this way.

8. Frieda Forall, head of nursing, is insistent that employees at her for-profit hospital should complete questionnaires about the proposed computer system at home, on their own time, not the hospital's.

   a. Write a paragraph to convince Frieda that administering the questionnaire in a way other than self-administration off the premises would garner better results and be a worthwhile use of employees' time.

   b. Nurse Forall is wavering in her position on self-administration but as yet remains unconvinced. List some incentives that can motivate managers to administer a questionnaire properly the first time.

GROUP PROJECTS

1. Using the interview data you gained from the group exercise on Maverick Transport in Chapter 5, meet with your group to brainstorm the design of a questionnaire for the hundreds of truck drivers which Maverick Transport employs. Recall Maverick is interested in implementing a satellite system for tracking freight and drivers. There are other systems that may impact the drivers as well. As your group constructs the questionnaire, consider the drivers' likely level of education and any time constraints the drivers are under for completing such a form.

2. Using the interview data you gained from the group exercise on Maverick Transport in Chapter 5, your group should meet to design a questionnaire for surveying the company's 20 programmers (15 of

whom have been hired in the past year) about their skills, ideas for new or enhanced systems, and so on. As your group constructs the programmer questionnaire, consider what you have learned about users in the other interviews, as well as what vision the director of information technology holds for the company.

SELECTED BIBLIOGRAPHY

Babbie, E. R. *Survey Research Methods*. Belmont, CA: Wadsworth Publishing Company, Inc., 1973.

Dillman, D. A. *Mail and Telephone Surveys*. New York: John Wiley & Sons, 1978.

Emory, C. W. *Business Research Methods*, 3rd ed. Homewood, IL: Richard D. Irwin, Inc., 1985.

THE QUEST CONTINUES...

Anna sits at her desk, reviewing the interview summaries and the memos that were gathered during the summer. There are several stacks of papers neatly filed in expansion folders.

"We have so much information," she remarks to Chip. "Yet I sense that we are only working with the tip of the iceberg. I don't have a solid feeling for the difficulties of faculty members and research staff. Are they experiencing some of the problems that came out in the memos and interviews? Are there additional problems that we haven't heard about?"

Chip looks up from his work of trying to extract key points for defining the problems. "I wonder if we should do more interviews, or perhaps gather more documents," he says.

"That would be a good idea, but how many interviews should we conduct and who should we interview?" Anna replies. "Suppose we interview several staff members and base the new system on the results. We could interview the wrong people and design a system to satisfy only their needs, missing key problems that the majority of faculty and staff need solved."

"I see what you mean," Chip answers. "Perhaps we should design a questionnaire and survey the faculty and research staff. Most of them would return the survey if it was easy to complete, especially people with major concerns."

"Great idea!" Anna says. "How should we decide which questions to include on the survey?"

"Let's speak with some key people and base the survey on the results. A good starting point would be Hy Perteks, since he is always talking with the faculty and staff. I'll give him a call and arrange a meeting," Chip says.

Chip arranged the meeting for the following morning, in a conference room adjacent to the Information Center.

"Thanks for meeting with us on such short notice," Chip opens. "We're thinking about surveying the faculty and research staff to obtain additional information that will help us define the system concerns."

"I think it's a tremendous idea," Hy replies. "I would also like some information that would give me a clue as to what type of software should be available in the Information Center and the type of training we should provide."

"What type of software information do you think we should obtain?" asks Anna.

"Certainly the major package types used," Hy answers. "Word-processing software is extremely popular. We should find out which package each user likes and, equally important, which *version* of the package. I know that some are using WordPerfect while others are using Wordstar, Word, and PFS Write. I have a few folks using PC Write and one person using Friendly Writer, since it's so simple to use. Database software also varies. Many are using dBASE, while others are involved with Paradox, R Base, or PC File. Same for spreadsheets, with Lotus being the most popular."

"Another consideration would be what type of specialized software is being used by groups of faculty members," muses Hy. "Many of the math department faculty are using Exp, a math word processor. Others are using various software packages for a number of courses. For instance, the information science people are using Excelerator. I've also heard that we're getting some biology and astronomy software. And the Art Department is moving strongly into the Mac arena for full-color production."

"Other than software packages and versions, what types of information should we capture?" asks Chip.

"I would like to know what level of expertise each person has," responds Hy. "No doubt, some are beginners while others have a good knowledge but have not mastered all of the features of a particular package. Some are experts, without question. They know the software inside and out. I'm interested in the beginners and intermediate users, since we should be providing different training for them. And I would really like to know who the experts are. Then I could contact them and ask if they would be willing to conduct a training session or serve as a resource if someone has a problem with an advanced feature of the software."

"Is there anything else you feel we should find out on the survey?" asks Chip.

"The only other thing that I worry about are problems that result in a faculty or staff member not using the software." Hy replies.

"What do you mean?" asks Chip.

"Well, suppose a person has the software but it is installed incorrectly, or displays a message, such as "Too many files open," replies Hy. "I've had some inquiries about this matter recently. One person said that they couldn't use dBASE except for simple tasks since they always got the too-many-files message. It turned out that the system was not configured for the maximum files and buffers in a standard file called the CONFIG.SYS. It was a simple matter to fix the problem, but it had been going on for years! Other such problems must exist, and I'd like to know what they are. This will make our whole staff more productive and comfortable with using microcomputers."

"Do you know of a representative faculty or staff member that we should interview?" Anna inquires.

"Yes, there's a faculty member in math, Rhoda Booke, who has consistently shown interest in hardware and software issues. I've helped her a number of times, and she's always friendly and grateful."

"Thanks once again for all of your help," says Chip. "We'll get back to you later with the results of the survey."

Anna arranges a meeting with Rhoda and explains the nature of the project and why she was selected as a faculty representative. The meeting was held in a small conference room in the math department.

"Thanks for meeting with us," says Anna after introductions had been made. "We'd like to have the faculty perspective on problems encountered with microcomputers and the associated software. Our goal is to provide faculty with the best possible resources with the least amount of problems."

"I'm really glad to be a part of the project," exclaims Rhoda. "I've been using software for about two years, and what a learning experience it has been! Thank goodness that Hy is available as a resource person. I've taken hours of his time, and it's been well worth the effort, I feel much more productive, and the students are using software that helps them grasp the material more thoroughly than simply doing math exercises and reading the text."

"That's good news. But are there some difficulties that you've been experiencing?" asks Chip.

"Well, becoming familiar with the software is a major hurdle. I spent a good portion of last summer, when I wasn't working on my book, learning how to use some of the classroom software for both algebra and calculus. The stuff's great, but I got stuck several times and had to call for help. It's necessary to understand the software in order to prepare lesson plans and explain to the students how to use it."

"How about problems with installing the software or hardware?" Anna asks.

"Oh, yes!" exclaims Rhoda. "I tried to install the software, and it went smoothly until the part where the screen asked what type of monitor was being used, monochrome text or graphics, and what type of resolution were the graphics, either CGA, MCGA, EGA, or VGA. I didn't even know what those letters meant," laughs Rhoda.

"Then there were setup problems," Rhoda continues. "I needed to change the CONFIG.SYS file to accommodate the number of files and buffers and had to modify the AUTOEXEC.BAT file to install the mouse driver when the computer first booted up. What a leaning experience that was. Some of the computers in the student lab gave us 'Not enough memory' error messages, and we learned that they had been installed with minimum main memory. I've heard that the physics faculty had the same problem.

"Are there any other concerns you have or feel that we should include on our survey to the faculty and research staff?" Chip asks.

"It would be useful to know who is using the same software in difference departments and what software is supplied by which vendor. Perhaps if we have many packages from one vendor, we could get a larger discount for software. The department software budget is already overwhelmed with requests," Rhoda says.

"Thanks for all of your help," Anna says. "If you think of any additional questions we should include on the survey, please do not hesitate to call us."

Back in their office, the analysts start compiling a list of the issues to be contained on the survey.

"We certainly need to ask about the software in use and about training needs," remarks Anna. "We should also address the problems that are occurring."

"Agreed," replies Chip. "I feel that we should include questions on software packages, vendors, versions, level of expertise, and training concerns. What I'm not so sure about is how to obtain information on problems the faculty and staff are encountering. How should we approach these issues?"

"Well," replies Anna, "we should focus on matters with which they are familiar. We might ask questions about the type of problems that are occurring but certainly not technical ones that they wouldn't find to be of interest. For example, we should not ask 'How much main memory is available on your machine?' because they may not know or care. They probably would not be familiar with the CONFIG.SYS or AUTOEXEC.BAT files either. And the survey should not ask any questions that we could easily look up answers to, such as 'Who is the vendor for the software?'"

"I see," replies Chip. "Let's divide the questions into categories. Some would be closed questions and some would be open-ended. Then there's the matter of which structure to use. . . ."

Exercises

E-1.   Based on the dialogue among Chip, Anna, Hy, and Rhoda, make a detailed list of concerns raised about hardware and software for faculty microcomputing.

E-2.   From the list of concerns, select the issues that would best be phrased as closed questions.

E-3.   From the list of concerns, select the issues that would best be phrased as open-ended questions.

E-4.   Based on problems 2 and 3, design a questionnaire to be sent to the faculty and research staff.

E-5.   Pilot your questionnaire by having other students in class fill it out. Based on their feedback and your capability to analyze the data you receive, revise your questionnaire.

OBSERVING DECISION-MAKER BEHAVIOR AND OFFICE ENVIRONMENT

KINDS OF INFORMATION SOUGHT

Observing the decision maker and the decision maker's physical environment are important information-gathering techniques for the systems analyst. Through observing activities of decision makers, the analyst seeks to gain insight about what is actually done, not just what is documented or explained. Additionally, through observation of the decision maker, the analyst attempts to see firsthand the relationships that exist between decision makers and other organizational members.

By observing the office environment, the systems analyst seeks the symbolic meaning of the work context for decision makers. The analyst examines physical elements of the decision maker's workspace for their influence on decision-making behavior. Further, through observation of the physical elements over which the decision maker has control (clothing, desk position, and so on), the analyst works to understand what messages the decision maker is sending. Finally, through observation, the analyst works to comprehend the influence of the decision maker on others in the organization. All of these kinds of information are summarized in Figure 7.1.

OBSERVING A DECISION MAKER'S BEHAVIOR

Systems analysts use observation for many reasons. One reason is to gain information about decision makers and their environments that is unavailable through any other method. Observing also helps to confirm or negate and reverse what has been found through interviewing, questionnaires, and other methods.

Observation must be structured and systematic if the findings are to be interpretable. Thus, it is of utmost importance that the systems analyst know *what* is being observed. Great care and thought must go into what and who will be observed, as well as when, where, why, and how. It is not enough simply to be aware of the need for observation.

FIGURE 7.1
Kinds of information sought
when observing decision-
maker behavior and office
environment.

Many observational schemes are available, each with its own objectives. Analysts are encouraged to draw from research as well as from their own experience to devise observational schemes that are workable.

Observing a Typical Manager's Decision-Making Activities

Managers' workdays have been described as a series of interruptions punctuated by short bursts of work. In other words, pinning down what a manager "does" is a slippery proposition even under the best of circumstances. In order for the systems analyst to grasp adequately how managers characterize their work, interviews and questionnaires are used, as discussed in Chapters 5 and 6. However, observation allows the analyst to see firsthand how managers gather, process, share, and use information to get work done.

The following steps aid in observing a manager's typical decision-making activities:

1. Decide what is to be observed (activities).
2. Decide at what level of concreteness activities are to be observed (that is, will the analyst observe that "The manager freely shared information with subordinates" or make a much more concrete observation such as "Manager sends a copy of the same memo to three subordinates"?). Determining the level of concreteness of observation will also dictate the amount of inference in each observation and subsequently the amount of interpretation needed once observations are made.
3. Create categories that adequately capture key activities.
4. Prepare appropriate scales, checklists, or other materials for observation.
5. Decide when to observe.

Deciding when to observe is covered in the next section.

Time and Event Sampling

Each approach to when to observe has its own advantages and tradeoffs. Time sampling allows the analyst to set up specific intervals at which to observe managers' activities. For example, time sampling might specify observing a decision maker during five randomly chosen ten-minute intervals throughout seven eight-hour days. The advantages of time sampling include cutting down on the bias that might otherwise enter into

	Time Sampling	Event Sampling
Advantages	• Cuts down on bias with randomization of observations • Allows a representative view of frequent activities	• Allows observation of behavior as it unfolds • Allows observation of an event designated as important
Disadvantages	• Gathers data in a fragmented fashion that doesn't allow time for a decision to unfold • Misses infrequent but important decisions	• Takes a great deal of analyst's time • Misses a representative sample of frequent decisions

FIGURE 7.2
Advantages and
disadvantages of time
versus event sampling.

observations made "just anytime." Time sampling also allows for a representative view of activities that occur fairly frequently.

The drawbacks of time sampling include gathering observational data in a piecemeal fashion that may not allow sufficient time for an event such as a decision to unfold in its entirety. A second problem with using time sampling to gather observational data is that rare or infrequent but important events (for example, a strategic decision on a five-year investment in a new management information system) may not be represented in the time that is sampled. Yet the decision is important and will have an impact.

Event sampling addresses both of these concerns by purposefully sampling entire events such as "a board meeting" or "a user training session," rather than sampling time periods randomly. Event sampling provides for observation of an integral behavior in its natural context. A drawback of event sampling is that it may not be possible to achieve a representative sample of frequent occurrences.

In light of the pros and cons of both approaches, analysts are encouraged to combine time and event sampling when deciding what, when, why, and how to observe decision-maker activities. A comparison and contrast of time versus event sampling is given in Figure 7.2.

As discussed in Chapter 2, decision making occurs on the operational, managerial, and strategic levels of the organization. The preceding discussion assumed that decision makers at all levels of the organization will interact with the information system and hence should be observed.

Observing a Decision-Maker's Body Language

The systems analyst subconsciously observes body language during the interviews and other interactions. This discussion is intended to bring that awareness to the conscious level, where it can be recognized and used by the analyst. Understanding body language enables the analyst to better understand the information requirements of the decision maker by adding dimension to what is being said. Nevertheless, although it is important to observe decision makers' body language, precise interpretation of it, movement for movement, is immensely difficult and also varies across cultures.

ADJECTIVE PAIRS AND CATEGORIES. Adjective pairs have become a popular way to record behavior. An example of decision-making behavior described in adjective pairs is: decisive/indecisive, confident/not confident, assertive/unassertive, and so on, as depicted in Figure 7.3.

FIGURE 7.3
A sample adjective-pairs
sheet for observing a decision
maker.

Name of Observer _Kendall, K_

Decision Maker _D. Side_

Date Observed _10/24/95_

Observed From _8 a.m. to 8:30 a.m._

From each pair, circle the one adjective that best describes the
decision maker during the time you were observing.

1. (Assertive) / Unassertive

2. Calm / (Excited)

3. (Credible) / Not Believable

4. (Outgoing) / Inward-looking

5. (Talkative) / Silent

6. (Articulate) / Inarticulate

7. Authoritative / (Uninformed)

8. (Self-started) / Unmotivated

9. (Goal-oriented) / Unfocused

10. (Problem Solver) / Problem Maker

Category systems for recording decision-making behavior were discussed briefly before. The analyst determines activity categories before observations are undertaken. An example of a concrete category is "Access database personally." Examples of a category system that asks for more analyst inference in recording observation are: "Uses internal sources of data," or "Shows initiative in accessing data." Forms listing categories are then copied in sufficient number and taken along to be completed as the analyst observes. A sample form illustrating the category system is shown in Figure 7.4.

THE ANALYST'S PLAYSCRIPT. Systems analysts can also use a technique called playscripting to record observed behavior. With this technique, the "actor" is the decision maker who is observed "acting" or making decisions. In setting up a playscript, the actor is listed in the left-hand column and all of his or her actions are listed in the right-hand column, as shown in Figure 7.5. All activities are recorded with action verbs so that a decision maker would be described as "talking," "sampling," "corresponding," and "deciding."

Playscript is an organized and systematic approach that demands that the analyst be able to understand and articulate the *action* taken by each decision maker observed. This approach eventually assists the systems analyst in determining information required for major and/or frequent decisions made by the people observed. For instance, from the quality assurance manager example in the playscript, it becomes clear that even though this decision maker is on the middle management level, he or she still requires a fair amount of external information to perform required activities of this specific job.

FIGURE 7.4
A sample observation form
employing categories of
decision-maker behavior.

Name of Observer __Kim McCabe__
Decision Maker __A.K.Stratton__
Date Observed ___6 / 10 / 95___
Observed From __8:30__ to __12:00__
(Start time to end time)

Each time the decision maker is observed engaging anew in the behavior listed, put 1 mark in the box beside the appropriate category. Mark only when you actually observe the decision maker in action. Fill out the first column ONLY when you are in the presence of the decision maker you are observing.

Behavior	Number of Times Behavior Occurs	Total	Percentage of Total
Instructs Subordinates	///	3	5
Instructs Peers	//	2	3
Instructs Superiors	/	1	2
Questions Subordinates	//	2	4
Questions Peers	///	3	5
Questions Superiors	/	1	2
Reprimands Subordinates		0	0
Reprimands Peers		0	0
Reprimands Superiors		0	0
Opens Mail	/////	5	9
Answers Phone	///// //	7	13
Makes Phone Call	///// /////	10	18
Reads External Information	///// ///// ///	13	23
Reads Internal Information	///	3	5
Processes Own Information	//	2	4
Asks Others to Process Information	///	4	7
		56	100%

OBSERVING THE PHYSICAL ENVIRONMENT

Observing decision makers' activities is just one way to assess their information requirements. Observing the physical environment in which decision makers work also reveals much about their information requirements. Most often, this means systematically examining the offices of decision makers, since offices constitute their primary workplace. Decision makers influence and are in turn influenced by their physical environments.

Structured Observation of the Environment

Film critics sometimes use a structured form of criticism called *mise-en-scène* analysis to systematically assess what is in a single shot of the film—looking at editing, camera angle, set decor, and the actors and their costumes to find out how they are shaping the meaning of the film as intended by the director. Sometimes the film's *mise-en-scène* will contradict what is said in dialogue. For information requirements analysis, the systems analyst

| **Playscript Analysis** | Company: | Solid Steel Shelving | Scenario: | Quality Assurance |
| | Analyst: | L. Bracket | Date: | 9/3/95 |

Decision Maker (Actor)	**Information-Related Activity (Script)**
Quality Assurance Manager	Asks shop floor supervisor for the day's production report
Shop Floor Supervisor	Prints out daily computerized production report
	Discusses recurring problems in production runs with quality assurance (QA) manager
Quality Assurance Manager	Reads production report
	Compares current report with other reports from the same week
	Inputs data from daily production run into QA model on micro
	Observes on-screen results of QA model
	Calls steel suppliers to discuss deviations from quality standards
Shop Floor Supervisor	Attends meeting on new quality specifications with quality assurance manager and vice president of production
Quality Assurance Manager	Drafts letter to inform suppliers on new quality specifications agreed upon in meeting
	Sends draft to vice president via E-mail
Vice President of Production	Reads drafted letter
	Returns corrections and comments via E-mail
Quality Assurance Manager	Reads corrected letter on E-mail
	Rewrites letter to reflect changes

can take on a role similar to that of the film critic. It often is possible to observe particulars about the surroundings that will confirm or negate the organizational narrative (or dialogue) that is found through interviews or questionnaires.

The method for *STRuctured OBservation of the Environment* is referred to as STROBE. It is systematic because (1) it provides a standard methodology and standard classification for analysis of organizational elements that influence decision making; (2) it allows other systems analysts to apply the same analytic framework to the same organization; and (3) it limits analysis to the organization as it exists during the current stage in its life cycle.

A correspondence exists between the elements of analysis for film criticism and those used in the STROBE assessment of the decision makers' information requirements. This correspondence makes it possible for

Filmic Elements	Organizational Elements
Set location	Office location
People positioned within a frame	Decision maker's placement in an office (i.e., desk placement)
Stationary objects	File cabinets, bookshelves, and equipment for storing information
Props (movable objects)	Calculators, VDT's, and other items used for processing information
External objects (brought in from other scenes)	Trade journals, newspapers, and items used for external information
Lighting and color	Office lighting and color
Costumes	Clothing worn by decision makers

the systems analyst to remember easily the analogy as pictured in Figure 7.6. A more detailed discussion of each of these elements follows.

STROBE Elements. There are seven concrete elements that are easily observable by the systems analyst. These elements can reveal much about the way a decision maker gathers, processes, stores, and shares information, as well as about the decision maker's credibility in the workplace. The seven observable elements are described in the following paragraphs.

Office location. One of the first elements a systems analyst should observe is the location of a particular decision maker's office with respect to other offices. Accessible offices tend to increase interaction frequency and informal messages, while inaccessible offices tend to decrease the interaction frequency and increase task-oriented messages. Offices distributed along the perimeter of the building usually result in a report or memo being held up in one of the offices, while office clusters encourage information sharing. It is also likely that the people whose offices are separated from others may tend to view the organization differently and so drift further apart from other organization members in their objectives.

Placement of the decision maker's desk. Placement of a desk in the office can provide clues to the exercise of power by the decision maker. Executives who enclose a visitor in a tight space with their back to the wall, while allowing themselves a lot of room, put themselves into the strongest possible power position. An executive who positions his or her desk facing the wall with a chair at the side for a visitor is probably encouraging participation and equal exchanges. The systems analyst should notice the arrangement of the office furniture and in particular the placement of the desk.

Stationary office equipment. File cabinets, bookshelves, and other large equipment for storing items are all included in the category of

FIGURE 7.7
Observe a decision maker's
office for clues of his or her
personal storage, processing,
and sharing of information.

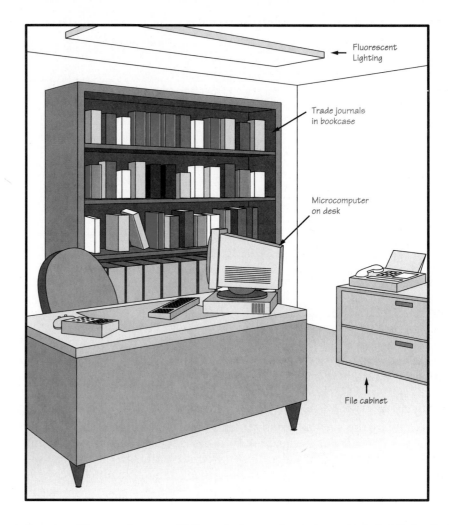

stationary office equipment. If there is no such equipment, it is likely that the decision maker stores very few items of information personally. If there is an abundance of equipment, it is presumed that the decision maker stores and values much information.

Props. Props (an abbreviation of the stage/film term properties) refers to all of the small equipment used to process information. This includes calculators, VDTs, pens, pencils, and rulers. The presence of calculators and VDTs suggests that a decision maker who possesses such equipment is more likely to use it personally than one who must leave the room to use it.

Trade journals and newspapers. A systems analyst needs to know what type of information is used by the decision maker. Observation of the type of publications stored in the office can reveal whether the decision maker is looking for external information (found in trade journals, newspaper clippings about other companies in the industry, and so on) or relies more on internal information (company reports, intra-office correspondence, policy handbooks).

Office lighting and color. Lighting and color play an important role in how a decision maker gathers information. An office lighted with warm,

Characteristics of Decision Makers	Corresponding Elements in the Physical Environment
Gathers information informally	Warm, incandescent lighting and colors
Seeks extraorganizational information	Trade journals present in office
Processes data personally	Calculators, VDTs present in office
Stores information personally	Equipment/files present in office
Exercises power in decision making	Desk placed for power
Exhibits credibility in decision making	Wears authoritative clothing
Shares information with others	Office easily accessible

FIGURE 7.8
A summary of decision-maker characteristics that correspond to observable elements in the physical environment.

incandescent lighting indicates a tendency toward more personal communication. An executive in a warmly lit office will gather more information informally, while another organizational member working in a brightly lit, brightly colored office may gather information through more formal memos and official reports. Figure 7.7 shows a decision maker's office equipment, props, trade journals, office lighting, and color.

Clothing worn by decision makers. Much has been written about the clothing worn by executives and others in authority. The systems analyst can gain an understanding of the credibility exhibited by managers in the organization by observing the clothing they wear on the job. The formal three-piece suit for a male or the skirted suit for a female represents the maximum authority according to some researchers who have studied perceptions of executive appearance. Casual dressing by leaders tends to open the door for more participative decision making but often results in some loss of credibility in the organization if the predominant culture values traditional, conservative clothing.

Through use of STROBE, the systems analyst can gain a better understanding of how managers gather, process, store, and use information. A summary of the characteristics exhibited by decision makers and the corresponding observable elements is shown in Figure 7.8. The following section examines options available to the systems analyst for recording and documenting observations.

APPLICATION ALTERNATIVES. Analysts may choose among many application strategies when using the STROBE approach. These strategies vary from very structured (such as taking photographs for later analysis) to unstructured. Four strategies are described in the following paragraphs.

Analysis of photographs. Photographing the environments of decision makers and then analyzing the photographs for elements of STROBE is most closely allied with the original use of *mise-en-scène* for film criticism. Interestingly, this application has parallels in much earlier management work. Since at the turn of the century Frank Gilbreth used film in his famous time-motion studies, analyzing frame-by-frame what motions were necessary to complete a task.

CONSULTING OPPORTUNITY 7.1

Don't Bank on Their Self-Image
or
Not Everything Is Reflected in a Mirror

"I don't want any power here," demurs Dr. Drew Charles, medical director of the regional blood center where your systems group has just begun a project. "I'm up to my neck in work just keeping the regional physicians informed so they follow good bloodbanking practices," he says, as he shields his eyes from the bright sunlight streaming into his office. He clicks off the monitor connected to his microcomputer and turns his attention to you and the interview.

Dr. Charles is dressed in a conservative, dark wool suit, and is wearing a red-striped silk necktie. He continues, "In fact, I don't make decisions. I'm here purely in a positive support role." He pulls out the organizational chart shown below to illustrate his point. "It is as clear as a fracture. The administrator is the expert on all administrative matters. I am the medical consultant only."

Dr. Charles' office is stacked high not only with medical journals such as *Transfusion*, but also with *BYTE* magazine and *Business Week*. Each is opened to a different page as if the doctor were in the process of devouring each new morsel of information. However, the overflow journals are not stored meticulously on metal bookshelves as expected. In sharp contrast to the gleaming, new equipment you saw being used in the donor rooms, the journals are piled a foot high on an old blood-donating bed that has been long retired from its intended use.

Next, you decide to interview the chief administrator, Craig Bunker, to whom Dr. Charles has alluded. Fifteen minutes after your scheduled appointment, Bunker's secretary, Dawn Upshaw, finally allows you to enter his office. Bunker, who has just finished a phone call, is dressed in a light-blue sport coat, checkered slacks, light-blue shirt, and a necktie. "How are you doing? I've just been checking around to see how everything's perking along," Bunker says by way of introduction. He is outgoing and very friendly.

As you glance around the room, you notice that there are no filing cabinets, nor is there a microcomputer such as Dr. Charles was using. There are lots of photos of Craig Bunker's family, but the only item resembling a book or magazine is the center's newsletter, *Bloodline*. As the interview begins in earnest, Bunker cheerfully launches into stories about the Pennsylvania Blood Center, where he held the position of assistant administrator six years ago.

Finally, you descend the stairs to the damp basement level of the Heath Lambert Mansion. The bloodmobiles have just returned, and processed blood has been shipped to area hospitals. You decide to talk with Sang Kim, a bloodmobile driver; Jenny McLaughlin, the distribution manager; and Roberta Martin, a lab technician who works the night shift.

Roberta begins, "I don't know what we'd do without the doctor." But in the same vein, Sang feeds the conversation by remarking, "Yeah, he helped us by thinking up a better driving schedule last week."

Jenny adds, "Dr. Charles is invaluable in setting the levels for each hospital, and if it wasn't for him, we wouldn't have word processing yet, let alone our new computer."

As one of the systems analysis team members assigned to the blood center project, use STROBE to help systematically interpret the observations you made about the offices of Dr. Charles and Craig Bunker. Consider any disparities between a decision maker's clothing, what a decision maker states, and what is said by others; office location and what is stated; and office equipment and policies stated. Additionally, suggest possible follow-up interviews and/or observations to help settle any unresolved questions.

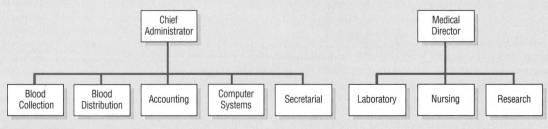

FIGURE 7.C1
Organization chart of the regional blood center.

Photographic applications of STROBE have some distinct advantages. One is that a document is made that can be referred to repeatedly. This can be extremely helpful when organizational visits must be limited due to time, distance, or expense.

A second advantage is that the photographer can focus specifically on pertinent elements of STROBE and thereby exclude extraneous elements. Additionally, using photography for STROBE allows a side-by-side comparison of organizations since the limitations of time and space are overcome by photography. A fourth advantage is that a photograph can supply detail that is easily overlooked during personal contact, when the systems analyst is not only observing, but is also conducting an interview or investigating hard data.

There are also drawbacks to using photography for implementing STROBE. First and foremost may be deciding what to photograph. Unlike the human eye, photographs are very limited as to what they can aim at and "take in."

The second drawback is that photography, although it may prove unobtrusive in the long term, is initially obtrusive. The systems analyst will face problems of decision makers posing, as well as intentionally or unintentionally changing their environments in attempting to make them somehow more acceptable to the analyst.

Checklist/Likert scale approach. A second application of STROBE is a less-structured technique than photography, a checklist/Likert scale approach. Researchers developed five-point Likert-type scales relating to seven decision-maker characteristics that were observable through physical elements in decision makers' organizational environments, as shown in Figure 7.9.

In the original study using this scale to assess sixteen blood administrators and medical directors from the United States and Canada, researchers found convergent and discriminant validity of the information gained through the STROBE scales and the information gained through interviewing and behavioral scales. The same Likert-type scales are recommended to systems analysts, who can use them as an application of STROBE in conjunction with more traditional methods.

Anecdotal list (with symbols). A third, and even less-structured way to implement STROBE is through the use of an anecdotal checklist with meaningful shorthand symbols. This approach to STROBE was useful in ascertaining the information requirements for four key decision makers in a midwestern blood center.

As can be seen in Figure 7.10, five shorthand symbols were used by the systems analysts to evaluate how observation of the elements of STROBE compared with the organizational narrative generated through interviews. The five symbols are:

1. A checkmark that means the narrative is confirmed.
2. A cross that means the narrative is reversed.
3. An oval or eye-shaped symbol that serves as a cue for the systems analyst to look further.
4. A square that means observation of the elements of STROBE modifies the narrative.
5. A circle that means the narrative is supplemented by what is observed.

FIGURE 7.9
Likert-type scales for use in
observing the physical environment of decision makers
with STROBE.

STROBE Scales for Observing the Physical Environment

1. Office lighting, walls, paintings and graphics are warm-toned, creating an informal arena for information exchange.

   Fluorescent lights, cool-colored walls, no decorations   *Incandescent lights, warm-colored wall, warm graphics*

   1   2   3   4   5

2. Office contains various forms of information brought in from outside the organization, including trade journals, association newsletters, and business newspapers.

   No outside sources of information   *Four or more journals or newspapers*

   1   2   3   4   5

3. Aids for processing of information are present in the office and are easily accessible.

   No calculators or CRTs visible   *Calculator or CRT accessible without leaving a chair*

   1   2   3   4   5

4. Office houses many pieces of equipment used for storing information.

   No storage cabinets in office   *Four or more file cabinets or shelves*

   1   2   3   4   5

5. Desk is placed to maximize territory for administrator and limit visitor space.

   Desk placed against wall   *Desk used as barrier with little space for visitor*

   1   2   3   4   5

6. Wears authoritative business suits rather than casual or sporty clothing.

   Wears casual or sporty clothing   *Wears conservative business suits*

   1   2   3   4   5

7. Administrator's office is easily accessible.

   Office located on separate floor from subordinates   *Office within 50 feet of subordinates*

   1   2   3   4   5

When STROBE is implemented in this manner, the first step is to determine key organizational themes growing out of interviews. Next the elements of STROBE are systematically observed, and then a matrix is constructed that lists major ideas from the organizational narrative about information gathering, processing, storing, and sharing on one axis and elements of STROBE on the other. When narrative and observations are compared, one of the five appropriate symbols is then used to characterize the relationship between the narrative and the relevant element observed. The analyst thus creates a table that first documents and then aids in analysis of observations.

Observation/narrative comparison. The fourth way to implement STROBE is also the least-structured method. Although filmgoers rarely attend a film with a *mise-en-scène* checklist in hand, few of its elements fail to make at least a subconscious impact on them. As long as the systems ana-

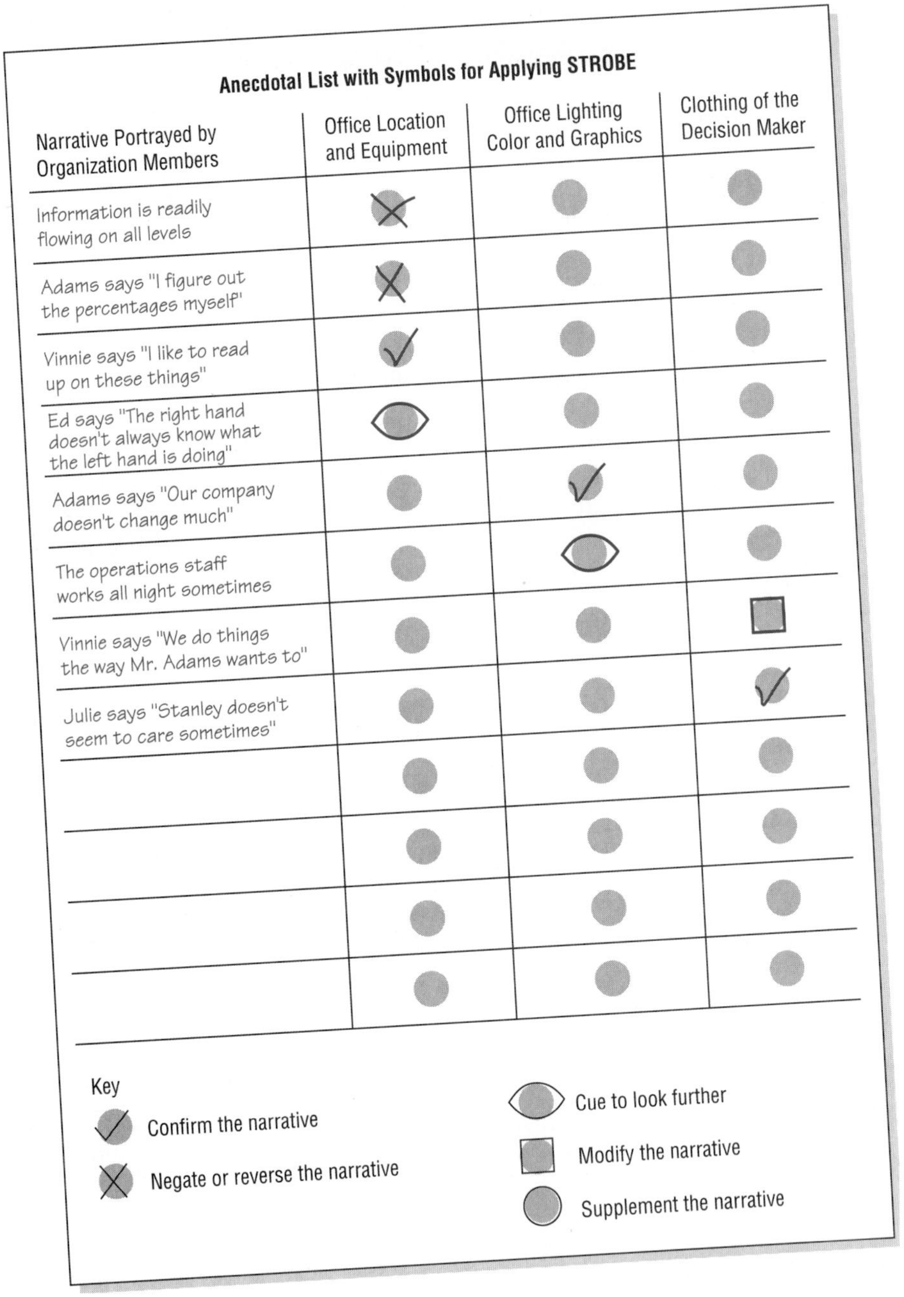

Anecdotal List with Symbols for Applying STROBE

Narrative Portrayed by Organization Members	Office Location and Equipment	Office Lighting Color and Graphics	Clothing of the Decision Maker
Information is readily flowing on all levels	Negate (✕)	Supplement (●)	Supplement (●)
Adams says "I figure out the percentages myself"	Negate (✕)	Supplement (●)	Supplement (●)
Vinnie says "I like to read up on these things"	Confirm (✓)	Supplement (●)	Supplement (●)
Ed says "The right hand doesn't always know what the left hand is doing"	Cue to look further (👁)	Supplement (●)	Supplement (●)
Adams says "Our company doesn't change much"	Supplement (●)	Confirm (✓)	Supplement (●)
The operations staff works all night sometimes	Supplement (●)	Cue to look further (👁)	Supplement (●)
Vinnie says "We do things the way Mr. Adams wants to"	Supplement (●)	Supplement (●)	Modify (■)
Julie says "Stanley doesn't seem to care sometimes"	Supplement (●)	Supplement (●)	Confirm (✓)
	Supplement (●)	Supplement (●)	Supplement (●)
	Supplement (●)	Supplement (●)	Supplement (●)
	Supplement (●)	Supplement (●)	Supplement (●)
	Supplement (●)	Supplement (●)	Supplement (●)

Key

✓ Confirm the narrative

✕ Negate or reverse the narrative

👁 Cue to look further

■ Modify the narrative

● Supplement the narrative

FIGURE 7.10
An anecdotal list with symbols for use in applying STROBE.

lyst is *aware* of the elements of *mise-en-scène* and these are consciously observed, valuable insights can be gained, even without the aid of a checklist. Examining the organization from a heightened awareness of the elements of STROBE affords a base for making structured observations. These observations can be used later in assessing information requirements.

SUMMARY

Analysts use observation as an information-gathering technique. Through observation, they earn insight as to what is actually done; see firsthand the relationships among decision makers in the organization; understand the influence of the physical setting on the decision maker; interpret the

"We're proud of our building here in Tennessee. In fact, we used the architectural firm of I. M. Paid to carry the same theme, blending into the local landscape while still reaching out to our clients, throughout all of the branches. We get lots of people coming through just to admire the building, once they catch on to where it is exactly. In fact, by Tennessee standards, we get so many sightseers that it might as well be the pyramids! Well, you can see for yourself as you go through. The East Atrium is my favorite place. Plenty of light, lots of louvered blinds to filter it. But it has always fascinated me that the building and its furnishings might tell quite a different story than its occupants.

"Sometimes employees complain that the offices all look the same. But the public rooms are spectacular. Even the lunch room is inviting. Most people can't say that about their cafeterias at work. You'll notice that everyone personalizes their office, anyway. So even if the offices were of the "cookie cutter" kind, their occupants' personalities seem to take over as soon as they have been here awhile. What have you seen? Was there anything that surprised you so far?"

HYPERCASE QUESTIONS

1. Use STROBE to compare and contrast Snowden Evans' and Ketcham's offices. What sort of conclusion about each person's use of information technology can you draw from your observations?

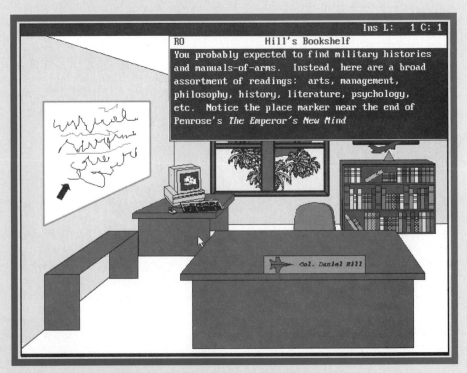

FIGURE 7.HC1
There are hidden clues in HyperCase. Use STROBE.

How compatible do Evans and Ketcham seem in terms of the systems they use? What other clues to their storage, use, and sharing of information can you draw based on your observations of their offices?

2. Carefully examine Kathy Blandford's office. Use STROBE to confirm, reverse, or negate what you have learned during your interview with her. List anything you found out about Ms. Blandford from observing her office that you did not know from the interview.

3. Carefully examine the contents of the MRE reception area using STROBE. What inferences can you make about the organization? List them. What interview questions would you like to ask, based on your observations of the reception area? Make a list of people you would like to interview and the questions you would ask each of them.

4. Describe in a paragraph the process you would go through in applying STROBE to observing an MRE office setting. List all elements in the MRE offices that seem important to understanding the users' decision-making behavior.

messages sent by the decision maker through clothing and office arrangement; and comprehend the influence of the decision maker on others.

Using time or event sampling, the analyst observes typical decision-maker activities and body language. There are numerous systems, for recording such observations, including category systems, checklists, scales, field notes, and playscripts.

In addition to observing a decision maker's behavior, the systems analyst should observe the decision maker's surroundings. A method for *STRuctured OBservation of the Environment* is called STROBE. A systems analyst uses STROBE in the same way that a film critic uses a method called *mise-en-scène* analysis to analyze a shot in a film.

Several concrete elements in the decision maker's environment can be observed and interpreted. These elements include (1) office location; (2) placement of the decision maker's desk; (3) stationary office equipment; (4) props, such as calculators and VDTs; (5) trade journals and newspapers; (6) office lighting and color; and (7) clothing worn by the decision maker. STROBE can be used to gain a better understanding of how decision makers actually gather, process, store, and share information.

There are a number of alternatives for applying STROBE in an organization. These include analysis of photographs, using a checklist based on Likert scales, adopting an anecdotal list with symbols, and simply writing up an observation/narrative comparison. Each method has certain advantages as well as drawbacks that the analyst needs to weigh when choosing one alternative over the other.

KEYWORDS AND PHRASES

systematic observation   STROBE
time sampling   office location

event sampling

decision maker's body language

adjective pairs

category systems

analyst's playscript

placement of decision maker's desk

stationary office equipment

props

trade journals and newspapers

clothing worn by decision makers

office lighting and color

REVIEW QUESTIONS

1. List three reasons why observation is useful to the systems analyst in the organization.

2. Why is it important that observation of decision makers be structured and systematic?

3. List five steps to help the analyst observe the decision maker's typical activities.

4. What are the advantages of using time sampling of observations?

5. What are the disadvantages of using event sampling of observations?

6. Compare the use of adjective pairs versus the analyst's playscript.

7. What three attributes make STROBE a systematic approach to observing the decision maker's physical environment?

8. List the seven concrete elements of the decision maker's physical environment that can be observed by the systems analyst using STROBE.

9. What are four different application strategies for using STROBE?

PROBLEMS

1. "I think I'll be able to remember most everything he does," says Ceci Awll. Ceci is about to interview Biff Welldon, vice president of strategic planning of OK Corral, a steak restaurant chain with 130 stores. "I mean, I've got a good memory. I think it's much more important to listen to what he says than to observe what he does anyway." As one of your systems analysis team members, Ceci has been talking with you about the desirability of writing down her observations of Biff's office and activities during the interview.

   a. In a paragraph, persuade Ceci that listening is not enough in interviews and that observing and recording those observations is also important.

   b. Ceci seems to have accepted your idea that observation is important but still doesn't know *what* to observe. Make a list of items and behaviors to observe, and in a sentence beside each behavior, indicate what information Ceci should hope to gain through observation of it.

   c. Ceci is uncomfortable writing down observations during her interviews. In a paragraph, suggest two methods for recording observations that do not require that they be used as the observation occurs. Now recommend *one* of the methods, and in a sentence or two, justify why you feel it would be a good method for Ceci in particular to try.

2. "We're a progressive company—always looking to be ahead of the power curve. We'll give anything a whirl if it'll put us ahead of the competition, and that includes every one of us to a man," says I. B. Daring, an executive with Michigan Manufacturing (2M). You are interviewing Daring as a preliminary step in a systems project in which his subordinates have expressed interest. As you listen to I. B., you look around his office to see that most of the information he has stored on shelves can be classified as internal procedures manuals. Additionally, you notice a PC on a back table of I. B.'s office. The monitor's screen is covered with dust, and the manuals stacked beside the PC are still encased in their original shrink wrap. You look up behind I. B.'s massive mahogany desk to see on the wall five framed oil portraits of 2M's founders, all clustered around a gold plaque bearing their corporate slogan, "Make sure you're right, then go ahead."

   a. What is the organizational narrative or storyline as portrayed by I. B. Daring? Rephrase it in your own words.

   b. List the elements of STROBE that you have observed during your interview with I. B.

   c. Next to each element of STROBE that you have observed, write a sentence on how you would interpret it.

   d. Construct a matrix with the organizational storyline down the left-hand side of the page and the elements of STROBE across the top. Using the symbols from the "anecdotal list" application of STROBE, indicate the relationship between the organizational storyline as portrayed by I. B. and each element you have observed (that is, indicate whether each element of STROBE confirms, reverses, causes you to look further, modifies, or supplements the narrative).

   e. Based on your observations of STROBE and your interview, state in a paragraph what problems you are able to anticipate in getting a new system approved by I. B. and others. In a sentence or two, discuss how your diagnosis might have been different if you had just talked to I. B. over the phone, or read his written comments on a systems proposal.

GROUP PROJECTS

1. Arrange to visit a local organization that is expanding or otherwise enhancing its information systems. To allow your group to practice the various observation methods described in this chapter, assign one of the following techniques to each group member: time sampling, event sampling, observing decision makers' body language, developing the analyst's playscript, and using STROBE. Many of these strategies can be employed during one-on-one interviews, while some require formal organizational meetings. Try to accomplish several objectives during your visit to the organization by scheduling it at an appropriate time to permit all team members to try their assigned method of observation. Using multiple methods such as interviewing and observation (often simultaneously) is the only cost-effective way to get a true, timely picture of the organization's information requirements.

2. Your group should meet and discuss their findings. Were there any surprises? Did the information garnered through observation confirm,

reverse, or negate what was learned in interviews? Were any of the findings from the observational methods in direct conflict with each other. Work with your group to develop a list of ways to address any puzzling information (for example, by doing follow-up interviews).

SELECTED BIBLIOGRAPHY

Kendall, K. E., and J. E. Kendall. "Structured Observation of the Decision-Making Environment: A Validity and Reliability Assessment," *Decision Sciences,* Vol. 15, No. 1, 1984.

Kendall, K. E., and J. E. Kendall. "STROBE: A Structured Approach to the Observation of the Decision-Making Environment." *Information & Management,* Vol. 7, No. 1, 1984.

Kendall, K. E., and J. E. Kendall. "Observing Organizational Environments: A Systematic Approach for Information Analysts." *Management Information Systems Quarterly,* Vol. 5, No. 1, 1981.

Runkel, P. J., and J. E. McGrath. *Research on Human Behavior: A Systematic Guide to Method.* New York: Holt, Rinehart and Winston, Inc., 1972.

Shultis, R. L. "'Playscript'—A New Tool Accountants Need." *NAA Bulletin,* August 1964, Vol. 45, No. 12, pp. 3–10.

Weick, K. E. "Systematic Observational Methods." In G. Lindzey and E. Aronson (eds.), *The Handbook of Social Psychology,* 2nd ed., Vol II. Reading, MA: Addison-Wesley Publishing Company, 1968.

SEEING IS BELIEVING

"Chip, I know the interviews took a long time, but they were worth it," Anna says defensively as Chip enters her office with a worried look on his face.

"I'm sure of *that*." Chip says. "You really made a good impression on them. People have stopped me in the hall and said they're glad we're working on the new system. I'm not worried about the interviews themselves. But I was concerned that we didn't have time to discuss observations before you did them."

"Rest assured, I was all eyes," Anna laughs. "I used a technique called STROBE (*STR*uctured *OB*servation of the *E*nvironment) to systematically see our decision maker's habitats. You'll be interested in these notes I wrote up for each person I interviewed," says Anna, as she hands Chip her written, organized observations from each interview.

Observations of Decision Makers' Offices

Decision maker	Dot Matricks
Office location	An enclosed office in the Administrative Data Processing area.The door is usually open. Large windows are located opposite the door with a beautiful view.
Placement of desk	Center of the room with a chair across the desk from Dot and another chair at the side of the desk.
Stationary equipment	There are two large bookcases containing a variety of books. One is ceiling height and another is desk height.
Decorations	On the lower bookcase are pictures of Dot's children. There are several pictures on the walls. One is a farm scene from the last century with a horse and buggy and two riders trotting up a dirt road.
Props	A mainframe/microcomputer workstation, turned on with a sign-on screen displayed. A stack of reports is on the left side. Several pens and a printer calculator are above the reports.
Trade journals and newspapers	Several copies of *Computerworld* and the *Journal of Management Systems* are on top of the bookcase. The latest *Computerworld* issue is on the desk.

Allen Schmidt,
Julie E. Kendall, and
Kenneth E. Kendall

Office lighting/color	Brightly lit, warm tan walls with a brown accent stripe.
Clothing	A dress, authoritatively jacketed with a navy blazer.
Decision maker	Mike Crowe
Office location	Workroom near the mainframe computer complex. A desk is in a cubicle partitioned at one end of the room.
Placement of desk	Against the wall. A chair is at the side of the desk and is piled high with technical manuals.
Stationary equipment	A file cabinet and a half-size bookcase. A long, low workbench covered with micros and parts.
Decorations	Posters of a magnified microchip showing the circuitry. Several posters of railroad trains.
Props	The bookcase is stacked high with papers, magazines, manuals, software packages, and diskettes. An IBM 486 microcomputer is on the desk. Displayed on it are several open windows overlapping each other.
Trade journals and newspapers	There are numerous catalogues for parts and a stack of *PC Tech Journals* in evidence.
Office lighting/color	The office is well lit with large overhead fluorescent lights as well as desk and work-area lighting.
Clothing	Dark slacks, a lightly striped shirt, and a dark tie accenting the shirt stripes.
Decision maker	Cher Ware
Office location	Within Administrative Data Processing. Cubicle, near the center of the microcomputer area.
Placement of desk	Facing a wall of the cubicle with a chair behind the desk and at the side of the desk. An old sofa is against another wall.
Stationary equipment	A bookcase and a file cabinet. The bookcase contains a variety of books referencing microcomputer software and hardware.
Decorations	Posters of mountain scenery, tranquil lakes, a forest, and one that says "Flower Power."

Props	The desk is rather cluttered with paper, pencils, coffee cups, and the like. A microcomputer is on the desk, with a wordprocessing screen and some partially keyed text displayed.
Trade journals and newspapers	Several internal reports. The latest copy of Word Perfect Corporate Report is stacked next to two microcomputer magazines. Each is folded back, exposing a product review page.
Office lighting/color	The cubical has burgundy walls and is warmly lit with ceiling and desk lighting.
Clothing	A flowered, pastel blouse and a denim skirt.
Decision maker	Paige Prynter
Office location	Administration building, an enclosed office. Located near other decision makers. The office door is normally closed. Thin vertical windows are part of the wall to the hallway.
Placement of desk	Close to the door. Expansive space behind the desk. Chair of visitor is against the wall and directly across the desk from Paige's chair.
Stationary equipment	A file cabinet is in the corner. There is a bookcase containing bound sets of books neatly organized.
Decorations	A framed print of an English landscape is on the wall.
Props	A terminal sits on the desk. It is turned off. A gold pen set is the only other object on the desk.
Trade journals and newspapers	A copy of the *Wall Street Journal* and some educational journals are visible on a small bookcase. No journals or reports are on the desk.
Office lighting/color	Lighting is fluorescent. The colors of the office are grey and mauve.
Clothing	Skirted suit with white blouse.
Decision maker	Hy Perteks
Office location	In the Information Center. A faculty and staff resource room with microcomputer and

several mainframe terminals. The office is partitioned off at one end of the room.

Placement of desk	The desk has its side against the partition wall with a chair to the side of it. The space behind and in front of the desk are fairly balanced.
Stationary equipment	There are two desk-height bookcases and several four-drawer file cabinets.
Decorations	The walls are covered with numerous posters, and artwork that his children have created. The posters are of astronomical objects, distant countries, and interesting surrealistic-looking computer artwork, some depicting fractals.
Props	The desk has a microcomputer with a menu of options displayed. There are pens and a metal printer-spacing ruler on the desk. Several smoke-colored boxes of diskettes are on a shelf.
Trade journals	Several issues of *PC Magazine* and a *Macintosh* journal are on the bookcase. The latest issue of *Byte* is on the desk.
Office lighting/color	The office is well lit with desk and overhead fluorescent lamps. The colors are a warm off-white.
Clothing	A sport jacket with a pale yellow shirt and dark tie. Dress slacks that coordinate with his jacket.

Exercises

E-1. Based on Anna's written observation of Dot's office and clothing, use STROBE to analyze Dot as a decision maker. In two paragraphs, compare and contrast what you learned in Dot's interview (Chapter 5) and what you learned via STROBE.

E-2. After examining Anna's written observations about Mike Crowe's office, use STROBE to analyze Mike as a decision maker. What differences (if any) did you see between Mike in his interview (Chapter 5) and Mike in the observations made? Use two paragraphs to answer.

E-3. Use STROBE to analyze Anna's written observations about Cher Ware and Paige Prynter. Use two paragraphs to compare and contrast the decision-making style of each as it is revealed by their offices and clothing.

E-4. Use STROBE to analyze Anna's written observations about Hy Perteks. Now compare your analysis with Hy's interview in Chapter 5. Use two paragraphs to discuss whether STROBE confirms, negates, reverses, or serves as a cue to look further in Hy's narrative. (Include any further questions you would ask Hy to clarify your interpretation.)

8

PROTOTYPING

KINDS OF INFORMATION SOUGHT

Prototyping of information systems is a worthwhile technique for quickly gathering specific information about users' information requirements. As will become evident in the second section of this chapter, there are four basic approaches to prototyping. Generally speaking, effective prototyping should come early in the systems development life cycle, during the requirements determination phase. However, prototyping is a complex technique that requires knowledge of the entire systems development life cycle before it is successfully accomplished.

initial reaction
user suggestion
innovation
revision

Prototyping is included at this point in the text to underscore its importance as an information-gathering technique. When using prototyping in this way, the systems analyst is seeking initial reactions from users and management to the prototype, user suggestions about changing or cleaning up the prototyped system, possible innovations for it, and revision plans detailing which parts of the system need to be done first or which branches of an organization to prototype next. Figure 8.1 shows the four kinds of information that analysts seek during prototyping.

INITIAL USER REACTIONS

As the systems analyst presenting a prototype of the information system, you are keenly interested in users' and management's reactions to the prototype. You want to know in detail how they react to working with the prototype and how good the fit is between their needs and the prototyped features of the system. Reactions are gathered through observation, interviews, and feedback sheets (possibly questionnaires) designed to elicit each person's opinion about the prototype as he or she interacts with it. Through such user reactions, the analyst discovers many perspectives on the prototype, including whether users seem happy with it and whether there will be difficulty in selling or implementing the system.

FIGURE 8.1
Kinds of information sought
when prototyping.

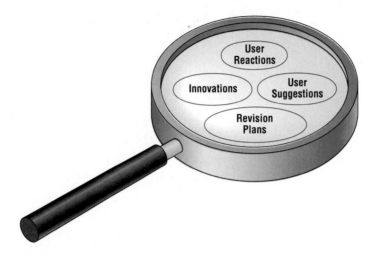

User Suggestions

The analyst is also interested in user and management suggestions about refining or changing the prototype presented. Suggestions are garnered from those experiencing the prototype as they work with it for a specified period. The time that users spend with the prototype is usually dependent on their dedication to and interest in the systems project.

Suggestions are the product of users' interaction with the prototype as well as their reflection on that interaction. The suggestions obtained from users should point the analyst toward ways of refining, changing, or "cleaning up" the prototype so that it better suits users' needs.

Innovations

Innovations for the prototype (which, if successful, will be part of the finished system) are part of the information sought by the systems analysis team. Innovations are new system capabilities that have not been thought of prior to interaction with the prototype. They go beyond the current prototyped features by adding something new and innovative.

Revision Plans

Prototypes preview the future system. Revision plans help identify priorities for what should be prototyped next. In situations where many branches of an organization are involved, revision plans help to determine which branches to prototype next.

Information gathered in the prototyping phase allows the analyst to set priorities and redirect plans inexpensively, with a minimum of disruption. Because of this, prototyping and planning go hand in hand.

APPROACHES TO PROTOTYPING

Kinds of Prototypes

The word *prototype* is used in many different ways. Rather than attempting to synthesize all of these into one definition or trying to mandate one correct approach to the somewhat controversial topic of prototyping, we will illustrate how each of several conceptions of prototyping may be usefully applied in a particular situation.

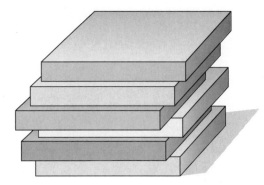

FIGURE 8.2
A patched-up prototype
works but is not efficient,
nor is it elegant.

PATCHED-UP PROTOTYPE. The first kind of prototyping has to do with constructing a system that works but is patched up or patched together. In engineering, this approach is referred to as breadboarding—creating a patched-together, working model of an (otherwise microscopic) integrated circuit.

An example in information systems is a working model that has all necessary features but is inefficient. In this instance of prototyping, users can interact with the system, getting accustomed to the interface and types of output available. However, the retrieval and storage of information may be inefficient since programs were written rapidly with the objective of being workable rather than efficient. A patched-up prototype may be envisioned as illustrated in Figure 8.2.

Another example of a patched-up prototype is an information system that has all the proposed features but is really a basic model that will eventually be enhanced.

NONOPERATIONAL PROTOTYPE. The second conception of a prototype is that of a nonworking scale model for the purposes of testing certain aspects of the design. An example of this approach is a full-scale model of an automobile for use in wind tunnel tests. The size and shape of the auto are precise, but the car is not operational. In this case, only features of the automobile essential to wind tunnel testing are included.

A nonworking scale model of an information system might be made when the coding required by the applications is too extensive to prototype, yet a useful idea of the system can be gained through prototyping of the input and output only. The kind of prototype is shown conceptually in Figure 8.3. In this instance, processing, because of undue cost and time, would not be prototyped. However, some decisions on the utility of the system could still be made based on prototyped input and output.

FIRST-OF-A-SERIES PROTOTYPE. A third conception of prototyping involves creating a first full-scale model of a system, often called a pilot. An example is prototyping the first airplane of a series. The prototype is completely operational and is a realization of what the designer hopes will be a series of airplanes with identical features.

This type of prototyping is useful when many installations of the same information system are planned. The full-scale working model allows realistic interaction with the new system, yet minimizes the cost of overcoming any problems that it presents. This sort of prototype is depicted in Figure 8.4.

FIGURE 8.3
A nonoperational prototype
may seek users' opinions on
the interfaces (input and
output).

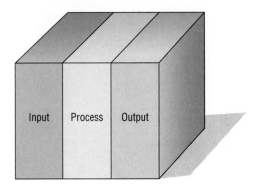

For example, when a retail grocery chain intends to use the same computerized system to check in vendors' shipments in a number of outlets, a full-scale model might be installed in one store in order to work through any problems before it is implemented in all the others.

Another example is found in banking installations for electronic funds transfer. A full-scale prototype is installed in one or two locations first, and if successful, duplicates are installed at all locations based on customer usage patterns and other key factors.

SELECTED FEATURES PROTOTYPE. A fourth conception of prototyping concerns building an operational model that includes some, but not all, of the features that the final system will have. An analogy would be a new retail complex that opens before all construction is complete.

In a newly opened retail mall, essential functions such as being able to purchase some goods, eating in a fast-food restaurant, and parking nearby are possible, although not all space is occupied and not all goods that will ultimately be for sale are available when the complex first opens. Nonetheless, from initial contact with the retail complex, it is possible to gain a good understanding of what future visits will be like.

When prototyping information systems in this way, some, but not all, essential features are included. For example, a system menu may appear on-screen that lists six features: add a record, update a record, delete a record, search a record for a keyword, list a record, or scan a record. However, in the prototyped system, only three of the six may be available for use so that the user may add a record (feature 1), delete a record (feature 3), and list a record (feature 5), as illustrated in Figure 8.5.

FIGURE 8.4
A first-of-a-series prototype is
a working model that will be
used elsewhere if it is
successful.

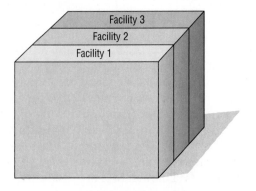

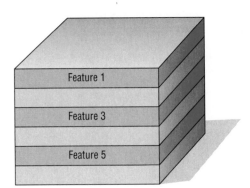

When this kind of prototyping is done, the system is accomplished in modules, so that if the features prototyped are evaluated as successful, they can be incorporated into the larger, final system without undertaking immense work in interfacing. Prototypes done in this manner are part of the actual system. They are *not* just a mock-up as in the first definition of prototyping considered previously.

Prototyping as an Alternative to the Systems Development Life Cycle

Some analysts argue that prototyping should be considered as an alternative to the systems development life cycle (SDLC). Recall that the SDLC, introduced in Chapter 1, is a logical, systematic approach to follow in the development of information systems.

Complaints about going through the SDLC center around two main concerns, which are interrelated. The first concern is the extended time required to go through the development life cycle. As the investment of analyst time increases, the cost of the delivered system rises proportionately.

The second concern about using the SDLC is that user requirements change over time. During the long interval between the time user requirements are analyzed and the finished system is delivered, user requirements are evolving. Thus, because of the extended development cycle, the resulting system may be criticized for inadequately addressing current user information requirements.

It is apparent that the concerns are interrelated, since they both pivot on the time required to complete the SDLC and the problem of falling out of touch with user requirements during subsequent development phases. If a system is developed in isolation from users (after initial requirements analysis is completed), it will not meet their expectations.

A corollary of the problem of keeping up with user information requirements is the suggestion that users cannot really know what they do or do not want until they see something tangible. And in the traditional SDLC, it often is too late to change an unwanted system once it is delivered.

To overcome these problems, some analysts propose that prototyping be used as an alternative to the systems development life cycle. When prototyping is used in this way, the analyst effectively shortens the time between ascertainment of information requirements and delivery of a workable system. Additionally, using prototyping instead of the traditional systems development life cycle might overcome some of the problems of accurately identifying user information requirements.

FIGURE 8.6
Certain factors determine
whether a system is more or
less suitable for prototyping.

With a prototype, users can actually see what is possible and how their requirements translate into hardware and software. Any of the four kinds of prototyping discussed earlier might be used.

Drawbacks to supplanting the systems development life cycle with prototyping include prematurely shaping a system before the problem or opportunity being addressed is thoroughly understood. Also, using prototyping as an alternative may result in producing a system that is accepted by specific groups of users but which is inadequate for overall system needs.

The approach we advocate here is to use prototyping as a part of the traditional systems development life cycle. In this view, prototyping is considered as an additional, specialized method for ascertaining users' information requirements.

DEVELOPING A PROTOTYPE

In this section, guidelines for developing a prototype are advanced. Prototyping is taken in the sense of the last definition that was discussed—that is, a selected features prototype that will include some but not all features, and if successful, will eventually be part of the larger, final system delivered.

When deciding whether to include prototyping as a part of the systems development life cycle, the systems analyst needs to consider what kind of problem is being solved and in what way the system presents the solution. Different types of systems and their suitability for prototyping are depicted in Figure 8.6. A straightforward payroll or inventory system, which solves a highly structured problem in a traditional manner, is not a good candidate for prototyping because the outcome of the system as a solution is well-known and predictable.

Rather, consider the novelty and complexity of the problem and its solution. A novel and complex system that addresses unstructured or semi-structured problems in a nontraditional way is a perfect candidate for prototyping. Decision support systems, which are the subject of Chapter 12, are personalized information systems that support users in semistructured decision making. As such, DSS are well-suited to prototyping.

The systems analyst must also evaluate the environmental context for the system when deciding whether to prototype. If the system will exist in an environment that is stable for long periods, prototyping may be unnecessary. However, if the environment for the system changes rapidly, then prototyping should be seriously considered. By their nature, prototypes are evolutionary and can absorb many revisions.

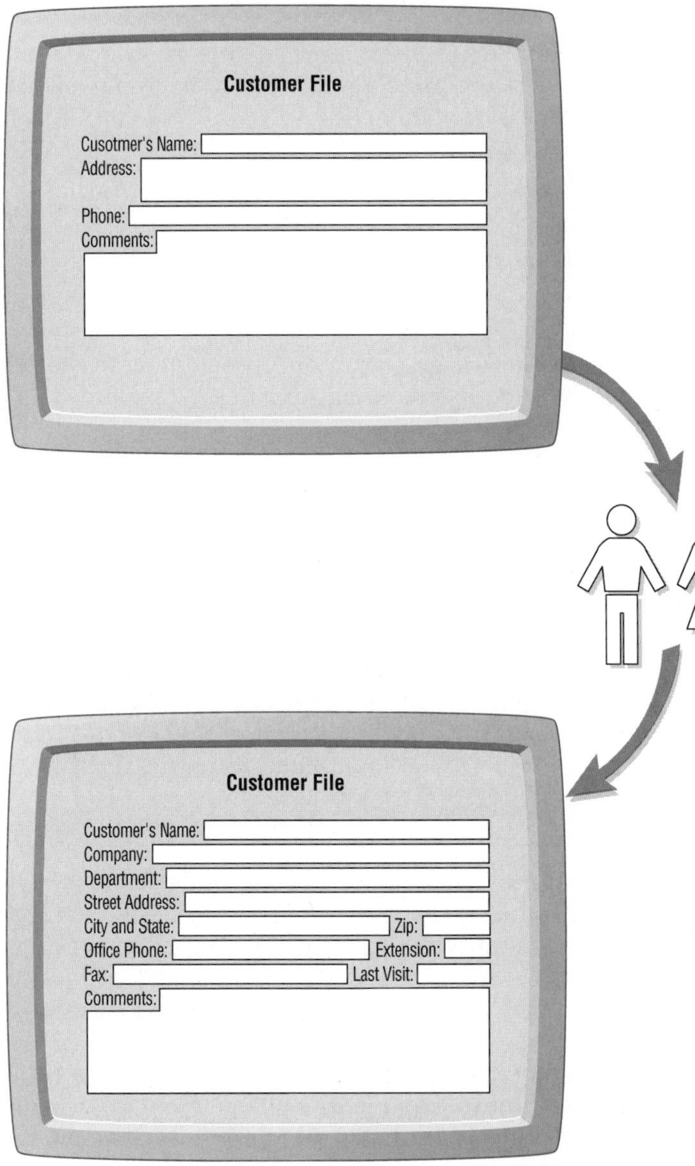

FIGURE 8.7
Eliciting user feedback
results in improved screens
that better address user
requirements.

Customer File

Cusotmer's Name:
Address:

Phone:
Comments:

Customer File

Customer's Name:
Company:
Department:
Street Address:
City and State: Zip:
Office Phone: Extension:
Fax: Last Visit:
Comments:

The prototype system is actually an operational portion of the eventual system that you will build. It is not a complete system since you will strive to build it quickly; only some essential functions will be included in the model. However, it is important to envision and then build the prototype as part of the actual system with which the user will interact. It must incorporate enough representative functions to allow users to understand that they are interacting with a real system.

Prototyping is a superb way to elicit feedback about the proposed system and how readily it is fulfilling the information needs of its users, as depicted in Figure 8.7. The first step of prototyping is to estimate the costs involved in building a module of the system. If costs of programmers' and analysts' time, as well as equipment costs, are within the budget, then building of the prototype can proceed. Prototyping is an excellent way to facilitate the integration of the information system into the larger system of the organization.

Guidelines for Developing a Prototype

Once the decision to prototype has been made, there are four main guidelines to observe when integrating prototyping into the requirements determination phase of the systems development life cycle:

1. Work in manageable modules.
2. Build the prototype rapidly.
3. Modify the prototype in successive iterations.
4. Stress the user interface.

As you can see, the guidelines suggest ways of proceeding with the prototype that are necessarily interrelated. Each guideline is explained in the following subsections.

WORKING IN MANAGEABLE MODULES. When prototyping some of the features of a system into a workable model, it is imperative that the analyst work in manageable modules. One of the distinct advantages of prototyping is that it is not necessary or desirable to build an entire, working system for prototype purposes.

An example of manageable modules was discussed in an earlier section. Recall that a manageable module is one that allows interaction with its key features, yet can be built separately from other system modules. Module features that are deemed less important are purposely left out of the initial prototype.

BUILDING THE PROTOTYPE RAPIDLY. Speed is essential to successfully prototyping an information system. Recall that one of the complaints voiced against following the traditional systems development life cycle is that the interval between requirements determination and delivery of a complete system is far too long to effectively address evolving user needs.

Analysts can use prototyping to shorten this gap by using traditional information-gathering techniques to pinpoint salient information requirements, then quickly making decisions that bring forth a working model. In effect, the user sees and uses the system very early in the systems development life cycle instead of waiting for a finished system to gain hands-on experience.

After brief analysis of information requirements using traditional methods such as interviewing, observation, and research into archival data, working models for the prototype are constructed. The prototype should take less than a week to put together; two or three days is preferable and possible. Remember that in order to build a prototype this quickly you must use special tools, such as an existing database management system, and software that allows generalized input and output, interactive systems, and so on. All of these tools permit speed of construction that is impossible with traditional programming.

It is important to emphasize that at this stage in the life cycle, the analyst is still gathering information about what users need and want from the information system. The prototype becomes a valuable extension of traditional requirements determination. The analyst assesses user feedback about the prototype in order to get a better picture of overall information needs.

Putting together an operational prototype rapidly, early in the systems development life cycle, allows the analyst to gain valuable insight into how the remainder of the project should go. By showing users very early in the process how parts of the system actually perform, rapid prototyping guards against overcommitting resources to a project that may eventually become unworkable.

MODIFYING THE PROTOTYPE. A third guideline for developing the prototype is that its construction must support modifications. Making the prototype modifiable means creating it in modules that are not highly interdependent. If this guideline is observed, less resistance is encountered when modifications in the prototype are necessary.

The prototype is generally modified several times, going through several iterations. Changes in the prototype should move the system closer to what users say is important. Each modification necessitates another evaluation by users.

As with the initial development, modifications must be accomplished swiftly, usually in a day or two, in order to keep the momentum of the project going. However, the exact timing of modifications depends on how dedicated users are to interacting with modified prototypes. Systems analysts must encourage users to do their share by evaluating changes rapidly.

The prototype is not a finished system. Entering the prototyping phase with the idea that the prototype will require modification is a helpful attitude that demonstrates to users how necessary their feedback is if the system is to improve.

STRESSING THE USER INTERFACE. The user's interface with the prototype (and eventually the system) is very important. Since what you are really trying to achieve with the prototype is to get users to further articulate their information requirements, they must be able to interact easily with the system's prototype. For many users the interface *is* the system. It should not be a stumbling block.

For example, at this stage, the goal of the analyst is to design an interface that allows the user to interact with the system with a minimum of training and that allows a maximum of user control over represented functions. Although many aspects of the systems will remain undeveloped in the prototype, the user interface must be well developed enough so that users can pick up the system quickly and not be put off. Online, interactive systems using screen output are ideally suited to prototypes. Chapter 18 describes in detail the considerations that are important in designing the user interface.

Many of the intricacies of interfaces must be streamlined or ignored altogether in the prototyping phase. However, if prototype interfaces are not what users need or want, or if systems analysts find that the interfaces do not adequately allow system access, then they, too, are candidates for modification.

Disadvantages of Prototyping

As with any information-gathering technique, there are several disadvantages to prototyping. The first is that it can be quite difficult to manage prototyping as a project within the larger systems effort. The second disadvantage is that users and analysts may adopt a prototype as a completed system when it is in fact inadequate and was never intended to serve as a finished system.

The analyst needs to weigh these disadvantages against the known advantages when deciding whether to prototype, when to prototype, and how much of the system to prototype.

MANAGING THE PROJECT. All of the systems analysts' management skills that you leaned in Chapter 3 come into play again as your systems analysis team constructs and modifies a prototype. All of the possible problems that project management is subject to are relevant here.

Although several iterations of the prototype may be necessary, extending the prototype indefinitely also creates problems. It is important that the systems analysis team devise and then carry out a plan regarding how feedback on the prototype will be collected, analyzed, and interpreted. Set up specific time periods during which you and management decision makers will use feedback to evaluate how well the prototype is performing. Even though the prototype is prized for its evolutionary nature, the analyst cannot permit prototyping to overtake other phases in the systems development life cycle.

Elicit feedback from users periodically, not just once, and ask them if previous suggestions for improvements or changes have been acted upon satisfactorily. Feedback is directed to the systems analysis team for their reaction and possible modification of the prototype to better fit user needs. Recall that modifications to the prototype should be managed on a tight schedule of only a day or two each throughout the successive iterations.

Adopting an Incomplete System as Complete. A second major disadvantage of prototyping is that if a system is needed badly and welcomed readily, the prototype may be accepted in its unfinished state and pressed into service without necessary refinement. While superficially this may seem an appealing way to short-cut the development effort, it works to the business' and team's disadvantage.

Users will develop interaction patterns with the prototype system that are not compatible with what will actually occur with the complete system. Additionally, a prototype will not perform all necessary functions. Eventually, when deficiencies are realized, user backlash may develop if the prototype has been mistakenly adopted and integrated into the business as if it were a complete system.

Advantages of Prototyping

Prototyping is not necessary or appropriate in every systems project, as we have seen. However, the advantages should also be given consideration when deciding whether to prototype. The three major advantages of prototyping are: the potential for changing the system early in its development, the opportunity to stop development on a system that is not working, and the possibility of developing a system that more closely addresses users' needs and expectations. All three advantages are interrelated.

Changing the System Early in its Development. Successful prototyping depends on early and frequent user feedback to help modify the system and make it more responsive to actual needs. As with any systems effort, early changes are less expensive than changes made late in the project's development.

Since the prototype can be changed many times, and since flexibility and adaptation are the heart of prototyping, using feedback to change the system is often the action taken. Feedback will help tell you if changes are warranted in the input, process, or output, or if all three need adjustment.

When changing a prototype, analysts do not need to worry about wasting many man-hours of their efforts and those of programmers who have developed a full-blown system only to find that it needs modifications. Although the prototype represents an investment of time and money, it is always considerably less expensive than a completed system. Concomitantly, system problems and oversights are much easier to trace and detect in a prototype with limited features and limited interfaces than they are in a complex system.

Scrapping Undesirable Systems. A second advantage of using prototyping as an information-gathering technique is the possibility of scrapping a system that is just not what users and analysts had hoped. Once again, the issue of time and money spent arises. A prototype represents much less of an investment than a completely developed system.

Permanently removing the prototype system from use is done when it becomes apparent that the system is not useful and does not fulfill the information requirements (and other objectives) that have been set. Although scrapping the prototype is a difficult decision to make, it is infinitely better than putting increasing sums of time and money into a project that is plainly unworkable.

DESIGNING A SYSTEM FOR USERS' NEEDS AND EXPECTATIONS. A third advantage of prototyping is that the system being developed should be a better fit with users' needs and expectations. Many studies of failed information systems indict the long interval between requirements determination and the presentation of the finished system, precisely because it is common for systems analysts to develop systems while sequestered away from users during this critical period.

It is better practice to interact with users throughout the systems development life cycle. If your team makes a commitment to ongoing user involvement in all phases of the project, then the prototype can be used as an interactive tool that shapes the final system to accurately reflect users' requirements.

Users who take early ownership of the information system work harder to ensure its success. One way to foster early user support is to involve users actively in prototyping.

If your evaluation of the prototype indicates that the system is functioning well, within the guidelines that have been set, the decision should be to keep the prototype going and continue expanding it to include other functions as planned. This then is considered an operational prototype. The decision is made to keep the prototype functioning if the prototype is

Disadvantages to Prototyping	Advantages to Prototyping
• Difficult to manage prototyping as a project within a larger systems effort • Users and analysts may adopt a prototype as a completed system when it is inadequate	• Potential exists for changing the system early in its development • Opportunity exists to stop development on a system that is not working • May address user needs and expectations more closely

FIGURE 8.8
Disadvantages and
advantages of prototyping.

within the budget set for programmers' and analysts' time, users find the system worthwhile, and it is meeting the information requirements and objectives that have been set. A list comparing disadvantages and advantages of prototyping is given in Figure 8.8.

USERS' ROLE IN PROTOTYPING

The users' role in prototyping can be summed up in two words: honest involvement. Without user involvement, there is little reason to prototype. The precise behaviors necessary for interacting with a prototype can vary, but it is clear that the user is pivotal to the prototyping process. Realizing the importance of the user to the success of the process, the systems analysis team must encourage and welcome input and guard against their own natural resistance to changing the prototype.

Interaction with the Prototype

There are three main ways a user can be of help in prototyping:

1. Experimenting with the prototype
2. Giving open reactions to the prototype
3. Suggesting additions to and/or deletions from the prototype

All of the foregoing stem from the users' initial and successive interaction with the prototype.

EXPERIMENTING WITH THE PROTOTYPE. Users should be free to experiment with the prototype. Unlike a mere list of systems features, the prototype allows users the reality of hands-on interaction.

Users need to be encouraged to experiment with the prototype. The final system will be delivered with documentation stating how the system is to be used, and this in effect constrains experimentation. But in the prototyping stage, the user is free from all but minimal instruction on how to use the system. When this is the case, experimentation becomes necessary to make the prototype work.

Analysts need to be present at least part of the time when experimentation is occuring. They can then observe users' interactions with the system, and they are bound to see interactions they never planned. A form for observing user experimentation with the prototype is shown in Figure 8.9. Some of the variables you should observe include user reactions to the prototype, their suggestions for changing or expanding the prototype, their innovations for using the system in completely new ways, and any revision plans for the prototype that aid in setting priorities. When revising the

FIGURE 8.9
An important step in prototyping is to properly record
user reactions, user suggestions, innovations, and
revision plans.

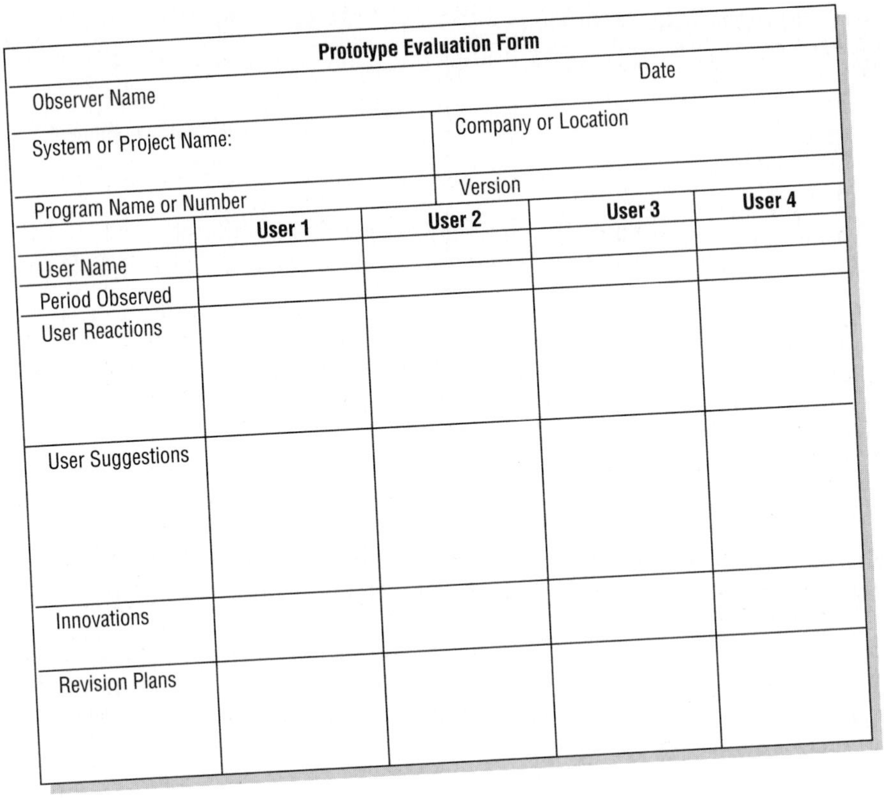

Prototype Evaluation Form				
Observer Name		Date		
System or Project Name:		Company or Location		
Program Name or Number		Version		
	User 1	User 2	User 3	User 4
User Name				
Period Observed				
User Reactions				
User Suggestions				
Innovations				
Revision Plans				

prototype, analysts should circulate their recorded observations among
team members so that everyone is fully informed.

GIVING OPEN REACTIONS TO THE PROTOTYPE. Another aspect of the users'
role in prototyping requires that they give open reactions to the prototype.
Unfortunately, this is not something that occurs on demand. Rather, making
users secure enough to give an open reaction is part of the relationship
between analysts and users that your team works to build.

Additionally, if users feel wary about commenting on or criticizing
what may be a pet project of organizational superiors or peers, it is unlikely that open reactions to the prototype will be forthcoming. Providing a
private (relatively unsupervised) period for users to interact with and
respond to the prototype is one way to insulate them from unwanted organizational influences.

SUGGESTING CHANGES TO THE PROTOTYPE. A third aspect of the users'
role in prototyping is to suggest additions to and/or deletions from the features being tried. The analysts' role is to elicit such suggestions by assuring
users that the feedback they provide is taken seriously, by observing users
as they interact, and by conducting short, specific interviews with users
concerning their experiences with the prototype.

Although users will be asked to articulate suggestions and innovations for the prototype, in the end it is the analyst's responsibility to weigh
these and translate them into workable changes where necessary. Users
need to be encouraged to brainstorm about possibilities and be reminded

that their input during the prototyping phase helps determine whether to save, scrap, or modify the system. In other words, users should never be resigned to accepting something less than what they want in the prototype stage. Systems analysts must remember to stress to users and management alike that prototyping is the most appropriate time for system changes.

In order to facilitate the prototyping process, the analyst must clearly communicate the purposes of prototyping to users, along with the idea that prototyping is valuable only when users are meaningfully involved.

SUMMARY

Prototyping is an information-gathering technique useful for supplementing the traditional systems development life cycle. When systems analysts use prototyping, they are seeking user reactions, suggestions, innovations, and revision plans in order to make improvements to the prototype and thereby modify system plans with a minimum of expense and disruption. Systems that support semistructured decision making (as decision support systems do) are prime candidates for prototyping.

The term *prototyping* carries several different meanings, four of which are commonly used. The first definition of prototyping is that of constructing a patched-up prototype. A second definition of prototyping is a nonoperational prototype that is used to test certain features of the design. A third conception of prototyping is creating the first-in-a-series prototype that is fully operational. This kind of prototype is useful when many installations of the same information system (under similar conditions) are planned. The fourth kind of prototyping is a selected features prototype that has some, but not all, of the essential system features. It uses self-contained modules as building blocks, so that if prototyped features are successful, they can be kept and incorporated into the larger, finished system.

The four major guidelines for developing a prototype are to: (1) work in manageable modules, (2) build the prototype rapidly, (3) modify the prototype, and (4) stress the user interface.

One disadvantage of prototypes is that managing the prototyping process is difficult because of the rapidity of the process and its many iterations. A second disadvantage is that an incomplete prototype may be pressed into service as if it were a complete system.

Although prototyping is not always necessary or desirable, it should be noted that there are three main, interrelated advantages to using it: (1) the potential for changing the system early in its development, (2) the opportunity to stop development on a system that is not working, and (3) the possibility of developing a system that more closely addresses users' needs and expectations.

Users have a distinct role to play in the prototyping process. Their main concern must be to interact with the prototype through experimentation. Systems analysts must work systematically to elicit and evaluate users reactions to the prototype, then work to incorporate worthwhile user suggestions and innovations into subsequent modifications.

KEYWORDS AND PHRASES

prototype	building the prototype rapidly
patched-up prototype	modifying the prototype
nonoperational prototype	stressing the user interface
first-in-a-series prototype	user involvement with prototyping
selected features prototype	manageable modules

REVIEW QUESTIONS

1. What four kinds of information is the analyst seeking through prototyping?
2. What is meant by the term "patched-up prototype"?
3. Define a prototype that is a "nonworking scale model."
4. Give an example of a prototype that is a "first full-scale model."
5. Define what is meant by a prototype that is a model with some, but not all, essential features.
6. List the advantages and disadvanges of using prototyping to *replace* the traditional systems development life cycle.
7. Describe how prototyping can be used to augment the traditional systems development life cycle.
8. What are the criteria for deciding whether a system should be prototyped?
9. List four guidelines that the analyst should observe in developing a prototype.

"Thank goodness it's the time of year when everything is new. I love spring, it's the most exhilarating time here at MRE. The trees are so green, with leaves in so many different shades. So many new projects to do, too; so many new clients to meet. It's really exciting. It reminds me of prototyping. Or what I know about prototyping, anyway. It's something new and fresh, a quick way to find out what's happening.

"In fact, I believe that we have a few prototypes already going here. The best thing about them is that they can change. I don't know anyone who's really been satisfied with a first pass at a prototype. But it is fun to be involved with something that is happening fast, and something that will change."

HYPERCASE QUESTIONS

1. Locate the prototype currently proposed for use in one of MRE's departments. Suggest a few modifications that would make this prototype even more responsive to the unit's needs.

2. Using a word processor, construct a nonoperational prototype for a Training Unit Project Reporting System. If you have a hypertext program available, attempt to create partial functionality by making the menus functional. *Hint*: See sample screens in Chapters 15 and 16 to help you in your design.

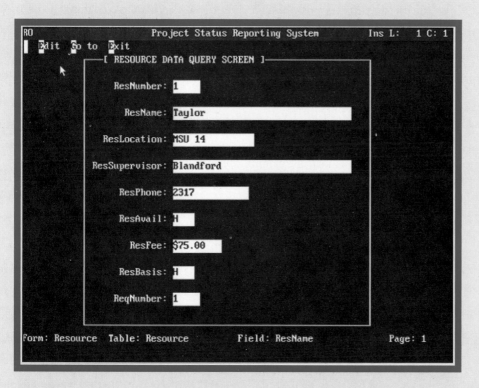

FIGURE 8.HC1
One of the many prototype screens found in HyperCase.

10. What are the two main problems identified with prototyping?

11. List the three main advantages in using prototyping.

12. What are three ways that a user can be of help in the prototyping process?

PROBLEMS

1. As part of a larger systems project, Clone Bank of Clone, Colorado, wants your help in setting up a new monthly reporting form for their checking and savings account customers. The president and vice presidents are very attuned to what customers in the community are saying. They feel that their customers want a checking account summary that looks like the one offered by the other three banks in town. However, they are unwilling to commit to that form without a formal summary of customer feedback that supports their decision. Feedback will not be used to change the prototype form in any way. They want you to send a prototype of one form to one group and to send the old form to another group.

   a. In a paragraph, discuss why it probably is not worthwhile to prototype the new form under these circumstances.

   b. In a second paragraph, discuss a situation under which it would be advisable to prototype a new form.

2. C. N. Itall has been a systems analyst for Tun-L-Vision Corporation for many years. When you came on board as part of the systems analysis team and suggested prototyping as part of the SDLC for a current project, C. N. said, "Sure, but you can't pay any attention to what users say. They have no idea what they want. I'll prototype, but I'm not 'observing' any users."

   a. As tactfully as possible, so as not to upset C. N. Itall, make a list of the reasons that support the importance of observing user reactions, suggestions, and innovations in the prototyping process.

   b. In a paragraph, describe what might happen if part of a system is prototyped, but no user feedback about it is incorporated into the successive system.

3. "Every time I think I've captured user information requirements, they've already changed. It's like trying to hit a moving target. Half the time I don't think they even know what they want themselves," exclaims Flo Chart, a systems analyst for 2 Good 2 Be True, a company that surveys product use for the marketing divisions of several manufacturing companies.

   a. In a paragraph, explain to Flo Chart how prototyping can help her to better define users' information requirements.

   b. In a paragraph, comment on Flo's observation: "Half the time I don't think they even know what they want themselves." Be sure to explain how prototyping can actually help users better understand and articulate their own information requirements.

4. Harold, a district manager for the multioutlet chain of Sprocket's Gifts, thinks that building a prototype can mean only one thing: a nonworking scale model. He also believes that this is too cumbersome a way to prototype information systems and thus is reluctant to do so.

   a. Briefly (in two or three paragraphs) compare and contrast the other three kinds of prototyping that are possible, so that Harold has an understanding of what prototyping can mean.

b. Harold has an option of implementing one system, trying it, and then having it installed in five other locations of Sprocket's if it is successful. Name a type of prototyping that would fit well with this approach, and in a paragraph defend your choice.

5. "I've got the idea of the century!" proclaims Bea Kwicke, a new systems analyst with your systems group. "Let's skip all of this SDLC garbage and just prototype everything. Our projects will go alot more quickly, we'll save time and money, and all of the users will feel as if we're paying them attention instead of going away for months on end and not talking to them."

    a. List the reasons that you (as a member of the same team as Bea) would give her to dissuade her from trying to scrap the SDLC and prototype every project.

    b. Bea is pretty disappointed with what you have said. In order to encourage her, use a paragraph to explain the situations that you feel would lend themselves to prototyping.

6. The following remark was overheard at a meeting between managers and a systems analysis team at the Fence-Me-In fencing company: "You told us the prototype would be finished three weeks ago. We're still waiting for it!"

    a. In a paragraph, comment on the importance of rapid delivery of a portion of a prototyped information system.

    b. List three elements of the prototyping process that must be controlled in order to assure prompt delivery of the prototype.

    c. What are some elements of the prototyping process that are difficult to manage? List them.

7. Nordic Designs, a chain of stores specializing in contemporary furniture from Scandinavia, has been circulating a corporate newsletter bragging about the prototype of their shipping information system. The newsletter story proclaims, "Our shipping information system prototype was put into service as soon as it was delivered. With absolutely no changes necessary, managers say it's the perfect solution to tracking furniture shipments. Watch for the prototype in your store soon."

    a. How has the writer of the story apparently misunderstood the concept of prototyping? Explain in a paragraph.

    b. List the problems faced by designers of prototypes if users expect that "absolutely no changes are necessary."

GROUP PROJECTS

1. Divide your group into two smaller subgroups. Have Group 1 follow the processes specified in this chapter for creating prototypes. Using a CASE tool or a word processor, Group 1 should devise two nonworking prototype screens using the information collected in the interviews with Maverick Transport employees accomplished in the group exercise in Chapter 5. Make any assumptions necessary to create two screens for truck dispatchers. Group 2 (playing the roles of dispatchers) should react to the prototype screens and provide feedback about desired additions and deletions.

2. Group 1 should revise the prototype screens based on the user comments they received. Group 2 should respond with comments about

how well their initial concerns were addressed with the refined prototypes.

3. As a united group, write a paragraph discussing your experiences with prototying for ascertaining information requirements.

SELECTED BIBLIOGRAPHY

Alavi, M. "An Assessment of the Prototyping Approach to Information Systems Development." *Communications of the ACM.* June 1984, Vol. 27, No. 6, pp. 556–63.

Avison, D., and D. N. Wilson. "Controls for Effective Prototyping." *Journal of Management Systems.* 1991, Vol. 3, No 1.

Davis, G. B., and M. H. Olson. *Management Information Systems, Conceptual Foundations, Structure, and Development*, 2nd ed. New York: McGraw-Hill Book Company, 1985.

Dearnley, P., and P. Mayhew. "In Favour of System Prototypes and their Integration into the Systems Development Cycle." *The Computer Journal.* February 1983, Vol. 26, pp. 36–42.

Gremillion, L. L., and P. Pyburn. "Breaking the Systems Development Bottleneck."*Harvard Business Review.* March–April 1983, pp. 130–37.

Harrison, T. S. "Techniques and Issues in Rapid Prototyping," *Journal of Systems Management.* June 1985, Vol. 36, No. 6, pp. 8–13.

Naumann, J. D., and A. M. Jenkins. "Prototyping: The New Paradigm for Systems Development." *Management Information Systems Quarterly.* September 1982, pp. 29–44.

REACTION TIME

"We need to get a feel for some of the output needed by the users," Anna comments. "It will help to firm up some of our ideas on the information they require."

"Agreed," replies Chip. "It will also help us determine the necessary input. From that we can design corresponding data entry screens. Let's create prototype reports and screens and get some user feedback."

Anna starts by developing the Preventive Maintenance Report prototype. Based on interview results, she sets to work creating the report she feels Mike Crowe will need.

"This report should be used to predict when machines should have preventive maintenance," Anna thinks. "It seems to me that Mike would need to know *which* machine needs work performed as well as *when* the work should be scheduled. Now let's see, what information would identify the machine clearly? The inventory number, brand name, and model would identify the machine. I imagine that the room and campus should be included to quickly locate the machine. A calculated maintenance date would tell Mike when the work should be completed. What sequence should the report be in? Probably the most useful would be by location."

The Report Prototype Design screen showing the completed PREVENTIVE MAINTENANCE REPORT is shown in Figure E8.1. Notice that function keys are shown in the pull-down menus at the top of the screen. CAMPUS CODE and ROOM NUMBER are printed only once for each location. The MICROCOMPUTER INVENTORY NO., BRAND NAME, MODEL, and

```
┌─────────────────── PREVENTIVE MAINTENANCE REPORT ──────────── ▼ ▲ ┐
│ Options                                                              │
│ Column  10....+...20....+...30....+...40....+...50....+...60..,.+...70....+...│
│ Repeat  /06/95          PREVENTIVE MAINTENANCE REPORT        PAGE  1 │
│ Field                        WEEK OF 01/06/95                        │
│                                                                      │
│ Exit        ROOM    MICROCOMPUTER      BRAND          MODEL     MAINTENANCE  DONE│
│    CODE    NUMBER   INVENTORY NO.      NAME                        DATE       │
│                                                                      │
│   XXXX    XXXXX      99999999      XXXXXXXXXX    XXXXXXXXXXX   Z9-99-99   ____ │
│                     99999999      XXXXXXXXXX    XXXXXXXXXXX   Z9-99-99   ____ │
│ 10                  99999999      XXXXXXXXXX    XXXXXXXXXXX   Z9-99-99   ____ │
│                     99999999      XXXXXXXXXX    XXXXXXXXXXX   Z9-99-99   ____ │
│                     99999999      XXXXXXXXXX    XXXXXXXXXXX   Z9-99-99   ____ │
│                     99999999      XXXXXXXXXX    XXXXXXXXXXX   Z9-99-99   ____ │
│                     99999999      XXXXXXXXXX    XXXXXXXXXXX   Z9-99-99   ____ │
│                                                                      │
│   XXXX    XXXXX      99999999      XXXXXXXXXX    XXXXXXXXXXX   Z9-99-99   ____ │
│                     99999999      XXXXXXXXXX    XXXXXXXXXXX   Z9-99-99   ____ │
│                     99999999      XXXXXXXXXX    XXXXXXXXXXX   Z9-99-99   ____ │
│                     99999999      XXXXXXXXXX    XXXXXXXXXXX   Z9-99-99   ____ │
│ 20                  99999999      XXXXXXXXXX    XXXXXXXXXXX   Z9-99-99   ____ │
│                                                                      │
│ TOTAL MICROCOMPUTERS SCHEDULED FOR PREVENTIVE MAINTENANCE    ZZZ,ZZ9 │
└──────────────────────────────────────────────────────────────────────┘
```

FIGURE E8.1
Report Prototype examples, PREVENTIVE MAINTENANCE REPORT.

*Allen Schmidt,
Julie E. Kendall, and
Kenneth E. Kendall*

Prototype Evaluation Form				
Observer Name Chip Puller			Date 1/06/95	

System or Project Name		Company or Location	
Microcomputer System		Central Pacific University	
Program Name or Number Prev. Maint.		Version 1	

	User 1	User 2	User 3	User 4
User Name	Mike C.	Dot M.		
Period Observed	1/06/95 AM	1/06/95 AM		
User Reactions	Generally favorable, got excited about project	Excellent!		
User Suggestions	Add the date when maintenance was performed.	Place a form number on top for reference. Place word WEEKLY in title.		
Innovations				
Revision Plans	Modify on 1/08/95. Review with Dot and Mike.			

FIGURE E8.2
Prototype Evaluation Form.

MAINTENANCE DATE are repeated downward to create columns. The Xs and 9s are codes, similar to those used in programming languages, which show the type of entry, either alphanumeric or numeric.

The report prototype is soon finished. After printing the final copy, Anna takes the report to both Mike Crowe and Dot Matricks. Their observations are recorded on the Prototype Evaluation Form shown in Figure E8.2. Mike Crowe is enthusiastic about the project and wants to know when the report will be in production. Dot is similarly impressed.

Several changes come up. Mike wants an area to write in the Completion Date of the preventive maintenance so the report can be used to reenter the dates into the computer. Dot wants the report number assigned by data control to appear at the top of the form for reference purposes. She also suggests that the report title be changed to WEEKLY PREVENTIVE MAINTENANCE REPORT. The next step is to modify the prototype report to reflect the recommended changes, then have both Mike and Dot review the result.

The report is easily modified and printed. Dot is pleased with the final result. "This is really a fine method for designing the system," she comments. "It's so nice to feel that we are a part of the development process and that our opinions count. I'm starting to feel quite confident that the final system will be just what we've always wanted."

Mike has similar praise, observing, "This will make our work so much smoother. It eliminates the guesswork about which machines need to be maintained. And sequencing them by room is a fine idea. We won't have to spend so much time returning to rooms to work on machines."

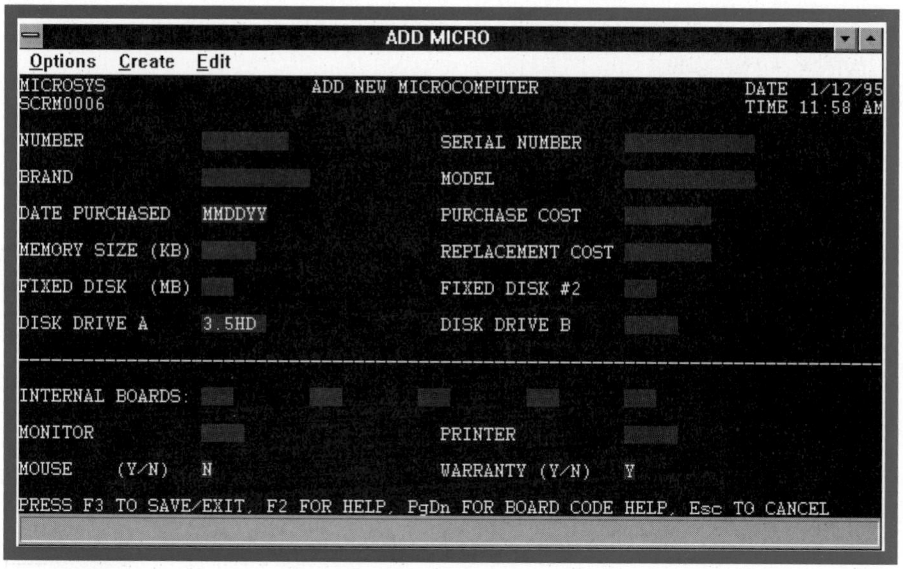

FIGURE E8.3
Design drawing screen, ADD NEW MICROCOMPUTER.

Chip and Anna next turned their attention to screen prototypes. "Since I like the hardware aspect of the system, why don't I start working on the Add New Microcomputer screen design," offers Chip.

"Sounds good to me," Anna replies. "I'll focus on the software aspects."

Chip analyzes the results of detailed interviews with Dot and Mike. He compiles a list of elements that each user would need when adding a microcomputer. Other elements, such as location and maintenance information, would update the MICROCOMPUTER MASTER later, after the machine was installed.

Excelerator's design screen, with the completed ADD NEW MICRO-COMPUTER prototype, is shown in Figure E8.3. Placed on the top of the screen are the current date and time as well as a centered screen title. Field captions are placed on the screen, with the left characters aligned. After all the captions are on the screen, Chip uses Excelerator's **FIELD** option to transfer XLDictionary element description to the screen.

A **FIELD DEFINITION SCREEN** area is displayed on the bottom of the screen, as shown in Figure E8.4. There are areas for a **Field Name** and for control of screen attributes such as **Bright** (high intensity), **Reverse** (reverse video), **Underline,** and **Blink.** The **Default** contains any information that should appear in the data field when the screen is first displayed. **Edit rules** limit what may be entered, and the **Help** message will display if the function key F2 is pressed.

"Having data dictionary elements defined sure helps to make quick prototypes," Chip comments. "It didn't take very long to complete the screen. Would you like to watch me test the prototype?"

"Sure," replies Anna. "This is my favorite part of prototyping."

Chip uses Excelerator to execute the screen design. Anna, Mike, and Dot watch as the screen is displayed, and Chip easily enters data.

"I really like this," Dot says. "May I try adding some data?"

"Be my guest," replies Chip. "Try to add both invalid and valid data. And be sure to press F2 to view some of the help messages."

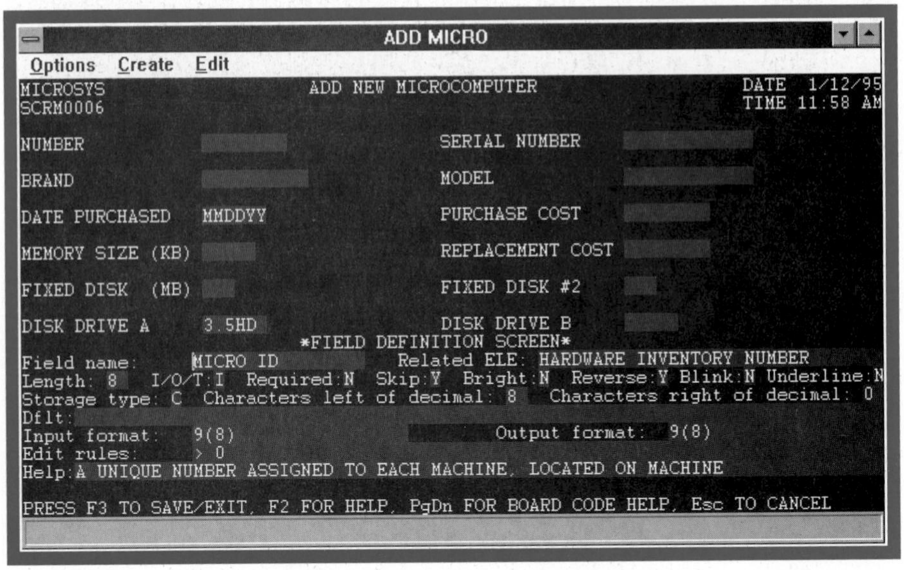

FIGURE E8.4
Design Field Definition screen, ADD NEW MICROCOMPUTER.

Dot is plainly enjoying herself as she enters data and tests the screen. Mike also spends time testing the screen. Both users state that they have a good understanding of the system and how it will operate when complete. Enthusiasm for the project is taking on a life of its own. Figure E8.5 is an example of the ADD NEW MICROCOMPUTER screen showing test data.

Anna returns to her desk and creates the ADD SOFTWARE RECORD screen design. The process is considerably slower, since she has not cre-

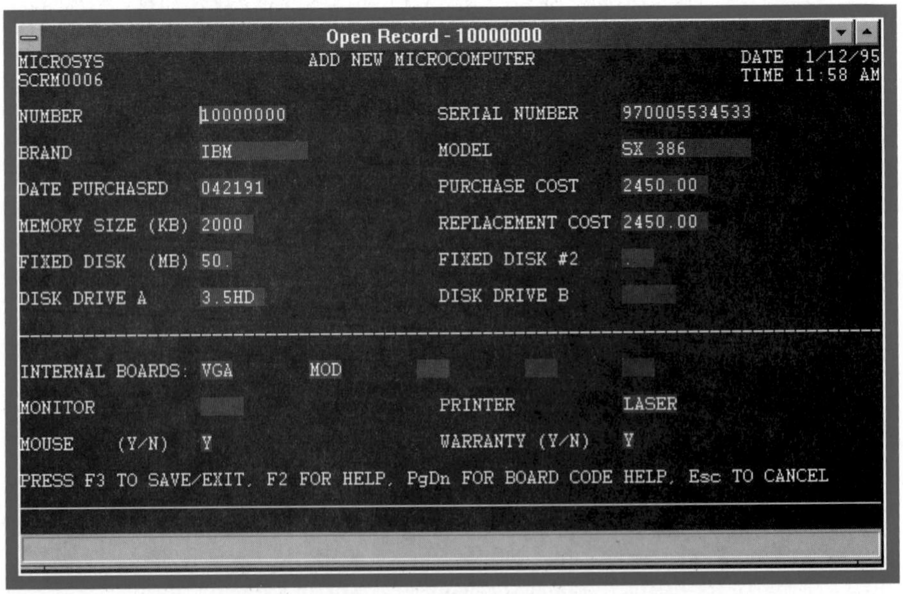

FIGURE E8.5
ADD NEW MICROCOMPUTER screen design with test data.

```
┌─────────────────────────────────────────────────────────────────────┐
│ ═      │            ADD SOFTWARE REC              │           ▼ ▲     │
│  Options   Create   Edit                                              │
│ MICROSYS                   ADD SOFTWARE RECORD            DATE 01/15/95│
│ SCRM0007                                                  TIME 11:01 AM│
│                                                                        │
│ NUMBER            ▓▓▓▓▓                                                │
│                                                                        │
│ TITLE             ▓▓▓▓▓▓▓▓▓▓▓▓▓▓▓▓      VERSION    ▓▓▓▓▓              │
│                                                                        │
│ PUBLISHER         ▓▓▓▓▓▓▓▓▓▓▓▓▓▓▓▓      CATEGORY   ▓▓▓▓              │
│                                                                        │
│ NUM. DISKETTES    ▓▓▓                   DISK SIZE  ▓▓▓               │
│                                                                        │
│ SITE LICENSE   N                        NUM COPIES 1 ▓               │
│ ─────────────────────────────────────────────────────────────────── │
│                   HARDWARE REQUIRED FOR SOFTWARE                       │
│                                                                        │
│ COMPUTER BRAND    ▓▓▓▓▓▓▓            MODEL        ▓▓▓▓▓▓▓            │
│                                                                        │
│ MEMORY REQD.      ▓▓▓▓                                                 │
│                                                                        │
│ MONITOR           ▓▓▓               PRINTER       ▓▓▓                │
│                                                                        │
│ XXXXXXXXXXXXXXXXXXXX  OPERATOR MESSAGE XXXXXXXXXXXXXXXXXXXXXXXXXXXXXXX │
│ XXXXXXXXXXXXXXXXXXXX  ERROR MESSAGE   XXXXXXXXXXXXXXXXXXXXXXXXXXXXXXXX │
└─────────────────────────────────────────────────────────────────────┘
```

FIGURE E8.6
ADD SOFTWARE RECORD prototype screen.

ated any data dictionary elements for software fields. As she describes each field on the screen, the length, help messages, pictures, and other attributes must be entered.

When Anna completes the screen design, she asks Cher to test the prototype. Cher keys information in, exercises the editing criteria, and views help messages.

"I really like the design of this screen and how it looks," remarks Cher. "However, it lacks some of the fields that would normally be included when a software package is entered, like the computer brand and model that the software runs on, the memory required, monitor, and the printer or plotter required."

"Those are all doable. I'll make the changes and get back to you," replies Anna, making some notes to herself.

A short time later, Cher again tests the ADD SOFTWARE RECORD screen. It includes all of the features that she requires. The completed screen design is shown in Figure E8.6. Notice that there is a line separating the software information from the hardware entries required.

"Watch this, Chip!" calls Anna. Chip walks over to Anna's desk. "With Excelerator's **Transform** feature, I can create data dictionary entries from the screen design."

As the **Transform** feature is invoked, an action screen provides feedback on the record and elements that are created. An example, using the ADD SOFTWARE RECORD screen design, is shown in Figure E8.7. After Anna confirms that all the entries are correct, the XLDictionary entries are created from the screen design. The entries with an action of **Skip** are ignored, since they already exist in the dictionary.

Anna and Chip continued to work on prototypes by designing, obtaining user feedback, and modifying the design to accommodate user changes. Now that the work is complete, they have a solid sense of the requirements of the system.

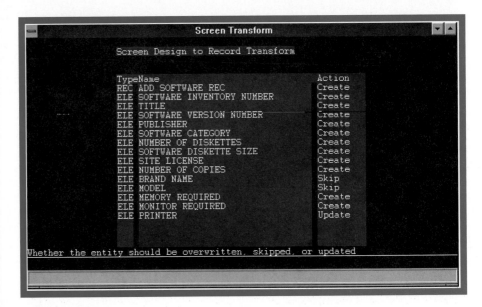

FIGURE E8.7
Transform Action screen.

Exercises*

Modify or create the report and screen prototypes for the following problems. Have your instructor or team member review the prototypes and suggest appropriate changes. Record the changes on a copy of the Prototype Evaluation Form (see Figure E8.2). Modify and print the final prototypes.

⊟ **E-1.** Use Excelerator to view the ADD MICRO/screen design prototype.

⊟ **E-2.** Modify the Preventive Maintenance Report prototype with the changes suggested by Mike and Dot.

⊟ **E-3.** Modify the Hardware Inventory Listing Report. Add the date and page number. Use the COLUMN feature to propagate all columns downward except the campus and room location. Include the total number of machines at the bottom of the report. Remember that the report should have page breaks for each room.

⊟ **E-4.** Modify the Software Investment Report. Add the date and page number. Use the REPEAT feature to create a block of columns filling the page. Each line on the report should be double spaced. The last line of the report should contain a count of the number of unique software titles and a grand total invested for all software.

---

* The exercises preceded by a disk icon require the program Excelerator (or another CASE tool). A disk is provided free of charge to any professor adopting this book. The examples on the disk may be imported into Excelerator and then used by students.

🖫 **E-5.** Modify the Installed Microcomputer Report. Add the following new columns to the right of the partially completed report:

MEMORY	DISK DRIVE A	DISK DRIVE B
FIXED DISK	FIXED DISK 2	MONITOR
PRINTER	MOUSE	BOARDS (Up to 5)

🖫 **E-6.** Create a prototype for Microcomputer Problem Report containing the following elements. The report should be produced for all microcomputers whose repair costs are over a predetermined limit.

HARDWARE INVENTORY NUMBER	BRAND NAME NUMBER OF REPAIRS
MODEL	WARRANTY
COST OF REPAIRS	TOTAL NUMBER OF
TOTAL COSTS	MACHINES

🖫 **E-7.** Produce the Software Installation Listing. Elements on the report are:

SOFTWARE INVENTORY NUMBER	TITLE NUMBER OF DISKETTES
VERSION NUMBER	HARDWARE INVENTORY
DISKETTE SIZE	NUMBER
CAMPUS LOCATION	ROOM LOCATION

🖫 **E-8.** Create the prototype for the Software Cross-Reference Report, showing on which machines each software package is located. The elements are:

TITLE	VERSION NUMBER
PUBLISHER	CAMPUS LOCATION
ROOM LOCATION	HARDWARE INVENTORY
BRAND NAME	NUMBER
	MODEL

Group print the TITLE, VERSION NUMBER, and PUBLISHER. For each group, print the total number of software copies available.

🖫 **E-9.** Modify the DELETE MICRO/screen design. Print and test the final result. The screen displays an entry area for the MICRO-COMPUTER INVENTORY NUMBER. Once the number is keyed, the program obtains a matching record and displays identifying information on the screen. The entry area has been created and captions are included on the screen. Complete the design by adding the following data fields to the right of the captions, aligned under the INVENTORY NUMBER: SERIAL NUMBER, BRAND, MODEL, DATE PURCHASED, MEMORY SIZE, CAM-PUS, and ROOM LOCATION. Change the OPERATOR MESSAGE to "PRESS ENTER TO DELETE RECORD, F1 TO CANCEL."

🖫 **E-10.** Mike Crowe needs a screen to enable him to change maintenance information about microcomputers. Sometimes these are routine changes, such as the LAST PREVENTIVE MAINTE-NANCE DATE or the NUMBER OF REPAIRS, but other changes may occur only sporadically, such as the expiration of a warranty. The HARDWARE INVENTORY NUMBER is entered, and the matching MICROCOMPUTER RECORD is read. The BRAND and MODEL are displayed for feedback. The operator may then change the WARRANTY, MAINTENANCE INTERVAL, NUMBER OF REPAIRS, LAST PREVENTIVE MAINTENANCE DATE, and TOTAL COST OF REPAIRS. The screen design has been partially completed with entry area and captions. Your task is to modify the UPDATE/MAINT Information screen design. Add the data fields to the right of the captions to finish the screen. Save and print the design. Review the finished product with your teammates or instructor.

E-11. Cher Ware would like a screen that would enable her to delete obsolete software, such as older versions of word-processing or database programs. The DELETE SOFTWARE screen is partially completed with an entry area for the SOFTWARE INVENTORY NUMBER. Add captions and data field areas for TITLE, VERSION, PUBLISHER, and SITE LICENSE. Print your design and have fellow students or your instructor critique the final result.

E-12. Create and test the Update Microcomputer Record screen. The screen elements are:

HARDWARE INVENTORY NUMBER	BRAND NAME
	ROOM LOCATION
CAMPUS LOCATION	MOUSE
FIXED DISK 2	BOARDS INSTALLED
PRINTER	(Up to 5 boards)

E-13. Build and test the Change Microcomputer Record prototype. This screen should allow the user to change all information on the Microcomputer Master except the primary key, HARDWARE INVENTORY NUMBER. Since there are many elements on the master file, create two linked screen.

E-14. Design a screen to enter Software Expert records. Software experts are persons within the university who have expertise in the particular software package and may be queried for advice. The screen design elements are:

EXPERT NAME	EXPERT TELEPHONE
EXPERT CAMPUS	EXPERT ROOM
EXPERT DEPARTMENT	LOCATION
EXPERT EMPLOYEE NUMBER	EXPERT TITLE
	SOFTWARE TITLE
VERSION NUMBER (*Note:* Use ALL as a default)	

Use the Transform option to create the XLDictionary record and elements for the Expert, Skip all elements that currently exist in the XLDictionary.

E-15. Design the Software Location Inquiry screen. The screen entry field is the TITLE and VERSION NUMBER. The output portion of the screen consists of a series of lines, with each line containing the CAMPUS LOCATION, ROOM LOCATION, HARDWARE

INVENTORY NUMBER, BRAND NAME, and MODEL. A message should be displayed informing the operator that there is another page of information.

⊟ **E-16.** Construct the Hardware Characteristic Inquiry screen design. The entry fields are BRAND NAME, GRAPHICS TYPE, MONITOR, and PRINTER. Entries may be placed in one or more of these fields to locate the corresponding records. The display portion of the inquiry screen consists of CAMPUS LOCATION, ROOM LOCATION, and HARDWARE INVENTORY NUMBER.

## 9

USING DATA FLOW DIAGRAMS

The systems analyst needs to make use of the conceptual freedom afforded by data flow diagrams (DFD), which graphically characterize data processes and flows in a business system. In their original state, data flow diagrams depict the broadest possible overview of system inputs, processes, and outputs, which correspond to those of the general systems model discussed in Chapter 2. A series of layered data flow diagrams may also be used to represent and analyze detailed procedures within the larger system.

THE DATA FLOW APPROACH TO REQUIREMENTS DETERMINATION

When systems analysts attempt to understand the information requirements of users, they must be able to conceptualize how data moves through the organization, the processes or transformation that the data undergoes, and what the outputs are. Although interviews and investigation of hard data provide a verbal narrative of the system, a visual depiction can crystallize this information in a useful way.

Through a structured analysis technique called data flow diagrams (DFD), the systems analyst can put together a graphical representation of data processes throughout the organization. The data flow approach emphasizes the logic underlying the system. By using combinations of only four symbols, the systems analyst can create a pictorial depiction of processes that will eventually provide solid system documentation.

Advantages of the Data Flow Approach

The data flow approach has four chief advantages over narrative explanations of the way data moves through the system. The advantages are:

1. Freedom from committing to the technical implementation of the system too early.
2. Further understanding of the interrelatedness of systems and subsystems.

3. Communicating current system knowledge to users through data flow diagrams.
4. Analysis of a proposed system to determine if the necessary data and processes have been defined.

Perhaps the biggest advantage lies in the conceptual freedom found in the use of the four symbols (which are covered in the upcoming section on DFD conventions). None of the symbols specifies the physical aspects of implementation. For instance, although an analyst will signify that data are stored at a particular point, the data flow approach does not dictate specifying the medium for storage. This allows the systems analyst to conceptualize necessary data flows and to avoid committing too quickly to their technical realization.

The data flow approach has the additional advantage of serving as a useful exercise for systems analysts, enabling them to better understand the interrelatedness of the system and its subsystems. Recall that in Chapter 2 we stressed the importance of being able to differentiate the system from its environment by locating its boundaries. It requires discipline and true understanding to conceptualize the system in a broad overview and then explode it into its functional subsystems.

A third advantage of the data flow approach is that it can be used as a tool to interact with users. An interesting use of DFD is to show them to users as incomplete representations of the analyst's understanding of the system. Users can then be asked to comment on the accuracy of the analyst's conceptualization, and the analyst can incorporate changes that more accurately reflect the system from the users' perspectives.

Although many texts tout the ease of communicating to users through data flow diagrams, this does not occur automatically. If you want to use DFD for interaction, you must assume responsibility for educating users about their purposes. Necessary background must be provided to users before data flow diagrams will be meaningful rather than confusing.

The last advantage of using data flow diagrams is that they allow analysts to describe each component used in the diagram. Analysis can then be performed to ensure that all necessary output may be obtained from the input data and processing logic reflected in the diagram. Detecting and correcting errors and design flaws of this nature in the earlier stages of the systems development life cycle is far less costly than in the later phases of programming, testing, and implementation.

Conventions Used in Data Flow Diagrams

Four basic symbols are used to chart data movement on data flow diagrams. They are a double square, an arrow, a rectangle with rounded corners, and an open-ended rectangle (closed on the left side and open-ended on the right), as shown in Figure 9.1. An entire system and numerous subsystems can be depicted graphically with these four symbols in combination.[1]

The double square is used to depict an external entity (another department, a business, a person, or a machine) that can send data to or receive data from the system. The external entity is also called a source or destination of data, and is considered to be external to the study. Each external entity is labeled with an appropriate name. Although it interacts with the system, it is

---

[1] Diagramming symbols used for data flow diagrams are based on work by C. Gane and T. Sarson. *Structured Systems Analysis and Design Tools and Techniques* (Englewood Cliffs, N.J.: Prentice-Hall, Inc., 1979).

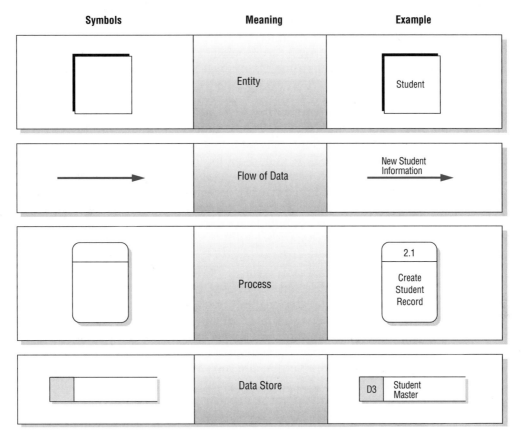

Symbols	Meaning	Example
	Entity	Student
→	Flow of Data	New Student Information →
	Process	2.1 Create Student Record
	Data Store	D3 Student Master

FIGURE 9.1
The four basic symbols used in data flow diagrams, their meanings, and examples.

considered as external to the boundaries of the system. External entities should be named with a noun. The same external entity may be used more than once on a given data flow diagram to avoid crossing data flow lines.

The arrow shows movement of data from one point to another, with the head of the arrow pointing toward the data's destination. Data flows occurring simultaneously can be depicted doing just that through the use of parallel arrows. Since an arrow represents data about a person, place, or thing, it too should be described with a noun.

A rectangle with rounded corners is used to show the occurrence of a transforming process. Processes always denote a change in or transformation of data; hence, the data flow leaving a process is *always* labeled differently from the one entering it. Processes represent work being performed within the system and should be named using one of the following formats. A clear name makes it easier to understand what the process is accomplishing.

1. Assign the name of the whole system when naming a high-level process. An example is INVENTORY CONTROL SYSTEM.

2. To name a major subsystem, use a name such as INVENTORY REPORTING SUBSYSTEM.

3. Use a verb-adjective-noun format for detailed processes. The verb describes the type of activity, for example, COMPUTE, VERIFY, PREPARE, PRINT, or ADD. The noun indicates what the major outcome of the process is, for instance, REPORT or RECORD. The adjective

illustrates which specific output such as BACKORDERED or INVENTORY, is produced. Examples of complete process names are: COMPUTE SALES TAX, VERIFY CUSTOMER ACCOUNT STATUS, PREPARE SHIPPING INVOICE, PRINT BACKORDERED REPORT, and ADD INVENTORY RECORD.

Processes must also be given a unique identifying number indicating the level of the diagram. This organization is discussed later in this chapter. Several data flows may go into and out of each process. Examine processes with a single flow in and out for missing data flows.

The last basic symbol used in data flow diagrams represents a data store and is an open-ended rectangle. This is drawn with two parallel lines, which are closed by a short line on the left side and open-ended on the right. These symbols are drawn only wide enough to allow identifying lettering between the parallel lines. In data flow diagrams, the type of physical storage (for example, tape, diskette, etc.) is not specified. At this point, the data store symbol is simply showing a depository for data that allows addition and retrieval of data.

The data store may represent a manual store, such as a filing cabinet, or a computerized file or database. Since data stores represent a person, place or thing, they are named using a noun. Temporary data stores, such as scratch paper or a temporary computer file are not included on the data flow diagram. Neither are any blank forms or blank diskettes included, even though they may be necessary for a business activity. Give each data store a unique reference number, such as D1, D2, D3, and so on to identify its level as described in the following section.

DEVELOPING DATA FLOW DIAGRAMS

Data flow diagrams can and should be drawn systematically. Figure 9.2 summarizes the steps involved in successfully completing data flow diagrams. First, the systems analyst needs to conceptualize data flows from a top-down perspective.

To begin a data flow diagram, collapse the organization's system narrative into a list with the four categories of external entity, data flow, process, and data store. This list in turn helps determine the boundaries of the system you will be describing. Once a basic list of data elements has been compiled, begin drawing a context diagram.

Creating the Context Diagram

With a top-down approach to diagramming data movement, the diagrams move from general to specific. While the first diagram helps the systems analyst grasp basic data movement, its general nature limits it usefulness. The initial context diagram should be an overview including basic inputs, the general system, and outputs. This will be the most general diagram—really a bird's-eye view of data movement in the system and the broadest possible conceptualization of the system.

The context diagram is the highest level in a data flow diagram and contains only one process, representing the entire system. The process is given the number zero. All external entities are shown on the context diagram, as well as major data flow to and from them. The diagram does not contain any data stores and is fairly simple to create, once the external entities and the data flow to and from them are known to analysts from interviews with users and document analysis.

FIGURE 9.2
Steps in developing data flow
diagrams.

**Developing Data Flow Diagrams
Using A Top-Down Approach**

✓ 1   Make a list of business activities and use it to determine various
   - External Entities
   - Data Flows
   - Processes
   - Data Stores

✓ 2   Create a context diagram which shows external entities and data flows to and from the system. Do not show any detailed processes or data stores.

3   Draw Diagram 0, the next level. Show processes, but keep them general. Show data stores at this level.

4   Create a child diagram for each of the processes in Diagram 0.

5   Check for errors and make sure the labels you assign to each process and data flow are meaningful.

6   Develop a physical data flow diagram from the logical data flow diagram. Distinguish between manual and automated processes, describe actual files and reports by name, and add controls to indicate when processes are complete or errors occur.

7   Partition the physical data flow diagram by separating or grouping parts of the diagram in order to facilitate programming and implementation.

Drawing Diagram 0 (The Next Level)

More detail than the context diagram permits is achievable by "exploding the diagrams." Inputs and outputs specified in the first diagram remain constant in all subsequent diagrams. However, the rest of the original diagram is exploded into close-ups involving three to nine processes and showing data stores and new lower-level data flows. The effect is that of taking a magnifying glass to view the original data flow diagram. Each exploded diagram should use only a single sheet of paper. By exploding DFDs into subprocesses, the systems analyst begins to fill in the details about data movement. The handling of exceptions is ignored for the first  two or three levels of data flow diagramming.

Diagram 0 is the explosion of the context diagram and may include up to nine processes. Including more processes at this level will result in a cluttered diagram that is difficult to understand. Each process is numbered with an integer, generally starting from the upper left-hand corner of the diagram and working toward the lower right-hand corner. The major data stores of the system (representing master files) and all external entities are included on Diagram 0. Figure 9.3 schematically illustrates both the context diagram and Diagram 0.

FIGURE 9.3
Context diagrams (above) can
be "exploded" into Diagram 0
(below). Note the greater
detail in Diagram 0.

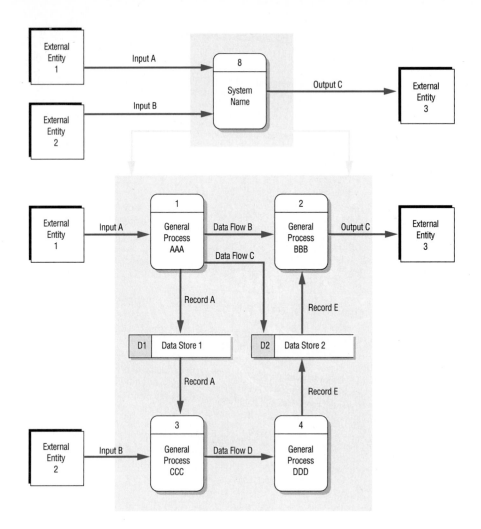

Since a data flow diagram is two-dimensional (rather than linear), you
may start at any point and work forward or backward through the diagram. If
you are unsure of what you would include at any point, take a different external entity, process, or data store and start drawing the flow from it. You may:

1. Start with the data flow from an external entity on the input side. Ask
   questions, such as: What happens to the data entering the system? Is
   it stored? Is it input to several processes?

2. Work backwards from an output data flow. Examine the output fields
   on a document or screen. (This approach is easier if prototypes have
   been created.) For each field on the output, ask: Where does it come
   from? Is it calculated or stored on a file? For example, when the output is a PAYCHECK, the EMPLOYEE NAME and ADDRESS would be
   located on an EMPLOYEE file, the HOURS WORKED would be on a
   TIME RECORD, and the GROSS PAY and DEDUCTIONS would be
   calculated. Each file and record would be connected to the process
   that produces the paycheck.

3. Examine the data flow to or from a data store. Ask: What processes
   put data into the store? What processes use the data? Note that a data
   store used in the system you are working on may be produced by a

Go with the Flow

"Let's see. We've got a clerk adding up the day's receipts from the cash register tape by calculator. After she adds them initially, she separates them into separate departments including juvenile, maternity, and infants. Then she gives her departmental subtotals and total on scratch paper to me," says Luis Asperilla.

Pamela Coburn, a systems analyst who is working with a group of twenty-six franchise clothing stores called Bonton's, is talking to the South Street store's manager, Luis, trying to understand the data flows within the store. Luis continues the narrative: "Then I recheck the day's receipts, looking for any discrepancies. Next, I enter the day's breakdown of the day's receipts, their departments, and the total day's receipts, into the ledger, and fill out the deposit for the bank. All daily receipt information is stored in one place, in the ledger in my office."

Pamela asks, "Do you keep a copy anywhere?" Luis pauses, then replies, "Well, there is a weekly report that summarizes all of the weekly information for the head of the franchising in New York. They enter it into their computers and we get sent a printout at the end of the month. So if I wait five weeks, I do in effect get a copy back. Except that I keep the printouts and reconcile it against my own monthly summary that I do by hand. You'd be surprised at how often there is a mistake in what they send back. Then I write them a letter and try to get it corrected so my six-month inventories come out right. I keep copies of all correspondence to New York in a file drawer. I'm always writing to them on something they've screwed up. And I need a copy to prove I sent in a correction."

Luis continues, "Computers in New York seem worth it, I suppose, but I think they introduce an awful lot of errors if you don't use common sense when you enter the numbers in. But the ledger book does get heavy to pull down from the shelf by the end of the year."

"I keep a lot of what happens in the store in my head, too," Luis adds thoughtfully. "It's so hard to write everything down, we get so busy. Like which customers are allowed layaway privileges and that. I keep a few notes in my desk. I think you'll find that I'm really organized compared to the other managers in town."

What are the advantages of drawing a data flow diagram of Luis' description of the store's data flows? What are some of the specific physical barriers to implementation that Pamela can overcome by representing the store's data flow in a data flow diagram?

different system. Thus, from your vantage point, there may not be any data flow into the data store.

4. Analyze a well-defined process. Look at what input data the process needs and what output it produces. Then connect the input and output to the appropriate data stores and external entities.

5. Take note of any fuzzy areas where you are unsure of what should be included, or what input or output is required. Awareness of problem areas will help you formulate a list of questions for follow-up interviews with key users.

Creating Child Diagrams (More Detailed Levels)

Each process on Diagram 0 may in turn be exploded to create a more detailed child diagram. The process on Diagram 0 that is exploded is called the *parent process*, and the diagram that results is called the *child diagram*. The primary rule for creating child diagrams, vertical balancing, dictates that a child diagram cannot produce output or receive input that the parent process does not also produce or receive. All data flow in or out of the parent process must be shown flowing in or out of the child diagram.

The child diagram is given the same number as its parent process in Diagram 0. For example, process 3 would explode to Diagram 3. The processes on the child diagram are numbered using the parent process number, a decimal point, and a unique number for each child process. On Diagram 3, the processes would be numbered 3.1, 3.2, 3.3, and so on. This convention allows the analyst to trace a series of processes through many levels of explosion. If Diagram 0 depicts processes 1, 2, and 3, then the child diagrams 1, 2, and 3 are all on the same level.

External entities are usually not shown on the child diagrams below Diagram 0. Data flow that matches the parent flow is called an *interface data flow* and is shown as an arrow from or into a blank area of the child diagram. If the parent process has data flow connecting to a data store, the child diagram may include the data store as well. Additionally, this lower-level diagram may contain data stores not shown on the parent process. For example, a file containing a table of information such as a tax table, or a file linking two processes on the child diagram may be included. Minor data flow, such as an error line, may be included on a child diagram but not on the parent.

Processes may or may not be exploded, depending on their level of complexity. When a process is not exploded, it is said to be functionally primitive and is called a *primitive process*. Logic is written to describe these processes and will be discussed in detail in Chapter 11. Figure 9.4 illustrates detailed levels within a child data flow diagram.

Checking the Diagrams for Errors

Numerous errors may occur when drawing flow diagrams. Some of the more common mistakes are shown in Figure 9.5.

It is useful to see how mistakes can come about in a data flow diagram. Figure 9.6 is an example of a data flow diagram that, if implemented, would produce an employee paycheck with many flaws. Several common errors made when drawing data flow diagrams are:

1. Forgetting to include a data flow or pointing an arrowhead in the wrong direction. An example is a process drawn showing all of its data flow as input or as output. Each process transforms data and must receive input and produce output. Usually this type of error occurs when the analyst has forgotten to include a data flow or placed an arrowhead pointing in the wrong direction. Process 1 has only input because the GROSS PAY arrow is pointing in the wrong direction. This error also affects Process 2, CALCULATE WITHHOLDING AMOUNT, which is additionally missing a data flow representing input for the withholding rates and the number of dependents.

2. Connecting data stores and external entities directly to each other. Data stores and entities may not be connected to each other; data stores and external entities must connect only with a process. A file does not interface with another file without the help of a program or a person moving the data, so the EMPLOYEE MASTER cannot directly produce the CHECK RECONCILIATION file. External entities do not directly work with files. For example, you would not want a customer rummaging around in the customer master file. Thus in Figure 9.6 the EMPLOYEE does not create the EMPLOYEE TIME FILE. If two external entities are directly connected, it indicates that they wish to communicate with each other. This connection is not included on the data flow diagram unless the system is facilitating the communication. Producing a report is an instance of this sort of communication. However, a process must still be interposed between the entities to produce the report.

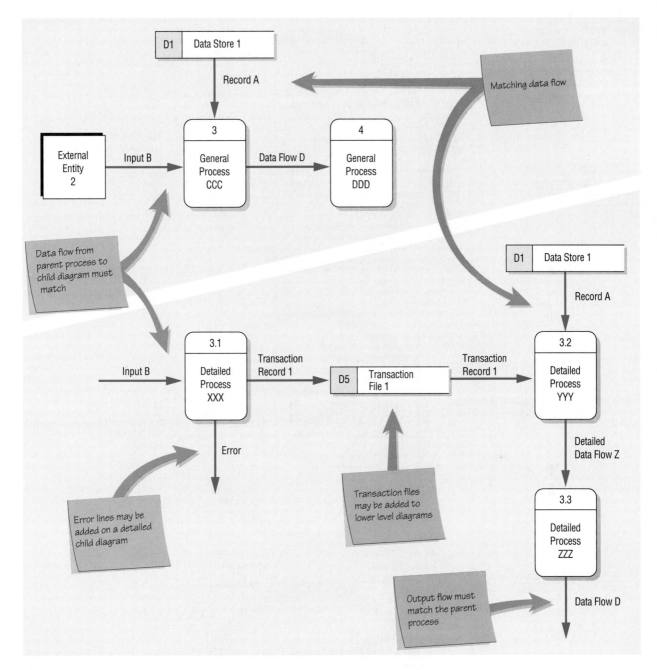

FIGURE 9.4
Differences between the parent diagram (above) and the child diagram (below).

3. Incorrectly labeling processes and/or data flow. Inspect the data flow diagram to ensure that each object or data flow is properly labeled. A process should indicate the system name or use the verb-adjective-noun format. Each data flow should be described with a noun.

4. Including more than nine processes on a data flow diagram. This creates a cluttered diagram that is confusing to read and hinders rather then enhances communication. If more than nine processes are involved in a system, group some of the processes that work together into a subsystem and place them in a child diagram.

FIGURE 9.5
Don't break the rules when
drawing data flow diagrams.

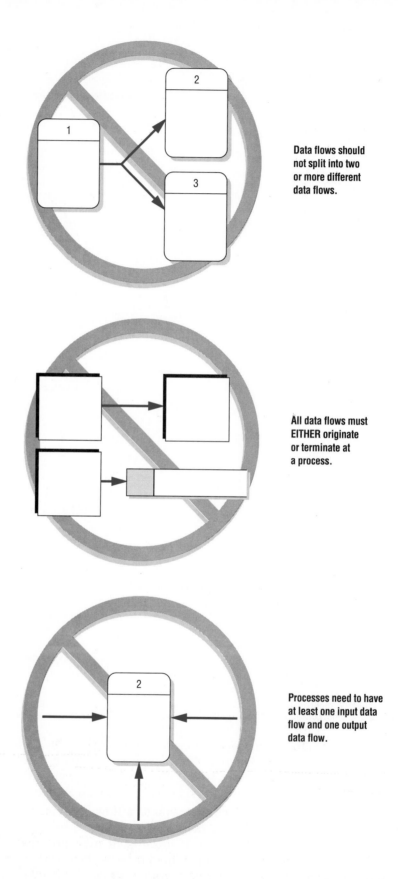

Data flows should
not split into two
or more different
data flows.

All data flows must
EITHER originate
or terminate at
a process.

Processes need to have
at least one input data
flow and one output
data flow.

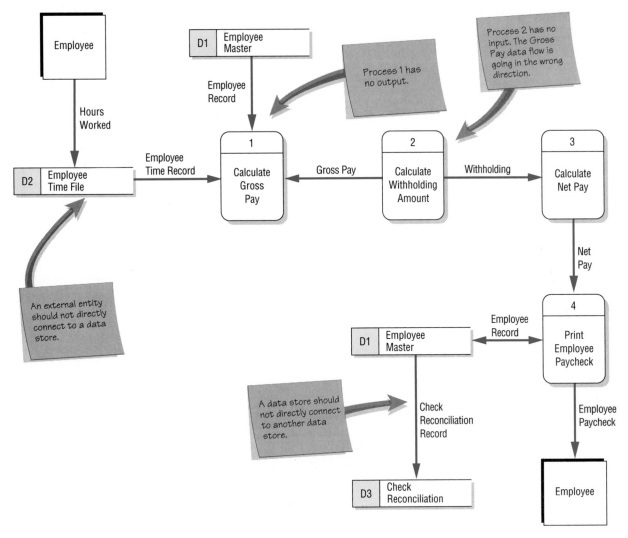

FIGURE 9.6
Typical errors that can occur in a data flow diagram (payroll example).

5. Omitting data flow. Examine your diagram for linear flow, that is, data flow where each process has only one input and one output. Except in the case of very detailed child data flow diagrams, linear data flow is somewhat rare. Its presence usually indicates that the diagram has missing data flow. For instance, in Figure 9.6 the process CALCULATE WITHHOLDING AMOUNT needs the number of dependents that an employee has and the WITHHOLDING RATES as input. In addition, NET PAY cannot be calculated solely from the WITHHOLDING, and the PAYCHECK cannot be created from the NET PAY alone. It also needs to include an EMPLOYEE NAME and the current and year-to-date payroll and WITHHOLDING figures.

6. Creating unbalanced decomposition in child diagrams. Each child diagram should have the same input and output data flow as the parent process. An exception to this rule is minor output, such as error lines, which are included only on the child diagram. The data flow diagram in Figure 9.7 is correctly drawn. Note that, though the data

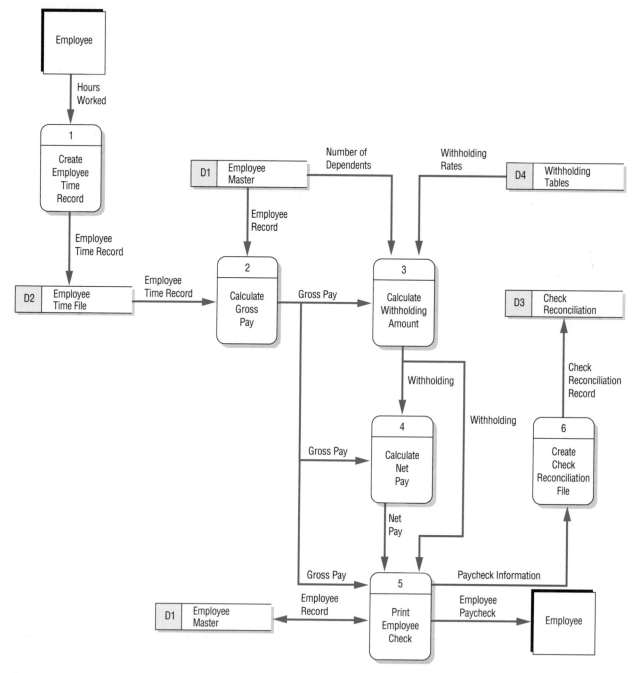

FIGURE 9.7
The correct data flow diagram for the payroll example.

flow is not linear, you can clearly follow a path directly from the source entity to the destination entity.

LOGICAL AND PHYSICAL DATA FLOW DIAGRAMS

Data flow diagrams are categorized as either logical or physical. A logical data flow diagram focuses on the business and how the business operates. It is not concerned with how the system will be constructed. Instead, it

Design Feature	Logical	Physical
What the model depicts	How the business operates	How hue system will be implemented (or how the current system operates)
What the processes represent	Business activities	Programs, program modules and manual procedures
What the data stores represent	Collections of data, regardless of how the data is stored	Physical files and databases, manual files
Type of data stores	Show data stores representing permanent data collections	Master files, transaction files. Any processes that operate at two different times must be connected by a data store
System controls	Show business controls	Show controls for validating input data, for obtaining a record (record found status), for ensuring successful completion of a process and for system security (example: journal records)

FIGURE 9.8
Features common of logical and physical data flow diagrams.

describes the business events that take place and the data required and produced by each event. Conversely, a physical data flow diagram shows how the system will be implemented, including the hardware, software, files, and people involved in the system. The chart shown in Figure 9.8 contrasts the features of logical and physical models. Notice that the logical model reflects the business, while the physical model depicts the system.

Ideally, systems are developed by analyzing the current system (the current logical DFD), then adding features that the new system should include (the proposed logical DFD). Finally the best methods to implement the new system should be developed (the physical DFD).

Developing a logical data flow diagram for the current system affords you a clear understanding of how the current system operates and thus a good starting point for developing the logical model of the current system. This time-consuming step is often omitted in order to go straight to the proposed logical DFD.

One argument in favor of taking the time to construct the logical data flow diagram of the current system is that it can be used to create the logical data flow diagram of the new system. Processes that will be unnecessary in the new system may be dropped and new features, activities, output, input, and stored data may be added. This approach provides a means of ensuring that the essential features of the old system are retained in the new system. Additionally, using the logical model for the current system as a basis for the proposed system provides for a gradual transition to the design of the new system. After the logical model for the new system has

FIGURE 9.9
The progression of models
from logical to physical.

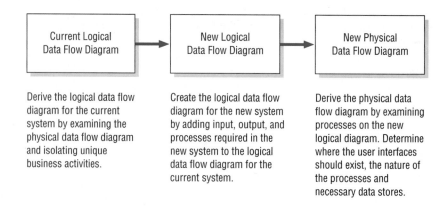

Current Logical Data Flow Diagram	New Logical Data Flow Diagram	New Physical Data Flow Diagram
Derive the logical data flow diagram for the current system by examining the physical data flow diagram and isolating unique business activities.	Create the logical data flow diagram for the new system by adding input, output, and processes required in the new system to the logical data flow diagram for the current system.	Derive the physical data flow diagram by examining processes on the new logical diagram. Determine where the user interfaces should exist, the nature of the processes and necessary data stores.

been developed, it may be used to create a physical data flow diagram for the new system. The progression of these models is illustrated in Figure 9.9.

Figure 9.10 shows a logical data flow diagram and a physical data flow diagram for a grocery store cashier. The CUSTOMER brings the ITEMS to the register; PRICES for all ITEMS are LOOKED UP, and then totaled; next, PAYMENT is given to the cashier; finally, the CUSTOMER is given a receipt. The logical data flow diagram illustrates the processes involved without going into detail about the physical implementation of activities. The physical data flow diagram shows that a bar code—the UPC PRICE code found on most grocery store items—is used. In addition, the physical data flow diagram mentions manual processes such as scanning, explains that a temporary file is used to keep a subtotal of items, and indicates that the PAYMENT could be made by CASH, CHECK, or DEBIT CARD. Finally, it refers to the receipt by its name, CASH REGISTER RECEIPT.

Developing Logical Data Flow Diagrams

First, construct a logical data flow diagram for the current system. There are a number of advantages to using a logical model, including:

1. Better communication with users
2. More stable systems
3. Better understanding of the business by analysts
4. Flexibility and maintenance
5. Elimination of redundancies and easier creation of the physical model

A logical model is easier to use when communicating with users of the system because it is centered on business activities. Users will thus be familiar with the essential activities and many of the information requirements of each activity.

Systems formed using a logical data flow diagram are often more stable than those that are not because they are based on business events and not on a particular technology or method of implementation. Logical data flow diagrams represent features of a system that would exist no matter what the physical means of doing business are. Examine the business activities listed for the FilmMagic video rental system in Figure 9.12. These will occur regardless of whether the system implemented is totally manual or fully automated. A logical data flow diagram has a business emphasis and helps the analyst to understand the business being studied, to grasp why procedures are performed, and to determine the expected result of performing a task.

Logical Data Flow Diagram

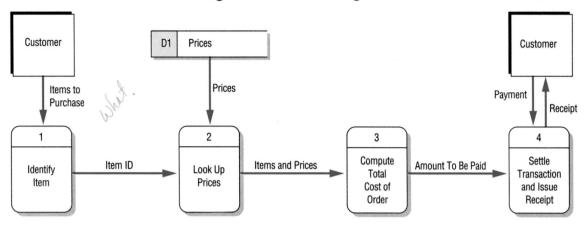

Physical Data Flow Diagram

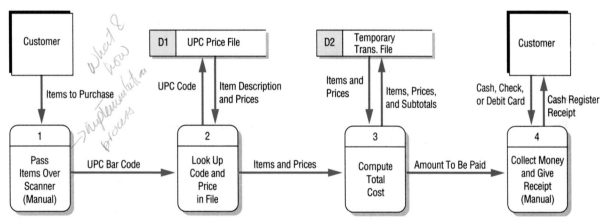

FIGURE 9.10
The physical data flow diagram (below) shows certain details not found on the logical data flow diagram (above).

The new system will be more flexible and easier to maintain if its design is based on a logical model. Business functions are not subject to frequent change. Physical aspects of the system change more frequently than do business functions.

Examining a logical model may help you to create a better system by eliminating redundancies and inefficient methods that exist in the current system. Additionally, the logical model is easy to create and simpler to use because it does not often contain data stores other than master files or a database.

Developing Physical Data Flow Diagrams

When the logical model of the new system is complete, it may be used to create a physical data flow diagram for the new system. The physical data

FIGURE 9.11
Physical data flow diagrams
contain many items not found
in logical data flow diagrams.

Contents of Physical Data Flow Diagrams

- Manual processes
- Processes for adding, deleting, changing, and updating records
- Data entry and verifying processes
- Validation processes for ensuring accurate data input
- Sequencing processes to rearrange the order of records
- Processes to produce every unique system output
- Intermediate data stores
- Actual file names used to store data
- Controls to signify completion of tasks or error conditions

flow diagram shows how the system will be constructed. Just as logical data flow diagrams have certain advantages, physical data flow diagrams have others, including:

1. Clarifying which processes are manual and which are automated
2. Describing processes in more detail than do logical DFDs
3. Sequencing processes that have to be done in a particular order
4. Identifying temporary data stores
5. Specifying actual names of files and printouts
6. Adding controls to ensure the processes are done properly

Figure 9.11 lists the contents of physical data flow diagrams. Notice that the list includes manual processes such as opening mail orders, creating a batch of forms for keying, visually inspecting a form, and so on. Also included are processes for adding, deleting, changing, and updating records. Each master file should link to one corresponding process for each of these tasks. Data entry processes such as keying (either batch or online) and verifying are also part of physical data flow diagrams.

Since much of the work performed in a system involves validation, such processes for ensuring accurate input should be included. It is estimated that 50–90 percent of program code is related to validation. Sequencing processes such as sorting and merging may also be included. Processes to produce every unique system output should be added, since each report or screen should be produced by a separate process.

Physical data flow diagrams also have intermediate data stores—often, a transaction file. Transaction or master files or a database are required to link any two processes that operate at different times. For example, a program may be used to process customer orders on a minute-by-minute basis. The information that program generates may then have to be stored on a monthly file for sending customer bills and on an annual file for producing an annual sales summary report. Also part of physical data flow diagrams are physical data stores. These are designated by the actual names of the files or database (for example, CUSTOMER MASTER FILE, rather than the label CUSTOMERS used on a logical data flow diagram), and may be further described by including the data set name, number of records, and other key attributes.

Controls are also included in physical data flow diagrams. Among them are: editing input data, "record found" status when accessing a file or database, security and backup controls such as a journal record, and batch update controls to ensure that files produced by one process are correctly transmitted to the next process. Make distinctions in the physical data flow diagram between which processes are manual and which are automated.

Manual processes should be documented with written procedures that instruct employees on how to accomplish the tasks at hand. Automated procedures require computer programs, either written in-house or purchased from a vendor. Processes that are automated should be described in the diagram either as on line or batch, and timing information may also be included. For example, an edit program must be run before an update program. Updates must be performed before producing a summary report. Note that because of such considerations a physical data flow diagram may appear more linear than a logical model.

Intermediate data stores often consist of transaction files used to store data between processes. Since most processes that require access to a given set of data are unlikely to execute at the same instant in time, transaction files must hold the data from one process to the next. An easily understood example of this concept is found in the everyday experience of grocery shopping. The activities are:

1. Selecting items from shelves
2. Checking out and paying the bill
3. Transporting the groceries home
4. Preparing a meal
5. Eating the meal

Each of these five activities would be represented by a separate process on a physical data flow diagram and occurs at a different time. For example, you would not typically transport the groceries home and eat them at the same time. Therefore a "transaction data store" is required to link each task. When you are selecting items, the transaction data store is the shopping cart. After the next process (checking out), the cart is unnecessary. The transaction data store linking checking out and transporting the groceries home is the shopping bag (cheaper than letting you take the cart home!). Bags are an inefficient way of storing the groceries once they are home, so cupboards and a refrigerator are used as a transaction data store between the activity of transporting the goods home and preparing the meal. Finally a plate, bowl, and cup are the link between preparing and eating the meal.

Create the physical data flow diagram for a system by analyzing its output and input. Determine which data fields or elements need to be keyed. These are called *base elements* and must be stored on a file. Elements that are not keyed but are rather the result of a calculation or logical operation are called *derived elements*. When examining the output, determine whether the information must immediately be displayed or made available to numerous users. The processes that produce such output are usually on line. Processes that involve a high volume of transactions, such as billing or check processing, or a large number of records that need to be summarized, are usually batch processes, meaning that the documents are keyed as a group, edited as a group, or printed as a group. Printed reports are usually produced by batch processes, and screens tend to be on line processes.

Analyze the output data flows and ask the question, "Is the information output coming from base elements on input flows or from calculations?" Often, determining this is easier after you have an understanding of the project data dictionary, discussed in Chapter 10. Regardless, create a process for each distinct output. If the stored information necessary for the report or screen is located on several files, show each file as an input data flow. If the output data needs to appear in a specific sequence, check to see if the files need to be sorted or indexed to match the sequence. Sorting is usually included on a lower-level child diagram as a separate process. Also analyze the input. On a lower-level diagram, include processes for keying, input record validation, and verification. Finally, be sure to add processes for updating master files with input data.

Sometimes it is not clear how many processes to place on one diagram and when to create a child diagram. One suggestion is to examine each process and count the number of data flows entering and leaving it. If the total is greater than four, the process is a good candidate for a child diagram. Physical data flow diagrams will be illustrated in the example later in this chapter.

PARTITIONING DATA FLOW DIAGRAMS

Partitioning is the process of examining a data flow diagram and determining how it should be divided into collections of manual procedures and collections of computer programs. Analyze each process to determine whether it should be a manual or automated procedure. Group automated procedures into a series of computer programs. A dashed line is often drawn around a process or group of processes that should be placed into a single computer program.

A process performed by people rather than by computers is a manual process. Filling out or inspecting forms, picking order items, and so on, are examples of manual processes. Written procedures should be developed for training new employees and developing operational consistency, so that each person performs a given procedure in the same way.

Automated processes use computer technology for performing the work even if such processes include some human activity such as keying or verifying input data. These processes become either a batch or an on line program as the system is developed. To determine whether a process is to be batch or on line, examine the data flow in and out of the process. If the data flow both in and out of the process is composed entirely of stored information generated and accessed by the computer, requiring no human intervention, the process is a batch process. Using a transaction or master file to produce a report is an example of a batch process.

If some of the input or output is entered or examined by people, the process may be either batch or on line. For example, keying new customer information could be performed as a batch by a data entry department or on line by the users. The data flow that links a manual process or an external entity to an automated process represents a person–computer interaction that requires a user interface, a means for an individual to work with the information technology. Typically, this interface is on line and it may consist of a screen, a report, or a hand-held optical scanner like those commonly used in retail stores.

Batch processes are usually used when programs process a high volume of data. For example, a large amount of data may need to be entered when processing a mailbag containing customer orders in a mail-order company. Batch processes are also used when a large amount of data must be read and summarized, or otherwise processed, to produce output. An example is reading an entire file of a bank's customers to determine overdrawn accounts.

Another consideration the analyst must address on the physical data flow diagram is whether several batch processes should be combined into one computer program or job stream. A *job stream* is several programs written separately but running back-to-back. On-line programs are usually reserved for low-volume transactions or inquiries or cases in which an employee is working directly with a customer, such as a telephone inquiry about the current status of a bank account.

To develop a collection or group of computer programs and manual procedures, examine each process and ask questions about the nature of the work being done. An element of experimentation or play may enter the design process at this time. Think about each process on the data flow diagram and see if it could be both batch and on line. Reflect on which option would be better for the user community. Describe the processes as manual, batch, or on line.

There are six reasons for partitioning data flow diagrams:

1. Different user groups. Are the processes performed by several different user groups, often at different physical locations within the company? If so, they should be partitioned into different computer programs. An example is the need to process customer returns and customer payments in a department store. Both processes involve obtaining financial information that is used to adjust customer accounts (subtracting from the amount the customer owes) but they are performed by different user groups at different locations. The counter handling items returned by customers is usually located at a desk near the store entrance. The payment counter is located somewhat in the interior of the store (for security) and is staffed by security personnel. Each group needs a different screen for recording the particulars of the transaction—either a credit screen or a payment screen.

2. Timing. Examine the timing of the processes. If two processes execute at different times, they cannot be grouped into one program.

3. Similar tasks. If two processes perform similar tasks and both are batch processes, they may be grouped into one computer program. For example, in a monthly run to adjust customer balances, both return item credits and customer payments are subtracted from the customer balance due. These two adjustment processes may readily be combined into one program.

4. Efficiency. Several batch processes may be combined into one program for efficient processing. For example, if a series of reports needs to use the same large input files, producing them from the same batch program may save considerable computer run time.

5. Consistency of data. Processes may be combined into one program for consistency of data. For example, an accounts receivable report needs to be printed periodically showing the amount due from each customer. The same figures must also be included on bills sent to the customers. If these two distinct outputs were produced in separate computer runs and the customer master file was updated between the runs, and the bills would have different data. The result is an unreliable, inconsistent system.

6. Security. Processes may be partitioned into different programs for security reasons. An example is a system with a process for adding a new customer and a process for changing customer financial information. Each process should have a separate program because, whereas only one

person (or several in a large organization) should have password access to the program that changes customer financial data, many persons may be needed and authorized to add new customer records.

A DATA FLOW DIAGRAM EXAMPLE

The corporation in our example is FilmMagic, a video rental chain founded by three people with expertise in the video rental business. The plan is to have a series of stores scattered strategically around a metropolitan area. The company has also adopted a unique policy of giving free rentals and videos to their high-volume customers in an attempt to gain a large market share. According to one of the company's owners, "If the airlines can have frequent flyer programs, our video stores can have a recurrent rental program." Consequently, a monthly customer bonus program will be part of the system.

Creating the Context Diagram

A summary of the business activities obtained from interviews with the owners of FilmMagic is illustrated in Figure 9.12. The context-level data flow diagram, representing an overview of the entire system, appears in Figure 9.13. Since the system must keep track of the number of videos a customer has rented, the external entity CUSTOMER has the most data flow to and from it. Note that the context diagram is relatively simple.

Drawing Diagram 0

Diagram 0, shown in Figure 9.14, depicts the major activities for the FilmMagic video rental system. Note that there is one process for each major activity. Each process is analyzed to determine the data required and the output produced. Process 1, RENT VIDEO ITEMS, summarizes the main function of the system and is thus a complex process. Notice the many input and output data flows.

To correctly draw the data flow diagram, questions must be asked such as, "What information is needed to rent a video?" A VIDEO RENTAL ITEM (which may be either a video cassette or a video game), a PAYMENT, and a CUSTOMER ID (a rental card) are required from the CUSTOMER. The VIDEO RENTAL ITEM is used to find matching information about the video, such as the price and description. The process creates a CASH TRANSACTION, that will eventually produce information about the total cash received. The CUSTOMER RECORD is obtained and updated with the total amount of the rental. A double-headed arrow indicates that the CUSTOMER RECORD is obtained from and replaced in the same file location. The RENTAL RECEIPT and video are given to the CUSTOMER. RENTAL INFORMATION such as the date and the item rented is produced for later use to generate MANAGEMENT REPORTS.

The other processes are simpler, with less input and output. Process 3, CHECK IN CUSTOMER VIDEO RETURN, updates the CUSTOMER data store indicating that items are no longer checked out. New customers must be added to the CUSTOMER data store before a video may be checked out. Process 5, ADD NEW CUSTOMER, takes NEW CUSTOMER INFORMATION and issues the customer a VIDEO RENTAL CARD. The card must be presented each time a customer wishes to check out a video.

Processes 2 and 4 produce useful information to manage the business and make decisions, such as when to lower the price of videos that are in

FIGURE 9.12
Start with a list of business
activities, which will help
you identify processes, external entities, and data flows.

Summary of Business Activities
Customer Rental System

1. Customers apply for a video rental card. They fill out a form and provide a means of verifying their identity. They are issued a video rental card.

2. Customers rent videos by giving the clerk their video rental card and the video cassettes or video games. The clerk totals the amount of the rental, which is received from the customers. The customer is given a receipt with the due date on it. A record is created for each item rented.

3. Customers return video cassettes or video games. If the video is returned late a note and the amount of the late fee is made on their record.

4. If a customer has a late fee they are required to pay the amount the next time they rent an item.

5. The company has several special policies designed to provide a competitive edge in the video rental market. Once a month the customer rental records are reviewed for customers that have rented more than the bonus level, currently set at $50. Bonus customers are sent a letter thanking them for their business as well as issuing them several free rental coupons (depending on the amount of rental for the month).

6. Once a year, the customer records are examined for persons that have rented more than a yearly bonus level (currently set at $250). A letter, free rental coupons, and a certificate for a free video (if they have rented over two times the bonus level) are sent to the customer.

demand and when to advertise to draw more customers, thereby increasing cash flow. Processes 6 and 7 use CUSTOMER data store information to PRODUCE MONTHLY and YEARLY CUSTOMER BONUS LETTERS. Notice that the names of the data flows going into and out of the processes are different, indicating that something has transformed input data to produce output. All processes start with a verb such as RENT, PRODUCE, or ADD.

Creating a Child Diagram

Figure 9.15 is the child diagram of Process 1, RENT VIDEO ITEMS, in the FilmMagic example. The input data flow VIDEO INFORMATION is connected only to the process GET VIDEO RECORD. The source of this input is a blank area on the drawing. This incomplete interface flow matches the flow into process 1 on Diagram 0. The same is true for VIDEO RENTAL, PAYMENT, and CUSTOMER ID.

FIGURE 9.13
Context level diagram for the
FilmMagic video rental
stores.

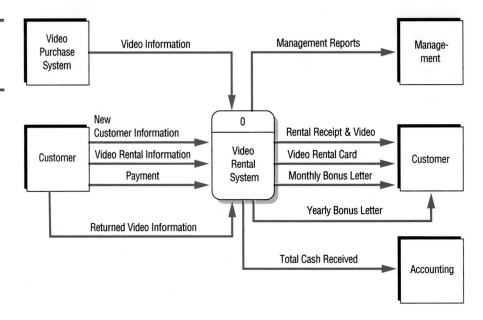

The CUSTOMER RECORD is also an interface data flow but is connected on Diagram 1 to the CUSTOMER data store, since data stores on the parent diagram may also be included on the child diagram. The output data flows CASH TRANSACTION and RENTAL RECEIPT are interface flows that match the parent process output. The flow NOT FOUND ERROR is not depicted in the parent process since an error line is considered a minor output.

Child diagram processes are more detailed, illustrating the logic required to produce the output. The process GET VIDEO RECORD uses VIDEO RENTAL, indicating which video the customer wishes to rent, to find the matching VIDEO INFORMATION (title, price, and so on). Process 1.5, FIND CUSTOMER RECORD, uses the CUSTOMER ID on the video rental card to locate the CUSTOMER record. The CUSTOMER NAME AND ADDRESS are printed on the RENTAL RECEIPT printed from process 1.4.

Creating a Physical Data Flow Diagram

Figure 9.16 is the physical data flow diagram corresponding to the FilmMagic logical Diagram 0 data flow diagram. Notice that the data flow names have been changed to reflect the method of implementation. The customer now supplies a VIDEO RENTAL BAR CODE and a CUSTOMER ID BAR CODE to process 1, RENT VIDEO ITEMS. The external entity VIDEO PURCHASE SYSTEM has been replaced with a VIDEO MASTER FILE, since files are used to communicate between systems. There are now two transaction files: CASH TRANSACTIONS and the RENTAL TRANSACTION FILE. The RENTAL TRANSACTION FILE is used to store information from the time the videos are rented until they are returned. The CASH TRANSACTIONS file is necessary since videos are rented throughout the day and the CASH RECEIVED REPORT is produced once a week. When customers return a video, data is entered using the RETURNED VIDEO SCREEN (to determine any late charges) and updates the RENTAL TRANSACTION FILE. New customers fill out the NEW CUSTOMER FORM, whereas on the logical data flow diagram this step is simply called NEW CUSTOMER INFORMATION.

An example of a physical child data flow diagram is Diagram 1 of the FilmMagic example, illustrated in Figure 9.17. Notice that there are processes

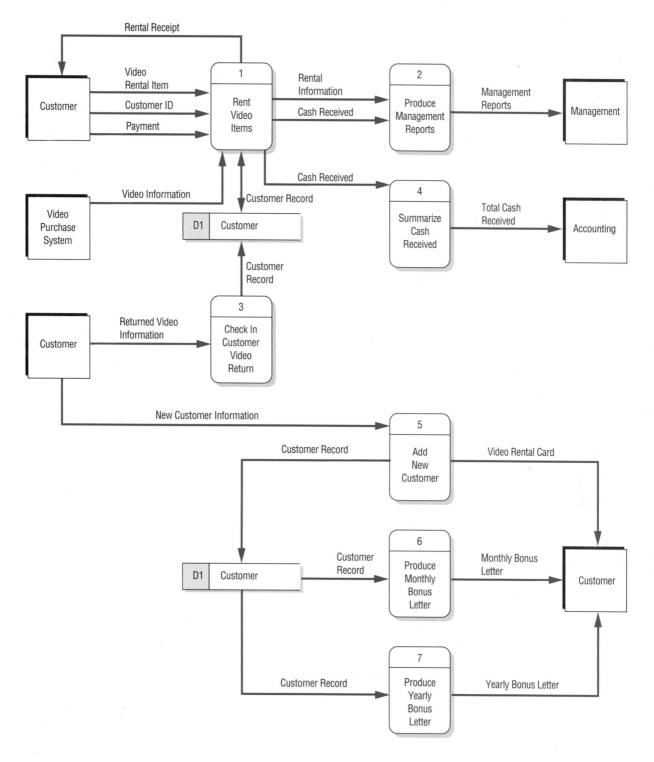

FIGURE 9.14
Diagram 0 for the FilmMagic video rental system shows seven major processes.

for scanning bar codes, displaying screens, locating records, and creating and updating files. The sequence of activities is important here, since the emphasis is on how the system will work and in what order events happen.

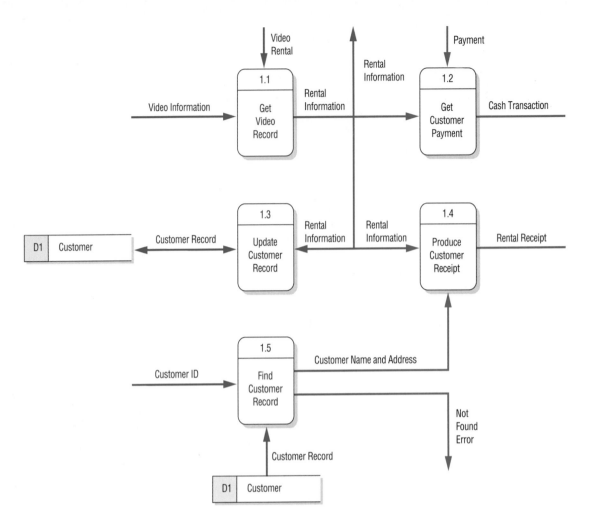

FIGURE 9.15
The child diagram for process 1 shows more detail than does Diagram 0.

Partitioning the Data Flow Diagram

Figure 9.18 illustrates partitioning for the FilmMagic physical data flow diagram. Notice the use of a dotted line to indicate which processes should be in separate programs. The process RENT VIDEO ITEMS operates on a minute-by-minute basis. The process CHECK IN CUSTOMER VIDEO RETURN also operates on a minute-by-minute basis. However, returns are handled at a later time than the rental process, and both procedures should thus be in separate programs.

The PRODUCE CASH RECEIVED REPORT process is weekly and therefore must also be in a separate program. Since the CASH TRANSACTION that goes into this process and the CASH RECEIVED REPORT coming out of the process are both computer information, the process should be implemented as a batch program. The same is true for process 4, PRODUCE MANAGEMENT REPORTS, for process 6, PRODUCE MONTHLY BONUS LETTER, and for process 7, PRODUCE YEARLY BONUS LETTER.

Process 5, ADD NEW CUSTOMER, could be either batch or on line. Since the customer is probably waiting for the video rental card on the other side of a counter, an on-line process would provide the best customer service.

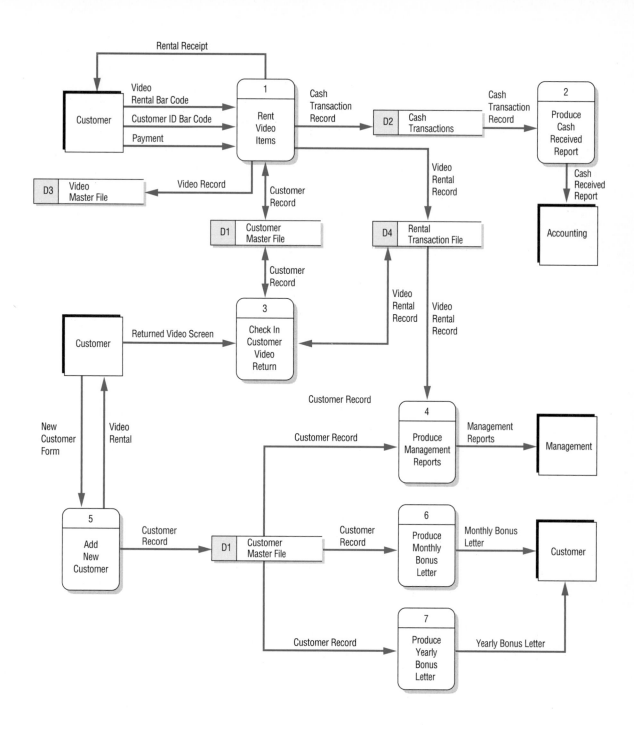

FIGURE 9.16
This physical data flow diagram matches logical Diagram 0.

A SECOND DATA FLOW DIAGRAM EXAMPLE

Often, a person's first exposure to data flow diagrams seems confusing because there are so many new concepts and definitions. This example is intended to illustrate the development of a data flow diagram by selectively

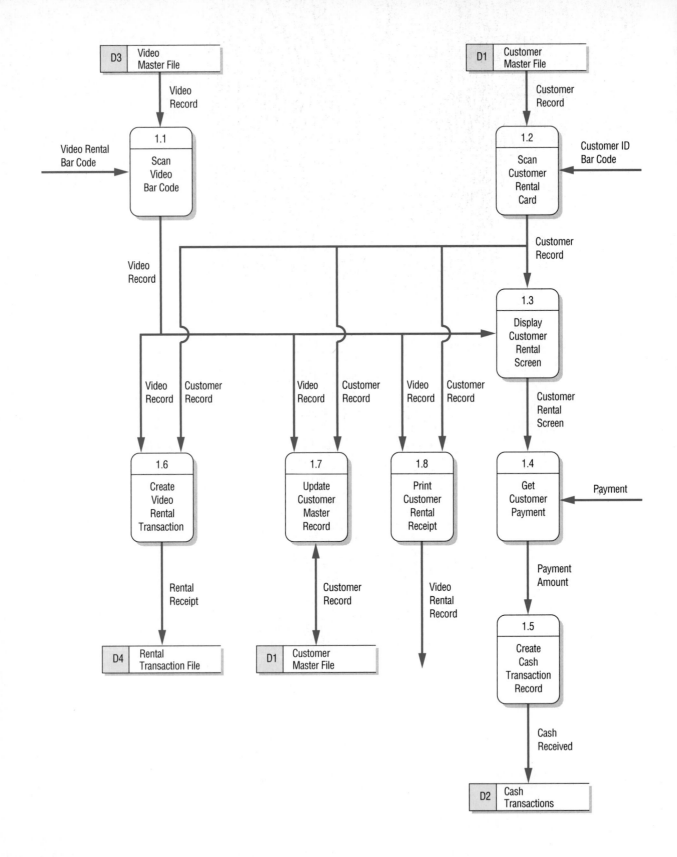

FIGURE 9.17
This physical child data flow diagram shows details such as scanning bar codes.

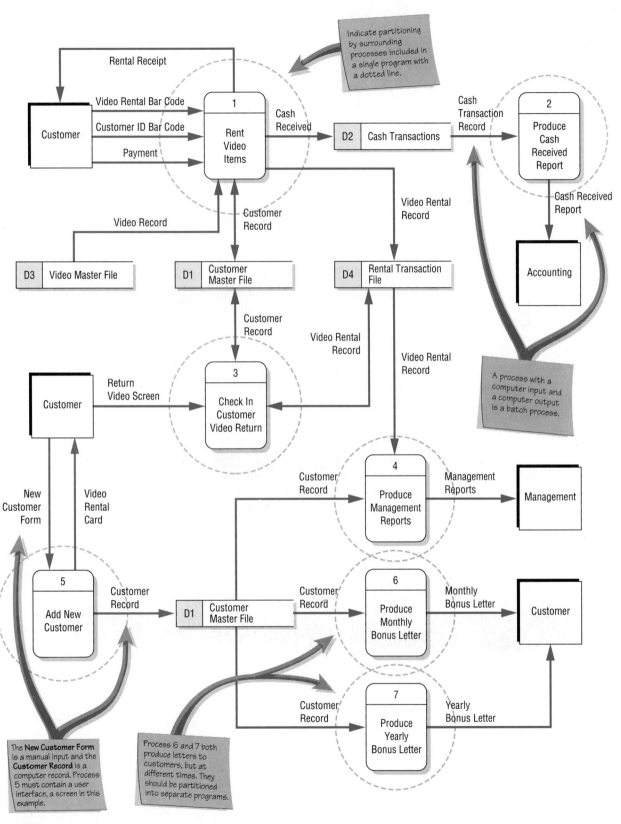

Within the figure, the following text labels appear:

Indicate partitioning by surrounding processes included in a single program with a dotted line.

Rental Receipt

Video Rental Bar Code
Customer ID Bar Code
Payment

Customer

1
Rent Video Items

Cash Received

D2 Cash Transactions

Cash Transaction Record

2
Produce Cash Received Report

Cash Received Report

Accounting

A process with a computer input and a computer output is a batch process.

Video Record

Customer Record

Video Rental Record

D3 Video Master File

D1 Customer Master File

D4 Rental Transaction File

Customer Record

Video Rental Record

Video Rental Record

Return Video Screen

Customer

3
Check In Customer Video Return

4
Produce Management Reports

Customer Record

Management Reports

Management

New Customer Form

Video Rental Card

5
Add New Customer

Customer Record

D1 Customer Master File

Customer Record

6
Produce Monthly Bonus Letter

Monthly Bonus Letter

Customer

Customer Record

7
Produce Yearly Bonus Letter

Yearly Bonus Letter

Customer

The New Customer Form is a manual input and the Customer Record is a computer record. Process 5 must contain a user interface, a screen in this example.

Process 6 and 7 both produce letters to customers, but at different times. They should be partitioned into separate programs.

FIGURE 9.18
Partitioning the FilmMagic physical data flow diagram.

FIGURE 9.19
A summary of business
activities for World's Trend
Catalog Division.

World's Trend
1000 International Lane
Cornwall, CT 06050

World's Trend is a mail order supplier of high quality, fashionable clothing. Customers place orders either by telephone, faxing, or mailing in an order form included with each catalog.

List of Business Activities

1. Add new customers to the customer master file. When customers are added to the master file, they are assigned a customer number, which is used when placing subsequent orders.

2. Perform inquiries to let customers know the current selling price of an item and the quantity available for sale.

3. Process customer orders by verifying that all order information is accurate and that a record exists for the customer placing the order. If a customer record does not exist, it is added to the master file. As orders are entered, customer and item master record fields are updated.

4. If a customer orders more of an item than is currently available in stock, backordered item information is sent to the inventory control department. When backordered items are received from World's Trend suppliers, they are shipped to the customers.

5. Orders are sent to the warehouse where they are filled.

6. A shipping statement is attached to the filled order. Mailing labels are prepared and the order is shipped to the customer.

7. Order information is used to produce a billing statement for all customers charging their goods to their World's Trend account.

8. Order information is used to produce an Accounts Receivable report for the Accounting department.

looking at each of the components we explored earlier in this chapter. The example, called "World's Trend Catalog Division," will also be used to illustrate concepts covered in Chapters 10 and 11.

A list of business activities for World's Trend can be found in Figure 9.19. You could develop this list using information obtained through interviews, investigation, and observation. The list can be used to identify external entities like CUSTOMER, ACCOUNTING, and WAREHOUSE and data flows such as ACCOUNTS RECEIVABLE REPORT and CUSTOMER BILLING STATEMENT. Later (when developing level 0 and child diagrams), the list can be used to define processes, data flows, and data stores.

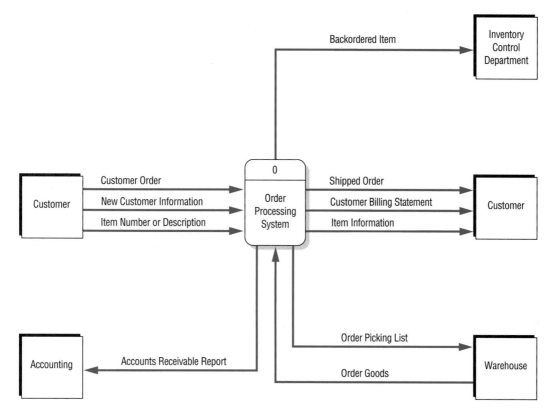

FIGURE 9.20
A context level data flow diagram for the order processing system at World's Trend.

Once this list of activities is developed, create a context diagram as shown in Figure 9.20. This diagram shows the ORDER PROCESSING CENTER in the middle (no processes are described in detail in the context level diagram) and five external entities (the two entities called CUSTOMER are really one and the same). The data flows that come from and go to the external entities are shown as well (for example, CUSTOMER ORDER and ORDER PICKING LIST).

Next, go back to the activity list and make a new list of as many processes and data stores as you can find. You can add more later, but start making the list now. If you think you have enough information, draw a level 0 diagram such as the one found in Figure 9.21. Call this Diagram 0 and keep the processes general so as not to overcomplicate the diagram. Later, you can add detail. When you are finished drawing the seven processes, draw data flows between them and to the external entities (the same external entities shown in the context diagram). If you feel there needs to be a data store such as ITEM MASTER or CUSTOMER MASTER, draw those in and connect them to processes using data flows. Now take the time to number the processes and data stores. Pay particular attention to making the labels meaningful. Check for errors and correct them before moving on.

At this point try to draw a child diagram (sometimes also called a level 1 diagram). Number your child diagrams Diagram 1, Diagram 2, and so on, in accordance with the number you assigned to each process in the level 0 diagram. When you draw Diagram 1 (as shown in Figure 9.22), make a list of subprocesses first. A process such as ADD CUSTOMER

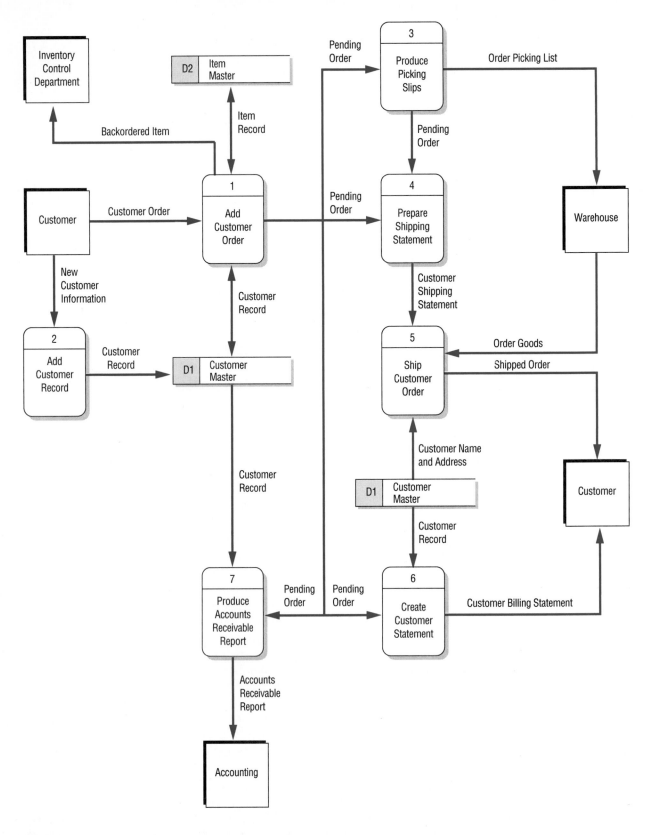

FIGURE 9.21
Diagram 0, of the order processing system for World's Trend Catalog Division.

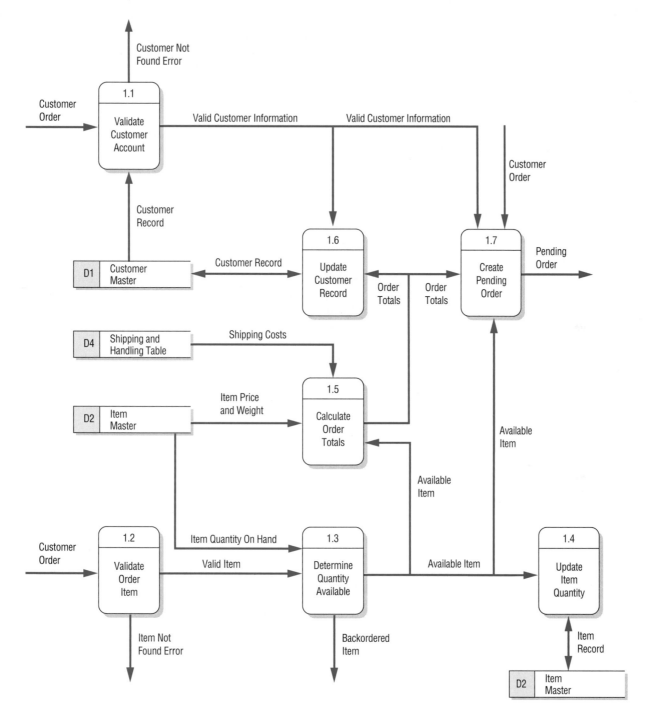

FIGURE 9.22
Diagram 1, of the order processing system for World's Trend Catalog Division.

ORDER can have subprocesses (in this case, there are seven). Connect these subprocesses to one another and also to data stores when appropriate. Subprocesses do not have to be connected to external entities, since we can always refer to the parent (or level 0) data flow diagram to identify these entities. Label the subprocesses 1.1, 1.2, 1.3, and so on. Take the time to check for errors and make sure the labels make sense.

If you want to go beyond the logical model and draw a physical model as well, look at Figure 9.23, which is an example of a physical data flow child diagram of Process 3, PRODUCE PICKING SLIPS. When you label a physical model, take care to describe the process in great detail. For example, Subprocess 3.3 in a logical model could simply be SORT ORDER ITEM, but in the physical model, a better label is SORT ORDER ITEMS BY LOCATION WITHIN CUSTOMER. When you write a label for a data store, refer to the actual file or database, such as CUSTOMER MASTER FILE or SORTED ORDER ITEM FILE. When you describe data flows, describe the actual form, report, or screen. For example, when you print a slip for order picking, call the data flow ORDER PICKING SLIP.

Finally, take the physical data flow diagram and suggest partitioning, combining or separating the processes. As stated earlier, there are many reasons for partitioning: identifying distinct processes for different user groups, separating processes that need to be performed at different times, grouping similar tasks, grouping processes for efficiency, combining processes for consistency, or separating them for security. Figure 9.24 shows that partitioning is useful in the case of World's Trend Catalog Division. You would first group Processes 1 and 2 because it would make sense to add new customers at the same time their first order was placed. You would then put Processes 3 and 4 in two separate partitions. Though both are batch processes, they must be done at different times from one another and thus cannot be grouped into a single program.

This completes the process of developing a data flow diagram from the top down, drawing a companion physical data flow diagram to accompany the logical data flow diagram, then partitioning the data flow diagram by grouping or separating the processes. The World's Trend example will be used again in Chapters 10 and 11.

USING DATA FLOW DIAGRAMS

Data flow diagrams are useful throughout the analysis and design process. Use original, unexploded data flow diagrams early when ascertaining information requirements. At this stage, they can help provide an overview of data movement through the system, lending a visual perspective unavailable in narrative data.

Tradeoffs are involved in deciding how far the data streams should be exploded. Time may be wasted and understandability sacrificed if data flow diagrams are overly complex. On the other hand, if the data flow diagrams are under-exploded, errors of omission could occur eventually that might affect the system being developed.

If data flow diagrams are used as a tool to solicit more specific information requirements from users, they should not be highly exploded or finalized in any medium before users have had a chance to walk through them with the systems analyst. Changes need to be incorporated after getting users' input. Overly exploded diagrams may not be helpful to users. And if data flow diagrams are too complex before presentation to users, the systems analyst is more likely to defend the representation than to welcome any user corrections.

After exploding the original data flow diagrams, use them as a tool for further interaction with users. At this stage, the data flow diagram shows your own conceptualization of the business data streams. Educate key users about the conventions used in data flow diagrams, then go through

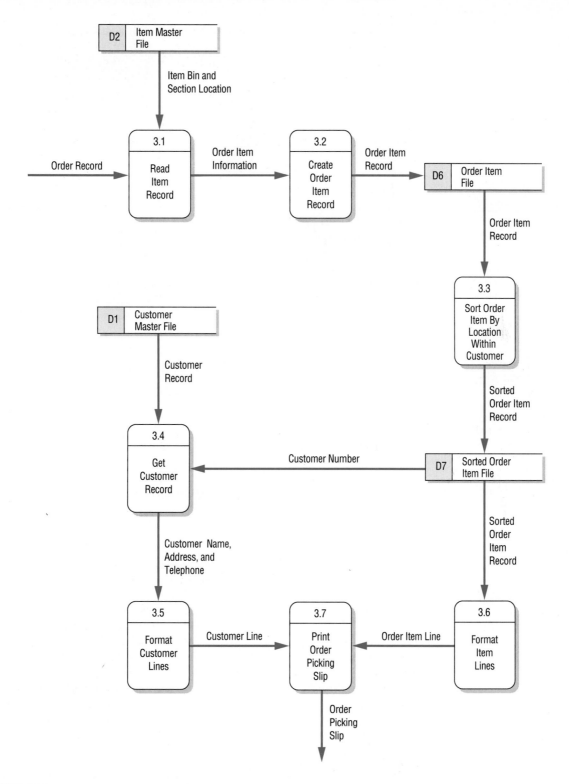

FIGURE 9.23
A physical data flow child diagram for World's Trend Catalog Division.

the successive levels with them. Ask for changes that they may suggest to
clarify processes or to make the diagrams more accurate in some way.

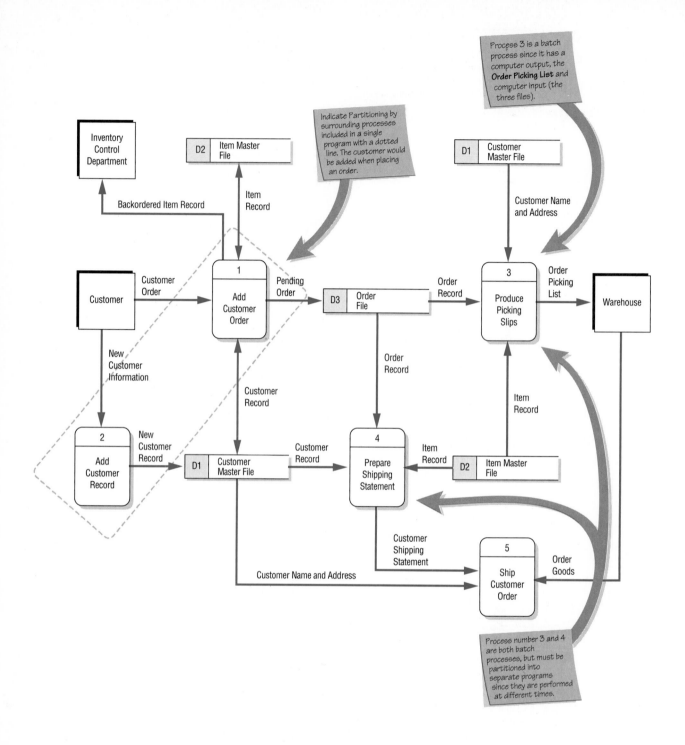

FIGURE 9.24
Partitioning the data flow diagram (Showing part of Diagram 0).

After user modifications are added, users and the systems analysis team approve the data flow diagrams as accurate reflections of the organization's data flows. The data flow diagrams can then be finalized and drawn using a CASE tool as in Figure 9.25.

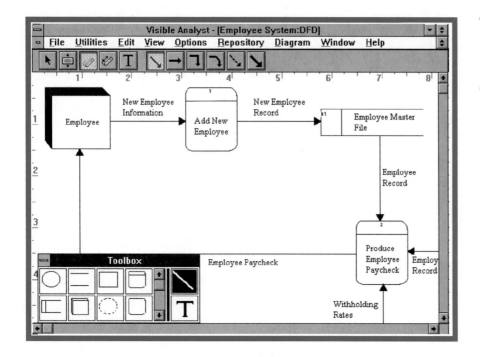

FIGURE 9.25
A Visible Analyst Workbench (VAW) screen showing a data flow diagram.

Once their content is clarified, the data flow diagrams need to be redrawn and relabeled in a meaningful way. The systems analyst might be quite competent at sketching through the logic of the data stream for data flow diagrams, but to make the diagrams truly communicative, meaningful labels for all data components are also required. Labels should not be generic, since then they do not tell us enough about the situation at hand. All general systems models bear the configuration of input, process, and output, so labels for a data flow diagram need to be more specific than that.

Consider effective naming as a top priority, so that someone unfamiliar with the system will be able to pick up a data flow diagram and, with a little training, understand what it depicts. Make labels as specific yet concise as possible. Try to avoid using the same term to mean two different things. Conversely, consolidate terms wherever possible, using only a few terms for the data item. Part of the reason data flow diagrams are effective is that they are consistent from page to page (recall the requirement that inputs and outputs remain constant between diagrams). The same sort of consistency should be evident in labeling.

Finally, remember that data flow diagrams are used as documentation of the system. Assume that data flow diagrams will be around longer than the people who drew them—this is, of course, always true if an external consultant is drawing them. Data flow diagrams can be used for documenting high or low levels of analysis and helping to substantiate the logic underlying the data flows of the organizations.

SUMMARY

In order to better understand the logical movement of data throughout a business, the systems analyst draws data flow diagrams (DFDs). Data flow diagrams are structured analysis and design tools that allow the analyst to comprehend the system and subsystems visually as a set of interrelated data flows.

CONSULTING OPPORTUNITY 9.2

There's No Business Like Flow Business

The phone at Merman's rings, and Annie Oaklea, head of costume inventory, picks it up and answers a query by saying, "Let me take a look at my inventory cards. Sorry, it looks as if there are only two male bear suits in inventory—with extra-growly expression at that. We've had a great run on bear. When do you need them? Perhaps one will be returned. No, can't do it, sorry. Would you like these two sent, regardless? The name of your establishment? Theatre in the Square? Right.

Delightful company! I see by our account card that you've rented from us before. An how long will you be needing the costumes?"

Figure 9.C1 is a data flow diagram that sets the stage for processing of costume rentals from Merman's. It shows rentals like the one Annie is doing for Theatre in the Square.

After conversing for another few moments about shop policy on alterations, Annie concludes her conversation by saying, "You are very lucky to get the

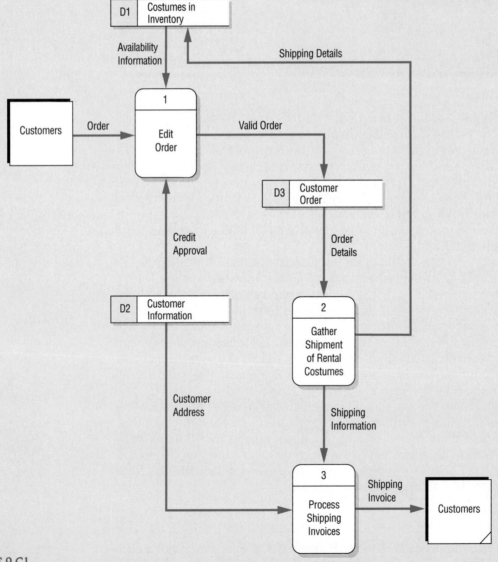

FIGURE 9.C1
A data flow diagram for Merman's Costume Rentals.

bears on such short notice. I've got another company reserving them for the first week in July. I'll put you down for the bear suits, and they'll be taken to you directly by our courier. As always, prompt return will save enormous trouble for us all."

Merman's costume rental enterprise is located in London's world-famous West End theatre district. When a theatre or television production company lacks the resources (either time or expertise) to construct a costume in their own shop, the cry goes up to "Ring up Merman's!" and they proceed to rent what they need with a minimum of fuss.

The shop (more aptly visualized as a warehouse) goes on for three floors full of costume racks, holding thousands of costumes hung together by historical period, then grouped as to whether they are for men or women, and then by costume size.[1] Most theatre companies are able to locate precisely what they need, through Annie's capable assistance.

Now tailor-make the *rental return* portion of the data flow diagram given earlier. Remember that timely returns are critical for keeping the spotlight on costumes rented from Merman's.

---

[1] Western Costume Company in Hollywood, California, is said to have more than 1 million costumes worth about $40 million.

Graphical representations of data movement storage, and transformation are drawn with the use of four symbols: a rounded rectangle to depict data processing or transformations; a double square to show an outside data entity (source or receiver of data); an arrow to depict data flow; and an open-ended rectangle to show a data store.

The systems analyst extracts data processes, sources, stores, and flows from early organizational narrative and uses a top-down approach to first draw a context diagram of the system within the larger picture. Then a level 0 logical data flow diagram is drawn. Processes are shown and data stores are added. Next, the analyst creates a child diagram for each of the processes in Diagram 0. Inputs and outputs remain constant but the data stores and sources change. Exploding the original data flow diagram allows the systems analyst to focus on ever more detailed depictions of data movement within the system. The analyst then develops a physical data flow diagram from the logical data flow diagram, partitioning it to facilitate programming. Each process is analyzed to determine whether it should be a manual or automated procedure. Automated procedures are subsequently grouped into a series of computer programs, designated as either batch or on line. Six considerations for partitioning data flow diagrams include whether: there are processes performed by different user groups, processes execute at the same times, processes perform similar tasks, batch processes can be combined for efficient processing, processes may be combined into one program for consistency of data, or whether processes may be partitioned into different programs for security reasons.

The advantages of data flow diagrams include the simplicity of notation; using them to gain clearer information from users; allowing the systems analyst to conceptualize necessary data flows without being tied to a particular physical implementation; allowing analysts to better conceptualize the interrelatedness of the system and its subsystems, and to analyze a proposed system to determine if the necessary data and processes have been defined.

"You take a very interesting approach to the problems we have here at MRE. I've seen you sketching diagrams of our operation almost since the day you walked in the door. I'm actually getting used to seeing you doodling away now. What did you call those? Oh, yes. Context diagrams. And flow charts? Oh, no. Data flow diagrams. That's it, isn't it?"

HYPERCASE QUESTIONS

1. Find the data flow diagrams already drawn in MRE. Make a list of those you found and add a column to show where in the organization you found them.
2. Draw a context diagram modeling the Training Unit Project Development process based on case interviews with relevant Training Unit staff. Then draw a level 0 diagram detailing the process.

FIGURE 9.HC1
In HyperCase® you can see who is using CASE tools and explore further.

KEYWORDS AND PHRASES

data-oriented systems	vertical balancing
context diagram	interface data flow
data flow diagrams	functionally primitive

level 0 diagram
external entity
   (source or destination)
transforming process
data store
exploding
top-down approach
parent process

primitive process
logical model
physical model
physical data stores
batch processes
on-line processes
transaction data store
child diagram

REVIEW QUESTIONS

1. What is one of the main methods available for the analyst to use in analyzing data oriented systems?

2. What are the three advantages of using a data flow approach over narrative explanations of data movement?

3. What are the four data items that can be symbolized on a data flow diagram?

4. What is a context diagram? Contrast it to a level 0 DFD.

5. Define the top-down approach as it relates to drawing data flow diagrams.

6. Describe what "exploding" data flow diagrams means.

7. What are the tradeoffs involved in deciding how far data streams should be exploded?

8. Why is labeling data flow diagrams so important? What can effective labels on data flow diagrams accomplish for those unfamiliar with the system?

9. What is the difference between a logically and physically oriented data flow diagram?

10. List three reasons for creating a logically oriented data flow diagram.

11. List five characteristics found on a physical data flow diagram that are not on a logical data flow diagram.

12. When are transaction files required in the system design?

13. What is partitioning and how is it used?

14. How can an analyst determine when a user interface is required?

15. List three ways of determining partitioning on a data flow diagram.

16. List three ways to use completed data flow diagrams.

PROBLEMS

1. Pamela Coburn, a systems analyst, has worked for some time with Luis Asperilla, the manager of the South Street Bonton's clothing store, observing him in action during the day and talking with him whenever business slows. Pamela is feeling fairly sure of the store's processes now and wants to capture what she's learned on paper.

   a. Draw a context diagram for Bonton's.

   b. Draw a level 0 data flow diagram of data movement at Bonton's on South Street, as Pamela might.

   c. Explode one of the processes from your first-level diagram into more detail, adding data stores and data flows. Make reasonable assumptions about the operation of a retail clothing store, if necessary, to finish the diagrams.

    d. In a paragraph, write a description of the process you exploded in problem 1, part c. What assumptions, if any, did you have to make in order to draw the second-level diagram?

2. In two paragraphs, defend the statement that "An advantage of data flow diagrams is that they free the systems analyst from premature commitment to technical implementation of the system." Use an example to support what you write.

3. Up to this point, you seem to have had excellent rapport with Kathy Kline, one of the managers who will use the system you are proposing. However, when you showed her the data flow diagrams you drew, she did not understand them.

    a. In a paragraph, write down in general terms how to explain to a user what a data flow diagram is. Be sure to include a list of symbols and what they mean.

    b. It takes some effort to educate users about data flow diagrams. Is it worthwhile to share them with users? Why or why not? Defend your response in a paragraph.

4. One common experience that students in every college and university share is enrolling in a college course.

    a. Draw a first-level data flow diagram of data movement for enrollment in a college course. Use a single sheet and label each data item clearly.

    b. Explode one of the processes in your original data flow diagram into subprocesses, adding data flows and data stores.

    c. List the parts of the enrollment process that are "hidden" to the outside observer and about which you have had to make assumptions to complete a second-level diagram.

5. Figure 9.EX1 is a level 1 data flow diagram of data movement in a Niagara Falls tour agency called Marilyn's Tours. Read it over, checking for any inaccuracies.

    a. List and number the errors that you have found on the diagram.

    b. Redraw and label the data flow diagram of Marilyn's so that it is correct. Be sure that your new diagram employs symbols properly in order to cut down on repetitions and duplications where possible.

6. Perfect Pizza wants to install a system to record orders for pizza and Buffalo chicken wings. When regular customers call Perfect Pizza on the phone, they are asked their phone number. When the number is typed into a computer, the name, address, and last order date is automatically brought up on the screen. Once the order is taken, the total, including tax and delivery, is calculated. Then the order is given to the cook. A receipt is printed. Occasionally, special offers (coupons) are printed so the customer can get a discount. Drivers who make deliveries give customers a copy of the receipt and a coupon (if any). Weekly totals are kept for comparison with last year's performance. Write a summary of business activities for taking an order at Perfect Pizza.

7. Draw a context diagram for Perfect Pizza (problem 6).

8. Explode the context-level diagram in problem 7 showing all the major processes. Call this Diagram 0. It should be a logical data flow diagram.

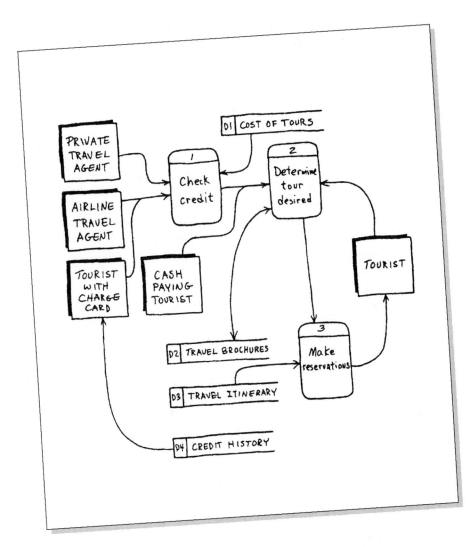

FIGURE 9.EX1
A hand-sketched data flow
diagram for Marilyn's Tours.

9. Draw a logical child diagram for Diagram 0 in problem 8 for the process that adds a new customer if he or she is not in the database currently (has never ordered from Perfect Pizza before).

10. Draw a physical data flow diagram for problem 8.

11. Draw a physical data flow diagram for problem 9.

12. Partition the physical data flow diagram in problem 8, grouping and separating processes as you deem appropriate. Explain why you partitioned the data flow diagram in this manner. (Remember that you do not have to partition the entire diagram, only the parts that make sense to partition.)

13. **a.** Draw a logical child diagram for process 6 in Figure 9.21.
    b. Draw a physical child diagram for process 6 in Figure 9.21.

14. Draw a physical data flow diagram for process 1.1 in Figure 9.22.

15. Create a context diagram for a real estate agent trying to match up buyers with potential houses.

16. Draw a logical data flow diagram showing general processes for problem 15. Call it Diagram 0.

17. Create a context diagram for billing in a dental office. External entities include the patients and insurance companies.

18. Draw a logical data flow diagram showing general processes for problem 17. Call it Diagram 0.

19. Create a data flow diagram for the following situation:

Technical Temporaries

Technical Temporaries is a company that specializes in placing employees in businesses for short periods of time. The company specializes in "temporaries" who have a high degree of proficiency in working with microcomputer software, such as word processing and spreadsheets, as well as other technical areas. Each employee must pass proficiency tests for areas in which they wish to be certified. The system described below is responsible for matching employees with short term openings that are available.

List of Business Activities

a. Businesses telephone the company to request temporaries to fill specific positions. The requests are used to create a Temporary Employment Request record. If the business requesting the temporary employee is not on the Employer Master file, a record is created for them.

b. Employees are selected to fill the temporary positions based on employee qualifications and availability. The Temporary Employee Master and the Temporary Employment Request files are used to list all qualified candidates.

c. Contracts are sent to the selected temporaries. Information is printed from the Employee Master, Employer Master, and Temporary Employment Request files.

d. Returned contracts are used to update the Employee Master file. The Temporary Employment Request file is updated with scheduling and personnel information.

e. Monthly schedules are printed for each employee. They contain information from the Employee Master, Employer Master, and the Temporary Employment Request files and are sequenced by employment date for each employee.

f. Notification is sent to the business requesting the temporary employees confirming the date and qualifications of the workers as well as their names.

20. Create a physical child data flow diagram for the following situation:

The Fastbase Corporation develops microcomputer database software products that are sold for both the domestic and international market. Customers receiving the products are sent a set of additional fonts if they return a warranty registration care included with the software and documentation. The diagram represents a batch process and is the child of process 5, ADD CUSTOMER REGISTRATION. The following tasks are included:

a. Inspect the Warranty Registration Card received from the customer to ensure that the information is complete and accurate. Incomplete cards are placed in a reject box.

b. Data entry operators key the Warranty Registration Card creating a Warranty Registration File.

c. A different data entry operator verifies the keyed data by reentering the Warranty Registration Card information. The data entry terminal compares the data previously keyed with the entry made by the second operators. Discrepancies are displayed.

d. The Warranty Registration File is input to a batch edit program. Each record is checked for accuracy. Errors are printed on a Warranty Validation Report and valid records are placed on a Valid Warranty Registration File.

e. The Valid Warranty Registration File is used as input, along with the Customer Master File, into the Customer Warranty Update Program. Records are added or updated, depending on whether the customer already exists on the Customer Master File.

f. The Valid Warranty Registration File is used to print a series of mailing labels for sending the font software to the customer.

21. Use the principles of partitioning to determine which of the processes in Problem 20 should be included in separate programs.

22. Create a physical child data flow diagram for the following situation: The local Personal Computer Users Group (PCUG) holds meetings once a month with informative speakers, door prizes, and sessions for special interest groups. A laptop computer is taken to the meetings for adding names of new members to the group. The diagram represents an on-line process and is the child of Process 1, ADD NEW MEMBERS. The following tasks are included:

a. Key the new member information.

b. Validate the information. Errors are displayed on the screen.

c. When all the information is valid, a confirmation screen is displayed. The operator visually confirms that the data are correct and either accepts the transaction or cancels it.

d. Accepted transactions add new members to the Membership Master file, stored on the laptop hard drive.

e. Accepted transactions are written to a Membership Journal file, stored on a diskette.

GROUP PROJECTS

1. Meet with your group to develop a context diagram for Maverick Transport (first introduced in Chapter 5). Use any data you have subsequently generated with your group about Maverick Transport. (*Hint*: concentrate on one of their functional areas, rather than trying to model the entire organization.)

2. Using the context diagram developed in problem 1, develop with your group a level 0 logical data flow diagram for Maverick Transport. Make any assumptions necessary to draw it.

3. With your group, choose one key process and explode it into a logical child diagram. Make any assumptions necessary to draw it. List follow-up questions and suggest other methods to get more information about processes which are still unclear to you.

4. Use the work your group has done to date to create a physical data flow diagram of a portion of the new system you are proposing for Maverick Transport.

SELECTED BIBLIOGRAPHY

Colter, M. "A Comparative Examination of Systems Analysis Techniques." *Management Information Systems Quarterly*, June 1984, Vol. 8, No. 1, pp. 51–66.

Davis, G. B., and M. H. Olson. *Management Information Systems, Conceptual Foundations, Structure and Development*, 2nd ed. New York: McGraw-Hill Book Company, 1985.

Gane, C., and T. Sarson. *Structured Systems Analysis and Design Tools and Techniques.* Englewood Cliffs, NJ: Prentice-Hall, Inc., 1979.

Gore, M., and J. Stubbe. *Elements of Systems Analysis*, 3rd ed. Dubuque, IA: William C. Brown Co., 1983.

Leeson, M. *Systems Analysis and Design.* Chicago, IL: Science Research Associates, Inc., 1985.

Lucas, H. *Information Systems Concepts for Management*, 3rd ed. New York: McGraw-Hill Book Company, 1986.

McFadden, F. R., and J. A. Hoffer. *Data Base Management.* Menlo Park, CA: The Benjamin/Cummings Publishing Company, 1985.

Martin, J. *Strategic Data-Planning Methodologies.* Englewood Cliffs, NJ: Prentice-Hall, Inc., 1982.

Senn, J. A. *Analysis and Design of Information Systems.* New York: McGraw-Hill Book Company, 1984.

Sprague, R. H., and E. D. Carlson. *Building Effective Decision Support Systems.* Englewood Cliffs, NJ: Prentice-Hall, Inc., 1982.

JUST FLOWING ALONG

After the results of interviews, questionnaires, and prototyping are gathered and analyzed, Anna and Chip move to the next step—modeling the system. Their strategy is to create a layered set of data flow diagrams and then describe the components.

Modeling starts with analyzing the context diagram of the current microcomputer system. This diagram is simple to create and is the foundation for successive levels because it describes the external entities and major data flow.

"Shall we create a physical data flow diagram of the current system?" asks Chip.

Anna replies, "No, it's fairly simple to understand, and we wouldn't gain any significant new knowledge of how the system operates. Let's start by creating a logical model of the current system."

The logical data flow diagrams are complete within a few days. Anna and Chip hold an afternoon meeting to review the diagrams and give each other feedback. "These look good," remarks Chip. "We can clearly see the business events that comprise the current system."

Anna replies, "Yes, let's take the current logical data flow diagrams and add all the requirements and desired features of the new system. We can also eliminate any of the unnecessary features that wouldn't be implemented in the new system."

Anna takes the context level diagram (shown in Chapter 2) and adds many of the reports, inquiries, and other information included in the new system. The finished context level diagram is shown in Figure E9.1. Notice that there are many new data flows. The maintenance department will receive reports that currently are not available. There are reports, for example, that automate hardware inventory and another that shows which software is located on which machines, the SOFTWARE CROSS-REFERENCE REPORT.

Chip reviews the finished diagram, commenting, "This is more art than science. It looks like all of the requirements of the new system are included. But this is far more complex than I originally thought it would be."

Anna replies, "Let's expand this to Diagram 0 for the new system. This will be a logical data flow diagram since we want to focus on the business needs. Perhaps it would be best if we work in a team for this diagram."

After several hours that afternoon and a good portion of the next morning, the diagram is complete. It is reviewed and modified with some minor changes. The finished Diagram 0 is shown in Figures E9.2, E9.3, E9.4, and E9.5. Since this is a logical diagram, it shows no keying or validation operations, nor any temporary data stores or transaction files. Timing is not a consideration, an example being the ADD NEW MICROCOMPUTER PROCESS, where it appears that orders are updated and reports simultaneously produced.

"This finally looks right," muses Chip. "All the major processes, data flow, and data stores are accounted for. And the overall diagram doesn't look too complicated."

Allen Schmidt,
Julie E. Kendall, and
Kenneth E. Kendall

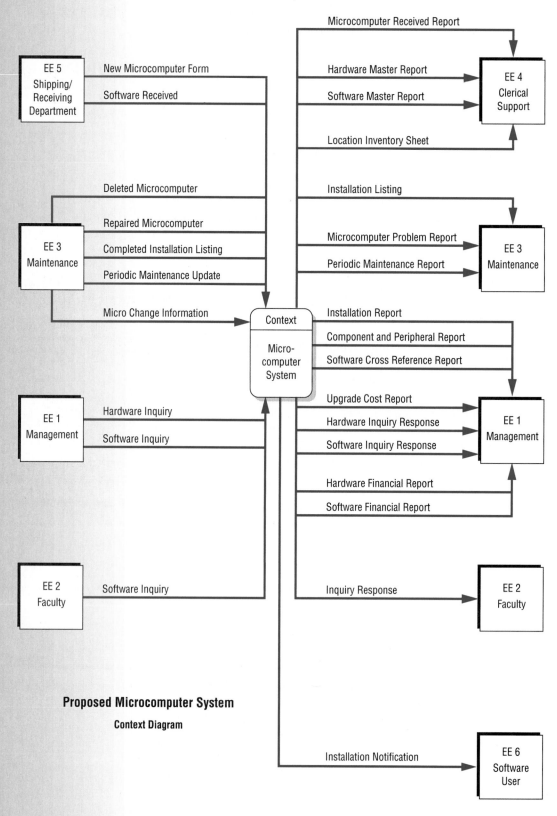

Proposed Microcomputer System

Context Diagram

FIGURE E9.1
Context level data flow diagram, Proposed System.

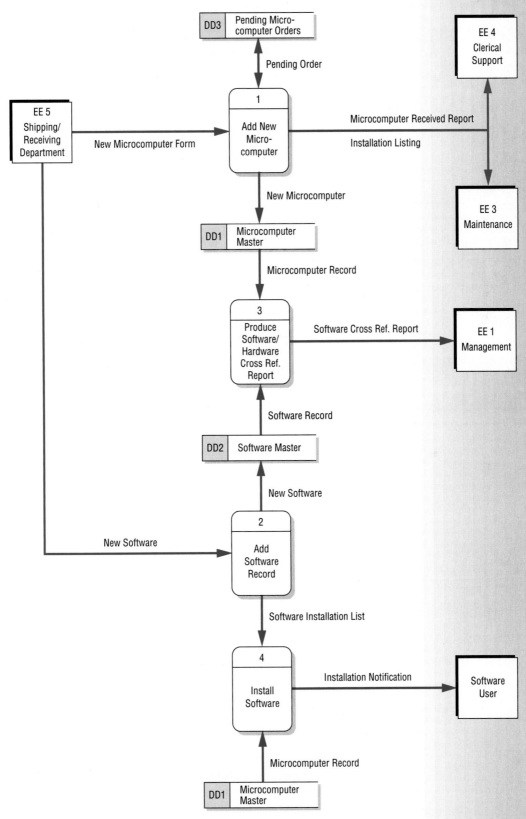

FIGURE E9.2
Diagram 0: Proposed Microcomputer System (part 1).

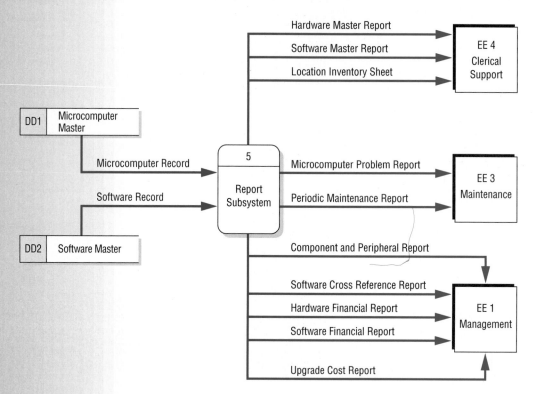

FIGURE E9.3
Diagram 0: Proposed Microcomputer System (part 2).

"Putting all of the inquiries into one subsystem and all the reports into another helped. Remember how complex the original diagram was?" asks Anna.

"I sure do," Chip replies. "I started to think we were tackling too much at once with this system. At least it's more manageable now. Since this is finished, what's the next step?"

"We need to decide how to implement the data flow diagram into a series of steps, shown on the physical data flow diagram." Anna says. "This logical data flow diagram shows the business tasks, or *what* should be accomplished. Now we need to show *how* the system will work. Keying, validation, information on whether programs are on line or batch, and transaction files need to be added."

Chip and Anna divide up the work by major tasks to be accomplished. Chip starts working on the ADD MICROCOMPUTER process.

When Chip draws the diagrams, he sees that he is drawing a level 0 diagram and then exploding it into many level 1 diagrams. Just as a parent may have many children, there may be many level 1 diagrams for a specific level 0 diagram. For this reason some analysts refer to these as parent and child diagrams.

Chip and Anna decide to abbreviate level 0 diagram as Diagram 0. The details are shown on a child diagram, Diagram 1. The external entities do not appear on the diagram since they are only shown on the context diagram and Diagram 0, the context diagram explosion.

Figure E9.6 is the finished version of Diagram 1, a batch process for adding new microcomputers. The NEW MICROCOMPUTER FORM is an input interface flow that matches the parent diagram. The MICROCOM-

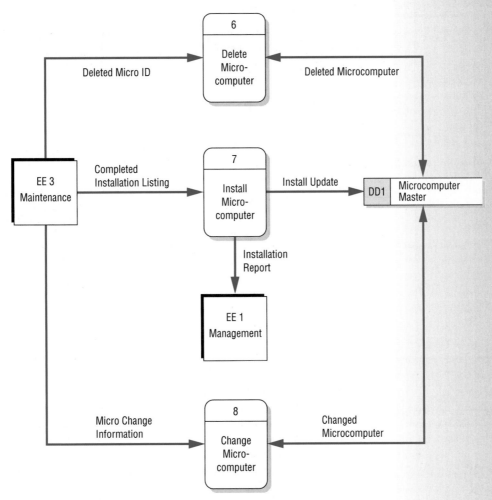

FIGURE E9.4
Diagram 0: Proposed Microcomputer System (part 3).

PUTER RECEIVED REPORT and INSTALLATION LISTING are output interface flows. Notice that several transaction files are needed to hold data between each process that runs at a different time. Errors are also shown, as a minor interface flow, which need not be present on the parent diagram. Keying, validation, and sorting processes are included, since they are necessary for implementation of the design.

Chip has some difficulty creating the diagram. The starting point is the input flow, NEW MICROCOMPUTER FORM. This has to be keyed, and since this is a batch process, the forms should be rekeyed by a separate operator to catch any keying errors. The results are stored on a transaction file.

Chip is unsure what activities will take place next so he decides to work backward from the MICROCOMPUTER MASTER data store. The records must be added to the master file. This means an update program is necessary. "Would the input to the ADD MICROCOMPUTER RECORD process be the keyed transactions?" Chip wonders to himself. "No. The data must be edited to ensure validity. The edit program should check all records for syntax errors and confirm that a record for the same microcomputer does not already exist on the master file."

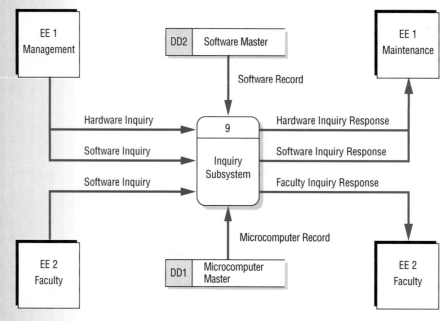

FIGURE E9.5
Diagram 0: Proposed Microcomputer System (part 4).

"Should the edit and update activities be accomplished in the same process?" Chip wonders. After some thinking the answer becomes clear. "We need to have a file of the new transactions for printing the INSTAL-LATION LISTING and the MICROCOMPUTER RECEIVED REPORT. It makes sense to separate the programs and create a VALID MICROCOM-PUTER TRANSACTION file out of the edit program."

Chip then decides to work backward from the INSTALLATION LIST-ING interface flow. "It needs to be printed, but what is the sequence of the prototype report? Ah, here it is!" he exclaims softly. Since the INSTALLA-TION LISTING needs to be in sequence by the manufacturer and model, it needs to be sorted. A sort process was added with the MICROCOMPUTER TRANSACTION as input. This same sequence was needed for the MICRO-COMPUTER RECEIVED REPORT. "All done," thinks Chip. "One more review and . . . whoops, forgot about updating the PENDING MICROCOM-PUTER ORDERS data store." One last change, and then the diagram was completed.

Anna reviews the diagram for omissions and errors. "I can see that you've put a great deal of thought into this," she exclaims. "It's really well designed. I've been working on Diagram 2, an explosion of Process 2, ADD SOFTWARE RECORD. Perhaps you would like to review the finished result."

"Sure," replies Chip. "I'll check it for omissions and errors."

Diagram 2 is shown in Figure E9.7. Since this is an on-line process, there are no key and verify operations. Instead, NEW SOFTWARE INFORMA-TION is keyed and edited by the same program. Errors are reported on the screen and corrected by the operator. After all errors have been corrected, the operator has a chance to sight-verify the data. If correct, the operator presses a key to accept the data; otherwise the transaction may be canceled or corrected.

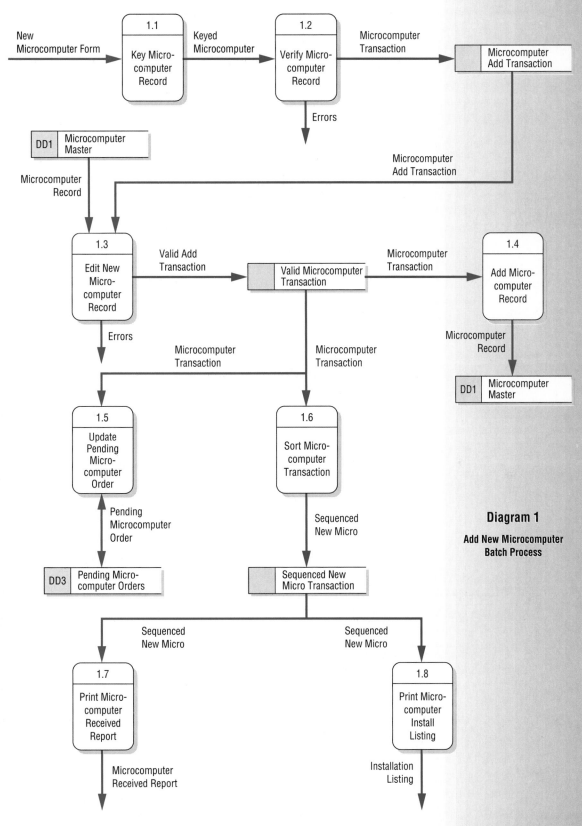

FIGURE E9.6
Diagram 1: Proposed Microcomputer System.

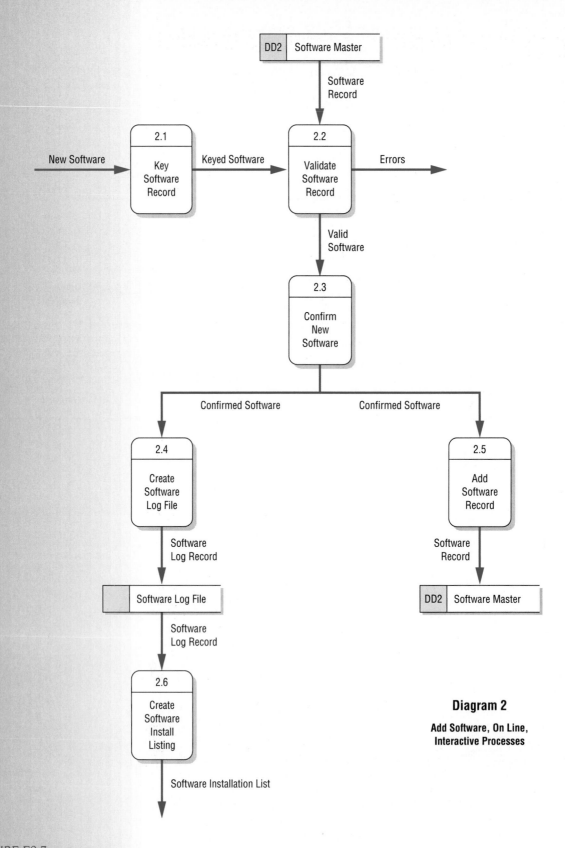

FIGURE E9.7
Diagram 2: Proposed Microcomputer System.

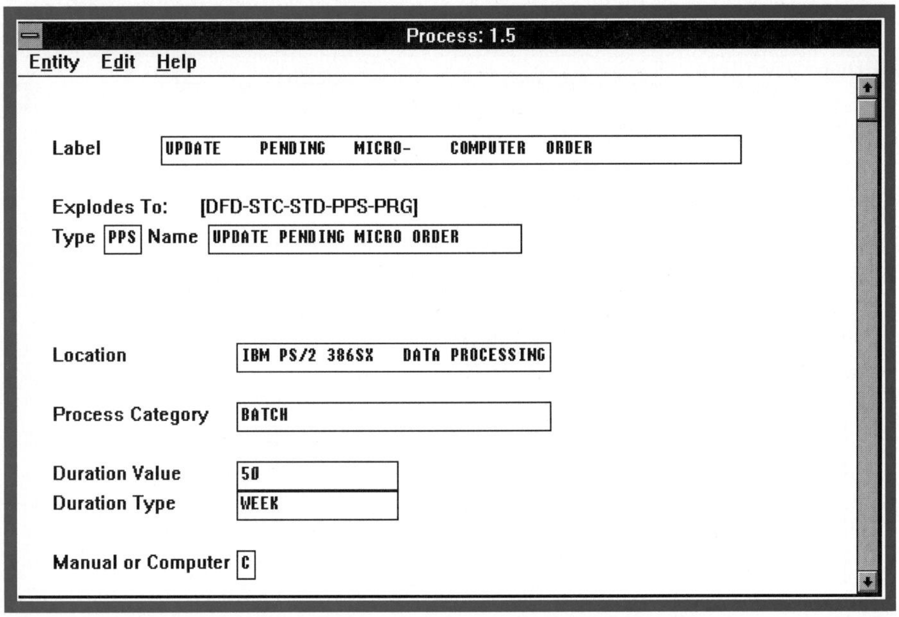

FIGURE E9.8
Process description screen, UPDATE PENDING ORDER.

Confirmed data is added to the SOFTWARE MASTER file and is used to create a SOFTWARE LOG RECORD. This record contains all of the keyed information as well as the date, time, and user ID of the person entering the transaction. In the ADD SOFTWARE diagram, this record is used to create the SOFTWARE INSTALLATION LIST as well as providing a backup of all new transactions and an audit trail of entries.

Since Chip and Anna are using Excelerator to create the data flow diagrams, all the components of the diagram may be described in Excelerator's repository, the XLDictionary. Chip starts by working on the ADD MICROCOMPUTER data flow diagram.

The description for Process 1.5, UPDATE PENDING MICROCOMPUTER ORDER is shown in Figure E9.8. The **Label** area contains the text that appears on the diagram. The **Explodes To:** entry is one of the most important entry areas. In the example shown, Chip has the process exploding to a **PPS**, a code for Primitive Process Specifications, which contains the detailed logic for updating the PENDING MICROCOMPUTER ORDER. Chip may easily explode the process to display these details or later use the XLDictionary feature to report on any or all Primitive Process Specifications.

Using a second description screen shown in Figure E9.9, Chip further links the update process to the user requirement UPDATE PENDING MICROCOMP. FILE and the test plan PENDING MICROCOMP. FILE UPDATE. All microcomputer hardware descriptions are grouped into the category MICROCOMPUTER INFORMATION.

Similarly, Chip describes Process 1 from the parent data flow diagram. This process is printed using Excelerator commands, as illustrated in Figure E9.10. The explosion path is to a DFD for Data Flow Diagram and the name DIAGRAM 1. This allows Chip to **Explode** or easily move from one diagram to another within Excelerator. Notice that when an entity is printed, the information from several screens is included on one easy-to-read report.

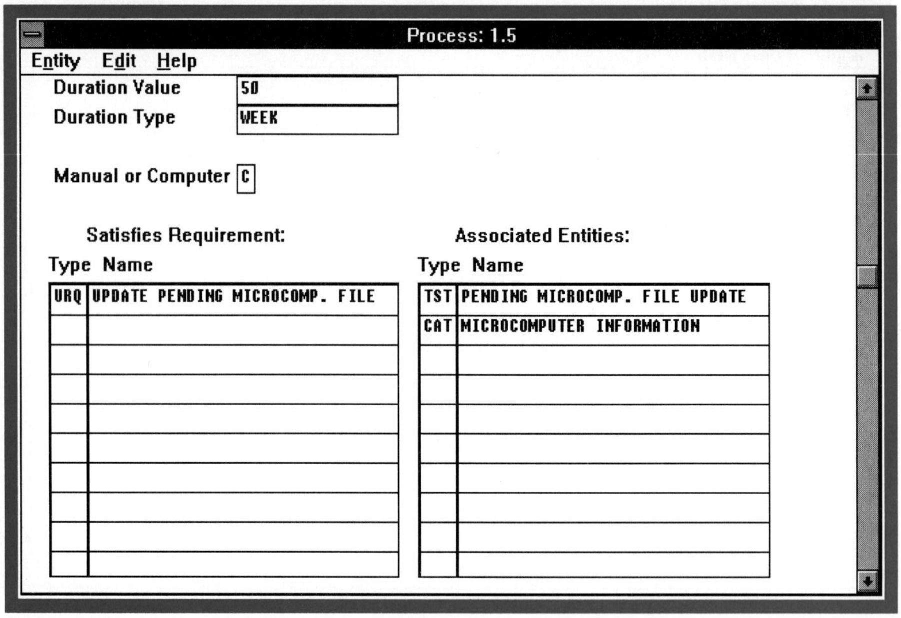

FIGURE E9.9
Process description screen, UPDATE PENDING ORDER, showing associated entities.

Anna describes the SOFTWARE MASTER data store, shown in Figure E9.11. This data store explodes to the record SOFTWARE MASTER. The record description contains details of the fields and smaller records composing the data store. There is also an entry area for **Index Elements** or key fields.

These provide both documentation for the data store and input to some of Excelerator's superb analysis options.

The NEW MICROCOMPUTER data flow designed by Chip is shown in Figure E9.12. This data flow explodes to a record containing NEW MICROCOMPUTER FORM details. The **Access Type** is A for an add transaction. Other components are similarly described.

It takes time to enter descriptions for all of the objects, but once the entries are complete Excelerator will provide comprehensive analysis of the design. Data Flow Diagram analysis provides several important features for validating the data flow diagram, the explosion diagrams, and descriptions of objects and connections.

When a specified data flow diagram is analyzed, the resultant report may reveal that any of the following data flow diagram syntax errors exist in that DFD:

1. The data flow diagram must have at least one process and must not have any freestanding objects or objects connected to themselves.
2. A process must receive at least one data flow and create at least one data flow. Processes with all input or all output should not occur.
3. A data store should be connected to at least one process.
4. A data store must contain, as part of its structure, the input and output data flow.
5. External entities should not be connected to each other. Although they communicate independently, that communication is not part of the system being designed.

```
DATE: 28-NOV-93      PROCESS - OUTPUT                    PAGE    1
TIME: 00:25          NAME: 1                          Excelerator

TYPE Process                         NAME 1

  Label      ADD NEW   MICRO-    COMPUTER

  Explodes To:     [DFD-STC-STD-PPS-PRG]
  Type DFD Name   DIAGRAM 1


  Location          IBM PS2 MODEL 385SX

  Process Category   BATCH

  Duration Value     50
  Duration Type      WEEK

  Manual or Computer C


        Satisfies Requirement:              Associated Entities:
  Type  Name                           Type  Name
  URQ ADD NEW MICROCOMPUTERS           CAT MICROCOMPUTER INFORMATION
  URQ MAINTAIN MICROCOMPUTER MASTER    TST ADD NEW MICROCOMPUTER
                                       TST PENDING MICROCOMP. FILE UPDATE


                    Description
  THIS PROCESS IS THE PORTION OF THE MICROCOMPUTER SYSTEM THAT ADDS NEW
  MICROCOMPUTERS TO THE MICROCOMPUTER MASTER FILE.  SEVERAL REPORTS ARE
  PRODUCED.  DETAILS ARE PROVIDED IN DIAGRAM 1.


  Modified By   CHIP          Date Modified  950401    # Changes  4
  Added By      ALLEN         Date Added     930702
  Last Project  MICRO
  Locked By                   Date Locked    0         Lock Status
```

FIGURE E9.10
Process description print, PROCESS 1.

Excelerator does not show the following errors or check the standards set by Chip and Anna for the project:

1. Data flow names in and out of a process should change (with exceptions).

2. Linear flow (several processes with only one input and output) is rarely found. Except in very low-level processes, it is a warning sign that some of the processes may be missing input or output flow.

3. External entities should not be connected directly to data stores. For example, you would not let an employee rummage through the Employee master file!

4. Process names should contain a verb describing the work being performed (with exceptions, such as INQUIRY SUBSYSTEM). Data flow names should be nouns.

Chip and Anna both use Excelerator to verify that the data flow diagram syntax is correct. Figure E9.13 shows a data flow diagram that has

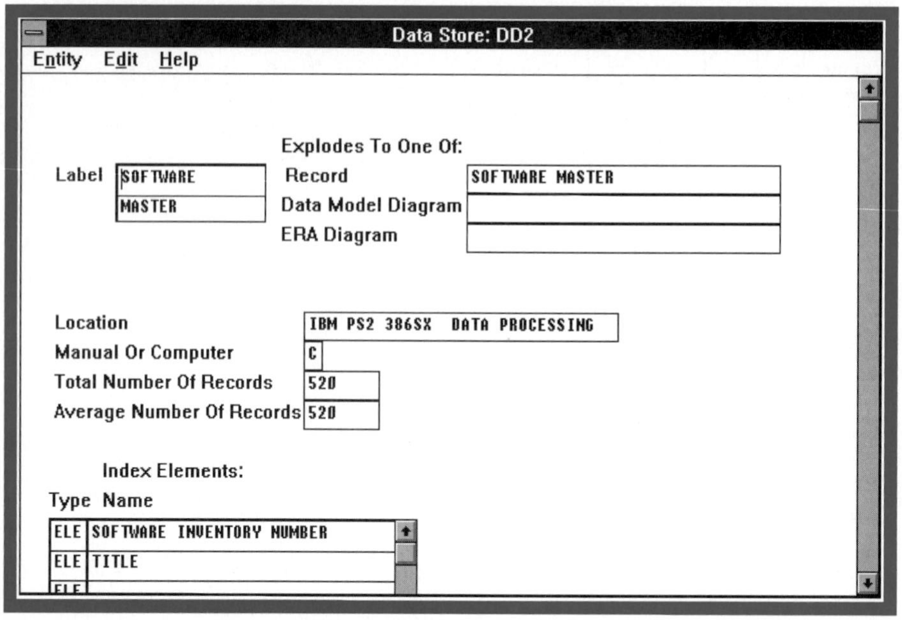

FIGURE E9.11
Data store description screen, SOFTWARE MASTER.

syntactical errors. The analysis report is shown in Figure E9.14. Notice that columns show the object type, the label or XLDictionary ID, and an error message.

Excelerator will also check that the levels balance among data flow diagram processes and the child diagrams. Inputs and outputs that do not match are shown.

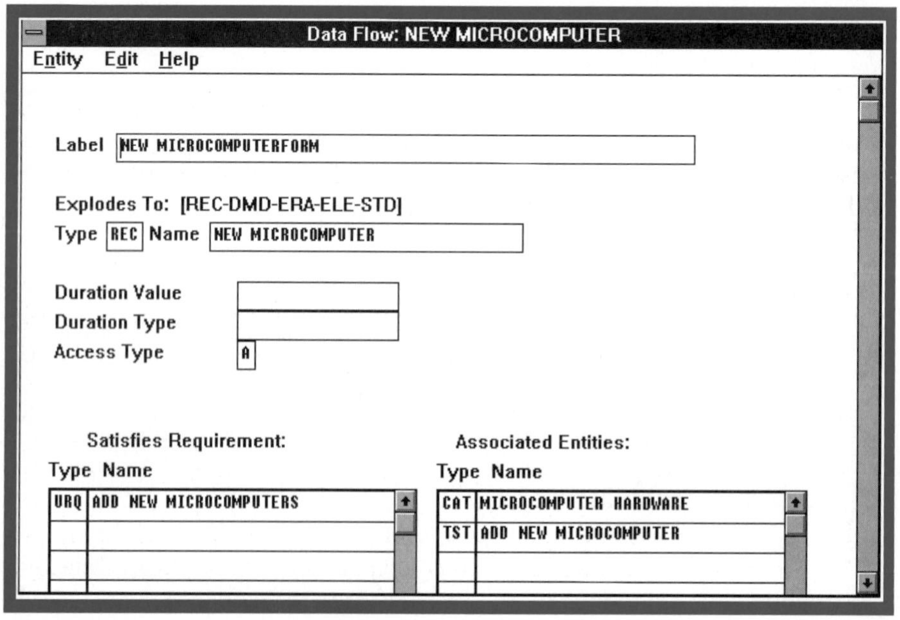

FIGURE E9.12
Data flow description screen, NEW MICROCOMPUTER

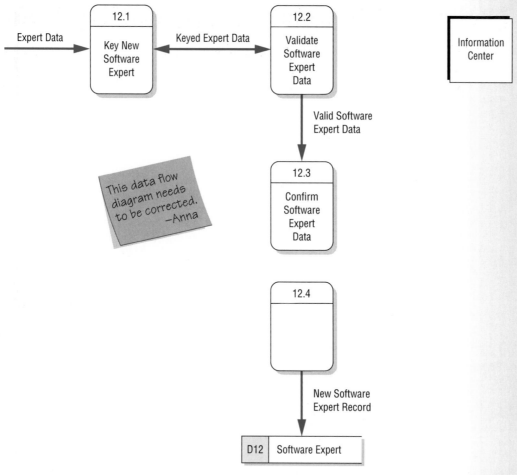

FIGURE E9.13
Data flow diagram with errors.

An **Undescribed Graph Entities** report shows the entities, the data stores, processes, and data flow that are found on a diagram but are not described in the XLDictionary. Chip and Anna found this report very useful for showing them design work that was incomplete.

Exercises [*]

▢ **E-1.** Use Excelerator to view the context diagram for the Proposed Microcomputer System. Experiment with ZOOM to view the diagram on different levels. Use the DESCRIBE option to view some of the data stores and the central process. Explode the central process to Diagram 0. Examine the data store descriptions. Zoom to CLOSE UP and use the orientation map to view different regions of the drawing screen. Print a window containing Process 9, Inquiry Subsystem. Explode Process 1 to view Diagram 1. Use the OTHER/RETURN feature to return to Diagram

---

[*] The exercises preceded by a disk icon require the program Excelerator (or another CASE tool). A disk is provided free of charge to any professor adopting this book. The examples on the disk may be imported into Excelerator and then used by students.

```
DATE: 21-FEB-95              DATA FLOW DIAGRAM              PAGE     1
TIME: 12:21                                                Excelerator
PROJECT NAME: CENTRAL PACIFIC UNIVERSITY


GRAPH NAME:  DIAGRAM 12


Data Flow Diagram Exceptions:

 TYPE      I/L  OBJECT ID OR LABEL                MESSAGE
 -----------------------------------------------------------------------
 -
|X-ENTITY | L | INFOR- MATION CENTER        | Is a free standing object  |
|PROCESS  | L | KEY NEW SOFTWARE EXPERT      | Does not produce DAF or CTF |
|PROCESS  | L | VALIDATE SOFTWARE EXPERT DATA| Does not receive DAF        |
|PROCESS  | L | CONFIRM SOFTWARE EXPERT DATA | Does not produce DAF or CTF |
|PROCESS  |   |       ** not labeled **      | Does not receive DAF        |
|                                                                        |
 -----------------------------------------------------------------------
 -
```

FIGURE E9.14
Data flow diagram validation report.

0. Explode Process 2 to view Diagram 2. Use OTHER/RETNTOP to return to the context diagram. Exit without saving.

E-2. Modify Diagram 0 of the Proposed Microcomputer System. Add Process 10, UPDATE SOFTWARE RECORD. Describe the process, including the explosion path DIAGRAM 10. Print a window showing the completed work.

Input:	1.	Software Changes, from Clerical Support
	2.	Software Delete ID, from Management
Output:	1.	Software Record, an update from the Software Master data store

E-3. Modify Diagram 10, UPDATE SOFTWARE RECORD. Add Process 10.2, Delete Software Record. Create the interface data flow, SOFTWARE DELETE ID. Connect to the SOFTWARE MASTER using a double-headed arrow. (*Hint:* Change the profile for this.) Print the final diagram.

E-4. Modify Diagram 4, INSTALL SOFTWARE. Add the following processes, describing each in the XLDictionary. Zoom to close up and check your diagram for a professional appearance. Print the final result, using the window option.

Process:		4.2 Install Microcomputer Software
Description:		Manual process, place software on machine
Input:	1.	Microcomputer Location, from Process 4.1
	2.	Software Title and Version, from Process 4.1
Output:	1.	Installed software form
Process:		4.3 Create Installed Software Transaction
Description:		Batch data entry process of creating

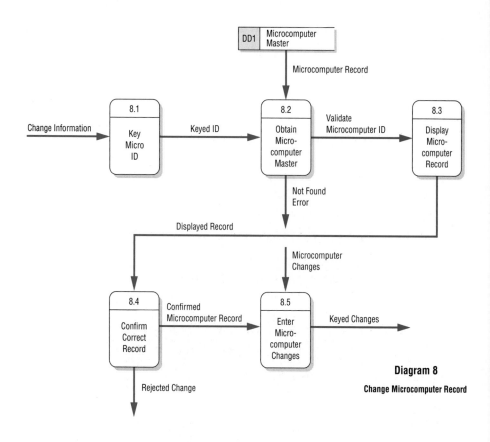

FIGURE E9.15
CHANGE MICROCOMPUTER data flow diagram.

		installed software transactions, including validation
Input:	1.	Installed software form
Output:	1.	Installed Software transaction, to Installed Software data store

Process:		4.4 Update Software Master
Description:		Random update of the SOFTWARE MASTER data store with update information
Input:	1.	Installed Software Transaction
Output:	1.	Software Master, update

Process:		4.5 Produce Installation Notification
Description:		Produce an installation notification informing users on which machines the software has been installed
Input:	1.	Installed Software Transaction
	2.	Software Master, from the SOFTWARE MASTER data store
	3.	Hardware Master, from the HARDWARE MASTER data store
Output:	1.	Installation Notification listing, an interface flow

E-5. Modify Diagram 8, Change Microcomputer Record, which is shown in Figure E9.15. This is an interactive, online program to change microcomputer information. Add the following three processes. Use DESCRIBE to add them to the XLDictionary. Describe the data flow. When completed, ZOOM to CLOSE UP, use the MOVE command to change the connections labels for a professional-looking graph, and print the diagram.

a. Process 8.6, VALIDATE CHANGES. This process edits each change field for validity. The input is the KEYED CHANGES. The output fields are CHANGE ERRORS (interface flow) and VALID CHANGES (to Process 8.7).

b. Process 8.7, CONFIRM CHANGES. This is a visual confirmation of the changes. The operator has a chance to reject the changes or accept them. Input is the VALID CHANGES. The output fields are REJECTED CHANGES (interface flow) and CONFIRMED CHANGES (to Process 8.8).

c. Process 8.8, REWRITE MICROCOMPUTER MASTER. This is a rewrite of the Microcomputer Master record with the changes on the record. Input is the CONFIRMED CHANGES. Output flow is the MICROCOMPUTER MASTER record, to the MICROCOMPUTER MASTER data store.

E-6. Create the explosion data flow diagram for Process 6, DELETE MICROCOMPUTER. The following table summarizes input, process, and output. Describe each process and data flow. When completed, ZOOM to CLOSE UP, use the MOVE command to change the connections labels for a professional-looking graph, and print the diagram.

Process:	6.1	—Key Delete ID
Description:		The microcomputer ID is keyed interactively
Input:	1.	Deleted Micro ID
Output:	1.	Keyed Delete

Process:	6.2	—Obtain Microcomputer Record
Description:		The Microcomputer Master record is read to ensure that it exists
Input:	1.	Keyed Delete (interface)
	2.	Microcomputer record, from the Microcomputer Master data store
Output:	1.	Not Found Error (interface)
	2.	Valid Microcomputer record

Process:	6.3	—Confirm Microcomputer Deletion
Description:		The microcomputer information is displayed on the screen for operator confirmation or rejection
Input:	1.	Valid Microcomputer record
Output:	1.	Rejected Deletion (interface)
	2.	Confirmed Deletion

Process: 6.4   —Delete Microcomputer Record
Description: The microcomputer record is *logically*
                       (not physically) deleted from the
                       Microcomputer master file by rewriting
                       the record with an I for inactive in the
                       Record Code field
Input: 1.   Confirmed Deletion
Output: 2.   Deleted Microcomputer, a double-headed
                       arrow to the Microcomputer Master
                       data store

E-7. Run the data flow diagram Graph Validation report for each of the data flow diagrams described in previous problems. Examine the diagrams and note the problems detected.

E-8. Produce the Level Balancing report for the diagrams created in the previous problems. Examine and interpret the information provided.

E-9. Run the Underscribed Graph Entities report for the diagrams produced in previous problems. Make note of the corrections that need to be made for the design material to be complete.

## 10

ANALYZING SYSTEMS USING DATA DICTIONARIES

After successive levels of data flow diagrams are complete, systems analysts use them to help catalog the data processes, flows, stores, structures, and elements in a data dictionary. Of particular importance are the names used to characterize data items. When given an opportunity to name components of data-oriented systems, the systems analyst needs to work at making the name meaningful yet exclusive of other existing data component names. This chapter covers the data dictionary, which is another method to aid in the analysis of data-oriented systems.

THE DATA DICTIONARY

The data dictionary is a specialized application of the kinds of dictionaries used as references in everyday life. The data dictionary is a reference work of data about data (that is, metadata) compiled by systems analysts to guide them through analysis and design. As a document, the data dictionary collects, coordinates, and confirms what a specific data term means to different people in the organization. The data flow diagrams covered in Chapter 9 are an excellent starting point for collecting data dictionary entries.

Systems analysts must be aware of and catalog different terms that refer to the same data item. This helps to avoid duplication of effort, allows better communication between organizational departments sharing a database, and makes maintenance more straightforward. The data dictionary can also serve as a consistent standard for data elements.

Automated data dictionaries (also part of the CASE tools mentioned earlier) are valuable for their capacity to cross-reference data items, thereby allowing necessary program changes to all programs sharing a common element. This feature supplants changing programs on a haphazard basis or waiting until the program won't run because a change has not been implemented across all programs sharing the updated item. Clearly, automated data dictionaries become important for large systems that produce several thousand data elements requiring cataloging and cross-referencing.

Need for Understanding the Data Dictionary

Many database management systems now come equipped with an auto-mated data dictionary. These dictionaries can be either elaborate or simple. Some computerized data dictionaries automatically catalog data items when programming is done; others simply provide a template to prompt the person filling in the dictionary to do so in a uniform manner for every entry.

Despite the existence of automated data dictionaries, understanding what data composes a data dictionary, the conventions used in data dictionaries, and how a data dictionary is developed are issues that remain pertinent for the systems analyst during the systems effort. Small systems with up to 1,000 entries can still be kept effectively in a manual data dictionary. Understanding the process of compiling a data dictionary can aid the systems analyst in conceptualizing the system and how it works. The upcoming sections allow the systems analyst to see the rationale behind what exists in automated data dictionaries as well as manual ones.

In addition to providing documentation and eliminating redundancy, the data dictionary may be used to:

1. Validate the data flow diagram for completeness and accuracy.
2. Provide a starting point for developing screens and reports.
3. Determine the contents of data stored in files.
4. Develop the logic for data flow diagram processes.

THE DATA REPOSITORY

While the data dictionary contains information about data and procedures, a larger collection of project information is called a repository. The repository concept is one of the many impacts of CASE tools and may contain the following:

1. Information about the data maintained by the system including data flow, data stores, record structures, and elements.
2. Procedural logic.
3. Screen and report design.
4. Data relationships, such as how one data structure is linked to another.
5. Project requirements and final system deliverables.
6. Project management information, such as delivery schedules, achievements, issues that need resolving, and project users.

The data dictionary is created by examining and describing the contents of the data flow, data stores, and processes, as illustrated by Figure 10.1. Each data store and data flow should be defined and then expanded to include the details of the elements it contains. The logic of each process should be described using the data flowing in or out of the process. Omissions and other design errors should be noted and resolved.

The four data dictionary categories—data flows, data structures, data elements, and data stores—should be developed to promote understanding of the data of the system. Procedural logic will be presented in Chapter 11.

To illustrate how data dictionary entries are created we will refer to an example for World's Trend Catalog Division. This company sells clothing and other items by mail order. A sample order form can be seen in Figure 10.2.

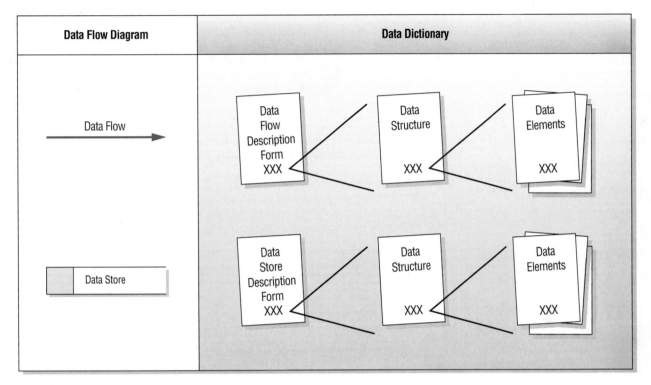

Data Flow Diagram	Data Dictionary

FIGURE 10.1
How data dictionaries relate to data flow diagrams.

This example gives some clues about what to enter into a data dictionary. First, you need to capture and store the name, address, and telephone number of the person placing the order. Then you need to address the details of the order: the item description, size, color, price, quantity, and so on. The customer's method of payment must also be determined. Once you have done this, these data may be stored for future use. This example will be used throughout this chapter to illustrate each part of the data dictionary.

Defining the Data Flow

Data flow is usually the first component to be defined. System inputs and outputs are determined from interviewing, observing users, and analyzing documents and other existing systems. The information captured for each data flow may be summarized using a form containing the following information:

1. ID, an optional identification number. Sometimes the ID is coded using a scheme to identify the system and the application within the system.
2. A unique descriptive name for this data flow. This name is the text that should appear on the diagram and be referenced in all descriptions using the data flow.
3. A general description of the data flow.
4. The source of the data flow. This could be an external entity, a process, or a data flow coming from a data store.

FIGURE 10.2
An order form from World's
Trend Catalog Division.

World's Trend
1000 International Lane
Cornwall, CT 06050
Customer Order

Please print clearly. See reverse side for item size codes. If the payment is made using a bank credit card, please include the credit card number and expiration date. Use charts on the reverse side for size codes and to determine postage. Connecticut residents must include sales tax.

Name (first, Middle, Last)					
Gilbert Sullivan					
Street			Apartment		
115 Buttercup Lane					
City		State	Zip		Country
Penzance		PA	17057		
Customer number (if known)		Catalog no.	Order Date (MM/DD/YY)		Telephone (Incl. Area Code)
09288		9401A	03/12/94		(215) 747-2837

Quantity	Item Number	Item Description	Size	Color	Price	Item Total
1	12343	Jogging Suit	M	BL	35.50	35.50
4	54224	Cushion impact socks/pair	M	WH	4.25	17.00
1	10617	Running shorts	M	BL	12.25	12.25
1	10617	Running shorts	M	GR	12.25	12.25

Method of Payment					
☐ Check	☑ Charge	☐ Money Order			

Fill in for credit card purchase only
☑ World's Trend ☐ AmExpress ☐ Discover ☐ MC ☐ Visa

Credit Card Number - Not required for World's Trend Charges   Expiration Date-MM/YY

Merchandise Total	77.00
Tax (CT Only)	
Shipping and Handling	9.80
Order Total	86.80

Form Number 0001 03/94

5. The destination of the data flow (same items listed under the source).

6. An indication of whether the data flow is a record entering or leaving a file, or containing a report, form, or screen. If the data flow contains data that are used between processes, it is designated as *internal*.

7. The name of the data structure describing the elements found on this data flow. For a simple data flow, this could be one or several elements.

8. The volume per unit of time. This could be records per day or any other unit of time.

9. An area for further comments and notations about the data flow.

Once again we can use our World's Trend Catalog Division example from Chapter 9 to illustrate a completed form. Figure 10.3 is an example of the data flow description representing the screen used to add a new CUSTOMER ORDER and to update the customer and item files. Notice that the external entity CUSTOMER is the input and that PROCESS 1 is the destina-

FIGURE 10.3
An example of a data flow
description from World's
Trend Catalog Division.

Data Flow Description

ID _____

Name _Customer Order_

Description _Contains customer order information and is used to update the_
customer master and item files and to produce an order record.

Source	Destination

Type of Data Flow

☐ File   ☑ Screen   ☐ Report   ☐ Form   ☐ Internal

Data Structure Traveling with the Flow	Volume/Time
Order Information	10/hour

Comments _An order record information for one customer order. The order_
may be received by mail, FAX or by the customer telephoning the order
processing department directly.

tion, providing linkage back to the data flow diagram. The checked box for "Screen" indicates that the flow represents an input screen. The detailed description of the data flow would not appear on this form, but would appear as a data structure.

Data flow for all input and output should be described first, followed by the intermediate data flow and the data flow to and from data stores. The detail of each data flow is described using a data structure, a group of elements sometimes called fields. A simple data flow may be described using a single element, for example, a customer number used by an inquiry program to find the matching customer record. An example of an electronic form is shown in Figure 10.4. Visible Analyst was used to create the form.

Describing Data Structures

Data structures are usually described using algebraic notation. This allows the analyst to produce a view of the elements that make up the data structure, along with information about those elements. For instance, the analyst will denote whether there are many of the same element within the data structure (a repeating group) or whether two elements may exist mutually exclusive of each other. The algebraic notation uses the following symbols:

1.   An equal sign (=) means "is composed of."
2.   A plus sign (+) means "and."
3.   Braces { } indicate repetitive elements, also called repeating groups or tables. There may be one repeating element or several within the group. The repeating group may have conditions, such as a fixed number of repetitions or upper and lower limits for the number of repetitions.

Define Item

Label: Customer Order

Entry Type: Data Flow

Description: Contains customer order information and is used to update the customer master and item files and to produce an order record.

Alias:

Composition: Order information

Notes: An order record contains information for one customer order. The order may be received by mail, FAX or by the customer telephoning the order processing department directly.

Help | Delete | Next | Save | Search | Jump | Page Two
Erase | Prior | Exit | Expand | File | Search Criteria...

4. Brackets [ ] represent an either/or situation. Either one element may be present or another, but not both. The elements listed between the brackets are mutually exclusive.

5. Parentheses ( ) represent an optional element. Optional elements may be left blank on entry screens and may contain spaces or zeros for numeric fields on file structures.

Figure 10.5 is an example of the data structure for adding a customer order at World's Trend Catalog Division. Each NEW CUSTOMER SCREEN consists of the entries found on the right side of the equal sign. Some of the entries are elements, but others, such as CUSTOMER NAME, ADDRESS, and TELEPHONE, are groups of elements or structural records. For example, CUSTOMER NAME is made up of FIRST NAME, MIDDLE INITIAL, and LAST NAME. Each structural record must be further defined until the entire set is broken down into its component elements. Notice that following the definition for the customer order screen are definitions for each structural record. Even a field as simple as the TELEPHONE NUMBER is defined as a structure so that the area code may be processed individually.

Structural records and elements that are used within many different systems are given a non-system specific name, such as street, city, and zip, that does not reflect the functional area within which they are used. This allows the analyst to define these records once and use them in many different applications. For example, a city may be a customer city, supplier city, or employee city. Notice the use of parentheses to indicate that (MIDDLE INITIAL), (APARTMENT), and (ZIP EXPANSION) are optional

FIGURE 10.5
Data structure example for
adding a customer order at
World's Trend Catalog
Division.

```
Customer Order =        Customer Number +
                        Customer Name +
                        Address +
                        Telephone +
                        Catalog Number +
                        Order Date +
                        {Available Order Items} +
                        Merchandise Total +
                        (Tax) +
                        Shipping and Handling +
                        Order Total +
                        Method of Payment +
                        (Credit Card Type) +
                        (Credit Card Number) +
                        (Expiration Date)

Customer Name =         First Name +
                        (Middle Initial) +
                        Last Name

Address =               Street +
                        (Apartment) +
                        City +
                        State +
                        Zip +
                        (Zip Expansion) +
                        (Country)

Telephone =             Area Code +
                        Local Number

Available Order Items = Quantity Ordered +
                        Item Number +
                        Item Description +
                        Size +
                        Color +
                        Price +
                        Item Total

Method of Payment =     [Check ¦ Charge ¦ Money Order]

Credit Card Type =      [World's Trend ¦ Amer. Express ¦ Discover ¦ MasterCard ¦ Visa]
```

ORDER (but not more than one). Indicate the OR condition by enclosing the options in square brackets and separating them with the symbol |.

Logical and Physical Data Structures

When data structures are first defined, only the data elements that the user would see, such as a name, address, and balance due are included. This stage is the logical design, showing what data the business needs for day-to-day operation. Using the logical design as a basis, the analyst then designs the physical data structures. These include additional elements necessary for implementing the system. Examples of physical design elements are:

FIGURE 10.6
Physical elements added to a
data structure.

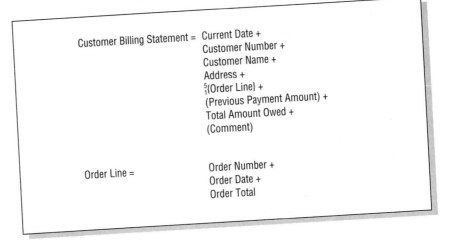

Customer Billing Statement = Current Date +
Customer Number +
Customer Name +
Address +
$^5_1${Order Line} +
(Previous Payment Amount) +
Total Amount Owed +
(Comment)

Order Line =
Order Number +
Order Date +
Order Total

1. Key fields used to locate records in a file. An example is an item number, which is not required for a business to function but is necessary for identifying and locating computer records.

2. Codes to identify the status of master records, such as whether an employee is active (currently employed) or inactive, maintained on files for producing tax information.

3. Transaction codes are used to identify types of records when a file contains different record types. An example is a credit file containing records for returned items as well as payments.

4. Repeating group entries containing a count of how many items are in the group.

5. Limits on the number of items in a repeated group.

Figure 10.6 is an example of the data structure for a Customer Billing Statement, showing that the Order Line is both a repeating item and a structural record. The Order Line limits are from 1 to 5, indicating that the customer may order from one to five items on this screen. Additional items would appear on subsequent orders.

The repeating group notation may have several other formats. If the group repeats a fixed number of times, that number is placed next to the opening brace, as in 12 {Monthly Sales}, where there are always 12 months in the year. If no number is indicated, the group repeats indefinitely. An example is a file containing an indefinite number of records, such as Customer Master File = {Customer Records}.

The number of entries in repeating groups may also depend on a condition, such as an entry on the Customer Master Record for each item ordered. This condition could be stored in the data dictionary as {Items Purchased} 5, where 5 is the number of items.

Data Elements

Each data element should be defined once in the data dictionary and may also be entered previously on an element description form such as the one illustrated in Figure 10.7. Characteristics commonly included on the element description form are:

Element Description Form

ID _____
Name _Customer Number_
Alias _Client Number_
Alias _Receivable Account Number_
Description _Uniquely identifies a customer that has made any business_
transaction within the last five years.

Element Characteristics

Length _6_   Dec. Pt. _____   ☐ Alphabetic
Input Format _9 (6)_   ☐ Alphanumeric
Output Format _9 (6)_   ☐ Date
Default Value _____   ☑ Numeric
☑ Continuous or ☐ Discrete   ☐ Base or ☑ Derived

Validation Criteria

Continuous	Discrete Value	Meaning
Upper Limit _<999999_		
Lower Limit _>0_		

Comments _The customer number must pass a modulus-11 check digit test._

1. Element ID. This optional entry allows the analyst to build automated data dictionary entries.

2. The name of the element. This should be descriptive, unique, and based on what the element is commonly called in most programs or by the major user of the element.

3. Aliases, which are synonyms or other names for the element. These are names used by different users within different systems. For example, a CUSTOMER NUMBER may also be called a RECEIVABLE ACCOUNT NUMBER or a CLIENT NUMBER.

4. A short description of the element.

5. Whether the element is base or derived. A base element is one that is initially keyed into the system, such as a customer name, address or city. Base elements must be stored on files. Derived elements are created by processes as the result of calculations or logic. An example is the total amount that a customer owes or an employee's gross pay. Analysis of base and derived elements differs and this difference provides a means of determining areas of the system that may need further work.

6. The length of an element. This should be the *stored* length of the item. The on-screen and printed lengths of the item may differ from this value, but the programs responsible for displaying the item on

the screen or printing it in a report will insert any additional formatting characters required. An important consideration is how long to make an element. Some elements have standard lengths. In the United States, for example, lengths for state name abbreviations, zip codes, and telephone numbers are all standard. For other elements the length may vary, and the analyst and user community must jointly decide the final length based on the following considerations:

a. Numeric amount lengths should be determined by figuring the largest number the amount will probably contain and then allowing reasonable room for expansion. Lengths designated for totals should be large enough to accommodate the sum of the numbers accumulated into them.

b. Name and address fields may be given lengths based on the following table. For example, a last name field of 11 characters will accommodate 98 percent of the last names in the U.S.

Field	Length	Percent of data that will fit (U.S.)
Last Name	11	98
First Name	18	95
Company Name	20	95
Street	18	90
City	17	99

c. For other fields, it is often useful to examine or sample historical data found within the organization to determine a suitable field length. For example, scanning a list of item descriptions would allow the analyst to find the largest description as well as a reasonable average length.

7. The type of data: numeric, date, alphabetic, or alphanumeric. Alphanumeric fields may contain a mixture of letters, numbers, and special characters. If the element is a date, its format—for example, MMDDYYYY—must be determined. If the element is numeric, its storage type should be determined. There are three standard formats: zoned decimal, packed decimal, and binary. The zoned decimal format is used for printing and displaying data. The packed decimal format is commonly used to save space on file layouts and for elements that require a high level of arithmetic to be performed on them. The binary format is suitable for the same purposes as packed decimal format but is less commonly used.

8. Input and output formats should be included, using special coding symbols to indicate how the data should be presented. These symbols and their use are illustrated in Figure 10.8. Each symbol represents one character or digit. If the same character repeats several times, the character followed by a number in parentheses indicating how many times the character repeats is substituted for the group. For example, XXXXXXXX would represent as X(8).

9. Validation criteria for ensuring that accurate data are captured by the system. Elements are either discrete, meaning they have certain fixed values, or continuous, with a smooth range of values. Here are common editing criteria:

a. A range of values is suitable for elements that contain continuous data. For example, in the U.S. a student grade point average may be

Formatting Character	Meaning
X	May enter or display / print any character
9	Enter of display only numbers
Z	Display leading zeros as spaces
,	Insert commas into a numeric display
.	Insert a period into a numeric display
/	Insert slashes into a numeric display
-	Insert a hyphen into a numeric display
V	Indicate a decimal position (when the decimal point is not included)

FIGURE 10.8
Format character codes.

from 0.00 through 4.00. If there is only an upper or lower bound to the data, a limit is used instead of a range.

b. A list of values is indicated if the data are discrete. Examples are codes representing the colors of items for sale in World's Trends' catalog.

c. A table of codes is suitable if the list of values is extensive (for example, state abbreviations, telephone country codes, or U.S. telephone area codes).

d. For key or index elements, a check digit is often included.

10. Any default value the element may have. The default value is displayed on entry screens and is used to reduce the amount of keying that the operator may have to do. Usually, several fields within each system have default values.

11. An additional comment or remarks area. This might be used to indicate the format of the date, special validation that is required, the check digit method used (explained in Chapter 9), and so on.

An example of a Visible Analyst data element description form can be found in Figure 10.9. As shown on the form, the CUSTOMER NUMBER may be called CLIENT NUMBER elsewhere in the system (perhaps old code written with this alias needs to be updated). The form is also useful because we can tell from it that the element is a numeric variable with a length of 6 characters. This variable can be as large as 999999 but cannot be less than zero.

Another kind of data element is an alphabetic element. In the case shown in Figure 10.10, the element is a discrete variable assigned certain codes. At World's Trend Catalog Division codes are used to describe colors: BL for blue, WH for white, and GR for green. When this element is implemented a table will be needed in order for users to look up the meanings of these codes. (Coding will be discussed further in Chapter 19.)

Data Stores

All base elements must be stored within the system. Derived elements, such as the employee year-to-date gross pay, may also be stored in the system. Data stores are created for each different data entity being stored. That is, when data flow base elements are grouped together to form a structural record, a data store is created for each unique structural record.

Since a given data flow may only show part of the collective data that a structural record contains, you may have to examine many different data flow structures to arrive at a complete data store description. For example,

FIGURE 10.9
Visible Analyst Workbench
(VAW) screens showing an
element description. Two
pages are required to
define an element.

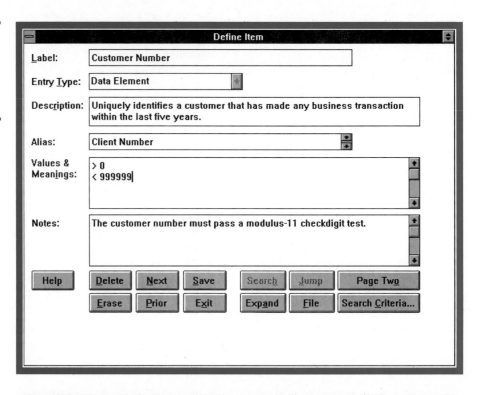

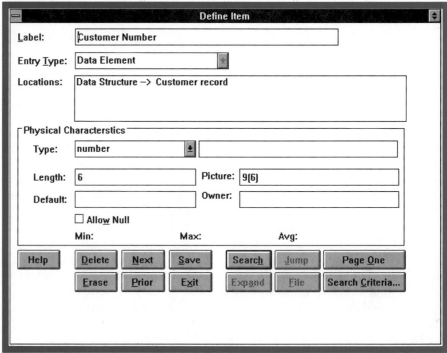

when adding a customer, you may initially include only information
known when the record is first created. Running balances, transaction
dates, and other information added to the Customer data store only after
business has progressed would be on different data flows.

Figure 10.11 is a typical form used to describe a data store. The information included on the form is:

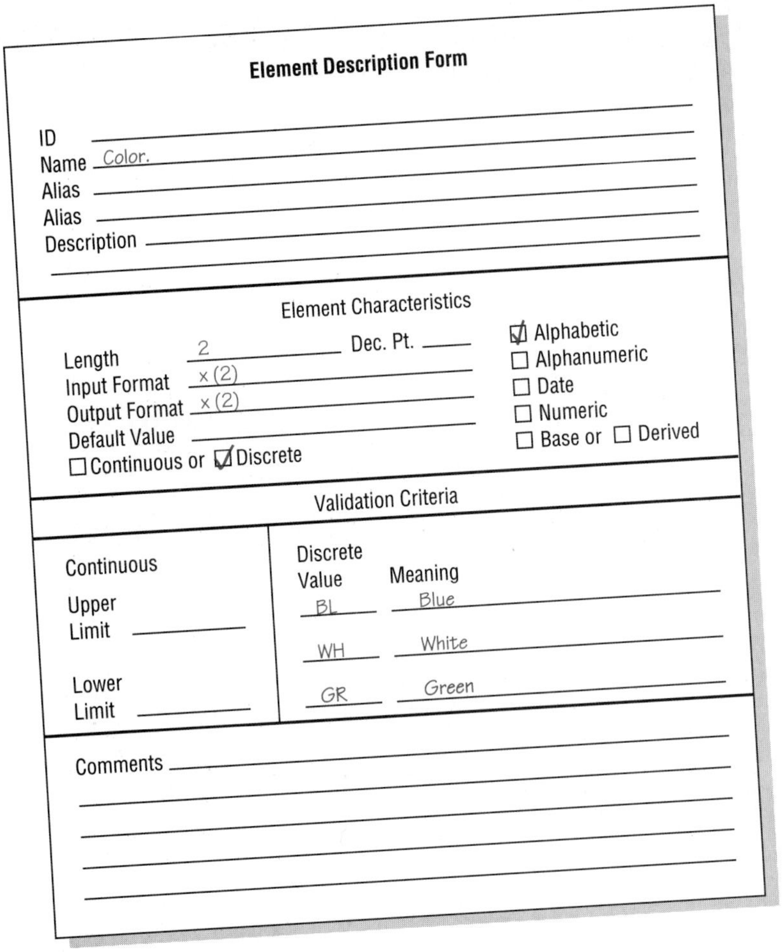

FIGURE 10.10
An example of an alphabetic element description form from World's Trend Catalog Division.

Element Description Form

ID _____
Name _Color._____
Alias _____
Alias _____
Description _____
_____

Element Characteristics

Length _____2_____ Dec. Pt. _____   ☑ Alphabetic
Input Format _x (2)_____   ☐ Alphanumeric
Output Format _x (2)_____   ☐ Date
Default Value _____   ☐ Numeric
☐ Continuous or ☑ Discrete   ☐ Base or ☐ Derived

Validation Criteria

Continuous	Discrete Value	Meaning
Upper Limit _____	BL	Blue
	WH	White
Lower Limit _____	GR	Green

Comments _____
_____
_____
_____
_____
_____

1. The Data Store ID. This is often a mandatory entry to prevent the analyst from storing redundant information. An example would be D1 for the CUSTOMER MASTER FILE.

2. The Data Store Name, descriptive and unique.

3. An Alias for the file, such as CLIENT MASTER FILE for the CUSTOMER MASTER FILE.

4. A short description of the data store.

5. The file type, either manual or computerized.

6. If the file is computerized, the file format designates whether the file is a database file or has the format of a traditional flat file. (File formats are detailed in Chapter 17.)

7. The maximum and average number of records on the file, as well as the growth per year. This information helps the analyst to predict the amount of disk space required for the application and is necessary for hardware acquisition planning.

8. The data set name specifies the file name, if known. In the initial design stages, this item may be left blank. An electronic form produced using Visible Analyst is shown in Figure 10.12. This example shows that the CUSTOMER MASTER FILE is stored on a computer in the form of a database with a maximum number of 45,000 records. (Records and the keys used to sort the database will be explained in Chapter 17.)

Data Store Description Form

ID _____ D 1 _____
Name _____ Customer Master File _____
Alias _____ Client Master File _____
Description _____ Contains a record for each customer. _____

Data Store Characteristics

File Type ☑ Computer ☐ Manual ☐ Sequential ☐ Direct
File Format ☑ Database ☐ Indexed

Record Size (Characters): _____ 200 _____ Block Size: _____ 4000 _____
Number of Records: Maximum _____ 45.000 _____ Average _____ 42,000 _____
Percent Growth per Year: _____ 6 _____ %

Data Set Name _____ Customer.MST _____
Copy Member _____ Custmast _____
Data Structure _____ Customer Record _____
Primary Key _____ Customer Number _____
Secondary Keys _____ Customer Name _____
_____ Zip _____
_____ Year to Date Amount Purchased _____

Comments _____ The Customer Master file records are copied to a history file and
purged if the customer has not purchased an item within the past
5 years. A customer may be retained even if he or she has not made a
purchase by requesting a catalog. _____

9. The data structure should use a name found in the data dictionary, providing a link to the elements for this data store. Primary and secondary keys must be elements (or a combination of elements) found within the data structure. In the example, the CUSTOMER NUMBER is the primary key and should be unique. The CUSTOMER NAME, ZIP, and YEAR-TO-DATE AMOUNT PURCHASED are secondary keys used to control record sequencing on reports and directly locate records. (Keys will be discussed in Chapter 17.)

CREATING THE DATA DICTIONARY

Data dictionary entries may be created after the data flow diagram has been completed or constructed as the data flow diagram is being developed. The use of algebraic notation and structural records allows the analyst to develop the data dictionary and the data flow diagrams using a top-down approach. For instance, the analyst may create Diagram 0 after the first few interviews and, at the same time, make the preliminary data dictionary entries. Typically, these consist of the data flow names found on the data flow diagram and their corresponding data structures. After several additional interviews have been conducted to learn the details of the system, the data flow diagram will be expanded and child diagrams created. The data dictionary is then modified to include the new

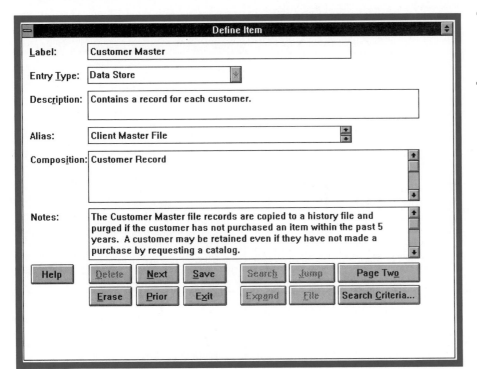

structural records and elements gleaned from further interviews, observation, and document analysis.

Each level of a data flow diagram should use data appropriate for the level. Diagram 0 should include only forms, screens, reports, and records. As child diagrams are created, the data flow into and out of the processes becomes more and more detailed, including structural records and elements. Thus each data flow diagram has data appropriate for the level of detail it is depicting. The data dictionary is needed because you would not want to show records and screens on a detailed child data flow diagram, nor scores of elements on a high-level data flow diagram.

Figure 10.13 illustrates a portion of two data flow diagram levels and corresponding data dictionary entries for producing an employee paycheck. Process 5, found on Diagram 0, is an overview of producing an EMPLOYEE PAYCHECK. The corresponding data dictionary entry for EMPLOYEE RECORD shows the EMPLOYEE NUMBER and four structural records, the view of the data obtained early in the analysis. Similarly, TIMEFILE RECORD and the EMPLOYEE PAYCHECK are also defined as series of structures.

If prototypes or sample documents are available, the complete data dictionary and set of data flow diagrams may be developed. If you have not previously obtained complete information, use the preliminary documentation to formulate questions such as "How is the payroll produced?" and "What fields are found on the paycheck?" for a second series of interviews with systems users. After each interview, the emerging system is documented by creating child diagrams and completing the corresponding data structures (Process 5.3 for example). This procedure is repeated until all data structures are completely defined.

As mentioned in Chapter 9, data flow diagrams must be balanced vertically between the parent process and the child diagram, yet each diagram should use

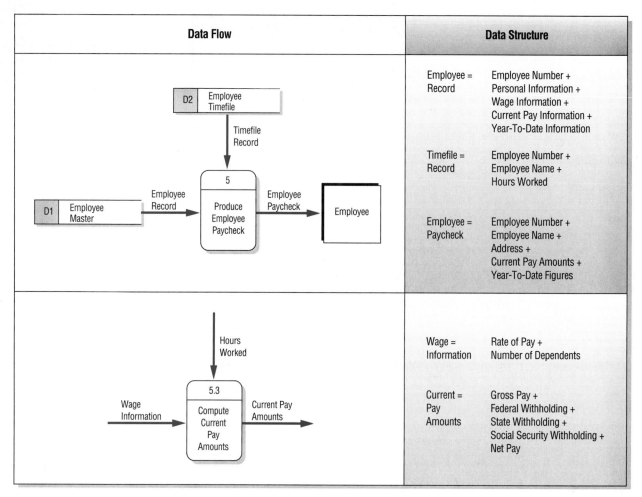

Data Flow	Data Structure

	Employee = Record	Employee Number + Personal Information + Wage Information + Current Pay Information + Year-To-Date Information
	Timefile = Record	Employee Number + Employee Name + Hours Worked
	Employee = Paycheck	Employee Number + Employee Name + Address + Current Pay Amounts + Year-To-Date Figures
	Wage = Information	Rate of Pay + Number of Dependents
	Current = Pay Amounts	Gross Pay + Federal Withholding + State Withholding + Social Security Withholding + Net Pay

FIGURE 10.13
Two data flow diagrams and corresponding data dictionary entries for producing an employee paycheck.

meaningful names for its level of data flow. For example, it would not make sense to use names such as EMPLOYEE RECORDS (input to Process 5.3.4, CALCULATE HOURLY GROSS PAY). Conversely, using the elements for calculating hourly gross pay on Diagram 0 would needlessly clutter that diagram.

Balancing data flow diagram levels is accomplished by using the data dictionary structures. Names do not have to match between the parent process and a corresponding child diagram. What is important is that the data flow names on the child data flow diagram are contained as elements or structural records within the data flow on the parent process. Returning to the example, WAGE INFORMATION (input into Process 5.3, COMPUTE CURRENT PAY AMOUNTS) is a structural record contained within the EMPLOYEE RECORD (input to Process 5). Similarly, GROSS PAY (output from Process 5.3.4) is contained within the structural record CURRENT PAY AMOUNTS (output from the parent Process 5.3, COMPUTE CURRENT PAY AMOUNTS).

Analyzing Input and Output

An important step in creating the data dictionary is to identify and categorize system input and output data flow. Input and output analysis forms

FIGURE 10.14
An input/output analysis
form example for World's
Trend Catalog Division.

Input and Output Analysis Form

Input/Output Name Customer Billing Statement

User Contact Susan Han

File Type ☑ Output ☐ Screen ☐ Undetermined

File Format ☑ Report

Sequencing Element(s) Zip Code (Page Sequence)
Order Number

Element Name	Length	B/D	Edit Criteria
Current Date	6	B	(System Supplied)
Customer Number	6	D	(Includes Check digit)
Customer First Name	20	B	Not Spaces
Customer Last Name	15	B	Not Spaces
Customer Middle Initial	1	B	A Through Z or Space
Street	20	B	Not Spaces
Apartment	20	B	Not Spaces
City	20	B	Not Spaces
State	2	B	Valid State Abbr.
Zip	9	B	Numeric, Last 4 Opt.
Order Number	6	D	> 0
Order Date	8	B	MM/DD/YY
Order Total	9	D	Format: 9 (7) V99
Previous Payment Amount	5	D	Format: 9 (7) V99
Total Amount Owed	9	D	Format: 9 (7) V99
Comment	60	B	

Comments Print one page for each customer. If there are more items
than will fit on a page, continue on a second page.

such as the one example shown in Figure 10.14 may be used to organize the information obtained from interviews and document analysis. Notice that this form contains the following commonly included fields:

1. A descriptive name for the input or output. If the data flow is on a logical diagram, the name should identify what the data are (for example, CUSTOMER INFORMATION). However, if the analyst is working on the physical design or if the user has explicitly stated the nature of the input or output, the name should include that information regarding the format. Examples are CUSTOMER STATEMENT and CUSTOMER DETAILS INQUIRY.

2. The user contact responsible for further details clarification, design feedback, and final approval.

3. Whether the data is input or output.

4. The format of the data flow. In the logical design stage, this may be undetermined.

5. Elements indicating the sequence of the data on a report or on a screen (perhaps in columns).

6. A list of elements, including their names, lengths, and whether they are base or derived, and their editing criteria.

Once the form has been completed, each element should be analyzed to determine whether the element repeats, whether it is optional, or whether

Want to Make It Big in the Theatre? Improve Your Diction(ary)!

As you enter the door of Merman's, Annie Oaklea greets you warmly, saying, "I'm delighted with the work you have done on the data flow diagrams. I would like you to keep playing the role of systems analyst for Merman's and see if you can eventually get a new information system for our costume inventory sewn up. Unfortunately, some of the terms you're using don't come off very well in the language of Shakespeare. Bit of a translation problem, I suspect."

Clinging to Annie's initial praise, you are undaunted by her exit line. You determine that a data dictionary based on the rental and return data flow diagrams would make a big hit.

Begin by writing entries for a manual system, in as much detail as possible. Prepare two data process entries, two data flow entries, two data store entries, one data structure entry, and four data element entries using the formats in this chapter. Portraying interrelated data items with preciseness will result in rave reviews. (Refer to Consulting Opportunity 9.2.)

---

it is mutually exclusive of another element. Elements that fall into a group or that regularly combine with several other elements in many structures should be placed together into a structural record.

These considerations can be seen in the completed Input and Output Analysis Form for World's Trend Catalog Division. In this example of a CUSTOMER BILLING STATEMENT, the CUSTOMER FIRST NAME, the CUSTOMER LAST NAME, and CUSTOMER MIDDLE INITIAL should be grouped together in a structural record.

Developing Data Stores

Another activity in creating the data dictionary is developing data stores. Up to now, we have determined what data needs to flow from one process to another. This information is described in data structures. The information, however, may be stored in numerous places and in each place the data store may be different. Whereas, data flows represent data in motion, data stores represent data at rest.

For example, when an order arrives at World's Trend it contains information of a temporary nature, that is, the information needed to fill that particular order. Meanwhile some of the information on the order form might be stored permanently. Examples of the latter include information about customers (so catalogs can be sent to them) and information about items (because these items will appear on many other customer's orders). Figure 10.15 shows that from a series of customer orders, information can be captured and stored into two data stores called CUSTOMER MASTER and the ITEM MASTER. An example of these data stores can be found in Figure 10.16.

Data stores contain information of a permanent or semi-permanent nature. An ITEM NUMBER, DESCRIPTION, and ITEM COST are examples of information that is relatively permanent. So is the TAX RATE. But when the ITEM COST is multiplied by the TAX RATE, the TAX CHARGED is calculated (or derived). Derived values do not have to be stored in a data store. When developing data stores it is acceptable to start with some information and then add more to the data store when you analyze more data flows and realize more information needs to be added.

When data stores are created for only one report or screen we can refer to them as "user views," because they represent the way that user

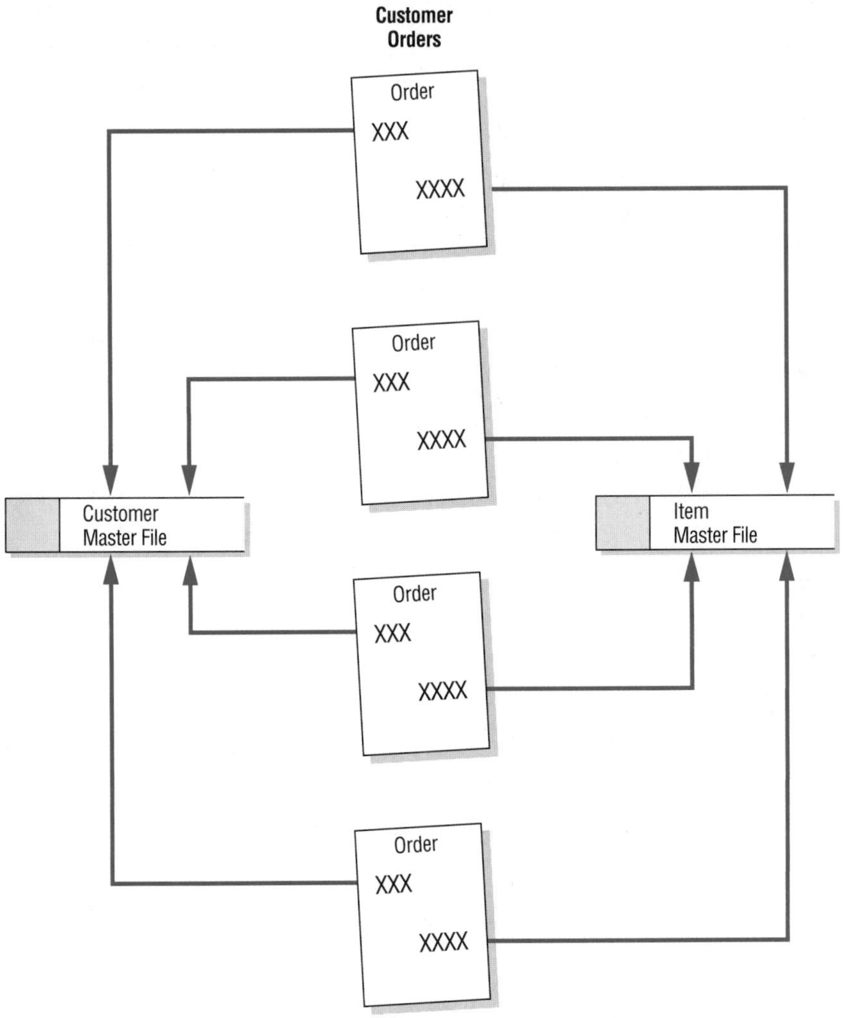

FIGURE 10.15
Information that comes from
customer orders may find
its way into different
data stores.

wants to see the information. A systems designer has to determine whether to set up individual files representing user views or set up a database representing many user views instead. The trade-offs associated with these two approaches are discussed in Chapter 17.

USING THE DATA DICTIONARY

The ideal data dictionary is automated, interactive, on line, and evolutionary. As the systems analyst learns about the organization's systems, data items are added to the data dictionary. On the other hand, the data dictionary is not an end in itself and must never become so. To avoid becoming sidetracked with the building of a complete data dictionary, the systems analyst should view it as an activity that parallels systems analysis and design.

To have maximum power, the data dictionary should be tied into a number of systems programs so that when an item is updated or deleted from the data dictionary it is automatically updated or deleted from the database. The data dictionary becomes only an historic curiosity if it is not kept current. Automated data dictionaries allow dramatic improvements in the upkeep of documentation. In doing so, they also change the work of the systems analyst.

FIGURE 10.16
Data stores derived from a
pending order at World's
Trend Catalog Division.

```
Customer Master =        Customer Number +
                         Customer Name +
                         Address +
                         Telephone +
                         Corporate Credit Card Number +
                         Expiration Date


Item Master =            Item Number +
                         Price +
                         Quantity On Hand


Order Record =           Customer Number +
                         Catalog Number +
                         Order Date +
                         {Available Order Items} +
                         Merchandise Total +
                         (Tax) +
                         Shipping and Handling +
                         Order Total +
                         Method of Payment +
                         (Credit Card Type) +
                         (Credit Card Number) +
                         (Expiration Date)


Available Order Items =  Item Number +
                         Quantity Ordered +
                         Quantity Shipped +
                         Current Price


Method of Payment =      [Check ¦ Charge ¦ Money Order]

Credit Card Type =       [World's Trend ¦ Amer. Express ¦ Discover ¦ MasterCard ¦ Visa]
```

Optional

selection

The data dictionary may also be used to create screens, reports, and forms. For example, examine the data structure for the World's Trend ORDER PICKING SLIP in Figure 10.17. Since the necessary elements and their lenghts have been defined, the process of creating physical documents consists of arranging the elements in a pleasing and functional way using design guidelines and common sense. Repeating groups become columns and structural records are grouped together on the screen, report, or form. The report layout for the World's Trends ORDER PICKING SLIP is shown in Figure 10.18. Notice that FIRST NAME and LAST NAME are grouped together in NAME and that QUANTITY (PICKED and ORDERED), SEC-TION, SHELF NUMBER, ITEM NUMBER, ITEM DESCRIPTION, SIZE, and COLOR form a series of columns, because they are the repeating elements.

The data structure and elements for a data store are commonly used to generate corresponding computer source language code, which is then incorporated into computer programs. The data dictionary may be used in conjunction with a data flow diagram to analyze the system design, detecting flaws and areas that need clarification. Some considerations are:

FIGURE 10.17
Data structure for an order
picking slip at World's Trend
Catalog Division.

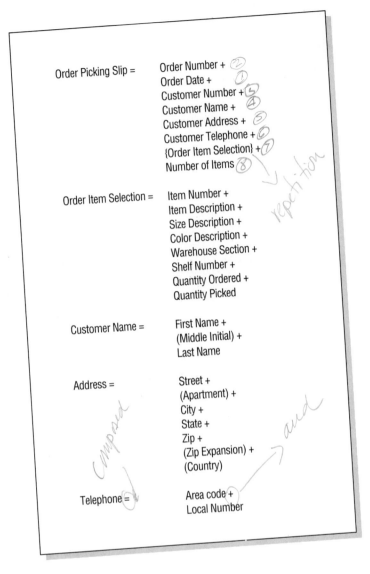

1. All base elements on an output data flow must be present on an input data flow to the process producing the output. Base elements are keyed and should never be created by a process.

2. A derived element must be created by a process and should be output from at least one process into which it is not input.

3. The elements that are present on a data flow coming into or going out of a data store must be contained within the data store.

Even though the trend is toward on-line automated data dictionaries, it is important to appreciate the importance of compiling even a manual data dictionary that is common to the organization. If begun early, a data dictionary can save many hours of time in the analysis and design phases. The data dictionary is the one common source in the organization for answering questions and settling disputes about any aspect of data definition. A current data dictionary can serve as an excellent reference for maintenance efforts on unfamiliar systems. Automated data dictionaries can serve as references for both people and programs.

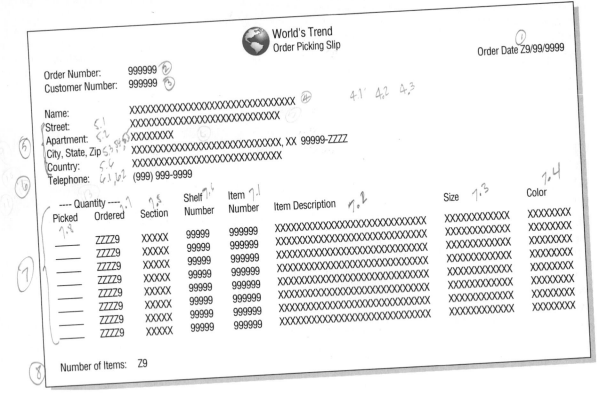

FIGURE 10.18
Order picking slip created from the data dictionary.

SUMMARY

Using a top-down approach, the systems analyst uses data flow diagrams to begin compiling a data dictionary, which is a reference work containing data about data, or "metadata," on all data processes, stores, flows, structures, and logical and physical elements within the system being studied. One way to begin is by including all data items from data flow diagrams.

A larger collection of project information is called a repository. CASE tools permit the analyst to create a repository that may include information about data flow, stores, record structures, and elements; procedural logic screen and report design; data relationships; project requirements and final system deliverables; and project management information.

Each entry in the data dictionary contains: the item name, English description, aliases, related data elements, range, length, encoding, and necessary editing information. The data dictionary is useful in all phases of analysis, design, and ultimately documentation, since it is the authoritative source on how a data element is used and defined in the system. Many large systems feature computerized data dictionaries, which cross-reference all programs in the database using a particular data element.

KEYWORDS AND PHRASES

data dictionary	repeating item
data structure	base element
data element	derived element

repository   zoned decimal
system deliverables   packed decimal
structural record   binary formats
physical data structures   repeating groups

REVIEW QUESTIONS

1. Define what is meant by the term *data dictionary.* Define *metadata.*
2. What are four reasons for compiling a complete data dictionary?
3. What are the chief differences between automated and manual data dictionaries?
4. What information is contained in the data repository?
5. What is a structural record?
6. List the seven specific categories that each entry in the data dictionary should contain. Briefly give the definition of each category.
7. What are the basic differences among data dictionary entries prepared for data stores, data structures, and data elements?
8. Why are structural records used?
9. What is the difference between logical and physical data structures?
10. Describe the difference between base and derived elements.
11. How do the data dictionary entries relate to levels within a set of data flow diagrams?
12. List the four steps to take in compiling a data dictionary.
13. Why shouldn't compiling the data dictionary be viewed as an end in itself?
14. What are the main benefits of using a data dictionary?

PROBLEMS

1. Based on Figure 9.EX1 in Chapter 9, Joe, one of your systems analysis team members, made the following entry for the manual data dictionary used by Marilyn's Tours:

   DATA ELEMENT = TOURIST* * * * PAYMENT
   ALIAS = TOURIST PAY
   CHARACTERS = 12–24
   RANGE = $5.00–$1,000
   VARIABLES = $5.00, $10.00, $15.00 up to $1,000, and anything in between in dollars and cents.
   TO CALCULATE = TOTAL COST OF ALL TOURS, ANY APPLICABLE N.Y. STATE TAX, minus any RESERVATION DEPOSITS made.

   a. Is this truly a data element? Why or why not?
   b. Rewrite the data dictionary entry for TOURIST PAYMENT, reclassifying it if necessary. Use the proper form for the classification you choose.

2. Pamela, the systems analyst, has made significant progress understanding the data movement at Bonton's clothing store. In order to share what she has done with other members of her team as well as the head of franchising in New York, she is manually composing a data dictionary.

"You're really doing very well. Snowden says you've given him all sorts of new ideas for running the new department. That's saying quite a lot, when you consider that he has a lot of his own ideas. By now I hope you've had a chance to speak with everyone that you would like to: certainly Snowden himself, Tom Ketcham, Daniel Hill, and Mr. Hyatt.

"Mr. Hyatt is an elusive soul, isn't he? I guess I didn't meet him until well into my third year. I hope you get to find out about him much sooner. Oh, but when you do get to see him, he cuts quite a figure, doesn't he? And those crazy airplanes. I've almost been conked on the head by one in the parking lot. But how can you get angry, when it's The Boss who's flying it? He's also got a secret—or should I say private—oriental garden off of his office suite. No, you'll never see it on the building plans. You have to get to know him very well before he'll show you that. But I would wager it's the only one like it in Tennessee—and maybe in the whole U.S. He fell in love with the wonderful gardens he saw in Southeast Asia as a young man. But it goes deeper than that. Mr. Hyatt knows the value of contemplation and meditation. If he has an opinion, you can be sure it has been well thought through."

HyperCase Questions

1. Briefly list the data elements that you have found on three different reports produced at MRE.

2. Based upon your interviews with Snowden Evans and others, list the data elements that you believe should be added to the Management Unit's project reporting systems to better capture important data on project status, project deadlines, and budget estimates.

3. Create a data dictionary entry for a new data store, a new data flow, and a new data process that you are suggesting based on your response to Question 2.

4. Suggest a list of new data elements that might be helpful to Jimmie Hyatt but are clearly not being made available to him currently.

   a. Write an entry in Pamela's data dictionary for one of the data flows that you depicted in your data flow diagram in problem 1 in Chapter 9. Be as complete as possible.

   b. Write an entry in Pamela's data dictionary for one of the data stores that you depicted in your data flow diagram in problem 1 in Chapter 9. Be as complete as possible.

3. Cecile, the manager of the bookstore that your systems analysis team has been working with to build a computerized inventory system, feels as if one of your team members is making a nuisance of himself by asking her extremely detailed questions about data items used in the system. For example, "Cecile, how much space, in characters, does listing of an ISBN number take?"

```
                           N                                                              5                    1
DATE Z9/99/99                       PRODUCT PART LISTING                                   •            PAGE ZZ9
   3  PRODUCT   PRODUCT DESCRIPTION  CREATION   PRODUCT    NUMBER    4 PART    PART DESCRIPTION   6 PART   WAREHOUSE
      NUMBER                         DATE       COST       OF PARTS    NUMBER  NUMBER             QUANTITY LOCATION

      999999    XXXXXXXXXXXXXXXXXX   Z9/99/99   ZZ,ZZ9.99      Z9     9999999  XXXXXXXXXXXXXXX      ZZ9     ZZZZ9
                                                                     9999999  XXXXXXXXXXXXXXX      ZZ9     ZZZZ9
                                                                     9999999  XXXXXXXXXXXXXXX      ZZ9     ZZZZ9
                                                                     9999999  XXXXXXXXXXXXXXX      ZZ9     ZZZZ9
                                                                     9999999  XXXXXXXXXXXXXXX      ZZ9     ZZZZ9
                                                                     9999999  XXXXXXXXXXXXXXX      ZZ9     ZZZZ9
                                                                     9999999  XXXXXXXXXXXXXXX      ZZ9     ZZZZ9
                                                                     9999999  XXXXXXXXXXXXXXX      ZZ9     ZZZZ9


      999999    XXXXXXXXXXXXXXXXXX   Z9/99/99   ZZ,ZZ9.99      Z9     9999999  XXXXXXXXXXXXXXX      ZZ9     ZZZZ9
                                                                     9999999  XXXXXXXXXXXXXXX      ZZ9     ZZZZ9
                                                                     9999999  XXXXXXXXXXXXXXX      ZZ9     ZZZZ9
                                                                     9999999  XXXXXXXXXXXXXXX      ZZ9     ZZZZ9
                                                                     9999999  XXXXXXXXXXXXXXX      ZZ9     ZZZZ9
                                                                     9999999  XXXXXXXXXXXXXXX      ZZ9     ZZZZ9

                            7  TOTAL NUMBER OF PRODUCTS ZZZZ9
```

FIGURE 10.EX1
A prototype of the Product-Part Listing.

---

a. What are the problems created by going directly to the manager with questions concerning data dictionary entries? Use a paragraph to list the problems you can see with your team member's approach.

b. In a paragraph, explain to your team member how he can better gather information for the data dictionary.

4. The Motion Manufacturing Company assembles bicycles, tricycles, scooters, roller blades and other outdoor sports equipment. Each outdoor product is built using many parts, which vary from product to product. Interviews with the head parts clerk have resulted in a list of elements for the Product-Part Listing, showing which parts are used in the manufacture of each product. A prototype of the Product-Part Listing is illustrated in Figure 10.EX1. Create a data structure dictionary entry for the Product-Part Listing. The head parts clerk has informed us that there are never more than 50 different parts for each product.

5. Analyze the elements found on the Product-Part Listing and create the data structure for the Product Master File and the Part Master File data stores.

6. Which of the elements on the Product-Part Listing are derived elements?

7. The Caribbean Cruise Company arranges cruise vacations of varying lengths at several locations. When customers call to check on the availability of a cruise, a Cruise Availability Inquiry, illustrated in Figure 10.EX2, is used to supply them with information. Create the data dictionary structure for the Cruise Availability Inquiry.

8. List the master files that would be necessary to implement the Cruise Availability Inquiry.

```
MM/DD/YY                    CRUISE AVAILABILITY            HH:MM
ENTER STATING DATE 99/99/99


----------------------------------------------------------------------

CRUISE INFORMATION:
CRUISE SHIP           XXXXXXXXXXXXXXXXXXX
LOCATION             XXXXXXXXXXXXXXXXXXX
STARTING DATE        Z9/99/99                  ENDING DATE Z9/99/99
NUMBER OF DAYS       ZZ9
COST                 ZZ,ZZZ.99
DISCOUNTS ACCEPTED   XXXXXXXXXXXX   XXXXXXXXXXXX   XXXXXXXXXXXXX
OPENINGS REMAINING ZZZZ9


XXXXXXXXXXXXXXXXXXXXXXXXXXXX COMMENTS XXXXXXXXXXXXXXXXXXXXXXXXXXXXXXXXXXX
F1 - HELP, F3 - MENU, F8 - NEXT CRUISE, F7 - PREVIOUS CRUISE, F10 - PORTS LIST
XXXXXXXXXXXXXXXXXXXXXXXXXX FEEDBACK MESSAGE XXXXXXXXXXXXXXXXXXXXXXXXXXXXXXXX
```

FIGURE 10.EX2
A VDT screen showing cruise availability

---

9. The following ports of call are available for the Caribbean Cruise
    Company:

Kingston	Port-au-Prince	Nassau
Montego Bay	St. Thomas	Freeport
Santo Domingo	Hamilton	Point-à-Pitre
San Juan	Port of Spain	St. Lucia

Create the PORT OF CALL element. Examine the data to determine the
length and format of the element.

GROUP PROJECTS

1. Meet with your group and use a CASE tool or a manual procedure to
    develop data dictionary entries for a process, data flow, data store,
    and data structure based on the data flow diagrams you completed for
    Maverick Transport in the Chapter 9 group exercises. As a group,
    agree on any assumptions necessary to make complete entries for
    each data element.
2. Your group should develop a list of methods to help you to make
    complete data dictionary entries for this exercise as well as for future
    projects. For example: Study existing reports; base them on new or
    existing data flow diagrams; and so on.

SELECTED BIBLIOGRAPHY

Colter, M. "A Comparative Examination of Systems Analysts Techniques."
    Management Information Systems Quarterly, June 1984, Vol. 8, No. 1,
    pp. 51–66.

Davis, G. B., and M. H. Olson. *Management Information Systems, Conceptual Foundations, Structure, and Development,* 2nd ed. New York: McGraw-Hill Book Company, 1985.

Gane, C., and T. Sarson. *Structured Systems Analysis and Design Tools and Techniques.* Englewood Cliffs, NJ: Prentice-Hall, Inc., 1979.

Gore, M., and J. Stubbe. *Elements of Systems Analysis,* 3rd ed. Dubuque, IA: William C. Brown Co., 1983.

Leeson, M. *Systems Analysis and Design.* Chicago, IL: Science Research Associates, Inc., 1985.

Lucas, H. *Information Systems Concepts for Management,* 3rd ed. New York: McGraw-Hill Book Company, 1986.

Martin, J. *Strategic Data-Planning Methodologies.* Englewood Cliffs, NJ: Prentice-Hall, Inc., 1982.

McFadden, F. R., and J. A. Hoffer. *Data Base Management.* Menlo Park, CA: The Benjamin/Cummings Publishing Company, 1985.

Semprevivo, P. C. *Systems Analysis and Design: Definition, Process, and Design.* Chicago, IL: Science Research Associates, Inc., 1982.

Senn, J. A. *Analysis and Design of Information Systems.* New York: McGraw-Hill Book Company, 1984.

Sprague, R.H., and E. D. Carlson. *Building Effective Decision Support Systems.* Englewood Cliffs, NJ: Prentice-Hall, 1982.

10 *Episode* CPU Case

DEFINING WHAT YOU MEAN

"We can use the data flow diagrams we completed to create data dictionary entries for all data flow and data stores," Chip says to Anna at their next meeting. Each of these components has a **Record** entry in the **Explodes To** area of the description screen. The records created for the Microcomputer System are thus linked directly to the data flow diagram components that describe data.

Anna and Chip meet to divide the work of creating records and elements. "I'll develop the data dictionary for the software portion of the system," Anna says.

"Good thing I enjoy doing the hardware," Chip kids her good-naturedly.

Records, or data structures, are created first. They may contain elements, the basic building blocks of the data structure, and may also contain other records within them called structural records. Program code may be easily generated using the dictionary. Excelerator also maintains relationships among graph components, records, and elements that may be used for analysis and reporting.

Using information from interviews and the prototype screens, Anna started to create the Software records. Since the output of a system will determine what data needs to be both stored and obtained via data entry screens, the starting point was the output data flow SOFTWARE INSTALLATION LIST. This prototype identifies some of the elements that should be stored within the Software Master file:

SOFTWARE INVENTORY NUMBER   DISKETTE SIZE
VERSION NUMBER   HARDWARE INVENTORY
NUMBER OF DISKETTES   NUMBER
CAMPUS LOCATION   ROOM LOCATION
TITLE

Other output prototype reports and screens were also examined. Additional elements were obtained when the ADD SOFTWARE prototype screen had been transformed into a record containing corresponding screen elements.

The final element list is shown in Figure E10.1. These elements were arranged into a logical sequence for the SOFTWARE MASTER file. The following standards for arranging elements within a record were used:

1. The major key element that uniquely identified the record. An example is the SOFTWARE INVENTORY NUMBER.
2. Descriptive information, such as TITLE, VERSION NUMBER, and PUBLISHER.
3. Information that is periodically updated, for example, the NUMBER OF COPIES.
4. Any repeating elements, such as HARDWARE INVENTORY NUMBER, denoting the machines on which the software has been installed.

```
DATE: 21-FEB-95      SOFTWARE ELEMENTS                        PAGE     1
TIME: 17:06                                                   Excelerator


ELE Name
-------------------------------
ACTIVE SOFTWARE CODE
COMPUTER BRAND
COMPUTER MODEL
DISKETTE SIZE
MEMORY REQUIRED
MONITOR REQUIRED
NUMBER OF COPIES
NUMBER OF DISKETTES
PRINTER REQUIRED
PUBLISHER
SITE LICENSE
SOFTWARE CATEGORY
SOFTWARE INVENTORY NUMBER
TITLE
VERSION NUMBER
```

FIGURE E10.1
Software element list.

Next, the SOFTWARE MASTER file record was created using Excelerator's **Record** entity. The description screen for creating a record is shown in Figure E10.2. Notice the entry area for an **Alternate Name**, or alias. Since each user may refer to the same record by a different name, all such names should be documented, resulting in enriched communication among users. **Normalized** should contain a Y if the data is in the third normal form.

Each element or structural record needs to be defined as part of the whole record. The name is keyed followed by the number of times the record or element repeats. The **Occ** or occurences column should contain the value 1 for all nonrepeating entries.

The **Type** column contains a code characterizing the entry, summarized as:

E   Elemental—not further subdivided.
R   Record—a structural record, one that is further subdivided.
K   Key—the primary key for the record. This is for a key that is not subdivided.

Alternate indexes may be specified in the **Sec-Keys** columns. The values that may be entered are:

S   Secondary key that is not subdivided
1–9   These numbers are for keys that are composed of several elementary items, that is, a *concatenated* key. The first field of the concatenated key should have the number 1; the second, field number 2; etc.

Examine the SOFTWARE MASTER file shown in Figure E10.2. It contains a primary key of SOFTWARE INVENTORY NUMBER and a secondary key of TITLE. A structural record, INSTALLATION MICROCOMPUTER contains hardware cross-reference information.

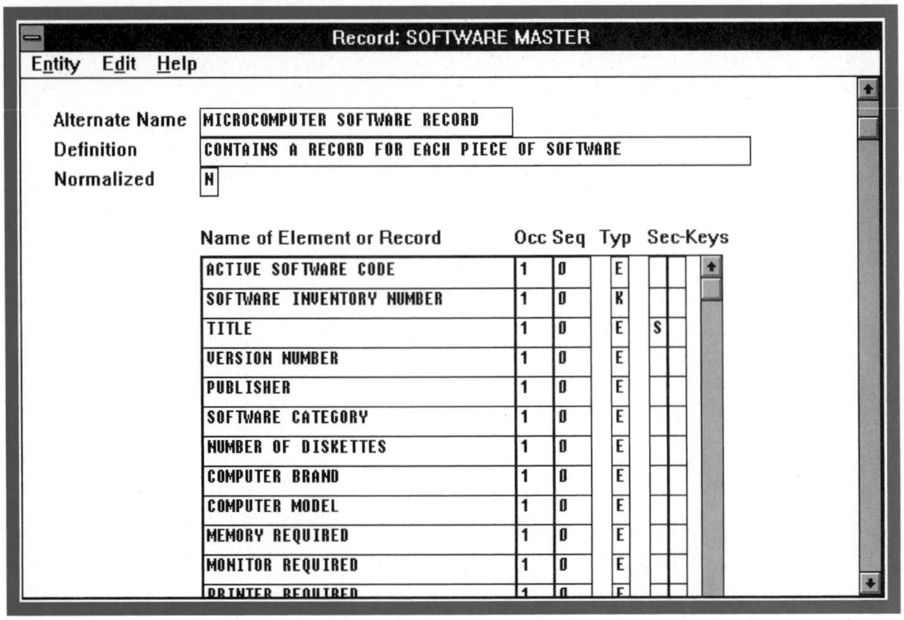

FIGURE E10.2
Record description screen, SOFTWARE MASTER file.

Excelerator allows you to easily describe each structural record or element composing the larger record. Anna places the cursor in each **Name** area and presses the F4 key. Further record and element screens are displayed and detailed information is entered.

"This is great!" Anna thinks to herself. "It's so easy to enter the details, and by using this method I won't accidentally forget to describe an element."

Chip is also impressed with the simplicity of creating the data dictionary. Following a process similar to Anna's, he creates a record description for the MICROCOMPUTER MASTER file. It contains a table of five internal boards and two structural records, PERIPHERAL EQUIPMENT and MAINTENANCE INFORMATION, illustrated in Figure E10.3. The area for entering Element or Record names is a scroll region, meaning that more lines may be keyed than will fit in the screen area. As entries are added to the bottom of the region, top entries scroll out of the area.

As elements are added to the record, Chip decides to describe each in detail. The Element description screen for the HARDWARE INVENTORY NUMBER is shown in Figure E10.4. Observe the areas for entering element attributes. Several alternate names may be included along with a definition, which is used as a help message when prototyping.

Input and output pictures are used to describe how the data are formatted. Each such picture is a coded entry, similar to those used in programming languages. Examples of some of the codes are:

9   Represents numeric data: Only numbers may be entered when prototyping.
A   Alphabetic: Only alphabetic characters may be entered.
X   Alphanumeric: Any characters may be entered.
Z   Zero suppression: Replace leading zeros with spaces.
$ Dollar sign: Replace leading zeros with a dollar sign.

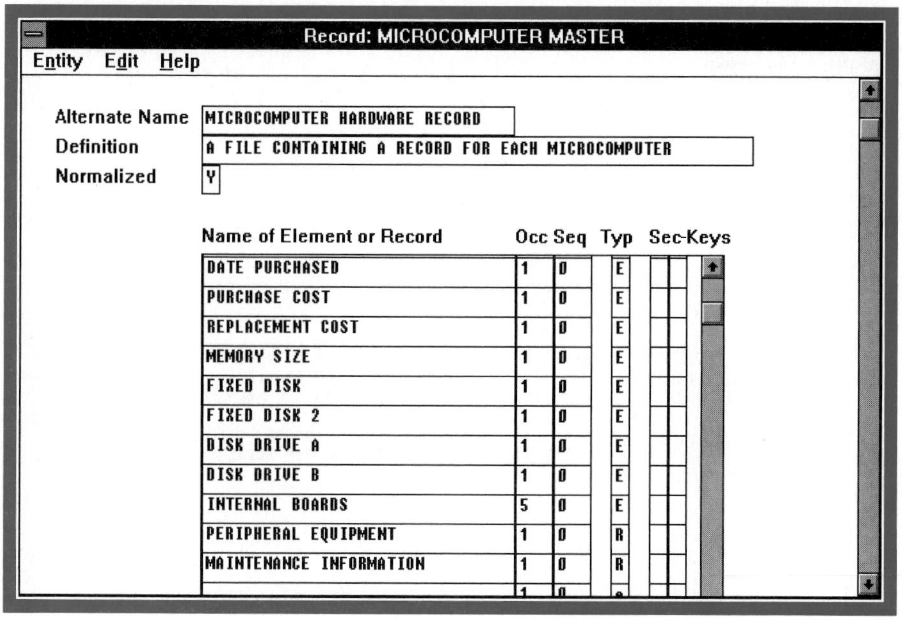

FIGURE E10.3
MICROCOMPUTER MASTER record description screen.

Chip is careful to include complete entries for the **Edit rules**, which define the allowable values that the element can have. These rules serve the dual purpose of providing documentation and limiting the values that may be entered when testing prototype screens.

The **Base** or **Derived** entry is another critical attribute that categorizes the data into one of two classes. A base (code B) element is an input field, one

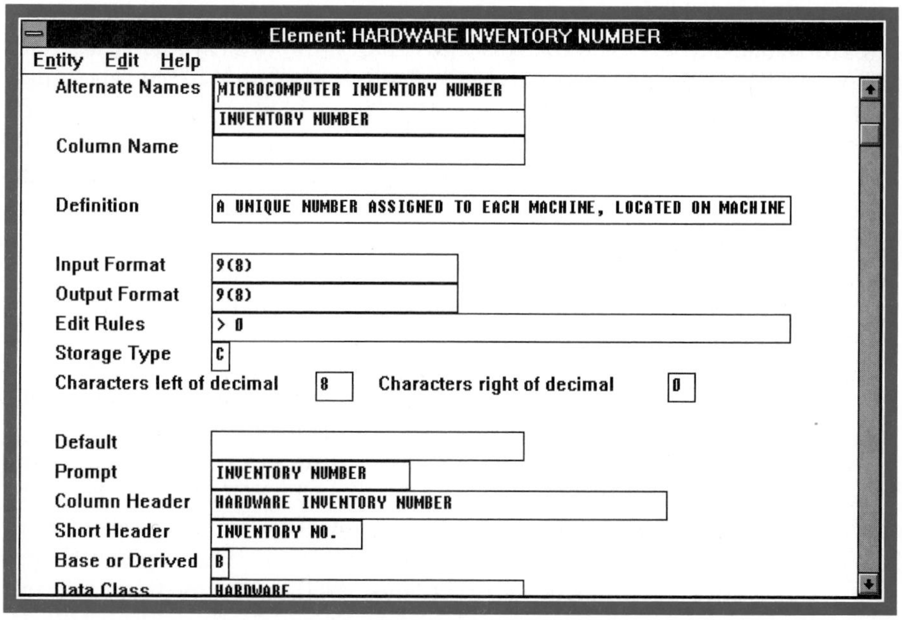

FIGURE E10.4
Element description screen, INVENTORY NUMBER.

```
┌─────────────────────────────────────────────────────────────────────┐
│ ═      Element: HARDWARE INVENTORY NUMBER                             ↑│
│ Entity  Edit  Help                                                    │
│ ┌──────────────────────┐      ┌──────────────────────┐              ↑│
│ │                      │      │                      │               │
│ │                      │      │                      │               │
│ │                      │      │                      │               │
│ │                      │      │                      │               │
│ │                      │      │                      │               │
│ │                      │      │                      │               │
│ │                      │      │                      │               │
│ └──────────────────────┘      └──────────────────────┘               │
│                      Description                                      │
│ ┌───────────────────────────────────────────────────────────────┐   │
│ │ THE HARDWARE INVENTORY NUMBER IS A UNIQUE NUMBER DESCRIBING ONE│   │
│ │ PARTICULAR MICROCOMPUTER.  THIS IS THE PRIMARY KEY FIELD FOR THE│  │
│ │ MICROCOMPUTER MASTER FILE.  IT IS PHYSICALLY ATTACHED TO THE MACHINE.│
│ │                                                               │   │
│ │ THE INVENTORY NUMBER IS A SEVEN DIGIT NUMBER WITH A CHECKDIGIT ATTACHED│
│ │ TO THE RIGHT.  WHEN ENTERING THE NUMBER, VALIDATE USING THE MODULUS-11│
│ │ CHECKDIGIT METHOD.                                            │   │
│ └───────────────────────────────────────────────────────────────┘  ↓│
└─────────────────────────────────────────────────────────────────────┘
```

FIGURE E10.5
HARDWARE INVENTORY NUMBER, description screen.

that has been keyed. Derived elements (code D) are those that have been calculated within a process. This information is used in conjunction with the data flow diagram to generate valuable analysis reports on the system design.

A second screen is completed with user requirements and the Associated Entities. The third screen provides an area for a long description to be entered. This description may contain any information that does not fit into the attributes areas on the first screen. Chip and Anna employ this screen to enter further edit criteria and other useful notation. The description for the HARDWARE INVENTORY NUMBER is shown in Figure E10.5. Notice that the description details how this HARDWARE INVENTORY NUMBER is used to physically keep track of the machines. Also, observe the notation on using a Modulus-11 check digit to verify the entry.

Anna and Chip repeat this process for all elements found on each record. This is a time-consuming but worthwhile effort. After the first few records are created, it becomes easier to create the remaining record structures. Excelerator automatically provides lists of the elements contained within the design.

"I think that we've designed a complete set of elements," Chip says at a checkpoint meeting.

"Yes," replies Anna. "There are reports that will show us the details of the data structures and help us to spot duplications and omissions. Let's put Excelerator to work producing record layouts for us."

The XLDictionary feature was used to print record layouts for each master file. Figure E10.6 is the output for the MICROCOMPUTER MASTER. Notice that all the elements are included along with the offset from the beginning of the record, calculated by Excelerator. The **Type** and number of times the record occurs are included as well as the length and definition from the **Element** description. Structural records such as PERIPHERAL EQUIPMENT are expanded to include their elements, and the total record length is printed.

```
DATE: 21-FEB-95                         RECORD - EXPLOSION                              PAGE    1
TIME: 16:57                             NAME: MICROCOMPUTER MASTER                      Excelerator


NAME:                    MICROCOMPUTER MASTER              DEFINITION:
ALIAS:                   MICROCOMPUTER HARDWARE RECORD     A FILE CONTAINING A  RECORD FOR EACH MICROCOMPUTER        Y


ELEMENT/RECORD                          OFF  OCC  TYPE  LEN  DEFINITION
--------------------------------------- ---  ---  ----  ---  ------------------------------------------------------------

RECORD CODE                             000  001   E    001  ACTIVE OR INACTIVE MICRO.  INACTIVE MEANS NO LONGER AVAILABLE

HARDWARE INVENTORY NUMBER               001  001   K    008  A UNIQUE NUMBER  ASSIGNED TO EACH MACHINE, LOCATED ON MACHINE

BRAND NAME                              009  001   E    010  THE NAME OF THE  MICROCOMPUTER

MODEL                                   019  001   E    012  THE PARTICULAR MODEL OF  MICROCOMPUTER

SERIAL NUMBER                           031  001   E    012  SERIAL NUMBER ASSIGNED BY  MANUFACTURER

CAMPUS LOCATION                         043  001   E    004  CAMPUS WHERE  MICROCOMPUTER IS LOCATED

ROOM LOCATION                           047  001   E    005  THE ROOM THE HARDWARE,  SOFTWARE OR EXPERT IS LOCATED WITHIN

DATE PURCHASED                          052  001   E    006  DATE THE MACHINE WAS  PURCHASED

PURCHASE COST                           058  001   E    004  THE COST TO PURCHASE THE  MICROCOMPUTER

REPLACEMENT COST                        062  001   E    004  COST TO REPLACE HARDWARE

MEMORY SIZE                             066  001   E    005  SIZE OF MICRO RAM MEMORY, IN  THOUSANDS OF CHARACTERS (K)

FIXED DISK                              071  001   E    002  MEMORY SIZE OF THE FIXED DISK IN  MILLIONS OF CHARACTERS (M)

FIXED DISK 2                            073  001   E    002  MEMORY SIZE OF THE FIXED DISK IN  MILLIONS OF CHARACTERS (M)

DISK DRIVE A                            075  001   E    006  THE SIZE OF DISKETTE DRIVE A, IN  INCHES AND DENSITY (LOW/HI)

DISK DRIVE B                            081  001   E    006  THE SIZE OF DISKETTE DRIVE B, IN  INCHES AND DENSITY (LOW/HI)

INTERNAL BOARDS                         087  005   E    003  THE OPTIONAL BOARDS THAT  ARE FOUND WITHIN THE MICROCOMPUTER

PERIPHERAL EQUIPMENT                    102  001   R         PERIPHERAL EQUIPMENT  STRUCTURAL RECORD                    Y
   MONITOR                              102  001   E    004  THE TYPE OF MONITOR ATTACHED   TO THE MICROCOMPUTER
   MOUSE                                106  001   E    001  MOUSE ATTACHED Y/N
   PRINTER                              107  001   E    005  A CODE FOR THE TYPE OF PRINTER  ATTACHED TO THE MICROCOMPUTER

MAINTENANCE INFORMATION                 112  001   R         MAINTENANCE PORTION OF  THE MICROCOMPUTER MASTER RECORD     Y
   WARRANTY                             112  001   E    001  IS A WARRANTY IN EFFECT (Y/N)
   MAINTENANCE INTERVAL                 113  001   E    002  THE LENGTH OF TIME   BETWEEN PREVENTIVE MAINTENANCE
   LAST PREVENT. MAINTENANCE DATE       115  001   E    008  THE DATE LAST   PREVENTIVE MAINTENANCE WAS PERFORMED
   NUMBER OF REPAIRS                    123  001   E    002  THE NUMBER OF TIMES THE  MICROCOMPUTER HAS BEEN REPAIRED
   COST OF REPAIRS                      125  001   E    004  THE TOTAL COST OF ALL REPAIRS

Record length is 129.
```

FIGURE E10.6
MICROCOMPUTER MASTER, record print.

"Anna, let's generate the computer program code for some of the records," Chip suggests. "It will be interesting to see how the code looks and perhaps produce some COPY library layouts."

A few selections with the mouse and several keystrokes later, the code is produced. Chip uses the Excelerator Code Generation screen, shown in Figure E10.7, to add a prefix of **CM-** to each entry and to select the computer language. Figure E10.8 is an example of code generated using COBOL language. Notice that Excelerator has replaced spaces in the element name with hyphens.

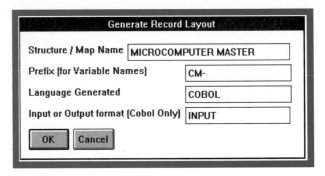

FIGURE E10.7
Generate record layout description screen.

RECORD AND ELEMENT ANALYSIS

"Now let's really put the power of Excelerator to use," Anna says. "Let's see how well we've really designed our data."

"What do you mean?" Chip asks.

"I've been studying the analysis features contained within Excelerator, and there's a wealth of options for checking our design for consistency and correctness," Anna replies. "The first step is to use Excelerator's XLDictionary to produce a summary report of the elements we've added. Then we can examine the list for duplications and redundancy."

Figure E10.9 is an example of the element summary report. Examine the contents carefully and look for redundancy, or elements defined more than once. These may be easy to spot since the list is sorted by element name. The elements HARDWARE INVENTORY NUMBER and HARD-WARE NUMBER, and SOFTWARE INVENTORY NUMBER and SOFT-WARE NUM, appear to be duplicate elements. Other duplicates, such as ROOM LOCATION and LOCATION, are harder to spot.

"Next we should use the XLDictionary **Relationships** option, which provides access to the many relationships maintained by Excelerator," Ann suggests, after a short break. "Each selection provides cross-reference information between two entities. Our first choice is **REC Contains ELE,** which shows the records and elements they contain. Notice that the available XLDictionary actions are different. We have two powerful choices for reporting. **Missing Entities** will show all the elements that need to be defined for a particular record, and **Summary Output** will list all elements for a particular record."

Figure E10.10 is the report produced for records containing elements that are missing entities. The first column shows records and the next column shows elements described on the records that are undefined in the XLDictionary.

"This is terrific!" exclaims Chip. "This Missing Elements report shows design work that needs to be completed. We should produce this for all the design components."

The undefined elements were added to the report. Producing the Missing Elements report a second time revealed no further undefined elements.

"Well, I guess that wraps up the data portion of the system design," Chip says.

"Guess again," replies Anna. "We've only begun to analyze. The Extended Analysis options will provide us with a lot of design information, both for analysis and for documentation."

```
*Record MICROCOMPUTER-MASTER Generated: 21-FEB-95
  01  MICROCOMPUTER-MASTER.
      05  CM-RECORD-CODE                   PIC X
                                  VALUE 'A'.
      05  CM-HARDWARE-INVENTORY-NUMBER
                                           PIC 9(8).
      05  CM-BRAND-NAME                    PIC X(10).
      05  CM-MODEL                         PIC X(12).
      05  CM-SERIAL-NUMBER                 PIC X(12).
      05  CM-CAMPUS-LOCATION               PIC XXXX.
      05  CM-ROOM-LOCATION                 PIC X(5).
      05  CM-DATE-PURCHASED                PIC 9(6).
      05  CM-PURCHASE-COST                 PIC 9(5).99
                       COMP-3.
      05  CM-REPLACEMENT-COST              PIC 9(5).99
                       COMP-3.
      05  CM-MEMORY-SIZE                   PIC 9(5).
      05  CM-FIXED-DISK                    PIC 999
                       COMP-3.
      05  CM-FIXED-DISK-2                  PIC 999
                       COMP-3.
      05  CM-DISK-DRIVE-A                  PIC X(6)
                                  VALUE '3.5HD'.
      05  CM-DISK-DRIVE-B                  PIC X(6).
      05  CM-INTERNAL-BOARDS               PIC XXX
                                        OCCURS 5 TIMES.
      05  CM-PERIPHERAL-EQUIPMENT.
          10  CM-MONITOR                   PIC X(4).
          10  CM-MOUSE                     PIC X
                                  VALUE 'N'.
          10  CM-PRINTER                   PIC X(5).
      05  CM-MAINTENANCE-INFORMATION.
          10  CM-WARRANTY                  PIC X
                                  VALUE 'Y'.
          10  CM-MAINTENANCE-INTERVAL  PIC 999
                       COMP-3.
          10  CM-LAST-PREVENT--MAINTENANCE-D
                                           PIC 9(6).
          10  CM-NUMBER-OF-REPAIRS         PIC 99.
          10  CM-COST-OF-REPAIRS           PIC 9(5).99
                       COMP-3.
```

FIGURE E10.8
MICROCOMPUTER MASTER generated code, COBOL language.

The analysts select **RECORD CONTENT ANALYSIS** as their first choice. The output of the Extended Analysis feature may take on two forms, either reports or matrices, a grid representation. The first option selected was **Empty Records**, which lists records without any structural records or elements. This option was chosen since it shows undefined records. Figure E10.11 is an example of the Empty Records report.

Corrections were made, and the **Recursive Records** report was produced, showing all records that contain themselves as a structural record at a lower level. Finally the **Equivalent Records** report was selected. It listed records that have the same lowest-level contents, that is, the same elements when all records have been expanded.

"I'm really impressed with this analysis," Chip says. "Since correcting the errors in our design, I've come to realize how easy it is to feel confident that the design has been completed when there are discrepancies and omissions still needing our attention."

ELEMENT NAME	ALTERNATE NAME	DEFINITION
ACTIVE SOFTWARE CODE		CODE TO DETERMINE IF SOFTWARE IS CURRENTLY IN USE
BRAND NAME	MICROCOMPUTER BRAND	THE NAME OF THE MICROCOMPUTER
CAMPUS LOCATION	CAMPUS CODE	CAMPUS WHERE MICROCOMPUTER IS LOCATED
CAMPUS LOCATION - LONG	FULL CAMPUS NAME	THE FULL CAMPUS NAME OBTAINED FROM THE CAMPUS TABLE
CATEGORY OF SOFT		A CODED ENTRY FOR THE TYPE OF SOFTWARE, REFER TO SOFTWARE CA
COMPUTER BRAND	HARDWARE REQUIRED	THE BRAND OF COMPUTER NECESSARY TO RUN THE SOFTWARE
COMPUTER MODEL		THE SPECIFIC MODEL NECESSARY TO RUN THE SOFTWARE
COST OF REPAIRS	TOTAL REPAIR COST	THE TOTAL COST OF ALL REPAIRS
COURSE ENROLLMENT LIMIT	ENROLLMENT LIMIT	THE MAXIMUM NUMBER OF PERSONS THAT MAY BE ENROLLED
COURSE INSTRUCTOR	INSTRUCTOR NAME	NAME OF THE INSTRUCTOR FOR A MICROCOMPUTER SOFTWARE COURSE
COURSE LENGTH	LENGTH OF CLASS	THE LENGTH OF THE COURSE IN DAYS
COURSE LEVEL		DIFFICULTY LEVEL: B BEGINNING, I INTER, A ADVANCED, P PROFES
COURSE TITLE	SOFTWARE TRAINING COURSE TITLE	THE TITLE OF A MICROCOMPUTER SOFTWARE TRAINING COURSE
DATE PURCHASED	ACQUISITION DATE	DATE THE MACHINE WAS PURCHASED
DEPARTMENT NAME	STAFF DEPARTMENT NAME	UNIVERSITY DEPARTMENT NAME
DISK DRIVE A	DISKETTE DRIVE A	THE SIZE OF DISKETTE DRIVE A, IN INCHES AND DENSITY (LOW/HI)
DISK DRIVE B	DISKETTE DRIVE B	THE SIZE OF DISKETTE DRIVE B, IN INCHES AND DENSITY (LOW/HI)
DISK SIZE		THE SIZE OF DISKETTE WITH THE ORIGINAL SOFTWARE PACKAGE
DISKETTE SIZE		THE SIZE OF DISKETTE WITH THE ORIGINAL SOFTWARE PACKAGE
FIXED DISK	FIXED DISK MEMORY	MEMORY SIZE OF THE FIXED DISK IN MILLIONS OF CHARACTERS (M)
FIXED DISK 2	FIXED DISK MEMORY - SECOND	MEMORY SIZE OF THE FIXED DISK IN MILLIONS OF CHARACTERS (M)
GRAND TOTAL MICRO INVESTMENT	HARDWARE INVESTMENT GRAND TOTAL	THE GRAND TOTAL AMOUNT INVESTED IN HARDWARE OR SOFTWARE
HARDWARE INVENTORY NUMBER	MICROCOMPUTER INVENTORY NUMBER	A UNIQUE NUMBER ASSIGNED TO EACH MACHINE, LOCATED ON MACHINE
HARDWARE NUMBER	MICROCOMPUTER INVENTORY NUMBER	A UNIQUE NUMBER ASSIGNED TO EACH MACHINE, LOCATED ON MACHINE
HARDWARE SUBTOTAL		TOTAL FOR ALL HARDWARE IN SELECTED GROUP
INTERNAL BOARDS	ADD ON BOARDS	THE OPTIONAL BOARDS THAT ARE FOUND WITHIN THE MICROCOMPUTER
LAST PREVENT. MAINTENANCE DATE	DATE OF LAST PREVENTIVE MAINT.	THE DATE LAST PREVENTIVE MAINTENANCE WAS PERFORMED
LOCATION	CAMPUS ROOM	THE ROOM THAT THE HARDWARE OR SOFTWARE IS LOCATED IN
MAINTENANCE INTERVAL	PREVENTIVE MAINTENANCE INTERVAL	THE LENGTH OF TIME BETWEEN PREVENTIVE MAINTENANCE
MEMORY REQUIRED	MEMORY REQUIRED	THE MEMORY SIZE REQUIRED TO RUN THE SOFTWARE, IN THOUSANDS,K
MEMORY SIZE		SIZE OF MICRO RAM MEMORY, IN THOUSANDS OF CHARACTERS (K)
MODEL	MICROCOMPUTER MODEL	THE PARTICULAR MODEL OF MICROCOMPUTER
MONITOR	VIDEO DISPLAY UNIT	THE TYPE OF MONITOR ATTACHED TO THE MICROCOMPUTER
MONITOR NAME	NAME OF VIDEO DISPLAY UNIT	THE NAME OF THE MONITOR CODED WITHIN HARDWARE RECORDS
MONITOR REQUIRED		THE TYPE OF MONITOR REQUIRED TO RUN THE SOFTWARE
MOUSE	LOGICAL POINTING DEVICE	MOUSE ATTACHED Y/N
NUMBER OF COPIES		THE NUMBER OF COPIES OF THE SOFTWARE PURCHASED
NUMBER OF DISKETTES		NUMBER OF DISKETTES INCLUDED WITH THE PACKAGE
NUMBER OF DISKS		THE NUMBER OF DISKETTES SUPPLIED WITH THE SOFTWARE PACKAGE
NUMBER OF MACHINES	MACHINE COUNT	A COUNT OF THE NUMBER OF MICROCOMPUTERS FOR A SPECIFIC MODEL
NUMBER OF REPAIRS	REPAIR FREQUENCY	THE NUMBER OF TIMES THE MICROCOMPUTER HAS BEEN REPAIRED
ORDER DATE		DATE THE ORDER FOR EQUIPMENT WAS PLACED
ORDER QUANTITY	QUANTITY ORDERED	QUANTITY OF HARDWARE ITEMS ORDERED
PREVENTATIVE MAINTENANCE DATE	DATE OF NEXT PREVENTATIVE MAINT.	THE CALCULATED DATE FOR NEXT PREVENTATIVE MAINTENANCE
PREVENTIVE MAINTENANCE DATE	DATE OF NEXT PREVENTIVE MAINT.	THE CALCULATED DATE FOR NEXT PREVENTIVE MAINTENANCE
PRINTER	MICROCOMPUTER PRINTER	A CODE FOR THE TYPE OF PRINTER ATTACHED TO THE MICROCOMPUTER
PRINTER REQUIRED		A CODE FOR THE PRINTER REQUIRED. MAY BE LEFT BLANK. REFER TO
PUBLISHER		THE MANUFACTURER OR PUBLISHER OF THE SOFTWARE
PURCHASE COST	MICROCOMPUTER COST	THE COST TO PURCHASE THE MICROCOMPUTER
PURCHASE ORDER NUMBER		SCHOOL PURCHASE ORDER NUMBER - UNIQUE FOR EACH ORDER PLACED
QUANTITY RECEIVED	QUANTITY SHIPPED	QUANTITY OF HARDWARE ITEMS RECEIVED FOR A PURCHASE ORDER
RECORD CODE	MICROCOMPUTER STATUS CODE	ACTIVE OR INACTIVE MICRO. INACTIVE MEANS NO LONGER AVAILABLE

FIGURE E10.9
Element summary output.

"We're not finished yet. There are some useful matrices that will provide documentation for any changes that may be made in the future. Let's produce the **Record Contains Element (One Level)** matrix, which shows records and their elements," Anna suggests.

Figure E10.12 shows a portion of this matrix produced for the Microcomputer system. Notice that records on the left are matched with elements on the top by the **Type**, whether a simple element or a key. The complete grid spans many pages.

"Now that the data design is complete and some of the problems have been corrected, we should produce some reports under the category **ELE-**

```
DATE: 21-FEB-95      REC CONTAINS ELE - MISSING ENTITY        PAGE    1
TIME: 19:27          NAME: *                                  Excelerator


Record Contains Missing Element                              Occ  Seq
------------------------------------------------------------ ---  ----
MICROCOMPUTER MAINTENANCE        PROBLEM DATE                 001  000
                                 PROBLEM DESCRIPTION          001  000
                                 PERSON REPORTING PROBLEM     001  000
                                 PHONE NUMBER                 001  000
                                 STATUS                       001  000
                                 REPAIR DATE                  001  000
```

FIGURE E10.10
Record contains element missing entities report example.

MENT ACCESS & DERIVATION ANALYSIS," says Anna. "Excelerator performs analysis on the elements that flow through a data flow diagram, following them in and out of processes and tracking how they are used within data flows and records.

"First we should run the **Unexploded Data Flows** option, which will list the data flows that do not explode to a record. Then we should run the **Unprocesses Elements** report showing elements that are not contained in any record. That way we'll catch any elements that were created using the XLDictionary, but that we forgot to include within records."

Figure E10.13 is the **Unprocessed Elements** report produced for the Microcomputer system. The elements listed were either deleted (because they were duplicates) or incorporated into records. After completing these corrections, Chip and Anna reconvene for further data analysis.

"There are many other reports and matrices that would be useful for us to produce," Anna says. "Some of these should be used later for documentation and tracking any proposed changes. There are two critical reports that we should produce at this time."

```
DATE: 21-FEB-95               EMPTY RECORDS              PAGE         1
TIME: 18:03                                              Excelerator
PROJECT NAME: CENTRAL PACIFIC UNIVERSITY


DESCRIPTION:   This report lists Records that contain no Elements or Records.

 EMPTY RECORDS
 -------------------------------------------------------------------------
|FACULTY INQUIRY RESPONSE                                                  |
|HARDWARE MASTER REPORT                                                    |
|INSTALLATION NOTIFICATION                                                 |
|INVENTORY SHEETS                                                          |
|MICROCOMPUTER RECEIVED REPORT                                             |
|                                                                          |
|PENDING MICROCOMPUTER ORDER                                               |
|SOFTWARE FINANCIAL REPORT                                                 |
|SOFTWARE RECEIVED                                                         |
|UPGRADE COST REPORT                                                       |
|                                                                          |
 -------------------------------------------------------------------------
```

FIGURE E10.11
Empty records report.

```
Record Contains Element (One Level)
--------------------------------------------------------------------------------
                                                         Feb21 95 18:04:15  C-1
    ... Continued

                                -------------------------------------------------
                                |E  |E  |E  |E  |E  |E  |E  |E  |E  |E  |E  |
                                |L  |L  |L  |L  |L  |L  |L  |L  |L  |L  |L  |
                                |E  |E  |E  |E  |E  |E  |E  |E  |E  |E  |E  |
                                |   |   |   |   |   |   |   |   |   |   |   |
                                |V  |C  |R  |W  |MI |LM |NR |C  |B  |M  |S  |
                                |E  |A  |O  |A  |AN |AA |UE |O  |R  |O  |E  |
                                |R  |M  |O  |R  |IT |SI |MP |S  |A  |D  |R  |
                                |S  |P  |M  |R  |NE |TN |BA |T  |N  |E  |I  |
                                |I  |U  |   |A  |TR |T  |EI |   |D  |L  |A  |
                                |O  |S  |L  |N  |EV |PE |RR |O  |   |   |L  |
                                |N  |   |O  |T  |NA |RN |S  |F  |N  |   |   |
                                |   |L  |C  |Y  |AL |EA |O  |   |A  |   |N  |
                                |N  |O  |A  |   |N  |VN |F  |R  |M  |   |U  |
                                |U  |C  |T  |   |C  |EC |   |E  |E  |   |M  |
                                |M  |A  |I  |   |E  |NE |   |P  |   |   |B  |
                                |B  |T  |O  |   |   |T  |   |A  |   |   |E  |
                                |E  |I  |N  |   |   |.D |   |I  |   |   |R  |
                                |R  |O  |   |   |   |A  |   |R  |   |   |   |
                                |   |N  |   |   |   |T  |   |S  |   |   |   |
                                |   |   |   |   |   |E  |   |   |   |   |   |
--------------------------      -------------------------------------------------
|REC ADD SOFTWARE REC     |     |   |   |   |   |   |   |   |   |   |   |
|-------------------------|     |---+---+---+---+---+---+---+---+---+---+---|
|REC HARDWARE             |     |   |   |   |   |   |   |   |   |   |   |
|INVESTMENT REPORT        |     |   |   |   |   |   |   |   |   |   |   |
|-------------------------|     |---+---+---+---+---+---+---+---+---+---+---|
|REC INSTALLATION         |     |   |   |   |   |   |   |   |   |   |   |
|MICROCOMPUTER            |     |   |   |   |   |   |   |   |   |   |   |
|-------------------------|     |---+---+---+---+---+---+---+---+---+---+---|
|REC INSTALLED SOFTWARE   |     | E | E | E |   |   |   |   |   |   |   |
|TRANSACTION              |     |   |   |   |   |   |   |   |   |   |   |
|-------------------------|     |---+---+---+---+---+---+---+---+---+---+---|
|REC MAINTENANCE          |     |   |   |   | E | E | E | E | E |   |   |
|INFORMATION              |     |   |   |   |   |   |   |   |   |   |   |
|-------------------------|     |---+---+---+---+---+---+---+---+---+---+---|
|REC MATCHING             |     |   | E | E |   |   |   |   |   | E | E |
|MICROCOMPUTER MASTER     |     |   |   |   |   |   |   |   |   |   |   |
|-------------------------|     |---+---+---+---+---+---+---+---+---+---+---|
|REC MICRO HARDWARE &     |     |   |   |   |   |   |   |   |   |   |   |
|SOFTWARE RECORD          |     |   |   |   |   |   |   |   |   |   |   |
|-------------------------|     |---+---+---+---+---+---+---+---+---+---+---|
|REC MICROCOMPUTER ADD    |     |   |   |   |   |   |   |   |   |   | E |
|TRANSACTION              |     |   |   |   |   |   |   |   |   |   |   |
|-------------------------|     |---+---+---+---+---+---+---+---+---+---+---|
|REC MICROCOMPUTER        |     |   |   |   |   |   |   |   |   | E | E |
|MAINTENANCE              |     |   |   |   |   |   |   |   |   |   |   |
|-------------------------|     |---+---+---+---+---+---+---+---+---+---+---|
|REC MICROCOMPUTER        |     |   | E | E |   |   |   |   |   | E | E | E |
|MASTER                   |     |   |   |   |   |   |   |   |   |   |   |
|-------------------------|     |---+---+---+---+---+---+---+---+---+---+---|
|REC PERIPHERAL           |     |   |   |   |   |   |   |   |   |   |   |
|EQUIPMENT                |     |   |   |   |   |   |   |   |   |   |   |
--------------------------      -------------------------------------------------
```

FIGURE E10.12
Record contains element matrix example.

The first report created was **Misused Base Elements**, showing the base elements that are input to the system and that leave but do not enter a process. This situation leads a potential "output without corresponding input" error. The report is extremely useful for analyzing the correctness of

```
DATE: 21-FEB-95        UNPROCESSED ELEMENTS IN RECORDS        PAGE        1
TIME: 09:08                                                  Excelerator
PROJECT NAME: CENTRAL PACIFIC UNIVERSITY

DESCRIPTION:   This report lists each Element contained in one or more
               Records where none of those Elements or Records explodes
               from a Data Flow.  Since none of these Elements is associated
               with any Data Flow, the Elements can not be used or produced
               by any Process in your Data Flow Diagrams.

  ELEMENT NAME
 ---------------------------------------------------------------------------
 |SOFTWARE TITLE                                                            |
 |SOFTWARE VERSION                                                          |
 |NUMBER OF DISKS                                                           |
 |PROBLEM DATE                                                              |
 |PROBLEM DESCRIPTION                                                       |
 |                                                                          |
 |PERSON REPORTING PROBLEM                                                  |
 |PHONE NUMBER                                                              |
 |STATUS                                                                    |
 |REPAIR DATE                                                               |
 |PURCHASE ORDER NUMBER                                                     |
 |                                                                          |
 |ORDER DATE                                                                |
 |ORDER QUANTITY                                                            |
 |QUANTITY RECEIVED                                                         |
 |                                                                          |
 ---------------------------------------------------------------------------
```

FIGURE E10.13
Unprocessed elements in records analysis report.

element descriptions and processes. Also listed are elements that are not described in the XLDictionary. An example of this report is shown in Figure E10.14.

A similar report is **Misused Derived Elements**, listing elements that are derived (calculated) but are not created by any process. Again, elements that are not described in the XLDictionary are included in the report.

Exercises[*]

🖫 **E-1.**   Use Excelerator to view the Microcomputer Master record. Browse the elements and structural records.

🖫 **E-2.**   Print the Software Master record using the Output command, Generate COBOL code for using the input pictures. Use the prefix **SR-** for Software Record.

[*] The exercises preceded by a disk icon require the program Excelerator (or another CASE tool). A disk is provided free of charge to any professor adopting this book. The examples on the disk may be imported into Excelerator and then used by students.

```
DATE: 21-FEB-95          MISUSED BASE ELEMENTS              PAGE        1
TIME: 09:08                                                Excelerator
PROJECT NAME: CENTRAL PACIFIC UNIVERSITY

DESCRIPTION:   This report lists Elements defined as base that are created by a
               Process. A base Element should not leave any Process it does not
               enter.

ELEMENT NAME    IS DERIVED BY    PROCESS NAME
-----------------------------------------------------------------------
|SOFTWARE INVENTORY NUMBER      |CONTEXT                           |
|PUBLISHER                      |CONTEXT                           |
|SOFTWARE CATEGORY              |2.5                               |
|DISKETTE SIZE                  |2.5                               |
|SITE LICENSE                   |CONTEXT                           |
|                                                                  |
|NUMBER OF COPIES               |CONTEXT                           |
|COMPUTER BRAND                 |CONTEXT                           |
|COMPUTER MODEL                 |CONTEXT                           |
|MEMORY REQUIRED                |2.5                               |
|MONITOR                        |1.4                               |
|                                                                  |
|PRINTER REQUIRED               |2.5                               |
|HARDWARE INVENTORY NUMBER      |CONTEXT                           |
|SOFTWARE EXPERT NAME           |CONTEXT                           |
|SOFTWARE EXPERT LOCATION       |2.5                               |
|TITLE                          |CONTEXT                           |
|                                                                  |
|VERSION NUMBER                 |CONTEXT                           |
|CAMPUS LOCATION                |1.4                               |
|ROOM LOCATION                  |CONTEXT                           |
|WARRANTY                       |1.4                               |
|MAINTENANCE INTERVAL           |1.4                               |
|                                                                  |
|LAST PREVENT. MAINTENANCE DATE |1.4                               |
|BRAND NAME                     |1.4                               |
|MODEL                          |1.4                               |
|SERIAL NUMBER                  |1.4                               |
|DATE PURCHASED                 |1.4                               |
|                                                                  |
|PURCHASE COST                  |1.4                               |
|MEMORY SIZE                    |1.4                               |
|INTERNAL BOARDS                |1.4                               |
|FIXED DISK                     |1.4                               |
|FIXED DISK 2                   |1.4                               |
|                                                                  |
|DISK DRIVE A                   |1.4                               |
|DISK DRIVE B                   |1.4                               |
|MOUSE                          |1.4                               |
|PRINTER                        |1.4                               |
|NUMBER OF DISKETTES            |2.5                               |
|                                                                  |
|ACTIVE SOFTWARE CODE           |2.5                               |
|MONITOR REQUIRED               |2.5                               |
|                                                                  |
-----------------------------------------------------------------------
```

FIGURE E10.14
Misused base elements report.

🖫 **E-3.** Use the Copy command to copy the Software Master to the New
Software record. Delete the following elements and structural
record:

ACTIVE SOFTWARE CODE
INSTALLATION MICRO
SOFTWARE EXPERT

E-4. Modify the Software Changes record, supplying changes to the Software Master record. The modifications are:

    a. Change the Software Inventory Number **Type** to K for Key.

    b. Add the following elements: Computer Brand, Computer Model, Memory Required, Monitor Required, Printer Required, Diskette Size, Site License, and Number of Copies.

    c. Change the **Normalized** code to Y for yes.

E-5. Modify the Microcomputer Add Transaction record, which contains new microcomputer records to be placed on the Microcomputer Master data store.

    a. Insert the Brand Name and Model above the Serial Number.

    b. Place the Campus Location and Room Location after the Serial Number.

    c. Add the following elements at the bottom of the list: Fixed Disk, Fixed Disk 2, Disk Drive A, and Disk Drive B.

    d. Delete the Internal Boards element, which will be determined after the microcomputer installation.

E-6. Modify the Installed Software Transaction, used to update the Software Master and produce the Software Installation Listing. Delete the Title and Version Number, since they may be obtained from the Software Master and are redundant keying. Add the Hardware Inventory Number, specifying the installation microcomputer. Delete the Campus Location and Room Location, since these are elements of the installation microcomputer.

E-7. View the data store entry for the Software Master. Use F4 to examine the Software Master record.

E-8. Modify the INSTALLED SOFTWARE data store. Add the Explosion Record INSTALLED SOFTWARE TRANSACTION. The location is IBM PC, Model 386 SX, D.P. The index elements are SOFTWARE INVENTORY NUMBER and HARDWARE INVENTORY NUMBER.

E-9. Define the data store SOFTWARE LOG FILE. This file is used to store information on the new software records plus the date, time, and user-ID of the person entering the record. The location is the DP Microcomputer Section, and the total and average number of records is 20. Index elements are SOFTWARE INVENTORY NUMBER, TITLE and VERSION (a concatenated key), and SOFTWARE CATEGORY.

E-10. Define the data store PENDING MICROCOMPUTER ORDERS. This file is created when a purchase order is made for ordering new microcomputers and is updated by the Microcomputer system. The location is the DP Microcomputer Section, and the total and average number of records is 100. Index elements are PURCHASE ORDER NUMBER and a concatenated key consisting of BRAND NAME and MODEL.

E-11. View the entry for the Software Record data flow. Use F4 to examine the Software Master record. Press F3 to return to the data flow description screen. Use F4 to view some of the User Requirements (your choice) and all of the Associated Entities.

⌨ **E-12.** Modify the SOFTWARE UPGRADE INFORMATION data flow. The explosion path is a record (**Type** REC) named SOFTWARE UPGRADE INFORMATION and the **Access Type** is **A** representing Add. Include the User Requirement MAINTAIN SOFTWARE INFORMATION and the following Associated Entities: Test; UPGRADE SOFTWARE; and Category, SOFTWARE.

⌨ **E-13.** Modify the SOFTWARE CROSS-REFERENCE REPORT data flow. The explosion path is the record SOFTWARE CROSS-REFERENCE REPORT and the **Acess Type** is **R** for Read. Add the User Requirement PRODUCE SOFTWARE/MICRO CROSS REF and the following Associated Entities: Test; PRODUCE HARDWARE/SOFTWARE XREF; Category, SOFTWARE; Category, MICROCOMPUTER INFORMATION; and Reference, Report Standards.

⌨ **E-14.** Create the data flow entity for INSTALL UPDATE. This flow updates the Microcomputer Master record with installation information. It explodes to the record INSTALL UPDATE and processes about 50 records per month. The **Access Type** is Update.

⌨ **E-15.** Explode the INSTALL UPDATE data flow to create the INSTALL UPDATE *record*. Provide a definition based on information supplied in the previous problem. Enter the following elements:

Name	Type	
HARDWARE INVENTORY NUMBER	K	
CAMPUS LOCATION	E	
ROOM	E	
INTERNAL BOARDS	E	Occurs 5 times
FIXED DISK 2	E	
MOUSE	E	
PRINTER	E	
MAINTENANCE INTERVAL	E	
DATE INSTALLED	E	

⌨ **E-16.** Create the data flow description for the SOFTWARE INSTALL LIST. This flow contains information on specific software packages and the machines on which the software should be installed. It explodes to the SOFTWARE INSTALLATION LISTING, and the duration value is 200 per day. The **Access Type** is Add.

⌨ **E-17.** Explode the SOFTWARE INSTALL LIST to create the SOFTWARE INSTALLATION LISTING record. The elements on the listing are:

Name	Type
SOFTWARE INVENTORY NUMBER	E
TITLE	E
VERSION NUMBER	E
NUMBER OF DISKETTES	E
DISKETTE SIZE	E
HARDWARE INVENTORY NUMBER	E
CAMPUS LOCATION	E
ROOM LOCATION	E

⌨ **E-18.** Modify and print the element HARDWARE SUBTOTAL. Change the **Output Format** to ZZ,ZZZ,ZZ9.99 and the **Storage Type** to P.

Add the **Characters right of decimal** value of 2. The **Prompt** and **Column Header** should be HARDWARE SUBTOTAL. Change the **Base or Derived** parameter to D.

E-19. Modify and print the MONITOR NAME element, the result of a table lookup using a monitor code. Add the **Input** and **Output Format** of X(30) and make the **Characters left of decimal** 30. Add the **Prompt** and **Headers** value MONITOR NAME.

E-20. Modify and print the STAFF DEPARTMENT element. **Edit Rules** should contain FROM "DEPARTMENT TABLE" and the **Input Format** is X(25). **Prompt** and **Column Header** should contain STAFF DEPARTMENT, with the **Short Header** entry of DEPART-MENT. Add the User Requirement MAINTAIN SOFTWARE EXPERT INFO. and the Associated Entity Category, SOFTWARE.

E-21. Create the following element descriptions. Use the values supplied in the table. Create any alternate names and definitions based on your understanding of the element. Prompts, column headings, and data classes should be entered to reflect the element.

Name	Purchase Order Number	Problem Description
Input Picture	9(7)	X(70)
Output Picture	ZZZZZZ9	X(70)
Edit Rules	> 0	
Storage Type	C	C
Chars. left/rt	7	70
Base/Derived	B	B
Source		MICRO CHANGE INFO.
Default		

Name	Total Microcomputer Cost	Next Preventive Maintenance Date
Input Picture	9(7) V99	MMDDYY
Output Picture	Z, ZZZ, ZZ9.99	MM-DD-YY
Edit Rules		
Storage Type	P	D
Chars. left/rt	7.2	6
Base/Derived	D	D
Source		
Default		

Name	Phone Number	Repair Status
Input Picture	9(10)	X
Output Picture	9(10)	X
Edit Rules	> 0	FROM 'REPAIR TABLE'
Storage Type	C	C
Chars. left/rt	10	1
Base/Derived	B	B
Source	REPAIRED MICROCOMPUTER FORM	REPAIRED MICROCOMPUTER FORM
Default		C

E-22. Generate the record layout for the INSTALL UPDATE record. Use COBOL and C language. Place the prefix **IUR-** in front of code data names and print the output.

E-23. Generate the record layout for the SOFTWARE INSTALLATION LISTING record. Create the code in COBOL and then BASIC. Use the prefix **SIL-** and print the output code.

E-24. Use the Relationships feature of the XLDictionary to produce the Missing Entities for the following categories. Examine each of the reports. In a paragraph, describe the information displayed and why the report is useful in analyzing the system design.

Relationship	XLD category	XLD entity
REC Contains ELE	REC/ELE	Record
REC Explodes-From DAS	REC/ELE	Record
DAF Explodes-To REC	DATA	Data Flow

E-25. Use the Relationships feature of the XLDictionary to produce the summary report for the following categories. Examine each of the reports, and in a paragraph, comment on where the information might be used.

Relationship	XLD category	XLD entity
ELE Access-Key-Of DAS	REC/ELE	Element
DAS Contained-In DFD	DATA	Data Store
DAS Sends-To PRC	DATA	Data Store
DAF Sent-By PRC	DATA	Data Flow

E-26. Use the Record Content option of Extended Analysis to produce the following reports and matrices. Explain in a paragraph where the information produced may be effectively used.

a. Empty Records report
b. Equivalent Records report
c. Record Contains Element (One Level) matrix
d. Record Contains Record (One Level) matrix

E-27. Produce the following reports and matrices from the Element Access & Derivation option of Extended Analysis. Explain in two paragraphs how the information could be used to analyze the design.

a. Unprocessed Elements report
b. Element Traceablility report
c. Misused Base Elements report
d. Misused Derived Elements report
e. Process Data Flows matrix
f. Process Element Access matrix

DESCRIBING PROCESS SPECIFICATIONS AND STRUCTURED DECISIONS

METHODS AVAILABLE

The systems analyst approaching process specifications and structured decisions has many options for documenting and analyzing them. In Chapters 9 and 10, you noted processes such as VERIFY AND COMPUTE FEES, but did not explain the logic necessary to do this. The methods available for documenting and analyzing the logic of decisions include structured English, decision tables, and decision trees. It is important to be able to recognize logic and structured decisions that occur in a business and how they are distinguishable from semistructured decisions. Then it is critical to recognize that structured decisions lend themselves particularly well to analysis with systematic methods that promote completeness, accuracy, and communication.

Decision analysis focuses on the logic of the decisions that are made, or need to be made, within the organization in order to carry out the objectives of the firm. This chapter covers the methods of structured English, decision tables, and decision trees for analyzing decisions and describing process logic, and in doing so complements the material on data flow diagrams from Chapter 9 and the data dictionary from Chapter 10.

OVERVIEW OF PROCESS SPECIFICATIONS

In order to determine the information requirements using a decision analysis strategy, the systems analyst must first determine the organization's objectives, using a top-down approach. The systems analyst must understand the principles of organizations (as covered in Chapter 2) and have a working knowledge of data-gathering techniques (as presented in Chapters 4 through 8). The top-down approach is critical because all decisions in the organization should be related, at least indirectly, to the broad objectives of the entire organization.

Process specifications—sometimes called minispecs, since they are a small portion of the total project specifications—are created for primitive processes on a data flow diagram as well as for some higher-level processes that explode to a child diagram. These specifications explain the decision-making logic and formulas that will transform process input data into output. Each derived element must have process logic to show how it is produced from the base elements or other previously created derived elements that are input to the primitive process.

The three goals of producing process specifications are:

1. Reduce the ambiguity of the process. This compels the analyst to learn details about how the process works. Any vague areas should be noted, written down, and consolidated for all process specifications. These observations form a basis and provide the questions for a follow-up interview with the user community.
2. Obtain a precise description of what is accomplished, which is usually included in a packet of specifications for the programmer.
3. Validate the system design. This includes ensuring that a process has all the input data flow necessary for producing the output. Additionally, all input and output must be represented on the data flow diagram.

You will find many situations where process specifications are not created. Sometimes the process is very simple, or the computer code already exists. This eventuality would be noted in the process description, and no further design would be required. Categories of processes that generally *do not* require specifications are:

1. Processes that represent physical input or output, such as read, write, and so on. These processes usually require only simple logic.
2. Processes that represent simple data validation, which is usually fairly easy to accomplish. The edit criteria are included in the data dictionary and incorporated into the computer source code. Process specifications may be produced for complex editing.
3. Processes that use prewritten code. These are generally included in a system as subprograms and functions.

Subprograms are computer programs that are written, tested, and stored on the computer system. They usually perform a general system function, such as validating a date or a check digit. These general purpose subprograms are written and documented only once but form a series of building blocks that may be used within many systems throughout the organization. Thus these subprograms appear as processes on many data flow diagrams. Functions are similar to subprograms but are coded differently. For example, a function library may be purchased for use in the C programming language or a database environment.

Process Specification Format

Process specifications link the process to the data flow diagram and the data dictionary, as illustrated in Figure 11.1. Each process specification should be entered on a separate form or into a CASE tool screen such as the one used for Excelerator and shown in the CPU case at the end of this chapter. Enter the following information:

1. The process number, which must match the process ID on the data flow diagram. This specification allows an analyst to work on or review any process and easily locate the data flow diagram containing the process.

Data Flow Diagram	Process Specification and Logic

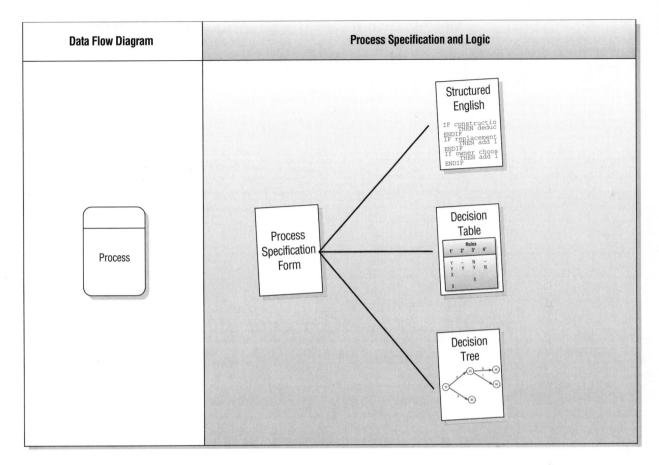

FIGURE 11.1
How process specifications relate to the data flow diagram.

2. The process name, which again must be the same as the name displayed within the process symbol on the data flow diagram.

3. A brief description of what the process accomplishes.

4. A list of data input flow, using the names found on the data flow diagram. Data names used in the formula or logic should match those in the data dictionary to ensure consistency and good communication.

5. The output data flow, also using data flow diagram and data dictionary names.

6. An indication of the type of process: batch, on line, or manual. All on-line processes require screen designs, and all manual processes should have well-defined procedures for employees performing the process tasks.

7. If the process uses prewritten code, include the name of the subprogram or function containing that code.

8. A description of the process logic that states policy and business rules in everyday language, not computer language pseudocode.

9. If there is not enough room on the form for a complete structured English description or if there is a decision table or tree depicting the logic, include the corresponding table or tree name.

FIGURE 11.2
An example of a completed
Process Specification form for
determining whether an item
is available.

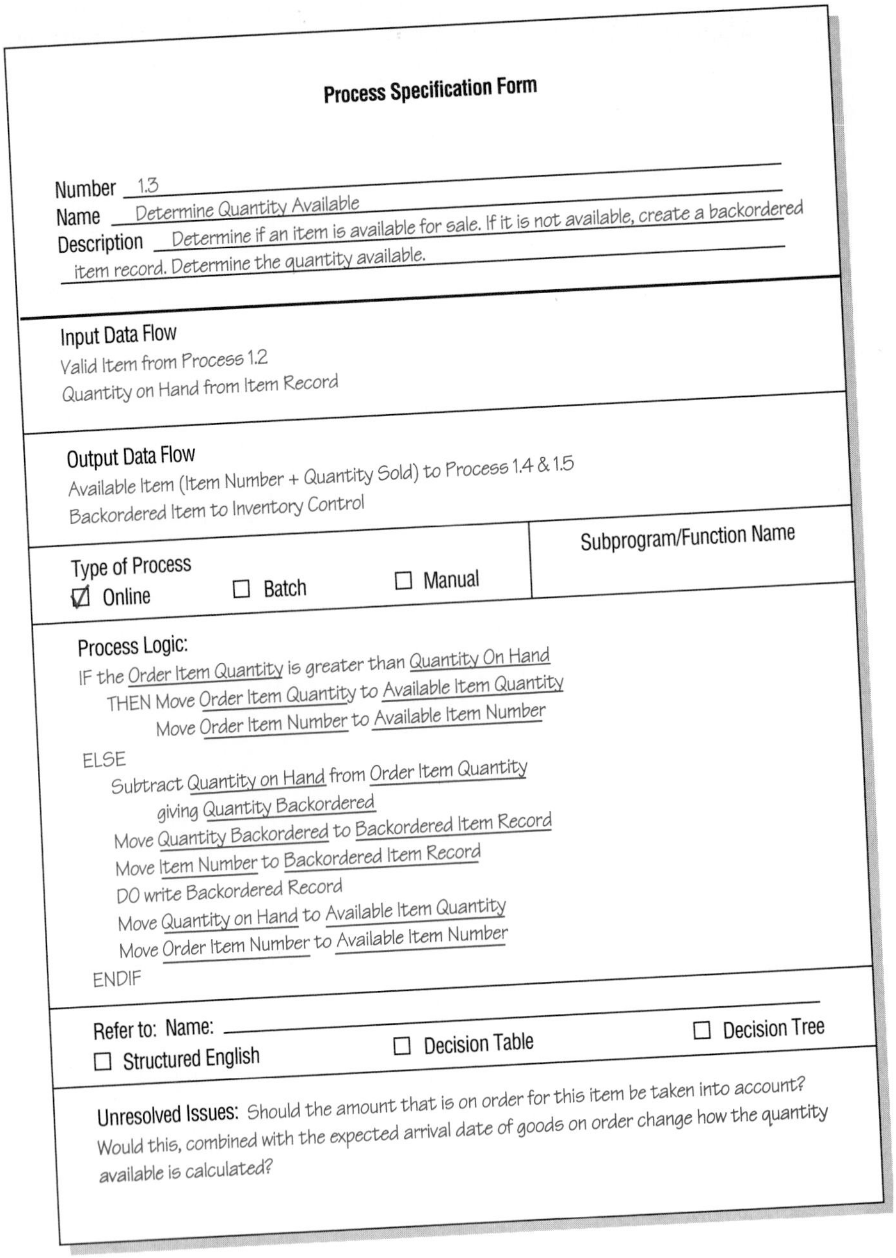

Process Specification Form

Number ___1.3_____

Name ___Determine Quantity Available_____

Description ___Determine if an item is available for sale. If it is not available, create a backordered
item record. Determine the quantity available._____

Input Data Flow

Valid Item from Process 1.2
Quantity on Hand from Item Record

Output Data Flow

Available Item (Item Number + Quantity Sold) to Process 1.4 & 1.5
Backordered Item to Inventory Control

Type of Process ☑ Online ☐ Batch ☐ Manual	Subprogram/Function Name

---

Process Logic:

IF the _Order Item Quantity_ is greater than _Quantity On Hand_
    THEN Move _Order Item Quantity_ to _Available Item Quantity_
        Move _Order Item Number_ to _Available Item Number_

ELSE
    Subtract _Quantity on Hand_ from _Order Item Quantity_
        giving _Quantity Backordered_
    Move Quantity Backordered to _Backordered Item Record_
    Move _Item Number_ to Backordered Item Record
    DO write Backordered Record
    Move _Quantity on Hand_ to _Available Item Quantity_
    Move _Order Item Number_ to _Available Item Number_

ENDIF

Refer to: Name: _____
☐ Structured English   ☐ Decision Table   ☐ Decision Tree

Unresolved Issues: Should the amount that is on order for this item be taken into account?
Would this, combined with the expected arrival date of goods on order change how the quantity
available is calculated?

---

10. List any unresolved issues, incomplete portions of logic, or other concerns. These issues form the basis of the questions used for follow-up interviews.

The above items should be entered to complete a process description form. These include a process number or name from the data flow diagram, as well as the eight other items shown in the World's Trend example (Figure 11.2). Notice that completing this form thoroughly facilitates linking the process to the data flow diagram and the data dictionary. When using an electronic form, such as the Visible Analyst screen shown in Figure 11.3, the description will not fit on one page. This disadvantage is offset by the ability to electronically search for key words.

FIGURE 11.3
Visible Analyst can be
used to describe process
specifications.

Define Item

Label: Determine Quantity Available

Entry Type: Process

Description: Determine if an item is available for sale. If it is not available, create a backordered item record. Determine the quantity available.

Process #: 1.3

Process Description:
```
IF the Order Item Quantity is greater than Quantity On Hand
        THEN Move Order Item Quantity to Available Item Quantity
              Move Order Item Number to Available Item Number
ELSE
```

Notes: Unresolved issues: Should the amount that is on order for this item be taken into account? Would this, combined with the expected arrival date of goods on order change how the quantity available is calculated?

[Help] [Delete] [Next] [Save] [Search] [Jump] [Page Two]
[Erase] [Prior] [Exit] [Expand] [File] [Search Criteria...]

Define Item

Label: Determine Quantity Available

Entry Type: Process

Process Description:
```
IF the Order Item Quantity is greater than Quantity On Hand
        THEN Move Order Item Quantity to Available Item Quantity
              Move Order Item Number to Available Item Number
ELSE
        Subtract Quantity On Hand from Order Item Quantity
            giving Quantity Backordered
        Move Quantity Backordered to Backordered Item Record
        Move Item Number to Backordered Item Record
        DO Write Backordered Record
        Move Quantity On Hand to Available Item Quantity
        Move Order Item Number to Available Item Number
ENDIF
```

[Help] [Delete] [Next] [Save] [Search] [Jump] [Page Two]
[Erase] [Prior] [Exit] [Contract] [File] [Search Criteria...]

Information Required for Structured Decisions

Conditions, condition alternatives, actions, and action rules must be known in order to design systems for structured decisions. The analyst first determines the conditions; that is, an occurrence that might affect the outcome of something else. In the next step, the systems analyst defines the condition alternatives as specified by the decision maker; these alternatives can be as simple as "yes" or "no," or they can be more descriptive, such as "less than $50," "between $50 and $100," and "greater than $100."

Next, actions are identified. These can include any instruction that needs to be carried out as a result of one or more of the above conditions.

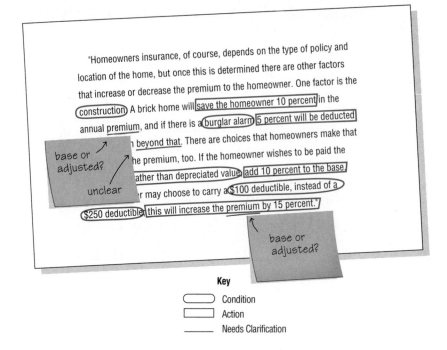

"Homeowners insurance, of course, depends on the type of policy and location of the home, but once this is determined there are other factors that increase or decrease the premium to the homeowner. One factor is the construction. A brick home will save the homeowner 10 percent in the annual premium, and if there is a burglar alarm 5 percent will be deducted ... beyond that. There are choices that homeowners make that ... he premium, too. If the homeowner wishes to be paid the ... ather than depreciated value add 10 percent to the base. ... r may choose to carry a $100 deductible, instead of a $250 deductible this will increase the premium by 15 percent."

base or adjusted?

unclear

base or adjusted?

Key

Condition
Action
Needs Clarification

Instructions to somehow manipulate or total numbers, print reports, or even disallow the transaction in question are all examples of potential actions. They are tied to the conditions by the action rules, which are directions to execute the required actions in order.

Examples of action rules are provided in this page from a rate document supplied to insurance agents from the Fortress Insurance Corporation:

> Homeowners insurance, of course, depends on the type of policy and the location of the home, but once this is determined there are other factors that increase or decrease the premium to the home-owner. One factor is the construction. A brick home will save the homeowner 10 percent in the annual premium, and if there is a burglar alarm, 5 percent will be deducted from the premium beyond that. There are choices that homeowners make that will increase the premium, too. If the homeowner wishes to be paid the replacement, rather than depreciated value, add 10 percent to the base. The homeowner may choose to carry a $100 deductible, instead of a $250 deductible; this will increase the premium by 15 percent.

This statement may seem clear at first, but a careful examination reveals ambiguities that need resolution before decision analysis is completed.

In Figure 11.4, this rate document was analyzed to determine the actions and conditions. A box was drawn around each action, and each condition was circled. (Boxes and circles will be used again later in the decision tree.) After this was done, questionable terms, ambiguities, unclear adjectives, and instances of "however" and "but" were underlined.

Problems occurred because (1) the "base" is not defined; (2) it isn't clear what the phrase "beyond that" refers to; (3) when the "premium" is modified, it is not clear if the deduction or increase is applied to the original premium or the adjusted premium, nor is it clear in what order this is

Number	Conditions	Condition Alternatives	Actions	Action Rule
1	Construction	Brick	Deduct 10% of Base* From Subtotal	Do This First
		Other	—	—
2	Home Has Burglar Alarm	Yes	Deduct 5% Off Adjusted Subtotal	Do This After Number 4
		No	—	—
3	Replacement Option is Chosen	Yes	Add 15% of Base* to Subtotal	Do This After Number 1
		No	—	—
4	Deductible	$100 Option	Add 10% of Subtotal to Subtotal	Do This After Number 3
		Standard $250	—	—

* Base is the original premium based on amount the home is insured for and the location of the home.

FIGURE 11.5
Organizing the decision process by specifying alternatives and actions, defining ambiguous terms, and describing and ordering action rules.

done. To clear up these details, an interview was conducted, and Figure 11.5 was drawn to organize the decision process. Notice that the alternatives are clearly specified; the actions are more specific; "base" is defined; and the action rules are described and ordered.

In the following sections, three alternatives for decision analysis of structured decisions will be explored. First, we will discuss structured English, then decision tables, and finally decision trees.

STRUCTURED ENGLISH

When the process logic involves formulas or iteration or when structured decisions are not complex, an appropriate technique for analyzing the decision process is the use of structured English. As the name implies, structured English is based on (1) structured logic, or instructions organized into nested and grouped procedures; and (2) simple English statements such as add, multiply, move, and so on.

The previous Fortress Insurance Corporation example provides us with a good use for structured English, and can be transformed into structured English, as shown in Figure 11.6, by putting the decision rules into their proper sequence and using the convention of IF-THEN-ELSE statements throughout.

Once this example is written in structured English, one can see that it is a rather simple sequential decision. Structured English can be more complex if blocks of instructions are nested within other blocks of instructions, as shown in Figure 11.7.

Writing Structured English

In order to write structured English, it is advisable to use the following conventions:

1. Express all logic in terms of sequential structures, decision structures, case structures, or iterations (see Figure 11.8 for examples of these).
2. Use and capitalize accepted keywords such as IF, THEN, ELSE, DO, DO WHILE, DO UNTIL, and PERFORM.
3. Indent blocks of statements to show their hierarchy (nesting) clearly.

Kit Chen Kaboodle, Inc.

"I don't want to get anyone stirred up, but I think we need to sift through our unfilled order policies," says Kit Chen. "I wouldn't want to put a strain on our customers. As you know already, Kit Chen Kaboodle is a mail-order cookware business specializing in 'klassy kitsch for kitchens,' like our latest catalog says. I mean, we've got everything you need to do gourmet cooking and entertaining: nutmeg grinders, potato whisks, egg separators, turkey basters, placemats with cats on 'em, ice cube trays in shamrock shapes, and more.

"Here's how we've been handling unfilled orders. We search our unfilled orders file once a week. If the order was filled this week, we delete the record, and the rest is gravy. If we haven't written to the customer in four weeks, we send 'em this cute card with a chef peeking into the oven, saying, 'Not ready yet.' (It's a notification that their item is still on backorder.)

"If the backorder date changed to greater than forty-five days from now, we send out a notice. But if the merchandise is seasonal (like Halloween treat bags, Christmas cookie cutters, or Valentine's Day cake molds) and the backorder date is thirty days or more, we send out a notice with a chef glaring at his egg timer.

"If the backorder date changed at all and we haven't sent out a card within two weeks, we send out a card with a chef checking his recipe. If the merchandise is no longer available, we send a notice (complete with chef crying in the corner) and delete the record.

"Thanks for listening to all of this. I think we've got the right ingredients for a good policy; we just need to blend them together and cook up something special."

Since you are the systems analyst that Kit hired, go through the narrative of how Kit Chen Kaboodle, Inc., handles unfilled orders, drawing boxes around each action she mentions and circling each condition brought up. Make notes of any ambiguities you would like to clarify in a later interview.

FIGURE 11.6
Using structured English for analyzing the decision process for a simple sequential decision.

```
Calculate Base Premium
IF construction is brick
    THEN deduct 10 percent of base to total
ENDIF
IF replacement option is chosen
    THEN add 10 percent of base to subtotal
ENDIF
If owner chooses $100 deductible
    THEN add 15 percent of subtotal
ENDIF
IF home has burglar alarm
    THEN deduct 5 percent of adjusted subtotal
ENDIF
```

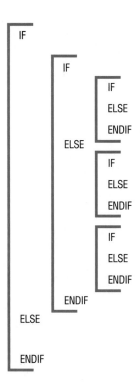

```
IF
    IF
            IF
            ELSE
            ENDIF
    ELSE
            IF
            ELSE
            ENDIF

            IF
            ELSE
            ENDIF
    ENDIF
ELSE

ENDIF
```

FIGURE 11.7
Proper use of structured English will involve nesting blocks of instructions within others.

Structured English Type	Example
Sequential Structure A block of instructions where no branching occurs	Action #1 Action #2 Action #3
Decision Structure Only IF a condition is true, complete the following statements otherwise jump to the ELSE	IF Condition A is True THEN implement Action A ELSE implement Action B ENDIF

Case Structure
A special type of decision structure where the cases are mutually exclusive (if one occurs the others cannot)
	IF Case #1 implement Action #1
	ELSE IF Case #2
	         implement Action #2
	ELSE IF Case #3
	         implement Action #3
	ELSE IF Case #4
	         implement Action #4
	ELSE print error
	ENDIF

Iteration Blocks of statements that are repeated until done	DO WHILE there are customers Action #1 ENDDO

FIGURE 11.8
Examples of logic expressed in a sequential structure, a decision structure, a case structure, and an iteration.

343

4. When words or phrases have been defined in a data dictionary (as in Chapter 10), underline those words or phrases to signify that they have a specialized, reserved meaning.

5. Be careful when using "and" and "or," and avoid confusion when distinguishing between "greater than" and "greater than or equal to" and like relationships. Clarify the logical statements now rather than waiting until the program coding stage.

A STRUCTURED ENGLISH EXAMPLE. The following example demonstrates how a spoken procedure for processing medical claims is transformed into structured English:

> We process all of our claims in this manner. First we determine whether the claimant has ever sent in a claim before; if not, we set up a new record. The claim totals for the year are then updated. Next we determine if a claimant has policy *A* or policy *B*, which differ in deductibles and copayments (the percentage of the claim claimants pay themselves). For both policies, we check to see if the deductible has been met ($100 for plan *A* and $50 for plan *B*). If the deductible has not been met, we apply the claim to the deductible. Another step adjusts for the copayment; we subtract the percentage the claimant pays (40 percent for plan *A* and 60 percent for plan *B*) from the claim. Then we issue a check if there is money coming to the claimant, print a summary of the transaction, and update our accounts. We do this until all claims for that day are processed.

In examining the foregoing statements, one notices some simple sequence structures, particularly at the beginning and end. There are a couple of decision structures, and it is most appropriate to nest these, first by determining which plan (*A* or *B*) to use and then subtracting the correct deductibles and copayments. The last sentence points to an iteration: either DO UNTIL all the claims are processed or DO WHILE there are claims remaining.

Realizing that it is possible to nest the decision structures according to policy plans, we can write the structured English for the foregoing example (see Figure 11.9). As one begins to work on the structured English, one finds that some logic and relationships that seemed clear at one time are actually ambiguous. For example, do we add the claim to the year-to-date (YTD) claim before or after updating the deductible? Is it possible that an error can occur if something other than plan *A* or *B* is stored in the claimant's record? We subtract 40 percent of what from the claim? These ambiguities need to be clarified at this point.

Besides the obvious advantage of clarifying the logic and relationships found in human languages, structured English has another important advantage: it is a communication tool. Structured English can be taught to and hence understood by others in the organization, so if communication is important, structured English is a viable alternative for decision analysis.

Data Dictionary and Process Specifications

All computer programs may be coded using the three basic constructs: sequence, selection (IF...THEN...ELSE and the case structure), and iteration or looping. The data dictionary indicates which of these constructs must be included in the process specifications.

FIGURE 11.9
Structured English for the
medical-claim processing
system. Underlining signifies
that the terms have been
defined in the data dictionary.

```
DO WHILE there are claims remaining
    IF claimant has not sent in a claim
        Set up new claimant record
    ELSE continue
    Add claim to YTD-Claim
    IF claimant has policy-plan A
        THEN IF deductible of $100.00 has not been met
            THEN subtract deductible-not-met from claim
            Update deductible
        ELSE continue
        ENDIF
        Subtract copayment of 40% of claim from claim
    ELSE IF claimant has policy-plan B
        THEN IF deductible of $50.00 has not been met
            THEN subtract deductible-not-met from claim
            Update deductible
        ELSE continue
        ENDIF
        Subtract copayment of 60% of claim from claim
    ELSE continue
    ELSE write plan-error-message
    ENDIF
    ENDIF
    IF claim is greater than zero
        Print check
    ENDIF
    Print summary for claimant
    Update accounts
ENDDO
```

If the data dictionary for the input and output data flow contains a series of fields without any iteration { } or selection [ ], the process specification will contain a simple sequence of statements, such as MOVE, ADD, SUBTRACT, and so on. Refer to the example of a data dictionary for the SHIPPING STATEMENT, illustrated in Figure 11.10. Notice that the data dictionary for the SHIPPING STATEMENT has the ORDER NUMBER, ORDER DATE, and the CUSTOMER NUMBER as simple sequential fields. The corresponding logic, shown in lines 3 through 5 in the corresponding structured English in Figure 11.11, consists of simple move statements.

A data structure with optional elements contained in parentheses or either/or elements contained within brackets will have a corresponding IF...THEN...ELSE statement in the process specification. Also, if an amount such as QUANTITY BACKORDERED is greater than zero, the underlying logic will be IF...THEN...ELSE. Iteration, indicated by braces on a data structure, must have a corresponding DO WHILE, DO UNTIL, or PERFORM UNTIL to control looping on the process specification. The data structure for the Order Items Lines allows up to five items in the loop. Lines 8 through 17 show the statements contained within the DO WHILE through the END DO necessary to produce the multiple Order Items.

Kneading Structure

Kit Chen has risen to the occasion and answered your questions concerning the policy for handling unfilled orders at Kit Chen Kaboodle, Inc. (with a minimum of yolking around). Based on those answers and any assumptions you need to make, pour Kit's narrative (from Consulting Opportunity 11.1) into a new mold by rewriting the recipe for handling unfilled orders in structured English.

DECISION TABLES

A decision table is a table of rows and columns, separated into four quadrants, as shown in Figure 11.12. The upper left quadrant contains the condition; the upper right quadrant contains the condition alternatives. The

FIGURE 11.10
Data structure for a shipping statement for World's Trend.

Shipping Statement =
Order Number +
Order Date +
Customer Number +
Customer Name +
Customer Address +
$_1^5${Order Item Lines} +
Number of Items +
Merchandise Total +
(Tax) +
Shipping and Handling +
Order Total

Customer Name =
First Name +
(Middle Initial) +
Last Name

Address =
Street +
(Apartment) +
City +
State +
Zip +
(Zip Expansion) +
(Country)

Order Item Lines =
Item Number +
Quantity Ordered +
Quantity Backordered +
Item Description +
Size Description +
Color Description +
Unit Price +
Extended Amount

Structured English

Format the shipping statement. After each line of the statement has been formatted, write the shipping line.

1. GET Order Record
2. GET Customer Record
3. Move Order Number to shipping statement
4. Move Order Date to shipping statement
5. Move Customer Number to shipping statement
6. DO format Customer Name (leave only one space between First/Middle/Last)
7. DO format Customer Address lines
8. DO WHILE there are items for the order
9.   GET Item Record
10.   DO Format Item Line
11.   Multiply Unit Price by Quantity Ordered giving Extended Amount
12.   Move Extended Amount to Order Item line
13.   Add Extended Amount to Merchandise Total
14.   IF Quantity Backordered is greater than zero
15.   Move Quantity Backordered to Order Item line
16.   ENDIF
17. ENDDO
18. Move Merchandise Total to shipping statement
19. Move 0 to Tax
20. IF State is equal to CT
21.   Multiply Merchandise Total by Tax Rate giving Tax
22. ENDIF
23. Move Tax to shipping statement
24. DO calculate Shipping and Handling
25. Move Shipping and Handling to shipping statement
26. Add Merchandise Total, Tax and Shipping and Handling giving Order Total
27. Move Order Total to shipping statement

FIGURE 11.12
The standard format used for
presenting a decision table.

Conditions and Actions	Rules
Conditions	Condition Alternatives
Actions	Action Entries

347

FIGURE 11.13
Using a decision table for
illustrating a store's policy of
customer checkout with four
sets of rules and four possible
actions.

Conditions and Actions	Rules			
	1	2	3	4
Under $50	Y	Y	N	N
Pays by check with 2 forms of ID	Y	N	Y	N
Uses credit card	N	Y	N	Y
Ring up sale	X			
Look up credit card in book		X		
Call supervisor for approval			X	
Call bank for credit authorization				X

lower half of the table contains the actions to be taken on the left side and the rules for executing the actions on the right. When a decision table is used to determine which action needs to be taken, the logic moves clockwise beginning from the upper left.

Suppose a store wanted to illustrate its policy on noncash customer purchases. The company could do so using a simple decision table as shown in Figure 11.13. Each of the three conditions (sale under $50 pays by check, and uses credit cards) have only two alternatives. The two alternatives are Y (yes, it is true) or N (no, it is not true). Four actions are possible:

1. Ring up the sale.
2. Look up the credit card number in a book before ringing up the sale.
3. Call the supervisor for approval.
4. Call the bank for credit card authorization.

The final ingredient that makes the decision table worthwhile is the set of rules for each of the actions. Rules are the combinations of the condition alternatives that precipitate an action.

For example, rule 3 says:

	IF
N	the total sale is NOT under $50.00
	and
Y	the customer paid by check and had two forms of ID
	and
N	the customer did not use a credit card
	THEN
X	call the supervisor for approval.

The foregoing example featured a problem with four sets of rules and four possible actions, but this is only a coincidence. The next example demonstrates that decision tables often become large and involved.

Developing Decision Tables

In order to build decision tables, the analyst needs to determine the maximum size of the table, eliminate any impossible situations, inconsistencies, or redundancies, and simplify the table as much as possible. The following steps provide the analyst with a systematic method for developing decision tables:

1. Determine the number of conditions that may affect the decision. Combine rows that overlap—for example, conditions that are mutually exclusive. the number of conditions becomes the number of rows in the top half of the decision table.

2. Determine the number of possible actions that can be taken. This becomes the number of rows in the lower half of the decision table.

3. Determine the number of condition alternatives for each condition. In the simplest form of decision table, there would be two alternatives (Y or N) for each condition. In an extended-entry table, there may be many alternatives for each condition.

4. Calculate the maximum number of columns in the decision table by multiplying the number of alternatives for reach condition. If there were four conditions and two alternatives (Y or N) for each of the conditions, there would be sixteen possibilities as follows:

Condition 1:	2 alternatives
Condition 2: ×	2 alternatives
Condition 3: ×	2 alternatives
Condition 4: ×	2 alternatives
	16 possibilities

5. Fill in the condition alternatives. Start with the first condition and divide the number of columns by the number of alternatives for that condition. In the foregoing example, there are sixteen columns and two alternatives (Y or N), so sixteen divided by two is eight. Then choose one of the alternatives, say Y, and write it in the first eight columns. Finish by writing N in the remaining eight columns as follows:

Condition 1:　Y Y Y Y Y Y Y Y N N N N N N N N

Repeat this for each condition, using a subset of the table:

Condition 1:　Y Y Y Y Y Y Y Y Y N N N N N N N N
Condition 2:　Y Y Y Y N N N N
Condition 3:　Y Y N N
Condition 4:　Y N

and continue the pattern for each condition:

Condition 1:　Y Y Y Y Y Y Y Y Y N N N N N N N N
Condition 2:　Y Y Y Y N N N N Y Y Y Y N N N N
Condition 3:　Y Y N N Y Y N N Y Y N N Y Y N N
Condition 4:　Y N Y N Y N Y N Y N Y N Y N Y N

6. Complete the table by inserting an X where rules suggest certain actions.

7. Combine rules where it is apparent that an alternative does not make a difference in the outcome; for example:

Condition 1:	Y Y
Condition 2:	Y N
Action 1:	X X

FIGURE 11.14
Constructing a decision table
for deciding which catalog to
send to customers who order
only from selected catalogs.

Conditions and Actions	Rules							
	1	2	3	4	5	6	7	8
Customer ordered from Fall catalog	Y	Y	Y	Y	N	N	N	N
Customer ordered from Christmas catalog	Y	Y	N	N	Y	Y	N	N
Customer ordered from special catalog	Y	N	Y	N	Y	N	Y	N
Send out this year's Christmas catalog		X		X		X		X
Send out special catalog			X				X	
Send out both catalogs	X				X			

can be expressed as:

Condition 1: Y
Condition 2: —
—————————————
Action 1: X

The dash [—] signifies that condition 2 can be either Y or N, and the action will still be taken.

8. Check the table for any impossible situations, contradictions, and redundancies. These will be discussed in more detail later.

9. Rearrange the conditions and actions (or even rules) if this makes the decision table more understandable.

A DECISION TABLE EXAMPLE. Figure 11.14 is an illustration of a decision table developed using the steps previously outlined. In this example, a company is trying to maintain a meaningful mailing list of customers. The objective is to send out only the catalogs from which customers will buy merchandise.

The company realizes that certain loyal customers order from every catalog and some people on the mailing list never order. These ordering patterns are easy to observe, but deciding which catalogs to send customers who order only from selected catalogs is more difficult. Once these decisions are made, a decision table is constructed for three conditions (C1: customer ordered from fall catalog; C2: customer ordered from Christmas catalog; and C3: customer ordered from specialty catalog), each having two alternatives (Y or N). Three actions can be taken: A1: send out this year's Christmas catalog; A2: send out the new specialty catalog; and A3: send out both catalogs. The resulting decision table has six rows (three conditions and three actions) and eight columns (two alternatives × two alternatives × two alternatives).

The decision table is now examined to see if it can be reduced. There are no mutually exclusive conditions, so it is not possible to get by with fewer than three condition rows. No rules allow the combination of actions. It is possible, however, to combine some of the rules as shown in Figure 11.15. For instance, rules 2, 4, 6, and 8 can be combined since they all have two things in common:

1. They instruct us to send out this year's Christmas catalog (action 1).
2. The alternative for condition 3 is always N.

Saving a Cent on Citron Car Rental

"We feel lucky to be this popular. I think customers feel we have so many options to offer that they ought to rent an auto from us," says Ricardo Limon, who manages several outlets for Citron Car Rental. "Our slogan is, 'You'll never feel squeezed at Citron.' We have five sizes of cars that we list as A through E.

A Subcompact
B Compact
C Midsize
D Full-size
E Luxury

Standard transmission is available only for A, B, and C. Automatic transmission is available for every size car.

"If a customer reserves a subcompact (A) and finds on arriving that we don't have one, that customer gets a free upgrade to the next-sized car, in this case a compact (B). Customers also get a free upgrade from their reserved car size if their company has an account with us. There's a discount for membership in any of the frequent flyer clubs through cooperating airlines, too. When customers step up to the counter, they tell us what size car they reserved, and then we check to see if we have it in the lot ready to go. They usually bring up any discounts, and we ask them if they want insurance and how long they will use the car. Then we calculate their rate, and write out a slip for them to sign right there."

Ricardo has asked you to computerize the billing process for Citron, so that customers can get their car quickly and still be billed correctly. Draw a decision table that represents the conditions, condition alternatives, actions, and rules you gained from Ricardo's narrative that will guide an automated billing process.

It doesn't matter what the alternatives are for the first two conditions, so it is possible to insert dashes [—] in place of the Y or N.

The remaining rules, 1, 3, 5, and 7, cannot be reduced to a single rule because two different actions remain. Instead, rules 1 and 5 may be combined; likewise for rules 3 and 7.

Conditions and Actions	Rules							
	1	2	3	4	5	6	7	8
Customer ordered from Fall catalog	Y	Y	Y	Y	N	N	N	N
Customer ordered from Christmas catalog	Y	Y	N	N	Y	Y	N	N
Customer ordered from special catalog	Y	N	Y	N	Y	N	Y	N
Send out this year's Christmas catalog		X		X		X		X
Send out special catalog			X				X	
Send out both catalogs	X				X			

Conditions and Actions	Rules		
	1'	2'	3'
Customer ordered from Fall catalog	–	–	–
Customer ordered from Christmas catalog	Y	–	N
Customer ordered from special catalog	Y	N	Y
Send out this year's Christmas catalog		X	
Send out special catalog			X
Send out both catalogs	X		

FIGURE 11.15
Combining rules to simplify the customer-catalog decision table.

Conditions and Actions	Rules			
	1'	2'	3'	4'
Customer ordered from Fall catalog	–	–	–	–
Customer ordered from Christmas catalog	Y	–	N	–
Customer ordered from special catalog	Y	N	Y	–
Ordered $50 or more	Y	Y	Y	N
Send out this year's Christmas catalog		X		
Send out special catalog			X	
Send out both catalogs	X			
Do not send out any catalog				X

Checking for Completeness and Accuracy

Checking over your decision tables for completeness and accuracy is essential. Four main problems can occur in developing decision tables: incompleteness, impossible situations, contradictions, and redundancy.

Assuring that all conditions, condition alternatives, actions, and rules are complete is of utmost importance. Suppose an important condition had been left out of the catalog store problem discussed earlier: If a customer ordered less than $50. The whole decision table would change because a new condition, new set of alternatives, new action, and one or more new rules would have to be added. Suppose the rule is: IF the customer did not order more than $50, THEN do not send any catalogs. A new rule 4 would be added to the decision table, as shown in Figure 11.16.

When building decision tables as outlined in the foregoing steps, it is sometimes possible to set up impossible situations. An example of this is shown in Figure 11.17. Rule 1 is not feasible, since a person cannot earn greater than $50,000 per year and less than $2,000 per month at the same time. The other three rules are valid. The problem went unnoticed because the first condition was measured in years and the second condition in months.

Contradictions occur when rules suggest different actions but satisfy the same conditions. The fault could lie with the way the analyst constructed the table or with the information the analyst received. Contradictions often occur if dashes [—] are incorrectly inserted into the table. Redundancy occurs when identical sets of alternatives require the exact same action. Figure 11.18 is an illustration of a contradiction and a redundancy. The analyst has to determine what is correct and resolve the contradiction or redundancy.

Conditions and Actions	Rules			
	1	2	3	4
Salary > $50,000/year	Y	Y	N	N
Salary < $2,000/month	Y	N	Y	N
Action 1				
Action 2				

This is an impossible situation.

352

Conditions and Actions	Rules						
	1	2	3	4	5	6	7
Condition 1	Y	Y	Y	Y	Y	N	N
Condition 2	Y	Y	Y	N	N	Y	N
Condition 3	–	N	–	–	–	N	Y
Action 1	X			X	X		
Action 2			X			X	
Action 3		X					X

Contradiction ———— Redundancy

FIGURE 11.18
Checking the decision table
for inadvertent contradictions
and redundancy is important.

More Advanced Decision Tables

Decision tables can become very burdensome because they grow rapidly as the number of conditions and alternatives increases. A table with only seven conditions with yes or no alternatives would have 128 columns. One way to reduce the complexity of unwieldy decision tables is to use extended entries, use the ELSE rule, or construct multiple tables.

Notice in the following Y or N table that the conditions are mutually exclusive.

C1: Did not order	Y	N	N	N
C2: Ordered once	N	Y	N	N
C3: Ordered twice	N	N	Y	N
C4: Ordered more than twice	N	N	N	Y

Therefore, they can be written in extended-entry form as follows:

C1: Number of times customer ordered   0 1 2 >2

The number of columns and rows necessary decreases while the understandability increases. Instead of using four rows for the number of times a customer orders, only one row is needed.

An example of a structured inventory ordering policy is shown in Figure 11.19. The cost of an item can be less than $10, between $10 and $50 inclusive, or greater than $50. In addition, the order quantity can be less than 50 units per order, between 50 and 100 units, or over 100 units. The decision table only has two condition rows, and the alternatives are written in words in the upper right-hand quadrant. By using extended-entry tables, the probability of redundancy and contradiction becomes smaller.

Another useful technique in building decision tables is to use the ELSE column. This technique is useful in helping to eliminate many repetitious rules requiring the exact same action. It is also useful in preventing errors of omission. Figure 11.20 shows how the automatic inventory ordering policy can take advantage of the ELSE rule.

Multiple tables are used to control the size of the table. A structured approach to building decision tables would avoid the use of GOTOs (jumping to another table) and instead use the instruction PERFORM. The PERFORM action allows orderly transfer from the original to another table and return to the original table. Figure 11.21 shows how transfer is made between tables using PERFORM.

FIGURE 11.19
Using extended-entry tables
reduces the possibility of
redundancy and contradic-
tion.

Conditions and Actions	Rules					
	1	2	3	4	5	6
Cost of the Item	–	Less than $10	Between $10 and $50 Inclusive	Greater than $50	Less than or Equal to $50	Greater than $50
Order Quantity	Less than 50 Units	Between 50 and 100 Units Inclusive	Between 50 and 100 Units Inclusive	Between 50 and 100 Units Inclusive	Over 100 Units	Over 100 Units
Order Immediately			X			
Wait Until Regular Order is Placed	X	X				
Check With Supervisor				X	X	
Send to Purchasing for Bid						X

Decision tables are an important tool in the analysis of structured decisions. One major advantage of using decision tables over other methods is that tables help the analyst ensure completeness. It is also easy to check for possible errors, such as impossible situations, contradictions, and redundancy. Decision table processors, which take the table as input and provide computer program code as output, are also available.

DECISION TREES

Decision trees are used when complex branching occurs in a structured decision process. Trees are also useful when it is essential to keep a string of decisions in a particular sequence. Although the decision tree derives its name from natural trees, decision trees are most often drawn on their side, with the root of the tree on the left-hand side of the paper, branching out to the right. This orientation allows the analyst to write on the branches in order to describe conditions and actions.

Unlike the decision tree used in management science, the analyst's tree does not contain probabilities and outcomes because in systems analysis trees are used mainly for identifying and organizing conditions and actions in a completely structured decision process.

Drawing Decision Trees

It is useful to distinguish between conditions and actions when drawing decision trees. This distinction is especially relevant when conditions and actions take place over a period of time and their sequence is important. For

Conditions and Actions	Rules 1	2	3	4	ELSE
Cost of the Item A cost < $10 B $10 ≤ cost ≤ $50 C cost > $50	–	A	B	C	
Order Quantity D quantity < 50 E 50 ≤ quantity ≤ 100 F quantity > 100	D	E	E	F	
Order Immediately			X		
Wait Until Regular Order is Placed	X	X			
Send to Purchasing for Bid				X	
Check with Supervisor					X

FIGURE 11.20
The ELSE rule can be used to eliminate repetitive rules requiring the same action.

DECISION TABLE 1.0

CONDITIONS AND TRANSACTION	1	2	3	4	5
C1:					
C2:					
C3:					
A1:					
PERFORM TABLE 1.1					X
A5:					
A6:					

DECISION TABLE 1.1

CONDITIONS AND TRANSACTION	1	2	3	4	5
C4:					
C5:					
C6:					
A2:					
A3:					
A4:					
RETURN					X

FIGURE 11.21
Use PERFORM to transfer to another decision table and RETURN to come back.

FIGURE 11.22
Conventions for drawing a
decision tree where circles
can be thought of as meaning
IF and squares meaning
THEN.

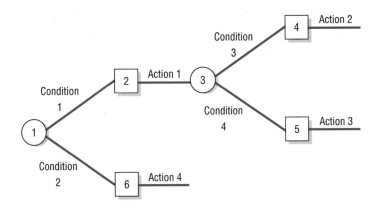

this purpose, use a square node to indicate an action and a circle to represent a condition, as shown in Figure 11.22. Using notation makes the decision tree more readable, as does numbering the circles and squares sequentially. Think of a circle as signifying IF while the square means THEN.

When decision tables were discussed in an earlier section, a point-of-sale example was used to determine the purchase approval actions for a department store. Conditions included the amount of the sale (under $50) and whether the customer paid by check or credit card. The four actions possible were to ring up the sale, look up the credit card in a book, call the supervisor for approval, or call the bank for credit card authorization. Figure 11.23 illustrates how this example can be drawn as a decision tree. In drawing the tree:

1. Identify all conditions and actions and the order and timing of these (if they are critical).
2. Begin building the tree from left to right while making sure you are complete in listing all possible alternatives before moving over to the right.

This simple tree is symmetrical, and the four actions at the end are unique. A more complex example follows to demonstrate that the tree does not have to be balanced and identical actions may appear more than once.

A COMPLEX DECISION TREE EXAMPLE. A systems analyst was hired to help Festival-on-the-Lake, a very popular theatre festival, fill requests for tickets. Here is part of an interview with the box office manager:

> When patrons request seats for a play, we try to fill their request, but often the seat they would like on their first performance date preference is sold out. On our order form, we ask the patron to choose three performance dates in order of preference, to indicate whether they prefer orchestra or balcony, and finally, to select the price of the seat they would like. We have three prices, $25, $20, and $15, and each price is available in both orchestra and balcony.
>
> Since we fill most of our ticket orders by mail, we have to assume a number of things and try to come as close as possible to the desires of the patron.
>
> If orchestra is not available, we assign balcony and vice versa, but if the first night selected is unavailable in the price requested

A Tree for Free

"I know you've got a plane to catch, but let me try to explain it once again to you, sir," pleads Glen Curtiss, a marketing manager for Premium Airlines. Curtiss has been attempting (unsuccessfully) to explain the airline's new policy for accumulating miles for awards (such as upgrades to first class, free flights, etc.) to a member of Premium's "Flying for Prizes" club.

Curtiss takes another pass at getting the policy off the ground, saying, "You see, sir, the traveler (that's you, Mr. Icarus) will be awarded the miles actually flown. If the actual mileage for the leg was less than 500 miles, the traveler will get 500 miles credit. If the trip was made on a Saturday, the actual mileage will be multiplied by 2. if the trip was made on a Tuesday,

the multiplication factor is 1.5. If this is the ninth leg traveled during the calendar month, the mileage is doubled no matter what day, and if it is the seventeenth leg traveled, the mileage is tripled.

"I hope that clears it up for you, Mr. Icarus. Enjoy your flight, and thanks for flying Premium."

Icarus, whose desire to board the Premium plane has all but melted away during Curtiss' long explanation, fades into the sea of people wading through the security lanes, without so much as a peep in reply.

Develop a decision tree for Premium Airline's new policy for accumulating award miles, so that the policy becomes clearer, is easier to grasp visually, and hence is easier to explain.

---

either in orchestra or balcony, we look at the second night. If the second night is unavailable, we look for options on the third. If the third night is unavailable, we select the next lower price and repeat the process. If the patron originally selected the lowest price, we must issue a notice that the ticket request could not be filled.

The foregoing interview suggests the use of a decision tree for two reasons: (1) The process is accomplished in stages ("First we try this, and if it doesn't work, we try this"); and (2) the logic is asymmetrical, lending itself to decision trees rather than decision tables.

The steps in building the decision tree are as follows:

1. Identify the conditions:
   1st choice of dates
   2nd choice of dates
   3rd choice of dates
   1st price preference

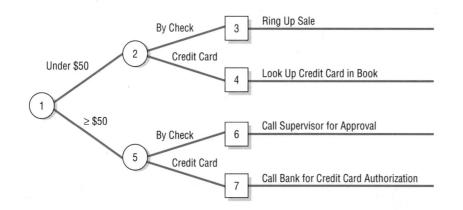

FIGURE 11.23
Drawing a decision tree to show the noncash purchase approval actions for a department store.

2nd price preference
3rd price preference
orchestra preference
balcony preference

2. Identify the condition alternatives:
   available
   not available

3. Identify the actions:
   assign seats
   issue tickets
   check 1st choice of dates
   check 2nd choice of dates
   check 3rd choice of dates
   repeat process for next lower price category
   check location preference
   issue sold out notice

4. Identify action rules (in order):
   start with ideal choice
   assign seats if available
   issue tickets if assigned
   check alternate location (orchestra/balcony)
   look at next choice of dates
   look at next price category
   issue notice if order is unfilled

The decision tree for the theatre festival is found in Figure 11.24. Actions are represented by the square nodes, and conditions are depicted by the circles. Notation of this sort keeps the processes clearer: The circles represent "IF," and the squares represent "THEN."

In building the tree, focus on the first action that should be taken, place it on the extreme left side, and then build from left to right with conditions or further actions. In the theatre example, choose ideal price and location on first choice of dates. If this ideal choice is available, two actions are taken: (1) The seat is assigned; and (2) tickets are issued. If the ideal choice is not available, the action taken is to check on availability of the alternate location (orchestra or balcony). If this is not available, the second choice of dates is examined, and so forth.

One caution about decision trees bears mentioning. the tree takes up considerable space, and consequently a minimum amount of description on conditions and actions is written on the tree. Instructions such as "assign seats" are not spelled out in enough detail at this point. the systems analyst needs to be aware of the implications of this brief statement; in this case, reserve the seats chosen, so they cannot be assigned to more than one patron; match the seat numbers with the patron, so they can be mailed. Furthermore, data requirements are not specified on the tree, only the conditions and actions.

The decision tree has three main advantages over a decision table. First, it takes advantage of the sequential structure of decision tree branches, so the order of checking conditions and executing actions is immediately noticeable.

Second, conditions and actions of decision trees are found on some branches but not on others, unlike decision tables where they are all part of

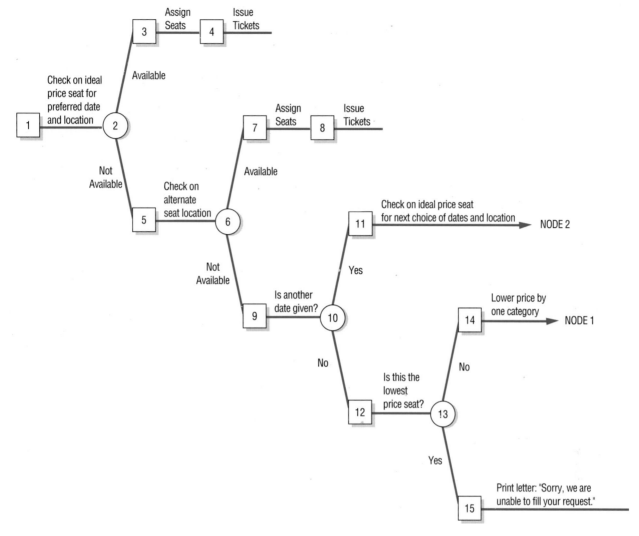

FIGURE 11.24
Building a decision tree for a process accomplished in stages whose logic is asymmetrical.

the same table. Those conditions and actions that are critical are connected directly to other conditions and actions, while those conditions that do not matter are absent. In other words, the tree does not have to be symmetrical.

Third, compared to decision tables, decision trees are more readily understood by others in the organization. Consequently, they are more appropriate as a communication tool.

CHOOSING A STRUCTURED DECISION ANALYSIS TECHNIQUE

We have examined the three techniques for analysis of structured decisions: structured English, decision tables, and decision trees. Although they need not be used exclusively, it is customary to choose one analysis technique for a decision rather than employing all three. The following guidelines provide you with a way to choose which of the three techniques to use for a particular case:

1. Use structured English when
   a. There are many repetitious actions.
      OR
   b. Communication to end users is important.
2. Use decision tables when
   a. Complex combinations of conditions, actions, and rules are found.
      OR
   b. You require a method that effectively avoids impossible situations, redundancies, and contradictions.
3. Use decision trees when
   a. The sequence of conditions and actions is critical.
      OR
   b. When not every condition is relevant to every action (the branches are different).

PHYSICAL AND LOGICAL PROCESS SPECIFICATIONS

The remaining sections in this chapter are advanced topics that may be explored further if you wish. The first topic shows how a data flow diagram can be transformed into process specifications. The second section explains how process specifications can, in turn, be used to balance (and correct) a data flow diagram.

Each data flow diagram process expands to a child diagram, a structure chart (discussed in Chapter 20), or process specifications (as structured English). If the process is primitive, the specifications show the logic, arithmetic, or algorithm for transforming the input into output. These specifications are a portion of the logical model—the business rules—which would exist regardless of the type of system used to implement the business. Business rules are often the basis of creating procedural language when using code generators.

For example, we observe that an auction house has a computer system to keep track of successful customer bids (process 4) and produce a payment statement for the person supplying the auctioned item (process 3).

If the process expands to a child diagram or a structure chart, the process specification describes the order and conditions under which the child diagram processes will execute. This control logic is a part of the physical model and would be created after the method of implementation (either batch or online) for the process has been determined. Figure 11.25 shows the auction system Diagram 4, an explosion of process 4, RECORD CUSTOMER BID. Figure 11.26 illustrates the structured English format for process 4. Note that most of the logic involves IF and PERFORM statements, which are typical of controlling program modules.

Using Process Specifications: Horizontal Balancing

Process specifications, whether on paper or captured using a CASE tool, may be used for generating computer language source code and for analyzing the system design. Computer programs are indicated by partitioning on a data flow diagram. All of the individual process specifications for a program are consolidated to become the processing details in a program specification packet.

To attempt to write the specifications for a program without examining each process may lead to omissions and errors. Since process specifications are developed on a small scale, one process at a time, each one may

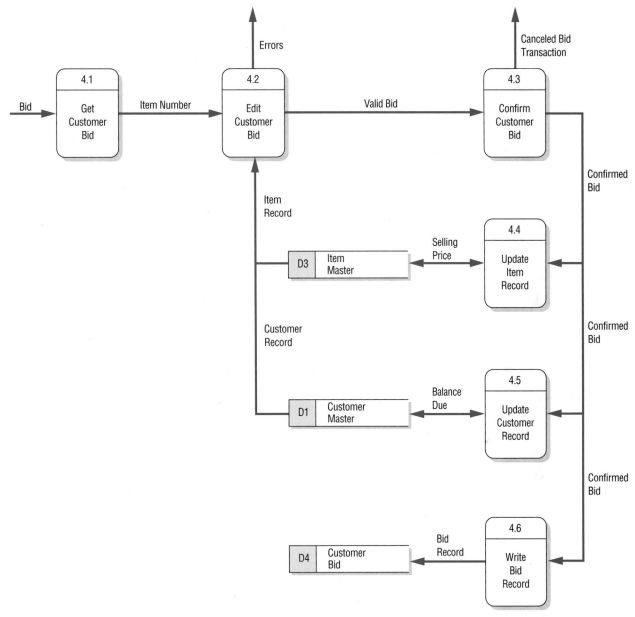

FIGURE 11.25
Data flow diagram explosion of process 4, RECORD CUSTOMER BID.

be analyzed for complete and correct logic. When the analysis is finished
and corrections are made for all processes within a program, the final program specifications should be complete and accurate.

Horizontal Balancing

Process specifications may be used to analyze the data flow diagram and
data dictionary through a method called horizontal balancing. Horizontal
balancing dictates that all output data flow elements must be obtained
from the input elements and process logic. Base elements on an output data
flow must be present on the input flow and derived elements on an output
flow must be either present on an input data flow or created using the

FIGURE 11.26
Structured English for a
process that explodes to a
child diagram.

Process Specification Form

Number __4__
Name ___RECORD CUSTOMER BID___
Description ___Operators key the customer bid. If the entries are correct, the___
___Item Master and Customer Master files are updated.___
___A Bid Record is created.___

Input Data Flow
Bid
Customer Record Balance Due
Item Record

Output Data Flow
Bid Record
Customer Record Balance Due
Item Record

Type of Process	Subprogram/Function Name
☑ Online ☐ Batch ☐ Manual	

Process Logic:
DO Get Customer Bid Screen
DO Edit Customer Bid
    Until Valid Bid
   Or Operator Cancel
IF Valid Bid
    DO Confirm Customer Bid (Visual confirm of the data)
    IF Confirmed
        DO Update Customer Record
        DO Update Inventory Record
        DO Write Bid Record
    ENDIF
ENDIF

Refer to: Name: _____
☐ Structured English   ☐ Decision Table   ☐ Decision Tree

Unresolved Issues:

process specifications. Unresolved areas should be summarized into a series of interview questions. Be sure to pose these questions during follow-up interviews with key users.

Figure 11.27 illustrates Diagram 3, an explosion of the Auction System process 3, PRODUCE SUPPLIER PAYMENT STATEMENT. Figure 11.28 shows the corresponding data dictionary entries. Figure 11.29 is the structured English for process 3.4, CALCULATE SUPPLIER NET BID, and for process 3.5, PRINT BID LINE. Figure 11.30 is the structured English for process 3.6, PRINT SUPPLIER TOTAL DUE LINE.

The output from process 3.4 is the NET BID for each item, a derived element. The logic for the process requires as input the SUPPLIER TYPE and ITEM BID AMOUNT, both used in the NET BID calculation. Checking the data flow diagram reveals that both these elements are input to process 3.4. However, only the NET BID is shown as output from the process. The AMOUNT PAID TO SUPPLIER, included in the structured English, is not

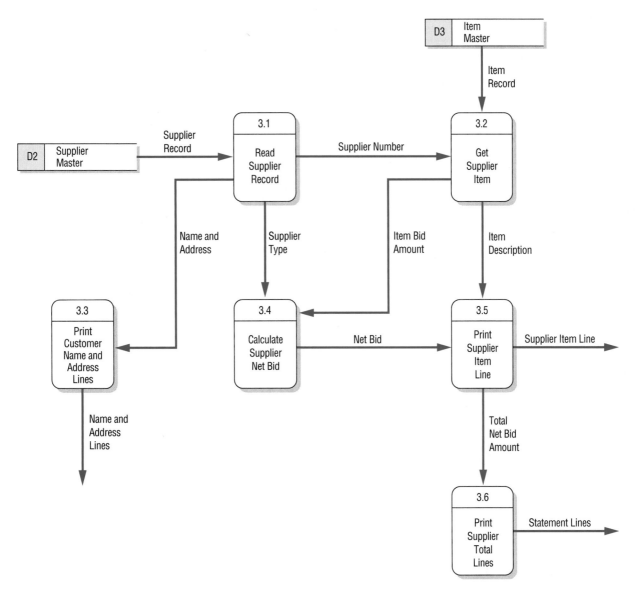

FIGURE 11.27
Diagram 3, Produce Supplier Payment Statement.

shown on the data flow diagram, nor is the ITEM MASTER data store. The YEAR-TO-DATE NET BID is not included in the data dictionary for the SUPPLIER RECORD, nor is it shown on the data flow diagram. The data flow diagram and data dictionary must be updated to include these missing components. Figure 11.31 shows Diagram 3 with the necessary corrections.

Examine the output from process 3.5. The SUPPLIER ITEM LINE contains four elements: ITEM DESCRIPTION, ITEM BID AMOUNT, NET BID, and DATE SOLD. The ITEM DESCRIPTION and NET BID are input to process 3.5, but DATE SOLD and ITEM BID AMOUNT, which are base elements, are not on any input flow. They must be added to the data flow diagram. To avoid having three input flows (ITEM DESCRIPTION, ITEM BID AMOUNT, and DATE SOLD) traveling from process 3.2 to 3.3, the entire item record is passed between the two processes. The final process to be

FIGURE 11.28
Data dictionary entries for
producing the Supplier
Sales Receipt.

```
Supplier Sales Receipt =     Current Date +
                             Supplier Type +
                             Supplier Name +
                             Address +
                             {Supplier Item Line} +
                             Auction Surcharge+
                             Total Amount Paid to Supplier


Supplier Item Line =         Item Description +
                             (Item Bid Amount) +
                             (Net Bid) +
                             (Date Sold)


Supplier Record =            Supplier Number +
                             Supplier Type +
                             Supplier Name +
                             Address


Item Record =                Item Number +
                             Item Description +
                             (Item Bid Amount) +
                             (Amount Paid to Supplier) +
                             (Date Sold) +
                             Supplier Number
```

examined is 3.6. The structured English requires that SUPPLIER TYPE and
TOTAL NET BID AMOUNT be present as input flow. Since only the
TOTAL NET BID AMOUNT is present, process 3.6 has missing input.

SUMMARY

Once the analyst identifies data flows and begins constructing a data dictionary, it is time to turn to process specification and decision analysis. The
three methods for decision analysis and describing process logic discussed
in this chapter are: structured English, decision tables, and decision trees.

Process specifications (or minispecs) are created for primitive processes
on a data flow diagram, as well as for some higher-level processes that
explode to a child diagram. These specifications explain the decision-
making logic and formulas that will transform process input data into output. The three goals of process specification are: to reduce the ambiguity
of the process, to obtain a precise description of what is accomplished,
and to validate the system design.

A large part of a systems analyst's work will involve structured decisions; that is, decisions that can be automated if identified conditions occur.
In order to do this, the analyst needs to define four variables in the decision
being examined: conditions, condition alternatives, actions, and action rules.

One way to describe structured decisions is to use the method
referred to as structured English, where logic is expressed in sequential
structures, decision structures, case structures, or iterations. Structured

FIGURE 11.29
Structured English description for processes 3.4
and 3.5.

Structured English: Processes 3.4, CALCULATE SUPPLIER NET BID

BEGIN CASE
IF the Supplier Type is a charitable organization
    THEN Commission Rate = 10%
ELSE IF the Supplier Type is a governmental unit
    THEN Commission Rate = 15%
ELSE IF the Supplier Type is a bankruptcy
    THEN Commission Rate = 18%
ELSE IF the Supplier Type is an estate
    THEN Commission Rate = 20%
ELSE Commission Rate = 25%
END CASE
Multiply Item Bid Amount by Commission Rate giving Commission
Subtract Commission from Item Bid Amount giving Net Bid
Move Net Bid to the Amount Paid to Supplier on the Item Record
Rewrite the Item Record
Add Net Bid to Year to Date Net Bid on the Supplier Record
Rewrite the Supplier Record

Structured English: Processes 3.5, PRINT BID LINE

Move Item Description to Supplier Item Line
Move Date Sold to Supplier Item Line
Move Item Bid Amount to Supplier Item Line
Move Net Bid to the Supplier Item Line
Write Supplier Item Line
Add Net Bid to Total Net Bid Amount

English uses accepted keywords such as IF, THEN, ELSE, DO, DO WHILE, and DO UNTIL to describe the logic used and indents to indicate the hierarchical structure of the decision process.

Decision tables provide another way to examine, describe, and document decisions. Four quadrants (viewed clockwise from the upper left-hand corner) are used to: (1) describe the conditions; (2) identify possible decision alternatives (such as Y or N); (3) indicate which actions should be performed; and (4) describe the actions. Decision tables are advantageous since the rules for developing the table itself, as well as the rules for eliminating redundancy, contradictions, and impossible situations, are straightforward and manageable. The use of decision tables promotes completeness and accuracy in analyzing structured decisions.

The third method for decision analysis is the decision tree, consisting of nodes (a square for actions and a circle for conditions) and branches. Decision trees are appropriate when actions must be accomplished in a certain sequence. There is no requirement that the tree be symmetrical, so only those conditions and actions that are critical to the decisions at hand are found on a particular branch.

FIGURE 11.30
Structured English description for process 3.6.

Structured English: Processes 3.6, PRINT SUPPLIER TOTAL DUE LINE

Note: The Auction Surcharge is a one-time cost per auction to cover set-up costs

```
BEGIN CASE
IF the Supplier Type is a charitable organization
        THEN Auction Surcharge = $200
ELSE IF the Supplier Type is a governmental unit
        THEN Auction Surcharge = $500
ELSE IF the Supplier Type is a bankruptcy
        THEN Auction Surcharge = $400
ELSE IF the Supplier Type is an estate
        THEN Auction Surcharge = $300
ELSE Auction Surcharge = $500
END CASE
Move Total Net Bid Amount to Statement Line
Write Statement Line
Move Auction Surcharge to Statement Line
Write Statement Line
Subtract Auction Surcharge from Total Net Bid Amount giving Payment Total
Move Payment Total to Statement Line
Write Statement Line
```

Each of the decision analysis methods has its own advantages and should be used accordingly. Structured English is useful when many actions are repeated and when communicating with others is important. Decision tables provide complete analysis of complex situations while limiting the need for change attributable to impossible situations, redundancies, or contradictions. Decision trees are important when proper sequencing of conditions and actions is critical and when each condition is not relevant to each action.

Each data flow diagram process expands to a child diagram, a structure chart, or process specifications (as structured English). If the process is primitive, the specifications show the logic, arithmetic, or algorithm for transforming the input into output. These logical model specifications are part of the business rules (which are often used as the basis of creating procedural language when using code generators).

If the process expands to a child diagram, or a structure chart, the process specification describes the order and conditions under which the child diagram processes will execute. This control logic is part of the physical model.

Process specifications may be used to analyze the data flow diagram and data dictionary through a method called horizontal balancing, which dictates that all output data flow elements must be obtained from the input elements and process logic. Unresolved areas can be posed as questions in follow-up interviews.

KEYWORDS AND PHRASES

structured decision   incompleteness
conditions   contradictions

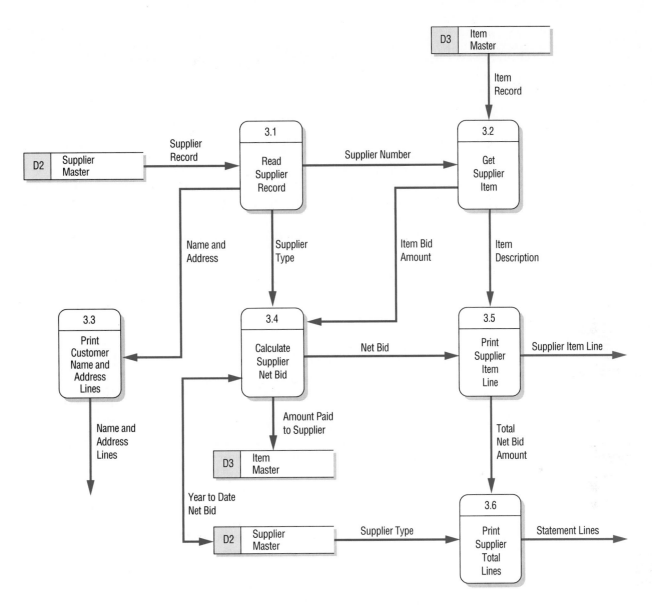

FIGURE 11.31
Corrected data flow diagram, an explosion of process 3, Produce Supplier Payment Statement.

action rules
condition alternatives
actions
impossible situations
structured English
decision tables

redundancy
decision trees
minispecs
process specifications
horizontal balancing

REVIEW QUESTIONS

1. List three reasons for producing process specifications.
2. Define what is meant by a structured decision.
3. What four elements must be known in order for the systems analyst to design systems for structured decisions?

"It's really great that you've been able to spend all of this time with us. One thing's for sure, we can use the help. And clearly, from your conversations with Snowden and others, you must realize we all believe that consultants have a role to play in helping companies change. Well, most of us believe it anyway.

"Sometimes structure is good for a person. Or even a company. As you know, Snowden is keen on any kind of structure. That's why some of the Training people can drive him wild sometimes. They're good at structuring things for their clients, but when it comes to organizing their own work, it's another story. Oh well, let me know if there's any way I can help you."

HYPERCASE QUESTIONS

1. Assume you will create the specifications for an automated project tracking system for the Training employees. One of the system's functions will be to allow project members to update or add names, addresses, and phone/fax numbers of new clients. Using structured English, write procedure for carrying out the process of entering a new client name, address, and phone/fax number. (*Hint:* The procedure should ask for a client name, check to see if the name is already in an existing client file, and let the user either validate and update the current client address and phone/fax (if necessary) or add a new client's address and phone/fax number to the client file.)

4. What are the two building blocks of structured English?
5. List five conventions that should be followed when using structured English.
6. What is the advantage of using structured English to communicate with people in the organization?
7. Which quadrant of the decision table is used for conditions? Which is used for condition alternatives?
8. What is the first step to take in developing a decision table?
9. List the four main problems that can occur in developing decision tables.
10. What is one way to reduce the complexity of unwieldy decision tables?
11. What is one of the major advantages of decision tables over other methods of decision analysis?
12. What are the main uses of decision trees in systems analysis?
13. List the four major steps in building decision trees.
14. What three advantages do decision trees have over decision tables?
15. Under what two situations should you use structured English?
16. In which two situations do decision tables work best?
17. Under what two situations are decision trees preferable?

18. How do data dictionary structures help in determining the type of structured English statements for a process?

19. What is horizontal balancing? Why is it desirable to balance each process?

PROBLEMS

1. Clyde Clerk is reviewing his firm's expense reimbursement policies with the new salesperson, Trav Farr. "Our reimbursement policies depend on the situation. You see, first we determine if it is a local trip. If it is, we only pay mileage of 18.5 cents a mile. If the trip was a one-day trip, we pay mileage and then check the times of departure and return. In order to be reimbursed for breakfast, you must leave by 7:00 A.M., lunch by 11:00 A.M., and have dinner by 5:00 P.M. To receive reimbursement for breakfast, you must return later than 10:00 A.M., lunch later than 2:00 P.M., and have dinner by 7:00 P.M. On a trip lasting more than one day, we allow hotel, taxi, and airfare, as well as meal allowances. The same times apply for meal expenses." Write structured English for Clyde's narrative of the reimbursement policies.

2. Draw a decision tree depicting the reimbursement policy given in problem 1.

3. Draw a decision table for the reimbursement policy given in problem 1.

4. A computer supplies firm called True Disk has set up accounts for countless businesses in Dosville. True Disk sends out invoices monthly and will give discounts if payments are made within ten days. The discounting policy is as follows: If the amount of the order for computer supplies is greater than $1,000, subtract 4 percent for the order; if the amount is between $500 and $1,000, subtract a 2 percent discount; if the amount is less than $500, do not apply any discount. Any special order (computer furniture, for example) is exempt from all discounting.

   Develop a decision table for True Disk discounting decisions, where the condition alternatives are limited to Y and N.

5. Develop an extended-entry decision table for the True Disk company discount policy described in problem 4.

6. Develop a decision tree for the True Disk company discount policy presented in problem 4.

7. Write structured English to solve the True Disk company situation in problem 4.

8. Premium Airlines has recently offered to settle claims for a class action suit, which was originated for alleged price fixing of tickets. The proposed settlement is stated as follows:

   "Initially, Premium Airlines will make available to the settlement class a main fund of $25 million in coupons. If the number of valid claims submitted is 1.25 million or fewer, the value of each claim will be the result obtained by dividing $25 million by the total number of valid claims submitted. For example, if there are 500,000 valid claims, each person submitting a valid claim will receive a coupon with a value of $50.

   "The denomination of each coupon distributed will be in a whole dollar amount not to exceed $50. Thus, if there are fewer than

500,000 valid claims, the value of each claim will be divided among two coupons or more. For example, if there are 250,000 valid claims, each person submitting a valid claim will receive two coupons, each having a face value of $50, for a total coupon value of $100.

"If the number of valid claims submitted is between 1.25 million and 1.5 million, Premium Airlines will make available a supplemental fund of coupons, with a potential value of $5 million. The supplemental fund will be made available to the extent necessary to provide one $20 coupon for each valid claim.

"If there are more than 1.5 million valid claims, the total amount of the main fund and the supplemental fund, $30 million, will be divided evenly to produce one coupon for each valid claim. The value of each such coupon will be $30 million divided by the total number of valid claims."

Draw a decision tree for the Premium Airlines settlement.

9. Write structured English for Premium Airlines in problem 8.

10. "Well, it's sort of hard to describe," says Sharon, a counselor at Less Is More Nutrition Center. "I've never had to really tell anybody about the way we charge clients or anything, but here goes.

"When clients come into Less Is More, we check to see if they've ever used our service before. Unfortunately for them, I guess, we have a lot of repeat clients who keep bouncing back. Repeat clients get a reduced rate (pardon the pun) of $100 for the first visit if they return within a year of the end of their program.

"Everyone new pays an initial fee, which is $200 for a physical evaluation. The client may bring in a coupon at this time, and then we deduct $50 from the upfront fee. Half of our clients use our coupons and find out about us from them. But we just give our repeaters their $100 off—they can't use a coupon, too! Clients who transfer in from one of our centers in another city get $75 off their first payment fee, but the coupon doesn't apply. Customers who pay cash get 10 percent off the $200, but they can't use a coupon with that."

Create a decision table with Y and N conditions for the client charge system at Less Is More Nutrition Center.

11. Reduce the decision table in Figure 11.EX1 to the minimum number of rules.

GROUP PROJECTS

1. Each group member (or each subgroup) should choose to become an "expert" and prepare to explain how and when to use one of the following structured decision techniques: structured English, decision tables, or decision trees. Each group member or subgroup should then make a case for the usefulness of their assigned decision analysis technique for studying the types of structured decisions made by the Maverick Transport company on dispatching particular trucks to particular destinations. Each group should make a presentation of their preferred technique.

2. After hearing each presentation, the group should reach a consensus on *which* technique is most appropriate for analyzing the dispatching decisions of Maverick Transport and *why* that technique is best in this instance.

Conditions and Actions	Rules															
	1	2	3	4	5	6	7	8	9	10	11	12	13	14	15	16
Sufficient Quantity on Hand	Y	Y	Y	Y	Y	Y	Y	Y	N	N	N	N	N	N	N	N
Quantity Large Enough for Discount	Y	Y	Y	Y	N	N	N	N	Y	Y	Y	Y	N	N	N	N
Wholesale Customer	Y	Y	N	N	Y	Y	N	N	Y	Y	N	N	Y	Y	N	N
Sales Tax Exemption Filed	Y	N	Y	N	Y	N	Y	N	Y	N	Y	N	Y	N	Y	N
Ship Items and Prepare Invoice	X	X	X	X	X	X	X	X								
Set up Backorder									X	X	X	X	X	X	X	X
Deduct Discount	X	X														
Add Sales Tax			X	X	X		X	X								

FIGURE 11.EX1
A decision table for a warehouse.

SELECTED BIBLIOGRAPHY

Adam, E. E., Jr., and R. J. Ebert. *Production and Operations Management*, 3rd ed. Englewood Cliffs, NJ: Prentice-Hall, Inc., 1986.

Awad, E. M. *Systems Analysis and Design*, 2nd ed. Homewood, IL: Richard D. Irwin, Inc., 1985.

Gane, C., and T. Sarson. *Structured Systems Analysis and Design Tools and Techniques*. Englewood Cliffs, NJ: Prentice-Hall, Inc., 1979.

Hartman, W., H. Matthes, and A. Proeme. *Management Information Systems Handbook*. New York: McGraw-Hill Book Company, 1968.

TABLING A DECISION

Processes that do not explode to any further child diagrams are called *primitive processes*. The logic of these processes, called a minispec or process specification, is usually described. For a given program, the sum of all the minispecs becomes the program specifications.

After doing many follow-up interviews with Dot Matricks, Anna tells Chip, "I've determined the logic needed to update the PENDING MICRO-COMPUTER ORDERS data store. Since many micros may be ordered on the same purchase order, as each microcomputer is entered the matching record is located and one is subtracted from the number of outstanding micros per purchase order."

Anna shows Chip the PRIMITIVE PROCESS SPECIFICATION print (depicted in Figure E11.1). "The name of the corresponding process, UPDATE PENDING MICROCOMPUTER ORDER (process 1.5), links the process specification to the data flow diagram," she explains. Inputs and outputs are listed and should match the data flow into the process. "The **Type** may be either ELE for element, or REC for record. The MICROCOMPUTER TRANSACTION record is input, and the updated PENDING MICROCOMPUTER ORDER is the output flow."

"That will be useful," Chip says. "Even though it took a while to untangle it all."

Anna points out that "The **Process Description** area contains the logic, shown in structured English. Constants necessary for calculations may also be entered.

"For example," she continues, "a sales tax rate or maximum hours worked before paying an overtime rate may be entered."

When the logic is complete, Anna further enters the UPDATE PENDING MICROCOMP. FILE User Requirement (URQ) which was satisfied by the process specification. Her plan is to link every component of the system back to the needs of each user. A Test Plan (TST) entry, PENDING MICROCOMP. FILE UPDATE has also been created. Even though the details of the test plan have not been determined, Anna will have a complete list of all the testing needs of the system. These may be reported on and completed in the later stages of analysis.

The last entity linked to the process specification is CAT for category. All microcomputer system components are grouped under the MICRO-COMPUTER INFORMATION category. When all the process specifications are completed, they will be printed and included as part of the program specification packet provided.

A decision table may be created for control or process logic. Before keying the decision table, it is a good idea to create it on paper and optimize the table. This way only the essential conditions and actions will be entered.

"I've been busy too," Chip assures Anna. "I've spoken with Cher Ware several times since you interviewed her. I've finally captured some of the logic for calculating the cost of a software upgrade.

"Cher indicated three different conditions affecting the cost. The site license provides unlimited copies and is used for popular software

Allen Schmidt,
Julie E. Kendall, and
Kenneth E. Kendall

installed on many micros. An educational discount is provided by many publishers, and a discount for quantity is usually available," Chip says.

"First I determined the values for the conditions and the number of combinations," Chip continues. He set out the three conditions and their values as follows:

Condition	Values	Number of Values
SITE LICENSE	Y/N	2
EDUCATIONAL DISCOUNT	Y/N	2
DISCOUNT FOR QUANTITY	Y/N	2

"The total number of combinations is found by multiplying the number of values for each of the conditions, $2 \times 2 \times 2 = 8$. The next step is to decide which conditions should be first." Chip continues, "I reason that a SITE LICENSE would not have a discount for quantity or an additional educational discount, since the actual site license cost already reflects this kind of discount. Therefore the SITE LICENSE should be the first condition. Each of the two other conditions would not have any particular advantage over the other, so the order is unimportant.

"Since the total number of conditions is eight and the SITE LICENSE condition has two possible values, the repeat factor would be 8/2 or 4." Chip continues by noting that the first row of the decision table would be:

Condition	1	2	3	4	5	6	7	8
SITE LICENSE	Y	Y	Y	Y	N	N	N	N

"The next condition is EDUCATIONAL DISCOUNT, which also has two values. Dividing these two into the previous factor of four yields: $4/2 = 2$ for the next repeat factor." Chip notes that the decision table now expands to:

Condition	1	2	3	4	5	6	7	8
SITE LICENSE	Y	Y	Y	Y	N	N	N	N
EDUCATIONAL DISCOUNT	Y	Y	N	N	Y	Y	N	N

Chip continues, "The last condition, DISCOUNT FOR QUANTITY, also has two values, and dividing these two into the previous repeat factor of two gives $2/2 = 1$, which should always be the repeat factor for the last row of the conditions." He notes that the completed condition entry is:

Condition	1	2	3	4	5	6	7	8
SITE LICENSE	Y	Y	Y	Y	N	N	N	N
EDUCATIONAL DISCOUNT	Y	Y	N	N	Y	Y	N	N
DISCOUNT FOR QUANTITY	Y	N	Y	N	Y	N	Y	N

Chip points out that when the actions are included, the completed decision table is:

Condition	1	2	3	4	5	6	7	8
SITE LICENSE	Y	Y	Y	Y	N	N	N	N
EDUCATIONAL DISCOUNT	Y	Y	N	N	Y	Y	N	N
DISCOUNT FOR QUANTITY	Y	N	Y	N	Y	N	Y	N

Actions

COST = SITE LICENSE COST	X X X X
COST = EDUCATIONAL COST × COPIES	X
COST = DISCOUNT COST × COPIES	X
COST = UPGRADE COST × COPIES	X
COST = (EDUC COST – DISC) × COPIES	X

"I have proceeded to reduce some of the redundant actions, specifically those occurring when a SITE LICENSE has been obtained," Chip continues. "Since the actions are the same for SITE LICENSE values of Y, the educational and quantity discounts are meaningless to the condition and don't have to be considered. Rules 1 through 4 may be reduced to one rule." Chip concludes by noting that the final optimized decision table is:

Condition	1	2	3	4	5
SITE LICENSE	Y	N	N	N	
EDUCATIONAL DISCOUNT	—	Y	Y	N	N
DISCOUNT FOR QUANTITY	—	Y	N	Y	N

Actions

	1	2	3	4	5
COST = SITE LICENSE COST	X				
COST = EDUCATIONAL COST × COPIES		X			
COST = DISCOUNT COST × COPIES			X		
COST = UPGRADE COST × COPIES				X	
COST = (EDUC COST - DISC) × COPIES		X			

"With the decision table in its final form," Chip tells Anna, "I used Excelerator to produce the decision table and include it in the system specifications."

The Excelerator **Structured Decision Table** description screen shown in Figure E11.2 contains the optimized decision table. The **Initial Condition** reflects what must be present before the decisions can be made, and in this case the SOFTWARE RECORD needs to have been read. There are three conditions: whether a site license, an educational discount, or a quantity discount is available. The **C** in the left column indicates a condition; **A** is for action. The actions show how the UPGRADE COST is determined for each condition, indicated by an **X** in the rule columns.

A second screen allows Requirements, Associated Entities, and a Description to be entered. The printed decision table is illustrated in Figure E11.3. Again, the decision table is linked to the user requirement, DETERMINE SOFTWARE UPGRADE COST. A Category and Test Plan entity are also created for later design work. The **Description** area contains a reference to process 5.10.3 that the logic represents.

Exercises[*]

🖫 **E-1.** Use Excelerator to view the Primitive Process Specification UPDATE PENDING MICRO ORDER.

---

[*] The exercises preceded by a disk icon require the program Excelerator (or another CASE tool). A disk is provided free of charge to any professor adopting this book. The examples on the disk may be imported into Excelerator and then used by students.

```
DATE: 28-NOV-93     PRIMITIVE PROCESS SPECIFICATION - OUTPUT        PAGE     1
TIME: 13:14         NAME: UPDATE PENDING MICRO ORDER               Excelerator


TYPE Primitive Process Specification    NAME UPDATE PENDING MICRO ORDER

            Inputs:                              Outputs:
    Type  Name                          Type  Name
    REC MICROCOMPUTER TRANSACTION        REC PENDING MICROCOMPUTER ORDER


                     Process Description
FOR EVERY MICROCOMPUTER TRANSACTION:

    FIND THE MATCHING MICROCOMPUTER ORDER RECORD.  USE THE PURCHASE
       ORDER NUMBER TO RANDOMLY READ THE FILE.

    SUBTRACT ONE FROM THE COUNT OF MICROS ORDERED.

    IF THE DATE ON THE MICROCOMPUTER TRANSACTION RECORD IS GREATER THAN
       THE DATE RECEIVED ON THE PENDING MICROCOMPUTER ORDER RECORD,
       MOVE THE TRANSACTION DATE TO THE MICROCOMPUTER DATE RECEIVED.
    REWRITE THE PENDING MICROCOMPUTER ORDER RECORD.

        Constants:
    Type  Name



        Satisfies Requirement:              Associated Entities:
    Type  Name                          Type  Name
    URQ UPDATE PENDING MICROCOMP. FILE   TST PENDING MICROCOMP. FILE UPDATE
                                         CAT MICROCOMPUTER INFORMATION


    Modified By   ALLEN        Date Modified  950401    # Changes  2
    Added By      ANNA         Date Added     950116
    Last Project  TEST FINAL
    Locked By                 Date Locked    0         Lock Status
```

FIGURE E11.1
Primitive Process Specifications print, UPDATE PENDING MICROCOMPUTER
ORDER.

⊞ **E-2.**   Modify and print the ACCUMULATIVE HARDWARE SUBTO-
TALS Primitive Process Specification. Add the **Process
Description** "Accumulate the hardware subtotals. These include
the number of machines for each hardware brand." Link the
Primitive Process Specification to the User Requirement
UPDATE PENDING MICROCOMP. FILE and the Associated
Entities Test, PENDING MICROCOMP. FILE UPDATE, and
Category MICROCOMPUTER INFORMATION.

⊞ **E-3.**   Modify and print the CONFIRM MICROCOMPUTER DELETION
Primitive Process Specification. Add the following:

Inputs:	REC MICROCOMPUTER RECORD
	REC SCREEN DELETION CONFIRMATION
Outputs:	REC CONFIRMED DELETION
	REC REJECTED DELETION

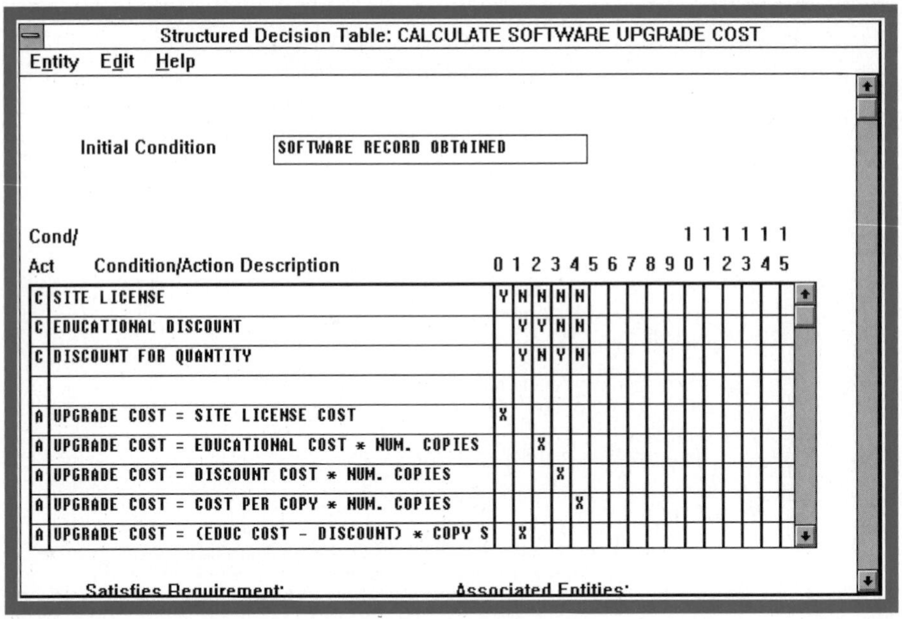

Structured Decision Table: CALCULATE SOFTWARE UPGRADE COST

Entity   Edit   Help

Initial Condition   SOFTWARE RECORD OBTAINED

Cond/ Act	Condition/Action Description	0	1	2	3	4	5	6	7	8	9	10	11	12	13	14	15
C	SITE LICENSE	Y	N	N	N	N											
C	EDUCATIONAL DISCOUNT		Y	Y	N	N											
C	DISCOUNT FOR QUANTITY		Y	N	Y	N											
A	UPGRADE COST = SITE LICENSE COST	X															
A	UPGRADE COST = EDUCATIONAL COST * NUM. COPIES			X													
A	UPGRADE COST = DISCOUNT COST * NUM. COPIES				X												
A	UPGRADE COST = COST PER COPY * NUM. COPIES					X											
A	UPGRADE COST = (EDUC COST - DISCOUNT) * COPY S		X														

Satisfies Requirement: Associated Entities:

FIGURE E11.2
Structured Decision Table description screen, UPGRADE COST.

Add the User Requirement MAINTAIN MICROCOMPUTER INFO. and the Associated Entities Test, DELETE MICROCOMPUTER RECORD, and Category, MICROCOMPUTER INFORMATION.

E-4. Create Primitive Process Specifications for process 8.6, VALIDATE MICROCOMPUTER CHANGES. Details of the process are:

Inputs:	REC - KEYED MICROCOMPUTER CHANGES
Outputs:	REC - VALID MICROCOMPUTER CHANGES
	REC - MICROCOMPUTER CHANGE ERRORS
Logic:	Validate the changes to the MICROCOMPUTER MASTER. Include a note to use the edit criteria established for each element. Provide the following additional editing criteria:

The ROOM LOCATION must be valid for a particular campus.

The MONITOR must not be a lower grade than the graphics board. An example of this error would be a VGA (higher resolution) graphics board paired with a CGA (lower resolution) monitor.

There must not be a second fixed disk without the first one.

The LAST PREVENTIVE MAINTENANCE DATE must not be greater than the current date.

The DATE PURCHASED must not be greater than the LAST PREVENTIVE MAINTENANCE DATE or greater than the current date.

```
DATE: 28-NOV-93      STRUCTURED DECISION TABLE - OUTPUT        PAGE    1
TIME: 13:29          NAME: CALCULATE SOFTWARE UPGRADE COST     Excelerator


TYPE Structured Decision Table      NAME CALCULATE SOFTWARE UPGRADE COST

      Initial Condition   SOFTWARE RECORD OBTAINED


Cond/                                               1 1 1 1 1 1
Act        Condition/Action Description    0 1 2 3 4 5 6 7 8 9 0 1 2 3 4 5
C SITE LICENSE                             Y N N N
C EDUCATIONAL DISCOUNT                     Y Y N N
C DISCOUNT FOR QUANTITY                    Y N Y N

A UPGRADE COST = SITE LICENSE COST            X
A UPGRADE COST = EDUCATIONAL COST * NUM. COPIES   X
A UPGRADE COST = DISCOUNT COST * NUM. COPIES        X
A UPGRADE COST = COST PER COPY * NUM. COPIES          X
A UPGRADE COST = (EDUC COST - DISCOUNT) * COPY S  X


        Satisfies Requirement:            Associated Entities:
   Type  Name                          Type  Name
   URQ DETERMINE SOFTWARE UPGRADE COST  CAT SOFTWARE
                                        TST PRODUCE SOFTWARE UPGRADE COST


                     Description
   THIS DECISION TABLE PROVIDES DETAILS FOR PROCESS 5.10.3, CALCULATE
   SOFTWARE UPGRADE COST.


   Modified By   ANNA        Date Modified  931127   # Changes  1
   Added By      CHIP        Date Added     950205
   Last Project  TEST FINAL
   Locked By                 Date Locked    0        Lock Status
```

FIGURE E11.3
Structured Decision Table print, UPGRADE COST.

The MODEL must conform to the type supported by the BRAND name.

No changes may be made to an inactive record.

E-5. Create Primitive Process Specifications for process 2.4, CREATE SOFTWARE LOG FILE. Use the data flow diagram examples to determine inputs and outputs. Process details are:

Format the SOFTWARE LOG RECORD from the following information:

The confirmed NEW SOFTWARE RECORD elements.

The following system elements: System date, System time, User ID, Microcomputer ID.

When the record has been formatted, write to the SOFTWARE LOG FILE.

E-6. Produce process specifications for process 5.7.2, FIND MATCHING HARDWARE RECORD. This is part of a program producing a report showing all microcomputers on which each software package would be located. Use Excelerator to view data flow diagram 5.7 and obtain the input and output records. Use structured English to depict the following logic:

For each software package record, loop while there is a matching hardware inventory number. Within the loop, accomplish the following tasks:

Randomly read the MICROCOMPUTER MASTER file.

If a record is found, format the MATCHING MICROCOMPUTER RECORD information.

If no record is found, format a NO MATCHING error line.

Further, if the found MICROCOMPUTER RECORD is inactive, indicating that it has been removed from service, format an INACTIVE MATCHING MICROCOMPUTER error line.

⊟ **E-7.** Use Excelerator to view the CALCULATE SOFTWARE UPGRADE COST decision table.

⊟ **E-8.** Modify the FIND SOFTWARE LOCATION decision table, representing the logic for an inquiry program for displaying all locations for a given SOFTWARE TITLE and VERSION. The conditions have been created and optimized, resulting in five rules. Enter the actions that need to be entered and an X in the column related to the conditions. Print the final decision table. The conditions and actions are represented by the following logic:

The SOFTWARE MASTER file is located for the specified TITLE. If the matching record is not found, an error message is displayed. Since there may be several versions, the VERSION NUMBER on the record is checked for a match to the version entered. If the requested version is not found, further records are read for using the alternate index. If all records are read and the version number is not found, an error message VERSION NOT AVAILABLE is displayed.

Once the correct software has been located, a matching MICROCOMPUTER MASTER record is obtained. If the MICROCOMPUTER MASTER is not found, the error message MACHINE NOT FOUND is displayed. For each matching machine, the CAMPUS TABLE is searched for the CAMPUS LOCATION code. If the code is not found, the message CAMPUS CODE NOT FOUND is displayed.

If no errors occur, the requested information is displayed.

⊟ **E-9.** Create a decision table for a batch update of the MICROCOMPUTER MASTER FILE. There are three types of updates: Add, Delete, and Change.

The MICROCOMPUTER MASTER record must be read. If the transaction is an Add and the master is not found, format and write the new microcomputer master record. Print a valid transaction line on an UPDATE REPORT. For a Change or Delete transaction, print a CHANGE ERROR LINE or a DELETE ERROR LINE if the master record is not found.

If the master record is found, check the active code. If the record is inactive and the transaction is an Add, format and rewrite the new microcomputer master record. Print a valid transaction line on an UPDATE REPORT. For a Change or Delete transaction, print a CHANGE ERROR LINE or a DELETE ERROR LINE.

If the **MICROCOMPUTER MASTER RECORD** is active and the transaction is an Add, print an ADD ERROR LINE. For a Change transaction, format the changes and rewrite the MICROCOMPUTER MASTER RECORD. Print the VALID TRANSACTION LINE. For a Delete transaction, change the ACTIVE CODE to inactive and rewrite the MICROCOMPUTER MASTER RECORD. Print the VALID TRANSACTION LINE.

Add the User Requirement, MAINTAIN MICROCOMPUTER INFO.

Add the **Associated Entities**:

　　Test Plan BATCH MAINTENANCE TEST

　　Category MICROCOMPUTER INFORMATION

In the **Description** area add the names of any codes used in the rule columns, such as A for ADD, D for DELETE, and C for CHANGE.

12

ANALYZING SEMISTRUCTURED DECISION SUPPORT SYSTEMS

METHODS AVAILABLE

Three major concerns arise when analyzing semistructured decision support systems. The systems analyst needs to know (1) whether decision makers are primarily analytic or heuristic; (2) how decisions are made in the three problem-solving phases of intelligence, design, and choice; and (3) the multiple-criteria methods useful in solving semistructured problems.

Decision support systems (DSS) can function in many ways. They can organize information for decision situations; interact with decision makers; expand the decision makers' horizons; present information for decision makers' understanding; add structure to decisions; and use multiple-criteria decision-making models. Multiple-criteria models include tradeoff processes, weighting methods, and sequential elimination methods, which are all well suited to handling the complexity and semistructured nature of many problems supported through DSS. This chapter covers what the systems analyst needs to know about analytic and heuristic decision makers, the three phases of problem solving supported by DSS, and multiple-criteria methods necessary to solve semistructured problems.

DECISION SUPPORT SYSTEMS

Decision support systems possess many characteristics that differentiate them from other, more traditional management information systems. End users of DSS, by virtue of the types of problems they address and the learning they undergo, also possess special characteristics that need to be considered.

381

Characteristics of a Decision Support System

First and foremost, a decision support system is a way to organize information intended for use in decision making. It involves the use of a database for a specific decision-making purpose. A DSS does not just automate transformations performed on data nor simply provide output in the form of reports. Rather, a decision support system supports the decision-making process through presentation of information designed for the decision maker's problem-solving approach and application needs. It neither displaces judgment nor makes a decision for the user.

A DSS allows the decision maker to interact with it in a natural manner via careful design of the user interface. A useful DSS will challenge and eventually change a decision maker. By contrast, an MIS provides output but no real impetus for change in the person receiving it. Interacting with a DSS will prove new and challenging for most decision makers and will provide new perspectives on the decision-making process that are attractive and understandable, yet innovative. By furnishing a new way to see problems and opportunities, a DSS eventually changes the user's decision-making process and, along with it, the user.

Decision support systems are designed to help support decisions involving complex problems that are formulated as semistructured. Because such problems remain resistant to complete computerization, a solution *per se* is not the goal of the DSS; instead a DSS supports the decision process that leads to a solution.

A DSS may be constructed to support one-time decisions, those that are infrequent, or those that occur routinely. The type of problem or opportunity best addressed through use of a DSS is one that ultimately requires human judgment—either because humans feel it is inappropriate to relinquish their judgment or because the problem cannot be fully automated—and that it is complex enough to benefit from the time savings to be gained through partial automation. Medical decisions involving differential diagnosis are a good example of such problems.

A decision support system is typically designed for either a particular decision maker or a group of decision makers. This high degree of individualization allows the system designer to customize important system features to adapt to the type of representations (graphs, tables, charts, and so on) and interface that the user understands best.

Rather than building a specific DSS "from scratch," a systems analyst can use a package of interrelated hardware and software called a DSS generator (DSSG). There has been considerable growth in the sales of DSS generators because they can lessen the time and cost associated with building a case-specific DSS. Hardware and software designated as "DSS tools" aid in the building of both specific DSS and DSS generators.

A decision support system is best conceptualized as a process instead of a product. Figure 12.1 contrasts the product orientation of traditional MIS with the process-oriented DSS. Notice that the focus of the DSS is on the decision maker's interaction with the system, and not on the output generated. As discussed in Chapter 2, processes are ways to transform inputs into outputs. In the instance of a DSS, the process works to transform the user—the decision maker—by changing and improving upon his or her decision-making performance.

What this process orientation means is that DSS are evolutionary in nature. Decision support systems change as the needs of the end-user change, and the decision maker changes through interacting with the DSS process.

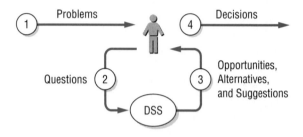

FIGURE 12.1
Decision support systems
have a process orientation
focusing on the decision
maker's interaction with the
system.

Decision Support System Users

Decision making in organizations occurs on three main levels: the strategic, the managerial, and the operational, as discussed in Chapter 2. Many of the decisions required on the operational level can be successfully and thoroughly automated. The same can be said for many routine managerial decisions. However, when problems and opportunities cannot be totally structured and human judgment and experience are required to make a decision, traditional management information systems are often considered inadequate for the task. It is in the solution of semistructured, complex problems that a DSS can be of use. This kind of problem most often occurs on the strategic and managerial levels.

Although use of a decision support system is not limited to middle- and upper-level managers or chief executive officers, these individuals are most often the primary users. They bring with them differing decision-making styles, differing needs, and differing levels of sophistication. The DSS designer therefore needs to take specific decision-making attributes into consideration so that it is possible for the user to interact successfully with the DSS. If the end user is too busy or too threatened by the prospect of interacting with the DSS, a technical go-between or assistant may be used to interact with the computer. In this way, the decision maker is free to analyze and react to the process, not to the mechanics of it.

Since DSS are designed specifically for a user or a group of users (as in group DSS, commonly abbreviated GDSS), systems analysts need to be acutely aware of how a decision maker's style might influence DSS design. In the following section, we discuss several concepts pertinent to decision support systems, including decision making under risk; decision-making style; and how decisions can be classified as structured, unstructured, and semistructured.

DECISION-MAKING CONCEPTS RELEVANT TO DSS

Many concepts help inform us about the relationship between decision making and decision support systems, including theories about certainty, uncertainty, and risk and how they help shape a decision maker's style as either analytic or heuristic. The three problem-solving phases of intelligence, choice, and design as they are supported by decision support systems are also of interest here.

Decision Making under Risk

Classical decision-making theory usually assumes that decisions are made under three sets of conditions: certainty, uncertainty, and risk. Certainty means that we know everything in advance of making our decision. A common management science model that assumes conditions of certainty is linear programming, where all the resources, rates of consumption, constraints, and profits are all assumed to be known and correct. Uncertainty implies just the opposite; we know nothing about the probabilities or the consequences of our decisions.

Between the two extremes of certainty and uncertainty lies the huge set of conditions called risk. Decisions made under risk assume that we are somewhat knowledgeable about our alternatives (controllable variables), what we cannot control but only estimate (environmental variables), and what the outcomes will be (dependent variables). Not only can we estimate the environmental variables, we can also estimate the probability that they will occur. This information can be 100 percent accurate, partially accurate, or false; but we still attempt to base the decision on the information we have. Most business decisions are made under risk.

AN EXAMPLE OF UNCERTAINTY, CERTAINTY, AND RISK. To help understand these three sets of conditions, suppose you had to decide whether to carry an umbrella into work one morning. There is only one circumstance that represents complete certainty; it is raining now. If you open the door, look outside, and it is raining, you know you must use an umbrella or you will get drenched. If the sun is out now, it still might rain in the afternoon.

Risk implies that we have an idea about the alternatives, probabilities, and outcomes. If we listen to the weather forecast on television and the forecaster says there is a 40 percent chance of rain, we can use that information to make our decision about whether to carry an umbrella.

To understand conditions of complete uncertainty, visualize being locked in a room without windows or visitors. Furthermore, your television cable company is having service problems, your radio's batteries are corroded, and your newspaper has been lost en route. In this situation, all of your sources of information about the outside weather would be gone.

But is this uncertainty? If all of your sources of information were taken away, wouldn't you still be able to make a decision under risk? Most everyone would be able to, because most people would realize where they were and what time of year it was. In other words, we know from experience what the probability of rain is in our location at this time of year. This example suggests that experience, as well as information, helps us to make decisions.

The relationship among certainty, uncertainty, and risk along with the resources of information and experience is shown in Figure 12.2. Some individuals rely more heavily on information, while others prefer to base

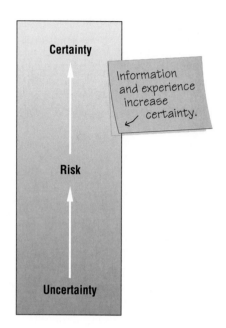

FIGURE 12.2
Decisions are made under
certainty, uncertainty, and
risk, which are determined by
availability of information
and experience.

their decisions on experience. The next section builds upon this relationship as it discusses decision-making style.

Decision-Making Style

The way in which information is gathered, processed, and used forms the parameters of decision-making style, together with the manner in which decisions are communicated and implemented. Decision makers are often characterized as being either analytic or heuristic.

ANALYTIC DECISION MAKING. An analytic decision maker relies on information that is systematically acquired and systematically evaluated to narrow alternatives and make a choice that is information based. As shown in Figure 12.3, analytic decision makers learn by analyzing a particular situation. They are methodical, using step-by-step procedures to make decisions. Analytic decision makers value quantitative information and the models that generate and use it.

Additionally, decision makers with an analytic style use mathematics to model problems and algorithms to solve them. An analytic decision maker seeks optimal, rather than completely satisfying solutions, being content with answers which satisfy most but not all requirements. Analytic decision makers use decision techniques such as graphing, probability models, and mathematical techniques to ensure a sound decision-making process. These methods, however, require that the information employed is: (1) available, (2) reasonable, (3) complete, and (4) accurate.

An example of an analytic decision maker is a manager who, when faced with a problem, employs a computerized management science model to resolve conflicts in an optimal way. To accomplish this, the manager determines an objective function and constraints, builds mathematical relationships, gathers information for the model, and solves the problem.

HEURISTIC DECISION MAKING. A decision maker who uses heuristics is making decisions with the aid of some guidelines (or rules of thumb),

Analytic Decision Maker	Heuristic Decision Maker
• Learns by analyzing	• Learns by acting
• Uses step-by-step procedure	• Uses trial and error
• Values quantitative information and models	• Values experience
• Builds mathematical models and algorithms	• Relies on common sense
• Seeks optimal solution	• Seeks satisficing solution

although they may not always be applied consistently or systematically. Heuristics are generally experience-based.

Heuristic decision makers learn by acting. They use trial and error to find a solution. Because of this they value experience, relying on common sense to guide them.

An example is a manager deciding heuristically from which company to purchase raw materials. Based on past experience, the manager knows that materials shipped from the East Coast tend to arrive at the plant on time. Formulating that experience as a heuristic, or rule of thumb, the manager decides to try and pick a supplier of raw materials from the East Coast.

The decision-making style of managers relates back to the openness and closedness of organizational systems. If information in the business is free-flowing, the opportunities for use of decision aids and systematic analysis may be greater. If timely information is difficult to acquire, the organization may be encouraging managers (albeit unwillingly) toward a more heuristic style.

IMPLICATIONS FOR DEVELOPMENT OF DECISION SUPPORT SYSTEMS. Analytic decision makers are systematic in their evaluation of alternatives in a decision situation. A DSS for an analytic decision maker should include several mathematical and graphical models that allow desired comparisons. It is also important to make supporting evidence for alternatives available through the DSS.

Heuristic decision makers are somewhat systematic in their approach to decision making, but they use rules of thumb for guidelines rather than carefully reasoning through each alternative each time it is presented. A decision support system supporting a heuristic thinker might present summary information on alternatives rather than detailing pros and cons in copious output. A DSS for heuristic decision makers might also display past decisions and their outcomes in support of the preference for experience-based data. Further discussions of DSS output are featured in Chapter 15, which deals with output design.

Problem-Solving Phases

Decision making (or problem solving) is a process and is conceived of in phases, rather than steps. In phases, the occurrence of behavior swells and tapers off, with some overlap between each phase. In stepped behavior, one step occurs independently of the next and is completed before the next step is carried out.

Walking into Open Arms

"I helped start Open Arms four years ago, after I earned my MBA," says Maria Ewing-Barton, the 36-year-old administrator of a health-care referral service. "When the County Medical Society realized that the health-care services here in Laramie weren't being fully utilized, a group of us thought about what we could do to fill the gap. We aim to match up patients with appropriate health-care providers. For various reasons (transiency, poverty, newly transferred to the city), patients have no regular contact with a health-care provider. I see anywhere from five to twenty patients a day. Some have chronic illnesses such as alcoholism; some have a common cold. I assess what level of treatment is relevant, what funding is possible, and decide what the next step for the patient will be. For example, should they see a private physician today or schedule an appointment with an eye doctor sometime in the future? I called you in to help me strengthen and justify the decision process I go through in making referrals, maybe through the creation of a DSS.

"I'd like to have a lot of information at my fingertips so that I can make decisions quickly. Although most cases are not life or death, some are serious. Also, I don't have much time to spend with each patient. I want to be sure I can justify my referral decisions, since some local doctors think I'm usurping their decision-making power. Most of the people in health care here trust my judgment, but the occasional physician is still skeptical of my qualifications. They resent the fact that my training is in management, not health care.

As an upshot, I have to be very methodical in defending my referral decisions to them.

"I keep statistics on the patients we've referred, and I read everything I can get my hands on in the medical and health-care administration journals, although they don't bear directly on what we do. I also talk to other administrators to keep current on the services their facilities are offering. What's frustrating is that the services available change so often. It seems as if local hospitals are only concerned with marketing their profitable specialties.

"I've been playing with the data I've accumulated, looking for patterns and trying to create some sort of model for the way Open Arms is working. As you can see, I have an old PC computer here in my office, and I've spent many evenings entering data to help formulate reasonable models of Open Arms. Although accurate records are important, I want to do more with the data than merely store it.

"Quite frankly, a large part of my decision on whether to refer is based on how I size up a person initially. I know it's important to be objective, but with so little time to make a decision, I usually go with my heart and not my head. Eventually, I would like to rely on the numbers I generate with my PC to match patients with health-care providers. Then I can justify my decisions when necessary. It's a way to make more effective matches, too, that are fairer to everyone."

What type of decision maker is Maria? Which of her characteristics lead to this viewpoint? Describe what you think is Maria's typical decision-making process regarding patient referrals.

The three phases of problem solving are intelligence, design, and choice (Simon, 1965). The decision maker begins with the intelligence phase, with design and choice following in phased succession. Let's examine each phase as it relates to decision-maker behavior.

INTELLIGENCE. Intelligence is awareness of a problem or opportunity. In this phase, the decision maker searches the external and internal business environments checking for decisions to make, problems to solve, or opportunities to examine. Intelligence means an active awareness of changes in environments that call for action.

Intelligence translates to vigilance: continual searching and scanning. The intelligence phase provides the impetus for the other two phases and always precedes them.

DESIGN. In the design phase, the decision maker formulates a problem and analyzes several alternative solutions. The design phase allows the decision maker to generate and analyze alternatives for their potential applicability.

Choice. The choice phase is characterized by the decision maker choosing a solution to the problem or opportunity identified in the intelligence phase. This choice follows from the foregoing analysis in the design phase and is reinforced by information gained in the choice phase. It also includes implementation of the decision maker's choice. Other authors have added separate phases for implementation and evaluation.

SEMISTRUCTURED DECISIONS

Many people conceive of decisions as existing on a continuum from structured to unstructured. Structured decisions are those where all or most of the variables are known and can be totally programmed. Decisions that are structured are routine and require little human judgment once the variables are programmed. Analysis of structured decisions is covered extensively in Chapter 11.

Unstructured decisions are those that are currently resistant to computerization and depend primarily on intuition. Semistructured decisions are those that are partially programmable, but still require human judgment. Decision support systems are most powerful when addressing semistructured decisions, since a DSS supports the decision maker in all phases of decision making but does not mandate one final answer.

It is hypothesized that all decisions may contain "deep structure"; that is, structure that is present but not yet apparent. If this is true, then eventually all decisions could be treated as semistructured, and the usefulness of a DSS would be substantially broader.

An argument used in support of the presence of deep structure is that the game of tic-tac-toe appears to be unstructured to a five-year-old child. While the child is learning to play the game, it isn't clear which move is the best, and the game itself seems suspenseful and exciting. As the child grows up, however, it soon becomes apparent that there is indeed a structure. If certain rules are applied, the outcome can be maximized by guaranteeing at least a tie.

However, tic-tac-toe is not like a business situation. First, the rules for tic-tac-toe are simple: Place an X in one of the spaces and wait until your opponent responds. Second, the objective is simple: Tie, or perhaps win, by placing three Xs in a row if your opponent makes an error. The only factor that makes the game unstructured is the decision skill of the decision maker. That is, the average child doesn't yet possess the analytical skills or experience needed to win the game.

Dimensions of Semistructured Decisions

Decisions are called semistructured or unstructured for a number of reasons. It is useful to visualize the dimensions of structured decisions as a cube, as illustrated in Figure 12.4. The three dimensions are:

1. The degree of decision-making skill required.
2. The degree of problem complexity.
3. The number of decision criteria considered.

In the tic-tac-toe example, the five-year-old child would not see the game as structured even though there was a single criterion and very simple rules, because the child's decision-making skill has not sufficiently developed.

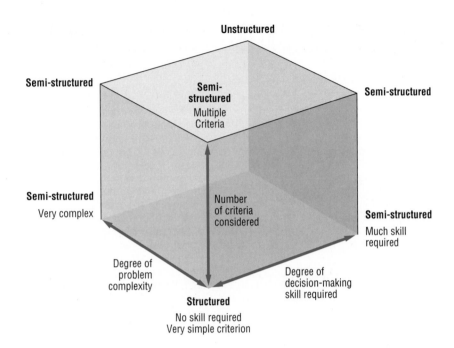

FIGURE 12.4
Visualizing structured decisions as a cube with three
dimensions: degree of decision-making skill required,
degree of problem complexity, and the number of decision criteria required.

DEGREE OF DECISION-MAKING SKILL REQUIRED. The degree of decision-making skill relates back to the concepts of analytic and heuristic decision makers. Decision-making skill is measured in the analytic and experience-based maturity of the decision maker. A DSS could help upgrade decision-making skill by providing easy-to-comprehend models (for the analytic thinker) or analogies (for the heuristic thinker).

THE DEGREE OF PROBLEM COMPLEXITY. If a problem is highly complex, it seems semistructured or even unstructured. A DSS can help in this regard by encouraging the decision maker to define the boundary of the system by clearly defining the problem and limiting the number of variables. In addition, the DSS should provide support in helping the decision maker systematically eliminate some alternatives. Decision support systems are needed to organize information, track variables, and present the problems, alternatives, and choices in a manner easily understandable to the manager.

NUMBER OF CRITERIA CONSIDERED. A manager concerned with a single decision criterion is dealing with a structured problem, but most real-world problems have multiple, conflicting goals and multiple decision criteria. Consequently, they are by nature semistructured. An example of a decision maker dealing with multiple conflicting objectives is a production manager deciding on a production schedule with objectives such as keeping costs to a minimum, maximizing customer satisfaction by meeting the delivery schedule, keeping quality high, and minimizing idle time. The production manager cannot optimize one of these objectives unless other objectives are sacrificed.

A decision involving multiple criteria is choosing a software package that is powerful, has clear documentation, and is user-friendly but inexpensive. Since it is unlikely that any single product fulfills all of the requirements,

The Proof Is in the Pizza

"I really enjoy my current position," says 53-year-old Hal Lupino. He is the district manager for the Calliope chain of seven Nebraska pizza palaces, which his father and uncle founded and still run. There are four stores in Lincoln (where the business started), two in Omaha, and one in Grand Island. They have expanded from small take-out places to sit-down restaurants that feature a giant, electronically controlled calliope that plays music while pizza eaters dine. However, the main attraction of the chain is still a secret family pizza recipe.

"Some people think I'm too old to be a district manager, but I have the best of both worlds in this job," Hal continues. "I've got a lot of decision-making power, with Dad and Uncle Reg getting up in years. But I still talk with lots of customers, too. The stores' profits have been increasing since 1964. We added the last store in Lincoln in 1984.

"Everyone, inside and out, has been sort of pressuring us to expand again. My son is an MBA student and he recommended you to help me set up a DSS to support location decisions.

"My thinking is that we should make the most of the delivery network we already have set up, since it's so darn expensive to move the ingredients we need. With the rotten luck the farmers are having and the fact that there are more sand dunes than people in western Nebraska, I think expansion there is out. My gut reaction is that competition is too fierce to get anything else going in Omaha.

"But I'll let managers and customers be my guide on where to locate next. I'm a people person. Why not ask someone a question rather than read a report about it? My father and uncle are different, though. Those guys love numbers. So if I don't give them some numbers to back up my decisions, I'll have a hard time getting them implemented. I've been humoring them by passing out questionnaires on new locations to our customers. Someday I'll have my secretary tally what they wrote. I've been reading their open-ended comments though; they're more interesting to me.

"I keep notes about what I hear from customers and managers on the bulk napkins we buy for the restaurants. They go in here (he indicates an in-basket piled with napkins) when I've read them. Otherwise, I keep 'em in my folder. I don't throw much away, but finding a key comment is a task.

"I guess I'm a slow-poke when it comes to making a decision. I go over and over what I've seen in the markets we serve and review all my experience in the business and all the talks with our customers. I keep going back to our last location decision when we opened the new store in Lincoln. If the proof is in the pudding, then Lincoln may just be the spot for the new one, too."

How can a decision support system make Hal a better decision maker? In particular what features of his style could it support? What features of his style might a decision support system change?

---

the decision maker must assign importance (rank or weight) to each criterion. Decision support systems are invaluable in helping decision makers handle multiple criteria. A more extensive discussion of multiple-objective and multiple-criteria models follows in a later section of this chapter.

Semistructured Decisions in Intelligence, Design, and Choice

No matter what the decision is, the decision has to go through each of the three phases (intelligence, design, and choice) in the decision-making process. Semistructured decisions are made in each of the phases of decision making. Sometimes the decision is easy and other times very cumbersome, but rarely do we encounter a problem in which every decision-making phase holds difficulty.

Figure 12.5 identifies some of the bottlenecks that occur in each of the three phases of the decision-making process. Bottlenecks in the intelligence phase occur because the decision maker is unable to identify a problem, define it, or set priorities for tackling the problem. During the design phase, bottlenecks can occur because the decision maker cannot generate feasible alternatives, assign values and/or outcomes to the alternatives, or

Intelligence	Unable to identify the problem
	Unable to define the problem
	Unable to prioritize the problem

Design	Unable to generate alternatives
	Unable to quantify or describe alternatives
	Unable to assign criteria, values, weights, and rankings

Choice	Unable to identify a choice method
	Unable to organize and present information
	Unable to select alternatives

establish performance criteria to compare alternatives. The choice phase can present bottlenecks, too, when the decision maker is unable to choose a decision method, organize and present information, or select an alternative. The following discussion focuses on how decision support systems can alleviate bottlenecks and thus assist the decision maker.

INTELLIGENCE PHASE DECISION SUPPORT SYSTEMS. Decision making is often difficult because the problem itself is difficult to identify. Problems are noticed only if appropriate performance measures are put in place to highlight them. Suppose a clothing store set a goal of selling $30,000 worth of merchandise in a week and always exceeded that goal; no problem would be identified. But what if more information revealed that, for the square footage leased, the store needs to make a minimum of $35,000 per week to stay in business? Without the additional information, the problem goes unnoticed. An effective DSS, therefore, must contain mechanisms for recognizing problems.

Once a problem is identified, it needs to be defined. A DSS could help the decision maker determine the scope of the problem to prevent being burdened with an overly complex decision. A store manager might choose to limit the problem to strategic pricing or strategic advertising. Other possible approaches such as firing employees or changing the merchandise mix would not be considered.

The final step in the intelligence phase is to assign a priority to the problem. The problem may be of an immediate nature, or it may be a future opportunity that could be pursued if other, more pressing, problems are addressed first. For example, an opportunity to expand may look very attractive initially, but may be delayed because of more pressing problems in the original store. Decision support systems are needed for problem and project selection.

DESIGN PHASE DECISION SUPPORT SYSTEMS. In a relationship that parallels the one just discussed, alternatives need to be identified. A decision support system can aid in generating alternatives that might not have occurred to the decision maker. Experience-based DSS can compare the current situation with similar scenarios and guide the manager through the maze of alternatives. Some alternative situations for the clothing manager to investigate include varying types and amounts of advertising or changing the prices of certain merchandise to attract more customers.

Next the alternatives need to be quantified or described. A decision maker could retrieve data from a database, collect new data, and manipulate data. A more heuristic decision maker might take an extra-organizational approach, build analogies, and seek opinions or consider various scenarios. The clothing store manager could gather quantitative information on, for example, costs and effectiveness of advertising, competitor's pricing, and price elasticity. The manager could also gather information from employees and customers. This information could be compiled and summarized for decision-making purposes.

Once alternatives are generated and organized, performance criteria need to be established. Then the decision maker can assign values, risks, weights, and/or a rank to each alternative. The clothing store manager may set weekly sales volume as one criterion, but may also want to include weekly costs, as well as intangibles such as customer satisfaction and employee morale. Spreadsheets are excellent ways to list various alternatives, and graphs provide vivid visuals to limit the number of alternatives being considered.

Decision support systems can represent possible choices to decision makers in ways that may not conform to their typical way of seeing the world. For example, if a problem solver is not accustomed to considering other alternatives, the DSS can suggest them. In essence, the DSS can expand the field of vision for the decision maker.

The interaction between DSS and the decision maker is strong in this phase. It is entirely feasible to build a DSS that will work through several "What-if?" scenarios with numerous variables, something that is too complex for lone decision makers to do. In this way, a DSS enhances the design phase by greatly expanding the number of possible actions that can be considered in detail, as well as suggesting new alternatives that the decision maker might otherwise overlook.

CHOICE PHASE DECISION SUPPORT SYSTEMS. Choosing a solution is obviously important, and in semistructured decisions the choice must be left up to the judgment of the decision maker with the support of the DSS. First, the DSS can be of help by reminding the decision maker what methods of choice are appropriate for the problem. This means the DSS can include suggestions for analytic techniques (which management science models to rely on) or heuristic techniques (how best to display information when making a choice). For example, our store manager may want to approach the problem on a simple cost-benefit basis, since the approaches being considered do not involve a great many intangibles (unlike the approaches to firing employees or changing store hours).

The decision support system can also help the decision maker organize and present the information. For one decision maker this might mean defining variables and formulating constraints that make up a management science model. For another manager, this may mean selecting the type of graph (line, bar, or pie chart), the scale, or range of data to consider. For our clothing store example, the manager might prefer to see the information displayed on a personal computer's spreadsheet.

The History of Scheduling

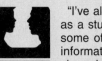

"I like my work here at the university," Stuart Dent admits. At age twenty-two, he is younger than many of the students and staff he deals with in his job of scheduling classes for the approximately 27,000 students who attend regular semester sessions. "I've been here two years, ever since I graduated in art history," Stu Dent continues.

"The person who had the job before me generated a whole stack of computer reports that showed each department's course schedule, availability of faculty, how often courses needed to be offered, what day they were offered on last, student preferences for course days, and availability of rooms. All that was a jumble, so I called you in to help. I know you teach a DSS course on campus.

"I want to schedule each required course at a time that is satisfactory to both faculty and students. I think the larger picture is important. Courses that occur in a cycle (for example, many graduate-level courses) should be offered when promised. I want to eliminate double-bind situations where a student is unable to take a course because its prerequisite hasn't ever been offered.

"I guess I'm pretty idealistic. I like thinking about historical trends and trying to characterize them. I asked my coworkers about the scheduling problem, but they keep sending me to the mountain of computer reports made by the guy who had my job before me. I'm so sick of their advice that I've 'joined the enemy' and decided to actually do something for the students. I've been interviewing a handful of students from each college on campus.

"I've also reviewed my own scheduling hassles as a student, in case they offer a key. Here are some of the charts I've sketched to summarize information from my experiences and the interviews, but as you can see, it's slow going.

"Although the old computer reports seem virtually useless, I've been careful to inventory them and maintain them. In fact, I labeled them and put them on a shelf here in my office. I know the value of history. The tapes I have of student interviews contain enough 'horror stories' about five-year undergrads being standard because of poor scheduling that they may be potentially damaging to the administration. I've duplicated them, and both sets of tapes are at home.

"I want to make my decisions quickly, since scheduling for each semester is done well in advance, and must be done twice a year. The students accept me and respect that I'm trying to do a good job. But Cyril, my boss, likes numbers, and I know he'll never go along with my suggestions for scheduling unless I back up my intuition with some quantitative data. The people I work with think I'm overwhelmed by the volume of data this department generates. They're doing what they always do and ignoring me until I sort everything out. But I'm confident in my ability to make good decisions."

In what ways can a decision support system help Stu? Describe how it can help in the intelligence, design, and choice phases of his decision making.

Finally, the decision support system needs to be able to handle multiple-criteria decision problems. The DSS would ideally carry out cumbersome manipulations but leave the decision up to the personal judgment of the decision maker. Since our store manager preferred information in the form of a spreadsheet, a tradeoff or weighting technique might be appropriate. Due to the increasing importance of making decisions based on multiple criteria, the subject is covered in more detail in the next section.

MULTIPLE-CRITERIA DECISION MAKING

Even in problems with complete information, a limited number of variables can be semistructured. These problems have numerous, often conflicting objectives, and are of much interest to the DSS designer. In modeling these decisions as realistically as possible, researchers have developed numerous approaches to evaluating multiple-objective or multiple-criteria problems.

Multiple-criteria approaches allow decision makers to set their own priorities, and most allow the decision maker to perform sensitivity analysis

	A	B	C	D
1	RENTAL		PURCHASE	
2				
3	NO CAPITAL IS TIED UP	1	TAX ADVANTAGES	1
4	NO FINANCING REQUIRED	1	OWN SYSTEM OUTRIGHT	1
5	EASY TO CHANGE SYSTEMS	1	FULL CONTROL	1
6	MAINTENANCE INCLUDED	1	SAVES 20,000 OVER 6 YEARS	1
7	KNOW RENTAL COMPANY WELL	1		
8	INSURANCE INCLUDED	1		
9				
10				
11				
12		6		4
13				
14				
15				
16				
17				
18				
19				
20				

by asking "what-if" types of questions. These methods include the tradeoff process, weighting methods, the conjunctive constraints approach, and goal programming. When included in DSS or MIS, multiple-criteria decision-making models allow the decision maker a more powerful way to evaluate alternatives in the design phase of decision making.

Using a Tradeoff Process

The tradeoff approach is often referred to as a favorite of the statesman Benjamin Franklin. When he had a difficult problem to solve he said that he drew a line to divide a sheet of paper into two columns. On one side, he wrote all of the reasons pro, and on the other all of the reasons con. Then he would begin to cross out any pros that were equal to any cons. Sometimes it would take two pros to equal a con, or vice versa.

The designer of decision support systems can use an updated version of this method in designing a decision support system. An example of this approach is depicted in Figure 12.6. Here we have two alternatives available to the decision maker, in this case a rent or buy decision. The advantages of each alternative are listed in columns *A* and *C* of the spreadsheet. In columns *B* and *D*, a number 1 is entered to indicate that the advantage is still a consideration.

As the decision maker analyzes the problem, any advantages in the *A* column are compared with advantages in column *C*. If the advantages are considered equal, the 1s are changed to 0s. Sometimes the decision maker may want to zero out a group of advantages, perhaps three on one side and two on the other. The process continues until either column *B* or *D* totals 0, as in Figure 12.7. The tradeoff approach has obvious limitations, but it still must not be overlooked as a decision aid for solving difficult problems.

FIGURE 12.7
Zeroing out advantages that
are equal to each other in
order to decide on an
alternative.

	A	B	C	D
1	RENTAL		PURCHASE	
2				
3	NO CAPITAL IS TIED UP	1	TAX ADVANTAGES	0
4	NO FINANCING REQUIRED	1	OWN SYSTEM OUTRIGHT	0
5	EASY TO CHANGE SYSTEMS	0	FULL CONTROL	0
6	MAINTENANCE INCLUDED	0	SAVES 20,000 OVER 6 YEARS	0
7	KNOW RENTAL COMPANY WELL	0		
8	INSURANCE INCLUDED	1		
9				
10				
11				
12		3		0
13				
14				
15				
16				
17				
18				
19				
20				

Using Weighting Methods

Students encounter a weighting method in every course they take when their grade is computed. Various components of the course are worth a certain percentage; for instance, 20 percent each for the first and second exams, 20 percent for the term paper, and 40 percent for the final examination. Numerical scores for each component are then multiplied by the percentages, and the final grade is calculated.

A spreadsheet example of a weighting approach is depicted in Figure 12.8. Here a purchase decision is needed regarding three database packages appropriate for a business. Each of the attributes is assigned a value by the decision maker. After examining the software packages, the decision maker assigns a grade to each attribute for each package; in this case, a grade of 1 to 10. The total score is then calculated in the last row of the spreadsheet, and the decision maker chooses the package with the highest total score. The decision maker has the opportunity to change some of the values for attributes, or even the scores assigned to each package in case "what-if" analysis is desired.

Using Sequential Elimination by Lexicography

Sometimes decision makers feel weighting methods disguise the best features of an alternative by taking a weighted average of all attributes. One method that features the importance of individual attributes is sequential elimination by lexicography. This method is less demanding than weighting because the attributes are simply ranked in order of importance rather than assigned weights. Intra-attribute values are still specified as in weighting.

An example of lexicography is found in Figure 12.9. A matrix of attributes and alternatives is entered into a spreadsheet. The spreadsheet is sorted, first by attribute from top (most important) to bottom (least important).

FIGURE 12.8
Using a weighting approach to grade software on a spread-sheet.

	A	B	C	D	E
1	%	ATTRIBUTES	DATAQUIX	BIGBASE	FLEXI FILE
2					
3	.20	FAST RESPONSE TIME	10	6	5
4	.05	MANY OUTPUT OPTIONS	6	4	7
5	.25	EASY TO USE	5	8	7
6	.20	EASY ERROR RECOVERY	10	7	6
7	.05	FLEXIBILITY	10	8	10
8	.10	GOOD DOCUMENTATION	8	9	10
9	.05	HOT LINE SUPPORT	8	10	5
10	.10	ABLE TO HANDLE BIG FILES	2	10	5
11					
12					
13					
14					
15		TOTALS	7.45	7.60	6.55
16					
17					
18					
19					
20					

Next, the alternatives are sorted row by row. Only those alternatives that have the highest possible score (in this case 10) for the first attribute are considered further. In other words, only 5, 7, 3, and 4 are potential answers. Then the second attribute is considered, and only 5 and 4 are considered further as shown in Figure 12.10.

FIGURE 12.9
Using sequential elimination by lexicography, which ranks the importance of individual attributes.

	A	B	C	D	E	F	G	H
1	ATTRIBUTE	RANK	CAR 5	CAR 7	CAR 3	CAR 4	CAR 2	CAR 1
2								
3	PRICE	1	10	10	10	10	5	4
4	MILEAGE	2	10	8	5	10	3	2
5	SAFETY	3	5	3	8	3	10	10
6	RESALE	4	7	9	10	5	5	10
7	COMFORT	5	10	3	2	10	2	3
8								
9								
10								
11								
12								
13								
14								
15								
16								
17								
18								
19								
20								

The data is sorted by rank (1 is most important).

FIGURE 12.10
Narrowing alternatives
through the use of sequential
elimination by lexicography.

	A	B	C	D	E	F	G	H
1	ATTRIBUTE	RANK	CAR 5	CAR 4	CAR 7	CAR 3	CAR 2	CAR 1
2								
3	PRICE	1	10	10	10	10	5	4
4	MILEAGE	2	10	10	8	5	3	2
5	SAFETY	3	5	3	3	8	10	10
6	RESALE	4	7	5	9	10	5	10
7	COMFORT	5	10	10	3	2	2	3
8								
9								
10								
11								
12								
13								
14								
15								
16								
17								
18								
19								
20								

Car 5 is chosen after the first three attributes are considered.

The final result is that alternative 5 is best because the score for the third attribute is higher for alternative 5 than for alternative 4. Once again, the decision maker can perform sensitivity analysis and rerun the sorting procedure to see if the answer changes.

Using Sequential Elimination by Conjunctive Constraints

Another sequential elimination technique is conjunctive constraints. As its name implies, the decision maker sets constraints, or standards, and then proceeds to eliminate all alternatives that do not satisfy the set of all constraints. If the constraints are set too tight, all of the alternatives are eliminated, but if they are not tight enough, many alternatives still remain. To use this method, the decision maker is required to employ an interactive approach.

Figure 12.11 shows a spreadsheet approach to sequential elimination by conjunctive constraints. In this example, the decision maker is trying to choose the most appropriate company vehicle. The attributes are listed in column *A*, the direction of constraints are placed in column *B*, and the value of the constraints in column *C*. Columns *D*, *F*, and *H* are used to contain any numerical values, and columns *E*, *G*, and *I* are used to show if the relationship is true or false. At the bottom of the spreadsheet, an "and" condition is set up so that all of the constraints must be met for the relationship at the bottom to be true.

At first, many alternatives may be feasible, so the decision maker then proceeds to change the values in column *C* until only one alternative remains. In the example shown in Figure 12.12, the decision maker changes the mileage from 18 to 20 miles per gallon, leaving car 3 as the only remaining alternative.

FIGURE 12.11
An example of a spreadsheet
approach to using sequential
elimination by conjunctive
constraints.

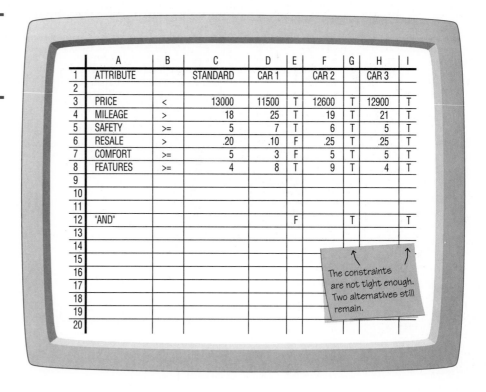

	A	B	C	D	E	F	G	H	I
1	ATTRIBUTE		STANDARD	CAR 1		CAR 2		CAR 3	
2									
3	PRICE	<	13000	11500	T	12600	T	12900	T
4	MILEAGE	>	18	25	T	19	T	21	T
5	SAFETY	>=	5	7	T	6	T	5	T
6	RESALE	>	.20	.10	F	.25	T	.25	T
7	COMFORT	>=	5	3	F	5	T	5	T
8	FEATURES	>=	4	8	T	9	T	4	T
9									
10									
11									
12	"AND"				F		T		T
13									
14									
15									
16									
17									
18									
19									
20									

The constraints are not tight enough. Two alternatives still remain.

The usefulness of this approach becomes apparent when you realize that a person often trades off attributes by interactively relaxing or tightening one or more constraints. This explains why people are willing to spend a little more money than they said initially, even though they rank price as the most important constraint.

FIGURE 12.12
Using sequential elimination
by conjunctive constraints
allows the decision maker to
trade off attributes by tightening one or more constraints.

	A	B	C	D	E	F	G	H	I
1	ATTRIBUTE		STANDARD	CAR 1		CAR 2		CAR 3	
2									
3	PRICE	<	13000	11500	T	12600	T	12900	T
4	MILEAGE	>	20	25	T	19	F	21	T
5	SAFETY	>=	5	7	T	6	T	5	T
6	RESALE	>	.20	.10	F	.25	T	.25	T
7	COMFORT	>=	5	3	F	5	T	5	T
8	FEATURES	>=	4	8	T	9	T	4	T
9									
10									
11									
12	"AND"				F		F		T
13									
14									
15									
16									
17									
18									
19									
20									

When the mileage is changed to 20 mpg, the number of alternatives is reduced to one.

Shelving Your Concerns

"I never know what to do. Sometimes one supplier's quality is good, but their cost is too high. Then I've got one who isn't that reliable, but when they can deal, their price makes it a steal. I'm just drawn to some suppliers like a magnet. It's rough to know how to decide. I mean, we literally go through tons of steel to make our shelves, and I've got to decide who to buy it from. We're the largest manufacturer of adjustable and nonadjustable shelving for retailers. Sometimes I think we could conquer the world with wall-to-wall shelves," says Abel Gance, director of purchasing for Gaul's Shelving.

"I've been trying to figure out a system for rating our steel suppliers, but most of my data just winds up sitting on a shelf because we're so busy with other stuff." Abel hands you the following breakdown of how he's been rating the suppliers (see the chart below).

What sort of approach would you recommend for Abel in determining which supplier to purchase steel from? Could you quantify the responses Mr. Gance gave you regarding the criteria? What type of multiple-criteria approach would you recommend? Why?

Supplier	Quality of Product	Cost of Items	Reliable Service	Merchandise Out-of-Stock	Return Policy
Bona Parts	Above average	Very high	Always reliable	Sometimes	Excellent
Waterloo	Average	Low	Seldom Reliable	Often	Satisfactory
Corsica Corp.	Above average	Average	Often reliable	Never	Poor
Josephine's Supplies	Below Average	Low	Often reliable	Never	Satisfactory
Wellington General Stores	Above average	Average	Always reliable	Sometimes	Excellent

PRIORITY 1 Do not exceed the total budget of $200,000
PRIORITY 2 Meet or exceed the contract of at least 40 TV spots
PRIORITY 3 Schedule at least 100 total (TV and radio) spots
PRIORITY 4 Keep the radio advertisements to 60 or less

Minimize $P_1 d_1^+ + P_2 d_2^- + P_3 d_3^- + P_4 d_4^+$

s.t. Budget $400 x_1 + 200 x_2 + d_1^- + d_1^+ = 20{,}000$
     TV Spots $x_1 + \qquad\quad d_2^- + d_2^+ = 40$
     Total Spots $x_1 + \qquad\quad d_3^- + d_3^+ = 100$
     Radio Spots $\qquad\quad x_2 + d_4^- + d_4^+ = 60$

Where x_1 is the number of television spots
x_1 is the number of radio spots

Priorities are taken in order, starting with P_1. The d^+ means that the number on the right-hand side will not be exceeded if the priority can be met. The d^- means that the number on the right-hand side will not be underachieved. Since there are multiple, conflicting goals, not all of the priorities will be met.

FIGURE 12.13
A goal-programming model for supporting the decision on allocating money for radio and television advertising.

Using Goal Programming

A discussion of multiple-criteria decision making is not complete without a discussion of goal programming, which has been widely applied to numerous problems in profit and nonprofit organizations. Goal programming, an example of which is featured in Figure 12.13, is similar in construct to linear programming, and therefore has the same assumptions and limitations.

A goal-programming model contains decision variables, deviational variables, priorities, and sometimes weights. Consequently, the decision maker must not only set goals for each of the goal equations in the problem, but also choose priorities for minimizing the deviational variables. Goal programming is a valuable technique when the information required is readily available and the decision maker is knowledgeable and confident about goals and priorities. In addition, the decision maker must be skilled at formulating goal equations—not a simple task.

SUMMARY

Decision support systems (DSS) are a special class of information systems that emphasize the process of decision making and changing DSS users through their interaction with the system. Decision support systems are well suited for addressing semistructured problems where human judgment is still desired or required. Decision support systems do not come up with one solution for users, rather they support the decision-making process by helping the user explore alternatives and consider their ramifications through different modeling techniques.

Users of DSS or group decision support systems (GDSS) come from all three management levels of the organization; however, semistructured decisions are most often required on the middle managerial and strategic levels. Users of a DSS are eventually changed through the process of interacting with the system.

The decision-making style of users can be categorized as either analytic or heuristic. Analytic decision makers tend to break down problems into quantitative components and use mathematical models to make a decision, while heuristic decision makers rely on experience. Decision support systems can be designed with the decision maker's predominant style in mind, so that analytical thinkers are supplied with quantitative models and heuristic decision makers are provided with summary information and memory aids that allow them to recall how they used heuristics in the past.

Semistructured decisions are those where human judgment is still required or considered desirable. Some decisions are considered to be semistructured because the decision maker doesn't possess the decision-making skills to make the decision. Also, if a problem is too complex it is classified as semistructured. Finally, a problem could be called semistructured if multiple criteria must be addressed. Decision support systems are especially well suited to help solve semistructured problems.

In all problem solving, decision makers go through three phases: intelligence, choice, and design. In the intelligence phase, the decision maker is scanning external and internal business environments for potential problems and opportunities. The design phase consists of articulating the problem or opportunity by discovering and creating alternatives, evaluating them, and examining their implications. The choice phase is comprised of choosing an alternative from among those that have been considered and

"So many decisions are made here. You'd be surprised at the types of things even the administrative assistants like me are asked to decide. And at the spur of the moment, not after long hours of analysis. And they are not trivial questions by any means. It seems as if the computers could help us decide most things, if we would just plan for it. But it's all of these *ad hoc* decisions we make that could use some support. I think Snowden would be all for it. I can certainly see the benefits."

HYPERCASE QUESTIONS

1. Where might a decision support system (DSS) fit in at MRE?
2. Who (which MRE employees) would be most likely to benefit from a DSS? Defend your choices.
3. Identify three semistructured decisions that are being made in the Management Systems and Training Unit. Choose one to support with a DSS. Explain your choice.

determining reasons and rationales for the adoption of that solution. Decision support systems should be designed to support decisions in all three phases of problem solving.

A complete decision support system should be able to support multiple-criteria decision making. The decision maker using this kind of DSS has a large repertoire of methods available, including a tradeoff process, weighting method, sequential elimination by lexicography, sequential elimination by conjunctive constraints, and goal programming.

KEYWORDS AND PHRASES

decision support system (DSS)
decision support system
  generators (DSSG)
group decision support system
 (GDSS)
decision making under certainty
decision making under
  uncertainty
decision making under risk
analytic decision making
heuristic decision making
intelligence phase
design phase

choice phase
semistructured decision
deep structure
decision-making skill
problem complexity
multiple criteria
tradeoff process
weighting methods
sequential elimination by
  lexicography
sequential elimination by
  conjunctive constraints
goal programming

REVIEW QUESTIONS

1. List the functions of decision support systems.
2. Define a decision support system and compare it to a management information system.

3. What is a DSS generator?

4. What type of problem or opportunity is best addressed through use of a decision support system?

5. Why is a decision support system best conceptualized as a process rather than a product?

6. How does a decision support system change its user?

7. Define the concept of decision making under risk.

8. Define the concept of decision making under certainty.

9. Define the concept of decision making under uncertainty.

10. Describe the characteristics of an analytic decision maker.

11. Describe the characteristics of a heuristic decision maker.

12. What are some features a decision support system for an analytic decision maker should include?

13. What are some features a decision support system for a heuristic decision maker should include?

14. Define what is meant by the intelligence phase of problem solving. How can a DSS support the intelligence phase?

15. Define what is meant by the design phase of problem solving. How can a DSS support the design phase?

16. Define what is meant by the choice phase of problem solving. How can a DSS support the choice phase?

17. What is meant by characterizing a decision as structured?

18. What is meant by characterizing a decision as semistructured?

19. Define the concept of deep structure in decisions.

20. What does decision-making skill mean? How can a DSS help in upgrading decision-making skill?

21. What does degree of problem complexity mean? How can a DSS decrease problem complexity?

22. List three multiple-criteria approaches to decision making.

23. Define what is meant by the term *weighting method* as it applies to decision making.

24. Define sequential elimination by lexicography.

25. Define sequential elimination by conjunctive constraints.

26. List the elements that compose a goal-programming model. Why is goal programming of limited use as a standard DSS tool?

PROBLEMS

1. While you are working on a large information systems project for a pharmaceutical company, Bob, a newly hired production supervisor, mentions to you that he heard about decision support systems in an MBA class. He would like to have you work on one for him as a sort of subsystem of the larger project. As a production supervisor, Bob reports to a production manager, but he makes routine decisions about production schedules, has input into purchase of ingredients, and manages line workers. He feels a DSS would be helpful in supporting these functions.

   a. In a paragraph, deny Bob's request for a decision support system. Provide reasons for not pursuing a DSS for supporting Bob's decision-making functions.

b. What changes in Bob's decision-making situation might make a DSS appropriate? Respond in a paragraph.

2. Mary Wren is owner of five Wren's Auto Supply Stores, a chain that sells all manner of auto parts to wholesale and retail customers. She currently uses a small computer rigged up by a friend who was interested in electronics to help her decide what to stock in each of the stores, which are located in five population centers. When her father was alive, he visited each store and based his orders on what managers said was selling well. Mary still visits stores, but she also inputs sales figures into a computer model that displays buying trends for each store. The model also has "what-if" capabilities so that Mary can experiment with different scenarios such as falling oil prices, increasing length of original car ownership, and increasing popularity of customizing kits. Mary does not rely solely on the computer to make her ordering decisions; she also uses her own observations about what is selling well to make ordering decisions for each store.

   a. Would you characterize the ordering decisions Mary must make for her five auto supply stores as semistructured? Why or why not? What are some of the variables involved? Respond in two paragraphs.

   b. What features of the information system Mary is using would support the assertion that it is more of a decision support system than a traditional management information system? List them.

   c. How is Mary's decision process improved upon by the DSS she is using? (Compare it to the way her father made decisions.) Respond in a paragraph.

3. After watching customer patterns for the first few weeks in her new business, Anita knows that most of her customers arrive in the early morning (before 9:30 A.M.) or in the late afternoon (between 3:30 P.M. and 5:00 P.M.). Based on this information, she has decided to close her fabric shop at 5:30 P.M.

   a. Is Anita making her decision under conditions of certainty, uncertainty, or risk? Explain in two sentences.

   b. Is her information most likely based on information or experience? Explain in two sentences.

4. "If this doesn't work, I can do something else. I just keep experimenting with different glazes for the figurines I sculpt. If they don't look pretty when they come out of the kiln, or if they blow up, or if no one buys them, I can try something else. Live and learn," says Emmy Potts, a sculptor who has a growing business selling custom-made ceramics.

   a. Would you characterize Emmy as an analytic or heuristic decision maker?

   b. Write a paragraph supporting your choice in 4a.

   c. Emmy wants a system to keep track of her reactions (and her customers' reactions) to different glazes and ceramics molds for the eventual purpose of ordering supplies and deciding what pieces to make (that is, what pieces will sell even thought they are not commissioned). What features would you incorporate into a decision support system for Emmy? List the features and write a sentence giving the reason for each.

5. Emmy's husband, Buddy, is retiring from his position as a district manager for a chain of hardware stores. For several years, he has been doing market research for the stores. He is systematic in the way he approaches problems and has long used mathematical formulas to project sales and so on. Although her business has been doing well in the last year and a half, Emmy is getting too bogged down in backlogged orders to use the decision support system you built for her. Buddy has agreed to take over the management aspects of her shop so that she can concentrate on artistic aspects.

   a. How would you characterize Buddy as a decision maker? Explain in a paragraph.

   b. What features could you include in a DSS to support Buddy's decision-making style? List them and write a sentence supporting each feature.

6. Louis, a systems analyst, has designed and implemented a decision support system for Scott Weidenfeed, owner of Grass That Grows, a huge suburban lawn care service. Part of the system is designed to flag any unusual problems that are reported by the numerous lawn crews. Some problems are of critical importance (detection of Dutch Elm disease, for example), since they will affect much of the community and must be addressed as soon as they are recognized. Resolving them will mean deciding on reassignment of crews from regular lawn care, extra expense to the company in terms of chemicals needed, and so on.

   a. Which of the three phases of problem solving is this part of the DSS supporting? Explain in a paragraph.

   b. Extend the lawn care example and describe in two paragraphs how the decision support system might support the two phases of problem solving that you did not list in part a. Make any assumption necessary about the company.

7. Howie Johnson is the president of the regional data-processing association. He is trying to choose a hotel to host the regional convention for the association.

   a. Make a list of eight to ten criteria for a good convention hotel.

   b. Choose a multiple-criteria decision method for selecting a hotel.

   c. In a paragraph, defend the method you chose.

8. Jo Pshop wants to determine how to sequence orders that are coming into her specialized invitation shop (invitations for weddings, parties, etc.). Business has been heavy lately, and sequencing of jobs is critical. Her choices are:

   1. First come, first served.

   2. Shortest processing time (the easiest jobs are done first).

   3. Due date (do them in the order promised).

   Since her decision is semistructured, you have suggested a tradeoff approach. List some criteria and explain how this technique would work.

9. Cary Farr has the job of deciding which of five shipping companies would be best to use for his business. This is the information he has gathered on the shipping companies' attributes:

	Cost	Damage	Percentage on Time	Complaints	Courteous
All American	2	4	5	3	1
United Truckers	4	3	2	3	4
Rapido Lines	1	1	3	4	3
Carefree Shippers	3	4	5	5	5
We-Do-It-All	4	3	4	3	3

The numbers are estimates based on the following scale:

1	2	3	4	5
much worse than average		average		much better than average

Cary gives the order of importance for each criterion as follows:

> Least cost (most important)
> Least damage
> Largest percentage on time
> Least complaints
> Most courteous (least important)

Help Cary by choosing a shipping company. Solve this problem using sequential elimination by lexicography.

10. Solve problem 9 using sequential elimination by lexicography, given the following order of importance:

> Least damage (most important)
> Largest percentage on time
> Least complaints
> Least cost
> Most courteous (least important)

11. Assume that in problem 9 weights were assigned for each of the criteria as follows:

Cost	.4
Damage	.2
Percentage on Time	.2
Complaints	.1
Courteous	.1
	1.0

Solve using the weighting method.

12. Solve problem 9 using sequential elimination by conjunctive constraints given the following constraints (remember, 3 = average, 5 = much above average).

Cost	Must be average or better
Damage	Must be average or better
Percentage on time	Does not matter
Complaints	Must be better than average
Courteous	Must be average or better

SELECTED BIBLIOGRAPHY

Alter, S. *Decision Support Systems: Current Practices and Continuing Challenges*. Reading, MA: Addison-Wesley, 1980.

Bennett, J. L. (ed.). *Building Decision Support Systems*. Reading, MA: Addison-Wesley, 1982.

Davis, G. B., and M. H. Olson. *Management Information Systems, Conceptual Foundations, Structure, and Development*, 2nd ed. New York: McGraw-Hill Book Company, 1985.

Keen, P. W., and M. S. Scott Morton. *Decision Support Systems. An Organizational Perspective*. Reading, MA: Addison-Wesley, 1978.

Kendall, K. E., and B. A. Schuldt. "Decentralizing Decision Support Systems: A Field Experiment with Drug and Criminal Investigators." *Decision Support Systems*, vol. 9, 1993, pp. 259–268.

Kendall, K. E., and B. A. Schuldt. "Case Progression Decision Support System Improves Drug and Criminal Investigator Effectiveness." *Omega*, vol. 21, no. 3, 1993, pp. 319–328.

Simon, H. *The Shape of Automation for Men and Management*. New York: Harper & Row, 1965.

Sprague, R. H., Jr., and E. D. Carlson. *Building Effective Decision Support Systems*. Englewood Cliffs, NJ: Prentice-Hall, Inc., 1982.

Sprague, R. H., Jr., and B. C. McNurlin. *Information Systems Management in Practice*. Englewood Cliffs, NJ: Prentice-Hall, Inc., 1986.

Turban, E. *Decision Support and Expert Systems: Management Support Systems*. New York: Macmillan Publishing Company, 1993.

Watson, H., and R. Sprague, (eds.). *Decision Support Systems: Putting Theory into Practice*, 3rd ed. Englewood Cliffs, NJ: Prentice-Hall, Inc., 1993.

AWAITING A WEIGHTY DECISION

"Now that the data flow diagrams, data dictionary, and process logic have been clearly defined, we should spend some time looking at the physical design alternatives for the new microcomputer system," says Chip. "We need to look at which of the several different designs is the best for Dot, Mike, Cher, Paige, and Hy."

"Yes," Anna replies, "and since this is not a problem of economics, we have no cost-benefit figures that would make the choice of the new system obvious. I suggest that we use a weighted method for determining which solution will be the best for the user group."

"That's an excellent idea!" exclaims Chip. "We already have a problem definition with weights assigned by the users. We should list the objectives for each problem and then analyze each alternative, determining the quality of the solution for the users."

Chip and Anna created three alternative solutions:

1. A mainframe batch solution, utilizing the data entry department for entering all system input. Updates are periodically performed. This alternative has a lower development cost and takes advantage of the rapid keying ability of the data-entry operators.

2. An on-line mainframe solution, with terminals installed in the user areas. This alternative has increased reliability since keyed data would immediately update master files. Inquiries would reflect changes made seconds ago.

3. A microcomputer solution using a local area network to provide access to a centralized database. This provides a high degree of reliability and quick response time. Each user could use the microcomputer for other tasks.

The microcomputer system has ten criteria that must be addressed. These objectives are summarized in Figure E12.1.

"Of the ten system objectives, the highest priority is to provide software and hardware cross-reference information," asserts Chip. "Let's start with this issue and examine how each of the solutions would satisfy it."

"The batch solution would print a report listing each machine and the software installed on it," says Anna. "The on-line system could also provide a similar report or have an inquiry screen to display the information. The microcomputer solution could also have reports or inquiries."

"Why don't we each determine a performance weight, using a scale from one to ten, on how the three solutions compare. Then we can average them together," Chip suggests.

Anna agrees, and the resulting performance weights for the first criterion are:

1. Batch solution scores a 7, a lower score than the others since it lacks the reliability of the up-to-date inquiry information that the on-line and microcomputer solutions provided. Any recent changes would be

Allen Schmidt,
Julie E. Kendall, and
Kenneth E. Kendall

407

Objectives	Weight
Provide software/hardware cross-reference.	10
Maintain complete microcomputer information.	9
Automate software installation procedure.	8
Provide software upgrade installation machine information.	7
Provide preventive and other maintenance information.	7
Maintain up-to-date accurate software information.	6
Provide complete cost information for microcomputer inventory.	5
Provide information on the cost to upgrade software.	5
Design a process for performing accurate and efficient physical microcomputer inventory.	3
Maintain and provide training and software expert information.	2

FIGURE E12.1
Microcomputer system objectives.

reflected on the screens, but not on the report, which would be printed only after a batch of updates was processed.

2. On-line solution scores a 10.
3. Microcomputer solution scores a 10.

Anna and Chip continue to analyze the quality of each of the three alternatives for the remaining issues. The results are shown in Figure E12.2, which depicts each of the ten system objectives and the weight or importance assigned to the objectives by the users.

Each solution has a brief narrative explaining how the solution will achieve the objective and a performance weight indicating the quality of the solution. The weight for each objective is then multiplied by the performance to determine a score for each solution fragment. The resulting scores are finally summed to provide an overall measure for the solution.

Exercises

E-1. Calculate the total score for solution 2, the mainframe on-line solution.

E-2. Calculate the final score for solution 3, the microcomputer local area network.

E-3. Which solution should be designed and implemented to solve the users' problems? Describe the system in a paragraph. If some of the performances were incorrectly estimated by a small amount, would a different solution be chosen? Explain your reasoning in a paragraph.

		MICROCOMPUTER SYSTEM PROPOSAL: System Alternatives						
		SOLUTION 1		SOLUTION 2		SOLUTION 3	
Objectives	Weight	Mainframe Batch	Performance	Mainframe On line	Performance	Microcomputer LAN	Performance
Provide software/hardware cross-reference.	10	Print cross-reference report after batch update.	7	Software location inquiry screen. Provide a cross reference report when requested.	10	Software location inquiry screen. Provide a cross-reference report when requested.	10
Maintain complete microcomputer information.	9	Send forms to data entry, key and verify. Batch update of indexed files.	5	Screens to add, delete, and change microcomputer information. Immediate update.	9	Screens to add, delete, and change microcomputer information. Screens to change maintenance data.	10
Automate software installation procedure.	8	Produce a list of all machines that must contain the upgraded software. Update files using data entry.	5	Use inquiry screens to determine which machines should contain the software. Automatically update master files.	9	Inquiry screens to determine installation machines. Update files automatically with overrides for exceptions.	10
Provide complete cost information for microcomputer hardware.	5	Produce reports providing cost detail and summary information.	7	Provide detail and summary cost reports. Include cost information on inquiry screens.	9	Provide detail and summary cost reports. Include cost and summary information on inquiry screens.	10
Provide information on the cost to upgrade software.	5	Produce report to show upgrade cost for all software.	4	On-line selection of package to be upgraded. Cost figures calculated based on number of upgrades.	10	On-line selection of package to be upgraded. Cost figures calculated based on number of upgrades. User may calculate individual departmental costs.	10
Design a process for performing accurate and efficient physical microcomputer inventory.	3	Inventory forms printed. Physical inventory completed and report used for data entry.	7	Physical inventory listing printed and used as a turn-around document. On-line update of changes.	9	Physical inventory listing printed. On-site entry of changes using local microcomputer.	10
Maintain and provide training and software expert information.	2	Batch add of software expert and training information.	5	On-line update of software expert and training courses. Inquiry screens to locate experts. Training listing printed.	9	On-line update of software expert and training courses. Inquiry screens provide expert information. Training listings printed.	10
Provide software upgrade installation machine information.	7	List all machines containing the software to be upgraded. Send changes to data entry.	6	Print report of all machines containing software. Note any installation exceptions and use screens to modify upgrade records.	8	A single screen to automatically upgrade all records. Use a micro in the installation room to immediately update any upgrade exceptions.	10
Provide preventive and other maintenance information.	7	Reports showing which machines require preventive maintenance. Update records via data entry.	7	Reports sorted by location for all machines requiring preventive maintenance. On-line update reflecting work completed.	8	Reports sorted by location for all machines requiring preventive maintenance. On-site creation of records using local microcomputer.	10
Maintain up-to-date accurate software information.	6	Weekly batch update of all additions, changes, and deletes.	4	On-line add, delete, and change programs. Automatic deletion of old versions when software is upgraded.	10	Screens for additions, deletions, and changes.	9

FIGURE E12.2

Three microcomputer system alternatives. Weight is the user-assigned weight, indicating importance of the objective. Performance is the performance weight, indicating the quality of the solution.

13

PREPARING THE SYSTEMS PROPOSAL

METHODS AVAILABLE

The systems proposal is a distillation of all that the systems analyst has learned about the business and what is needed to improve its performance. In order to address information requirements adequately, the systems analyst must use systematic methods for acquiring hardware and software, identify and forecast future costs and benefits, and perform cost-benefit analysis. All of these methods are used in preparing systems proposal material.

Information needs of users drive the selection of computer hardware, data storage media, and any prepackaged software. The hardware and software system that is eventually proposed is the analyst's response to users' information needs. This chapter provides the methods necessary to project future needs systematically and then weigh current hardware and software alternatives. Forecasting, guidelines for hardware and software acquisition, and cost-benefit analysis are also considered.

ASCERTAINING HARDWARE AND SOFTWARE NEEDS

In this section, we cover the process of estimating the present and future workloads of a business and the process involved in evaluating the ability of computer hardware and software to handle workloads adequately. Figure 13.1 shows the steps the systems analyst takes in ascertaining hardware and software needs. First, all current computer hardware must be inventoried to discover what is on hand and what is usable. Then current and future system workloads must be estimated. Following this, an evaluation of available hardware and software is undertaken.

The systems analyst needs to work along with users to determine what hardware will be necessary. Hardware determinations can come only in conjunction with determining information requirements. Knowledge of the organizational structure (as discussed in Chapter 2) can also be helpful in

FIGURE 13.1
Steps in choosing hardware
and software.

**Steps in Acquiring Computer
Hardware and Software**

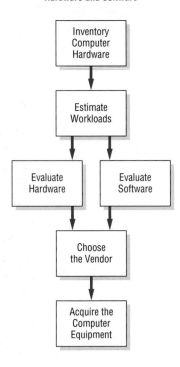

hardware decisions. Only when systems analysts, users, and management have a good grasp of what kinds of tasks must be accomplished, can hardware options be considered.

Inventorying Computer Hardware

Begin by inventorying what computer hardware is already available in the organization. As will become apparent, some of the hardware options involve expanding or recycling current hardware, so it is important to know what is on hand.

If an updated computer hardware inventory is unavailable, the systems analyst needs to set up one quickly and carry through on it. You need to know:

1. Type of equipment—model number, manufacturer.
2. Status of equipment operation—on order, operating, in storage, in need of repair.
3. Estimated age of equipment.
4. Projected life of equipment.
5. Physical location of equipment.
6. Department or person considered responsible for equipment.
7. Financial arrangement for equipment—owned, leased, or rented.

Figure 13.2 provides an example of a hardware inventory form that can be given to the relevant people. It should be easy to fill out, and should explicitly request that peripherals such as disk drives and VDTs be enumerated separately.

	First Computer	Second Computer	Third Computer

1. Equipment
  a. CPU/type/
    manufacturer/model
  b. Storage/type/
    manufacturer/model
  c. Input/type/
    manufacturer/model
  d. Output/type/
    manufacturer/model
  e. Communications/type/
    manufacturer/model			

2. Status
   On order
   Fully operational
   In need of repair
   In storage			

3. Estimated Age of Equipment			
4. Projected Life			
5. Located			

6. Name of individual
   responsible for equipment
     Purchase
     Operation
     Maintenance			

7. Financial Agreement
     Owned
     Rented
     Leased			

FIGURE 13.2
Using a form for taking inventory of equipment currently available in the organization.

Ascertaining the current hardware available will aid in a sounder decision-making process when hardware decisions are finally made, since much of the guesswork about what exists will be eliminated. Through your earlier interviewing, questionnaires, and research of archival data, you will already know the number of people available for data processing as well as their skills and capabilities. Use this information to project how well the staffing needs for new hardware can be met.

Estimating Workloads

The next step in ascertaining hardware needs is to estimate workloads. This means that systems analysts formulate numbers that represent both current and projected workloads for the system, so that any hardware obtained will possess the capability to handle current and future workloads.

FIGURE 13.3
Comparisons of workloads
between existing and
proposed systems.

	Existing System	Proposed System
Task	Monthly summary of shipments to distribution warehouses	Same
Method	Manual	Computer
Personnel	Distribution Manager	Computer Operator
Cost/Hour	$20.00	$10.00
When and How	Daily: files shipping receipts for each warehouse Monthly: summarizes daily records using calculator and prepares report	Daily: runs program that totals shipments and writes to disk Monthly: runs program that summarizes and prints reports
Human Time Requirements	Daily: 20 minutes Monthly: 8 hours	Daily: 4 minutes Monthly: 20 minutes
Computer Time Requirements	None	Daily: 4 minutes Monthly: 20 minutes

If estimates are accomplished properly, the business should not have to replace hardware solely due to unforeseen growth in system use. (However, other events, such as superior technological innovations, may dictate hardware replacement if the business wants to maintain its competitive edge.)

Out of necessity, workloads are sampled rather than actually put through several computer systems. The guidelines given on sampling in Chapter 4 can be of use here, since in workload sampling the systems analyst is taking a sample of necessary tasks and computer resources required to complete them.

Figure 13.3 is a comparison of the times required by an existing and a proposed information system to handle a given workload. Notice that the company is currently using a manual system to make a monthly summary of shipments to their distribution warehouses, and a computer system is being suggested. The workload comparison looks at cost per hour of each system, when and how each process is done, how much human time is required, and how much computer time is needed.

Evaluating computer hardware is the shared responsibility of management, users, and systems analysts. Although vendors will be supplying details about their particular offerings, analysts need to oversee the evaluation process personally since they will have the best interests of the business at heart. Additionally, systems analysts may have to educate users and management about general advantages and disadvantages of hardware before they can capably evaluate it.

Based on current inventory of computer equipment and adequate estimates of current and forecast workload, the next step in the process is to consider kinds of equipment available that appear to meet projected needs. Information from vendors on possible systems and system configurations become more pertinent at this stage and should be reviewed with management and users.

Additionally, workloads can be simulated and run on different systems, including those already used in the organization. This process is referred to as benchmarking.

Criteria that the systems analysts and users should use to evaluate performance of different systems hardware include time required for average transactions (including how long it takes to input data and how long it takes to receive output); total volume capacity of the system (how much can be processed at the same time before a problem arises); idle time of the central processing unit; and size of memory provided.

Some criteria will be shown in formal demonstrations; some cannot be simulated and must be gleaned from manufacturers' specifications. It is important to be clear about required and desired functions before getting too wrapped up in vendors' claims during demonstrations.

Once functional requirements are known and the current products available are comprehended and compared with what already exists in the organization, decisions are made by the systems analysts in conjunction with users and management about whether obtaining new hardware is necessary. Options can be thought of as existing on a continuum from using only equipment already available in the business all the way to obtaining entirely new equipment. In between are options to make minor or major modifications to the existing computer system.

COMPUTER SIZE AND USE. The rapid advance of technology dictates that the systems analyst research types of computers available at the particular time that the systems proposal is being written. Computer sizes range all the way from the smallest notebook-sized microcomputers to room-sized supercomputers. Each has different attributes to consider when deciding how to implement a computer system.

Acquisition of Computer Equipment

The three main options for acquisition of computer hardware include buying, leasing, or renting it. There are advantages and disadvantages to weigh for each of the decisions, as shown in Figure 13.4. Some of the more influential factors to consider in deciding which option is best for a particular installation include initial versus long-term costs; whether the business can afford to tie up capital in computer equipment; and whether the business desires full control of and responsibility for the computer equipment.

Buying implies that the business itself will own the equipment. One of the main determinants of whether to buy is the projected life of the system. If the system will be used longer than four to five years (with all other factors held constant), the decision is usually made to buy. Notice in the example in Figure 13.5 that the cost of purchase after six years is dramatically lower than that of leasing or renting. As systems become smaller and distributed

FIGURE 13.4
Comparing the advantages and disadvantages of buying, leasing, and renting computer equipment.

	Advantages	Disadvantages
Buying	• Cheaper than leasing or renting over the long run • Ability to change system • Provides tax advantages of accelerated depreciation • Full control	• Initial cost is high • Risk of obsolescence • Risk of being stuck if choice was wrong • Full responsibility
Leasing	• No capital is tied up • No financing is required • Leases are lower than rental payments	• Company doesn't own the system when lease expires • Usually a heavy penalty for terminating the lease • Leases are more expensive than buying
Renting	• No capital is tied up • No financing is required • Easy to change systems • Maintenance and insurance are usually included	• Company doesn't own the computer • Cost is very high because vendor assumes the risk (most expensive option)

systems become increasingly popular, more businesses are deciding to purchase equipment.

Leasing, rather than buying, computer hardware is another possibility. Leasing equipment from the vendor or a third-party leasing company is more practical when the projected life of the system is less than four years. Additionally, if significant change in technology is imminent, leasing is a better choice. Leasing also allows the business to put its money elsewhere, where it can be working for the company, rather than being tied up in capital equipment. Over a long period, however, leasing is not an economical way to acquire computer power.

Rental of computer hardware is the third main option for computer acquisition. One of the main advantages of renting is that none of the company's capital is tied up. Hence, no financing is required. Also, renting computer hardware makes it easier to change system hardware. Finally,

FIGURE 13.5
Comparison of alternatives for computer acquisition.

Rental	
Monthly rental	$170
x 36 months	
Total cost over 3 years	$6,120

Lease	
Monthly lease	$150
x 36 months	
Subtotal	5,400
Initial payment	500
Total cost over 3 years	$5,900

Purchase	
Purchase price	$6,000
Scrap value	− 500
Total cost over 3 years	$5,500

416

FIGURE 13.6
Guidelines for vendor
selection.

Vendor Selection Criteria

- Hardware Support
  Full line of hardware
  Quality products
  Warranty
- Software Support
  Complete software needs
  Custom programming
  Warranty
- Installation and Training
  Commitment to schedule
  In-house training
  Technical assistance
- Maintenance
  Routine maintenance procedures
  Specified response time in emergencies
  Equipment loan while repair is being done

maintenance and insurance are usually included in rental agreements. However, because of the high costs involved and the fact that the company will not own the rented equipment, rental should be contemplated only as a short-term move to handle nonrecurring or limited computer needs or technologically volatile times.

EVALUATION OF VENDOR SUPPORT FOR COMPUTER HARDWARE. There are several key areas to evaluate when weighing the support services available to businesses from vendors. Most vendors offer testing of hardware upon delivery and a 90-day warranty covering any factory defects, but you must ascertain what else the vendor has to offer. Vendors with comparable quality frequently distinguish themselves from others by the range of support services they offer.

A list of key criteria to check when evaluating vendor support is provided in Figure 13.6. Most of the extra vendor support services listed there are negotiated separately from hardware lease or purchase contracts.

Support services include routine and preventive maintenance of hardware; specified response time (within six hours, next working day, etc.) in case of emergency equipment breakdowns; loan of equipment in the event that hardware must be permanently replaced or off-site repair is required; and in-house training, or off-site group seminars for users. Remember that it may be more difficult to obtain training for unique hardware that is not widely used by other organizations. While the possibility of a customized installation may be attractive, the prospects for its long-term support may be diminished. Peruse the support services accompanying the purchase or lease of equipment and remember to involve appropriate legal staff before signing contracts for equipment or services.

Unfortunately, evaluating computer hardware is not as straightforward as simply comparing costs and choosing the least expensive option. Some other eventualities commonly brought up by users and management include (1) the possibility of adding on to the system if the need comes up later; (2) the possibility of interfacing with equipment from other vendors if the system needs to grow; (3) the benefits of buying more memory than is

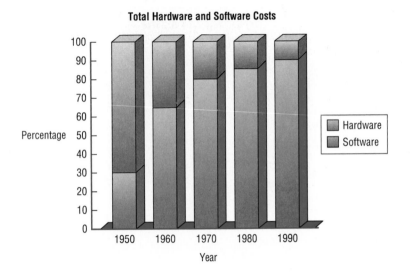

Total Hardware and Software Costs

projected as necessary, with the expectation that business will eventually "grow into it"; and (4) corporate stability of the vendor.

Adding on to the existing system is often the spur for systems projects. Installing a system with add-on capability is a worthwhile way to proceed. Although it takes a little extra planning, it is cheaper and more flexible than the third approach obtaining excess memory and carrying it in inventory for a number of years.

Competition among vendors has made the idea of producing hardware that is compatible with a competitor's important for vendors' survival. However, before becoming convinced that buying cheaper compatibles is the way to endow your system with add-on capability, do enough research to feel confident that the original vendor is a stable corporate entity.

Software Evaluation

Packaged software, rather than application programs specifically written for an installation, are becoming more readily available and certainly should be given careful consideration. Many hours of valuable programmer time can be saved if packaged software is deemed suitable for part or all of the system and extensive customizing isn't necessary. The bar chart in Figure 13.7 shows the cost of software (projected as ever-increasing) as part of total hardware and software costs.

Once again, you will be dealing with vendors who may have their own best interests at heart. You must be willing to evaluate software along with users and not be unduly influenced by vendors' sales pitches. Specifically, there are six main categories on which to grade software, as shown in Figure 13.8: performance effectiveness, efficiency, ease of use, flexibility, quality of documentation, and manufacturer support.

Evaluate packaged software based on a demonstration with test data from the business considering it and an examination of accompanying documentation. Vendors' descriptions alone will not suffice. Vendors typically certify that software is working when it leaves their supply house, but they will not guarantee that it will be error-free in every instance or will not "crash" when incorrect actions are taken by users. Obviously, they will not guarantee their packaged software if used in conjunction with faulty hardware.

FIGURE 13.8
Guidelines for evaluating
software.

Software Evaluation

- Performance Effectiveness
  - Able to perform all required tasks
  - Able to perform all tasks that may be desired at some time in the future
  - Well-designed VDT screens
  - Adequate capacity
- Performance Efficiency
  - Fast response time
  - Efficient input
  - Efficient output
  - Efficient storage of data
  - Efficient back-up
- Ease of Use
  - Satisfactory user interface
  - Help menus available
  - Flexible interface
  - Adequate feedback
  - Good error recovery
- Flexibility
  - Options for input
  - Options for output
  - Usable with other software
- Quality of Documentation
  - Good organization
  - Adequate tutorial
  - Answers questions adequately
- Manufacturer Support
  - Hot line
  - Newsletter
  - Frequent (low-cost) updates

The need for multiple copies or network versions of software (for use at several microcomputer workstations, for instance) means negotiating a multiple-use agreement with the vendor so that copyrights are not infringed through the creation of illegal copies. This often means purchase of one software package at its regular price and purchase of any additional copies at a reduced price.

It is also possible to negotiate a special vendor services contract covering support for purchased software. This might include extended technical assistance, emergency and preventive maintenance, free or reduced-price updates, additional copies of documentation, and special user training.

IDENTIFYING AND FORECASTING COSTS AND BENEFITS

Costs and benefits of the proposed computer system must always be considered together, since they are interrelated and often interdependent. Although the systems analyst is trying to propose a system that fulfills various information requirements, decisions to continue with the proposed system will be based on a costs and benefits analysis, not on information requirements. In many ways, benefits are measured by costs, as will become apparent in the next section.

Veni, Vidi, Vendi or I Came, I Saw, I Sold

"It's really some choice. I mean, no single package seems to have everything we want. Some of them come darn close, though," says Roman, an advertising executive for *Empire Magazine*, with whom you have been working on a systems project. Recently, the two of you have decided that packaged software would probably suit the advertising department's needs and stem its general decline.

"The last guy's demo we saw, you know, the one who worked for Data Coliseum, really had a well-rounded pitch. And I like their brochure. Full-color printing, on card stock. Classic," Roman asserts.

"And what about those people from Vesta Systems? They're really fired up. And their package was easy to use with a minimum of ceremony. Besides, they said they would train all twelve of us, on-site, at no charge. But look at their advertising. They just take things off their printers."

Roman fiddles in his chair as he continues his ad-hoc review of software and software vendors. "That one package from Mars, Inc., really sold me all on its

own, though. I mean, it had a built-in calendar. And I like the way the menus for the screen displays could all be chosen by Roman numerals. It was easy to follow. And the vendor isn't going to be hard to move on price. I think they're already in a price war.

"But, do you want to know my favorite?" Roman asks archly. "It's the one put out by Jupiter, Unlimited. I mean, it has everything, doesn't it? It costs a little extra coin, but it does what we need it to do, and the documentation is heavenly. They don't do any training of course—they think they're above it."

You are already plotting that in order to answer Roman's burning questions by your March 15 deadline, you need to evaluate the software systematically, as well as the vendors, and then render a decision. Evaluate each vendor and package based on what Roman has said so far (assume you can trust his opinions). What are Roman's apparent biases when evaluating software and vendors? What further information do you need about each company and its software before making a selection?

Forecasting Costs and Benefits

Systems analysts are required to predict certain key variables before the proposal is submitted to the client. To some degree, a systems analyst will rely on a "what-if" analysis; for example, "What if labor costs rise only 5 percent per year for the next three years, rather than 10 percent?" However, the systems analyst should realize that you cannot rely on "what-if" analysis for everything if the proposal is to be credible, meaningful, and valuable.

The systems analyst has many forecasting models available. The main condition for choosing a model is the availability of historical data. If they are unavailable, the analyst must turn to one of the judgment methods: estimates from the salesforce, surveys to estimate customer demand, Delphi studies (a consensus forecast developed independently by a group of experts through a series of iterations), creating scenarios, or drawing historical analogies.

If historical data are available, the next differentiation between classes of techniques involves whether the forecast is conditional or unconditional. Conditional implies that there is an association among variables in the model or that such a causal relationship exists. Common methods in this group include correlation, regression, leading indicators, econometrics, and input-output models.

Unconditional forecasting means the analyst isn't required to find or identify any causal relationships. Consequently, systems analysts find these methods are low-cost, easy-to-implement alternatives. Included in this group are graphical extrapolation, moving averages, and analysis of time

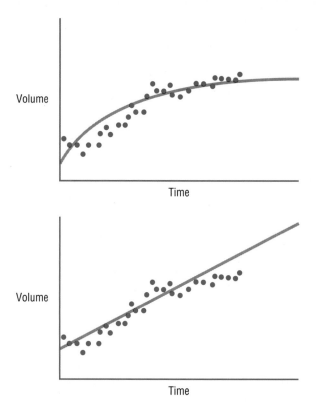

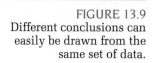

FIGURE 13.9
Different conclusions can
easily be drawn from the
same set of data.

series data. Since these methods are simple, reliable, and cost-effective, the remainder of the section focuses on them.

ESTIMATION OF TRENDS. Trends can be estimated in a number of different ways. The most widely used techniques are: (1) graphical judgment, (2) the method of least squares, and (3) the moving average method. A brief explanation of these techniques is in order.

Graphical judgment. The simplest way to identify a trend and forecast future trends is by graphical judgment. This is accomplished by simply looking at the graph and estimating freehand an extension of a line or curve. An example of graphical judgment is illustrated in Figure 13.9.

The disadvantages of this method are obvious from looking at the graphs in the figure. The extension of the line or curve may depend too much on individual judgment and may not represent the real situation. The graphical judgment method is useful, however, because the ability to perform sensitivity analysis (what-if) has increased with the introduction of electronic spreadsheets.

The method of least squares. When a trend line is constructed, the actual data points will fall on either side of that line. The objective in estimating a trend using the least squares method is to find the "best-fitting line" by minimizing the sum of the deviations from a line. Once the best-fitting line is found, it can be graphed, and the line can be extended to forecast what will happen.

The best-fitting line, or least square line, is developed from the data points $(X_1, Y_1), (X_2, Y_2), \ldots (X_N, Y_N)$, where the X coordinates signify the

FIGURE 13.10
The objective of the least
squares method is to find the
"best-fitting line."

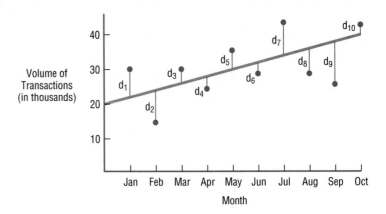

time periods and the Y coordinates represent the variable the systems analyst is trying to predict. The equation for the least square line is expressed
in the form

$$Y = m * X + b$$

where the variable m represents the slope of the line and b represents the Y
intercept, the point at which the line intercepts the Y axis.

An example of a least square line is drawn in Figure 13.10. In this
illustration, the least square line is drawn to estimate a trend in transactions from January to October. The volume starts at 21,000 in January and
rises an average of 2,000 units per month.

We recommend a more computationally efficient method to find the
least square equation by calculating the center of gravity of the data by taking
$x = X - \bar{X}$ and $y = Y - \bar{Y}$ and then calculating the least square line as

$$y = \left(\frac{\Sigma xy}{\Sigma x^2}\right) * x$$

finally substituting back the $X - \bar{X}$ for x and $Y - \bar{Y}$ for y.

Moving averages. The method of moving averages is useful because
some seasonal, cyclical, or random patterns may be smoothed, leaving the
trend pattern. The principle behind moving averages is to calculate the
arithmetic mean or data from groups of periods, using the equation

$$\frac{Y_1 + Y_2 + \cdots + Y_N}{N}$$

and then to calculate the next arithmetic mean by discarding the oldest
period's data and adding data from the next period

$$\frac{Y_2 + Y_3 + \cdots + Y_{N+1}}{N}$$

and in this manner say the average is moving.

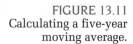

FIGURE 13.11
Calculating a five-year
moving average.

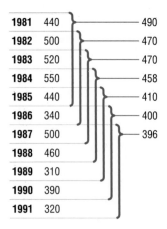

1981	440		490
1982	500		470
1983	520		470
1984	550		458
1985	440		410
1986	340		400
1987	500		396
1988	460		
1989	310		
1990	390		
1991	320		

Figure 13.11 shows one type of moving average. Here five years' data are averaged and the resulting figure is indicated. Notice that years 1981 through 1985 inclusive are averaged to represent 1983, then the years 1982 through 1986 are averaged to get a representative figure for 1984 and so on. When the results are graphed as in Figure 13.12, it is easily noticeable that the widely fluctuating data are smoothed.

The moving average method is useful for its smoothing ability, but at the same time it has many disadvantages. First, the data at the very beginning and end are lost. In the preceding example, we lost data for 1981 and 1982 at the beginning and years 1990 and 1991 at the end. The trend line must be extended from 1989, rather than from 1991 as would have been the case in least squares. Furthermore, moving averages are more strongly affected by extreme values than the methods of graphical judgment and least squares.

Many worthwhile forecasting packages are available for microcomputers as well as for mainframes. The analyst should learn forecasting well, as it often provides information valuable in justifying the entire project.

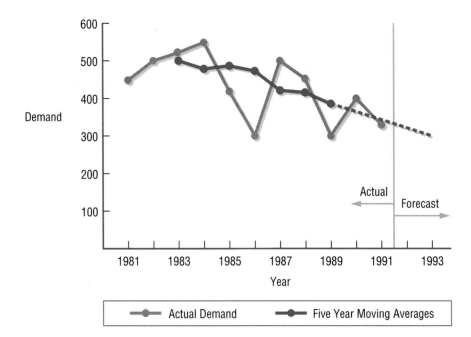

FIGURE 13.12
A five-year moving average smooths widely fluctuating data.

The Birth of a System

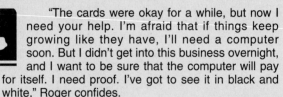

"Yup, what little there is is all mine. I started in this business because I couldn't keep my hands off of the stuff. I loved tinkering with our electronic equipment, taking apart TVs and VCRs. Ask my wife, Carol. Then I started helping friends with their projects, and they thought I was pretty good. When I inherited some money, I opened this little shop selling and repairing TVs and VCRs and renting videotapes," says Roger Corman, owner of a video rental and repair store.

"Right now," Roger continues as he tours you around the small store, "we use a manual system for keeping track of rental videotapes. We make a 3 X 5 card for each title we own and the name of the person renting the tape is recorded on this card.

"The cards were okay for a while, but now I need your help. I'm afraid that if things keep growing like they have, I'll need a computer soon. But I didn't get into this business overnight, and I want to be sure that the computer will pay for itself. I need proof. I've got to see it in black and white," Roger confides.

"I was interested enough to keep a log of demand for rental tapes for the past eighteen months," Roger continues. "Here it is."

Hoping to catch up on some movies you've missed recently, you agree to do a small systems project for Roger in return for a fee and some free videotaped films. Using the methods you have learned so far, forecast the demand for tape rentals and for new titles.

Month	Number of rentals	Number of titles
January	1000	70
February	1200	100
March	1400	130
April	1800	140
May	2200	150
June	2000	160
July	1800	170
August	1800	180
September	2500	200
October	2800	220
November	3000	280
December	3500	260
January	4000	280
February	4600	300
March	4800	320
April	5200	340
May	5700	360
June	5000	380
July	4800	400
December	3500	260
January	4000	280
February	4600	300
March	4800	320
April	5200	340
May	5700	360
June	5000	380
July	4800	400

Einstein discovers that time is actually money.

Identifying Benefits and Costs

Benefits and costs can be thought of as either tangible or intangible. Both tangible and intangible benefits and costs must be taken into account when systems are considered.

TANGIBLE BENEFITS. Tangible benefits are advantages measurable in dollars that accrue to the organization through use of the information system. Examples of tangible benefits are: an increase in speed of processing, access to otherwise inaccessible information, access to information on a more timely basis than was possible before, the advantage of the computer's superior calculating power, and decreases in the amount of employee time needed to complete specific tasks. And there are still others. Although measurement is not always easy, tangible benefits can actually be measured in terms of dollars, resources, or time saved.

INTANGIBLE BENEFITS. Some benefits that accrue to the organization from use of the information system are difficult to measure but are important nonetheless. These are known as intangible benefits.

Intangible benefits include improving the decision-making process, enhancing accuracy, becoming more competitive in customer service, maintaining a good business image, and increasing job satisfaction for employees by eliminating tedious tasks. As you can judge from the list given, intangible benefits are extremely important and can have far

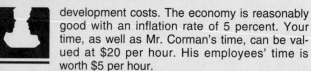
reaching implications for the business as it relates to people outside the organization as well as within it.

While intangible benefits of an information system are important factors in deciding whether to proceed with a system, a system built solely for its intangible benefits will not be successful. You must discuss both tangible and intangible benefits in your proposal. Since presenting both will allow decision makers in the business to make a well-informed decision about the proposed system.

TANGIBLE COSTS. The concepts of tangible and intangible costs present a conceptual parallel to the tangible and intangible benefits discussed already. Tangible costs are those that can be accurately projected by the systems analyst and the business' accounting personnel.

Included in tangible costs are the cost of equipment such as computers and terminals, costs of resources, cost of systems analysts' time, cost of programmers' time, and other employees' salaries. These costs are typically well-established or can be found out quite easily and are the costs that will require a cash outlay of the business.

INTANGIBLE COSTS. Intangible costs are difficult to estimate and may not be known. They include losing a competitive edge, losing the reputation for being first with an innovation or the leader in a field, declining company

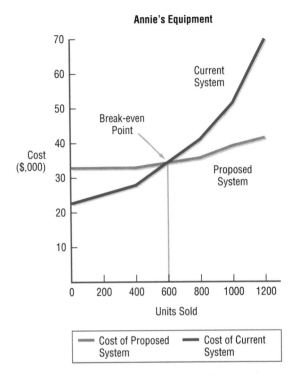

Annie's Equipment

Cost ($,000)

Units Sold

Current System

Break-even Point

Proposed System

— Cost of Proposed System   — Cost of Current System

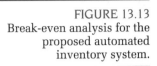

image due to increased customer dissatisfaction, and ineffective decision making due to untimely or inaccessible information. As you can imagine, it is next to impossible to accurately project a dollar amount for intangible costs. In order to aid decision makers who want to weigh the proposed system and all of its implications, you must include intangible costs, even though they are not quantifiable.

COMPARING COSTS AND BENEFITS

There are many well-known techniques for comparing the costs and benefits of the proposed system. They include break-even analysis, payback, cash-flow analysis, and present value. All of these techniques provide straightforward ways of yielding information to decision makers about the worthiness of the proposed system.

Break-even Analysis

By comparing costs alone, this kind of analysis allows the systems analyst to determine the break-even capacity of the proposed information system. The point at which total costs of the current system and of the proposed system intersect represents the break-even point—where it becomes profitable for the business to get the new information system.

Total costs include the costs that recur during operation of the system plus the developmental costs that occur only once (one-time costs of installing a new system)—that is, the tangible costs that were just discussed. Figure 13.13 is an example of break-even analysis on a small store that maintains inventory using a manual system. As volume rises, the costs of the manual system rise at an increasing rate. A new computer system would cost a substantial sum up front, but the incremental costs for higher volume would be rather small. The graph shows that the computer system would be cost-effective if the business sold about 600 units per week.

FIGURE 13.14
Payback analysis showing a
payback period of three and a
half years.

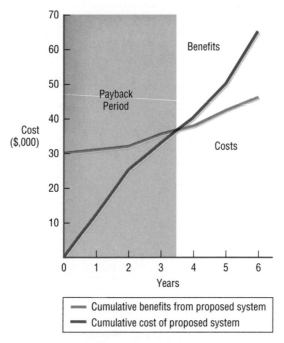

Year	Cost	Cumulative Costs	Benefits	Cumulative Benefits
0	30,000	30,000	0	0
1	1,000	31,000	12,000	12,000
2	2,000	32,000	12,000	24,000
3	2,000	35,000	8,000	32,000
4	3,000	38,000	8,000	40,000
5	4,000	42,000	10,000	50,000
6	4,000	46,000	15,000	65,000

Break-even analysis is useful when a business is growing and volume is a key variable in costs. One disadvantage of break-even analysis is that benefits are assumed to remain the same, regardless of which system is in place. From our study of tangible and intangible benefits, we know this is clearly not the case.

Payback

Payback is a simple way to assess whether a business should invest in a proposed information system based on how long it will take for the benefits of the system to pay back the costs of developing it. Briefly, the payback method determines the number of years of operation that the information system needs to pay back the cost of investing in it. Figure 13.14 illustrates a system with a payback period of three and a half years.

Payback can be determined in one of two ways—either by increasing revenues or increasing savings. A combination of the two methods can also be used. Since this is a popular way to assess alternative investments, businesses will typically have a set time period for payback assessments (three years, for example). This is something you can find out from the accounting personnel with whom you are working on the systems project.

	Year 1 Quarter 1	Quarter 2	Quarter 3	Quarter 4	Year 2 Quarter 1
Revenue	5,000	20,000	24,960	31,270	39,020
Software Development	10,000	5,000			
Personnel	8,000	8,400	8,800	9,260	9,700
Training	3,000	6,000			
Equipment Lease	4,000	4,000	4,000	4,000	4,000
Supplies	1,000	2,000	2,370	2,990	3,730
Maintenance	0	2,000	2,200	2,420	2,660
Total Costs	26,000	27,400	17,370	18,670	20,090
Cash Flow	-21,000	-7,400	7,590	12,600	18,930
Cumulative Cash Flow	-21,000	-28,400	-20,810	-8,210	10,720

FIGURE 13.15
Cash-flow analysis for the computerized mail-addressing system.

If the proposed system has a projected payback of six years in a company that adheres to a three-year maximum payback on projects involving fast-changing technology, the system will be rejected. Payback that is made within the range used by the business but is still longer than typical (for example, four years instead of three) may not be rejected outright but may be subject to scrutiny through other methods.

Although the payback method offers a well-known and simple way to assess the worthiness of the information system, it has three drawbacks that limit its usefulness. One drawback is that it is strictly a short-term approach to investment and replacement decisions; the second is that it does not consider the importance of how repayments are timed; and the third is that the payback method does not consider the total returns from the proposed systems project that may go well beyond the payback year. Other forms of analysis should be used to augment the payback method and overcome some of these flaws.

Cash-flow Analysis

Cash-flow analysis examines the direction, size, and pattern of cash flow that is associated with the proposed information system. If you are proposing the replacement of an old information system with a new one and the new information system will not be generating any additional cash for the business, only cash outlays are associated with the project. If this is the case, the new system cannot be justified on the basis of new revenues generated and must be examined closely for other tangible benefits if it is to be pursued further.

Figure 13.15 shows a small company that is providing a mailing service to other small companies in the city. Revenue projections are that only $5,000 will be generated in the first quarter, but after the second quarter revenue will grow at a steady rate. Costs will be large in the first two quarters and then level off. Cash-flow analysis is used to determine when a company will begin to make a profit (in this case, it is the third quarter with a cash flow of $7,590) and when it will be "out of the red"—that is, when revenue has made up for the initial investment (in the first quarter of year two, when accumulated cash flow changes from a negative amount to a positive $10,720).

FIGURE 13.16
Without considering present
value, the benefits appear to
outweigh the costs.

| | Year | | | | | | |
	1	2	3	4	5	6	Total
Costs	40,000	42,000	44,100	46,300	48,600	51,000	272,000
Benefits	25,000	31,200	39,000	48,700	60,800	76,000	280,700

The proposed system should have increased revenues along with cash outlays. Then the size of cash flow must be analyzed along with the patterns of cash flow associated with the purchase of the new system. You must ask when cash outlays and revenues will occur, not only for the initial purchase but over the life of the information system as well.

Present Value

Present value analysis helps the systems analyst to present to business decision makers the time value of the investment in the information system as well as the funds flow (as discussed in the previous section). Present value is a way to assess all of the economic outlays and revenues of the information system over its economic life and to compare costs today with future costs and today's benefits with future benefits.

In Figure 13.16, system costs total $272,000 over six years and benefits total $280,700. Therefore, we might conclude that benefits outweigh the costs. However, benefits only started to surpass costs after the fourth year, and dollars in the sixth year will not be equivalent to dollars in year one.

For instance, a dollar investment at 7 percent today will be worth $1.07 at the end of the year and will double in approximately ten years. The present value, therefore, is the cost or benefit measured in today's dollars and depends on the cost of money. The cost of money is the opportunity cost, or the rate that could be obtained if the money invested in the proposed system was invested in another (relatively safe) project.

The present value of $1.00 at a discount rate of i is calculated by determining the factor

$$\frac{1}{(1 + i)^n}$$

where n is the number of periods. Then the factor is multiplied by the dollar amount, yielding present value as shown in Figure 13.17. In this example, the cost of money—discount rate—is assumed to be .12 (12 percent) for the entire planning horizon. Multipliers are calculated for each period: $n = 1$, $n = 2$, . . . $n = 6$. Present values of both costs and benefits are then calculated using these multipliers. When this is done, the total benefits (measured in today's dollars) are $179,484—less than the costs (also measured in today's dollars). The conclusion to be drawn is that the proposed system is not worthwhile if present value is considered.

Although this example, which used present value factors, is useful in explaining the concept, all electronic spreadsheets have a built-in present value function. The analyst can directly compute present value using this feature.

Guidelines for Analysis

The use of the methods discussed in the preceding section depends on the methods employed and accepted within the organization itself. However, for general guidelines it is safe to say:

gible (quantifiable) or intangible (nonquantifiable and resistant to direct comparison).

A systems analyst has many methods for analyzing costs and benefits. Break-even analysis examines the cost of the existing system versus the cost of the proposed system. The payback method determines the length of time it will take before the new system is profitable. Cash-flow analysis is appropriate when it is critical to know the amount of cash outlays, while present value takes into consideration the cost of borrowing money. These tools help the analyst examine the alternatives at hand and make a well-researched recommendation in the systems proposal.

KEYWORDS AND PHRASES

vendor support	intangible benefits
forecasting	tangible costs
analysis of time series data	intangible costs
graphical judgment	break-even analysis
method of least squares	payback
moving averages	cash-flow analysis
tangible benefits	present value

REVIEW QUESTIONS

1. List the elements that should be included on a computer hardware inventory form.
2. What is meant by the words *estimated workload*?
3. List four criteria for evaluating system hardware.
4. What are the three main options for acquisition of computer hardware?
5. Under what conditions is rental of computer hardware appropriate?
6. List four extra support services that are negotiable with vendors of computer hardware.
7. List the six main categories on which to grade software.
8. Why is forecasting a useful tool for the systems analyst?
9. Define unconditional forecasting.
10. What is a disadvantage of graphical judgment?
11. What is the objective in estimating a trend using the least squares method?
12. Why is the method of moving averages a useful one?
13. Define tangible costs and benefits. Give an example of each.
14. Define intangible costs and benefits. Give and example of each.
15. List four techniques for comparing costs and benefits of a proposed system.
16. When is break-even analysis useful?
17. What are the three drawbacks of using the payback method?
18. When is cash-flow analysis used?
19. Define present value analysis.
20. As a general guideline, when should present value analysis be used?

"Sometimes the people who have been here some time are surprised at how much we have actually grown. And yes, I do admit that it isn't easy to keep track of what each person is up to, or even what purchases each department has made in the way of hardware and software. We're working on it, though. Snowden would like to see more accountability for computer purchases. He wants to make sure that we know what we have, where it is, why we have it, who's using it, and if it's boosting MRE productivity or, as he so delicately puts it, 'to see whether it's just an expensive toy' that we can live without."

HyperCase Questions

1. Using the form provided in Chapter 13, complete a computer equipment inventory form for the Training and Management Systems Unit.

2. Using the "Guidelines for Evaluating Software" in Chapter 13, do a brief evaluation of the Project Status Reporting System (PSRS) used by the Management Systems employees. In a paragraph, briefly critique this custom-made software by comparing it to off-the-shelf software such as Lotus' "Organizer," or Microsoft's "Project." (Both are mentioned in Chapter 3.)

3. List the intangible costs and benefits of the PSRS as reported by employees of MRE.

4. Briefly describe the two alternatives Snowden is considering for the proposed project tracking and reporting system.

5. What organizational and political factors should Snowden consider in proposing his new system at MRE? (In a brief paragraph, discuss three central conflicts.)

PROBLEMS

1. Delicato, Inc., a manufacturer of precise measuring instruments for scientific purposes, has presented you with a list of attributes that its managers think are probably important in selecting a vendor for computer hardware and software. The criteria are not listed in order of importance.

    1. Low price.
    2. Precisely written software for engineering applications.
    3. Vendor performs routine maintenance on hardware.
    4. Training for Delicato employees.

    a. Critique their list of attributes in a paragraph.
    b. Using their initial input, help Delicato, Inc., draw up a more suitable list of criteria for selecting computer hardware and software vendors.

2. SoftWear Silhouettes is a rapidly growing mail-order house specializing in all-cotton clothing. Management is contemplating purchase of microcomputers and software to help with supplier and customer

accounts. Company offices are located in a small, isolated New England town, and the employees have little computer training.

    a. Considering the company's situation, draw up a list of software attributes that SoftWear Silhouettes should emphasize in their choice of software.

    b. List the variables that contributed to your response in part a above.

3. Below is ten years' demand for YarDarts, an outdoor game for the whole family that is part of the 65-game product line of Open Air, Ltd., a manufacturer specializing in outdoor games that can be played in a small area.

Year	Demand
1985	20,900
1986	31,200
1987	28,000
1988	41,200
1989	49,700
1990	46,400
1991	51,200
1992	52,300
1993	49,200
1994	57,600

    a. Graph the demand data for YarDarts.

    b. Forecast the demand for YarDarts for the next five years using the graphical judgment approach.

4.   **a.** Determine the linear trend for YarDarts demand using the least squares method.

    b. Estimate the demand for YarDarts for the next five years using the trend you determined.

5.   **a.** Determine the linear trend for YarDarts using a three-year moving average.

    b. Use least squares on the averages in part 3a to determine a linear trend.

    c. Estimate demand for YarDarts for the next five years by extending the linear trend found in part 3b.

6. Does the data for YarDarts appear to have a cyclical variation? Explain.

7. Interglobal Paper Company has asked your help in comparing their present computer system with a new one its board of directors would like to see implemented. Proposed system and present system costs are listed in the table at the top of the next page.

    a. Using break-even analysis, determine the year in which Interglobal Paper will break even.

    b. Graph the costs and show the break-even point.

	Proposed System Costs	Present System Costs
Year 1		
Equipment Lease	$20,000	$11,500
Salaries	30,000	50,000
Overhead	4,000	3,000
Development	30,000	—
Year 2		
Equipment Lease	$20,000	$10,500
Salaries	33,000	55,000
Overhead	4,400	3,300
Development	12,000	—
Year 3		
Equipment Lease	$20,000	$10,500
Salaries	36,000	60,000
Overhead	4,900	3,600
Development	—	—
Year 4		
Equipment Lease	$20,000	$10,500
Salaries	39,000	66,000
Overhead	5,500	4,000
Development	—	—

8. Below are system benefits for Interglobal Paper Company (from problem 7):

Year	Benefits
1	$55,000
2	75,000
3	80,000
4	85,000

    a. Use the costs of Interglobal's proposed system from problem 7 to determine the payback period (use the payback method).

    b. Graph the benefits versus the costs and indicate the payback period.

9. Glenn's Electronics, a small company, has set up a computer service. The table at the top of the next page shows the revenue expected for the first five months of operation, in addition to the costs for office remodeling, and so on.

    Determine the cash flow and accumulated cash flow for the company. When is Glenn's expected to show a profit?

	Month				
	July	August	September	October	November
REVENUE	35,000	36,000	42,000	48,000	57,000
COSTS					
Office remodeling	25,000	8,000			
Salaries	11,000	12,100	13,300	14,600	16,000
Training	6,000	6,000			
Equipment Lease	8,000	8,480	9,000	9,540	10,110
Supplies	3,000	3,150	3,300	3,460	3,630

10. Alamo Foods of San Antonio wants to introduce a new computer system for its perishable products warehouse. The costs and benefits are listed below.

Years	Costs	Benefits
1	$33,000	$21,000
2	34,600	26,200
3	36,300	32,700
4	38,100	40,800
5	40,000	51,000
6	42,000	63,700

    a. Given a discount rate of 8 percent (.08) perform present value analysis on the data for Alamo Foods. (*Hint*: Use the formula

$$\frac{1}{(1 + i)^{n}}$$

to find the multipliers for years 1 to 6.)

    b. What is your recommendation for Alamo Foods?

11. **a.** Suppose the discount rate in problem 10 changes to 13 percent (.13). Perform present value analysis using the new discount rate.

    b. What is you recommendation to Alamo Foods now?

    c. Explain the difference between problem 10, part b and problem 11, part b.

12. Solve problem 7 using an electronic spreadsheet program such as LOTUS 1-2-3, Excel, or Quattro.

13. Use a spreadsheet program to solve problem 9.

14. Solve problem 10 using a function for net present value—for example: @NPV (*x*, range) in LOTUS 1-2-3.

SELECTED BIBLIOGRAPHY

Buffa, E. S. *Modern Production/Operations Management*, 6th ed. New York: John Wiley & Sons, 1980.

Cleland, D. I., and W. R. King. *Systems Analysis and Project Management*, 2nd ed. New York: McGraw-Hill Book Company, 1975.

Lazzaro, V. "Outlining for Conducting and Implementing a Systems Study." In V. Lazarro (ed.), *Systems and Procedures: A Handbook for Business and Industry*, 2nd ed. Englewood Cliffs, NJ: Prentice-Hall, Inc., 1968.

Lucas, H. *Information Systems Concepts for Management*, 3rd ed. New York: McGraw-Hill Book Company, 1986.

Meredith, J. R., and T. E. Gibbs. *The Management of Operations*, 2nd ed. New York: John Wiley & Sons, 1984.

Sumner, M. *Computers, Concepts and Uses*. Englewood Cliffs, NJ: Prentice-Hall, Inc., 1985.

Voich, D., Jr., H. J. Mottice, and W. A. Shrode. *Information Systems for Operations and Management*. Cincinnati: South-Western Publishing Company, 1975.

PROPOSING TO GO FORTH

"Since we chose to design and implement the new microcomputer system using microcomputers linked with a local area network, we should work on preparing the systems proposal," Anna begins. She and Chip are meeting to plan the next phase of the design.

"Yes," replies Chip, "we need to make some hardware and software decisions as well as ensure that the users are aware of the benefits the new system will provide."

"We should determine which software will be required to implement the system and the hardware requirements for each user of the system," notes Anna. "Why don't you work on the hardware portion, and I'll investigate software?"

"Sure," Chip replies. "I plan to meet with each of the users again. When I have all of the information, I'll produce a summary report."

Chip proceeds to work with each user to determine what equipment would be required. Some of his findings are:

Mike Crowe has an IBM 486 microcomputer on the desk. This is more than adequate for serving the needs of the new system. Additional equipment necessary is a portable microcomputer for creating transactions when performing physical inventory and preventive maintenance work.

Dot Matricks has an IBM PS/2 Model 70 386 combination mainframe/microcomputer workstation. This is adequate for the new system.

Hy Perteks has an older microcomputer on his desk. Recommend that it be replaced with an IBM PS/2 Model 386SX microcomputer.

Paige Prynter has a mainframe terminal. Recommend replacing the terminal with an IBM PS/2 Model 70 386 workstation. Purchase software to run terminal emulation on the workstation.

Cher Ware has an older microcomputer. Recommend that it be upgraded with an IBM PS/2 Model 386SX.

Other equipment and supplies: a server microcomputer to manage the network. This should be a PS/2 Model 386SX or better fitted with communication boards. A higher-speed laser printer with font cartridges attached directly to the server and smaller personal laser printers for all microcomputers attached to each microcomputer should be provided. Additionally, cable must be purchased to connect each of the users on the network.

Chip uses Excelerator to capture and print information on the hardware devices. From the XLDictionary, he uses the System Device entity to add both existing and new microcomputers to be used in the proposed system. The description screen for the microcomputer currently installed in Mike Crowe's area is shown in Figure E13.1.

Notice that there are areas for entering identifying and configuration information for the microcomputer. The **Attribute** entry area is used to enter information about peripheral devices and internal boards. The description screen for Paige Printer is shown in Figure E13.2. Notice that the **Serial Number** attribute contains the text "NEW," indicating a machine to be purchased.

When all the entries are complete, Chip will use the Report Writer feature of Excelerator to list all microcomputers to be purchased—those

*Allen Schmidt,
Julie E. Kendall, and
Kenneth E. Kendall*

439

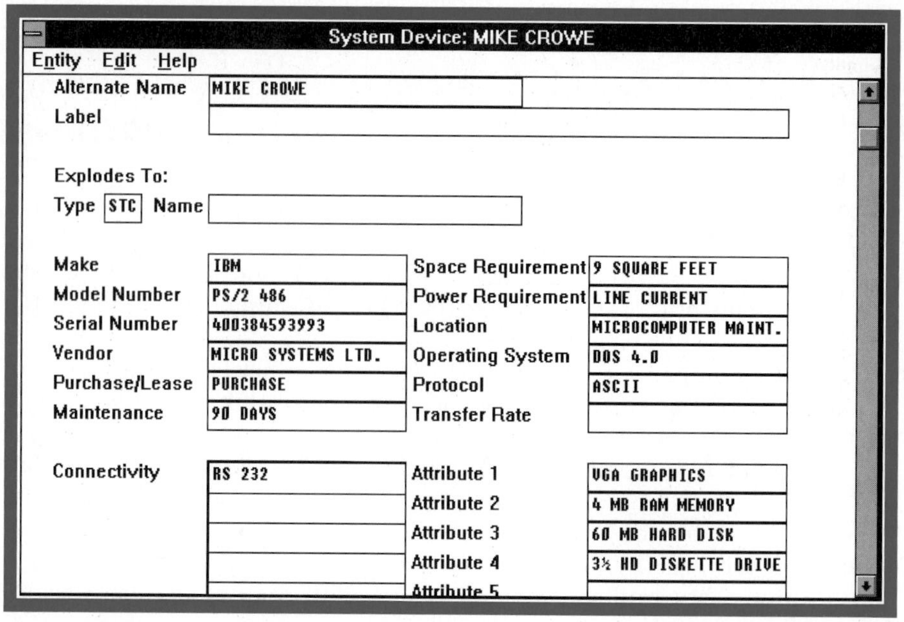

FIGURE E13.1
System Device description screen—existing microcomputer, MIKE CROWE.

containing the word "NEW" in the **Serial Number** field. Another report shows all the existing microcomputers.

Meanwhile, Anna is determining the software that would be necessary to implement the system. Since each of the users would be receiving software developed by programmers, the major task was to decide what software would be needed for system development and to network the microcomputers. After researching software options, Anna made the following recommendations:

1. Development software to create the system. Two options are available:
   a. Use a microcomputer-based COBOL package, which would need to be purchased. The versions used in the classroom are the result of a grant and are limited to educational use only.
   b. Use a database package and write programming code. Compile the database programs into executable code. Currently dBASE is available, but a compiler such as Clipper would have to be purchased. Other database packages should be evaluated.
2. Network software is required to establish and make the local area network "user-friendly" with menu selections.

Chip and Anna sit at a work table and examine each other's findings.

"I suppose the next task is to obtain some cost figures for the hardware and software selection," Anna says. "What do you think is our best source of cost information?"

"There are several sources of information," Chip replies. "One would be to examine trade journals for prices. There are many mail-order houses that would have posted prices. We should also call or visit dealers and obtain quotes, especially with educational discounts. The manufacturers

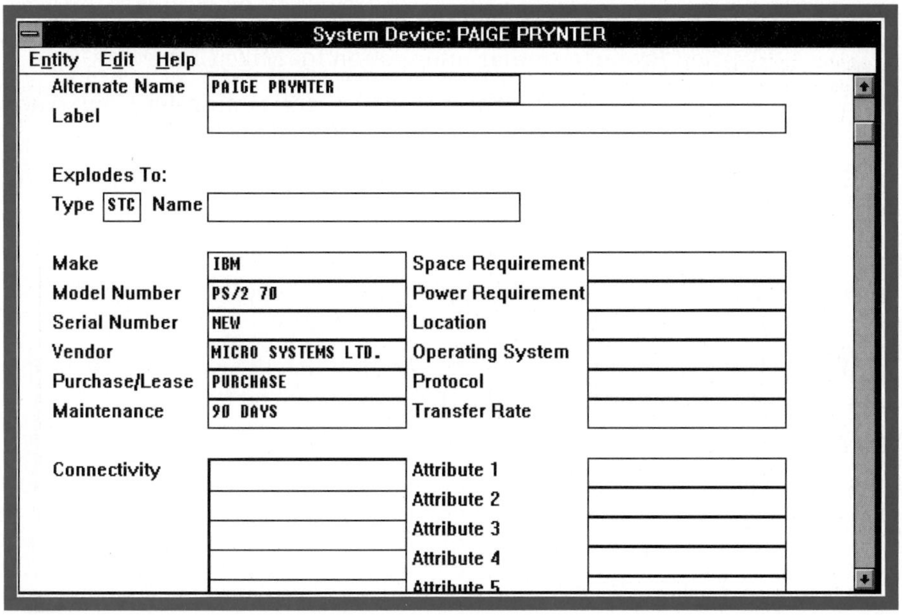

FIGURE E13.2
System device description screen—new microcomputer, PAIGE PRYNTER.

may have special programs available. We'll check with the university purchasing officer, too. Once we have all the cost information, we can produce a document as part of the systems proposal."

Exercises*

E-1. Use microcomputer periodicals in your library to investigate costs for each of the machines and peripheral devices to be purchased. Make a comparison list for each machine.

E-2. Visit a local computer retail store and obtain cost information for each of the microcomputers listed in this episode. Include printers and VGA-quality monitors. Make a comparison list for each machine.

E-3. Investigate three different network costs. Include hardware, software, network boards, and 500 feet of cable to connect the machines. Write a list or use a spreadsheet to summarize your work.

E-4. Scan trade journals and summarize your findings comparing three different database packages, their features, and costs.

E-5. Investigate the features and prices for microcomputer COBOL packages. Make a summary list of your findings.

E-6. View the System Device entity for Mike Crowe.

---

* The exercises preceded by a disk icon require the program Excelerator (or another CASE tool). A disk is provided free of charge to any professor adopting this book. The examples on the disk may be imported into Excelerator and then used by students.

E-7. Modify and print the System Device description for Paige Prynter. Produce similar information for Mike Crowe.

E-8. Modify and print the System Device description for Cher Ware. Again, produce similar information for Mike Crowe.

E-9. Copy the System Device entity for Mike Crowe to that of Hy Perteks. Modify and print the description based on information supplied in this chapter.

E-10. Based on information supplied in this chapter, create and print the System Device entity for Dot Matricks.

E-11. Use the Report Writer feature to produce the NEW MICROCOMPUTER EQUIPMENT report.

E-12. Use the Report Writer feature to produce the EQUIPMENT TO BE UPGRADED report.

WRITING AND PRESENTING THE SYSTEMS PROPOSAL

METHODS AVAILABLE

The written proposal serves as a summary of the systems analyst's work in the business up to that point, and as such it is essential that great care is given to writing and presenting it. Through the use of three methods, the analyst can create a successful systems proposal. These methods are effectively organizing the content, writing in a professional style, and orally presenting the proposal in an informative way.

THE SYSTEMS PROPOSAL

Organizing the Systems Proposal

Once you have gathered the material to be included in your systems proposal, you need to piece it together in a logical and visually effective way. This means including ten main functional sections, using an effective writing style, using figures to supplement your writing, and attending to the visual details of the written proposal.

WHAT TO INCLUDE IN THE SYSTEMS PROPOSAL. There are ten main sections comprising the written systems proposal, as shown in Figure 14.1. Each part has a particular function, and the eventual proposal should be arranged in the following order:

1. Cover letter.
2. Title page of project.
3. Table of contents.
4. Executive summary (including recommendations).
5. Outline of systems study with appropriate documentation.
6. Detailed results of systems study.

FIGURE 14.1
Each systems proposal should
contain ten main sections,
each serving a unique
function.

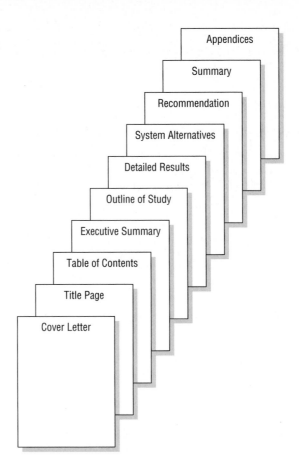

7. Systems alternative (3 or 4 possible solutions).
8. Systems analysts' recommendations.
9. Summary.
10. Appendices (assorted documentation, summary of phases, correspondence, etc.).

Cover letter. A cover letter to management and the MIS task force should accompany the systems proposal. It should list the people who did the study and summarize the objectives of the study. The cover letter can also include the prearranged time and place for the oral presentation of the systems proposal. Keep the cover letter concise (one page maximum) and friendly, since its function is to reacquaint management with the systems project.

Title page. Include on the title page the name of the project, the names of the systems analysis team members, and the date the proposal is submitted. Keep the title page uncluttered in appearance.

Titling a project is more art than science. The proposal title must accurately express the content of the proposal, but it can also exhibit some imagination. Alliteration, using the same letter to begin each work ("The

Simon Says System"), can work sometimes, but there are many other ideas that will serve as well, such as using the main title with a subtitle and separating them with a colon. If the project has developed an acronym that is recognized and respected in the organization, it can be used in the title. The main point is that titling is important in getting your reader to open the proposal, and it should not be done as an afterthought.

Table of contents. The table of contents can be enormously useful to readers of long proposals. If the proposal is very short (less than ten pages), omit the table of contents since it is superfluous on such a short document.

The key to producing a useful table of contents occurs much earlier in proposal preparation when the analyst writes sections and subsections with expressive headings and subheadings to indicate the contents of each. The more concise yet telling these are, the more useful will be the resulting table of contents.

Executive summary. Executive summaries are so well known in the business world that they have become a cliché that conjures up a harried businessperson who is only able to grasp the rudimentary elements of organizational functioning available in such summaries. We can laugh at the cliché while still acknowledging that a well-written executive summary is critical to the systems proposal.

The executive summary, in 250 to 375 words, provides the who, what, when, where, why, and how of the proposal—just as would the first paragraph in a newspaper story. It goes right to the heart of the systems project, so that anyone reading it will have an accurate concept of what is going on. It should also include the recommendations of the systems analysts and desired management action, since some people will only have time to read the summary.

The executive summary is difficult to write since it is content-laden, yet concise. It should be written only after the remainder of the proposal is complete, since only then will the analyst have an adequate, overall picture of what is being proposed.

Outline of systems study. This section provides information about all of the methods used in the study and who or what was studied. Any questionnaires, interviews, sampling of archival data, observation, or prototyping used in the systems study should be discussed in this section.

Detailed results of systems study. This section details what the systems analyst has found out about the system through all of the methods described in the preceding section. Any conclusions about systems problems that have come to the fore through the study should be noted here. This includes kinds and rates of errors; current and projected work volume; and how work is being handled by the current system.

This section presents problems with the existing system. The material included here should raise the problems or opportunities that call forth the alternatives presented in the next section.

Systems alternative. In this portion of the proposal, the analyst presents two or three alternative solutions that directly address the aforementioned problems. Although more than three solutions are usually possible, preliminary analyses should leave you with the best two or three alternatives for inclusion here. Among the alternatives you should present is that of keeping the system the same.

Each alternative (even that of preserving the *status quo*) should be explored separately. Describe the costs and benefits of each situation. This is an excellent place to insert graphs clearly comparing costs and benefits of each solution. Since there are usually tradeoffs involved in any solution, be sure to include the advantages and disadvantages of each.

Each alternative must clearly indicate what management must do to implement it. This should be written as clearly as possible—for example, "Buy PCs for all middle managers"; "Purchase packaged software to manage inventory"; "Modify the existing system through funding in-house programming efforts"; and so on.

Systems analysts' recommendations. After the systems analysis team has weighed the alternatives, it will have a definite professional opinion about which solution is most workable. This section expresses the *recommended* solution. Include the reasons supporting the team's recommendation, so that it is easy to understand why it is being made. The recommendation should flow logically from the preceding analysis of alternative solutions.

Proposal summary. The proposal summary is a brief statement that mirrors the content of the executive summary. It should not quote the material from the executive summary verbatim, however. It gives the objectives of the study and the recommended solution. It also allows the analyst one

An Inflammatory Appendage

A new member of your systems analysis team has just handed you a rough draft of the table of contents for the team's system proposal. Without even reading the rest of the proposal, you are getting worried. The page below is what you have read so far:

What are some of the items that are causing you to feel some pain? Based on what you can diagnose from the table of contents alone, what are some cuts you would make to the systems proposal? Consider your clients and the purposes of the systems proposal (*not* to anesthetize them) in making your revision.

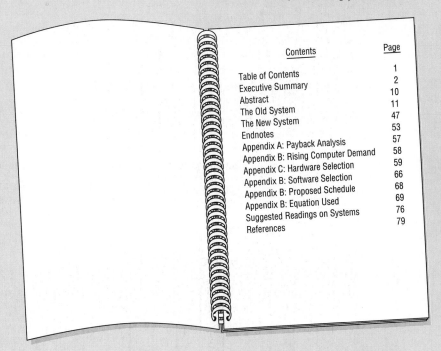

FIGURE 14.C1
A table of contents from the proposal.

more chance to stress the project's importance and feasibility along with the value of the recommendations. Conclude the proposal on a positive note.

Appendices. This is the last part of the systems proposal and it can include any information that the systems analyst feels may be of interest to specific individuals, but which is not essential for understanding the systems study and what is being proposed. Appendices might include pertinent correspondence, a summary of phases completed in the study, detailed graphs for analysis purposes, or even previously done systems studies.

While it is important to be complete, do not overkill with large volumes of meaningless data in the appendices. If material is not important enough to be in the body of the proposal, perhaps it should not be included at all.

It is difficult to provide useful heuristics about the appropriate length of the systems proposal. Keep in mind that the proposal's size is directly related to the size of the modification or system being proposed. A minor systems alteration should not evoke a 300-page tome.

Once the systems proposal is written, carefully select who should receive the report. Not everyone needs a copy or should get one. Personally hand the report to the people you have selected. This is a way to impress upon them your continuing enthusiasm for and involvement in the project. Your visibility is important for the acceptance and eventual success of the system.

Choosing a Writing Style

Although a business style of writing is most often appropriate for writing a systems proposal, your choice of a writing style will ultimately be determined by what you have already witnessed in the organization's own publications. If the people who compose your target audience favor a certain style, use it to write your proposal.

Keeping the audience in mind means presenting information in a way that is easily comprehensible to them without being condescending. This requires finesse since there should be enough detail for management to make informed decisions without being overwhelmed. Keep references to a minimum and do not use footnotes. Where appropriate, use examples, illustrations, diagrams, tables, figures, and graphs to support main points of the proposal.

Using Figures for Effective Communication

The emphasis so far in this chapter has been on considering your audience when composing the systems proposal. Tables and graphs as well as words are important in capturing and communicating the proposed system. In fact, much of the information that the analyst collects can be communicated more readily through a combination of figures and words than through words alone.

Integrating figures into your proposal helps demonstrate that you are responsive to the different ways people absorb information. Figures within the report supplement written information and must always be interpreted in words. Tables and graphs never stand alone.

EFFECTIVE USE OF TABLES. Although tables are not technically termed *visual aids,* they provide a different way of grouping and presenting analyzed data that the analyst wants to communicate to the proposal reader. Tables are more similar to figures than they are to written text and are therefore discussed here.

Tables use labeled columns and rows to present statistical or alphabetical data in an organized way. Each table must be numbered according to the order in which it appears in the proposal and should be meaningfully titled. Figure 14.2 shows appropriate layout and labeling for a table. Some guidelines for tables include:

1. Type only one table per page and integrate it into the body of the proposal rather than relegating it to the end of the proposal.
2. Try to fit the entire table vertically on a single page if possible.

FIGURE 14.2
Guidelines for creating effective tables.

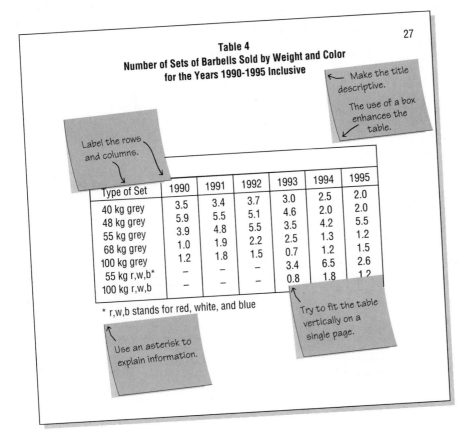

Table 4
Number of Sets of Barbells Sold by Weight and Color
for the Years 1990-1995 Inclusive

Make the title descriptive.

The use of a box enhances the table.

Label the rows and columns.

Type of Set	1990	1991	1992	1993	1994	1995
40 kg grey	3.5	3.4	3.7	3.0	2.5	2.0
48 kg grey	5.9	5.5	5.1	4.6	2.0	2.0
55 kg grey	3.9	4.8	5.5	3.5	4.2	5.5
68 kg grey	1.0	1.9	2.2	2.5	1.3	1.2
100 kg grey	1.2	1.8	1.5	0.7	1.2	1.5
55 kg r,w,b*	–	–	–	3.4	6.5	2.6
100 kg r,w,b	–	–	–	0.8	1.8	1.2

* r,w,b stands for red, white, and blue

Try to fit the table vertically on a single page.

Use an asterisk to explain information.

3. Number and title the table at the top of the page. Make the title descriptive and meaningful.

4. Label each row and column. Use more than one row for a title if necessary.

5. Use a boxed table if room permits. Vertically ruled columns will enhance the readability.

6. Use an asterisk if necessary to explain detailed information contained in the table.

Several methods for comparing costs and benefits were presented in Chapter 13. Tabled results of those comparisons should appear in the systems proposal. If a break-even analysis is done, a table illustrating results of the analysis should be included. Payback can be shown in tables that serve as additional support for graphs. A short table comparing computer systems or options might also be included in the systems proposal.

EFFECTIVE USE OF GRAPHS. This section covers different kinds of graphs including line graphs, column charts, bar graphs, and pie charts. Line, column, and bar graphs compare variables, while pie charts illustrate the composition of 100 percent of an entity.

The guidelines for including effective graphs in a proposal are:

1. Draw only one graph to a page unless you want to make a critical comparison between graphs.

CHAPTER 14:
WRITING AND PRESENTING
THE SYSTEMS PROPOSAL

FIGURE 14.3
Guidelines for drawing
effective line graphs.

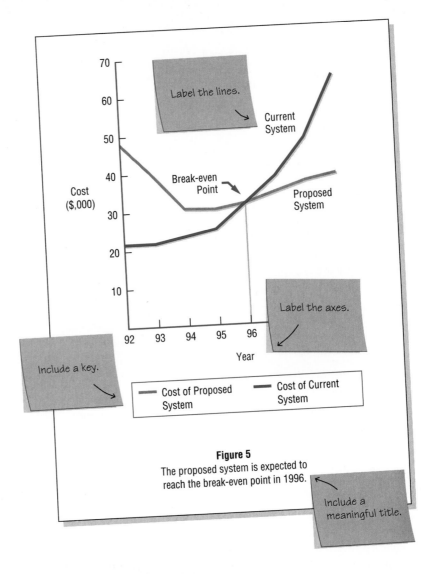

Figure 5
The proposed system is expected to
reach the break-even point in 1996.

2. Integrate the graph into the body of the proposal.
3. Give the graph a sequential figure number and a meaningful title.
4. Label each axis, and any lines, columns, bars, or pieces of the pie on the graph.
5. Include a key to indicate differently colored lines, shaded bars, or crosshatched areas.

An example of how a graph would appear on a page in a systems proposal is shown in Figure 14.3. Our explanation of graphs will begin with the simplest type, called a line graph.

Line graphs. Line graphs are used primarily to show change over time. No other type of graph shows a trend more clearly than a line graph. Changes in a single variable or up to five variables can be illustrated in a single line graph.

There are times, however, when a line graph is used to show something other than time on the horizontal axis. This situation occurs when

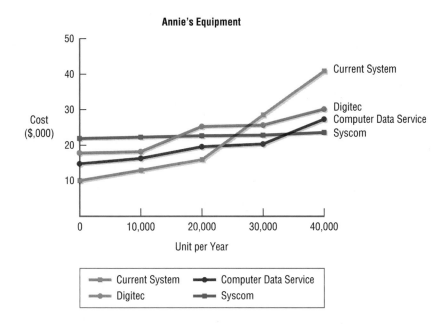

FIGURE 14.4
Depicting each variable with
a different kind of line
on the line graph.

one has to estimate when two or more lines intersect, as shown in Figure 14.4. In this example, the current system is the least expensive until Annie's Equipment grows to approximately 22,000 units per year. Then Computer Data Service offers the least expensive option. Later we find that Syscom becomes the least expensive option if Annie's were to grow to over 34,000 units annually. Any other type of graph (column, bar, or pie—all to be discussed in following sections) would not be able to estimate the point between 30,000 units and 40,000 units.

A dramatic method of visual comparison, in the same general family as line graphs, is the area chart. Figure 14.5 shows the growth of the video-cassette industry over the time period 1989–1994. In this area chart, the total gross receipts consist of both sales (the darker area) and rentals (the lighter area). The area chart is very useful when the difference between two variables expands greatly.

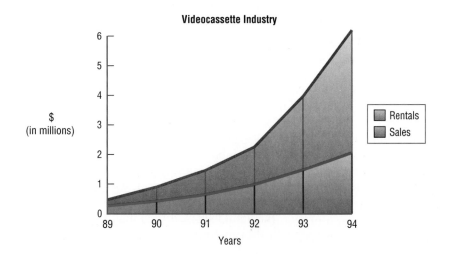

FIGURE 14.5
An area chart is a form of line
graph that may make more of
an impact.

FIGURE 14.6
A familiar icon such as a
diskette can be used to create
columns on a column chart.

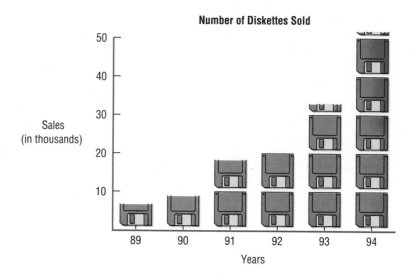

In Chapter 13, the importance of forecasing for justifying the systems project was stressed. Line graphs are excellent ways of showing proposal readers how demand on the computer system may change within a certain number of years or how demand for the products or services of a business may change within a specific time period.

Line graphs are also useful for representing results of payback analysis or break-even analysis to decision makers. Graphic display of payback period is an excellent way to portray the economic feasibility of the proposed system, as is a graph of break-even results.

Column charts. Other familiar kinds of graphs are column charts. Column charts can depict a comparison between two or more variables over time but they are used more often to compare different variables at a particular point in time. Although they do not show trends as well as line graphs, nor can one easily estimate value between columns using them, many people find column charts easier to understand than line graphs.

A simple column chart is shown in Figure 14.6. In this example, the columns consist of diskettes. One way to attract the reader, particularly someone who disdains statistics and graphs, is to make the graph more human. A familiar icon, such as a diskette, can be useful in this regard.

Figure 14.7 shows a column chart with more than one variable. When this occurs, draw the columns in different colors or shades to distinguish between the variables. Notice that there is space between each of the two classes (HQ and Troops A, B, C, D, and E) but no space between the two variables, "current strength" and "minimum required."

There are also special forms of column charts. A 100-percent stacked column chart is shown in Figure 14.8. This type of chart is used to show the relationship between two variables that make up 100 percent of an entity. Here, sporting goods sales are made up of competitive sporting equipment and individual achievement equipment. The chart depicts the competitive sporting equipment as shrinking as a percentage of total sales. (It does not show, however, the actual sales, which may indeed be growing even though the percentage is diminishing.)

Nebraska State Patrol Uniform Division

Another special type of column chart is the deviation column chart. This type of chart is useful for emphasizing years that show a loss or pointing out the year in which the company intends to break even. Furthermore, the chart can be drawn to show the deviation from an average. An example of a deviation column chart is shown in Figure 14.9, where the differences in above- and below-average months are emphasized.

Bar charts. Bar charts are similar to column charts, but are never used to show a relationship over a period of years. Rather, they are used to show one or more variables within certain classes or categories during a specific time period.

The bars themselves may be organized in many different ways. They can be in alphabetical, numerical, geographical, or progressive order, or they can be sorted by magnitude.

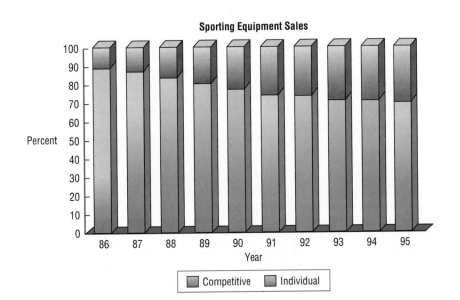

Sporting Equipment Sales

FIGURE 14.8
A 100-percent column chart can be used to show the percentage share over time.

453

FIGURE 14.9
A deviation column chart can
be more effective in showing
which months have above-
average transactions.

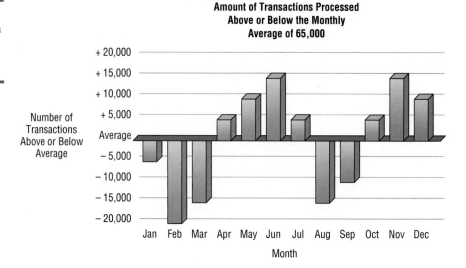

**Amount of Transactions Processed
Above or Below the Monthly
Average of 65,000**

For instance, in a systems proposal, a bar chart would be useful in comparing the volumes of shipping invoices, customer accounts, and vendor invoices processed by the computer system during July, as shown in Figure 14.10. A bar chart is one of the most widely known forms of graphs and can make a comparison in a straightforward way.

There are special types of bar charts, just as there are special column charts. One example, shown in Figure 14.11, is a 100-percent subdivided bar chart. This is the equivalent of a 100-percent stacked column chart and is used to demonstrate what percentages of males and females rent certain categories of videotapes.

Pie charts. Another commonly used type of graph is the circle or pie chart. It is used to show how 100 percent of a commodity is divided at a particular point in time, as in Figure 14.12. The data display begins at 12 o'clock on the circle and works clockwise, placing the largest percentage (or wedge of pie) next to the second largest, all the way down to the smallest. Observe this convention unless you want to show dramatic contrasts in percentages by placing the largest and smallest percentages side by side.

FIGURE 14.10
A bar chart is like a column
chart, but is mainly used to
compare different items at a
specific point in time.

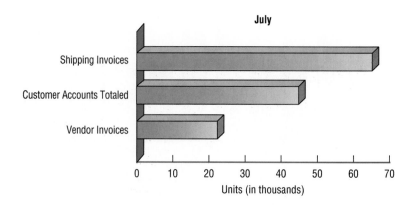

July

454

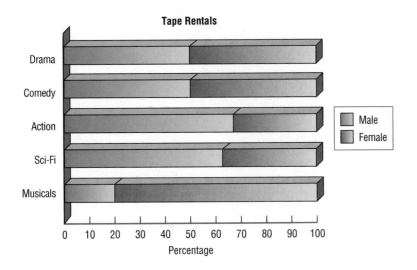

Tape Rentals

FIGURE 14.11
A 100-percent bar chart makes the items appear to be of equal importance so it is easier to analyze the percentages visually.

In this example, a pie chart is used to show the market share of three computer software companies. Computer Data Systems has the largest share at approximately 45 percent of the total market, while Digidec has the second biggest share at 35 percent. Finally, Syscom has only 20 percent of the market. If for some reason we want to emphasize one aspect of the data—a company in this example—we can separate that piece of the pie from the remainder.

Pie charts are easier to read than 100-percent stacked column charts or 100-percent subdivided bar charts. Their main disadvantage is that they take up a lot of room on a page. If an analyst wanted to show more than six categories, one of the previously mentioned 100-percent charts would be preferable to drawing six individual pie charts.

EFFECTIVE USE OF SCHEDULING CHARTS AND DIAGRAMS. In Chapter 3, Gantt charts generated via project management software were recommended for use in scheduling systems projects. Include a summary Gantt chart of the kind shown in Figure 14.13 in the systems proposal. This chart graphically shows when the project will be completed, and also shows estimates of time required for each analysis and design activity.

PERT charts, as discussed in Chapter 3, are another specialized kind of graph for a more technical audience. It is possible to include a

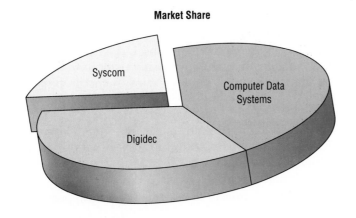

Market Share

FIGURE 14.12
A visually appealing way to display how 100 percent of an entity is divided up at a particular time is a pie chart.

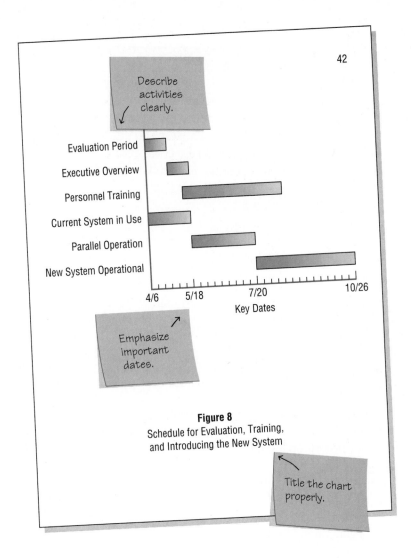

Figure 8
Schedule for Evaluation, Training,
and Introducing the New System

computer-generated PERT chart in the systems proposal appendix to illustrate more precisely the work path that is planned for the systems analysis team. Technical readers reviewing the proposal may use the PERT charts you provide to see if dates for critical activities conflict with other organizational deadlines.

GUIDELINES FOR USING FIGURES IN THE SYSTEMS PROPOSAL. Figures (tables and graphs) can communicate in a way that is not possible in words alone. When preparing the systems proposal, remember to take advantage of the graphs and tables that you are already using for planning purposes. The following guidelines help enhance the systems proposal through the use of figures:

1. Whenever possible, integrate the figure into the body of the proposal itself. The figure may be placed on the page following its first reference. If your first thought is to relegate the figure to an appendix, it may not be important enough to include at all.

2. Always introduce figures in the text before they appear.

Should This Chart Be Barred?

"Gee, I'm glad they hired you guys, I know the Redwings will be better next season because of you. My job'll be a lot easier, too," says Andy Skors, ticket manager for the Kitchener, Ontario, hockey team, the Kitchener Redwings. Andy has been working with your systems analysis team on analyzing the systems requirements for computerizing ticket sales.

Recall that when we last heard from the systems analysis team, consisting of Hy Sticking (your leader), Rip Shinpadd, Fiona Wrink, and yourself, you were wrestling with whether to expedite the project and setting team productivity goals (in Consulting Opportunities 3.2 and 3.3, respectively).

Andy is talking with the team about what to include in the systems proposal to make it as persuasive as possible to Redwings' management. "I know they're going to like this chart," Andy continues, "It's a little something I drew up after you asked me all of those questions on past ticket sales, Rip."

Andy hands the bar chart to Rip, who looks at it and suppresses a slight smile. "As long as we have you here Andy, why don't you explain it for us?"

Like a player fresh out of the penalty box, Andy skates smoothly into his narrative of the graph, "Well our ticket sales reached an all-time high in 1990. We

were real crowd pleasers that year. Could've sold seats on the scoreboard if they let me. Unfortunately, ticket sales were at an all-time low in 1994. I mean, we're talking about a disaster. Tickets moved slower than a glacier. I had to convince the players to give tickets away when they made appearances at the shopping mall. Why, just look at this table, it's terrible.

"I think computerizing the ticket sales will help us pick out who our season supporters are. We've got to figure out who they are and get them back. Get them to stick with us. That would be a good goal to shoot for," Andy concludes.

As Andy's presentation finally winds down, Hy looks as if he thought the twenty-minute period would never end. Picking up on his signal, Fiona says, "Thanks for the data, Andy. We'll work on getting them into the report somehow."

As Fiona and Rip head out of the room with Andy, Hy realizes the bench has emptied so he asks you, the fourth team member, to coach Andy on his bar chart by making a list of the problems you see with it. Hy would also like to sketch some alternate ways to graph the data on ticket sales so that a correct and persuasive graph of ticket sales can be included in the systems proposal.

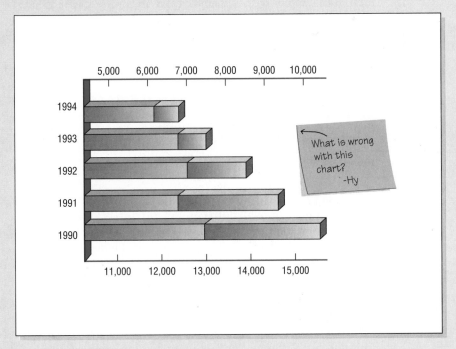

FIGURE 14.C2
An incorrectly drawn graph.

Status	Year	Average tickets sold per game	Season tickets sold per season
Best year	1990	15,643	7,505
	1991	14,880	6,808
	1993	13,254	6,735
Worst year	1994	12,690	6,351

3. Always interpret figures in words; never leave them to stand on their own.

4. Title all figures, label each axis, and provide legends where necessary.

5. Use more that one figure if necessary, so that the point you make is clear and figures are uncluttered.

This has been a cursory glance at using tables and graphs to help you make a point within the systems proposal. For a more detailed, in-depth discussion of the use of figures, see Chapter 15 on designing effective output.

Adopting a Unifying Proposal Style

VISUAL AND FORMATTING CONSIDERATIONS. Proposals are persuasive documents. All the best arguments for proceeding in a specific way are brought to the fore when writing the systems proposal. By the same token, the proposal must be visually persuasive. Content and style go hand in hand, and neglecting this relationship only defeats the proposal's purpose. Figure 14.14 shows how visual elements can be used to offset the written material.

Use of white space. White space distributed throughout the text of the systems proposal helps to set off ideas, assuring that they will be noticed. Write concisely so that white space can be used without bloating the proposal to an overly long document. Leave margins of one inch at the top, bottom, left, and right of each page. Leave one and a half inches if you intend to bind the left side. Double-space the entire report.

Use of headings and subheadings. Use of headings and subheadings is critical, especially if the proposal is long. Headings set apart each section and point the reader to a main section. If imaginatively written, headings help readers to follow the logic of the writing and maintain interest. Subheadings function in much the same way, but refer to more specific points. When taken altogether, headings and subheadings should provide a useful and instructive outline of the entire proposal.

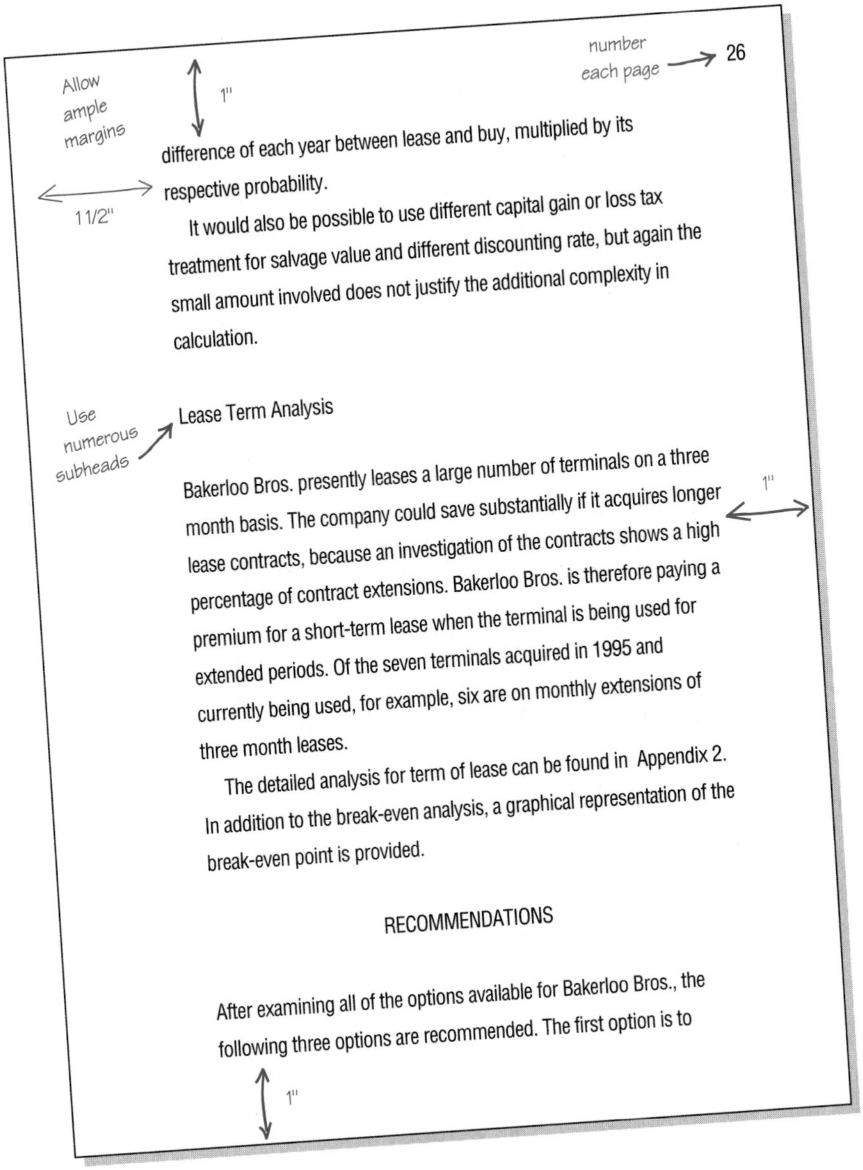

FIGURE 14.14
Guidelines for using visual
elements to enhance the content of the systems proposal.

number
each page → 26

Allow
ample
margins

1"

1 1/2"

difference of each year between lease and buy, multiplied by its

respective probability.

It would also be possible to use different capital gain or loss tax

treatment for salvage value and different discounting rate, but again the

small amount involved does not justify the additional complexity in

calculation.

Use
numerous
subheads

Lease Term Analysis

Bakerloo Bros. presently leases a large number of terminals on a three

month basis. The company could save substantially if it acquires longer

1"

lease contracts, because an investigation of the contracts shows a high

percentage of contract extensions. Bakerloo Bros. is therefore paying a

premium for a short-term lease when the terminal is being used for

extended periods. Of the seven terminals acquired in 1995 and

currently being used, for example, six are on monthly extensions of

three month leases.

The detailed analysis for term of lease can be found in Appendix 2.

In addition to the break-even analysis, a graphical representation of the

break-even point is provided.

RECOMMENDATIONS

After examining all of the options available for Bakerloo Bros., the

following three options are recommended. The first option is to

1"

Headings can be set off in many ways to alert readers typographically to a change in sections. Common methods are using all capital letters, centering, indenting, underlining, bold and double-strike printing, or any combination of these.

Headings and subheadings should be distinguishable from each other not only by content, but by placement on the page or by use of one of the other treatments previously listed. For headings and subheadings to be effective, the analyst must be consistent in their use throughout the proposal. Follow a style manual or employ a personal style, but be consistent in its application to maximize the impact of headings and subheadings.

Page numbering. It is important to number every page, since page numbers are the quickest way for readers to find their places. Page numbers can be in four places: either in the right-hand corner of the page; alternating left and right-hand corners if material is printed back-to-back and bound; at the bottom of the page; or at the top of the page. Whichever position you choose, be consistent. Page numbers of proposal pages on which major headings occur should be listed in the table of contents.

References and appendices. Keeping references to external support materials to a minimum is appreciated by most organizational audiences who will read the systems proposal. If necessary, you may include references, double-spaced and in consistent format, at the end of your report.

Proposal readers are usually of diverse organizational interests. If the proposal seeks to address technical as well as other users, the addition of appendices including technical specifications may be wise. A separate, more detailed proposal addressing technical concerns is also an option, although time costs must be considered before too much custom tailoring is done on the proposal.

You should request times to present the systems proposal orally. These occasions are excellent opportunities to sell your ideas and the system, as well as to answer any questions that arise. Oral presentations help you to retain your visibility in the organization, and they are essential.

PRESENTING THE SYSTEMS PROPOSAL

The topic of the presentation is obviously the systems proposal itself (or some part of it). The next considerations include who will compose the audience for the presentation and how to organize, support, and deliver the oral presentation. All of these areas are interrelated, but for the sake of clarity we will begin by examining each separately.

Understanding the Audience

Just as the audience for the written proposal helps dictate writing style, level of detail, the type of figures, the audience for the oral presentation helps the speaker discover how formal to be, what to present, and what types of visual aids to include. It is imperative that you know *who* you will be addressing.

Organizing the Systems Proposal Presentation

Page through the data collected from the organization that is summarized in the written proposal. Find four to six main points that capsulize the proposal. In particular, check the executive summary, the recommendation sections, and the proposal summary. If the time allotted for the oral presentation is longer than half an hour, main points can be expanded to nine or more. However, for most brief oral presentations, four to six main points are all that can be absorbed by the listener.

Each main point of the oral report needs support to back up any assertions that are made. It is incorrect to assert a main point and not justify it. There are many options for supporting main points. They include examples, illustrations, quotations of testimony or authority, and statistics.

PLANNING THE INTRODUCTION AND CONCLUSION. Once main points and supporting points are worked out, an introduction and conclusion can be written. Notice that writing of the introduction comes last, not first. That is because the introduction should preview the proposal's four to six main points, which are impossible to determine at the outset. The preview cues the audience to listen for what is coming up.

Manufacturer	Product
Aldus	Persuasion
Lotus Corporation	Freelance Graphics
Micrografx	Charisma
Microsoft Corporation	PowerPoint
Software Publishing	Harvard Graphics
WordPerfect Corporation	WordPerfect Presentations

FIGURE 14.15
Slide presentation packages permit users to choose a template style, format and insert text, and include graphics and video.

The introduction should also include a "hook," something that will get the audience intrigued with what is coming next. This should be a creative approach to the proposal that directly unites the audience's interests with the new material being presented. For example, an anecdote, an analogy, a quotation, poetry, or even a joke can open a presentation successfully, while avoiding a dull or trite beginning. If humor is used, it should be directly relevant to the topic, and should make a point for the analyst about what is coming up.

As noted before, the introduction and conclusion for an oral presentation are written in parallel. Recall that this approach is similar to the way the executive summary and proposal summary are handled for the written proposal. The reason for this is that conclusions should mirror introductions. Conclusions should review main points in a manner similar to the introduction's preview. The analyst shouldn't quote verbatim from the introduction, but the main ideas should be reiterated, and a closing thought (similar to the creative hook of the introduction) should be given. For instance, if you began with analogizing the growth of a system with the way a plant grows, return to the analogy for the close. The definite closure provided is reasonable and satisfying to the audience.

FIELDING QUESTIONS. Questions can be taken either during or after the presentation. Answering questions during the presentation itself makes for a more informal, relaxed meeting. However, if there is a serious challenge, it could derail the proposal prematurely. In order to maintain control and communicate your points effectively, it is permissible to request that questions be saved until the end.

USING VISUALS. Visuals used in an oral presentation function similarly to figures in the written proposal—they supplement and enliven material. Consider enlarging some of the key figures from the proposal for use in the presentation. Visuals should be as professional-looking as possible (if an artist is available to create visuals for you, all the better). All printing on visuals should be uniform and legible from anywhere in the audience. For this occasion, visuals should be prepared ahead of time, not drawn while you are speaking.

Use PC-based packages to produce visuals for your presentation and report. A list of selected PC packages can be found in Figure 14.15. Now there are services that make high-resolution slides and overheads from text and graphics produced on microcomputers. One such company is Magicorp. You can draw a diagram in Micrografx Designer or some other graphics package, transmit it via modem, and Magicorp will produce and send out the 35 mm slide within the same day.

Practice using visuals so that any ineptness with the equipment doesn't become the focus of the audience's attention. Make sure that necessary display equipment will be available on the day of your presentation. Remember to look directly at the audience, not at the visual, when you speak.

Taking a PC into the Presentation. One of the most effective visuals you can use is a VDT display powered by a portable PC. If you are building a microcomputer system, this is doubly true.

There are some logistics to be aware of when taking a PC into the proposal meeting. If possible, try to use a large-screen projector system so that everyone in the room is able to see the VDT display at the same time. If this is not possible, use of multiple PCs and accompanying VDTs should be considered. No more than five onlookers to a VDT screen is a useful heuristic.

Microcomputers are valuable for presenting the slide shows discussed previously, as well as spreadsheets with "what-if" capability. For example, "What if the interest rate drops dramatically? How will that affect the payback period?" A PC and a properly set up spreadsheet can allow decision makers to entertain numerous "what-if" scenarios during the meeting itself.

The system that you are proposing may involve PCs. In this instance, microcomputers can act as a prototype, and users and decision makers in the meeting will be provided with an early, concrete realization of the system to come. Do not hesitate to let people other than the presenters use the computer. In our experience, this has worked very well; even people lacking computer experience have found it appealing.

On the other hand, do not put the entire burden of your systems presentation on the microcomputer. Even if you take a PC into the presentation, you will still need to explain what you are doing. Also, things can and do go wrong. You must plan a backup method for presenting material just in case you encounter software or hardware problems that are not solvable on the spot.

Systems analysts can also make presentations go smoothly by using professional hypermedia programs such as HyperWriter by Ntergaid. Hypermedia allows the audience to explore certain areas more deeply. Hypermedia can also be used for tutorials and training later on.

Now that audiences, supporting materials, and visuals have been discussed, we turn to oral delivery of the systems proposal. This is where the systems presentation departs radically from the written systems proposal.

Using Presentation in Graphics Packages

One of the most exciting ways to present your systems proposal is to make a slide show using a presentation software package such as Freelance Graphics for Windows by Lotus. An easy to use, professional-looking template called SmartMasters includes an icon and a way to organize text on the slide (a bulleted list or other designation). Figure 14.16 is an example of a beginning slide for a presentation that the user is making to update the audience with new information.

Basically, you are asked to choose a look for your presentation from among several professionally designed templates. Notice that in our example, the user has chosen a notebook template that makes it look as if the

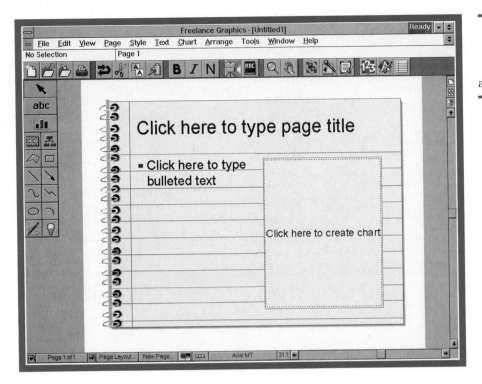

FIGURE 14.16
Use any of the thousands of
library clip art available to
enliven slide presentations
and reinforce your key points.

information is displayed on a spiral-bound notebook page. Color can also be added to support this effect. The choice of a notebook template is appropriate to a rather informal, educational presentation.

The next step in creating a slide show is to select page layout from the multiple choices of professionally designed templates. In our example, a bulleted list with a chart has been chosen. The user could also have chosen a numbered list or one of many other format options. The next step is to fill in the content of the presentation for each slide. Notice that you can add a graphic or clip art to the slide. If you use a program such as Charisma, you can even add a video clip to enhance your presentation.

In Figure 14.17 the user has chosen a different template and then included three different pieces of library clip art to reinforce the points being made in the text. Notice that a variety of interesting and engaging clipboard art is available to users. Remember to choose images that help to creatively enliven what you are trying to communicate. If you have CD-ROM capability, your choices and the combinations you can create are virtually limitless, since the clip art library discs that are purchased with software can include over 12,000 images, symbols, and fonts.

Using the slide software presentation package to create your talk permits you to rearrange the order of your presentation, as shown in Figure 14.18. This becomes important if you want to tailor your presentation to suit different audiences. Additionally, you may want to add or delete slides to shorten or expand the time it takes to present your talk, depending on time constraints for your meeting. A page of thumbnail views of the slides can be printed, copied, and distributed to audience members after your talk to serve as notes of your presentation. For legibility—and to leave room for additional audience members' notes—limit the number of slide images per page to half a dozen or so for thumbnail views. If views are too small, they will not be readable.

FIGURE 14.17
Use color to make your slideshow charts more understandable. In this example, drawn using Lotus Corporation's Freelance Graphics, a key is included to help the audience distinguish among three treatments.

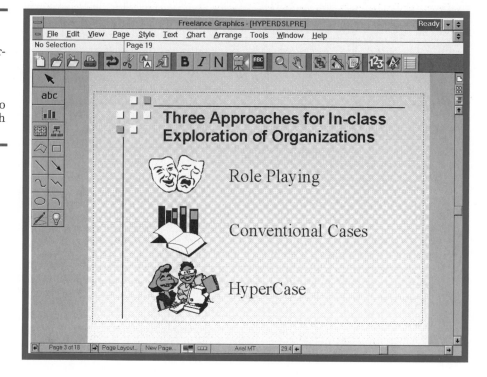

In the lower left-hand corner of this example, you can see that users have the option of taking advantage of multimedia capabilities by including sound in their slideshow. Again, use your creativity to employ sound in a memorable way. For example, launching a new project may call for the sound of a rocket blast-off countdown or the sound of the blast-off itself. Music and, in some cases, full-motion video can be used to highlight a presentation as well.

FIGURE 14.18
Rearrange the order of your slide presentation to suit a specific audience or to compress or expand the time it takes to present your talk. The lower right-hand corner of the screen shows an option for taking advantage of multimedia capabilities by including sound in your slideshow.

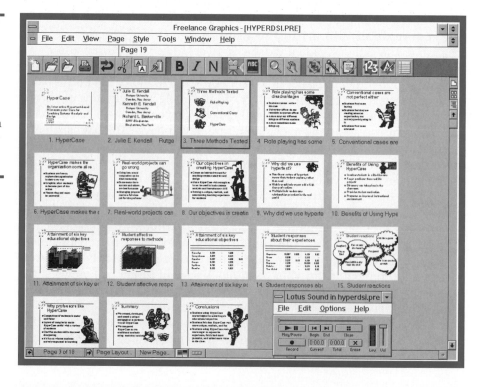

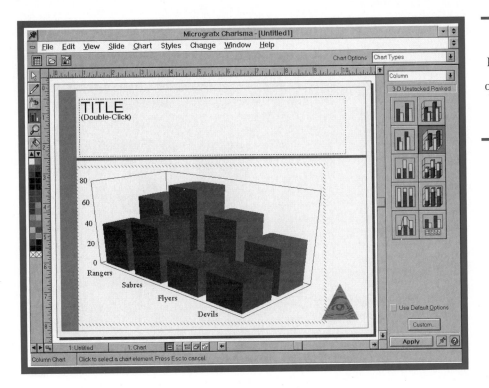

All of the material you have learned about graphics and graphical displays can be put to use with the help of a presentation package such as Micrografx Charisma. Remember to include charts and graphs in your slideshow where appropriate. They are easy to do and make your point nicely, with meaningful graphics, when words just cannot say it all. In Figure 14.19, the user has chosen a type of bar chart to show a relationship among four sports teams. Notice that on the right-hand side of the screen ten charting options are graphically previewed. The chart can be labeled, and each axis can be labeled as well. Additionally, the user can add color or shading to help the audience distinguish among columns.

Sometimes you will address a more technical audience, who will need to see precise views of material. When that is the case, you can use a package such as Micrografx Designer, which permits you to do three-dimensional drawing. Notice that in Figure 14.20 Micrografx Designer has been used to add dimension and detail to the objects portrayed by permitting the user to specify from which direction the light source falls. The overall effect is not only very pleasing, but helpful in ensuring that your points will be clearly made.

There are a few guidelines to follow when creating a slideshow. Though many of the design lessons you will learn in Chapters 15 and 16 will be helpful, some criteria are unique to this situation. When creating a slideshow, remember to:

1. Use the templates provided by most packages for a well-designed, consistent effect as well as to save time.

2. Use a combination of graphics and text to communicate. Data can be charted in many different ways for effective display. Fonts and font sizes should be chosen for readability and appropriateness.

FIGURE 14.20
When more precise 3-D drawings are required or when you are addressing a technical audience, use a package such as Micrografx Designer to add dimension and detail to the objects portrayed.

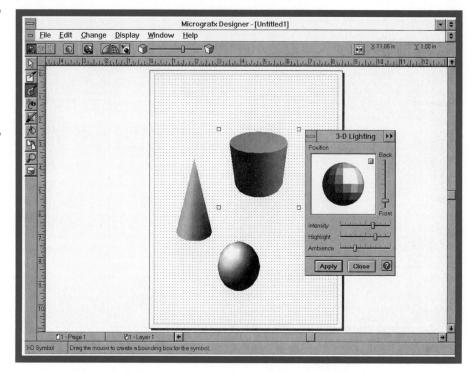

3. Keep a clean look to each slide and guard against clutter. Include no more than five key points per slide.

4. Use color in a meaningful way. Provide a color key for complicated visuals such as charts.

5. Use clip art with text to add humor and reinforce your points.

6. Use sound to help reinforce the points of your presentation. Judicious use of sound will help your audience recall your talk.

7. Take a multimedia approach to your presentation, integrating slides, video, and sound via hypermedia to communicate in a memorable way.

Using presentation software to create a slideshow results in an interesting, consistent, and easy-to-follow presentation with many potential uses. Save the slides you create on disk because they can be presented and used in many different ways. Presentation options include showing the slides on a single monitor; projecting them to a group via projection hardware and creating a multimedia show; or printing them out to create overhead transparencies or audience notes (four to eight per page). Many speakers like to use a combination approach, perhaps projecting their slideshow and then reinforcing it with an audience handout. You may want to include copies of the presentation charts you have created in the systems proposal document itself.

Principles of Delivery

Knowing who is in the audience will tell the analyst how formal to make the presentation. If the chief executive officer is included in the meeting, chances are it will be quite formal. If primary users, rather than executives, compose the audience, perhaps a less formal, workshop-type presentation will be more appropriate.

FIGURE 14.21
Guidelines for the effective
oral delivery of the
systems proposal.

One of the best ways to gauge the formality of presentations is by observing many different organizational meetings prior to the systems proposal presentation. This helps in understanding implicit organizational expectations. Expectations are usually based on customs and culture, and may dictate that every presenter must use an overhead projector, show professionally made 35mm slides, or provide an outline of his or her remarks. Although these customs may not be articulated by organizational members, observing them may be important to whether a presentation is judged to be successful.

The rules for delivery, shown in Figure 14.21, are basic:

1. Project loud enough so that the audience can hear you.
2. Look at each person in the audience as you speak.
3. Make visuals large enough so that the audience can see them.
4. Use gestures that are natural to your conversational style.
5. Introduce and conclude your talk confidently.

The very thought of getting up in front of people can make presenters extremely nervous—in fact, the greatest fear of males is said to be public speaking (it's the second greatest fear of females). Four guidelines that can help presenters overcome anxiety are: (1) be yourself; (2) be prepared; (3) speak naturally (do not memorize or read); and (4) breath deeply before your presentation. Each of these guidelines is discussed in the upcoming sections.

THE FIRST GUIDELINE: BE YOURSELF. "Be yourself" means that the persona of the speaker is very important in persuading an audience. Presenters need to develop themselves in all aspects of personality—intellectually, emotionally, spiritually. The ancient Greeks held to the idea that speakers had to earn the right to address the audience through development of a complete self.

Modern audiences may not seem as demanding, and yet a fully developed personality puts the presenter in an excellent position to cope with any contingencies of the speaking situation, such as challenging questioners, taking unfavorable stands, or something as mundane as overcoming faulty equipment. It is also a great source of insight when attempting to put a creative twist on uninspiring material.

THE SECOND GUIDELINE: BE PREPARED. Being prepared means that the more thoroughly the analyst knows his or her material, the easier it will be to deliver it. One excellent speaker we know goes on what she calls "automatic pilot." She admits to paralyzing stage fright, but overcomes it by thoroughly knowing her main points. When presenting, she seemingly allows her subconscious to deliver her well-prepared talk. This translates into the necessity of adequate rehearsal time for presenters. Few, if any, speakers are so gifted as to be able to ad lib a talk. Being prepared gives speakers confidence that they do indeed have something important to tell the audience and that they will do anything (including overcoming anxiety) to communicate with them.

THE THIRD GUIDELINE: SPEAK NATURALLY. Speaking naturally, not memorizing or reading, may seem antithetical to being prepared since a speaker reading from a prepared text has little risk of departing from his or her key points. However, reading destroys speaker credibility by taking away opportunities for vital eye contact. Memorizing a talk lessens chances for successfully adapting to a particular audience. And when a speaker loses his or her place in a memorized talk, it is nearly impossible to recover gracefully. Those who memorize their talks tend to concentrate on getting the presentation letter perfect rather than on communicating the content. Analysts who memorize or read their presentations are in danger of losing an audience's interest very rapidly.

Instead of reading or memorizing, know your five or six key points very well. Be confident that you have a message to deliver, and know what it is. Know what support materials accompany each main point, but do not write them out. If time is short, or if the audience is different than you had expected, you can change your supporting material on the spot and still communicate key points. The notes for your oral presentation should be limited to an easily readable listing of main points, perhaps with a symbol to indicate when to show a visual. Short notes prevent speakers from falling into the trap of reading if they become nervous.

THE FOURTH GUIDELINE: REMEMBER TO BREATHE. Reminding the presenter to breathe is meant to be only slightly facetious, since we breathe without even considering it. However, an excellent way to achieve a strong speaking voice is to become aware of the breathing process. Take long, deep breaths immediately before addressing the group. Allow yourself to breathe between sentences and during normal pauses in your speaking. It is physiologically impossible to breathe deeply and still be nervous.

SUMMARY

The systems analyst has three main steps to follow for putting together an effective systems proposal: functionally organizing the proposal content, writing the proposal in an appropriate business style, and orally presenting an informative systems proposal. Since the proposal is the embodiment of the work that has been done thus far and the proposed effort, it is a critical document for selling the system. To be effective, the proposal should be written in a clear and understandable manner, and its content should be divided into ten functional sections. It should have an appropriate title that catches the interest of readers and clearly portrays what is forthcoming. The proposal should feature an executive summary that offers a concise overview of the systems project and analysts' recommendations.

Visual considerations are important when putting together a proposal that communicates well. Use enough white space to set off text; be generous when including headings and subheadings; number all pages; and keep references and appendices to a minimum.

Much of what is important in the systems proposal can be enhanced through the correct use of figures, including tables and graphs. Graphs compare two or more variables over time or at a particular point in time. Figures are always accompanied with a written interpretation in the proposal. The graphs and tables used for planning prior to the proposal can be incorporated into it when relevant.

The oral presentation of the system is based on the written proposal and is another way of effectively selling the system. One option for presentation

"I know it's hard to get your feet wet, but you've been here long enough that we're all curious about what you've come up with so far. We're especially interested in what you think of us! Are we one big happy family or is this a zoo? Seriously, Snowden would like it very much if you gave a brief oral presentation of a preliminary proposal for a new automated project reporting system for the Training Group. Who should we include? Well, Mr. Torrey, Dan Hill, Tom Ketcham, and Snowden, of course, will want to be there. Let's see . . . I've got the executive calendar on the screen here. Everyone we need is free a week from Thursday at 3:00. You can bring your whole team along if you want. That room has multimedia capabilities, if you want to get fancy, but keep it to about 15 minutes at the most. Oh, one more thing, I'm sure Mr. Hyatt will want to come. Have fun!"

HYPERCASE QUESTIONS

1. Prepare an outline of the preliminary proposal for a new automated project reporting system for the Training Group. Include enough detail so that it would be possible to use your outline as speaking notes during a presentation.

2. Use a software package such as Freelance Graphics by Lotus Corporation to create a short (3–5 slides) slideshow to illustrate the preliminary proposal for the automated project reporting system you outlined in problem 1.

3. Have your teammates role play the parts of Warren Torrey, Dan Hill, Tom Ketcham, and Snowden Evans (the part of Mr. Hyatt is optional). Present your brief preliminary proposal for the new automated project reporting system to them. Use the slideshow you have created for problem 2.

4. Write a two-paragraph report based on feedback received on the preliminary proposal during the role playing in problem 3. What questions arose? What changes will you make?

is to create a slideshow using presentation software. Also, graphics presentation packages and clip art can be used to enhance visual presentation of the systems proposal. In order to give a strong oral presentation, the analyst should know four elements ahead of time: who will compose the audience; the topic (presumably the systems proposal or some part of it); time allotted for the presentation; and equipment available (including room setup). All four elements are interrelated, and each needs to be thought through and planned to ensure success.

KEYWORDS AND PHRASES

systems proposal	bar charts
executive summary	pie charts
analysts' recommendations	oral presentation
line graphs	visuals
column charts	principles of delivery

REVIEW QUESTIONS

1. What are the three steps the systems analyst must follow to put together an effective systems proposal?
2. List the ten main sections of the systems proposal.
3. Which sections of the systems proposal should include the solution the analyst thinks is *most* workable?
4. What relationships does a line graph depict?
5. What relationships does a column chart depict?
6. What relationships does a bar graph depict?
7. What relationships does a pie chart depict?
8. List the five guidelines for using figures effectively in the systems proposal.
9. What purpose do headings and subheadings serve in the written systems proposal?
10. What sort of support material should be included in an oral presentation of the systems proposal to executive audiences?
11. When should the introduction for an oral presentation of the systems proposal be written?
12. How can a microcomputer be used as a visual aid in an oral presentation of the systems proposal?
13. List the seven guidelines for creating a slideshow on your computer.
14. List the five rules for effective oral delivery of the systems proposal.

PROBLEMS

1. "I think it's only fair to write up *all* of the alternatives you've considered," says Lou Cite, a personnel supervisor for Day-Glow Paints. "After all, you've been working on this systems thing for a while now, and I think my boss and everyone else would be interested to see what you've found out." You are talking with Lou as you prepare to put together the final systems proposal that your team will be presenting to upper management.

    a. In a paragraph, explain to Lou why your proposal will not (and should not) contain all of the alternatives that your team has considered.

    b. In a paragraph, discuss the sorts of alternatives that should appear in the final systems proposal.

2. In going over the data you have collected for your proposal for Linder's Machine Parts, of Duluth, Minnesota, you find a forecast of demand for parts for the next five years, as well as the forecast of the number of companies purchasing parts. You would like to include the data in your systems proposal to help support the need for a new system and the numbers currently given in this narrative are: "The columns show that demand of 120,000 will increase to 130,000 in year 2, go up 20,000 in year 3, go up 40,000 in year 4, and level off in year 5. Although demand for parts will be going up, the total number of companies who will be buying will be down from 700 in year 1 by 50 companies each year through the next five years."

    a. Based on the narrative, draw a bar graph to depict demand over the next five years for Linder's Machine Parts.

b. Based on the narrative, draw a column chart to depict demand over the next five years for Linder's Machine Parts.

c. Based on the narrative, draw a bar graph to show the decline in total number of companies ordering machine parts from Linder's.

d. Based on the narrative, draw a line graph to depict the increase in demand and the decrease in total number of companies purchasing parts together.

3. "I was thinking of how I'll handle my portion of the presentation to management," says Margaret, a member of your systems analysis team. "Even though some of them told us the 'haven't been keeping up with computers,' I think they need to know the technical aspects of our recommended system inside and out, otherwise they may not accept it. So I'll begin by defining basic terms like 'byte' and 'program code,' and then turn the meeting into a short tutorial on computing. What do you think?"

a. In a paragraph, critique Margaret's approach to the systems proposal presentation to the executive audience.

b. In a paragraph, suggest a different way to approach the executive audience for the systems proposal presentation. Be sure to include types of support, as well as topics, that would be more appropriate than what Margaret has in mind.

SELECTED BIBLIOGRAPHY

Di Salvo, V. S. *Business and Professional Communication*. Columbus: Charles E. Merrill Publishing Company, 1976.

Himstreet, W. C., and W. M. Baty. *Business Communication Principles and Methods*, 6th ed. Boston: Kent Publishing Company, 1981.

Lewis, P. V., and W. H. Baker. *Business Report Writing*. Columbus: Grid, Inc., 1978.

Stefik, M., G. Foster, D. G. Bobrow, K. Kahn, S. Lanning and L. Suchman. "Beyond the Chalkboard: Computer Support for Collaboration and Problem Solving in Meetings." *Communications of the ACM*, Vol. 30, no. 1, January 1987, pp 32–47.

"That completes the list," Anna says. "I've contacted each user of the system as well as management. The presentation meeting for the proposed new microcomputer system is scheduled for 10 A.M. next Tuesday. We have most of the materials ready, so let's put the finishing touches on the documentation."

Chip looks up from the task of creating an executive summary. "It seems hard to believe that we're almost finished with the analysis stage. I'm a little apprehensive about the meeting. I hope everything goes well."

"I'm sure it will," Anna says reassuringly. "We've been thorough in our analysis, and the proposal seems to be coming along nicely too."

Chip completes the executive summary, shown in Figure E14.1. This is the document that gives an overview of the nature of the system and the recommended solution. After completing the executive summary, he proceeds to create the outline of the study. This document, shown in Figure E14.2, is another summary, since many of the persons reviewing the proposal have been involved in the interviews and prototypes. It provides a concise review of the methods that have been used in analyzing the needs of the microcomputer system.

Meanwhile, Anna was working on polishing the results section of the analysis, called the *problem definition*. Earlier in the analysis, she had taken information from the interviews, survey, and prototypes and produced ten concise points reflecting system needs. These points had been reviewed by the users and modified with minor changes to clarify them. Each user was then requested to rank the issues on relative importance, using a scale from one to ten. These final ranks were then averaged to become weights, indicating overall importance. The completed problem definition is shown in Figure E14.3.

Alternatives for the proposed system have already been created and evaluated (refer to Chapter 12). The recommended solution is a microcomputer local area network.

"We should include information showing how we are going to evaluate the installed system," Chip says. "How do you feel we should create evaluation criteria?"

"Well . . ." Anna replies thoughtfully, "perhaps we should restate the objectives in more concise terms. The original objectives were broadly stated, allowing us to be more flexible and creative in our choice of solutions. The new objectives would be measurable, describing deliverables: the specific screens, reports, and other products of system development."

Chip and Anna work together to develop the measurable objectives. They start with the first objective and work down the list, point by point. Following are the broadly stated objectives:

1. Provide software/hardware cross-reference.
2. Maintain complete microcomputer information.
3. Automate software installation procedure.
4. Provide information on software upgrade installation by machine.

Allen Schmidt,
Julie E. Kendall, and
Kenneth E. Kendall

Microcomputer System Proposal
Executive Summary

The system for managing microcomputer hardware and software is inadequate for the current level of devices and software packages. The designers of the original system, installed in the early 1980's, could not foresee the rapid development of products culminating in the tremendous variety presently available.

Analysts Anna Liszt and Chip Puller have conducted extensive interviews with system users. Persons interviewed include Mike Crowe, Dot Matricks, Hy Perteks, Paige Prynter, and Cher Ware. The problems determined from these interviews include missing information and a lack of cross-referencing hardware and software information. As software and hardware demands escalate in the future, this lack of information will result in an increase in redundant information and a duplication of costly services.

We recommend a Microcomputer System with a local area network linking all parties involved in the system. Menu screens will allow users to select options to update hardware and software information. Reports will be periodically produced and a variety of inquiry screens made available.

Additional benefits include improved cost information, automating the preventive maintenance scheduling, ease of updating software versions, and improved techniques for performing physical device inventory.

Programs and data will be secured by requiring users to enter a user identification number and password. The user ID will further control who has access to the various system functions: update, report generation, or inquiry.

Training sessions will be conducted prior to final installation of the Microcomputer System. It is recommended that at least two persons should be trained for each system aspect.

The estimated completion date is August 19, 1995. The estimated time for development is 8 person months at an expense of $50,000. Hardware expenditures should not exceed $15,000.

FIGURE E14.1
Executive Summary.

5. Provide preventive and other maintenance information.
6. Maintain up-to-date, accurate software information.
7. Provide complete cost information for microcomputer hardware.
8. Provide information on the cost to upgrade software.
9. Design a process for performing accurate and efficient physical microcomputer inventory.
10. Maintain and provide training and software expert information.

"How do you think we can restate, 'Provide software/hardware cross-reference' as a measurable objective?" asks Chip.

"Let's look at the data flow diagrams, data dictionary records, and prototypes to review how we plan to provide the cross-reference information," responds Anna. "How about 'Provide a software inquiry listing the

Microcomputer System Proposal
Outline of Systems Study

The Microcomputer System has been thoroughly investigated using a series of interviews, examination of memos, a survey of the faculty and staff, and a series of prototype screens and reports.

The memos examined included a period from July through August of 1994. These provided initial information on the nature of the problems inherent in the current system.

A series of initial and follow-up interviews was conducted with the following individuals: Mike Crowe, Microcomputer Specialist; Dot Matricks, Manager of Microcomputer Systems; Hy Perteks, Information Center Director; Paige Prynter, Financial Analyst, and Cher Ware, Software Specialist.

The results of the interviews became the basis of a questionnaire administered to the faculty and research staff. This confirmed the rapid expansion of microcomputer hardware and software in almost every discipline as well as confirming the need for training.

Prototypes were designed to elicit feedback from system users. These were carefully constructed, demonstrated, and modified based on the comments of users.

FIGURE E14.2
Outline of a systems study.

machine and its location for each copy of the software. Produce hardware/software cross-reference report on demand?"

"Sounds good," says Chip, "The next one, 'Maintain complete microcomputer information,' could be stated as 'Add maintenance, preventive maintenance, boards, cost, and peripheral information to the HARDWARE MASTER file. Create separate online programs for adding, deleting, changing, and modifying maintenance information.'"

Chip and Anna work together to restate the third objective, "Automate software installation procedure," as "Create an online inquiry screen to determine the location of suitable microcomputers. Use the screen to choose locations. Print the location list. Provide automatic update of files after insallation."

Chip takes the completed measurable objectives section and enters it all into Excelerator's **Deliverable** entity. Figure E14.4 is an example of the Deliverable description screen for PROVIDE SOFTWARE/HARDWARE CROSS-REFERENCE REPORT. The description area contains a longer narrative.

A second screen, shown in Figure E14.5, expands the deliverable into detailed components. Listed are the SOFTWARE MASTER and HARDWARE MASTER records, the SOFTWARE/HARDWARE XREF REPORT, and the SOFTWARE LOCATE inquiry screen. The **Assigned To** and **Status** (Not Started, Started, or Complete) are left blank and will be updated after the project has been approved. The bottom half of the screen is reserved for information supplied for those using ABT's Project Workbench software.

The deliverables may be incorporated into the **Work Breakdown Structure** graph, created after approval of the project to determine work

Microcomputer System Proposal
Detailed Results – Problem Definition

The Microcomputer System has become inadequate to handle the current volume of microcomputers, their peripheral devices and software installed upon them. Additional information needs to be added to existing files and there is a lack of cross-referencing software packages installed upon machines.

The Microcomputer Maintenance department has difficulty determining which machines require preventive maintenance and a physical inventory of microcomputers and the peripheral devices is not regularly performed.

Cost information is not accurately maintained or reported.

	Issues–Present Situation	Weight
1.	There is a lack of information about which software is installed on any given microcomputer.	10
2.	Incomplete information is maintained for each microcomputer	9
3.	The present system does not provide microcomputer capacity information used to determine which machine software may be installed upon.	8
4.	There is no method of determining which machines contain software scheduling for an upgrade.	7
5.	Preventive and other maintenance information is not acquired. There is no reliable method for predicting preventive maintenance dates.	7
6.	Software information is missing and out of date, with redundant records for older versions.	6
7.	Cost information is incomplete for microcomputers.	5
8.	Software upgrade cost data is unavailable.	5
9.	The process for performing physical microcomputer inventory is inaccurate and inefficient.	3
10.	There is no method for maintaining training and software expert information.	2

FIGURE E14.3
Problem definition.

assignments and monitor progress. Reports may be produced showing all deliverables that are not complete or not assigned to a programmer or analyst.

Anna works on a presentation graph portraying the microcomputers linked in the network. The finished graph is shown in Figure E14.6. Notice the server with main files in the center, indicating that one centralized database will be maintained.

Tuesday morning finds Chip and Anna in the conference room. Copies of the proposal are neatly placed on the table in front of each seat. The overhead transparencies are arranged in the correct sequence, and all is ready for the presentation.

"I'm feeling a few butterflies in my stomach," murmurs Chip. "Even though I've spoken with all these people before, this is different somehow."

"I'm a little nervous myself," answers Anna. "It's normal to feel that way. But don't worry, we're well prepared and we'll take turns presenting different topics and features."

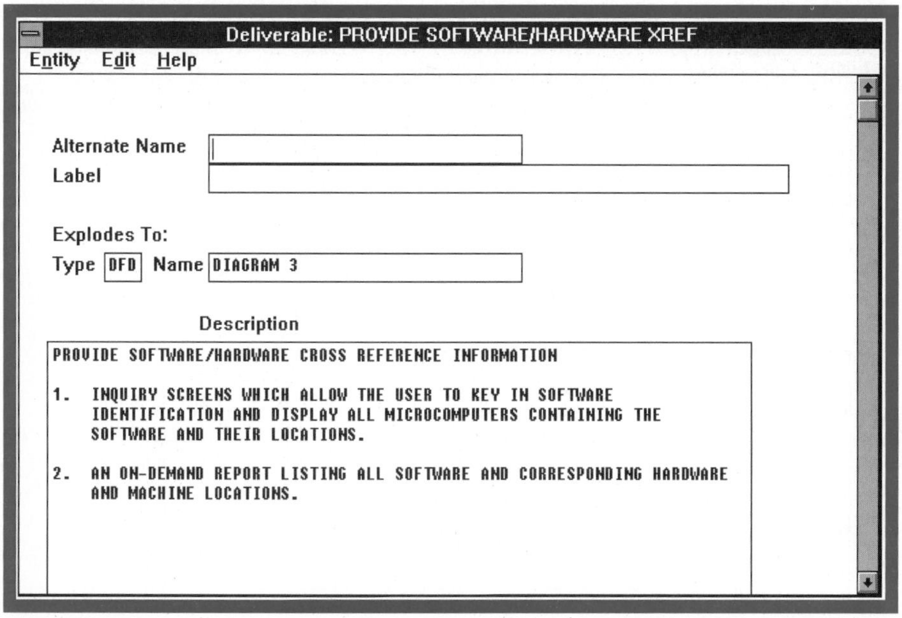

FIGURE E14.4
Deliverable entity, first screen, PROVIDE SOFTWARE/HARDWARE CROSS-REFERENCE.

The users arrive the presentation begins. Anna starts with opening remarks and an introductory summary. Chip takes a deep breath and walks to the front of the room. He gains confidence as he reviews some of the problems and displays the graphs showing the increase in software and hardware over the past ten years. The audience is listening intently, visibly interested in what he is saying.

The presentation lasts about an hour. User feedback is detailed and enthusiastic. Chip and Anna are delighted when the users unanimously approve their recommendation.

Exercises*

E-1. Rewrite the last seven broadly stated objectives as measurable objectives.

E-2. Use Excelerator to view the PROVIDE SOFTWARE/HARDWARE XREF deliverable.

E-3. Modify and print the COMPLETE MICROCOMPUTER INFO. deliverable. Include the following Deliverable Components on the second screen:

a. REC PERIPHERAL EQUIPMENT

b. REC MICROCOMPUTER MAINTENANCE

c. SCD CHANGE MICRO

d. SCD DELETE MICRO

e. SCD ADD MICRO

---

* The exercises preceded by a disk icon require the program Excelerator (or another CASE tool). A disk is provided free of charge to any professor adopting this book. The examples on the disk may be imported into Excelerator and then used by students.

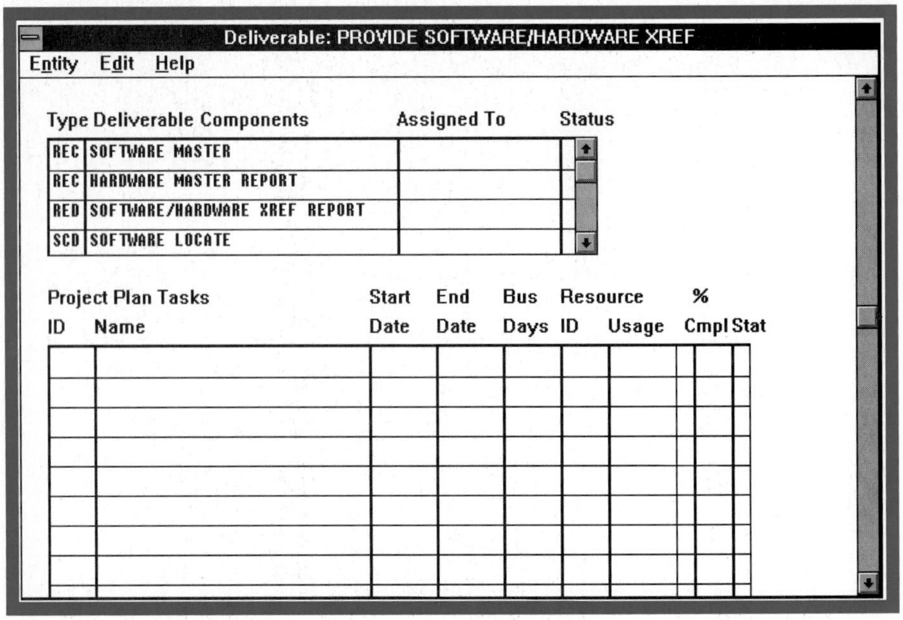

FIGURE E14.5
Deliverable entity, second screen, PROVIDE SOFTWARE/HARDWARE CROSS-REFERENCE.

E-4. Modify and print the AUTOMATE SOFTWARE INSTALLA-TION deliverable. Add the following **Explodes To** information on the first screen: DFD DIAGRAM 4. Include the following Deliverable Components on the second screen:

a. REC SOFTWARE MASTER

b. REC INSTALLED SOFTWARE TRANSACTION

c. SCD CHANGE SOFTWARE

d. SCD MACHINE BY CATEG

e. RED SOFTWARE INSTALLATION LISTING

E-5. Create and print a deliverable entity for the PROVIDE SOFT-WARE UPGRADE INSTALLATION INFORMATION objective. The objective is accomplished by a program to list the machines that will have software upgraded and a screen to automatically upgrade all software records. Upgrade exceptions may be entered on the screen.

The deliverable explodes to the data flow diagram DIAGRAM 10, UPGRADE SOFTWARE. Include the following components:

a. SOFTWARE UPGRADE LISTING report design

b. UPGRADE SOFTWARE screen design

c. SOFTWARE MASTER record

E-6. Create and print the PROVIDE MAINT. INFO. deliverable. It explodes to the data flow diagram, DIAGRAM 5.4, PRINT PERIOD-IC MAINTENANCE REPORT. Include the following components:

a. Report design, PREVENTIVE MAINTENANCE REPORT

b. Report design, PROBLEM MACHINE REPORT

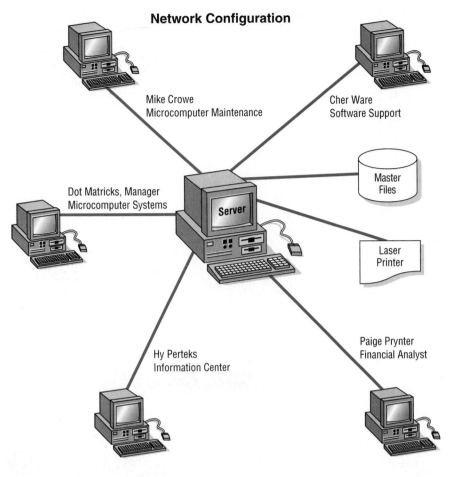

Network Configuration

Mike Crowe
Microcomputer Maintenance

Cher Ware
Software Support

Dot Matricks, Manager
Microcomputer Systems

Server

Master
Files

Laser
Printer

Hy Perteks
Information Center

Paige Prynter
Financial Analyst

FIGURE E14.6
Microcomputer network configuration.

---

        c. Screen design, MAINTENANCE DET.

        d. Screen design, CHANGE MICRO.

E-7. Use Excelerator to view the MICROCOMPUTER GROWTH presentation graph.

E-8. Modify and print the SOFTWARE GROWTH presentation graph. Add diskette symbols to reflect the following total number of software packages for each of the following years:

Year	Cumulative Software Packages
1994	871
1995	1002
1996	1469
1997	2192

E-9. Modify the MICROCOMPUTER CONFIGURATION presentation graph. Include the portable microcomputer that Mike Crowe will use to update records from remote locations.

15

DESIGNING EFFECTIVE OUTPUT

OUTPUT DESIGN OBJECTIVES

Output is information delivered to users through the information system. Some data require extensive processing before they become suitable output; other data are stored, and when they are retrieved, they are considered output with little or no processing. Output can take many forms: the traditional hard copy of printed reports, and soft copy such as VDT screens, microforms, and audio output. Users are reliant on output in order to accomplish their tasks and they often judge the merit of the system solely by its output. In order to create the most useful output possible, the systems analyst works closely with the user through an interactive process until the result is considered to be satisfactory.

Since useful output is essential to ensuring use and acceptance of the information system, there are several objectives that the systems analyst tries to attain when designing output. As shown in Figure 15.1, there are six objectives for output:

1. Design output to serve the intended purpose.
2. Design output to fit the user.
3. Deliver the appropriate quantity of output.
4. Assure that the output is where it is needed.
5. Provide the output on time.
6. Choose the right output method.

Designing Output to Serve the Intended Purpose

All output should have a purpose. It is not enough that a report or screen is made available to users because it is technologically possible to do so. During the information requirements determination phase of analysis, the systems analyst finds out what purposes must be served. Output is then designed based on those purposes.

481

FIGURE 15.1
Six objectives for the
design of output.

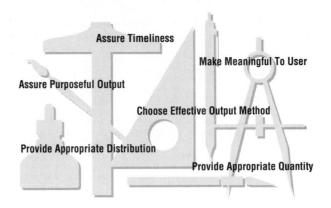

You will see that you have numerous opportunities to supply output simply because the application permits you do so. However, remember the rule of purposiveness. If the output is not functional, it should not be created, since there are costs of time and materials associated with all output from the system.

Designing Output to Fit the User

With a large information system serving many users for many different purposes, it is difficult to personalize output. Based on interviews, observations, cost considerations, and perhaps prototypes, it will be possible to design output that addresses what many, if not all, users need and prefer.

Generally speaking, it is more practical to create user-specific output when designing it for a decision support system or other highly interactive applications. However, it is still possible to design output to fit a user's function in the organization, which leads us to the next objective.

Delivering the Appropriate Quantity of Output

More is not always better, especially where the amount of output is concerned. Part of the task of designing output is deciding what quantity of output is correct for users. You can see that this is a very difficult task, since information requirements are in continuing flux.

A useful heuristic is that the system must provide what each person needs to complete his or her work. However, this is still far from a total solution, since it may be appropriate to display a subset of that information at first and then provide a way for the user to access additional information easily. For example, rather than cluttering a screen with an entire year's sales, each of twelve screens might provide a month's sales with subsequent months and summary information available on separate screens.

The problem of information overload is so prevalent as to have become a cliché, but it remains a valid concern. No one is served if excess information is given only to flaunt the capabilities of the system. Always keep the decision makers in mind when deciding about quantity of output. Often they will not need great amounts of output, especially if there is an easy way to access more.

Making Sure the Output Is Where It Is Needed

Output is printed on paper, displayed on screens, piped over speakers, and stored on microforms. Output is often produced at one location (for example, in the data-processing department) and then distributed to the user.

The increase in on-line, screen-displayed output that is personally accessible has cut down somewhat on the problem of distribution, but appropriate distribution is still an important objective for the systems analyst. To be used and useful, output must be presented to the right user. No matter how well-designed reports are, if they are not seen by the pertinent decision makers they have no value.

Providing the Output on Time

One of the most common complaints of users is that they do not receive information in time to make necessary decisions. The systems analysts' objectives for output are thus compounded. Not only do you have to be conscientious about who is receiving what output, you must also be concerned about the timing of output distribution.

Although timing isn't everything, it does play a large part in how useful output will be to decision makers. By this phase in the systems development life cycle, you have learned what output is necessary, and at what time, to drive each stage of the organization's processes. Many reports are required on a daily basis, some only monthly, others annually, others only by exception. Accurate timing of output can be critical to business operations.

Choosing the Right Output Method

As mentioned earlier, output can take many forms including printed paper reports, information on VDT screens, audio with digitized sounds that simulate the human voice, and microforms. Choosing the right output method for each user is another objective in designing output.

For many people, the term output still conjures up the vision of stacks of paper computer printouts, but this is changing rapidly. With the movement to on-line systems, much output now appears exclusively on display screens. The analyst needs to recognize the tradeoffs involved in choosing an output method. Costs differ, as do the flexibility, life span, distribution, storage and retrieval possibilities, transportability, and overall impact of the data on the user. Choice of output methods is not trivial, nor is it usually a foregone conclusion.

RELATING OUTPUT CONTENT TO OUTPUT METHOD

The content of output from information systems must be considered as interrelated to the output method. Whenever you design output, you need to think of how function influences form and how the intended purpose will influence the output method that you choose.

Output should be thought of in a general way, so that any information put out by the computer system that is useful to people in some way can be considered output. It is possible to conceptualize output as either external (going outside the business) or internal (staying within the business).

External output is familiar to you through utility bills, advertisements, paychecks, annual reports, and myriad other communications that organizations have with their customers, vendors, suppliers, industry, and competitors. Some of this output, such as utility bills, is designed by the systems analyst to serve double duty as a turnaround document. Figure 15.2 is a gas bill that is a turnaround document for the gas company's data processing. In other words, the output for one stage of processing becomes the input for the next. When the customer

FIGURE 15.2
A turnaround document for
Minigasco's data processing.

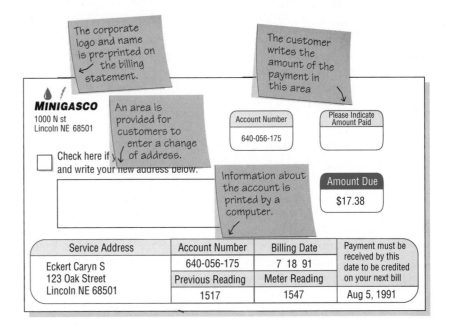

returns the designated portion of the document, it is optically scanned and used as computer input.

External output differs from internal output not only in its distribution, but often in its design and appearance as well. Many external documents must include instructions to the recipient if they are to be used correctly. Additionally, many external outputs are placed on preprinted forms bearing the company logo and corporate colors.

Internal outputs include various reports to decision makers. These range all the way from short summary reports to lengthy, detailed reports. An example of a summary report is a report summarizing monthly sales totals. A detailed report might give weekly sales by salesperson.

Other kinds of internal reports include historical reports that recount an occurrence and exception reports that are output only at the time an exception (a deviation from the expected) occurs. Examples of exception reports are a listing of all employees with no absences for the year; a listing of all salespeople who did *not* meet their monthly sales quota; or a report on consumer complaints made in the last six months.

In this section, different output technologies (the processes whereby output is produced) are covered. In addition, the factors involved in choosing a particular output method are discussed. The effects of different kinds of output on users are then considered. Finally, guidelines are given for presenting output to users.

Choosing Output Technology

Producing different types of output requires use of different technologies. For printed computer output, the options include impact and nonimpact printers. For screen output, the options include attached or stand-alone cathode ray tubes or liquid crystal displays. Audio output can be amplified over a loudspeaker or listened to through small speakers on a PC. Microforms of output are created by specially equipped camera and film in

Output Method	Advantages	Disadvantages
Printer	• Affordable for most organizations • Flexible in types of output, location, and capabilities • Handles large volumes of output • Reaches many inexpensively • Highly reliable with little down time	• May be noisy • Compatibility problems with computer software • May require special, expensive supplies • Still requires some operator intervention • Depending on model may be slow
Specialty Printers (Label makers, envelope printers, etc.)	• Can easily accomplish special tasks that would be difficult on a standard printer • Speeds up the job at hand	• Incurs additional cost of printer and specialty labels • Adds clutter to desks • Cannot be networked
VDT Screen	• Interactive • Works in on-line, real time transmission through widely dispersed network • Quiet • Takes advantage of computer capabilities for movement within databases and files • Good for frequently accessed, ephemeral messages	• Requires cabling and setup space • Still may require printed documentation • Can be expensive if required for many users
Audio Output	• Good for individual user • Good for transient messages that will be acted upon and then discarded • Good where worker needs hands free for other tasks • Good if output is highly repetitive	• Is expensive to develop • Needs dedicated room where output will not interfere with other tasks • Has limited application • Is not yet perfected
Microform	• Handles large volumes of information • Reduces space required for storage • Preserves fragile but frequently used materials • Avoids problems of paging through physically cumbersome reports	• Requires special software for easy accessibility • Needs special equipment for printing hard copy • Can be expensive initial investment
CD-ROM	• Has large capacity • Allows multimedia output • Has speedy retrieval compared to paper and microforms • Is less vulnerable to damage	• Is expensive to develop • Is more difficult to update • Is more difficult to use on a network
Electronic Output (E-mail, faxes, and bulletin boards)	• Reduces Paper • Can be updated very easily • Eliminates "telephone tag" • Can be "broadcast"	• Has generally lower resolution • Is not conducive to formatting (e-mail) • Is difficult to convey context of messages (e-mail)

FIGURE 15.3
A comparison of output methods.

microfiche and microfilm. As you can see, the choices are numerous. Figure 15.3 is a comparison of output methods.

PRINTERS. Since printed reports are still the most common kind of output, it is logical to assume that in any large organization printers are ubiquitous. Although other types of output are gaining popularity, for the foreseeable future it is likely that businesses will still desire printed output.

As a systems analyst, it is up to you to keep current on the available output technology through experience and trade journals. Printers are changing so rapidly that any list of them is outdated the next year. For instance, the nation's largest manufacturer of computers has seventy printers in its printer line alone. However, it is possible to review some general features of printers that are currently available, as well as some trends in the technology.

The trend in printers for mainframe computer systems as well as for personal computers is toward increased flexibility. This translates into expanding the options for the location of the printing site itself; accommodating different numbers of characters per page; numerous type styles and type fonts; changeable positioning of print on the page; more graphics capability (including the use of color); quieter printing; reduction in inventory of preprinted forms; simplified operator tasks; and less overall operator intervention. Even when printers are dedicated to one particular use, vendors are stressing flexibility to facilitate that use.

Together with users, the systems analyst must determine the purpose for the printer. Once this is established, there are three key factors to keep in mind. They are the printer's:

1. Reliability.
2. Compatibility with software and hardware.
3. Manufacturer support.

Reliability means that the printer can be counted upon to do what it was acquired to do over a period of time, with a tolerable amount of repairs. A reliable printer is extremely important when large volumes of materials (such as customer account bills) are being prepared to meet a particular deadline.

Compatibility of the printer with software and hardware is important when you consider that many times systems are modified or networked with other smaller systems. Severe compatibility problems may result in systems not being used at all.

As with the purchase, rental, or leasing of computers themselves, manufacturer support of printers is typically negotiated separately from other agreements. However, it is important that manufacturers be willing to service printers on-site the same day problems occur or to provide reasonable equipment loans while a printer is being repaired.

SPECIALTY PRINTERS. Users have long been plagued by problems with laser printers when attempting to use them to generate labels inexpensively. Mailing labels are some of the most commonly used system output. Recently, a number of new specialty printers dedicated to a single task have been developed. Specialty printers are inexpensive, highly useful desktop technology. High-quality label printers such as CoStar's Label Writer have become immensely popular and accept text from most standard office applications.

Envelopes and mailing labels present another output design opportunity for the analyst. Notice in Figure 15.4 that with specialty technology you can design a desired layout form that will include a bar code and

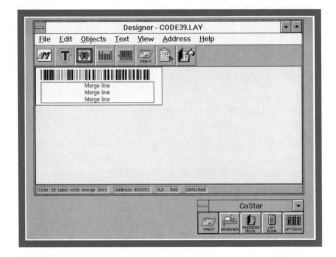

FIGURE 15.4
Creating labels is easy using a
Label Writer II printer and
software from CoStar
Corporation.

merge lines of text from a word processor or most other applications that the user would use routinely. Corporate logos or other meaningful icons can also be added to envelopes and labels. Since addresses and other information are captured directly from the original source, keying errors are prevented. Additionally, expensive printer resources are not tied up with a small job. Disadvantages of this technology include possible proliferation of specialty printers and resulting additional desktop clutter and difficulties in networking them.

SCREENS AS OUTPUT. Screens are an increasingly popular output technology. Once used mostly for data entry, screens are becoming a feasible technology for many other uses as well, as their size and price decrease and their capability with other system components increases.

In addition to their initial equipment cost, screens require adequate and correct cabling to connect to the system, as well as space for their proper positioning at work stations. Even though they resemble printers in this regard, screens have distinct advantages over printers because of their quietness and potential for interactive user participation. In the latter regard, screen output (depending, of course, on systems design) can afford flexibility in allowing the user to change output information in real time either through deletion, addition, or modification. Screens also allow review of stored output via access to and display of items from a relevant database. This permits individual decision makers to move away from storing redundant printouts.

Conversely, screens may provide an ideal output technology for information that is needed only once and that need never be stored. For example, output concerning whether all system terminals are currently in use is pertinent for a user trying to get on the system only in real time. In other words, screen output can be ephemeral, and this fleeting quality works to the user's advantage so that output is obtained, acted upon for a momentary decision, and never used again. In this instance, the message "All terminals are in use, please try the system later" led the user to quit the system and try again later in the workday. In Chapter 18, we discuss another potential drawback—the health concerns recently raised about the soundness of prolonged video display terminal (VDT) use on the job.

AUDIO OUTPUT. In a way, audio output could be thought of as the exact opposite of printed output. Audio output is transient, whereas the printed word is permanent. It is usually output for the benefit of one user, whereas printed output is often widely distributed.

Audio output is interpreted by the human ear as speech, although it is actually produced by discrete digital sounds that are then put together in such a way as to be perceived as continuous words. Telephone systems were among the first businesses to use audio output for customers.

To produce audio output the content for a particular application must be determined first; then a vocabulary is recorded and then translated into digital signals that are stored. When a user interfaces with the computer an appropriate response is located in memory and sent over the audio output device for the user to hear.

The systems designer needs to be aware of the value of sound output. Programs such as Wired for Sound, by Aristosoft, Inc., are useful to the personal computer user because verbal confirmation sometimes allows a user to work more quickly and with more confidence. Sound also gives the user time cues (Talking Clock), verbal confirmation of typing (Talking Calculator), and verbal confirmation when deleting files (Talking Graveyard). Even a simple confirmation of "OK" and "Cancel" is sometimes useful.

Sound can also enhance a presentation. Public domain music and sound effects are readily available. Presentation packages like Freelance Graphics (Lotus Corp.) and Charisma (Micrografx) allow users to insert sound—Charisma even allows videos to be inserted. Sound files come in various formats, but one of the most common for the IBM compatible is the .WAV files that can be played in Microsoft Windows. These .WAV files can be obtained from various bulletin boards and are also available on CD-ROM.

Even speech synthesis has come to the personal computer, making it possible to proof a document or spreadsheet by listening to the words as well as reading them on paper. A sound board and programs such as Monologue make it possible to accomplish these and other sound output options.

Audio output is being used to "staff" toll-free catalog numbers twenty-four hours a day. By using a digital phone, consumers can call the number, and in response to instructions via audio output, enter the item number, quantity, price, and their credit card number. This means that stores are capturing sales that would otherwise be missed, since hiring actual employees might be too expensive to justify offering a twenty-four-hour number.

MICROFORMS. Microforms, including microfilm and microfiche (a sheet of microfilm), are ways to store large volumes of information in approximately one percent of the space that the printed material would take. Microforms are ideal for large volumes of output such as cataloged parts or customer lists, and they can significantly reduce the physical space required for storage.

Special machines are needed to take magnetic computer tapes and create microfilm. Projector-like machines are then used to magnify the images so that they can be read. It is possible to purchase computer-assisted retrieval systems for microfilm that index and quickly retrieve desired material.

Your Cage or Mine?

"Why can't they get this right? It's driving me to distraction. The zoo in Colombia is writing to me about a tiger that has been on loan from our place since 1983. They should be writing to Tulsa," trumpets Ella Fant, waving a letter in the air. Ella is general curator in charge of the animal breeding program at the Gotham Zoo.

She is talking with the zoo's five-person committee about the proposals before them. The committee meets every month to decide which animals to loan to other zoos, and which animals to get on loan in order to breed them. The committee is composed of Ella Fant, the general curator; Ty Garr, the zoo's director; two zoo employees, Annie Malle and Mona Key; and a layman, Rex Lyon, who is a businessman in the community.

Ty Garr paces in front of the group and continues the meeting, saying, "We have the possibility of loaning out two of our gold lion tarmarins. And we have the opportunity to play matchmaker for two lesser pandas. Since three of you are new to the committee, I'll briefly discuss your responsibility. As you know, Ella and I would pounce on any chance to lure animals in for the breeding program. Your duties are to assess the zoo's financial resources, and look at our zoo's immediate demands. You also must consider the season and our shipping capability, as well as that of the zoo's we're considering. The other zoos charge us nothing for loan of their animals for the breeding program. We pay the shipping for any animal being loaned to us and then maintain them, and that gets expensive."

"We are linked, via computer network, into an inventory system of selected species with 164 other zoos," says Ella as she picks up the story from Ty. "My office has a computer equipped with video screen. We can access the records of all captive animals in the system, including those from the two zoos we are negotiating with right now."

As the committee works they begin asking questions. "I need to read some information, get some meat to sink my teeth into, before I'm ready to decide whether the loan of the lesser pandas is a good idea. Where is the data on the animals we're considering?" growls Rex.

Annie replies, "We have to go to Ella's office to get to it. Mostly, the other employees who need to know just use the screen. We've been waiting for other users for our computer so that we could justify a better printer. Right now the one we're using is just for numbers and the printout doesn't copy very well."

Mona Key gets into the swing of the discussion and says, "Some information on the current state of the budget would be divine, too. I'll go bananas with new expenditures until we at least have a summary of what we're spending. I bet it's a bunch."

Ty answers saying, "We don't mean to monkey around, but frankly we feel trapped. Costs of reproducing all of the financial data seem high to us. We'd rather put our money into reproducing rare and endangered species! Paperwork multiplies on its own."

The group laughs nervously together, but there is an air of expectancy in the room. The consensus is that they need more information about the zoo's financial status and the prospective loan animals.

Ella, aware that the group cannot be tamed in the way the previous one was, suggests, "The old committee preferred to get their information informally, through chattering with us. Let's spend this first meeting discovering what kinds of documents you feel you need to do your work as a committee."

What are some of the problems related to output that the committee is experiencing? What suggestions do you have for improving output to the committee? How can the budget constraints of the zoos be met while still allowing the committee to receive the output they need to function? Comment on the adequacy of the output technology that is currently in use at the zoo. Suggest alternatives or modifications to output and output technology that would enhance what is being done.

The drawbacks of using microfilmed output are the necessity of acquiring and maintaining new equipment as well as training users on it. A hard copy of microfilmed material is often needed, which means that copy equipment must also be acquired. As you can see, it is difficult to get away from creating a paper copy. Finally, without the benefits of a computer-aided retrieval system, accessing microfilmed documents can be time-consuming and frustrating.

The advantages of microforms are saving a great deal of space, maintaining required records without needing massive storage, preservation of frequently used but fragile materials, and avoiding the trouble of physically paging through voluminous reports.

CD-ROM. With demand for multimedia output growing, the display of material on CD-ROMs has become increasingly widespread. Once used almost exclusively for reference works because of their large storage capacity, CD-ROMs are being used to output any information that is voluminous and somewhat stable in content. For example, CD-ROM displays are used to supply parts numbers for auto manufacturers and to provide extended training courses for consultants.

Retrieval of CD-ROM output is faster compared with older methods of accessing paper and microforms. Additionally, CD-ROM discs are less vulnerable to damage from human handling than other output. CD-ROMs can include full color text and graphics, as well as music and full motion video, so as an output medium they provide a designer maximum creativity. Drawbacks of designing content for CD-ROM output is that it is very time-consuming and therefore expensive. Additionally, because of its read-only format it is more troublesome to update than other forms of output. It is also more difficult to use on a network.

ELECTRONIC OUTPUT. Many of the new systems you design will have the capability of sending electronic output in the form of e-mail, faxes, and bulletin board messages that can be sent from one computer to another without the necessity of hard copy. Many of the advances in electronic output are paving the way for what is often called the "information superhighway. While we leave it to you to trace out the far-reaching social implications of these shifts, in a very practical way, as an analyst, you are already involved with them.

Some of the advantages of electronic output can be realized by looking at the example in Figure 15.5, a fax sent via Delrina's WinFax Pro.

Notice that the recipient of the fax was able to electronically mark up the text with revisions and corrections, then fax it back to the source with the changes electronically included. No paper output was exchanged, and yet the revision process was facilitated. Part of your task when designing electronic output may be to help the organization develop guidelines about what constitutes a "legal" electronic signature for such signed documents.

Electronic mail is an exchange of messages between computers, which you can set up and run internally within the organization or which can be set up through communication companies or on-line services such as CompuServe or Prodigy. By designing e-mail systems you can support communication throughout the organization, help reduce paper waste, cut down on the tiresome game of telephone tag, help users broadcast messages to many others, and provide a means of update output very easily. A useful and flexible e-mail system can form the basis of support for work groups. In Chapter 21, we cover groupware in detail.

The disadvantages of e-mail (in particular, Internet) output include difficulty in formatting control, the potential for abusing the system (for example incorrectly using the "Reply" function and thereby broadcasting a message meant for a particular person), difficulties in developing a useful protocol for handling "junk" e-mail, and the need to develop organizational policies for acceptable usage. Printed output can use fonts very effectively, and denote the serious nature of a memo or report or convey a casual style to encourage informality. This is not easy to do using e-mail because formatted documents must be sent as files in rich text format or an equivalent. This is a cumbersome process, which products like Acrobat by Adobe have been developed to handle effectively.

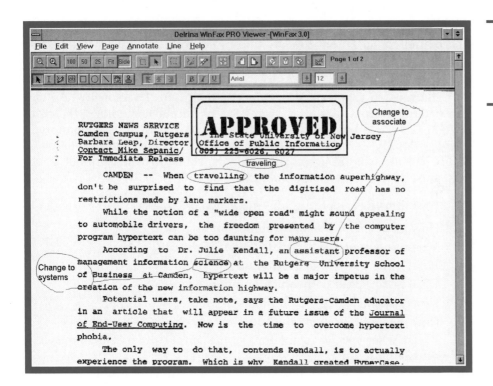

FIGURE 15.5
Users can annotate a fax and
send it back to the sender
without paper output using
Delrina's WinFax Pro.

It is also difficult to express your mood or the intent of your message via e-mail, perhaps because e-mail seems by its nature more informal and conversational than printed output. Thus humor, for example, is often misunderstood in e-mail messages, and symbols have been developed over the years to allow the user to say "This statement is in jest." A case in point is the symbol: -) at the end of a sentence, meaning that the sentence was a joke. (Turn the page sideways to see a face.) Designers of e-mail output need to take these and similar concerns into consideration.

The most popular function on the Internet is international e-mail, which is very fast and low in cost in comparison to many other e-mail systems. (Internet can be thought of as a "network of networks," since at last count 11,000 networks were connected to it.) In addition to e-mail, an almost overwhelming amount of information may also be accessed on the Internet, including several hundred libraries worldwide, bulletin boards, and free, high-quality software. Though a network provider can help you facilitate physically connecting the organization to Internet, doing so requires careful planning (in addition to administrative paperwork) to envision how the existing LAN structure, as well as the organizational culture, can support this important link. Once connected, a systems designer may help the organization make use of information services such as Gopher or electronic conferencing lists such as Listserve.

INTEGRATED OUTPUT OFFICE MACHINES. In the future the process of selecting and directing output to a particular device should be made easier. In 1994, Microsoft announced "Microsoft at Work" (MAW) architecture, a system that would allow all commonly used office machines such as copiers, fax machines, printers, computers, and telephones to work together in harmony. This technology would require changes in all relevant equipment and perhaps the combination of certain features into a single machine—for instance, faxes would be automatically distributed via e-mail, and output could be sent directly to a copier rather than first to a printer and subsequently to the copier.

FACTORS TO CONSIDER WHEN CHOOSING OUTPUT TECHNOLOGY. As you can determine from this brief discussion of output technology, there are several factors to consider when choosing it. Although the technology changes rapidly, certain usage factors remain fairly constant in relation to technological breakthroughs. These factors, some of which present trade-offs, must be considered. They include:

1. Who will use (see) the output (requisite quality)?
2. How many people need the output?
3. Where is output needed (distribution/logistics)?
4. What is the purpose of the output?
5. What is the speed with which output is needed?
6. How frequently will the output be needed?
7. How long will (or must) the output be stored?
8. Under what special regulations is the output produced, stored, and distributed?
9. What are the initial and ongoing costs of maintenance and supplies?
10. What are the environmental requirements (noise absorption, controlled temperature, space for equipment, and cabling) for output technologies?

Examining each factor separately will allow you to see the interrelationships and how they may be traded off for one another in a particular system.

Who will use the output? Discovering who will use the output is important because job requirements help dictate what output method is appropriate. For example, when district managers must be away from their desks for extended periods, they need printed output that can travel with them as they visit the managers in their region. Alternatively, screen output is excellent for people such as truck dispatchers who are deskbound for long periods.

Also, different standards apply depending on whether a recipient of output is internal or external to the business. External recipients of output (clients and customers, vendors and suppliers, shareholders and regulatory agencies) will require different output than users within the business. Clients and customers often have difficulty accessing electronic output, since they simply do not have the equipment. In this event, you must provide printed output for them or develop another common interface (such as a touchtone phone) whereas screen, audio, or print output all might be viable options for internal use.

Knowing who will be using the output should also help you determine the requisite quality of output. Standard, lined computer paper printout is considered acceptable by many internal users, but letter-quality output is required for adequate business correspondence with external publics. Therefore, while a line printer will serve as a satisfactory output method for much internal work, a letter-quality printer is still necessary for most external contacts. Special forms such as computerized turnaround documents (output that becomes input when turned around or sent back by customers) will be covered in an upcoming section.

How many people need the output? Choice of output technology is also influenced by how many users need the output. If many people need output, printed copies are probably justified. If only one user needs output, a screen, microform, or even audio may be more suitable.

If many users in the business need different output at different times for short periods and they need it quickly, then screens connected to online terminals able to access database contents are a viable option.

Where is output needed? Another factor influencing choice of output technology is the physical destination of the output. Information that will remain close to its point of origin, that will be used by a few users within the business, and that may be stored or referred to frequently can safely be printed. An abundance of information that must be transmitted to users at great distances in branch operations may be better distributed electronically, with the recipient deciding whether to print output, display it on screens, or store it. One example of such information is documentation for an application.

Sometimes federal or state regulations dictate that a printed form remain on file at a particular location for a specified period of time. In those instances, it is the responsibility of the systems analyst to see that the regulation is observed for any new or modified output that is designed.

What is the purpose of the output? The purpose of the output is another factor to consider when choosing output technology. If the output is intended to be a report with the purpose of attracting shareholders to the business by allowing them to peruse corporate finances at their leisure, then well-designed, printed output such as an annual report is desirable. If the purpose of the output is to provide fifteen-minute updates on stock market quotations and the material is highly encoded and changeable, then screen displays or even audio is preferable.

What is the speed with which output is needed? As we go down through the three levels of strategic, middle, and operations management within the organization, we find decision makers at the lowest level of operations management need output rapidly so that they can quickly adjust to events such as a stopped assembly line, raw materials that have not arrived on time, or a worker who is absent unexpectedly. On-line, on-screen output may be useful here.

As we ascend up the management levels, we observe that strategic managers are much less likely to need output rapidly. They are more in need of output for a specific time period, which helps in forecasting business cycles and trends.

Additionally, particular businesses are more likely to need rapid output of the sort which is often provided on screen, via on-line systems. A case in point is an intensive care unit, where a nurse continually surveys a heart-attack victim's pulse via a monitor connected to a video display terminal versus a doctor reading the printout from and EKG during a healthy patient's routine physical examination. The first is literally a life-or-death situation; the second presumably is not. In the intensive care unit, reaction time to output is everything. Therefore, real-time output is needed. In the second situation, there is likely a time lapse between the accomplishment of the EKG and the reading of the results, with no criticality involved. Fortunately, most technological decisions on output are not life-or-death, but this example does point up the burden on the systems analyst to make reasonable choices.

How often will the output be accessed? The more frequently output is accessed, the more important is its display on screens connected to on-line systems. Infrequently accessed output which is needed by only a few users is well-suited to microforms such as microfiche or microfilm. For example, university librarians at U.S. schools make observations about the frequency of use when deciding to microfilm daily newspapers from foreign countries.

Output that is accessed frequently is a good candidate for incorporation into online systems, with display on screens. Adopting this type of technology allows users easy access and alleviates physical wear and tear that deteriorates frequently handled printed output.

How long must the output be stored? As just noted, output printed on paper deteriorates rapidly with age. Output preserved on microforms and microfilms is not as prone to succumb to environmental disturbances such as light, humidity, and human handling. Therefore, in order to store output for long periods, it may be necessary to microfilm it.

The business in question may be subject to governmental regulations on local, state, or federal levels that dictate how long output must be kept on file. Organizations themselves also enact policies about how long output must be retained. For example, some universities require professors to retain student work (output) for a full semester after a final grade for the student has been recorded. While student papers may take a lot of storage space, the short retention period does not justify the cost of microfilming them.

Under what special regulation is the output produced? The appropriate format for some output is actually regulated by the government. For example, an employee's W-2 form must be printed; its final form cannot be a screen or microform output. Each business exists within a different complex of regulations under which it produces output. To that extent, appropriate technology for some functions may be dictated by law.

However, much of this regulation is industry-dependent. For example, a regional blood system is required by federal law to keep a medical history of a blood donor, as well as his or her name, on file. The exact output form is not specified, but the content is strictly spelled out. Other governmental regulations may require the printing and storing of output on standardized forms. The analyst must be aware of these regulations and make sure the business is in compliance.

What are the initial costs and continuing costs of maintenance and supplies? The initial costs of purchasing or leasing equipment must be considered as yet another factor that enters into the choice of output technology. Most vendors will help you estimate initial purchase or lease costs of computer hardware, including the cost of printers and video display terminals.

A Right Way, a Wrong Way, and a Subway

"So far so good. Sure, there have been some complaints, but any new subway will have those. The 'free ride' gimmick has helped attract some people who never would have ridden otherwise. I think there are more people than ever before interested in riding the subway," says Bart Rayl. "What we need is an accurate fix on what ridership has been so far so we can make some adjustments on our fare decisions and scheduling of trains."

Rayl is an operations manager for S.W.I.F.T., the newly built subway for Western Ipswich and Fremont Transport that serves a major northeastern city in the United States. He is speaking with Benton Turnstile, who reports to him as operations supervisor of S.W.I.F.T. The subway system is in its first month of operation, offering limited lines. Marketing people have been giving free rides on the subway in order to increase public awareness of S.W.I.F.T.

"I think that's a good idea," says Turnstile. "It's not just a token effort. We'll show them we're really on the right track. I'll get back to you with ridership information soon," he says.

A month later, Rayl and Turnstile meet to compare the projected ridership with the new data. Turnstile proudly presents a two-inch-high stack of computer printouts to Rayl. Rayl looks a little surprised but proceeds to go through it with Turnstile. "What all is in here?" Rayl asks, fingering the top page of the stack hesitantly.

"Well," says Turnstile training his eyes on the printout, "It's a list of all of the tickets that were sold from the computerized machines. So it tells us how many tickets were bought and what kind of tickets were bought. The guys from Systems That Think, Inc., told me that this report would be the most helpful for us, just like it was for the operations people in Buffalo and Pittsburgh," says Turnstile, turning quickly to the next page.

"Maybe, but remember those subway systems began with really limited service. We're bigger. And what about the sales from the three manned ticket booths in the Main Street Terminal?" asks Rayl.

"The clerks in the booth can get information summarizing ticket sales on-screen any time they want it. But it's not included here. Remember we projected only 10 percent of our sales would be from the booths anyway. Let's go with our original idea, and add that to the printout," suggests Benton.

Rayl replies, "But I've been observing riders. Half of them seem to be afraid of the computerized ticket machines. Others start using them, get frustrated reading the directions, or don't know what to do with the ticket that comes out, and wind up at the ticket booth blowing off steam. Furthermore, they can't understand the routine information posted on the kiosks, which is all in graphics. They wind up asking clerks what train goes where." Rayl pushes the printout holding the ticket sales to one side of the conference table and says, "I don't have much confidence in this report. I feel as if we're sitting here trying to operate the most sophisticated subway system in the U.S. by peering down a tunnel instead of at the information as we should be."

What are some of the specific problems with the output that the systems consultants and Benton Turnstile gave to Bart Rayl? Evaluate the media that are being used for output, as well as the timing of its distribution. Comment on the external output that users of the computerized ticket machines are apparently receiving. Suggest some changes in output: to help Rayl get the information he needs to make decisions on fares and scheduling of trains and to help users of the subway system get the information they need.

However, many vendors do not provide information about how much it costs to keep a printer working (paper, toner, photoelectric unit, repairs, and maintenance). So it falls to the analyst to research the costs of operating different output technologies over time.

Beyond that, the systems analyst may need to gather cost information about other, less-used alternatives such as audio output and microforms. Both may cost substantially more than traditional output methods, but their costs can decrease with use so that in the long run the user would be better off financially with an audio system. As you have seen, original and maintenance costs are far from the only factors influencing the choice of output method.

What are the environmental requirements for output technologies? As noted earlier, printers require a dry, cool environment to operate properly. Monitors for screen-displayed output require space for setup and cabling to connect them to the database being accessed. Audio output requires a relatively quiet place that allows the user to make sense of digitized sounds.

Output technologies themselves actually create environmental disturbances. The systems analyst must be careful with the choice of technology because of this. Audio output requires a quiet environment to be heard and it should not be audible to employees (or customers) who are not using it. This means that the analyst should not specify audio output for a work situation where many employees are engaged in a variety of tasks unrelated to the output. For example, grocery store managers using microprocessor-based audio output attached to scanners at checkstands have found that cashiers working side-by-side with many other checkers often turn down the volume on their speakers (which name aloud each item scanned and its price) to avoid irritation and errors. Unfortunately, this defeats the audio doublecheck.

Conversely, some output technologies are prized for their unobtrusiveness. Libraries that emphasize silence in the workplace make extensive use of display screens. This choice is much quieter than having a patron physically check the stacks for a book.

REALIZING HOW OUTPUT BIAS AFFECTS USERS

Whatever form it takes, output is not just a neutral product that is subsequently analyzed and acted upon by decision makers. Output affects users in many different ways. The significance of this fact for the systems analyst is that great thought and care must be put into designing the output in order to avoid biasing it.

Recognizing Bias in the Way Output Is Used

It is a common error to assume that once the systems analyst has signed off of a system project, his or her impact in ended. Actually, the analyst's influence is long-lasting. Much of the information on which organizational members base their decisions is determined by what analysts perceive is important to the business.

Bias is present in everything that humans create. This is not to adjudge bias as bad, but to make the point that it is inseparable from what we (and consequently our system) produce. The concerns of systems analysts are to avoid unnecessarily biasing output and to make users aware of the possible biases in the output they receive.

There are three main ways in which presentations of output are unintentionally biased:

1. How information is sorted.
2. Setting of acceptable limits.
3. Choice of graphics.

Each source of bias is discussed separately in the following subsections.

INTRODUCING BIAS WHEN INFORMATION IS SORTED. Bias is introduced to output when the analyst makes choices about how information is sorted for a report. Common sorts include alphabetical, chronological, and cost.

Information presented alphabetically may overemphasize the items that begin with the letters A and B, since users tend to pay more attention to information presented first. For example, if past suppliers are listed alphabetically, companies such as "Aardvark Printers," "Advent Supplies," and "Barkley Office Equipment" are shown to the purchasing manager first.

Bias is also unintentionally introduced into reports that are arranged chronologically. Once again, users' attention is drawn to the events listed first, which are those things that occurred first. So in reviewing the use of computing time, and MIS manager who uses output presented chronologically may be biased toward examining usage for January, February, and March and slighting the figures for November and December.

A third type of sorting, by cost, may also bias the output. Presenting information by cost alone (or by any single factor) can be extremely misleading. Providing a context for cost such as listing benefits, the time period during which cost was assessed, or other variables considered are ways to correct for this particular bias.

INTRODUCING BIAS BY SETTING LIMITS. A second major source of bias in output is the predefinition of limits for particular values being reported. Many reports are generated on an exception basis only, which means that when limits on values are set beforehand, only exceptions to those values will be output. Exception reports make the decision maker aware of deviations from satisfactory values. There are four general problems with setting limits that may bias output:

1. Limit set too low.
2. Limit set too high.
3. Range of exceptions output too narrow.
4. Range of exceptions output too wide.

Limits that are set too low for exception reports can bias the user's perception. For example, and insurance company that generates exception reports on all accounts one week overdue has probably set too low a limit on overdue payments. The decision maker receiving the output will be overwhelmed with "exceptions" that are not really cause for concern. The one-week overdue exception report leads to the user's misperception that there are a great many overdue accounts. A more appropriate limit for generating an exception report would be accounts thirty days overdue.

Users can also be biased by output that is printed in an exception report when too high a limit is to be met before information is included. For example, a quality assurance manager for a large manufacturer receives an exception report if more than 10 lots out of 100 of rubber hose produced are defective according to specifications such as tensile strength. Typically, the manager can expect 3 lots to be defective. However, the limit is too high to be of any tangible value because the problem could have been detected earlier as the defective rate began to rise. For the information to be useful, limits on allowable defects must be tightened. The resultant bias of setting too high a limit is that a false sense of security is generated. In fact, there is little, if any, timely output when allowances are set at unrealistically high limits.

A third way that setting limits can introduce bias is if the range of information output in an exception report is set too narrowly. For example, if the marketing department of a food manufacturer generates reports on the number of consumers between ages eight and ten who send in for offers from the back of cereal boxes, they may not be generating much useful

FIGURE 15.6
A misleading graph that
might bias the user.

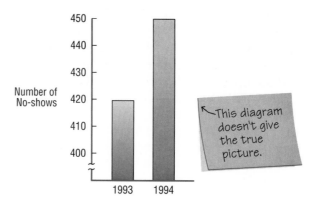

information. A too narrowly defined range may mean losing the very information that you were originally attempting to pinpoint.

Conversely, setting too wide a range for information output on an exception report can also bias users. For example, if the gas company generates an exception report on its high-volume residential users, but employs a range of all residential customers using between 6 and 2,600 cubic feet of gas per month, the output will be overwhelming. The range of usage is too broad to get a grasp of high usage; rather, the report includes just about all of the gas company's residential customers. Output generated within too broad a range can bias the user into magnifying the existence of "exceptions" or problems.

INTRODUCING BIAS THROUGH GRAPHICS. Output is subject to a third type of presentation bias, which is brought about by the analyst's choice of graphics for output display. Bias can occur in the selection of the graphic size, its color, the scale used, and even the type of graphic.

Graphic size must be proportional, so that the user is not biased as to the importance of variables presented. For example, Figure 15.6 shows a column chart comparing the number of no-shows for hotel bookings in 1993 with no-shows for hotel bookings in 1994. Notice that the vertical axis is broken, and it appears that the number of no-shows for 1994 is twice as much as the number of no-shows in 1993, although the number of no-shows has actually gone up only slightly.

Choice of graphic color is also important as it, too, may unduly bias the user. The analyst needs to be aware that any colored output naturally claims more user attention than black-and-white printed or displayed output. Certain colors may be assigned meanings within business, and those should not be changed by the analyst without good cause. For instance, red might be used to indicate a problem, such as a budget that is "in the red," as part of an exception report. Some colors are not easily legible (see Chapter 16 on input design for specifics on screen color), so they should be avoided. Otherwise, users will be biased against even reading information or related graphics.

The scale of graphics used for output also bears the potential of biasing the user. Most users perceive that the larger the item, the greater its importance. For example, if a pictograph shows a small icon of a ship to represent overseas trade in one year and, on the same graph, shows a larger icon to represent the same amount of shipping a year later, it may bias the user's interpretation by suggesting that overseas trade has grown, when only the year has changed.

Users also perceive that when more of an item is displayed, it is more important. Graphic output that always show an icon symbolizing 10 units produced is automatically interpreted as meaning "30 units were produced" if three icons are shown. Users might thus be biased if the icon were used in a cluster of three on a newly developed output screen to denote that the user was seeing a production report.

The type of graphic chosen for output is also a potential source of bias for users. A pie chart is inappropriate if percentages of a whole are not the point. Bar and column charts can overexaggerate differences between variables. As discussed in Chapter 14, if more that two variables are to be shown over time, it is more appropriate to depict them on a line chart than on a bar chart. A poor choice of graph along with an inappropriate presentation can bias the user as to the meaning of the output. Graphics for oral presentation were covered in Chapter 14, and a more detailed discussion is presented in a later section of this chapter on designing graphics for a decision support system.

Avoiding Bias in the Design of Output

There are specific strategies that systems analysts can use to avoid biasing the output they design:

1. Awareness of the sources of bias.
2. Interactive design of output that includes users.
3. Working with users so that they are informed of the output's biases.
4. Creating output that is flexible and that allows users to modify limits and ranges.
5. Training users to rely on multiple output for conducting "reality tests" on system output.

All of these (except the first) focus on the relationship between the systems analyst and the user as it involves output. It is necessary that systems analysts realize the potential impact of output and be aware of the possible ways in which output is unintentionally biased.

Interactive design of output means that output cannot be successfully designed in a vacuum. Rather, the systems analyst must actively solicit user feedback regarding output. The design process will require several iterations before users feel output is useful. Unavoidably, users will incorporate their own biases into output, but they will also be clearer about how to interpret output that they help design.

The third way to avoid unintentional bias is to work with users so that they are informed of the output's biases. This is done in training sessions, as well as in the documentation. Output (especially screens) can include information about the way the information has been generated, thus pinpointing potential biases included in the report.

Biased output can also be avoided (or at least made explicit) if users are able to modify the limits and ranges set for output. This approach is especially suited to on-line, interactive systems. The drawback is that there may be a lack of consistency in output that could lead to problems if future comparisons are necessary. Flexibility in output may also lead to communication problems among users who, for example, may be using different ranges of values to spot problems.

A fifth way to help avoid unintentional bias in output is to train users to conduct "reality tests" on the output they receive. This includes comparing

Franchise Store Information
Ranked by Earnings in Dollars
For the Month Ending MM/DD/YY
Page 2

F NO	Store Name	DIV	Dist	Rank	Sales Dollar 000's	Gross Profit 000's	%	Other Income 000's	%	Allocated Expenses 000's	%	Earnings Dollars	%
C 5112	Front Royal, VA	20	23	51	126	5	3.93	2	1.8	5	4.0	2,144	1.7
S 4311	Rockville, MD	40	41	52	144	6	4.27	0	0.3	4	3.1	2,062	1.4
R 3021	Middleburg, VA	20	22	53	95	4	4.29	2	1.9	4	4.0	2,057	2.2
S 5021	Culpeper, VA	20	26	54	219	8	3.78	3	1.5	10	4.4	2,005	0.9
R 2820	Waldorf, MD	40	42	55	72	3	4.69	1	1.2	2	3.3	1,903	2.6
C 4424	Fairfax-Lee Hgwy	20	22	56	131	5	4.16	2	1.3	5	4.0	1,869	1.4
C 4423	Baileys X-Roads	20	22	57	98	5	4.70	2	1.7	5	4.6	1,727	1.8
S 3821	Herndon, VA	20	23	58	221	7	3.35	4	1.7	9	4.2	1,703	0.8
C 7126	Frederick, MD	30	32	59	125	5	4.04	2	1.6	5	4.3	1,615	1.3
S 8029	Centreville, VA	20	27	60	175	7	3.73	3	1.9	8	4.7	1,593	0.9
R 5029	Minnieville, VA	20	34	61	34	2	5.28	1	3.3	1	4.0	1,572	4.7
S 7520	Mount Vernon	20	24	62	90	5	5.22	2	1.7	5	5.2	1,558	1.7
C 4712	D.C. M Street	40	44	63	235	10	4.35	4	1.8	13	5.5	1,489	0.6
S 4716	Annandale	20	25	64	126	6	4.52	0	0.1	4	3.5	1,457	1.2
S 7922	Vienna, VA	20	25	65	177	9	4.86	2	1.2	9	5.3	1,447	0.8
R 4491	Great Falls	20	24	66	86	4	4.39	2	1.9	4	4.7	1,364	1.6
R 3926	Harper's Ferry	30	33	67	68	3	4.80	0	0.3	2	3.1	1,325	1.9
C 2422	Falls Church	20	27	68	144	6	4.06	2	1.4	7	4.6	1,322	.9
R 3024	Clifton, VA	20	23	69	53	3	5.17	1	1.6	2	4.3	1,273	2.4
C 4511	Silver Spring, MD	20	42	70	121	5	4.06	1	1.2	5	4.3	1,237	1.0
R 5120	Olney, MD	30	31	71	43	2	4.60	1	2.2	2	4.0	1,217	2.8
C 4527	D.C Connecticut Ave	40	45	72	110	5	4.28	0	0.2	4	3.4	1,200	1.1
C 4526	Pennsylvania Ave	40	42	73	134	6	4.55	0	0.2	5	4.0	1,073	0.8
S 2923	Manassas	20	25	74	198	7	3.54	0	0.1	6	3.1	1,057	0.5
	City Stores				6,025	255	4.23	67	1.1	190	3.2	69,987	1.2
	Suburban Stores				3,402	171	5.03	54	1.6	133	3.9	35,020	1.0
	Rural Stores				2,018	92	4.56	27	1.3	47	2.3	43,223	2.1
	Total (All Stores in Region)				11,445	518	4.52	148	1.3	370	3.2	148,230	1.3

FIGURE 15.7
A printed output report for divisional managers of a food wholesaler.

output with their own experience and expectations (does what they are reading make sense in a practical way) and using multiple output from different sources (daily and monthly reports, observation and speaking with others in the business, etc.) to arrive at an understanding of what is actually happening in the organization. Such checks prevent overreliance on any one source of output and help correct for bias by introducing other perspectives.

DESIGNING PRINTED OUTPUT

Using the information gained through the information requirements determination phase, and having decided to use printed output, the systems analysts is ready to begin its physical design. The source of information to be included in reports is the data dictionary, the compilation of which was covered in Chapter 10. Recall that the data dictionary includes names of data elements as well as the required field length of each entry.

Guidelines for Printed Report Design

Figure 15.7 is an output report that is intended for divisional managers of a food wholesaler that supplies a number of franchise grocery stores. We will focus on different aspects of the report as we cover the tools, conventions, and functional and stylistic design attributes of printed output reports.

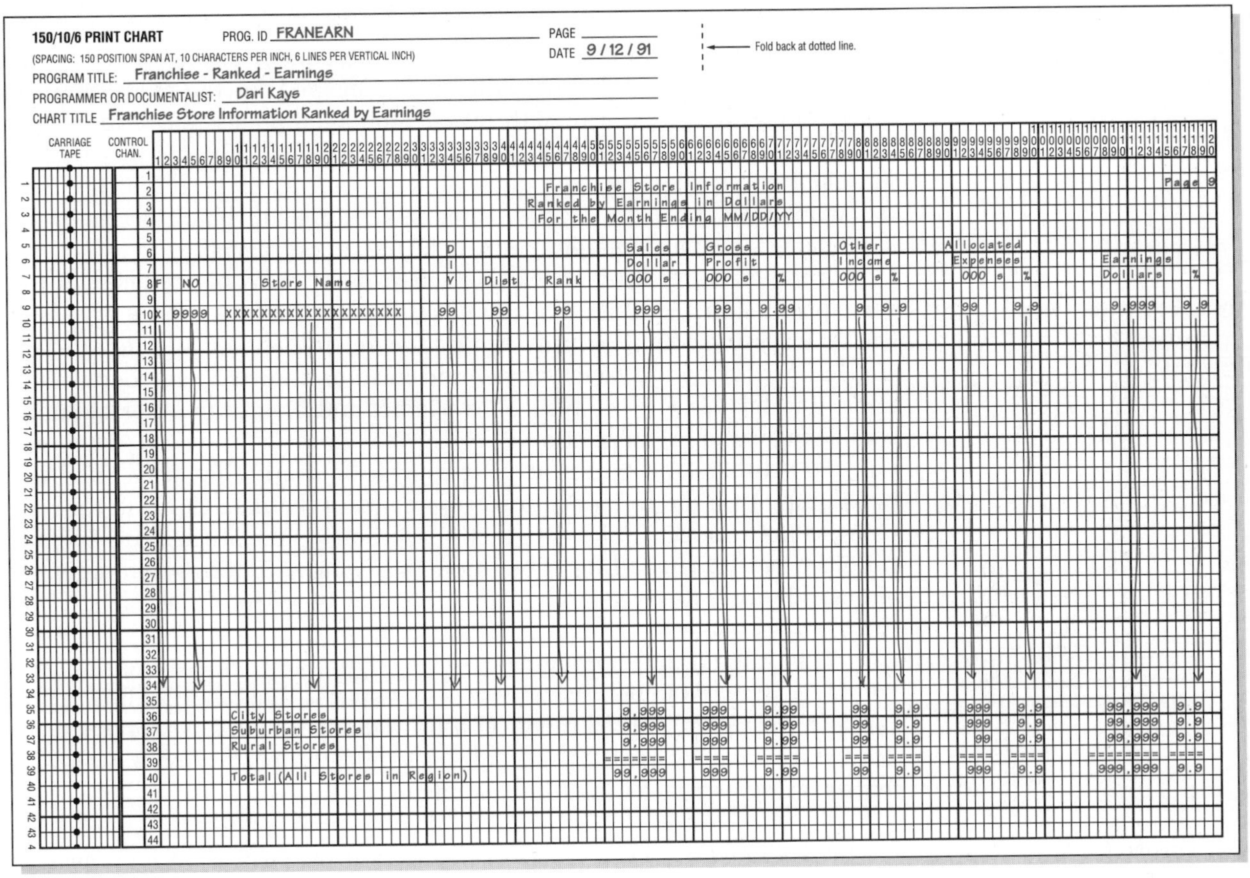

FIGURE 15.8
A printer layout form showing conventions to follow in designing printed output.

REPORT DESIGN CONVENTIONS. Conventions to follow when filling in the layout worksheet include how to signify the type of data (alphabetic, special, or numeric) that will appear in each position; showing the exact size of the form being prepared; and showing the way to indicate a continuation of data on consecutive layout forms. Each of the conventions is illustrated in Figure 15.8.

Constant information is information that remains the same whenever the report is printed. To indicate constant information, the analyst writes it in on the layout form, one character per space. The title of the report and all of the column headings are written in as constant information.

Variable information is information that can vary each time the report is printed out. In our example, the sales figures in thousands of dollars will change, and hence it is indicated as variable information.

In order to signify a space that the computer will fill with either an alphabetic character (A-Z and a-z) or a special character such as an asterisk (*), dollar sign ($), or ampersand (&), write X in the space (just as was done in the data dictionary). For example, in order to show the field length for the store's name, which can be up to 21 alphabetic characters long, you would put X in each of 21 grid spaces. An alternative (and equally acceptable) convention would be to put an X in the beginning space with a line through the following spaces and an X to anchor the last space occupied by the item, so that the store's name is signified by X_____X.

In order to show that the computer will fill in the space with a numeric character (0-9), a 9 is written in the correct space on the worksheet. For example, to indicate the spaces needed for the store number, you would fill in the grid with 9999. This symbolizes that a four-digit number will be printed in that position on the report. Spaces that will be left blank in order to separate data should be left blank on the printer layout worksheet. In our example, three spaces are left blank between the store name and the store number to make the report readable.

Another convention holds that when data are to be repeated in the same position in a column, it is not necessary to continue putting details in each successive space. Simply draw a wavy line (called the *detail line*) continuing downward from the column head as shown by the detail line, under the headings Store No., Store Name, and all of the other columns containing variable information.

To estimate the width of your report, determine for each field the maximum of (1) the field length requirements of the data elements you are using as they appear in the data dictionary, and (2) the longest line in your proposed column heading. Then add two spaces to allow for room on either side for better readability. Finally, sum these field estimates to get the width estimate.

This calculation is demonstrated in Figure 15.9 where the reported width is estimated to be a minimum of 114 spaces. We have to allow a few spaces for margins, but the report will fit in the 120 spaces we set as a goal. With the variety of font types, font sizes, and the proportional nature of fonts spacing becomes difficult to estimate exactly.

PAPER QUALITY, TYPE, AND SIZE. Output can be printed on innumerable kinds of paper. The overriding constraint is usually cost. Paper that is treated in any special way—either preprinted, inked in color, multipart with carbon interleaves, or carbonless transfer—is more expensive than plain paper.

However, the kind of paper used has a predictable effect on the user, so that investing in special papers may be justifiable. For example, using bond to print letters of appreciation to employees would be a way of showing that the letter has special content and differs in importance from everyday internal memos. Other examples are the use of security paper for checks and check envelopes, and documents that must bear official, inalterable seals such as passports, birth certificates, and many others.

Paper also differs as to its weight, depending on the rag (cotton) content. More cotton means better quality, durability, and a higher price, but a business may still want particular correspondence to be printed on cotton bond in order to present a more distinguished image.

Common lengths for reports in the U.S., whether they appear on preprinted forms or computer printouts, are 3 1/2, 3 2/3, 5 1/2, 6, 7 1/2, and 11 inches. The width of the report is determined by the number of characters necessary to title each column, along with the number of characters necessary between columns and in margins to make the form readable and aesthetically pleasing.

SPECIAL OUTPUT FORMS. The variety of special output forms is seemingly endless, since virtually any color ink or paper can be used. Many options on positioning of headings and logotypes are open. The systems analyst lays out the content of the report on a preprinted form in the same manner as on the computer-prepared report.

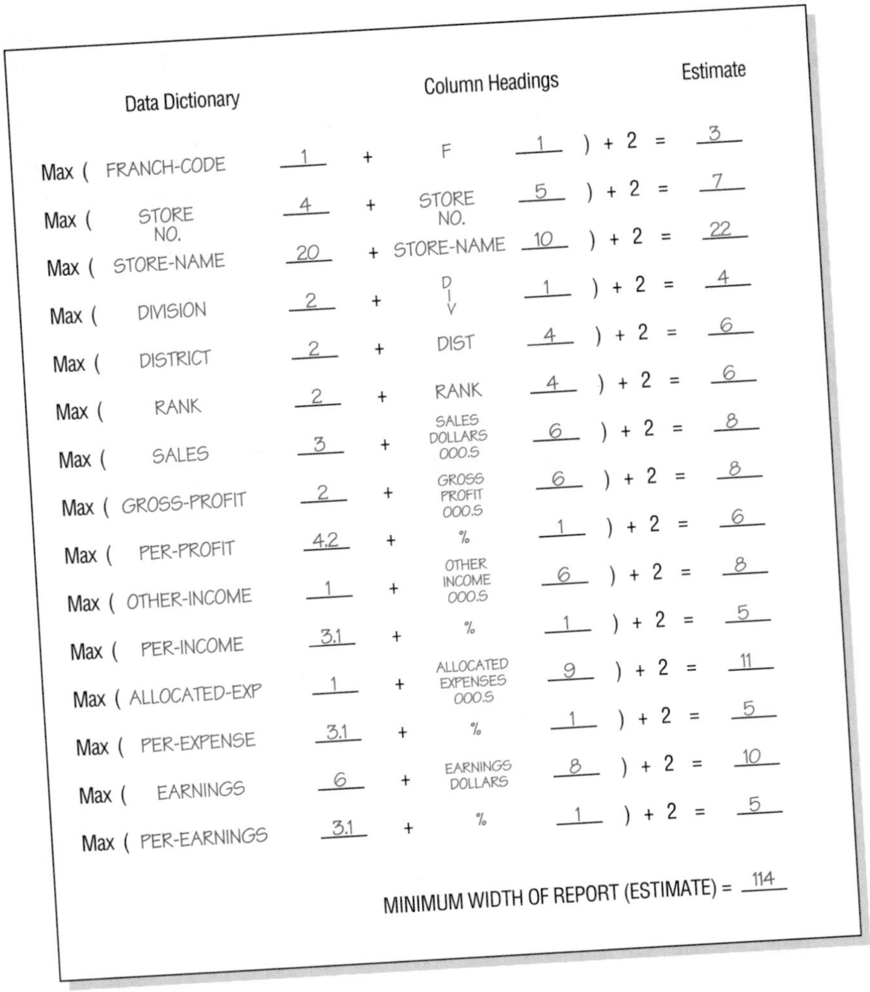

Data Dictionary
Column Headings
Estimate
Max (FRANCH-CODE 1 + F 1) + 2 = 3
Max (STORE NO. 4 + STORE NO. 5) + 2 = 7
Max (STORE-NAME 20 + STORE-NAME 10) + 2 = 22
Max (DIVISION 2 + D I V 1) + 2 = 4
Max (DISTRICT 2 + DIST 4) + 2 = 6
Max (RANK 2 + RANK 4) + 2 = 6
Max (SALES 3 + SALES DOLLARS 000.S 6) + 2 = 8
Max (GROSS-PROFIT 2 + GROSS PROFIT 000.S 6) + 2 = 8
Max (PER-PROFIT 4.2 + % 1) + 2 = 6
Max (OTHER-INCOME 1 + OTHER INCOME 000.S 6) + 2 = 8
Max (PER-INCOME 3.1 + % 1) + 2 = 5
Max (ALLOCATED-EXP 1 + ALLOCATED EXPENSES 000.S 9) + 2 = 11
Max (PER-EXPENSE 3.1 + % 1) + 2 = 5
Max (EARNINGS 6 + EARNINGS DOLLARS 8) + 2 = 10
Max (PER-EARNINGS 3.1 + % 1) + 2 = 5
MINIMUM WIDTH OF REPORT (ESTIMATE) = 114

FIGURE 15.9
A page from a data dictionary combined with predicted column headings used to estimate size of a printed report.

Preprinted forms are used for many purposes, among them to send to customers as turnaround documents. Preprinted forms can easily convey a distinctive corporate image through use of corporate colors and design. Using innovative shapes, colors, and layouts are also dramatic ways of drawing users' attention to the report that is contained on the preprinted form.

The chief drawback of preprinted forms is their cost. They are extremely expensive in comparison to computer-generated report forms, sometimes costing three times as much. Also, more forms must be kept in inventory. However, the expense may be justified, especially in instances where creating interest is of competitive importance.

Design Consideration. In designing the printed report, the systems analyst incorporates both functional and stylistic or aesthetic considerations so that the report supplies the user with necessary information in a readable format. Since function and form reinforce each other, one should not be emphasized at the expense of the other.

Functional attributes. The functional attributes of a printed report include the heading or title of the report, the page number, the date of

Is Your Work a Grind?

"I want everything I can get may hands on. And the tighter the information is packed the better. Forget that stuff you hear about information overload. It's not in my vocabulary. I want it all. And not in a bunch of pretty looking, half-page reports either. All together, packed on one sheet that I can take into a meeting in case I need to look something up. And I need it every week," proclaims Stephen Links, vice president of a large, family-owned sausage company.

During an interview, Links has been grilling Paul Plishka, who is part of the systems analysis team that is busy designing a management information system for Links Meats. Although Paul is hesitant about what Links has told him, he proceeds to design a printed report that includes all of the important items the team has settled on during the analysis phase.

However, when a prototype of the new report, designed to his specifications, is handed to Stephen there appears to be a change of heart. Links says in no uncertain terms that he can't find what he needs.

"This stuff looks terrible. It looks like scraps. My kindergartner makes better reports in crayon. Look at this: It's all ground up together. I can't find anything. Where's the summary of the number of pork items sold in each outlet? Where is the total volume of items sold for *all* outlets? How about the information on our own shop downtown?" says Links, slicing at the report.

The report clearly needs to be redesigned. How should Paul Plishka go about designing a report that better suits Stephen Links? What tack can the analyst take in suggesting more reports with a less-crowded format? Comment on the difficulty of implementing user suggestions that go against your design training. What are the tradeoffs involved (as far as information overload goes) in generating numerous reports versus generating one large report containing all of the information, such as Stephen wanted? Devise a heuristic concerning display of report information on one report versus generation of numerous reports.

---

preparation, the column headings, grouping of related data items together, and the use of control breaks. Each of these serves a distinctive purpose for the user.

The heading or the title of the report immediately orients users to what it is they are reading. The title should be descriptive, yet concise. It is often redundant to include the word "report" in the title.

Each page should be numbered so that the user has an easy point of reference when discussing output with others or locating important figures. Also, if pages of output become separated, page numbers are invaluable in reconstructing the document.

Include the date of report preparation on each printout. Sometimes this helps users estimate the value of the output. Often, the more timely the output, the more valuable it is.

Column heading serve to further orient the user as to the report contents. Each data item must have a heading. Headings should be short and descriptive. It is permissible to use abbreviations if they are common to users and meaningful to them. Check that abbreviations are not used elsewhere in the organization with a meaning different from that intended in the report.

Data items that are related to one another should be grouped together on the report. This facilitates understanding for the user, and in many instances fulfills their expectations of where items should appear. In our sample worksheet, store name and store number are grouped together because divisional managers use them interchangeably in referring to stores.

Use control breaks (which are breaks in data where summaries occur) to help readability. Separate these breaks from the rest of the data with additional lines of space. For example, if 200 franchise grocery stores are grouped by division, the report might feature a control break at the end of each division.

Stylistic/aesthetic attributes. There are several stylistic or aesthetic considerations for the systems analyst to observe when designing a printed report. If printed output is difficult to read and unappealing, it will not be used effectively or may not be used at all. The upshot is uninformed decision makers and a waste of computer time, as well as other organizational resources.

Printed reports should be well organized, following the way that the eye sees. In this culture, that means the report should read from top to bottom and left to right. As mentioned before, related data items should be grouped together.

Use of control breaks was brought up earlier as a functional, consideration, but the manner in which they are set off on a page of a report can also be considered aesthetic. Draw attention to control breaks, summaries, and other important information by boxing them off with special characters such as asterisks or extra spaces. This makes it easier to find critical information. Avoid printing out long, unbroken columns of information.

Additional blank spaces between columns also contribute to the readability of a report. Users should be able to locate key figures easily on a page; adding blank spaces will facilitate this.

As with the systems proposal report discussed in Chapter 14, printed output reports require ample margins on the right and left, as well as on the top and bottom. These serve to focus the user's attention on the material centered on the page and make reading easier. Since the point of creating output is that it be used, the importance of organization, readability, and ease of use cannot be overstated.

Other stylistic elements that can be used to distinguish printed output are the use of color coding, organizational logos, or preprinted forms that feature these. Graphics are also a possibility for printed output. They are covered in the section on designing output for decision support systems. Do not show users the printer layout worksheet itself. Rather, show them a prototype of the output report so they can make changes. The mock-up should look as realistic as possible.

Steps in Preparing the Printer Layout Worksheet

The following is a step-by-step guide for preparing the printer layout worksheet:

1. Determine the need for the report.
2. Determine the users.
3. Determine data items to be included.
4. Estimate the number of spaces necessary and decide on the overall size of the report. (Or, use a computer-aided design tool.)
5. Title the report.
6. Number the pages of the report.
7. Include the preparation date on the report.
8. Label each column of data appropriately.
9. Define the detail line for variable data by indicating whether each space is to be used for an alphabetic, special, or numeric character.

10. Indicate the positioning of summaries (control breaks).
11. Review prototype reports with users and programmers for feasibility, usefulness, readability, understandability, and aesthetic appeal.

Your expertise as a systems analyst enters in when you are required to design printed reports that bring content and form together in a meaningful way. Printed output is the embodiment of your belief about what users need to know to make decisions. There is a tradeoff involved between wanting decision makers to have all available information and designing a useful report that does not overwhelm them with extraneous details.

DESIGNING SCREEN OUTPUT

Chapter 16 covers designing screens for input, and the same guidelines also apply here for designing screen output, although the contents will change. Notice that screen output differs from printed output in a number of ways. It is ephemeral—that is, a VDT display is not "permanent" in the same way that printouts are—it can be more specifically targeted to the user, it is available on a more flexible schedule, it is *not* portable in the same way, and sometimes it can be changed through direct interaction.

Additionally, users must be instructed on which keys to press when they want to continue reading further screens, how to end the display, and how to interact with the display (if possible). Access to screen displays may be controlled through the use of a password, whereas distribution of printed output is controlled by other means.

Guidelines for Screen Design

There are four guidelines to facilitate the design of screens. To summarize, they are:

1. Keep the screen simple.
2. Keep screen presentation consistent.
3. Facilitate user movement among screens.
4. Create an attractive screen.

Two examples of output screens are shown in Figures 15.10 and 15.11. Notice the difference between the readability of the two screens. On the first, the district number is listed in every instance for the voting register. The readability of the screen is improved when the district number is listed only once and repeating information is avoided. This section concentrates on how this kind of graphical and tabular output is created for on-screen display. Chapter 16 covers specific information on how to achieve the four guidelines.

A SCREEN DESIGN EXAMPLE. Just as the printer layout worksheet is used to plan the spacing for printed output, a similar form is used to plan screens and communicate that detail to programmers. Basically, the same conventions of notation are followed for screen layout as for printed output layout. Differences in screen design include the necessity of putting instructions on screen for changing screens, moving between screens, and terminating the display of output.

Voter Registration Records
New Rochelle Office

Dist.	Number	Street	Last Name	First	Party	Last
69	11413	Bonny Meadow Lane	Petrie	Laura	D	11/93
69	11413	Bonny Meadow Lane	Petrie	Robert	D	11/91
69	11414	Bonny Meadow Lane	Helper	Jerry	D	11/91
69	11414	Bonny Meadow Lane	Helper	Millicent	D	06/92
69	11415	Bonny Meadow Lane	Brady	Alan	R	11/91
69	11416	Bonny Meadow Lane	Sorel	Buddy	D	11/89
69	11416	Bonny Meadow Lane	Sorel	Pickles	D	11/89
69	11417	Bonny Meadow Lane	Coolie	Melvin	R	06/93
69	11418	Bonny Meadow Lane	Rogers	Sally	D	11/92
69	11341	Elm Street	Cleaver	June	R	06/93
69	11341	Elm Street	Cleaver	Ward	R	06/93

Press the PGDN key to continue
F1 = Help   F2 = Return to the Main Menu   F3 = Change Party
F4 = Change Name   F5 = Add a Voter   F6 = Change Last Voted

FIGURE 15.10
Poorly designed screen output that repeats redundant information.

Voter Registration Records
New Rochelle Office
District Number 69

Street	Number	Last Name	First	Party	Last
Bonny Meadow Lane	11413	Petrie	Laura	D	11/93
			Robert	D	11/91
	11414	Helper	Jerry	D	11/91
			Millicent	D	06/92
	11415	Brady	Alan	R	11/91
	11416	Sorel	Buddy	D	11/89
			Pickles	D	11/89
	11417	Coolie	Melvin	R	06/93
	11418	Rogers	Sally	D	11/92
Elm Street	11341	Cleaver	June	R	06/93
			Ward	R	06/93

Press the PGDN key to continue
F1 = Help   F2 = Return to the Main Menu   F3 = Change Party
F4 = Change Name   F5 = Add a Voter   F6 = Change Last Voted

FIGURE 15.11
An improved screen report that eliminates redundant information.

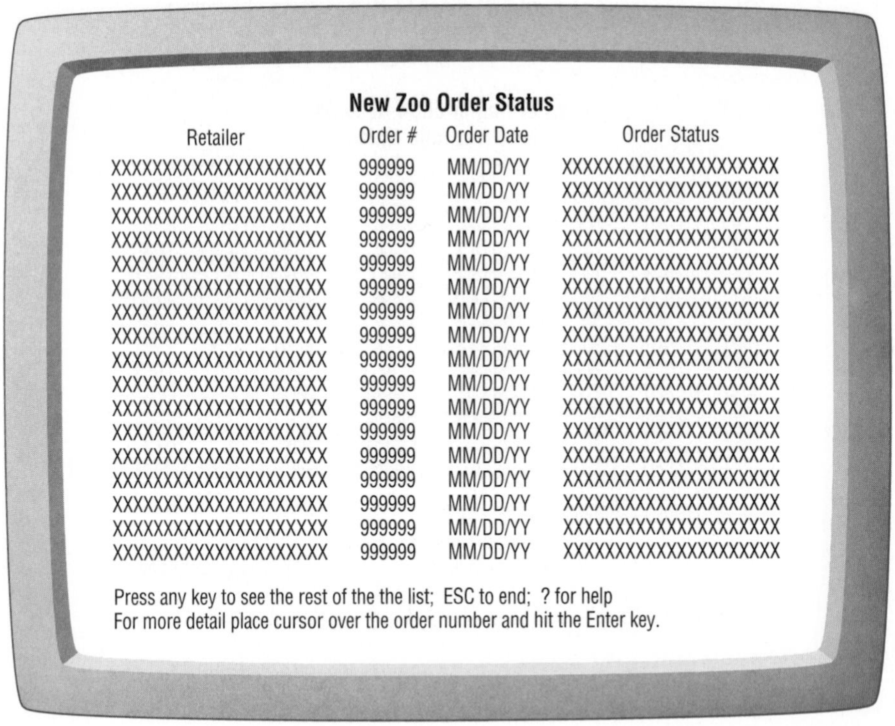

FIGURE 15.12
An electronic form used for
planning a screen layout.

New Zoo Order Status

Retailer	Order #	Order Date	Order Status
XXXXXXXXXXXXXXXXXXX	999999	MM/DD/YY	XXXXXXXXXXXXXXXXXXX
XXXXXXXXXXXXXXXXXXX	999999	MM/DD/YY	XXXXXXXXXXXXXXXXXXX
XXXXXXXXXXXXXXXXXXX	999999	MM/DD/YY	XXXXXXXXXXXXXXXXXXX
XXXXXXXXXXXXXXXXXXX	999999	MM/DD/YY	XXXXXXXXXXXXXXXXXXX
XXXXXXXXXXXXXXXXXXX	999999	MM/DD/YY	XXXXXXXXXXXXXXXXXXX
XXXXXXXXXXXXXXXXXXX	999999	MM/DD/YY	XXXXXXXXXXXXXXXXXXX
XXXXXXXXXXXXXXXXXXX	999999	MM/DD/YY	XXXXXXXXXXXXXXXXXXX
XXXXXXXXXXXXXXXXXXX	999999	MM/DD/YY	XXXXXXXXXXXXXXXXXXX
XXXXXXXXXXXXXXXXXXX	999999	MM/DD/YY	XXXXXXXXXXXXXXXXXXX
XXXXXXXXXXXXXXXXXXX	999999	MM/DD/YY	XXXXXXXXXXXXXXXXXXX
XXXXXXXXXXXXXXXXXXX	999999	MM/DD/YY	XXXXXXXXXXXXXXXXXXX
XXXXXXXXXXXXXXXXXXX	999999	MM/DD/YY	XXXXXXXXXXXXXXXXXXX
XXXXXXXXXXXXXXXXXXX	999999	MM/DD/YY	XXXXXXXXXXXXXXXXXXX
XXXXXXXXXXXXXXXXXXX	999999	MM/DD/YY	XXXXXXXXXXXXXXXXXXX
XXXXXXXXXXXXXXXXXXX	999999	MM/DD/YY	XXXXXXXXXXXXXXXXXXX
XXXXXXXXXXXXXXXXXXX	999999	MM/DD/YY	XXXXXXXXXXXXXXXXXXX

Press any key to see the rest of the the list; ESC to end; ? for help
For more detail place cursor over the order number and hit the Enter key.

Figure 15.12 is an example of screen layout from Excelerator that is being prepared for outputting tabular reports for use by the shipping department of a stuffed animal manufacturer called NewZoo. The shipping department is currently using a manual system to keep track of shipments, but with the growth in outlets they have experienced in the past year this approach is no longer practical. The shipping department would like a running summary of shipping activity so that any problems can be handled quickly, especially during the heavy shipping season in September.

Notice that the screen is generally divided into three parts. The top gives the title or heading of the screen report, "NEWZOO ORDER STATUS." Just as the columns were all given headings on the paper printout, so too are they given headings on the screen. Note, too, that the screen reads from top to bottom, and from left to right.

Continuing our analysis of this example, the columns are written in exactly as they are to appear on the screen. RETAILER, ORDER #, ORDER DATE, and ORDER STATUS are all columns that will appear on the screen. In the RETAILER column, notice that the output is designated as alphabetic characters, whereas ORDER # is shown as numeric with the use of 9s. ORDER STATUS is also noted as alphabetic characters.

Notice that the two bottom lines of the screen are used for instructions to the user. When the user positions the cursor over any ORDER #, it will automatically bring up another screen that gives more detailed information about that particular retailer's shipment.

When the screen is in a preliminary design phase, before it is finalized, it is wise to show a prototype screen to users and get their feedback about changes or improvements that they would like to see. This interactive process continues until users feel satisfied that the output provides what they need to see in a usable format. Just as with printed output, good screen cannot be created in isolation. Systems analysts need the feedback

FIGURE 15.13
The resulting screen shows
how the information actually
appears.

New Zoo Order Status

Retailer	Order #	Order Date	Order Status
Animals Unlimited	933401	09/05/94	Shipped On 09/29
	934567	09/11/94	Shipped On 09/21
	934613	09/13/94	Shipped On 09/21
	934691	09/14/94	Shipped On 09/21
Bear Bizarre	933603	09/02/94	Partially Shipped
	933668	09/08/94	Scheduled For 10/03
	934552	09/18/94	Scheduled For 10/03
	934683	09/18/94	Shipped On 09/28
Cuddles Co.	933414	09/12/94	Shipped On 09/18
	933422	09/14/94	Shipped On 09/21
	934339	09/16/94	Shipped On 09/26
	934387	09/18/94	Shipped On 09/21
	934476	09/25/94	Backordered
Stuffed Stuff	934341	09/14/94	Shipped On 09/26
	934591	09/18/94	Partially Shipped
	934633	09/26/94	Backordered
	934664	09/29/94	Partially Shipped

Press any key to see the rest of the the list; ESC to end; ? for help
For more detail place cursor over the order number and hit the Enter key.

of users to design worthwhile screens. Once approved by users, the screen layout can be finalized.

The screen produced from the Excelerator screen design display is pictured in Figure 15.13. Notice that the screen is uncluttered, yet gives a basic summary shipping status. The display orients the user as to what they are looking at with the use of a heading. Instructions at the bottom of the screen provide the user with several options, including continuing the present display, ending the display, getting help, or getting more detail.

Output screens within an application should display information consistently from screen to screen. Figure 15.14 shows the screen that results when the user positions the cursor over the ORDER # for a particular retailer. The new screen presents more details on Bear Bizarre. In the body of the screen, the user can see the retailer's order number, complete address, the order date, and the status. Additionally, a detailed breakdown of the shipment and a detailed status of each part of the shipment are given. A contact name and phone number are supplied, along with the account balance, credit rating, and shipment history. Notice that the bottom portion of the screen advises the user of options, including more details, ending the display, or getting help.

Rather than crowding all retailer information onto one screen, the analyst has made it possible for the user to bring up a particular retailer if a problem or question arises. If, for example, the summary screen indicates that an order was only "partially shipped," the user can check further on the order by calling up a detailed retailer screen and then following up with appropriate action. So far, we have been discussing general tabular output for information system screen displays. Although there is much overlap, some aspects of interaction with displays, as well as how the decision maker uses them, change as we turn to designing tabular output specifically for decision support systems.

FIGURE 15.14
If users want more details
regarding the shipping status,
they can call up a separate
screen.

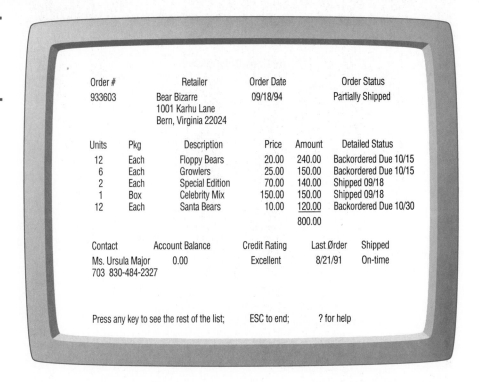

Order #		Retailer	Order Date		Order Status
933603		Bear Bizarre	09/18/94		Partially Shipped
		1001 Karhu Lane			
		Bern, Virginia 22024			

Units	Pkg	Description	Price	Amount	Detailed Status
12	Each	Floppy Bears	20.00	240.00	Backordered Due 10/15
6	Each	Growlers	25.00	150.00	Backordered Due 10/15
2	Each	Special Edition	70.00	140.00	Shipped 09/18
1	Box	Celebrity Mix	150.00	150.00	Shipped 09/18
12	Each	Santa Bears	10.00	120.00	Backordered Due 10/30
				800.00	

Contact	Account Balance	Credit Rating	Last Ørder	Shipped
Ms. Ursula Major	0.00	Excellent	8/21/91	On-time
703 830-484-2327				

Press any key to see the rest of the list;   ESC to end;   ? for help

Tabular Output for Decision Support Systems

In Chapter 12, information systems that were designed to support decision makers in semistructured decision systems, called decision support systems (DSS) were introduced. A DSS helps the decision maker to make a decision through interaction with the system. The DSS often uses screen output with a mouse or keyboard interface in order to accomplish that interaction. Output designed for decision support systems is thus characterized by modifiability and flexibility, which are not as important in output from a traditional MIS.

Figure 15.15 shows a screen for the Nebraska State Patrol Manpower Planning Decision Support System. The screen is from a Lotus spreadsheet, so the rows are numbered in the left margin, and the columns are indicated by the letters in the fourth row. There are also two menu-command rows at the top of the screen. Data are entered by viewing the output screen, placing the cursor over the cell the decision maker wants to change, and typing in a new value.

The performance measures for response time of the State Patrol troops are shown in Figure 15.16. Once again, the rows are numbered and the columns are indicated by letters. The response times are listed in a matrix by type of call and troop. Notice the instruction at the bottom of the screen that tells the user to page down for more information.

Graphical Output for Decision Support Systems

All throughout the analysis process, the systems analyst has been using graphs: to organize information through the use of data flow diagrams; to schedule activities with PERT charts; and to inform management about recommendations on the proposed information system. In Chapter 14, we covered the use of line graphs, bar, column, and pie charts in the written and oral systems proposal. Refer to that chapter for details on the effects of different kinds of graphs on decision makers.

SUMMARY

Output is any useful information or data delivered by the information system or decision support system to the user. Output can take virtually any form including print, screen, audio, microforms, CD-ROM, and electronic.

The systems analyst has six main objectives in designing output. They are to design output to serve the intended purpose and to fit the user, to deliver the right quantity of output, to deliver it to the right place, to provide output on time, and to choose the right output method.

It is important that the analyst realize that output content is related to output method. Output of different technologies affects users in different ways. Output technologies also differ in their speed, cost, portability, flexibility, and storage and retrieval possibilities. All of these factors must be considered when deciding among print, on-screen, audio, microforms, or electronic output, or a combination of these output methods.

The presentation of output can bias users in their interpretation of it. Analysts must be aware of the sources of bias, interact with users to design output, inform users of the possibilities of bias in output, create flexible and modifiable output, and train users to use multiple output to help verify the accuracy of any particular report.

Printed reports are designed with the use of on-screen or paper printer layout sheets. The data dictionary serves as the source for necessary data on each report. Mock-ups or prototypes of reports are shown to users before report design is completed, and any necessary changes are made.

"I'd say the reception you received (or should I say that your team received) for your proposal presentation was quite warm. How did you like meeting Mr. Hyatt? What? He didn't come? Oh (*laughing*), he's his own man. Anyway, don't worry about that too much. The reports I got from Snowden were encouraging. In fact, now he wants to see some preliminary designs from you all. Can you have something on his desk (or screen) in two weeks? He'll be in Singapore on business next week, but then when he recovers from the jet lag, he'll be looking for those designs. Thanks."

HYPERCASE QUESTIONS

1. Consider the reports from the Training Unit. What are Snowden's complaints about these reports. Explain in a paragraph.

2. Using either a layout paper form or a CASE tool, design a prototype output screen based on the Training Unit's reports that will summarize the following information for Snowden:

   Number of accepted projects in the training unit.
   Number of projects currently being reevaluated.
   Training subjects areas for which a consultant is being requested.

3. Design an additional output screen that you believe will support Snowden in the kind of decision making he does frequently.

4. Show your screens to three classmates. Get written feedback from them about how to improve the output screens you have designed.

5. Redesign the screens to capture the improvements suggested by your classmates. In a paragraph, explain how you have addressed each of their concerns.

The systems analyst uses the layout sheet or screen to communicate physical design to the programmer.

VDT screens, which are an especially important form of output for decision support systems as well as for traditional MIS, are designed using on-screen layout forms. Once again, aesthetics and usefulness are important to creating a well-designed screen. It is important to produce prototypes of screens that allow users to make changes where desired.

On-screen graphical output is becoming increasingly popular, especially for decision support systems. The systems analyst must consider the effect of graphs on users, the kind of data to be displayed, the purpose of the graphs, and their intended audience. Many software packages devoted to graphics are available. It is essential that decision makers receive training in how to interpret graphs if graphs are to be useful to them.

KEYWORDS AND PHRASES

internal output	output bias
external output	Internet
VDT screen	output design
audio output	control break
microforms	detail line

electronic output
e-mail
electronic bulletin boards
CD-ROM

constant information
variable information
printer layout worksheet

REVIEW QUESTIONS

1. List six objectives the analyst pursues in designing system output.
2. Contrast external output with internal output produced by the system.
3. What are three situations that point to printers as the best choice for output technology?
4. Give two instances that indicate that on-screen output is the best solution for the choice of output technology.
5. What are two of the drawbacks to audio output?
6. Cite two instances in which microforms would be a worthwhile choice for output.
7. List potential multimedia and electronic output methods.
8. What are the drawbacks of multimedia and electronic output?
9. List ten factors that must be considered when choosing output technology.
10. What output type is best if frequent updates are a necessity?
11. What kind of output is desirable if many readers will be reading, storing, and reviewing output over a period of years?
12. List three main ways in which presentations of output are unintentionally biased.
13. What are five ways the analyst can avoid biasing output?
14. What is the difference between constant and variable information presented on a report?
15. Why is it important to show users a prototype output report rather than the printer layout worksheet?
16. List six functional elements of printed reports.
17. List five stylistic/aesthetic elements of printed reports.
18. In what ways do screen and printed output differ?
19. List four guidelines to facilitate the design of good screen output.
20. What differentiates output for a DSS from that of a more traditional MIS?
21. What are the four primary considerations the analyst has when designing graphical output for decision support systems?

PROBLEMS

1. "I'm sure they won't mind if we start sending them the report on these oversized computer sheets. All this time we've been condensing it, retyping it, and sending it to our biggest accounts, but we just can't now. We're so understaffed, we don't have the time," says Otto Breth. "I'll just write a comment on here telling them how to respond to this, and then we can send it out."
   a. What potential problems do you see in casually changing external output? List them.
   b. Discuss in a paragraph how internal and external output can differ in appearance and function.

2. "I don't need to see it very often, but when I do I have to be able to get at it quickly. I think we lost the last contract because the information I needed was buried in a stack of paper on someone's desk somewhere," says Luke Alover, an architect describing the company's problems to one of the analysts assigned to the new systems project. "What I need is instant information about how much a building of that square footage cost the last time we bid it; what the basic materials such as steel, glass, and concrete cost now from our three top suppliers; who our likely competition on this type of building might be; and who composes the committee that will be making the final decision on who gets the bid. But right now, it's in a hundred reports somewhere. I have to look all over for it."

   a. Given the limited details you have here, use a paragraph to suggest an output method for Luke's use that will solve some of his current problems. In a second paragraph, explain your reasons for choosing the output method you did. (*Hint*: Be sure to relate output method to output content in your answer.)

   b. Luke's current thinking is that no paper record of the output discussed above need be kept. In a paragraph, discuss what factors should be weighed before screen output is used to the exclusion of printed reports.

   c. Make a list of five to seven questions concerning the output's function in the organization that you would ask Luke and others before deciding to do away with any printed reports currently being used.

3. Here are several situations calling for decisions about output content, output methodology, distribution, etc. For each situation, note the appropriate output decision.

   a. A large, well-regarded supplier of key raw materials to your company's production process requires a year-end summary report of totals purchased from them. Output method?

   b. Internal "brainstorming" memos are circulated via staff regarding plans for company picnic/fundraiser. Output method?

   c. A summary report of financial situation is needed by a key decision maker to use in presenting a proposal to potential external backers. Output method?

   d. A listing of current night's hotel room reservations is needed for front desk personnel. Output method?

   e. A listing of current night's hotel room reservations is needed for the use of local police. Output method?

   f. A real-time count of people passing through the gates of Wallaby World (an Australian theme park) will be used by parking lot patrols. Output method?

   g. An inventory system must register an item each time it has been scanned by a wand. Output method?

   h. A summary report of merit pay increases allotted to each of 120 employees, will be used by 22 supervisors during joint supervisors' meeting and subsequently when explaining merit pay increases to their own departmental employees. Output method?

i. Competitive information is needed by three strategic planners in the organization, but it is industrially sensitive if widely distributed. Output method?

j. Historical files of actual documents filed are kept for a period of seven years, as mandated by federal regulations. Output method?

4. "I think I see now where that guy was coming from, but he had me going for a minute there," say Miss deLimit. She is discussing a prototype of screen output, designed by the systems analyst, that she has just seen. "I mean, I never considered it a problem before if even as much as 20 percent of the total class size couldn't be fit into a class. We know our classes are in demand, and since we can't hire more faculty to cover the areas we need, the adjustment has to come in the student demand. He's got it highlighted as a problem if only 5 percent of the students who want a class can't get in. But that's okay. Now that I know what he means, I'll just ignore it when the computer beeps."

a. In a sentence or two, describe the problem Miss deLimit is experiencing with the screen output.

b. Is her solution to "ignore the beeps" a reasonable one given that output is in the prototype stage?

c. In a paragraph, explain how the screen output for this particular problem can be changed so that it better reflects the rules of the system Miss deLimit is using.

5. Here is a log sheet for a patient information system used by nurses at a convalescent home to record patient visitors and activities during their shifts. Design a printed report (50 lines long by 120 columns wide maximum) that provides a summary for the charge nurse of each shift and a report for the activities coordinator at the end of a week. Be sure to use proper conventions to indicate constant and variable data, and so on. These reports will be used to determine staffing patterns and future activities offerings.

Date	Patient	Visitors	Relationship	Activities
2/14	Clarke	2	Mother, father	walked about halls, attended chapel, meals in cafeteria
	Coffey	6	Coworkers	played games, party in room
	Martine	0	—	meals in room
	Laury	4	husband and friends	games in sunroom, watched TV
	Finney	2	parents	conversation, meals in cafeteria
	Cartwright	1	sister	conversation, crafts room
	Goldstein	2	sister, brother	conversation, games out of room, whirlpool

6. Design a screen for problem 5, using a screen layout form (80 columns by 24 rows). Make any assumptions about system capability necessary, and follow screen design conventions for on-screen instructions. (*Hint*: You can use more than one screen if you wish.)

   a. In a paragraph discuss why you designed each report as you did in problems 5 and 6. What are the major differences in your approach to each? Can the printed reports be successfully transplanted to the screen without changes? Why or why not?

7. Clancy Corporation manufactures uniforms for police departments worldwide. Their uniforms are chosen by many groups because of their low cost and simple, yet dignified design. You are helping to design a DSS for Clancy Corp., and they have asked for tabular output that will help them in making various decisions about what designers to use, where to market their uniforms, and what changes to make to uniforms to keep them looking up to date. Here are some of the data they would like to see output in tables, including uniform style names, and example buyer group of each style, and which designers design which uniform styles:

   a. Prepare an example of on-screen tabulator output that incorporates the foregoing data about Clancy's. Follow proper conventions for on-screen tabular output. Use codes and a key where appropriate.

Style Name	Example buyer	Designers
full military	(NYPD)	Claudio, Rialtto, Melvin Mine
half military	(LAPD)	Rialtto, Calvetti, Duran, Melvin Mine
formal dress	Australian Armed Forces	Claudio, Dundee, Melvin Mine
casual dress	("Miami Vice")	Johnson, Melvin Mine

8. Clancy's is also interested in graphical output for their DSS. They want to see a graphical comparison of how many of each style of uniform is being sold each year.

   a. Choose an appropriate graph style and design and on-screen graph that incorporates the following data:

      1991 full military (57 percent of all sales)
      1992 full military (59 percent of all sales)
      1993 casual dress (62 percent of all sales)
      1994 casual dress (55 percent of all sales)
      1995 casual dress (40 percent) and half military (22 percent)
      Be sure to follow proper screen design conventions. Use codes and a key if necessary.

   b. Chose a second method of graphing that might allow the decision makers at Clancy's to see a trend in purchase of particular uniform styles over time. Draw an on-screen graph for use as part of the output for

Clancy's DSS. Be sure to follow proper screen design conventions. Use codes and a key if necessary.

c. In a paragraph, discuss the differences in the two on-screen graphs you have chosen. Defend your choices.

GROUP PROJECTS

1. Brainstorm with your team members about what types of output are most appropriate for a variety of employees of Maverick Transport. Include a list of environments, or decision making situations and type of output. In a paragraph discuss why the group suggested particular options for output.

2. Have each group member design an output screen or form for the output situations you listed in problem 1. (Use either a CASE tool or paper layout form to complete each screen or form.)

3. Share each output screen or form among your team members. Using the feedback gathered, improve the screens or forms you have designed.

SELECTED BIBLIOGRAPHY

Davenport, T. H. "Saving IT's Soul: Human-Centered Information Management." *Harvard Business Review,* March–April, 1994, pp. 119–131.

Davis, G. B., and H. M. Olson. *Management Information Systems, Conceptual Foundations, Structure, and Development*, 2nd ed. New York: McGraw-Hill Book Company, 1985.

IBM, "The Finishing Touch," brochure on printing, 1986, pp. 14–24.

Jarvenpaa, S. L., and G. W. Dickson. "Myth vs. Facts About Graphics in Decision Making," *Spectrum,* vol. 3, no 1., February 1986, pp. 1–3.

Laudon, K. C. and Laudon, J. P. *Management Information Systems,* 3rd ed. New York: Macmillan Publishing Company, 1994.

McCombie, K. "Connecting Your Enterprise LAN to the Internet," *Internet World*, June 1994.

Quarterman, J. S., "What Can Businesses Get Out of Internet." *Computerworld*, February 22, 1993.

Senn, J. A. *Analysis and Design of Information Systems*, 2nd ed. New York: McGraw-Hill Book Company, 1987.

Whitten, J. L., L. D. Bentley, and V. M. Barlow. *Systems Analysis and Design*, 3rd ed. Barr Ridge, IL: Irwin, 1994.

REPORTING ON OUTPUTS

"Let's create output specifications and then work backward through the data flow to determine the corresponding input data," says Anna during her next meeting with Chip.

"Of course," Chip agrees.

Output was separated into two categories: reports and screens. Reports were further defined as external reports, such as the User Software Notification, or internal reports like the Hardware Inventory Listing. Each report was further classified as a detailed, exception, or summary report.

Based on conversations with Paige Prynter, the analysts believe that the HARDWARE INVESTMENT REPORT has the highest priority. It is need as soon as possible because the budget process will soon reach a critical phase and there are many requests for new hardware.

The process used for creating the HARDWARE INVESTMENT REPORT is similar to creating all reports. Chip examines the data flow diagrams for the new system and locates the data flow labeled HARDWARE FINANCIAL REPORT. This exploded to the record shown in Figure E15.1, HARDWARE INVESTMENT REPORT, providing a list of all the elements on the report.

The element list is used to create the report layout. Since the elements are described in the XLDictionary, they are easily selected for inclusion on the report. Page titles and column headings are added, with careful attention to centering, and the whole report is examined for a professional appearance. Minor adjustments are made and the sample printed.

The next step is crucial—Chip asks Paige to review the report and make any changes she likes. Chip asks, "Are there any additional columns or other data missing that would make for a more useful report? Is all the data on the report necessary?"

Paige studies the output for a few minutes and remarks, "Subtotals for each BRAND, including the NUMBER OF MACHINES and grand totals, are necessary. We receive requests for different types of machines, and knowing how many of each machine may help determine what is purchased."

Chip returns to his microcomputer and makes the necessary changes. The final HARDWARE INVESTMENT REPORT layout is shown in Figure E15.2. This is again reviewed by Paige, and she signs off on the layout as complete.

The logic for this summary report is outlined in a process specification. The MICROCOMPUTER MASTER file is sorted by MODEL within BRAND. Records are read from the MICROCOMPUTER MASTER file, and totals for each BRAND and MODEL are accumulated. When either BRAND or MODEL changes, a report line is printed. When a change in BRAND occurs, BRAND SUBTOTALS are printed. GRAND TOTALS are printed after all records are processed.

Excelerator also may be used to create reports, either from XLDictionary information or by entering data into prototype screen designs. Since the Add Microcomputer prototype screen has already been developed,

Allen Schmidt,
Julie E. Kendall, and
Kenneth E. Kendall

```
DATE: 21-FEB-95                         RECORD - EXPLOSION                                    PAGE    1
TIME: 12:35                             NAME: HARDWARE INVESTMENT REPORT                       Excelerator

NAME:                           HARDWARE INVESTMENT REPORT       DEFINITION:
ALIAS:                          MICROCOMPUTER INVESTMENT REPORT CONTAINS ELEMENTS FOUND ON THE MICROCOMPUTER INVEST. RPT.N

ELEMENT/RECORD                                  OFF  OCC  TYPE  LEN  DEFINITION
----------------------------------------------  ---  ---  ----  ---  -------------------------------------------------------

COMPUTER BRAND                                  000  001   E    010  THE BRAND OF COMPUTER NECESSARY TO RUN THE SOFTWARE

COMPUTER MODEL                                  010  001   E    012  THE SPECIFIC MODEL NECESSARY TO RUN THE SOFTWARE

NUMBER OF MACHINES                              022  001   E    004  A COUNT OF THE NUMBER OF MICROCOMPUTERS FOR A SPECIFIC MODEL

TOTAL INVESTMENT                                026  001   E    006  THE TOTAL AMOUNT INVESTED IN HARDWARE OR SOFTWARE

SUBTOTAL - MICRO BRAND INVESTED                 032  001   E    006  THE TOTAL AMOUNT INVESTED IN HARDWARE OR SOFTWARE

GRAND TOTAL MICRO INVESTMENT                    038  001   E    006  THE GRAND TOTAL AMOUNT INVESTED IN HARDWARE OR SOFTWARE

Record length is 44.
```

FIGURE E15.1
HARDWARE INVESTMENT REPORT record.

Anna uses the screen design to add records to an Excelerator-created data file.

After several records are entered, the **Screen Data Reporting** feature is used to create the report. Figure E15.3 is an example of the screen used to specify the report characteristics. Areas are available for selecting records for the report, determining the format of the report, and specifying the sort sequence. This direct link to the data entered on screens is a valuable aid to determining if the screens are correctly designed and functional in producing appropriate report data.

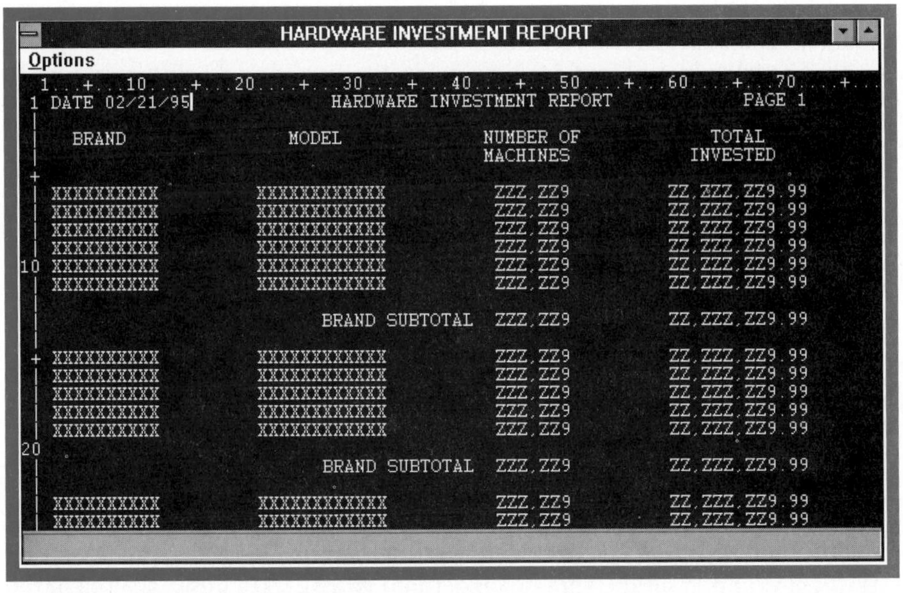

FIGURE E15.2
HARDWARE INVESTMENT REPORT layout.

FIGURE E15.3
MICROCOMPUTER INSTALLATION report.

The fields found on the screen data file are listed in the middle columns and simply need to be selected to create the final report. Headers, column widths, and a report title may be created and modified. Other selections allow the designer to add counts and totals.

The field selections were made, and the report was produced. A copy of the report is taken to Mike Crowe to get his feedback. Mike notes that two additional columns are needed: one column to indicate whether a mouse is necessary and one column to indicate the type of monitor. A few keystrokes and several mouse clicks later, the final report, shown in Figure E15.4, is produced.

A similar method may be used for producing other Excelerator reports. Chip must determine the elements found on the NEW MICRO-COMPUTER FORM and decides to let Excelerator tell him the information, Complete system elements were added earlier in the design phase, including an entry area titled **Source** referring to the form from which the element is keyed.

Chip selects the **Report Writer** option and proceeds to create the list of fields on the form. Figure E15.5 is an example of the selection screen, similar to that for producing screen data-entry reports. Columns are created, and the selection criteria picked only those records with a **Source** entry of NEW MICROCOMPUTER FORM. The report produced is shown in Figure E15.6.

Anna spends some time speaking with Cher Ware about her report needs. Several printed reports were outlined when Cher asks the question, "Will I get reports on the screen, ones that I can quickly view, that have the latest information?" The discussion that followed resulted in the creation of several screen reports.

DATE: 21-FEB-95 MICROCOMPUTER INSTALLATION REPORT PAGE 1
TIME: 12:34 Excelerator

SERIAL NUMBER	BRAND	MODEL	MEMORY SIZE	FIXED DISK	DISK DRIVE A	MOUSE	MONITOR
002999459952	APPLE	MAC II CX	2000	50.	3.5HD		
002389698342	APPLE	MAC II CX	2000	50.	3.5HD		
002387232222	APPLE	MAC II CX	2000	50.	3.5HD		
333444555666	IBM	PS2 50Z	2000	30.	3.5HD		VGA
668984983448	IBM	PS2 50Z	1000	30.	3.5HD		
974564564533	IBM	SX 386	2000	50.	3.5HD		
974598734533	IBM	SX 386	2000	50.	3.5HD		
974598734533	IBM	SX 386	2000	50.	3.5HD		
970005534533	IBM	SX 386	2000	50.	3.5HD	Y	
974598734533	IBM	SX 386	2000	50.	3.5HD		
239729387234	IBM	SX 386	2000	40.	3.5HD		MOD

FIGURE E15.4
MICROCOMPUTER INSTALLATION REPORT.

SOFTWARE BY CATEGORY, the first screen report created, is presented in Figure E15.7. The screen has no entry fields, since there is no selection of data and the entire report is to be displayed. The Software Category is group displayed with four other columns: software title, version, publisher, and the number of copies. If a site license is available, the COPIES column contains a value of 999. The CATEGORY column is also

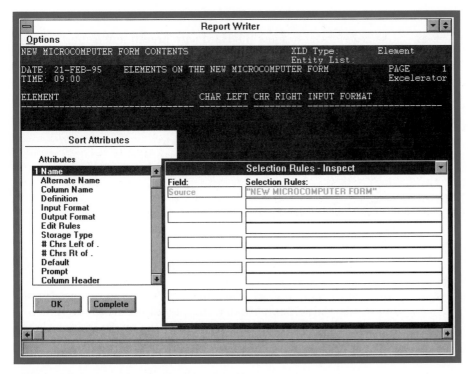

FIGURE E15.5
NEW MICROCOMPUTER FORM element report selection.

```
DATE: 28-NOV-93      ELEMENTS ON THE NEW MICROCOMPUTER FORM            PAGE    1
TIME: 12:16                                                            Excelerator


ELEMENT                                CHAR LEFT CHR RIGHT INPUT FORMAT
--------------------------------       --------- --------- ------------------------
BRAND NAME                                   10         0 X(10)
DATE PURCHASED                                6         0 9(6)
DISK DRIVE A                                  6         0 X(6)
DISK DRIVE B                                  6         0 X(6)
FIXED DISK                                    3         0 999
FIXED DISK 2                                  3         0 999
HARDWARE INVENTORY NUMBER                     8         0 9(8)
INTERNAL BOARDS                               3         0 XXX
MEMORY SIZE                                   5         0 9(5)
MODEL                                        12         0 X(12)
MONITOR                                       4         0 X(4)
PRINTER                                       5         0 X(5)
PURCHASE COST                                 5         2 9(5).99
SERIAL NUMBER                                12         0 X(12)
WARRANTY                                      1         0 X
```

FIGURE E15.6
NEW MICROCOMPUTER FORM element report.

displayed as a code. The reason for using coded information is that a
screen report is limited to eighty characters in width.

There is no feedback message on the screen report, since no data are
keyed. However, the operator message must provide instructions on how
to scroll to the next or previous page and how to exit the report.

Exercises[*]

⊟ **E-1.** Use Excelerator to view the Hardware Investment Report.

⊟ **E-2.** Chip, Dot, and Mike participated in several brainstorming sessions resulting in the outlining of several reports. A HARD-
WARE MASTER REPORT has been partially completed. Modify
the report to include the following columns. This is a large
report, and you will have to scroll to the right on the screen to
add columns. Print the completed report.

MEMORY
FIXED DISK
FIXED DISK 2
DISKETTE A
DISKETTE B
MONITOR
MOUSE
PRINTER

⊟ **E-3.** After meeting with Cher Ware and Hy Perteks to discuss reporting needs, Anna has partially completed the USER NOTIFICA-
TION NEW SOFTWARE report. Modify the report to include the

[*] The exercises preceded by a disk icon require the program Excelerator (or another CASE
tool). A disk is provided free of charge to any professor adopting this book. The examples on
the disk may be imported into Excelerator and then used by students.

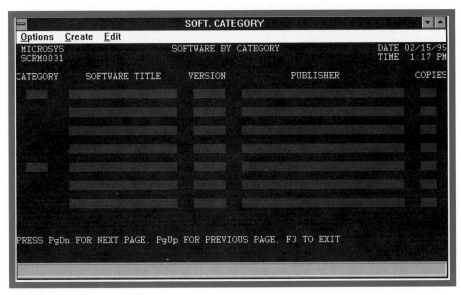

FIGURE E15.7
SOFTWARE BY CATEGORY screen report.

following columns and print your results. Headings have been provided on the report for the missing columns.

CAMPUS LOCATION (fully spelled out not, the coded entry)
CAMPUS ROOM
MICROCOMPUTER BRAND
MICROCOMPUTER MODEL
NUMBER OF COPIES

Is the report a summary or detailed report? In a paragraph, outline the logic that you feel the report-producing program must use.

E-4. Both Dot and Mike need to know when new microcomputers have been received. Create the NEW MICROCOMPUTER RECEIVED REPORT. The data flow MICROCOMPUTER RECEIVED REPORT has been exploded to the record NEW MICROCOMPUTER RECEIVED RPT. Print or view the record to determine the columns that must be printed on the report.

E-5. Create the SOFTWARE MASTER REPORT, containing pertinent information that helps Cher and Hy to easily locate the various copies of any software package. The elements necessary to produce the report are located on the SOFTWARE MASTER REPORT record.

The TITLE, VERSION, PUBLISHER, and CATEGORY should be group printed. Totals are to be included for each Title/Version combination. Print the completed report design.

E-6. View and print the Excelerator report NEW SOFTWARE FORM. Use the **Report Writer** feature found within the **ANALYSIS** option.

E-7. Use the **Screen Data Reporting** feature to view and print the MICRO INSTALLATION REPORT based on data entered in the ADD MICRO screen prototype.

⊟ **E-8.** View the SOFTWARE BY CATEGORY screen report. The screen design name is SOFT. CATEGORY. Use the **Screen Data Entry** feature to view the sample data on the screen. The data entry file name is SOFTWARE BY CATEGORY. Press PgDn and PgUp to view next and previous pages of output.

⊟ **E-9.** Modify the SOFTWARE BY MACHINE screen report. The screen name is SOFT. BY MACH. Heading lines have been provided, and the first data field of each column is included. Use cut-and-paste techniques to create the columns. Eliminate the feedback message and change the operator message to: PRESS PgDn FOR NEXT PAGE, PgUp FOR PREVIOUS, F3 TO EXIT. When the report is finished, copy the screen to SOFT. BY MACH. 2. Use the **Inspect** option to test the screen. Create sample data and enter it onto the screen. Press Esc when finished.

⊟ **E-10.** Create the OUTSTANDING PURCHASE ORDERS FOR MICRO-COMPUTERS report. This would be produced for all PURCHASE ORDER records that have a purchase order code of M101, representing microcomputers, with the further condition that the QUANTITY ORDERED on the record must be greater than QUANTITY RECEIVED.

Include the following columns:
ORDER NUMBER
BRAND
MODEL
ORDER DATE
QUANTITY ORDERED
QUANTITY RECEIVED

In a paragraph, state whether this is a summary, exception, or detailed report. Explain.

DESIGNING EFFECTIVE INPUT

INPUT DESIGN OBJECTIVES

The quality of system input determines the quality of system output. It is vital that input forms and screens be designed with this critical relationship in mind. By insisting on well-designed input, the systems analyst is acknowledging that poor input calls into question the trustworthiness of the entire system.

Well-designed input forms and visual display terminal (VDT) screens should meet the objectives of effectiveness, accuracy, ease of use, consistency, simplicity, and attractiveness, as depicted in Figure 16.1. All of these objectives are attainable through the use of basic design principles, knowledge of what is needed as input for the system, and an understanding of how users respond to different elements of forms and screens.

Effectiveness means that input forms and screens serve specific purposes in the management information system, while accuracy refers to design that assures proper completion. Ease of use means that forms and screens are straightforward and require no extra time to decipher. Consistency in this case means that forms and screens group data similarly from one application to the next, while simplicity refers to keeping forms and screens purposely uncluttered in a manner that focuses the user's attention. Attractiveness implies that users will enjoy using, or even be drawn to using, forms and screens through their appealing design.

GOOD FORM DESIGN

Although an in-house forms specialist may be available, the systems analyst should be capable of designing a complete and useful form. It is also important to be able to recognize poorly designed, overlapping, or unnecessary forms that are wasting the organization's resources and therefore should be eliminated.

FIGURE 16.1
Six objectives for the design
of input.

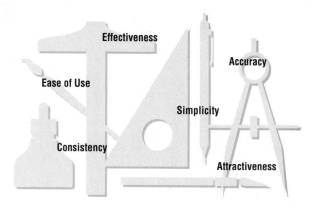

Forms are important instruments for steering the course of work. By definition, they are preprinted or duplicated papers that require people to fill in responses in a standardized way. Forms elicit and capture information required by organizational members that will often input to the computer. Through this process, forms often serve as source documents for data entry personnel.

Four Guidelines for Form Design

Four guidelines for form design should be observed in order to design useful forms:

1. Make forms easy to fill out.
2. Ensure that forms meet the purpose for which they are designed.
3. Design forms to assure accurate completion.
4. Keep forms attractive.

There are a number of means to achieve each guideline for form design. Each of the four guidelines is considered separately in the following subsections.

Making Forms Easy to Fill Out

To reduce error, speed completion, and facilitate entry of data, it is essential that forms be easy to fill out. This guideline is based on more than well-placed empathy for the user. The cost of the forms is minimal compared to the cost of the time employees spend filling them out and inputting data to the computer.

FORM FLOW. Designing a form with proper flow can minimize the time and effort expended by employees in form completion. Forms should flow from left to right and top to bottom, as shown in the police incident report depicted in Figure 16.2

The flow of the incident report works because it is based on the way people in the Western culture read a page. The incident report is designed so that the attending officer first fills in the date, then the time, then continues on to the bottom of the form, which elicits suggestions on further handling of the situation.

Illogical flow takes extra time and is frustrating. A form that requires people to go directly to the bottom of the form and then skip back up to the top for completion exhibits poor flow.

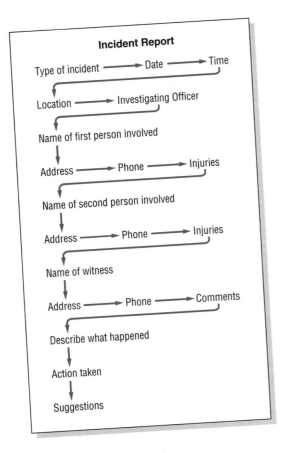

FIGURE 16.2
Good form flow makes the
form easy to use.

SEVEN SECTIONS OF A FORM. A second technique that makes it easy for people to fill out forms correctly is logical grouping of information. The seven main sections of a strong form are:

1. Heading.
2. Identification and access.
3. Instructions.
4. Body.
5. Signature and verification.
6. Totals.
7. Comments.

Ideally, these sections should appear on a page grouped as they are in Figure 16.3. Notice that the seven sections cover basic information required on most forms. The top quarter of the form is devoted to three sections: the heading, the identification and access section, and the instructions section.

The heading section usually includes the name and address of the business originating the form. The identification and access section includes codes that may be used to file the report and gain access to it at a later date. (In Chapter 17 we discuss in detail how to access specially keyed information in a database.) This information is very important when an organization is required to keep the document for a specified number of

FIGURE 16.3
Seven sections found in well-
designed forms.

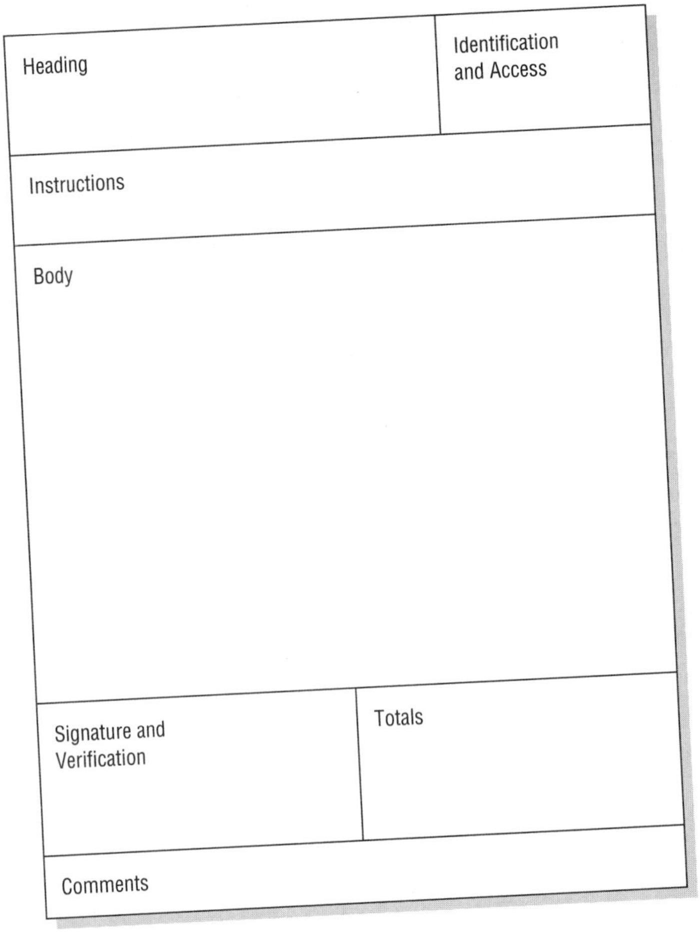

Heading	Identification and Access
Instructions	
Body	
Signature and Verification	Totals
Comments	

years. The instructions section tells how the form should be filled out and where it should be routed when complete.

The middle of the form is its body, which composes approximately half of the form. This is the part of the form that requires the most detail and development from the person completing it. The body is the part of the form most likely to contain explicit, variable data. For example, on a parts requisition form this section might include data such as the firm ordering the part, part number, quantity ordered, and price.

The bottom quarter of the form is composed of three sections: signature and verification, totals, and comments. By requiring a signature in this part of the form, the designer is echoing the design of other familiar documents, such as letters. Requiring ending totals and a summary of comments is a logical way to provide closure for the person filling out the form.

CAPTIONING. Clear captioning is yet another technique that can make easy work of filling out a form. Captions tell the person completing the form what to put on a blank line, space, or box. Several options are available for captioning, as shown in Figure 16.4. Notice that two types of line captions and two types of check-off captions are shown.

The advantage of putting the caption below the line is that there is more room on the line itself for data. The disadvantage is that it is sometimes unclear which line is associated with the caption: the line above or

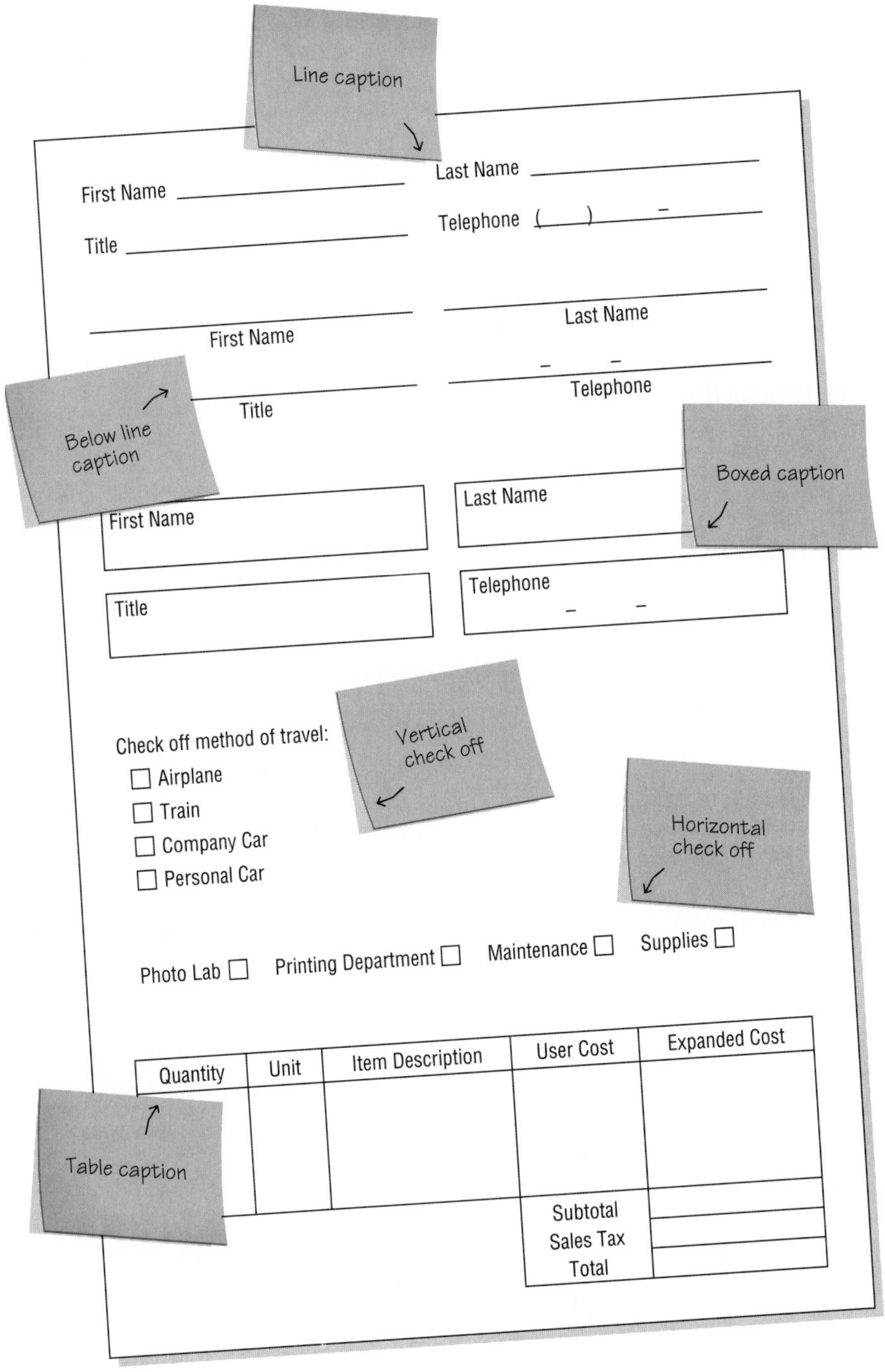

FIGURE 16.4
Major captioning alternatives.

below the caption. The person filling out the form may realize that the wrong line has been used and will subsequently have to complete a new form.

Line captions can be to the left of blanks and on the same line, or they can be printed below the line where data will be entered.

Another way to caption is to provide a box for data instead of a line. Captions can be placed inside, above, or below the box. Boxes on forms help people enter data in the correct place, and also make reading the form easier for the form's recipient. The caption should use a small type point size, so that it does not dominate the entry area. Small vertical "tick marks" may be included in the box if the data is intended for entry into a computer system. If there is not enough room on a record for the data, the person filling out the form, rather than the data entry operator, has the freedom to determine how the data should be abbreviated. Captions may also include small clarification notes to help the user correctly enter the information, such as: Date (MM/DD/YY) or Name (Last, First, Middle Initial).

Whatever styles of line caption are chosen, it is important to employ them consistently. For instance, it is confusing to fill out a form that has both above- and below-line captions.

Check-off captions are superior when response options are necessarily restricted. Notice the list of travel methods shown for the vertical check-off example in the previous figure. If employee expenses for business travel are reimbursed only for those travel methods listed, a check-off system is more expedient that a blank like. It has the added advantage of reminding the person who is verifying the data to look for an airline ticket stub or other receipt.

A horizontal check-off caption is also superior to a line caption when information required is routine and constant. An example is a form that would request services from one of the following departments: Photo Lab, Printing Department, Maintenance, or Supplies. The departments routinely provide service to others in the organization and are not likely to change quickly.

Table captions work well in the body of a form where details are required. When and employee properly fills out a form with table captions he or she is creating a table for the next person receiving the form, thereby helping to organize data coherently.

A combination of captions can also be used effectively. For example, table captions can be used to specify categories such as quantity, and line captions to indicate where the subtotal, sales tax, and total should be typed. Since different captions serve different purposes, it is generally necessary to employ several caption styles in each form.

Meeting the Intended Purpose

Forms are created to serve one or more purposes in the recording, processing, storing, and retrieving of information for businesses. Sometimes it is desirable to provide different information to different departments or users, yet still share some basic information. This situation is where specialty forms are useful.

One example of a specialty form can be found in Figure 16.5, a three-part form with each part serving a specific purpose. This form is a purchase invoice for Annie's Equipment, a gymnastic and exercise equipment retailer. The form is actually a three-part preprinted form with two pull-out carbon sheets.

By virtue of its functional design, the invoice serves accounting and salespeople in the store, the bank that processes customers' credit-card charges, and the customer. The top copy of the invoice is the store's copy. Notice that it requires the most detailed information of the three copies. The store copy includes the store number as well as the customer card number and the approval code for the charge. All of this information is used by a data entry person to ensure proper billing.

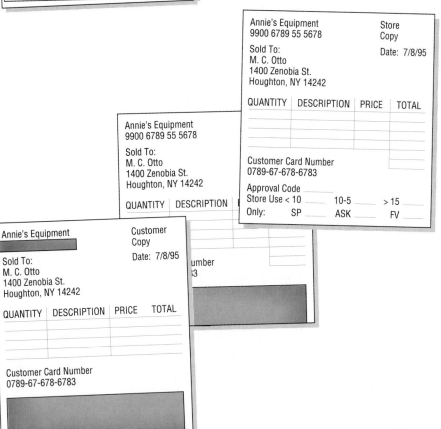

FIGURE 16.5
A three-part specialty form.

Some of the unique entries required on the store copy are used to track productivity of Annie's eight salespeople. Since these data might be bothersome to anyone outside of the store, instructions for proper completion of the bottom blanks are not printed, but rather provided orally.

The bottom of the store copy requires the salesperson to check off how much time was necessary to make the sale: less than 10 minutes, 10 to 15 minutes, or more than 15 minutes. It also requires the salesperson (SP) to initial the form, check off whether the customer asked (ASK) for them by name, and whether it was the customer's first visit (FV) to Annie's.

The second copy of the three-part invoice is route to the bank holding the customer's credit-card account. Notice that the bank still needs store and customer account numbers, but the sales performance data are omitted through use of a short carbon. Wherever the carbon is cut or blocked out, nothing will be printed.

The customer copy of the invoice is the simplest. It copies essential information that fills customer needs, such as date, description of equipment purchased, price paid, and credit card used. However, the customer copy uses a specially shaded box to block out Annie's store number, which would be unnecessary for the customer. Sales performance data are also omitted from the customer copy.

The term *specialty form* can also refer solely to the way forms are prepared by the stationer. Examples of stationers' specialty forms are multiple-part forms to create instant triplicates of data, continuous-feed forms that run through the printer without intervention, and perforated forms that leave a stub behind as a record when they are separated. Use of such forms must be judicious; they are costly, and users can quickly be strangled with the red tape generated by meaningless multiple-part forms.

Assuring Accurate Completion

Error rates typically associated with collecting data will drop sharply when forms are designed to assure accurate completion. Design is important in making people do the right thing with the form, whether it is the first or four-hundredth time they are using it.

The Bakerloo Brothers employee expense voucher, shown in Figure 16.6, goes a long way toward securing accurate form completion. Many of the form design techniques we have discussed are utilized in this sample expense voucher. The form design implements the correct flow: top to bottom, and left to right. It also observes the idea of seven main sections or information categories. Additionally, the employee expense voucher uses a combination of clear captions and instructions.

Since Bakerloo Brothers employees are reimbursed only for actual expenses, getting a correct total expenditure is essential. The form design provides an internal double check with column totals and row totals expected to sum to the same number. If the row and column totals don't sum to the same number, the employee filling out the form knows there is a problem and can correct it on the spot. An error is prevented, and the employee can be reimbursed the amount due; both outcomes are attributable to a suitable form design.

Keeping Forms Attractive

Although attractiveness of forms is dealt with last, its order of appearance is not meant to diminish its importance. Rather, it is addressed last because making forms appealing is accomplished by applying the techniques discussed in the preceding sections. Aesthetic forms draw people into them and encourage completion. This means that people who fill out the forms will be more satisfied and that the forms will be completed.

Forms should look uncluttered. They should appear organized and logical after they are filled in. Providing enough space for typewritten or handwritten responses will help in this regard. Typewritten entries require a minimum of 1/6-inch spacing between lines, and handwritten entries require approximately 1/4-inch. Forms designed for completion by either hand or typewriter should allow about 1/3-inch intervals between lines. A

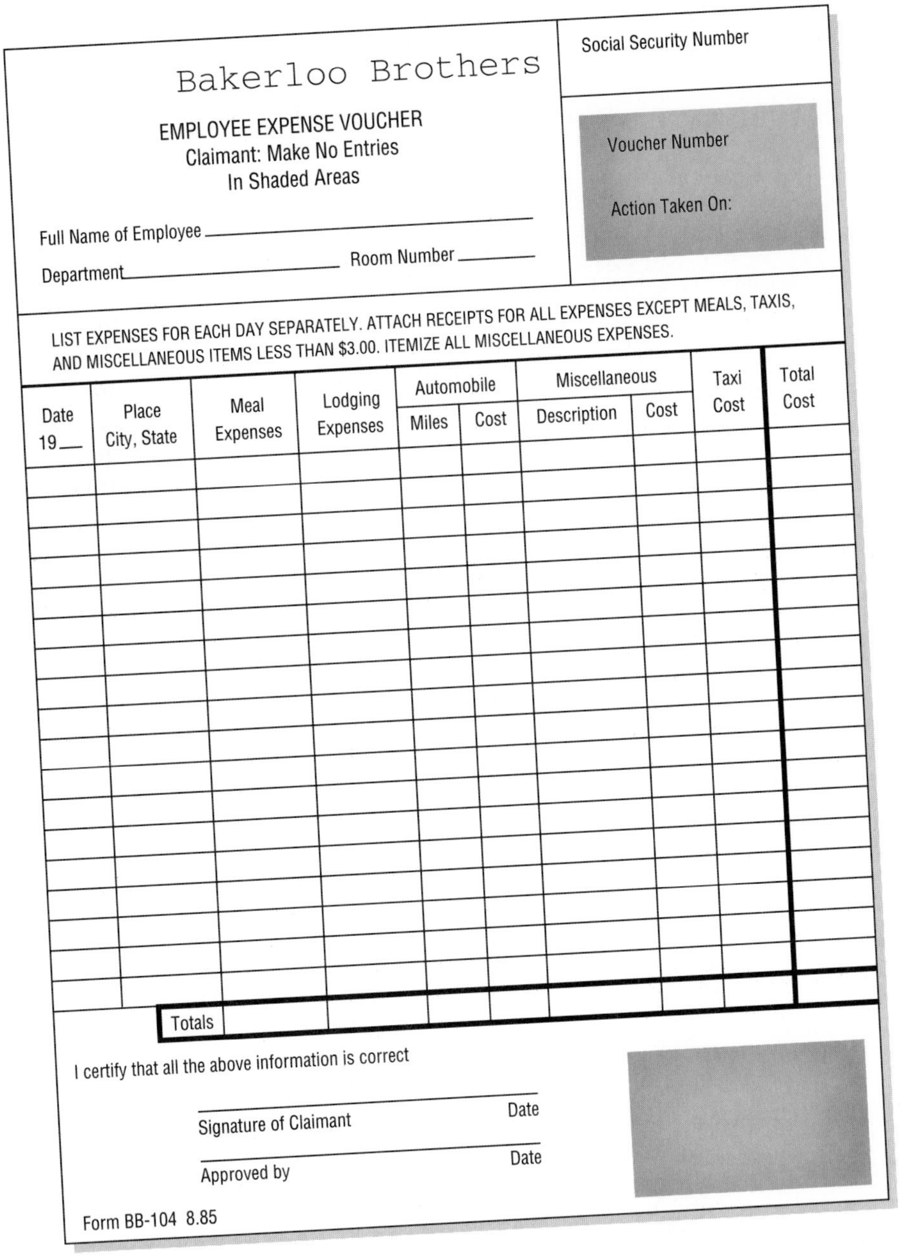

FIGURE 16.6
A form that encourages
accurate completion.

Bakerloo Brothers

Social Security Number

EMPLOYEE EXPENSE VOUCHER
Claimant: Make No Entries
In Shaded Areas

Voucher Number

Action Taken On:

Full Name of Employee _____

Department _____ Room Number _____

LIST EXPENSES FOR EACH DAY SEPARATELY. ATTACH RECEIPTS FOR ALL EXPENSES EXCEPT MEALS, TAXIS, AND MISCELLANEOUS ITEMS LESS THAN $3.00. ITEMIZE ALL MISCELLANEOUS EXPENSES.

Date 19__	Place City, State	Meal Expenses	Lodging Expenses	Automobile		Miscellaneous		Taxi Cost	Total Cost
				Miles	Cost	Description	Cost		
Totals									

I certify that all the above information is correct

_____   _____
Signature of Claimant   Date

_____   _____
Approved by   Date

Form BB-104 8.85

useful heuristic for gauging the appropriate length of lines is allowing for five handwritten or eight typewritten characters per inch. Allowing ample room invites completion.

To be attractive, forms should elicit information in the expected order: convention dictates asking for name, street address, city, state, and zip or postal code, and country if necessary. Proper layout and flow contribute to a form's attractiveness.

Using different fonts for type within the same form can help make it appealing to fill in. Separating categories and subcategories with thick and thin lines can also encourage interest in the form. Type fonts and line weights are useful design elements for capturing attention and making people feel secure that they are filling in the form correctly.

This Form May Be Hazardous to Your Health

Figure 16.C1 is a printed medical history form that Dr. Mike Robe, a family practitioner, has his receptionist give to all new patients. All patients must fill it out before they see the doctor.

The receptionist is getting back many incomplete and/or confusing responses. This makes it difficult for Dr. Robe to review the forms and understand why the new patient is there. Additionally, the poor responses make it time-consuming for the receptionist to enter new patients into the files.

Medical History Form

Name _____ Employer _____ Age _____

Address _____ Zip _____ Phone _____ Office _____

Insurer _____ Is this [ ] your policy [ ] your spouse's policy

Blue Cross [ ]   State Physician's Service [ ]   Other [ ]   (state) _____

- -

Have you ever had surgery?   Yes____   No____   If so, when? _____

Describe the surgery _____

Have you ever been hospitaziled?   Yes____   No____   If so, when? _____

Why? _____

Complete the following...

	I have had	Family history
Diabetes	☐	☐
Heart trouble	☐	☐
Cancer	☐	☐
Seizure	☐	☐
Fainting	☐	

What have you been immunized for? _____

Family: _____ _____ _____
            Spouse or next of kin   Relationship   Address

Date of last exam ___/___   Who refered you? _____

Why are you seeing the doctor today?

Are you currently having pain? _____ Constant _____ Sporadic _____

How long does it last? _____ Please give us your soc. sec. # _____

IMPORTANT! We need your correct insurance carrier number _____

FIGURE 16.C1
Your help in improving this form is greatly appreciated.

Computer-Assisted Form Design

Numerous form design packages are available for microcomputers. These packages are listed in Figure 16.7. One of the best packages at the time of this writing is called FormFlow by Delrina. FormFlow runs in the Windows environment and its GUI interface is familiar to anyone who uses Windows.

FormFlow was used to draw the Job Application form in Figure 16.8. Notice the floating toolbar. Company logos can be imported, bar codes can be used, and photos can be stored as well. Judicious use of these features allows forms to be designed with great precision.

Controlling Business Forms

Controlling business forms is an important task. Businesses often have a forms specialist who controls forms, but sometimes it falls to the systems analyst to set up and implement forms control.

Basic duties for controlling forms include making sure that each form in use fulfills its specific purpose and that the specified purpose is integral to organizational functioning; preventing duplication of information collected and the forms that collect it; designing effective forms; deciding on how to get forms reproduced in the most economical way; and establishing stock control and inventory procedures that make forms available when needed at the lowest possible cost. A unique form number and revision date (month/year) should be included on each form.

Even if a form specialist is available, control of paperwork is still an area that must be double checked by the systems analyst. Improvement and change in information systems is highly dependent on managerial information activities, many of which derive from data originally captured on forms.

Manufacturer	Product	Paper Forms	Electronic Forms
Beyond Inc.	BeyondMail Forms Designer	No	Yes
Delrina Corp.	FormFlow	Yes	Yes
JetForm Corp.	JetForm	Yes	Yes
Microsoft Corp.	Microsoft Electronic Forms Designer	No	Yes
WordPerfect Corp.	WordPerfect Informs	Yes	Yes

FIGURE 16.7
Selected forms design software for personal computers. Some packages allow the user to design paper forms as well as electronic forms.

537

FIGURE 16.8
Designing forms using
FormFlow by Delrina.

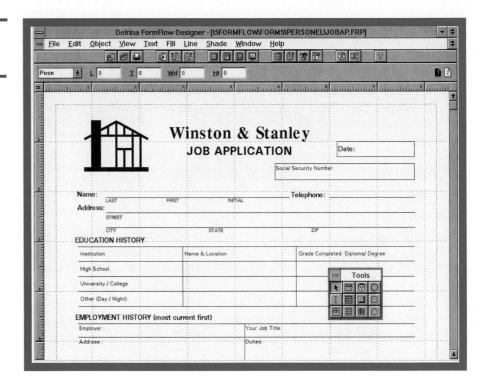

GOOD SCREEN DESIGN

Much of what we have already said about good form design is transferable to screen design. Once again, the user must remain foremost in the analyst's thoughts during the design of visual display terminal (VDT) screens.

There are differences, however, and systems analysts should strive to realize the unique qualities of screen displays rather than blindly adopting conventions of paper forms. One big difference is the constant presence of a cursor (a block of light or other pointer) on the screen, which orients the user to the current data-entry position. As data are entered on screen, the cursor moves one character ahead, pointing the way.

In this section, we present guidelines for effective screen design. These are presented in order to aid the attainment of the overall input design goals of effectiveness, accuracy, ease of use, consistency, simplicity, and attractiveness.

Four Guidelines for Screen Design

The four guidelines for screen design are important but not exhaustive. As noted in Chapter 15, they include:

1. Keep the screen simple.
2. Keep the screen presentation consistent.
3. Facilitate user movement among screens.
4. Create an attractive screen.

In the next subsections, we develop each of these guidelines along with presenting many design techniques for observing the four guidelines.

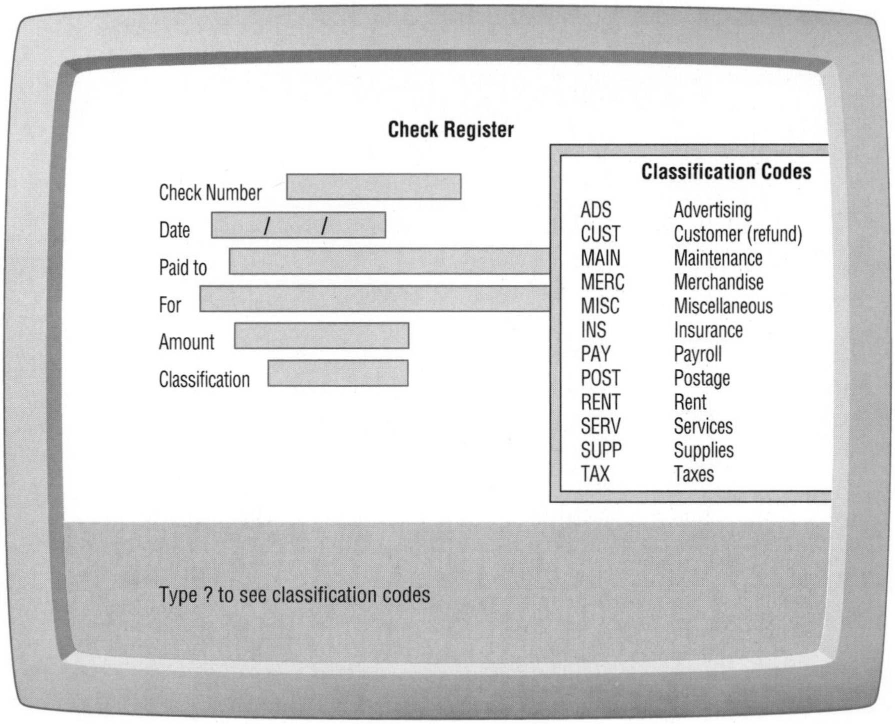

FIGURE 16.11
A window can keep the
screen simple.

producing the window if the code entered was incorrect. This helps prevent errors that might have occurred if all classification codes were accepted by the system.

Windows have almost limitless applications. For instance, they may allow users to stop data entry and check another file; get details on how data entry should proceed; calculate a value on-screen and then return to data entry to enter the sum calculated; set an alarm clock for an appointment reminder; or perform a number of other possible actions.

Since multiple windows are possible, any or all of the preceding functions could appear in varying sizes on a VDT screen at the same time. Clicking the right mouse button might bring up more window options. Entering another command or pressing a predefined key might allow the operator to clear the windowed information from the screen and return to the original display.

One of the main disadvantages of windows is that they allow the user to overcomplicate a simple screen. By including too many windowing operations, the designer may be inviting the creation of a chaotic-looking screen that subsequently results in a user who is lost and frustrated by all of the clutter. Windows must be used judiciously when they will support the purpose of the user, not hinder it.

Keeping the Screen Consistent

The second guideline for good screen design is to keep the screen display consistent. If users are working from paper forms, screens should follow what is shown on paper. Screens can be kept consistent by locating information in the same area each time a new screen is accessed. Also, information that logically belongs together should be consistently grouped together: Name and address go together, not name and zip code.

FIGURE 16.12
The first screen shows
columns A to D. To see more
the user must scroll.

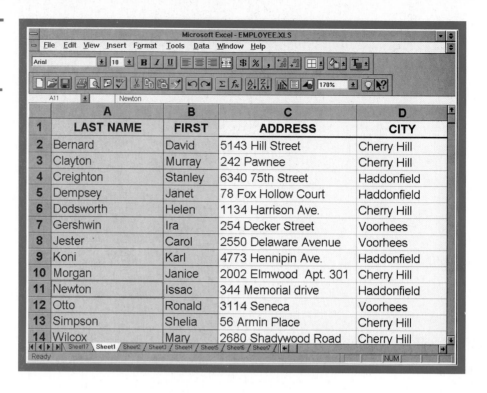

The check register depicted earlier helps users input data correctly because it requests data that is consistent with familiar paper checks. For example, "Date," "Paid to," and "Amount" are all expected to be found on a check.

When the user accesses the next screen in order to input the next check, "Check Number," "Date," and "Paid to" are all in the same place as on the previous screen. Keeping the data entry fields in the same place for every screen helps maintain consistency. Recalling and using the three sections of a screen presented previously will also help designers keep screens consistent.

Facilitating Movement

The third guideline for good screen design is to make it easy to move from one screen to another. One common method for movement is to have users feel as if they are physically moving to a new screen. There are at least three ways this illusion of physical movement among screens is developed.

SCROLLING. An example of effective scrolling is shown in Figure 16.12, which depicts employee records with name, address, and city displayed on the first screen. This example is from an Excel spreadsheet. The screen designer used the command "freeze pane" to ensure that row 1 and columns A and B will always be displayed no matter which way the user scrolls, as shown in Figure 16.13.

Another method mimicking physical movement from screen to screen is to employ keys already assigned on the computer keyboard. PC keyboards have keys labeled "Pg Up" for page up and "Pg Dn" for page down, which in effect take the user to a new page (screen display). This is an extremely easy way for inexperienced users to change screens, although it

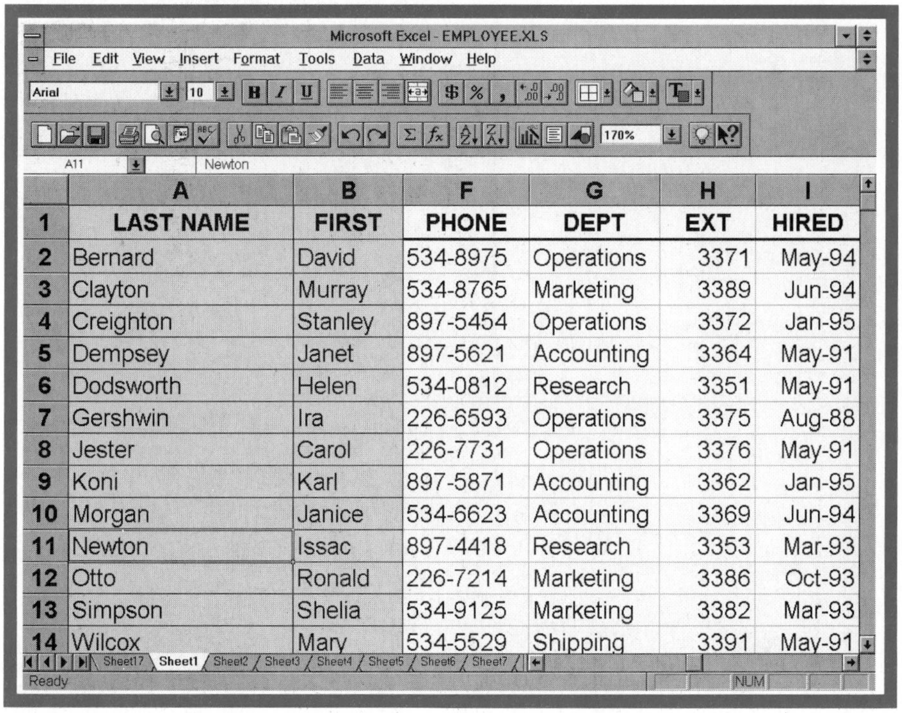

FIGURE 16.13
After scrolling, the user still
sees columns A and B and
also sees columns F to I.

The spreadsheet in the figure shows the following data:

	A	B	F	G	H	I
1	**LAST NAME**	**FIRST**	**PHONE**	**DEPT**	**EXT**	**HIRED**
2	Bernard	David	534-8975	Operations	3371	May-94
3	Clayton	Murray	534-8765	Marketing	3389	Jun-94
4	Creighton	Stanley	897-5454	Operations	3372	Jan-95
5	Dempsey	Janet	897-5621	Accounting	3364	May-91
6	Dodsworth	Helen	534-0812	Research	3351	May-91
7	Gershwin	Ira	226-6593	Operations	3375	Aug-88
8	Jester	Carol	226-7731	Operations	3376	May-91
9	Koni	Karl	897-5871	Accounting	3362	Jan-95
10	Morgan	Janice	534-6623	Accounting	3369	Jun-94
11	Newton	Issac	897-4418	Research	3353	Mar-93
12	Otto	Ronald	226-7214	Marketing	3386	Oct-93
13	Simpson	Shelia	534-9125	Marketing	3382	Mar-93
14	Wilcox	Mary	534-5529	Shipping	3391	May-91

does take up additional keyboard space and forces users to take their hands off the alphabetic keyboard to use the keypad.

CALLING UP MORE DETAIL. Another general approach to movement between screens allows users to call up another screen quickly by using cursor positioning along with a specific command. For example, Figure 16.14 exhibits a screen devoted to employee records. In order for the human resources manager to call up a specific employee record, he just positions the cursor over the chosen employee's number and hits Enter.

That command brings up the next screen of a detailed employee record, as shown in Figure 16.15. The manager sees a photograph of the employee and can scroll downward to obtain more information.

ON-SCREEN DIALOG. Displaying prompts facilitates a special kind of user movement between screens. Prompts are extremely useful in applications such as telemarketing. The initial screen used by Summerfest volunteers at public station DETV for their summer fund drive is shown in Figure 16.16. Volunteer phone answerers are facing this first screen when the phone rings. The left side of the screen shows the dialog (prompts) that the volunteer should use. The right-hand side of the screen shows default (most likely) responses for each question.

The phone answerer begins a call by asking if the person is calling to contribute. If "yes," the default response (the Enter key, for instance) is pressed, and the volunteer continues the dialog with the second question. The volunteer types the caller's last name into the database that contains active contributors.

The next question should confirm what the caller has said about contributing. If the person never before contributed to DETV, a window is pulled up on the screen as shown in Figure 16.17. The prompt reminds the

FIGURE 16.14
An overview screen of
employee records designed
using Delrina's FormFlow.

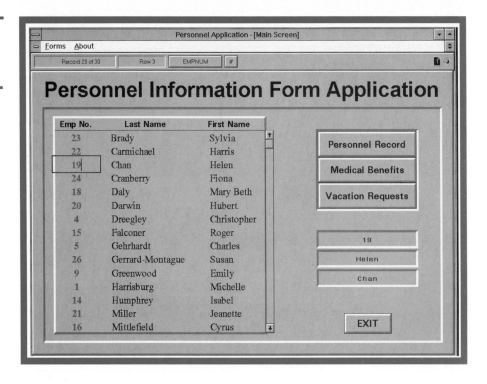

volunteer to ask for and enter the caller's address, then inquire about the existence of an apartment number.

Alternatively, if the caller responds that he or she has contributed before, a different window is called up as shown in Figure 16.18. This screen provides the caller's last-known address, then prompts the volunteer to ask if

FIGURE 16.15
Calling up more detail on an
employee (screen design
using FormFlow by Delrina).

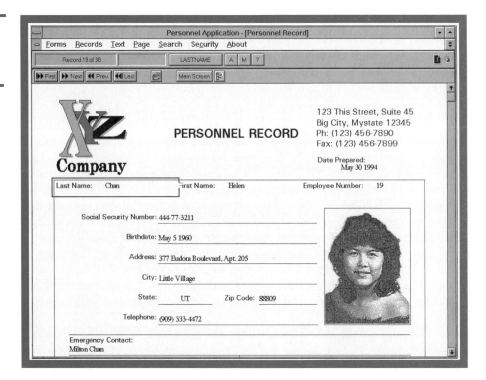

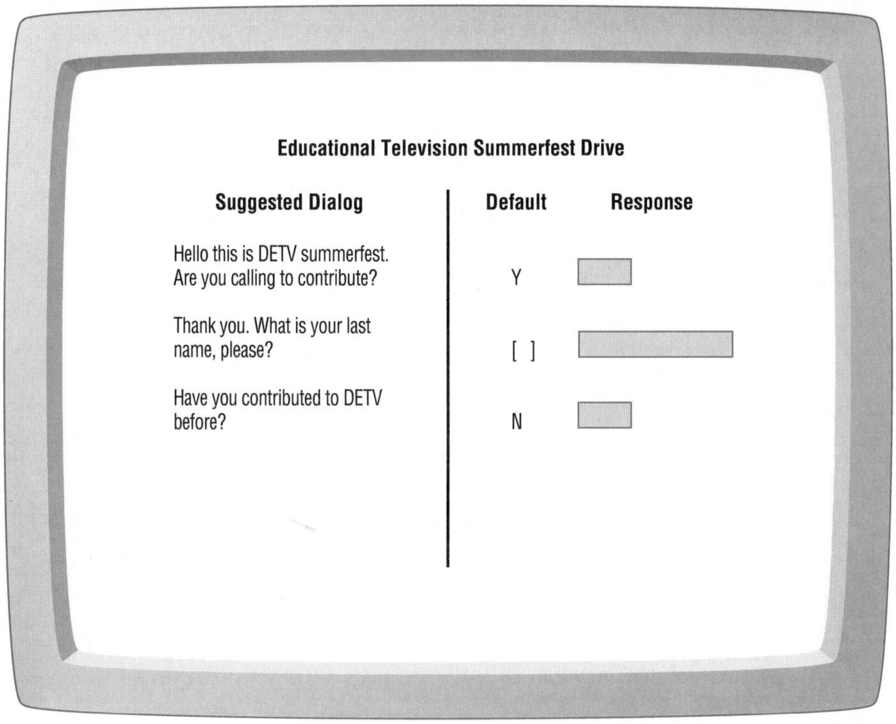

FIGURE 16.16
First screen for public broad-
casting station DETV's
Summerfest drive.

Educational Television Summerfest Drive

Suggested Dialog	Default	Response

Hello this is DETV summerfest.
Are you calling to contribute?   Y

Thank you. What is your last
name, please?   [ ]

Have you contributed to DETV
before?   N

it is still correct. The dialog proceeds until the contribution amount and method of payment are finalized. All throughout the contribution process, the volunteer has used split-screen dialog prompts and defaults to move from screen to screen in order to procure and enter the correct data.

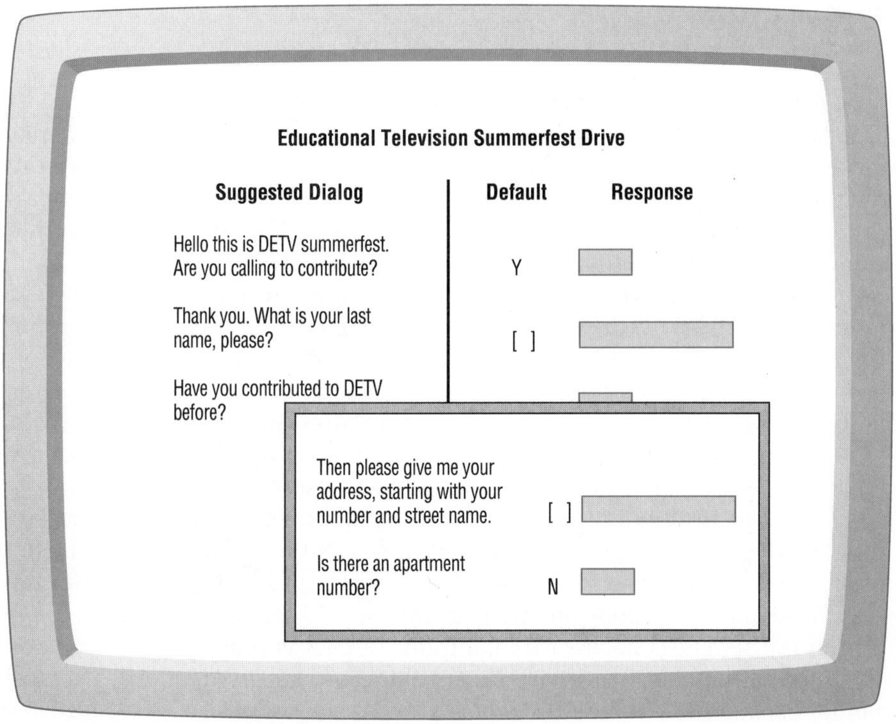

FIGURE 16.17
Window displayed if the
caller has not contributed to
DETV before.

Educational Television Summerfest Drive

Suggested Dialog	Default	Response

Hello this is DETV summerfest.
Are you calling to contribute?   Y

Thank you. What is your last
name, please?   [ ]

Have you contributed to DETV
before?

Then please give me your
address, starting with your
number and street name.   [ ]

Is there an apartment
number?   N

FIGURE 16.18
Windows displayed if the
caller has contributed to
DETV before.

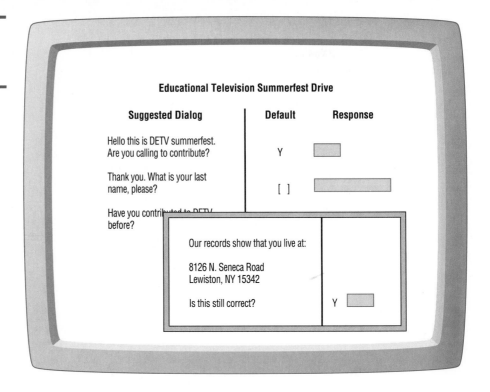

An interesting method of creating the feel of physically moving from screen to screen is direct manipulation (a graphical user interface that will be discussed in detail in Chapter 18). An example is designing a cursor to look like a human hand. This on-screen hand would be used to push forward to a new screen or back to a previous one by use of a mouse in a way that is analogous to pushing a piece of paper upward or downward on a desk.

Designing an Attractive Screen

The fourth guideline for good screen design is to create an attractive screen for the user. If users find screens appealing, they are likely to be more productive, need less supervision, and make fewer errors. Some of the design principles used for forms apply here, too, and some aesthetic principles have already come up in a slightly different context.

Screens should draw the user into them and hold their attention. This is accomplished with the use of plenty of open area surrounding data-entry fields, so the screen achieves and uncluttered appearance. You would never crowd a form; similarly you should never crowd a screen. You are far better off using multiple screens and windows than jamming everything onto one. By creating screens that are easy to grasp at first glance, you appeal to both inexperienced and experienced users.

Use logical flow in the plan to your screens. Organize screen material to take advantage of the way people function so that they can easily find their way around the screen. Also, consistently partition information into the three smaller sections detailed earlier.

If the screen is necessarily complex, appeal is heightened by separating information categories with lines composed of periods, dashes, ampersands, exclamation points, or boxes. The check register screen shown in

FIGURE 16.19
A check register screen that
shows balanced design.

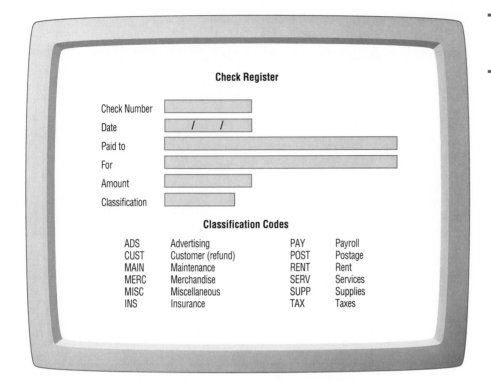

Check Register

Check Number

Date

Paid to

For

Amount

Classification

Classification Codes

ADS	Advertising	PAY	Payroll
CUST	Customer (refund)	POST	Postage
MAIN	Maintenance	RENT	Rent
MERC	Merchandise	SERV	Services
MISC	Miscellaneous	SUPP	Supplies
INS	Insurance	TAX	Taxes

Figure 16.19 uses boxes to define data-entry fields. Note that the boxes are left-justified, which results in an orderly look for the screen.

Thickness of separation lines between subcategories can also be varied to add further distinctions. This helps the user to see quickly the purpose of the screen and what data items are required.

With the advent of Graphical User Interfaces (GUI), it is possible to make input screens very attractive. By using color or shaded boxes and creating three-dimensional boxes and arrows, forms can be made user-friendly and fun to use. Figure 16.20 shows an example of an order entry screen that is particularly effective.

INVERSE VIDEO AND BLINKING CURSORS. Other techniques can also effectively enhance the attractiveness of screens but only if they are used sparingly. They include inverse video, blinking cursor or fields, and type fonts in various styles and sizes.

When you are considering use of these techniques, simplicity is still the watch-word. Design the basic screen that will include basic information first. Then, if greater differentiation is still needed, the basics can be embellished. Fortunately, additional enhancements may not be as costly for screen design as they are for forms.

Inverse video swaps the foreground color for the background color. This is an excellent way to highlight an important field, but employing it risks the chance that the users will be overwhelmed with the brightness of the inverse to the point that they ignore other fields.

Blinking video displays, when used for a cursor, are one way to alert an inexperienced user to its location. Blinking can also be used for error control by calling attention to a field that was skipped. Some users find blinking video annoying, imagining that the computer is impatiently awaiting the next entry.

FIGURE 16.20
You can design an attractive
screen with a 3-dimensional
effect using Delrina's
FormFlow.

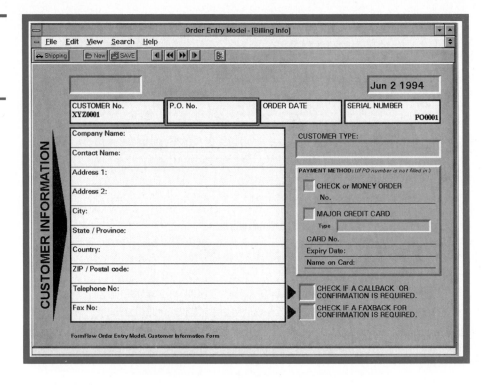

USING DIFFERENT TYPE FONTS. State-of-the-art computer systems and software allow type fonts of different styles and sizes. Type fonts are another way to make screens attractive to users. Different styles enhance differentiation among categories. For instance, thick, sans serif type style can be used to denote main categories and give screens a modern look. Larger type can indicate captions for data-entry fields. Thinner type with serifs can be used to designate subcategories on the same screen and provide a more conservative look.

When contemplating use of different type styles and sizes, ask yourself if they truly assist the user in understanding and liking the screen. If they draw undue attention to the art of screen design, or serve as a distraction, leave them out.

Differences in Mainframe and Microcomputer Screen Design

Mainframe and microcomputer design have much in common, but there are some critical differences between them. A mainframe computer is designed to work with many terminals, whereas a microcomputer is a self-contained processing unit and terminal. To increase mainframe efficiency, screens are sent as a whole, rather than as a series of individual keystrokes. Conversely, a microcomputer is designed to respond to any keystroke.

When using a PC, the user may be prompted to press a certain key, and the program responds by displaying information. For example, most spreadsheet programs allow the user to press a slash (/) to bring up a menu of options. A microcomputer program may pause for the user to examine the screen and display the message "Press any key to continue." When the user presses a key, the program continues.

A mainframe computer operates differently. The data entered on the screen is stored at the terminal and not transmitted to the mainframe until the user presses one of several keys designated as transmission keys. These

Squeezin' Isn't Pleasin'

The Audiology Department in a large veteran's hospital is using a VDT so that audiology technicians can enter data directly into the computer. After talking with Earl Lobes, one of the technicians, you determine that the screen design is a major problem.

"We used a form at one time, and that was decent," said Mr. Lobes. "But the screen doesn't make sense. I guess they had to squeeze everything on there, and that ruined it."

You have been asked to redesign the 80-column by 24-row screen (Figure 16.C2) to capture the same information, but to simplify it and, by doing so, reduce the errors that have been plaguing the technicians. You realize that squeezing isn't the only problem with the screen.

Explain your reasons for changing the screen as you did. You may use more than one screen if you think it is necessary.

AUDIOLOGICAL EXAMINATION REPORT

Patient last name   First   middle initial
Examining Station   Date of exam
Patient number   Social Security number
First exam   Claim number

AIR CONDUCTION

		Right ear						Left ear		
500	1000	2000	4000	6000		500	1000	2000	4000	6000
☐	☐	☐	☐	☐		☐	☐	☐	☐	☐

BONE CONDUCTION

		Right ear						Left ear		
500	1000	2000	4000	6000		500	1000	2000	4000	6000
☐	☐	☐	☐	☐		☐	☐	☐	☐	☐

SPEECH AUDIOMETRY SECT.   Comments [
SPEECH RECEP. THRESHOLD
Right Ear [ ]
Left Ear [ ]   Referred by [   ]
RIGHT EAR DISCR.   Reason for referral
% [ ] Masking [ ]   Examining Audiologist
LEFT EAR DISCRIM.   Exam. Audiologist's No.
% [ ] Masking [ ]   Next Appt.

FIGURE 16.C2
This screen can be designed to be more user-friendly.

---

keys (on an IBM mainframe) are called AID keys, for **A**ttention **ID**entifier, and include the Enter key, the Clear key, function keys 1 to 24 (PF1-24), and three **P**rogram **A**ttention keys called PA1 through PA3. When one of these keys is pressed, the screen data, along with whichever of the keys has been pressed, is transmitted to the mainframe. By utilizing AID keys, the mainframe does not have to respond to each terminal keystroke, and each user thus benefits from improved response time. (Response time is the time that elapses between the moment the user presses an AID key and appearance of a new screen generated by the computer.)

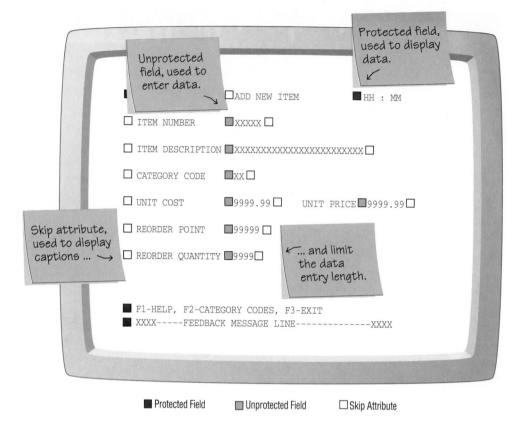

FIGURE 16.21
A screen showing attribute characters.

Another technique used in mainframe systems is to transmit only the data fields on a screen that have been altered—that is, those fields in which the user has entered new data or changed existing data. Clearly defining the screen fields ensures that only the minimal number of characters are transmitted from each terminal to the central computer, and response time again is thereby improved.

ATTRIBUTES. The data fields on a screen are defined using a field attribute character. The attribute character occupies one screen position, immediately preceding the data field, and always appears as a blank (invisible) character on the screen. Figure 16.21 illustrates a screen used to enter new item information with the attribute characters indicated by small rectangles. Notice that these rectangles are located before, and sometimes after, each screen data field.

Attribute characters control the characteristics of the screen field to the right of them and include the following qualities:

1. Protection.
2. Intensity.
3. Shift and extended attributes.

These are described in the following sections.

Protection. Protection determines whether the user may enter data into the screen field or not. There are three types of protection: unprotected, which allows any users to enter data; protected, used for output display information such as an operator message; and auto skip, used for captions, titles, and other screen features that do not change. The cursor will only be placed in unprotected areas of the screen.

On the ADD NEW ITEM screen, there is a protected attribute in front of the date, the time, the operator message (indicating the function key assignments), and the feedback message line. As the program processes input data, different information will be sent to these fields, but the user will not be allowed to key any data into them.

The title ADD NEW ITEM and the captions—ITEM NUMBER, ITEM DESCRIPTION, CATEGORY CODE, and so on—all have the skip attribute, since these displays do not change on the ADD NEW ITEM screen.

The Xs representing where the ITEM NUMBER, ITEM DESCRIPTION, and CATEGORY CODE, as well as the 9s representing areas where numeric data is to be entered, are all designated as unprotected. After each unprotected screen field there is another auto skip attribute character. This is used to control the number of characters the user may enter for each screen field. As each character is entered, the cursor advances to the right. When the auto skip attribute character is reached, the cursor "jumps" to the next unprotected screen field. When the last entry field is completed, the cursor wraps around to the first screen field.

Intensity. Intensity is how bright a screen field will appear. Three choices are available: normal, generally used for displaying captions, titles, date, time, and other fixed information and for entering data; bright, or high-intensity, often used when displaying error messages and to highlight an error in a field; and invisible, usually reserved for passwords. A combination of protected or unprotected and normal or bright intensities provides different screen colors for data and captions: usually white, green, blue, and red.

Shift and Extended Attributes. The shift attribute limits data fields to numeric or alphanumeric entries when keying data. If a screen field uses the numeric shift attribute, data entered as 123 in an 8-character field will become right-justified in the field and padded with zeros on the left after the Enter key has been pressed, resulting in 00000123. This attribute is frequently used for numeric data-entry fields. Extended attributes may be included, which provide for reverse video, underline, extra color, and blinking.

ATTRIBUTE CHARACTER CONSIDERATIONS. When designing mainframe terminal screens for entering data, the attribute character must be taken into consideration. At least one space must be reserved between captions and data entry areas for the attribute character. Normally, dates are entered without any slashes, spaces, or hyphens separating the month, the day, and the year. The reason for not entering a slash, for example, is that either the operator would have to key the slash or the program would have to display the slash. Having the operation key the slash slows the data entry process and may lead to inconsistent entry of dates. Some users might enter dates with slashes while other users might forget to enter the slashes.

If the program displays the slashes and the entire date entry field is unprotected, the operator may accidentally overtype the slashes. If the slashes are placed on the screen as protected entry fields, there must be an attribute byte before and after each slash to protect them. The field would have the following attribute character format: **uMMs/uDDs/uYYs** where **u** represents the unprotected attribute character necessary for entering a month, day, or year and **s** represents the auto skip attribute for jumping the cursor over the slashes. The data would appear to be spread out across the screen and would display as MM / DD / YY.

This consideration is also taken into account when designing entry fields for other fields that have editing characters in them, such as a standard U.S. telephone number—(nnn) nnn-nnnn—Social security numbers are another case in point. Finally, including a fixed screen location for the placement of the decimal point in amount fields is a common example of the need for attribute characters.

SCREEN CODE GENERATION. Screens may be designed using a number of CASE tools. Excelerator screens may be used to generate COBOL and other language code. A commonly used IBM mainframe screen programming language is CICS (Customer Information Control System, sometimes pronounced "kicks"). CICS code makes extensive use of attribute character control and is one of the most efficient means for sending and receiving mainframe screens. Many of the powerful CASE code generators, such as Texas Instruments IEF (Information Engineering Facility) and Knowledgeware's IEW (Information Engineering Workbench), generate CICS code. Excelerator may be linked through an additional interface product to Micro Focus, which will generate CICS code for an Excelerator screen. This code may be tested and executed on a microcomputer and then ported to the mainframe.

Micro Focus has a powerful toolset called Dialog System 3270. This code generation software will take a mainframe CICS screen and automatically generate a Windows, OS/2, or one of several other screen formats which function as entry or display screens. This provides great flexibility when creating systems. A program may run on a mainframe, a microcomputer, or other system without rewriting program code. This flexibility is often used in a client/server architecture, where the database may reside on the mainframe and the screen interface my exist on a microcomputer or as a mainframe program.

Figure 16.22 is an example of a mainframe CICS screen for adding customer payments. A CUSTOMER NUMBER is entered, and customer information (NAME, STREET, BALANCE DUE, and so on) is displayed using data from the CUSTOMER MASTER file. An INVOICE NUMBER, CHECK NUMBER, and PAYMENT AMOUNT are entered on the lower portion of the screen. Figure 16.23 is an example of the corresponding Windows or OS/2 screen that is generated using the Micro Focus Dialog System. Notice that all entry or protected display fields are surrounded by rectangles, the standard entry field for a graphical user interface screen. Captions do not have a rectangle, since they do not change as various payments are entered. Protection, color, and so on are all translated onto the graphical screen.

Using Icons in Screen Design

Icons are pictorial, on-screen representations symbolizing computer actions that users may select using a mouse, keyboard, lightpen, or joystick. Icons

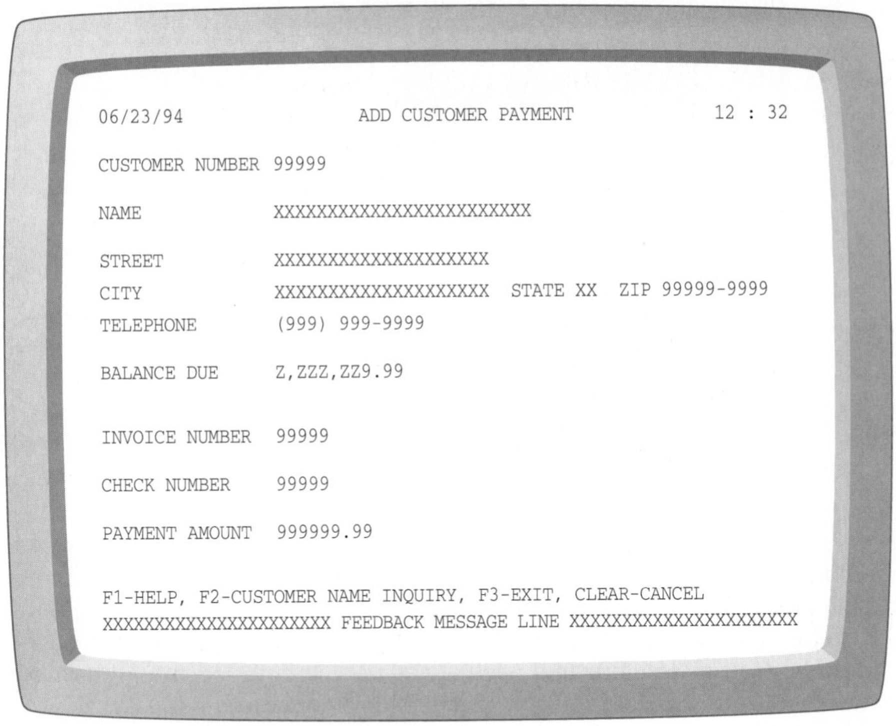

FIGURE 16.22
Mainframe screen for adding customer payments.

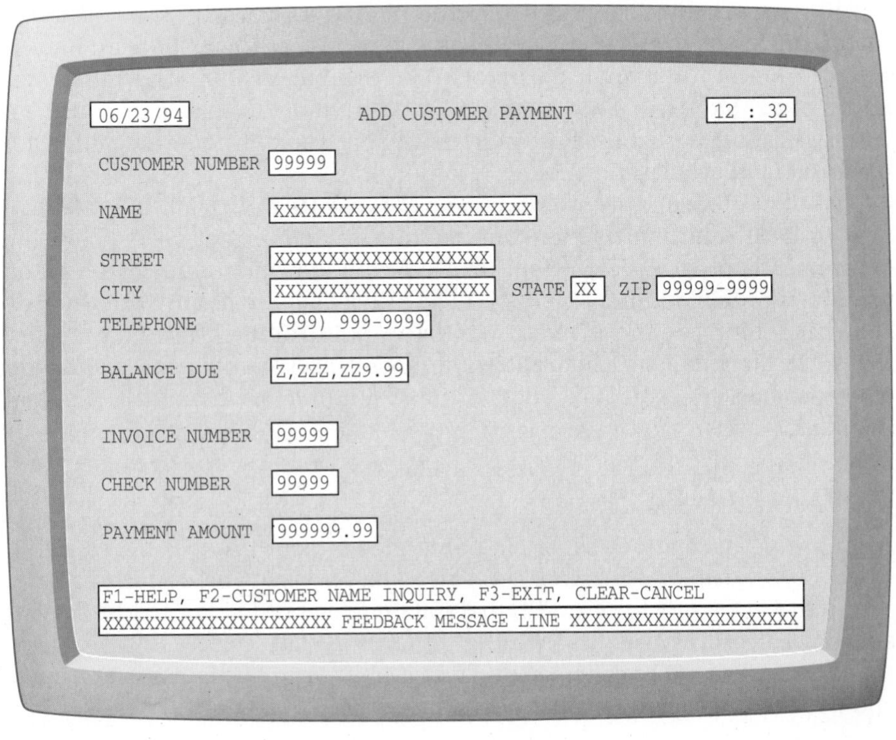

```
06/23/94              ADD CUSTOMER PAYMENT           12 : 32

CUSTOMER NUMBER  99999

NAME             XXXXXXXXXXXXXXXXXXXXXXXX

STREET           XXXXXXXXXXXXXXXXXXXX
CITY             XXXXXXXXXXXXXXXXXXXX   STATE XX   ZIP 99999-9999
TELEPHONE        (999) 999-9999

BALANCE DUE      Z,ZZZ,ZZ9.99

INVOICE NUMBER   99999

CHECK NUMBER     99999

PAYMENT AMOUNT   999999.99

F1-HELP, F2-CUSTOMER NAME INQUIRY, F3-EXIT, CLEAR-CANCEL
XXXXXXXXXXXXXXXXXXXXXX FEEDBACK MESSAGE LINE XXXXXXXXXXXXXXXXXXXXXXX
```

FIGURE 16.23
Windows or OS/2 screen generated from the mainframe screen.

```
06/23/94              ADD CUSTOMER PAYMENT           12 : 32

CUSTOMER NUMBER  99999

NAME             XXXXXXXXXXXXXXXXXXXXXXXX

STREET           XXXXXXXXXXXXXXXXXXXX
CITY             XXXXXXXXXXXXXXXXXXXX   STATE XX   ZIP 99999-9999
TELEPHONE        (999) 999-9999

BALANCE DUE      Z,ZZZ,ZZ9.99

INVOICE NUMBER   99999

CHECK NUMBER     99999

PAYMENT AMOUNT   999999.99

F1-HELP, F2-CUSTOMER NAME INQUIRY, F3-EXIT, CLEAR-CANCEL
XXXXXXXXXXXXXXXXXXXXXX FEEDBACK MESSAGE LINE XXXXXXXXXXXXXXXXXXXXXXX
```

FIGURE 16.24
Icons from Microsoft
Excel 5.0.

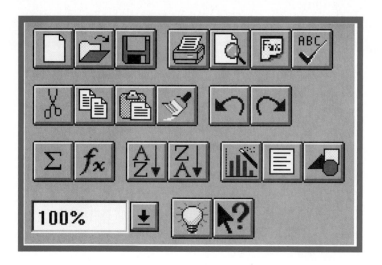

serve functions similar to those of words and may replace them in many menus, since their meaning is more quickly grasped than words. Icons designed for the spreadsheet for Excel 5.0 shown in Figure 16.24.

There are some guidelines for the design of effective icons. Shapes should be readily recognizable, so that the user is not required to master a new vocabulary. Numerous icons are already known to most users. Use of standard icons can quickly tap into this reservoir of common meaning. A user may point to a file cabinet, "pull out" a file folder icon, "grab" a piece of paper icon, and "throw it" in the wastebasket icon. By employing standard icons, designers and users all save time.

Icons for a particular application should be limited to around twenty recognizable shapes so that icon vocabulary is not overwhelming and a worthwhile coding scheme can still be realized.

Use icons consistently throughout applications where they will appear together. This ensures continuity and understandability. Standardizing icon usage can be taken even further. Some software houses are developing their own corporate icon system so that when different application packages are purchased from them, the user can count on employing familiar icons. Researchers are also attempting to invent a standardized icon system.

Generally, icons are useful if they are meaningful. Their chief advantage so far has been attracting and exciting inexperienced users about the computer's potential. Experienced users may become annoyed with the pseudo-simplicity and cuteness of icons or become impatient with the way in which icons tend to mask what the computer is actually doing. However, it is conceivable that experienced users prefer command language (discussed in the next chapter) more out of habit than out of any real dislike for icons.

Graphical User Interface Design

A graphical user interface (GUI, pronounced "gooey") uses a Windows, OS/2, Macintosh, or other graphics screen for entering and displaying data. While these screens have traditional data entry and display fields, several additional features are also included in the screen design. These are illustrated in Figure 16.25. The screen shown is used to add a customer order and has been designed to illustrate many of the GUI features.

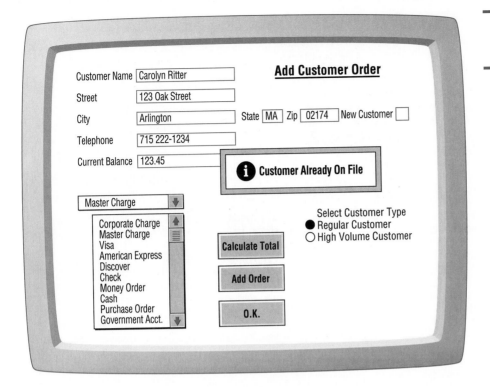

FIGURE 16.25
Illustration of GUI
components.

Rectangles, as mentioned previously, are used to outline data entry and display fields. A check box is used to indicate a new customer. Check boxes contain an X or are empty, corresponding to whether the user selected or did not select the option; they are used for nonexclusive choices, where one or more of the options may be checked. An alternative notation is to use a square button with a check mark ( ) to indicate that the option has been selected. Note that check box text is usually placed to the right of the box.

A circle, called a radio button, is used to select exclusive choices: either one or the other option can be chosen, but not both. An example of this device are the buttons located under the caption SELECT CUS-TOMER TYPE. The customer is either a REGULAR CUSTOMER or a HIGH-VOLUME CUSTOMER, but not both. The selected button has a darkened center. Choices are again listed to the right of the button.

A list box is one which displays several options that may be selected with the mouse. A drop-down list box is used when there is little room available on the screen. (In the figure a drop-down list box is used for selecting the method of payment.) A single rectangle exists with an arrow pointing down toward a line, located on the right side of the rectangle. Selecting this arrow causes a list box to be displayed. In the ADD CUS-TOMER ORDER example, the method of payment may be chosen from this list. The scroll bars on the right side of the list box are used if there are more choices than will display within the box. Once a choice has been made, it is displayed in the drop-down selection rectangle, and the list box disappears. As illustrated, the previous credit card choice in this example was MasterCard.

A command button performs an action when the user selects it with the mouse. CALCULATE TOTAL, ADD ORDER, and O.K. are examples of

What's That Thing Supposed to Be?

Art Istik flips off his VDT with a loud click. "I've just about had it," he says, turning impatiently to his colleague. Looking at Art with mock sympathy, Sim Ball says, "New system is too much for you, isn't it?" Art replies, "No, it's not. But I'll tell you what's really wrong. It's these silly pictures."

Art clicks on his newly installed microcomputer, rebooting a database management program that appears on his VDT. The first screen shows icons shaped like a Sherlock Holmes cap, some kind of tree, a pair of socks, an apple, a door, and a rabbit. Sim, leaning over Art's shoulder, takes one look at the screen and laughs uncontrollably.

Art says sarcastically, "I knew you would be able to help." Sim manages to stop laughing long enough to point to the pair-of-socks icon and demands, "What's that thing supposed to be?"

Art replies, "I have no idea. All I know is that this database management package is from some West Coast company called 'Organic Outputs.' The software is called 'DATAPIX: The icon-based database' by a guy named Drew Ikahn. Maybe we ought to call him up. His idea of a good screen is way out. No way can I learn all these crazy pictures." Sim returns to his desk saying. "Yeah. But at least it's entertaining."

As a last resort, Art turns to the DATAPIX user's manual, which provides the translation of the unconventional icons.

Based on Art Istik's and Sim Ball's comments (and laughter), describe what you feel is amiss with the DATAPIX icons, (Figure 16.C3). To what do Art and Sim seem to attribute some of the problems with their database management program? Applying some of the information you learned about using icons effectively, redraw the DATAPIX icons to improve them.

Icon		Meaning
Apple		**Create** a file (as in Adam and Eve)
Door		**Enter** data (as you would a door)
Sherlock's Cap		**Find** (after Holmes' famous investigative powers)
Pair of Socks		**Sort** (as in laundry)
Tree		**Print** (a gentle reminder that printing destroys the trees)
Rabbit		**Copy** a file (for making multiple copies)

FIGURE 16.C3
These DATAPIX icons can be improved.

command buttons. The text is centered inside the button, which has a rectangular shape. If there is a default action, such as the O.K. button, the text is generally surrounded with a dashed line. The button may also be shaded to indicate that it is the default. The user may press the Enter key to select the default button.

Several other symbols are often used on GUI screens, to send important messages to the user. Each should be within a rectangular window and should clearly spell out the message. An "i" within a circle represents "information" and alerts the user with a message. The information symbol in the figure is used to alert the user that the customer is already on file. An exclamation point within a circle indicates a warning message, and a stop sign is used for a critical error or other action message.

Using Color in Screen Design

Color is an appealing and proven way to facilitate computer input. Appropriate use of color on the VDT screen allows contrast of foreground and background; highlighting of important fields on forms; featuring of errors; special coding of input; and attention to many other special attributes.

Highly contrasting colors should be used for foreground and background. This helps users grasp what is presented quickly without straining. Also, background color will affect perception of foreground color. For example, dark green may look like a different color if taken off a white background and placed on a yellow one. Specifically, the top five most legible combinations of foreground lettering on background are (starting with the most legible combination):

1. Black on yellow.
2. Green on white.
3. Blue on white.
4. White on blue.
5. Yellow on black.

The least legible are red on green and blue on red. As can be gathered from these possible foreground and background combinations, bright colors should be used for foregrounds, with less bright colors for the background. Strongly contrasting colors should be assigned first to fields that must be differentiated; then other colors can be assigned.

Use color to highlight important fields on screens. Fields that are important can be colored differently from the rest. Alternatively, important fields and data can be programmed in a brighter color than those that are less important. Fields that are used often should be colored differently from other fields.

Like colors can mean similar situations, so that the red end of the spectrum (red, pink, fuchsia) might, for example, indicate dangerous or error situations. As is shown in Figure 16.26, red may mean that entering data at the time of its display will permanently alter a file.

On this screen the column depicting June's sales data for all car salespeople is red on a white background, which means it is ready to be updated. The programmer has also highlighted headings for the rows and columns in blue so that the user can easily distinguish them from other material. In this instance, blue means "headings." It is important to assign only one meaning to each color.

Color can assist in the special coding of input and should be used in addition to a well-formatted screen. Color coding is of great help in assisting users with searching and counting tasks. Alphanumeric blocks, groups, or columns are usefully distinguished through use of color. If displays are high-density, it is wise to use a double coding strategy employing both color and shape or color and patterns. Many applications now permit users to customize colors.

FIGURE 16.26
Color enhancement of a VDT
screen.

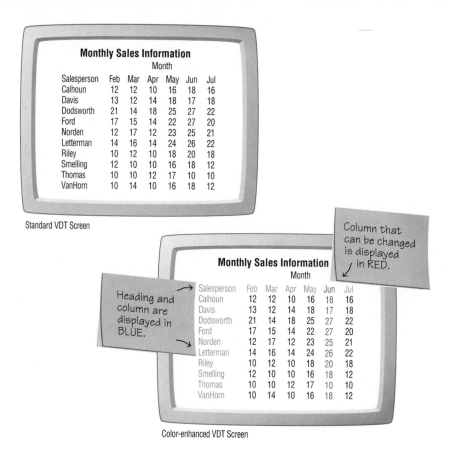

Standard VDT Screen

Color-enhanced VDT Screen

As with any enhancement, screen designers need to question the added value of using color. Use of color can be overdone; a useful heuristic is no more than four colors for new users, and only up to seven for experienced ones. Irrelevant colors distract users and detract from their performance. However, there are numerous instances where color has been shown to facilitate use in very specific ways. Color should be considered an important way to contrast foreground and background, highlight important fields and data, point out errors, and allow special coding of input.

SUMMARY

This chapter has covered elements of input design for forms and VDT screens. Well-designed input should meet the goals of effectiveness, accuracy, ease of use, consistency, and attractiveness. Knowledge of many different design elements will allow the systems analyst to reach these goals.

The four guidelines for well-designed input forms are:

1. Forms must be easy to fill out.
2. Forms must meet the purpose for which they are designed.
3. Forms must be designed to assure accurate completion.
4. Forms must be attractive.

Design of useful forms and screens overlaps in many important ways, but there are some distinctions. Screens display a cursor which continually orients the user. Screens often provide assistance with input, whereas beyond preprinted instructions, it may be difficult to get additional assistance with a form.

The four guidelines for well-designed VDT screens are:

1. Screens must be kept simple.
2. Screens must be consistent from screen to screen.
3. Screen design must facilitate movement between screens.
4. Screens must be attractive.

Many different design elements allow the systems analyst to meet these guidelines.

Proper flow of both forms and screens is important. Forms should group information logically into seven categories, and screens should be divided into three main sections. Captions on forms and screens can be varied, as can type fonts and the weights of lines dividing subcategories of information. Multiple-part forms are another way to ensure that forms meet their intended purposes. Designers can use windows, prompts, dialog boxes, and defaults on-screen to assure the effectiveness of design. There are many similarities, but some critical differences, between screen design for mainframe systems and screen design for microcomputers. To increase efficiency, mainframe screens are sent as a whole, rather than as a series of individual keystrokes.

Data fields on a mainframe screen are defined using a field attribute character, which controls the qualities of protection, intensity, shift, and extended attributes. The attribute character must be considered when designing mainframe terminal screens.

Screens can be designed using a number of CASE tools. A commonly used IBM mainframe screen programming language is CICS (Customer Information Control System). Many of the powerful CASE code generators generate CICS code. Icons, color, and graphical user interfaces can also be used to enhance user understanding of input screens.

KEYWORDS AND PHRASES

form and screen flow	specialty forms
three screen sections	facilitating screen movement
seven sections of a form	control of business forms
windows for screens	response time
line captions	visual display terminal (VDT)
scrolling on screen	attribute characters
box captions	CICS
on-screen dialog	on-screen icons
horizontal check-off captions	on-screen color
inverse video	screen color combinations
vertical check-off captions	cursor
blinking cursor	

REVIEW QUESTIONS

1. What are the design objectives for both input forms and screens?
2. List the four guidelines for good form design.

"Isn't Spring the most beautiful season here? The architect really captured the essence of the landscape, didn't he? I mean, you can't go anywhere in the building without seeing another beautiful vista through those huge windows. When Snowden came back, he looked at your output screens. The good news is, he thinks they'll work. The project is blossoming, just like the flowers and trees. When Snowden returns from Finland, would you have some input screens ready to demonstrate? He doesn't want things to slow down just because he's out of the country. By the way, the Singapore trip was very successful. Maybe MRE will be worldwide someday."

HyperCase Questions

1. Using either a paper layout form or software such as Delrina's FormFlow, design a prototype paper form that captures client information for the Training Unit.

2. Test your form on three classmates by having each of them fill it out. Ask them for a written critique of the form.

3. Redesign your input form to reflect your classmates' comments.

4. Using either a paper layout form, or a CASE tool such as Excelerator, design a prototype screen form that captures client information for the Training Unit.

5. Test your input screen on three classmates, by having each of them try it out. Ask them for a written critique of the screen's design.

6. Redesign the input screen based on the comments you receive. In a paragraph, explain how you have addressed each comment.

3. What is proper form flow?

4. What are the seven sections of a good form?

5. List four types of captioning for use on forms.

6. What is a specialty form? What are some disadvantages of using specialty forms?

7. List the guidelines for spacing of handwritten forms and typewritten forms.

8. What are the basic duties involved in controlling forms?

9. List the four guidelines for good VDT screen design.

10. What are the three sections useful for simplifying a screen?

11. What are the advantages of using on-screen windows?

12. What are the disadvantages of using on-screen windows?

13. List two ways screens can be kept consistent.

14. Give three ways to facilitate movement between screens.

15. What are the differences between mainframe and microcomputer screen design?

16. What is an attribute character? Where is it used?

17. What screen characteristics are stored in an attribute character?

18. List four graphical interface design elements. Along side each, describe when it would be appropriate to incorporate each of these in a screen design.

19. Define what is meant by on-screen icons. When are icons generally useful?

20. List the five most legible foreground and background color combinations for VDT use.

21. What are three situations where color may be useful in screen design?

PROBLEMS

1. Here are captions used for a state census form:

   Name
   ----

   occupation
                        ----

   address ----------------------------------

                        zip code

   Number of people in household?

   Age of head of household
                              ----

   a. Redo the *captions* so that the state census bureau can capture the same information requested on the old form without confusing respondents.
   b. Redesign the form so it exhibits proper flow. (*Hint:* Make sure to provide an access and identification section so that the information can be stored in the state's computers.)

2. Elkhorn College needs to keep better track of the books checked out from its Buck Memorial Library.
   a. Design and draw a form on 4-1/4 by 5-1/2 inch-long paper to use for checking out library books. Label the seven sections of a form that you included.
   b. Design and draw a representation of a VDT screen to accomplish the same thing. The screen has 80 columns and 24 rows. Label the three sections of a screen that you included.

3. Refer to Figure 16.24 which shows the icons from Excel 5.0, the spreadsheet program from Microsoft, and try to explain what each of the icons mean. Propose new icons if the actual ones are confusing.

4. Take a look at Figure 16.EX1. These are icons from Freelance Graphics, a presentation package from Lotus Development Corporation. Try to guess what the icons mean. Does the light bulb have the same meaning as the Microsoft application in problem 3? Explain. Suggest other icons that are better.

5. Speedy Spuds is a fast-food place offering all manner of potatoes. The manager has a thirty-second rule for serving customers. Servers say they could achieve this if the form they must fill out and give to the

kitchen crew were simplified. The information from the completed form is keyed into the computer system at the end of the day, when the data entry person needs to enter the kind of potato purchased, additional toppings purchased, the quantity, and the price charged. The current form is difficult for servers to scan and fill out quickly.

   a. Design and draw a form (you choose the size, but be sensible) that lists possible potatoes and toppings in a manner that is easy for servers and kitchen crew to scan and can also be used as input for the accounting system. (*Hint*: Remember to observe *all* of the guidelines for good form design.)

   b. Design and draw a representation of a VDT screen (in this case 40 columns by 24 rows) that can be used by the data entry operator to fill in the information captured on the form.

   c. List three changes you made in the form to adapt it to guidelines for good screen design.

6. Sherry's Meats, a regional meat wholesaler/retailer, needs to collect up-to-date information on how much of each meat product they have in each store. They will then use that information to schedule deliveries from their central warehouse. Currently, customers entering the store fill out a detailed form specifying their individual order. The form lists over 150 items; meat and meat products available in different amounts. At the end of the day, between 250 and 400 customer orders are tabulated and deducted from the store's inventory. Then the office worker in each store phones in an order for the next day. Store employees have a difficult time tabulating sales because of the mistakes customers make in filling out their forms.

   a. It is not possible to have the solitary office worker in each store fill out the numerous customer order forms. Change the form (3-1/2 inches by 6 inches *either* horizontal or vertical) and draw it so that it is easier for customers to fill out correctly and for office workers to tabulate.

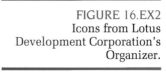

FIGURE 16.EX2
Icons from Lotus
Development Corporation's
Organizer.

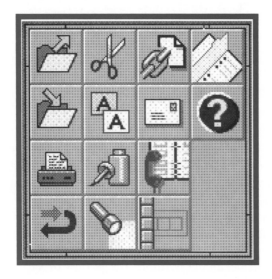

b. Design and draw a specialty form of the same size that will meet the needs of Sherry's customers, office workers, and warehouse workers.

c. Design and draw two different forms of the same size to meet the purposes in part *b,* since Sherry's carries both pork and beef products. (*Hint*: Think about ways to make forms easy to distinguish visually.)

7. R. George's, a fashionable clothing store that also has a mail-order business, would like to keep track of the customers coming into the store in order to expand their mailing list.

   a. Design and draw a simple form that can be printed on 3 x 5-inch cards and given in-store customers to fill out. (*Hint*: The form must be aesthetically appealing to encourage R. George's upscale clientele to complete it.)

   b. Design and draw a representation of a VDT screen (80 columns by 24 rows) that captures in-store customer information from the cards in part *a.*

   c. Design and draw an on-screen window for use with the screen in part *b* that allows comparison between in-store customer information and a listing of customers who hold R. George's credit cards.

   d. Design and draw a second on-screen window to compare in-store customers with mail-order customers.

8. Zero Corp. likes what you have achieved for them in forms control, but would like to set up an in-house forms specialist to continue your work. Compose a concise job description for an in-house forms specialist that lists four of their most important job responsibilities.

9. Figure 16.EX2 depicts the icons from a personal information manager (PIM) we discussed in Chapter 3, called Organizer. See if you can guess what each of the icons mean. Why do you think that good icon design is important? Explain in a paragraph why you think (or do not think) that these icons conform to the principles of good design.

10. Design a system of on-screen icons with readily recognizable shapes that allows account executives in brokerage houses to determine at a glance what actions (if any) need to be taken on a client's account.

a. Draw icons that correspond to:
  i. Transaction completed on same day.
  ii. Account needs updating.
  iii. Client has requested information.
  iv. Account in error.
  v. Account inactive for two months.
  vi. Account closed.

b. Some of the brokers have color screens. Redraw and color the six icons to show how you would use color to enhance their meaning.

11. My Belle Cosmetics is a large business that has sales well ahead of any other regional cosmetics firm. As an organization, they are very sensitive to color, since they introduce new color lines in their products every fall and spring. They have recently begun using technology to electronically show in-store customers how they appear in different shades of cosmetics without the bother of actually applying the cosmetics. They are also considering purchase of color display screens for their executive offices to aid in decision making.

a. Design and draw a representation of a VDT screen (80 columns by 24 rows) that depicts current sales as they would be shown on a regular screen.

b. Design and draw representation of a VDT screen of the same size that is the equivalent to the one in part *a* but which vividly demonstrates to decision makers in My Belle how color improves the understandability of the screen.

12. The Home Finders Reality Corporation specializes in locating homes for prospective buyers. Home information is stored in a database and is to be displayed on an inquiry screen. Design a graphical user interface (GUI) screen to enter the following data fields which are used to select and display homes matching the criteria. Keep in mind the features that are available for a GUI screen. The screen elements (which are not in any particular sequence) are:

  A. Minimum size (in square feet)
  B. Maximum size (optional, in square feet).
  C. Minimum number of bedrooms.
  D. Minimum number of bathrooms.
  E. Garage size (optional, number of cars).
  F. School district (a limited number of school districts are available for each area).
  G. Swimming pool (yes/no, optional).
  H. Setting (either city, suburban, or rural).
  I. Fireplace (yes/no, optional).
  J. Energy efficient (yes/no).

GROUP PROJECTS

1. Maverick Transport is considering updating its mainframe screens. With your team, brainstorm about what should appear on input screens for mainframe terminals of operators who are entering delivery load data as loads are approved. Fields will include date of delivery, contents, weight, special requirements (for example, whether contents are perishable) and so on.

2. Each team member should design an appropriate input screen using either a CASE tool or paper layout form. Share your results with your team members.

3. Make a list of other input screens that Maverick Transport should develop. Remember to include dispatcher screens, as well as screens to be accessed by customers and drivers. Indicate which should be microcomputer screens and which should be mainframe screens.

SELECTED BIBLIOGRAPHY

Dahlboom, B., and L. Mathiassen. *Computers in Context.* Cambridge, MA: NCC Blackwell, 1993.

Gibbs, M. "Forms Design and Control." In V. Lazarro (ed.), *Systems and Procedures: A Handbook for Business and Industry,* 2nd ed. Englewood Cliffs, NJ: Prentice-Hall, Inc., 1968.

Ives, B. "Graphical User Interfaces for Business Information Systems." *Management Information Systems Quarterly* (Special Issue), December 1982, pp. 15-48

Reisner, P. "Human Factors Studies of Data Base Query Languages: A Survey and Assessment." *Computing Surveys,* Vol. 4, no. 1, 1981.

The, L., "Stress Tests for GUI Programs." *Datamation,* September 1992.

FORMING SCREENS AND SCREENING FORMS

CPU Pooling information from the output design, and reviewing their progress, Chip and Anna proceeded to the next stage, the design of input. "Forms and screens must be designed to easily and accurately capture input information," remarks Anna.

Chip replies, "Special attention should be placed on creating input screens that are easy to use and require minimal operator entry."

Chip goes on to explain that each element defined using Excelerator has an attribute called **Source.** As the elements are created, the name of the form, or source document, is entered into this area. Using the **Report Writer** feature, a list of all the elements to be included on the form is printed, as shown in Figure E16.1. The form is then zoned to group logically related elements, which are arranged in a manner that would allow the user to easily complete the form. Since a prototype of the data-entry screen was previously approved, the task of designing the form is considerably simplified.

```
DATE: 28-NOV-93       MICROCOMPUTER MASTER ELEMENT LIST          PAGE     1
TIME: 12:18                                                      Excelerator


Name
--------------------------------
BRAND NAME
CAMPUS LOCATION
COST OF REPAIRS
DATE PURCHASED
DISK DRIVE A
DISK DRIVE B
FIXED DISK
FIXED DISK 2
HARDWARE INVENTORY NUMBER
INTERNAL BOARDS
LAST PREVENT. MAINTENANCE DATE
MAINTENANCE INTERVAL
MEMORY SIZE
MODEL
MONITOR
MOUSE
NUMBER OF REPAIRS
PRINTER
PURCHASE COST
RECORD CODE
REPLACEMENT COST
ROOM LOCATION
SERIAL NUMBER
WARRANTY
```

Allen Schmidt,
Julie E. Kendall, and
Kenneth E. Kendall

566

FIGURE E16.1
ADD MICROCOMPUTER FORM element list.

Add New Microcomputer

Complete for every microcomputer received. Inventory number is located on the tag supplied by Maintenance. Monitor, Printer and Boards are coded items. See reverse side for values. Second Fixed Disk and Second Diskette Drive are optional entries.

Inventory Number | Serial Number

Brand name – Manufacturer

Date Purchased MM-DD-YY | Purchase Cost

Memory (KB) | Replacement Cost

Drive Unit Size

Fixed Disk (MB) | Second Fixed Disk (MB)

Diskette Drive (KB) — Check If High Density | Second Diskette Drive (KB) — Check If High Density

Internal Board Codes

Monitor | Printer | Mouse (Y/N) | Warranty (Y/N)

Form MS-001 2/92

FIGURE E16.2
ADD MICROCOMPUTER form.

Chip schedules a meeting with Dot to review the form. She looks thoughtfully at the document for a few minutes and remarks, "This looks very good. I can see you've considered our viewpoint when designing the form. The only change I would recommend is to separate the initial information we have when the microcomputer is received from the data that is supplied as we make decisions on which printer, monitor, or mouse to attach."

Chip revises the form with the suggested changes and obtains final approval from Dot. The completed form is shown in Figure E16.2. Notice the zoning and the use of tick marks indicating the number of characters to be keyed. These help the user decide how to abbreviate data that would not fit within the file or database field length.

With the form complete, Chip starts working on modifying the screen used to enter the form data. The screen design matched the form, with fields on the screen in the same order and rough placement as on the form. The ADD NEW MICROCOMPUTER entry screen is shown in Figure E16.3.

```
┌─────────────────────────────────────────────────────────────────────┐
│ ─                        ADD MICRO                              ▼ ▲   │
│  Options   Create   Edit                                              │
│ MICROSYS                  ADD NEW MICROCOMPUTER          DATE  1/12/95 │
│ SCRM0006                                                 TIME 11:58 AM │
│                                                                        │
│ NUMBER            ▓▓▓▓▓        SERIAL NUMBER      ▓▓▓▓▓                │
│                                                                        │
│ BRAND             ▓▓▓▓▓        MODEL             ▓▓▓▓▓▓                │
│                                                                        │
│ DATE PURCHASED    MMDDYY       PURCHASE COST      ▓▓▓▓                 │
│                                                                        │
│ MEMORY SIZE (KB)  ▓▓▓▓         REPLACEMENT COST   ▓▓▓▓▓                │
│                                                                        │
│ FIXED DISK  (MB)  ▓▓▓          FIXED DISK #2      ▓▓▓                  │
│                                                                        │
│ DISK DRIVE A      3.5HD        DISK DRIVE B       ▓▓▓▓                 │
│ ─────────────────────────────────────────────────────────────────── │
│                                                                        │
│ INTERNAL BOARDS:  ▓▓▓  ▓▓▓   ▓▓▓   ▓▓▓   ▓▓▓                          │
│                                                                        │
│ MONITOR           ▓▓▓          PRINTER            ▓▓▓                  │
│                                                                        │
│ MOUSE    (Y/N)    N            WARRANTY (Y/N)     Y                   │
│ PRESS F3 TO SAVE/EXIT, F2 FOR HELP, PgDn FOR BOARD CODE HELP, Esc TO CANCEL│
│                                                                        │
└─────────────────────────────────────────────────────────────────────┘
```

FIGURE E16.3
ADD NEW MICROCOMPUTER screen.

One of the considerations of the entry screen is the availability of help. New employees would not be familiar with the operation of the system or what is required for a particular field entry. F2 was chosen as the function key to press to display an individual data field help message. Chip also designs several help screens that could be invoked at the touch of different keys. The BOARD CODE HELP SCREEN, shown in Figure E16.4, was the first designed. This would allow the users to obtain codes for internal microcomputer boards. The information is coded to facilitate quick keying and to reduce the size of the files. Data on the help screen is for display only, with control returning to the previous screen after exiting the help screen.

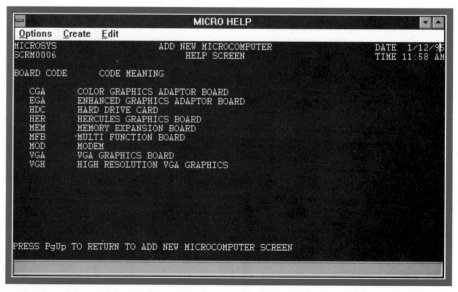

FIGURE E16.4
BOARD CODE HELP screen.

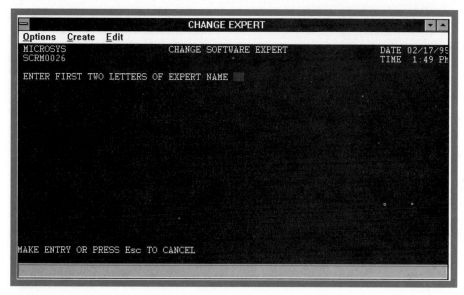

FIGURE E16.5
CHANGE EXPERT screen, obtain starting letter.

Dot reviews the completed screen and uses Excelerator's **Prototyping** feature to enter some test data. "I'm really impressed!" she exclaims. "This is much smoother than I ever expected. When can we expect the rest of the system?" Chip smiles with appreciation and remarks that great progress is being made. "I do hope that the rest of the system is as clear to use and easy to operate!" Dot says appreciatively.

Meanwhile Anna is meeting with Hy Perteks, who is desperately seeking help. "I'm swamped with requests for help on software packages! Is there any way to design a portion of the system for maintaining information on the available software experts?" asks Hy. "I have names written on scraps of paper and I keep misplacing them. Often I find out who these experts are only after someone else finds them first."

Anna asks some questions about what information would be required and how Hy would like to maintain and display the records. Hy replies, "There is so much expertise available, but the only way I have of locating the person's information is by using their name as an index. And I confess, I'm awful at remembering the correct spelling of the first name, let alone the last name." Anna assures him that there will be an easy-to-use system available soon.

Back at her desk, Anna thinks about the problem. "The ADD screen would be easy to create, but what about the CHANGE screen?" She wonders, "How can I?" then thinks, "Ah ha!" and snaps her fingers. The design becomes clear. There would be three screens. The first screen, shown in Figure E16.5, would contain an entry area for the first two letters of the expert's last name. The operator would have only two choices, to enter the letters or cancel the action.

These two letters would be used to start reading the EXPERT file, sequenced by LAST NAME. For every match found, the name of the expert would be displayed on the second screen, as in Figure E16.6. If more than one screenful of names exist for the given letters, additional name selection screens would be presented.

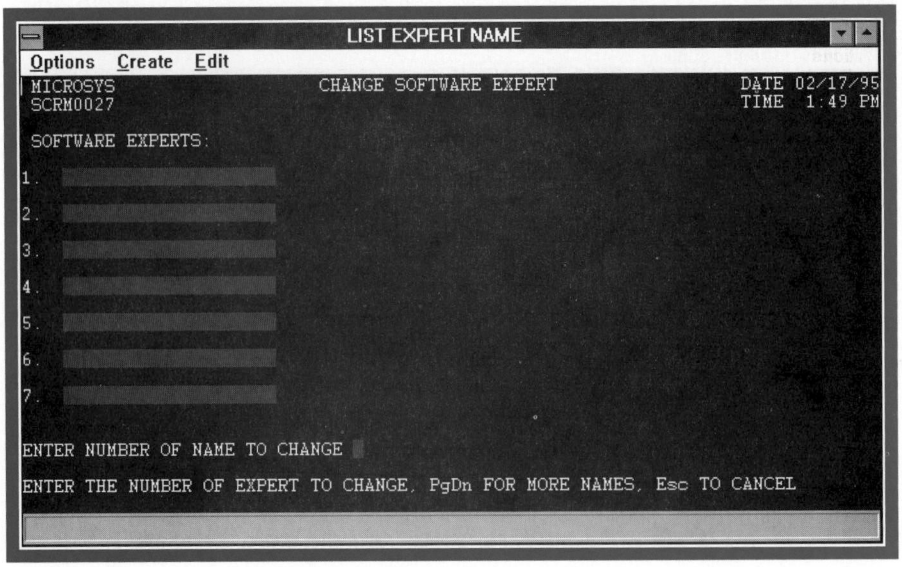

FIGURE E16.6
CHANGE EXPERT screen, name selection.

The operator would simply enter the number in front of the desired expert name and the corresponding record would be obtained. The third screen, shown in Figure E16.7, would allow Hy to change any of the data on file. To provide good feedback, the data on the file would be displayed for the operator to view. Any changes are made by simply keying the new data over existing data. The operator could also cancel the changes if the wrong name was inadvertently selected.

The problem of deleting Software Expert records of employees who retired or resigned had a different approach. Anna reasoned that this

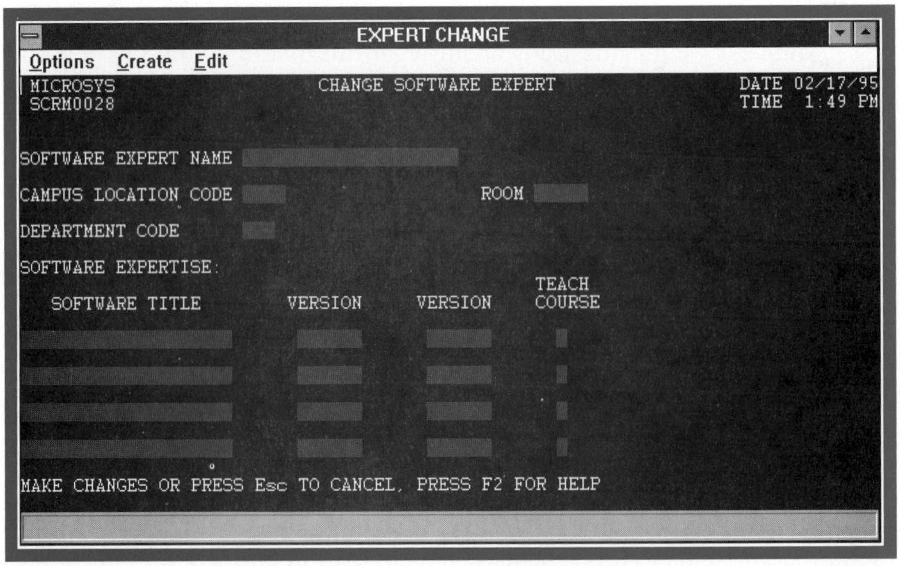

FIGURE E16.7
CHANGE EXPERT screen.

```
┌─────────────────────────────────────────────────────────────────┐
│ ▬              DELETE EXPERT                          ▼ ▲         │
│ Options  Create  Edit                                             │
│ ┌───────────────────────────────────────────────────────────────┐│
│ │ MICROSYS              DELETE SOFTWARE EXPERT      DATE 02/18/95 ││
│ │ SCRM0029                                          TIME  2:17 PM ││
│ │ ENTER SOFTWARE EXPERT NAME  ▓▓▓▓▓▓▓▓▓▓▓▓▓▓▓▓▓                   ││
│ │                                                                ││
│ │ ──────────────────────────────────────────────────────────────││
│ │ RECORD FOR EXPERT IS:                                          ││
│ │                                                                ││
│ │ CAMPUS LOCATION        ▓▓▓▓▓▓▓▓▓▓▓▓      ROOM  ▓▓▓▓▓            ││
│ │                                                                ││
│ │ DEPARTMENT             ▓▓▓▓▓▓▓▓▓▓▓▓▓▓▓▓▓▓                       ││
│ │                                                                ││
│ │ SOFTWARE TITLES:       ▓▓▓▓▓▓▓▓▓▓▓▓                            ││
│ │                                                                ││
│ │                        ▓▓▓▓▓▓▓▓▓▓▓▓                            ││
│ │                                                                ││
│ │                        ▓▓▓▓▓▓▓▓▓▓▓▓                            ││
│ │                                                                ││
│ │                        ▓▓▓▓▓▓▓▓▓▓▓▓                            ││
│ │                                                                ││
│ │                                                                ││
│ │ PRESS ENTER TO CONFIRM DELETE OR Esc TO CANCEL, F2 FOR HELP    ││
│ │ ▓▓▓▓▓▓▓▓▓▓▓▓▓▓▓▓▓▓▓▓▓▓▓▓▓▓▓▓▓▓▓▓▓▓▓▓▓▓▓▓▓▓▓▓▓▓▓▓▓▓▓▓▓▓▓▓▓▓▓▓▓▓▓▓││
│ └───────────────────────────────────────────────────────────────┘│
└─────────────────────────────────────────────────────────────────┘
```

FIGURE E16.8
DELETE EXPERT screen.

would be a rather rare occurrence and felt that the full name should be entered to delete a record. This would prevent accidentally deleting the wrong record. The name could be obtained from a printed report or an inquiry screen.

After the name is entered, the DELETE EXPERT program would read the SOFTWARE EXPERT record and display pertinent information. All codes on the file, such as CAMPUS LOCATION and DEPARTMENT, would be replaced with the full code meaning. The operator would have the opportunity to review the record and either delete or cancel the delete action. The final screen is shown in Figure E16.8.

Hy is delighted with the prototype screens. As he tests each of them, he remarks, "You don't know how easy it's going to be for me to answer help requests. This is fabulous!" He pauses for a long moment and then asks, "I have a lot of requests to provide periodically scheduled training courses. Do you think that we could work on a system to . . ."

Exercises*

🖫 **E-1.**   Cher Ware has remarked several times that a good form would make the task of adding new software much easier. It would also provide permanent paper documentation for software additions.

Design a form to add software to the SOFTWARE MASTER file. Use Excelerator to produce a list of elements on the form. The report selection criteria has already been created and needs only to be printed. View the NEW SOFTWARE FORM criteria and print the form.

---

* The exercises preceded by a disk icon require the program Excelerator (or another CASE tool). A disk is provided free of charge to any professor adopting this book. The examples on the disk may be imported into Excelerator and then used by students.

E-2. Hy Perteks would like a form to fill out as he learns about new Software Experts. Use the Excelerator **Report Writer** feature to view and print the ADD EXPERT FORM report. This report contains the entry fields used for the form.

E-3. Test the ADD MICRO data-entry screen. Use the **Screen Data Entry** feature of Excelerator to add several hardware records. Create test data by using equipment located in the room containing Excelerator. Enter both correct and incorrect data, observing error messages. Press F2 for individual data field help messages.

E-4. View the DELETE EXPERT screen design. Why are codes replaced with their meaning when providing feedback on the record to be deleted?

E-5. View the CHANGE EXPERT screen. Use the **Screen Data Entry** feature with the **Modify** option to change some of the data stored on the file. The data file name is CHANGE SOFTWARE EXPERT. Press the Enter key (when prompted for a name) to obtain a selector list of record keys. Use PgDn to move to successive screens.

E-6. On a change screen, why is it important to have selection for *records* to be changed when text, such as a name or description, is the key for locating a record? Answer in a paragraph.

E-7. Modify the CHANGE SOFTWARE screen design. This screen allows Cher Ware to modify data that have been incorrectly entered as well as information that routinely changes, such as SOFTWARE EXPERT and NUMBER OF COPIES. The SOFTWARE INVENTORY NUMBER is the primary key and may not be changed. Add the following data fields to be modified:

> MEMORY REQUIRED
> DISKETTE SIZE
> SOFTWARE EXPERT NAME
> MONITOR REQUIRED
> SITE LICENSE
> PRINTER REQUIRED
> NUMBER OF COPIES

Use the **Inspect** feature to test the screen. Include valid and invalid data. Examine the help messages by pressing F2.

E-8. Hy Perteks is constantly receiving requests for microcomputer software training classes, which are periodically scheduled. He would like to maintain a list of training courses available for faculty and staff.

Modify the ADD SOFT COURSE screen design. Elements to be added are:

> COURSE TITLE
> ENROLLMENT LIMIT
> LEVEL
> Up to 4 INSTRUCTORS
> CLASS LENGTH

Test the screen by using the **Inspect** feature.

E-9. Cher Ware and Anna spent the better part of a morning working out details on the software portion of the system. Plagued by the problem of providing consistent software upgrades for all machines, Cher would like an easy method of upgrading. A few older versions of software may also be retained for special needs.

Part of the solution is to produce a report, sorted by location, of all machines containing the software to be upgraded. As the new software is installed, a check mark is placed on the report after each machine.

Create and print the UPGRADE SOFTWARE screen design. The key fields are SOFTWARE TITLE and the old VERSION NUMBER, with an area provided to enter the new VERSION NUMBER. The update program will display a line for each machine containing the old version of the software installed. Lines are sorted by CAMPUS LOCATION and ROOM LOCATION.

Columns are CAMPUS LOCATION, ROOM LOCATION, MACHINE ID, MODEL, UPGRADE, and RETAIN OLD VERSION. The UPGRADE column contains a default of Y (Yes) which may be overridden. The RETAIN OLD VERSION is N (No) by default and may also be changed. Modify the operator message to indicate the following controls:

F3	EXIT/SAVE
Esc	CANCEL
PgDn	NEXT SCREEN
PgUp	PREVIOUS SCREEN

E-10. Explain why the UPGRADE SOFTWARE screen would display machines instead of having Cher enter the machine IDs. In a paragraph, discuss why the screen displays records in a CAMPUS/ROOM sequence.

E-11. Hy Perteks is concerned that old courses for obsolete versions of software are cluttering the disks. Create and print the Delete Software Course screen.

Entry fields are the SOFTWARE TITLE and VERSION NUMBER. The program displays a line for each course taught for the software version. The first column contains an entry field with a D (for Delete) presented as a default. Placing a space in the field will prevent the record from being deleted. The other columns for each line are: COURSE TITLE, LEVEL, and CLASS LENGTH. Add a meaningful operator message.

E-12. Use a paragraph to explain why it is a good idea to use default values on screens such as UPGRADE SOFTWARE and DELETE SOFTWARE COURSE.

## 17

DESIGNING THE
FILE OR DATABASE

Database

DESIGN OBJECTIVES

Data storage is considered by some to be the heart of an information system. The general objectives in the design of data storage organization are shown in Figure 17.1.

First, the data has to be available when the user wants to use it. Second, the data must be accurate and consistent (it must possess integrity). Beyond this, the objectives of database design include efficient storage of data as well as efficient updating and retrieval. Finally, it is necessary that information retrieval be purposeful. The information obtained from the stored data must be in a form useful for managing, planning, controlling, or decision making.

CONVENTIONAL FILES AND DATABASES

There are two approaches to the storage of data in a computer-based system. The first method is to store the data in individual files, each unique to a particular application. Figure 17.2 illustrates an organization with a number of information systems using conventional, separate files: SALES-FILE, which contains historical sales information; CURRENT-ACTIVITY, which is updated often; and PERSONNEL-FILE, which contains addresses, titles, and so on.

Notice that the NUM and NAME exist in each file. Besides the extra effort needed to input the NAME three times, a name change (because of a change in marital status, for instance) would require updating three separate files.

The second approach to the storage of data in a computer-based system involves building a database. A database is a formally defined and centrally controlled store of data intended for use in many different applications. Figure 17.3 shows that different users in different departments within the organization can share the same database. A user may select a portion of the database as shown in data set 1, or certain rows in data set 2.

minimized. Wl
sary informatic
ting data will
the file, there
the data.

An analy:
ing applicatio
development
cannot take or
database appl
limit the scop
new applicati

Processii
choose the op
but it is impo
tasks. Conseq
tem for one
utmost conce
that purpose.

575

FIGURE 17.1
Five objectives for
of data storage.

The use of individual files has many consequences. One major problem is the lack of potential for files to evolve. Files are often designed only with immediate needs in mind. When it becomes important to query the system for a combination of some of the attributes, these attributes may be contained in separate files or may not even exist. Redesigning files often implies that programs that access the files must be rewritten accordingly. This translates into expensive programmers' time for file and program development and maintenance.

A system using conventional files implies that stored data will be redundant. Furthermore, updating files is more time-consuming. Data integrity is a concern, since a change in one file will also require modification of the same data in other files. Seldom-used files may be neglected when it is time for updating.

Databases

Databases are not merely a collection of files. Instead, a database is a central source of data meant to be shared by many users for a variety of applications. The heart of a database is the DBMS (database management system), which allows the creation, modification, and updating of the database; the retrieval of data; and the generation of reports. The person who ensures that the database meets its objectives is called the database administrator.

The effectiveness objectives of the database include:

1. Ensuring that data can be shared among users for a variety of applications.
2. Maintaining data that are both accurate and consistent.
3. Ensuring that all data required for current and future applications will be readily available.
4. Allowing the database to evolve and the needs of the users grow.
5. Allowing users to construct their personal view of the data without concern for the way the data are physically stored.

FIGURE 17.2
The use of separ
means that the s
often are stored
one place.

The foregoing list of objectives provides us with a reminder of the advantages and disadvantages of the database approach. First, the sharing of the data means that data need to be stored only once. This in turn helps achieve data integrity, since changes to data are accomplished more easily and reliably if the data appear once rather than in many different files.

When a user needs particular data, a well-designed database anticipates the need for such data (or perhaps it has already been used for another application). Consequently, the data have a better chance of being available in a database than in a conventional file system. A well-designed database can also be more flexible than separate files—that is, a database can evolve as the needs of users and applications change.

Finally, the database approach has the advantage of allowing users their own view of the data. Users need not be concerned with the actual structure of the database or its physical storage.

The first disadvantage of the database approach is that all of the data are stored in one place. Therefore, data are more vulnerable to catastrophes and require complete backup. There is a risk that the database administrator becomes the only one privileged or skilled enough to go near the data. The bureaucratic procedures required to modify or even update the database can seem insurmountable.

Other disadvantages come about when attempting to achieve two efficiency objectives for the management of the data resource:

1. Keeping the time required to insert, update, delete, and retrieve data to a tolerable amount.
2. Keeping the cost of storing the data to a reasonable amount.

Remember that a database cannot be optimized for retrieving data for a specific application, since it may be shared by many users for various applications. Furthermore, additional software for the DBMS is required, and occasionally a larger computer is required.

The database approach is a concept that is becoming increasingly important. The use of relational databases (covered later in this chapter) on networked PCs means that the concept is becoming understandable to many users. Many users are extracting parts of the central database from mainframes and downloading them onto personal computers. These smaller databases are then used to generate reports or answer queries specific to the end user.

Relational databases for PCs have improved dramatically over the last few years. The leaders—Paradox, DBase, and Access—have remained competitive. All are extremely flexible in designing reports and labels. All allow the end user to read in databases from other software programs. All have good query capability. Some are more user friendly than others.

One major technological change has been the design of database software to take advantage of the graphical user interface. With the advent of Microsoft Access 2.0, users can drag and drop fields between two or more tables. Developing relational databases has been made relatively easy.

FIGURE 17.4
Reality, data, and metadata.

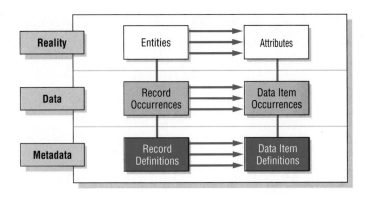

DATA CONCEPTS

Before considering the use of files or the database approach, it is important to understand how data are represented. In this section critical definitions are covered, including the abstraction of data from the real world to the storage of data in files.

Reality, Data, and Metadata

The real world itself will be referred to as reality. Data collected about people, places, or events in reality will eventually be stored in the file or database. In order to understand the form and structure of the data, information about the data itself is required. The information that describes data is referred to as metadata.

The relationship between reality, data, and metadata is pictured in Figure 17.4. Within the realm of reality, there are entities and attributes; within the realm of actual data, there are record occurrences and data item occurrences; within the realm of metadata, there are record definitions and data item definitions. The meanings of these terms are discussed in the following section.

ENTITIES. Any object or event about which someone chooses to collect data is an entity. An entity may be a person, place, or thing—for example, a salesperson, a city, or a product. Any entity can also be an event or unit of time such as a machine breakdown, a sale, or a month or year.

RELATIONSHIPS. Relationships are associations between entities (sometimes they are referred to as data associations). Figure 17.5 is an entity-relationship diagram that shows various types of relationships.

The first type of relationship is a one-to-one relationship (designated as 1:1). The diagram shows that there is only one PRODUCT PACKAGE for each PRODUCT. The second one-to-one relationship shows that each EMPLOYEE has a unique OFFICE. Notice that all of these entities can be described further (a PRODUCT PRICE would not be an entity, nor would a phone extension).

The second type of relationship is a one-to-many (1:M) association. As shown in the figure, a PHYSICIAN in a health-maintenance organization is assigned many PATIENTS, but a PATIENT is assigned only one PHYSICIAN. Another example shows that an EMPLOYEE is a member of only one DEPARTMENT, but each DEPARTMENT has many EMPLOYEES(s).

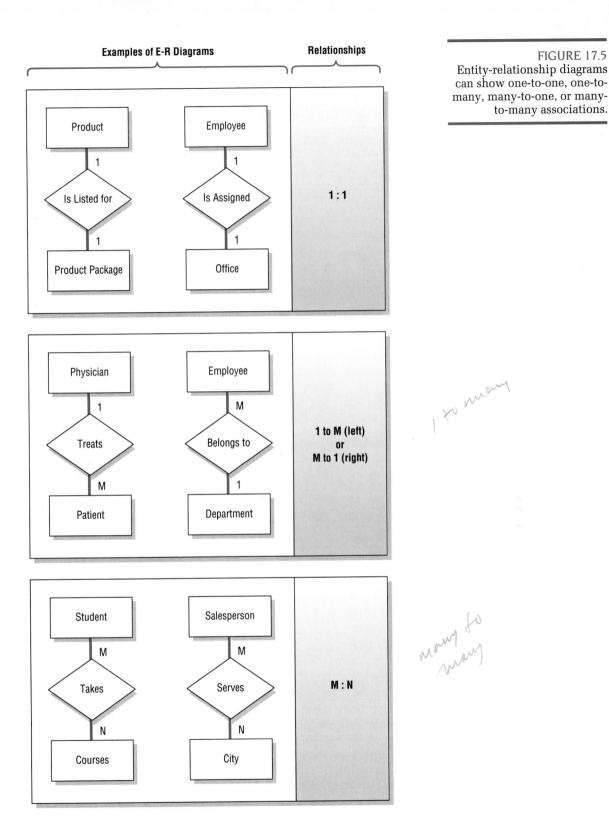

Finally, a many-to-many relationship (designated as M:N) describes the possibility that entities may have many associations in either direction. For example, a STUDENT can have many COURSES, while at the same

FIGURE 17.6
Typical values assigned to
data items may be numbers,
alphabetic characters, special
characters, and combinations
of all three.

Entity	Data Item	Value
Salesperson	Salesperson Number Salesperson Name Company Name Address Sales	87254 Kaytell Music Unlimited 45 Arpeum Circle $20,765
Package	Width Height Length Weight Mailing Address Return Address	2 16 16 3 765 Dulcinea Drive P.O. Box 341 Spring Valley, MN
Order	Product(s) Description(s) Quantity Ordered Last Name of Person Who Placed the Order First Initial Street Address City State Zip Code Credit Card Number Date Order Was Placed Amount Status	B521 "My Fair Lady" compact disc 1 Kiley R. 765 Dulcinea Drive La Mancha CA 93407 65-8798-87 05/01/94 $6.99 Backordered

time a COURSE may have many STUDENT(s) enrolled in it. The second example shows that a SALESPERSON can call on many cities, and a CITY can be a sales area for many SALESPERSON(s).

ATTRIBUTES. An attribute is some characteristic of an entity. There can be many attributes for each entity. For example, a patient (entity) can have many attributes such as last name, first name, street address, city, state, and so on. The date of the patient's last visit, as well as the prescription details, are also attributes. When the data dictionary was constructed in Chapter 9, the smallest particular described was called a data element. When files and databases are discussed, these data elements are generally referred to as data items. Data items are in fact the smallest units in a file or database. The words *data item* are also used interchangeably with attribute.

Data items can have values. These values can be of fixed or variable length; they can be alphabetic, numeric, or alphanumeric. Examples of data items and their values can be found in Figure 17.6.

Sometimes a data item is also referred to as a field. A field, however represents something physical, not logical. Therefore, many data items can be packed into a field; the field can be read and converted to a number of data items. A common example of this is to store the date in a single field as MM/DD/YY. In order to sort the file in order by date, three separate data items are extracted from the field and sorted first by YY, then by MM, and finally by DD.

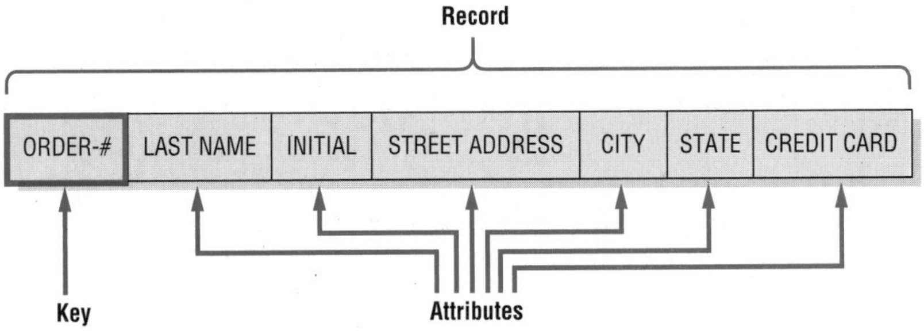

Record

ORDER-# | LAST NAME | INITIAL | STREET ADDRESS | CITY | STATE | CREDIT CARD

Key

Attributes

FIGURE 17.7
A record has a primary key
and may have many
attributes.

RECORDS. A record is a collection of data items that have something in common with the entity described. Figure 17.7 is an illustration of a record with many related data items. The record shown is for an order placed with a mail-order company. The <u>ORDER-#</u>, LAST NAME, INITIAL, STREET-ADDRESS, CITY, STATE, and CREDIT CARD are all attributes. Most records are of fixed length, so there is no need to determine the length of the record each time.

Under certain circumstances (for instance, when space is at a premium), variable-length records are used. A variable-length record is used as an alternative to reserving a large amount of space for the longest possible record, say the maximum number of visits a patient has made to a physician. Each visit would contain many data items that would be part of the patient's full record (or file folder in a manual system). Later in this chapter, normalization of a relation is discussed. Normalization is a process to eliminate repeating groups found in variable-length records.

KEYS. A key is one of the data items in a record that is used to identify a record. When a key uniquely identifies a record, it is called a primary key. For example, <u>ORDER-#</u>, can be a primary key because only one number is assigned to each customer order. In this way, the primary key identifies the real-world entity (customer order).

A key is called a secondary key if it cannot uniquely identify a record. Secondary keys can be used to select a group of records that belong to a set (for example, orders that come from the state of Virginia).

When it is not possible to identify a record uniquely by using one of the data items found in a record, a key can be constructed by choosing two or more data items and combining them. This is called a concatenated key. When a data item is used as a key in a record, the description is underlined. Therefore, in the ORDER RECORD (<u>ORDER-#</u>, LAST NAME, INITIAL, STREET-ADDRESS, CITY, STATE, CREDIT CARD) the key is <u>ORDER-#</u>. If an attribute is a key in another file, it should be underlined with a <u>dashed line</u>.

METADATA. Metadata is data about the data in the file or database. Metadata describes the name given and the length assigned each data item. Metadata also describes the length and composition of each of the records.

Figure 17.8 is an example of metadata for a database. The length of each data item is indicated according to a convention whereby 5.2 means that 5 spaces are reserved for the number, two of which are to the right of the decimal point. The letter N signifies "numeric," the A stands for alphanumeric. The D stands for "date" and is automatically in the form

Data Item	Value	
Salesperson Number	N	5
Salesperson Name	A	20
Company Name	A	26
Address	A	36
Sales	N	9.2
Width	N	2
Height	N	2
Length	N	2
Weight	N	2
Mailing Address	A	36
Return Address	A	36
Product(s)	A	4
Description(s)	A	30
Quantity Ordered	N	2
Last Name of Person Who Placed the Order	A	24
First Initial	A	1
Street Address	A	28
City	A	12
State	A	2
Zip Code	N	9
Credit Card Number	N	10
Date Order Was Placed	D	8 MM/DD/YY
Amount	$	7.2
Status	A	22

Fields
N Numeric
A Alphanumeric
D Date MM/DD/YY
$ Currency
M Memo

Special formats for fields may be specified.

7.2 means that the field takes up 7 digits, two of which are right of the decimal.

MM/DD/YY. Some programs, such as Paradox, use a $ to denote a currency field that places decimal points and commas in the right place. It is also possible in some database packages to specify an acceptable data format, where numbers, letters, dashes, and so on must appear in a particular place. The order of the data items is the logical order in the record; if a record is displayed, the data items are in the order indicated from top to bottom.

AN ENTITY-RELATIONSHIP EXAMPLE. An entity-relationship diagram containing many entities, many different types of relations, and numerous attributes is featured in Figure 17.9. Here, a PHYSICIAN treats many PATIENTS (1:M) who subscribe to their own INSURANCE CARRIER. Of course, the PATIENT is only one of many patients that subscribe to that particular INSURANCE CARRIER (M:1).

To complete the PHYSICIAN's records, the physician needs to keep information about the treatments a PATIENT has. Many PATIENTS experience many TREATMENTS, making this a many-to-many (M:N) relationship. TREATMENTS can include the taking of prescriptions, and likewise this is a M:N relationship because many treatments may call for combinations of pharmaceuticals and many drugs may work for many treatments.

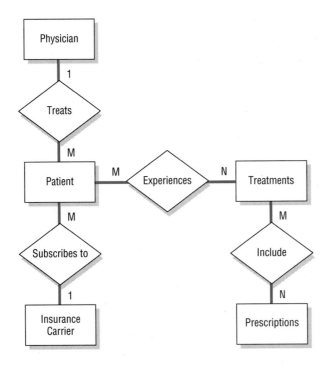

Some detail is then filled in for the attributes in Figure 17.10. The attributes are listed next to each of the entities and the key is underlined. For example, the entity PRESCRIPTIONS has a PRODUCT-NAME, DOSAGE, MANUFACTURER, and AMOUNT. Ideally, it would be beneficial to design a database in this fashion, using entity-relationship diagrams and then filling in the details concerning attributes. This is a desirable, top-down approach, but it is sometimes very difficult to achieve.

File Organization

A file contains groups of records used to provide information for operations, planning, management, and decision making. The types of files used are discussed first, followed by a description of the many ways conventional files can be organized.

FILE TYPES. Files can be used for storing data for an indefinite period of time, or they can be used to store data temporarily for a specific purpose. Master files and table files are used to store data for a long period. The temporary files are usually called transaction files, work files, or report files.

Master files. Master files contain records for a group of entities. The attributes may be updated often, but the records themselves are relatively permanent. These files tend to have large records containing all information about a data entity. Each record usually contains a primary and several secondary keys. Often, master files are stored as indexed or indexed-sequential files. While the analyst is free to arrange the data elements within a master file in any order, a standard arrangement is usually to place the primary key field first, followed by descriptive elements, and finally, elements that reflect the business and change frequently with business activities. This allows

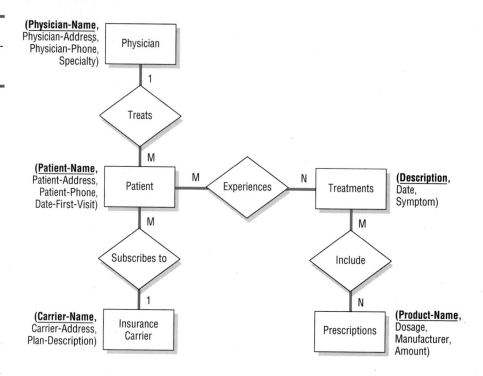

FIGURE 17.10
Attributes can be listed along-side the entities. In each case the key is underlined.

(Physician-Name, Physician-Address, Physician-Phone, Specialty)

Physician

1

Treats

M

(Patient-Name, Patient-Address, Patient-Phone, Date-First-Visit)

Patient

M   Experiences   N   Treatments   **(Description,** Date, Symptom)

M

Subscribes to

M

Include

1

(Carrier-Name, Carrier-Address, Plan-Description)

Insurance Carrier

N

Prescriptions   **(Product-Name,** Dosage, Manufacturer, Amount)

analysts or other operational people to identify records easily when a file is listed with a print utility.

Descriptive information is data that does not change with business events, such as an item description, customer name, address, or employee department. These elements are usually changed by maintenance programs using direct access methods. Generally, these elements contain alternate keys or indexes, and the data are in display format.

Business information elements are those that periodically change with business events, such as year-to-year gross pay, grade point average, customer account balance, and the customer date of last purchase. These elements are changed by update programs, usually by reading both files and sequentially matching records for efficiency. The record elements are modified only when the data is in error, by correction programs using random update methods. Often the dollar amount fields are in a compressed data format called packed decimal to save room on files and speed up program execution time.

If the master file is stored using conventional file methods, an expansion area is reserved at the end of each record. This provides room for adding new fields to the record as business needs change. If the file is part of a database structure, expansion area is not required. Examples of a master file include patient records, customer records, a personnel file, or a parts inventory file.

Table files. A table file contains data used to calculate more data or performance measures. One example is a table of postage rates to determine the shipping costs of a package. Another example is a tax table. Table files usually are read only by a program.

Transaction files. A transaction file is used to enter changes for updating the master file and producing reports. Suppose a newspaper subscriber master file needs to be updated; the transaction file would contain the subscriber number, a transaction code such as E for extending the subscription, C for canceling the subscription, or A for address change. Then only information relevant to the updating needs to be entered; that is, the renewal length if E, and the address if A. No additional information would be needed if the subscription was canceled. The rest of the information already exists in the master file. As a result, transaction files are usually kept to a minimum length. Transaction files may contain several different types of records, such as the three used for updating the newspaper subscription master, with a code on the transaction file indicating the type of transaction.

Work files. A program can sometimes run more efficiently if a work file is used. A common example of a work file is a file that is resorted so that records may be accessed more quickly.

Report files. When it is necessary to run a program, but no printer is available (or a printer is busy printing other jobs), a report file is used. Sending the output to a file rather than a printer is called spooling. Later, when the device is ready, the document can be printed. Report files are very useful, because users can take files to other computer systems and output to specialty devices such as plotters, laser printers, microfiche units, and even computerized typesetting machines.

SEQUENTIAL ORGANIZATION. When records are physically in order in a file, the file is said to be a sequential file. When a sequential file is updated, it is necessary to go through the entire file. Since records cannot be inserted in the middle of the file, a sequential file is usually copied over during the updating process.

Figure 17.11 illustrates a file of current orders for a mail-order company that sells compact discs and phonograph albums. The file contains twelve records and is stored sequentially according to the ORDER-#. If we want to look up order 13432, we would start at the beginning and read through the file until we arrived at order 13432.

Sequential master files are used when the hardware requires it (remember that a magnetic tape is a sequential device) or when the normal access requires that most of the records be accessed. In other words, when we need to read or update only a few records, it is inefficient to use a sequential structure, but when many records need to be read or modified, sequential organization would make sense. Sequential organization is normally used for all types of files except master files.

LINKED LISTS. When files are stored on direct-access devices such as a disk or drum, the options are expanded. Records can be sorted logically, rather than physically, using linked lists. Linked lists are achieved by using a set of pointers to direct you to the next logical record located anywhere in the file.

Figure 17.12 shows the compact disc ordering file with an additional attribute used to store the pointer. Since the file is already stored in sequential order according to ORDER-#, the pointer is used to point to records in logical (alphabetical) order by LAST NAME. This example

FIGURE 17.11
A sequential file sorted by
ORDER-#.

	ORDER-#	LAST NAME	I	STREET-ADDRESS	CITY	ST	CREDIT-CARD
1	10784	MacRae	G	2314 Curly Circle	Lincoln	NE	45-4654-76
2	10796	Jones	S	34 Dream Lane	Oklahoma City	OK	45-9876-74
3	11821	Preston	R	1008 Madison Ave.	River City	IA	34-7642-64
4	11845	Channing	C	454 Harmonia St.	New York	NY	34-0876-87
5	11872	Kiley	R	765 Dulcinea Drive	La Mancha	CA	65-8798-87
6	11976	Verdon	G	7564 K Street	Chicago	IL	67-8453-18
7	11998	Rivera	C	4342 West Street	Chicago	IL	12-2312-54
8	12765	Orbach	J	1345 Michigan Ave.	Chicago	IL	23-4545-65
9	12769	Steele	T	3498 Burton Lane	Finnian	NJ	65-7687-09
10	12965	Crawford	M	1986 Barnum Cir.	London	NH	23-0098-23
11	13432	Cullum	J	354 River Road	Shenandoah	VT	45-8734-33
12	13542	Mostel	Z	65 Fiddler Street	Anatevka	ND	34-6723-98

shows an obvious advantage of using linked lists: Files can be sorted logically in many different ways by using a variety of pointers.

HASHED FILE ORGANIZATION. Direct-access devices also permit access to a given record by going directly to its address. Since it is not feasible to reserve a physical address for each possible record, a method called hashing is used. Hashing is the process of calculating an address from the record key.

Suppose that there were 500 employees in an organization and we wanted to use the social security number as a key. It would be inefficient to reserve 999,999,999 addresses, one for each social security number. Therefore, we could take the social security number and use it to derive the address of the record.

There are many hashing techniques. A common one is to divide the original number by a prime number that approximates the storage locations, and then to use the remainder as the address, as follows: begin with the Social Security Number 053-4689-42. Then divide by 509, yielding 105047. Note that 105047 multiplied by 509 does not equal the original number, but equals 53468923 instead. The difference between the original

FIGURE 17.12
A linked list uses pointers to
designate the logical order of
the records.

ORDER FILE

START = 4

	ORDER-#	LAST NAME	I	STREET-ADDRESS	CITY	ST	CREDIT-CARD	POINTER
1	10784	MacRae	G	2314 Curly Circle	Lincoln	NE	45-4654-76	12
2	10796	Jones	S	34 Dream Lane	Oklahoma City	OK	45-9876-74	5
3	11821	Preston	R	1008 Madison Ave.	River City	IA	34-7642-64	7
4	11845	Channing	C	454 Harmonia St.	New York	NY	34-0876-87	10
5	11872	Kiley	R	765 Dulcinea Drive	La Mancha	CA	65-8798-87	1
6	11976	Verdon	G	7564 K Street	Chicago	IL	67-8453-18	END
7	11998	Rivera	C	4342 West Street	Chicago	IL	12-2312-54	9
8	12765	Orbach	J	1345 Michigan Ave.	Chicago	IL	23-4545-65	3
9	12769	Steele	T	3498 Burton Lane	Finnian	NJ	65-7687-09	6
10	12965	Crawford	M	1986 Barnum Cir.	London	NH	23-0098-23	11
11	13432	Cullum	J	354 River Road	Shenandoah	VT	45-8734-33	2
12	13542	Mostel	Z	65 Fiddler Street	Anatevka	ND	34-6723-98	8

number, 534688942, and the dividend, 53468923, is the remainder, and equals 19. The storage location of the record for an employee whose social security number is 053-4689-42 would thus be 19.

A problem arises, however, when a person with a different social security number (say, 472-3840-86) has the same remainder. When this occurs, the second person's record has to be placed in a special overflow area.

INDEXED ORGANIZATION. An index is different from a pointer since it is stored in a file that is separate from the data file. Figure 17.13 shows that four separate index files are generated on the ORDER FILE for compact discs.

The numerous index files have practical applications. If we want to list the details of the order placed by "Cullum," we can look up "Cullum" in the LAST-NAME INDEX file and go directly to record 11. The CITY INDEX could be used for a mailing list; the STATUS INDEX could be used to write notices to people with backordered items; and so on.

When the number of index files increases, it is possible to use index files for storing much of the data. The amount of information in the index files can be quite large. In this case, the structure is referred to as an inverted list.

Inverted lists are most appropriate when used to find information on a specific combination of keys. For example, a query such as "Who in Chicago still has an item that is backordered?" could be answered efficiently. Inverted lists, however, are difficult to maintain. Hence, inverted lists are more appropriate for a file that is rarely updated.

INDEXED-SEQUENTIAL ORGANIZATION. A widely used method of file organization is called indexed-sequential organization, or ISAM (for indexed-sequential access method). In an ISAM file, the records are arranged in blocks. The records within blocks are stored in order physically, but the blocks of records may be in any order. Therefore, an index is needed to locate the blocks of records.

A newer organizational format used for mainframe computers is the VSAM (virtual storage access method), a more modern and efficient method for handling indexed-sequential files. Indexed-sequential files allow programs to read records directly (that is, randomly) without reading other records in the file. Records written using an indexed-sequential method are placed in sequence within the file. When organized in this way, records may be deleted or rewritten without reading other records as well. When a record is rewritten, it is physically placed on the disk in the same location from which the original record was obtained.

Database Organization

LOGICAL AND PHYSICAL VIEWS OF DATA. A database, unlike a file, is intended to be shared by many users. It is clear that each user sees the data in different ways. We refer to the way a user pictures and describes the data as a user view. However, the problem is that different users have different user views. These views are examined, and an overall logical model of the database needs to be developed. Finally, the logical model of the database must be transformed into a corresponding physical database

FIGURE 17.13
Inverted lists can have many indices.

LAST-NAME INDEX

Channing	4
Crawford	10
Cullum	11
Jones	2
Kiley	5
MacRae	1
Mostel	12
Orbach	8
Preston	3
Rivera	7
Steele	9
Verdon	6

CITY INDEX

Anatevka			12
Chicago	6	7	8
Finnian			9
La Mancha			5
Lincoln			1
London			10
New York			4
Oklahoma City			2
River City			3
Shenandoah			11

CREDIT-CARD INDEX

12-2312-54	7
23-0098-23	10
23-4545-65	8
34-0876-87	4
34-6723-98	12
34-7642-64	3
45-4654-76	1
45-8734-33	11
45-9876-74	2
65-7687-09	9
65-8798-87	5
67-8453-18	6

STATUS INDEX

Backordered	5	8	9	12
In Process	3	4	10	11
Shipped 5/12	1	6	7	
Shipped 5/14	2			

ORDER FILE

	ORDER-#	LAST NAME	I	STREET-ADDRESS	CITY	ST	CREDIT-CARD	STATUS
1	10784	MacRae	G	2314 Curly Circle	Lincoln	NE	45-4654-76	Shipped 5/12
2	10796	Jones	S	34 Dream Lane	Oklahoma City	OK	45-9876-74	Shipped 5/14
3	11821	Preston	R	1008 Madison Ave.	River City	IA	34-7642-64	In process
4	11845	Channing	C	454 Harmonia St.	New York	NY	34-0876-87	In process
5	11872	Kiley	R	765 Dulcinea Drive	La Mancha	CA	65-8798-87	Backordered
6	11976	Verdon	G	7564 K Street	Chicago	IL	67-8453-18	Shipped 5/12
7	11998	Rivera	C	4342 West Street	Chicago	IL	12-2312-54	Shipped 5/12
8	12765	Orbach	J	1345 Michigan Ave.	Chicago	IL	23-4545-65	Backordered
9	12769	Steele	T	3498 Burton Lane	Finnian	NJ	65-7687-09	Backordered
10	12965	Crawford	M	1986 Barnum Cir.	London	NH	23-0098-23	In process
11	13432	Cullum	J	354 River Road	Shenandoah	VT	45-8734-33	In process
12	13542	Mostel	Z	65 Fiddler Street	Anatevka	ND	34-6723-98	Backordered

design. Physical design is involved with how data are stored and related, as well as how they are accessed.

In database literature, the views are referred to as schema. Figure 17.14 shows how the user reports and user views (user schema) are related to the logical model (conceptual schema) and physical design (internal schema).

There are three main types of logically structured databases: hierarchical, network, and relational.

HIERARCHICAL DATA STRUCTURES. Hierarchical data structures imply that an entity can have no more than one owning entity. Therefore, it is a structure made up of many 1:M or 1:1 associations. Other associations such as M:1 or M:N are not allowed.

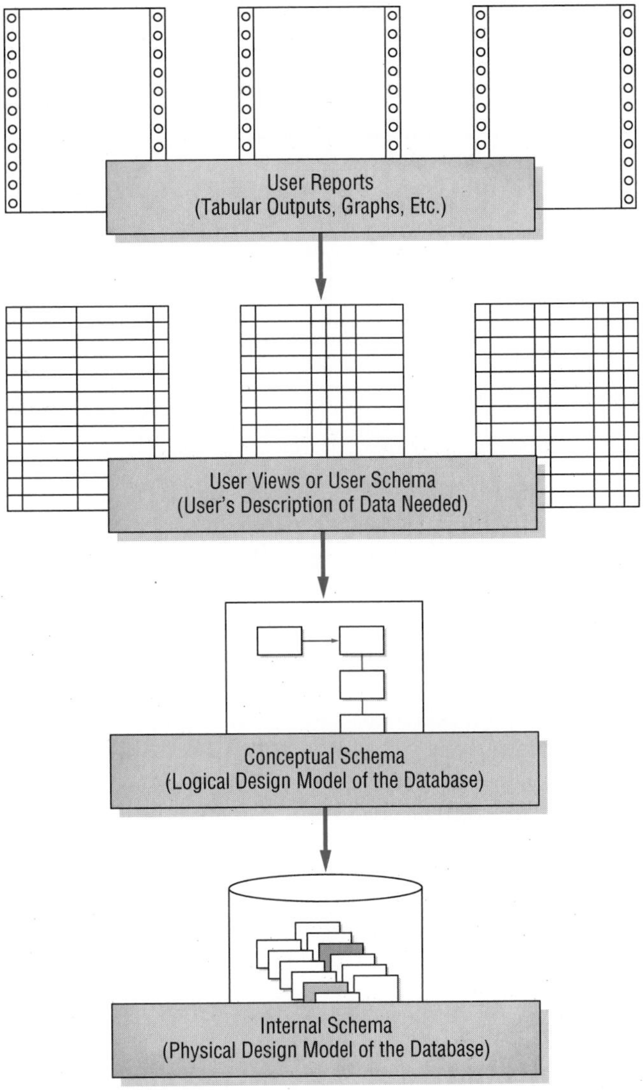

FIGURE 17.14
Database design includes syn-
thesizing user reports, user
views, and logical and
physical designs.

User Reports
(Tabular Outputs, Graphs, Etc.)

User Views or User Schema
(User's Description of Data Needed)

Conceptual Schema
(Logical Design Model of the Database)

Internal Schema
(Physical Design Model of the Database)

Hierarchical structures are sometimes called trees because the subordinates connected to the owning entities resemble the branches of a tree but are usually drawn upside down, as shown in Figure 17.15.

Sometimes it is very easy to retrieve information from a hierarchical database. As an example, consider the hierarchical structure in Figure 17.16. In this example, each compact disc (ITEM) has one or more subordinates (CUSTOMERS). If we wanted to see who ordered the CD "42nd Street," we would go to the owning entity B894 only and look at each subordinate (in this case, 11845 and 11872) to find the names "Channing" and "Kiley."

Sometimes, however, operations may become difficult. For example, if we found an error in the credit-card number of "G. MacRae," we would have to search through each owning entity to ensure that we find every occurrence of "G. MacRae." Notice also that we cannot add a new customer until a specific item is chosen. This is one of the disadvantages of the hierarchical structure.

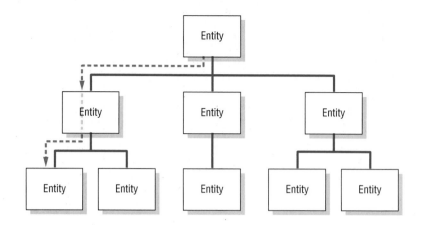

NETWORK DATA STRUCTURES. A network structure allows any entity to have any number of subordinates or superiors. A network structure is shown in Figure 17.17. Entities are connected using network links, which are data items common to both of the connected entities. Some of the problems inherent in hierarchical structures can be alleviated using the network structure, but the network structure is more complex.

An example of the compact disc ordering database using a network structure is shown in Figure 17.18. The entities (ITEM-DESCRIPTION and ORDER-DETAILS) are connected by network links (STATUS-LINK). Updating a record (such as correcting a person's credit-card number) is easier than in the hierarchical structure, because the order record (10784 for "MacRae") appears only once. It is also possible to insert records for customers who have not yet placed orders (for instance, if they wish to be

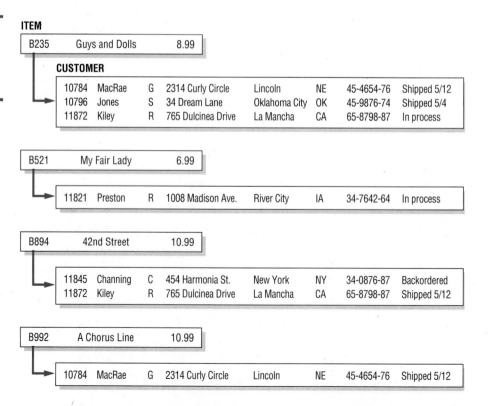

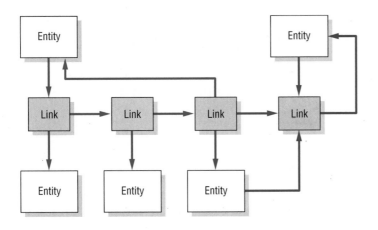

FIGURE 17.17
Network structures allow the
entity to have any number of
subordinates or superiors,
and entities are connected by
common links.

on a catalog mailing list). The appropriate ITEM-DESCRIPTION can be
added at a later date, when the order is placed.

RELATIONAL DATA STRUCTURES. A relational structure consists of one
or more two-dimensional tables, which are referred to as relations. The
rows of the table represent the records, and the columns contain attributes.

The compact disc ordering database is depicted as a relational structure in Figure 17.19. Here, three tables are needed to (1) describe the
items and keep track of the current price of compact discs (ITEM-PRICE),

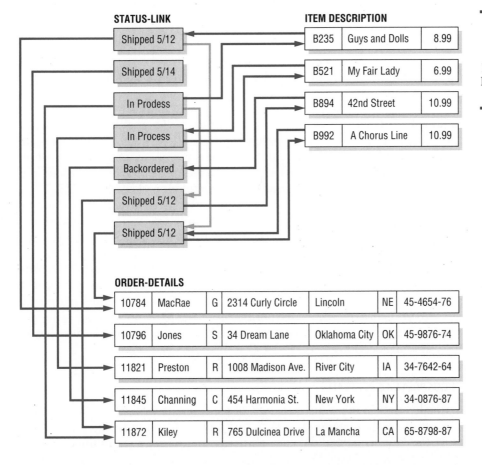

FIGURE 17.18
The status is used in this
example to link the ITEM-
DESCRIPTION to the ORDER-
DETAILS in this network data
structure.

FIGURE 17.19
In a relational data structure,
data are stored in many
tables.

ITEM-PRICE

ITEM-#	TITLE	PRICE
B235	Guys and Dolls	8.99
B521	My Fair Lady	6.99
B894	42nd Street	10.99
B992	A Chorus Line	10.99

ORDER

ORDER-#	LAST NAME	I	STREET-ADDRESS	CITY	ST	CHARGE-ACCT
10784	MacRae	G	2314 Curly Circle	Lincoln	NE	45-4654-76
10796	Jones	S	34 Dream Lane	Oklahoma City	OK	44-9876-74
11821	Preston	R	1008 Madison Ave.	River City	IA	34-7642-64
11845	Channing	C	454 Harmonia St.	New York	NY	34-0876-87
11872	Kiley	R	765 Dulcinea Drive	La Mancha	CA	65-8798-87

ITEM-PRICE

ITEM-#	ORDER-#	STATUS
B235	10784	Shipped 5/12
B235	19796	Shipped 5/14
B235	11872	In Process
B521	11821	In Process
B894	11845	Backordered
B894	11872	Shipped 5/12
B992	10784	Shipped 5/12

(2) describe the details of the order (ORDER), and (3) identify the status of the order (ITEM-STATUS).

To determine the price of an item, we need to know the item number to be able to find it in the relation ITEM-PRICE. To update "G. MacRae's" credit-card number, we can search the ORDER relation for MacRae and correct it only once, even though he ordered many compact discs. To find out the status of part of an order, however, we must know the ITEM-# and ORDER-#, and locate that information in the relation ITEM-STATUS.

Maintaining the tables in a relational structure is usually quite simple compared to maintaining a hierarchical or network structure. One of the primary advantages of the relational structures is that ad-hoc queries are efficiently handled.

When relational structures are discussed in the database literature, different terminology is often used. A file is called a relation, a record is usually referred to as a tuple, and the attribute value set is called a domain.

In order for relational structures to be useful and manageable, the relational tables must first be "normalized." Normalization is detailed in the following section.

NORMALIZATION

Normalization is the transformation of complex user views and data stores to a set of smaller, stable data structures. In addition to being simpler and more stable, normalized data structures are more easily maintained.

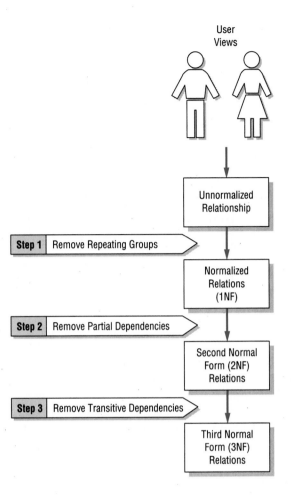

FIGURE 17.20
Normalization of a relation is
accomplished in three
major steps.

User
Views

Unnormalized
Relationship

Step 1 Remove Repeating Groups

Normalized
Relations
(1NF)

Step 2 Remove Partial Dependencies

Second Normal
Form (2NF)
Relations

Step 3 Remove Transitive Dependencies

Third Normal
Form (3NF)
Relations

The Three Steps of Normalization

Beginning with either a user view or a data store developed for a data dictionary (see Chapter 9), the analyst normalizes a data structure in three steps, as shown in Figure 17.20. Each step involves an important procedure to simplify the data structure.

The relation derived from the user view or data store will most likely be unnormalized. The first stage of the process includes removing all repeating groups and identifying the primary key. In order to do this, the relation needs to be broken up into two or more relations. At this point, the relations may already be of the third normal form, but more likely more steps will be needed to transform the relations to the third normal form.

The second step ensures that all nonkey attributes are fully dependent on the primary key. All partial dependencies are removed and placed in another relation.

The third step removes any transitive dependencies. A transitive dependency is one in which nonkey attributes are dependent on other nonkey attributes.

A Normalization Example

Figure 17.21 is a user view for the Al S. Well Hydraulic equipment company. The report shows (1) the SALESPERSON-NUMBER, (2) the SALESPERSON-NAME, and (3) the SALES-AREA. The body of the report shows the

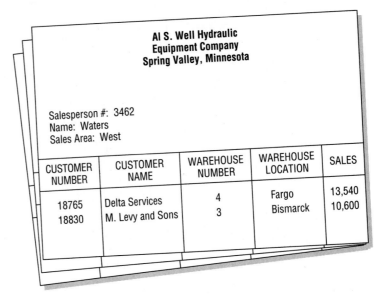

**Al S. Well Hydraulic
Equipment Company
Spring Valley, Minnesota**

Salesperson #: 3462
Name: Waters
Sales Area: West

CUSTOMER NUMBER	CUSTOMER NAME	WAREHOUSE NUMBER	WAREHOUSE LOCATION	SALES
18765	Delta Services	4	Fargo	13,540
18830	M. Levy and Sons	3	Bismarck	10,600

(4) CUSTOMER-NUMBER and (5) CUSTOMER-NAME. Next is (6) the WAREHOUSE-NUMBER that will service the customer, followed by (7) the WAREHOUSE-LOCATION, which is the city in which the company is located. The final information contained in the user view is (8) the SALES-AMOUNT. The rows (one for each customer) on the user view show that items 4 through 8 form a repeating group.

If the analyst was using a data flow/data dictionary approach, the same information in the user view would appear in a data structure. Figure 17.22 shows how the data structure would appear at the data dictionary stage of analysis. The repeating group is also indicated in the data structure by an asterisk (*) and indentation.

Before proceeding, note the data associations of the data elements in Figure 17.23. This type of illustration is called a bubble diagram or data model diagram. Each entity is enclosed in an ellipse, and arrows are used to show the relationships. Although it is possible to draw these relationships with an E-R diagram, sometimes it is easier to use the simpler bubble diagram to model the data.

FIGURE 17.22
The analyst would find a data structure (from a data dictionary) useful in developing a database.

SALESPERSON-NUMBER
SALESPERSON-NAME
SALES-AREA
CUSTOMER-NUMBER* (1-)
   CUSTOMER-NAME
     WAREHOUSE-NUMBER
      WAREHOUSE-LOCATION
       SALES-AMOUNT

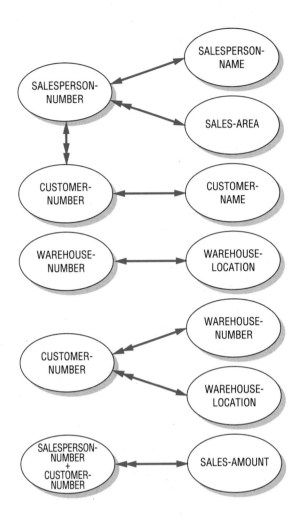

FIGURE 17.23
Drawing data model diagrams
for data associations sometimes helps analysts appreciate the complexity of data
storage.

In this example there is only one SALESPERSON-NUMBER assigned to each SALESPERSON-NAME, and that person will cover only one SALES-AREA, but each SALES-AREA may be assigned to many salespeople: hence, the double arrow notation from SALES-AREA to SALESPERSON-NUMBER. For each SALESPERSON-NUMBER, there may be many CUSTOMER-NUMBER(s).

Furthermore, there would be a one-to-one correspondence between CUSTOMER-NUMBER and CUSTOMER-NAME; the same is true for WAREHOUSE-NUMBER and WAREHOUSE-LOCATION. CUSTOMER-NUMBER will have only one WAREHOUSE-NUMBER and WAREHOUSE-LOCATION, but each WAREHOUSE-NUMBER or WAREHOUSE-LOCATION may service many CUSTOMER-NUMBER(s). Finally, in order to determine the SALES-AMOUNT for one salesperson's calls to a particular company, it is necessary to know both the SALESPERSON-NUMBER and the CUSTOMER-NUMBER.

The main objective of the normalization process is to simplify all of the complex data items that are often found in users' views. For example, if the analyst were to take the user view discussed above and attempt to make a relational table out of it, the table would look like Figure 17.24. Since this is a relation based on our initial user view, we will refer to it as SALES-REPORT.

FIGURE 17.24
If the data were listed in an
unnormalized table, there
could be repeating groups.

SALESPERSON NUMBER	SALESPERSON NAME	SALES AREA	CUSTOMER NUMBER	CUSTOMER NAME	WAREHOUSE NUMBER	WAREHOUSE LOCATION	SALES AMOUNT
3462	Waters	West	18765	Delta Systems	4	Fargo	13540
			18830	A. Levy and Sons	3	Bismarck	10600
			19242	Ranier Company	3	Bismarck	9700
3593	Dryne	East	18841	R. W. Flood Inc.	2	Superior	11560
			18899	Seward Systems	2	Superior	2590
			19565	Stodola's Inc.	1	Plymouth	8800
etc.							

SALES-REPORT is an unnormalized relation since it has repeating groups. It is also important to observe that a single attribute such as SALESPERSON-NUMBER cannot serve as the key. The reason for this is clear when one examines the relationships between SALESPERSON-NUMBER and the other attributes in Figure 17.25. Although there is a one-to-one correspondence between SALESPERSON-NUMBER and two attributes (SALESPERSON-NAME and SALES-AREA), there is a one-to-many relationship between SALESPERSON-NUMBER and the other five attributes (CUSTOMER-NUMBER, CUSTOMER-NAME, WAREHOUSE-NUMBER, WAREHOUSE-LOCATION, and SALES-AMOUNT).

SALES-REPORT can be expressed in the following shorthand notation:

SALES REPORT   (SALESPERSON-NUMBER,
                                SALESPERSON-NAME, SALES-AREA,
                                (CUSTOMER-NUMBER,
                                CUSTOMER-NAME,
                                WAREHOUSE-NUMBER,
                                WAREHOUSE-LOCATION,
                                SALES-AMOUNT))

where the inner set of parentheses represent the repeated group.

FIRST NORMAL FORM (1NF). The first step in normalizing a relation is to remove the repeating groups. In our example, the unnormalized relation SALES-REPORT will be broken up into two separate relations. These new relations will be named SALESPERSON and SALESPERSON-CUSTOMER.

Figure 17.26 shows how the original, unnormalized relation SALES-REPORT is normalized by separating the relation into two new relations. Notice that the relation SALESPERSON contains the primary key <u>SALESPERSON-NUMBER</u> and all of the attributes that were not repeating (SALESPERSON-NAME and SALES-AREA).

The second relation, SALESPERSON-CUSTOMER, contains the primary key from the relation SALESPERSON (the primary key of SALESPERSON is SALESPERSON-NUMBER) as well as all of the attributes that were part of the repeating group (CUSTOMER-NUMBER, CUSTOMER-NAME, WARE-HOUSE-NUMBER, WAREHOUSE-LOCATION, and SALES-AMOUNT). However, knowing the SALESPERSON-NUMBER is insufficient to know the CUSTOMER-NAME, SALES-AMOUNT, WAREHOUSE-LOCATION, and so on. In this relation, one must use a concatenated key (both <u>SALESPERSON-</u>

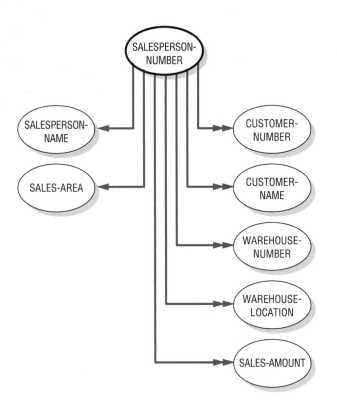

FIGURE 17.25
A data model diagram shows
that in the unnormalized relation, the SALESPERSON-
NUMBER has a 1:M associa-
tion with some attributes.

NUMBER and CUSTOMER-NUMBER to access the rest of the information.
It is possible to write the relations in shorthand notation as follows:

SALESPERSON   (SALESPERSON-NUMBER, SALESPERSON-NAME,
                     SALES-AREA)

and

SALESPERSON-CUSTOMER   (SALESPERSON-NUMBER,
                              CUSTOMER-NUMBER,
                              CUSTOMER-NAME,
                              WAREHOUSE-NUMBER,
                              WAREHOUSE-LOCATION,
                              SALES-AMOUNT)

The relation SALESPERSON-CUSTOMER is a first normal relation, but it is
not in its ideal form. Problems stem from the fact that some of the attributes
are not functionally dependent on the primary key, SALESPERSON-NUM-
BER, CUSTOMER-NUMBER. In other words, some of the nonkey attributes
are dependent only on CUSTOMER NUMBER, and not on the concatenated key. The data model diagram in Figure 17.27 shows that SALES-
AMOUNT is dependent on both SALESPERSON-NUMBER and CUS-
TOMER-NUMBER, but the other three attributes are dependent only on
CUSTOMER-NUMBER.

   SECOND NORMAL FORM (2NF). In the second normal form, all of the
attributes will be functionally dependent on the primary key. Therefore,
the next step is to remove all of the partially dependent attributes and

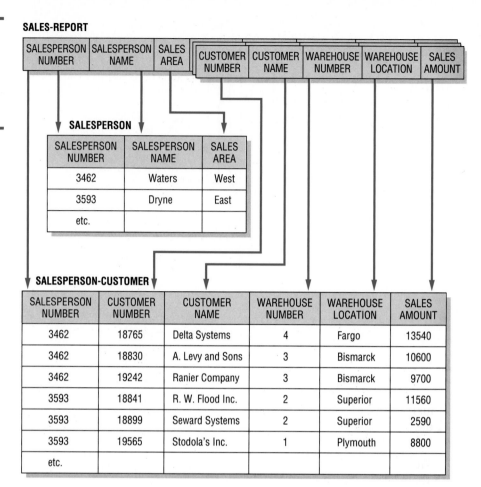

FIGURE 17.26
The original unnormalized relation SALES-REPORT is separated into two relations, SALESPERSON (3NF) and SALESPERSON-CUSTOMER (1NF).

place them in another relation. Figure 17.28 shows how the relation SALESPERSON-CUSTOMER is split into two new relations: SALES and CUSTOMER-WAREHOUSE. These relations can also be expressed as:

SALES   (<u>SALESPERSON-NUMBER</u>, <u>CUSTOMER-NUMBER</u>, SALES-AMOUNT)

and

CUSTOMER-WAREHOUSE   (<u>CUSTOMER-NUMBER</u>, CUSTOMER-NAME, WAREHOUSE-NUMBER, WAREHOUSE-LOCATION)

The relation CUSTOMER-WAREHOUSE is in the second normal form. It can still be simplified further because there are additional dependencies within the relation. Some of the nonkey attributes are dependent not only on the primary key, but also on a nonkey attribute. This dependency is referred to as a transitive dependency.

Figure 17.29 shows the dependencies within the relation CUSTOMER-WAREHOUSE. In order for the relation to be a second normal form, all of the attributes must be dependent on the primary key <u>CUSTOMER-NUM-BER</u>, as shown in the diagram. However, WAREHOUSE-LOCATION is

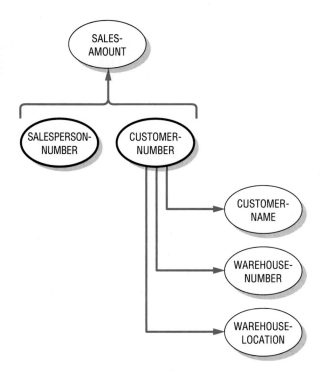

obviously dependent on WAREHOUSE-NUMBER also. To simplify this relation, another step is required.

THIRD NORMAL FORM (3NF). A normalized relation is third normal if all of the nonkey attributes are fully functionally dependent on the primary key and there are no transitive (nonkey) dependencies. In a manner similar to the previous steps, it is possible to break apart the relation CUSTOMER-WAREHOUSE into two relations, as shown in Figure 17.30.

The two new relations are called CUSTOMER and WAREHOUSE and can be written as follows:

CUSTOMER   (<u>CUSTOMER-NUMBER</u>, CUSTOMER-NAME,
                WAREHOUSE-NUMBER)

and

WAREHOUSE   (<u>WAREHOUSE-NUMBER</u>,
                WAREHOUSE-LOCATION)

The primary key for the relation CUSTOMER is <u>CUSTOMER-NUMBER</u>, and the primary key for the relation WAREHOUSE is <u>WAREHOUSE-NUMBER</u>.

In addition to these primary keys, we can identify WAREHOUSE-NUMBER to be a foreign key in the relation CUSTOMER. A foreign key is any attribute that is nonkey in relation, but a primary key in another relation. We designate that WAREHOUSE-NUMBER is a foreign key in the previous notation and in the figures by underscoring it with a dashed line.

Finally, the original, unnormalized relation SALES-REPORT has been transformed into four third normal (3NF) relations. In reviewing the relations

SALESPERSON-CUSTOMER

SALESPERSON NUMBER	CUSTOMER NUMBER	CUSTOMER NAME	WAREHOUSE NUMBER	WAREHOUSE LOCATION	SALES AMOUNT

CUSTOMER-WAREHOUSE

CUSTOMER NUMBER	CUSTOMER NAME	WAREHOUSE NUMBER	WAREHOUSE LOCATION
18765	Delta Systems	4	Fargo
18830	A. Levy and Sons	3	Bismarck
19242	Ranier Company	3	Bismarck
18841	R. W. Flood Inc.	2	Superior
18899	Seward Systems	2	Superior
19565	Stodola's Inc.	1	Plymouth
etc.			

SALES

SALESPERSON NUMBER	CUSTOMER NUMBER	SALES AMOUNT
3462	18765	13540
3462	18830	10600
3462	19242	9700
3593	18841	11560
3593	18899	2590
3593	19565	8800
etc.		

FIGURE 17.29
A data model diagram shows that a transitive dependency exists between WAREHOUSE-NUMBER and WAREHOUSE-LOCATION.

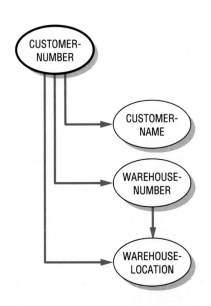

602

CUSTOMER-WAREHOUSE

CUSTOMER NUMBER	CUSTOMER NAME	WAREHOUSE NUMBER	WAREHOUSE LOCATION

CUSTOMER

CUSTOMER NUMBER	CUSTOMER NAME	WAREHOUSE NUMBER
18765	Delta Systems	4
18830	A. Levy and Sons	3
19242	Ranier Company	3
18841	R. W. Flood Inc.	2
18899	Seward Systems	2
19565	Stodola's Inc.	1
etc.		

WAREHOUSE

WAREHOUSE NUMBER	WAREHOUSE LOCATION
4	Fargo
3	Bismarck
2	Superior
1	Plymouth
etc.	

FIGURE 17.30
The relation CUSTOMER-WAREHOUSE is separated into two relations called CUSTOMER (1NF) and WAREHOUSE (1NF).

shown in Figure 17.31, one can see that the single relation SALES-REPORT was transformed into the following four relations:

SALESPERSON   (SALESPERSON-NUMBER, SALESPERSON-NAME, SALES-AREA)

SALES   (SALESPERSON-NUMBER, CUSTOMER-NUMBER, SALES-AMOUNT)

CUSTOMER   (CUSTOMER-NUMBER, CUSTOMER-NAME, WAREHOUSE-NUMBER)

and

WAREHOUSE   (WAREHOUSE-NUMBER, WAREHOUSE-LOCATION)

The third normal form is adequate for most database design problems. The simplification gained from transforming an unnormalized relation into a set of 3NF relations is a tremendous benefit in the insertion, deletion, and updating of information in the database. An entity-relationship diagram for the database is shown in Figure 17.32.

Using the Entity-Relationship Diagram to Determine Record Keys

The entity relationship diagram may be used to determine the keys required for a record or a database relation. The first step is to construct the entity-relationship diagram and label a unique (primary) key for each data entity. Figure 17.33 shows and entity-relationship diagram for a customer order system. There are three data entities: CUSTOMER, with a prime key of CUSTOMER-NUMBER; ORDER, with a key of ORDER-NUMBER;

FIGURE 17.31
The complete database con-
sists of four 1NF relations
called SALESPERSON,
SALES, CUSTOMER, and
WAREHOUSE.

SALESPERSON

SALESPERSON NUMBER	SALESPERSON NAME	SALES AREA
3462	Waters	West
3593	Dryne	East
etc.		

SALES

SALESPERSON NUMBER	CUSTOMER NUMBER	SALES AMOUNT
3462	18765	13540
3462	18830	10600
3462	19242	9700
3593	18841	11560
3593	18899	2590
3593	19565	8800
etc.		

CUSTOMER

CUSTOMER NUMBER	CUSTOMER NAME	WAREHOUSE NUMBER
18765	Delta Systems	4
18830	A. Levy and Sons	3
19242	Ranier Company	3
18841	R. W. Flood Inc.	2
18899	Seward Systems	2
19565	Stodola's Inc.	1
etc.		

WAREHOUSE

WAREHOUSE NUMBER	WAREHOUSE LOCATION
4	Fargo
3	Bismarck
2	Superior
1	Plymouth
etc.	

FIGURE 17.32
An entity-relationship
diagram for the Al S. Well
Hydraulic Company database.

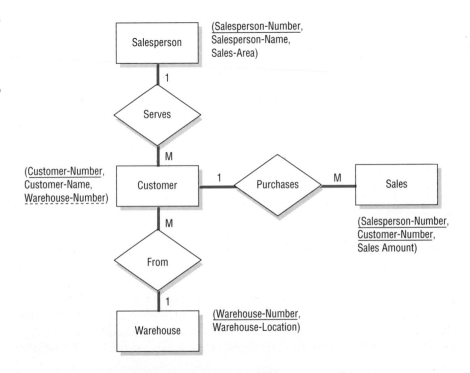

FIGURE 17.33
An entity-relationship diagram for customer orders.

and ITEM, with ITEM-NUMBER as the prime key. One CUSTOMER may place many orders, but each ORDER can be placed by one CUSTOMER only, so the relationship is one-to-many. Each ORDER may contain many ITEMS, and each ITEM may be contained within many ORDERS, so the ORDER-ITEM relationship is many-to-many.

A foreign key, however, is a data field on a given file which is the primary key of a different master file. For example, a DEPARTMENT-NUMBER indicating a student's major may exist on the STUDENT MASTER file. DEPARTMENT-NUMBER could also be the unique key for the DEPARTMENT MASTER file.

One-to-Many Relationship

A database file cannot contain a repeating group or table, but a traditional indexed-sequential file may have one. The file on the "many" end may have foreign keys stored in a table on the file at the "one" end. For example, the CUSTOMER MASTER FILE may be designed to contain a table of outstanding order numbers. The disadvantage of using such a table is that all the table entries may be filled with order numbers, and the analyst is then faced with the decision to expand the table (which is expensive and time-consuming) or lose some of the data in the table.

Many-to-Many Relationship

When the relationship is many-to-many, three files are necessary: one for each data entity and one for the relationship. The ORDER and ITEM entities in our example have a many-to-many relationship. The prime key of each data entity is stored as a foreign key of the relational file. The relational file may simply contain the prime keys for each data entity or may contain additional data, such as the grade received for a course or the quantity of an item ordered. Refer to the file layout illustrated in Figure 17.34. The ORDER ITEM FILE contains information about which order contains which items and provides a link between the ORDER FILE and the ITEM MASTER FILE.

The relationship file should be indexed on each foreign key—one for each of the files in the relationship—and may have a prime key consisting of a combination of the two foreign keys. To find many records from a second file given the first file, directly read the relational file for the desired key. Locate the matching record in the second "many" file. Continue to loop through the relational file until the desired key is no longer found. For example, to find records in the ITEM MASTER for a specific record in the ORDER MASTER FILE, directly read the ORDER ITEM FILE using the

FIGURE 17.34
When the relationship is
many-to-many, three files are
necessary.

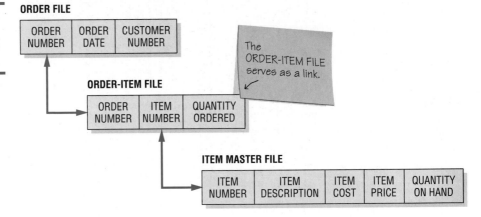

ORDER-NUMBER as the index. Records are logically sequenced based on the data in the index, so all records for the same ORDER-NUMBER are grouped together. For each ORDER ITEM record that matches the desired ORDER-NUMBER, directly read the ITEM MASTER FILE using the ITEM-NUMBER as an index.

The logic is the same for the reverse situation, for example, finding all the orders for a backordered item that has been received. Use the desired ITEM-NUMBER to directly read the ORDER ITEM FILE. The ORDER ITEM INDEX is set to the ITEM-NUMBER. For all matching ORDER ITEM records, use the ORDER-NUMBER to directly read the ORDER FILE. Finally, directly read the CUSTOMER MASTER FILE to obtain the CUSTOMER-NAME and ADDRESS using the CUSTOMER-NUMBER on the ORDER FILE.

FIGURE 17.35
When using indexed-sequential files, one of the files may contain a table of keys.

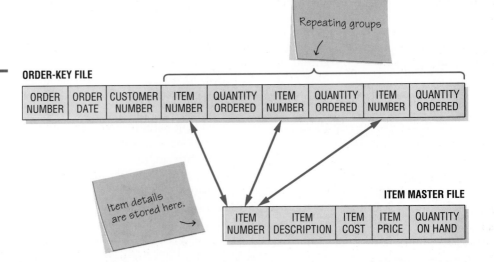

FIGURE 17.36
Example of a poorly designed
item master file.

Item Record =   Item Number +
                 Item Description +
                 Item Category +
                 Unit Cost +
                 Unit Price +
                 Reorder Point +
                 Reorder Quantity +
                 Month Sales +
                 Month Backordered +
                 Year To Date Sales +
                 Year To Date Backordered +
                 Vendor Name +
                 Vendor Street +
                 Vendor City +
                 Vendor State +
                 Vendor Zip +
                 Vendor Contact Person

When using indexed-sequential files, one of the files may contain a table of keys for the other file, eliminating the need for a relational file. Refer to the example illustrated in Figure 17.35. The ORDER KEY FILE has a table of order item information. Each element in the table contains an ITEM-NUMBER and the QUANTITY-ORDERED. The remaining information about all items is found in the ITEM MASTER FILE which is organized sequentially by ITEM-NUMBER. The disadvantage of this method is that it is difficult and time-consuming to find the orders that match a specific item number. Many conventional file systems utilize tables on master file records.

GUIDELINES FOR FILE/DATABASE RELATION DESIGN

The following guidelines should be taken into account when designing master files or database relations:

1. Each separate data entity should create a master file. Do not combine two distinct entities on one file. For example, items are purchased from vendors. The ITEM MASTER FILE should contain only item information and the VENDOR MASTER FILE should contain only vendor information. Figure 17.36 illustrates the data dictionary for a poorly designed ITEM MASTER FILE, which includes information about the vendor. There may be many items purchased from one vendor, and the VENDOR NAME and ADDRESS in this arrangement

FIGURE 17.37
The improved item and vendor master files.

Item Record =   Item Number +
                 Item Description +
                 Item Category +
                 Unit Cost +
                 Unit Price +
                 Reorder Point +
                 Reorder Quantity +
                 Month Sales +
                 Month Backordered +
                 Year To Date Sales +
                 Year To Date Backordered +
                 Vendor Number

Vendor Record = Vendor Number +
                 Vendor Name +
                 Vendor Street +
                 Vendor City +
                 Vendor State +
                 Vendor Zip +
                 Vendor Contact Person

would be stored on many records. If a vendor changes its address, multiple item records would have to be modified. If some were modified and others were not, the system would produce inconsistent results, such as purchase orders for one item going to the old address and other purchase orders being sent to the new address. Figure 17.37 illustrates the data dictionary for the improved ITEM MASTER FILE and VENDOR MASTER FILE.

2. A specific data field should exist only on one master file. For example, the CUSTOMER NAME should exist only on the CUSTOMER MASTER FILE, not the ORDER FILE or any other master file. The exceptions to this guideline are the key or index fields, which may be on as many files as necessary. If a report or screen needs information from many files, the indexes should provide the linkage to obtain the required records.

3. Each master file or database relation should have programs to Create, Read, Update and Delete (abbreviated CRUD) the records. Ideally, only one program should add new records, and one program should delete specified records. Data records may be changed—for instance, to change an address or correct an incorrect customer balance—by one program or several, depending on the data. These file maintenance programs are responsible for infrequent, unpredictable changes to the data.

Usually many update programs are responsible for changing data fields in the course of normal business activities. For example, a customer master file may have a CURRENT BALANCE field that is increased by the ORDER

TOTAL within the order processing program and decreased by a PAY-MENT AMOUNT or an AMOUNT RETURNED, using output by two additional programs.

MAKING USE OF THE DATABASE

Steps in Retrieving and Presenting Data

There are eight steps in the retrieval and presentation of data:

1. Choose a relation from the database.
2. Join two relations together.
3. Project columns from the relation.
4. Select rows from the relation.
5. Derive new attributes.
6. Index or sort rows.
7. Calculate totals and performance measures.
8. Present data.

The first and last steps are mandatory, but the six steps in between are optional, depending on how data are to be used. Figure 17.38 is a visual guide to the steps, which are described in the following section.

CHOOSE A RELATION FROM THE DATABASE. The first and obvious step is to choose a relation from the database. A good way to accomplish this is to keep a directory of user views as a memory aid. Even if the user wants an ad-hoc query, it is useful to have similar views available.

JOIN TWO RELATIONS TOGETHER. The operation join is intended to take two relations and put them together to make a larger relation. In order for two relations to be joined, they must have a common attribute. For instance, take two relations from our example:

CUSTOMER   (<u>CUSTOMER-NUMBER</u>, CUSTOMER-NAME,
                  WAREHOUSE-NUMBER)

and

WAREHOUSE   (<u>WAREHOUSE-NUMBER</u>,
                  WAREHOUSE-LOCATION)

Suppose we join these relations over WAREHOUSE-NUMBER to get a new relation, CUSTOMER-WAREHOUSE-LOCATION. The joining of these relations is illustrated in Figure 17.39. Also note that the new relation is not 3NF.

The operation join may also go one step further; that is, it may combine files for rows that have an attribute that meets a certain condition. Figure 17.40 shows an example in which two relations, SALES and QUOTA, are joined by satisfying the condition that a salesperson has met or exceeded predetermined quotas.

Join is an important operation because it can take many 3NF relations and combine them to make a more useful relation. Together with the operations below it, join is a powerful operation.

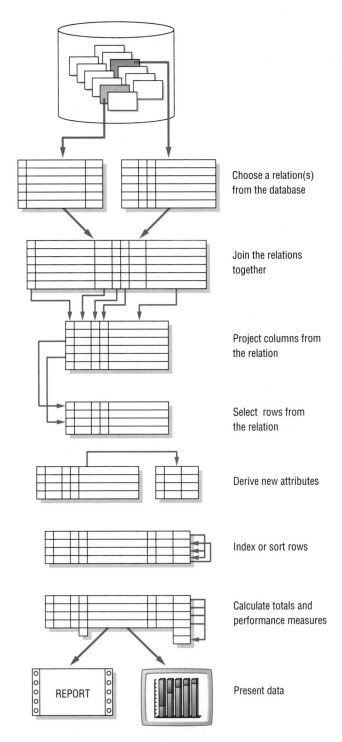

Choose a relation(s)
from the database

Join the relations
together

Project columns from
the relation

Select rows from
the relation

Derive new attributes

Index or sort rows

Calculate totals and
performance measures

REPORT

Present data

FIGURE 17.38
Data are retrieved and presented in eight distinct steps.

PROJECT COLUMNS FROM THE RELATON. Projection is the process of building a smaller relation by choosing only relevant attributes from an existing relation. In other words, projection is the extraction of certain columns from a relational table.

FIGURE 17.39
The operation join takes two
relations and puts them
together to form a single
relation.

CUSTOMER

CUSTOMER NUMBER	CUSTOMER NAME	WAREHOUSE NUMBER
18765	Delta Systems	4
18830	A. Levy and Sons	3
19242	Ranier Company	3
18841	R. W. Flood Inc.	2
18899	Seward Systems	2
19565	Stodola's Inc.	1
etc.		

WAREHOUSE

WAREHOUSE NUMBER	WAREHOUSE LOCATION
4	Fargo
3	Bismarck
2	Superior
1	Plymouth
etc.	

Join

CUSTOMER-WAREHOUSE-LOCATION

CUSTOMER NUMBER	CUSTOMER NAME	WAREHOUSE NUMBER	WAREHOUSE LOCATION
18765	Delta Systems	4	Fargo
18830	A. Levy and Sons	3	Bismarck
19242	Ranier Company	3	Bismarck
18841	R. W. Flood Inc.	2	Superior
18899	Seward Systems	2	Superior
19565	Stodola's Inc.	1	Plymouth
etc.			

An example of projection is featured in Figure 17.41. The relation:

CUSTOMER-WAREHOUSE-LOCATION   (CUSTOMER-NUMBER,
CUSTOMER-NAME,
WAREHOUSE-NUMBER),
WAREHOUSE-LOCATION

is projected over CUSTOMER-NUMBER and WAREHOUSE-LOCATION,
and during the projection process, duplicate records are removed.

SELECT ROWS FROM THE RELATION. The operation referred to as selection is similar to projection, but instead of extracting columns it extracts rows. Selection creates a new (smaller) relation by extracting records that contain an attribute meeting a certain condition.

Figure 17.42 illustrates how the selection operation works. Selection is performed on the relation PERSONNEL to extract salaried employees only. There is no need to remove duplicate records here as there was in the previous illustration of projection.

FIGURE 17.40
Relations can be joined subject to certain conditions.

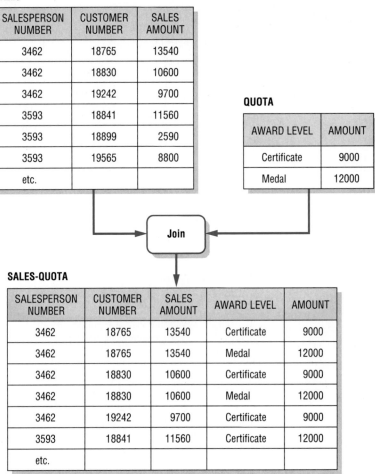

SALES

SALESPERSON NUMBER	CUSTOMER NUMBER	SALES AMOUNT
3462	18765	13540
3462	18830	10600
3462	19242	9700
3593	18841	11560
3593	18899	2590
3593	19565	8800
etc.		

QUOTA

AWARD LEVEL	AMOUNT
Certificate	9000
Medal	12000

Join

SALES-QUOTA

SALESPERSON NUMBER	CUSTOMER NUMBER	SALES AMOUNT	AWARD LEVEL	AMOUNT
3462	18765	13540	Certificate	9000
3462	18765	13540	Medal	12000
3462	18830	10600	Certificate	9000
3462	18830	10600	Medal	12000
3462	19242	9700	Certificate	9000
3593	18841	11560	Certificate	12000
etc.				

Selection may also be performed for a more complex set of conditions. For example: Select all of the employees who are salaried *and* who
make more than $40,000 annually, or employees who are hourly *and*
make more than $15.00 per hour. Selection is an important operation for
ad-hoc queries.

DERIVE NEW ATTRIBUTES. The fifth step involves the manipulation of
the existing data plus some additional parameters (if necessary) to derive
new data. New columns are created for the resulting relation. An example
of derivation of new attributes can be found in Figure 17.43. Here, two new
attributes are determined: (1) GIRTH (by multiplying the sum of width and
height by 2 and adding it to length), and (2) SHIPPING-WEIGHT (which
depends on the girth).

INDEX OR SORT ROWS. People require data to be organized in a certain
order so they can locate items in a list more easily or group and subtotal
items more easily. Two options for ordering data are available: indexing
and sorting.

Indexing is the logical ordering of rows in a relation according to
some key. As discussed in the previous section, the logical pointer takes

CUSTOMER-WAREHOUSE-LOCATION

CUSTOMER NUMBER	CUSTOMER NAME	WAREHOUSE NUMBER	WAREHOUSE LOCATION
18765	Delta Systems	4	Fargo
18830	A. Levy and Sons	3	Bismarck
19242	Ranier Company	3	Bismarck
18841	R. W. Flood Inc.	2	Superior
18899	Seward Systems	2	Superior
19565	Stodola's Inc.	1	Plymouth
etc.			

Projection

CUSTOMER-LOCATION

CUSTOMER NUMBER	WAREHOUSE LOCATION
18765	Fargo
18830	Bismarck
19242	Bismarck
18841	Superior
18899	Superior
19565	Plymouth
etc.	

FIGURE 17.41
Projection creates a smaller relation by choosing only relevant attributes (columns) from the relation.

up space, and listing the relation by using an index is slower than if the relation were in the proper physical order. The index, however, takes up far less space than a duplicate file.

Sorting is the physical ordering of a relation. The result of physical sorting is a sequential file as discussed earlier in the chapter. Figure 17.44 illustrates indexing and sorting of the relation <u>PERSONNEL</u> by employee name in alphabetical order.

CALCULATE TOTALS AND PERFORMANCE MEASURES. Once the appropriate subset of data is defined and the rows of the relation are ordered in the required manner, totals and performance measures can be calculated. Figure 17.45 shows how calculation is performed.

PRESENT DATA TO THE USER. The final step in the retrieval of data is presentation. Presentation of the data abstracted from the database can take many forms. Sometimes the data will be presented in tabular form, sometimes in graphs, and other times as a single-word answer on a screen. Output design, as covered in Chapter 15, provides a more detailed look at presentation objectives, forms, and methods.

FIGURE 17.42
Selection extracts the relevant
records (rows) from the
relation.

PERSONNEL

NUMBER	EMPLOYEE NAME	DEPARTMENT	S/H	GROSS
72845	Waters	Outside Sales	S	48960
72888	Dryne	Outside Sales	S	37200
73712	Fawcett	Distribution	H	23500
80345	Well, Jr.	Marketing	S	65000
84672	Piper	Maintenance	H	20560
89760	Acquia	Accounting	H	18755
etc.				

Selection

SALARIED-EMPLOYEES

NUMBER	EMPLOYEE NAME	DEPARTMENT	S/H	GROSS
72845	Waters	Outside Sales	S	48960
72888	Dryne	Outside Sales	S	37200
80345	Well, Jr.	Marketing	S	65000
etc.				

SUMMARY

How to store data is often an important decision in the design of an information system. There are two approaches to storing data. The first approach is to store data in individual files, one file for each application. The second approach is to develop a database that can be shared by many users for a variety of applications as the need arises. Dramatic improvements have been made in the design of database software to take advantage of the graphical user interface.

The conventional file approach may at times be a more efficient approach since the file can be application-specific. On the other hand, the database approach may be more appropriate because the same data need to be entered, stored, and updated only once.

To understand data storage, it is necessary to have a grasp of three realms: reality, data, and metadata. An entity is any object or event for which we are willing to collect and store data. Attributes are the actual characteristics of these entities. Data items can have values and can be organized into records that can be accessed by a key. Metadata describes the data and can contain restrictions about the value of a data item (such as numeric only).

Examples of conventional files include master files, table files, transaction files, work files, and report files. They can have a sequential organization, linked lists, hashed file organization, indexed organization, or

PACKAGE NUMBER	WIDTH	HEIGHT	LENGTH	WEIGHT
A3456	4	3	26	4
A3457	12	12	20	10
A3458	10	20	34	20
A3459	15	15	22	18
A3460	10	10	40	40
A3461	10	20	34	22
A3462	5	10	15	30
A3463	8	14	44	35

FIGURE 17.43
Derivation creates new attributes (columns) in the relation by manipulating the data contained in existing attributes.

Some Examples: GIRTH = 2 (WIDTH + HEIGHT) + LENGTH

Derivation

IF GIRTH > 84 AND WEIGHT < 25
THEN SHIPPING WEIGHT = WEIGH
ELSE SHIPPING WEIGHT = WEIGH1

PACKAGE NUMBER	WIDTH	HEIGHT	LENGTH	WEIGHT
A3456	4	3	26	4
A3457	12	12	20	10
A3458	10	20	34	20
A3459	15	15	22	18
A3460	10	10	40	40
A3461	10	20	34	22
A3462	5	10	15	30
A3463	8	14	44	35

GIRTH	SHIPPING WEIGHT
50	4
68	10
94	25
82	18
80	40
90	25
45	30
88	35

indexed-sequential organization. A more modern and efficient way to handle indexed-sequential files is the VSAM. Databases can have hierarchical, network, or relational structures.

Normalization is the process that takes user views and transforms them into less complex structures called normalized relations. There are three steps in the normalization process. First, all repeating groups are removed. Second, all partial dependencies are removed. Finally, the transitive dependencies are taken out. After these three steps, the result is the creation of numerous relations that are of third normal form (3NF).

The entity-relationship diagram may be used to determine the keys required for a record or a database relation. The three guidelines to follow when designing master files or database relations are: (1) each separate data entity should create a master file. Do not combine two distinct entities on one file; (2) a specific data field should exist only on one master file; and (3) each master file or database relation should have programs to create, read, update, and delete.

The process of retrieving data may involve as many as eight steps: (1) a relation or relations are chosen and (2) joined; (3) projection and

FIGURE 17.44
Sort orders the records (rows) in the relation so that records can be displayed in order and can be grouped for subtotals. Here the PERSONNEL relation is sorted alphabetically according to EMPLOYEE NAME.

PERSONNEL

NUMBER	EMPLOYEE NAME	DEPARTMENT	S/H	GROSS
72845	Waters	Outside Sales	S	48960
72888	Dryne	Outside Sales	S	37200
73712	Fawcett	Distribution	H	23500
80345	Well, Jr.	Marketing	S	65000
84672	Piper	Maintenance	H	20560
89760	Acquia	Accounting	H	18755

Sort

EMPLOYEES-BY-NAME

NUMBER	EMPLOYEE NAME	DEPARTMENT	S/H	GROSS
89760	Acquia	Accounting	H	18755
72888	Dryne	Outside Sales	S	37200
73712	Fawcett	Distribution	H	23500
84672	Piper	Maintenance	H	20560
72845	Waters	Outside Sales	S	48960
80345	Well, Jr.	Marketing	S	65000

(4) selection are performed on the relation to extract the relevant rows and columns; (5) new attributes may be derived; (6) rows are sorted or indexed; (7) totals and performance measures are calculated; and finally (8) the results are presented to the user.

KEYWORDS AND PHRASES

data storage
conventional file
database
database management
   system (DBMS)
database administrator
data model diagram
record
key
master file
table file
transaction file

work file
report file
sequential organization
linked list
hashed file organization
indexed organization
indexed-sequential
   organization
indexed-sequential access
   method (ISAM)
virtual storage access
   method (VSAM)

SHIPPING-WEIGHT

PACKAGE NUMBER	WIDTH	HEIGHT	LENGTH	WEIGHT	GIRTH	SHIPPING WEIGHT
A3456	4	3	26	4	50	4
A3457	12	12	20	10	68	10
A3458	10	20	34	20	94	25
A3459	15	15	22	18	82	18
A3460	10	10	40	40	80	40
A3461	10	20	34	22	90	25
A3462	5	10	15	30	45	30
A3463	8	14	44	35	88	35

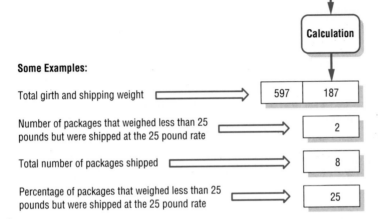

Calculation

Some Examples:

Total girth and shipping weight ⟹ | 597 | 187 |

Number of packages that weighed less than 25 pounds but were shipped at the 25 pound rate ⟹ 2

Total number of packages shipped ⟹ 8

Percentage of packages that weighed less than 25 pounds but were shipped at the 25 pound rate ⟹ 25

FIGURE 17.45
Calculation provides subtotals, totals, and other performance.

"I hear very good things about your team from the people in Management Systems. You even got some hard-earned praise from Training people. You know, Tom Ketcham isn't easy to please these days. Even *he* is seeing some possibilities. I think you'll pull us together yet. Unless we all go off in different directions again . . . I'm just teasing you. I told you to think about whether we are a family, a zoo, or a war zone. Now's the time to start designing systems for us that fit us. You've been here long enough now to form those opinions. I hope they're favorable. I think our famous Southern hospitality should help influence you, don't you? I was so busy persuading you that we're worth the effort, that I almost forgot to tell you. Tom and Snowden have agreed to think about moving toward a database of some sort. Would you have this ready in the next two weeks? Tom is at a conference in Minneapolis, but when he returns you should have some database ideas worked up for Snowden and him to discuss it. Keep at it."

HyperCase Questions

1. Assume your team members have used the Training Unit Client Characteristics Report to design a database table to store the relevant information contained on this report, with the following result:

Table name: CLIENT_TABLE

COLUMN NAME	DESCRIPTION
CLIENT-ID (primary key)	Mnemonic made up by user like STHSP for State Hospital
CLIENT-NAME	The actual, full client name
ADDRESS	The client's address
CONTACTS	The names of contact persons
PHONE-NUMBER	The phone numbers of contact persons
CLASS	The type of institution (VA hospital, clinic, other, etc.)
STAFF-SIZE	Size of client staff (number)
TRAINING-LEVEL	Minimum required expertise level of the staff (as defined by the class)
EQUIP-QTY	The number of medical machines that the client has
EQUIP-TYPE	The type of medical machines (e.g., x-ray, MRI, CAT)
EQUIP-MODEL-YR	The model and year of each medical machine

2. Apply normalization to the table your team has developed to remove repeating groups. Display your results.

3. Remove transitive dependencies from your table, and show your resulting database table.

REVIEW QUESTIONS

1. What are the advantages of organizing data storage as separate files?
2. What are the advantages of organizing data storage using a database approach?
3. What are the effectiveness measures of database design?
4. What are the efficiency measures of database design? Why do they conflict with each other?
5. List some examples of entities and their attributes.
6. Define the term *metadata.* What is its purpose?
7. List file types of commonly used conventional files. Which of these are temporary files?
8. What is a linked list?
9. What often occurs when a hashed file organization is used?
10. What is an inverted list? When is it valuable to have an inverted list?
11. Name the three main types of database organization.
12. Define the term *normalization.*
13. What is removed when a relation is converted to the first normal form?
14. What is removed when a relation is converted from 1NF to 2NF?
15. What is removed when a relation is converted from 2NF to 3NF?
16. List the eight steps for retrieving, presorting, and presenting data.
17. What does join do? What is projection? What is selection?
18. State the differences between "sort" and "index."
19. List two ways of storing a many-to-many relationship and the differences between the two methods.
20. What types of programs must be included in the system design for each master file?

PROBLEMS

1. Given the following file of renters:

Record #	Last name	Apartment Number	Rent	Lease Expires
41	Warkentin	102	550	4/30
42	Buffington	204	600	4/30
43	Schuldt	103	550	4/30
44	Tang	209	600	5/31
45	Cho	203	550	5/31
46	Yoo	203	550	6/30
47	Pyle	101	500	6/30

   a. Develop a linked list by apartment number in ascending order.
   b. Develop a linked list according to last name in ascending order.

2. Develop an inverted file. Develop an index for each of the attributes.

3. The following is an example of a grade report for two students at the University of Southern New Jersey:

	USNJ Grade Report			
	Spring Semester 1995			

Name: I. M. Smarte   Major: MIS
Student: 053-6929-24   Status: Senior

Course Number	Course Title	Professor	Professor's Department	Grade
MIS 403	Systems Analysis	Kendall, K.	DESC	A
MIS 411	Conceptual Foundations	Kendall, J.	DESC	A
MIS 420	Human Factors in IS	Kendall, J.	DESC	B
CIS 412	Database Design	Sibley, E.	CIS	A
DESC 353	Management Models	Kelly, D.	DESC	A

	USNJ Grade Report			
	Spring Semester 1995			

Name: E. Z. Grayed   Major: MIS
Student: 472-6124-59   Status: Senior

Course Number	Course Title	Professor	Professor's Department	Grade
MIS 403	Systems Analysis	Kendall, K.	DESC	B
MIS 411	Conceptual Foundations	Kendall, J.	DESC	A

Draw a hierarchical data structure for this user view. Focus on each individual course and follow the approach used in Figure 17.15.

4. Draw a network data structure for the user view in problem 3. Use grade as a link and follow the approach in Figure 17.17.

5. Draw a data model diagram with associations for the user view in problem 3.

6. Convert the user view in problem 3 to a 3NF relation. Show each step along the way.

7. Draw an entity-relationship diagram for the following:

Many students play many different sports. One person, called the head coach, assumes the role of coaching all of these sports. Each of the entities have a number and a name. (Make any assumptions necessary to complete a reasonable diagram. List your assumptions.)

8. The entity relationship diagram you drew in problem 7 represents the data entities necessary to implement a system for tracking students and the sports teams that they play. List the files necessary to implement

the system, along with primary, secondary, and foreign keys that are required to link the files.

9. Draw an entity-relationship diagram for the following situation:

   A commercial bakery makes many different products. These include breads, desserts, specialty cakes, and many other baked goods. Ingredients such as flour, spices, milk, and so on are purchased from vendors. Sometimes an ingredient is purchased from a single vendor and other times an ingredient is purchased from many vendors. The bakery has commercial customers, such as schools and restaurants, that regularly place orders for baked goods. Each baked good has a specialist that oversees the setup of the bake operation and inspects the finished product.

10. List the files and keys necessary to implement the commercial bakery system.

SELECTED BIBLIOGRAPHY

Avison, D. F. *Information Systems Development: A Database Approach,* 2nd ed. London: Blackwell Scientific Publications, 1992.

Everest, G. C. *Database Management: Objectives, System Functions, and Administration.* New York: McGraw-Hill Book Company, 1985.

Gane, C., and T. Sarson. *Structured Systems Analysis: Tools and Techniques.* Englewood Cliffs, NJ: Prentice-Hall, Inc., 1979.

McFadden, F., and J. A. Hoffer. *Modern Database Management,* 4th ed. Redwood City, CA: The Benjamin/Cummings Publishing Company, Inc., 1994.

BACK TO DATA BASICS

After numerous interviews, prototypes, data flow diagrams, and data dictionary entries had been completed, Anna and Chip both start work on the data model. "I'll be responsible for creating a Data Model Diagram," Anna promises. Chip volunteers to complete an entity-relationship diagram. "Let's compare the two diagrams for accuracy and consistency when we're done," Anna suggests, and so they did.

Figure E17.1 shows the entity-relationship diagram for the microcomputer system. Excelerator names each of the rectangles a *data entity*. This is distinct from an external entity, which represents a source or recipient of information on a data flow diagram. The data entity represents a file of information stored within the system, corresponding to a data store on the data flow diagram. Each of the diamonds represents a relationship between the data entities.

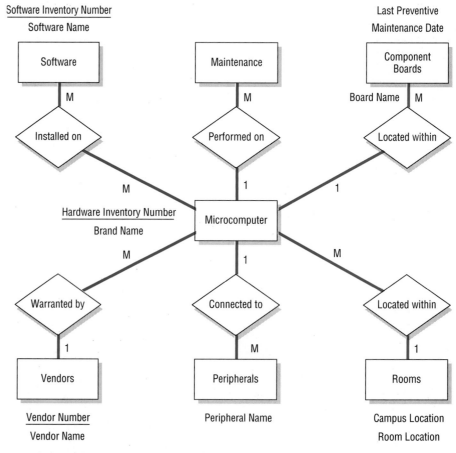

FIGURE E17.1
Entity-relationship diagram, Microcomputer System.

Allen Schmidt,
Julie E. Kendall, and
Kenneth E. Kendall

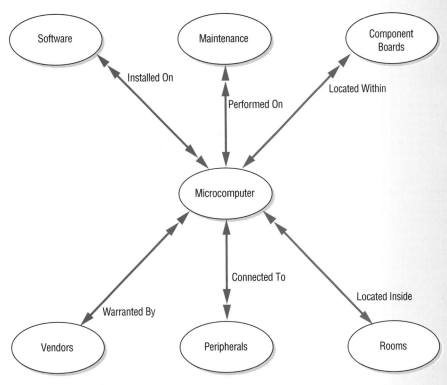

FIGURE E17.2
Data Model Diagram, Microcomputer System.

"When I created the entity-relationship diagram, I started with the simplest portions of the system," Chip tells Anna. "The first data entities created were SOFTWARE and HARDWARE. The relationship is that software is installed on the hardware. Next I determined the cardinality of the relationship. Since one software package could be installed on many microcomputers, this relationship is one-to-many. Each microcomputer may also have many different software packages installed on it, also providing a one-to-many relationship. Since there is a one-to-many relationship for each of the data entities, the full relationship between them becomes many-to-many."

Chip continues by saying, "I kept on diagramming data entities, working on MAINTENANCE, COMPONENT BOARDS, and the other data entities and their relationships. When all the diagram components were drawn, attributes were added. To keep the diagram from becoming cluttered, only key attributes for each data entity were included. The other attributes are defined in records that are linked to the data entity."

"I've been busy, too," Anna confides. She has created a data model diagram. Her finished product is shown in Figure E17.2. "I did as you did, Chip," she said. "I started with the obvious portions of the system, the hardware and software. I chose to use double-headed arrows or a trident, a small three-pronged symbol, to represent the *many* end of the connection. Notice that the general design of the Data Model Diagram is the same as the entity-relationship diagram."

Each of the data entities was described in the XLDictionary of Exelerator. Figure E17.3 is an example of the description screen completed for the MICROCOMPUTER data entity. A key component is the link to the

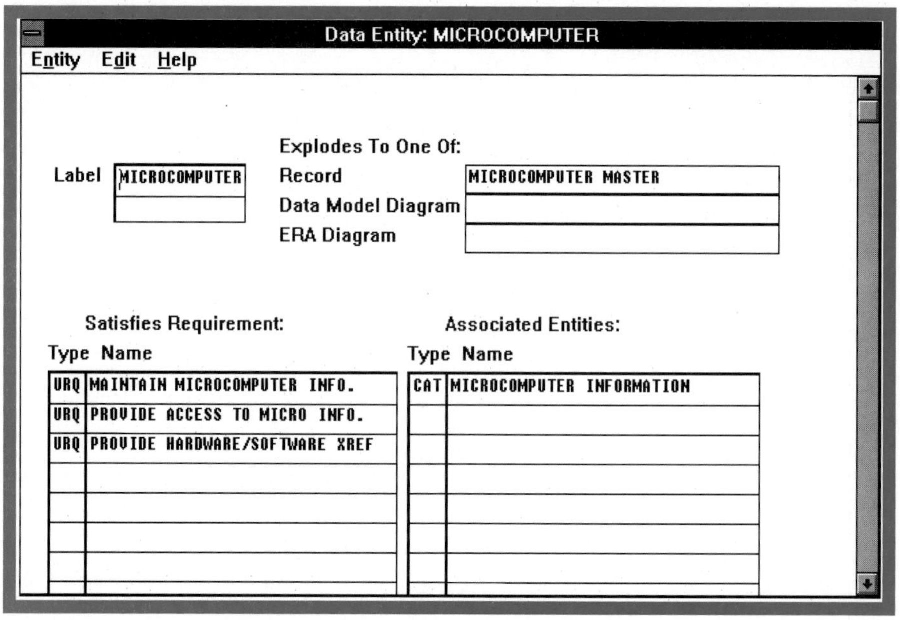

FIGURE E17.3
Data Entity description screen, MICROCOMPUTER.

MICROCOMPUTER MASTER record in the **Explodes To One Of** area. This allows Excelerator later to perform analysis on the data model design. The data entity is also linked to user requirements (URQ) and grouped under the MICROCOMPUTER INFORMATION category.

After spending time comparing diagrams, both Anna and Chip are satisfied that the relationships between the data have been accurately portrayed. Next they decided how to design the files or database from the diagrams. A critical choice had to be made: whether to use files or a database. "I think a series of indexed files and COBOL language is best," Chip says.

Anna says, "The system should be implemented using dBASE, since a database structure would easily accommodate the many relationships."

The HARDWARE/SOFTWARE relationship is analyzed first. Since there is a many-to-many relationship between these two data entities, it may be implemented in one of two forms:

1. Use three indexed files, which is the database solution. These are:
    a. HARDWARE MASTER.
    b. SOFTWARE MASTER.
    c. A hardware/software relationship file. This would contain the key fields for the HARDWARE and SOFTWARE master file for all software installed on all machines.
2. While the preceding database solution could also be used when designing a COBOL-indexed file structure, a better alternative would be to use a repeating group on one of the files, referencing the other master file. This is easier for accomplishing file maintenance and producing information. The files would be:
    a. A HARDWARE MASTER file.
    b. A SOFTWARE MASTER file with a repeating group or table of HARDWARE INVENTORY NUMBERS, the key field of the MICROCOMPUTER MASTER on which the software would be

```
DATE: 21-FEB-95                     RECORD - EXPLOSION                              PAGE    1
TIME: 12:28                         NAME: MICROCOMPUTER MASTER                      Excelerator

NAME:                       MICROCOMPUTER MASTER       DEFINITION:
ALIAS:                      MICROCOMPUTER HARDWARE RECORD   A FILE CONTAINING A RECORD FOR EACH MICROCOMPUTER       Y

ELEMENT/RECORD                            OFF  OCC  TYPE  LEN  DEFINITION
-----------------------------------       ---  ---  ----  ---  ------------------------------------------------------------

RECORD CODE                               000  001  E     001  ACTIVE OR INACTIVE MICRO. INACTIVE MEANS NO LONGER AVAILABLE

HARDWARE INVENTORY NUMBER                 001  001  K     008  A UNIQUE NUMBER ASSIGNED TO EACH MACHINE, LOCATED ON MACHINE

BRAND NAME                                009  001  E     010  THE NAME OF THE MICROCOMPUTER

MODEL                                     019  001  E     012  THE PARTICULAR MODEL OF MICROCOMPUTER

SERIAL NUMBER                             031  001  E     012  SERIAL NUMBER ASSIGNED BY MANUFACTURER

CAMPUS LOCATION                           043  001  E     004  CAMPUS WHERE MICROCOMPUTER IS LOCATED

ROOM LOCATION                             047  001  E     005  THE ROOM THE HARDWARE, SOFTWARE OR EXPERT IS LOCATED WITHIN

DATE PURCHASED                            052  001  E     006  DATE THE MACHINE WAS PURCHASED

PURCHASE COST                             058  001  E     004  THE COST TO PURCHASE THE MICROCOMPUTER

REPLACEMENT COST                          062  001  E     004  COST TO REPLACE HARDWARE

MEMORY SIZE                               066  001  E     005  SIZE OF MICRO RAM MEMORY, IN THOUSANDS OF CHARACTERS (K)

FIXED DISK                                071  001  E     002  MEMORY SIZE OF THE FIXED DISK IN MILLIONS OF CHARACTERS (M)

FIXED DISK 2                              073  001  E     002  MEMORY SIZE OF THE FIXED DISK IN MILLIONS OF CHARACTERS (M)

DISK DRIVE A                              075  001  E     006  THE SIZE OF DISKETTE DRIVE A, IN INCHES AND DENSITY (LOW/HI)

DISK DRIVE B                              081  001  E     006  THE SIZE OF DISKETTE DRIVE B, IN INCHES AND DENSITY (LOW/HI)

INTERNAL BOARDS                           087  005  E     003  THE OPTIONAL BOARDS THAT ARE FOUND WITHIN THE MICROCOMPUTER

PERIPHERAL EQUIPMENT                      102  001  R          PERIPHERAL EQUIPMENT STRUCTURAL RECORD              Y
  MONITOR                                 102  001  E     004  THE TYPE OF MONITOR ATTACHED TO THE MICROCOMPUTER
  MOUSE                                   106  001  E     001  MOUSE ATTACHED Y/N
  PRINTER                                 107  001  E     005  A CODE FOR THE TYPE OF PRINTER ATTACHED TO THE MICROCOMPUTER

MAINTENANCE INFORMATION                   112  001  R          MAINTENANCE PORTION OF THE MICROCOMPUTER MASTER RECORD   Y
  WARRANTY                                112  001  E     001  IS A WARRANTY IN EFFECT (Y/N)
  MAINTENANCE INTERVAL                    113  001  E     002  THE LENGTH OF TIME BETWEEN PREVENTIVE MAINTENANCE
  LAST PREVENT. MAINTENANCE DATE          115  001  E     008  THE DATE LAST PREVENTIVE MAINTENANCE WAS PERFORMED
  NUMBER OF REPAIRS                       123  001  E     002  THE NUMBER OF TIMES THE MICROCOMPUTER HAS BEEN REPAIRED
  COST OF REPAIRS                         125  001  E     004  THE TOTAL COST OF ALL REPAIRS

Record length is 129.
```

FIGURE E17.4
MICROCOMPUTER MASTER record print.

installed. This table could also be included on the HARDWARE MASTER file, referencing the SOFTWARE INVENTORY NUMBER for each software package installed on the machine.

"I finally see your way of thinking," Chip says. After a lengthy discussion, they decide to go ahead with the database solution. It will be easier for the programmers to design, code, implement, and maintain the system. Further, the file structures will be easy to modify as the system evolves.

The next key step is the normalization of the data records. These were created earlier in the design and were not analyzed for violations of the third normal form. Excelerator has several normalization analysis options, which are only available for the Data Model Diagram. The MICROCOMPUTER MASTER is shown in Figure E17.4. SOFTWARE in Figure E17.5. Each of these files is linked to the corresponding data entities on the Data Model Diagram.

```
    DATE: 21-FEB-95                           RECORD - EXPLOSION                              PAGE     1
    TIME: 12:31                               NAME: SOFTWARE MASTER                           Excelerator

    NAME:                        SOFTWARE MASTER              DEFINITION:
    ALIAS:                       MICROCOMPUTER SOFTWARE RECORD  CONTAINS A RECORD FOR EACH PIECE OF SOFTWARE         N

    ELEMENT/RECORD                               OFF   OCC  TYPE  LEN  DEFINITION
    ------------------------------------------   ---   ---  ----  ---  ------------------------------------------------

    ACTIVE SOFTWARE CODE                         000   001  E     001  CODE TO DETERMINE IF SOFTWARE IS CURRENTLY IN USE

    SOFTWARE INVENTORY NUMBER                    001   001  K     008  UNIQUE SOFTWARE IDENTIFICATION NUMBER

    TITLE                                        009   001  E     020  SOFTWARE TITLE

    VERSION NUMBER                               029   001  E     005  VERSION OF THE SOFTWARE

    PUBLISHER                                    034   001  E     030  THE MANUFACTURER OR PUBLISHER OF THE SOFTWARE

    SOFTWARE CATEGORY                            064   001  E     004  THE CATEGORY OF SOFTWARE, EG. WORD PROCESSING - CODED ENTRY

    NUMBER OF DISKETTES                          068   001  E     002  NUMBER OF DISKETTES INCLUDED WITH THE PACKAGE

    COMPUTER BRAND                               070   001  E     010  THE BRAND OF COMPUTER NECESSARY TO RUN THE SOFTWARE

    COMPUTER MODEL                               080   001  E     012  THE SPECIFIC MODEL NECESSARY TO RUN THE SOFTWARE

    MEMORY REQUIRED                              092   001  E     005  THE MEMORY SIZE REQUIRED TO RUN THE SOFTWARE, IN THOUSANDS,K

    MONITOR REQUIRED                             097   001  E     003  THE TYPE OF MONITOR REQUIRED TO RUN THE SOFTWARE

    PRINTER REQUIRED                             100   001  E     005  A CODE FOR THE PRINTER REQUIRED. MAY BE LEFT BLANK. REFER TO

    DISKETTE SIZE                                105   001  E     006  THE SIZE OF DISKETTE WITH THE ORIGINAL SOFTWARE PACKAGE

    SITE LICENSE                                 111   001  E     001  WHETHER OR NOT A SOFTWARE SITE LICENSE HAS BEEN OBTAINED

    NUMBER OF COPIES                             112   001  E     004  THE NUMBER OF COPIES OF THE SOFTWARE PURCHASED

    INSTALLATION MICROCOMPUTER                   116   001  R                                                          Y
      HARDWARE INVENTORY NUMBER                  116   999  E     008  A UNIQUE NUMBER ASSIGNED TO EACH MACHINE, LOCATED ON MACHINE
      SOFTWARE EXPERT NAME                       8108  001  E     020  SOFTWARE PACKAGE EXPERT
      SOFTWARE EXPERT LOCATION                   8128  001  E     004  CAMPUS LOCATION OF STAFF PERSON

    Record length is 8132.
```

FIGURE E17.5
SOFTWARE MASTER record print not normalized.

Chip and Anna choose the **ANALYSIS** and **Extended Analysis** options. From the Extended Analysis menu displayed, the first choice was **Data Model Validation Analysis.** This was chosen because Excelerator will automatically update the Data Relation descriptions linking the data entities with data entity and cardinality information. An example of the updated Data Relationship for INSTALLED ON between SOFTWARE and HARDWARE is shown in Figure E17.6. The entity names and the cardinality are supplied by Excelerator. There are also reports that list both undescribed Data Relationships and the Data Relationships modified by Excelerator.

There is one matrix available for reporting or viewing, **Data Relationships,** which is an excellent summary of how data entities are related to each other. Figure E17.7 is the Data Relationships matrix for the Microcomputer System.

Another **Extended Analysis** feature is **Data Normalization,** which helps to ensure that the records are in the third normal form. Analysis is on record

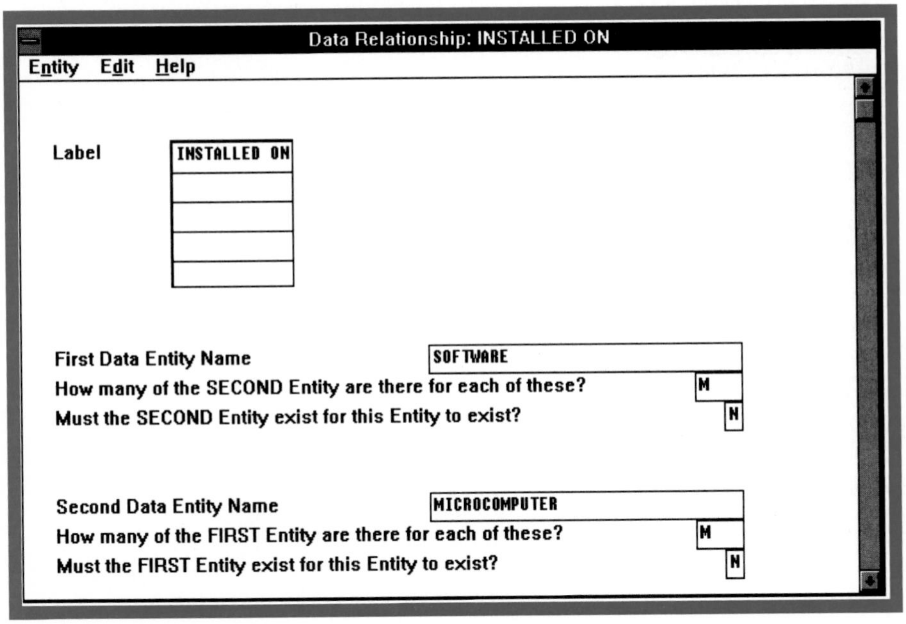

FIGURE E17.6
Data Relationship description screen, INSTALLED ON.

keys and the Data Model Diagram. The analysis does not normalize the records; it only reports on the errors in the design that prevent the records from being fully normalized. This option is run late in analysis, after the design is complete. Records, the Data Model Diagram, and Data Entities should be complete. If in doubt, run the Undescribed Graph Entities and Data Model Diagram Analysis first. Then use Record Content and Key Validation Analysis to determine any missing or contradictory information. Make corrections before running the Data Normalization reports and matrices. The following options are available for Data Normalization reports:

Repeating Groups
Element Access Conflicts
Matching Key Records
Record Dependencies
Data Entity Exceptions
Data Model Relationships
DAR/Record Conflicts

Repeating groups shows any repeating groups (for example, tables) that are within records declared to be normalized, meaning that the Normalized field on the record description contains a **Y.**

Figure E17.8 is the report produced for the microcomputer system, which Anna ran before running other reports. Notice that both the MICRO-COMPUTER MASTER and the SOFTWARE MASTER have repeating groups that need to be eliminated. Anna and Chip decide to create a relational file containing the HARDWARE INVENTORY NUMBER and the SOFTWARE INVENTORY NUMBER. Figure E17.9 shows the structure of this record. Also the INTERNAL BOARDS table was removed from the MICROCOMPUT-ER MASTER file, resulting in a relational file containing the elements HARDWARE INVENTORY NUMBER and a code for the INTERNAL BOARD.

Data Relationships

Feb21 95 13:02:14 A-1

	DAE SOFTWARE	DAE MICROCOMPUTER	DAE MAINTENANCE	DAE COMPONENT BOARDS	DAE VENDORS	DAE PERIPHERALS	DAE ROOMS
DAE SOFTWARE		M					
DAE MICROCOMPUTER	M		M	M	M	M	M
DAE MAINTENANCE		M					
DAE COMPONENT BOARDS		M					
DAE VENDORS		M					
DAE PERIPHERALS		M					
DAE ROOMS		M					

FIGURE E17.7
Data Relationships Matrix print.

Elemental Access Conflicts shows each element, other than key fields, found within several records, or redundant data. Records analyzed are those declared to be normalized. The report for the microcomputer system did not have any of these errors.

Matching Key Records lists potential errors where a single record contains the whole key of another record, thus the *key* of both records is identical. Both records are assumed to be normalized. The records shown may be valid or they may be duplicate or similar records. The report produced for the microcomputer system did not show any matching key errors.

```
DATE: 21-FEB-95              REPEATING GROUPS           PAGE        1
TIME: 13:10                                              Excelerator
PROJECT NAME: CENTRAL PACIFIC UNIVERSITY

DESCRIPTION:   This report identifies Records that violate 1st Normal Form by
               containing Records and Elements that occur more than once. The
               report lists the repeated contents.

 RECORD NAME                    RECORDS/ELEMENTS REPEATED    | OCC | TYPE|
 -----------------------------------------------------------+-----+-----
|INSTALLATION MICROCOMPUTER    |HARDWARE INVENTORY NUMBER    | 999 |  E  |
|                              |                             |     |     |
|MICROCOMPUTER MASTER          |INTERNAL BOARDS              | 005 |  E  |
|                              |                             |     |     |
 -----------------------------------------------------------------------
```

FIGURE E17.8
Repeating Groups analysis report.

Record Dependencies shows the records that are described as normalized and whose key is contained as an element of another record. These records have a one-to-many relationship that may be valid. Examine the records to see if the relationship is valid and make any necessary corrections to the design. A valid record dependency was shown as existing between the SOFTWARE MASTER-NORMALIZED and the relational file MICRO HARDWARE & SOFTWARE RECORD.

Data Entity Exceptions provides a list of Data Entities problems that prevent further analysis. It lists which Data Entities do not have a record defined for them, which Data Entity records are not normalized (they do not contain a **Y** in the Normalized field), which do not have keys, which Data Entity records have repeating groups, and which Data Entities explode to a lower-level record defined as a type **R** in a higher-level record description, called a structural record. Figure E17.10 is an example of this report for the Microcomputer System.

Removing the hardware table from the SOFTWARE MASTER left it in the first normal form as printed in Figure E17.11. Since there is a single primary key with all attributes dependent on it, the record is in the second normal form. However, there is a transitive dependency, since the SOFTWARE EXPERT NAME and SOFTWARE EXPERT LOCATION are both on

```
DATE: 21-FEB-95                     RECORD - EXPLOSION                               PAGE     1
TIME: 12:30                         NAME: MICRO HARDWARE & SOFTWARE RECORD           Excelerator

NAME:                     MICRO HARDWARE & SOFTWARE RECORDDEFINITION:
ALIAS:                    HARDWARE/SOFTWARE RELATIONSHIP  RELATIONSHIP RECORD FOR MICRO SOFTWARE AND HARDWARE      Y

ELEMENT/RECORD                      OFF  OCC  TYPE  LEN  DEFINITION
-----------------------------       ---  ---  ----  ---  ------------------------------------------------------------

HARDWARE INVENTORY NUMBER           000  001   K    008  A UNIQUE NUMBER ASSIGNED TO EACH MACHINE, LOCATED ON MACHINE

SOFTWARE INVENTORY NUMBER           008  001   E    008  UNIQUE SOFTWARE IDENTIFICATION NUMBER

Record length is 16.
```

FIGURE E17.9
MICROCOMPUTER HARDWARE & SOFTWARE record print.

```
DATE: 21-FEB-95              DATA ENTITY EXCEPTIONS        PAGE        1
TIME: 13:42                                                Excelerator
PROJECT NAME: CENTRAL PACIFIC UNIVERSITY

DESCRIPTION:   This report lists Data Entities that cannot be further
               analyzed.  Asterisks indicate whether each Data Entity
               explodes to no Record, to a Record not flagged as Normalized,
               to a structural Record, to a Record with repeating groups,
               or to a Record with no key.

                                    |    |REC  |     |    | REC| REC
                                    | NO |NOT  |STRUC|    | REP| NO
          DATA ENTITY NAME          | REC|NORML|REC  |GROUP| KEY
          -----------------------------------------------------------
          |MICROCOMPUTER            |    |     |     |    | *  |
          |PERIPHERALS              |    |     |     | *  |    |
          |SOFTWARE                 |    | *   |     |    | *  |
          |ROOMS                    |    | *   |     |    |    |
          |COMPONENT BOARDS         |    | *   |     |    |    |
          |                         |    |     |     |    |    |
          |MAINTENANCE              |    |     |     |    |    | *  |
          |VENDORS                  |    | *   |     |    |    |
          |                         |    |     |     |    |    |
          -----------------------------------------------------------
```

FIGURE E17.10
Data Entity Exceptions analysis report.

the record. To place the record in the third normal form, the SOFTWARE EXPERT LOCATION was removed to an EXPERT FILE.

Several useful matrices are available under the Data Normalization analysis option. One is the **Record Dependencies,** shown in Figure E17.12. It shows records and how they are related to other records, either one or many.

Another useful matrix is **Data Entity Records** which provides information on Data Entities and the records to which they explode. Figure E17.13 is an example of the useful overview provided by this grid.

Exercises*

E-1. Use Excelerator to view the entity-relationship diagram for the Microcomputer System.

E-2. Add the SOFTWARE EXPERT to the entity-relationship diagram. It has the relationship SERVICES to software. What is the cardinality?

E-3. Create the Data Model Diagram shown in Figure E17.2. Be sure to use DESCRIBE to link the data entities to the already existing XLDictionary descriptions.

E-4. Use the Extended Analysis option of Excelerator to run the Data Model Validation Analysis. Produce the Modified Data Relationships report. Use the XLDictionary to view the Data Relationships. How have they changed?

E-5. Produce the following reports from the Data Normalization feature. Comment on what the information is telling you and how it may help to place the records in the third normal form.

```
DATE: 21-FEB-95                    RECORD - EXPLOSION                              PAGE    1
TIME: 13:15                        NAME: SOFTWARE MASTER - NORMALIZED              Excelerator


NAME:               SOFTWARE MASTER - NORMALIZED    DEFINITION:
ALIAS:              MICROCOMPUTER SOFTWARE RECORD   CONTAINS A RECORD FOR EACH PIECE OF SOFTWARE        Y


ELEMENT/RECORD                              OFF  OCC  TYPE  LEN  DEFINITION
---------------------------------------     ---  ---  ----  ---  -----------------------------------------------------------

ACTIVE SOFTWARE CODE                        000  001   E    001  CODE TO DETERMINE IF SOFTWARE IS CURRENTLY IN USE

SOFTWARE INVENTORY NUMBER                   001  001   K    008  UNIQUE SOFTWARE IDENTIFICATION NUMBER

TITLE                                       009  001   E    020  SOFTWARE TITLE

VERSION NUMBER                              029  001   E    005  VERSION OF THE SOFTWARE

PUBLISHER                                   034  001   E    030  THE MANUFACTURER OR PUBLISHER OF THE SOFTWARE

SOFTWARE CATEGORY                           064  001   E    004  THE CATEGORY OF SOFTWARE, EG. WORD PROCESSING - CODED ENTRY

NUMBER OF DISKETTES                         068  001   E    002  NUMBER OF DISKETTES INCLUDED WITH THE PACKAGE

COMPUTER BRAND                              070  001   E    010  THE BRAND OF COMPUTER NECESSARY TO RUN THE SOFTWARE

COMPUTER MODEL                              080  001   E    012  THE SPECIFIC MODEL NECESSARY TO RUN THE SOFTWARE

MEMORY REQUIRED                             092  001   E    005  THE MEMORY SIZE REQUIRED TO RUN THE SOFTWARE, IN THOUSANDS,K

MONITOR REQUIRED                            097  001   E    003  THE TYPE OF MONITOR REQUIRED TO RUN THE SOFTWARE

PRINTER REQUIRED                            100  001   E    005  A CODE FOR THE PRINTER REQUIRED. MAY BE LEFT BLANK. REFER TO

DISKETTE SIZE                               105  001   E    006  THE SIZE OF DISKETTE WITH THE ORIGINAL SOFTWARE PACKAGE

SITE LICENSE                                111  001   E    001  WHETHER OR NOT A SOFTWARE SITE LICENSE HAS BEEN OBTAINED

NUMBER OF COPIES                            112  001   E    004  THE NUMBER OF COPIES OF THE SOFTWARE PURCHASED

SOFTWARE EXPERT NAME                        116  001   E    020  SOFTWARE PACKAGE EXPERT

Record length is 136.
```

FIGURE E17.11
SOFTWARE MASTER file print normalized.

---

    a. Repeating Groups.

    b. Element Access Conflicts.

    c. Matching Key Records.

    d. Record Dependencies.

    e. Data Entity Exceptions.

    f. Data Model Relationships.

    g. DAR/Record Conflicts.

E-6. Print the following Data Normalization matrices. In a paragraph, comment on the usefulness of these in analyzing and documenting the system.

    a. Record Dependencies.

    b. Data Entity Records.

E-7. Explain in a paragraph why you think a table would be acceptable on a record in an indexed file system written in COBOL.

---

* The exercises preceded by a disk icon require the program Excelerator (or another CASE tool). A disk is provided free of charge to any professor adopting this book. The examples on the disk may be imported into Excelerator and then used by students.

```
Record Dependencies
--------------------------------------------------------------------------------
                                                 Feb21 95 13:04:17  A-1


                                        -------
                                       |R   |R  |
                                       |E   |E  |
                                       |C   |C  |
                                       |    |   |
                                       |MS  |S- |
                                       |IO  |O  |
                                       |CF  |FN |
                                       |RT  |TO |
                                       |OW  |WR |
                                       | A  |AM |
                                       |HR  |RA |
                                       |AE  |EL |
                                       |R   | I |
                                       |DR  |MZ |
                                       |WE  |AE |
                                       |AC  |SD |
                                       |RO  |T  |
                                       |ER  |E  |
                                       | D  |R  |
                                       |&   |   |
                                        -------
  --------------------------           -------
 |REC MICRO HARDWARE &        |   |   | 1 |
 |SOFTWARE RECORD             |   |   |   |
 |---------------------------|   |---+---|
 |REC SOFTWARE MASTER -       |   | M |   |
 |NORMALIZED                  |   |   |   |
  --------------------------           -------
```

FIGURE E17.12
Record Dependencies matrix print.

```
Data Entity Records
--------------------------------------------------------------------------------
                                          Feb21 95 13:08:18  A-1


                           ---------------------------
                          |R  |R  |R  |R  |R  |R  |R  |
                          |E  |E  |E  |E  |E  |E  |E  |
                          |C  |C  |C  |C  |C  |C  |C  |
                          |   |   |   |   |   |   |   |
                          |MM |PE |S  |LI |CI |MM |V  |
                          |IA |EQ |O  |ON |ON |IA |E  |
                          |CS |RU |F  |CF |MF |CI |N  |
                          |RT |II |T  |AO |PO |RN |D  |
                          |OE |PP |W  |TR |OR |OT |O  |
                          |CR |HM |A  |IM |NM |CE |R  |
                          |O  |EE |R  |OA |EA |ON |   |
                          |M  |RN |E  |NT |NT |MA |R  |
                          |P  |AT |   |  I|TI |PN |E  |
                          |U  |L  |M  |O  |O  |UC |C  |
                          |T  |   |A  | N | N |TE |O  |
                          |E  |   |S  |   |   |E  |R  |
                          |R  |   |T  |   |   |R  |D  |
                          |   |   |E  |   |   |   |   |
                          |   |   |R  |   |   |   |   |
                           ---------------------------
 ---------------------------    ---------------------------
|DAE MICROCOMPUTER         |   | X |   |   |   |   |   |   |
|--------------------------|   |---+---+---+---+---+---+---|
|DAE PERIPHERALS           |   |   | X |   |   |   |   |   |
|--------------------------|   |---+---+---+---+---+---+---|
|DAE SOFTWARE              |   |   |   | X |   |   |   |   |
|--------------------------|   |---+---+---+---+---+---+---|
|DAE ROOMS                 |   |   |   |   | X |   |   |   |
|--------------------------|   |---+---+---+---+---+---+---|
|DAE COMPONENT BOARDS      |   |   |   |   |   | X |   |   |
|--------------------------|   |---+---+---+---+---+---+---|
|DAE MAINTENANCE           |   |   |   |   |   |   | X |   |
|--------------------------|   |---+---+---+---+---+---+---|
|DAE VENDORS               |   |   |   |   |   |   |   | X |
 ---------------------------    ---------------------------
```

FIGURE E17.13
Data Entity Records matrix print.

18

DESIGNING THE USER INTERFACE

USER INTERFACE OBJECTIVES

The interface *is* the system for most users. However well or poorly designed, it stands as the representation of the system, and, by reflection, your competence as a systems analyst.

Your goal must be to design interfaces that help users and businesses get the information they need in and out of the system by addressing the following objectives:

1. Effectiveness as achieved through design of interfaces that allow users to access the system in a way that is congruent with their individual needs.

2. Efficiency as demonstrated through interfaces that increase speed of data entry and reduce errors.

3. User consideration as demonstrated in designing suitable interfaces and providing appropriate feedback to users from the system.

4. Productivity as shown through following ergonomically sound principles of design for user interfaces and workspaces.

With these in mind, we move to more detailed discussions of how each of the objectives, as shown in Figure 18.1, can be met.

TYPES OF USER INTERFACE

In this section, several different kinds of user interface are described, including natural-language interfaces, question-and-answer inquiries, menus, form-fill interfaces, command language, and graphical user interfaces (GUIs). The user interface has two main components: presentation language, which is the computer-to-human part of the transaction, and action language, which characterizes the human-to-computer portion. Together both concepts cover the form and content of the term *user interface*.

FIGURE 18.1
The four user interface
objectives.

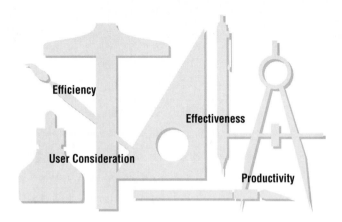

Natural-Language Interfaces

Natural-language interfaces are perhaps the dream and ideal of inexperienced users, since they permit users to interact with the computer in their everyday or "natural" language. No special skills are required of the user, who interfaces with the computer using natural language.

The screen depicted in Figure 18.2 lists three natural-language questions from three different applications. Notice that interaction with each seems very easy. For instance, the first sentence—which says, "List all of the salespeople who met their quotas this month"—seems straightforward.

However, if natural language is taken to mean typical written or spoken English, the hope of using it to communicate with computers can quickly be dampened. The English language is ambiguous, replete with myriad exceptions to every rule.

Ambiguity works to communicators' advantage in many contexts, particularly when one is attempting to be diplomatic or does not want to supply a self-incriminating response. However, the subtleties and irregularities residing in the ambiguities of English produce an extremely exacting and complex programming problem.

There are some limited attempts at natural-language interfacing for particular applications where any other type of interface is nonfeasible. Implementation problems and extraordinary demand on computing resources have so far kept natural-language interfaces to a minimum. However, many programmers and researchers are working diligently on natural-language interfaces, so it is definitely an area that will continue to grow and therefore merits your continued monitoring.

Question-and-Answer Interfaces

In this kind of interface the computer displays a question to the user on the screen. In order to interact, the user enters an answer (usually via a keyboard), and the computer acts on that input information in a preprogrammed manner, typically by moving to the next question.

Many management science applications use a question-and-answer interface. A goal programming example is shown in Figure 18.3. As with most question-and-answer interfaces, the computer system directs the questioning sequence. The user responds to what is asked. For instance, in responding to the phrase "Now enter the number of constraints," the user types in an appropriate number.

FIGURE 18.2
Natural-language interfaces.

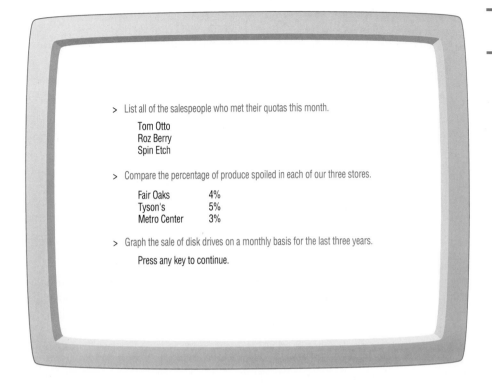

> List all of the salespeople who met their quotas this month.

    Tom Otto
    Roz Berry
    Spin Etch

> Compare the percentage of produce spoiled in each of our three stores.

Fair Oaks	4%
Tyson's	5%
Metro Center	3%

> Graph the sale of disk drives on a monthly basis for the last three years.

    Press any key to continue.

Another type of question-and-answer interface, called a dialog box, is shown in Figure 18.4. This acts as a question-and-answer interface within another application, in this case a PERT chart for a systems analysis project for the Bakerloo Brothers. Notice that the rectangle for YES is highlighted, indicating it is the most likely answer for this situation. The main interface for this application need not necessarily be question-and-answer. Rather, by incorporating a dialog box, the programmer has included an easy-to-use interface within a more complicated one.

Programmers attempt to phrase questions for display in a question-and-answer interface in a concise and understandable manner, but they also need to anticipate the kinds of answers the user will input and the system will accept. Greater latitude for user response translates directly into an increase in the complexity of the programming required.

When interfaces are designed, a decision is made on how much flexibility to allow the user in responding to questions. Users require instruction about how much flexibility they are being afforded. For instance, users must know if typing "Y" is an acceptable replacement for typing "Yes" as a response.

It is possible to include additional help or prompting to remind the user of acceptable responses, and many programmers do. This is important because if users expend too much additional effort in searching for responses or remembering how to respond, they could be dissatisfied and not want to use the system.

Experience suggests that as users become more proficient with the system they may become impatient with detailed, repetitive questions. They might prefer an option allowing responses to be abbreviated versions of the questions.

FIGURE 18.3
Question-and-answer
interface.

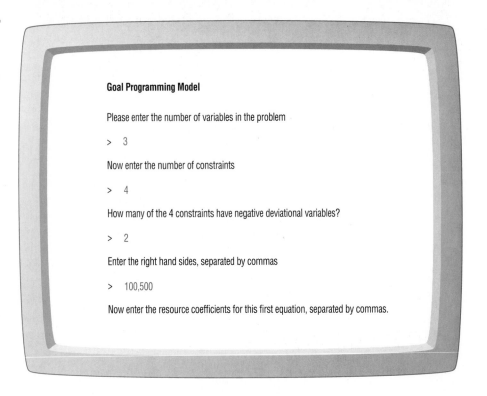

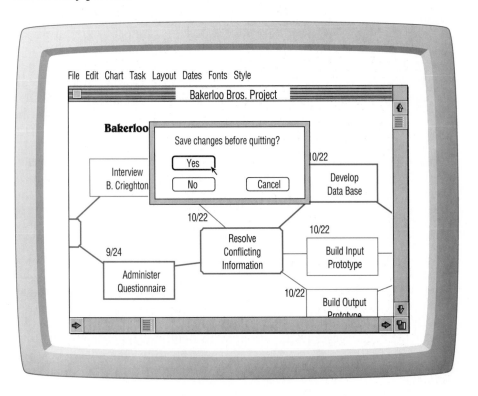

New users, unfamiliar with computers, may find question-and-answer interfaces most comfortable, quickly gaining confidence through their success. However, system designers need to guard against lulling an overly confident new user into expecting system capabilities above what are actually present.

FIGURE 18.4
A dialog box: one type
of question-and-answer
interface.

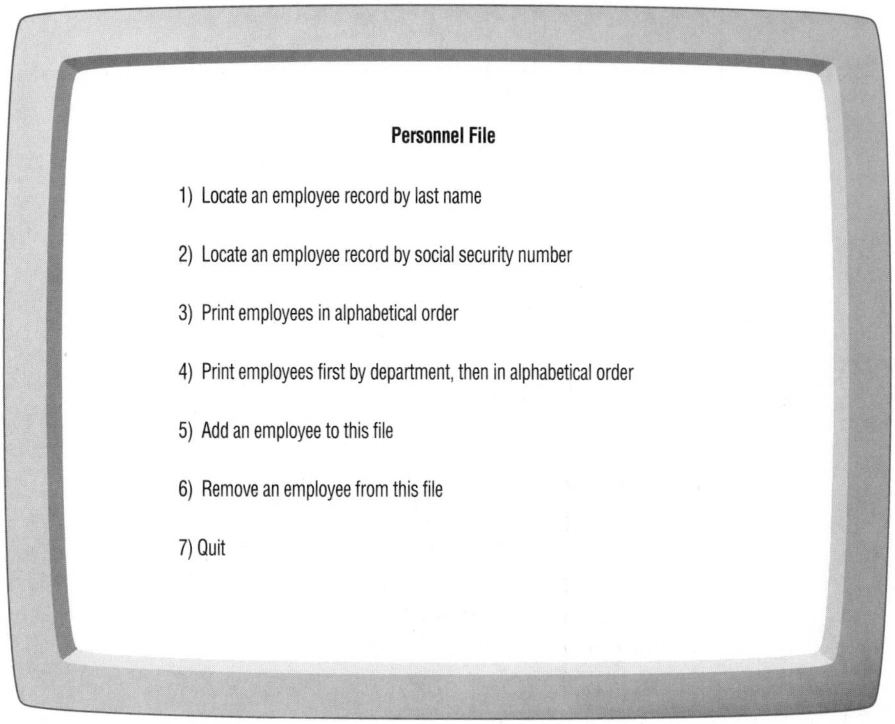

FIGURE 18.5
A menu using numbers to
select an action.

Personnel File

1) Locate an employee record by last name

2) Locate an employee record by social security number

3) Print employees in alphabetical order

4) Print employees first by department, then in alphabetical order

5) Add an employee to this file

6) Remove an employee from this file

7) Quit

Menus

This interface appropriately borrows its name from the list of dishes that can be selected in a restaurant. Similarly, a menu interface provides the user with an on-screen list of available selections.

In responding to the menu, a user is limited to the options displayed. The user need not know the system but *does* need to know what task should be accomplished. For example, with a typical word-processing menu users can choose "edit," "copy," or "print" options. However, to best utilize the menu users must know which task they desire to perform.

Menus as an interface are not hardware-dependent. Variations abound. Menus can be set up to use keyboard entry, lightpen, or mouse. Selections can be identified with a number, letter, or a keyword, or users can click on a selection with a mouse.

An example of a menu-driven program is shown in Figure 18.5. The user has a menu of seven different actions that may be taken on personnel files. In order to choose selection "5) Add an employee to this file," the user has only to type a 5. This takes the user to a new screen, which is ready for entry of new employee data.

Consistency is important in designing a menu interface. In order to access a menu selection, a user may be required to press the Enter key, or the computer may turn directly to the desired program when only a single key must be hit. For example, if the menu offers only the numbers 0 through 9, it is possible to use only one key stroke without hitting Enter. If more numbers are required, Enter is needed to distinguish whether the user intends to enter 1, 10, or 100, for example.

Menus can also be put aside until the user wants to employ them. Figure 18.6 shows how a pull-down menu is used while constructing a PERT chart for a systems analysis project being completed for the Bakerloo

FIGURE 18.6
A pull-down menu is there
when the user needs it.

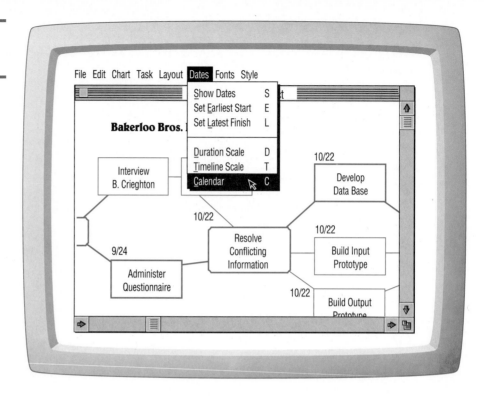

Brothers. The user puts the pointer on the word "dates" and pulls it down. Then the user puts the arrow on "calendar," selecting the option to display the project on a conventional monthly calendar.

Menus can be nested within one another to lead a user through options in a program. Nested menus have some advantages. They allow the screen to appear less cluttered, which is consistent with good screen design. Nested menus also allow users to avoid seeing menu options in which they have no interest, so irrelevant user information is reduced. Additionally, nested menus can move users quickly through the program.

When mainframe terminals are used, the menu is widely used to control the system. Pull-down menus and icons are generally used when the operator is using a PC.

Although generally a boon to the inexperienced, menus can present some problems for experienced users. Experienced users may grow impatient at picking their way through successive menus every time a program is used. One way to overcome this would be to give users an option of entering all necessary menus in a single-line command entry. This makes the system amenable to both experienced and inexperienced users.

Form-Fill Interfaces (Input/Output Forms)

Form-fill interfaces consist of on-screen forms displaying fields containing data items or parameters that need to be communicated to the user. The form often is a facsimile of the paper form already familiar to the user. This interface technique is also known as a form-based method and input/output forms.

Figure 18.7 is an example from Delrina's FormFlow. In this program the end user can go from field to field by pressing the Tab key or using the mouse.

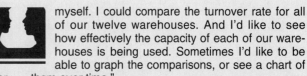
On-screen forms are set up to show what information should be input and where. Blank fields requiring information can be highlighted with inverse or flashing characters. The cursor is moved by the user from field to field by a single stroke of the arrow key, for instance. This arrangement allows movement one field backward or one field forward by hitting the arrow key.

Form input for screens can be simplified by supplying default values for fields and then allowing users to modify default information if necessary. For example, a database management system designed to show a form for inputting checks may supply the next sequential check number as a default when a new check form is exhibited. If checks are missing, the user changes the check number to reflect the actual check being input.

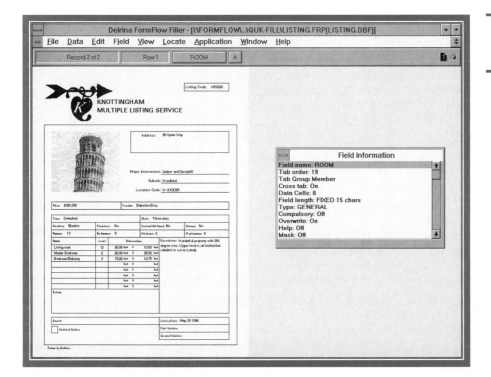

FIGURE 18.7
An example of the form-fill interface.

A powerful use of input/output forms is shown in Figure 18.8. In this example the programmer has set up a form for users in the State Motor Vehicle Division. But the form is more helpful than the typical input/output form, because it allows users who possess only a minimum of data to fill in the form partially. The computer will then take the data supplied (last name begins with McK, no valid license) and search the appropriate database to find information that completes the records already begun. The computer fills in the form with two names, McKinley and McKinnon. Notice that the computer does not pull up the record for McNeil, even though he fits the requirement of no valid driver's license. This is because McNeil does not fit the "McK" requirement the user previously stipulated.

Input for on-screen fields can be alphanumerically restricted, so that users can enter only numbers in a field requesting a social security number, or input only letters where a person's name is required. If numbers are input where only letters are allowed, the computer may alert the user that the field was filled out incorrectly. No matter what type of enforcement is employed to ensure that the form is filled out properly, users should be considered.

The chief advantage of the input/output form interface is that the printed version of the filled-in form provides excellent documentation. It shows field labels as well as the context for entries.

There are few disadvantages to input/output forms. The main drawback is similar to the "experienced user" problem discussed for question-and-answer interfaces and menus. Experienced users may become impatient with input/output forms and may want ways to enter data that are more efficient.

Command-Language Interfaces

A command-language interface allows the user to control the application with a series of keystrokes, commands, phrases, or some sequence of these. It is a popular interface that is more refined than those previously discussed.

Two application examples of command language are shown in Figure 18.9. The first example shows the user asking to use a file containing data on all salespeople and then asking the computer to display all last names, then first names, for all salespeople whose current sales (CURSALES) are greater than their quota. In the second example, the user asks to use a file called GROCER. Then the user directs the computer to calculate the spoilage (SPOILS) by subtracting produce sold from produce bought. After this is done, the user asks to go back to the top of the file and print out (LIST) the file.

Contrast the comprehension difficulty of the command language with that of the natural-language interface. The command language has no inherent meaning for the user, and that fact makes it quite dissimilar to the other interfaces discussed so far.

Command languages manipulate the computer as a tool by allowing the user to control the dialog. Therefore, command language affords the user more flexibility and control. When the user gives a command to the computer using command language, it is executed by the system immediately. Then the user may proceed to give it another command.

Command languages require memorization of syntax rules that may prove to be obstacles for inexperienced users (however, anyone can learn

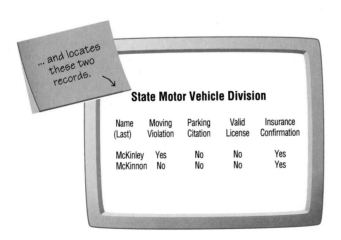

FIGURE 18.8
Input/output interface for
locating records in a state
motor vehicle database.

State Motor Vehicle Division

Name (Last)	Moving Violation	Parking Citation	Valid License	Insurance Confirmation
Mck.			No	

VEHICLE DATABASE

This query searches the database ...

NAME (LAST)	MOVING VIOLATION	PARKING VIOLATION	VALID LICENSE	INSURANCE CONFIRMATION
McKenzie	Yes	No	Yes	Yes
McKibben	No	No	Yes	Yes
McKinley	Yes	No	Yes	Yes
McKinnon	No	No	No	Yes
McMaster	Yes	No	Yes	Yes
McMichael	Yes	Yes	Yes	Yes
McNeil	No	No	Yes	Yes

... and locates these two records.

State Motor Vehicle Division

Name (Last)	Moving Violation	Parking Citation	Valid License	Insurance Confirmation
McKinley	Yes	No	No	Yes
McKinnon	No	No	No	Yes

them with practice). Other interfaces resemble human exchanges more
closely and are therefore more easily understood by users unaware of how
a computer functions. Experienced users tend to prefer command languages, possibly because of the faster completion time they allow.

Don't Slow Me Down

"I've seen 'em all." Carrie Moore tells you. "I was here when they got their first computer. I guess I've sort of made a career of this," she says cheerfully, pointing to the large stack of medical insurance claim forms she has been entering into the computer system. As a systems analyst, you are interviewing Carrie, a data-entry operator for HealthPlus, (a large, medical insurance company) about changes being contemplated in the computer system.

"I'm really fast compared to the others," she states as she nods toward the six other operators in the room. "I know because we have little contests all of the time, to see who's the fastest, with the fewest errors. See that chart on the wall? That shows how much we enter, how fast. The gold stars show who's the best each week."

"I don't really mind if you change computers, like I say, I've seen 'em all." She resumes typing on the terminal as she continues the interview. "But whatever you do, don't slow me down. One of the things I'm most proud of is, I can still beat the other operators. They're good too, though," Carrie adds.

Based on this partial interview with Carrie Moore, what type of user interface will you design for her and the other operators? Assume that the new system will still require massive amounts of data entry from various medical insurance forms sent in by claimants.

Compare and contrast interfaces such as natural language, question-and-answer, menus, and input/output form. Then choose and defend one alternative. What qualities possessed by Carrie and the other operators, and the data they will be entering, shaped your choice? Is there more than one feasible choice? Why or why not?

Graphical User Interfaces (GUIs)

Graphical User Interfaces (GUIs) allow direct manipulation of the graphical representation on the screen, which can be accomplished with keyboard input, a joystick, or a mouse. Direct manipulation requires more system sophistication than the interfaces discussed previously.

FIGURE 18.9
Command-language interfaces.

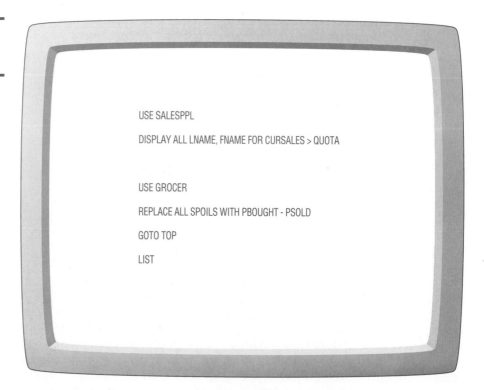

```
USE SALESPPL

DISPLAY ALL LNAME, FNAME FOR CURSALES > QUOTA


USE GROCER

REPLACE ALL SPOILS WITH PBOUGHT - PSOLD

GOTO TOP

LIST
```

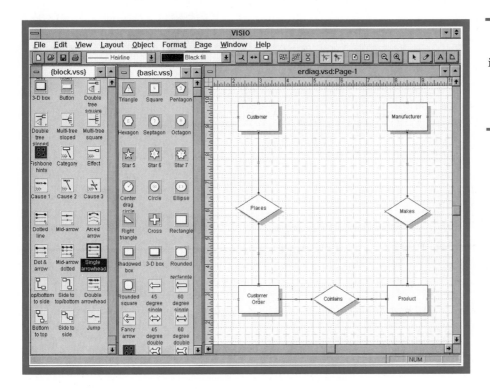

FIGURE 18.10
One common feature of GUI
interfaces is "drag-and-drop."
This entity relationship diagram was drawn by dragging
template symbols onto the
paper using Visio.

An example of the drag-and-drop feature of a GUI interface (sometimes simply called a drag-and-drop interface) is shown in Figure 18.10.
In this screen from Visio by Shapeware, the symbols arrayed on the left
are called templates. In order to draw with this interface, the user drags
and drops a master shape into their drawing (shown on the right of the
figure as a piece of paper.) This kind of interface makes the work of the
analyst, by creating entity relationship diagrams or other specialized drawings, much easier. Visio comes with many more stencils, for drawing data
flow diagrams, program flow charts, network diagrams, object oriented diagrams, and it even has templates for designing office spaces.

The key to GUI is the constant feedback on task accomplishment that
it provides. Continuous feedback on the manipulated object means that
changes or reversals in operations can be made quickly, without incurring
error messages. The concept of feedback for users is discussed thoroughly
in an upcoming section, "Feedback for Users."

An imaginative use of a graphical user interface utilizing icons is
shown in Figure 18.11. The top screen shows the layout of the city of
Lakewood, along with a pull-down menu listing available delivery drivers.
All possible routes, such as "Country Club" and "Botanical Gardens," are
shown as icons.

In order to assign one of the drivers, in this case, "Lewis, George,"
to the downtown delivery route, the scheduler moves Lewis's record,
via arrow keys or a mouse, directly over the downtown icon. Lewis is
then assigned to the downtown route. This is a quick, visual way to
assign drivers to routes, which does not demand that a user have long-
standing familiarity with the geographical layout of the city, the routes,
or the drivers.

Icons are used extensively when running Microsoft Windows, IBM
OS/2, or Apple Macintosh operating systems. By double-clicking the left

FIGURE 18.11
A GUI interface is used for
assigning drivers to routes.

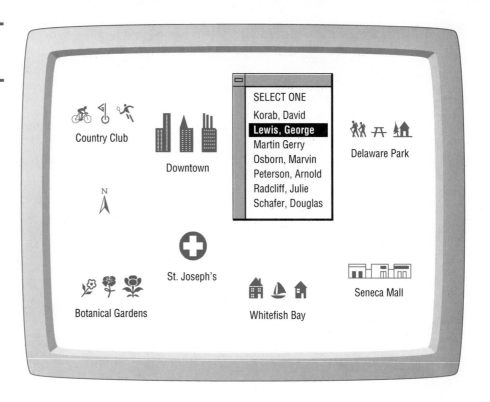

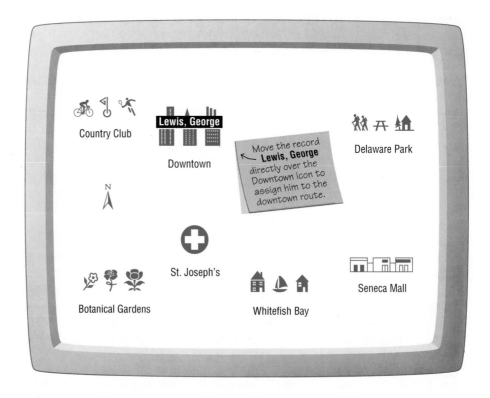

mouse button rapidly, the user selects an icon to run the corresponding program. Icons are often arranged within larger windows, called program groups or folders. When a program group icon is selected, the window

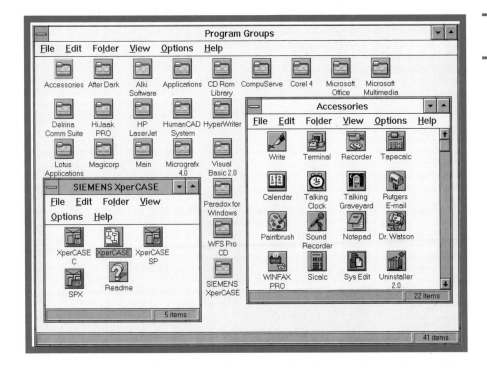

FIGURE 18.12
Icon program groups.

opens up, displaying the group icons. The analyst should design program groups with the same care used to design full-screen or pull-down menus. An example of group items and their corresponding program group windows is illustrated in Figure 18.12.

The creation of GUI interfaces poses a challenge, since an appropriate model of reality or acceptable conceptual model of the representation must be invented. This requires combining several skills in a way that stretches the capabilities of most systems analysts and programmers.

DIALOG AND DESKTOPS

Guidelines for Dialog Design

Dialog is the communication between the computer and a person. Well-designed dialog makes it easier for people to use a computer and leads to less frustration with the computer system. There are several key points for designing good dialog. Some of these were mentioned in Chapter 16.

1. Meaningful communication, so that the computer understands what people are entering and people understand what the computer is presenting or requesting.
2. Minimal user action.
3. Standard operation and consistency.

COMMUNICATION. The system should present information clearly to the user. This means presenting an appropriate title on each screen, minimizing the use of abbreviations, and providing clear user feedback. Inquiry programs should display code meanings as well as data in an edited format, for example, displaying slashes between the month, day, and year in a date field or commas and decimal points in an amount field. User instructions

FIGURE 18.13
An Order Help Screen with
hypertext links.

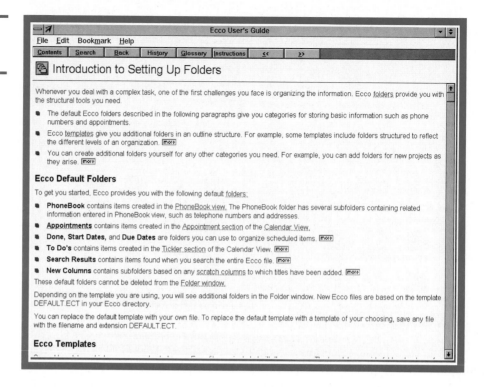

should be supplied (usually on one line only) regarding details such as available function key assignments. Displaying the instruction line using inverse video helps to draw the user's attention to the instructions.

In a graphical interface, the cursor may change shape depending on the work being performed. For example, in Excelerator, the cursor is an arrow when the user is creating a diagram and a rectangle or underscore when the user is working with text.

Easy-to-use help screens should be provided. Many microcomputer help screens have additional topics that may be directly selected using highlighted text displayed on the first help screen. These hypertext links are usually in a different color, which makes them stand out in contrast to the rest of the help text. They are usually selected using a mouse. Refer to the sample help screen in Figure 18.13. The boldface text indicates the links to further help screens. The bar on the right side of the screen is selected with a mouse for scrolling up and down to view the complete help text, since it will not fit on a single screen. Help should also be provided when codes are entered. Pop-up windows are a useful way to accomplish this.

The other side of communication is that the computer should "understand what the user has entered." This means that all data entered on the screen should be edited for validity.

MINIMAL USER ACTION. Keying is often the slowest part of a computer system, and good dialog will minimize the number of keystrokes required. You can accomplish this in a number of different ways.

1. Keying codes instead of whole words on entry screens. Codes are also keyed when using a command-language interface. An example is entering DIR, for Directory, to obtain a list of files on a personal computer, or CD for Change Directory.

2. Only entering data that is not already stored on files. For example, when changing or deleting item records, only the item number should be entered. The computer responds by displaying descriptive information that is currently stored on the item file. When entering an order for customers, the customer number is entered and the name and address is displayed, allowing the operator to sight verify that the customer number has been entered correctly.

3. Supplying the editing characters (for example, slashes as date field separators) via software for personal computers. Users should not have to enter formatting characters such as leading zeros, commas, or a decimal point when entering a dollar amount, or slashes or hyphens when entering a date. (On a mainframe terminal, these characters are omitted.)

4. Using default values for fields on entry screens. Defaults are used when a user enters the same value in a screen field for the majority of the records being processed. The values are displayed, and the user may press the Enter key to accept the default or overtype the default value with a new one. For example, an inventory control clerk may use a screen to generate purchase orders for items that are low in stock. The screen would display the reorder quantity from the item record as a default purchase quantity. Under typical circumstances, the user would simply press Enter to accept this quantity, but if the item were a popular sale item, the operator might choose to enter a higher amount to increase the quantity purchased.

If the software must be flexible enough to accommodate different user situations, it should be designed so that the preset defaults may be changed. The new defaults should display each time the software is invoked. An example would be changing the screen colors, which should not have to be manually reset each time the screen is used.

On graphical user interfaces, such as Microsoft Windows, a default value will be outlined with a dashed line. The user may press the Enter key to choose this option, rather than moving the mouse to the button and pressing a mouse key.

5. Designing an inquiry (or change or delete) program so that the user needs to enter only the first few characters of a name or item description. The program displays a list of all matching names, and when the operator chooses one, the matching record is displayed.

6. Providing keystrokes for selecting pull-down menu options. Often, these options are selected using a mouse, followed by some keying. This requires users to move their hand from the keyboard to the mouse and back to the keyboard. As users become familiar with the system, keystrokes often provide a faster method for manipulating the pull-down menus, since both hands remain on the keyboard. The combination of keys used is often displayed to the right of each menu option. On an IBM personal computer this usually involves pressing a function key or the Alt key followed by a letter. Refer to the pull-down menu for the Customer Order system illustrated in Figure 18.14. Notice that the U in Update Files is in boldface type, indicating a change in color or a high-intensity display on the screen. The user could either use a mouse or press the Alt key and the letter U to select this option. The user could also press the Alt key and the letter A to directly run the Add Customer program.

FIGURE 18.14
Example of a pull-down
menu with shortcut keys.

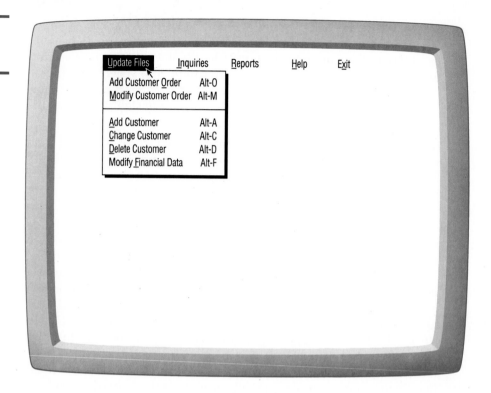

Any combination of these six approaches can help the analyst decrease the number of keystrokes required by the user, thereby speeding up data entry and minimizing errors.

STANDARD OPERATION AND CONSISTENCY. The system should be consistent throughout its set of different screens and in the mechanisms for controlling the operation of the screens. Consistency makes it easier for the users to learn how to use new portions of the system once they are familiar with one component. You can achieve consistency by:

1. Locating titles, date, time, and operator and feedback messages in the same places on all screens.
2. Exiting each program by the same key or menu option. It would be poor design to use function key 4 (F4) to exit the ADD CUSTOMER program and function key 6 (F6) to exit the CHANGE CUSTOMER program.
3. Canceling a transaction in a consistent way, usually the CLEAR key on a mainframe and the ESCAPE key on a microcomputer.
4. Obtaining help in a standardized way. The industry standard for help is function key 1 (F1), and most microcomputer software developers are adopting this convention.
5. Standardizing the color used for all screens. Error messages are typically displayed in red. Remember to keep the background screen color the same for all applications.
6. Standardizing the use of icons for similar operations when using a graphical user interface. For example, a small piece of paper with a bent upper corner often represents a document.

Function	Key	Comments
Help	F1	
Exit	F3	Exit With Save
Prompt	F4	
Refresh	F5	
Backward	F7	Scroll Up One Screen
Forward	F8	Scroll Down One Screen
Retrieve	F9	
Cancel	F12	Exit Without Save
Left	F19	Scroll Left One Screen
Right	F20	Scroll Right One Screen

FIGURE 18.15
Common user access function
key definitions.

To encourage software developers to develop a consistent user interface, IBM has produced standards called Common User Access, abbreviated CUA. These provide a consistent user view of screen formats, interaction techniques, and keyboard layouts for IBM personal, midrange, and mainframe computers. Some standard function key assignments have also emerged and are listed in Figure 18.15.

An example of good GUI interface design is the dialog box shown in Figure 18.16. This example is from Microsoft's Word for Windows 6.0. Note that the dialog box has two sides, the left consisting of four white lists with pull-down arrows. The upper left-hand side lists all files with a DOC extension. The large box in the middle lists the directories on the drive specified in the box beneath it. The bottom box lists the type of files. Each of these is in a separate section, and this convention is carried through in dialog boxes for other programs. The right side contains one-time control buttons (options such as OK, Cancel, Find File, or Help) and check-off boxes that remain in effect until the X is removed. The design is good because (1) the dialog box is gray so the user knows some action is required; (2) the control buttons are large; (3) the Xs in the check-off boxes are clear; and (4) the lists are uniform—that is the pull-down arrows are to the right. The box labeled "OK" doesn't make much sense to the novice, but the daily user soon understands that this box means "Accept the selections and the options and continue."

Customizing Desktops

People like to customize their own desktops. One way to accomplish this is to purchase a "shell" which they feel would improve what is normally offered in the way of a desktop by the operating system (e.g., Windows or Macintosh). Figure 18.17 is an example of a desktop shell called PC Tools for Windows from Central Point Software. The shell replaces the program manager that comes with Windows.

In this example three programs are currently running: (1) a clock that not only tells the time, but shows what part of the world is in darkness; (2) a Talking Calculator, by Aristosoft, Inc.; and (3) a program called Crash Guard, also by Central Point Software, that monitors systems resources so that the user knows when memory or disk space is getting low. When this shell is closed, it remembers which programs were running and restores them to the place at which the user left them the next time the shell is opened.

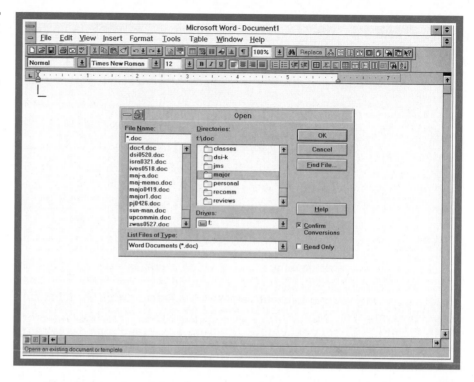

The desktop has other features, such as the "virtual desktop" at the
extreme right. Here the user has set up five different desktops (each a different color) and does certain work on each. Word processing may be done
on one desktop, maintenance can be done on a second, illustrations on a
third, etc. The user can jump from one desktop to another and move programs or icons between desktops. Other features include quick access to

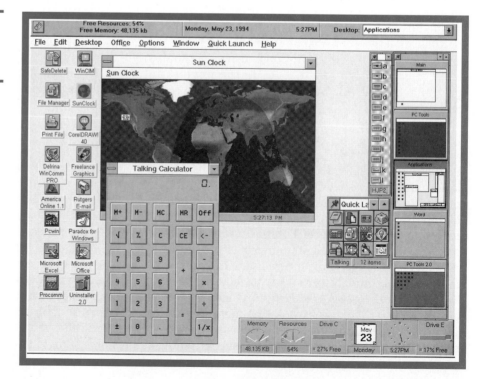

That's Not a Light Bulb

From your preliminary analysis, it appears that many reductions in error will be realized if sales clerks at Bright's Electric (which sells electrical parts, bulbs, and fixtures to wholesale customers) adopt an on-line system. The new system would allow sales clerks to withdraw a part from inventory and thereby update inventory, return a part to inventory, check on the inventory status, and check whether a part is backordered. Currently, in order to update inventory, sales clerks fill out a three-part form by hand. The customer gets one, inventory keeps one, and at the end of the day the originals are deposited in the front office.

The next morning, the first thing the lone office worker does is enter the data from the forms into the computer. Errors occur when she enters the wrong part numbers or quantities. Additional time is consumed when inventory workers go hunt for a part that they think might be in stock, but which is not. Updated inventory sheets are available to the sales clerks around noon, but by that time they have already taken from inventory twice the number of parts that will be taken out after noon. Clearly, a well-designed on-line system would help reduce these errors and also help with inventory control.

The owner, Mr. Bright, has entertained the idea of an on-line system and dropped it several times over the last five years. The chief reason is that the sales clerks, who would be the heaviest users of the system, do not think the systems analysts they've talked to can fulfill their needs.

M. T. Sockette, the sales clerk who has been with Bright's the longest, is the most vocal, telling you, "We know the parts, we know our customers. What we could do with a computer here would be great. But the guys they've brought in here to get it going! I mean, they say things like, 'You can step right up and type one 60-watt General Electric light bulb' into the computer."

"To us, that's not a light bulb, it's a GE60WSB. All of us know the part numbers here. We pride ourselves on it. Typing in all that junk will take all day."

After talking to Mr. Bright, you decide to implement an on-line system. You have talked to M. T. and the others and reassured them that the system will use the part numbers they're familiar with, and save them time. Although skeptical, they have been persuaded by you to give it a try.

What type of user interface will you design for the sales clerks? Compare and contrast natural language, question-and-answer, menus, input/output forms, and command language for their suitability as user interfaces at Bright's. Then choose one interface and explain why you find this the most appropriate based on what you know about Bright's sales clerks and their current system.

drives (note the list of available drives on this particular system), quick access to key programs via their corresponding icons which appear on the desktop at all times, and the ability to organize files into logical folders. Most desktops also support drag and drop functionality. It is easy to see why end users prefer to manage their own desktops, just as they like to take care of their physical workspace and organize their desks and file cabinets to suit them.

Other User Interfaces

Other user interfaces, while less common that those discussed previously, are growing in popularity. These interfaces include pointing devices such as lightpens, touch-sensitive screens, and speech recognition and synthesis. Each of these interfaces has its own special attributes that uniquely suit it to particular applications.

Pointing devices (most often a lightpen) are used to point to the VDT screen. The user may then select an item from the screen. Lightpens are more common in Japan, where keyboard entry of the thousands of complex characters composing people's names poses an awesome task. Some engineering applications allow use of a lightpen to actually "draw" on the screen, rather than just selecting a menu item.

Touch-sensitive screens allow a user to use a finger (or object) to activate the screen when it comes close to the screen surface. Coming close to the screen breaks a grid of light beams within or just over the screen's surface.

Touch-sensitive screens are useful in public information displays such as maps of cities and their sights posted in hotel lobbies; explanations of dioramas in museums; and even location of camping facilities in state parks. Touch-sensitive screens require no special expertise from users, and the screen is self-contained, requiring no special input device that might be broken or stolen.

Voice recognition has long been the dream of scientists and science fiction writers alike. It is intuitively appealing, since it seems to approximate human communication. With voice recognition, the user speaks to the computer, and the system is able to recognize an individual's vocal signals, convert them, and store the input. Voice recognition inventory systems are already in operation.

An advantage of voice recognition systems is that their use can speed data entry enormously, while freeing the user's hands for other tasks. Speech input adds still another dimension to the PC. It is now possible to add equipment and software that allows a personal computer user to say commands such as "Open File," or "Save File" to avoid using the keyboard. The obvious advantages of this technology are increased accuracy and greater speed than conventional mouse movements afford.

When evaluating the interfaces you have chosen, there are some standards to keep in mind:

1. The necessary training period for users should be acceptably short.
2. Users early in their training should be able to enter commands without thinking about them, or referring to a help menu or manual.
3. The interface should be "seamless," so that errors are few and those that do occur are not occurring because of poor design.
4. Time necessary for users and the system to bounce back from errors should be short.
5. Infrequent users should be able to relearn the system quickly.

There are many different interfaces available, and it is important to realize that an effective interface goes a long way toward successfully involving users. Users should want to use the system. In the next section, we discuss the importance of providing feedback for users in order to support and sustain their involvement with the system.

FEEDBACK FOR USERS

All systems require feedback in order to monitor and change behavior, as was discussed in Chapter 2. Feedback usually compares current behavior with predetermined goals and gives back information describing the gap between actual and intended performance.

Since humans themselves are complex systems, they require feedback from others to meet psychological needs. Feedback also increases human confidence. How much feedback is required is an individual characteristic.

When users interface with machines they still need feedback about how their work is progressing. As designers of user interfaces, systems ana-

FIGURE 18.18
Feedback is used in
many ways.

Feedback Is Needed to Tell the User That:
• The computer has accepted the input
• The input is in the correct form
• The input is not in the correct form
• There will be a delay in the processing
• The request has been completed
• The computer is unable to complete the request
• More detailed feedback is available (and how to get it)

lysts need to be aware of the human need for feedback and build it into the system. When we discuss feedback for users we typically refer to feedback from on-line systems.

Feedback to the user from the system is necessary in seven distinct situations, as shown in Figure 18.18. Feedback that is ill-timed or too plentiful is not helpful since we can process only a limited amount of information. Each of the seven situations where feedback is appropriate is explained in the upcoming subsections.

ACKNOWLEDGING ACCEPTANCE OF INPUT. The first situation in which users need feedback is to learn that the computer has accepted the input. For example, when a user enters a name on a line the computer provides feedback to the user by advancing the cursor one character at a time when the letters are entered correctly.

RECOGNIZING THAT INPUT IS IN THE CORRECT FORM. Users need feedback to tell them that input is in the correct form. For example, a user inputs a command, and the on-screen computer feedback is "READY" as the program progresses to a new point. A poor example of feedback to tell the user that input is in the correct form would be, "INPUT OK," since this takes extra space, is cryptic, and does nothing to encourage input of more data.

NOTIFYING THAT INPUT IS NOT IN THE CORRECT FORM. Feedback is necessary to warn users that input is not in the correct form. When data are incorrect, one way to inform the user is to generate a window that briefly describes the problem with the input and how the user can correct it, as shown in Figure 18.19.

Notice that the message concerning an error in inputting the length of subscription is polite and concise, but not cryptic, so that even inexperienced users will be able to understand it. The subscription length entered is wrong, but the feedback given does not dwell on the fact that the user made a mistake. Rather, it offers options (13, 26, or 52 weeks) so that the error can be corrected easily.

So far we have been discussing visual feedback, but many systems have audio feedback capabilities as well. When a user inputs data with incorrect form, as shown previously for subscription length, the system might beep instead of providing a window. Beeping, buzzing, or ringing that is set off by common data-entry errors causes users to become disgruntled or frustrated. Additionally, audio feedback alone is not descriptive, so

Waiting to Be Fed

"Yeah, we were sold a package all right. This one right here. Don't get me wrong, it gets the work done. We just don't know when."

You are talking with Owen Itt, who is telling you about the sales unit's recent purchase of new software for their microcomputers that allows input of sales data for each of their sixteen salespeople, provides output comparison data for them, and projects future sales based on past sales records.

"But we've had some odd experiences with this program," Owen continues. "It seems slow or something. For instance, we're never sure when it's done. I type in a command to get a file and nothing happens. About half a minute later (if I'm lucky), the screen I want might come up. But I'm never sure. If I ask it to save sales data, I just get a whirring sound. If it

works, I'm returned to where I was before. If it doesn't save data, I'm still returned to where I was before. It's confusing. And I never know what to do. There's nothing on the screen that tells me what to do next. See the manual that came with this? It's dog-eared because we have to keep thumbing through trying to figure out what to do next."

Based on what you've heard in the interview, take this opportunity to supplement the program by designing some on-screen feedback for Owen and his sales team. The feedback should address all of Owen's concerns, while following the guidelines for giving feedback to users and the guidelines for good screen design.

it is not as helpful to users as on-screen directions. Use audio feedback sparingly, perhaps to denote urgent situations.

EXPLAINING A DELAY IN PROCESSING. One of the most important kinds of feedback informs the user that there will be a delay in processing his or her request. Delays longer than 10 seconds or so require feedback so that the user knows the system is still working.

Figure 18.20 shows a screen providing feedback in a window for a user who has just requested a printout of the newspaper's subscription list. The screen displays a sentence reassuring the user that the request is being processed, as well as a sign in the upper-right-hand corner instructing the user to "WAIT" until the current command has been executed. The screen also provides a way to stop the operation if necessary.

One microcomputer system uses an icon for feeding back information on processing delays. The icon is in the familiar shape of a wristwatch or an hourglass and serves as visual reassurance that the system is working.

Timing feedback of this sort is critical. Too slow a system response could cause the user to input commands that impede or disrupt processing, and too quick a response may make users feel as if the pace of their work is being propelled by the system.

ACKNOWLEDGING THAT A REQUEST IS COMPLETED. Users need to know when their request has been completed and new requests may be input. Figure 18.21 shows a screen where the user has requested preparation of an index by name. When the indexing is finished, the system replies with "DONE." The user then knows it is safe to proceed.

Often a specific feedback message is displayed when an action has been completed by a user, such as "EMPLOYEE RECORD HAS BEEN ADDED," "CUSTOMER RECORD HAS BEEN CHANGED," or "ITEM NUMBER 12345 HAS BEEN DELETED."

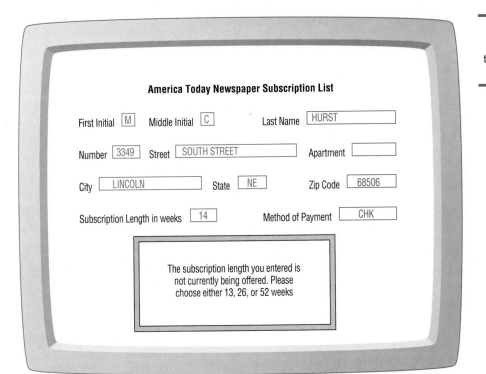

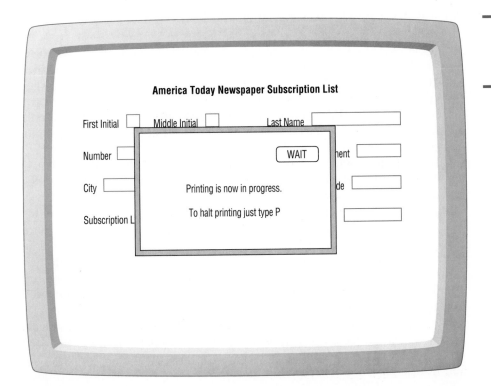

FIGURE 18.21
Feedback tells when input is
accepted, whether processing
is completed or not, and how
to ask for further assistance.

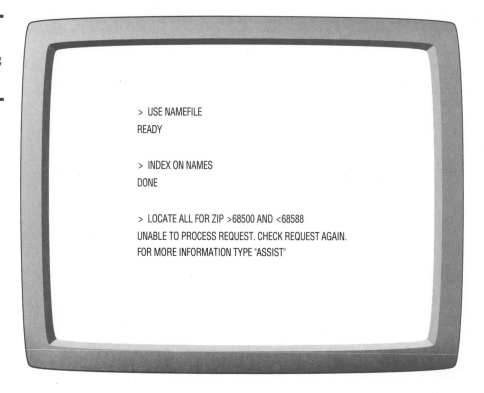

```
> USE NAMEFILE
READY


> INDEX ON NAMES
DONE


> LOCATE ALL FOR ZIP >68500 AND <68588
UNABLE TO PROCESS REQUEST. CHECK REQUEST AGAIN.
FOR MORE INFORMATION TYPE "ASSIST"
```

NOTIFYING THAT A REQUEST WAS NOT COMPLETED. Feedback is also needed to let the user know that the computer is unable to complete a request. Notice that in the last figure the system has displayed the message, "UNABLE TO PROCESS REQUEST. CHECK REQUEST AGAIN," in response to the user's request to locate subscribers by zip code. The user can then go back and check to see if the request has been input correctly, rather than continuing to enter commands that cannot be executed.

OFFERING THE USER MORE DETAILED FEEDBACK. In relation to this, users need to be reassured that more detailed feedback is available and shown how they can get it. Notice that the system has displayed a message instructing the user to type "ASSIST" for more information.

Other commands, such as INSTRUCT, EXPLAIN, and MORE, may also be employed. Or the user may type a question mark or point to an appropriate icon to get more feedback. Using the command HELP or having users hit the Escape key as ways to obtain further information has been questioned, since users may feel helpless or caught in a trap from which they must escape. However, both conventions are in use, and their familiarity to users may overcome these concerns.

Feedback is essential to all humans. Even when interfacing with machines, people still require it. Plan to provide feedback for users so that they are aware of: whether their input is being accepted; whether input is or is not in the correct form; whether processing is going on; whether requests can or cannot be processed; and whether more detailed information is available and how to get it.

It is well worth the systems analyst's time to provide user feedback. If used correctly, feedback can be a powerful reinforcer of users' learning processes, as well as serving to improve their performance with the system and increasing their motivation to produce.

A Variety of Help Options. Feedback on personal computers has developed over the years. "Help" originally started as a response to pressing a function key such as F1, and the GUI alternative is the pull-down help menu. But this approach was cumbersome, as end users had to navigate through a table of contents or search using an index. Next came context-sensitive help. End users could simply click on the right mouse button, and topics or explanations about the current screen or area of the screen would be revealed. Sometimes software manufacturers call these cue cards. The third type of help on personal computers occurs when the end user places the arrow over an icon and leaves it there for a couple of seconds. At this point some programs pop up a balloon similar to those found in comic strips. This balloon explains a little bit about the icon.

The fourth type of help has been the wizards, which ask the end user a series of questions and then make a decision accordingly. Wizards have been used in narrowing a search in an encyclopedia such as Encarta, designing a chart in Freelance or PowerPoint, or choosing a style for a word-processing memo.

Besides help built into the software, software manufacturers offer help lines (most customer service telephone lines are not toll-free, however). Some manufacturers offer a fax-back system. An end user can request a catalog of various help documents to be sent by fax and then order from the catalog by entering the item number with a push-button phone.

Finally, software forums exist on CompuServe, America Online, or bulletin boards maintained by the software company itself. An end user will often get information from the software manufacturer's technical support staff, but sometimes the end user can also get valuable information from other users of the product. This type of support is, of course, unofficial, and the information thus obtained may be true, partially true, or may even lead the user astray. The principles regarding the use of software forums are the same for those mentioned in Chapter 20, where FOLKLORE is discussed. Read this section before you accept what is said on bulletin boards. Beware!

Besides informal help on software, bulletin boards are extremely useful for updating drivers, viewers, and the software itself. Most computer magazines have some sort of "driver watch" or "bug report" that monitors the bulletin boards for useful programs to download.

DESIGNING QUERIES

Query Types

The questions we pose concerning data from our database are referred to as queries. There are six basic query types. Each query involves three items: an entity, an attribute, and a value. In each case, two of these are given, and the intent of the query is to find the remaining item.

Query Type 1. "In the first type of query, the entity and one of the entity's attributes are given. The purpose of the query is to find the value. The query can be expressed as:

What is the value of a specified attribute for a particular entity?

Sometimes it is more convenient to use notation to help formulate the query. This query can be written as:

$$V \longleftarrow (E, A)$$

where V stands for the value, E for entity, A for attribute, and the variables in parenthesis are given.

The following question:

What did employee number 73712 make in year 1994?

can be stated more specifically as:

What is the value of the attribute YEAR-94 for the entity EMPLOYEE-NUMBER 73712?

Basic query type 1 is illustrated in Figure 18.22. The record containing employee number 73712 was found, and the answer to the query was $27,100.

QUERY TYPE 2. The intent of query type 2 is to find an entity or entities when an attribute and value are given. Query type 2 can be stated as follows:

What entity has a specified value for a particular attribute?

Since values can also be numeric, it is possible to search for a value equal to, greater than, less than, not equal to, greater than or equal to, and so on. An example of this type of query is:

What employee(s) earned more than $50,000 in 1994?

or more specifically:

What entities (EMPLOYEE-NUMBER) have the value > 50,000 for the attribute YEAR-94?

The notation for query type 2 is:

$$E \longleftarrow (V, A)$$

Figure 18.23 illustrates query type 2. In this case, three employees made more than $50,000, so the response turned out to be a listing of the employee numbers for the three employees.

QUERY TYPE 3. The purpose of query type 3 is to determine which attribute(s) fits the description provided when the entity and value are given. It can be stated as:

What attribute(s) has a specified value for a particular entity?

This query is useful when there are many similar attributes that have the same property. The example below has similar attributes (specific years) that contain the annual salaries for the employees of the company:

What years did employee #72845 make over $50,000?

FIGURE 18.22
Query type 1 finds the value of an attribute for a given entity.

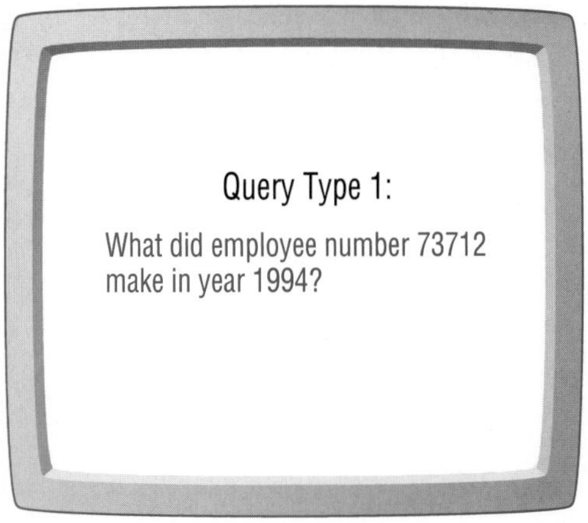

Query Type 1:

What did employee number 73712 make in year 1994?

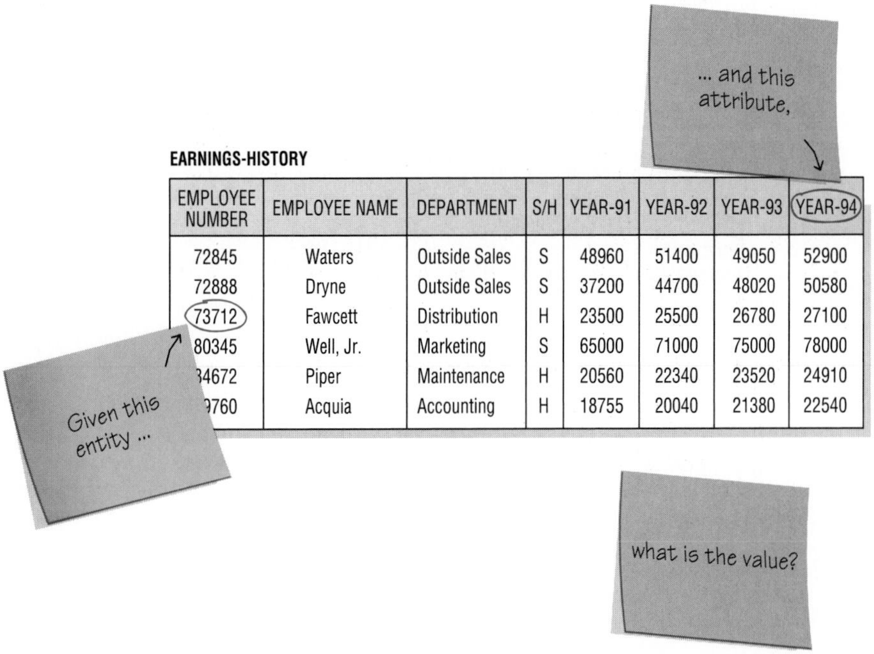

... and this attribute,

EARNINGS-HISTORY

EMPLOYEE NUMBER	EMPLOYEE NAME	DEPARTMENT	S/H	YEAR-91	YEAR-92	YEAR-93	YEAR-94
72845	Waters	Outside Sales	S	48960	51400	49050	52900
72888	Dryne	Outside Sales	S	37200	44700	48020	50580
73712	Fawcett	Distribution	H	23500	25500	26780	27100
80345	Well, Jr.	Marketing	S	65000	71000	75000	78000
84672	Piper	Maintenance	H	20560	22340	23520	24910
9760	Acquia	Accounting	H	18755	20040	21380	22540

Given this entity ...

what is the value?

Response:
$27,100

661

FIGURE 18.23
Query type 2 finds the entities
that satisfy a specific value for a
particular attribute.

Query Type 2:
What employee(s) earned more
than $50,000 in 1994?

Given a value
> 50000 ...

... for this
attribute,

EARNINGS-HISTORY

EMPLOYEE NUMBER	EMPLOYEE NAME	DEPARTMENT	S/H	YEAR-91	YEAR-92	YEAR-93	YEAR-94
72845	Waters	Outside Sales	S	48960	51400	49050	52900
72888	Dryne	Outside Sales	S	37200	44700	48020	50580
73712	Fawcett	Distribution	H	23500	25500	26780	27100
80345	Well, Jr.	Marketing	S	65000	71000	75000	78000
84672	Piper	Maintenance	H	20560	22340	23520	24910
89760	Acquia	Accounting	H	18755	20040	21380	22540

what are the
entities?

Response:
Employee numbers:
72845
72888
80345

or more precisely,

> What attributes {YEAR-91, YEAR-92, YEAR-93, YEAR-94} have a value > 50,000 for the entity EMPLOYEE-NUMBER = 72845?

where the optional list in braces { } is the set of eligible attributes.

The notation for query type 3 is:

$$A \longleftarrow (V, E)$$

An illustration of query type 3 is given in Figure 18.24. In this example, Waters (#72845) made over $50,000 for two years. These years are listed in the response. Query type 3 is rarer than either type 1 or type 2 due to the requirement of having similar attributes exhibiting the same properties.

QUERY TYPE 4. This query is similar to query type 1. The difference is that the values of all attributes are desired. Query 4 can be expressed as:

> List all the values for all of the attributes for a particular entity.

Examples of query 4 include:

> List all the details in the earnings history file for employee number 72888.

or

> List all of the information regarding the inventory status on part HV-5678.

The notation for query type 4:

$$\text{all } V \longleftarrow (E, \text{all } A)$$

An illustration of query type 4 is shown in Figure 18.25. The response for this query was simply the record for the employee named Dryne (#72888).

QUERY TYPE 5. The fifth type is another global query, but it is similar in form to query type 2. Query type 5 can be stated as:

> List all entities that have a specified value for all attributes.

An example of query type 5 is:

> List all of the employees whose earnings exceeded $50,000 in any of the years available.

The notation for query type 5 is:

$$\text{all } E \longleftarrow (V, \text{all } A)$$

An example of query type 5 is shown in Figure 18.26.

QUERY TYPE 6. The sixth query type is similar to query type 3. The difference is that query type 6 requests a listing of the attributes for all entities rather than one particular entity. Query type 6 can be stated as:

> List all the attributes that have a specified value for all entities.

FIGURE 18.24
Query type 3 finds the
attributes when the entity
and value are given.

Query Type 3:

What year(s) did employee
number 72845 make
over $50,000?

... and a value
GT 50000,

EARNINGS-HISTORY

EMPLOYEE NUMBER	EMPLOYEE NAME	DEPARTMENT	S/H	YEAR-91	YEAR-92	YEAR-93	YEAR-94
72845	Waters	Outside Sales	S	48960	51400	49050	52900
72888	Dryne	Outside Sales	S	37200	44700	48020	50580
73712	Fawcett	Distribution	H	23500	25500	26780	27100
0345	Well, Jr.	Marketing	S	65000	71000	75000	78000
572	Piper	Maintenance	H	20560	22340	23520	24910
0	Acquia	Accounting	H	18755	20040	21380	22540

Given this
entity ...

what are the
attributes?

Response:

Year-92
Year-94

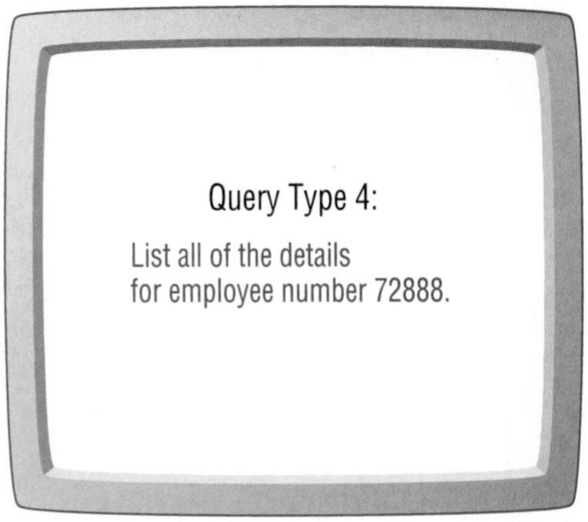

FIGURE 18.25
Query type 4 lists all the
values for all attributes
of a particular entity.

Query Type 4:

List all of the details
for employee number 72888.

... for ALL
attributes,

EARNINGS-HISTORY

EMPLOYEE NUMBER	EMPLOYEE NAME	DEPARTMENT	S/H	YEAR-91	YEAR-92	YEAR-93	YEAR-94
72845	Waters	Outside Sales	S	48960	51400	49050	52900
72888	Dryne	Outside Sales	S	37200	44700	48020	50580
73712	Fawcett	Distribution	H	23500	25500	26780	27100
80345	Well, Jr.	Marketing	S	65000	71000	75000	78000
4672	Piper	Maintenance	H	20560	22340	23520	24910
760	Acquia	Accounting	H	18755	20040	21380	22540

Given this
entity ...

list ALL of
the values.

Response:

72888 Dryne Outside Sales S 37200 44700 48020 50580

665

FIGURE 18.26
Query type 5 lists all of the
entities that satisfy a value
for all attributes described.

Query Type 5:

List all of the employees
whose earnings exceeded $50,000
in any of the years available.

Given a value
> 50000 ...

... for ALL
attributes,

EARNINGS-HISTORY

EMPLOYEE NUMBER	EMPLOYEE NAME	DEPARTMENT	S/H	YEAR-91	YEAR-92	YEAR-93	YEAR-94
72845	Waters	Outside Sales	S	48960	51400	49050	52900
72888	Dryne	Outside Sales	S	37200	44700	48020	50580
73712	Fawcett	Distribution	H	23500	25500	26780	27100
80345	Well, Jr.	Marketing	S	65000	71000	75000	78000
84672	Piper	Maintenance	H	20560	22340	23520	24910
89760	Acquia	Accounting	H	18755	20040	21380	22540

list ALL of the
entities.

Response:

Employee numbers:

72845
72888
80345

The following is an example of query type 6:

List all of the years for which earnings exceeded $20,000 for all employees in the company.

The notation for query type 6 is:

$$\text{all } A \longleftarrow (V, \text{all } E)$$

An illustration of query type 6 can be found in Figure 18.27. As with query 3, query type 6 is not used as much as other types.

BUILDING MORE COMPLEX QUERIES. The preceding six query types are only building blocks for more complex queries. Expressions referred to as Boolean expressions can be formed for queries. One example of a Boolean expression is:

List all of the customers who have zip codes greater than or equal to 60001 and less than 70000 and who have ordered more than $500 from our catalogs or have ordered at least 5 times in the past year.

One of the difficulties with this statement is in determing which operator (for example, AND) belongs with which condition, and the order in which the parts of the expression should be carried out. The following may help to clarify this problem:

LIST ALL CUSTOMERS HAVING (ZIP-CODE GE 60001 AND ZIP-CODE LT 70000) AND (AMOUNT-ORDERED GT 500 OR TIMES-ORDERED GE 5)

Now some of the confusion is eliminated. The first improvement is that the operators are expressed more clearly as GE, GT, LT than as English phrases such as "at least." Second, the attributes are given distinct names such as AMOUNT-ORDERED and TIMES-ORDERED. In the earlier sentence, these attributes were both referred to as "have ordered." Finally, parentheses are used to indicate the order in which the logic is to be performed. Whatever is in parentheses is done first. Figure 18.28 shows how a more complex query is performed on a relation.

Operators are generally performed in a predetermined order of precedence. Arithmetic operators are usually performed first (exponentiation, then either multiplication or division, and then addition or subtraction). Next comparative operators are performed. These include GT (greater than), LT (less than), and others. Finally, the Boolean operators are performed (first AND and then OR). Within the same level, the order generally goes from left to right. The precedence is summarized in Figure 18.29.

PRODUCTIVITY AND ERGONOMICS DESIGN

Users might avoid using a system or become dissatisfied with it simply because the systems analyst has not bothered to visualize what it would be like to sit at a workstation and enter data into the system day in and day out. The powerful influence of the workstation on user involvement with the system

FIGURE 18.27
Query type 6 lists all of the
attributes that have a specified value for all entities.

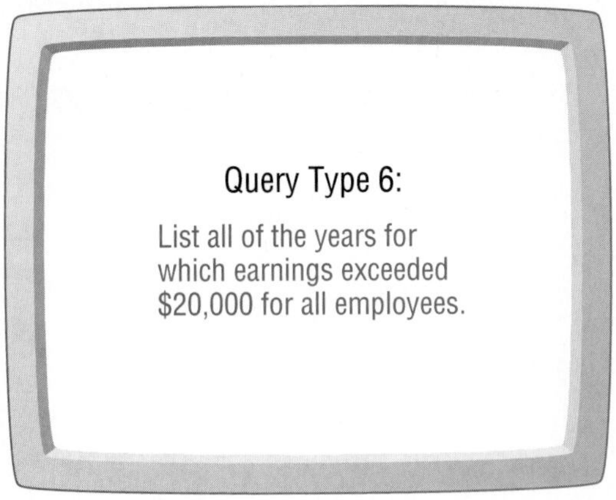

Query Type 6:

List all of the years for
which earnings exceeded
$20,000 for all employees.

... given a value
> 20000,

EARNINGS-HISTORY

EMPLOYEE NUMBER	EMPLOYEE NAME	DEPARTMENT	S/H	YEAR-91	YEAR-92	YEAR-93	YEAR-94
72845	Waters	Outside Sales	S	48960	51400	49050	52900
72888	Dryne	Outside Sales	S	37200	44700	48020	50580
73712	Fawcett	Distribution	H	23500	25500	26780	27100
80345	Well, Jr.	Marketing	S	65000	71000	75000	78000
84672	Piper	Maintenance	H	20560	22340	23520	24910
89760	Acquia	Accounting	H	18755	20040	21380	22540

For **ALL**
entities ...

list **ALL** of the
attributes.

Response:
Year-92
Year-93
Year-94

FIGURE 18.28
Complex queries can be
created using Boolean logic.

Query:

List all customers who have
zip codes greater or equal to
60001 and less than 70000 AND
(have either ordered more than
$500 from catalogs OR have
ordered a least 5 times
in the past year).

GE 60001
and
LT 70000

GT 500

GE 5

ORDER-TIMES

ORDER-#	LAST NAME	I	STREET-ADDRESS	CITY	ST	ZIP	AMOUNT	TIMES
10784	MacRae	G	2314 Curly Circle	Lincoln	NE	68506	322	8
10796	Jones	S	34 Dream Lane	Oklahoma City	OK	73118	47	2
11821	Preston	R	1008 Madison Ave.	River City	IA	52101	36	1
11845	Channing	C	454 Harmonia St.	New York	NY	10453	98	4
11872	Kiley	R	765 Dulcinea Drive	La Mancha	CA	93407	125	7
11976	Verdon	G	7564 K Street	Chicago	IL	60637	187	5
11998	Rivera	C	4342 West Street	Chicago	IL	60625	559	10
12765	Orbach	J	1345 Michigan Ave.	Chicago	IL	60616	58	3
12769	Steele	T	3498 Burton Lane	Finnian	NJ	07860	323	6
12965	Crawford	M	1986 Barnum Cir.	London	NH	03570	145	2
13432	Cullum	J	354 River Road	Shenandoah	VT	05201	237	4
13542	Mostel	Z	65 Fiddler Street	Anatevka	ND	58501	38	1

OR

AND

List **ALL** entities
that satisfy the
conditions.

Response:
10784
11976
11998

FIGURE 18.29
Arithmetic, comparative, and
Boolean operators are
processed in a hierarchical
order of precedence unless
parentheses are used.

Type	Level	Symbol
Arithmetic Operators	1	**
	2	* /
	3	+ –
Comparative Operators	4	GT LT EQ NE GE LE
Boolean Operators	5	AND
	6	OR

must be considered. Continued use, user productivity, comfort, and satisfaction with the system are all related to how ergonomically well-designed the workspace is. (Ergonomics refers to application of biological and engineering data to the problems relating to people and the machines they use in work.)

Systems analysts can skillfully utilize their knowledge about the influence of well-designed workstations to support the behavior they want from users—productive use of the system. An example from a typical university computer room serves to underscore how workstation design determines use of computers.

Universities often allow free use of VDTs, but one or two VDTs will have time restrictions posted. These VDTs are for use by someone who has only minor changes to make to their computer program. The concept is similar to a grocery store express lane, but instead of "Eight items or less," the sign in the computer room posted about the restricted VDTs states "Five minutes or less." Policing this concept, however, is difficult. This is where the design takes over. Rather than monitoring usage of the VDTs and cutting off users after five minutes, designers solve the problem by making users stand, rather than sit. No chairs are provided for the "express" VDTs. And there is rarely a problem with the five-minute rule. Comfortable seating is just one of the variables in getting users to use the system.

Sometimes what exists in the user workspace will not be under your control as a systems analyst. However, if the opportunity arises, you should be able to recommend ergonomically sound workstation designs. The user's office/workstation should be viewed as an improvable context that must be adapted to the individual if you want the system to be used. The workspace variables important to consider include: room color and lighting; VDT screens and user keyboards; computer desks; and user seating.

Computer Room Color and Lighting

Computer rooms should be painted in muted colors with flat paints that do not assault the senses of their inhabitants nor give off a glare. Some colors and decoration schemes produce negative effects on users. Painting every wall in a light, bright color (brighter than the brightest possible VDT screens) should be avoided, since it increases glare on VDT screens. Decorating computer rooms in several different colors should also be avoided. Too many wall colors distract users from their tasks and can be confusing.

Rooms where computers or terminals are used should avoid use of fluorescent light, which is too bright for VDT use and has an almost imper-

CONSULTING OPPORTUNITY 18.5

Hey, Look Me Over—Reprise

You have been called back to take another look at Merman's Costumes. Here is part of the database created for Annie Oaklea of Merman's (whom you last worked with in Consulting Opportunities 9.2 and 10.1). The database contains information such as the cost of the rental, date checked out, date due back, and the number of days the costume has been rented since the beginning of the year (YTD DAYS OUT) (see Figure 18.C1).

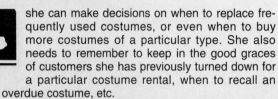

Analyzing Annie's typical day in the costume rental business, you realize that there are several queries that she must make of the database so that she can make decisions on when to replace frequently used costumes, or even when to buy more costumes of a particular type. She also needs to remember to keep in the good graces of customers she has previously turned down for a particular costume rental, when to recall an overdue costume, etc.

Formulate several queries that will help her get the information she needs from the database (*Hint:* Make any assumptions necessary about the types of information she needs to make decisions, and use as many of the different query types discussed in this chapter as you can.)

COSTUME-RENTAL

COSTUME NUMBER	DESCRIPTION	SUIT NUMBER	COLOR	COST OF RENTAL	DATE CHECKED OUT	DUE DATE	YTD DAYS OUT	TYPE OF COSTUME	REQUESTS TURNED DOWN
0003	Lady MacBeth F, SM	01	Blue	15.00	10/15	11/30	150	Standard	2
0128	Lady Di F, SM	01	Royal Blue	18.00	09/07	09/12	150	Trendy	6
1342	Bear F, MED	01	Dk. Brown	12.50	10/24	11/09	26	Standard	0
1344	Bear F, MED	02	Dk. Brown	12.50	10/24	11/09	115	Standard	0
1347	Bear F, LG	01	Black	12.50	10/24	11/09	22	Standard	0
1348	Bear F, LG	02	Black	12.50	11/01	11/08	10	Standard	0
1400	Goldilocks F, MED	01	Light Blue	7.00	10/24	11/09	140	Standard	0
1402	Goldilocks F, MED	02	Light Blue	7.00	10/28	11/09	10	Standard	0
1852	Hamlet M, MED	01	Dark Green	15.00	11/02	11/23	115	Standard	3
1853	Ophelia F, SM	01	Light Blue	15.00	11/02	11/23	22	Standard	0
4715	Prince M, LG	01	White/purple	10.00	11/04	11/21	145	Standard	5
4730	Frog M, SM	01	Green	7.00	11/04	11/21	175	Standard	2
7822	Jester M, MED	01	Multi	7.50	11/10	12/08	12	Standard	0
7824	Jester M, MED	02	Multi	7.50	11/09	11/15	10	Standard	0
7823	Executioner M, LG	01	Black	7.00	11/19	12/05	21	Standard	0
8645	Dr. Spock N, LG	01	Orange	18.00	09/07	09/12	150	Trendy	4
9000	Pantomime F,LG	01	Red	7.00	08/25	09/15	56	Standard	0
9001	Pantomime M, MED	01	Blue	7.00	08/25	09/15	72	Standard	0
9121	Juggler M, MED	01	Multi	7.00	11/05	11/19	14	Standard	0
9156	Napoleon M, SM	01	Blue/white	15.00	10/26	11/23	56	Standard	1
9942	Ronald Reagan M, LG	01	Navy Blue	15.00	11/03	11/10	140	Trendy	3

FIGURE 18.C1
A portion of the database from Merman's costume rental shop.

ceptible, yet continuous, flicker. It is better to provide incandescent lamps that produce more natural light or lamps that use halogen bulbs. Rooms with VDTs should be about half as bright as rooms in typical offices where people process paperwork.

Do not allow VDTs to be placed where direct window light can hit the screen, as this creates tremendous glare. Ideally, VDT users should be furnished with adjustable task lights at their workstations.

FIGURE 18.30
Position of the VDT and desk
height are key factors in user
satisfaction and productivity.

Visual Display Terminals and Keyboards

The design of efficient and effective screen displays was covered in the preceding chapter, along with design of user input, and use of screen color and icons. But there are some remaining ergonomic specifications and health considerations that also figure into use of visual display terminals (VDTs).

Researchers have found that the following guidelines will enhance user comfort when viewing a VDT. Generally, flexibility and adjustability for individual preferences are the watchwords. The more control given users over the features of their VDTs the better.

1. VDT screens should be within comfortable sightlines, as pictured in Figure 18.30. That means setting VDTs at an angle 10 to 15 degrees from the vertical, away from the user. The user should look slightly downward; the screen should be 5 to 35 degrees from the horizontal.

2. VDT screens should be perceived as continuous images. This means no glare, flickering of images, or bleeding of characters into one another.

3. VDT screens should provide sharp contrast, with adjustable brightness and crisp image resolution.

Concerns have been voiced about possible health risks for VDT users, some of whom have complained of physical symptoms ranging from headaches, eyestrain, and backaches, to problem pregnancies and early onset of cataracts. Studies of the effects of VDTs' extremely low-frequency radiation have been controversial to date.

Until the controversy is settled and regulations of manufacture are set up, users working regularly with VDTs must take personal responsibility for checking up on any physical symptoms they feel are related to use of the VDT. Although recommending frequent breaks (fifteen minutes away from the screen for every two hours in front of it) and regular eye exams for VDT users, trade unions in the U.S. have approved use of VDTs by their members. Good-quality liquid crystal displays (LCDs) are available for portable computers. LCDs should cut down on some of the health concerns traditionally associated with VDTs.

User keyboards for computer interface should be as flexible and adjustable as possible. Early microcomputers featured built-in keyboards, but detachable keyboards are now the rule. Detachability and light weight allow changes in sitting position for users, who need a break from doing data entry in a continuous pose. Most users naturally change position about every ten minutes.

Users should not have to reach up or down to access the keyboard. Forearms should form a right angle to the elbow, and the user should reach slightly downward to the keyboard. Following these guidelines can help prevent repetitive motion injuries of the fingers or wrists.

Computer Furniture

Computer furniture includes the desks or stands on which computers and keyboards rest. Many times computers are put into existing furniture setups. This can work if, for example, a microcomputer with a built-in keyboard is put into a former typewriter setup. Typewriting desks and stands are designed to a 26-inch height standard. This is a good height for long periods of data entry.

Putting a keyboard for data entry on an already existing desktop is not a good idea. The standard desktop height of 29 inches is too high for continuous keyboard use, which at that height causes back, neck, and arm strain. If users have both a desk and a computer table, the desk should be 29 inches high, and the computer table 26 inches high. Both can be joined into an L-shaped configuration for ease of access.

As we saw in the example at the beginning of this section, user seating is important enough to influence whether systems are used, and with what satisfaction. Getting the correct chair can also increase user comfort and productivity. Well-designed seating often looks as if it had been sculpted around a person. Users' chairs should be armless with firm upper- and lower-back support (preferably adjustable for the individual) and a firm seat cushion providing back support. Chairs with five casters provide excellent balance and mobility.

Seating height should be adjustable for the individual, but clearly it should preserve the prescribed relationship between the user's gaze and the VDT screen, as well as preserving the relationship between the user's posture and the keyboard. In order to get users to use the system, well-designed workstations are essential.

SUMMARY

We have focused on system users, their interface with the computer, their need for feedback, and the design of their workstation in this chapter. The success of the systems you design depends on user involvement and acceptance. Therefore, thinking about users in systematic and empathic ways is of utmost importance, and not a peripheral issue for systems analysts.

Various types of user interfaces and input devices were covered in this chapter. Some interfaces are particularly well-suited to inexperienced users such as: natural-language, question-and-answer, menus, form-fill,

"I have no problem with using a mouse, or any other rodent you throw my way. Really, though, whatever Snowden needs is what I try to do. But everyone is different. I've seen people here go out of their way to avoid using a computer altogether. Other people would prefer not to talk with a human. In fact, they would be as happy as a puppy chewing on a new bedroom slipper if they could use command language to interact. I have a hunch they would prefer not talking to people at all. But that's just an impression. Most of the folks we have here are open to new things. Otherwise they wouldn't be here at MRE. We do pride ourselves on our creativity. I have you signed up for a meeting with people from the Training group, including Tom Ketcham, Melissa Smith, and Kathy Blandford. You can invite anyone else you think should be included. Snowden may sit in as well, if he has time. That's why he asked me to relay the message, I guess. They'll be very curious to see what kind of interface you are suggesting for them on the new project reporting system."

HyperCase Questions

1. Write a short proposal describing what type of user interface would be appropriate for the users of the project reporting system who are in the Training group. Include reasons for your decision.

FIGURE 18 HC.1
In HyperCase® you can see how users process information in order to create a more effective user interface.

2. Design a user interface using a CASE tool such as Excelerator or paper layout forms. What are the key features that address the needs of the people in the Training group?
3. Demonstrate your interface to a group of students who can role play as members of the Training group. Ask for reactions.
4. Redesign the interface based on the feedback you have received. Write a paragraph to say how your new design addresses any comments you have received.

graphical user interfaces, the mouse, lightpens, and touch-sensitive screens. Command language is better suited to experienced users.

Combinations of interfaces can be extremely effective. For example, using pull-down menus with graphical user interfaces or employing nested menus within question-and-answer interfaces yields interesting combinations. Each interface poses a different level of challenge for programmers, with natural language being the most difficult to program.

Users' need for feedback from the system was also stressed. System feedback is necessary to let users know if their input is being accepted; if input is or is not in the correct form; if processing is going on; if requests can or cannot be processed; and if more detailed information is available and how to get it. Audio feedback can also be effective.

Queries are designed to allow users to extract meaningful data from the database. There are six basic types of queries, and they can be combined using Boolean logic to form more complex queries.

Finally, we considered how users' workspaces influence their willingness to use the system, and how workstations can be improved through implementation of relevant ergonomic principles. There are specific productivity and comfort guidelines on construction and position of VDTs, keyboards, computer stands, and users' seating, but generally all of them should be flexible enough to permit adjustment for individual use.

KEYWORDS AND PHRASES

graphical user interface (GUI)	natural-language interfaces
question-and-answer interfaces	menus
pull-down menus	nested menus
form-fill interfaces	input/output form
command-language interfaces	lightpens
touch-sensitive screen	speech recognition and synthesis
queries	Boolean operators
seven kinds of feedback for users	ergonomic specifications

REVIEW QUESTIONS

1. What are the four objectives for designing user interfaces?
2. Define natural-language interfaces. What is their major drawback?

3. Explain what is meant by question-and-answer interfaces. What kind of users are they best suited to?

4. Describe how users use on-screen menus.

5. What is a nested menu? What are its advantages?

6. Define on-screen input/output forms. What is their chief advantage?

7. Explain what command-language interfaces are. What types of users are they best suited to?

8. Define graphical user interfaces. What is the key difficulty they present for programmers?

9. For what type of user is a GUI interface particularly effective?

10. What are the three guidelines for designing good screen dialog?

11. List five standards to aid in evaluating user interfaces.

12. What are the seven situations that require feedback for users?

13. What is an acceptable way of telling the user that input was accepted?

14. Why is it unacceptable to notify the user that input is not correct solely through use of beeping or buzzing?

15. When a user is informed that his or her input is not in the correct form, what additional feedback should be given at the same time?

16. When a request is not completed, what feedback should be provided to the user?

17. List in shorthand notation the six basic query types.

18. Give three guidelines for setting up VDTs for user productivity and comfort.

19. What is the preferred height for VDT desks? Why is the height important?

20. List four ways for achieving the goal of minimal operator action when designing a user interface.

21. When should it be appropriate to include a default value in an entry field?

22. What are hypertext links? Where should they be used?

PROBLEMS

1. Design a nested menus interface for a hotel reservation, check-in, and check-out system. Use numbers to select a menu item. Show how each menu would look on an 80-column by 24-row screen.

2. Design a form-fill interface for inventory control of a musical CD and tape wholesale company for use on an 80-column by 24-row screen.

3. Design a command-language interface that a travel agent would use to book seats for an airline.
   a. Show what it would look like on an 80-column by 24-row screen.
   b. Make a list of commands needed to book an airline seat, and write down what each command means.

4. Design a graphical user interface for an executive desktop. Use icons for file cabinets, wastebasket, telephone, and so on. Show how they would appear on the VDT screen.

5. Design a screen (80 columns by 24 rows) that provides appropriate feedback for a user whose command cannot be executed.

6. Design a screen (80 columns by 24 rows) for a payroll software package that displays information telling the user how to get more detailed feedback.

7. Design a screen (80 columns by 24 rows) that displays an acceptable way to tell users that their input was accepted.

8. Write six different queries for the file in problem 1 in Chapter 17.

9. Write six different queries for the 3NF relation in problem 6 in Chapter 17.

GROUP PROJECTS

1. With your group members, create a pull-down menu for an employment agency that matches professional candidates to position openings. Include a list of keystrokes that would directly invoke the menu options using the ALT-X format. The menu has the following options:

Add employee	Add employer	Add position
Change employee	Change employer	Change position
Delete employee	Delete employer	Delete position
Employee inquiry	Match employee to opening	
Position inquiry	Print open positions report	
Employer inquiry	Print successful matches report	

2. In a paragraph, describe the problems your group faced in creating this menu.

3. Figure 18.EX1 shows how the drag-and-drop feature used in GUI interfaces allows the user to move sentences around in a word processing package. As a group, suggest how drag-and-drop can be used to its fullest potential in the following applications:

   a. Project management software (Chapter 3)
   b. Relational database program (Chapter 17)
   c. Screen or forms designer (Chapter 16)
   d. Presentation package (Chapter 14)
   e. Spreadsheet program (Chapter 12.)
   f. CASE tool for drawing data flow diagrams (Chapter 9)
   g. Fax program (Chapter 15)
   h. File management program (Chapter 18)
   i. Personal information manager (PIM) (Chapter 3)
   j. Illustration in a drawing package (Chapter 14)
   k. CASE tool for developing data dictionaries (Chapter 10)
   l. Decision tree drawing program (Chapter 11)

   For each solution your group designs, draw the screen and show movement by using an arrow.

FIGURE 18.EX1
GUI interfaces allow users to rearrange interview questions in a word processing package by using the "drag-and-drop" feature.

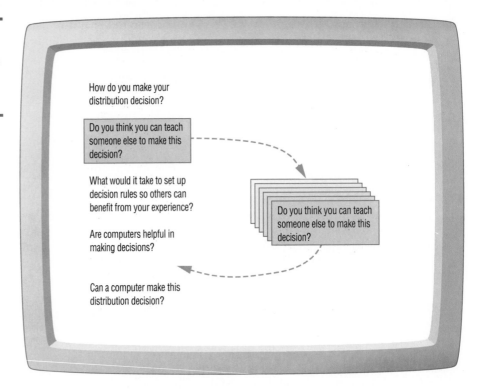

How do you make your distribution decision?

Do you think you can teach someone else to make this decision?

What would it take to set up decision rules so others can benefit from your experience?

Are computers helpful in making decisions?

Can a computer make this distribution decision?

Do you think you can teach someone else to make this decision?

SELECTED BIBLIOGRAPHY

Benbesat, I., and R. G. Schroeder. "An Experimental Investigation of Some MIS Design Variables." *Management Information Systems Quarterly,* Vol. 2, No. 2, 1978, pp. 43–54.

Bennett, J. L. *Building Decision Support Systems.* Reading, MA: Addison-Wesley Publishing Company, 1983.

Davis, G. B., and M. H. Olson. *Management Information Systems: Conceptual Foundations, Structure, and Development.* New York: McGraw-Hill Book Company, 1985.

Dietsch, D. "Ergo, Ergonomics." *A+*, Vol. 3, Issue 6, 1985.

Gane, C., and T. Sarson. *Structured Systems Analysis: Tools and Techniques.* Englewood Cliffs, NJ: Prentice-Hall, 1979.

Kleiner, A., Ed. "The Health Hazards of Computers." *Whole Earth Review,* No. 48, 1985, pp.80–93.

Laudon, K. C., and J. P. Laudon. *Management Information Systems,* 3rd ed. New York: Macmillan Publishing Company, 1994.

UP TO THE USERS

"Let's take our prototypes and some new screens, reports, and forms to create the final user interface," Anna says to Chip. "It's about time, isn't it?" replies Chip. He was all too aware of the importance of designing a good interface.

After talking awhile, they set up the following screen dialog guidelines:

1. Well-designed screens should:
   Communicate actions and intentions clearly to users.
   Show options available to operators. Examples would be:
   MAKE CORRECTIONS OR PRESS ESC TO CANCEL
   ENTER HARDWARE INVENTORY NUMBER OR PRESS F10 TO EXIT
   PRESS ENTER KEY
   PRESS ENTER TO CONFIRM DELETE, ESC TO CANCEL
   Standardize use of any abbreviations.
   Avoid the use of codes, substituting the code meaning.
   Provide help screens for complicated portions of the dialog.

2. Feedback should be provided to the users. This includes:
   Titles to show the current screen.
   Actions successfully completed messages, such as:
   RECORD HAS BEEN ADDED
   RECORD HAS BEEN CHANGED
   Error messages. Examples are:
   INVALID DATE
   CHECKDIGIT IS INVALID
   SOFTWARE IS NOT ON FILE
   Processing delay messages similar to:
   PLEASE WAIT—REPORT IS BEING PRODUCED

3. There should be consistency in the design, including:
   Location of the OPERATOR MESSAGE—line 23 on every screen.
   Location of the FEEDBACK MESSAGE line—chosen as line 24.
   Date, time, system name, and screen reference number should appear in heading lines.
   Consistent exit of all screens; for example, through use of the same function key.
   Standard use of keys, such as PgDn and PgUp, to display a next or previous screen within a multiple-screen display.
   A consistent method of canceling an operation; for example, through use of the Escape key (Esc).
   Standardized use of color and high-intensity display; for example, all error messages would appear in red.

4. Minimum operator actions should be required to use the system. Some examples are:
   The use of **Y** and **N** as Yes and No replies. The use of the plus and minus signs on the number pad as a substitute for **Y** and **N**.

Allen Schmidt, Julie E. Kendall, and Kenneth E. Kendall

679

When changing or deleting records, only the record key need be specified. The system would obtain the record and display pertinent information.

When names are required as key entries, only the first few letters of the name need be entered. The program should find all matching record key names and present these for selection by the operator.

Data-entry screens should allow the entry of codes.

All numeric entries may omit leading zeros, commas, or a decimal point.

As each data field is completed, the cursor should advance to the next entry field.

After each option is completed, the same screen, with blank entry areas, should be redisplayed until the exit key is pressed.

an option is exited, the previous menu is to be displayed.

5. Data entering the system should be validated. Guidelines are:

Specific fields should be verified according to edit criteria.

As errors are detected, operators should be given a chance to either correct the error or cancel the transaction.

When no errors have been detected in a transaction, the screen should be presented to the operator for visual confirmation. The operator should have the opportunity to either accept the screen or make corrections to the data entered.

Since the system is to be written using dBASE, Chip and Anna decide to use a menu to control the system. The advantage of using a menu is that all the options may be written as independent programs and linked under the menu structure. It also allows the flexibility of easy expansion as the system evolves. Conferring with the users, a consensus was obtained that a menu was indeed the best choice. Only Hy Perteks was strongly in favor of using a mouse and Windows for controlling the system. Mike Crowe also was in favor of the Windows approach but said that whatever was good for others was fine with him. Other users objected to the use of a mouse since many did not have a mouse interface. Dot was strongly in favor of the menu-controlled system since it was easy for new employees to learn.

Upon examining the many screens and reports (over thirty in all), Chip and Anna decide to split the menu into several smaller menus. The main menu will have four choices, hardware update, software update, inquiries, and reports, as illustrated in Figure E18.1. Each of these options will be represented by a submenu, such as the MICROCOMPUTER SYSTEM REPORT MENU shown in Figure E18.2.

The menu interactions will be represented in a hierarchical structure, with screens shown as rectangles and the primary menu represented by the rectangle on the top. Each secondary menu will be shown beneath the primary menu, with screen programs at the lowest level. Figure E18.3 is the screen hierarchy for the microcomputer system.

"Here's what I think the guidelines for the update programs should be," Anna tells Chip. "The key focus is on accuracy, with comprehensive editing for each data field. Add programs will display an entry screen and allow either Hardware or Software records to be created. After all entries are complete, a visual confirmation of the data is requested. A record could be added only if the primary key for the record does not already exist.

"Delete screens must have a simple, primary key entry such as HARDWARE INVENTORY NUMBER," Anna continues. "The corresponding

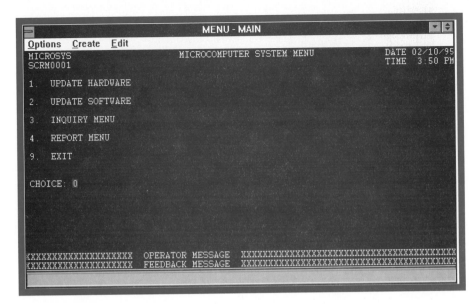

FIGURE E18.1
Microcomputer System Main Menu print.

record is read and the information displayed. Operators are prompted to confirm the delete. If the operator confirms NO, the delete action is canceled. How does all this sound?" she asks Chip.

"So far, so good," he replies. "Anything on change screens?"

"Yes. Change screens have a primary key for the record entered and the matching record read. Record information is to be displayed, allowing the operator to overtype the data with changes. All changes are to be validated with full editing. When all change fields are valid, the screen is displayed for visual confirmation of the changes. The operator may proceed to

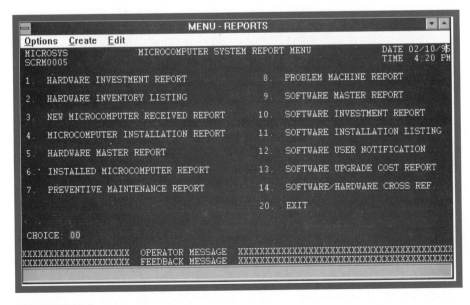

FIGURE E18.2
Microcomputer System Reports Menu.

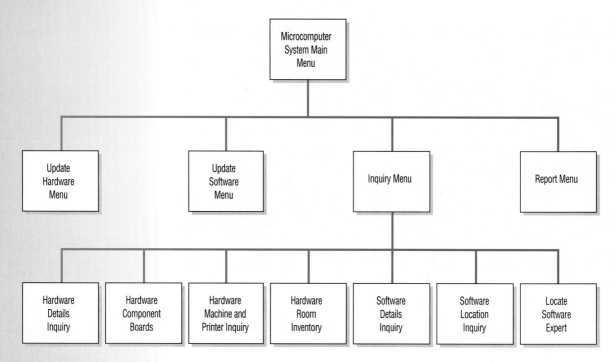

FIGURE E18.3
Screen Hierarchy, microcomputer system.

update the record or make corrections to the data entered. Is that clear enough for the user?" Anna asks.

"I think it's very good," Chip acknowledges.

Chip is responsible for the inquiry portion of the system. The focus on these programs is speed. A short entry is obtained from the operator and, after minimal editing, the corresponding records are read. Information is formatted for maximum communication and displayed. "I've met with various users," he tells Anna. "Here's a list of inquiry programs." (These are shown in Figure E18.4, the INQUIRY MENU.) Each of the inquiry screens is designed, along with the database files needed and possible errors that could occur.

"The first screen I designed was the HARDWARE INQUIRY," Chip continues. "I produced a rough layout and met with Dot to obtain feedback on the design. After pointing out some minor corrections, she mentioned that the maintenance details should be included, providing complete information for each microcomputer. To prevent overcrowding of a single screen, I decided to place the maintenance details on a second screen, with paging between the two screens." (The resulting screens are shown in Figures E18.5 and E18.6.)

The program logic is to use the HARDWARE INVENTORY NUMBER as the only entry field on the screen. The record is located in the database. If it is not found, the feedback message is HARDWARE RECORD NOT FOUND. Once the record is located, the matching board records are read. Board records contain a code for the type of board, and the BOARD CODE TABLE is searched for the matching code. If the code is found, the meaning of the code should be formatted on the screen; otherwise the display should contain two asterisks, a space, and the code.

"I selected the SOFTWARE LOCATION inquiry as the next screen to develop," Chip tells Anna. "After talking at length with Cher, I produced

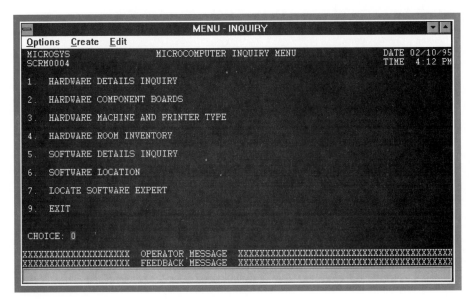

FIGURE E18.4
Inquiry Menu, microcomputer system.

the details. The entry fields are the software TITLE and the VERSION. Five columns of information are displayed: HARDWARE INVENTORY NUMBER, BRAND NAME, MODEL, CAMPUS, and ROOM. This allows Cher to quickly locate a machine containing the desired software. She seems to be happy with this idea so far," Chip adds.

Figure E18.7 shows the SOFTWARE LOCATION inquiry screen. The program reads the SOFTWARE MASTER file using the alternate key TITLE. If the matching record is not found, an error message is displayed. Since there may be several versions, the VERSION NUMBER on the record

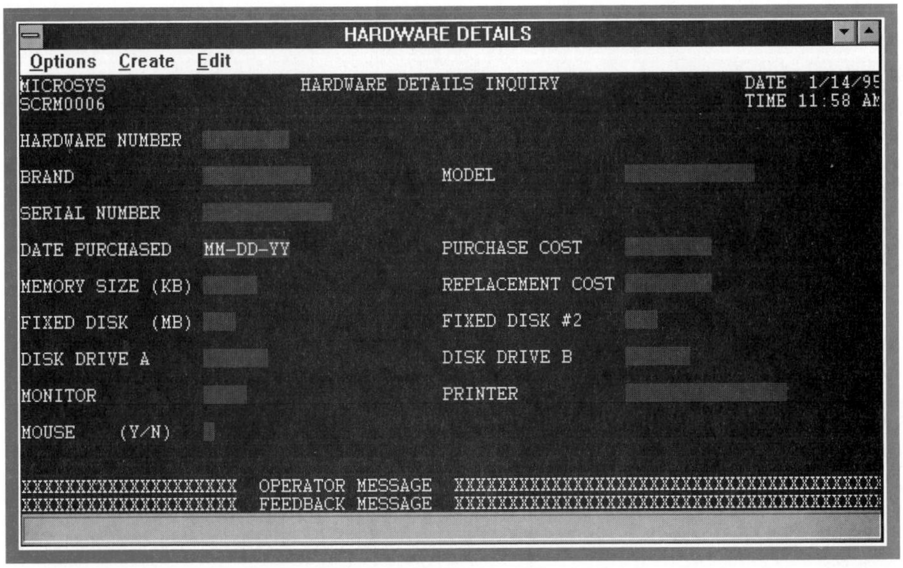

FIGURE E18.5
HARDWARE INQUIRY, first screen.

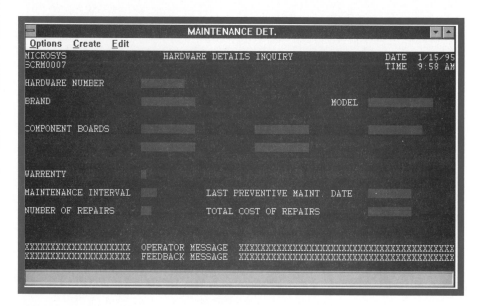

FIGURE E18.6
HARDWARE INQUIRY, second screen.

is checked for a match to the version entered. If the requested version is not found, further records are read for using the alternate index. If all records are read and the version number is not found, an error message, VERSION NOT AVAILABLE, is displayed.

Once the correct software has been obtained, the relational file is read using the SOFTWARE INVENTORY NUMBER. This relational file contains the SOFTWARE INVENTORY NUMBER and the matching HARDWARE INVENTORY NUMBER, which is used as a primary key to read the MICRO-COMPUTER MASTER file. If the MICROCOMPUTER MASTER is not found, the message MACHINE appears in the HARDWARE INVENTORY

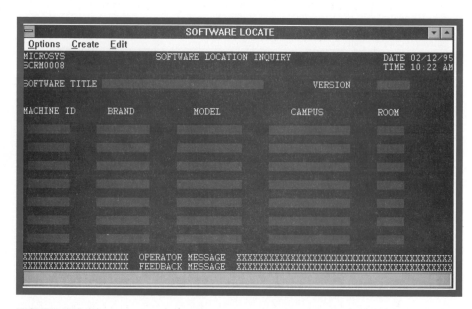

FIGURE E18.7
SOFTWARE LOCATION inquiry screen.

NUMBER column and the text NOT FOUND in the BRAND column. Other columns for this entry would contain spaces.

For each matching machine, the CAMPUS TABLE is searched for the CAMPUS LOCATION code. If the code is not found, the text NOT FOUND is displayed in the CAMPUS column. After twelve machine location lines have been created, the program pauses and the operator may press the page down (PgDn) key another twelve lines. This may be repeated until all matching machines are displayed.

"I think we've got a good start on designing our user interfaces," Anna comments. Chip nods in agreement.

Exercises*

💾 **E-1.** Use Excelerator's prototyping feature, SCREENS & REPORTS, to modify the Hardware Update menu. Print the completed menu, which should include the following options:

3. DELETE MICROCOMPUTER RECORD
4. UPDATE INSTALLED MICROCOMPUTER
5. UPDATE MAINTENANCE INFORMATION
9. EXIT

💾 **E-2.** Create and print the menu for updating software. Include the following choices:

ADD SOFTWARE PACKAGE
CHANGE SOFTWARE INFORMATION
DELETE SOFTWARE RECORD
UPGRADE SOFTWARE
CHANGE SOFTWARE MACHINE LOCATION
EXIT

(*Hint:* Use the copy option to copy one of the other menus and then modify the contents.)

E-3. Examine the HARDWARE INQUIRY shown in Figures E18.5 and E18.6. Explain the inquiry **type** using the value, entity, and attribute (V, E, A) notation.

E-4. In a paragraph explain why a data-entry screen should have an emphasis on accuracy while an inquiry screen emphasizes how fast results may be displayed.

💾 **E-5.** Modify and print the hierarchy chart representing the Hardware Update menu. Add rectangles to represent the following menu options.

CHANGE MICROCOMPUTER
DELETE MICROCOMPUTER RECORD
UPDATE INSTALLED MICROCOMPUTER

---

* The exercises preceded by a disk icon require the program Excelerator (or another CASE tool). A disk is provided free of charge to any professor adopting this book. The examples on the disk may be imported into Excelerator and then used by students.

E-6. Use Excelerator to draw a hierarchy chart representing the options found on the UPDATE SOFTWARE menu. Start with the top rectangle representing the UPDATE SOFTWARE menu.

E-7. In a paragraph explain why the program producing the HARDWARE INQUIRY would use two asterisks, a space, and the code to represent the code not found in the BOARD CODE TABLE error, rather than the feedback line (line 24) commonly used to report screen errors.

E-8. Discuss in a paragraph why more than one screen would be needed to produce the SOFTWARE LOCATION inquiry.

E-9. Modify and print the SOFTWARE DETAILS inquiry screen. The entry field is SOFTWARE INVENTORY NUMBER and all Software information, with the exception of Expert and Machines Installed On, should be displayed. Add the following data fields after the captions provided on the screen. Be sure to align data display fields for a pleasing appearance.

> DISK SIZE
> SITE LICENSE
> NUMBER OF COPIES
> COMPUTER BRAND
> MODEL REQUIRED
> MEMORY REQUIRED
> MONITOR REQUIRED
> PRINTER REQUIRED

E-10. When scheduling classrooms for student use, Cher Ware needs to know all the software packages in a given room. She would like to enter the CAMPUS LOCATION and the ROOM on an inquiry screen. The display fields would be TITLE, VERSION, SITE LICENSE, and NUMBER OF COPIES. This inquiry has been partially completed by Chip.

Modify the screen design and print the completed inquiry. The screen has the entry areas and the first line of the display columns. Complete the design by copying each display field to complete columns of output data. The display lines should be double-spaced, with the first column partially completed to serve as an example.

E-11. Mike Crowe needs to know which component boards are installed in each machine. Use Excelerator to create and print the COMPONENT BOARD inquiry. The input field is the HARDWARE INVENTORY NUMBER. Output fields are: BRAND NAME, MODEL, and up to five BOARDS. The logic is to randomly read the MICROCOMPUTER MASTER using the HARDWARE INVENTORY NUMBER. If the record is not found, display an error message to that effect. Find the matching BOARD records. Write the notation using value, entity, and attribute (V, E, A) for the type of inquiry.

E-12. Every so often Hy Perteks receives a request for help concerning a given software package. Staff members and students need to perform advanced options or transfer data to and from different packages, and are having difficulties. Hy would like to enter the software TITLE and VERSION NUMBER. The resulting display would show the SOFTWARE EXPERT NAME, and his or her CAMPUS LOCATION and ROOM NUMBER. Create and print the screen design for the LOCATE SOFTWARE EXPERT inquiry. Describe the logic and files needed to produce the inquiry. Write the notation for this inquiry using value, entity, and attribute (V, E, A).

💾 **E-13.** In a follow-up interview with Cher Ware, it was determined that she needs to know what machines are available to install any software package, given its graphics requirements. The example provided was Excelerator, which had the minimum requirement of EGA graphics.

Produce an inquiry that would allow Cher to enter the monitor code and, optionally, a graphics board and campus location for the software. Four columns should be displayed:

HARDWARE INVENTORY NUMBER
CAMPUS LOCATION
ROOM LOCATION
GRAPHICS BOARD

Write a paragraph describing the logic of obtaining the results. Include the type of inquiry using value, entity, and attribute (V, E, A) notation.

💾 **E-14.** Both Cher and Hy expressed an interest in finding machines of a specified brand connected to different printers. Sometimes the engineering students need a plotter, whereas other situations demand a laser or postscript printer.

Design and print an inquiry that would have the PRINTER and BRAND NAME of the microcomputer as input fields. Output would be two columns: CAMPUS LOCATION (full name, not a code) and ROOM LOCATION.

Briefly describe the logic used in producing the output. Would this inquiry need multiple pages to display all the information? Why or why not? Use a paragraph to describe the type of inquiry using value, entity, and attribute (V, E, A) notation.

19

DESIGNING ACCURATE DATA-ENTRY PROCEDURES

DATA-ENTRY OBJECTIVES

Making sure that data are entered into the system accurately is of the utmost importance. It is by now axiomatic that the quality of data input determines the quality of information output. The systems analyst can support accurate data entry through achievement of three broad objectives, as shown in Figure 19.1. They are effective coding, effective and efficient data capture and entry, and assuring quality through validation.

The quality of data is a measurement of how consistently correct the data are within certain preset limits. Effectively coded data facilitates accurate data entry by cutting down on the sheer quantity of data and thus the time required to enter it.

When data are being entered efficiently, data entry is meeting predetermined performance measures that give the relationship between time spent on entry and number of data items entered. Efficient data entry also means that data to be input are quickly and easily decipherable by data-entry operators. Effective coding, effective and efficient data capture and entry, and assuring data quality through validation procedures are all data-entry objectives covered in this chapter.

EFFECTIVE CODING

One of the ways that data can be entered more accurately and efficiently is through the knowledgeable employment of various codes. The process of putting ambiguous or cumbersome data into short, easily entered digits or letters is called coding (not to be confused with program coding).

Coding aids the systems analyst in reaching the objective of efficiency, since data that are coded require less time to enter and reduce the number of items entered. Coding can also help in appropriate sorting of data at a later point in the data transformation process. Additionally, coded data can save valuable memory and storage space. In sum, coding is a way of being eloquent but succinct in capturing data.

Effective and Efficient Data Entry

Effective Coding

Assuring Quality Through Validation

Besides providing accuracy and efficiency, codes should have a purpose. Specific types of codes allow us to treat data in a particular manner. Purposes for coding include:

1. Keeping track of something.
2. Classifying information.
3. Concealing information.
4. Revealing information.
5. Requesting appropriate action.

Each of these purposes for coding is discussed in the following sections, along with some example of codes.

Keeping Track of Something

Sometimes we want merely to identify a person, place, or thing in order to keep track of it. For example, a shop that manufactures custom-made upholstered furniture needs to assign a job number to a project. The salesperson needs to know the name and address of the customer, but the job shop manager or the workers who assemble the furniture need not know who the customer is. Consequently, an arbitrary number is assigned to the job. The number can be either random or sequential, as described in the following subsection.

SIMPLE SEQUENCE CODES. The simple sequence code is a number that is assigned to something if it needs to be numbered. It therefore has no relation to the data itself. Figure 19.2 shows how a furniture manufacturer's orders are assigned an order number. This is an easy reference number so the company can keep track of the order in process. It is more efficient to enter job "5676" than "That brown and black rocking chair with the leather seat for Arthur Hook, Jr."

Using a sequence code rather than a random number has some advantages. First, it eliminates the possibility of assigning the same number. Second, it gives users an approximation of when the order was received.

Sequence codes should be used when order of processing requires knowledge of the sequence in which items enter the system or the order in which events unfold. An example is found in the situation of a bank running a special promotion that makes it important to know when a person applied for a special, low-interest home loan, since (all other things being

Order #	Product	Customer
5676	Rocking Chair/with Leather	Arthur Hook, Jr.
5677	Dining Room Chair/Upholstered	Millie Monice
5678	Love Seat/Upholstered	J. & D. Pare
5679	Child's Rocking Chair/Decals	Lucinda Morely

FIGURE 19.2
Using a simple sequence code
to indicate the sequence in
which orders enter a custom
furniture shop.

equal) the special mortgage loans will be granted on a first-come, first-served basis. In this case, assigning a correct sequence code to each applicant is important.

ALPHABETIC DERIVATION CODES. There are times when it is undesirable to use sequence codes. The most obvious instance is when you do *not* wish to have someone read the code to figure out how many numbers have been assigned. Another situation in which sequence codes may not be useful is when a more complex code is desirable to avoid a costly mistake. One possible error would be to add a payment to account 223 when you meant to add it to account 224, by typing an incorrect digit.

The alphabetic derivation code is a commonly used approach in identifying an account number. The example in Figure 19.3 comes from a mailing label for a magazine. The code becomes the account number. The first five digits come from the first five digits of the subscriber's zip code; the next three are the first three consonants in the subscriber's name; the next four numbers are the street address; and the last three make up the code for the magazine. The main purpose of this code is to identify an account. Notice that the expiration date is not part of the account number, as that can change more frequently than the other data.

Classifying Information

Coding affords the ability to distinguish between classes of items. Classifications are necessary for many purposes—for example, reflecting what parts of a medical insurance plan an employee carries or showing which student has completed the core requirements of his or her coursework.

To be useful, classes must be mutually exclusive. For example, if a student is in class F, meaning freshman, having completed 0 to 36 credit hours, he or she should not also be classifiable as a sophomore (S). Overlapping classes would be F = 0–36 credit hours and S = 32–64 credit hours, and so on. Data are unclear and not as readily interpretable when coding classes are not mutually exclusive.

CLASSIFICATION CODES. Classification codes are used to distinguish one group of data with special characteristics from another. Classification codes can consist of either a single letter or a number. They are a shorthand way of describing a person, place, thing, or happening.

Classification codes are listed in manuals or posted so that users can locate them easily. Many times users become so familiar with frequently used codes that they memorize them. A user classifies an item, then enters its code directly into the terminal of an on-line system or onto a source document of a batch system.

FIGURE 19.3
Identifying the account of a
magazine subscriber with an
alphabetic derivation code.

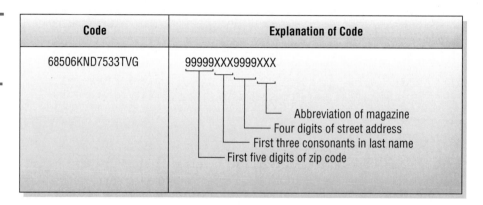

Code	Explanation of Code
68506KND7533TVG	99999XXX9999XXX — Abbreviation of magazine — Four digits of street address — First three consonants in last name — First five digits of zip code

An example of classification coding is the way you may wish to group tax-deductible items for the purpose of completing your income taxes. Figure 19.4 shows how codes are developed for items such as interest, medical payments, contributions, and so on. The coding system is simple: Take the first letter of each of the categories. Contributions are C; interest payments are I; supplies are S.

All goes well until we get to other categories, such as computer items, insurance payments, and subscriptions, that begin with the same letters we used previously. Figure 19.5 demonstrates what happens in this case. The coding was stretched so that we could use the P for comPuter; the N for iNsurance; and the B for suBscriptions. Obviously, this is far from being perfect. One way to avoid the confusion of this type is to allow for codes longer than one letter. This will be discussed later in this chapter, under the subheading of mnemonic codes.

BLOCK SEQUENCE CODES. Earlier, we discussed sequence codes. The block sequence code is an extension of the sequence code. Figure 19.6 shows how a business assigns numbers to microcomputer software. Main categories of software are spreadsheets, database packages, word-processing packages, and presentation packages. These were assigned sequential numbers in the following "blocks" or ranges: spreadsheets 100–199, database 200–299, and so forth. The advantage of the block sequence code is that the data are grouped according to common characteristics, while still taking advantage of the simplicity of assigning the next available number (within the block, of course) to the next item needing identification.

FIGURE 19.4
Grouping tax-deductible
items through use of a one-
letter classification code.

Code	Tax Deductible Item
I	Interest Payments
M	Medical Payments
T	Taxes
C	Contributions
D	Dues
S	Supplies

Code	Tax Deductible Item
I	Interest Payments
M	Medical Payments
T	Taxes
C	Contributions
D	Dues
S	Supplies
S	Subscriptions
C	Computer
I	Insurance
M	Miscellaneous
B	Subscriptions
P	Computer
N	Insurance
X	Miscellaneous

These duplicate codes...

...are corrected by "forcing" the codes to fit.

FIGURE 19.5
Problems in using a one-letter classification code occur when categories share the same letter.

Concealing Information

Codes may be used to conceal or disguise information we do not wish others to know. There are many reasons why a business may want to do this. For example, a corporation may not want information in a personnel file to be accessed by data-entry workers. A store may want its salespeople to know the wholesale price to show them how low a price they can negotiate, but they may encode it on price tickets to prevent customers from finding that out. A restaurant may want to capture information about the service

Code	Name of Software Package	Type
100	Quatro	Spreadsheet
101	Lotus	
102	Excel	
.	.	
200	Access	Database
201	Paradox	
202	dBASE	
.	.	
300	Word for Windows	Word Processing
301	Wordperfect	
.	.	
400	Charisma	Presentation
401	Freelance	
402	Powerpoint	

FIGURE 19.6
Using a block sequence code to group similar software packages.

FIGURE 19.7
Encoding markdown prices
with a cipher code is a way of
concealing price information
from customers.

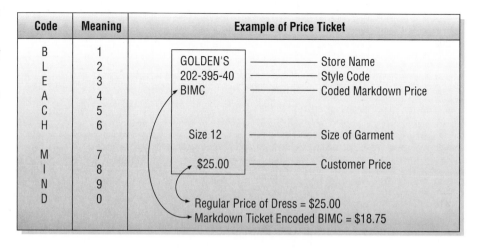

Code	Meaning	Example of Price Ticket
B	1	
L	2	GOLDEN'S ——— Store Name
E	3	202-395-40 ——— Style Code
A	4	BIMC ——— Coded Markdown Price
C	5	
H	6	
		Size 12 ——— Size of Garment
M	7	
I	8	$25.00 ——— Customer Price
N	9	
D	0	

Regular Price of Dress = $25.00
Markdown Ticket Encoded BIMC = $18.75

without letting the customer know the name of the server. The following is an example of concealing information through codes.

CIPHER CODES. Perhaps the simplest coding method is the direct substitution of one letter for another, one number for another, or one letter for a number. A popular type of puzzle called a cryptogram is an example of letter substitution. Figure 19.7 is an example of a cipher code taken from a Buffalo, New York, department store that coded all markdown prices with the words BLEACH MIND. No one really remembered why whose words were chosen, but all the employees knew them by heart, and so the cipher code was successful. Notice in this figure that an item with a retail price of $25.00 would have a markdown price of BIMC, or $18.75 when decoded letter by letter.

Revealing Information

Sometimes it is desirable to reveal information through a code. In a clothing store, information about the department, product, color, and size is printed along with the price on the ticket for each item. This helps the salespeople and stockpeople locate the place for the merchandise.

Another reason for revealing information through codes is to make the data entry more meaningful. A familiar part number, name, or description supports more accurate data entry. The examples of codes in the following section explain how these concepts can be realized.

SIGNIFICANT-DIGIT SUBSET CODES. When it is possible to describe a product via its membership in many subgroups, we can use a significant-digit subset code to help describe it. The clothing-store price ticket example in Figure 19.8 is an example of an effective significant-digit code.

To the casual observer or customer, the item description appears to be one long number. To one of the salespeople, however, the number is made up of a few smaller numbers, each having a meaning of its own. The first three digits represent the department, the next three the product, the next three the color, and the last three the size.

Significant-digit subset codes may consist of information that actually describes the product (for example, the number 10 means size 10) or numbers that are arbitrarily assigned (for instance, 202 is assigned to mean the maternity department). In this case, the advantage of using a significant-digit subset code is the ability to locate items that belong to a certain group

Code	Merchandise Described	Explanation of Code
2023954010	Red maternity dress, style 395, size 10	202 - 395 - 40 - 10 ↑ Department (Maternity) ↑ Product (Dress Style 395) ↑ Color (Red) ↑ Size (Size 10)
4142191912	Beige winter coat, style 219, size 12	414 - 219 - 19 - 12 ↑ Department (Winter Coats) ↑ Product (Coat Style 219) ↑ Color (Beige) ↑ Size (Size 12)

FIGURE 19.8
Using a significant-digit sub-set code to help employees locate items belonging to a particular department.

or class. For example, if the store's manager decided to mark down all winter merchandise for an upcoming sale, salespeople could locate all items belonging to departments 310 through 449.

MNEMONIC CODES. A mnemonic (pronounced nî-môn´-ĭk) is a memory aid. Any code that helps the data-entry person remember how to enter the data or the end user remember how to use the information can be considered a mnemonic. Using a combination of letters and symbols affords a strikingly clear way to code a product so that the code is easily seen and understood.

The city hospital codes used by the Buffalo regional blood center are mnemonic, as shown in Figure 19.9. The simple codes were invented precisely because the blood-bank administrators and systems analysts wanted to ensure that hospital codes were easy to memorize and recall. Mnemonic codes for the hospitals helped lessen the possibility of blood being shipped to the wrong hospital.

Requesting Appropriate Action

Codes are often necessary for instructing either the computer or the decision maker about what action to take. Such codes are generally referred to as "function codes" and they typically take the form of either sequence or mnemonic codes.

FUNCTION CODES. The functions that the analyst or programmer desires the computer to perform with data are captured in function codes. Spelling out precisely what activities are to be accomplished is replaced by the use of a short numerical or alphanumeric code.

Figure 19.10 shows examples of a function code for updating inventory. Data required for input vary depending on what function is needed. For

FIGURE 19.9
Mnemonic codes function as
memory aids by using a
meaningful combination of
letters and numbers.

Code	City Hospitals
BGH	Buffalo General Hospital
ROS	Roswell Park Memorial Institute
KEN	Kenmore Mercy
DEA	Deaconess Hospital
SIS	Sisters of Charity
STF	Saint Francis Hospital
STJ	Saint Joseph's Hospital
OLV	Our Lady of Victory Hospital

example, appending or updating a record would require only the record key and function code, whereas adding a new record would require all data elements to be input, including the function code.

General Guidelines for Coding

In the previous section, we examined the purposes for using different types of codes to enter and store data. Next, we examine a few heuristics for establishing a coding system. These rules are highlighted in Figure 19.11.

BE CONCISE. Codes should be concise. Overly long codes mean more keystrokes and consequently more errors. Long codes also mean that storing the information in a database will require more memory.

Short codes are easier to remember and easier to enter. If codes must be long, they should be broken up into subcodes. For example, 5678923453127 could be broken up with hyphens as follows: 5678-923-453-127. This is a much more manageable approach and takes advantage of the way people are known to process information in short chunks.

KEEP THE CODES STABLE. Stability means that the identification code for a customer should not change each time new data are received. Earlier, we presented an alphabetic derivation code for a magazine subscription list. The expiration date was not part of the subscriber identification code because this was likely to change.

Don't change the code abbreviations in a mnemonic system. Once you have chosen the code abbreviations, do not try to revise them since this makes it extremely difficult for data-entry personnel to adapt.

FIGURE 19.10
Function codes compactly
capture functions that the
computer must perform.

Code	Function
1	Delivered
2	Sold
3	Spoiled
4	Lost or Stolen
5	Returned
6	Transferred Out
7	Transferred In
8	Journal Entry (Add)
9	Journal Entry (Subtract)

In Establishing a Coding System the Analyst Should:
• Keep codes concise
• Keep codes stable
• Make codes that are unique
• Allow codes to be sortable
• Avoid confusing codes
• Keep codes uniform
• Allow for modification of codes
• Make codes meaningful

FIGURE 19.11
There are eight general guidelines for establishing a coding
system.

ASSURE THAT CODES ARE UNIQUE. In order for codes to work, they must be unique. Make a note of all codes used in the system in order to assure that you are not assigning the same code number or name to the same items. Code numbers and names are an essential part of the entries in data dictionaries, as discussed in Chapter 9.

ALLOW CODES TO BE SORTABLE. If you are going to manipulate the data usefully, the codes must be sortable. For example, if you decided to code the data as MMMDDYY—where the first three symbols were the month as a three-letter abbreviation, the second two were the date as a number, and the last two digits were the year—and then tried to sort by date in ascending order, you would get the results shown in Figure 19.12. Both years and months would be out of order. Make sure that you can do what you intend to do with the codes you create. Numerical codes are much easier to sort than alphanumerics; therefore, consider converting to numerics wherever practical.

Incorrect Sorting Using Alphanumeric Code MMMDDYY	Correct Sorting Using Numeric Code YYMMDD
Apr0487	850501
Aug2887	851226
Dec2587	860108
Dec2685	860206
Feb0686	860315
Feb2387	860611
Jan0886	860716
Jul0487	860915
Jul1686	861018
Jun0487	861110
Jun1186	870223
Jun1287	870404
Mar1586	870517
May0185	870604
May1787	870612
Nov1086	870704
Oct1886	870828
Oct2487	871024
Oct3187	871031
Sep1586	871225

FIGURE 19.12
Plan ahead in order to be able
to do something useful with
data that have been entered.
In this example the person
creating the codes did not
realize the data would have to
be sorted.

It's a Wilderness in Here

"I can't stand this. I've been looking for this (he swings a coonskin cap by its tail above his head) for the last forty-five minutes," complains Davey, one of the new warehouse workers for Crockett's, a large catalog-sales firm. "The catalog slip calls it a Coo m5-9w/tl. Good thing you told me Coo stands for coonskin. Then, of course, I thought about caps and looked over here. I found it here in this bin labeled BOYS/CAP. Wouldn't it be easier if the catalog matched the bins? To me, this invoice says, 'Cookware, metallic, 5–9-piece set with Teflon.' I've been stranded in the cookware sets the whole time."

Daniel, Davey's coworker, barely listens to him as he hurriedly pulls items out of bins to fill another order. "You get used to it. They've got to have it this way so the computers can understand the bill later. Mostly, I look at the catalog page number on the invoice, then I look it up in the book and sort of translate it to back here . . . unless I remember it from finding it before," Daniel explains.

Davey persists saying, "But computers are smart. And we have to fill so many orders. We should tell the people up in billing the names we've got on our bins."

Daniel replies cynically, "Oh, sure. They're dying to know what we think." Then he continues in a quieter tone, "You know, we used to have it like that. But when they got all the new computers, and went to 24-hour phone orders it all changed. Said the operators had to know more about what they were selling. So they changed their codes to be more like a story."

Davey, surprised at Daniel's revelation, asks, "What's the story for the one I was working on?"

Inspecting the code on the cap's invoice, Daniel replies, "The one you were working on was 'Coo m5-9w/tl.' After looking it up real fast on her computer the operator can tell the customer, 'It's a coonskin cap (Coo) for boys (m for male) ages 5–9 with a real tail (w/tl).' We can't see the forest for the trees because of their codes, but you know Crockett's—they've got to make the sale."

How important is it that the warehouse bins and invoices are encoded inconsistently? What are some of the problems created when a code appears to be mnemonic but employees are never given an appropriate "key" to decoding them? What changes would you make to invoice/warehouse coding for Crockett's?

AVOID CONFUSING CODES. Try to avoid using coding characters that look or sound alike. Characters O (the letter oh) and 0 (the number zero) and easily confused, as are the letter I and the number 1, and the letter Z and the number 2. Therefore, codes such as B1C and 280Z are unsatisfactory.

One example of a potentially confusing code is the Canadian Postal Code, as shown in Figure 19.13. The code format is X9X 9X9, where X stands for a letter and 9 stands for a number. One advantage to using letters in the code is to allow more data in a six-digit code (there are twenty-six letters, but only ten numbers). Since the code is used on a regular basis by Canadians, the code makes perfectly good sense to them. To foreigners sending mail to Canada, however, it may be difficult to tell if the second-to-the-last symbol is a Z or a 2.

KEEP THE CODES UNIFORM. Codes need to follow readily perceived forms most of the time. Codes used together, such as BUF-234 and KU-3456, are poor because the first contains three letters and three numbers, while the second has only two letters followed by four numbers.

When you are required to add dates, try to avoid using the codes MMD-DYY in one application, YYDDMM in a second and MMDD19YY in a third. It is important to keep codes uniform among as well as within programs.

In the past, uniformity meant that all codes be kept the same length. With the introduction of on-line systems, the length is not as important as it once was. In a batch system, cards were keypunched and data generally had to be kept in distinct columns on the card. If most codes were four characters in length, a three-character code would require a blank. With on-line systems,

Code Format for Canadian Postal Code X9X 9X9			
Handwritten Code	**Actual Code**	**City, Providence**	**Problem**
L8S 4M4	L8S 4M4	Hamilton, Ontario	S looks like a 5
T3A Z 5	T3A 2E5	Calgary, Alberta	2 looks like a Z 5 looks like an S
LOS IJO	LOS 1J0	Niagara-on-the-Lake, Ontario	Zero and Oh look alike S looks like a 5 1 looks like an I

FIGURE 19.13
Combining lookalike characters in codes can result in errors.

the Enter key is hit after data entry is verified by the operator as correct, so it doesn't make much difference if the code is three or four characters long.

ALLOW FOR MODIFICATION. Adaptability is a key feature of a good code. The analyst must keep in mind that the system will evolve over time, and the coding system should be able to encompass change. The number of customers should grow, customers will change names, and suppliers will modify the way they number their products. The analyst needs to be able to forecast the predictable and anticipate a wide range of future needs when designing codes.

MAKE CODES MEANINGFUL. Unless the analyst wants to hide information intentionally, codes should be meaningful. Effective codes not only contain information, they also make sense to people using them. Meaningful codes are easier to understand, work with, and recall. The job of data entry becomes more interesting when working with meaningful codes instead of just entering a series of meaningless numbers.

EFFECTIVE AND EFFICIENT DATA CAPTURE

In order to assure the quality of data entered into the system, it is important to capture data effectively. Data capture has received increasingly more attention as the point in information processing at which excellent productivity gains can be made. Great progress in improving data capture has been made in the past two decades, as we have moved from a multiple-step, slow, and error-prone system such as keypunching to sophisticated, optical character recognition, bar codes, and point-of-sale terminals.

Deciding What to Capture

The decision of what to capture precedes the user interacting with the system. Indeed it is vital in making the eventual interface worthwhile, for the adage "Garbage in, garbage out" is still true.

Decisions about what data to capture for system input are made among systems analysts and systems users. Much of what will be captured is specific to the particular business. Capturing data, inputting it, storing it, and retrieving it are all costly endeavors, mostly due to the labor costs involved. All that considered, what to capture becomes an important decision.

Catching a Summer Code

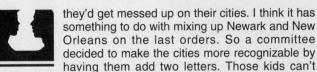

Vickie takes her fingers off her terminal's keyboard and bends over her workstation to verify the letters on the invoices stacked in front of her. "What on earth?" Vickie says aloud as she further scrutinizes the letters that encode cities where orders are to be shipped.

Shelly Overseer, her supervisor, who usually sits a couple of workstations away, is passing by and sees Vickie's consternation. "What's the matter? Did the salesman forget to write in the city code again?"

Vickie swings around in her chair to face Shelly. "No, there are codes here. But they're weird. We usually use a three-letter code, right? Like CIN for Cincinnati, SEA for Seattle, MIN for Minneapolis, BUF for Buffalo. But they're all *five*-letter codes here."

"Look," Vickie says, lifting the invoice to show Shelly. "CINNC, SEATT, MINNE. It'll take me all day to enter these. Not to mention the storage space they'll take. No kidding, it's really slowing me down. Maybe there's a mistake. Can't I just use the standard?"

Shelly backs away from Vickie's terminal as if the problem was contagious. Excusing herself apologetically, Shelly says, "It's the part-timers. They are learning sales now, and management was worried that

they'd get messed up on their cities. I think it has something to do with mixing up Newark and New Orleans on the last orders. So a committee decided to make the cities more recognizable by having them add two letters. Those kids can't learn everything we know overnight, even though they try. But it's just until August 19, until the part-timers go back to school."

As Vickie glumly turns back to her keyboard, Shelly puts her hand sympathetically on Vickie's shoulder and says, "I know it's a strain and it's making you feel miserable, but don't worry. You'll get over it. It's just a summer code."

What general guidelines of coding has management overlooked in their decision to use a summer code for cities? What is the effect on full-time data-entry personnel of changing codes for the ease of temporary help? What future impact could the temporary change in codes have on sorting and retrieving data entered during the summer period? What changes can you suggest so that the part-timers don't get mixed up on codes in the short term? How can this be accomplished without marring the productivity of data-entry personnel?

There are two types of data to enter: data that *change* or vary with every transaction, and data that concisely *differentiate* the particular item being processed from all other items.

An example of changeable data is the quantity of supplies purchased each time an advertising firm places an order with the office supply wholesaler. Since quantities change depending on the number of employees at the advertising firm and how many accounts they are servicing, quantity data must be entered each time an order is placed.

An example of differentiation data would be inclusion on a patient record of the patient's social security number and the first three letters of his or her last name. In this way, the patient is uniquely differentiated from other patients in the same system.

Letting the Computer Do the Rest

When considering what data to capture for each transaction and what data to leave to the system to enter, it is important to take advantage of what computers do best. In the preceding example of the advertising agency ordering office supplies, it is not necessary for the operator entering the stationery order to reenter each item description each time an order is received. The computer can store and access this data easily.

Computers can automatically handle repetitive tasks, such as recording the time of the transaction, calculating new values from input, and storing and retrieving data on demand. By deploying the best features of computers, efficient data capture design avoids needless data entry. This, in turn, alleviates much human error and boredom.

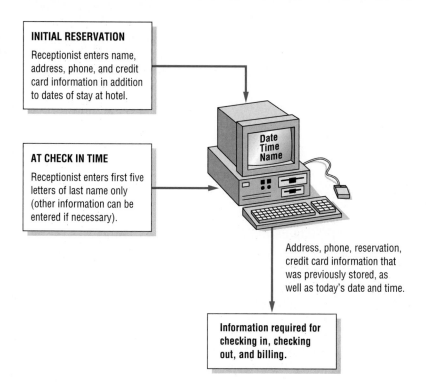

FIGURE 19.14
Automatically recording date
and time in a hotel reservation system eliminates unnecessary data entry.

INITIAL RESERVATION
Receptionist enters name, address, phone, and credit card information in addition to dates of stay at hotel.

AT CHECK IN TIME
Receptionist enters first five letters of last name only (other information can be entered if necessary).

Date
Time
Name

Address, phone, reservation, credit card information that was previously stored, as well as today's date and time.

Information required for checking in, checking out, and billing.

Software can be written to indicate automatically the date of data entry so that the person inputting data does not have to bother with this for every transaction processed. Alternatively, the computer program can be written to ask the user to enter today's date. Once entered, the system proceeds to use that date on all transactions processed in that data-entry session.

Part of a VDT screen for hotel reservations and guest check-ins is shown in Figure 19.14. Notice that when a reservation is made initially, the guest's name and credit-card number are entered. When the guest checks in, the desk clerk calls up the record without having to entirely reenter name or number. The system also automatically records date and time, saving further data entry.

As you can see, it is unnecessary to enter data for each transaction that can be easily retrieved by the computer from storage. A prime example is that of the on-line computer library center used by over 4,000 libraries in the United States. Using thirteen mainframes hooked up to numerous mini- and microcomputers, OCLC was built upon the idea that each item bought by a library should only have to be cataloged once for all time. Once an item is entered, cataloging information goes into the huge OCLC database and is shared with participating libraries. In this case, implementation of the simple concept of entering data only once has saved enormous data-entry time.

The calculating power of the computer should also be taken into account when deciding what *not* to reenter. Computers are adept at long calculations, using data already entered.

For example, the person doing data entry may enter the flight numbers and account number of an air trip taken by a customer belonging to a frequent-flight incentive program. The computer then calculates the number of miles accrued for each flight, adds it to the miles already in the customer's account, and updates the total miles accrued to the account. The computer may also flag an account that, by virtue of the large number of miles flown, is now eligible for a prize. Although all of this information may print out on the customer's updated account sheet, the only new data entered were flight numbers of flights flown.

Although users will have suggestions about what data are unnecessary, these decisions should not be made at the time of entry. Rather, the decision is best made by the systems analyst in conjunction with users at an earlier stage in the process. Through your prior analyses, you will possess the larger picture of what is being input to the system and for what purpose. When analyses are complete, unnecessary input becomes apparent, as do redundancies.

Avoiding Bottlenecks and Extra Steps

A bottleneck in data entry is an apt allusion to the physical appearance of a bottle. Data are poured rapidly into the wide mouth of the system only to be slowed in its "neck" because of an artificially created instance of insufficient processing for the volume or detail of the data being entered. One way a bottleneck can be avoided is by ensuring that there is enough capacity to handle the data that are being entered.

Ways to avoid extra steps are determined not only at the time of analysis, but also when users begin to interact with the system. The fewer steps involved in inputting data, the fewer chances there are for the introduction of errors. So beyond the obvious consideration of saved labor, avoiding extra steps is also a way to preserve quality of data. Once again, use of an on-line, real-time system that captures customer data without necessitating filling out a form is an excellent example of saving steps in data entry.

Starting with a Good Form

Effective data capture is achievable only if prior thought is given to what the source document should contain. The data-entry operator inputs data from the source document (usually some kind of form); this document is the source of a large amount of all system data. On-line systems (or special data-entry methods such as bar codes) may circumvent the need for a source document, but often some kind of paper form such as a receipt is created anyway.

Effective forms do not require reentry of information that the computer has already stored or of data such as time or date of entry, which the computer can determine automatically. Chapter 15 discusses in detail how a form or source document should be designed to maximize its usefulness for capturing data and to minimize the time users need to spend entering data from it.

Choosing a Data-Entry Method

Keypunching used to be the workhorse of the data-processing world, but now it has been supplanted by more efficient and more accurate methods. Keypunching was cumbersome, and the data on the cards had to be typed twice—once for the actual punching and a second time for verification. Besides, if cards were submitted out of order, the computer job or data wouldn't make sense.

Several more efficient data-entry methods are available, and choosing among them is shaped by many factors including the need for speed, accu-

To Enter or Not to Enter: That Is the Question

"I've just taken on the presidency of Elsinore Industries," says Rose N. Krantz. "We're actually part of a small cottage industry that manufactures toy villages for children seven years and up. Our tiny hamlets consist of various kits that will build what children want from interlocking plastic cubes; essentials like city hall, the police station, the gas station, a hot dog stand, and so on. Each kit has a unique part number from 200 to 800 (not every number is used, however). The wholesale price varies from $54.95 for the city hall to $1.79 for a hot dog stand.

"But I've been melancholy over what I've found out since signing on at Elsinore. 'Something is rotten' here, to quote a famous playwright. In fact, the invoicing system was so out of control that I've been working around the clock with our bookkeeper, Gilda Stern," Krantz soliloquizes.

"I would like you to help straighten things out," Rose continues. "We ship to twelve distribution warehouses around the country. Each invoice we write out includes the warehouse number (1–12), its street address, and the zip code. We also put on each invoice the date we fill the order, code numbers for the hamlet kits they order, a description of each kit, the price per item, and the quantity of each kit ordered. Of course, we also include the subtotals of kit charges, shipping charges, and the total that the warehouse owes us. No sales tax is added, since they resell what we send them to toy stores in all fifty states. I want you to help us design a computerized data-entry system that will be part of the invoicing system for Elsinore Industries."

For your design of a data-entry system for Elsinore, take into consideration all of the objectives for data entry discussed throughout this chapter. How can you make the data-entry system efficient? Specify what data can be stored and retrieved, and what data must be entered anew for each invoice. How can unnecessary work be avoided? How can data accuracy be assured?

---

racy, and operator training; cost of the data-entry method (whether it is materials- or labor-intensive); and the methods currently in use in the organization.

KEY TO STORAGE. Key to storage—including key-to-tape, key-to-disk, and key-to-floppy diskette—provides improvements over keypunching for data entry. All three methods require a keyboard for entering data, hence the similarities in their names.

Key-to-tape is the oldest of the three methods and is a way to enter great amounts of data efficiently. From a keyboard, an operator enters data onto a magnetic tape. This circumvents the problem of mixed up or lost paper cards encountered in the older data-entry method of keypunching. Additionally, key-to-tape recorder systems can be programmed to verify entries, search for previously stored material, and gather productivity data. Tapes can be transported to the processing center or transmitted on line.

Similar to key-to-tape recorder data entry is key-to-disk data entry, which uses disks rather than tapes as the storage medium. Additionally, operators use a VDT to access instructions about their work. Key-to-disk also allows for transport of finished disks to processing centers, or systems can be made to transmit in an on-line mode.

Key-to-floppy diskettes is growing in popularity and use. Ease of updating and changing files on diskettes, along with their transportability, make them an excellent choice for smaller jobs, while limited storage makes them impractical for larger ones. Floppy diskettes, which come in 3 1/2 inch, 5 1/4-inch and 8-inch sizes, are reusable, unlike the earliest paper punch cards.

CHAPTER 19:
DESIGNING ACCURATE
DATA-ENTRY PROCEDURES

FIGURE 19.15
Optical character recognition
(OCR) of special-character
source documents facilitates
data entry.

This type of data entry requires a microcomputer and software to permit editing and control functions; a VDT, which provides operator instructions; disk drives; and system-compatible diskettes. Data entry can be made on a stand-alone basis, without using the mainframe's CPU, or can go on line if so equipped in order to speed the process.

OPTICAL CHARACTER RECOGNITION. Optical character recognition (OCR) is a way to read input from a source document with an optical scanner rather than off of the magnetic media we have been discussing so far. Using OCR devices can speed data input from 50 to 75 percent over the keying methods already discussed.

What is needed is a source document that can be optically scanned when it is filled out, either through special block printing or by hand, as shown in Figure 19.15. How the source document is filled in depends on the requirements of the particular hardware and software.

The increased speed of OCR comes through not having to encode or key in data from source documents. It eliminates many of the time-consuming and error-fraught steps of other input devices. In doing so, OCR demands few employee skills and commensurately less training. This results in fewer errors and less time spent by employees in redundant efforts, and decentralizes responsibility for quality data directly to the unit that is generating it. Optical character recognition, which has become available to all, has one additional, highly practical use: the transformation of faxes into documents that can be edited.

OTHER METHODS OF DATA ENTRY. Other methods of data entry are also becoming more widely employed. Most of these methods reduce labor costs by requiring few operator skills or little training, move data entry closer to the source of data, and eliminate the need for a source document. In doing so, they have become fast and highly reliable data-entry methods. The data-entry methods discussed in the following sections include magnetic ink character recognition, mark-sense forms, punch-out forms, bar codes, and data strips.

Magnetic ink character recognition (MICR). Magnetic ink characters are found on the bottom of bank checks and some credit-card bills. This method is akin to OCR in that special characters are read, but its use is limited. Data entry through magnetic ink character recognition (MICR) is done through a machine that reads and interprets a single line of material encoded with ink made up of magnetic particles.

DIRECTIONS FOR MARKING

Use #2 or #2½ pencil only DO NOT use ink or ballpoint
Make heavy black marks that fill the circle completely
erase cleanly any answer you wish to change–make no stray marks

Examples of PROPER marks   Examples of IMPROPER marks

1. What levels of people do you <u>primarily</u> serve in your work?
   managers
   supervisors; foremen
   other salaried
   hourly
   volunteers

2. Total size of the organization you serve:
   less than 1,000   15,000-25,000
   1,000-5,000   more than 25,000
   5,000-15,000

5. A most Significant Part
4. A Major Part
3. A Substantial Part
2. A Smaller Part
1. A Minor Part
0. Does Not Apply

3. What training and development techniques
   do you use? (please mark each technique)

Technique	0	1	2	3	4	5
lecture with or without media	0	1	2	3	4	**5**
films	0	**1**	2	3	4	5
videotape closed-circuit TV	0	1	2	3	**4**	5
discussions (cases, issues, etc.)	0	1	2	3	4	**5**
role playing	0	1	2	**3**	4	5
behavior modeling	**0**	1	2	3	4	5
simulation; advanced gaming	0	1	**2**	3	4	5
on-the-job training	0	1	2	**3**	4	5
job rotation	0	**1**	2	3	4	5
internships; assistantships	**0**	1	2	3	4	5
organization development techniques	0	1	**2**	3	4	5
Other	0	1	2	3	4	5

Some advantages of using MICR are (1) it is reliable, high-speed, not susceptible to accepting stray marks since they are not encoded magnetically; (2) if it is required on all withdrawal checks, it serves as a security measure against bad checks; and (3) data-entry personnel can see the numbers making up the code if it is necessary to verify it.

Mark-sense forms. Mark-sense forms allow data entry through use of a scanner to sense where marks have been made by lead pencil on special forms. A common usage is for scoring answer sheets for survey questionnaires, as shown in Figure 19.16. Little training of entry personnel is necessary, and a high volume of forms can be processed quickly.

Drawbacks of mark-sense forms include the fact that, while the readers can determine whether a mark has been made, they cannot interpret the mark in the way that optical character readers do. Stray marks on forms can thus be entered as incorrect data. Additionally, choices are limited to the answers provided on the mark-sense form; forms have difficulty in capturing alphanumeric data because of the space required for a complete set of letters and numbers; and it is easy for those filling out mark-sense forms to get confused and put a mark in an incorrect position.

Punch-out forms. Punch-out forms are a quick and convenient way of capturing and entering limited data. Figure 19.17 shows an example of a punch-out form used for balloting purposes, where the voter uses a stylus to make a hole or deep indentation by the name of their chosen candidate. Punch-out forms are used for balloting purposes when votes must be tallied quickly.

Bar codes. Bar codes typically appear on product labels, but also appear on patient identification bracelets in hospitals and in almost any context in which a person or object needs to be checked into and out of any kind of inventory system. Bar codes can be thought of as "metacodes," or codes encoding codes, since they appear as a series of narrow and wide bands on a label which encodes numbers or letters. These symbols in turn have access to product data stored in computer memory. A beam of light from a scanner or lightpen is drawn across the bands on the label either to confirm or record data about the product being scanned.

A bar-coded label such as the one shown in Figure 19.18 includes coding for a particular grocery product: the manufacturer identification number, the product identification number, a code to verify the scan's accuracy, and codes to mark the beginning and end of the scan.

Bar coding affords an extraordinarily high degree of accuracy for data entry. It saves labor costs for retailers in that each item does not have to be individually price-marked. Additionally, bar coding allows automatic capturing of data that can be used for reordering, more accurate inventory tracking, and forecasting future needs. Sale prices or other changes in the meaning of the bar codes are entered into the central processor, saving the trouble of marking down numerous items.

New input devices are constantly being developed. Of course it has been possible to transfer photographic images for some time now using

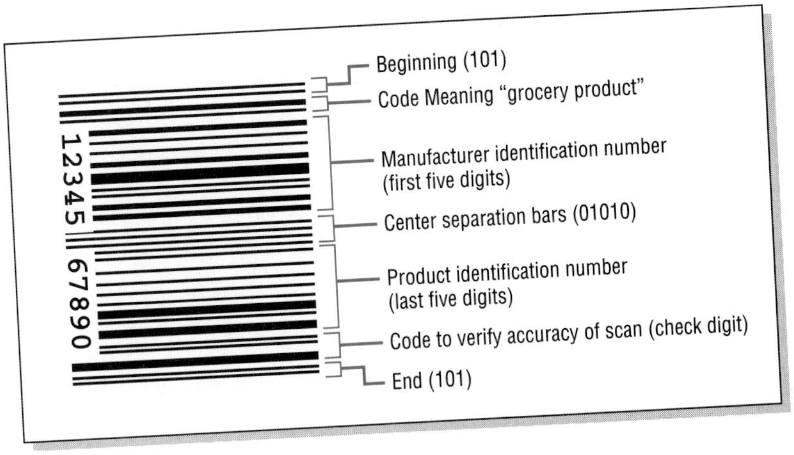
12345 67890
Beginning (101)
Code Meaning "grocery product"
Manufacturer identification number
(first five digits)
Center separation bars (01010)
Product identification number
(last five digits)
Code to verify accuracy of scan (check digit)
End (101)

FIGURE 19.18
Bar coding, as shown in this label for a grocery product, affords highly accurate data entry. Used with the permission of the Uniform Code Council, Dayton, Ohio.

systems like the Kodak Photo CD process, but a digital camera such as Apple computer's QuickTake would cut out the middle step of digitizing your photographs.

Using Intelligent Terminals. Intelligent terminals can be considered a step above dumb terminals and a step below intelligent workstations and portable microcomputers in their capabilities. In many instances, intelligent terminals can do away with the need for a source document.

The biggest advantage of using intelligent terminals is that, through use of a microprocessor, they are able to relieve the CPU of many of the burdens of editing, controlling, transforming, and storing data, which the dumb terminals require. Dumb terminals rely on the CPU for all data manipulation including editing, updating, and so on.

The configuration for intelligent terminals is a microprocessor, VDT screen, and a keyboard. The intelligent terminal has access to the CPU through a communication link and can be either on line or deferred on line. In an on-line intelligent terminal, all of the steps in entry, processing, verifying, and output are done immediately with the customer present. The closer data entry is to the source of the data, the more accurate it is likely to be. A well-known example of an on-line intelligent terminal is the airline ticketing system.

Deferred on line intelligent terminals allow data to be entered and verified immediately, but processing is batched and done later (which is less expensive). Electronic cash registers combine these attributes, with both input and output capabilities as point-of-sale terminals.

ASSURING DATA QUALITY THROUGH INPUT VALIDATION

So far, we have discussed assuring the effective capturing of data onto source documents and its efficient entry into the system through various input devices. Although these are necessary conditions for assuring quality data, they alone are not sufficient.

Errors cannot be ruled out entirely, and the critical importance of catching errors during input, *prior* to processing and storage, cannot be overemphasized. The web of problems created by incorrect input can be a nightmare, not the least of which is that many problems take a long time to surface.

This Type of Validation:	Can Prevent These Problems
Validating Input Transactions	Submitting the wrong data Data submitted by an unauthorized person Asking the system to perform an unacceptable function
Validating Input Data	Missing data Incorrect field length Data has unacceptable composition Data are out of range Data are invalid Data does not match with stored data

You cannot imagine everything that will go awry with input, but you must cover the kinds of errors that give rise to the largest percentage of problems. A summary of potential problems that must be considered when validating input are given in Figure 19.19.

Validating Input Transactions

Validating input transactions is largely done through software, which is the programmer's responsibility, but it is important that the systems analyst know what common problems might invalidate a transaction. Businesses committed to quality will include validity checks as part of their routine software.

Three main problems can occur with input transactions: submitting the wrong data to the system, submitting of data by an unauthorized person, or asking the system to perform an unacceptable function.

SUBMITTING THE WRONG DATA. An example of submitting the wrong data to the system would be attempting to input a patient's social security number into a hospital's payroll system. This error is usually an accidental one; however, it should be flagged before data are processed.

SUBMITTING OF DATA BY AN UNAUTHORIZED PERSON. The system should also be able to discover if otherwise correct data are submitted by an unauthorized person. For instance, only the supervising pharmacist should be able to enter inventory totals for controlled substances in the pharmacy. Invalidation of transactions submitted by an unauthorized individual apply to privacy and security concerns surrounding payroll systems and employee evaluation records that determine pay levels, promotions, or discipline; files containing trade secrets; and files holding classified information such as national defense data.

ASKING THE SYSTEM TO PERFORM AN UNACCEPTABLE FUNCTION. The third error that invalidates input transactions is asking the system to perform an unacceptable function. For instance, it would be logical for a human resources manager to update the existing record of a current employee; however, it would be invalid to ask the system to create a new file rather than merely to update an existing record.

Validating Input Data

It is essential that the input data itself, along with the transactions requested, be valid. Several tests can be incorporated into software to assure this. We will consider seven possible ways to validate input.

TEST FOR MISSING DATA. The first kind of validity test examines data to see if there are any missing items. For some situations, *all* data items must be present. For example, a social security file for paying out retirement or disability benefits would be invalid if it did not include the payee's social security number.

Additionally, the record should include the key data that distinguishes one record from all others and the function code telling the computer what to do with the data. The systems analyst needs to interact with users to determine what data items are essential and to find out whether exceptional cases ever occur that would allow data to be considered valid even if some data items were missing.

TEST FOR CORRECT FIELD LENGTH. A second kind of validity test checks input to assure that it is of the correct length for the field. For example, if the Omaha, Nebraska, weather station reports into the national weather service computer, but mistakenly provides a two-letter city code (OM) instead of the national three-letter city code (OMA), the input data might be deemed invalid and hence would not be processed.

TEST FOR CLASS OR COMPOSITION. This type of validity test checks to see that data fields that are supposed to be exclusively composed of numbers do not include letters, and vice versa. For example, a credit-card account number for American Express should not include any letters. Using a composition test, the program should not accept an American Express account number that includes both letters and numbers.

TEST FOR RANGE OR REASONABLENESS. These validity tests are really a common-sense measure of input that answers the question of whether data fall within an acceptable range or whether they are reasonable within predetermined parameters. For instance, if a user was trying to verify a proposed shipment date, the range test would not permit a shipping date on the thirty-second day of October, nor would it accept shipment in the thirteenth month, the respective ranges being 1 to 31 days and 1 to 12 months.

A reasonableness test ascertains whether the item makes sense for the transaction. For example, entering an age of 120 years would not be reasonable when adding a new employee to the payroll.

TEST FOR INVALID VALUES. Checking input for invalid values works if there are only a few valid values. This test is nonfeasible for situations in which values are not restricted and predictable. This kind of test is useful for checking responses where data are divided into a limited number of classes. For example, a brokerage firm divides accounts into three classes only: class 1 = active account; class 2 = inactive account; class 3 = closed account. If data are assigned to any other class through an error, the values are invalid.

TEST FOR COMPARISON WITH STORED DATA. The next test for validity of input data that we will consider is comparing it with data that the computer

Do You Validate Parking?

"What are we going to do, Mercedes?" Edsel asks wearily. Together Mercedes and Edsel are reviewing the latest billing printout for their firm, Denton & Denton Parking Garages. They have been purchasing batch billing services from a small, local computer services company since they acquired three parking garages in a medium-sized metropolitan area. Denton & Denton Parking Garages rent daily, monthly, and yearly parking places to corporations and individuals.

Mercedes replies, "I'm not sure what our next move is. But the billing is all wrong. Maybe we should try to talk to the computer people."

"They said they could figure out how to compute these charges from looking at what the old owners did by hand before, and said they didn't want to run the old and new systems in parallel," Edsel remarks, shaking his head. "But this isn't right. At least I can't figure it out. Maybe you can."

Mercedes accepts the notion of chasing the suspect output and starts looking at the report in detail. "Well, for one thing, they don't realize we get cars from all over in here. Wherever we've got a car with plates that aren't in-state it seems as if the computer stops figuring. Look, our plates start with a number and then a letter, right? Well this one from New York begins with three letters. The computer can't handle it," she says.

Edsel catches on and starts to think about the business as he looks at the printout. "Yeah, and look here. This person doesn't have a yearly account number, just a monthly one, so no bill came out," he says. "We've got monthlies, too, and the computer doesn't know it?"

"And look at this. It still made daily charges for the three days in November when we told them right out there weren't any vacancies for daily customers. It isn't reasonable," Mercedes asserts.

Edsel continues paging through the printout but Mercedes stops him, saying, "But don't look any further. I'm calling the computer people so we can get this straightened out."

How would you characterize the problems being encountered with the current garage billing system? What are some tests for validity of data that could be included in the software for a revised billing system for the parking garages? What could the programmer/analysts for the computer services company have done differently, so that the customer was not faced with correcting the poor-quality output?

---

has already stored. For example, a newly entered part number can be compared with the complete parts inventory in order to assure that the number exists and is being entered correctly.

SETTING UP SELF-VALIDATING CODES. Another method for assuring the accuracy of data, particularly identification numbers, is to use a check digit in the code itself. This procedure involves beginning with an original numerical code, performing some mathematics to arrive at a derived check digit, and then adding the check digit to the original code. The mathematical process involves multiplying each of the digits in the original code by some predetermined weights, summing these results, and then dividing this sum by a modulus number. The modulus number is needed because the sum usually is a large number, and we need to reduce the result to a single digit. Finally, the remainder is subtracted from the modulus number, giving us the check digit.

Figure 19.20 shows how a five-digit part number for a radiator hose (54823) is converted to a six-digit number containing a check digit. In this example, the weights chosen were the "1-3-1" system; in other words, the weights alternate between 1 and 3. After the digits 5, 4, 8, 2, and 3 were multiplied by 1, 3, 1, 3 and 1, they became 5, 12, 8, 6, and 3. These new digits sum to 34. Next, 34 is divided by the chosen modulus number, 10, with the result of 3 and a remainder of 4. The remainder, 4, is subtracted from the modulus number, 10, giving a check digit of 6. The digit 6 is now

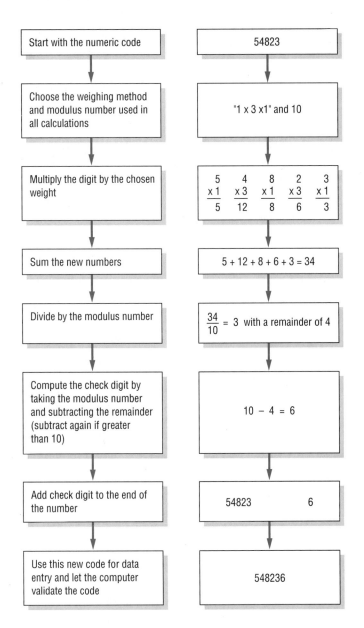

Start with the numeric code	54823
Choose the weighing method and modulus number used in all calculations	"1 x 3 x1" and 10
Multiply the digit by the chosen weight	$\begin{array}{ccccc} 5 & 4 & 8 & 2 & 3 \\ \times 1 & \times 3 & \times 1 & \times 3 & \times 1 \\ \hline 5 & 12 & 8 & 6 & 3 \end{array}$
Sum the new numbers	5 + 12 + 8 + 6 + 3 = 34
Divide by the modulus number	$\frac{34}{10}$ = 3 with a remainder of 4
Compute the check digit by taking the modulus number and subtracting the remainder (subtract again if greater than 10)	10 – 4 = 6
Add check digit to the end of the number	54823 6
Use this new code for data entry and let the computer validate the code	548236

tacked on to the end of the original number, giving us the official product code for the radiator hose (548236).

Using check digits. The check digit system works in the following way. Suppose we had the part number 53411. This number has to be typed into the system, and while that is being done, different types of errors can occur. One possible error is the single digit miskey. For example, the clerk types in 54411 instead of 53411. Only the digit in the thousand place is incorrect, but this error may result in the wrong part being shipped.

A second type of error is a transposed digit. It commonly occurs that the intended number 53411 gets typed in as number 54311 instead, just because two keys are pressed in reverse order. Transposition errors are also difficult for humans to detect.

These errors are avoidable through use of a check digit because each of these numbers—the correct one and the error—would have a different

FIGURE 19.21

Avoiding common data-entry errors through use of a check digit.

Status	Original Code	Check Digit	New Code
Correct	5 3 4 1 1	8	534118
Single Digit Mispunch	5 ④ 4 1 1	5	544115
Transpose	5 ④③ 1 1	6	543116

check digit number, as shown in Figure 19.21. Now if part number 53411 was modified to 534118 (including the check digit 8) and either of the two errors just described occurred, the mistake would be caught. If the second digit was miskeyed as a 4, the computer would not accept 544118 as a valid number, since the check digit for 54411 would be 5, not 8. Similarly, if the second and third digits were transposed, as in 543118, the computer would also reject the number because the check digit for 54311 would be 6, not 8.

The systems analyst chooses the weights and the modulus number, but once chosen they must not change. Some examples of weighting methods and modulus numbers can be found in Figure 19.22.

The check digit system is not foolproof. It is conceivable that two part numbers (732463 and 732413, for example) may have the same check digit. A single miskey in the second digit from the right would not be detected in that case.

The check digit system also has a cost. The added space taken up by the check digit must be considered, as well as the added computation involved in calculating and verifying the check digit. The check digit approach is useful when the original codes are five or more digits, codes are simple numerics with no meaning, and the cost of making miskey and transposition errors is high.

The seven tests for checking on validity of input can go a long way toward protecting the system from entry and storage of erroneous data. Always assume that errors in input are more likely than not to occur. It is your responsibility to understand which errors will invalidate data and how to use the computer to guard against those errors and thus limit their intrusion into system data.

SUMMARY

Assuring the quality of the data input to the information system is critical to assuring quality output. The quality of data entered can be improved through attainment of the three major data-entry objectives: effective coding, effective and efficient data capture, and validating data.

One of the best ways to speed data entry is through effective use of coding, which puts data into short sequences of digits and/or letters. Both simple sequence codes and alphabetic derivation codes can be used to follow the progress of a given item through a system. Classification codes and block sequence codes are useful for distinguishing classes of

Check Digit Method	Calculations for Check Digit to be Added to the Original Number 29645
Modulus 10 "2-1-2"	$\begin{array}{ccccc} 2 & 9 & 6 & 4 & 5 \\ \times 2 & \times 1 & \times 2 & \times 1 & \times 2 \\ \hline 4 & +9 & +12 & +4 & +10 \end{array}$ = 39/10 = 3 remainder $\begin{array}{r} 10 \\ (9) \\ \hline 1 \end{array}$ Check digit equals Code with check digit is 296451.
Modulus 10 "3-1-3"	$\begin{array}{ccccc} 2 & 9 & 6 & 4 & 5 \\ \times 3 & \times 1 & \times 3 & \times 1 & \times 3 \\ \hline 6 & +9 & +18 & +4 & +15 \end{array}$ = 52/10 = 5 remainder $\begin{array}{r} 10 \\ (2) \\ \hline 8 \end{array}$ Check digit equals Code with check digit is 296458.
Modulus 11 "Arithmetic"	$\begin{array}{ccccc} 2 & 9 & 6 & 4 & 5 \\ \times 6 & \times 5 & \times 4 & \times 3 & \times 2 \\ \hline 12 & +45 & +24 & +12 & +10 \end{array}$ = 103/11 = 9 remainder $\begin{array}{r} 11 \\ (4) \\ \hline 7 \end{array}$ Check digit equals Code with check digit is 296457.
Modulus 10 "Geometric"	$\begin{array}{ccccc} 2 & 9 & 6 & 4 & 5 \\ \times 32 & \times 16 & \times 8 & \times 4 & \times 2 \\ \hline 64 & +144 & +48 & +16 & +10 \end{array}$ = 282/11 = 25 remainder $\begin{array}{r} 11 \\ (7) \\ \hline 4 \end{array}$ Check digit equals Code with check digit is 296454.

FIGURE 19.22
Examples of weighting methods and modulus numbers.

items from each other. Codes such as the cipher code are also useful to conceal information that is sensitive or is restricted to personnel within the business.

Revealing information is also a worthwhile use of codes since it can enable business employees to locate items in stock and can also make data entry more meaningful. Significant-digit subset codes use subgroups of digits to describe a product. Mnemonic codes also reveal information by serving as memory aids for helping a data-entry operator enter data correctly or helping the end user in using information. Codes that are useful for informing computers or people about what functions to perform or what actions to take are called function codes; they circumvent having to spell out in detail what actions are necessary.

Another part of assuring effective data entry is attention to the input devices being used. A well-designed, effective form to serve as a source document (where needed) is the first step. Data can be input through many different methods, each with varying speed and reliability. Efficiency improvements on key-to-tape have been realized through the invention of key-to-disk and key-to-floppy diskette systems. Optical character recognition (OCR) allows reading of input data through use of special software, which eliminates some steps and also requires fewer employee skills.

"Sometimes I think I'm the luckiest person on Earth. Even though I've been here five years, I still enjoy the people I meet and what I do. Yes, I know Snowden's demanding. You've experienced some of that, haven't you? He, for one, loves codes. I, for another, think that they are a pain. I always forget them or try to make up new ones or something. But some of the physicians think they're great. Must be all of those Latin abbreviations they study in their med school classes. I hear that your most pressing assignment this week has to do with actually getting the information into the project reporting system. The Training Unit wants your ideas, and they want them fast. Good luck with it. Oh, and when Snowden gets back from Thailand, I'm certain he'll want to take a peek at what your team has been up to."

HYPERCASE QUESTIONS

1. Using a CASE tool such as Excelerator or a paper layout form, design a data-entry procedure for the proposed project reporting system for the Training Unit. Assume we are particularly concerned about the consulting physicians staff, who don't want to spend a great deal of time keying in large amounts of data when using the system.

2. Test your data-entry procedure on three teammates. Ask for feedback concerning the appropriateness of the procedure, given the type of users the system will have.

3. Redesign the data-entry procedure to include the feedback you have received. Explain in a paragraph how your changes reflect the comments you were given.

Other data-entry methods include magnetic ink character recognition, used by banks to encode customer account numbers; mark-sense forms used for high-volume data entry; and punch-out forms used on ballots. Bar codes (applied to products and then scanned) also speed data entry and improve data accuracy and reliability. New input technologies such as digital cameras are also being developed. Intelligent terminals are input devices (often microprocessor-based) with a VDT, keyboard, and a communication link to the CPU. They permit transactions to be entered and completed in real time.

Along with appropriate coding, data capture, and input devices, accurate data entry can be enhanced through the use of input validation. The systems analyst must assume that errors in data *will* occur and must work with users in designing input validation tests to prevent erroneous data from being processed and stored.

Input transactions should be checked to assure that the transaction requested is acceptable, authorized, and correct. Input data can be validated through inclusion in the software of several types of tests that check for missing data, length of data item, range and reasonableness of data, and invalid values for data. Input data can also be compared with stored data for validation purposes. Once numerical data are input, they can be checked and corrected automatically through the use of check digits.

KEYWORDS AND PHRASES

coding
simple sequence code
alphabetic derivation code
classification code
block sequence code
cipher code
significant-digit subset code
mnemonic code
function code
redundancy in input data
bottlenecks
key to storage
optical character recognition (OCR)
magnetic ink character
    recognition (MICR)

digital camera
mark sense
punch outs
bar codes
intelligent terminals
validating input
test for missing data
test for correct field length
test for class or composition
test for range or reasonableness
test for invalid values
test for comparison with
    stored data
self-validating codes
check digits

REVIEW QUESTIONS

1. What are the three primary objectives of data entry?
2. List the five general purposes for coding data.
3. Define the term *simple sequence code.*
4. When is an alphabetic derivation code useful?
5. Explain what is accomplished with a classification code.
6. Define the term *block sequence code.*
7. What is the simplest type of code for concealing information?
8. What are the benefits of using a significant-digit subset code?
9. What is the purpose of using a mnemonic code for data?
10. Define the term *function code.*
11. List the eight general guidelines for proper coding.
12. What is changeable data?
13. What is differentiation data?
14. Define the term *bottleneck* as it applies to data entry.
15. What is one specific way to reduce redundancy of data being entered?
16. What three repetitive functions of data entry can be done more efficiently by the computer than by the data-entry operator?
17. List eight data-entry methods.
18. List the three main problems that can occur with input transactions.
19. What are the seven tests for validating input data?
20. Which test checks to see whether data fields are correctly filled in with either numbers or letters?
21. Which test would not permit a user to input a date such as October 32?
22. Which test assures data accuracy by incorporation of a number in the code itself?

PROBLEMS

1. A small, private university specializing in graduate programs wants to keep track of when a particular student actually enrolls. Suggest a kind of code for this purpose and give an example of its use in the university that demonstrates its appropriateness.

2. The military has been using a simple sequence code to keep track of new recruits. However, there have been some upsetting mixups between recruit files because of similar-looking recruit numbers.

   a. In a paragraph, suggest a different coding scheme that will help uniquely identify each recruit and explain how it will prevent mix-ups.

   b. The military is concerned that confidential information in their coding of new recruits (such as IQ score and rating of physical condition upon entering the service) *not* be revealed to clerks without appropriate clearance, but will still be encoded on a recruit's identification number so that those conducting basic training are immediately aware of the type of recruit they are training. Suggest a type of code (or combination of codes) that can accomplish this, and give an example.

3. A code used by an ice cream store to order its products is 12DRM215-220. This code is deciphered in this manner: 12 stands for the count of items in the box, DRM stands for DREAMCICLES (a particular kind of ice cream novelty), and 215-220 indicates the entire class of low-fat products carried by the distributor.

   a. What kind of code is this? Describe the purpose behind each part (12, DRM, 215-220) of the code.

   b. Construct a coded entry using the same format and logic for an ice cream novelty called Pigeon Bars, which come in a six-count package and are *not* low-fat.

   c. Construct a coded entry using the same format and logic for an ice cream novelty called Airwhips, which come in a 24-count package and are low-fat.

4. The data-entry operators at Cataldo's Construction have been making errors in entering the codes for residential siding products, which are: U = stUcco, A = Aluminum, R = bRick, M = Masonite, EZ = EZ colorlok enameled masonite, N = Natural wood siding, AI = pAInted finish, SH = SHake SHingles. Only one code per address is permitted.

   a. List the possible problems with the coding system that could be contributing to erroneous entries. (*Hint:* Are the classes mutually exclusive?)

   b. Devise a mnemonic code that will help the operators understand what they are entering and subsequently help their accuracy.

   c. How would you redesign the classes for siding materials? Respond in a paragraph.

5. This is a code for one product in an extensive cosmetic line: L02002Z621289. L means that it is a lipstick; 0 means it was introduced without matching nail polish; 2002 is a sequence code indicating in what order it was produced; Z is a classification code indicating that

the product is hypoallergenic; and 621289 is the number of the plant (there are fifteen plants) where the product is produced.

    a. Critique the code by listing the features that might lead to inaccurate data entry.

    b. Designer Melvin Mine owns the cosmetic firm that uses this coding scheme. Always interested in new design, Melvin is willing to look at a more elegant code that encodes the *same* information in a better way. Redesign the coding scheme and provide a key for your work.

    c. Write a sentence for each change you have suggested indicating what data-entry problem (from part *a*) the change will eliminate.

6. Melvin Mine's cosmetic firm requires its salespeople to use lap-top microcomputers to enter orders from retail department stores (their biggest customers). This information is then relayed to warehouses, and orders are shipped on a first-come, first-served basis. Unfortunately, the stores are aware of this policy and are extremely competitive about which one of them will offer a new Melvin Mine product first. Many retailers have taken the low road and persuaded salespeople to falsify their order date on sales forms by making it earlier than it actually was.

    a. This problem is creating havoc at the warehouse. Disciplining any of the personnel involved is not feasible. How can the warehouse computer be used to certify when orders are actually placed? Explain in a paragraph.

    b. Salespeople are complaining that they have to ignore their true job of selling so that they can key in order data. List the data items relating to sales of cosmetics to retailers that should be stored in and retrieved from the central computer, rather than keyed in for every order.

7. List the best data-entry method and your reason for choosing it for each of the five situations listed below:

    a. Turnaround document for a utility company that wants notification of change in customer address.

    b. Data retrieval allowed only if there is positive machine identification of party requesting data.

    c. Not enough trained personnel available to interpret long written responses, many forms submitted that capture answers to multiple-choice examinations, high reliability necessary, fast turnaround not required.

    d. Warehouse set up for a discount record operation; record bins are labeled with price information but individual albums are not; and few skilled operators available to enter price data.

    e. Poison control center that maintains a large database of poisons and antidotes; needs a way to enter data on poison taken; also enter weight, age, and general physical condition of victim when person calls the center's toll-free number for emergency advice.

8. One of your systems analysis team members surprises you by asserting that when a system uses a test for correct field length, it is redundant also to include a test for range or reasonableness. In a paragraph, give an example that demonstrates that your team member is mistaken on this one.

9. Several retailers have gotten together and begun issuing a "state" credit card that is good only in stores within their state. As a courtesy, sales clerks are permitted to transcribe the 15-digit account number by hand (after getting it from the accounting office) if the customer is not carrying his or her card. The only problem with accounts that retailers have noticed so far is that sometimes erroneous account numbers are accepted into the computer system and a bill is issued to a nonexistent account. What sort of validity test would clear up the problem? How? Respond in a paragraph.

10. The following are part numbers:

    38902
    38933
    39402
    35693
    35405
    39204

    Develop a check digit for the preceding part numbers using 1-3-1-3-1 multipliers and modulus 11. Use the method presented in this chapter. Why do some numbers have the same check digit?

11. Develop a check digit system for the preceding part numbers using 5-4-3-2-1 multipliers and modulus.

12. Why would a check digit system such as 1-1-1-1-1 not work as well as other methods? What errors would it miss?

GROUP PROJECTS

1. Along with your group members, read Consulting Opportunity 19.3, "To Enter or Not to Enter: That is the Question," earlier in this chapter. Design an appropriate data entry system for Elsinore Industries. Your group's design should emphasize efficiency and accuracy. Additionally, distinguish between data that are changeable and that which differentiates the item being entered from all others.

2. Divide your group into analysts and Elsinore Industries employees in order to role play. The analysts should present the new data entry system. Ask for feedback on the design from Elsinore employees.

3. Write a brief paragraph describing how to improve the original data entry design based on the comments received.

SELECTED BIBLIOGRAPHY

Davis, G. B., and M. H. Olson. *Management Information Systems, Conceptual Foundations, Structure, and Development,* 2nd ed. New York: McGraw-Hill Book Company, 1985.

Galitz, W. O. *Human Factors in Office Automation.* Atlanta: GA. Life Office Automation Management Association, 1980.

Miller, G. A. "The Magical Number Seven, Plus or Minus Two: Some Limits on Our Capability for Processing Information." *The Psychological Review,* Vol. 63, No. 2, March 1956, pp. 81–97.

Owsowitz, S., and A. Sweetland. "Factors Affecting Coding Errors." *Rand Memorandum RM-4346-PR.* Santa Monica: The Rand Corporation, 1965.

Robey, D., and W. Taggart. "Human Processing in Information and Decision Support Systems." *Management Information Systems Quarterly,* Vol. 6, No. 2, June 1982, pp. 61–73.

Sumner, M. *Computers, Concepts and Uses.* Englewood Cliffs, NJ: Prentice-Hall, Inc., 1985.

ENTERING NATURALLY

Tuesday afternoon finds Anna and Chip having their weekly analysis and design review session. Chip waves toward a large stack of documents that are neatly organized on a large table. "I can't believe that we're almost finished with the design of this system," he remarks. "It's been a long process, but I'll bet we've obtained enough user feedback to ensure a high-quality system. All that's left is the design of the data-entry procedures, and we'll be ready to start packaging the specs for the programmers."

"Yes," replies Anna. "The end is in sight. Let's start by examining the design of the input portion of the system." The data flow diagram shown in Figure E19.1 represents a portion of two Add programs. The top diagram depicts adding new microcomputers using a batch process.

"Since this is to be performed by data entry, we should use key-to-diskette data entry," remarks Anna. "The microcomputers are usually ordered for an entire lab, so they often arrive in shipments of twenty or more. We can take advantage of the keying speed of the data-entry operators. The new microcomputer information is on easy-to-enter forms that will be keyed by one operator and then rekeyed by a different person to verify the data. The results will be stored on a transaction file for use by the edit and update programs."

"The Add Software process will have a different design," notes Chip. "Since software does not arrive in a batch, the add program is on line. Instead of a key-and-verify operation, the operator will have to search-verify each transaction. After all data fields have been edited for accuracy, a message will appear on the bottom of the screen. It will prompt the operators to check the data on the screen for accuracy against the form and press the Enter key if correct. The operators will have a chance to make changes if the data are keyed incorrectly. This method may not be keyed as fast as data entry, but the errors are corrected by the person seeing the data, which speeds up the actual updating of the files."

Regardless of the method for adding information, every data field must be edited for accuracy. As Chip noted, "In the long run, it's better to have complete editing for accuracy in the programs, rather than finding erroneous data has been stored on master files and printed on reports."

The strategy for field editing is to check the data in the following order:

1. Syntax, whether the data is numeric or alphabetic, and the length of the data. An example is the HARDWARE INVENTORY NUMBER, which must be eight characters in length and numeric.

2. The contents of the field, including range, limit, and values for the data. When validating the DATE PURCHASED, the month must be from 1 to 12. This check should occur only after the month has been verified as numeric.

Allen Schmidt,
Julie E. Kendall, and
Kenneth E. Kendall

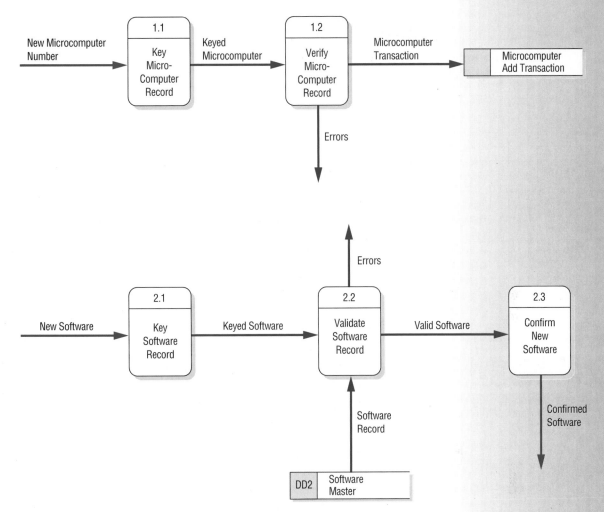

FIGURE E19.1
Data flow diagram portions, add programs.

3. Cross-reference checks between two or more data elements. When checking the day portion of the DATE PURCHASED, a table of the number of days possible for each month was used for an upper limit. This table could not be used if the month number was not from 1 to 12. Check digits are another example of a cross-reference edit.

4. External edits, such as reading a file to verify if the record to be added already exists on the file. Reading records is slower than editing, which is performed in main memory, and should occur only after the data successfully pass all other edits.

Edit criteria have been entered on the Excelerator Element Description screen as the elements were added to the design. These elements include simple editing criteria and table checking. Figure E19.2 shows the editing criteria for the HARDWARE INVENTORY NUMBER. Notice that the **Input Format** is 9(8), with 9's indicating that the data should be numeric. The limit check is shown as greater than zero.

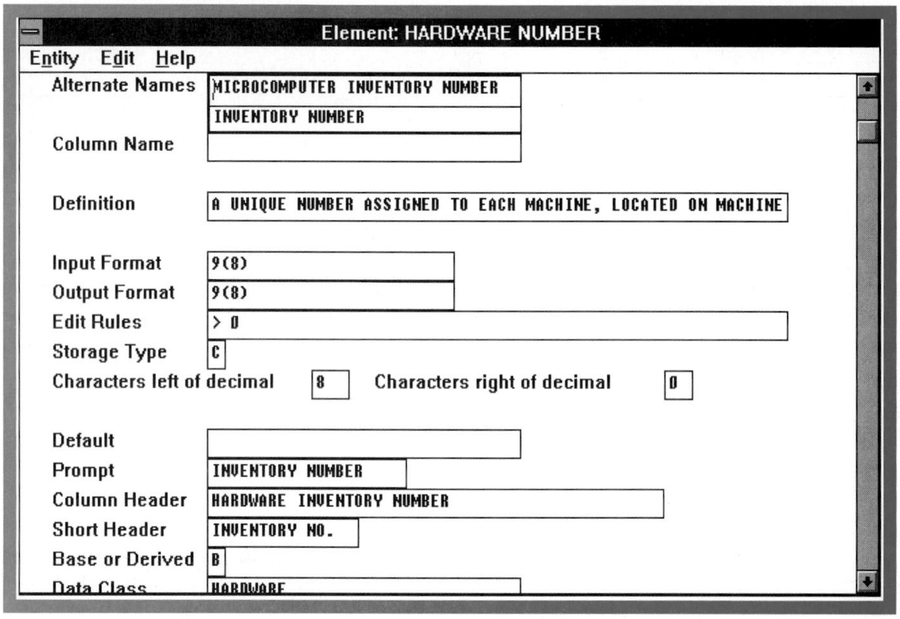

FIGURE E19.2
Element description screen showing edit criteria, HARDWARE INVENTORY
NUMBER.

The **Description** area provided may be used to enter additional editing criteria. The HARDWARE INVENTORY NUMBER description shown in Figure E19.3 includes a reference for using the modulus-11 method of verifying the check digit portion of the number. Further, when adding a new microcomputer, the MICROCOMPUTER MASTER file must be read to ensure that a record does not already exist with the same HARDWARE INVENTORY NUMBER.

"I think these reports will be useful," Chip tells Anna. "The first report involves creating several Excelerator Entity Lists, which are combined to produce a final list of all the elements found both on the MICRO-COMPUTER MASTER file and the structural records contained within the master. The Entity List is used by the Report Writer feature to produce a report containing the elements, their input format, and edit rules. (This report is shown in Figure E19.4.)

"I produced another report showing the elements that had entries in the **Description** area," Chip continues. "Together these reports were used to produce the edit criteria table, which became part of our program specs." (This table is shown in Figure E19.5.)

Several of the elements have edit rules referring to tables. An example is the INTERNAL BOARDS element with the edit rule **FROM "BOARD TABLE" OPT.** The OPT, for optional, indicates the entry may contain spaces.

"I'll produce a list of all tables we'll require," Anna offers. Again, the **Report Writer** feature supplies the necessary information. A list of all elements containing edit criteria starting with the word FROM was printed, as shown in Figure E19.6. Included on the list is the Input Format, showing the length of the code. Using the list, tables are created.

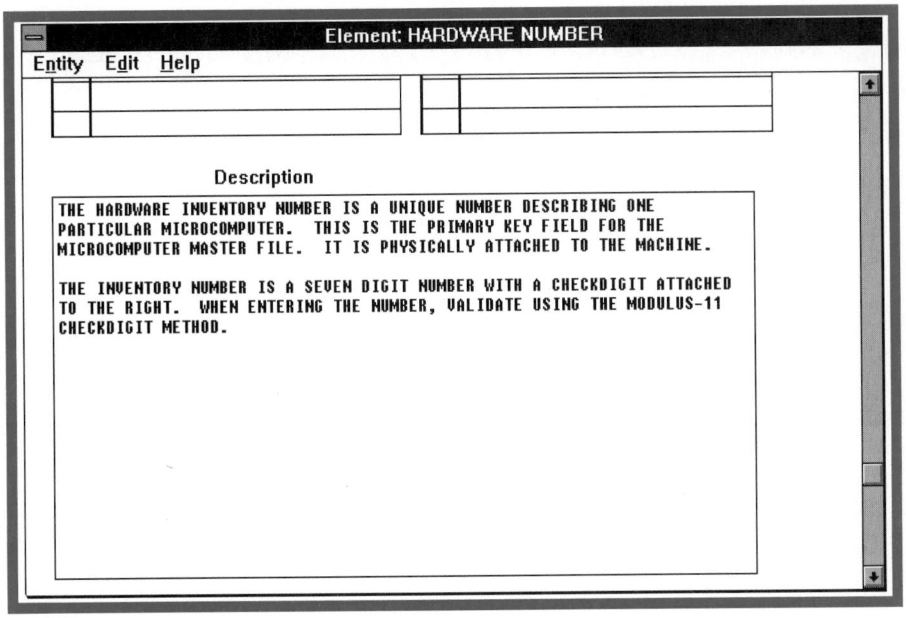

FIGURE E19.3
Element description with descriptive edit criteria, HARDWARE INVENTORY NUMBER.

Each table is defined using the **Table of Codes** feature of Excelerator. Chip and Anna each spend time working on the tables. A mnemonic code is chosen for BOARDS and MONITORS since these would be easy for maintenance personnel to work with. Mnemonic codes are also used to represent the SOFTWARE CATEGORY, since these will be easy for users to remember.

"There are a wide variety of printers available," remarks Chip. "I think a significant-digit coding scheme would be the best here. The first digit represents the type of printer, laser and so on. The next two digits are for manufacturer, and the last two a sequence number representing different model numbers."

Anna agrees, "That's good, Chip. That strategy can also be used for the campus buildings. The first digit for the campus location, and the remaining two digits representing individual buildings within the campus."

Chip designs the codes used for the BOARD TABLE. The entry screen is shown in Figure E19.7. Two entry areas are used to define codes. The left column contains the code, and the right column the meaning of the code. This entry area is a *scroll* region. As the bottom line is entered, all lines scroll upward, providing room for up to 100 table entries. If more entries are needed, the table may be linked to another **Table of Codes.**

"Here's the SOFTWARE CATEGORY Table of Codes I created," says Anna. (The output is illustrated in Figure E19.8.) "This report will become part of the permanent documentation of the microcomputer system. Now anyone needing a list of codes may copy it, and the table is updated with new codes as they become available."

"That's a valuable component of the system," Chip comments. "It provides consistency for all codes and their meanings."

```
Name                             Edit Rules
------------------------------   --------------------------------------------------------------
ACTIVE SOFTWARE CODE             VALUES ARE "A", "I"
BRAND NAME                       NOT " "
CAMPUS LOCATION                  FROM "CAMPUS CODE TABLE"
CAMPUS LOCATION - LONG
CATEGORY OF SOFT                 FROM "SOFTWARE CATEGORY TABLE"
COMPUTER BRAND                   FROM "HARDWARE BRAND TABLE"
COMPUTER MODEL
COST OF REPAIRS
COURSE ENROLLMENT LIMIT          > 5
COURSE INSTRUCTOR                NOT " "
COURSE LENGTH                    > 0
COURSE LEVEL                     VALUES ARE "B", "I", "A", "P"
COURSE TITLE                     NOT " "
DATE PURCHASED                   > 0
DEPARTMENT NAME                  NOT " "
DISK DRIVE A                     VALUES ARE "3.5DD", "3.5HD", "5.25DD", "5.25HD"
DISK DRIVE B                     VALUES ARE "3.5DD", "3.5HD", "5.25DD", "5.25HD" OPT
DISK SIZE                        VALUES ARE "3.5DD", "3.5HD", "5.25DD", "5.25HD"
DISKETTE SIZE                    VALUES ARE "3.5DD", "3.5HD", "5.25DD", "5.25HD"
FIXED DISK                       0, >19
FIXED DISK 2                     0, >19
GRAND TOTAL MICRO INVESTMENT
HARDWARE INVENTORY NUMBER        > 0
HARDWARE NUMBER                  > 0
HARDWARE SUBTOTAL
INTERNAL BOARDS                  FROM "BOARD TABLE" OPT
LAST PREVENT. MAINTENANCE DATE   > 0
LOCATION                         NOT " "
MAINTENANCE INTERVAL             VALUES ARE FROM 7 THRU 250
MEMORY REQUIRED                  > 0
MEMORY SIZE                      >255
MODEL                            NOT " "
MONITOR                          FROM "MONITOR TABLE"
MONITOR NAME
MONITOR REQUIRED                 FROM "MONITOR TABLE"
MOUSE                            VALUES ARE "Y", "N"
NUMBER OF COPIES                 > 0
NUMBER OF DISKETTES              > 0
NUMBER OF DISKS                  > 0, < 50
NUMBER OF MACHINES
NUMBER OF REPAIRS
ORDER DATE
ORDER QUANTITY                   > 0
PREVENTIVE MAINTENANCE DATE      > 0
PREVENTIVE MAINTENANCE DATE      > 0
PRINTER                          FROM "PRINTER TABLE"
PRINTER REQUIRED                 FROM "PRINTER TABLE"
PUBLISHER                        NOT " "
PURCHASE COST                    >500
PURCHASE ORDER NUMBER            > 0
QUANTITY RECEIVED
RECORD CODE                      VALUES ARE 'I', 'A'
REPLACEMENT COST                 0, >500
ROOM LOCATION                    NOT " "
SERIAL NUMBER                    NOT " "
```

FIGURE E19.4
Add Microcomputer program edit rules report.

MICROCOMPUTER MASTER ELEMENT LIST	NUMERIC	ALPHABETIC	LENGTH	DATE	LIMIT	RANGE	TABLE	CHECK DIGIT	CROSS REFER	FILE CHECK
ELEMENT NAME										
BRAND NAME			<0				X			
CAMPUS LOCATION							X			
COST OF REPAIRS	X									
DATE PURCHASED	X		6	X					2	
DISK DRIVE A						3				
DISK DRIVE B						3			4	
FIXED DISK	X				5					
FIXED DISK 2	X				5				6	
HARDWARE INVENTORY NUMBER	X		8		1			X		X
INTERNAL BOARDS							X			
LAST PREVENT. MAINTENANCE DATE	X		6	X						
MAINTENANCE INTERVAL	X					7				
MEMORY SIZE	X				8					
MODEL			>0							
MONITOR							X			
MOUSE		X	1			X				
NUMBER OF REPAIRS	X									
PRINTER						X				
PURCHASE COST	X				1					
RECORD COST		X	1			10				
REPLACEMENT CODE	X									
ROOM LOCATION			>0							
SERIAL NUMBER			>0							
WARRANTY		X	1			9				

Legend of codes:
1 Limit: Must be greater than 0
2 Date must be greater than current date
3 Values are 3.5DD, 3.5HD, 5.25DD, 5.25HD
4 Disk drive A must exist
5 Value is either 0 or greater than 19
6 First fixed disk must exist
7 Range: 7 to 250
8 Limit: Greater than 255
9 Values are Y or N
10 Values are A or I

FIGURE E19.5
Microcomputer master element list.

Chip and Anna finish their work the next morning, at about 11:30. They glance around the room happily, frequently reexamining the final design. The months of analysis, design work, consultation with the users, and careful adherence to standards are finally complete.

```
DATE: 28-NOV-93     MICROCOMPUTER SYSTEM - TABLE LIST              PAGE    1
TIME: 12:21                                                        Excelerator


ELEMENT                  TABLE NAME                         Input Format
-----------------------  ---------------------------------  ---------------
CAMPUS LOCATION          FROM "CAMPUS CODE TABLE"           XXXX
CATEGORY OF SOFT         FROM "SOFTWARE CATEGORY TABLE"     X(4)
COMPUTER BRAND           FROM "HARDWARE BRAND TABLE"        X(10)
INTERNAL BOARDS          FROM "BOARD TABLE" OPT             XXX
MONITOR                  FROM "MONITOR TABLE"               X(4)
MONITOR REQUIRED         FROM "MONITOR TABLE"               XXX
PRINTER                  FROM "PRINTER TABLE"               X(5)
PRINTER REQUIRED         FROM "PRINTER TABLE"               X(5)
SOFTWARE CATEGORY        FROM "SOFTWARE TYPE TABLE"         XXXX
```

FIGURE E19.6
Add Microcomputer program edit table.

"I feel really good about this project," says Anna.
Chip agrees, "I'm proud of the quality we put in."

*Exercises**

E-1. Explain the difference between verifying input data in a batch data entry situation and in an on-line program.

E-2. Modify and print the following elements with edit criteria (continued on the following pages).

	Element	Edit Criteria
a.	SOFTWARE CATEGORY	FROM "SOFTWARE CATEGORY TABLE"
b.	NUMBER OF COPIES	>0
c.	PRINTER REQUIRED	FROM "PRINTER TABLE"
d.	ACTIVE SOFTWARE CODE	VALUES ARE "A", "I"
e.	DISKETTE SIZE	VALUES ARE "3.5DD", "3.5HD", "5.25DD", "5.25HD"
f.	PUBLISHER	NOT " "
g.	SITE LICENSE	VALUES ARE "Y", "N"

E-3. Modify and print the following elements with edit criteria placed in the **Description** area:

a. Element: SOFTWARE INVENTORY NUMBER

Description: A modulus-11 check digit must be verified when entering the number. The ADD SOFTWARE program creates the check digit.

The ADD SOFTWARE program should also check the SOFTWARE MASTER file to ensure that a record with the same inventory number does not already exist.

---

* The exercises preceded by a disk icon require the program Excelerator (or another CASE tool). A disk is provided free of charge to any professor adopting this book. The examples on the disk may be imported into Excelerator and then used by students.

```
┌──────────────────────────────────────────────────────────────────┐
│ ─                    Table of Codes: BOARD TABLE                   │
│ E̲ntity  E̲dit  H̲elp                                                 │
│   Alternate Name  │INTERNAL BOARDS                    │          ▲ │
│   Definition      │CODES FOR THE COMPONENT BOARDS LOCATED WITHIN MICROCOMPUTERS│
│                                                                    │
│      Next Table of Codes:                                          │
│   Type  Name                                                       │
│   │TAB│ │                                    │                     │
│                                                                    │
│              Code     Meaning                                      │
│              │MOD │  │MODEM                            ▲│           │
│              │EGA │  │EGA GRAPHICS BOARD                │           │
│              │CGA │  │CGA GRAPHICS BOARD                │           │
│              │VGA │  │VGA GRAPHICS BOARD                │           │
│              │HER │  │HERCULES GRAPHICS BOARD           │           │
│              │MEM │  │MEMORY EXPANSION BOARD            │           │
│              │HDC │  │HARD DRIVE CARD                   │           │
│              │MFB │  │MULTI FUNCTION BOARD              │           │
│              │VGH │  │VGA HIGH RESOLUTION BOARD        ▼│         ▼ │
└──────────────────────────────────────────────────────────────────┘
```

FIGURE E19.7
Table of Codes Description screen, BOARD TABLE.

---

b. Element: DATE PURCHASED

Description: Verify that the DATE PURCHASED is less than or equal to the current date.

c. Element: QUANTITY RECEIVED

Description: Verify that the QUANTITY RECEIVED is less than or equal to the QUANTITY ORDERED.

d. Element: SOFTWARE UPGRADE VERSION

Description: Ensure that the upgrade version is greater than the current version.

e. Element: FIXED DISK 2

Description: FIXED DRIVE 2 may exist only if there is an entry for FIXED DISK.

E-4. View and print the Report Writer selections used to produce edit criteria for the ADD SOFTWARE program. The name of the report is ADD SOFTWARE ELEMENTS. Then print the ELEMENTS WITH A DESCRIPTION report. Use the results of these reports to produce an edit table for the ADD SOFTWARE program.

E-5. View the SOFTWARE CATEGORY Table of Codes.

E-6. Modify and print the BOARD TABLE Table of Codes. Add the following codes (continued on the following pages).

SER   SERIAL PORT
SSR   SECOND SERIAL PORT
ACC   ACCELERATOR CARDS
SIX   AST SIX PACK PLUS

727

MAT	MATH CO-PROCESSOR CHIP
FAX	FAX BOARD

⊟ **E-7.** Modify and print the PRINTER TABLE Table of Codes. The format of this significant digit code is:

TMMSS where

T is the type of printer
M is the manufacturer
S represents a sequence number, a higher number indicating an improved model

Values for the type of printer are:

0	☐	Dot matrix
1	☐	Daisy wheel
2	☐	Ink jet
3	☐	Thermal
4	☐	Laser
5	☐	Postscript
6	☐	Plotter

Values for the manufacturer are:

01	☐	IBM
02	☐	Epson
03	☐	Hewlett-Packard
04	☐	Panasonic
05	☐	Star Micronics
06	☐	Okidata
07	☐	Kodak
08	☐	Texas Instruments

Add the following codes:

Code	Meaning
20301	Hewlett-Packard DeskJet PLUS
50801	Texas Instruments microLaser PS 17
40201	Epson Laser EPL-6000
40305	Hewlett-Packard LaserJet III
40401	Panasonic KX-p4420

⊟ **E-8.** Create and print the MONITOR TABLE Table of Codes, using the mnemonic form. Add the following entries:

Code	Meaning
VGA	VGA GRAPHICS MONITOR
EGA	ENHANCED GRAPHICS MONITOR
CGA	COLOR GRAPHICS MONITOR
MONO	MONOCHROME MONITOR-GREEN
ORAN	MONOCHROME MONITOR-ORANGE

```
DATE: 21-FEB-95      TABLE OF CODES - OUTPUT                    PAGE      1
TIME: 12:32          NAME: SOFTWARE CATEGORY TABLE              Excelerator


TYPE Table of Codes                    NAME SOFTWARE CATEGORY TABLE

   Alternate Name
   Definition      TABLE OF SOFTWARE CATEGORY CODES

         Next Table of Codes:
   Type  Name
   TAB

                   Code       Meaning
                   ACCN       ACCOUNTING
                   DB         DATABASE
                   CAD        COMPUTER AIDED DESIGN
                   DPUB       DESKTOP PUBLISHING
                   COM        COMMUNICATIONS
                   EDUC       EDUCATIONAL
                   FNCL       FINANCIAL
                   GRPH       GRAPHICS
                   INTG       INTEGRATED
                   PGM        PROGRAMMING LANGUAGES
                   SS         SPREADSHEETS
                   TRNG       TRAINING
                   UTIL       UTILITIES
                   WP         WORD PROCESSING



   Modified By    ANNA          Date Modified   950324    # Changes   3
   Added By       ANNA          Date Added      930905
   Last Project   TEST FINAL
   Locked By                    Date Locked     0         Lock Status
```

FIGURE E19.8
SOFTWARE CATEGORY table print.

> HVGA   HIGH-RESOLUTION VGA MONITOR
> PLSM   PLASMA MONITOR

E-9. After speaking with Dot Matricks and Mike Crowe, it has become apparent that the campus codes must be sortable for installing hardware and software, as well as creating inventory sheets. Create and print the CAMPUS CODE TABLE. The first digit represents the campus location. Values are:

1   Central Campus
2   Waterford Campus
3   Hillside Campus

The next three digits represent buildings within the campus, with the following building codes:

001	Administration	010	Environmental Studies
002	Admissions	011	Geology
003	Agricultural	012	Library
004	Astronomy	013	Law
005	Business	014	Mathematics

006	Chemical Engineering	015	Medicine
007	Computer Science	016	Physics
008	Education	017	Psychology
009	Engineering	018	Zoology

Use a combination (your choice) of campus and building codes to build the final table of codes. Include the meaning of the code.

20

QUALITY ASSURANCE THROUGH SOFTWARE ENGINEERING

APPROACHES TO QUALITY

Quality has long been a concern of businesses, as it should be for systems analysts in the analysis and design of information systems. It is too risky to undertake the entire analysis and design process without using a quality assurance approach. The three approaches to quality assurance through software engineering are: (1) securing total quality assurance through designing systems and software with a top-down, modular approach; (2) documenting software with appropriate tools; and (3) testing, maintaining, and auditing software.

Two thoughts guide quality assurance. The first is that the user of the information system is the single most important factor in establishing and evaluating its quality. The second is that it is far less costly to correct problems in their early stages than it is to wait until a problem is articulated through user complaints or crises.

We already have learned about the huge investment of labor and other business resources that are required to launch a system successfully. Using quality assurance throughout the process is a way to minimize risks and helps ensure that the resulting system is what is needed and wanted and that it will demonstrably improve some aspect of business performance. This chapter provides the analyst with three major approaches to quality.

THE TOTAL QUALITY MANAGEMENT APPROACH

Total quality management (TQM) is essential through all of the systems development steps. According to Dean and Evans (1994) the primary elements of TQM are meaningful only when occurring in an organizational context that supports a comprehensive quality effort. It is within this context that the elements of customer focus, strategic planning and leadership, continuous improvement, and empowerment and teamwork become united to change employees' behavior and ultimately, the organization's course.

731

Notice that the concept of quality has broadened over the years to reflect an organizational, rather than an exclusively production, approach. Instead of conceiving of quality as controlling the number of defective products produced, quality is now thought of as an evolutionary process toward perfection that is otherwise referred to as total quality management.

The emphasis on quality has moved up from the shop floor through the ranks to top management. A combination of factors has contributed to rising corporate concern for quality on all levels. These factors include increased availability of performance data, emulation of successful Japanese management techniques, and increased attention to white-collar productivity.

Performance data within businesses are becoming more readily available to employees on all levels. The acceptance of "management by objectives" and the espousal of participatory management techniques have made employees themselves concerned about how their performance is being measured. This employee awareness is important in relation to total quality management, since the concept can work only if each individual is committed to quality work.

Keen trade competition with Japan has made managers in the United States curious about the management techniques that the Japanese are using to succeed. Although many factors have been discussed, the internalized commitment to quality seems to carry great influence.

Finally, we consider the increasing focus on white-collar productivity as helping to foster adoption of TQM in many businesses. When productivity on production lines improved markedly, demand for higher white-collar productivity also rose. Pressure for increasing management productivity was supported by the development of new techniques for measuring what managers actually do. A movement for greater accountability from upper-level employees whose companies are being downsized also pushed forward the desire for improved management productivity.

Systems analysts must be aware of the factors that are driving the interest in quality. It is important to realize that increasing commitment of businesses to TQM fits extraordinarily well into the overall objectives for systems analysis and design.

Responsibility for Total Quality Management

The somewhat surprising lesson garnered from total quality management in production situations is that the customer is the single most important factor in establishing and evaluating the quality of products. This development is paralleled in MIS and DSS research findings that point to the critical importance of the user for ensuring successful systems implementation.

Practically speaking, a large portion of the responsibility for the quality of information systems rests with systems users and management. Two things must happen for TQM to become a reality with systems projects. First, the full organizational support of management must exist—a departure from merely endorsing the newest management gimmick. This means establishing a context for management to consider seriously how quality of information systems and information itself affects their work.

Early commitment to quality from the analyst and the business is necessary to achieve the goal of quality, as shown in Figure 20.1. This results in exerting an evenly paced effort toward quality throughout the systems

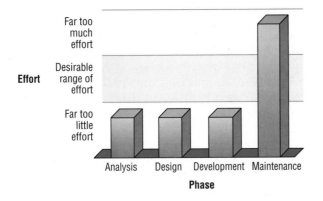

FIGURE 20.1
To prevent unnecessary
maintenance, an evenly
paced effort toward quality
throughout the systems development life cycle is the
analyst's goal.

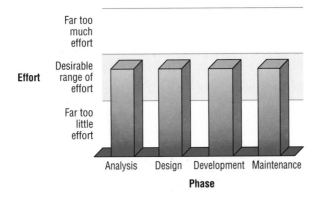

development life cycle, rather than having to pour huge amounts of effort into ironing out problems at the end of the project.

Organizational support for quality in management information systems can be achieved through providing on-the-job time for quality circles, consisting of six to eight organizational peers specifically charged with considering how to improve management information systems and how to implement improvements.

Alternatively, total quality management of MIS and DSS can be centralized through the organization's information center (discussed in detail in Chapter 21). The center can serve as the repository for quality guidelines drawn up by internal MIS quality circles or proposed in competing organizations within the particular industry.

Through work in MIS quality circles or through other mechanisms already in place, management and users must develop guidelines for quality standards of MIS. Preferably, standards will be reshaped every time a new system or major modification is to be formally proposed by the systems analysis team.

It is not a problem if users drawing up quality guidelines possess little or no expertise in computing systems. Users are expected to contribute their knowledge of how their department operates and what they consider acceptable quality for system input, processing, and output.

Hammering out quality standards is not easy, but it is possible and it has been done. Part of the systems analyst's job is encouraging users to crystallize their expectations about information systems and their interactions with them.

Departmental quality standards must then be communicated through feedback to the systems analysis team. The team is often surprised at what has developed. Expectations typically are less complex than what experienced analysts know could be done with a system. Additionally, issues that have been overlooked or underrated by the analyst team may be designated as extremely pressing in users' quality standards. Getting users involved in spelling out quality standards for MIS will help the analyst avoid expensive mistakes in unwanted or unnecessary systems development.

Structured Walkthrough

One of the strongest quality management actions the systems analysis team can take is to routinely do structured walkthroughs. Structured walkthroughs are a way to use peer reviewers to monitor the system's programming and overall development, point out problems, and allow the programmer or analyst responsible for that portion of the system to make suitable changes.

Structured walkthroughs involve at least four people, including the person responsible for the part of the system or subsystem being reviewed (a programmer or analyst); a walkthrough coordinator; a programmer or analyst peer; and a peer to take notes about suggestions. Others might include an organizational peer attuned to user needs, and someone aware of organizational standards. Management is neither involved in the structured walkthrough nor told of the specific problems that are discussed. Typically, management is informed that a structured walkthrough has been completed, when it was done, the names of those participating, and whether the system work was accepted as found, needs revision, or needs revision and a follow-up walkthrough.

Each person attending a walkthrough has a special role to play. The coordinator is there to ensure that the others adhere to any roles assigned and to assure that any activities scheduled are accomplished. The program author or analyst is there to listen, not to defend his or her thinking, rationalize a problem, or argue. The peer is present to point out errors or potential problems, not to specify how the problems should be remedied. The note-taker records what is said so that the others present can interact without encumbrance.

Structured walkthroughs can be done whenever a portion of coding, a subsystem, or a system is finished. Just be sure that the subsystem under review is comprehensible outside of its larger context. Structured walkthroughs fit well within a total quality management approach when accomplished throughout the systems development life cycle. The time they take should be short—half an hour to an hour at most—which means that they must be well coordinated. Figure 20.2 shows a form useful in organizing the structured walkthrough as well as reporting its results. Since walkthroughs take time, do not overuse them.

Use structured walkthroughs as a way to obtain (and then act on) valuable feedback from a perspective that you lack. As with all of the quality assurance measures, the point of walkthroughs is to evaluate the product systematically on an ongoing basis, rather than waiting until completion of the system.

Systems Design and Development

In this section we define the bottom-up and top-down design of systems as well as the modular approach to programming. We discuss advantages of

Report to Management on Structured Walkthrough

Date of Walkthrough: / /

Time:

Project Name:

Project Number

Portion (Description) of Work Examined

Walkthrough Coordinator:
List of Participants:

Comments:

Action Recommended (Check One):
( ) ACCEPT WORK AS FOUND
( ) REVISE WORK
( ) REVISE WORK AND CONDUCT
( ) FOLLOW-UP WALKTHROUGH
( ) REJECT WORK

Signature of Coordinator:

Date Report is Filed: / /

each, as well as the precautions that should be observed when employing either a top-down or modular approach. We also discuss the appropriateness of the top-down and modular approaches for aiding in quality assurance of systems projects.

BOTTOM-UP DESIGN. Bottom-up design refers to identifying the processes that need computerization as they arise, analyzing them as systems, and either coding them or purchasing packaged software to meet the immediate problem. The problems that require computerization most frequently are on the lowest level of the organization. Furthermore, problems on the lowest level of the organization are initially the only problems for which computerization is cost-effective. Hence, the name bottom-up refers to the bottom level on which computerization was first introduced. Businesses often take this approach to systems development by going out and acquiring, for example, software packages for accounting, a different package for production scheduling, and another one for marketing.

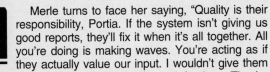
When in-house programming is done with a bottom-up approach, it is difficult to interface the subsystems so that they perform smoothly as a system. Interface bugs are enormously costly to correct and many of them are not uncovered until programming is complete, when analysts are trying to meet a deadline in putting the system together. At this juncture, there is little time, budget, or user patience to allow debugging of delicate interfaces that have been ignored.

Although each subsystem appears to get what it wants, when the overall system is considered there are severe limitations to taking a bottom-up approach. One is that there is a duplication of effort in purchasing software and even entering data. Another is that much worthless data are entered into the system. A third, and perhaps the most serious drawback of the bottom-up approach, is that overall organizational objectives are not considered and hence cannot be met.

TOP-DOWN DESIGN. It is easy to visualize what the top-down approach refers to; it means looking at the large picture of the system and then exploding it into smaller parts or subsystems, as shown in Figure 20.3. Top-down design allows the systems analyst to ascertain overall organizational objectives first, along with ascertaining how they are best met in an overall system. Then the analyst moves to dividing that system into subsystems and their requirements.

Top-down design is compatible with the general systems thinking that was discussed in Chapter 2. When systems analysts employ a top-down approach they are thinking about the interrelationships and interdependencies

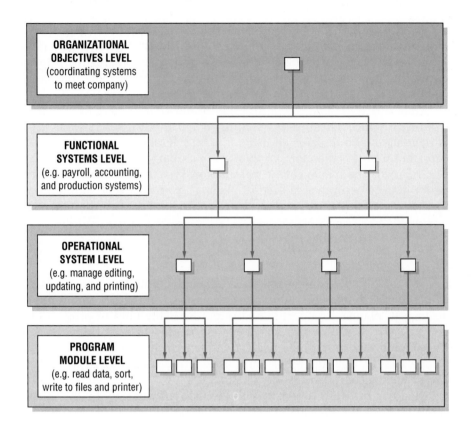

FIGURE 20.3
Using the top-down approach
to first ascertain overall
organizational objectives.

ORGANIZATIONAL OBJECTIVES LEVEL
(coordinating systems to meet company)

FUNCTIONAL SYSTEMS LEVEL
(e.g. payroll, accounting, and production systems)

OPERATIONAL SYSTEM LEVEL
(e.g. manage editing, updating, and printing)

PROGRAM MODULE LEVEL
(e.g. read data, sort, write to files and printer)

of subsystems as they fit into the existing organization. The top-down approach also provides desirable emphasis on synergy or the interfaces that systems and their subsystems require, which is lacking in the bottom-up approach.

The advantages of using a top-down approach to systems design include avoiding the chaos of attempting to design a system "all at once." As we have seen, planning and implementing a management information system is incredibly complex. Attempting to get all subsystems in place and running at once is agreeing to fail.

A second advantage of taking a top-down approach to design is the ability to have separate systems analysis teams working in parallel on different but necessary subsystems. This can save a great deal of time. The use of teams for subsystems design is particularly well suited to a total quality assurance approach.

A third advantage resides in avoiding a major problem associated with a bottom-up approach. That is, using a top-down approach prevents systems analysts from getting so mired in detail that they lose sight of what the system is supposed to do.

There are some pitfalls of top-down design that the systems analyst needs to be aware of. The first is the danger that the system will be divided into the "wrong" subsystems. Attention must be paid to overlapping needs and sharing of resources so that the partitioning of subsystems makes sense for the total systems picture. Further, it is important that each subsystem address the correct problem.

A second danger is that once subsystem divisions are made, their interfaces may be neglected or ignored. Responsibility for interfaces needs to be detailed.

A third caution that accompanies the use of top-down design is that eventually subsystems must be reintegrated. Mechanisms for reintegration need to be put in place at the beginning. One suggestion is regular information trading between subsystem teams; another is using tools that permit flexibility if changes to interrelated subsystems are required.

Total quality management and the top-down approach to design can go hand in hand. The top-down approach provides the systems group with a ready-made division of users into task forces for subsystems. Task forces set up in this manner can then serve a dual function as quality control circles for the management information system. The necessary structure for quality assurance is then in place, as is proper motivation for getting the subsystem to accomplish the departmental goals important to the users involved.

Modular Development

Once the top-down design approach is taken, the modular approach is useful in programming. This approach involves breaking the programming into logical, manageable portions, or modules. This kind of programming fits well with top-down design because it emphasizes the interfaces between modules, rather than neglecting them until later in systems development. Ideally, each module should be functionally cohesive, so that it is charged with accomplishing only one function.

Modular program design has three main advantages. First, modules are easier to write and debug because they are virtually self-contained. Tracing an error in a module is less complicated, since a problem in one module should not cause problems in others.

A second advantage of modular design is that modules are easier to maintain. Modifications usually will be limited to a few modules, not spread over an entire program.

A third advantage of modular design is that modules are easier to grasp since they are self-contained subsystems. This means that a reader can pick up a code listing of a module and understand its function.

Some guidelines for modular programming include:

1. Keep each module to a manageable size (ideally including only one function).
2. Pay particular attention to the critical interfaces (the data and control variables that are passed to other modules).
3. Minimize the number of modules the user needs to modify when making changes.
4. Maintain the hierarchical relationships set up in the top-down phases.

Modularity in the Windows Environment

Modularity is becoming increasingly important. Microsoft developed two systems to link programs in its Windows environment. The first is called Dynamic Data Exchange (DDE), which shares code by using dynamic link library (DLL) files. Using DDE, a user can store data in one program—perhaps a spreadsheet such as Excel—and then use that data in another program such as, a word-processing package like Word for Windows. The program that contains the original data is called the server, while the program that uses the data is called the client (other terms for *client* are container and host). The DDE link can be set up so that whenever the client word-processing file is opened the data are automatically updated and any changes made to the server spreadsheet file since the word-processing file was last opened will be reflected.

One of the most commonly used DLL files is COMMDLG.DLL, which contains Windows' File Open, File Save, Search, and Print dialog boxes. One advantage of using this file is that programs will have the same look and feel as other Windows programs. It also speeds development, because programmers do not have to write the code contained in common DLL files.

There is a big disadvantage in using a file such as COMMDLG.DLL, however: It is limited in features. Perhaps a systems designer thinks that it is important for the user to have the ability to create a subdirectory, or move or rename files, when saving a file. Maybe it is important to search for a file when you try to open a file. In such cases it becomes necessary to design your own File Open and File Save commands. The main disadvantage to using common DLL files is that these programs tend to use the least common denominator rather than taking advantage of potentially powerful features; therefore they appeal to the average user rather than the power user.

A second approach to linking programs in Windows is called Object Linking and Embedding (OLE). This method of connecting programs is superior to DDE for tying in application data and graphics. While DDE uses a cut-and-paste approach to linking data and does not retain formatting, OLE retains all of the properties of the originally created data. This object-oriented approach (see Chapter 22 for a discussion of object-oriented principles) allows the end user to remain in the client application and still edit the original data in the server application. With OLE 2.0, when an end user clicks on the embedded object a toolbar pops up to allow visual editing. Figure 20.4 shows how a user can edit a graphic produced using PowerPoint while remaining in Word for Windows.

Structure Charts

The recommended tool for designing a modular, top-down system is called a structure chart. A structure chart is simply a diagram consisting of rectangular boxes, which represent the modules, and connecting arrows.

Figure 20.5 shows three modules labeled 1, 1.1, and 1.2. As noted earlier with data flow diagrams, the number to the right of the decimal point in 1.1 and 1.2 signifies that these modules are subsets of module 1.

Structure charts created using the program, Visio, can be seen in Figure 20.6. An alternative notation for the three modules is shown. These are labeled 100, 110, and 120 and are connected using right-angle lines. Higher-level modules are numbered by 100s or 1000s while lower-level modules are numbered by 10s or 100s. This allows programmers to insert modules using a number between the adjacent module numbers. For example, a module inserted between modules 110 and 120 would receive number 115. If two modules were inserted, the numbers might be 114 and 117. These numbering schemes vary, depending on the organizational standards used.

Off to the sides of the connecting lines, two types of arrows are drawn. The arrows with the empty circles are called *data couples,* while the arrows with the filled-in circles are called *control flags* or *switches.* A switch is the same as a control flag except that it is limited to two values: either "yes" or "no." These arrows indicate that something is passed either down to the lower module or back up to the upper one.

FIGURE 20.4
Visual editing allows a user
to change data in one application while remaining in
another.

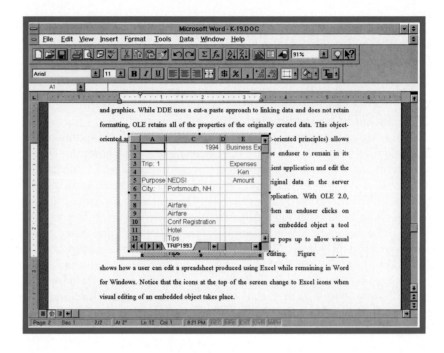

Ideally, the analyst should keep this coupling to a minimum. The fewer data couples and control flags one has in the system, the easier it is to change the system. When these modules are actually programmed, it is important to pass the least number of data couples between modules.

Even more important, numerous control flags should be avoided. Control is designed to be passed from lower-level modules to those higher in the structure. However, on rare occasions, it will be necessary to pass control downward in the structure. Control flags govern which portion of a module is to be executed and are associated with IF...THEN...ELSE... and other similar types of statements. When control is passed downward, a low-level module is allowed to make a decision, and the result is a module that performs two different tasks. This violates the ideal of a functional module: It should perform only one task.

FIGURE 20.5
A structure diagram
encourages top-down design
using modules.

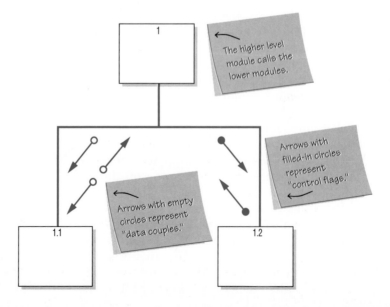

FIGURE 20.6
An alternative style for structure charts.

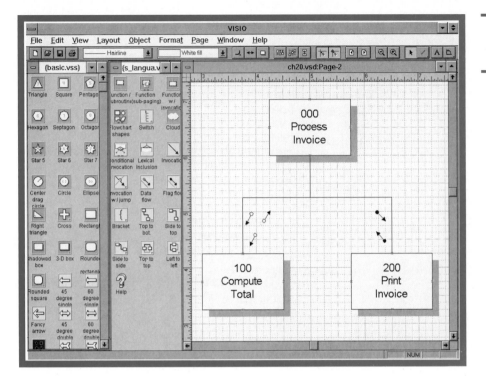

Figure 20.7 illustrates a portion of a structure chart for adding new employees. The program reads an EMPLOYEE TRANSACTION FILE and verifies that each record in the file contains only acceptable data. Separate reports are printed for both valid and invalid records, providing an audit trail of all transactions. The report containing invalid records is sent to the users for error correction. Records that are valid are placed on a valid

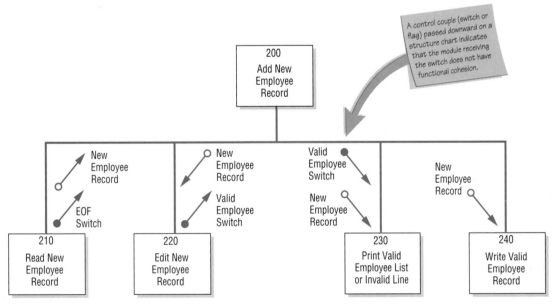

FIGURE 20.7
This structure chart illustrates control moving downward and also shows non-functional modules.

FIGURE 20.8
Pseudocode for module 230
illustrating the effect of
passing a switch downward.

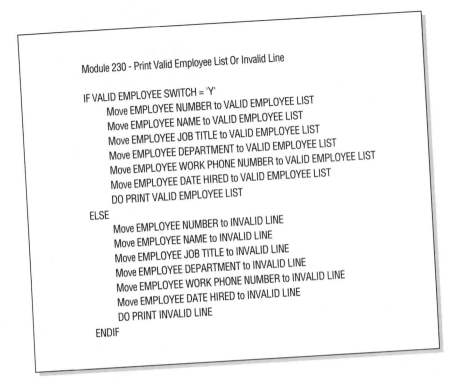

```
Module 230 - Print Valid Employee List Or Invalid Line

IF VALID EMPLOYEE SWITCH = 'Y'
      Move EMPLOYEE NUMBER to VALID EMPLOYEE LIST
      Move EMPLOYEE NAME to VALID EMPLOYEE LIST
      Move EMPLOYEE JOB TITLE to VALID EMPLOYEE LIST
      Move EMPLOYEE DEPARTMENT to VALID EMPLOYEE LIST
      Move EMPLOYEE WORK PHONE NUMBER to VALID EMPLOYEE LIST
      Move EMPLOYEE DATE HIRED to VALID EMPLOYEE LIST
      DO PRINT VALID EMPLOYEE LIST
ELSE
      Move EMPLOYEE NUMBER to INVALID LINE
      Move EMPLOYEE NAME to INVALID LINE
      Move EMPLOYEE JOB TITLE to INVALID LINE
      Move EMPLOYEE DEPARTMENT to INVALID LINE
      Move EMPLOYEE WORK PHONE NUMBER to INVALID LINE
      Move EMPLOYEE DATE HIRED to INVALID LINE
      DO PRINT INVALID LINE
ENDIF
```

transaction file, which is passed to a separate program for updating the Employee master file. Module 200, ADD NEW EMPLOYEE RECORD, represents the logic of adding one record. Since module 230 is used to print both reports, a control flag must be sent down to tell the module which report to print. The logic of module 230 is thus entirely controlled by an IF statement, illustrated in Figure 20.8.

Figure 20.9 shows the correct way to design the structure underneath module 200, ADD NEW EMPLOYEE RECORD. Here, each print function

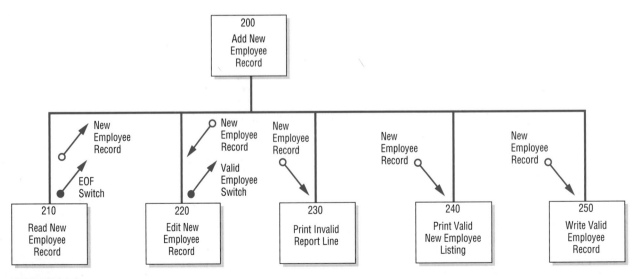

FIGURE 20.9
An improved structure chart showing control flowing upward.

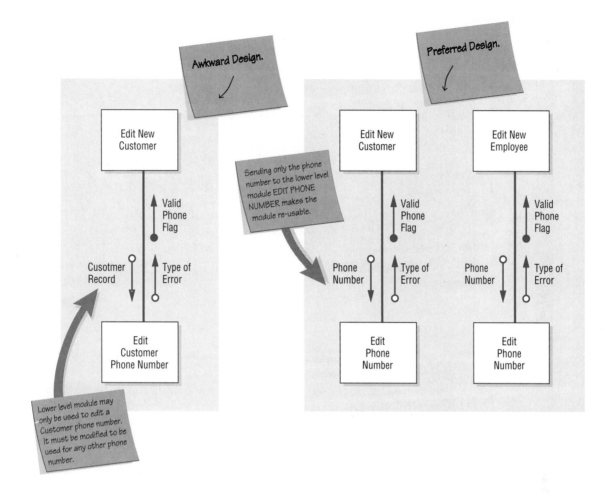

FIGURE 20.10
Creating reusable modules.

has been placed in a separate module, and control flags are only passed up the structure to the higher-level module.

The data that are passed via data couples must also be examined. It is best to pass only the data required to accomplish the function of the module. This approach is called "data coupling." Passing excessive data is called "stamp coupling," and while it is relatively harmless, it reduces the possibility of creating a reusable module. Figure 20.10 illustrates this concept. Here, the module EDIT NEW CUSTOMER passes the CUSTOMER RECORD to the EDIT CUSTOMER PHONE NUMBER module, where PHONE NUMBER, an element found within the CUSTOMER RECORD, is validated and a control flag is passed back to the EDIT NEW CUSTOMER module. The TYPE OF ERROR (if any), containing an error message such as "INVALID AREA CODE" or "PHONE NUMBER IS NOT NUMERIC," is also passed upward. The message may be either printed or displayed on a screen.

While such modules are fairly easy to create and modify every time a phone number from a different source record needs to be edited, a new module, similar to EDIT CUSTOMER PHONE NUMBER must be created. Further, if the way the phone number is being validated changes, as occurs

FIGURE 20.11
Iterations are depicted on
structure charts by drawing a
loop.

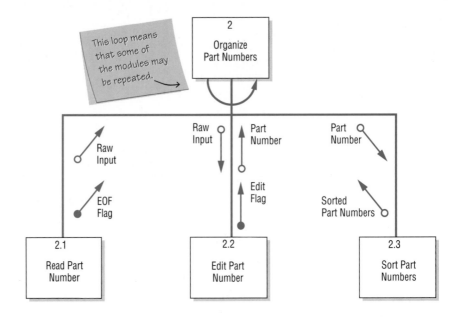

when a new area code or an international country code must be added, each of these lower-level modules must be modified.

Since the lower-level module does not require any of the other elements on the CUSTOMER RECORD, the solution is to pass only the PHONE NUMBER to the lower-level module. The name of the module in this scenario changes to EDIT PHONE NUMBER, and it may be used to edit *any* phone number: a customer phone number or an employee phone number. The modules on the right side of the figure illustrate this concept. When the rules for validating the phone number change, only EDIT PHONE NUMBER needs to be modified, regardless of how many programs utilize that module. Often these general-purpose modules are placed in a separately compiled program, called a subprogram, function, or procedure in various computer languages.

FIGURE 20.12
The small diamond in a
structure chart indicates that
certain modules are to be
performed only when a
specified condition exists.

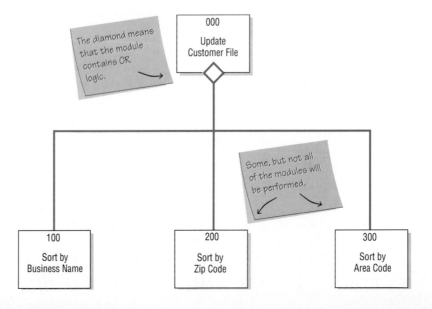

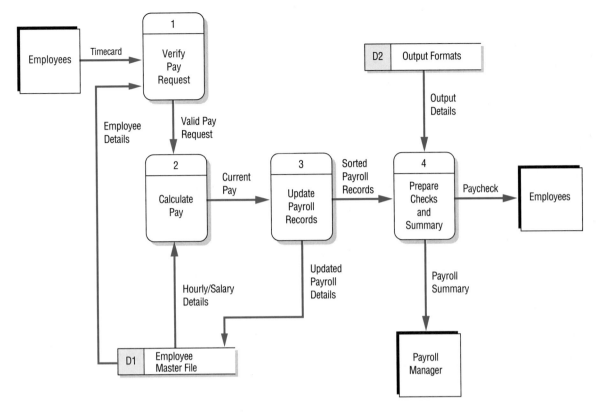

FIGURE 20.13
The data flow diagram for a payroll system is linear.

Another symbol used in structure charts is the loop, as shown in Figure 20.11. This symbol indicates that some procedures found in modules 2.1 and 2.2 are to be repeated until finished. In this example of organizing part numbers, the processes "read part number" and "edit part number" are repeated until there are no more numbers. Then the numbers are sorted in module 2.3. In this example, the data couples are "raw input," "part numbers," and "sorted part numbers." Notice that some of these data couples occur twice, once going up to the main module 2 and once going down to the submodule. The control flags are "E-O-F flag" and "Edit flag."

Still another symbol used in structure charts is the small diamond. The diamond appears on the bottom of one of the rectangles, as shown in Figure 20.12, and signifies that only some of the modules below the diamond will be performed. Notice that the diamond doesn't indicate which modules will be selected, nor does the loop indicate which modules will be repeated. They are meant to be general, not specific.

DRAWING A STRUCTURE CHART. Obviously, structure charts are meant to be drawn from the top down, but where does one start to find the processes that are to become the modules? Most likely, the best place to find this information is in the data flow diagram (see Chapter 9).

Figure 20.13 is a data flow diagram of a payroll system. The entities are the EMPLOYEES and the PAYROLL MANAGER. Four processes are drawn in the data flow diagram:

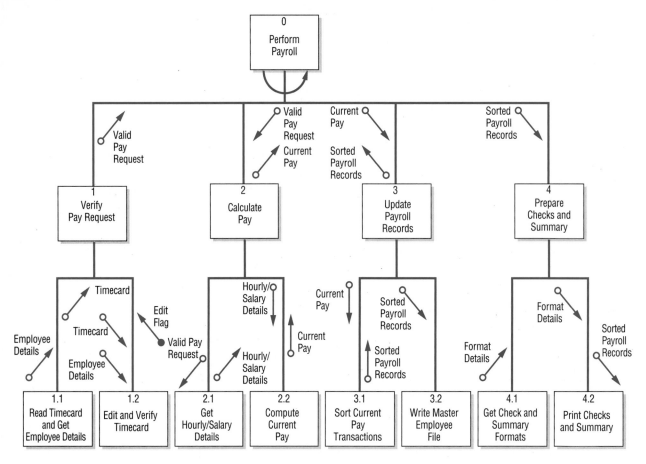

FIGURE 20.14
The structure chart for the payroll example shows hierarchy: data couples and
control flags are kept to a minimum.

1. Verify pay request.
2. Calculate pay.
3. Update payroll records.
4. Prepare checks and summary.

Notice that there are two data stores and many data flows. More important-ly, observe that the data flow diagram is laid out in a linear fashion. Now the data flow diagram will be used to draw the hierarchical structure chart.

The structure chart is shown in Figure 20.14. The main process at the top of the chart is called "Perform payroll" and represents the module that controls everything underneath. The modules on the second level bear the same names and perform the same processes shown in the data flow diagram. Since the data flow diagram is intended to be a logical representation of the system, it is not unusual that the modules derived from the diagram are the same.

The modules on the second level will control the operations of the modules on the third level. These third-level modules accomplish separate functions such as "READ TIMECARD and get EMPLOYEE DETAILS," "EDIT and VERIFY TIMECARD," and so on. Each of these modules contains only one function, which is the ideal case.

The data flows on a data flow diagram turn into the data couples found on a structure chart. Notice that the TIMECARD, VALID PAY REQUEST, and other data are present on both diagrams.

In this example, the data couples and control flags are kept to a minimum. The hierarchical structure makes the structure chart appear to be an inverted tree, but the symmetry is only a coincidence. This example is said to be "transform-centered," because all of the transactions follow the same path.

When all of the transactions do *not* follow the same path, the structure chart is said to be "transaction-centered." A simple example of a transaction-centered structure chart is shown in Figure 20.15. The two diagrams accomplish the same thing, but the top diagram is awkward because the same decision is made in two places. The bottom design is preferred because it can reduce the number of decisions (or alternatively, reduce the number of control flags that have to be passed between modules).

A data flow diagram for a transaction-centered system is shown in Figure 20.16. Here, the major metropolitan newspaper company publishes a variety of newspapers such as the *Morning Star,* the *Daily Planet,* and the special *Weekend Nova.* Depending on the transaction the subscriber wants, a different set of actions will be taken. This sort of transaction-centered system is often drawn as a second-level data flow diagram.

The resulting structure chart can be seen in Figure 20.17. It is important that the decision be made at a high level in the structure chart. One module simply determines the transaction type. Following this, one of the actions is performed. Notice that the module entitled "UPDATE AND PRINT SUBSCRIBERS" is common to all transactions.

This particular structure chart served the main objectives of drawing structure charts; that is:

1. To encourage a top-down design.
2. To support the concept of modules and identify the appropriate modules.
3. To identify and limit as much as possible the data couples and control flags that pass between modules.

When transforming a data flow diagram into a structure chart, there are several additional considerations to keep in mind. The data flow diagram will indicate the sequence of the modules in a structure chart. If one process provides input to another process, the corresponding modules must be performed in the same sequence. Figure 20.18 is a data flow diagram for preparing a student report card. Notice that process 1, READ GRADE RECORD, provides input to process 2, READ COURSE RECORD, and process 3, READ STUDENT RECORD. The structure chart created for this diagram is illustrated in Figure 20.19. Notice that module 110, READ GRADE RECORD, must be executed first. Processes 2 and 3 must be executed next, but since they do not provide input to each other, the order of these modules in the structure chart is unimportant and may be reversed without any effect on the final results. Processes 2 and 3 provide input to process 4, CALCULATE GRADE POINT AVERAGE. Process 5, PRINT STUDENT REPORT CARD, receives data flow from all the other processes and must be the last module to be performed.

If a process explodes to a child data flow diagram, the module corresponding to the parent process will have subordinate modules that correspond to the processes found on the child diagram. Process 5, PRINT

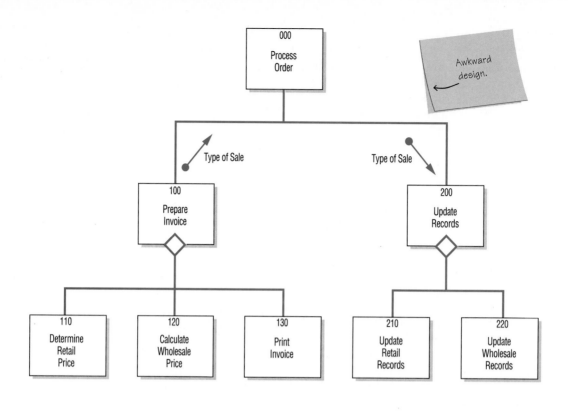

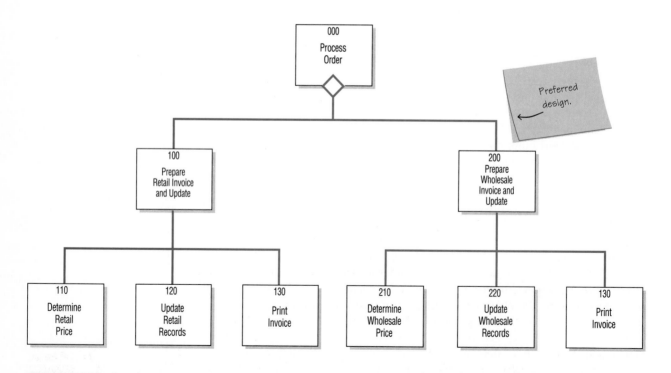

FIGURE 20.15
To prevent redundant decisions (or the passing of a control flag such as type of sale), the structure chart can be redrawn to make the decision at the top.

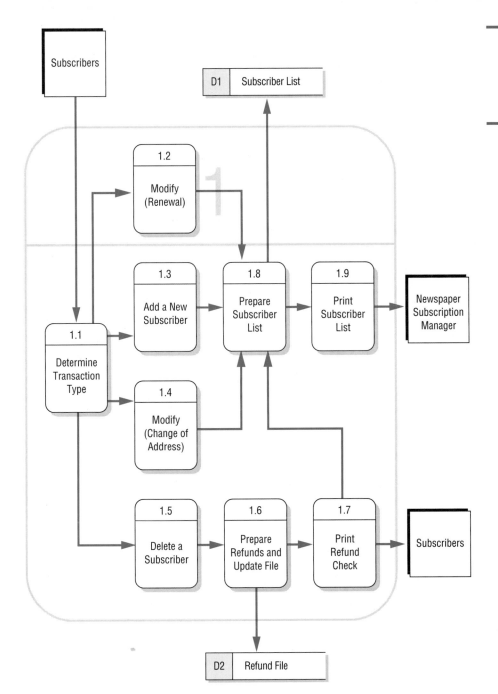

STUDENT REPORT CARD, has four input data flows and one output and is therefore a good candidate for a child diagram. Figure 20.20 illustrates Diagram 5, the details of process 5. The processes on Diagram 5 translate to the modules subordinate to module 150, PRINT STUDENT REPORT CARD.

Types of Modules

Structure chart modules fall into one of three general categories: control, transformational (sometimes called worker), and functional or specialized. When producing a structure chart that is easy to develop and modify, care should be taken not to mix the different types of modules.

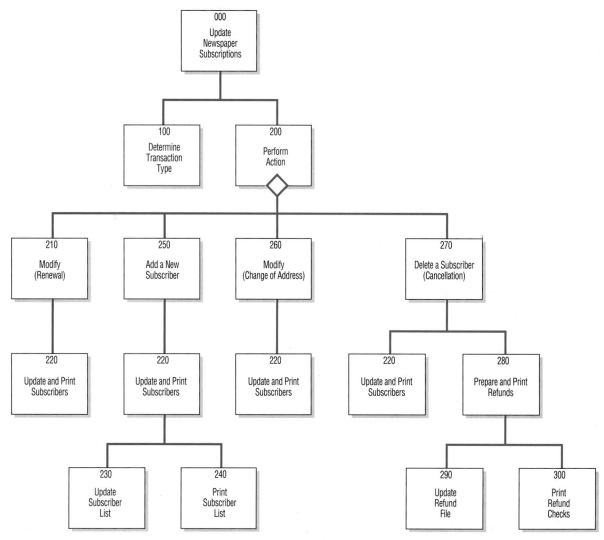

FIGURE 20.17
A structure chart for a transaction-centered system can branch out from a diamond and then later share the same module.

Control modules are usually found near the top of the structure chart and contain the logic for performing the lower-level modules. The control modules may or may not be represented on the data flow diagram. The types of statements that are usually in control modules are IF, PERFORM, and DO. Detailed statements such as ADD and MOVE are usually kept to a minimum. Control logic is usually the most difficult to design, and therefore control modules should not be very large in size. If a control module has more than seven to nine subordinate modules, new control modules should be created that are subordinate to the original control module. The logic of a control module may be determined from a decision tree or decision table. A decision table with too many rules is split into several decision tables, with the first table performing the second table. Each decision table would create a resulting control module. (See Chapter 11 for more on decision trees and tables.)

Transformational modules are those created from a data flow diagram. They usually perform only one task, although several secondary

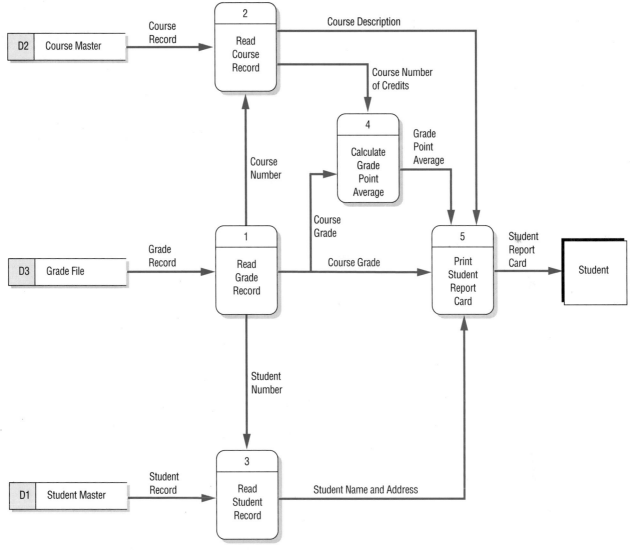

FIGURE 20.18
Data flow diagram for printing a student report card.

tasks may be associated with the primary task. For example, a module named PRINT CUSTOMER TOTAL LINE may format the total line, print the line, add to the final totals, and finally set the customer totals to zero in preparation for accumulating the amounts of the next customer. Transformational modules usually have mixed statements, a few IF and PERFORM or DO statements, and many detailed statements such as MOVE, ADD, and so on. These modules are lower in the structure than control modules.

Functional or specialist modules are the lowest in the structure, with a rare subordinate module beneath them. They perform only one task such as formatting, reading, calculating, writing, and so on. Some of these modules are found on a data flow diagram, but others may have to be added, such as reading a record or printing an error line.

Figure 20.21 represents the structure chart for adding reservations for hotel guests. Modules 000, ADD GUEST RESERVATIONS, and 100,

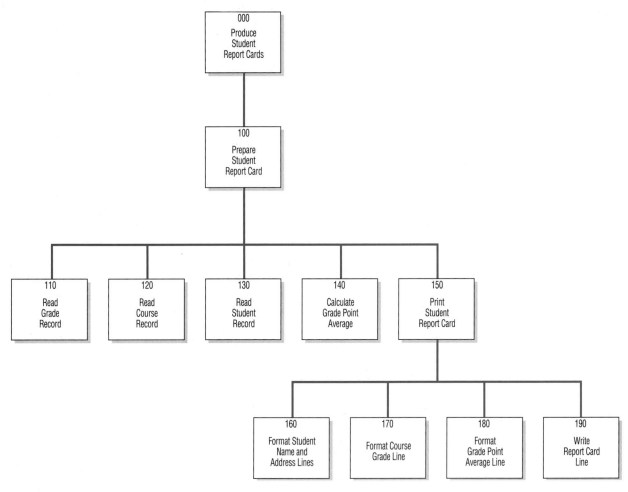

FIGURE 20.19
A structure chart for producing student report cards.

ADD ROOM RESERVATION, are control modules, representing the entire program (module 000) and the control necessary for making one room reservation (module 100). Module 110, DISPLAY RESERVATION SCREEN, is a functional module responsible for displaying the initial reservation screen. Modules 120, GET VALID ROOM RESERVATION, and 160, CONFIRM ROOM RESERVATION, are lower-level control modules.

Module 120, GET VALID ROOM RESERVATION, is performed iteratively until the reservation data is valid or until the reservation operator cancels the transaction. This type of GET VALID... module relieves the 100 module of a fair amount of complex code. The modules subordinate to GET VALID ROOM RESERVATION are functional modules responsible for receiving the reservation screen, editing or validating the room reservation, and displaying an error screen if the input data are not valid. Since these modules are in a loop, control remains in this portion of the structure until the screen data are valid.

Module 160, CONFIRM ROOM RESERVATION, is also performed iteratively and allows the operator to sight-verify that the correct information has been entered. In this situation, the operator will inspect the screen and press a

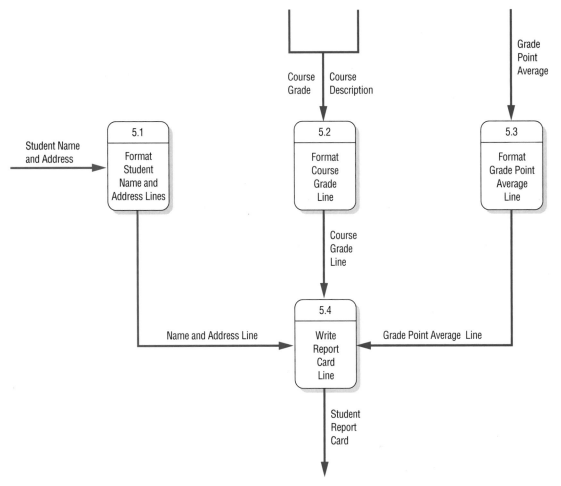

FIGURE 20.20
Child diagram for process 5, PRINT STUDENT REPORT CARD.

specified key, such as the Enter key if the data are correct or a different key to modify or cancel the transaction. Again, the program will remain in these modules, looping until the operator accepts or cancels the reservation.

Module 190 is a transformational module that formats the RESERVA-TION RECORD and performs module 200 to write the RESERVATION RECORD. Modules 130, 140, 150, 170, 180, and 200 are functional modules, performing only one task: accepting a screen, displaying a screen, or editing or writing a record. These modules are the easiest to code, debug, and maintain.

Module Subordination

A subordinate module is one lower on the structure chart called by another module higher in the structure. Each subordinate module should represent a task that is a part of the function of the higher-level module. Allowing the lower-level module to perform a task not required by the calling module is called improper subordination. In such a case, the lower module should be moved higher in the structure.

Figure 20.22 illustrates this concept using a structure chart for changing a customer master file. Examine module 120, READ CUSTOMER

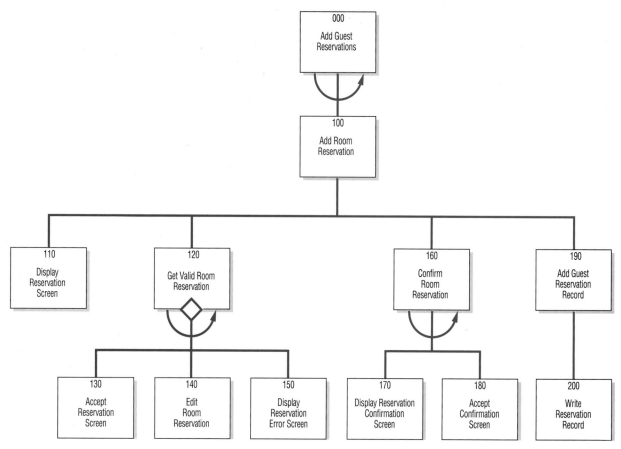

FIGURE 20.21
A structure chart for adding hotel guest reservations on line.

MASTER. It has the task of using the CUSTOMER NUMBER from the CHANGE TRANSACTION RECORD to directly obtain the matching CUSTOMER RECORD. If the record is not found, an error line is printed. Otherwise, the CUSTOMER MASTER is changed, and the record is rewritten. This should be a functional module, simply reading a record, but instead it has three subordinate modules. The question must be asked, "Does an error line have to be printed to accomplish reading the CUSTOMER MASTER?" Further, "Does the new CUSTOMER MASTER RECORD have to be formatted and rewritten in order to read the CUSTOMER MASTER?" Since the answer to both questions is "No," modules 130, 140, and 150 should not be subordinate to READ CUSTOMER MASTER.

Figure 20.23 shows the corrected structure chart. Control statements are moved out of the READ CUSTOMER MASTER record and into the primary control module, CHANGE CUSTOMER RECORD. READ CUSTOMER MASTER becomes a functional module.

Even when a structure chart accomplishes all of the purposes for which it was drawn, the structure chart cannot stand alone as the sole design/documentation technique. First, it doesn't show the order in which the modules should be executed (a data flow diagram will accomplish this). Second, it doesn't show enough detail (Nassi-Shneiderman charts,

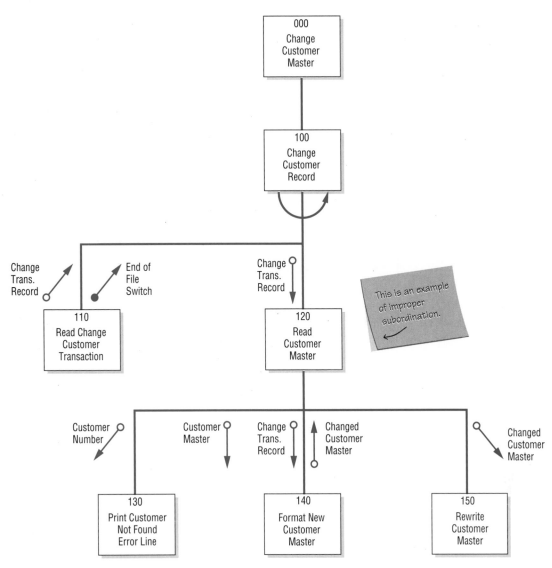

FIGURE 20.22
A structure chart illustrating the principle of improper subordination.

Warnier-Orr diagrams, and pseudocode will accomplish this). The remainder of this chapter will discuss these more detailed design/documentation techniques for software development, using the newspaper subscription problem presented earlier, which we will now view in more detail.

SOFTWARE ENGINEERING AND DOCUMENTATION

Planning and control are essential elements of every successful system. In developing software for the system, planning takes place in the design before programming is even begun. We need techniques to help us set program objectives, so that our programs are complete. We also need design techniques to help us break apart the programming effort into manageable modules.

It is not satisfactory, however, to try to get by with just the planning stages. After programs are completed they must be maintained, and

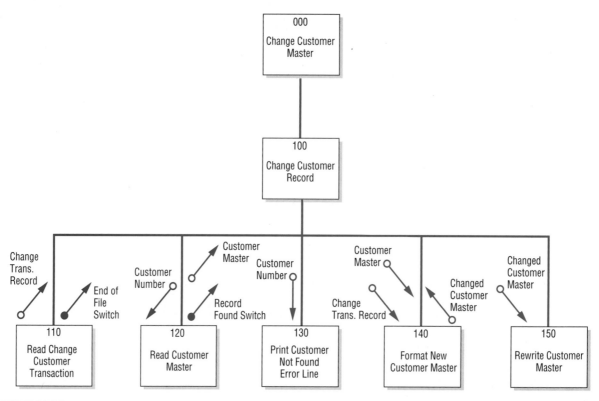

FIGURE 20.23
A corrected structure chart showing proper subordination.

maintenance efforts typically outweigh the effort expended on the original design and programming.

The techniques described in the upcoming section are meant not only to be used initially in the design of software, but also in its maintenance. Since most systems are not considered disposable, they will need to be maintained. The total quality assurance effort requires that programs be documented properly.

Software and procedures are documented so that they are encoded into a format that can be easily accessed. Access to procedures is necessary for new people learning the system and as a reminder to those who use the program infrequently. Documentation allows users, programmers, and analysts to "see" the system, its software, and procedures without having to interact with it.

Some documentation provides an overview of the system itself, while procedural documentation details what must be done to run software on the system, and program documentation details the program code used.

Turnover of information service personnel has traditionally been high in comparison to other departments, so chances are that the people who conceived of and installed the original system will not be the same ones who maintain it. Consistent, well-kept-up documentation will shorten the number of hours required for new people to learn the system before performing maintenance.

There are many reasons why systems and programs are undocumented or underdocumented; some of the problems reside with the systems and programs themselves, others with systems analysts and programmers.

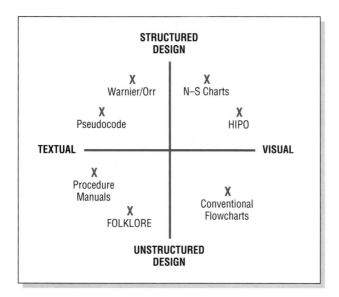

FIGURE 20.24
Each software design and
documentation technique is
unique in how visual it is and
how structured it is.

Some old systems were written before the business standardized its documentation techniques but are still in use (*sans* documentation). Many other systems have tolerated major and minor modifications and patches over the years, but their documentation has not been modified to reflect them. Some systems featuring specialized programs were purchased for their important applications despite their lack of accompanying documentation.

Systems analysts may fail to document systems properly because they do not have time or are not rewarded for time spent documenting. Some analysts do not document because they dread doing so or feel that it is not their real work. Further, many analysts are reticent about documenting systems that are not their own, perhaps fearing reprisals if they include incorrect material about someone else's system. Documentation accomplished via a CASE tool during the analysis phases can address many of these problems.

Design and Documentation Techniques

There is no single standard design and documentation technique in use today. In this section, we discuss several different techniques that are currently in use. Each technique has its own advantages and disadvantages, because each has unique properties. Figure 20.24 shows how each technique compares to the others if we plot them according to two attributes: (1) how structured the technique is and (2) how visual the technique is.

Next, we discuss each of these techniques, starting from the upper right-hand quadrant in the figure, where the most highly structured, very visual techniques appear.

The HIPO Method

HIPO is an acronym for Hierarchy (plus) Input/Process/Output. The acronym provides us with a description and a memory aid for what this technique is about.

First, it is hierarchical because the entire programming system consists of smaller subsystems. This technique supports a top-down design approach and also reduces the perceived complexity of the system because each of the subcomponents can be addressed separately.

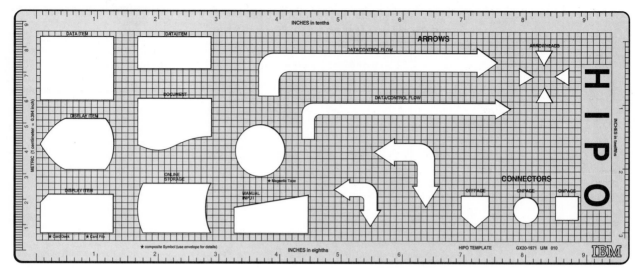

FIGURE 20.25
The standard HIPO template.

Second, the acronym reminds us of the three main parts of any system: input, process, and output. Once the hierarchy chart is completed, other HIPO diagrams are drawn on pages divided vertically into three sections, with the input section on the left, the process section in the middle, and the output section on the right.

HIPO is a visual technique. The main benefit of visual techniques derives from ease in reading the standardized symbols they use to depict types of data entry, data storage, and data output devices. HIPO was developed by IBM, and therefore HIPO templates (see Figure 20.25) and worksheets are obtainable from IBM.

There are three main types of diagrams in the HIPO system:

1. VTOC or visual table of contents.
2. Overview IPO (input/process/output) diagrams.
3. Detailed IPO diagrams.

Each of these types is discussed in the upcoming subsections.

THE VTOC (VISUAL TABLE OF CONTENTS). The VTOC is the hierarchy chart. It provides a map that allows the reader to locate a program module within the main system. Notice in Figure 20.26 that the numbers in each of the boxes follow a pattern so that one can easily see the relationship between two modules. That is, modules 2.1 (Transaction Entry) and 2.4 (Update File) belong to the same system component 2.0 (Inventory Update), but modules 3.1 (Generate Daily Report) and 3.2 (Generate Summaries) belong to component 3.0 (Report Processing). These same numbers are used in the overview IPO diagrams and detailed IPO diagrams.

The hierarchy chart in the VTOC appears similar to a traditional organizational chart; it will take on the shape of a pyramid. Below the chart, there is room for a more complete description of the boxes within it.

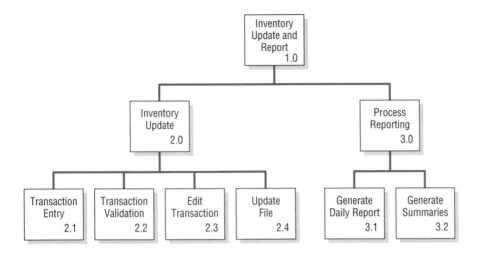

FIGURE 20.26
The VTOC chart maps the
main system for the reader,
who can then locate a
program module within it.

1.0 INVENTORY UPDATE AND REPORT SYSTEM (Main Program Module)
Coordinates all processing of other program modules.

2.0 INVENTORY UPDATE
Process all transactions and updates the inventory file.

   2.1 TRANSACTION ENTRY
   Enters all transactions involving units added, sold, spoiled, or lost.

   2.2 TRANSACTION VALIDATION
   Checks to determine whether transaction type and part number are valid.

   2.3 EDIT TRANSACTION
   Allows the editing to correct transaction types or part numbers.

   2.4 UPDATE FILE
   Adds and deletes items and quantities in inventory file.

3.0 REPORT PROCESSING PROGRAM
Runs daily and summary report modules.

   3.1 GENERATE DAILY REPORT
   Totals and prints daily report of inventory.

   3.2 GENERATE SUMMARIES
   Totals and prints inventory summary report.

OVERVIEW IPO DIAGRAMS. The next type of diagram in the HIPO system allows a macro view of input, process, and output, and hence it is referred to as an overview diagram. At this point, it is useful to list all of the inputs, processes, and outputs in the three sections of the paper without drawing in the specialized symbols.

An example of an overview IPO diagram can be found in Figure 20.27. Notice that this particular diagram encompasses all of module 3.0. Inputs include the old inventory file and transaction record. Processing includes both modules 3.1 and 3.2. Output from this part of the system includes the new inventory file, backorder file, daily inventory report, and summary report.

DETAILED IPO DIAGRAMS. In order to make them more useful, the overview diagrams must be broken apart into diagrams for each of the modules contained within them. Therefore, the overview diagram for 2.0 will be broken up into separate diagrams for modules 2.1, 2.2, 2.3, and 2.4.

FIGURE 20.27
An example of an overview
IPO diagram for 3.0 that gives
a macro view of input,
process, and output.

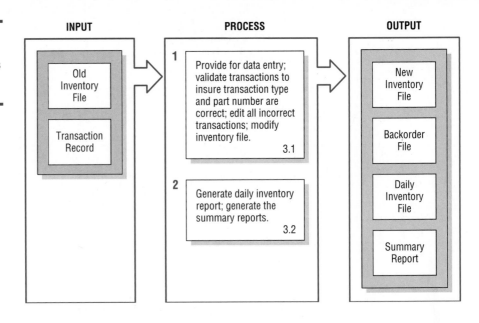

At this point, it facilitates understanding to add symbols for input and output media. Figure 20.28 shows how a detailed diagram would be used in the system we described. Disk symbols are used to indicate how the "transaction file" and the "transaction file sorted by part number" are stored. Part numbers are stored on magnetic tape, as shown. Finally, the list of invalid transactions are output to a display.

FIGURE 20.28
A detailed IPO diagram for
2.2 that uses symbols for
input and output media.

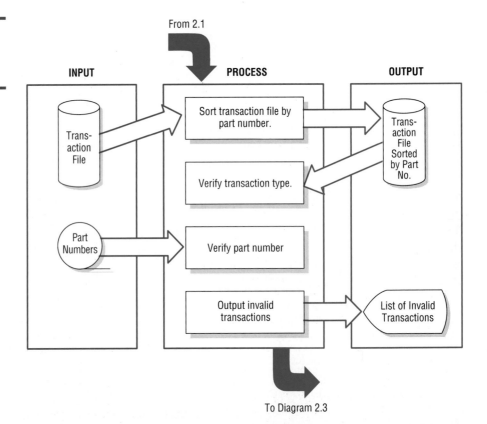

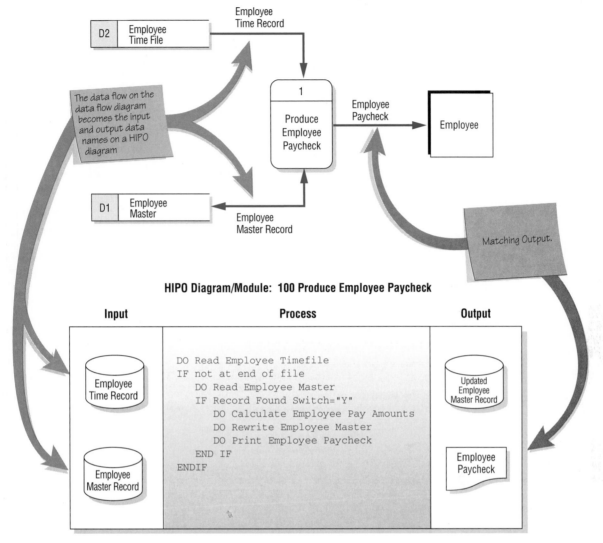

FIGURE 20.29
Linking the data flow diagram to a HIPO diagram.

The data flow diagram may be used to create a HIPO diagram. Data flow is represented as the data listed in the Input and Output columns. Data stores translate into the disk or tape symbols, and printed data flows sent to the user become report symbols. Refer to Figure 20.29, showing the data flow diagram and corresponding HIPO diagram for creating an employee paycheck. This same input and output is included on a structure chart as the coupling passed between modules.

HIPO Strengths and Weaknesses. HIPO is a highly visual, somewhat structured technique for design and documentation. When analysts become familiar with the symbols used, HIPO becomes a valuable tool. Too often, however, others in the organization are unfamiliar with the symbols, so HIPO turns out to be too specialized a tool for explaining how a system or program works.

HIPO takes up a considerable amount of space on paper. In order to see a whole program, it is necessary to flip through a number of pages. The

FIGURE 20.30
Similar symbols are used for documenting systems and programs in conventional flowcharting.

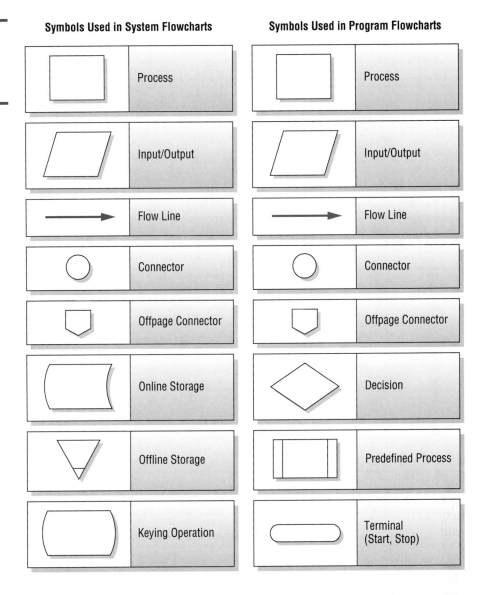

Symbols Used in System Flowcharts	Symbols Used in Program Flowcharts
Process	Process
Input/Output	Input/Output
Flow Line	Flow Line
Connector	Connector
Offpage Connector	Offpage Connector
Online Storage	Decision
Offline Storage	Predefined Process
Keying Operation	Terminal (Start, Stop)

numerous pages may end up losing the reader. The various levels of diagrams also take up space, and it is sometimes difficult to follow program flow. Thus HIPO diagrams are most often used to represent the details of each module on a structure chart and to prepare computer program code.

However, HIPO is also useful in documenting programs. It provides an avenue for the program author to return readily to the program after a long period of time. Other programmers who understand the standardized symbols also appreciate the value of HIPO diagrams, and they are commonly used in structured walkthroughs.

Flowcharts

Another visual, but unstructured approach to program design and documentation is the use of ordinary flowcharts. Examples of the symbols for documenting both systems and programs can be found in Figure 20.30. Notice that some symbols are common to both systems and programs. In Figure 20.31, examples of more specific symbols are used to identify the form of input (paper document, magnetic tape, drum, disk, manual input, and VDT display).

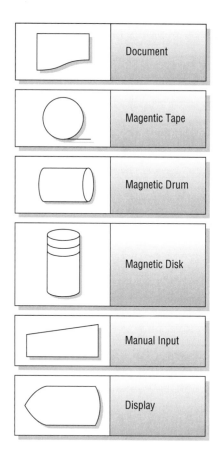

	Document
	Magentic Tape
	Magnetic Drum
	Magnetic Disk
	Manual Input
	Display

FIGURE 20.31
Identify input media with the more specific symbols used in flowcharting.

A sample flowchart paralleling the HIPO chart described in the previous section is shown in Figure 20.32. The flowchart is linear; therefore, not as much attention is paid to input and output. Notice that the "file of transactions" and "file of sorted transactions" are drawn on the main flow line with the processes, and consequently do not stand out.

There are many disadvantages to using ordinary flowcharts. First, they are not drawn according to the fundamentals of structured programming, so they depict the flow of the program, but not its structure. Like HIPO, flowcharts take up considerable space, so the reader has to turn many pages to grasp what the program does. There are so many branches coming from each of the decisions on a flowchart that there are many different ways to draw them. Each author uses a unique style and therefore finds it difficult to read another author's flowchart. There is also an extensive list of symbols to understand and memorize, which makes flowcharts more difficult to use.

Perhaps the best reason for using flowcharts is that they have been used for a long time, and people who have been promoted within a company over the years may understand ordinary flowcharts better than newer techniques. If this is an important consideration, ordinary flowcharts may be an appropriate documentation technique.

Nassi-Shneiderman Charts

A more structured but somewhat less visual approach for design and documentation is the Nassi-Shneiderman (N-S) chart. The main advantage of the N-S chart is that it adopts the philosophy of structured programming. Second, it uses a limited number of symbols so that the flowchart takes up

FIGURE 20.32
A system flowchart is a visual
but unstructured way to
design and document
systems.

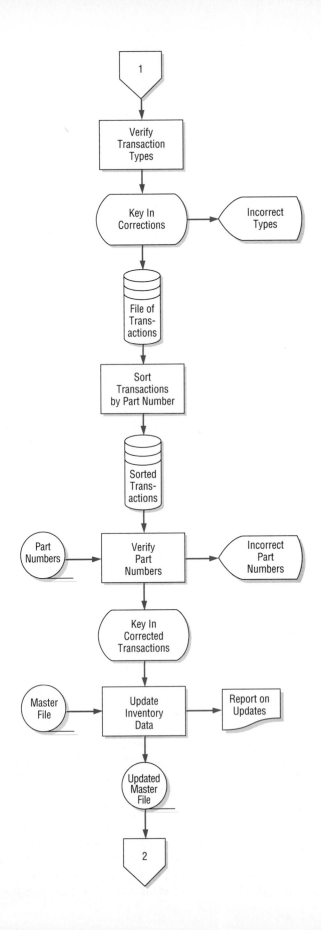

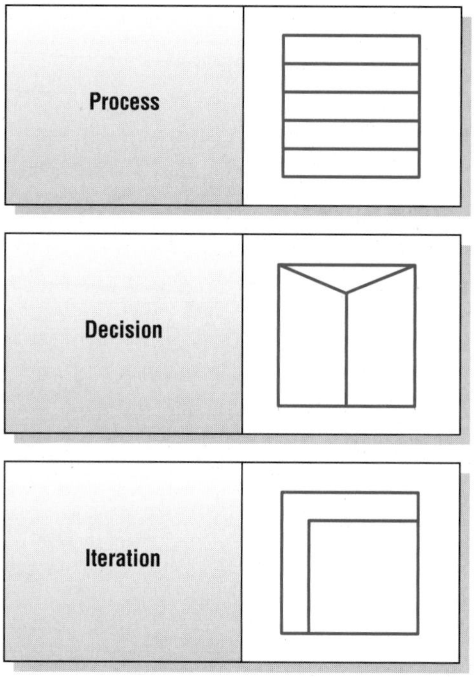

FIGURE 20.33
The three basic symbols used
to draw Nassi-Shneiderman
charts.

less space and can be read by someone unfamiliar with symbols used in other types of flowcharts. Figure 20.33 shows the three basic symbols that are used in N-S charts.

The first symbol is a box, used to represent any process in the program. The second symbol is a column-splitting triangle to represent a decision (notice the similarity to a diamond in traditional flowcharting). The most basic form of a decision, "true" or "false," is shown in this figure, but any form of a decision including several condition alternatives can be depicted using this symbol. The third symbol is the box-within-a-box symbol used to show that an iteration takes place. The box-within-a-box also appears as an indentation on the whole chart.

In structured programming, a top-down approach is used. This means that the analyst would begin by drawing the major loops first and then indent to complete the inner loops later.

A newspaper subscription updating system is depicted in the N-S chart in Figure 20.34. The example shows that a process is repeated for every newspaper on a daily basis. Within each newspaper iteration, a number of operations such as clearing newspaper totals, printing the date, and printing the newspaper name are performed. Then another loop is encountered; this loop is performed for every subscriber update. A search for the subscriber record is performed and, depending on whether the transaction is a (1) renewal, (2) new subscription, (3) cancellation, or (4) change of address, a different action is taken. Other tasks (such as updating totals and printing information) are performed, and the iterations are continued while there are subscribers and newspapers to update.

Nassi-Shneiderman charts must be complete and comprehensive in order to be understood. This is somewhat of a disadvantage in comparison to other methods, since the fear of being incomplete might prevent analysts and programmers from even starting a N-S chart. If changes to the system will be made regularly, N-S charts may not be appropriate. Since they must

FIGURE 20.34
Using a Nassi-Shneiderman
chart to depict a daily subscription updating service for
newspapers.

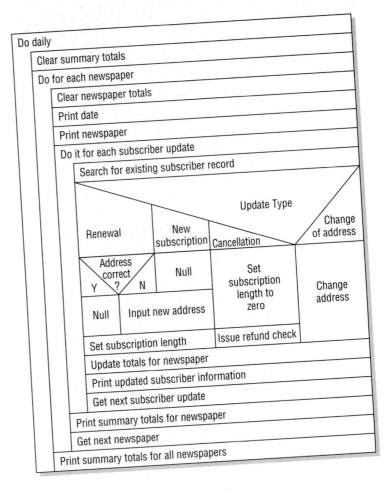

be entirely redrawn to accommodate change, N-S charts are not easily modified.

On the other hand, the benefits of using N-S charts are many. They provide analysts with a tool for aiding the program design and development process because they are compatible with structured programming. The N-S chart is easy to read because no knowledge of complex symbols is required. It does not take up precious space either. In summary, the N-S chart can be a very valuable tool for the analyst, and it is supported by some CASE tools such as XperCASE.

Warnier-Orr Diagrams

Another structured technique is the Warnier-Orr diagram. The approach is similar to that of HIPO and N-S charts in that a hierarchical or top-down approach is also taken. The Warnier-Orr diagram is not as visual as the N-S chart, as brackets are the only symbols it uses.

The brackets and other notation can be found in Figure 20.35. Brackets are used to represent sets and subsets, and variables such as *M* and *N* are used to represent the number of times an iteration is performed. When one condition is either met or not met, the notation (0, 1) is used, and a + signifies that the list of items are possible alternatives. PERFORM is used to branch to another part of the program.

Symbol	Meaning
{ { {	Signify sets and subsets
(M)	Means do the set M times
(0, 1)	Means the condition must be either true or false
+	Implies the statements above and below the + are mutually exclusive alternatives
PERFORM	Is used to jump to another part of the diagram

The left side of the Warnier-Orr diagram represents the overview. As the analyst moves from left to right, the system is decomposed into smaller subsystems. Development of Warnier-Orr diagrams is unique because, once the general structure is defined, the analyst starts with the output and works backwards. Unlike the N-S chart, sufficient room can be left to make any necessary modifications.

The same newspaper update procedure discussed in the N-S chart section is used as an example here. In Figure 20.36, the analyst or programmer starts with the broadest item (daily update) and uses brackets to denote the beginning, middle, and end of the daily update procedure. Within the middle bracket is the newspaper loop performed N times, and it too has a beginning, middle, and end.

The middle section is once again exploded to show the subscriber update loop, performed S times. Within this loop, the transaction can be one of the following: a renewal, new subscriber, change of address, or cancellation. The (0,1) denotes that all of these transactions are either true or false, while the + signifies that they are indeed mutually exclusive.

The next step is to add the detailed operations to the Warnier-Orr diagram, as in Figure 20.37. Compare the Warnier-Orr diagram to the N-S chart.

Warnier-Orr diagrams are useful because they are compatible with structured programming techniques and are easy to develop. Since they also show program flow from the top to the bottom of a page, they are superior to HIPO diagrams. Warnier-Orr diagrams are easy to read and easier to modify than N-S charts. They do not have to be complete before they are useful (unlike the N-S charts described earlier) because Warnier-Orr diagrams are developed backwards from system outputs.

FIGURE 20.36
Using a Warnier-Orr diagram
to depict a daily subscription
service for newspapers.

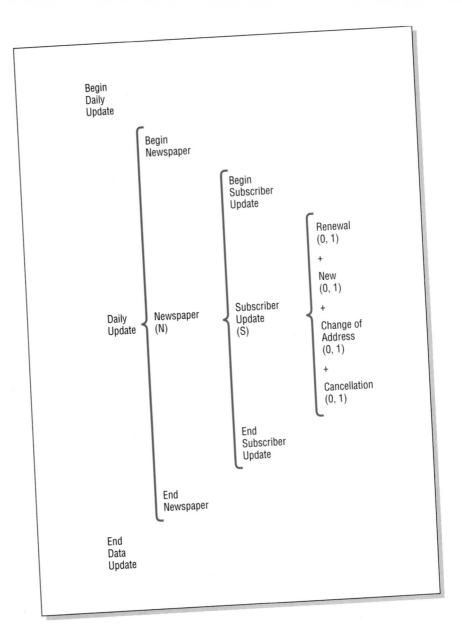

Pseudocode

In Chapter 11, we introduced the concept of structured English as a technique of analyzing decisions. Pseudocode is similar to structured English in that it is not a particular type of programming code, but it can be used as an intermediate step for developing program code. Pseudocode for the newspaper example is given in Figure 20.38.

The use of pseudocode is common in the industry, but lack of standardization will prevent it from being accepted by everyone. Since pseudocode is so close to program code, it is naturally favored by programmers and consequently not as favored by business analysts.

Pseudocode is frequently used to represent the logic of each module on a structure chart. Often, it is incorporated into the process logic of a HIPO diagram. When there is not enough time to create formal HIPO diagrams, pseudocode is used for structured walkthroughs.

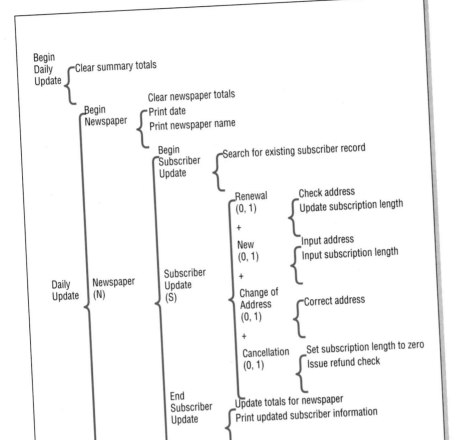

FIGURE 20.37
Adding detailed operations to
the newspaper service
Warnier-Orr diagram.

The data flow diagram may be used to write the pseudocode logic. When used at a program level, rather than a system level, the data flow diagram may incorporate several additional symbols. The asterisk (∗), meaning "and," is used to indicate that both data flows named must be present. Refer to the portion of a data flow diagram that is illustrated in Figure 20.39. If the input data flows are from different records, the presence of the "and" connector signifies that the process receiving the flow must perform some sort of file matching. This is either a sequential match, reading all the records from both files, or an indexed read of a second file using a key field obtained from the first file.

The plus sign enclosed in a circle ⊕ represents an exclusive "or" and indicates that one or the other data flow is present at any given time. Use of this symbol implies that the process receiving or producing the data flow must have

FIGURE 20.38
Using pseudocode to depict a
daily subscription update
service for newspapers.

```
Open Files
Summary.total = 0
Read the first newspaper.name
DO WHILE there are more newspaper.name(s)
     PRINT date
     PRINT newspaper.name
     Newspaper.total = 0
     Read first subscriber.record
     DO WHILE there are more subscriber.record(s)
          IF Action = Renewal
               THEN subs.length = subs.length + num.weeks
               IF address < > cur.address
                    THEN PERFORM Address.change
               ELSE continue
          ELSE IF Action = New
                    THEN PERFORM Address.change
                    subs.length - num.weeks
          ELSE IF Action = Cancellation
                    subs.length = 0
                    PERFORM Refund
          ELSE IF Action = Address.change
                    PERFORM Address.change
          ELSE PERFORM Action.error
          ENDIF
          Newspaper.total = Newspaper.total + 1
          PERFORM Print.subscriber
          Read another subscriber.record
     ENDDO
     PERFORM Print.newspaper
     Get next newspaper.name
ENDDO
Close Files
```

a corresponding IF...THEN...ELSE statement. In the figure, process 1, EDIT
EMPLOYEE CHANGES, must have an IF statement to determine if the change
transaction is valid or not. Process 2, UPDATE EMPLOYEE RECORD, must
have both the VALID EMPLOYEE TRANSACTION and the EMPLOYEE MAS-
TER RECORD, and must match the records somehow to produce the output.

Procedure Manuals

Procedure manuals are common organizational documents that most people have seen. They are the English component of documentation,
although they may also contain program codes, flowcharts, and so on.
Manuals are intended to communicate to those who use them. They may
contain background comments, steps required to accomplish different
transactions, instructions on how to recover from problems, and what to
do next if something isn't working (troubleshooting). Many manuals are
now available on line, with hypertext capability that facilitates use.

Getting a Leg Up

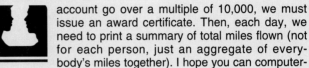

"I think it's magnificent," proclaims Glen. He's been taking a bird's eye view of the decision tree you drew of Premium Airline's 'Flying for Prizes' policies. "This will help me straighten up and fly right when I'm explaining our program to everyone. You've put us on course, all right. Now if you can just get the computers to cooperate! No, I'm just kidding you. But you know, something else has come up since you've talked with the ticket agents. We've got new instructions on handling fliers' accounts.

"Basically, they say that on a daily basis we must update each 'Flying for Prizes' account, for each flier, for each leg they travel (an example of a leg is from Omaha to Chicago; another one would be from Chicago to New York). If the miles flown in an account go over a multiple of 10,000, we must issue an award certificate. Then, each day, we need to print a summary of total miles flown (not for each person, just an aggregate of everybody's miles together). I hope you can computerize this for us. They've got pretty lofty expectations, but I guess it's good to aim high. Let us know if it's just pie in the sky, though."

Premium Airlines has asked you to help them further with their "Flying for Prizes" system. First, draw an overview Warnier-Orr diagram that depicts the functions Glen has just described to you.

Enhance your understanding by taking the next step and drawing a second, detailed Warnier-Orr diagram. Use the logic details given in Consulting Opportunity 11.4 to draw your second diagram.

A straightforward, standardized approach to writing manuals is desirable. A business will often make a person or even an entire department responsible for producing and maintaining manuals. It is essential that manuals are thought of as current rather than historical documents. To be useful, manuals must be kept up to date. Many software developers therefore include "read me" files with applications to document changes in the software that occurred too late in its development to be included in the accompanying printed user's manual.

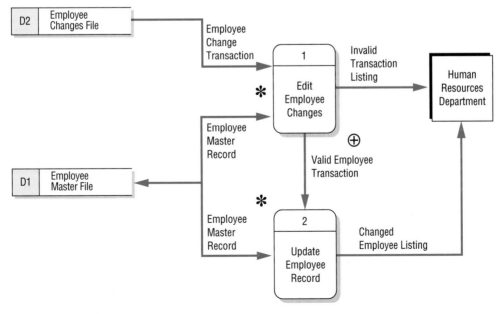

FIGURE 20.39
Use of "and" (∗) and "or" ⊕ connectors to determine program logic.

FIGURE 20.40
Table of contents of the procedure manual for a program called EZsort.

TABLE OF CONTENTS

Section 1 Introducing EZSORT	1
1. About EZSORT	2
2. Starting Up	3
3. The Basics	5
4. A Short Tutorial	
Section 2 Using EZSORT	12
1. Data Entry	13
2. Sorting Using EZSORT	17
3. Sorting Options	20
4. Output	25
5. Advanced Sorting Using EZSORT	30
Section 3 What to Do If...	41
1. Some Common Problems	42
2. Staying Out of Trouble	47
Section 4 Reference	50
1. Input Parameters	51
2. Sorting Options	53
3. Output Parameters	55
4. List of Error Messages	58
5. Glossary	62
6. Hardware Constraints	66
Index	75

Manuals should not contain overblown rhetoric touting the benefits of the application, the contents of the manual, or what the manual documents. Remember that the manual is not an advertisement.

A good manual will be used repeatedly as a reference. As such, it needs to be organized in a logical way with careful thought given to the circumstances that would call forth use of the manual. If an on-line manual uses a hypertext interface, users will be able to access documentation that is context-specific.

The example of a table of contents for a manual shown in Figure 20.40 lists key sections necessary for a good manual. The biggest complaints with procedure manuals are: (1) they are poorly organized; (2) it is hard to find needed information; (3) the specific case in question does not appear in the manual; and (4) the manual is not written in plain English.

In addition to the manual's organization and clarity, careful thought should be given to the kinds of people who will be using the manual. In an upcoming section on testing, we discuss the importance of having users "test" systems manuals before the manuals are finalized.

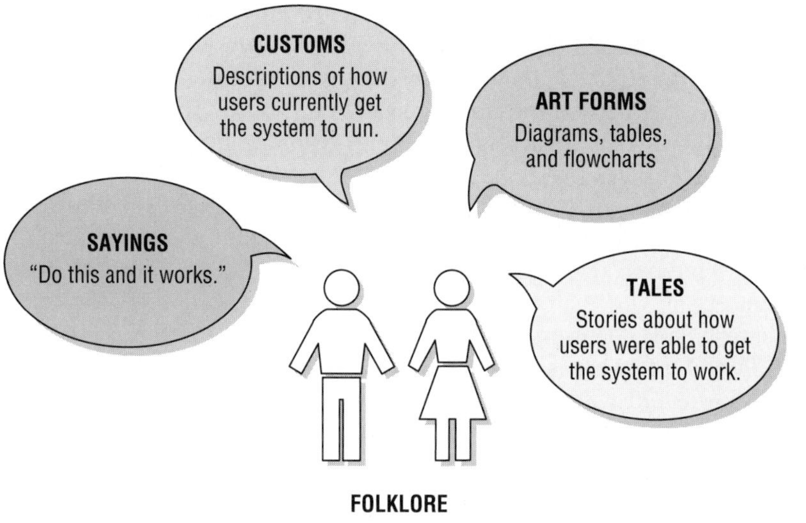

FIGURE 20.41
Customs, tales, sayings, and
art forms used in the
FOLKLORE method of
documentation apply to
information systems.

CUSTOMS
Descriptions of how
users currently get
the system to run.

ART FORMS
Diagrams, tables,
and flowcharts

SAYINGS
"Do this and it works."

TALES
Stories about how
users were able to get
the system to work.

FOLKLORE

The FOLKLORE Method

FOLKLORE is a system documentation technique that was created to supplement some of the techniques just covered. Even with the plethora of techniques available, many systems are inadequately documented or not documented at all. FOLKLORE gathers information that is often shared among users but is seldom written down.

FOLKLORE is a systematic technique, based on traditional methods used in gathering folklore about people and legends. This approach to systems documentation requires the analyst to interview users, investigate existing documentation in files, and observe the processing of information. The objective is to gather information corresponding to one of four categories: customs, tales, sayings, and art forms. Figure 20.41 suggests how each category relates to documentation of information systems.

When documenting customs, the analyst (or other folklorist) tries to capture in writing what users are currently doing to get all programs to run without problems. An example of a custom is: "Normally, we take two days to update the monthly records because the task is quite large. We run commercial accounts on day one and save the others for the next day."

Tales are stories that users tell regarding how the systems worked. The accuracy of the tale, of course, depends on the user's memory and is at best an opinion about how the program worked. The following is an example of a tale:

> The problem occurred again in 1985. This time the LIB409 job (monthly update) was run with only the "type 6" records in it. Because of this, there were no financial records in the LIBFIN file. When we tried to read the empty file it was immediately closed, and the totals were consequently reported as zero. We were able to correct this problem by adding a "type 7" record and rerunning the job.

Tales normally have a beginning, a middle, and an end. In this instance, we have a story about a problem (the beginning), a description of the effects (the middle), and the solution (the end).

Sayings are brief statements representing generalizations or advice. We have many sayings in everyday life, such as "April showers bring May flowers" or "A stitch in time saves nine." In systems documentation, we have many sayings, such as, "Write-protect the original before you try to back it up," or "Omit this section of code and the program will bomb," or "Always back up frequently." Users like to give advice, and the analyst should try to capture this advice and include it in the FOLKLORE documentation.

Gathering art forms is another important activity of traditional folklorists, and the systems analyst should understand its importance, too. Flowcharts, diagrams, and tables that users draw sometimes may be better or more useful than flowcharts drawn by the original system author. Analysts will often find such art posted on bulletin boards, or they may ask the users to clean out their files and retrieve any useful flowcharts and diagrams.

The FOLKLORE approach works because it can help fill the knowledge gap created when a program author leaves. Contributors to the FOLKLORE document do not have to document the entire system, only parts they know about. Finally, it is fun for users to contribute, taking some of the burden from analysts. Recently, FOLKLORE was automated in Finland to aid in documentation of a new system.

The danger of relying on FOLKLORE is that the information gathered from users may be correct, partially correct, or even incorrect. However, unless someone takes the time to redo program documentation entirely, the description of customs, tales, sayings, and art forms may be the only written information about how a set of programs works.

Choosing a Design and Documentation Technique

The techniques discussed in this chapter are extremely valuable as design tools, memory aids, productivity tools, and as a means of reducing dependencies on key staff members. However, the systems analyst is faced with a difficult decision regarding which method to adopt. The following is a set of guidelines to help the analyst use the appropriate technique.

Choose a technique that:

1. Is compatible with existing documentation.
2. Is understood by others in the organization.
3. Allows you to return to working on the system after you have been away from it for a period of time.
4. Is suitable for the size of the system you are working on.
5. Allows for a structured design approach if that is considered to be more important than other factors.
6. Allows for easy modification.

CODE GENERATION AND DESIGN REENGINEERING

Code generation is the process of using software, often a lower or integrated CASE product, to create all or a part of a computer program. Many different code generators exist for almost every popular computer language and every platform from the microcomputer to midrange and mainframe computers.

Full code generators require a formal methodology for entering all data, business rules, screen designs, and so on. Otherwise, much of the computer program code must be entered into the CASE toolset. Partial code generators generate only specific pieces of code that may be incorporated into a program being constructed by programmers. An example of partial code generation is Excelerator's ability to generate record layouts

Write Is Right

"It's so easy to understand. I say if everybody uses HIPO, we won't have trouble, you know, with things not being standardized," said Al Gorithm, a new programmer who will be working with your systems analysis team. Al is speaking to an informal meeting among three members of the systems analysis team, a six-person MIS task force from the advertising department, and two programmers who were all working to develop an MIS for advertising personnel.

Philip, an advertising account executive and one of the members of the MIS task force, looks up in surprise. "What is this thing called?" The two programmers reply at the same time, "HIPO." Philip looks unimpressed and says, "That doesn't say anything to me."

Neeva Phail, one of the systems analysts, begins explaining, "HIPO stands for Hierarchy plus Input Process Output. It's a way to document programs. It probably won't matter one way or the other what we use, if..."

Flo Chart, another systems analyst, breaks in saying, "HIPO takes a lot of paper. I hate looking through those things. Even I get lost." She looks hopefully at the programmers, "I'm sure we can agree on a better technique."

Allan, an older advertising executive, seems slightly upset, stating, "I learned about flowcharting from the first systems analysts we had years ago. Don't you people do that anymore? I think they work best."

What was at first a friendly meeting suddenly seems to have reached an impasse. The participants are looking warily at each other. As a systems analyst who has worked on many different projects with many different kinds of people, you realize that the group is looking to you to make some reasonable suggestions.

Based on what you know about the various documentation techniques, what technique or techniques would you propose to the group? How will the technique(s) you proposed overcome some of the concerns they have voiced? What process will you use to decide on appropriate techniques?

---

and screen design layouts. (For details, refer to the examples in the CPU case at the end of Chapter 10.) With add-on products (such as Microfocus interface module), Excelerator can generate COBOL paragraph names from a structure chart, as well as mainframe screen design code.

One advanced approach to code generation is a set of programs called XperCASE by Siemens AG Österreich. With this sophisticated set of tools, the systems analyst can not only generate program code, but also reengineer existing code. Reengineering (or reverse engineering) allows the analyst to take existing computer code, convert it to a standard structured tool such as a Nassi-Shneiderman chart, modify the logic, and output it as computer code in a different language. An example of reengineering occurs when an analyst begins with existing COBOL code, converts it to a Nassi-Shneiderman chart, adds new features, and outputs it in C++.

Figure 20.42 is a segment of a COBOL program used to print a simple control break report. COBOL has been used in this example because of its similarity to pseudocode; however, C or xBASE (dBASE, Paradox, Foxpro, and so on) code could also have been used.

The report generated in this example is a summary report. Therefore, each line in the report represents the total sales for a particular customer no matter how many times the customer has ordered from the company. The program logic goes as follows: the program reads a file of sales records, SALES-HISTORY-FILE, sorted by customer number, and accumulates total sales for each customer. When a new customer number is detected, the program prints a line showing the current customer number and the total sales figure. Then the program moves on to the next customer and starts accumulating total sales for that customer. Once all the customer records are read and processed, the company total sales figures are printed.

CHAPTER 20:
QUALITY ASSURANCE
THROUGH SOFTWARE
ENGINEERING

```
        PROCEDURE DIVISION.
   *
        000-PREPARE-SALES-REPORT.
   *
            OPEN INPUT    SALES-HISTORY-FILE
            OPEN OUTPUT PRINT-FILE.
            PERFORM 100-FORMAT-HEADING-DATES.
            PERFORM 200-PRODUCE-SALES-LINE
                 UNTIL SALES-REC-EOF.
            PERFORM 300-PRINT-COMPANY-TOTAL-LINE.
            CLOSE SALES-HISTORY-FILE
                 PRINT-FILE.
            STOP RUN.
   *



        200-PRODUCE-SALES-LINE.
   *
            PERFORM 210-READ-SALES-RECORD.
            IF FIRST-RECORD
                 MOVE SR-CUST-NO      TO-OLD-CUST-NO
                 MOVE 'N' TO FIRST-RECORD-SW
            ELSE
                 IF SR-CUST-NO GREATER THAN OLD-CUST-NO
                      PERFORM 230-PRINT-CUSTOMER-LINE.
            IF NOT SALES-REC-EOF
                 PERFORM 220-ACCUMULATE-CUSTOMER-TOTALS.
   *
```

Two modules are illustrated, 000-PREPARE-SALES-REPORT, responsible for producing the entire report, and 200-PRODUCE-SALES-LINE,
which has the logic to read, accumulate, and print the customer total line
when all the records have been read for a particular customer.

This program was reengineered using a product by Siemens of Austria,
Vienna called XperCASE in the United States. (XperCASE is called
EasyCASE in other parts of the world.) XperCASE uses Nassi-Shneiderman
charts to depict program logic. Figure 20.43 is a Nassi-Shneiderman chart
created from the COBOL paragraph 000-PREPARE-SALES-REPORT. Notice
that the PERFORM UNTIL code has been translated into a sideways "L"
shape, indicating iteration.

Figure 20.44 is the diagram created from paragraph 200-PRODUCE-
SALES-LINE. Each PERFORM statement from the COBOL program, such as
210-READ-SALES-RECORD, is isolated in a rectangle with vertical bars at
each end. IF...THEN...ELSE statements are transformed into the standard
Nassi-Shneiderman format using angle lines to separate the IF actions from
the ELSE actions. Refer to the block containing the IF logic to see if the new
sales history customer number is greater than the old customer number
(indicating that all of the records for the customer have been accumulated).

Once the program code has been reverse engineered, the design may
be modified, eliminating unused features and adding new features to the

program. Figure 20.45 illustrates the Windows screen for inserting a new construct into the existing diagram. Notice the variety of statement structures that may be added, such as an IF-THEN-ELSE, a PARAGRAPH, or a PERFORM. The PERFORM option has an arrow pointing to the right, indicating that more options will appear once it is selected. Some examples are PERFORM BEFORE TEST, PERFORM OUTLINE, PERFORM INLINE, and PERFORM *n* TIMES.

Figure 20.46 illustrates the screen for editing existing portions of the diagram. Sections such as an IF-THEN-ELSE may be copied or moved to a new location, deleted, or enclosed (that is, surrounded by a new PERFORM UNTIL or other structure). Selecting Push down (Ctrl+D) moves the structure into a lower-level module within the diagram.

The diagram was modified to add another level of subtotals. The old version of the SALES REPORT contained only customer totals and a final total. Modifications were made to add an intermediate subtotal for each salesperson. If the salesperson number changes, lines are printed for both the customer and salesperson. If the salesperson number does not change, but the customer number does, a line is printed only for the customer. Figure 20.47 illustrates the new Nassi-Shneiderman diagram with the salesperson IF logic and subtotals included.

The COBOL code for the updated Nassi-Shneiderman diagram was regenerated. Figure 20.48 shows the resulting program code for the 200 module, PRODUCE-SALES-LINE. Notice that the IF statement to check for a change in salesperson number has been generated, along with the two PERFORMs, 230-PRINT-CUST-LINE and 240-PRINT-SLSPN-LINE. Another benefit of code regenerating is that the resulting code has been upgraded to the latest version of COBOL. The original code (shown earlier) was written using COBOL 74. The regenerated program is in the latest version, COBOL 85, and contains statements, such as END-IF that are not part of the older version of COBOL.

FIGURE 20.44
An XperCASE example of a
Nassi-Shneiderman chart cre-
ated from 200-PRODUCE-
SALES-LINE.

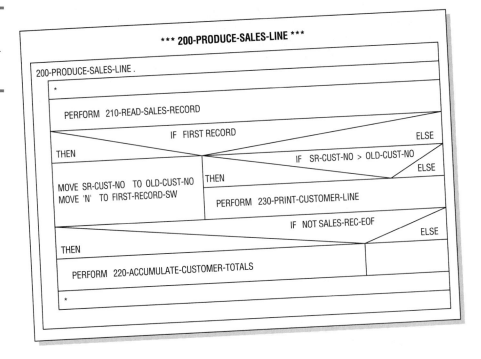

TESTING, MAINTENANCE, AND AUDITING

The Testing Process

All of the system's newly written or modified application programs, as
well as new procedural manuals, new hardware, and all system interfaces, must be tested thoroughly. Haphazard, trial-and-error testing will
not suffice.

FIGURE 20.45
An XperCASE example of
inserting a new construct
into an existing diagram.

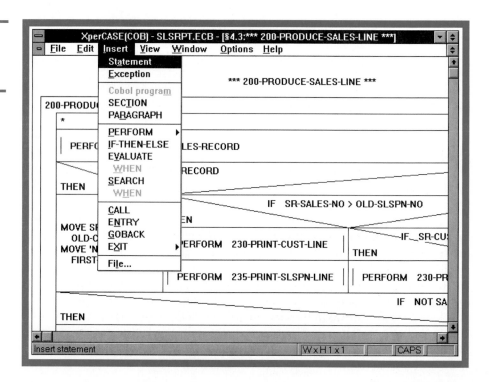

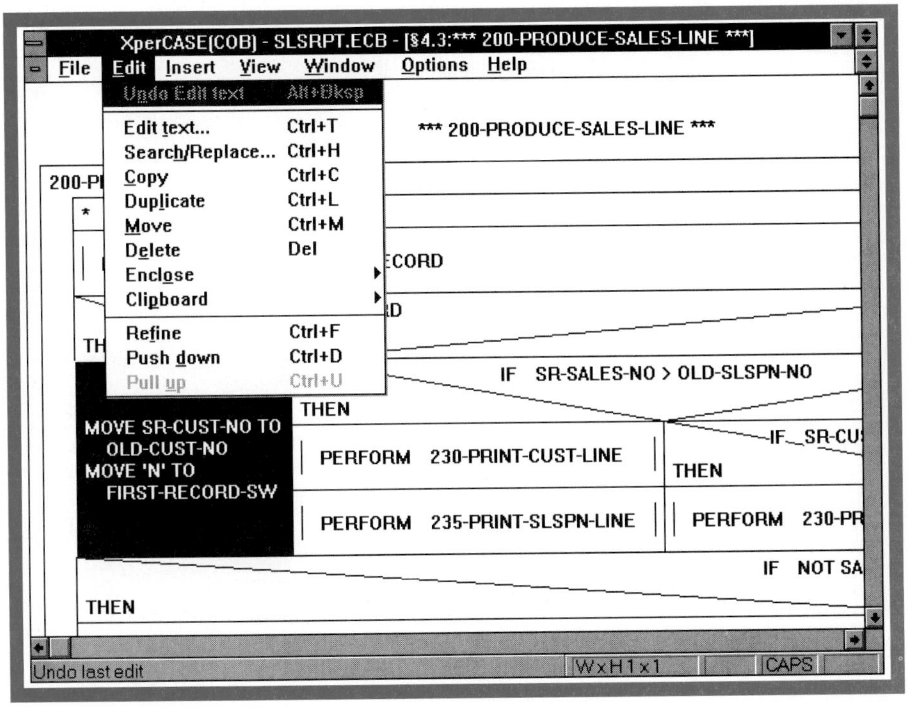

FIGURE 20.46
An XperCASE example of
editing the Nassi-
Shneiderman diagram.

Testing is done throughout systems development, not just at the end. It is meant to turn up heretofore unknown problems, not to demonstrate the perfection of programs, manuals, or equipment.

Although testing is tedious, it is an essential series of steps that helps assure the quality of the eventual system. It is far less disruptive to test beforehand than to have a poorly tested system fail after installation. Testing is accomplished on subsystems or program modules as work progresses. Testing is done on many different levels at various intervals. Before the system is put into production, all programs must be desk checked, checked with test data, and checked to see if the modules work together with one another as planned.

The system as a working whole must also be tested. This includes testing the interfaces between subsystems, the correctness of output, and the usefulness and understandability of system documentation and output. Programmers, analysts, operators, and users all play different roles in the various aspects of testing, as shown in Figure 20.49. Testing of hardware is typically provided as a service by vendors of equipment who will run their own tests on equipment when it is delivered on site.

PROGRAM TESTING WITH TEST DATA. Much of the responsibility for program testing resides with the original author(s) of each program. The systems analyst serves as an advisor and coordinator for program testing. In this capacity, the analyst works to ensure that correct testing techniques are implemented by programmers, but probably does not personally carry out this level of checking.

At this stage, programmers must first desk check their programs to verify the way the system will work. In desk checking, the programmer follows each step in the program on paper to check whether the routine works as it is written.

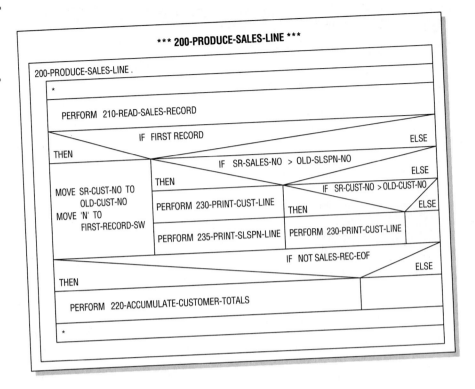

Next, programmers must create both valid and invalid test data. These data are then run to see if base routines work and also to catch errors. If output from main modules is satisfactory, then you can add more test data in order to check other modules. Created test data should test minimum and maximum values possible, as well as all possible variations in format and codes. File output from test data must be carefully verified. It should never be assumed that data contained in a file are correct just because a file was created and accessed.

Throughout this process, the systems analyst checks output for errors, advising the programmer of any needed corrections. The analyst will usually not recommend or create test data for program testing, but might point out to the programmer omissions of data types to be added in later tests.

LINK TESTING WITH TEST DATA. When programs pass desk checking and checking with test data, they must go through link testing, which is also referred to as string testing. Link testing checks to see if programs that are interdependent actually work together as planned.

A small amount of test data, usually designed by the systems analyst to test system specifications as well as programs, is used for link testing. It may take several passes through the system to test all combinations because it is immensely difficult to unravel problems if you try to test everything all at once.

The analyst creates special test data that cover a variety of processing situations for link testing. First, typical test data are processed to see if the system can handle normal transactions—those that would make up the bulk of its load. If the system works with normal transactions, then variations are added, including invalid data used to ensure that the system can properly detect errors.

```
* - - - - - - - - - - - - - - - - - - - - - - - - - - - - - - - - - -
# XPER *
        200-PRODUCE-SALES-LINE.
    *
            PERFORM 210-READ-SALES-RECORD
            IF FIRST-RECORD
            THEN
                    MOVE SR-CUST-NO TO
                    OLD-CUST-NO
                MOVE 'N' TO
                    FIRST-RECORD-SW
            ELSE
                IF SR-SALES-NO > OLD-SLSPN-NO
                THEN
                    PERFORM 230-PRINT-CUST-LINE
                    PERFORM 235-PRINT SLSPN-LINE
                ELSE
                    IF SR-CUST-NO > OLD-CUST-NO
                    THEN
                            PERFORM 230-PRINT-CUST-LINE
                    END-IF
                END-IF
            END-IF
            IF NOT SALES-REC-EOF
            THEN
                    PERFORM 220-ACCUMULATE-CUSTOMER-TOTALS
            END-IF
    *
                                                # XPER P
    *                                    - - - - - - - - - - - - - - -
* - - - - - - - - - - - - - - - - - - - - - - - - - -
# XPER )
```

FULL SYSTEMS TESTING WITH TEST DATA. When link tests are satisfactorily concluded, the system as a complete entity must be tested. At this stage, operators and end users become actively involved in testing. Test data, created by the systems analysis team for the express purpose of testing system objectives, are used.

As can be expected, there are a number of factors to consider when systems testing with test data:

1. Examining whether operators have adequate documentation in procedure manuals (hard copy or on line) to afford correct and efficient operation.

2. Checking whether procedure manuals are clear enough in communicating how data should be prepared for input.

3. Ascertaining if work flows necessitated by the new or modified system actually "flow."

4. Determining if output is correct and whether users understand that this is, in all likelihood, how output will look in its final form.

FIGURE 20.49
Programmers, analysts,
operators, and users all play
different roles in testing
software and systems.

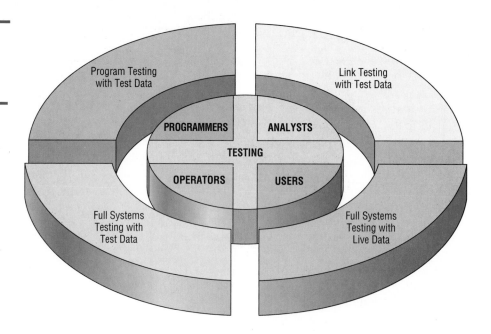

Remember to schedule adequate time for system testing. Unfortunately, this is a step that often gets dropped if system installation is lagging behind the target date.

Systems testing includes reaffirming quality standards for system performance that were set up when initial system specifications were made. Everyone involved should once again agree how to determine whether the system is doing what it is supposed to do. This will include measures of error, timeliness, ease of use, proper ordering of transactions, acceptable down time, understandable procedure manuals, and so on.

FULL SYSTEMS TESTING WITH LIVE DATA. When systems tests using test data prove satisfactory, it is a good idea to try the new system with several passes on what is called "live data"—data that have been successfully processed through the existing system. This step allows an accurate comparison of the new system's output with what you know to be correctly processed output, as well as a good feel for how actual data will be handled. Obviously, this step is not possible when creating entirely new outputs. As with test data, only small amounts of live data are used in this kind of system testing.

Testing is an important period for assessing how end users and operators actually interact with the system. Although much thought is given to user-system interaction (see Chapter 18), you can never fully predict the wide range of differences in the way users will actually interact with the system. It is not enough to interview users about how they are interacting with the system; you must observe them firsthand.

Items to watch for are ease of learning the system; the adjustment to ergonomic factors; and user reaction to system feedback, including what happens when an error message is received and what happens when the user is informed that the system is executing his or her commands. Be particularly sensitive to how users react to system response time and the language of responses. Also listen to what users say about the system as they encounter it. Any real problems need to be addressed before the system is put into production, not just glossed over as adjustments to the system that users and operators "ought" to make on their own.

As mentioned earlier, procedure manuals also need to be tested. Although manuals can be proofread by support staff and checked for technical accuracy by the systems analysis team, the only real way to test them is to have users and operators try them, preferably during full systems testing with live data. Have them use accurate but not final versions of the manuals.

It is difficult to communicate procedures accurately. Difficulty is compounded when a systems analyst or programmer has been working with a system for a long time. Recalling your own early experiences with intimidating or frustrating new systems can help focus your thinking on producing readable and useful documentation. Remember that manuals need to be organized in different ways for users who will interact with the system in countless ways. Too much information will be just as much a deterrent to system use as too little. Use of hypertext for on-line manuals can help in this regard. Consider and incorporate user and operator suggestions into the final versions of manuals and other forms of documentation.

Maintenance Practices

Your objective as a systems analyst should be to install or modify systems that have a reasonable useful life. You want to create a system whose design is comprehensive and farsighted enough to serve current and projected user needs for several years to come. Part of your expertise should be in projecting what those needs might be and then building flexibility and adaptability into the system. The better the system design, the easier it will be to maintain and the less money the business will have to spend on maintenance.

Reducing maintenance costs is a major concern, since software maintenance alone can devour upwards of 50 percent of the total data-processing budget for a business. Excessive maintenance costs reflect directly back on the system's designer, since approximately 70 percent of software errors have been attributed to inappropriate software design. From a systems perspective, it makes sense that detecting and correcting software design errors early on is less costly than letting errors remain unnoticed until maintenance is necessary.

Maintenance is performed most often to improve the existing software rather than to respond to a crisis or system failure. As users' requirements change, software and documentation should be changed as part of the maintenance work. Additionally, programs might be recoded to improve on the efficiency of the original program. Over half of all maintenance is comprised of such enhancement work.

Maintenance is also done to update software in response to the changing organization. This work is not as substantial as enhancing the software, but it must be done. Emergency and adaptive maintenance comprise less than half of all system maintenance.

Part of the systems analyst's job is to ensure that there are adequate channels and procedures in place to permit feedback about, and subsequent response to, maintenance needs. Users and operators must be able to communicate problems and suggestions easily to those who will be maintaining the system. It is very discouraging (sometimes so much so that the system will fall into disuse) if the system is not properly maintained.

Cramming for Your Systems Test

"We're strapped for time. Just look at this projection," says Lou Scuntroll, the newest member of your systems analysis team, showing you the PERT chart that the team has been using to project when the new system would be up and running. "We can't possibly make the July target date for testing with live data. We're running three weeks behind because of that slow equipment shipment."

As one of the systems analysts who have seen deadlines come and go on other projects, you try to remain calm and to size up the situation carefully before you speak. Slowly, you question Lou about the possibility of delaying testing.

Lou replies, "If we try to push the testing off until the first weeks of August, there are two key people from accounting who are going to be out on vacation." Lou is visibly upset at the possibility of missing the deadline.

Stan Dards, another junior member of your systems analysis team, enters Lou's office. "You two look terrible. Things are going okay, aren't they? I'm not reassigned to program a payroll application, am I?"

Lou looks up, obviously not appreciating Stan's sense of humor nor what seems like his single-minded self-concern. "Good thing you came in when you did. We've got some big decisions to make about scheduling." Lou holds up the PERT chart for Stan's inspection. "Notice the July test date. Notice that there is no way we can make it. Any bright ideas?"

Stan contemplates the chart momentarily, then states, "Something's got to go. Let's see here... Maybe move testing of the accounting module to—"

Lou interrupts, saying bluntly, "Nope, already thought of that, but Stanford and Binet from accounting are out of town in August. Maybe we can skip that portion of the testing. They've been really cooperative. I don't think they'd object if we just 'do it for real' and test as we actually go into production."

"I think that's a good idea, Lou," Stan agrees, trying to make up for his earlier jokes. "We haven't had any real trouble with that, and the programmers sure are confident. That way we could stay on schedule with everything else. I vote for *not* testing the accounting portion, just sort of winging it when it starts up."

As the most senior member of the team present, what can you do to convince Lou and Stan about the importance of testing the accounting module with live data? What can systems analysts do in planning their time in order to allow adequate time for testing with test and live data? What are some of the possible problems the team may encounter if they do not test the system completely with live data before putting the system into production? Realistically, are there steps in the system analysis and design process that can be collapsed in order to bring a delayed project in on time?

The systems analyst also needs to set up a classification scheme to allow users to designate the perceived importance of the maintenance being suggested or requested. Classifying requests enables maintenance programmers to understand how users themselves estimate the importance of their request. This viewpoint can then be taken into account along with other factors when scheduling maintenance.

Auditing

Auditing is yet another way of assuring the quality of the information contained in the system. Broadly defined, auditing refers to having an expert who is not involved in setting up or using a system examine information in order to ascertain its reliability. Whether or not information is found to be reliable, the finding on its reliability is communicated to others for the purpose of making the system's information more useful to them.

For information systems, there are generally two kinds of auditors: internal and external. Whether both are necessary for the system you design depends on what kind of system it is. Internal auditors work for the same organization that owns the information system, whereas external (also called "independent") auditors are hired from the outside.

Basically, external auditors are used when the information system processes data that influences a company's financial statements. External auditors audit the system to assure the fairness of the financial statements being produced. They may also be brought in if there is something out of the ordinary occurring that involves company employees, such as suspected computer fraud or embezzlement.

Internal auditors study the controls used in the information system to make sure that they are adequate and that they are doing what they are purported to be doing. They also test the adequacy of security controls. Although they work for the same organization, internal auditors do not report to the people responsible for the system they are auditing. The work of internal auditors is often more in-depth than that of external auditors.

SUMMARY

The systems analyst uses three broad approaches to total quality management (TQM) for analyzing and designing information systems: designing systems and software with a top-down, modular approach; designing and documenting systems and software using systematic methods; and testing systems and software so that they can be easily maintained and audited.

Users are critically important for establishing and evaluating the quality of several dimensions of management information systems and decision support systems. They can be involved in the entire evolution of systems through the establishment of MIS task forces or quality circles.

TQM can be successfully implemented by taking a top-down approach to design. This refers to looking at overall organizational objectives first, then decomposing them into manageable subsystem requirements. Modular development makes programming, debugging, and maintenance easier to accomplish. Programming in modules is well suited to taking a top-down approach.

Two systems that link programs in the Windows environment are DDE (Dynamic Data Exchange) which shares code by using dynamic link library (DLL) files. Using DDE a user can store data in one program and then use it in another. A second approach to linking programs in Windows is called OLE (for Object Linking and Embedding). This linking method is superior to DDE for linking application data and graphics due to its object-oriented approach.

A recommended tool for designing a top-down, modular system is called a structure chart. Two types of arrows are used to indicate the kinds of parameters that are passed between the modules. The first is called a data couple; the second is called a control flag. Structure chart modules fall into one of three categories: control, transformational (sometimes called worker), and functional or specialized.

Part of total quality management is to see that programs and systems are properly designed, documented, and maintained. Six of the many documentation and design techniques that can aid the systems analyst are HIPO, flowcharts, Nassi-Shneiderman charts, Warnier-Orr diagrams, pseudocode, procedure manuals, and FOLKLORE. Data flow diagrams can be used to create HIPO diagrams. Pseudocode is frequently used to represent the logic of each module or structure chart. Often it is incorporated into the process logic of a HIPO diagram. Pseudocode is used for structured walkthroughs when there is not enough time to create formal HIPO diagrams. Systems analysts must choose a technique that fits in well with what was previously used in the organization and that allows flexibility and easy modification.

"This is a fascinating place to work. I'm sure you agree now that you've had a chance to observe us. Sometimes I think it must be fun to be an outsider . . . Don't you feel like an anthropologist discovering a new culture? I remember when I first came here. Everything was so new, so strange. Why even the language was different. It wasn't a 'customer'; it was a 'client.' And we didn't have 'departments'; we have 'units.' It's not an employee cafeteria; it's the 'canteen.' That goes for the way we work, too. We all have our different ways to approach things. I think I'm getting the hang of what Snowden expects, but every once in a while I make a mistake, too. For instance, if I can give him work on disk, he'd just as soon see it that way than get a printed report. That's why I have two computers on my desk, too! I always see you taking so many notes . . . I guess it makes sense, though. You're supposed to document what *we* do with our systems and information, as well as what your team is doing, aren't you?"

HYPERCASE QUESTIONS

1. Use the FOLKLORE method to complete the documentation of the Management Systems Unit PSRS system. Be sure to include customs, tales, sayings, and art forms.

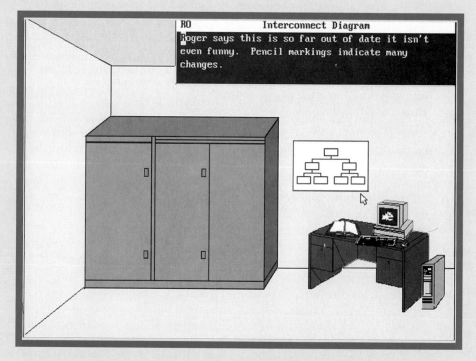

FIGURE 20.HC1
In HyperCase® use FOLKLORE to document art forms that users have created or collected to make sense of their systems.

2. In two paragraphs suggest a PC-based approach for capturing the elements of FOLKLORE, so that it is not necessary to use a paper-based log. Make sure that your suggested solution can accommodate graphics as well as text.

3. Design input and output screens for FOLKLORE that facilitate easy entry and provide prompting so that recall of FOLKLORE elements is immediate.

Code generation is the process of using software to create all or part of a computer program. Many code generators are now available commercially. Reengineering and reverse engineering refer to using software to analyze existing program code and create CASE design elements from the code. CASE design may then be modified and used to generate new computer program code.

Testing of specific programs, subsystems, and total systems is essential to quality. Testing is done to turn up any existing problems with programs and their interfaces before the system is actually used. Typically, testing is done in a bottom-up fashion with program codes being desk checked first. Following several intermediate test steps, testing of the full system with live data (actual data that has been successfully processed with the old system) is accomplished. This provides an opportunity to work out any problems that arise before the system is put into production.

System maintenance is an important consideration. Well-designed software can help reduce maintenance costs. Systems analysts need to set up channels for user feedback on maintenance needs, since systems that are not maintained will fall into disuse.

Both internal and external auditors are used to determine the reliability of the system's information. They communicate their audit findings to others in order to improve the usefulness of the system's information.

KEYWORDS AND PHRASES

total quality management (TQM)	external auditor
	MIS quality circles
structured walkthrough	desk check
bottom-up design	top-down design
modular development	dynamic data exchange (DDE)
dynamic link library (DLL)	object linking and embedding (OLE)
structure charts	data couples
control flags	stamp coupling
software documentation	HIPO method
overview IPO diagrams	detailed IPO diagrams
flowcharts	Nassi-Shneiderman charts
Warnier-Orr diagrams	pseudocode
FOLKLORE method	code generation

code generators

reengineering

link testing with test data

full systems testing with
live data

reverse engineering

program testing with test data

internal auditor

full systems testing with test data

software maintenance

REVIEW QUESTIONS

1. What are the three broad approaches available to the systems analyst for attaining quality in newly developed systems?

2. Who or what is the most important factor in establishing and evaluating the quality of information systems or decision support systems? Why?

3. Define the total quality management (TQM) approach as it applies to analysis and design of information systems.

4. What is an MIS quality circle?

5. Define what is meant by doing a structured walkthrough. Who should be involved? When should structured walkthroughs be done?

6. List the disadvantages to taking a bottom-up approach to design.

7. List the advantages of taking a top-down approach to design.

8. What are the three main disadvantages of taking a top-down approach to design?

9. Define modular development.

10. List four guidelines for correct modular programming.

11. How do structure charts help the analyst?

12. Name the two types of arrows used in structure charts.

13. Why do we want to keep the number of arrows to a minimum when using structure charts?

14. What are the two main types of structure charts?

15. Why should control flags be passed upward in a structure chart?

16. List two ways that the data flow diagram helps to build a structure chart.

17. List the three categories of modules. Why are they used in structure charts?

18. Give two reasons that support the necessity of well-developed system and software documentation.

19. What does the acronym HIPO signify?

20. List the three main types of diagrams in the HIPO system.

21. How does the VTOC help the reader locate a program module within the main system?

22. Do overview IPO diagrams provide a macro or micro view of input, process, and output?

23. List two drawbacks of the HIPO method.

24. List two advantages of the HIPO method.

25. What are the disadvantages of using flowcharts?

26. Give the two chief advantages of Nassi-Shneiderman charts.

27. What symbols are used to construct Warnier-Orr diagrams?

28. What advantages do Warnier-Orr diagrams have over Nassi-Shneiderman charts?

29. Define *pseudocode.*

30. List the four biggest complaints about procedure manuals.

31. In what four categories does the FOLKLORE documentation method collect information?

32. List six guidelines for choosing a design and documentation technique.

33. What are the advantages of using code generation and design reengineering for building systems?

34. Whose primary responsibility is it to test computer programs?

35. What is the difference between test data and live data?

36. What are the two types of systems auditors?

PROBLEMS

1. One of your systems analysis team members has been discouraging user input on quality standards, arguing that since you are the experts, you are really the only ones that know what constitutes a quality system. In a paragraph, explain to your team member why getting user input is critical to system quality. Use an example.

2. Draw a structure chart for the credit-reporting system in Figure 20.EX1.

3. Construct a structure chart for the payroll system in Figure 9.7 in Chapter 9.

4. Bestmonth Lumber Company is setting up a new payroll system. The system must:
   a. Prepare checks to employees.
   b. Prepare monthly reports to management.
   c. Prepare reports for taxes at year's end.
   d. Add employees to the payroll.
   e. Modify a record (give employee raises and change tax withholding if needed).
   f. Delete employees from the payroll.
   g. Accept input about sick days, half-days worked, etc.
   Draw a HIPO chart for Bestmonth of their new payroll system.

5. The employee files for Bestmonth are on magnetic tape; the transactions are keyed onto a disk. Draw a detailed IPO diagram for modifying a record.

6. Draw a Nassi-Shneiderman (N-S) chart to update your checkbook. Start with the balance the last time you balanced it. Subtract checks, electronic withdrawals, and any service charges. Add deposits and interest.

7. Draw a Warnier-Orr diagram for problem 6.

8. Write pseudocode for problem 6.

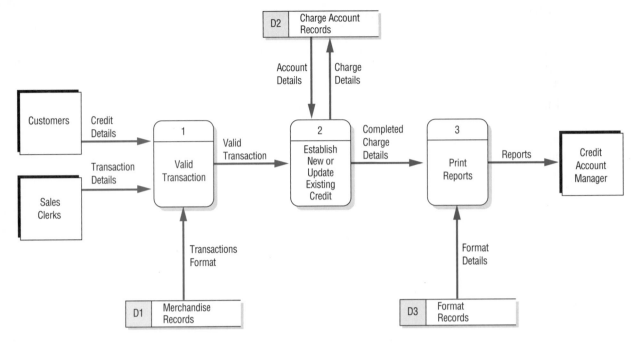

FIGURE 20.EX1
A data flow diagram for a credit reporting system.

9. Bestmonth Lumber Company is setting up a monthly payroll report. The report has the following information:

Heading	(left)	department number
		run date
	(center)	company name
		title of report
	(right)	page number
Body		last name
		first name
		monthly gross
		federal taxes
		state taxes
		FICA taxes
		other deductions
		monthly net

Draw a Warnier-Orr diagram to process the monthly report.

10. Draw an N-S chart for problem 9.

11. Write pseudocode for the Citron Car rental policy provided in Consulting Opportunity 11.3 in Chapter 11.

12. Write a detailed table of contents for a procedure manual on checking out software from your school's microcomputer laboratory. Make sure that the manual is written with the user in mind, not just the software librarian.

13. Your systems analysis team is close to completing a system for Meecham Feeds. Roger is quite confident that the programs that he has written for Meecham's inventory system will perform as necessary, since they are similar to programs he has done before. Your

team has been very busy and would ideally like to begin full systems testing as soon as possible.

This is what two of your junior team members have proposed:

a. Skip desk checking of the programs (since similar programs were checked in other installations; Roger has agreed).

b. Do link testing with large amounts of data to prove that the system will work.

c. Do full systems testing with large amounts of live data to show the system is working.

Respond to each of the three steps in their proposed test schedule. Use a paragraph to explain your response.

14. Propose a revised testing plan for the Meecham Feeds problem (problem 13). Break down your plan into a sequence of detailed steps.

GROUP PROJECTS

1. Divide your group into two subgroups. One subgroup should interview the other about their experiences encountered in registering for a class. Questions should be designed to elicit information on customs, tales, sayings, and art forms that will help document the registration process (manual and/or automated) at your school.

2. Reunite your group to create a short excerpt for a FOLKLORE manual that documents the process of registering for a class based on the folklore passed on in the interviews in problem 1. Remember to include examples of customs, tales, sayings, and art forms.

SELECTED BIBLIOGRAPHY

Dean, Jr., J. W., and J. R. Evans. *Total Quality.* Minneapolis/St. Paul: West Publishing Company, 1994.

Deming, W. E. *Management for Quality and Productivity.* Cambridge, MA: MIT Center for Advanced Engineering Study, 1981.

Katzan, H., Jr. *Systems Design and Documentation: An Introduction to the HIPO Method.* New York: Van Nostrand Reinhold Company, 1976.

Kendall, J. E., and P. Kerola. "A Foundation for the Use of Hypertext Based Documentation Techniques." *Journal of End-User Computing,* Winter, 1994.

Kendall, K. E., and R. Losee. "Information System FOLKLORE: A New Technique for System Documentation," *Information & Management,* vol. 10, no. 2, 1986.

Kendall, K. E., and S. Yoo. "Software Design with the PB (Pseudocode-Box) Diagram: Performance Evaluation Using a Quasi-Experimental Method." *Proceedings of the National Conference of the Decision Sciences Institute.* Honolulu, Hawaii, November 1986.

Lee, S. M., and M. J. Schniederjans. *Operations Management.* Boston: MA: Houghton-Mifflin Company, 1994.

Porter, W. T., and W. E. Perry. *EDP Controls and Auditing,* 2nd ed. Belmont, CA: Wadsworth Publishing Company, Inc., 1977.

Shelly, G. B., and T. J. Cashman. *Business Systems Analysis and Design.* Fullerton, CA: Anaheim Publishing Company, 1975.

Yourdon, E. *Managing the Structured Techniques,* 2nd ed. Englewood Cliffs, NJ: Prentice-Hall, Inc., 1977.

CHARTING THE STRUCTURE

"Here they are, as promised," Chip and Anna say triumphantly as they hand over their specifications to Mack Roe, the project programmer.

"Thanks," Mack says. "I've got a lot of work ahead."

Mack's first task is to produce an overview of the programs that would work together. Excelerator's Presentation Graphics are used to create system flowcharts of all the major programs that would operate together. The first system flow is the series of programs and manual processes depicting the installation of new microcomputers. The finished diagram is shown in Figure E20.1. Notice that all the programs and manual processes are centered in the drawing, identifying steps in the procedure.

NEW MICROCOMPUTER FORMS are sent to data entry, where they are keyed and verified. A VERIFICATION REPORT provides the first document in an audit trail of transactions. The MICROCOMPUTER ADD TRANSACTION is input into a validation program, ensuring that quality data enters the system. A second VALIDATION REPORT continues the audit trail, and a VALID ADD TRANSACTION file contains all records with no errors. This file is input to a program to add a new record to the MICROCOMPUTER MASTER file and a separate program to update the PENDING MICROCOMPUTER ORDER file.

VALID ADD TRANSACTIONS are sorted by MODEL within BRAND NAME for printing the MICROCOMPUTER RECEIVED REPORT and the MICROCOMPUTER INSTALLATION LISTING. This information will be used to determine which locations receive the machines.

Mack completes other system flowcharts for the remaining portions of the system. Next the programs on each system flowchart are designed. Mack starts by creating a structure chart for each program and then for each module design. The PRODUCE SOFTWARE CROSS-REFERENCE REPORT structure chart is shown in Figure E20.2. This is the first draft that Mack uses in a structured walkthrough with Dee Ziner, a senior programmer.

Dee Ziner has several important suggestions for improving the structure. She notes that, "Module 130, PRINT ERROR LINE, is improperly subordinate to the calling module 120, READ HARDWARE RECORD. The question may be asked, 'Must the program print an error line in order to accomplish reading a HARDWARE RECORD?' Since the answer is 'No,' the module should be placed at the same level as 120, READ HARDWARE RECORD."

She continues discussing the situation with Mack, saying, "The same is true concerning module 160, PRINT SUBTOTAL LINES. This is not a function of accumulating hardware subtotals, and should not be called from module 150, ACCUMULATE HARDWARE SUBTOTALS." Dee continues the walkthrough by asking the question, "May one SOFTWARE RECORD be located on many machines?" Mack responds that this is true, and another controlling module, PRINT SOFTWARE CROSS-REFERENCE LINES was included in the structure chart.

Mack proceeds to incorporate the changes to the structure chart. When the correct hierarchy is established, the coupling is added. Careful attention is given to pass minimal data and to only pass control *up* the

Written by Allen Schmidt, Jullie E. Kendall, and Kenneth E. Kendall

structure chart. The final version is illustrated in Figure E20.3. Module 116 is new, using the SOFTWARE/HARDWARE RELATIONAL file to link one SOFTWARE RECORD to many HARDWARE RECORDS. The SOFTWARE INVENTORY NUMBER is passed down to the module, and the relational file is randomly read. The HARDWARE INVENTORY NUMBER and control switch RELATION NOT FOUND are passed up the structure.

The final structure chart has a functional shape to it. A few control modules at the top of the structure, several worker modules in the middle, and a few specialist modules at the bottom provide a general fan-out, fan-in shape. The module names are all of the verb-adjective-noun form, describing what has been accomplished after the module has finished executing. For example, module 150 has the verb ACCUMULATE, describing the work accomplished by the module. SUBTOTALS, a noun, are being accumulated, and HARDWARE describes which subtotals are accumulated.

Each of the modules on the structure chart, called functions by Excelerator, were described in the XLDictionary. Figure E20.4 is a print of the function description for 100, PRODUCE SOFTWARE LINES. The function explodes in greater detail to the module PRODUCE SOFTWARE LINES. The location of the computer code, either microcomputer or mainframe disk, along with requirements and associated entities, is completed. A description area is used to list the module tasks. Since PRODUCE SOFTWARE LINES is a control module, its logic should consist of looping and decision making, with minimal statements concerning processing details such as ADD or READ.

Each function may explode to a module description. Figure E20.5 is an example of the module description for 120, READ HARDWARE RECORD. The project, author, and file name are specified. The version number assures control over multiple copies of the same module.

The number of lines is an important indicator of the complexity of a module. Control modules should be kept small in size—twenty-five lines or fewer. Worker modules, which transform input data to output, may be up to fifty lines. Specialist modules such as READ or WRITE are usually small, less than twenty-five lines. A definition and the location may be specified. **The Call Sequence/Input parameters** indicate the data passed to the module, the HARDWARE NUMBER. The **Return Values** show the data and control passed to the calling module, corresponding to the symbols on the Structure Chart. A second screen contains areas for requirements and the processing logic.

Figure E20.6 is a print of the module description for 160, PRINT SUBTOTAL LINES. Included are the data passed to and from the module and a description of the logic. Other modules are described, and together they are used to code the complete program.

As each major entity—data flow diagrams, system flowcharts, processes, and so on—is created, an associated entity of TST for test plan is also created. The test plan first exists only as a name and is later modified to create the actual test plan. This results in a complete list of test plans that are to be developed without getting sidetracked when creating the original entity.

Anna creates the ADD NEW MICROCOMPUTER data flow diagram and creates a TST entity shell at the same time. Chip has the task of creating detailed test plans later in the development stage. Figure E20.7 is the finished test plan for ADD NEW MICROCOMPUTERS. Notice the **Alternate Name, Test Purpose,** a **Test Type** of LINK, and **Test Method** of TEST CASES. The **Test Type** shows the level of testing: unit, link, system, or acceptance. **Test Method** indicates how the test is to be performed: test cases, test drivers, and so on.

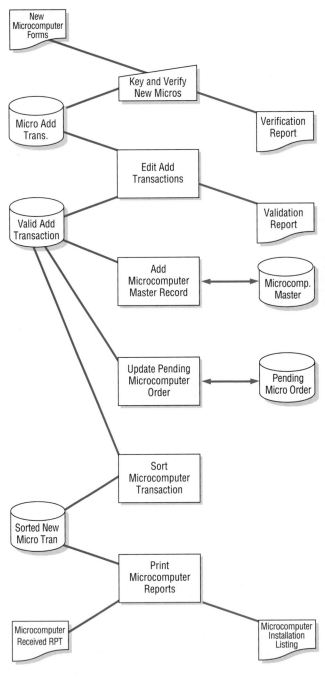

FIGURE E20.1
Microcomputer system flowchart.

"The **Test Description** area is used for entering the details of the test plan," Chip explains to Anna. "Since this test is for a larger group of programs, general statements are made for every program to be tested with a reference to further test plans for each program within the system."

As the test plans are completed, they are sent to Mack and Dee, who will create the actual test data. Invalid and valid data are included on each test file. The same is true for interactive systems, except that the test data are written on forms imitating the screen design. After Mack has finished testing

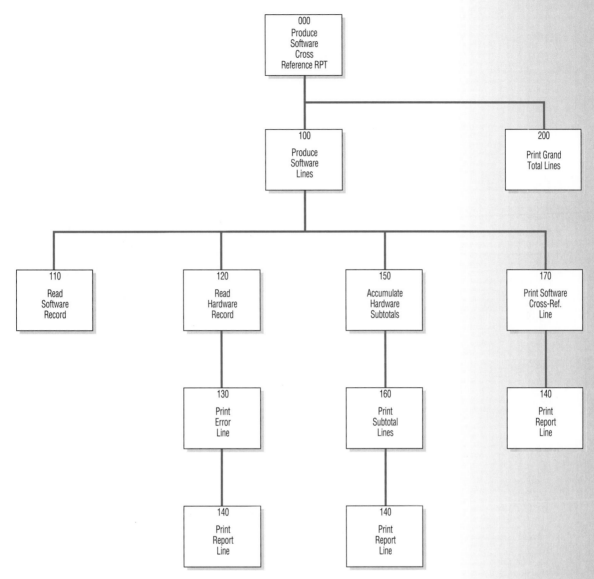

FIGURE E20.2
PRODUCE SOFTWARE CROSS-REFERENCE REPORT structure chart.

his programs and is satisfied that they are working correctly, he challenges
Dee to find any errors in the programs. In turn Dee has Mack test her programs in a round of friendly competition. They both realize that programmers may not always catch their own errors, since they are intimately familiar with their own programs and may not recognize subtle errors in logic.

Exercises [*]

💾 **E-1.** View the PRODUCE SOFTWARE CROSS-REF REP structure
chart. Use the **DESCRIBE** feature to examine some of the functions. Use the **BROWSE** key to explore a few of the modules.

---

* The exercises preceded by a disk icon require the program Excelerator (or another CASE
tool). A disk is provided free of charge to any professor adopting this book. The examples on
the disk may be imported into Excelerator and then used by students.

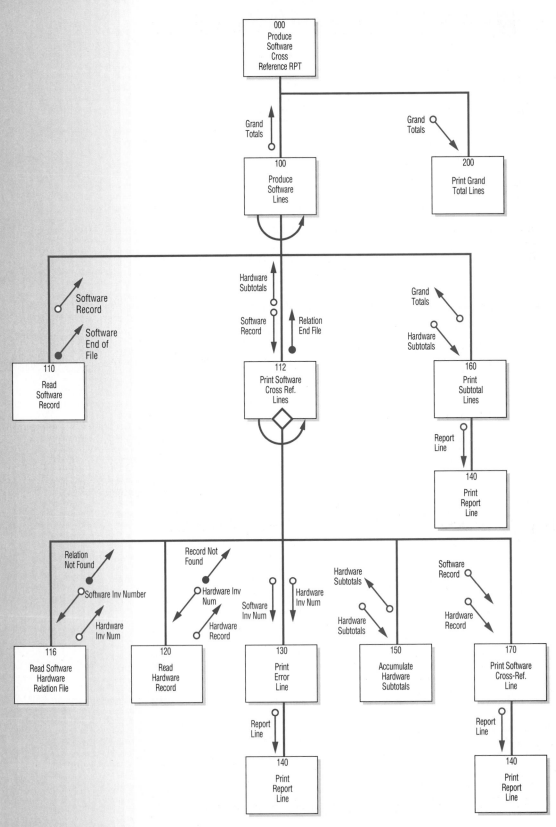

FIGURE E20.3
PRODUCE SOFTWARE CROSS-REFERENCE REPORT structure chart, with coupling.

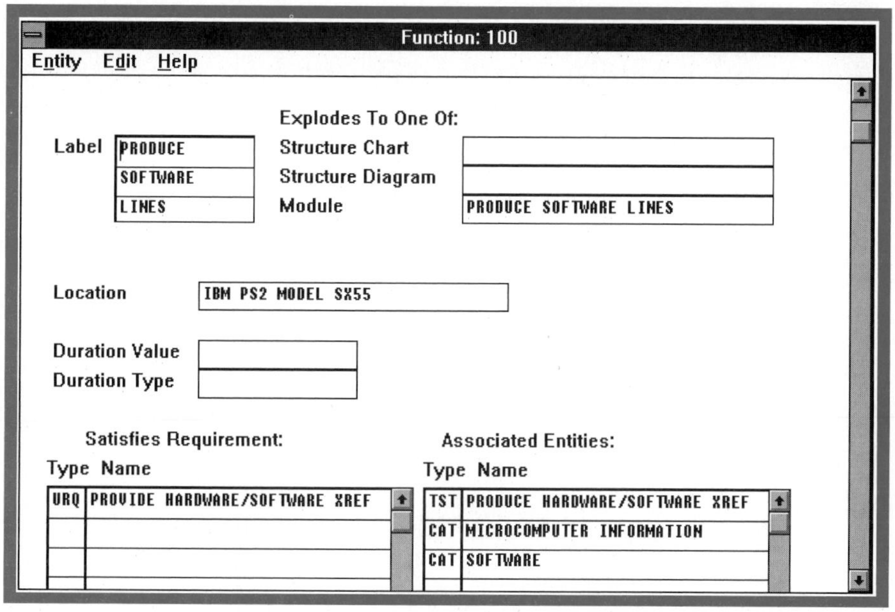

FIGURE E20.4
PRODUCE SOFTWARE LINES Function print.

☐ **E-2.** Modify the PRODUCE HARDWARE INVESTMENT RPT structure chart. Add the function PRINT INVESTMENT LINE in the
empty rectangle provided. Subordinate to this module is PRINT
HEADING LINES and WRITE REPORT LINE. Describe each
function in the XLDictionary.

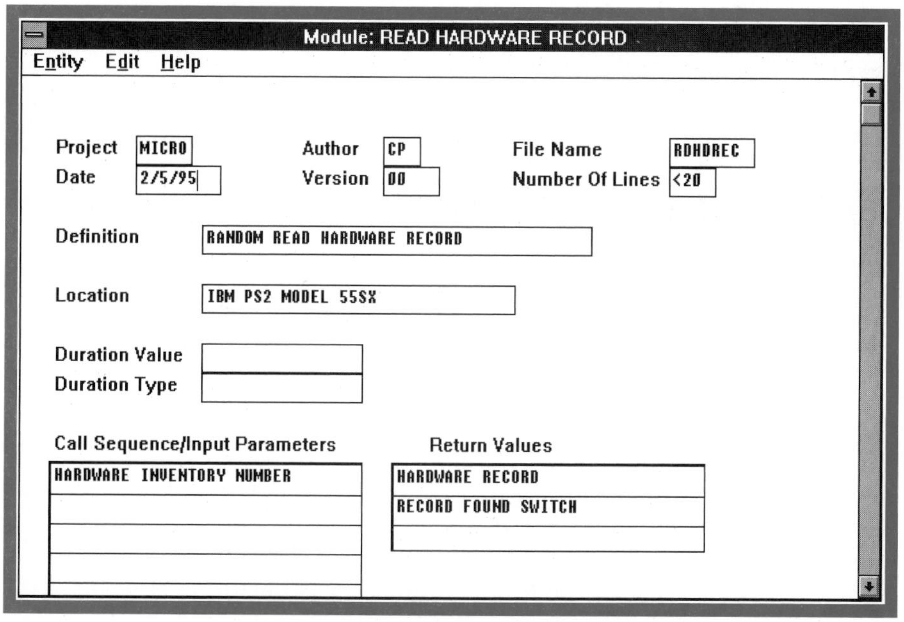

FIGURE E20.5
READ HARDWARE RECORD Module screen.

```
DATE: 21-FEB-95      MODULE - OUTPUT                        PAGE     1
TIME: 12:33          NAME: PRINT SUBTOTAL LINES             Excelerator


TYPE Module                           NAME PRINT SUBTOTAL LINES

   Project MICRO          Author  CP          File Name       PRTSTLLN
   Date    2/5/92         Version 00          Number Of Lines 35

   Definition    PRINT SUBTOTALS WHEN SOFTWARE CHANGES


   Location      IBM PS2 MODEL SX55 D.P.


   Duration Value
   Duration Type


   Call Sequence/Input Parameters          Return Values
   HARDWARE SUBTOTALS               GRAND TOTALS



        Satisfies Requirement:              Associated Entities:
   Type  Name                          Type  Name
   URQ PROVIDE HARDWARE/SOFTWARE XREF   TST PRODUCE HARDWARE/SOFTWARE XREF
                                        CAT MICROCOMPUTER INFORMATION
                                        CAT SOFTWARE



                           Description
   MODULE TASKS ARE:

   1.  FORMAT THE SUBTOTAL LINE USING THE MICROCOMPUTER COUNT
   2.  CALL PRINT REPORT LINE TO PRINT THE SUBTOTAL LINE
   3.  ADD THE SUBTOTAL COUNT TO THE GRAND TOTAL
   4.  ZERO THE SUBTOTAL COUNT


   Modified By    ANNA         Date Modified  950225   # Changes  1
   Added By       ANNA         Date Added     950222
   Last Project   TEST FINAL
   Locked By                   Date Locked    0        Lock Status
```

FIGURE E20.6
PRINT SUBTOTAL LINES Module print.

E-3. Modify the CHANGE MICROCOMPUTER FILE structure chart.
      Include the LOOP symbol and add the following modules subor-
      dinate to 160, CHANGE MICROCOMPUTER RECORD (also see
      the following page):

      A. DISPLAY CHANGE SCREEN
      B. ACCEPT MICROCOMPUTER CHANGES
      C. VALIDATE CHANGES
      D. DISPLAY ERROR MESSAGE (*Hint:* Use copy and
          module 150)
      E. CONFIRM CHANGES

      The following modules should be subordinate to 220, PUT
      MICROCOMPUTER RECORD:

      A. FORMAT MICROCOMPUTER RECORD
      B. REWRITE MICROCOMPUTER RECORD

```
─                    Test: ADD NEW MICROCOMPUTER
 Entity  Edit  Help
    Alternate Name       ADD NEW MICROCOMPUTER BATCH TEST                    ⬆

              Test Purpose
    ┌──────────────────────────────────────────────────────────────┐
    │ TEST TO DETERMINE IF NEW MICROCOMPUTERS ARE CORRECTLY ADDED TO THE │
    │ MICROCOMPUTER MASTER FILE.  INCLUDE VALIDATION OF THE ADD MICROCOMPUTER │
    │ INFORMATION, UPDATING THE PENDING MICROCOMPUTER ORDER FILE AND PRINTING │
    │ THE INSTALLATION LISTING.                                        │
    │                                                                  │
    └──────────────────────────────────────────────────────────────┘

    Test Type          ┌────────────────────┐
                       │ LINK               │
    Test Method        ├────────────────────┤
                       │ TEST CASES         │
                       └────────────────────┘

            Test Description
    ┌──────────────────────────────────────────────────────────────┐
    │ 1.   VALID AND INVALID TRANSACTIONS ARE TO BE CREATED TO TEST THE EDIT │
    │ ADD TRANSACTIONS PROGRAM.  ALL INVALID TRANSACTIONS SHOULD BE DETECTED │
    │ AND PRINTED.  VALID TRANSACTIONS ARE PLACED ON THE MICROCOMPUTER ADD │
    │ TRANSACTION FILE.                                                │
    │                                                                  │
    │ 2.   THE VALID ADD TRANSACTIONS FILE SHOULD CONTAIN RECORDS EXISTING ON │
    │ THE MASTER FILE AND THOSE THAT DO NOT.  ALL TRANSACTIONS THAT HAVE A │    ⬇
    └──────────────────────────────────────────────────────────────┘
```

FIGURE E20.7
ADD NEW MICROCOMPUTER Test plan.

⌨ **E-4.** Modify the ADD SOFTWARE RECORDS structure chart by adding a looping symbol and coupling for the connections. The following coupling should be placed on the connection line above each module (also see the following page):

- A. Module: DISPLAY ADD SOFTWARE SCREEN
  - Passed Up: ADD SOFTWARE SCREEN
- B. Module: ACCEPT ADD SOFTWARE SCREEN
  - Passed Up: EXIT INDICATOR (Control)
    ADD SOFTWARE SCREEN DATA
- C. Module: VALIDATE ADD SOFTWARE DATA
  - Passed Down: ADD SOFTWARE SCREEN DATA
  - Passed Up: CANCEL TRANSACTION (Control)
    VALID ADD SOFTWARE DATA
- D. Module: READ SOFTWARE RECORD
  - Passed Down: SOFTWARE INVENTORY NUMBER
  - Passed Up: RECORD FOUND (Control)
- E. Module: VALIDATE HARDWARE REQUIREMENTS
  - Passed Down: ADD SOFTWARE SCREEN DATA
  - Passed Up: VALID DATA (Control)
    ERROR MESSAGE
- F. Module: DISPLAY ERROR MESSAGE
  - Passed Down: ERROR MESSAGE
- G. Module: PUT NEW SOFTWARE RECORD
  - Passed Down: VALID ADD SOFTWARE DATA
- H. Module: FORMAT SOFTWARE RECORD
  - Passed Down: VALID ADD SOFTWARE DATA
  - Passed Up: FORMATTED SOFTWARE RECORD I.
  - Module: WRITE SOFTWARE RECORD
  - Passed Down: FORMATTED SOFTWARE RECORD

□ **E-5.** Create the PRINT PROBLEM MACHINE REPORT structure chart. An outline of the modules follows, with each subordinate module indented.

> PRINT PROBLEM MACHINE REPORT
>> PRINT PROBLEM MACHINE LINES
>>> READ MACHINE RECORD
>>> DETERMINE PROBLEM MACHINE
>>> PRINT PROBLEM MACHINE LINE
>>>> PRINT HEADING LINES
>>>> WRITE REPORT LINE
>> PRINT FINAL REPORT LINES
>>> WRITE REPORT LINE

□ **E-6.** Create the CHANGE SOFTWARE RECORD structure chart. Modules of the program are shown with subordinate modules indented.

> CHANGE SOFTWARE FILE
>> CHANGE SOFTWARE RECORDS
>>> GET SOFTWARE RECORD
>>>> DISPLAY SOFTWARE ID SCREEN
>>>> ACCEPT SOFTWARE ID SCREEN
>>>> FIND SOFTWARE RECORD
>>>> DISPLAY ERROR LINE
>>> OBTAIN SOFTWARE CHANGES
>>>> DISPLAY CHANGE SCREEN
>>>> ACCEPT SOFTWARE CHANGES
>>>> VALIDATE CHANGES
>>>> DISPLAY ERROR LINE
>>> PUT SOFTWARE RECORD
>>>> FORMAT SOFTWARE RECORD
>>>> REWRITE SOFTWARE RECORD

□ **E-7.** Create the SOFTWARE DETAILS INQUIRY structure chart. Modules are listed with subordinate modules indented (see next page).

> INQUIRE SOFTWARE DETAILS
>> INQUIRE SOFTWARE RECORD
>>> GET SOFTWARE RECORD
>>>> DISPLAY SOFTWARE ID SCREEN
>>>> ACCEPT SOFTWARE ID SCREEN
>>>> FIND SOFTWARE RECORD
>>>> DISPLAY ERROR LINE
>>> DISPLAY INQUIRY SCREEN
>>>> FORMAT SOFTWARE INQUIRY SCREEN
>>>> DISPLAY SOFTWARE INQUIRY SCREEN

□ **E-8.** View the ADD MICROCOMPUTER system flowchart. Use **DESCRIBE** to examine some of the object descriptions.

□ **E-9.** Modify the ADD SOFTWARE system flow. Add the following program rectangles below the INSTALL SOFTWARE manual process. Include input and output files and reports specified for each program.

<pre>
    Program: UPDATE SOFTWARE RELATIONAL FILE
    Input: UPDATED SOFTWARE INSTALLATION LIST,
                     document
                  UPDATE INSTALLED SOFTWARE SCREEN, display
    Output: SOFTWARE RELATIONAL FILE, disk
                  INSTALLED SOFTWARE TRANSACTION, disk
    Program: PRINT USER NOTIFICATION REPORT
    Input: INSTALLED SOFTWARE TRANSACTION, disk
    Output: USER NOTIFICATION REPORT, report
</pre>

▢ **E-10.** Create the ADD STAFF system flowchart. There are two pro-
grams. ADD STAFF and PRINT NEW STAFF LIST. Input to the
ADD STAFF program is a NEW STAFF listing and an ADD NEW
STAFF entry screen. The STAFF MASTER file is updated and a
NEW STAFF LOG FILE is produced. The NEW STAFF LOG
FILE is input to the PRINT NEW STAFF LIST program, produc-
ing the report NEW STAFF LIST.

▢ **E-11.** View the ADD NEW MICROCOMPUTER test entity. Use the
PgUp and PgDn commands to view the different screens. Select
the XLDictionary option **Relationships** to view the entities that
refer to the ADD MICROCOMPUTER test plan.

▢ **E-12.** Modify the ADD SOFTWARE RECORD test entity. Include a test
description reflecting the following test summary:

Test the ADD NEW SOFTWARE program by supplying both
valid and invalid data for all screen fields. Test function keys
for exiting and canceling the transaction.

Validate that new records are added to the SOFTWARE MAS-
TER file and the correct SOFTWARE LOG file records have
been created.

Verify that the SOFTWARE INSTALLATION LISTING has
been correctly produced.

Test the DETERMINE HARDWARE LOCATION INQUIRY program. Include valid and invalid records.

Create data to effectively test the UPDATE SOFTWARE RELA-
TIONAL file. Include valid and invalid cases.

Validate that the information printed on the USER NOTIFICA-
TION report is complete and correct.

▢ **E-13.** Modify the CHANGE MICROCOMPUTER RECORD test entity.
Include the **Test Type** of UNIT, and the **Test Method** of CASES.
Include the following test description:

Provide IDs for both existing and nonexisting MICROCOM-
PUTER MASTER records. For existing records, test that only
active records may be changed.

Include valid and invalid entries for all data fields on the
change screen. Examine error messages for content and correctness.

Test all function keys to ensure that the program may be correctly exited and transactions canceled.

E-14. Produce the PRINT INVENTORY LOCATION SHEET test entity. The **Test Type** is UNIT, with a **Test Method** of CASES. Include a description noting that the report should be printed with separate sheets for each location, sorted by room location within each campus. All input data is assumed valid.

E-15. Add the SOFTWARE LOCATION INQUIRY test data plan. The **Test Type** is UNIT and the **Test Method** is INTERACTIVE. The test description should include the following details:

The SOFTWARE INVENTORY NUMBER should be used to locate the matching SOFTWARE RECORD. Test for record found and not found. When records are found, the SOFTWARE HARDWARE RELATIONAL file is used to locate all HARDWARE INVENTORY NUMBERS for the given software ID. Test for no relational records and several relational records for one software ID.

When matching HARDWARE INVENTORY NUMBERS are found, test for matching MICROCOMPUTER MASTER records, including both records found and not found. For each matching MICROCOMPUTER MASTER record, search the CAMPUS TABLE for a matching code. Include codes on the table and not on the table.

Test all function keys.

E-16. Create the PRINT HARDWARE/SOFTWARE CROSS-REFERENCE REPORT test entity. The **Test Type** is UNIT, with a **Test Method** of CASES. Use the PRODUCE SOFTWARE CROSS-REFERENCE REPORT structure chart to determine a good test plan.

21

SUCCESSFULLY IMPLEMENTING THE INFORMATION SYSTEM

IMPLEMENTATION APPROACHES

The process of assuring that the information system is operational and then allowing users to take over its operation for use and evaluation is called implementation. The systems analyst has several approaches to implementation that should be considered as the changeover to the new system is being prepared. These include shifting more computer power to users via an information center and/or distributed processing; training users; converting from the old system; and evaluating the new one.

The first approach to implementation concerns the movement of computer power to individual users by setting up an information center (IC) or shifting computer power and responsibility to groups throughout the business with the help of distributed computing.

The second approach to implementation is using different strategies for training users and information center personnel, including taking them on their own level, using a variety of training techniques, and making sure that each user understands any new role that he or she must enact because of the new information system.

Another approach to implementation is choosing a conversion strategy. The systems analyst needs to weigh the situation and propose a conversion plan that is appropriate for the particular organization and information system.

The fourth approach to implementation involves evaluating the new or modified information system or information center. The analyst needs to formulate performance measures on which to evaluate the information center or system. Evaluations come from information center personnel, users, management, and analysts themselves.

803

ESTABLISHING AN INFORMATION CENTER

Throughout this book, the systematic development of computerized information systems using the systems development life cycle has been encouraged. However, the analyst knows that not all user needs are adequately addressed through a long-term, large-scale systems project.

Sometimes requirements change before the system is delivered; other times users cannot wait months or years for a solution. The realistic analyst also recognizes that users with short-term information needs should not be ignored because of the pressures of completing full-scale systems projects or project backlogs.

A New Role for the Information Systems Department

The creation and implementation of an information center is proposed as a way to make it easier for users to fulfill their short-term information needs while still receiving support from the information systems department. The information center is organized as an arm of that department.

Before the decision to create a center is made, a cost-benefit analysis must be completed. Executives must be shown that the information center can give a reasonable return on investment. Experiences with information centers suggest that a two-dollar return for every dollar invested in the information center can be expected. It is important that the information center hold its own as a contributor to the business. The four steps necessary to establishing an information center are listed in Figure 21.1.

INFORMATION CENTER OBJECTIVES. An information center has as its primary objective supporting internal organizational users in accessing data so that they are empowered to formulate, analyze, and solve their own business problems or questions through the use of computers. Initially, this requires a statement of commitment from users and information center personnel that the information center is a worthwhile concept. It also requires specifying the roles of information center personnel and users.

THE SYSTEMS ANALYST IN THE INFORMATION CENTER. The information center, as part of a larger information systems effort in a business, provides a management or support opportunity for the systems analyst. It is possible to begin an information center with a manager and two or three technical people. The manager must be committed to the information center concept and be willing to manage and promote it as a cost-justifiable branch of the information systems department.

Since people staffing the information center may supply the only personal contact users have with the systems department, the personality and image projected by center employees are extremely important. Above all, they must be genuinely adept at interacting with users, often on a one-to one basis, in a support role. Technical expertise, the willingness to learn new equipment, packages, and tools, and the capacity to communicate one's expertise to users are also important attributes of information center employees.

Information center personnel are present to educate and train users about how to access pertinent databases, to help users formulate a request, to demonstrate how to use available packages and tools, to help users at the terminal, and to encourage new users. For their part, in committing to

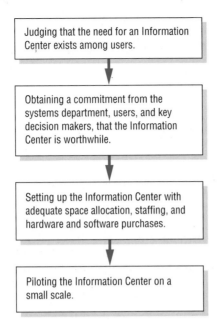

FIGURE 21.1
Four steps in establishing
information centers.

Judging that the need for an Information Center exists among users.

Obtaining a commitment from the systems department, users, and key decision makers, that the Information Center is worthwhile.

Setting up the Information Center with adequate space allocation, staffing, and hardware and software purchases.

Piloting the Information Center on a small scale.

the information center, users must accept responsibility for the fact that the resources they are using are not free, serve as experts on the business background of their problems, learn how to use equipment and software, and communicate their experiences to other users.

The information center is not intended to replace traditionally accomplished systems projects. Rather, it is intended to smooth the long-standing conflict between information systems personnel and users. Information systems personnel typically have a large backlog of projects and maintenance and are therefore loath to take on requests for immediate help on the basis of what seems like user whim. Users feel that many times their immediate information needs are being ignored because of the analysts' attention to a backlog of long-term systems projects.

By purposely deploying people to support users in learning how to use the information resource themselves, the information center frees analysts to work on larger systems development projects. This solution can reduce conflict between information systems people and users as well as reducing project backlog and maintenance.

ADVANTAGES OF THE INFORMATION CENTER TO USERS. Many advantages of the information center to organizational users can be realized. Since the whole center pivots on accessibility, a well-run facility allows greater access to information resources and technical support for the user. It also means that many needs can be filled quickly. As users learn more, they are less dependent on key information systems people. Additionally, knowledge of information systems and their uses is disseminated more rapidly into the organization at large.

ADVANTAGES TO THE INFORMATION SYSTEMS DEPARTMENT. As mentioned before, many of the advantages for the information systems group derive from reducing the pressure on them to handle small requests quickly, while simultaneously managing larger projects. Additionally, with information center support many users can design new output reflecting up-to-the-minute

FIGURE 21.2
Advantages and disadvan-
tages of information centers.

Advantages to Users of the Information Center	Advantages to the Systems Department
Greater access to the information resource Greater access to technical support Information needs can be filled quickly Users become less dependent Knowledge of information systems is disseminated more rapidly	Reduces pressure to handle simple requests quickly User designs output; frees analyst to design system Service orientation of department is made evident to users Users become less dependent

Potential Disadvantages of Information Centers
The information center may become the workhorse of the systems department if organizational positioning is poor Systems personnel and users must commit to changing their work relationships

needs, an outcome which frees analysts to design systems. Perhaps the biggest benefit is that the service orientation of the information systems department is made evident to users in a positive and convincing way through the establishment of a well-run information center.

DISADVANTAGES OF THE INFORMATION CENTER. As with any new enterprise, the creation of an information center is not without its disadvantages. Some problems can arise if the organizational positioning of the information center is not carefully thought through. It must not be seen as a mere workhorse for the information systems department. Neither should the center be positioned within one functional area (for example, accounting). It should be positioned so that it is equally accessible to all functional areas.

Another obstacle is that the information center calls for systems personnel and users to commit to changing their working relationships. This is easier said than done, and a center built without first establishing a two-way relationship has no real chance of success. Both of these obstacles are surmountable, but those involved in the creation of the center must be willing to spend adequate time in thinking through these issues. Advantages to users of the information center, advantages to the systems department of the IC, and disadvantages of the IC are summarized in Figure 21.2.

Information Center Practices

Several practices are helpful in setting up the information center. These include adequately staffing the center, planning for a proper physical setup, using available hardware, and examining software availability and limitations.

ADEQUATELY STAFFING THE INFORMATION CENTER. As mentioned briefly before, an information center carries with it many roles. Characteristics desirable for each role are given in Figure 21.3. Some personnel functions can be doubled up when a center is just beginning, but to conduct a fair

Title	Characteristics Needed
Manager	Good communications and managerial skills; training as a systems analyst
Product Specialist	Technical background, training as systems analyst, learns new software packages quickly, communicates knowledge to others
Technician	Excellent technical knowledge, learns quickly
Educator /Trainer	Knowledge of training techniques, likes interaction with users, learns quickly
Secretary/Documentor	Keeps information center communicating internally, maintains and updates manuals and other center documents

FIGURE 21.3
Required roles in the
information center.

test of the information center, personnel should not be spread too thinly. The center staff ideally will include:

1. A manager.
2. One or more product specialists.
3. Technical support.
4. Educator/trainer.
5. Secretarial/documentor support.

A manager who can do all of the traditional human resources planning and management in addition to strategic planning for the future of the information center is essential. This person must be capable of correctly positioning the information center in the larger organization without posing a threat to the information systems department.

The information center staff should include an analyst who is usually the first contact for the user. Among other things, this person must be able to help users formulate their requests and justify expending resources on them.

Additionally, the center staff should include one or more product specialists. The product specialist is the next person in line to work with the user in tackling his or her business problem. Product specialists help users frame a problem in terms of the software packages that the specialists support.

At least one technical support person is needed to install and maintain whatever software packages are supported by the product specialists in the information center.

The person filling the educator/trainer role helps users (and other center employees) learn about packages available through the center.

Secretarial/documentor support is also a key personnel role to be filled in the information center. This person provides secretarial and administrative support for the manager. The documentation aspect of this job is also important, as this person is charged with maintaining and updating manuals and other documents for the center. The person in this role is a conduit for communication within the center.

PLANNING THE PHYSICAL SETUP OF THE INFORMATION CENTER. It is critical that a proper physical setup be arranged for the information center. In order to be recognized as a serious entity, adequate, accessible, and secure space must be allocated for the information center.

Plan for an office for each of the full-time people who will be hired. Each person needs a PC (preferably with network access) in their office. Also provide a common workroom with PCs for users. Include space in the information center for a multimedia room that can be dedicated to educational efforts.

PILOTING THE INFORMATION CENTER. Piloting the information center means starting the center services on a small scale. This permits the IC staff to see where potential problems are and allows favorable user response to filter through the organization. It also means that you can begin an information center with two or three key personnel (for instance, a manager, two analysts, and a secretary).

When limiting staff, you must also limit the number of users. Pilot the information center with just a handful of users, perhaps five or six. Choose users carefully, targeting users who have a current need that you can meet well. Attempt to find a software package that they are somewhat familiar with, but with which they are not yet proficient. The package should also be something that a larger prospective user group will be interested in using eventually.

Try to get a good fit between the user, information center support, the package, and the problem being tackled (which should have a measurable outcome when solved). Controlling for these factors when piloting the information center increases the center's chance of organizational success in the longer term.

During the analysis of system needs, it is possible that the analyst will see the need to investigate the possibility of building electronic networks rather than just one system or a self-contained information center.

Implementing Distributed Systems

If the reliability of a telecommunications network is high, it is possible to have distributed systems for businesses, which can be conceived of as an application of telecommunications. The concept of distributed systems is used in many different ways. Here, it will be taken in a broad sense so that it includes workstations that can communicate with each other and data processors, as well as different hierarchical architectural configurations of data processors that communicate with each other and that have differing data-storage capabilities.

The information architecture model that will likely dominate networking in the next few years is that of the client/server. In this model, the processing functions are delegated either to "clients" (users) or to "servers," depending on which machines are most suitable for executing the work. In this type of architecture, the client portion of a network application will run on the client system, with the server part of the application running on the file server. With a client/server model, users interact with limited parts of the application including the user interface, data input, database queries and report generation. Functions such as controlling user access to centralized databases, retrieving or processing data, and other aspects such as managing peripheral devices are handled by the server.

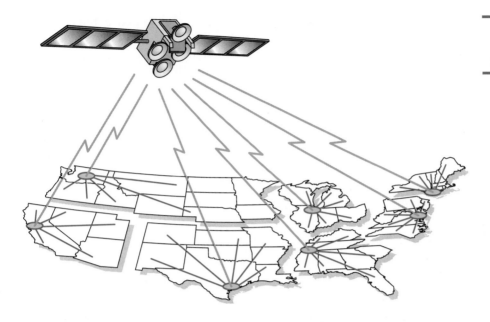

FIGURE 21.4
A distributed system can
span a country via satellites.

Applications for the client/server model must be written as two separate software components, each running on separate machines, but they must appear as if they are operating as one application. The client/server model is more expensive than other options such as the X terminal model, which uses terminals to access remote computers. However, using the client/server model affords greater computer power and greater opportunity to customize applications.

TYPES OF DISTRIBUTED SYSTEMS NETWORKS. While networks can be characterized by their shape or topology, they are also discussed in terms of their geographic coverage and the kinds of services they offer. Standard types of networks include a wide-area network (WAN), and a local area network (LAN). Local area networks are standard for linking local computers and/or terminals within a department, building, or several buildings of an organization. Wide-area networks can serve users over several miles or across entire continents. There are four main types of distributed systems networks: hierarchical, star, ring, and bus. Each requires different hardware and software and has different capabilities.

As shown in Figure 21.4, using a satellite allows the distributed system excellent access to numerous destinations in one country. One satellite can cover up to a third of the world, so efficiency is high.

Hierarchical networks. In a basic hierarchical configuration the host, a mainframe computer, controls all of the other nodes that include minicomputers and microcomputers. Notice that computers on the same level do not communicate with each other. The intention of this arrangement is that large-scale computing problems are handled by the mainframe and lesser computing demands are handled on the correct level by either minicomputers or microcomputers.

Star networks. Another popular configuration for distributed computing is the star network. A mainframe or microcomputer is designated the central node. As such, it communicates with the lesser nodes, but they cannot communicate directly with one another. A need for the microcomputers to communicate with each other would be met by one microcomputer sending data to the central node, which in turn would relay the data to a second microcomputer.

Ring networks. Ring networks are another possibility for distributed computing. There is no central computer for a ring. Rather, its shape reminds us that all of the nodes are of equal computing power. With the use of a ring network, all microcomputers can communicate directly with one another, passing along all the messages they read to their correct destinations on the ring.

Bus configurations. Another type of network for distributed processing is the bus configuration. Bus configurations work well in close quarters, such as a suite of offices where several different devices can be hooked together via a central cable. A bus configuration allows a great deal of change through permitting users to add or remove devices quite easily. In a bus configuration the single, central cable serves as the only path.

Network Modeling

Since networking has become so important, the systems designer needs to consider network design. Whether a systems designer gets involved with decisions about token rings or Ethernet networks, or worries about hardware like routers and bridges that must be in place when networks meet, the systems designer must always consider the logical design of networks. This is where network modeling enters in.

CASE tools such as Excelerator or Visible Analyst are not sufficient to help the systems designer with network modeling. It is possible to use some of the drawing tools in Excelerator's presentation graph feature, but forcing the data modeling tools to do network modeling just does not work. Therefore, we suggest using some sort of symbols (like the ones in Figure 21.5) to model the network. It is useful to have distinct symbols to distinguish among hubs, external networks, and workstations. It is also useful to adopt a convention for illustrating multiple networks and workstations.

Typically, a top-down approach is appropriate. The first step is to draw a network decomposition diagram that provides an overview of the system. Next, draw a hub connectivity diagram. Finally, explode the hub connectivity diagram to show the various workstations and how they are to be connected.

DRAWING A NETWORK DECOMPOSITION DIAGRAM. We can illustrate drawing a network decomposition model by referring once again to the World's Trend Catalog Division example from earlier chapters. Start by drawing a circle at the top and labeling it "World's Trend Network." Now draw a number of circles on the level below as shown in Figure 21.6. These circles represent hubs for the marketing division and each of the three order-entry and distribution centers (the U.S. Division, Canadian Division, and the Mexican Division).

We can extend this further by drawing another level. This time we can draw in the workstations. For example, the Marketing Division has two

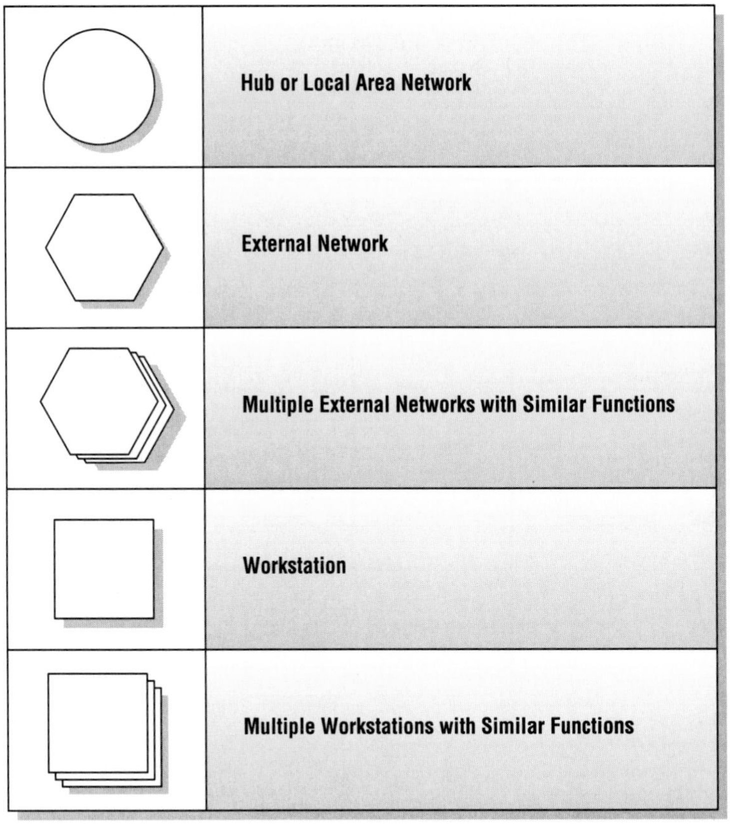

○	**Hub or Local Area Network**
⬡	**External Network**
⬡⬡	**Multiple External Networks with Similar Functions**
▢	**Workstation**
▢▢	**Multiple Workstations with Similar Functions**

FIGURE 21.5
Use special symbols when
drawing network decomposition and hub connectivity
diagrams.

workstations connected, while the U.S. Division has 33 workstations on its LAN (Administration, the U.S. Warehouse, the Order-Entry Manager, and 30 Order-Entry Clerks). This network is simplified for the purpose of providing a readily understandable example.

CREATING A HUB CONNECTIVITY DIAGRAM. The hub connectivity diagram is useful to show how the major hubs are connected. At World's Trend (see Figure 21.7), there are four major hubs that are all connected to one another. In addition, there are external hubs (suppliers) that need to be notified when inventory drops below a certain point, and so on. Each of the three divisions are connected to the 21 suppliers; however, the Marketing Division does not need to be connected to suppliers.

To produce an effective hub connectivity diagram, start by drawing all of the hubs. Then experiment (perhaps sketching it first on a sheet of paper) to see which links are necessary. Once this is done, you can redraw the diagram so it is attractive and communicates well to users.

EXPLODING THE HUB CONNECTIVITY DIAGRAM INTO A WORKSTATION CONNECTIVITY DIAGRAM. The purpose of network modeling is to show the connectivity of workstations in some detail. To do so we explode the hub connectivity diagram. Figure 21.8 shows each of the 33 workstations for the U.S. Division and how they are to be connected.

Draw the diagrams for this level by examining the third level of the network decomposition diagram. Group items such as "Order-Entry Manager" and "Order-Entry Clerks" together, since you already recognize

FIGURE 21.6
A network decomposition diagram for World's Trend.

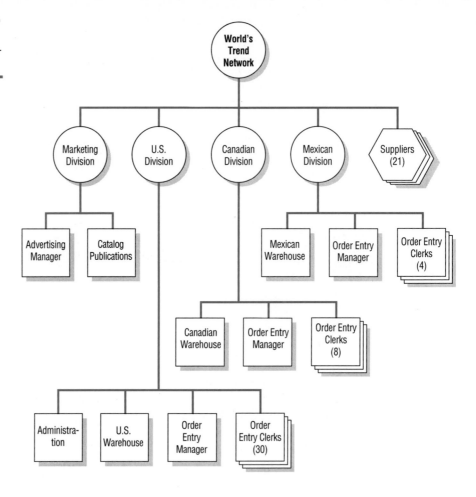

FIGURE 21.7
A hub connectivity diagram
for World's Trend.

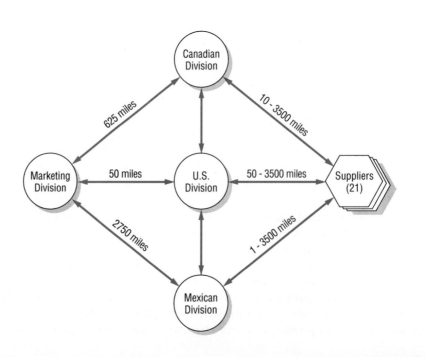

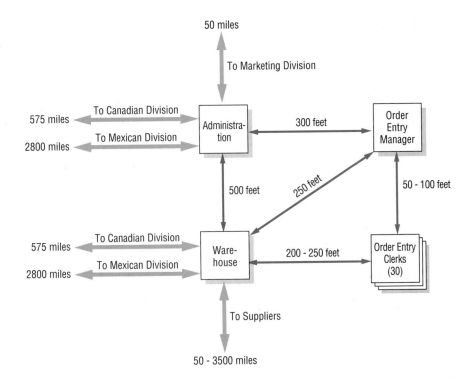

FIGURE 21.8
A workstation connectivity
diagram for World's Trend.

50 miles

To Marketing Division

To Canadian Division
575 miles

To Mexican Division
2800 miles

Administra-tion

300 feet

Order
Entry
Manager

500 feet

250 feet

50 - 100 feet

To Canadian Division
575 miles

To Mexican Division
2800 miles

Ware-house

200 - 250 feet

Order Entry
Clerks
(30)

To Suppliers

50 - 3500 miles

that they must be connected. Use a special symbol to show multiple work-stations and indicate in parentheses the number of similar workstations. In our example, there are 30 order entry clerks.

On the perimeter of the diagram, place workstations that must be connected to other hubs. In this way it will be easier to represent these connections using arrows. Draw the external connections in a different color or use thicker arrows. External connections are usually long-distance. For example, Administration is connected to the Marketing Division, 50 miles away, and also to the Canadian and Mexican Divisions. The warehouse needs to communicate directly with the Canadian and Mexican warehouses, in case it is possible to obtain the merchandise from another warehouse. Order-Entry Managers and Clerks do not have to be connected to anyone outside of their LAN.

Hub connectivity diagrams can be exploded to many levels. If doing so makes sense in your particular application, go ahead and draw it that way. There is no limit to the possible number of explosions.

Hub connectivity and workstation connectivity diagrams can be drawn using software packages as well. Although it may be difficult if you restrict yourself to using CASE tool software, it is relatively simple if you use flexible drag-and-drop software, such as Visio, by Shapeware (see Figure 21.9).

Visio even contains stencils that depict certain pieces of equipment if you wish to go into that much detail. Using specific stencils, an analyst could drag each symbol from the template to the piece of paper. Figure 21.10 shows how two networks are set up for a software manufacturer. The top part of the figure illustrates the program development sector's network of the organization, while the bottom part shows the sales department's network.

Additional detail is shown by zooming in on the program development network. In Figure 21.11 we can see that there are 3 IBM compatibles hooked up to a bus network that has a laser printer, scanner, a modem for connection to laptop computers, and a server. Packages, such as Visio, are

FIGURE 21.9
Analysts can draw hub connectivity diagrams using software like Visio.

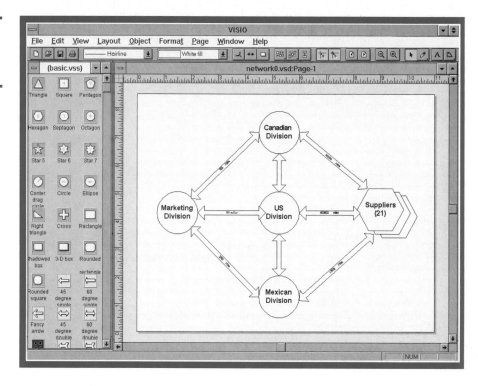

extremely useful to the systems analyst because they save time and enhance communication by using standard symbols.

Groupware

Writing applications either for an entire organization or a solitary decision maker has also begun to change dramatically. Recognizing that much of the

FIGURE 21.10
A more detailed diagram of two networks, drawn by selecting symbols from a template and dragging them to the piece of paper. This diagram was drawn using Visio from Shapeware.

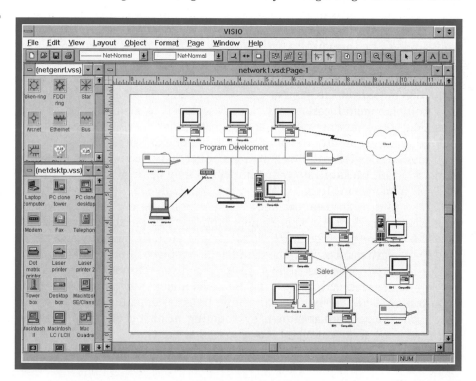

814

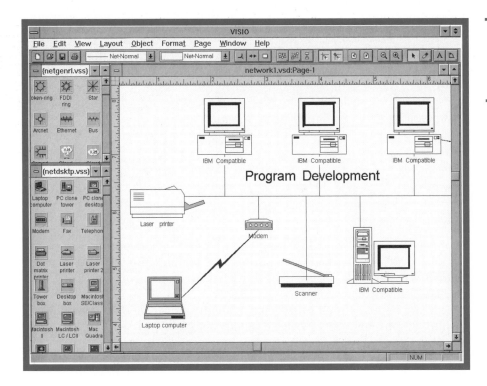

FIGURE 21.11
A closer view of the network shows what type of equipment is connected to the program development group.

organization's work is actually accomplished in groups or teams, there is now a powerful movement afoot to develop special software called "groupware" that supports people who work together in the organization. Groupware takes advantage of the potential synergies and power available from networked PCs in either local area networks (LANs) or wide-area networks (WANs). Groupware products can help group members to schedule and attend meetings, share data, create and analyze documents, communicate in unstructured ways with one another via e-mail, hold group conferences, do image management on the departmental level, and manage and monitor workflow.

We are still far from an integrated approach to groupware, which means that often developers will create a product which supports some combination but not all of the foregoing functions. At the heart of most groupware is a useful, easy-to-use, flexible e-mail system. If asked to develop workgroup applications you should first assess whether there is currently a usable e-mail system in place upon which to build other functions.

You can see from the wide range of capabilities possible that there is no standard definition for what comprises groupware. In fact, each software company seems to be putting forward a different vision of what kind of support groups need to function best.

The product that has defined groupware for many users is Lotus Notes, which Lotus corporate officers aptly refer to as "the Network GUI." Notes features a document-oriented database that has a wide range of options and far fewer restrictions than traditional databases. Group users working with Notes will find its fields can handle numerous fonts, text colors, scanned images, hypertext links to other documents in Notes, and even push buttons that are actually Notes macros. Using a simple, straightforward, "no-frills" interface, Notes helps novices get up and running quickly. All Notes databases use an identical interface, so that once a group member has learned one database, it is easy to use a new one.

Manufacturer	Product
Adaptive Software	PeopleScheduler
Beyond	Beyond Mail
Lotus Development Corp.	Lotus Notes, cc:Mail
Microsoft Corp.	Microsoft Mail, Microsoft Schedule+
Microsystem Software	CaLANdar
TEAM Software	Channels
Trax Softwork	TeamTalk 1.0
WordPerfect	WordPerfect Office 4.0

Additionally, Notes has been called "mail-integrated" and provides flexible, wide-ranging mail capabilities that support the way group members work, as well as letting them use mail in some novel way (for example, sending Notes messages to a database).

Many organizations experience difficulty in getting networked applications to run smoothly with adequate backups and security. In other words, many network applications purporting to be groupware do not deliver what has been promised because of initial faulty development, and subsequent poor implementation and backup. Lotus Notes has successfully addressed this pitfall by using a breakthrough replication technology that enables it to keep many copies of a database (whether they are on LANs or remote workstations) and to synchronize them by using background dial-up phone connections from time to time. Lotus Notes has been criticized as a very expensive, monolithic option for supporting group work, but it has attracted a large following.

While most software companies agree to the importance of supporting group work, they differ in their visions of what groups and individuals need for support. For example, Novell/WordPerfect currently offers groupware features such as e-mail, messaging, and calendaring in a networked environment. In the future, WordPerfect envisions supporting users with the capability to pull together a report containing objects gathered from anywhere on the network, regardless of what systems were used to create them. Thus a report could have text from the annual report, bar charts from last week's sales meeting, and scanned images of hand-drawn sketches that portray the latest departmental brainstorming session. In such a case, the computer would search out the various pieces, and the software would coordinate them for use in one document.

FIGURE 21.13
There are five main advantages to creating distributed systems.

Advantages of Distributed Systems
• Allow data storage out of the way of on-line, real-time transactions
• Allow less expensive media for data storage when all data are not needed all of the time by all users
• Lower equipment cost since not all system parts need to perform all functions
• Lower equipment cost by permitting flexibility in choice of manufacturer
• Less expensive than large systems initially since expansion can be planned for without actually purchasing hardware

Another approach to developing groupware has been taken by Microsoft, which is giving rudimentary workgroup capability to products such as Windows for Workgroups and Windows NT. New GUI interfaces dubbed Chicago and Cairo are also supposed to include an "object store" similar to the one currently available in Lotus Notes, so that Microsoft operating systems will have built-in workgroup capabilities. In the short term, Microsoft is working with smaller developers and consultants to develop workgroup application solutions. This bottom-up approach seems to be showing successful results as well. Different groupware offers different forms of support. Figure 21.12 gives a brief list of popular groupware products and their manufacturers.

ADVANTAGES OF DISTRIBUTED SYSTEMS. Distributed systems allow storage of data where they are not "in the way" of any on-line real-time transactions. For example, response time on inquiries might be improved if not all records must be searched through before a response is made. Additionally, not all data are needed by all users all of the time, and so they can be stored in less expensive media at a different site and only accessed when needed.

Use of distributed systems can also lower equipment costs, since not all parts of the system need to be able to perform all functions. Some capabilities, such as processing and storage, can be shared.

Distributed systems can also help lower costs by permitting flexibility in choice of manufacturer, since the whole focus of networks is communicating between nodes and therefore manufacturers make compatible components. This compatibility allows shopping for price as well as for function. Further, distributed systems can be initially less expensive than large systems in that it is feasible to plan for expansion without actually having to buy hardware at the time the system is implemented. Advantages of distributed systems are given in Figure 21.13.

DISADVANTAGES OF DISTRIBUTED SYSTEMS. Distributed systems pose some unique problems that centralized computer systems do not. The analyst needs to weigh these problems against the advantages just presented and to raise them with the concerned business as well.

The first problem is that of network reliability. In order to make a network an asset rather than a liability, it must be possible to transmit, receive, process, and store data reliably. If there are too many problems with system reliability, the system will be abandoned.

Distributing greater computing power to individuals increases the threat to security because of widespread access. The necessity of secret passwords, secure computer rooms, and adequate security training of personnel are all concerns that multiply when distributed systems are implemented.

Systems analysts creating distributed systems need to be wary of making several small, stand-alone systems with limited communication capability. It is important to focus on the network itself, or the synergistic aspect of distributed systems. Their power resides in their capabilities to interact as user work groups share data. If the relationship between subsystems is ignored or deemphasized, you are creating more problems than you are solving. Disadvantages of distributed systems are listed in Figure 21.14.

Partially in response to problems experienced in sharing software among departmental computers, there is a relatively new concept in the

FIGURE 21.14
There are four chief disadvantages to creating distributed systems.

Disadvantages of Distributed Systems
• Difficulty in achieving a reliable system
• Security concerns increase commensurately when more individuals have access to the system
• Analysts must emphasize the network and the interactions it provides and deemphasize the power of subsystems
• Choosing the wrong level of computing to support (i.e., individual instead of department, department instead of branch)

industry called "cooperative processing," which at this point is more of a philosophy than any particular hardware configuration. Cooperative processing attempts to do away with the departmental level of minicomputers by networking only two tiers of computers. Its emphasis is on accessing and sharing data rather than on supporting intradepartmental computing.

TRAINING USERS

Systems analysts engage in an educational process with users that is called training. Throughout the systems development life cycle, the user has been involved, so that by now the analyst should possess an accurate assessment of the users that must be trained. As we have seen, information centers retain trainers of their own.

In the implementation of large projects, the analyst will often be managing the training rather than being personally involved in it. One of the most prized assets the analyst can bring to any training situation is the ability to see the system from the users' viewpoint. The analyst must never forget what it is like to face a new system. Those recollections can help analysts empathize with users and facilitate their training.

Training Strategies

Training strategies are determined by who is being trained and who will train them. The analyst will want to ensure that anyone whose work is affected by the new information system is properly trained by the appropriate trainer.

WHO TO TRAIN. All people who will have secondary or primary use of the system must be trained. This includes everyone from data-entry personnel to those who will use output to make decisions without personally using a computer. The amount of training a system requires thus depends on how much someone's job will change because of the new system.

You must ensure that users of different skill levels and job interests are separated. It is certain trouble to include novices in the same training sessions as experts, since novices are quickly lost, and experts are rapidly bored with basics. Both groups are then lost.

PEOPLE WHO TRAIN USERS. For a large project, many different trainers may be used depending on how many users must be trained and who they are, as shown in Figure 21.15. Possible training sources include:

Possible Trainers	Who to Train	
	Primary Users	Secondary Users
Vendors		X
Systems Analysts	X	X
External Paid Trainers		X
In-House Trainers	X	
Other System Users	X	

The analyst has several options when considering which trainers to use.

The choice of trainer depends partially on who is being trained.

FIGURE 21.15
It may be possible to use many different trainers in a large systems project.

1. Vendors.
2. Systems analysts.
3. External paid trainers.
4. In-house trainers.
5. Other system users.

This list gives just a few of the options the analyst has in planning for and providing training.

Large vendors often provide off-site, one- or two-day training on their equipment for free. These sessions include both lecture and hands-on training in a focused environment.

Since systems analysts know the organization's personnel and the system, they can often provide good training. The use of analysts for training purposes depends on their availability, since they also are expected to oversee all of the implementation process.

External paid trainers are sometimes brought into the organization to help with training. They may have broad experience in teaching people how to use a variety of computers, but they may not give the hands-on training necessary for some users. Additionally, they may not be able to custom-tailor their presentations enough to make them meaningful to users.

Full-time, in-house trainers are usually familiar with personnel and can tailor materials to their needs. One of the drawbacks of in-house trainers is that they may possess expertise in other areas, but not information systems, and they may therefore lack the depth that users need.

It is also possible to have any of these trainers train a small group of people from each functional area that will be using the new information system. They in turn can then be used to train the remaining users. This approach can work well if the original trainees still have access to materials and trainers as resources when they themselves are providing training. Otherwise, it might degenerate into a trial-and-error situation rather than a structured one.

Guidelines for Training

The analyst has four major guidelines for setting up training. They are: (1) establishing measurable objectives, (2) using appropriate training methods, (3) selecting suitable training sites, and (4) employing understandable training materials.

TRAINING OBJECTIVES. Who is being trained in large part dictates the training objectives. Training objectives for each group must be spelled out clearly. Well-defined objectives are of enormous help in letting trainees know what is expected of them. Additionally, objectives allow evaluation of training when it is complete. For example, operators must know such basics as turning on the machine, what to do when common errors occur, basic troubleshooting, and how to end an entry.

TRAINING METHODS. Each user and operator will need slightly different training. To some extent, their jobs determine what they need to know, and their personalities, experience, and background determine how they learn best. Some users learn best by seeing, others by hearing, still others by doing. Since it is usually not possible to customize training for an individual, a combination of methods is often the best way to proceed. That way, most users are reached through one method or another.

Methods for those who learn best by seeing include demonstrations of equipment and exposure to training manuals. Those who learn best by hearing will benefit from lectures about procedures, discussions, and question-and-answer sessions among trainers and trainees. Those who learn

What IBM Calls It	What It Really Is
Planar Board	System Board
Micro Channel Architecture	Personal System/2 Bus
Asynchronous Communication Adapter	Serial Port
Dual Asynchronous Adapter	Two Serial Ports
Direct Access Storage Device (DASD)	A Disk
Fixed Disk	A Hard Disk
Fixed File	A Hard Disk
Data Migration Facility	A Cable
Memory Expansion Kit	Overpriced RAM Chips
Solution Pac	Bundled Hardware and Software
Operating System 2	DOS 5
Presentation Manager	Microsoft Windows
Systems Application Architecture	Compatibility
Topview 1.12	Unhealthy Nostalgia
IBM/Microsoft Joint Development Agreement	Arm-twisting
IBM-Designed VLSI	See You in Court

Using terms peculiar to analysts or vendors when attempting to train users creates more hurdles than it clears, as you can see from the translation (albeit a humorous one) required to make IBM jargon understandable. Reprinted from *PC Magazine*, May 26, 1987. Copyright © 1987 Ziff Communications Company.

best by doing need hands-on experience with new equipment. For jobs such as that of computer operator, hands-on experience is essential, whereas a quality assurance manager for a production line may only need to see output, learn how to interpret it, and know when it is scheduled to arrive.

TRAINING SITES. Training takes place in many different locations, some of which are more conducive to learning than others. Large computer vendors provide special off-site locations where operable equipment is maintained free of charge. Their trainers offer hands-on experience as well as seminars in a setting that allows users to concentrate on learning the new system. One of the disadvantages of off-site training is that users are away from the organizational context within which they must eventually exist.

On-site training within the users' organization is also possible with several different kinds of trainers. The advantage is that users see the equipment placed as it will be when it is fully operational. A serious disadvantage is that trainees often feel guilty about not fulfilling their regular job duties if they remain on-site for training. Thus, full concentration on training may not be possible.

Off-site training sites are also available for a fee through consultants and vendors. These can be set up in places with meeting space for rent such as a hotel, or they may even be permanent facilities maintained by the trainers. These arrangements allow workers to be free from regular job demands, but they may not provide equipment for hands-on training.

TRAINING MATERIALS. In planning for training of users, systems analysts must realize the importance of well-prepared training materials. These include training manuals; training cases, in which users are assigned to work through a case that incorporates most of the commonly encountered interactions with the system; and prototypes and mock-ups of output. Most packaged software provides on-line tutorials to illustrate basic functions.

Because the user's understanding of the system depends on them, training materials must be clearly written. This means training materials should be well indexed, written for the correct audience with a minimum of jargon, and available to everyone who needs them. A summary of considerations for training objectives, methods, sites, and materials is provided in Figure 21.16.

CONVERSION

A third approach to implementation is physically converting the old information system to the new or modified one. There are many conversion strategies available to analysts, and there is also a contingency approach that takes into account several organizational variables in deciding which conversion strategy to use. These is no single best way to proceed with conversion. The importance of adequate planning and scheduling of conversion (which often takes many weeks), file backup, and adequate security cannot be overemphasized.

Conversion Strategies

The five strategies for converting from the old system to the new are given in Figure 21.17.

Elements	Relevant Factors
Training Objectives	Depend on requirements of user's job
Training Methods	Depend on user's job, personality, background and experience; use combination of lecture, demonstration, hands-on, and study
Training Sites	Depend on training objectives, cost, availability; free vendor sites with operable equipment; in-house installation; rented facilities
Training Materials	Depend on users' needs; operating manuals, cases, prototypes of equipments and output; online tutorials

1. Direct changeover.
2. Parallel conversion.
3. Phased conversion.
4. Modular prototype.
5. Distributed conversion.

Each of the five conversion approaches is described separately in the upcoming sections.

DIRECT CHANGEOVER. Conversion by direct changeover means that, on a specified date, the old system is dropped and the new system is put into use. Direct changeover can only be successful if extensive testing is done

FIGURE 21.17
Five conversion strategies for information systems.

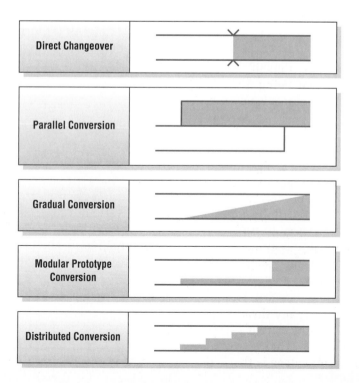

822

beforehand and it works best when some delays in processing can be tolerated. Sometimes direct changeover is done in response to a government mandate. An advantage of the direct changeover is that users have no possibility of using the old system rather than the new. Adaptation is a necessity.

Direct changeover is considered a risky approach to conversion, and its disadvantages are numerous. For instance, long delays might ensue if errors occur, since there is no alternate way to accomplish processing. Additionally, users may resent being forced into using an unfamiliar system without recourse. Finally, there is no adequate way to compare new results with old.

PARALLEL CONVERSION. This refers to running the old system and the new system at the same time, in parallel. This is the most frequently used conversion approach, but its popularity may be in decline because it works best when a computerized system replaces a manual one. Both systems are run simultaneously for a specified period of time, and the reliability of results is examined. When the same results can be gained over time, the new system is put into use, and the old one is stopped.

The advantages of running both systems in parallel include the possibility of checking new data against old data in order to catch any errors in processing in the new system. Parallel processing also offers a feeling of security to users, who are not forced to make an abrupt change to the new system.

There are many disadvantages to parallel conversion. These include the cost of running two systems at the same time and the burden on employees of virtually doubling their workload during conversion. Another disadvantage is that unless the system being replaced is a manual one, it is difficult to make comparisons between outputs of the new system and the old one. Supposedly, the new system was created to improve on the old one. Therefore, outputs from the systems should differ. Finally, it is understandable that employees who are faced with a choice between two systems will continue using the old one because of their familiarity with it.

GRADUAL CONVERSION. Gradual conversion attempts to combine the best features of the earlier two plans, without incurring all of the risks. In this plan, the volume of transactions handled by the new system is gradually increased as the system is phased in. The advantages of this approach include allowing users to get involved with the system gradually and the possibility of detecting and recovering from errors without a lot of down time. Disadvantages of gradual conversion include taking too long to get the new system in place and its inappropriateness for conversion of small, uncomplicated systems.

MODULAR PROTOTYPE CONVERSION. This approach to conversion uses the building of modular, operational prototypes (as discussed in Chapter 8) to change from old systems to new in a gradual manner. As each module is modified and accepted, it is put into use. One advantage is that each module is thoroughly tested before being used. Another advantage is that users are familiar with each module as it becomes operational.

The fact that prototyping is often not feasible automatically rules out this approach for many conversions. Another disadvantage is that special attention must be paid to interfaces so that the modules being built actually work as a system.

DISTRIBUTED CONVERSION. This refers to a situation in which many installations of the same system are contemplated, as is the case in banking or in franchises such as restaurants or clothing stores. One entire conversion is done (with any of the four approaches considered already) at one site. When that conversion is successfully completed, other conversions are done for other sites.

An advantage of distributed conversion is that problems can be detected and contained, rather than inflicted simultaneously on all sites. A disadvantage is that even when one conversion is successful, each site will have its own peculiarities to work through, and these must be handled accordingly.

A contingency approach to deciding on a conversion strategy is recommended—that is, the analyst considers many factors (including the wishes of clients) in choosing a conversion strategy. Obviously, no particular conversion approach is equally suitable for every system implementation.

Security

Security of computer facilities, stored data, and information generated is part of a successful conversion. Recognition of the necessity for security is a natural outgrowth of the belief that information is a key organizational resource, as discussed in Chapter 1.

It is useful to think of security of systems, data, and information on an imaginary continuum from totally secure to totally open. Although there is no such thing as a totally secure system, the actions analysts and users take are meant to move systems toward the secure end of the continuum by lessening the system's vulnerability. It should be noted that as more people in the organization gain greater computer power, security becomes increasingly difficult and complex. Sometimes organizations will hire a security consultant to work with the systems analyst when security is crucial to successful operations.

Security is the responsibility of all those who come in contact with the system and is only as good as the most lax behavior or policy in the organization. Security has three interrelated aspects: physical, logical, and behavioral. All three must work together if the quality of security is to remain high.

PHYSICAL SECURITY. Physical security refers to securing the computer facility, its equipment, and software through physical means. These can include controlling access to the computer room via machine-readable badges or a human sign-in/sign-out system; using closed circuit television cameras to monitor computer areas; and backing up data frequently and storing backups in a fireproof, waterproof area.

Additionally, small computer equipment should be secured so that a typical user cannot move it, and it should be guaranteed uninterrupted power. Alarms that notify appropriate people of fire, flood, or unauthorized human intrusion must be in working order at all times.

Decisions about physical security should be made when the analyst is planning for computer facilities and equipment purchase. Obviously, physical security can be much tighter if anticipated in advance of actual installation and if computer rooms are specially equipped for security when they are constructed rather than outfitted as an afterthought.

LOGICAL SECURITY. Logical security refers to logical controls within software itself. The logical controls familiar to most users are passwords or authorization codes of some sort. When used, they permit the user with the correct password to enter the system or a particular part of a database.

However, passwords are treated cavalierly in many organizations. Employees have been overheard yelling a password across crowded offices, posting passwords by taping them to their terminals, and sharing personal passwords with authorized employees who have forgotten their own.

Logical and physical controls are important but clearly not enough to provide adequate security. Behavioral changes are also necessary.

BEHAVIORAL SECURITY. The behavioral expectations of an organization are encoded in its policy manuals and even on signs posted on bulletin boards, as we saw in Chapter 4. But the behavior that organization members internalize is also critical to the success of security efforts.

Security can begin with screening employees who will eventually have access to computers, data, and information in order to ensure that their interests are consistent with the organization's interests and that they fully understand the importance of carrying through on security procedures. Policies regarding security must be written, distributed, and updated so that employees are fully aware of expectations and responsibilities. Typically, this is where the systems analyst will first have contact with the behavioral aspects of security.

Part of the behavioral facet of security is monitoring behavior at irregular intervals in order to ascertain that proper procedures are being followed and to correct any behaviors that may have eroded with time. Having the system log the number of unsuccessful sign-on attempts of users is one way of monitoring whether unauthorized users are attempting to sign on to the system. Periodic and frequent inventory of equipment and software is desirable. In addition, unusually long sessions or atypical after-hours access to the system should be examined.

Output generated by the system must be recognized for its potential to put the organization at risk in some circumstances. Controls for output include screens that can only be accessed via password; classification of information (that is, to whom it can be distributed and when); and secure storage of printed and magnetically stored documents.

In some cases, provision for shredding documents that are classified or proprietary must be made. Shredding or pulverization services can be contracted from an outside firm that, for a fee, will shred magnetic media, typewriter and printer cartridges, and paper. A large corporation may shred upwards of 76,000 pounds of output in a variety of media annually.

Other Conversion Considerations

Conversion also entails other details for the analyst, which include:

1. Ordering equipment (up to three months ahead of planned conversion).
2. Ordering any necessary materials that are externally supplied to the information system such as toner cartridges, paper, preprinted forms, and magnetic media.
3. Appointing a manager to supervise, or personally supervising the preparation of the installation site.
4. Planning, scheduling, and supervising programmers and data-entry personnel who must convert all old files and databases.

For many implementations, your chief role will be accurately estimating the time needed for each activity, appointing people to manage each subproject, and coordinating their work. For smaller projects, you will do much of the conversion work on your own. Many of the project management techniques learned in Chapter 3, such as Gantt charts, PERT, and successfully communicating with team members, are useful for planning and controlling implementation.

Organizational Metaphors and Their Relationship to Successful Systems

Be aware of organizational metaphors when you attempt to implement a system you have just developed. Our recent exploratory research has suggested that the success or failure of a system might have something to do with metaphors used by organizational members.

When people in the organization describe the company as a zoo, you can infer that the atmosphere is chaotic, while if it is described as a machine, everything is working in an orderly fashion. When the predominant metaphor is war, journey, or jungle, the environment is chaotic like the zoo. However, the war and journey are oriented toward an organization goal, while the zoo and jungle are not.

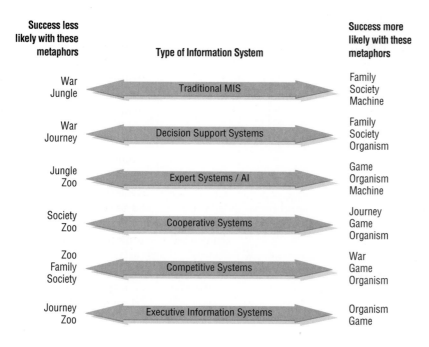

FIGURE 21.18
Organizational metaphors
may contribute to the success
or failure of an information
system.

Success less likely with these metaphors	Type of Information System	Success more likely with these metaphors
War Jungle	Traditional MIS	Family Society Machine
War Journey	Decision Support Systems	Family Society Organism
Jungle Zoo	Expert Systems / AI	Game Organism Machine
Society Zoo	Cooperative Systems	Journey Game Organism
Zoo Family Society	Competitive Systems	War Game Organism
Journey Zoo	Executive Information Systems	Organism Game

In addition to the machine, metaphors such as society, family, and the game all signify order and rules. While the machine and game are goal oriented, the society and zoo do not stress the company's goal, but instead allow the individuals in the corporation to set their own standards and rewards. Another metaphor, the organism, appears balanced between order and chaos, corporate and individual goals.

Our research suggests that the success or failure of a system may have something to do with the predominant metaphor. Figure 21.18 shows that traditional MIS will tend to succeed when the predominant metaphor is society, machine, or family, but might not succeed if the metaphor is war or jungle (two chaotic metaphors). Notice, however, that competitive systems will most likely succeed if the metaphor is war.

Positive metaphors appear to be the game, organism, and machine. Negative metaphors appear to be the jungle and the zoo. The others (journey, war, society, and family) show mixed success depending on the type of information system being developed. More research needs to be done in this area. In the mean time, the systems analyst should be aware that metaphors communicated in interviews could be meaningful and may even be a contributing factor towards the success of the information system implementation.

EVALUATION

Throughout the systems development life cycle, the analyst, management, and users have been evaluating the evolving information system (and/or information center) in order to give feedback for its eventual improvement. Evaluation is also called for following system implementation.

Evaluation Techniques

In recognition of the fact that ongoing evaluation of information systems (and information centers) is important, many evaluation techniques have been devised. These techniques include cost-benefit analysis (as discussed

Information Systems Modules	Form Utility	Time Utility	Place Utility	Possession Utility	Actualization Utility	Goal Utility
Inventory Lists	Good. Acronyms used were the same as shipping codes. As systems grew, too much information was presented; this overload called for summary information.	Good. Reports were received at least one hour before scheduled shipments on a daily basis.	Good. Inventory lists were printed at the regional blood center. Lists were delivered to hospitals with the current shipments.	Good. The same people who originally kept manual records received these reports.	Good. Implementation was easy since hospitals found the inventory lists to be extremely useful.	Good. Information about the location of particular units was made available.
Management Summary Reports	Good. Summary report was designed to exact format specifications of manual summary reports developed by the blood administrator for city hospitals.	Good. Same as listings	Good. Summary reports were printed at the center where they were needed.	Good. Blood administrators who originally kept manual reports for city hospitals received summary information.	Good. Blood administrators participated in the design of the reports.	Good. Summary reports helped reduce outdating and prevent shortages.
Short-Term Forecasting	Good. A forecast was issued for each blood type.	Good. Forecasts were updated daily.	Good. Printed at blood center.	Good. Administrators concerned with distribution and collections received the report.	Good. Output design could have been more participative.	Good. Shortages were prevented by calling in more donors.
Heuristic Allocation	Poor. The people who allocated blood mistrusted the mysterious numbers produced by the computer.	Good. Reports were provided one hour before allocation decisions were made.	Good. Printed at blood center.	Fair. Administrator responsible for daily blood allocation received the original.	Poor. Too many people were involved with the level of blood inventories to be able to participate in the design of the system. Hospitals were not prepared to participate with computer-based rationing of blood units.	Poor. Although consultants were concerned about reducing shipping costs, this was not an immediate goal of the blood region. Shipping costs were passed on to patients.
Decentralized Performance Measurement	Good. Peer review committee understood and accepted the reports.	Good. Monthly performance measures were available within one day after the month ended.	Good. Reports were mailed to the peer review committee.	Good. Performance reports were given to peer review committee and the regional blood administrator at the same time.	Fair. Trial period with peer committee was satisfactory, but the regional blood administration was unwilling to participate. Consulting team was unable to convince blood administrator that outdating should be kept low.	Good. Goals were consistent with regional objectives. The blood administrator did not consider minimizing blood outdating to be a priority goal, even though it is national blood policy.
Bloodmobile Scheduling	Good. Tabular form included sufficient detail while computer-produced graph provided summary information as well.	Good. Feedback within one day.	Good. Computer terminal was in the same building so assistant administrator could make changes himself.	Good. Assistant administrator used system for one year. When he left, improving scheduling was not considered a priority item.	Fair. Trial period was successful, but when assistant administrator left, no one else had the knowledge to run the system. Perhaps the origination was not ready for the refinement in this module.	Fair. Goals of this module were overshadowed by more immediate goals.
Policy Planning Model	Good. The form was the same as the bloodmobile scheduling output.	Good. Immediate feedback.	Not applicable.	Results were published in blood management and health care journals.	Not applicable.	Good. Goals were long range strategic planning alternatives.

FIGURE 21.19
Evaluating a blood inventory information and decision support system using the information system utility approach.

Mopping Up with the New System

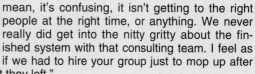

"I don't know what happened. When the new system was installed, the systems analysts made a clean get away as far as I can tell," says Marc Schnieder, waxing philosophic. Recall that he is owner of the Marc Schnieder Janitorial Supply Company. (You last met Marc in Consulting Opportunity 17.1, where you helped him with his data storage needs. In the interim, he has had a new information system installed.)

"The systems analysis team asked us some questions about how we liked the new system," Marc supplies eagerly. "We didn't really know how to tell them that the output wasn't as spotless as we'd like. I mean, it's confusing, it isn't getting to the right people at the right time, or anything. We never really did get into the nitty gritty about the finished system with that consulting team. I feel as if we had to hire your group just to mop up after what they left."

After further discussions with Stan Lessink, the company's chief programmer, you realize that the team that did the initial installation had no evaluation mechanism. Suggest a suitable framework for evaluating the kinds of concerns that Mr. Schnieder raised about the system. What are the problems that can occur when a system is not evaluated systematically?

in Chapter 13); models that attempt to estimate the value of a decision based on the effects of revised information using information theory; simulation or Bayesian statistics; user evaluations that emphasize implementation problems and user involvement; and information utility approaches that examine the properties of information.

Each type of evaluation serves a different purpose and has inherent drawbacks. Cost-benefit analysis may be difficult to apply since information systems provide information about objectives for the first time, making it impossible to compare performance before and after implementation of the system, information center, or distributed network. The revised decision evaluation approach presents difficulty since all variables involved with the design, development, and implementation of the information system cannot be calculated or quantified. The user involvement approach yields some insight for new projects by providing a checklist of potentially dysfunctional behavior by various organizational members, but it stresses implementation over other aspects of MIS design. The system utility approach to evaluation can be more comprehensive than the others if it is expanded and systematically applied.

The Information System Utility Approach

The information system utility approach for evaluating information systems can be a comprehensive and fruitful technique for measuring the success of a developed system. It also can serve as a guide in development of any future projects the analyst might undertake.

Utilities of information include possession, form, place, and time. In order to evaluate the information system comprehensively, these utilities must be expanded to include actualization utility and goal utility. Then the utilities can be seen to address adequately the questions of who (possession), what (form), where (place), when (time), how (actualization), and why (goal). An example of this information utility approach can be seen in the evaluation of a blood inventory system in Figure 21.19.

POSSESSION UTILITY. Possession utility answers the question of who should receive output—in other words, who should be responsible for making decisions. Information has no value in the hands of someone who lacks the power to make improvements in the system or someone who lacks the ability to use the information productively.

FORM UTILITY. Form utility answers the question of what kind of output is distributed to the decision maker. The documents must be useful for a particular decision maker, in terms of their format and the jargon used. Acronyms and column headings must be meaningful to the user. Furthermore, information itself must be in an appropriate form. For example, the user should not have to divide one number by another to obtain a ratio. Instead, a ratio should be calculated and prominently displayed. At the other extreme is the presentation of too much irrelevant data. Information overload certainly decreases the value of an information system.

PLACE UTILITY. Place utility answers the question of where information is distributed. Information must be delivered to the location where the decision is made. More detailed reports or previous management reports should be filed or stored to facilitate future access.

TIME UTILITY. Time utility answers the question of when information is delivered. Information must arrive before a decision is made. Late information has no utility. At the other extreme is the delivery of information too far in advance of the decision. Reports may become inaccurate or may be forgotten if delivered prematurely.

ACTUALIZATION UTILITY. Actualization utility involves how the information is introduced and used by the decision maker. First, the information system has value if it possesses the ability to be implemented. Second, actualization utility implies that an information system has value if it is maintained after its designers depart or if a one-time use of the information system obtains satisfactory and long-lasting results.

GOAL UTILITY. Goal utility answers the why of information systems by asking whether the output has value in helping the organization obtain its objectives. The goal of the information system must not only be in line with the goals of decision makers, but must also reflect their priorities.

Evaluating the System

An information system can be evaluated as successful if it possesses all six utilities. If the system module is judged as "poor" in providing one of the utilities, the entire module will be destined to failure. A partial or "fair" attainment of a utility will result in a partially successful module. If the information system module is judged as "good" in providing every utility, the module is a success.

The information system utility approach of "who, what, when, where, why, and how" used to evaluate the regional blood inventory management information system resulted in the subjective judgments concerning the utility of the information system summarized in the table. As you can see, four of the modules were rated as "good" in each category of utility, and consequently these modules were considered successful. Two were evaluated as partially successful, and one module was judged a failure after the trial period. Explanations of each judgment made for the seven modules are also provided.

The information system utility approach is a workable and straightforward framework for evaluating large-scale information systems projects and ongoing information center efforts. It also can be usefully employed as a checklist to monitor progress of systems under development. Further, evaluation following implementation allows the analyst to acquire ideas about how to proceed with future systems projects.

SUMMARY

Implementation is the process of assuring that the information system and/or information center is operational and then involving well-trained users in its operation. In large systems projects, the primary role of the analyst is overseeing implementation by correctly estimating the time needed, and then supervising the installation of equipment for traditional systems, information centers, or distributed processing, training of users, and converting files and databases to the new system.

An information center implemented within a business, as part of the larger systems department, is a way to make it easier for users to fulfill their short-term information needs. Through the information center, users learn to solve their own immediate business problems with available computer hardware and software and expert help from center specialists. Both users and information center personnel must commit to the idea that the information center is a worthwhile enterprise and be willing to play the new roles required in the center.

It is possible to begin an information center with a manager and two or three technical people (one or all of whom might be systems analysts). Employees of the center must be technically competent, but also must enjoy interacting with users in a support role. Users must accept responsibility for the resources they are using, want to learn, and be able to formulate their problems based on their own business background.

Distributed systems take advantage of telecommunications technology and database management to interconnect people manipulating some of the same data in meaningful but different ways. As hardware and software are evaluated, the systems analyst also needs to consider the costs and benefits of employing a distributed system to fulfill user requirements.

One of the most popular ways to approach distributed systems is through the use of a client/server model. Standard types of organizational networks include the local area network (LAN) and the wide area network (WAN). Using a top-down approach, analysts can use six symbols to help draw network decomposition and hub connectivity diagrams. New software, called groupware, is becoming more functional and more widespread. Its purpose is to help group members to work together via networks.

Training users and personnel to interact with the information system and/or the information center is an important part of implementation, since they must be able to run the system without the intervention of the analyst. The analyst needs to consider who needs to be trained, who will train them, objectives of training, methods of instruction to be used, sites, and materials.

Conversion is also part of the implementation process. The analyst has several strategies for changing from the old information system to the new. The five conversion strategies include direct changeover, parallel conversion, phased conversion, modular prototype conversion, and distributed conversion. Taking a contingency approach to conversion strategies can help the analyst in choosing an appropriate strategy to suit different system and organizational variables.

Recent exploratory research suggests that systems analysts can improve the chances that newly-implemented systems will be accepted if they develop systems with predominant organizational metaphors in mind. Nine main metaphors in use are: the family, society, machine, organism, journey, game, war, jungle, and zoo. For example, traditional MIS are more likely to succeed when metaphors such as the family, society, or machine are used, and less likely to succeed with organizational metaphors such as war and jungle.

After implementation, the new system or information center should be evaluated. Many different evaluation approaches are available, including cost-benefit analysis, the revised decision evaluation approach, and user involvement evaluations.

The information system utility framework is a direct way to evaluate a new system based on the six utilities of possession, form, place, time, actualization, and goal. These utilities correspond to, and answer the questions of who, what, where, when, how, and why in order to evaluate the utilities of the information system or newly created information center. Utilities can also serve as a checklist for systems under development.

KEYWORDS AND PHRASES

information center (IC)
end user
IC manager
distributed processing
hierarchical network
star network
ring network
bus configuration
client/server model
WAN
LAN
groupware
training objectives
training sites
training materials
parallel conversion
direct changeover
gradual conversion
modular prototype
distributed conversion
physical security

logical security
behavioral security
organizational metaphors
  family
  society
  machine
  organism
  journey
  game
  war
  jungle
  zoo
information system utility
approach to evaluation
  possession utility
  form utility
  place utility
  time utility
  actualization utility
  goal utility

REVIEW QUESTIONS

1. List the four approaches to implementation.
2. What is the main purpose for creating an information center?
3. What type of analysis must be completed before the decision to create an information center is made?

"As you know, Snowden is determined to implement some kind of automated tracking for the Training people. But even after having you and your team here at MRE for all of this time, it isn't clear to me how this will ever come about. You've probably noticed by now that people like Tom Ketcham are pretty set in their ways. But so is Snowden, and he definitely has the upper hand. I'm not telling you anything you don't know already, am I? I think that when Snowden comes back from Poland, you should be ready to show him how we can implement an automated tracking system for the Training group. But it really has to be acceptable to the new users. After all, they're the ones that have to live with it. I'll pencil you in for a meeting with Snowden two weeks from today."

HYPERCASE QUESTIONS

1. Develop an *implementation plan* that would be useful to the Training group in changing to an automated project tracking system. Use a paragraph to explain your approach. Be sure that what you are doing also meets Snowden's expectations.

2. In two paragraphs, discuss what *conversion* approach is appropriate to adopting a new automated project tracking system for the Training group.

3. Provide an outline of steps you would take to train the users in the Training group to use their new system. In a paragraph, discuss any obstacles you see to training the users in the Training group, and also list how you would overcome these problems.

4. What attributes are desirable in all information center personnel, as they relate to end users?

5. List the advantages of the information center for users.

6. List the advantages of the information center for the traditional systems department.

7. What are the disadvantages of establishing an information center?

8. List the staff that the ideal information center would include and give a brief job description for each position.

9. Briefly describe the kind of space and equipment necessary to set up a new information center adequately.

10. Review the critical aspects of setting up a pilot information center.

11. Describe what is meant by *distributed system*.

12. What is a hierarchical network?

13. Draw a star network and label the nodes appropriately.

14. How does a ring network differ from a star network?

15. What is a bus configuration for distributed processing?

16. What is the client/server model?

17. What is the purpose of groupware?

18. Who should be trained to use the new or modified information system?

19. List the possible sources of training for users of information systems.

20. Why is it important to have well-defined training objectives?

21. Some users learn best by seeing, others by hearing, still others by doing. Give an example of how each kind of learning can be incorporated into a training session.

22. State an advantage and a disadvantage of on-site training sessions.

23. List the attributes of well-executed training materials for users.

24. List the five conversion strategies for converting old information systems to new ones.

25. Define the terms physical, logical, and behavioral security and give an example of each that illustrates the differences among them.

26. List the nine organizational metaphors and the hypothesized success of each type of system given their presence.

27. List and describe the utilities of information systems that can be used to evaluate the information system or information center.

PROBLEMS

1. Cramtrack, the regional/commuter train system, is trying to train users of its newly installed computer system. In order for the users to get the proper training, the systems analysts involved with the project sent a memo to the heads of the four departments that include both primary and secondary users. The memo said in part, "Only people who feel as if they require training need to make reservations for off-site training; all others should learn the system as they work with it on the job." Only three of a possible forty-two users signed up. The analysts were satisfied that the memo effectively screened people who needed training from those who did not.

   a. In a paragraph, explain how the systems analysts got off the track in their approach to training.

   b. Outline the steps you would take to ensure that the right people at Cramtrack are trained.

2. A beautiful, full-color brochure arrived on Mel Cooley's desk describing DVD (Data Values Diversified) off-site training program and facilities in glowing terms, showing happy users at terminals and professional-looking trainers leaning over them with concerned looks. Mel ran excitedly into Sally's office and told her, "We've got to use these people. This place looks terrific!" Sally was not persuaded by the brochure but didn't know what to say in defense of the on-site training for users that she had already authorized.

   a. In a few sentences, help Sally argue the usefulness of on-site training with in-house trainers, versus off-site training with externally hired trainers.

   b. If Mel does decide on the DVD training, what should he do to verify that this is indeed the right place to train the company's information system users? Make a list of actions he should take.

3. "Just a little longer. I want to be sure this is working alright before I change over," says Buffy, the owner of three bathroom accessories boutiques called Tub 'n Stuff. Her accountant, who helped her set up a new accounting information system is getting desperate to persuade

Buffy to change over completely to the new system. Buffy has insisted on running the old and new systems in parallel for an entire year.

   a. Briefly describe the general problems involved in using a parallel conversion strategy for implementing a new information system.

   b. Use a paragraph to convince the owner of Tub 'n Stuff that a year of running a system in parallel is long enough. Suggest a way to end Tub 'n Stuff's dual systems that will provide enough reassurance to Buffy. (Assume that the new system is reliable.)

4. Ginny's Office Supplies Company recently had a new computerized information system installed to help its managers with inventory. In speaking with managers, you notice that they seemed disgruntled with the system output, which is a series of screens that show current inventory, customer and supplier addresses, and so on. All screens need to be accessed through several special commands and use of a secret password. The managers had several opinions about the system but had no systematic way to evaluate it.

   a. Devise a checklist or form that helps Ginny's managers evaluate the utilities of an information system.

   b. Suggest a second way to evaluate the information system. Compare it with what you did in part *a*.

GROUP PROJECT

1. With your group members, prepare for your final exam by completing the crossword puzzle in Figure 21.EX1. The clues are found in Figure 21.EX2. Notice that there are hints regarding where to learn more about the material.

SELECTED BIBLIOGRAPHY

Baskerville, R. L. "An Analytical Survey of Information Systems Security Design Methods: Implications for Information Systems Development." *Computing Surveys*, 1994.

Carlyle, R. E. "Squeezing the Middle." *Datamation*, Vol. 32, No. 10, 1986, pp. 26–28.

FitzGerald, J., and T. S. Eason. *Fundamentals of Data Communication.* New York: John Wiley & Sons, Inc., 1978.

Ginzberg, M. J. "Key Recurrent Issues in the MIS Implementation Process." *Management Information Systems Quarterly*, Vol. 5, No. 2, 1981, pp. 47–59.

Gore, M., and J. Stubbe. *Elements of Systems Analysis.* Dubuque: Wm. C. Brown Co. Publishers, 1983.

Hammond, L. W. "Management, Considerations for an Information Center." *IBM Systems Journal*, Vol. 21, No. 2, 1982, pp. 131–161.

Jessup, L. M., and J. S. Valacich. *Group Support Systems.* New York: Macmillan, 1993.

Kendall, J. E. "Using Metaphors for Knowledge Elicitation During Expert Systems Development." *Proceedings of the First International Meeting of the Decision Sciences Institute.* Brussels, June, 1991, pp. 153–155.

Kendall, J. E. "Using Metaphors to Enhance Intelligence in Information Systems: Rationale for an Alternative to Rule-Based Intelligence," *Information Processing 92, Volume III: Intelligent Systems and*

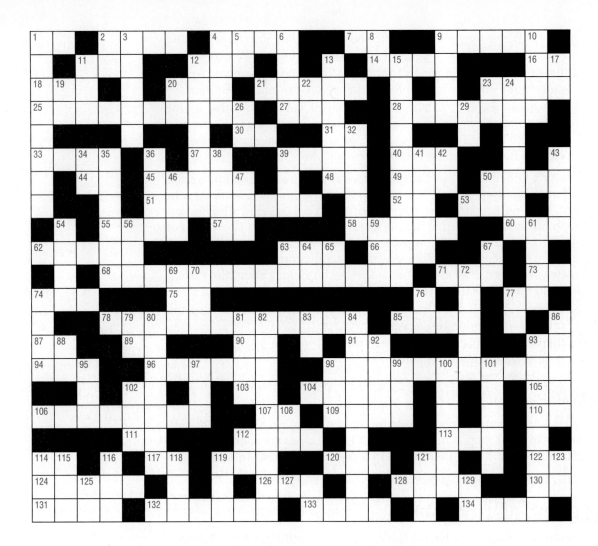

A comprehensive crossword puzzle for systems analysts.

Personal Computers, edited by F. Vogt, Amsterdam: Elsevier-North Holland, 1992, pp. 213–219.

Kendall, K. E. "Evaluation of a Regional Blood Distribution Information System." *International Journal of Physical Distribution and Materials Management*, Vol. 10, No. 7, 1980.

Kendall, J.E., and K.E. Kendall. "Metaphors and Methodologies: Living Beyond the Systems Machine." *MIS Quarterly*, Vol. 17, No. 2, June 1993, pp. 149–171.

Kendall, J. E., and K. E. Kendall. "Metaphors and their Meaning for Information Systems Development. *European Journal of Information Systems*, Vol. 3, No. 1, 1994, pp. 37–47.

Labriola, D. "Remote Possibilities." *PC Magazine*, June 14, 1994.

Shaffer, G. "Coping With Change." *PC Magazine*, June 14, 1994.

Swanson, E. B. *Information System Implementation*. Homewood, IL: Richard D. Irwin, Inc., 1988.

Zmud, R. W., and J. F. Cox. "The Implementation Process: A Change Approach." *Management Information Systems Quarterly*, Vol. 3, No. 2, 1979, pp. 35–44.

ACROSS

1 Always appears with ENDDO (Ch.11)
2 File operation (Ch. 17)
4 Type of file organization Abbr. (Ch. 17)
7 Systems Analyst: Abbr.
9 Opposite of Output (Ch. 16)
11 Important person
12 Executive Information System: Abbr. (Ch. 1)
14 Systems Development Life Cycle: Abbr. (Ch. 1)
16 Expert System (Ch. 1)
18 _____/CAM system
20 Like a beer
21 File operation (Ch. 17)
23 Opposite of East
25 Data gathering technique: Plural (Ch. 5)
27 Type of bar code (Ch. 19)
28 Overview in a DFD (Ch. 9)
30 Information Technology: Abbr.
31 Operating system: Abbr.
33 International Conference on Information Systems: Abbr.
37 Type of diagram: Abbr. (Chs. 2 and 17)
39 Project management technique (Ch. 3)
40 Big Blue
44 Foot: Abbr.
45 Not a renter (Ch. 13)
48 District Attorney: Abbr.
49 Warnier-_____ diagrams (Ch. 20)
50 _____ Utility (Ch. 21)
51 Type of diagram: 2 wds. (Ch. 9)
52 Doesn't apply: Abbr.
53 Check digit method: Abbr. (Ch. 19)
55 Follow rules
57 Research and development: Abbr.
58 Educate users (Ch. 21)
60 Shape in a bubble diagram (Ch. 17)
62 Sylvester Stallone character
63 CAD/_____ system
66 Vase
68 DFD symbol: 2 wds. (Ch. 9)
71 Quality approach: Abbr.
73 Symbol for gold in the periodic table of the elements
74 Female deer
75 Mnemonic postal code for Pennsylvania (Ch. 19)
77 Mnemonic postal code for Illinois (Ch. 19)
78 Its symbol is a diamond (Ch. 17)
85 Method for documenting structured decisions (Ch. 11)
87 Direction of a data flow (Ch. 9)
89 _____ UNTIL or _____ WHILE (Ch. 11)
90 _____ Box: Abbr.
91 Code for arsenic in the periodic table of the elements
93 Mnemonic postal code for Michigan (Ch. 19)
94 Noah's boat
96 A service on the Internet (Ch. 15)
98 Rapid development method (Ch. 8)
102 Spanish for yes
103 Mnemonic postal code for New Mexico (Ch. 19)
104 Type of scale (Ch. 6)
105 ___LSE ___F in structured English (Ch. 11)
106 Type of data flow diagram (Ch. 9)
107 Good _____ gold
109 River that flows North
110 Mnemonic postal code for Montana (Ch. 19)
111 Mnemonic postal code for Massachusetts (Ch. 19)
112 Data _____ (Ch. 9)
113 The C.P.U. case takes place in a computer _____
114 Mnemonic postal code for Washington (Ch. 19)
117 Los Angeles: Abbr.
119 Type of interface (Ch. 18)
120 Type of chart (Ch. 14)
121 To be or not to _____
122 Type of diagram: Abbr. (Ch. 20)
124 Electronic communication (Ch. 15)
126 Metaphor for a chaotic organization (Ch. 21)
128 Type of automated tool used by analysts (Ch. 1)
130 Information Center: Abbr. (Ch. 21)
131 Distortion of data (Chs. 4 and 15)
132 Part of the population (Ch. 4)
133 Type of type (Ch. 15)
134 Compact _____ (Ch. 15)

DOWN

1 _____ maker (Ch. 12)
2 Code for silicon in the periodic table of the elements
3 Puccini wrote many of these
4 User _____ of data (Ch. 17)
5 Social security: Abbr.
6 Type of interface (Ch. 18)
8 An adverb
9 Symbol used in Windows (Ch. 18)
10 Validating computer code (Ch. 19)
11 Type of display (Ch. 15)
12 Data _____, part of a data dictionary (Ch. 10)
13 Contains data (Ch. 17)
15 Data _____ (Ch. 10)
17 Street: Abbr.
19 Indefinite article
20 Artificial Intelligence: Abbr. (Ch. 1)
22 Data processing: Abbr. (Ch. 1)
23 Us
24 Describe a DFD process in greater detail (Ch. 9)
26 Code for silicon in the periodic table
29 Manufacturer of a CASE tool: Abbr. (Ch. 1)
32 Beginning
34 A word used in structured English (Ch. 11)
35 Method for structured observation (Ch. 7)
36 Cipher (Ch. 19)
38 Opposite of front
39 Delrina's WinFax _____ (Ch. 15)
41 Human computer
42 Mister: Abbr.
43 Control _____ (Ch. 20)
46 Custom or direction
47 Rural free delivery: Abbr.
50 CompuServe command
54 _____ effect (Ch. 6)
56 Type of caption (Ch. 16)
59 Groove or depression
61 _____ programming (Ch. 12)
63 Code for cerium in the periodic table of the elements
64 Systems _____alyst (Ch. 1)
65 Mnemonic postal code for Montana (Ch. 19)
67 Before noon
69 U.S. agency that protects the environment: Abbr.
70 Rodent, but not a mouse
72 Operation performed on a database (Ch. 18)
74 _____ store (Ch. 10)
76 Boolean operator (Ch. 18)
77 Information Analyst: Abbr.
79 Edward: Abbr.
80 Type of data flow diagram (Ch. 9)
81 Type of system (Ch. 2)
82 Transformation of user views and data stores (Ch. 17)
83 Laser printer manufacturer
84 To break apart data flow diagrams (Ch. 9)
86 Check _____ (Ch. 19)
88 Operations Research: Abbr.
92 Earth
93 Type of code (Ch. 19)
95 Data item used to identify a record (Ch. 17)
97 Buddy or friend
98 Skillet
99 Digit
100 Decision _____ : Plural (Ch. 11)
101 Type of question (Ch. 5)
102 Society for Information Management: Abbr.
108 _____ what!
112 Kung _____
114 Worldwide _____, electronic communication
115 _____ Pro, a word processing package
116 Type of system: Abbr. (Ch. 1)
118 Also known as: Abbr.
119 Rift
121 Type of chart (Ch. 14)
123 Mnemonic postal code for South Carolina (Ch. 19)
125 American Airlines: Abbr.
127 United States _____ America
128 Computer language
129 Edition: Abbr.

FIGURE 21.EX2
Clues for the crossword puzzle.

SEMPER REDUNDATE

 Mack Roe walks to Anna's desk where Chip is standing and says, "The last program has been tested and incorporated into the system test. The results indicate that the system is finally complete. Every program and subsystem is working as planned. The whole system checks out. Testing has been thorough and exacting, with all the problems and program bugs satisfactorily resolved. I've reviewed the deliverables, and each one has been developed into programs. I'll leave you two to install it and then celebrate."

"That's fantastic!" Anna replies as Mack leaves. "We've been anticipating this moment for a long time. We now have the task of installing the system. I've checked with Mike Crowe, and all the hardware has arrived and been installed. The microcomputers have been connected in a star configuration, and the network software has been installed. Why don't we make a list of the tasks to be completed?"

"Sure," answers Chip. "We'll need to train the users on the operation of the system. It would be good to provide some general training, followed by specific training for each user. We might want to train several people for each specific operation—the user and a backup person."

"That's all right with me," responds Anna. "But I don't think we should have a backup person for Paige Prynter. Somehow I don't feel that she would be fond of the idea."

"Speaking of backup," says Chip, "what about creating backups of master and other system files? We should design an automated procedure for creating these copies."

"Yes," replies Anna. "We also need to be concerned with system security. Who may access the data and who has clearance to update various database elements."

"I agree," remarks Chip. "Another consideration is converting the production files from the old system to the new format. We don't want to rekey all the records from the hardware and software master files."

"Why don't we have one of the programmers write a one-time program that will convert each file from the old format to the new?" suggests Anna. "The indexes could be automatically updated and additional fields initialized to spaces or zeros."

The programmers complete the file conversion programs within a short time. The new files are created and painstakingly verified for accuracy. This effort is rewarded with new master files that contain all of the necessary records loaded with correct information.

Training is scheduled to start in the Information Center. Hy Perteks is more than willing to reserve a block of time for installing the software and providing the training sessions. Chip and Anna alternated in providing instruction, each for portions of the system which they had created.

With the training sessions concluded, the last task is the conversion of the old system to the new. The phased method is selected as the best approach. First, the microcomputer hardware programs are installed. Records are updated with information for the additional elements included in the system design.

Allen Schmidt,
Julie E. Kendall, and
Kenneth E. Kendall

Next, the software update programs are installed. Again, updates to master file records are entered. When the records contain complete information, the inquiry screens are installed. Lastly, report and menu programs are added to the system.

"The installation is a great success," exults Chip. "Everything is working correctly, without a bug in the system. I guess we should knock on wood. Have you heard any comments from the users?"

"Yes," replies Anna. "They are happy and relieved to have their new system. Mike Crowe has already started to use the preventive maintenance feature and has his student help tackling one lab room at a time. Cher and Dot were running through the various screens and several times commented on how easy it is to perform tasks. I paid a visit to Paige Prynter, and she asked me what she should do with all her free time."

The analysts smile at each other. Chip says, "This has been a really great project to work on."

"It certainly has," answers Anna. "The best system we've ever created here at CPU."

"I've learned a lot about the university in my short time here, too. It's a great place to work," Chip muses.

"And as long as you remember our motto, you should do alright," Anna replies. "Semper redundate," she quotes to Chip.

"Yeah, I see it on all the letterhead. But I must admit, I never took Latin in school. What does the motto actually mean?" Chip asks.

"Always backup!" Anna says securely.

Exercises

E-1. Use a paragraph to speculate on why the star network configuration was used. Does the fact that users are in several different rooms have any consideration in the matter?

E-2. Describe procedures that should be designed to create automatic backup files. In your paragraph, be sure to consider pros and cons of these procedures.

E-3. List security measures that should be taken to prevent unauthorized persons from using the microcomputer system.

E-4. Explain in a paragraph why a phased conversion would be used to install the microcomputer system.

OBJECT-ORIENTED SYSTEMS ANALYSIS AND DESIGN

Object-oriented (O-O) concepts arise from developments in modern programming languages. These O-O languages have new structures that are felt to improve program maintenance and make large parts of programs reusable. The consequent recycling of program parts should reduce the costs of development in computer-based systems. It has already proved very effective in the development of graphical user interfaces and databases. Because O-O languages have different constructs, computer systems must be specified in such a way that the effective use of these constructs is maximized. This constraint has led to a number of new O-O systems analysis and design techniques. Given the possibility that much of the future programming workload could move to O-O programming, it is important for systems analysis and design students to become comfortable with O-O terminology and techniques.

In this chapter we consider the essential concepts of the systems analysis and design techniques that are related to object-oriented programming technology. This activity will extend the analysis and design knowledge you have already developed into simple O-O skills. For example, O-O design notation combine aspects of both entity-relationship diagrams and data flow diagrams. Furthermore, object specifications could employ flowcharts, structured English, decision tables, or any of the process specification notations that you have learned in earlier chapters as a point of departure.

Diverse approaches to O-O analysis and design have been published, perhaps best exemplified by Coad and Yourdon's "OOA-OOD" approach. We will use Coad and Yourdon's work for our consideration because it uses simple notation while retaining a very comprehensive O-O orientation, maintains a perspective on government standards, and uses the structured design presented in earlier chapters as its "point of departure."

Object-oriented techniques are believed to be better than older approaches to handling the increasing pace of change in many of today's

Richard L. Baskerville,
Julie E. Kendall, and
Kenneth E. Kendall

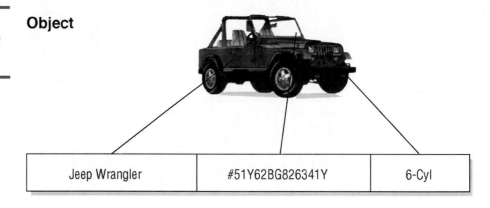

FIGURE 22.1
An example of the attributes of an object from the class "Automobile."

Object

Jeep Wrangler	#51Y62BG826341Y	6-Cyl

organizations. For example, many products are increasingly being made to order or manufactured in short-run batches as manufacturers seek greater concentration on customer satisfaction and penetration of niche markets. This trend means frequent changes to software bundled with these products. Also, many organizations are seeking to become more flexible through cross-functional teams, intercompany entrepreneurships, and virtual corporations. Constant shifting of people and responsibilities means an increasing need for rapid systems development and maintenance. O-O techniques are thought to work well in these kinds of situations where complicated information systems are undergoing continuous maintenance, adaptation, and redesign.

THE OBJECT-ORIENTED IDEA

Object-oriented analysis and design concepts were developed to support O-O programming technology. The development of this programming technology was not an instantaneous revolution, but rather the evolution of a collection of somewhat disconnected concepts that have been brought together to form a new paradigm for software engineering. For example, O-O programming draws its concept of encapsulation from the software engineering idea of data abstraction and its concept of inheritance from the database idea of generalization and specialization.

Since O-O analysis and design is strongly related to O-O programming, we should briefly explore this O-O programming context *before* proceeding to O-O analysis and design. Six basic ideas characterize O-O programming: (1) objects, (2) classes, (3) messages, (4) encapsulation, (5) inheritance, and (6) polymorphism.

Objects

An object is a computer representation of some real-world thing or event. Figure 22.1 shows how a computer might represent your car. For example, if you own a Jeep Wrangler, the computer would store the name of the model (Jeep Wrangler), the vehicle ID number (#51Y62BG826341Y), and the motor type (6-Cyl). Objects can have both attributes (such as the model, VIN, and motor type) and behaviors (such as "lights go on" and "lights go off").

Classes

A class is a category of similar objects. Objects are grouped into classes. Figure 22.2 shows how a group of objects representing automobiles might

Class

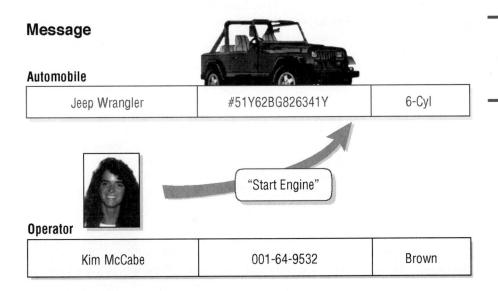

Automobile

Make/Model	VIN	Engine

FIGURE 22.2
Shared attributes of objects
grouped into the class
"Automobile."

be formed into a class called "Automobile." A class defines the set of shared attributes and behaviors found in each object in the class. For example, every automobile will have attributes for Make/Model, VIN, and Engine. The programmer must define the classes in the program. When the program runs, objects can be created from the established class. The term "instantiate" is used when an object is created from a class. For example, a program could instantiate the Jeep Wrangler as an object from the class Automobile.

Messages

Information can be sent by one object to another. In Figure 22.3, an object (Gloria) of the class "Operator" is sending a message to an object (Jeep) of the class "Automobile." The message is "Start Engine." These messages are not free-form in any sense; rather, the classes Operator and Automobile have been carefully programmed to send and receive a Start Engine message. The Operator class has been programmed to transmit a Start Engine message under certain conditions. The Automobile class has been programmed to react to a Start Engine message in some way.

Encapsulation

Typically, the information about an object is encapsulated by its behavior. This means that an object maintains data about the real-world things it

Message

Automobile

Jeep Wrangler	#51Y62BG826341Y	6-Cyl

"Start Engine"

Operator

Kim McCabe	001-64-9532	Brown

FIGURE 22.3
Example of the information
that can be sent by an object
of one class to an object of
another class.

843

FIGURE 22.4
Example illustrating how a
message from one object
causes another object from a
different class to change one
of its attributes.

Encapsulation

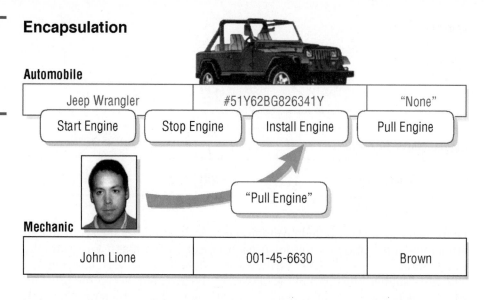

represents in a true sense. Typically an object must be "asked" or "told" to change its own data with a message, rather than waiting for such data from outside processes to change the nature of an object. In Figure 22.4, the Bruce object (class Mechanic) sends a Pull Engine message to the Jeep object (class Automobile). The Automobile class reacts to this message with a behavior (also called a "method" or "procedure") that changes the Engine attribute to None. This method is named Pull Eng. We see that the Jeep object reacts to the message by changing one of its attributes to None.

It may seem trivial whether an attribute of an object is changed by directly altering its data or by sending a message to the object to trigger internal behavior that changes that data. But this difference is an extremely important characteristic of O-O programs. Encapsulated data can be protected in such a way that only the object itself can make such changes through its own behavior. This construct makes it easier to build objects that are very reliable and consistent because they have complete control over their own attributes. It also makes program maintenance and change much easier. For example, the Mechanic class is isolated completely from the internal details of the Automobile class. The Automobile class can be totally reprogrammed without changing anything in the Mechanic class, as long as the Automobile class continues to receive a Pull Engine message properly. This isolation makes it much easier to change one part of a program without causing problems to cascade out into other parts of the program.

Inheritance

Classes can have "children"—that is, one class can be created out of another class. The original, or parent class is known as a "base class." The child class is called a "derived class." A derived class can be created in such a way that it will inherit all of the attributes and behaviors of the base class. In Figure 22.5, a derived class (Truck) is created such that it inherits all of the attributes of the base class Automobile. A derived class may have *additional* attributes and behaviors as well. For example, the class Truck not only has attributes for Make/Model, VIN, and Engine, but also has attributes for Cargo, Trailers, and Refridge. Automobile objects do not have these new attributes. Inheritance reduces programming labor by reusing

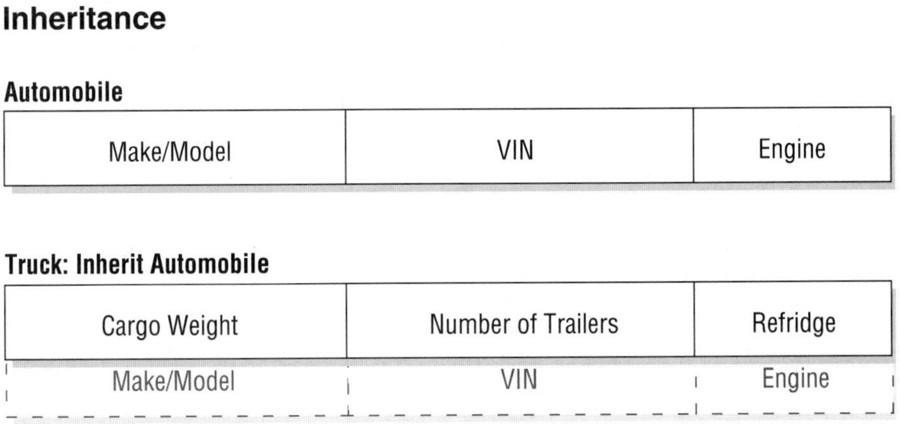

Inheritance

Automobile

Make/Model	VIN	Engine

Truck: Inherit Automobile

Cargo Weight	Number of Trailers	Refridge
Make/Model	VIN	Engine

FIGURE 22.5
Example of inheritance of
parent class attributes by a
child class.

old objects easily. The programmer only needs to declare that the Truck class inherits from the Automobile class and then provide any additional details about new attributes or behaviors (shown in the bold box in the figure). All of the old attributes and behaviors of the Automobile class are automatically and implicitly part of the Truck class (these are shown in the dashed box) and require no new programming at all.

Some O-O programming languages provide multiple inheritance. In these special cases, a derived class can be created so that it inherits all of the attributes and behaviors of more than one base class. For example, if there were both a class called Automobile and a class called Bicycle, we could create a derived class called Motorcycle that inherits all of the attributes and behaviors of Automobile *and* all of the attributes and behaviors of Bicycle.

Polymorphism

The term polymorphism regards alternative behaviors among related derived classes. When several classes inherit both attributes and behaviors, there can be cases where the behavior of a derived class might be different from that of its base class or its sibling derived classes. This means that a message may have different effects depending on exactly what class of object receives the message. In Figure 22.6 we see three classes: File, ASCII File, and Bitmap File. Both ASCII and Bitmap inherit all of the attributes of File *except* the Print behavior. A message to activate the Print behavior of an object of the generic parent File class might cause the File Size, File Type, and Date/Time attributes to be printed. The same message sent to an ASCII object might cause the text in the file to be sent to the printer. The same message sent to a Bitmap object might cause a graphic display program to execute.

OBJECT-ORIENTED ANALYSIS

The Coad and Yourdon approach to O-O analysis is based on a five-layer model. These layers consist of (1) class/object layer, (2) structure layer, (3) attribute layer, (4) service layer, and (5) subject layer. We can visualize the entire process of analysis and design as being the development and assembly of these five layers into one laminated design package. Figure 22.7 illustrates how the five layers interlock. These layers add a three-dimensional structure to the analysis and design notation that gives further power in representing the complexity in flexible systems. Each of

FIGURE 22.6
An example of polymorphism
among related classes.

Polymorphism

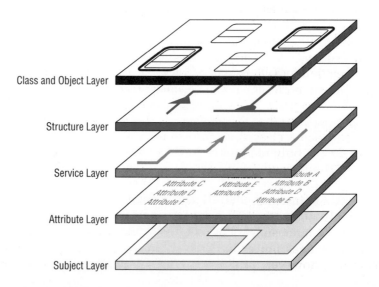

File

File Size	File Type	Date/Time	Print

Ascii File: Inherit File

Delimiter	Rec Size	Print

Bitmap File: Inherit File

Color/Mono	Resolution	Print

these layers will be discussed in more detail later in this chapter as we consider the activities of O-O analysis and design.

1. **THE CLASS/OBJECT LAYER.** This layer of the analysis and design denotes the classes and objects.
2. **THE STRUCTURE LAYER.** This layer captures various structures of classes and objects, such as one-to-many relationships and inheritance.
3. **THE SERVICE LAYER.** This layer denotes messages and object behaviors (services and methods).
4. **THE ATTRIBUTE LAYER.** This layer details the attributes of classes.
5. **THE SUBJECT LAYER.** This layer divides the design into implementation units or team assignments.

Analyzing Classes and Objects

Coad and Yourdon distinguish Class, Object, and Class-&-Object in the following ways:

Object: An abstraction of something in a problem domain, reflecting the capabilities of a system to keep information about it, interact with it, or

FIGURE 22.7
The five layers of object-
oriented analysis.

Class and Object Layer

Structure Layer

Service Layer

Attribute C   Attribute E   Attribute B
Attribute D   Attribute F   Attribute D
Attribute F   Attribute E

Attribute Layer

Subject Layer

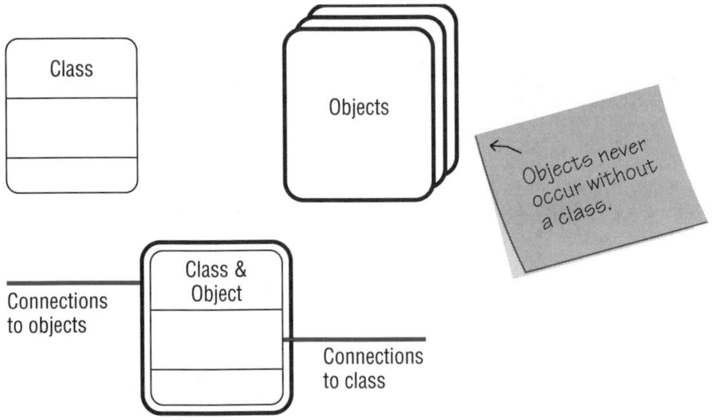

FIGURE 22.8
Notation representing the
concepts Class, Object, and
Class-&-Object.

both; an encapsulation of attribute values and their exclusive services. Synonym: an instance.

Class: A description of one or more objects with a uniform set of attributes and services, including a description of how to create new objects in the class.

Class-&-Object: A term referring to both the class and the objects that are instantiated in the class.

There are five general types of objects that can be discovered during analysis. Objects often represent *tangible things* such as vehicles, devices, and books. Sometimes objects represent *roles* enacted by persons or organizations. Roles include objects like customer, owner, or department. Objects may also be derived from *incidents* or events such as flight, accident, or meeting. Incidents typically happen at a specific time. Other objects may denote *interactions* such as a sale or a marriage. Interactions have a transaction or contract quality. Objects may also detail *specifications*. Specifications have standards or a definition quality and generally imply that other objects will represent instances of tangible things. For example, a class of object such as "insurance policy type" may have instances like "whole life," "term life," or "homeowners." Such a class of objects specifies qualities common to certain instances of another class of objects called "insurance policy."

The notation for Class, Object, and Class-&-Object is shown in Figure 22.8. Classes are represented by rounded rectangular boxes (bubtangles) divided into three parts. The name of the class is shown in the upper division of the box. The other two divisions are used for the attribute and service layers. When a class appears without Objects, it can only be a base class because the only reason for such an "objectless" class is a means of grouping attributes and services that will be inherited by several other classes.

Objects that instantiate the Class are represented by a shaded box surrounded by the class. Since Objects instantiate a Class, it is not possible for Objects to exist independently of their class. Because of this dependence, some notation does not distinguish between classes and objects. Coad and Yourdon, however, provide the Class-&-Object notation in order to graphically distinguish between structures and messages that are intended for the Class (such as a "create a new instance object" message) from structures and messages intended for the Object (such as "pull engine").

Techniques for discovering objects are basically the same as those discussed in earlier chapters for discovering processes and data entities. However, there are certain criteria that we can use to help determine whether a new class of objects is justified:

1. There is a need to remember the object. That is, the object can be described in a definite sense, and its attributes are relevant to the problem.

2. There is a need for certain behaviors of the object. That is, even though an object has no attributes, there are services that it must provide or object states that must be recalled.

3. Typically, an object will have multiple attributes. Objects that have only one or two attributes suggest over-analyzed designs.

4. Typically, a class will have more than one object instantiation unless it is a base class.

5. Typically, attributes will always have a meaningful value for each object in a class. Objects that produce a NULL value for an attribute or for which an attribute is not applicable usually imply a generalization-specialization structure (described later in this chapter).

6. Typically, services will always behave in the same way for every object in a class. Services that vary dramatically for some objects in a class or that return without action for some objects also suggest a generalization-specification structure.

7. Objects should implement requirements that are derived from the problem setting, not the solution technology. The analysis portion of the O-O project should not become dependent on a particular implementation technology such as a specific computer system or a specific programming language. Objects that address such technical details should not appear until very late in the design stage. Technology-dependent objects suggest that the analysis process is faulty.

8. Objects should not duplicate attributes and services that could be derived from other objects in the system. For example, an object that stores the age of an employee is superfluous when a separate employee object exists that maintains a date-of-birth attribute. The age object can be eliminated by an age service that is a component of the employee object.

Kayjay World Example 1

Kayjay World is a small vacation theme park that operates a circular, six-train monorail system connecting a parking lot, a theme park, a hotel, and a concert hall/restaurant complex. There are four stations, each with a ticket booth and a boarding queue. Passengers obtain a ticket for one of the three possible destination stations and enter the boarding queue. The boarding queue is arranged in such a way that every seat on a train will be filled before any passenger can be left at a station. Trains consist of an engine and one to six passenger cars, each car carrying 50 passengers.

As shown in Figure 22.9, the rail system consists of fifteen safety segments of track, and each train in service occupies one of these segments. A

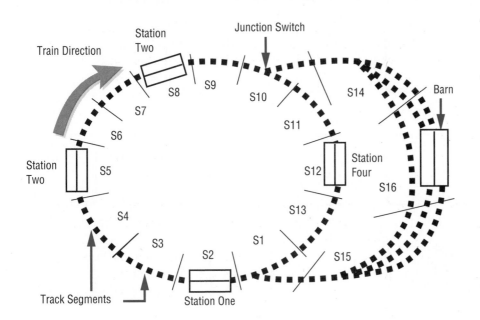

FIGURE 22.9
Diagram of the Kayjay World
monorail system.

Train Direction

Station Two

Junction Switch

S8 · S9 · S10 · S11 · S14 · Barn

S7

S6

Station Two · S5

S4 · S3 · S2 · S1

S12 · Station Four

S13 · S16 · S15

Track Segments · Station One

train may not enter a segment that is occupied by another train. Each station counts as one segment, and each link between stations is divided into two or three segments. There is a barn capable of storing all six trains with two access segments: one exit segment (S14) leading to the barn and yard, and one entrance segment (S15) departing from the barn and yard. There is only one junction switch, joining segment S10 to either segment S11 or S14. Segment S14 leads to the barn and thus is joined to the main circuit with the only system junction switch. The segment from the barn (S15) merges with the main track in a fixed junction and does not require a switch. When a train is on S13 and another is on S15, and both are thus competing for segment S1, the train on S15 is given priority.

The capacity manager initializes the system by ordering one train to leave the barn and thus be placed in service. At least one train remains in service until the capacity manager shuts down the system, ordering the last train out of service. However, when the excess capacity of every train in service falls below 50% and at least one train falls below 25%, another train leaves the barn and is placed in service. If the excess capacity of every train exceeds 50%, then one train is removed from service and sent to the barn. (This train accepts no new passengers beginning with station one and thus the remaining passengers alight at station three.) A yard manager declares out-of-service trains in the barn and yard either "operable" or "inoperable." Operable trains are rotated back into service on a first-in, first-out basis. The yard manager switches inoperable trains out of the automatic system by removing them from the service queue. The inoperable trains then enter a manually switched maintenance yard. Though each train usually has four cars, if an engine fails during high season the yard master may detach one or more of the inoperable train's cars, take an operable train into the service yard, and add one or more of the orphaned passenger cars to the operable train. An engine can pull six full cars, so the monorail can lose two engines and still operate at full capacity (1200 passengers). However, this event raises the minimum capacity of the system from 200 to 300 passengers.

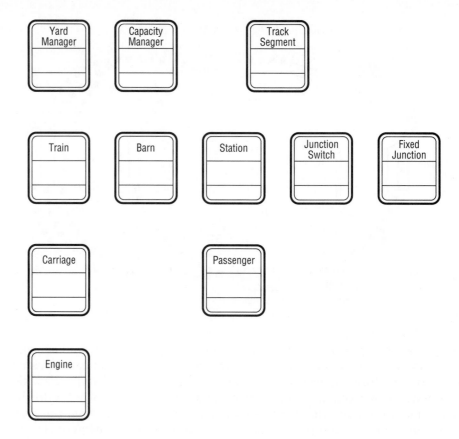

FIGURE 22.10
Initial outline of the Class-&-
Object layer of Kayjay
World's monorail system.

Based on the preceding problem description, we can sketch out a preliminary class and object analysis. At this early stage in this analysis, all of the objects are Class-&-Objects. As is typical of an early analysis, base classes will soon emerge from further analysis to come. Figure 22.10 is the initial outline of the Class-&-Object layer of the O-O design package.

Analyzing Structures

There are two basic types of structures that might be imposed on classes and objects. These are the Generalization-Specialization structure (known as "Gen-Spec") and the Whole-Part structure.

1. GEN-SPEC STRUCTURES. Inheritance is created with Gen-Spec structures. These relationships between classes are sometimes called classification, subtype, or ISA (pronounced " is-uh") relationships. Gen-Spec structures are denoted by a semicircle with its rounded edge toward the generalized class. These structures always connect class-to-class. They are typically of a hierarchical form. Figure 22.11 shows a Gen-Spec structure between Class-&-Objects in which the classes Bus and Motorcycle inherit all of the properties of the class Automobile.

2. WHOLE-PART STRUCTURES. These structures denote collections of different objects that compose another whole object. Such relationships between objects are sometimes called assemblies, aggregations, or HASA (pronounced "hǎs-uh") relationships. Whole-Part structures are noted by a triangle pointing toward the "whole" object. These

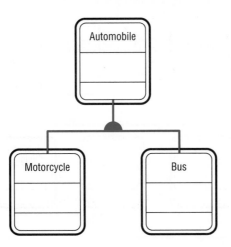

FIGURE 22.11
A Gen-Spec structure involving the relationship of the classes Motorcycle and Bus to the class Automobile.

structures always connect object-to-object. Figure 22.12 shows a Whole-Part structure in which vehicle objects are shown to be composed of two other objects: Motor and Chassis.

Whole-Part structures also have cardinality, as represented by one-to-many or many-to-many. This concept was discussed in the section on entity relationship models in Chapter 17. The notation "0,m" specifies that a Vehicle can have no motor (0), or one or more motors (m). The notation "0,1" specifies that a Motor can be part of no vehicle (0) or one vehicle (1), but never more than one. The "1,m" specifies that a Vehicle can have one or more Chassis, but never fewer than one. The "1" specifies that a Chassis is always related to one and only one Vehicle.

Kayjay World Example 2

We continue our work based on the problem description for Kayjay World given earlier by imposing a preliminary structure analysis, or structure layer, onto the Class-&-Object diagram. This structure analysis is shown in Figure 22.13. Note that the Barn, Station, Junction Switch, and Fixed Junction classes share similar functions with Track Segments. We can thus design a Gen-Spec structure between Track Segment and these other classes. This way, Station, and the other classes inherit all of the attributes and services of a Track Segment.

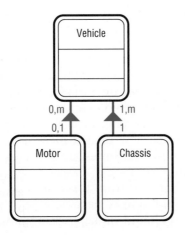

FIGURE 22.12
A Whole-Part structure illustrating the relationships of the objects Motor and Chassis to the object Vehicle.

FIGURE 22.13
Preliminary structure analysis
of Kayjay World's monorail
system.

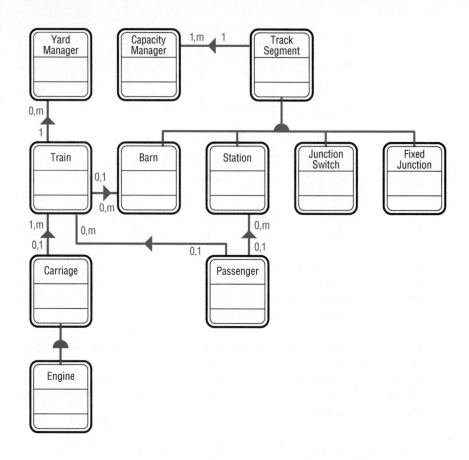

We can also design several Whole-Part structures. For instance, a Station object may have Passenger objects. Similarly, a Train object may have Carriage objects and Passenger objects. We can also decide that the Yard Manager will have all of the Train assemblies and the Capacity Manager will have all of the Track objects.

The relationship between Carriage and Engine is a tricky one. A train engine is just a special kind of train carriage—a kind of carriage that has a motor and very few seats. Also, it seems that the Barn object can have Train objects as part of it. This may create problems at implementation time because Train objects can then be part of both the Yard Manager and the Barn. But we will see how this seeming conflict can be sorted out during the design stage of the project.

Analyzing Attributes

The names of the attributes of a class are written in the center section of the class box in the design package. In Figure 22.14, the attributes Oname and Oaddress have been layered over the Owner object, and the attributes Model and Color have been layered over the Vehicle object. The basic idea of an attribute is unchanged from our earlier discussion of this topic in Chapter 17. However, three new related ideas are germane to our object-oriented perspective. First, attributes are always more prone to change than classes. If a structure or a set of classes seems to be getting cluttered because an object is changing from class to class, perhaps the Class-&-Object in question should simply become a set of attributes in another class. Second, attributes should be kept as high as possible in Gen-Spec

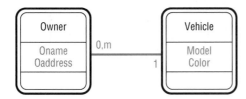

FIGURE 22.14
Depiction of two classes and
their respective attributes.

structures. This constraint reduces programming and maintenance because a change made in one Gen object will be automatically inherited by all of the Spec objects. Third, associations or relationships between objects (other than structures) should be detailed as instance connections rather than as foreign keys.

INSTANCE CONNECTIONS. The concept of primary and foreign keys was discussed earlier in Chapter 17. Rather than clutter up the design package with such implementation details, primary key attributes are not specified. Consequently, references between objects such as associations or relationships are denoted by a single line between objects with the same cardinality notation used in Whole-Part structures. Notice that instance connections always occur between objects, not classes. For example, an instance connection exists between owner and vehicle objects. The cardinality notes tell us that an owner may be related to zero, one, or more vehicles, but a vehicle must always be related to only one owner.

PRELIMINARY SPECIFICATION TEMPLATE. With the introduction of attributes, we need additional analysis details to support the layered diagram package. At this stage of the analysis, these details only regard descriptions of the attributes and constraints on their values. Coad and Yourdon recommend a specification template that provides an outline similar to a data dictionary. This template can then be expanded and modified as the analysis continues.

Kayjay World Example 3

The analysts for the Kayjay World project would next have to spend some time collecting information about the attributes of the monorail system's objects and the relationships between those objects, adding the attribute details and instance connections to the preliminary analysis. The attribute names and instance connections form the preliminary attribute layer of the O-O design package, as shown in Figure 22.15. We first spot the relationship between a Train and the Track Segment that it occupies. Also, carriages may be linked to other carriages when they form a train in a relationship called a self-association, represented with a line looping back to the same object. We continue by analyzing how passengers queue to buy tickets and board trains, so that each passenger is related to the preceding and the following passengers in the queue. We also note that Track Segments are related to other Track Segments in that one segment follows a preceding segment and precedes a following segment. Fixed Junctions are branch segments related to a Track Segment joining the main line. There are many alternative ways to design branch track lines like the line going to the yard and the barn. One good way is to ensure that a Junction Switch has a

FIGURE 22.15
Preliminary attribute layer of
the O-O design for Kayjay
World.

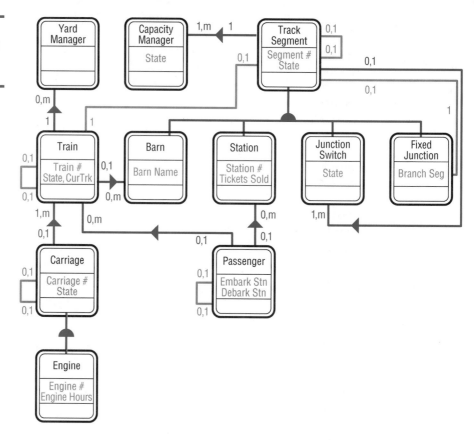

branch line, and that the line to the yard and barn belongs to the Junction Switch in a Whole-Part structure.

Now we can expand on the diagram of the attribute layer by creating a corresponding textual specification, as shown in Figure 22.16. This preliminary specification template contains more details about the attributes of the objects. It is called a template because it becomes the basic outline for the full specification that will be developed as the project continues.

Analyzing Services

Services—also called methods or procedures—become part of objects in much the same way as attributes. Because services frequently involve changes in the state of an object they are most commonly analyzed and designed using state diagrams. Consequently service analysis consists of three activities: object state analysis, service specification, and message specification.

OBJECT STATE ANALYSIS. We can discover state changes most easily by finding the attributes in each object which affect the object's behavior. As we examine each attribute, we ask, "Will the object behavior change when this attribute's value is changed?" Where no attributes change the object behavior, yet we know the object will behave differently under certain conditions, we should probably add a "state" attribute. For example, if we are analyzing a train carriage that will pick up and drop off passengers, we know that the train should behave differently in reaction to a "discharge passengers" message depending on whether the train is stopped at a station platform or careening down a straightaway track at ninety miles per hour.

Specification: Track Segment
    Attribute: Segment Number
    Attribute: State (Occupied/Free)
    Attribute: Next Segment
    Attribute: Previous Segment

Specification: Station
    Attribute: Station Number
    Attribute: Tickets Sold

Specification: Junction Switch
    Attribute: State (Normal/Branch); Normal means a connection to the Next Segment,
        Branch means a connection to Branch Segment

Specification: Fixed Junction
    Attribute: Branch Segment; The merging segment number

Specification: Barn
    Attribute: Barn Name

Specification: Train
    Attribute: Train Number
    Attribute: Service State (In/Out/Inop)

Specification: Carriage
    Attribute: Carriage Number
    Attribute: State (Operable/Inoperable)

Specification: Engine
    Attribute: Engine Number
    Attribute: Engine Hours

Specification: Passenger
    Attribute: Embarking Station
    Attribute: Destination Station

Specification: Capacity Manager
    Attribute: State (Operating/Closed)

Figure 22.17 illustrates a state diagram for a state variable for such a train carriage. The arrow at the top of the State = Stopped box shows that the initial state when the object is created is always Stopped. The other arrows show possible state changes, for example, from Stopped to Running or Stopped to Unloading. Notice that there is no way to change states from Running to Unloading. This logically prevents the object from discharging passengers while in motion. State diagrams are added as needed to the specification templates to document such state attributes.

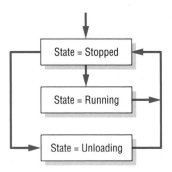

SERVICE SPECIFICATION. Services are categorized as either simple or complex. Simple services involve very few conditions or operations and often apply to every Class-&-Object in the system. These include such services as create-object, store-object, retrieve-object, connect-object (make an instance connection), access-object (get or set values for attributes), and delete-object. Simple services are implicit, sometimes specified once in the design and never mentioned again. Occasionally, very obvious simple services are not mentioned in the design at all, but are instead left for the programmers to build as needed during implementation. Simple services may appear in the specification templates but are not mentioned in the layered diagram package.

Complex services involve loops, many operations, or compound conditions. These services typically apply to only one Class-&-Object. Complex services frequently entail "companion" or "private" services that are similar to subroutine modules. Private services are internal subroutines that only the object itself knows about and can trigger. Companion services are subroutines used by complex services that can also be triggered as distinct services by messages from other objects in the system. Complex services are always depicted in the service layer of the layered diagram package. The names of such services appear in the lower section of class boxes. Figure 22.18 shows three complex services: Move in the Vehicle object, Emer.Stop in the Operating Sys object, and Emer.Stop in the Database object.

We specify complex services more completely in the specification template. Almost any of the procedural specification tools discussed earlier in the chapters on Software Engineering (Chapter 20) and Structured Decision Systems (Chapter 11) can be used, such as program flowcharts, Warnier-Orr diagrams, decision tables, or structured English.

MESSAGE SPECIFICATION. Messages detail how one object's behavior can trigger behavior in another object. That is, messages are generated by one object with the intention of triggering a service in another object. Essentially, messages document the dependence of one process on another process in a different object. Messages exist solely to communicate between services and entail both control flow and data flow.

Messages regarding simple services are not documented in the layered diagram package because they are typically implicit in the simple services. Messages directed to classes, such as create-object or delete-object, are typically not diagrammed either. Consequently, most diagrammed messages end up being from object to object rather than class to class or object to class.

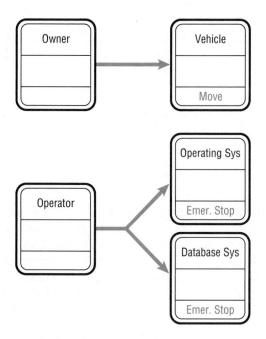

FIGURE 22.18
Examples of complex services
depicted in the service layer
of the layered diagram.

Messages are shown as broad arrows in the service layer of the layered diagram package. In the lower portion of the figure, a single message is being sent from one object to two objects. Conversely, the case may be that two services are needed independently by a single object. In this example, however, the Operator object generates a single message that triggers emergency shutdown behavior in both the Database and Operating Sys objects simultaneously.

Because messages detail complex services, they typically align with the sending service and the receiving service. However, even in moderately complex systems there will be very few complex services and consequently very few messages in the diagram. This fact naturally tends to highlight the really important functions of the system.

Complex services that are not triggered by messages tend to be triggered by timed events or human interaction. A class without an incoming message but with a complex service will typically need some sort of human interface.

Assembling the Specification Template

When we add service details to our O-O specification template, this portion of the analysis swells with detail. State diagrams, structured English, and flowcharts can be lengthy. The exact format of the specification can vary considerably from analysis to analysis. Figure 22.19 shows a basic specification template outline. We can add any important object details that need to be explicitly stated for the designers and programmers.

Kayjay World Example 4

Figure 22.20 shows the analysis of the Kayjay example with the Services layer added. There are three complex services among the objects: the Yard Manager's Assemble train/Disassemble train service, the Capacity Manager's Check service (Check determines whether to add or remove trains in the system), and the Move service in the Train object. Almost everything that happens in the system

FIGURE 22.19
The basic outline for a specification template.

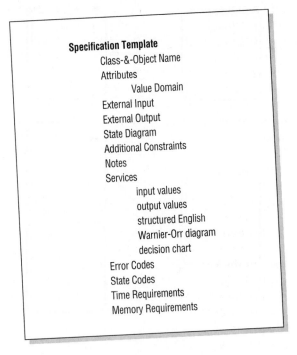

FIGURE 22.20
Layered diagram showing the
service layer of the Kayjay
World monorail system.

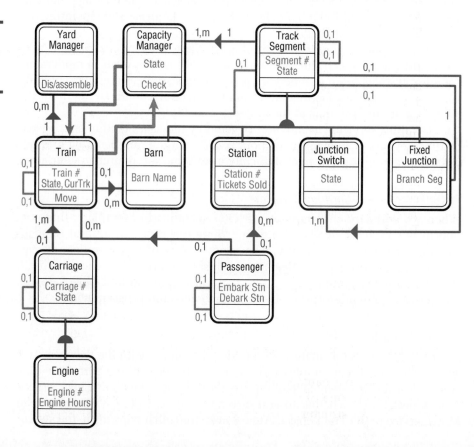

results from a train moving. Passengers might debark because a train moves into a station. A junction switch may change states because a train moves out of service. It seems odd that in a traditional design we might have assumed that the Yard Manager or Capacity Manager was central to the design. But in this O-O approach, the Train is the center of the universe.

The Move service is triggered by the Capacity Manager when the train is moved into service. After that the train Move service takes over. Each time a train moves, the Move service uses the opportunity to check the need to add or remove trains. Thus the Move Service triggers the Capacity Manager's Capacity Check service. Notice that there is no message in the diagram that triggers the Yard Manager's Dis/assemble service. During the O-O design activities later in this chapter, we will learn that this "missing" trigger message implies that the Yard Manager class includes a human interface. This human interface allows an operator to manually trigger this service.

Figures 22.21*A* and 22.21*B* show the partial specification for the Train Class services. The Move service also triggers four private complex services that do not appear in the layered diagram: One figures out where the train is, one handles setting the junction switch, one processes the train into the barn, and one handles the case of entering a fixed junction. In our example, we document two of these services using pseudocode. This partial specification also depicts the multiple inheritance from the List and Cell objects that arises in the first stages of O-O design activities. This is shown here because early prototyping of important objects and services during analysis is frequently useful to establish feasibility and proof of concept. This early prototyping required the reuse of library classes to handle list and data structures. The List and Cell classes are discussed further in the Kayjay World example of problem domain component design. It is not unusual in O-O projects for analysis and design activities to merge temporarily under opportunistic circumstances such as prototyping of our Train Move service.

Analyzing Subjects

In the case of very large systems, we can use an additional layer in the O-O layered diagram package to organize the work of analysis, design, and implementation. This layer provides a means of dividing a complex specification into logical work units. A subject layer is only necessary in large projects involving many classes. The subjects are noted by layering a broad shaded line that denotes the boundaries of a particular subject onto the O-O diagram. The name of the subject is noted in one corner of the subject box.

Usually, a subject will have an apparent "owner" class. This is a class that is centrally connected to all of the classes and objects in the subject space. Typically the subject is named after this class.

Kayjay World Example 5

Because of the amount of work involved in designing the Train, perhaps we should decide to divide the project into two subjects: (1) the Train Subject, including the Yard Manager, Passengers, Trains, and their components; and (2) the Railroad Subject, including the Capacity Manager and all forms of Tracks. Figure 22.22 shows the analysis of Kayjay World with the subject layer added.

We could have named the subjects "Yard Manager" and "Capacity Manager" because one of these classes was at the top of each of the two respective subject structures. However, these names don't match the way

FIGURE 22.21
A. Partial specification for the
Train class in the Kayjay
World system.

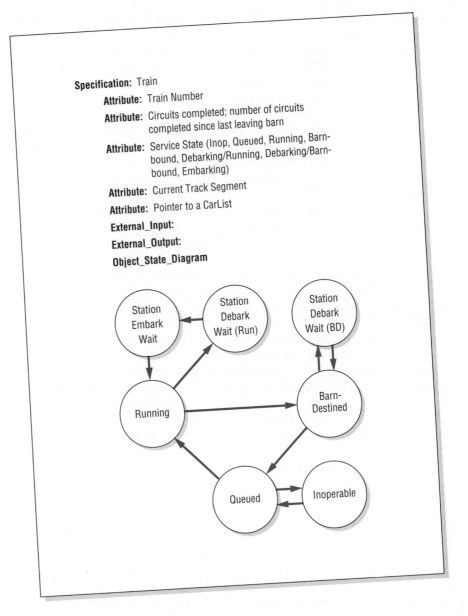

Specification: Train

    Attribute: Train Number

    Attribute: Circuits completed; number of circuits
              completed since last leaving barn

    Attribute: Service State (Inop, Queued, Running, Barn-
              bound, Debarking/Running, Debarking/Barn-
              bound, Embarking)

    Attribute: Current Track Segment

    Attribute: Pointer to a CarList

External_Input:

External_Output:

Object_State_Diagram

the users described the two general subjects. We choose to be more consistent with the users' language and name the Subjects "Railroad" and "Train." We could then divide our analysis and design project (and perhaps later, implementation) between two teams: the Railroad Subject team and the Train Subject team.

OBJECT-ORIENTED DESIGN

Design activities in the Coad and Yourdon approach carry the analysis tools forward into the complete set of specifications for implementation. Where the analysis is reasonably technology-independent, the design activities become increasingly oriented toward a particular O-O language and development environment.

O-O design activities are grouped into the four major components of the final system: the problem component, the human interface component, the data management component, and the task management component.

Additional_Constraints:

Notes: A train is a list of passengers. It is also related to the CARLIST object, which is a list of carriages.

Service: Create me
Service: Destroy me
Service: Access Train Number (read)
Service: Access Circuits completed (read, incr, zero)
Service: Access Service State (read, set states)
State Codes: Inoperable=0, Queued =1, Running=2, Barn-Destined=3,Station Debarking & Barn-Destined=4, Station Debarking & Running=5, Station Embarking=6
Return Codes: True=1, False=0
Error Codes: Success=0, Failure=-1
Train Service: enter station, debark & embark passengers
    enterStation (Station *) Service chart pseudocode
        Trigger "debark passengers" service
        IF train is "barnbound"
            THEN enterStation service is complete
        ELSE
            trigger "embark passengers" service
            enterStation service is complete
Train Service: enter barn, join queue of ready trains (Service chart pseudocode not shown).
Train Service: set switch, check if train is occupying a switch–set proper track branch for next move opportunity (Service chart pseudocode not shown)
Train Service: get track, determine which track segment is under train (Service chart pseudocode not shown)
Train Service: find fixed junction, finds track segment that is next for a train entering a fixed junction (Service chart pseudocode not shown)
Train Service: move train, moves train to next segment when possible
    moveTrain ( ) Service chart pseudocode
        IF states are not ok
            THEN return "fails" message
    trigger get track service
    IF get track fails
        THEN return "fails" message
    trigger getNext (in list base class) service
    IF getNext is "none"
        THEN trigger find fixed junction service
            IF find junction fails
            THEN setup next track with getHead (in list base class) service
        IF next track segment is not free
            THEN return "error"message
        IF next track is a barn
            THEN trigger enter barn service
            AND return "ok" message
    occupy next track
    set current track value
    free previous track
    IF next track is a station
        THEN trigger enter station service
    prepare for next move by doing
        trigger setSwitch service
        trigger check system capacity service
    return "ok"

FIGURE 22.21(*continued*)
B. Partial specification for the Train class in the Kayjay World system.

Market Changes

"They want the core of the customer service representative's user interface radically reprogrammed again!" fumes Alberto Santos, the Information Systems Development Director at Mandelbrot Mutual Funds. "Only eight months ago we completed a two-year development project of the CSR System—the Customer Service Representative System. During that entire project, we endured a nightmare of moving requirements. Every month, those guys in the Marketing Department would invent some competitive new customer service feature, and within a week, the CSR group would be down here with vast changes to the CSR System specification. I thought we'd never finish that project! Now it looks like we will have to start a new reprogramming project on a system less than a year old. We had forecast this system for a seven-year lifespan! Now I think it may be going into eternal reconstruction."

Alberto is downloading on Jessica Coates, the senior application systems analyst responsible for the CSR system, and Fletcher Henderson, the programmer who wrote most of the user interface. "Calm down Al," flushes Jessica. "This is not the fault of the kids in Marketing or CSR. The nature of our business has been affected by fast-paced competition. Marketing doesn't invent these changes out of boredom. They are often responding to new, computer-based customer services offered by our competition. We have to stay ahead, or at least keep up, or we'll all be looking for a new job!"

"Al, Jessie, I think you better know that the situation may be worse than you think," Fletcher chips in.

"The programmers have actually been making small changes in the CSR user interface for the past eight months anyway. The CSR users have been calling us directly and begging for help. They typically want just a small change to one isolated part of the system. However, this has created a high labor drain because we have to recertify the entire system. You know how the effects of a small change can ripple throughout a large program. We've billed the time to program maintenance on the grounds that we thought we were just fine-tuning the completed system. Although the changes have been gradual, in eight months we've pretty much rewritten about a quarter of the CSR user interface code already. The work has not been falling off. It's still pretty steady."

"So what you're telling me," says Alberto, nearly flaming, "is that we have system needs in this area that have been changing constantly while we tried to write specifications, tried to write program code, and tried to make a fixed solution work against a fluid problem. How can we afford to write programs if they will only last a few months without needing expensive maintenance?"

How can Alberto manage a systems development process that no longer has fixed or constant business processes as part of its goal set? Is there a way for Jessica to manage a specification and control maintenance costs when programmers are constantly asked to tinker with isolated parts of a large program? Keep in mind that an important goal is to provide good support for the users' needs and the organization's business strategies.

Each of the five layers of the O-O design is expanded as needed across the four implementation components. Figure 22.23 shows how these elements interact to complete the system design.

All of the analysis documentation should carry directly into the design stage. Few new tools are needed at this point. The layered diagram package and the specification template remain the major components of the design. These documents are not supplemented or replaced, but instead are expanded to include the remaining implementation details during the design phase.

We frequently use prototypes (as discussed earlier in Chapter 8) during the design phase. Rough versions of the objects are created and tested in their roles within the four components. This means that frequently the design package is sent forward to the programmers with portions of the program code already written. Designers will often use the expected implementation language (such as C++ or SmallTalk) as the mechanism to write complete specifications for the classes. For example, the designer may find it easy to copy the C++ class definition from an operational prototype into the specification. This may prove to mean less work for the designer and eliminates duplicate efforts on the part of designers and implementation programmers.

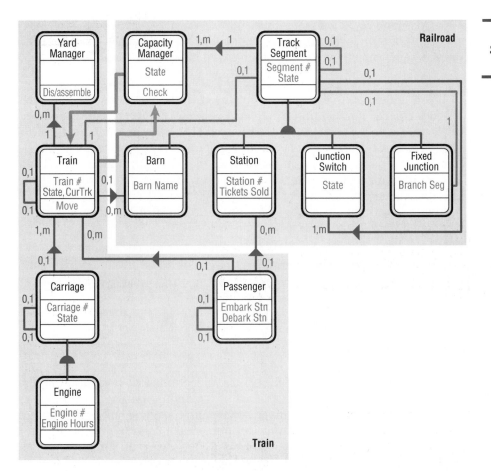

FIGURE 22.22
Subject layer for the analysis
of the Kayjay World system.

Designing the Problem Domain Component

The problem domain component (PDC) is the basic set of functional
objects that arrive from the analysis stage. These objects directly solve the
problems intended to be solved by the system we are building. The other
components, such as human interface and data management, are incidental
functions that must be added to the PDC in order to "get it working."

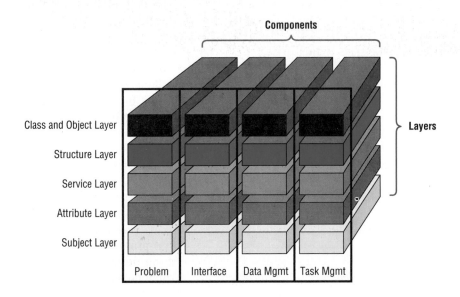

FIGURE 22.23
O-O design elements grouped
into components and layers.

Consequently, the design for the PDC is mostly completed in the analysis stage. Only three activities are needed to complete the design of the PDC: reuse design, implementation structures, and language accommodation.

REUSE DESIGN. We may want to add new classes to the PDC in order to reuse objects. For example, there are commercial packages of highly generalized classes for objects. An experienced O-O programming organization usually owns a library of classes developed in-house for objects. These libraries and packages may contain classes that have attributes and services to objects similar to those required in our design. We can add these reusable classes to our design as base classes in a Gen-Spec structure. The derived classes in these Gen-Spec structures are the classes originally developed in the analysis stage.

IMPLEMENTATION STRUCTURES. We may want to add other structures to our design purely for implementation reasons. Also, we may want to use aggregation structures to create natural entry points for lists or queues, or a Gen-Spec structure to permit several classes of objects to share a protocol or data structure. These structures use the inheritance concept to make the programming task much easier.

LANGUAGE ACCOMMODATION. We may need to fix the design so that the structures can be built in the chosen programming language, since these languages may have different inheritance patterns. Some languages support multiple inheritance; others only support single inheritance; still others support *no* inheritance. In the more restrictive cases, the inheritance patterns in the design must be modified to allow for the capabilities of the implementation language.

Kayjay World Example 6

About this time in the project, we would probably begin to prototype the PDC using the planned program implementation language. For purposes of this example, we choose C++. We could use some of the C++ library classes for lists and queues as base classes for structures that connected tracks, connected passengers, and connected carriages. After some experimentation, we could settle on two base classes from a typical in-house library: List and Cell. The Cell class typically has all of the attributes and services needed for a doubly linked list data structure. The List class typically provides an "anchor" entry point for Cell-based lists and provides services such that the list could also be manipulated as a queue data structure.

Figure 22.24 illustrates a design for the List and Cell Gen-Spec structures. Every object that heads a list inherits the services and attributes of the List class from the library. Every object that is a member of a list inherits the services and attributes of the Cell class from the library. Notice that the List and Cell classes are never instantiated with objects of their own. They use Class symbols in the diagram rather than the Class-&-Object symbols used by all of the other classes. Track Segment is a specialization of Cell, because it belongs to a list of track segments, and Passenger, which will belong to a list or queue of passengers. Likewise, Carriage belongs to a list of carriages in a train. Similarly, Station and Train are specializations of list because each may have a list of passengers. The Capacity Manager

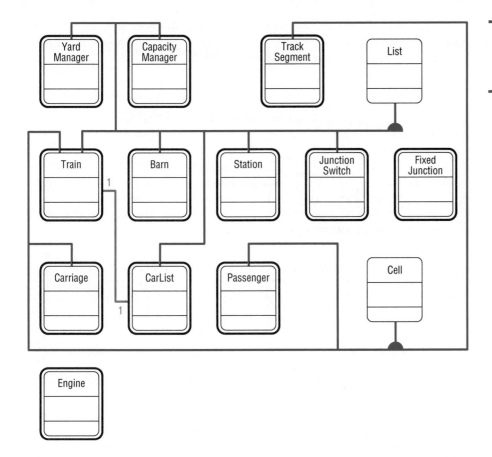

FIGURE 22.24
Design for the List and Cell
Gen-Spec structures for the
Kayjay World system.

and Junction Switch have lists of tracks. The Yard Manager and Barn have lists of trains.

Train has multiple inheritance from both Cell and List. (This was also noted on the partial specification shown earlier.) It may be a member of a list or the head of a list. That is, it may be a member of a list of trains in the barn, for instance, and at the same time, the head of a list of on-board passengers. But there is a new Class-&-Object here as well: CarList. CarList is the head of a list and has an instance connection with Train: a one-to-one relationship. CarList is necessary because the Train object is actually the head of two lists: a list of passengers and a list of carriages. There is no easy way in C++ for Train to participate in two Gen-Spec structures with List. The only way to get a second Gen-Spec structure was to create the new Class-&-Object, CarList, and connect it one-to-one with Train. Train is the head of a list of passengers and is directly related to one CarList, which is the head of a list of carriages.

Designing the Human Interface Component

In this activity we create the menus, reports, and interactive screens that people will use to work with the system. The activities are basically the same as those we discussed earlier in Chapter 18 on Designing the User Interface. However, in the O-O design context, this phase culminates in a specification for new Human Interface Component (HIC) classes that must be added to the design.

Typically, we can lean heavily on library classes in the design of the HIC classes. This is one area where the reusability of O-O classes has proven

FIGURE 22.25
Profiles of two users of the
Kayjay World monorail
system.

Kayjay World Monorail Control System User and Task Descriptions

1   I'm a Train Driver
   1.1   Purpose: I control the deadman switch and emergency door and brake controls.
           I also operate the radio and make announcements on the train's public address
             system.
   1.2   Characteristics
           Age: I'm 20 years old.
           Level Or education: I'm a high school grad with 2 years of college.
           Limitations: I don't have broad experience.
   1.3   Critical Success Factors
       I need to feel I am contributing.
       I like to interact with people.
   1.4   Skill level: Novice
   1.5   Task scenario
           Ride in front of train.
           Monitor status indicators.
           Operate deadman switch.
           Make scripted announcements.
           Follow emergency procedures.

2   I'm a Ticket Seller
   2.1   Purpose: I explain the destinations to customers, collect cash or vouchers, and
           issue tickets according to customers' requests
   2.2   Characteristics
           Age: I'm 17 years old.
           Level of education: I'm a high school student.
           Limitations: I don't have broad experience.
   2.3   Critical Success Factors
       I need to feel I am contributing.
       I like to interact with people.
   2.4   Skill level: Novice
   2.5   Task scenario
           Customer arrives at window from queue, and I explain the three destinations.
           I ask for destination & number in party.
           I ask for the proper coupons or a cash amount.
           If the coupons & cash are correct, I press the destination button and give
             tickets to customer.
           I tell the customer the next departure time and current train frequency (from
             the video screen).
           I direct customer to the boarding queue.

very effective. Library classes usually provide generalizations of menus, windows, mouse control, icons, font control, and cut-and-paste utilities.

Prototypes are very useful during the HIC design for smoothing out just how the library classes will work with the PDC objects. As we described earlier in Chapter 8 on Prototyping, user interaction with the prototypes can provide extremely useful information about the effectiveness of the design.

Kayjay World Example 7

We generally employ interview information or user reflections to compile profiles of the users involved in the monorail system. Two examples built from Kayjay World user roles appear in Figure 22.25.

Based on these and other profiles, we could choose a touch-screen control interface based on a control panel metaphor. One reason for this

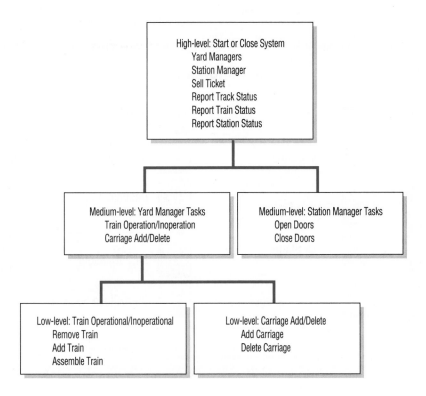

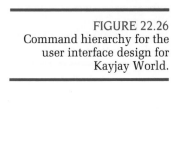

FIGURE 22.26
Command hierarchy for the
user interface design for
Kayjay World.

choice is that the users lack the experience and education needed for more complex interfaces based on keyboards and menus. We might also have discovered that typical work environments were noisy and distracting, which could lead to errors unless the interface displays were large and clear.

Two major activities would follow: work on a command hierarchy (Figure 22.26) and work toward a crude prototype to determine what new classes would be needed from the C++ libraries. In this example, we need only add a single library class, ControlPanel, which provides all of the touch-screen management services. A prototype would show that most of the HIC could be implemented as Menu objects derived from the ControlPanel Class.

The command hierarchy is carefully planned: The highest-level commands are directed to the lowest-level users. Ticket sales and status inquiries functions are most frequently used by young operators and station managers. Further down the hierarchy are functions for the Station and Yard Managers. At the very lowest level are sophisticated functions for assembling trains for the system.

Now we can design and prototype the touch screens. Figure 22.27 depicts the prototype of the main control screen, and Figure 22.28 shows the prototype of the main Yard Manager's screen.

Designing Task and Data Management Components

These two components are very strongly linked to the implementation technology. Task management is heavily determined by the computing hardware configuration, and data management is heavily determined by the systems software available when the system is actually running.

The Task Management Component (TMC) is most important when the system is running on multiple processors or computers. A "task" is a

FIGURE 22.27
Main control touch screen for
the Kayjay World system.

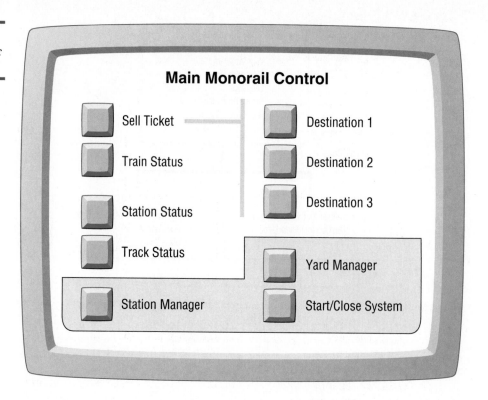

Main Monorail Control

Sell Ticket

Train Status

Station Status

Track Status

Station Manager

Destination 1

Destination 2

Destination 3

Yard Manager

Start/Close System

collection of related services that should run together (perhaps on the same processor). Tasks are triggered by elapsed time or an event. The objects of the TMC obey task triggers, processor assignments, and priorities when services are invoked.

FIGURE 22.28
Main screen for the Yard
Manager of Kayjay World.

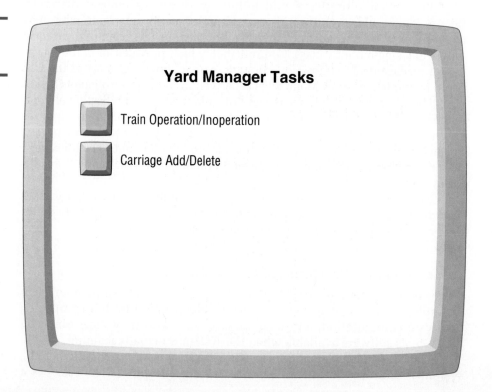

Yard Manager Tasks

Train Operation/Inoperation

Carriage Add/Delete

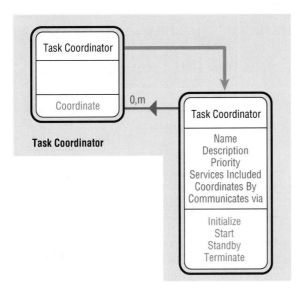

FIGURE 22.29
The task management components of O-O analysis and
design.

The TMC component typically appears as shown in Figure 22.29. This new TMC Subject is just added to the existing layered diagram package. The TMC component is then implemented by creating new Task objects as needed by the system.

The Data Management Component (DMC) typically regards classes and objects needed to store and retrieve the other objects in the system. The DMC varies considerably depending on whether the underlying run-time technology is an object-oriented database, a relational database, or an ordinary "flat" file system. In an object-oriented database environment, the DMC is almost completely provided by the database. In a relational database or a flat-file environment, the DMC must provide storage services to the system.

There are three different ways to design the DMC. One approach is to build storage services into each Class-&-Object in the design. This usually involves a considerable amount of additional design programming.

An alternative is to create an ObjectServer Class-&-Object that provides all database services. This alternative involves a very complex object that knows how to store or retrieve all objects in the system. Any storage requests are made via messages to this single object. Figure 22.30 shows the design for an ObjectServer.

A third method is to create a Storable Class. This third approach is a combination of the previous two approaches. The Storable Class includes basic store-me and retrieve-me services in a generalized form. Every object in the system that must be stored or retrieved is then connected in a Gen-Spec

FIGURE 22.30
Design for an ObjectServer
Class-&-Object.

FIGURE 22.31
Partial example of a Storable
Class.

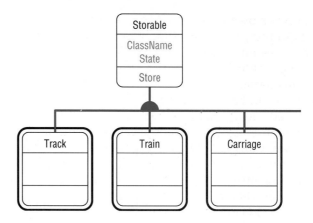

structure to the Storable Class. This will usually work only in those cases where multiple inheritance is available in the implementation technology. Figure 22.31 shows a partial example of a Storable Class.

Kayjay World Example 8

The final steps in our example regard the design of the TMC and the DMC. The TMC is necessary because each train will process its object on the processor on-board each engine. This means that the services connected with moving a Train would form a natural task for these processors. We could also design three independent tasks that would run on the monorail system's central computer. One of these is the task associated with moving a train into the system. Another such task is the collection of routine maintenance services. The third task running on the central computer is the task coordinator itself. The specifications for two of these task objects follow:

> **Task Name:** Coordinator
> > **Services:** Coordinate
> > **Processor:** Central

> **Task Name:** MoveTrain
> > **Description:** move train to next location
> > **Priority:** high
> > **Services:**
> > > train moves (train idle)
> > > switch branch or normal (empty train headed for barn arrives at switch)
> > > occupy track (train moves)
> > > passenger embark & debark (trains stops at station)
> > **Coordinates by:** event (train idle)
> > **Communicates via:** input & output lines
> > **Processor:** Engine

In our example we choose to use an ObjectServer approach to designing a DMC, since this could be easily implemented using the relational database already available to the monorail system computers. The ObjectServer will have to store and retrieve data about its own state and the state of the database as part of its processing. We must also design the relational table specifications for the objects Station, Junction Switch, Train, and Track, as well as the ObjectServer's own data (in a table named "StoreData"). We would likely have to prototype the ObjectServer, including the StoreData and Train tables, to make sure our design is feasible.

Prototyping would bring out some of the implementation problems more clearly. This design could be very difficult to implement for a variety of reasons. The C++ linked list structures and other object connections are probably all based on internal C++ pointers. These pointers would be meaningless when the object is stored in a database and deleted from the C++ memory heap. Consequently, the ObjectServer will have to translate such references into relational foreign keys during storage, and recreate the C++ linkages during retrieval. This is not a simple task and it demonstrates the importance of an O-O database management system as part of the run-time package for an O-O design.

Below are a partial set of DMC specifications for the Kayjay World example:

Specification: ObjectServer
      Attribute: MetadataTable
      External_Input:
      External_Output:
      Object_State_Diagram:
      Additional_Constraints:
      Notes: Relational Database
      Service: Create me
      Service: Destroy me
      Service: Access MTableName
      Service: StoreObject
            Exit if unchanged
            If delete
                  Switch on ClassName, each may
                      delete inherited object rows
                      delete object rows
                      delete object
            If Update or Insert
                  Switch on ClassName, each may
                      Replace embedded pointers
                      Add inherited pointers
                      Insert or Update rows
                      Set Storable State
      Service: RetrieveObject
            Switch on ClassName, each may
                Create Object
                Fetch & assign inherited rows
                Fetch & assign object row
                Set Storable State
      Service: Open
            For all TableNames in MTable
                Retrieve ClassName
                For all ObjIdNums in TableName
                    RetrieveObject
     StateCodes: 0-unchanged since read, 1-newly created object,
            2-updated since read, 3-deleted object

Table Specifications

Table: StoreData

Metadata for Monorail System

Column definitions
# Name	Type
1 ClassName	TEXT 25
Exact Class Name for object	
2 TableName	TEXT 20
Exact Database Table Name for Obj	
3 ColumnName	TEXT 20
Exact Database column name=Attrib	
4 AttribName	TEXT 25
Exact Attribute name stored	

Table: Train

Table for storing train objects

Column definitions
# Name	Type
1 TrainNumber	INTEGER
2 Circuits	INTEGER
Circuits Complete	
3 State	INTEGER
Service State (Op, Inop, etc)	
4 CurSeg	INTEGER
Current Track Segment Number	
5 CarList	INTEGER
ObjIdNum of related Car List	
6 Passengers	INTEGER
ObjIdNum of First Passenger	
7 ObjIdNum	INTEGER
ObjectIdNumber	

Table: Track

Table for storing track objects

Column definitions
# Name	Type
1 SegmentNumber	INTEGER
2 State	INTEGER
3 Us	INTEGER
ObjIdNumber of List of tracks	
4 PrevTrack	INTEGER
ObjIdNum of previous track	
5 NxtTrack	INTEGER
ObjIdNum of next track segment	
6 ObjIdNum	INTEGER
Object Id Number	

Recycling the Programming Environment

"I feel like I'm writing the same code over and over again," says Benito Pérez, a programmer working on a new automated warehouse design. "I have written so many programs lately that dealt with robotic-type things that control themselves: automated mailroom trolleys, building surveillance robots, automatic pool cleaners, automatic lawnmowers, monorail trains, and now warehouse trolleys. These are all variations on a theme."

Lisa Bernoulli, the project manager, had heard this sort of complaint for years: "Oh come on, Ben, these things aren't really that close. How can you compare a mailroom robot, an automated warehouse, and a monorail train? I'll bet less than ten percent of the code is the same."

"Look," says Benito, "all three involve machines that have to find a starting point, follow a circuitous route, make stops for loading and unloading, and eventually go to a stopping point. All three have to make decisions at branches in their routes. All three have to avoid colliding with things. I'm tired of redesigning code that is largely familiar to me.

"Hmmm," Lisa mused as she looked over the basic requirements for the warehouse system and remembered the monorail system she and Benito had worked on last year. The requirements regarded a small-lot electronics manufacturing firm that was automating its warehouse and product movement system. The warehouse contains incoming parts, work-in-progress, and finished goods. The automated warehouse uses a flatbed robot trolley. This robot is a four-wheel electric cart, similar to a golf cart, except that it has no seats. Flatbed robot trolleys have a flat, six-foot by four-foot cargo surface about three feet above ground level. These trolleys have a radio communications device that provides a real-time data link to a central warehouse computer. Flatbed trolleys have two sensors: a path sensor that detects a special type of paint and a motion sensor that detects movement. These trolleys follow painted paths around the factory floor. Special paint codes mark forks or branches in the paths, trolley start or stop points, and general location points.

The facility included three loading dock stations and ten workstations. Each station had a video terminal or computer connected to the central computer. When products are needed, or are ready to be collected from a workstation, the central computer is informed by the worker at the station. The central computer then dispatches trolleys accordingly. Each station has a drop point and a pickup point. Flatbed trolleys move about the factory picking up work at pickup points and dropping off work at drop points. The program that will run the trolleys must interact heavily with the existing job scheduling program that helps schedule workstation tasks.

How similar are the trolleys to the monorail trains in the Kayjay World examples? How should Lisa go about reusing Benito Pérez' work on the monorail in their current task of creating a trolley object?

Alternative Approaches and Notation

The O-O techniques presented here are based on one popular approach presented by Coad and Yourdon. There are several competing approaches which offer variations in the notation and types of analysis and design abstractions. None of these techniques is easily comparable to the others. However, the notation can be translated directly. For example, in Figure 22.32, you will find the notation for inheritance used by five of the authors noted in the bibliography. They are mostly quite similar. The important thing to realize here is that, once you understand the principles of inheritance, a change in notation is not difficult.

Techniques for O-O analysis and design, much the same as in O-O programming, are still somewhat in a developmental phase. Though it is not yet clear whether any single approach will become widely accepted, the techniques and notation that you have learned in this chapter certainly represent a good beginning for those interested in gaining further experience with the general concepts of object-oriented techniques.

SUMMARY

Object-oriented analysis and design techniques developed in response to the increasing use of O-O programming languages. O-O designs can effectively

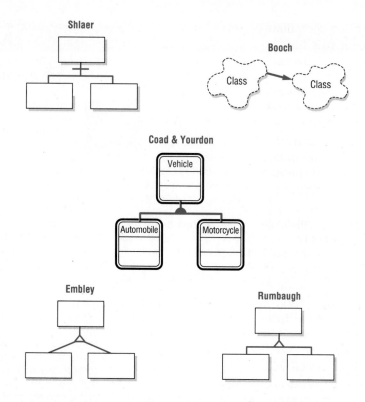

FIGURE 22.32
Comparative inheritance design notation of five different 0-0 analysis and design authors.

specify such new O-O programming structures as inheritance and polymorphism. There are a number of diverse approaches to O-O analysis and design. In this chapter we studied one such approach, devised by Peter Coad and Ed Yourdon.

The basic concepts underlying object-oriented analysis are objects, classes, messages, encapsulation, inheritance, and polymorphism. An object is a computer representation of some real-world thing or event. Similar objects are grouped into categories called classes. A class is the system specification for a group of similar (or related) objects. Objects communicate with each other through messages. A message is sent by one object to another object and is intended to stimulate some particular, predefined behavior by the receiver. Because all of an object's internal data is buffered from other objects by internal predefined processes (the object's behavior), objects are said to encapsulate their data. The only way to change data held by an object is by sending a message to that object that will stimulate the object to make such an internal change. The inheritance concept refers to the ability to create new (derived) classes based in part on old (base) classes. Derived classes can inherit all or part of the structure and behavior of base classes and extend these with new structures and behaviors. Inheritance opens the way for polymorphic objects. Polymorphism permits a base class to take the form of any of its derived classes when the circumstances demand it. Further, derived classes may substitute their own behavior in place of their base class's behavior in reaction to certain messages from other objects.

The Coad and Yourdon O-O model consists of five layers. Classes and objects are noted in the first layer. Second, a structure layer details relationships between classes or objects. Attributes of classes are noted in the third layer. A service layer details messages and object behaviors. Finally, a subject layer may be used to divide large models into project units.

Objects are computer representations of tangible things, roles, incidents, interactions, or specifications. Typically, objects embody: a need to be recalled or remembered; a distinct set of several attributes, each with a meaningful value; siblings with exactly the same behavior; and independence from their implementation technology.

Structures link classes or objects. Classes may be linked together in a Gen-Spec structure for inheritance. Objects may also be linked together in a Whole-Part structure for aggregation. Aggregation involves objects that are composed or assembled from other objects.

Attributes are the data fields maintained by and related to a class. In addition, the attribute specification may include instance connections between objects. Instance connections represent some nonstructural relationship between two objects, such as the relationship between a vehicle object and an owner object.

Services are the behavior of objects and typically embody mechanisms by which the object can change its state. Simple services, such as those that merely set a data value, are generally not documented in the O-O model. Complex services that involve conditional processes or subroutines are documented in a specification template, which may also include attribute and state details. Services are typically triggered by messages created by other objects' services. Again, messages that trigger simple services are generally not detailed in the O-O model.

The entire O-O design package maps the five-layered O-O model onto four major system components. The problem domain component contains the basic set of functions that accomplish the system's primary goals or purposes. The human interface component includes menus, interactive screens, and reports that represent the exchanges between computers in the system and people using the system. The task management component collects various services together into tasks that occur at related times or are related to a particular processing unit. The data management component provides mechanisms for retrieving and storing objects, classes, and system states. The task and data management components are closely dependent on implementation technologies such as the exact model and configuration of computer hardware and the exact vendor and version of database management programs used in the system.

O-O analysis, design, and programming has been developed in response to the need for flexibility in computer-based information systems. Encapsulation, inheritance, and polymorphism are intended to provide complex systems with mechanisms for fast, easy, and reliable program maintenance and change. Though O-O development typically involves a more extensive (and expensive) analysis and design phase, this investment pays off in lower operating costs for systems that are likely to require high maintenance activity.

KEYWORDS AND PHRASES

class
command hierarchy
data management component
encapsulation
generalization-specialization
human interface component

inheritance
instance connections
message
multiple inheritance
object
object-oriented

object-oriented database	specification template
polymorphism	state diagrams
problem component	subject
prototype	task management component
service	whole-part

REVIEW QUESTIONS

1. What are the six basic ideas that characterize object-oriented programming?
2. Describe the difference between an Object and a Class.
3. How does encapsulation change the manner in which data are updated by programs?
4. What two types of classes are involved in any inheritance relationship?
5. Multiple inheritance means that there will be multiple occurrences of which type of class in the inheritance relationship?
6. Does polymorphism only occur where there is inheritance?
7. What are five general types of objects?
8. How can you tell from Coad and Yourdon's notation whether a class has been instantiated with objects?
9. What are eight criteria used to determine whether a new class is justfied?
10. What are two basic types of structures that might be imposed on classes and objects?
11. What is the name of the notation used to denote a reference from one class to an unrelated class?
12. How can state changes be discovered easily in objects?
13. What are two categories of services?
14. How are messages denoted in the service layer of a Coad and Yourdon diagram?
15. What kind of project typically calls for the use of subject layers?
16. What four major components comprise the design activities?
17. What three activities take place in completing the problem domain component?
18. Which two design components are very strongly linked to implementation technology?
19. Define the term TMC.
20. What are three ways to design a Data Management Component?
21. Which approach to design of the Data Management Component involves a very complex additional object?

PROBLEMS

1. The Kayjay World Station Master is typically a college student in his or her early twenties. The Station Master's duties include supervising the Ticket Seller and Platform Guards at their respective stations. The Station Master actually operates some train controls, including the "door open," "door close," and "boarding complete" switches. "I

want a simple system," says Buffy Bronzebight, "one that I know will allow passengers to embark and debark safely. Confusion on the station platform is dangerous, and unexpected delays irritate the visitors. In the best of all worlds, the trains move regularly. Next best are delays you expect. You can announce them to the passengers, and then they don't get so mad. The worst delays are the unexpected ones. My job is pretty straightforward: When an arriving train comes to a complete halt, I press the 'door open' switch and allow train passengers to debark. After all passengers have debarked, I instruct the guards to allow the queued passengers to board the train. When all passengers have boarded, or the train seats have filled, I instruct the guards to check the platform for safety and press the 'door close' switch. I then check the train visually according to the safety procedure and press the 'boarding complete' switch so the train may leave."

Based on this information, write user and task descriptions for the Station Master.

2. The Kayjay World Capacity Manager is a full-time position typically held by an experienced person with a college degree, although this individual has only rarely been someone trained in computers or engineering. Sam Spindlefold has held this position for twelve years: "I monitor the operation of the monorail system and the barn, and watch over track conditions and station operations. It is my system: I'm in charge of starting and stopping the system and supervising all manual operations. I also have to be sure that the 'right' number of trains are operating. When the monorail was first installed, I spent three weeks with the contractor's engineers learning how it all worked. What matters most to me is that the system runs smoothly in bad conditions. Also, I should not be bothered with operational problems in typical conditions. I'm happy when the trains move smoothly around the system at peak hours and passengers are never delayed more than 7 minutes when waiting for a train. I usually work the startup shift: I select 'startup system' from my screen. As soon as the Train Driver presses the deadman switch (kind of like a throttle), the first train launches from the barn. Although I rarely work a closedown shift, those people only have to select 'closedown system' from their screen. All empty trains exit the system. I dread 'alarm' conditions, such as a train failure or driver release of the deadman switch. In such cases, I may have to manually override controls by issuing radio instructions to Train Drivers or Station Managers, having yard workers manually switch the junction, or sending the gasoline-powered yard engine out to tow a disabled train."

Based on this information, write user and task descriptions for the Capacity Manager.

3. The Kayjay World Yard Manager is in charge of the operating condition of the trains, monitoring their operating performance, coupling trains and placing them in service, and uncoupling trains and removing them for maintenance. Yard Managers also remove or add rolling stock when new cars are purchased or old ones are junked. Yard Managers are often trained mechanics or machinists, and most are very experienced. Billy Leroy has been working at Kayjay World since it opened fifteen years ago: "What I want most is a yard link that's easy to change and works all the time so's I can yank a train

over to the yard fast and get another train out in its place fast. I don't want a complicated computer system that gets in my way when I need to assemble trains from yard stock. I want to turn the doggone computer control off if I need to. I spend most of my day fixing broken train parts. For example, say a train is sent to the barn with a jammed door. First I look for a quick fix. There usually isn't one, and I have to select commands from the computer menu that tells the system that the train is inoperable. Then I manually set two yard switches in the barn queue and yard and use manual controls to drive the train onto one yard siding. Next I have to uncouple the train and use a gasoline yard engine to pull the bad car onto the repair rack. I can then recouple the remaining cars and use the computer menu to enter the new train configuration. Once again, I manually set two yard switches and return the short train to the barn queue, and then use the computer menu to tell the system that the train is again operable."

Based on this information, write user and task descriptions for the Yard Manager.

4. Draw a prototype touch screen for the "Train Operational Control" portion of the Kayjay World Command hierarchy.

5. Complete the Kayjay World Example 8 TMC specifications by writing the ExitBarn and Maintenance task specifications. ExitBarn would move a train into the system. Maintenance would handle a number of miscellaneous tasks, chiefly operating according to human input and control: train enters barn queue because it is going out of service; start system (a clock-driven process each morning); close system (a clock-driven process each evening); a train breaks (becomes inoperative); a train gets fixed (becomes operative); a train gets assembled from cars and engines; a new car is added to the rolling stock; an old car gets junked.

6. Complete Kayjay World Example 8 DMC ObjectServer specifications by writing definitions for "Close" and "Backup" Services. Close would write all objects to the database as part of the shut-down process. Backup would capture a "snapshot" of the current objects in case of a computer crash.

7. Complete the Kayjay World Example 8 DMC Relational Database Table Specifications by writing the Station and JuncSwitch Objects table definitions. Work from the attribute definitions and don't forget to add any necessary referential attributes.

8. Complete the Kayjay World Example 4 Specification by designing a service logic flow diagram (or other procedural specification) for the "enter barn" train service.

9. Complete the Kayjay World Example 4 Specification by designing a service logic flow diagram (or other procedural specification) for the "set switch" train service.

10. Complete the Kayjay World Example 4 Specification by designing a service logic flow diagram (or other procedural specification) for the "get Track" train service.

11. Complete the Kayjay World Example 4 Specification by designing a service logic flow diagram (or other procedural specification) for the "find fixed junction" train service.

SELECTED BIBLIOGRAPHY

Booch, G. *Object-Oriented Design with Applications.* Redwood City, CA: Benjamin/Cummings, 1991.

Coad, E., and E. Yourdon. *Object-Oriented Design.* Englewood Cliffs, NJ: Yourdon Press, 1991.

Coad, P., and E. Yourdon. *Object-Oriented Analysis,* 2nd ed. Englewood Cliffs, NJ: Yourdon Press, 1991.

Embley, D., B. Kurtz, and S. Woodfield. *Object-Oriented Systems Analysis, A Model-Driven Approach.* Englewood Cliffs, NJ: Yourdon Press, 1992.

Rumbaugh, J., M. Blaha, W. Premerlani, F. Eddy, and W. Lorensen. *Object-Oriented Modeling and Design.* Englewood Cliffs, NJ: Prentice-Hall, Inc., 1991.

Shlaer, S., and S. Mellor. *Object Lifecycles: Modeling the World in States.* Englewood Cliffs, NJ: Yourdon Press, 1992.

Shlaer, S., and S. Mellor. *Object-Oriented Systems Analysis: Modeling the World in Data.* Englewood Cliffs, NJ: Yourdon Press, 1988.

INDEX

Page numbers followed by an italic *f* refer to figures.

Integrated personal information managers. *See* PIMs

Intelligence phase, decision support systems, 387

Intelligent terminals, 707

Interdependence, organizations and, 28

Interface data flow, 236

Internal auditors, 784–785

Internal output, 484

Internet, 490–491

Interrelatedness, organizations and, 28

Interval scales, 153–54

Interviews, 109–132
  beginning the interview, 121–122
  concluding the interview, 122
  CPU-staff interviews, 134–144
  information sought, 109–110
  before the interview, 121
  interviewee
    feelings, 109–110
    goals, 110
    opinions, 109
  interview report, writing, 123, 124*f*
  Joint Application Design (JAD), 123–127
    benefits of using JAD, 126–127
    drawbacks of using JAD, 127
    participants in, 124–125
    planning the JAD session, 126
    structured analysis of project activities, 126
    when to use, 124
    where to hold JAD meetings, 126
  preparation for, 110–112
    decide on question types and structure, 111–112
    decide who to interview, 111
    establish objectives, 111
    prepare the interviewee, 111
    read background material, 110–111
  question arrangement, 115–17, 118*f*
    diamond-shaped structure, 117, 118*f*
    funnel structure, 117
    pyramid structure, 115–116
  question pitfalls
    double-barreled questions, 115
    leading questions, 115
  question types, 112–114
    bipolar, 113
    closed, 113–114
    open-ended, 112–13, 114*f*
    probes, 114, 115*f*
  recording the interview
    notetaking, 121
    tape recording, 120
  structured vs. unstructured, 117–118, 119*f*

Invalid values test, 709

Inventory, computer hardware, 412–413

Inverse video, 547

Investigation, 88–98
  abstracting archival document data, 96–98
  of hard data
    qualitative document analysis, 93–96
      guidelines, 93–95
      manuals, 95–96
      memos, 94*f*, 95
      policy handbooks, 96, 97*f*
      signs, 95
    quantitative document analysis, 89–92, 90, 94
      data capture forms, 90–92
      performance reports, 89–90
      reports for decision making, 89

Iteration, 343*f*

J

Joint Application Design (JAD), 123–127
  benefits of using JAD, 126–127
  drawbacks of using JAD, 127
  participants in, 124–125
  planning the JAD session, 126
  structured analysis of project activities, 126
  when to use, 124
  where to hold JAD meetings, 126

Joystick, 644

K

Kayjay World examples, 848–855, 857–861, 863–872

Keyboards, design of, 673

Key fields, 298

Keying
  data flow diagrams and, 244
  minimizing keystrokes, 648–650

Key reports, analyzing, 89

Keys, 583

Key-to-disk data entry, 703

Key to storage, 703–704

Key-to-tape recorder data entry, 703

Knowledge-based system, 3

Knowledge work systems (KWS), definition of, 2

L

Label printers, 485*f*, 486

Labels, data flow diagrams, 263

Language accommodation, 864

Laser printers, 486

Least squares method, trends estimation and, 421–422

Leniency, scaling and, 155

Lexicography, sequential elimination by, 395–397

Lighting, in computer room design, 670–671

Lighting and color, as STROBE element, 182–183

Lightpens, 653

Line captions, 530–531

Line graphs, 450–452

Linked lists, conventional files, 587–588

Local area networks (LANS), 815

Logical data flow diagrams, 240–243

Logical process specifications, 360–364

Logical security, 825

Logos, corporate, 487

Lotus Corporation, 63

Lotus Notes, 815–816

M

Magnetic ink character recognition (MICR), 704–705

Mainframe computers vs. microcomputers, 548–552

Maintenance practices, 783–784

Manageable modules, 206

Management
  implications for information systems development, 37–38
  middle, 36
  operations, 35–36
  strategic, 36–37

Management information systems (MIS) definition of, 2–3. *See also* Information system

Manual data dictionary, 292, 311

Manual processes, 245, 246

Manuals
  investigation and, 95–96
  procedure, 770–772